BECKETT
WRESTLING
ALMANAC

BECKETT - THE #1 AUTHORITY ON COLLECTIBLES

THE HOBBY'S MOST RELIABLE
AND RELIED UPON SOURCE ™

Founder: Dr. James Beckett III
Edited by Matt Bible and the Price Guide Staff of Beckett Media LLC

BECKETT is a registered trademark of BECKETT MEDIA LLC, DALLAS, TEXAS
Manufactured in the United States of America | Published by Beckett Media LLC

Beckett Media LLC
4635 McEwen Dr.
Dallas, TX 75244
972.991.6657
beckett.com

First Printing
ISBN: 978-1-953801-01-2

BECKETT WRESTLING ALMANAC

NUMBER 3
BECKETT - THE #1 AUTHORITY ON COLLECTIBLES

EDITORIAL
Mike Payne - Editorial Director

COVER DESIGN
Eric Knagg - Graphic Designer

ADVERTISING
Ted Barker - Advertising Director
972.448.9147, tbarker@beckett.com
Alex Soriano - Advertising Sales
Executive, 619.392.5299,
alex@beckett.com

**COLLECTIBLES DATA
PUBLISHING**
Brian Fleischer
Manager, | Sr. Market Analyst
Daniel Moscoso - Digital Studio
Lloyd Almonguera, Matt Bible,
Jeff Camay, Steve Dalton, Justin
Grunert, Badz Mercader, Eric Norton,
Kristian Redulla, Sam Zimmer
Price Guide Staff

BECKETT GRADING SERVICES
Jeromy Murray
VP, Grading & Authentication
jmurray@beckett.com
4635 McEwen Road, Dallas, TX 75244
Grading Sales – 972-448-9188 |
grading@beckett.com

**BECKETT GRADING SALES/
SHOW STAFF**
DALLAS OFFICE
4635 McEwen, Dallas, TX 75244
Derek Ficken - Midwest/Southeast
Regional Sales Manager
dficken@beckett.com
972.448.9144

NEW YORK OFFICE
Charles Stabile - Northeast Regional
Sales Manager
484 White Plains Rd, 2nd Floor,
Eastchester, N.Y. 10709
cstabile@beckett.com
914.268.0533

ASIA OFFICE
Dongwoon Lee - Asia/Pacific Sales
Manager, Seoul, Korea
dongwoonl@beckett.com
Cell: +82.10.6826.6868

GRADING CUSTOMER SERVICE:
972-448-9188 or grading@beckett.com

OPERATIONS
Amit Sharma – Manager - Business Analytics
Alberto Chavez - Sr. Logistics & Facilities
Manager

**EDITORIAL, PRODUCTION
& SALES OFFICE**
4635 McEwen Road,
Dallas TX 75244
972.991.6657
www.beckett.com

CUSTOMER SERVICE
Beckett Media, LLC
4635 Mc Ewen Road.
Dallas, TX 75244
Subscriptions, Address Changes,
Renewals, Missing or Damaged Copies
866.287.9383 • 239.653.0225

FOREIGN INQUIRES
subscriptions@beckett.com
Back Issues: www.beckettmedia.com

**BOOKS, MERCHANDISE,
REPRINTS**
239.280.2380
Dealer Sales & Production
dealers@beckett.com

BECKETT MEDIA, LLC
Sandeep Dua: President
Kevin Isaacson: Chief Operating Officer
Jeromy Murray: President - Beckett
Collectibles

COVER BACKGROUND: GETTY IMAGES

CONTENTS

BECKETT WRESTLING ALMANAC - NUMBER 3

KAMALA™

Road Warrior Animal™

SMACK DOWN

WRESTLING ALL STARS

PAT PATTERSON

SUPERSTAR

Topps

LUKE HARPER™

ABOUT THE AUTHOR

Based in Dallas, Beckett Media LLC is the leading publisher of sports and specialty market collectible products in the U.S. Beckett operates Beckett.com and is the premier publisher of monthly sports and entertainment collectibles magazines.

The growth of Beckett Media's sports mag-azines, **Beckett Baseball, Beckett Sports Card Monthly, Beckett Basketball, Beckett Football, Beckett Hockey** and **Beckett Vintage Collector**, is another indication of the unprecedented popularity of sports cards. Founded in 1984 by Dr. James Beckett, Beckett sports magazines contain the most extensive and accepted Price Guide, collectible superstar covers, colorful feature articles, the Hot List, tips for beginners, information on errors and varieties, autograph collecting tips and profiles of the sport's hottest stars. Published 12 times a year, **Beckett Baseball** is the hobby's largest baseball periodical.

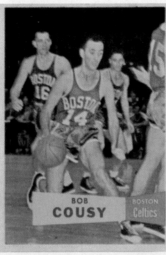

ALL-TIME TOP 20 WRESTLERS

1. HULK HOGAN

2. RIC FLAIR

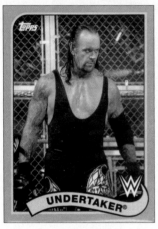

3. UNDERTAKER

4. STONE COLD STEVE AUSTIN

5. JOHN CENA

6. THE ROCK

7. SHAWN MICHAELS

8. BRUNO SAMMARTINO

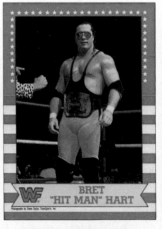

9. BRET "HIT MAN" HART

10. "MACHO MAN" RANDY SAVAGE

ALL-TIME TOP 20 WRESTLERS

11. CHRIS JERICHO

12. ANDRE THE GIANT

13. TRIPLE H

14. DUSTY RHODES

15. EDGE

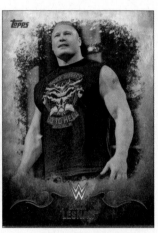

16. BROCK LESNAR

17. STING

18. CM PUNK

19. "ROWDY" RODDY PIPER

20. MICK FOLEY

ALL-TIME TOP 20 WOMAN WRESTLERS

1. TRISH STRATUS

2. CHARLOTTE FLAIR

3. CHYNA

4. THE FABULOUS MOOLAH

5. AWESOME KONG (KHARMA)

6. LITA

7. BETH PHOENIX

8. BECKY LYNCH

9. ALUNDRA BLAYZE (MADUSA)

10. SENSATIONAL SHERRI

ALL-TIME TOP 20 WOMAN WRESTLERS

11. WENDI RICHTER

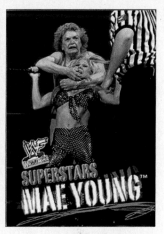

12. MAE YOUNG

13. SASHA BANKS

14. BULL NAKANO

15. RONDA ROUSEY

16. ALEXA BLISS

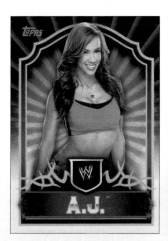

17. AJ LEE

18. NATALYA

19. LEILANI KAI

20. MICKIE JAMES

ALL-TIME TOP 10

VINTAGE ACTION FIGURES
(PRE-2000)

1. 1993 HASBRO WWF SERIES 7 KAMALA CRESCENT MOON BELLY

2. 1993 HASBRO WWF MAGAZINE SERIES UNDERTAKER

3. 1992 HASBRO WWF SERIES 3 BRUTUS THE BARBER BEEFCAKE ZEBRA TIGHTS

4. 1989 LJN WWF SUPERSTARS BLACK CARD RE-RELEASE MACHO MAN RANDY SAVAGE

5. 1987 LJN WWF WRESTLING SUPERSTARS SERIES 4 MISS ELIZABETH PURPLE SKIRT

6. 1991 HASBRO WWF SERIES 2 DUSTY RHODES

7. 1994 HASBRO WWF SERIES 11 1-2-3 KID

8. 1984 LJN WWF WRESTLING SUPERSTARS SERIES 1 HULK HOGAN

9. 1991 GALOOB WCW SUPERSTARS UK BIG JOSH

10. 1991 GALOOB WCW SUPERSTARS SERIES 1 STING ORANGE TIGHTS

ALL-TIME TOP 10

MODERN ACTION FIGURES
(2000-PRESENT)

1. 2004-08 JAKKS PACIFIC WWE ULTIMATE WARRIOR EXCLUSIVES

2. 2006 JAKKS PACIFIC WWE EXCLUSIVES HULK HOGAN/100* TOYFARE MAGAZINE

3. 2004 JAKKS PACIFIC WWE EMPLOYEE GIFT EXCLUSIVES RIC FLAIR/25*

4. 2004 JAKKS PACIFIC WWE EXCLUSIVES ROWDY RODDY PIPER/100* TOYFARE MAGAZINE

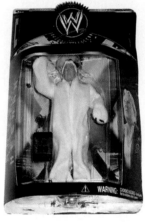

5. 2006 JAKKS PACIFIC WWE EXCLU-SIVES BOBBY THE BRAIN HEENAN WEASEL/100* TOY FAIR GIVEAWAY

6. 2008 JAKKS PACIFIC WWE EXCLUSIVES EDDIE GUERRERO/100* NYC TOY FAIR GIVEAWAY

7. 2007 JAKKS PACIFIC WWE EXCLU-SIVES ROWDY RODDY PIPER DELUXE STYLE/100* NYC TOY FAIR GIVEAWAY

8. 2008 JAKKS PACIFIC WWE EXCLUSIVES UNDERTAKER GITD/100* TOYFARE MAGAZINE

9. 2009 JAKKS PACIFIC WWE EXCLUSIVES REY MYSTERIO/100* TOYFARE MAGAZINE

10. 2009 JAKKS PACIFIC WWE EXCLUSIVES SUNNY/100* TOYFARE MAGAZINE

ALL-TIME TOP 20 AUTOGRAPH CARDS

1. 1998 DUOCARDS WWF AUTOGRAPHS THE ROCK

2. 1999 TOPPS WCW/NWO NITRO AUTHENTIC SIGNATURES "MACHO MAN" RANDY SAVAGE

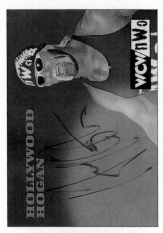

3. 1998 TOPPS WCW/NWO AUTHENTIC SIGNATURES HULK HOGAN

4. 2001 FLEER WWF WRESTLEMANIA SIGNATURE MOVES AUTOGRAPHS STONE COLD STEVE AUSTIN

5. 2001 FLEER WWF ULTIMATE DIVA COLLECTION SIGNED WITH A KISS TRISH STRATUS

6. 1998 TOPPS WCW/NWO AUTHENTIC SIGNATURES EDDIE GUERRERO

7. 2001 FLEER RAW IS WAR BOOTY AUTOGRAPHS UNDERTAKER

8. 2019 TOPPS WWE TRANSCENDENT VINCE MCMAHON

9. 1999 TOPPS WCW/NWO NITRO AUTHENTIC SIGNATURES MISS ELIZABETH

10. 2001 FLEER WWF CHAMPIONSHIP CLASH DIVAS PRIVATE SIGNING STEPHANIE MCMAHON-HELMSLEY

ALL-TIME TOP 20 AUTOGRAPH CARDS

11. 1999 TOPPS WCW/NWO NITRO AUTHENTIC SIGNATURES STING

12. 1998 DUOCARDS WWF AUTOGRAPHS OWEN HART

13. 2005 TOPPS HERITAGE WWE AUTOGRAPHS JOHN CENA

14. 2019 TOPPS WWE TRANSCENDENT SHANE MCMAHON

15. 1999 TOPPS WCW/NWO NITRO AUTHENTIC SIGNATURES GOLDBERG

16. 2015 TOPPS CHROME WWE NXT AUTOGRAPHS ALEXA BLISS

17. 1998 TOPPS WCW/NWO AUTHENTIC SIGNATURES BOBBY HEENAN

18. 1999 TOPPS WCW/NWO NITRO AUTHENTIC SIGNATURES CURT HENNIG

19. 1998 DUOCARDS WWF AUTOGRAPHS CHYNA

20. 1998 TOPPS WCW/NWO AUTHENTIC SIGNATURES CHRIS JERICHO

ALL-TIME TOP 10 CARD SETS

1. 1985 TOPPS WWF

2. 1979 RAX ROAST BEEF GULAS NWA MID AMERICA CHAMPIONSHIP WRESTLING

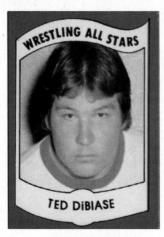

3. 1982 PWE WRESTLING ALL-STARS SERIES A

4. 1982 PWE WRESTLING ALL-STARS SERIES B

5. 1954-55 PARKHURST WRESTLING

6. 2019 TOPPS WWE TRANSCENDENT

7. 2015 TOPPS WWE UNDISPUTED

8. 2016 TOPPS WWE DIVAS REVOLUTION

9. 1987 TOPPS WWF

10. 1994 ACTION PACKED WWF

ALL-TIME TOP 10 FUNKO POPS

1. MACHO MAN RANDY SAVAGE PINK
(2015 WWE.COM EXCLUSIVE)

2. JOHN CENA THE U GREEN HAT
(2014 WWE.COM EXCLUSIVE)

3. REY MYSTERIO DARK
(2014 SDCC EXCLUSIVE)

4. HULK HOGAN HULK RULES
(2014 WWE.COM EXCLUSIVE)

5. ZACK RYDER GREEN TIGHTS/500*
(2017 FUNKO HQ EXCLUSIVE)

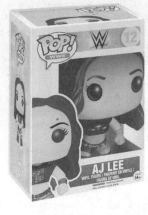

6. AJ LEE
(2014 WWE.COM EXCLUSIVE)

7. REY MYSTERIO BRIGHT BLUE
(2014 7-11 EXCLUSIVE)

8. CM PUNK PINK TRUNKS
(2014 HOT TOPIC EXCLUSIVE)

9. JOHN CENA BLACK PANTS
(2015 WWE.COM EXCLUSIVE)

10. DANIEL BRYAN PATTERNED
(2014 WWE.COM EXCLUSIVE)

Welcome to the Beckett® Wrestling Almanac. This 3rd edition is an enhanced and expanded volume with the addition of new releases, updated prices, and changes to older listings. The Beckett® Wrestling Almanac will do what no other publication has done -- give you the most complete and comprehensive collectible listings possible. The prices were added to the checklists just prior to printing and reflect not the author's opinions or desires, but the going retail prices for each collectible, based on the marketplace such as conventions and shows, hobby shops, online trading, auction results and other first-hand reports of realized sales.

What is the best price guide available on the market today? Of course sellers will prefer the price guide with the highest prices, while buyers will naturally prefer the one with the lower prices. Accuracy, however, is the true test. Compared to other price guides, The Beckett® Wrestling Almanac may not always have the highest or lowest values, but the accuracy of both our checklists and pricing – produced with the utmost integrity – will make it the most widely used reference book in the hobby.

LISTINGS AND SECTIONS

Listings and Sections

Each collection is personal and reflects the individuality of its owner. There are no set rules on how to collect. Since collecting is a hobby or leisure pastime, what you collect, how much you collect, and how much time and money you spend collecting are entirely up to you. The funds you have available for collecting and your own personal taste should determine how you collect.

It is not possible to collect every card and action figure ever produced. Therefore, beginners, as well as intermediate and advanced collectors, usually specialize in some way. One of the reasons this hobby is popular is that individual collectors can define and tailor their collecting methods to match their own tastes.

Many collectors select complete sets from particular years or acquire only certain wrestlers/athletes, while some collectors are only interested in collecting certain figures or autographs.

WHAT'S LISTED

Products listed in the Price Guide typically:
- Are produced by licensed manufacturers
- Are widely available
- Have market activity on single items
- International releases

HOW IT'S LISTED

Unlike regular Beckett® Almanacs, the sort order of this publication is somewhat unique. Like the others, all listings are organized 1) alphabetically then 2) chronologically.

WHAT THE COLUMNS MEAN

The LO and HI columns reflect current retail selling ranges. The HI column on the right generally represents the full retail selling price. The LO column on the left generally represents the lowest price one would expect to find with extensive shopping.

GRADING

All cards in the price guide are based on NrMint to Mint condition. Damaged cards are generally sold for 25 to 75 percent of Mint value. Toy prices are based on Mint condition.

Toys that are loose (out-of-package) are generally sold for 50 percent of the listed price, but may list for less/more depending on market sales.

CURRENCY

This price guide is intended to reflect the entire North American market. While not all of the cards are produced in the United States, they will reflect the market value in U.S. dollars.

GLOSSARY/LEGEND

Our glossary defines terms most frequently used in the collecting hobby. Some of these terms are common to other types of collecting while others may have several meanings depending on the use and context.

7-11	7-11 Exclusive
AMZ	Amazon Exclusive
ARGO	Argo's Exclusive
BJ	BJ's Exclusive
BL	Big Lots Exclusive
CAN	Issued in Canada
CH	Chase Figure
FB	Flashback
FCE	Fall Convention Exclusive
FHQ	Funko Headquarters Exclusive
FL	Foot Locker Exclusive
FP	First Piece in an Action Figure Line
FYE	fYe Exclusive
GITD	Glow-in-the-Dark
GS	GameStop Exclusive
HILLS	Hills Exclusive
HT	Hot Topic Exclusive
KB	Kay-Bee Toys Exclusive
KM	K-Mart Exclusive
LE	Limited Edition
MA	Mail-Away
MANIA TIX	WrestleMania Ticket Mail-In Exclusive
MEI	Meijer Exclusive
NYC TF	New York City Toy Fair Exclusive
NYCC	New York Comic Con
OL	Internet/Online Exclusive
PROFIG	Profigures.com Exclusive
RTWM21 TOUR	- Road to WrestleMania 21 Tour Giveaway Exclusive
RSC	Ringside Collectibles Exclusive
RSF	Ringside Fest Exclusive
SC	Sam's Club Exclusive
SCE	Summer Convention Exclusive
SDCC	San Diego Comic Con Exclusive
SE	Special Edition
TAR	Target Exclusive
TFM	Toyfare Magazine Exclusive
TRU	Toys R Us Exclusive
UK	Issued in United Kingdom
US	Issued in the United States
V	Vaulted (applies only to Funko products)
WG	Walgreens Exclusive
WM	Walmart Exclusive
WRMS	WrestleMania Shop Exclusive
WWE SZ	WWE Shopzone Exclusive

As with any new publication, we appreciate reader feedback. If you have any questions, concerns, corrections or suggestions, please contact us at: **nonsports@beckett.com**

Trading Cards

1994 Action Packed WWF

Subset within the set includes: CC = Colossal Crushers (30-42)

COMPLETE SET (42)	15.00	30.00
COMPLETE FACTORY SET (42)	15.00	30.00
UNOPENED BOX (24 PACKS)		
UNOPENED PACK (6 CARDS)		
COLOSSAL CRUSHERS (30-36)		
1 Bam Bam Bigelow	.20	.50
2 I.R.S.	.20	.50
3 Doink the Clown	.20	.50
4 Diesel	.20	.50
5 Razor Ramon	.25	.60
6 Ludvig Borga	.20	.50
7 Shawn Michaels	.40	1.00
8 Yokozuna	.20	.50
9 Head Shrinkers	.20	.50
10 Bushwhackers	.20	.50
11 Bob Backlund	.20	.50
12 Undertaker	1.25	3.00
13 Macho Man Randy Savage	.50	1.25
14 Adam Bomb	.20	.50
15 Bret Hit Man Hart	.60	1.50
16 Luna	.25	.60
17 1-2-3 Kid	.20	.50
18 Owen Hart	.30	.75
19 Lex Luger	.60	1.50
20 Bastion Booger	.20	.50
21 Quebecers	.20	.50
22 Marty Jannetty	.20	.50
23 Freddie Blassie	.25	.60
24 Stenier Brothers	.25	.60
25 Smoking Gunns	.20	.50
26 Andre the Giant	1.00	2.50
27 Paul Bearer	.30	.75
28 M.O.M.	.20	.50
29 Tatanka	.20	.50
30 Yokozuna CC	.20	.50
31 Diesel CC	.40	1.00
32 Adam Bomb CC	.20	.50
33 Bastion Booger CC	.20	.50
34 Earthquake CC	.20	.50
35 Mabel CC	.20	.50
36 Ludvig Borga CC	.20	.50
37 Razor Ramon	.40	1.00
38 Shawn Michaels	.40	1.00
39 Macho Man Randy Savage	.50	1.25
40 Bret Hit Man Hart	.40	1.00
41 Steiner Brothers	.25	.60
42 Undertaker/Paul Bearer CC	.60	1.50

1994 Action Packed WWF 24 Kt Gold Leaf

COMPLETE SET (6)	25.00	60.00
STATED ODDS 1:24		
1G Razor Ramon	15.00	40.00
2G Shawn Michaels	8.00	20.00
3G Macho Man Randy Savage	6.00	15.00
4G Bret Hit Man Hart	6.00	15.00
5G Steiner Brothers	5.00	12.00
6G Undertaker/Paul Bearer	10.00	25.00

1994 Action Packed WWF Autographed Prototypes

1 Macho Man Randy Savage	250.00	500.00
2 Undertaker	500.00	1000.00

1994 Action Packed WWF Prototypes

COMPLETE SET (2)	3.00	8.00
1 Macho Man Randy Savage	2.00	5.00
2 Undertaker	2.50	6.00

1995 Action Packed WWF

Subsets within the set include: DD = Dirtiest Dozen (25-36); HFR = High Flyers of the Ring (37-42)

COMPLETE SET (42)	15.00	40.00
COMPLETE FACTORY SET (42)	15.00	40.00
UNOPENED BOX (24 PACKS)		
UNOPENED PACK (6 CARDS)		
1 Bret Hit Man Hart	.30	.75
2 Undertaker	.75	2.00
3 Razor Ramon	.40	1.00
4 Diesel	.20	.50
5 Heavenly Bodies	.20	.50
6 Doink the Clown	.20	.50
7 Lex Luger	.25	.60
8 Alundra Blayze	.50	1.25
9 Yokozuna	.20	.50
10 Bam Bam Bigelow	.25	.60
11 British Bulldog	.25	.60
12 Crush	.20	.50
13 King Kong Bundy	.25	.60
14 Nikolai Volkoff	.20	.50
15 Tatanka	.20	.50
16 Paul Bearer	.30	.75
17 Head Shrinkers	.20	.50
18 Duke the Dumpster	.20	.50
19 Dink	.20	.50
20 Bushwhackers	.20	.50
21 Diesel	.20	.50
22 Mabel	.20	.50
23 Smoking Gunns	.20	.50
24 Undertaker	1.25	3.00
25 Shawn Michaels DD	.75	2.00
26 Owen Hart DD	.50	1.25
27 Jim The Anvil Neidhart DD	.25	.60
28 Mr. Fuji DD	.20	.50
29 IRS DD	.60	1.50
30 Luna DD	.40	1.00
31 Well Dunn DD	.20	.50
32 Jerry The King Lawler DD	.40	1.00
33 Double J Jeff Jarrett DD	.25	.60
34 Mr. Bob Backlund DD	.20	.50
35 Bull Nakano DD	.20	.50
36 Million Dollar Man Ted DiBiase DD	.30	.75
37 1-2-3 Kid HFR	.20	.50
38 Shawn Michaels HFR	.40	1.00
39 Adam Bomb HFR	.20	.50
40 Bob Spark Plugg Holly HFR	.25	.60
41 Bret "Hit Man" Hart HFR	.40	1.00
42 Bam Bam Bigelow HFR	.25	.60

1995 Action Packed WWF 24 Kt Gold Leaf

COMPLETE SET (12)	30.00	75.00
STATED ODDS 1:96		
G1 Shawn Michaels	6.00	15.00
G2 Owen Hart	6.00	15.00
G3 Jim The Anvil Neidhart	4.00	10.00
G4 Mr. Fuji	4.00	10.00
G5 IRS	4.00	10.00
G6 Luna	5.00	12.00
G7 Well Dunn	3.00	8.00
G8 Jerry The King Lawler	5.00	12.00
G9 Double J Jeff Jarrett	4.00	10.00
G10 Mr. Bob Backlund	4.00	10.00
G11 Bull Nakano	3.00	8.00
G12 Ted Dibiase	5.00	12.00

1995 Action Packed WWF Promos

LT1 Lawrence Taylor WMXI	6.00	15.00
MM1 Diesel	2.00	5.00
MM2 Undertaker	2.50	6.00

1952 Al Haft's Stars of the Mat

COMPLETE SET (16)	
NNO Argentine Rocca	
NNO Big Bill Miller	
NNO Buddy Rogers	
NNO Don Arnold	
NNO Don Eagle	
NNO Edmund Francis	
NNO Frankie Talaber	
NNO Gene Stanlee (Mr. America)	
NNO Honest Johnny Valentine	
NNO Jackie Nichols	
NNO Joe Scarpello	
NNO Lou Thesz	
NNO Luther Lindsey	
NNO Marvin Mercer	
NNO Professor Roy Shire	
NNO Ruffy Silverstein	

1953 Al Haft's Stars of the Mat

COMPLETE SET (16)	
NNO Argentina Rocca	
NNO Bob Geigel	
NNO Buddy Nature Boy Rogers	
NNO Daffy Ed Francis	
NNO Don Arnold	
NNO Don Eagle	
NNO Don Lewin	
NNO Dr. Big Bill Miller	
NNO Frankie Talaber	
NNO Joe Scarpello	
NNO Lou Thesz	
NNO Luther Lindsey	
NNO Marvin Mercer	
NNO Roy Professor Shire	
NNO Ruffy Silverstein	
NNO Vern Gagne	

1954 Al Haft's Stars of the Mat

COMPLETE SET (12)	
NNO Al Kashey	
NNO Andre Drapp	
NNO Bob Geigel	
NNO Carol Cook	
NNO Don Eagle	
NNO Dr. Big Bill Miller	
NNO Frankie Talaber	
NNO Great Scott	
NNO Jack Pesek	
NNO June Byers	
NNO Mary Jane Mull	
NNO Nell Stewart	

2018 All In Series 1

COMPLETE SET (36)	50.00	100.00
1 All In	.60	1.50
2 Cody	4.00	10.00
3 Brandi	2.50	6.00
4 Kenny Omega	5.00	12.00
5 Matt Jackson	2.50	6.00
6 Nick Jackson	2.50	6.00
7 Nick Aldis	1.25	3.00
8 Stephen Amell	2.00	5.00
9 Joey Janela	2.00	5.00
10 Penelope Ford	3.00	8.00
11 Tessa Blanchard	2.50	6.00
12 Kazuchika Okada	2.00	5.00
13 Kota Ibushi	2.00	5.00
14 Penta El Zero M	2.50	6.00
15 Rey Fenix	3.00	8.00
16 El Bandido	.60	1.50
17 Flip Gordon	.60	1.50
18 MJF	6.00	15.00
19 Adam Page	4.00	10.00
20 Joey Ryan	3.00	8.00
21 Rey Mysterio	1.50	4.00
22 Jerry Lynn	.60	1.50
23 Jay Lethal	2.00	5.00
24 Burnard	.60	1.50
25 Briscoe Brothers	.75	2.00
26 Best Friends	2.00	5.00
27 Chelsea Green	5.00	12.00
28 Britt Baker	5.00	12.00
29 Madison Rayne	2.50	6.00
30 Marty Scurll	.60	1.50
31 SoCal Uncensored	2.00	5.00
32 BTE	.60	1.50
33 Masa	.60	1.50

34 Bury	.60	1.50
35 Cracker Barrel	.60	1.50
36 Checklist	.75	2.00

1926 Allen's Candy Wrestlers

COMPLETE SET (24)

NNO Al Karasick
(Combination Bar & Toe Hold)
NNO Billy Edwards
NNO Billy Edwards
(Hammerlock & Leg Cradle Hold)
NNO Billy Meeske
NNO Billy Meeske
(Standing Reverse Wristlock)
NNO Clarence Weber
NNO John Kilonis
NNO John Kilonis
(Aeroplane Spin)
NNO John Kilonis
(Reverse Head and Armlock)
NNO Mike Yokel
NNO Mike Yokel
(Short Arm Scissors)
NNO Mike Yokel
(Standing Splits)
NNO Sam Clapham
NNO Sam Clapham
(Standing Wristlock)
NNO Sam Clapham
(Straight Arm Bar & Shoulder Twist)
NNO Sam Clapham vs. Mike Yokel
(Body Scissors & Armhold)
NNO Ted Thye
NNO Ted Thye
(Headlock)
NNO Ted Thye
(Reserve Wristlock)
NNO Ted Thye
(Standing Reverse Double Wristlock)
NNO Walter Miller
(Head & Armlock)
NNO Walter Miller
(Half Nelson)
NNO Walter Miller
(Head & Crotch Hold)
NNO Walter Miller
(Straight Arm Scissors)

1999 Artbox WWF MotionCardz

Subsets within the set include: SM = Signature Moves (1-8); Undertaker/Kane (9-16); D-Generation X (17-24); The Rock (25-32); and Stone Cold (33-40).

COMPLETE SET (40)	10.00	25.00
UNOPENED BOX (24 PACKS)		
UNOPENED PACK (8 CARDS)		
1 The Undertaker SM	.40	1.00
2 Stone Cold Steve Austin SM	.50	1.25
3 Kane SM	.40	1.00
4 Kane SM	.40	1.00
5 Road Dogg SM	.40	1.00
6 The Rock SM	.60	1.50
7 Stone Cold Steve Austin SM	.50	1.25
8 The Undertaker SM	.75	2.00
9 The Undertaker/Kane	.40	1.00
10 The Undertaker/Kane	.40	1.00
11 The Undertaker/Kane	.40	1.00
12 The Undertaker/Kane	.40	1.00

13 The Undertaker/Kane	.40	1.00
14 The Undertaker/Kane	.40	1.00
15 The Undertaker/Kane	.40	1.00
16 The Undertaker/Kane	.40	1.00
17 D-Generation X	.40	1.00
18 D-Generation X	.40	1.00
19 D-Generation X	.40	1.00
20 D-Generation X	.40	1.00
21 D-Generation X	.40	1.00
22 D-Generation X	.40	1.00
23 D-Generation X	.40	1.00
24 D-Generation X	.40	1.00
25 The Rock	.60	1.50
26 The Rock	.60	1.50
27 The Rock	.75	2.00
28 The Rock	.75	2.00
29 The Rock	.75	2.00
30 The Rock	.60	1.50
31 The Rock	.60	1.50
32 The Rock	2.00	5.00
33 Stone Cold Steve Austin	.50	1.25
34 Stone Cold Steve Austin	.50	1.25
35 Stone Cold Steve Austin	.50	1.25
36 Stone Cold Steve Austin	.50	1.25
37 Stone Cold Steve Austin	.50	1.25
38 Stone Cold Steve Austin	.50	1.25
39 Stone Cold Steve Austin	.50	1.25
40 Stone Cold Steve Austin	.50	1.25
R1 Sable Revealed	5.00	12.00

1999 Artbox WWF MotionCardz Attitudes

COMPLETE SET (4)	5.00	12.00
STATED ODDS 1:12		
AT1 Undertaker	2.50	6.00
AT2 No Holds Barred	2.00	5.00
AT3 Kane	1.25	3.00
AT4 D-Generation X	2.00	5.00

1999 Artbox WWF MotionCardz Temporary Tattooz

COMPLETE SET (8)	6.00	15.00
STATED ODDS 1:1		
WWF11 Stone Cold 3:16 Logo	1.25	3.00
WWF12 Kane	1.00	2.50
WWF13 Undertaker	1.25	3.00
WWF14 Stone Cold Skull Logo	1.25	3.00
WWF15 Stone Cold Skull Logo	1.25	3.00
WWF16 Stone Cold Skull Logo	1.25	3.00
WWF17 Raw Is War Logo	.75	2.00
WWF18 War Zone Logo	.75	2.00

1999 Artbox WWF MotionCardz Promos

P1 Val Venis/Taka Michinoku	4.00	10.00
P2 Undertaker/Road Dogg	5.00	12.00

2001 Artbox WWF Slams! MotionCardz

Subset within the set includes: FM = FULL Motion (3, 4, 5, 6, 8, 11, 14, 25, 35, 36)

COMPLETE SET (45)	12.00	30.00
COMPLETE SET W/O SP (40)		
UNOPENED BOX (24 PACKS)		
UNOPENED PACK (4 CARDS)		
SP 41-44 STATED ODDS 1:12		
SP 45 STATED ODDS 1:240		
1 Test	.25	.60
2 Rikishi vs. Val Venis	.25	.60
3 The Undertaker vs. HHH FM	1.00	2.50
4 Bradshaw vs. Edge FM	.60	1.50
5 Trish Stratus FM	1.50	4.00
6 HHH vs. Chris Jericho	1.00	2.50
7 The Rock vs. Chris Benoit	1.00	2.50
8 Scotty 2 Hotty/Grandmaster Sexay FM	.25	.60
9 Road Dogg vs. Chris Jericho FM	.40	1.00
10 Bradshaw vs. Edge	.60	1.50
11 The Rock FM	1.00	2.50
12 D-Von & Buh-Buh Ray vs. Edge	.60	1.50
13 Buh-Buh Ray Dudley vs. Christian	.40	1.00
14 Trish vs. Lita FM	1.50	4.00
15 Rikishi vs. Val Venis	.25	.60
16 Steve Blackman	.15	.40
17 Steve Blackman vs. Crash Holly	.15	.40
18 Kurt Angle vs. The Undertaker	.75	2.00
19 The Undertaker vs. HHH	1.00	2.50
20 Lita vs. Test	1.00	2.50
21 Edge and Christian vs. Kane	.60	1.50
22 Bob Hardcore Holly vs. Kurt Angle	.60	1.50
23 Buh-Buh Ray vs. Road Dogg	.25	.60
24 X-Pac vs. Buh-Buh Ray Dudley	.25	.60
25 Commissioner Foley FM	.60	1.50
26 Faarooq vs. X-Pac	.25	.60
27 X-Pac vs. Faarooq	.25	.60
28 Chyna vs. Edge	.60	1.50
29 Buh-Buh Ray Dudley vs. Edge	.60	1.50
30 Hardyz vs. Dudley Boyz	.40	1.00
31 Steve Austin vs. Mr. Ass #1	1.00	2.50
32 The Rock	1.00	2.50
33 Stephanie vs. Buh-Buh Ray Dudley	.75	2.00
34 The Rock vs. Shane McMahon	1.00	2.50
35 Mankind vs. Prince Albert FM	.60	1.50
36 Grandmaster Sexay vs. Test FM	.25	.60
37 Rock & Mick Foley vs. Chris Benoit	1.00	2.50
38 Chris Benoit vs. Eddie Guerrero	.60	1.50
39 Edge vs. Buh-Buh Ray Dudley	.60	1.50
40 Val Venis vs. Rikishi	.25	.60
41 Kurt Angle/Hardcore Holly SP	1.00	2.50
42 Kane vs. Kurt Angle SP	1.00	2.50
43 Steve Blackman/Shano Mac SP	1.00	2.50
44 Matt Hardy SP	1.00	2.50
45 The Godfather SP		

2001 Authentic Images WWF 24K Gold

COMPLETE SET (3)

NNO Hunter Hearst Helmsley
NNO Kurt Angle
NNO Stone Cold Steve Austin

1999 Authentic Images WWF 24K Gold Signature Series

COMPLETE SET (4)

1 The Rock
2 Sable
3 Stone Cold Steve Austin
4 Undertaker

2020 AWS Legends Vol. 1

1 Scorpio Sky
2 La Parka
3 Candice LeRae
4 Lil' Cholo
5 Al Katrazz

6 Los Chivos
7 Shocker
8 Mercedes Martinez
9 Babi Slymm
10 Peter Goodmean In Memoriam
11 Checklist

1999 Candy Planet WWF Poster Puzzle Cards

COMPLETE SET (5)

NNO Kane
NNO The Rock
NNO Sable
NNO Stone Cold Steve Austin
NNO The Undertaker

1997 Cardinal WWF Trivia Game Cards Series 1

These 30 photo cards were issued in the WWF Trivia board game. Each of the cards has a color photo with a yellow border on the front with the WWF logo surrounded by a number between 1 and 6 repeated consistantly across the back. These cards were used within the game to allow the player to assemble an All-Star team of wrestlers. There was a second printing in 1998 where the cards contain a thicker stock and lighter images.

COMPLETE SET (30)	500.00	750.00
1 Stone Cold Steve Austin	125.00	250.00
2 Justin Bradshaw	2.50	6.00
3 Brakus	2.00	5.00
4 British Bulldog	3.00	8.00
5 Crush	1.50	4.00
6 Diesel	2.00	5.00
7 Faarooq	1.50	4.00
8 Flash Funk	1.25	3.00
9 Doug Furnas	1.25	3.00
10 Henry Godwinn	1.25	3.00
11 Phineas Godwinn	1.25	3.00
12 The Goon	1.25	3.00
13 Bret Hit Man Hart	5.00	12.00
14 Owen Hart	3.00	8.00
15 Hunter Hearst-Helmsley	50.00	100.00
16 Bob Holly	2.00	5.00
17 Goldust	2.50	6.00
18 Ahmed Johnson	1.50	4.00
19 Philip LaFon	1.25	3.00
20 Jerry Lawler	2.00	5.00
21 Rocky Maivia	250.00	500.00
22 Mankind	4.00	10.00
23 Marc Mero	1.25	3.00
24 Shawn Michaels	3.00	8.00
25 Aldo Montoya	1.25	3.00
26 Papa Shango	1.25	3.00
27 Sycho Sid	2.00	5.00
28 The Sultan	1.25	3.00
29 Undertaker	15.00	40.00
30 Vader	2.00	5.00

1998 Cardinal WWF Trivia Game Cards Series 1

1 Stone Cold Steve Austin
2 Justin Bradshaw
3 Brakus
4 British Bulldog
5 Crush
6 Diesel

7 Faarooq
8 Flash Funk
9 Doug Furnas
10 Henry Godwinn
11 Phineas Godwinn
12 The Goon
13 Bret Hit Man Hart
14 Owen Hart
15 Hunter Hearst-Helmsley
16 Bob Holly
17 Goldust
18 Ahmed Johnson
19 Philip LaFon
20 Jerry Lawler
21 Rocky Maivia
22 Mankind
23 Marc Mero
24 Shawn Michaels
25 Aldo Montoya
26 Papa Shango
27 Sycho Sid
28 The Sultan
29 Undertaker
30 Vader

1998 Cardinal WWF Trivia Game Cards Series 2

1 Stone Cold Steve Austin
2 Justin Bradshaw
3 Brakus
4 British Bulldog
5 Crush
6 Diesel
7 Faarooq
8 Flash Funk
9 Doug Furnas
10 Henry Godwinn
11 Phineas Godwinn
12 The Goon
13 Bret Hit Man Hart
14 Owen Hart
15 Triple H
16 Bob Holly
17 Goldust
18 Ahmed Johnson
19 Philip LaFon
20 Jerry Lawler
21 The Rock
22 Mankind
23 Marc Mero
24 Shawn Michaels
25 Aldo Montoya
26 Papa Shango
27 Sycho Sid
28 The Sultan
29 Undertaker
30 Vader

2001 Cardinal WWF Trivia Game Cards Series 3

NNO	Al Snow	1.50	4.00
NNO	APA	1.50	4.00
NNO	The Big Show	2.00	5.00
NNO	Chris Benoit		
NNO	Chris Jericho		
NNO	Chyna	15.00	40.00
NNO	Debra		
NNO	Dudley Boyz	1.50	4.00

NNO	Edge & Christian	1.50	4.00
NNO	Hardy Boyz	3.00	8.00
NNO	Kane		
NNO	K-Kwik		
NNO	Kurt Angle	10.00	25.00
NNO	Lita	15.00	40.00
NNO	Perry Saturn w/Terri		
NNO	Rhyno		
NNO	Rikishi		
NNO	The Rock	50.00	100.00
NNO	RTC		
NNO	Steve Blackman	1.50	4.00
NNO	Stone Cold Steve Austin	15.00	40.00
NNO	Tazz		
NNO	Test		
NNO	Too Cool		
NNO	Triple H w/Stephanie McMahon-Helmsley		
NNO	Trish Stratus	25.00	60.00
NNO	Undertaker	8.00	20.00
NNO	Vince McMahon	4.00	10.00
NNO	William Regal	1.50	4.00
NNO	X-Pac	1.50	4.00

1995 CARDZ WCW Main Event

COMPLETE SET (100)		20.00	50.00
UNOPENED BOX (36 PACKS)		250.00	350.00
UNOPENED PACK (8 CARDS)		7.00	10.00
1	Wild Cat Willie	.20	.50
2	Hulk Hogan	.40	1.00
3	Ric Flair	.30	.75
4	Sting	.25	.60
5	Macho Man Randy Savage	.20	.50
6	Frank Andersson	.10	.25
7	Marcus Bagwell	.20	.50
8	The Patriot	.10	.25
9	Paul Roma	.10	.25
10	Paul Orndorff	.12	.30
11	Blacktop Bully	.10	.25
12	Bobby Eaton	.10	.25
13	Diamond Dallas Page	.25	.60
14	Meng	.10	.25
15	Bunkhouse Buck	.10	.25
16	Booker T	.20	.50
17	Stevie Ray	.10	.25
18	Brad Armstrong	.10	.25
19	Arn Anderson	.12	.30
20	Lord Steven Regal	.12	.30
21	Johnny B. Badd	.10	.25
22	Flyin Brian	.30	.75
23	Big Bubba	.10	.25
24	Dustin Rhodes	.12	.30
25	Jerry Sags	.10	.25
26	Brian Knobs	.10	.25
27	Kevin Sullivan	.10	.25
28	Vader	.12	.30
29	Stunning Steve Austin	20.00	50.00
30	Alex Wright	.10	.25
31	Avalanche	.10	.25
32	Butcher	.10	.25
33	Hacksaw Jim Duggan	.20	.50
34	Dave Sullivan	.10	.25
35	Nasty Boys	.10	.25
36	Harlem Heat	.12	.30
37	Pretty Wonderful	.10	.25
38	Stars & Stripes	.10	.25
39	Monster Maniacs	.40	1.00
40	Jimmy Hart	.20	.50
41	Sister Sherri	.12	.30

42	Harley Race	.10	.25
43	Colonel Parker	.10	.25
44	Gary Cappetta	.10	.25
45	Mean Gene Okerlund	.60	1.50
46	Bobby Heenan	.20	.50
47	Tony Schiavone	.10	.25
48	Eric Bischoff	.40	1.00
49	Gordon Solie	.10	.25
50	Larry Zbyszko	.12	.30
51	Nick Bockwinkel	.10	.25
52	Diamond Doll	.60	1.50
53	Das Wunderkind Alex Wright	.10	.25
54	Harlem Heat	.12	.30
55	Dave Sullivan	.10	.25
56	Atomic Leg Drop	.40	1.00
57	Scorpion Death Lock	.25	.60
58	Power Bomb	.12	.30
59	Bulldog	.12	.30
60	Sleeper	.10	.25
61	Sunset Flip	.10	.25
62	Hollywood & Vine	5.00	12.00
63	Vadersault	.12	.30
64	Pit Stop	.10	.25
65	Flying Elbow	.20	.50
66	Figure Four Leglock	.30	.75
67	Headlock	.40	1.00
68	Hulk Hogan/Ric Flair	.40	1.00
69	Hulk Hogan/Ric Flair	.12	.30
70	Hogan/Vader	.20	.50
71	Rhodes/Anderson	.20	.50
72	Macho Man Randy Savage	.40	1.00
73	Macho Man Randy Savage	.40	1.00
74	Macho Man Randy Savage	.40	1.00
75	Macho Man Randy Savage	.40	1.00
76	Ric Flair	.30	.75
77	Ric Flair	.30	.75
78	Ric Flair	.30	.75
79	Ric Flair	.30	.75
80	Sting	.30	.75
81	Sting	.30	.75
82	Sting	.30	.75
83	Hulk Hogan	.40	1.00
84	Hulk Hogan	.40	1.00
85	Hulk Hogan	.40	1.00
86	Hulk Hogan	.40	1.00
87	Hulk Hogan	.40	1.00
88	Hulk Hogan	.40	1.00
89A	Uncensored	.10	.25
89B	Spring Stampede	.10	.25
90	Starrcade 1994	.10	.25
91	Halloween Havoc 1994	.10	.25
92	Fall Brawl	.10	.25
93	Bash at the Beach	.10	.25
94	Slamboree 1994	.10	.25
95A	Superbrawl IV	.10	.25
95B	Superbrawl V	.10	.25
96	Arn Anderson	.12	.30
97	Harlem Heat	.10	.25
98	Vader	.12	.30
99	Hulk Hogan	.60	1.50
100	Checklist	.10	.25

1995 CARDZ WCW Main Event Promos

P1	Hulk Hogan	1.50	4.00
P2	Sting	1.25	3.00
NNO	Hogan vs. Flair TEK	2.00	5.00
NNO	Clash of the Champions KKLZ		

1986 Carnation Major League Wrestling

COMPLETE SET (6)		150.00	300.00
NNO	Kamala	15.00	40.00
NNO	The Koloffs	20.00	50.00
NNO	Ric Flair	75.00	150.00
NNO	Rick Martel	15.00	40.00
NNO	The Road Warriors	30.00	75.00
NNO	Sergeant Slaughter	25.00	60.00

2007 Carolina Independent Wrestling SuperStars

Subset included in this release: TT = Tag Teams (65-76)

COMPLETE SET (80)

1 Title Card
2 Kirby Mack
3 Xsiris
4 Corey Edsel
5 Josh Magnum
6 Damian Kage
7 Scab
8 Timber
9 Malachi
10 Derek Ryze
11 Dick Foley
12 Kohl McAbee
13 Adam Owens
14 Phil Shatter
15 Wicked
16 B.J. Hancock
17 Ric Converse
18 Damien Wayne
19 Zack Salvation
20 Shea Shea McGrady
21 Tre G
22 Brandon Powers
23 K.C. McKnight
24 Big Daddy Z
25 Bobby Houston
26 Donnie Dollar$
27 Mitch Conner
28 D.Z. Hyde
29 Tommy Vandal
30 Yoshi Hiroshima
31 Joey Silvia
32 Styxx
33 Jake Manning
34 Aslyum
35 Baja El Grande, Jr.
36 Scotty Matthews
37 Tito Rain
38 Marcellus King
39 Hangtime
40 Gluteus Maximus
41 Kamikazee Kid
42 Phillip Grant
43 Wallabee Joe
44 Willie Watts
45 Rob Killjoy
46 Xavier Night
47 Boomer Payne
48 Ken Magnum
49 Aaron Devil
50 Amber OlNeal
51 Charlie Dreamer
52 Jaheem The Dream

53 James Drake
54 Mark Slain
55 Danny Dollar
56 Chris Chance
57 Chris Chrisifix
58 Ostgard
59 Frank Nash
60 LAW
61 Pitt
62 Section 8
63 Jamie Lee
64 Derik Fliehr
65 The Neon Lions TT
66 Tank Lawson & Rob McBride TT
67 The New Age Freebirds TT
68 Maximum Exposure TT
69 Nu Skool TT
70 The New Age Sheepherders TT
71 Team EGO TT
72 The East Coast Avengers TT
73 Attention Deficit Disorder TT
74 Perfect Violence TT
75 The Italian Franchise TT
76 Team Maction TT
77 Card Listing #1
78 Card Listing #2
79 Card Listing #3
80 Card Listing #4

1992 Catcher Quartett WWF Series 1

COMPLETE SET (32)

A1 Macho Man Randy Savage
A2 Ultimate Warrior
A3 Undertaker
A4 Bret Hitman Hart
B1 Big Boss Man
B2 British Bulldog
B3 Sgt. Slaughter
B4 Tatanka
C1 El Matador
C2 Virgil
C3 Crush
C4 Natural Disasters
D1 Animal of the Legion of Doom
D2 Ric Flair
D3 Papa Shango
D4 Berzerker
E1 Shawn Michaels
E2 Skinner
E3 Nailz
E4 Repo Man
F1 The Mountie
F2 The Model Rick Martel
F3 Kamala
F4 Ted Di Biase of Money Inc.
G1 Beverly Brothers
G2 Nasty Boys
G3 Bushwhackers
G4 Hulk Hogan
H1 The Rocket Owen Hart of High Energy
H2 Razor Ramon
H3 Mr. Perfect
H4 Hacksaw Jim Duggan

1992 Catcher Quartett WWF Series 2

COMPLETE SET (32)

A1 Macho Man Randy Savage

A2 Ultimate Warrior
A3 Undertaker
A4 Bret Hitman Hart
B1 Big Boss Man
B2 British Bulldog
B3 Sgt. Slaughter
B4 Tatanka
C1 El Matador
C2 Virgil
C3 Crush
C4 Typhoon of the Natural Disasters UER
(spelled Thyphoon)
D1 Legion of Doom
D2 Ric Flair
D3 Papa Shango
D4 Berzerker
E1 Shawn Michaels
E2 Skinner
E3 Nailz
E4 Repo Man
F1 The Mountie
F2 The Model Rick Martel
F3 Kamala
F4 Money Inc.
G1 Beverly Brothers
G2 Brian Knobbs of the Nasty Boys
G3 Bushwhackers
G4 Hulk Hogan
H1 High Energy
H2 Razor Ramon
H3 Mr. Perfect
H4 Hacksaw Jim Duggan

1992 Catcher Quartett WWF Series 3

COMPLETE SET (32)

A1 Macho Man Randy Savage
A2 Ultimate Warrior
A3 Undertaker
A4 Bret Hitman Hart
B1 Big Boss Man
B2 British Bulldog
B3 Sgt. Slaughter
B4 Tatanka
C1 El Matador
C2 Virgil
C3 Crush
C4 Natural Disasters
D1 Legion of Doom
D2 Ric Flair
D3 Papa Shango
D4 Berzerker
E1 Shawn Michaels
E2 Skinner
E3 Nailz
E4 Repo Man
F1 The Mountie
F2 The Model Rick Martel
F3 Kamala
F4 Money Inc.
G1 Blake of the Beverly Brothers
G2 Jerry Sags of the Nasty Boys
G3 Bushwhackers
G4 Hulk Hogan
H1 High Energy
H2 Razor Ramon
H3 Mr. Perfect
H4 Hacksaw Jim Duggan

1992 Catcher Quartett WWF Series 4

COMPLETE SET (32)

A1 Macho Man Randy Savage
A2 Ultimate Warrior
A3 Undertaker
A4 Bret Hitman Hart
B1 Big Boss man
B2 British Bulldog
B3 Sgt. Slaughter
B4 Tatanka
C1 El Matador
C2 Virgil
C3 Crush
C4 Natural Disasters
D1 Hawk of the Legion of Doom
D2 Ric Flair
D3 Papa Shango
D4 Berzerker
E1 Shawn Michaels
E2 Skinner
E3 Nailz
E4 Repo Man
F1 The Mountie
F2 The Model Rick Martel
F3 Kamala
F4 Money Inc.
G1 Beverly Brothers
G2 Nasty Boys
G3 Bushwhackers
G4 Hulk Hogan
H1 High Energy
H2 Razor Ramon
H3 Mr. Perfect
H4 Hacksaw Jim Duggan

1993 Catcher Quartett WWF Series 5

COMPLETE SET (32)

A1 Bret Hit Man Hart
A2 Undertaker
A3 Hulk Hogan
A4 Crush
B1 Mr. Perfect
B2 Bam Bam Bigelow
B3 Kamala
B4 Money Inc.
C1 Doink
C2 Macho Man Randy Savage
C3 Big Boss Man
C4 Tatanka
D1 Virgil
D2 Papa Shango
D3 Shawn Michaels
D4 Repo Man
E1 Hacksaw Jim Duggan
E2 Razor Ramon
E3 Bushwhackers
E4 Nasty Boys
F1 Giant Gonzalez
F2 Head Shrinkers
F3 Beverly Brothers
F4 Damian Demento
G1 Bob Backlund
G2 Brutus The Barber Beefcake
G3 Lex Luger
G4 Steiner Brothers
H1 Yokozuna
H2 El Matador

H3 Paul Bearer
H4 Billy of the Smoking Gunns

1993 Catcher Quartett WWF Series 7

COMPLETE SET (32)

A1 Bret Hit Man Hart
A2 Undertaker
A3 Hulk Hogan
A4 Crush
B1 Mr. Perfect
B2 Bam Bam Bigelow
B3 Kamala
B4 Money Inc.
C1 Doink
C2 Macho Man Randy Savage
C3 Big Boss Man
C4 Tatanka
D1 Virgil
D2 Papa Shango
D3 Shawn Michaels
D4 Repo Man
E1 Hacksaw Jim Duggan
E2 Razor Ramon
E3 Bushwhackers
E4 Knobbs of the Nasty Boys
F1 Giant Gonzalez
F2 Head Shrinkers
F3 Beverly Brothers
F4 Damian Demento
G1 Bob Backlund
G2 Brutus The Barber Beefcake
G3 Lex Luger
G4 Steiner Brothers
H1 Yokozuna
H2 El Matador
H3 Paul Bearer
H4 The Smoking Gunns

1993 Catcher Quartett WWF Series 8

COMPLETE SET (32)

A1 Bret Hit Man Hart
A2 Undertaker
A3 Hulk Hogan
A4 Crush
B1 Mr. Perfect
B2 Bam Bam Bigelow
B3 Kamala
B4 Money Inc.
C1 Doink
C2 Macho Man Randy Savage
C3 Big Boss man
C4 Tatanka
D1 Virgil
D2 Papa Shango
D3 Shawn Michaels
D4 Repo Man
E1 Hacksaw Jim Duggan
E2 Razor Ramon
E3 Luke of the Bushwhackers
E4 Nasty Boys
F1 Giant Gonzalez
F2 Head Shrinkers
F3 Beverly Brothers
F4 Damian Demento
G1 Bob Backlund
G2 Brutus The Barber Beefcake
G3 Lex Luger

G4 Steiner Brothers
H1 Yokozuna
H2 El Matador
H3 Paul Bearer
H4 Billy of the Smoking Gunns

2008 Champions with Attitude Wrestling

COMPLETE SET (39)

NNO Abel Adams
NNO The Alabama Ambassador
NNO Amien Rios
NNO Asylum
NNO Awesome Kong
NNO Bill Hazelwood
NNO Black Pegasus
NNO Charles Culler
NNO Chris Hamrick
NNO Chris Mayne
NNO CWA Director of Authority
NNO CWA's Pro Wrestling Announcer Bill Hazelwood
NNO Daffney
NNO Danny Dollar
NNO Frank
NNO Gluteus Maximus
NNO Hexxon
NNO J.J. Jackson
NNO Jean Pierre Flex
NNO Joey Nuggs
NNO Josh Magnum
NNO Kimo
NNO Kirby Mack
NNO Malachi
NNO Matt Graves
NNO Mikael Judas
NNO Nicky
NNO Phill Shatter
NNO Roger Gleaton CWA CEO
NNO Rusty Young
NNO Shark Girl
NNO Sixx
NNO Snapp Ego
NNO T.J. Mack
NNO The Man Scout
NNO Timber
NNO Timber (w/barbwire bat)
NNO The Urban Legend Xavier Night
NNO Zack Salvation

1991 Championship Marketing WCW

COMPLETE SET (110)	12.00	30.00
UNOPENED BOX (36 PACKS)		
UNOPENED PACK (16 CARDS)		
1 Sting	.30	.75
2 Arn Anderson	.15	.40
3 Michael Hayes	.12	.30
4 Rick Steiner	.15	.40
5 The Fabulous Freebirds	.15	.40
6 The Steiner Brothers	.15	.40
7 Lex Luger	.15	.40
8 Ric Flair	.50	1.25
9 Tom Zenk	.12	.30
10 Sid Vicious	.12	.30
11 Brian Pillman	.12	.30
12 Ric Flair	.50	1.25
13 Sid Vicious	.12	.30
14 The Four Horsemen	.50	1.25
15 Jim Ross	.12	.30
16 Ron Simmons	.15	.40
17 Barry Windham	.12	.30
18 Sid Vicious	.12	.30
19 Sid Vicious	.12	.30
20 Sting and Ric	.50	1.25
21 Beautiful Bobby Punishes Opponent	.12	.30
22 New Champion/Sting	.30	.75
23 Paul E. with Mouth Open	.12	.30
24 Michael Hayes	.12	.30
25 Scott Steiner	.15	.40
26 Rick Steiner	.15	.40
27 World TV Champion/Arn Anderson	.15	.40
28 Barry Windham with Arms Raised	.12	.30
29 Tommy Rich	.12	.30
30 Ricky Morton	.12	.30
31 Horsemen Press Conference	.50	1.25
32 The Freebirds	.15	.40
33 Terry Taylor	.12	.30
34 Dirty Dutch Mantell	.15	.40
35 Nature Boy Ric Flair	.50	1.25
36 Lex Presses Ric	.50	1.25
37 Lex and Sting	.15	.40
38 Flyin' Brian	.12	.30
39 Ric Flair	.50	1.25
40 Sting and Lex	.30	.75
41 Missy Hyatt	.15	.40
42 Three Out of Four/Horsemen	.12	.30
43 Sid Vicious in Action	.12	.30
44 Terry Taylor vs. Z-Man	.12	.30
45 Southern Boys	.12	.30
46 Sting	.30	.75
47 What Did You Say?/Ric Flair	.50	1.25
48 Arn, Paul E. and Ric Flair	.50	1.25
49 Sting	.30	.75
50 Say Uncle/Sid Vicious	.12	.30
51 Paul E. Dangerously	.12	.30
52 Sting and Ric	.50	1.25
53 Sting, Jim and Lex	.30	.75
54 What a Belt!/Sting	.30	.75
55 Sting	.30	.75
56 Ric All In White	.50	1.25
57 Lex Presses Ric II	.50	1.25
58 El Gigante	.15	.40
59 Arn Says My Turn	.15	.40
60 Sid Vicious	.12	.30
61 Brian and Ric	.50	1.25
62 Flyin Brian	.12	.30
63 The Fabulous Freebirds	.15	.40
64 No Sid This High	.12	.30
65 El Gigante	.12	.30
66 Ric, Jim and Sting	.50	1.25
67 No It's Mine/Flair, JR & Sting	.50	1.25
68 Golden Nature Boy	.50	1.25
69 Missy and Scott	.15	.40
70 Ron Simmons	.15	.40
71 Telephone/Paul E. Dangerously	.12	.30
72 Jimmy Jam Garvin	.15	.40
73 Ric Flair in Pink Robe	.50	1.25
74 Beautiful Bobby	.12	.30
75 Lex Luger	.15	.40
76 Z-Man	.12	.30
77 Where's The Door?/Ric Flair	.50	1.25
78 El Gigante	.12	.30
79 What Do You Think?/Ric Flair	.50	1.25
80 6 Time World Champion/Ric Flair	.50	1.25
81 Missy Hyatt	.15	.40
82 The New Champion/Sting	.30	.75
83 Celebration/Sting	.30	.75
84 USA Sting	.30	.75
85 Sting Is Injured	.30	.75
86 Let's Get Busy/Sting	.30	.75
87 Courage of a Champion/Sting	.30	.75
88 No Hold the Anchovies Paul E. Dangerously	.12	.30
89 Lex Presses Ric III	.50	1.25
90 Barry Windham	.12	.30
91 Heads or Tails/Ric Flair & Lex Luger	.50	1.25
92 U.S. Heavyweight Champion/Lex Luger	.15	.40
93 Getting Ready For Battle/Lex Luger	.15	.40
94 Lex Wins the Title	.15	.40
95 Ric Goes Too Far	.50	1.25
96 El Gigante and the Champ/Sting	.30	.75
97 Z-Man	.12	.30
98 World Tag-Team Champions Doom with Teddy Long	.12	.30
99 Missy in Evening Gown	.15	.40
100 Missy Hyatt	.15	.40
101 Tony (Schiavone) in Front of Chicago Building	.12	.30
102 Ricky Morton	.12	.30
103 Flyin Brian	.12	.30
104 The Steiners Want Sting Revenge	.15	.40
105 Z-Man Tom Zenk	.12	.30
106 Southern Boys	.12	.30
107 Teddy R. Long	.12	.30
108 Arn Anderson in Action	.15	.40
109 Sting in Action	.30	.75
110 Doom	.12	.30

1991 Championship Marketing WCW Puzzle

COMPLETE SET (110)	6.00	15.00
STATED ODDS 1:1		
1 Puzzle Card	.12	.30
2 Puzzle Card	.12	.30
3 Puzzle Card	.12	.30
4 Puzzle Card	.12	.30
5 Puzzle Card	.12	.30
6 Puzzle Card	.12	.30
7 Puzzle Card	.12	.30
8 Puzzle Card	.12	.30
9 Puzzle Card	.12	.30
10 Puzzle Card	.12	.30
11 Puzzle Card	.12	.30
12 Puzzle-Card	.12	.30
13 Puzzle Card	.12	.30
14 Puzzle Card	.12	.30
15 Puzzle Card	.12	.30
16 Puzzle Card	.12	.30
17 Puzzle Card	.12	.30
18 Puzzle Card	.12	.30
19 Puzzle Card	.12	.30
20 Puzzle Card	.12	.30
21 Puzzle Card	.12	.30
22 Puzzle Card	.12	.30
23 Puzzle Card	.12	.30
24 Puzzle Card	.12	.30
25 Puzzle Card	.12	.30
26 Puzzle Card	.12	.30
27 Puzzle Card	.12	.30
28 Puzzle Card	.12	.30
29 Puzzle Card	.12	.30
30 Puzzle Card	.12	.30
31 Puzzle Card	.12	.30
32 Puzzle Card	.12	.30
33 Puzzle Card	.12	.30
34 Puzzle Card	.12	.30
35 Puzzle Card	.12	.30
36 Puzzle Card	.12	.30
37 Puzzle Card	.12	.30
38 Puzzle Card	.12	.30
39 Puzzle Card	.12	.30
40 Puzzle Card	.12	.30
41 Puzzle Card	.12	.30
42 Puzzle Card	.12	.30
43 Puzzle Card	.12	.30
44 Puzzle Card	.12	.30
45 Puzzle Card	.12	.30
46 Puzzle Card	.12	.30
47 Puzzle Card	.12	.30
48 Puzzle Card	.12	.30
49 Puzzle Card	.12	.30
50 Puzzle Card	.12	.30
51 Puzzle Card	.12	.30
52 Puzzle Card	.12	.30
53 Puzzle Card	.12	.30
54 Puzzle Card	.12	.30
55 Puzzle Card	.12	.30
56 Puzzle Card	.12	.30
57 Puzzle Card	.12	.30
58 Puzzle Card	.12	.30
59 Puzzle Card	.12	.30
60 Puzzle Card	.12	.30
61 Puzzle Card	.12	.30
62 Puzzle Card	.12	.30
63 Puzzle Card	.12	.30
64 Puzzle Card	.12	.30
65 Puzzle Card	.12	.30
66 Puzzle Card	.12	.30
67 Puzzle Card	.12	.30
68 Puzzle Card	.12	.30
69 Puzzle Card	.12	.30
70 Puzzle Card	.12	.30
71 Puzzle Card	.12	.30
72 Puzzle Card	.12	.30
73 Puzzle Card	.12	.30
74 Puzzle Card	.12	.30
75 Puzzle Card	.12	.30
76 Puzzle Card	.12	.30
77 Puzzle Card	.12	.30
78 Puzzle Card	.12	.30
79 Puzzle Card	.12	.30
80 Puzzle Card	.12	.30
81 Puzzle Card	.12	.30
82 Puzzle Card	.12	.30
83 Puzzle Card	.12	.30
84 Puzzle Card	.12	.30
85 Puzzle Card	.12	.30
86 Puzzle Card	.12	.30
87 Puzzle Card	.12	.30
88 Puzzle Card	.12	.30
89 Puzzle Card	.12	.30
90 Puzzle Card	.12	.30
91 Puzzle Card	.12	.30
92 Puzzle Card	.12	.30
93 Puzzle Card	.12	.30
94 Puzzle Card	.12	.30
95 Puzzle Card	.12	.30
96 Puzzle Card	.12	.30
97 Puzzle Card	.12	.30
98 Puzzle Card	.12	.30
99 Puzzle Card	.12	.30
100 Puzzle Card	.12	.30

101	Puzzle Card	.12	.30
102	Puzzle Card	.12	.30
103	Puzzle Card	.12	.30
104	Puzzle Card	.12	.30
105	Puzzle Card	.12	.30
106	Puzzle Card	.12	.30
107	Puzzle Card	.12	.30
108	Puzzle Card	.12	.30
109	Puzzle Card	.12	.30
110	Puzzle Card	.12	.30

1991 Championship Marketing WCW Promos

COMPLETE SET (12)

1 Sting
2 Arn Anderson
4 Rick Steiner
5 Fabulous Freebirds
7 Lex Luger
8 Ric Flair
9 Tom Zenk
10 Sid Vicious
11 Brian Pillman
12 Ric Flair
13 Sid Vicious
NNO Scott Steiner w/Smothers SP

2006-10 Chikara Wrestling

COMPLETE SET (30)

1 Shanesaw
2 Crossbones
3 Delirious
4 Claudio Castagnoli
5 Larry Sweeney
6 Hallowicked
7 Equinox
8 Chris Hero
9 Los Ice Creams
10 Gran Akuma
11 Mike Quackenbush
12 Chuck Taylor
13 Hydra
14 The Colony
15 Icarus
16 UltraMantis Black
17 Lince Dorado
18 Eddie Kingston
19 El Pantera
20 Shayne Hawke
21 Tim Donst
22 Osirian Portal
23 Mitch Ryder
24 Cheech Hernandez
25 Super Smash Bros.
26 Brodie Lee
27 Frightmare
28 The Batiri
29 Hatfield
30 Touchdown

2006-10 Chikara Wrestling Chase

NNO Toyota

1987 Circle K Coca-Cola WWF Supermatch

COMPLETE SET (20)		30.00	75.00
1	Hulk Hogan	10.00	25.00

2	Hercules and Bobby Heenan	2.00	5.00
3	The Hart Foundation	2.50	6.00
4	Randy Macho Man Savage	3.00	8.00
5	Koko B. Ware	1.25	3.00
6	George The Animal Steele	1.25	3.00
7	Ricky The Dragon Steamboat	1.50	4.00
8	The Honky Tonk Man	2.00	5.00
9	Hacksaw Jim Duggan	1.25	3.00
10	Kamala and Kimchee	2.50	6.00
11	Billy Jack Haynes	1.25	3.00
12	Junk Yard Dog	1.50	4.00
13	Jake The Snake Roberts	4.00	10.00
14	The Killer Bees	1.25	3.00
15	Tito Santana	1.25	3.00
16	The Can-Am Connection	1.25	3.00
17	Andre the Giant	6.00	15.00
18	Elizabeth	3.00	8.00
19	The British Bulldogs	2.00	5.00
20	The Iron Sheik	1.25	3.00

1990 Classic WWF

COMPLETE FACTORY SET (145)		10.00	25.00
UNOPENED BOX (36 PACKS)			
UNOPENED PACK (15 CARDS)			
1	Hulk Hogan	.60	1.50
2	Big Boss Man	.10	.25
3	Ravishing Rick Rude	.15	.40
4	Macho Man Randy Savage	.40	1.00
5	The Ultimate Warrior	.25	.60
6	Demolition	.10	.25
7	Jake The Snake Roberts	.25	.60
8	Million Dollar Man Ted DiBiase	.15	.40
9	Hacksaw Jim Duggan	.15	.40
10	Andre the Giant	.40	1.00
11	Miss Elizabeth	.15	.40
12	Brutus The Barber Beefcake	.15	.40
13	Rowdy Roddy Piper	.25	.60
14	Jimmy Superfly Snuka	.25	.60
15	Bushwhackers	.10	.25
16	Dusty Rhodes	.10	.25
17	Hercules	.10	.25
18	Sensational Queen Sherri	.15	.40
19	Mr. Perfect	.15	.40
20	Rick Martel	.10	.25
21	Tito Santana	.10	.25
22	Mr. Fuji	.10	.25
23	Jimmy Hart	.15	.40
24	Brother Love	.10	.25
25	Akeem	.10	.25
26	Bad News Brown	.10	.25
27	Honky Tonk Man	.15	.40
28	The Rockers	.15	.40
29	Koko B. Ware	.15	.40
30	Bobby The Brain Heenan	.15	.40
31	Dino Bravo	.10	.25
32	The Genius	.10	.25
33	Greg The Hammer Valentine	.15	.40
34	Virgil	.10	.25
35	Haku	.10	.25
36	Rugged Ronnie Garvin	.10	.25
37	Bret Hit Man Hart	.15	.40
38	Hart Foundation	.15	.40
39	Red Rooster	.10	.25
40	Hillbilly Jim	.10	.25
41	Slick		
42	The Widow Maker	.10	.25
43	The Ultimate Warrior	.25	.60
44	Honky Tonk Man	.15	.40

45	Bret Hit Man Hart	.15	.40
46	Jim Neidhart	.15	.40
47	Bushwhackers	.10	.25
48	Paul Roma	.10	.25
49	Barry Horowitz	.10	.25
50	Brooklyn Brawler	.10	.25
51	Mean Gene Okerlund	.10	.25
52	Gorilla Monsoon	.10	.25
53	Jesse The Body Ventura	.40	1.00
54	Sean Mooney	.10	.25
55	Danny Davis	.10	.25
56	Jack Tunney	.10	.25
57	Hulk Hogan	.60	1.50
58	Big Boss Man	.10	.25
59	Ravishing Rick Rude	.15	.40
60	Macho Man Randy Savage	.40	1.00
61	The Ultimate Warrior	.25	.60
62	Demolition	.10	.25
63	Jake The Snake Roberts	.25	.60
64	Million Dollar Man Ted DiBiase	.15	.40
65	Hacksaw Jim Duggan	.15	.40
66	Andre the Giant	.40	1.00
67	Miss Elizabeth	.15	.40
68	Brutus The Barber Beefcake	.15	.40
69	Jimmy Superfly Snuka	.25	.60
70	Bushwhackers	.10	.25
71	Dusty Rhodes	.10	.25
72	Hercules	.10	.25
73	Sensational Queen Sherri	.15	.40
74	Mr. Perfect	.15	.40
75	Jimmy Hart	.15	.40
76	Andre the Giant	.40	1.00
77	Brother Love	.10	.25
78	Akeem	.10	.25
79	Bad News Brown	.10	.25
80	Honky Tonk Man	.15	.40
81	The Rockers	.15	.40
82	Koko B. Ware	.15	.40
83	Bobby The Brain Heenan	.15	.40
84	Dino Bravo	.10	.25
85	The Genius	.10	.25
86	Greg The Hammer Valentine	.15	.40
87	Virgil	.10	.25
88	Haku	.10	.25
89	Rugged Ronnie Garvin	.10	.25
90	Hulk Hogan	.60	1.50
91	Red Rooster	.10	.25
92	Hillbilly Jim	.10	.25
93	The Widow Maker	.10	.25
94	Freddie Blassie	.10	.25
95	Bret Hit Man Hart	.15	.40
96	Jim Neidhart	.15	.40
97	Demolition	.10	.25
98	Paul Roma	.10	.25
99	Barry Horowitz	.10	.25
100	Brooklyn Brawler	.10	.25
101	Danny Davis	.10	.25
102	Hulk Hogan	.60	1.50
103	Big Boss Man	.10	.25
104	Ravishing Rick Rude	.15	.40
105	Macho Man Randy Savage	.40	1.00
106	The Ultimate Warrior	.25	.60
107	Demolition	.10	.25
108	Jake The Snake Roberts	.25	.60
109	Million Dollar Man Ted DiBiase	.15	.40
110	Hacksaw Jim Duggan	.15	.40
111	Andre the Giant	.40	1.00
112	Miss Elizabeth	.15	.40

113	Brutus The Barber Beefcake	.15	.40
114	Jimmy Superfly Snuka	.25	.60
115	Tito Santana	.10	.25
116	Bushwhackers	.10	.25
117	Honky Tonk Man	.15	.40
118	The Rockers	.15	.40
119	Koko B. Ware	.15	.40
120	Haku	.10	.25
121	The Rockers	.15	.40
122	Red Rooster	.10	.25
123	Bret Hit Man Hart	.15	.40
124	Jim Neidhart	.15	.40
125	Hulk Hogan	.60	1.50
126	Macho Man Randy Savage	.40	1.00
127	The Ultimate Warrior	.25	.60
128	Demolition	.10	.25
129	Hulk Hogan	.60	1.50
130	Andre the Giant	.40	1.00
131	Jimmy Superfly Snuka	.25	.60
132	Bushwhackers	.10	.25
133	Honky Tonk Man	.15	.40
134	The Rockers	.15	.40
135	Haku	.10	.25
136	Miss Elizabeth	.15	.40
137	Macho Madness	.40	1.00
138	Honky Tonk Man	.15	.40
139	The Ultimate Warrior	.25	.60
140	Million Dollar Man Ted DiBiase	.15	.40
141	Simply Ravishing	.15	.40
142	Big Boss Man	.10	.25
143	Brutus The Barber Beefcake	.15	.40
144	Koko B. Ware	.15	.40
145	Hulk Hogan Rules	.60	1.50

1990 Classic WWF History of WrestleMania

COMPLETE SET (150)		10.00	25.00
COMPLETE FACTORY SET (150)			
UNOPENED BOX (36 PACKS)			
UNOPENED PACK (15 CARDS)			
*TRADEMARK: .6X TO 1.5X BASIC CARDS			
1	Greg The Hammer Valentine	.12	.30
	Junk Yard Dog		
2	Tito Santana	.10	.25
	Masked Executioner		
3	Hulk Hogan	.50	1.25
4	Dream Team	.10	.25
	British Bulldogs		
5	Battle Royal	.10	.25
6	Battle Royal	.10	.25
7	Battle Royal	.10	.25
8	Brutus The Barber Beefcake	.12	.30
	British Bulldogs		
9	Tito Santana	.12	.30
	Junk Yard Dog/Funk Brothers		
10	Greg The Hammer Valentine	.12	.30
11	Hulk Hogan	.50	1.25
	King Kong Bundy		
12	Macho Man Randy Savage	.20	.50
	George The Animal Steele		
13	Macho Man Randy Savage	.20	.50
	George The Animal Steele		
14	Hulk Hogan	.50	1.25
	King Kong Bundy		
15	Hulk Hogan	.50	1.25
	King Kong Bundy		
16	Andre the Giant	.40	1.00
17	Slick	.10	.25

	Tito Santana		
18	Rowdy Roddy Piper	.20	.50
	Adrian Adonis		
19	Andre the Giant	.50	1.25
	Hulk Hogan		
20	Jim Neidhart	.10	.25
	Dynamite Kid		
21	Davey Boy Smith	.12	.30
	Danny Davis		
22	Slick	.10	.25
	Tito Santana		
23	Stadium Scene	.10	.25
24	Honky Tonk Man	.15	.40
	Jake The Snake Roberts		
25	Brutus The Barber Beefcake	.12	.30
	Adrian Adonis		
26	Hulk Hogan	.50	1.25
	Andre the Giant		
27	Hulk Hogan	.50	1.25
	Andre the Giant		
28	Hulk Hogan	.50	1.25
	Andre the Giant		
29	Million Dollar Man	.20	.50
	Macho Man Randy Savage		
30	Million Dollar Man	.20	.50
	Macho Man Randy Savage		
31	Million Dollar Man	.20	.50
	Macho Man Randy Savage		
32	Hulk Hogan	.50	1.25
	Macho Man Randy Savage		
33	Hulk Hogan	.50	1.25
	Macho Man Randy Savage		
34	Hulk Hogan	.50	1.25
	Andre the Giant		
35	Hulk Hogan	.50	1.25
	Andre the Giant		
36	Hulk Hogan	.50	1.25
	Andre the Giant		
37	Hulk Hogan	.50	1.25
	Andre the Giant		
38	Hulk Hogan	.50	1.25
	Andre the Giant		
39	Hulk Hogan	.50	1.25
	Andre the Giant		
40	Hulk Hogan	.50	1.25
41	Hulk Hogan	.50	1.25
42	Brutus The Barber Beefcake	.12	.30
43	Brutus The Barber Beefcake	.12	.30
	Honky Tonk Man		
44	Honky Tonk Man	.12	.30
	Brutus The Barber Beefcake		
45	Rick Martel	.10	.25
	Demolition		
46	Demolition	.10	.25
	Strike Force		
47	Ravishing Rick Rude	.15	.40
	Jake The Snake Roberts		
48	Hercules	.12	.30
	Ultimate Warrior		
49	The Hammer	.20	.50
	Macho Man Randy Savage		
50	The Hammer	.20	.50
	Macho Man Randy Savage		
51	Hulk Hogan	.50	1.25
52	Million Dollar Man	.40	1.00
	Virgil/Andre the Giant		
53	Hulk Hogan	.50	1.25
	Macho Man Randy Savage		
54	Macho Man Randy Savage	.20	.50
	Akeem		
55	Ring Scene	.10	.25
56	Bobby The Brain Heenan	.10	.25
	Koko B. Ware		
57	Battle Royal	.10	.25
58	Million Dollar Man	.12	.30
	Hacksaw Jim Duggan		
59	Dino Bravo	.10	.25
	Don Muraco		
60	Jake The Snake Roberts	.15	.40
	Rick Rude		
61	Hercules	.12	.30
	Ultimate Warrior		
62	Jake The Snake Roberts	.15	.40
	Rick Rude		
63	Hercules	.12	.30
	Ultimate Warrior		
64	Hercules	.12	.30
	Ultimate Warrior		
65	Hercules	.12	.30
	Ultimate Warrior		
66	Mr. Fuji	.10	.25
	Ax		
67	Demolition	.10	.25
	Tito Santana		
68	Rick Martel	.10	.25
	Smash		
69	Honky Tonk Man	.12	.30
	Brutus The Barber Beefcake		
70	Bret Hit Man Hart	.12	.30
	Bad News Brown		
71	Bret Hit Man Hart	.12	.30
	Bad News Brown		
72	Bret Hit Man Hart	.12	.30
	Bad News Brown		
73	Bad News Brown	.10	.25
74	Power of Pain	.10	.25
	Demolition		
75	Million Dollar Man	.12	.30
	Virgil		
76	Mr. Fuji	.10	.25
	Ax		
77	Demolition	.10	.25
78	Andre the Giant	.40	1.00
	Jake The Snake Roberts		
79	Bret Hit Man Hart	.12	.30
	Honky Tonk Man		
80	Brooklyn Brawler	.10	.25
81	King Haku	.10	.25
	Hercules		
82	King Haku	.10	.25
	Hercules		
83	Million Dollar Man	.12	.30
	Brutus The Barber Beefcake		
84	Dino Bravo	.10	.25
	Ronnie Garvin		
85	Bad News Brown	.12	.30
	Hacksaw Jim Duggan		
86	Bad News Brown	.12	.30
	Hacksaw Jim Duggan		
87	Bret Hit Man Hart	.12	.30
	Greg The Hammer Valentine		
88	Bret Hit Man Hart	.12	.30
	Honky Tonk Man		
89	Mr. Perfect	.12	.30
	Blue Blazer		
90	Bobby The Brain Heenan	.12	.30
91	Bushwhackers	.10	.25
	Rougeau Brothers		
92	Bushwhackers	.10	.25
	Rougeau Brothers		
93	Dino Bravo	.10	.25
	Ronnie Garvin		
94	Hulk Hogan	.50	1.25
	Macho Man Randy Savage		
95	Hulk Hogan	.50	1.25
	Macho Man Randy Savage		
96	Hulk Hogan	.50	1.25
	Macho Man Randy Savage		
97	Akeem	.15	.40
	Shawn Michaels		
98	The Rockers	.12	.30
	Akeem		
99	Hulk Hogan	.50	1.25
	Macho Man Randy Savage		
100	Hulk Hogan	.50	1.25
	Macho Man Randy Savage		
101	Hulk Hogan	.50	1.25
	Macho Man Randy Savage		
102	Hulk Hogan	.50	1.25
	Macho Man Randy Savage		
103	Hulk Hogan	.50	1.25
	Macho Man Randy Savage		
104	Ravishing Rick Rude	.12	.30
	Ultimate Warrior		
105	Ravishing Rick Rude	.12	.30
	Ultimate Warrior		
106	The Ultimate Warrior	.12	.30
107	Hulk Hogan	.50	1.25
	Macho Man Randy Savage		
108	Marty Jannetty	.10	.25
	Akeem		
109	Brutus The Barber Beefcake	.12	.30
	Virgil		
110	Ravishing Rick Rude	.12	.30
	Ultimate Warrior		
111	Ravishing Rick Rude	.12	.30
	Ultimate Warrior		
112	Ravishing Rick Rude	.12	.30
	Ultimate Warrior		
113	Haku	.40	1.00
	Andre the Giant		
114	Million Dollar Man	.15	.40
	Jake The Snake Roberts		
115	Barbarian	.10	.25
	Tito Santana		
116	Rick Martel	.10	.25
	Koko B. Ware		
117	Million Dollar Man Ted DiBiase	.12	.30
118	Hacksaw Jim Duggan	.12	.30
	Bravo		
119	Hacksaw Jim Duggan	.12	.30
	Bravo		
120	Hacksaw Jim Duggan	.12	.30
	Bravo		
121	Macho King	.10	.25
	Dusty Rhodes		
122	American Dream	.15	.40
	Sapphire/Miss Elizabeth		
123	Macho Man Randy Savage	.20	.50
124	Hart Foundation	.12	.30
125	Dusty Rhodes	.20	.50
	Macho Man Randy Savage		
126	American Dream	.12	.30
	Sapphire/Queen Sherri		
127	Bad News	.20	.50
	Rowdy Roddy Piper		
128	Brutus The Barber Beefcake	.12	.30
	Genius		
129	Sato	.10	.25
	Tanaka/Marty Jannetty		
130	Big Boss Man	.10	.25
	Akeem		
131	Sato	.15	.40
	Shawn Michaels		
132	Hulk Hogan	.50	1.25
	Ultimate Warrior		
133	Hulk Hogan	.50	1.25
	Ultimate Warrior		
134	Hulk Hogan	.50	1.25
	Ultimate Warrior		
135	Hulk Hogan	.50	1.25
	Immortal One		
136	The Ultimate Warrior	.12	.30
137	Rhythm and Blues	.10	.25
138	Ravishing Rick Rude	.15	.40
	Superfly Jimmy Snuka		
139	Rhythm and Blues	.12	.30
	Jimmy Hart		
140	Demolition	.10	.25
141	Andre the Giant	.40	1.00
	Bobby Heenan		
142	Haku	.10	.25
	Smash		
143	Smash	.10	.25
	Haku/Ax		
144	Brutus The Barber Beefcake	.12	.30
	Mr.Perfect		
145	Hulk Hogan	.50	1.25
	Ultimate Warrior		
146	Brutus The Barber Beefcake	.12	.30
147	The Ultimate Warrior	.12	.30
148	Bushwhackers	.10	.25
149	The Rockers	.12	.30
150	Dusty Rhodes	.10	.25

1991 Classic WWF Promos

NNO Brutus The Barber Beefcake
NNO The Bushwhackers
NNO Hulk Hogan
NNO Macho King Randy Savage
NNO Ultimate Warrior

1991 Classic WWF Superstars

	COMPLETE SET (150)	10.00	25.00
	COMPLETE FACTORY SET (150)		
	UNOPENED BOX		
	UNOPENED PACK (12 CARDS)		
	*EUROPEAN: SAME VALUE		
1	Hulk Hogan	.50	1.25
2	Ultimate Warrior	.30	.75
3	Texas Tornado	.12	.30
4	Jake The Snake Roberts	.20	.50
5	Big Boss Man	.10	.25
6	Hacksaw Jim Duggan	.12	.30
7	Davey Boy Smith	.12	.30
8	The Model Rick Martel	.10	.25
9	Million Dollar Man Ted DiBiase	.12	.30
10	Bobby Heenan	.12	.30
11	Rockers	.15	.40
12	Legion of Doom	.12	.30
13	Tugboat	.10	.25
14	Power & Glory	.10	.25

#				#			
15	Bushwackers	.10	.25	83	Bushwackers	.10	.25
16	Macho King Randy Savage	.30	.75	84	Macho King Randy Savage	.30	.75
17	Koko B. Ware	.10	.25	85	General Adnan	.10	.25
18	Superfly Jimmy Snuka	.15	.40	86	The Mountie	.10	.25
19	Davey Boy Smith	.12	.30	87	Rowdy Roddy Piper	.25	.60
20	Sensational Queen Sherri	.12	.30	88	Undertaker	.40	1.00
21	Barbarian	.10	.25	89	Mr. Perfect	.15	.40
22	Virgil	.10	.25	90	Sgt. Slaughter	.15	.40
23	Nasty Boys	.10	.25	91	Hulk Hogan	.50	1.25
24	Million Dollar Man Ted DiBiase	.12	.30	92	Earthquake	.10	.25
25	Big Boss Man	.10	.25	93	Paul Bearer	.12	.30
26	Sgt. Slaughter	.15	.40	94	Koko B. Ware	.10	.25
27	Barbarian	.10	.25	95	Superfly Jimmy Snuka	.15	.40
28	Nasty Boys	.10	.25	96	Sensational Queen Sherri	.12	.30
29	Mr. Perfect	.15	.40	97	Sgt. Slaughter	.15	.40
30	Undertaker	.40	1.00	98	Rowdy Roddy Piper	.25	.60
31	Rowdy Roddy Piper	.25	.60	99	Hulk Hogan	.50	1.25
32	The Mountie	.10	.25	100	Ultimate Warrior	.30	.75
33	Davey Boy Smith	.12	.30	101	Texas Tornado	.12	.30
34	General Adnan	.10	.25	102	The Model Rick Martel	.10	.25
35	Hulk Hogan	.50	1.25	103	Earthquake	.10	.25
36	Ultimate Warrior	.30	.75	104	Legion of Doom	.12	.30
37	Texas Tornado	.12	.30	105	Bret Hart	.12	.30
38	Hacksaw Jim Duggan	.12	.30	106	Undertaker	.40	1.00
39	Jake The Snake Roberts	.20	.50	107	Mr. Perfect	.15	.40
40	Hulk Hogan	.50	1.25	108	Sgt. Slaughter w/General Adnan	.15	.40
41	The Model Rick Martel	.10	.25	109	Big Boss Man	.10	.25
42	Earthquake	.10	.25	110	Million Dollar Man Ted DiBiase	.12	.30
43	Jimmy Hart	.15	.40	111	Hulk Hogan	.50	1.25
44	Rockers	.15	.40	112	Legion Of Doom	.12	.30
45	Slick	.10	.25	113	Mr. Perfect	.15	.40
46	Legion of Doom	.12	.30	114	Ultimate Warrior	.30	.75
47	Mr. Fuji	.10	.25	115	Big Boss Man	.10	.25
48	Tugboat	.10	.25	116	Hacksaw Jim Duggan	.12	.30
49	Power & Glory	.10	.25	117	Power & Glory w/Slick	.10	.25
50	Bushwackers	.10	.25	118	Macho King Randy Savage	.30	.75
51	Macho King Randy Savage	.30	.75	119	Bushwackers	.10	.25
52	Hulk Hogan	.50	1.25	120	Tugboat	.10	.25
53	Koko B. Ware	.10	.25	121	Mr. Perfect	.15	.40
54	Superfly Jimmy Snuka	.15	.40	122	Barbarian	.10	.25
55	Haku	.10	.25	123	Hulk Hogan	.50	1.25
56	Sensational Queen Sherri	.12	.30	124	Ultimate Warrior	.30	.75
57	Nasty Boys	.10	.25	125	Big Boss Man	.10	.25
58	Virgil	.10	.25	126	Hacksaw Jim Duggan	.12	.30
59	Million Dollar Man Ted DiBiase	.12	.30	127	Jake The Snake Roberts	.20	.50
60	Big Boss Man	.10	.25	128	The Model Rick Martel	.10	.25
61	Sgt. Slaughter	.15	.40	129	The Dragon Ricky Steamboat	.12	.30
62	Barbarian	.10	.25	130	Mr. Perfect	.15	.40
63	Mr. Perfect	.15	.40	131	Haku	.10	.25
64	Undertaker	.40	1.00	132	Million Dollar Man Ted DiBiase	.12	.30
65	Rowdy Roddy Piper	.25	.60	133	Texas Tornado	.12	.30
66	The Mountie	.10	.25	134	Macho King Randy Savage	.30	.75
67	General Adnan	.10	.25	135	Macho King Randy Savage	.30	.75
68	The Dragon Ricky Steamboat	.12	.30	136	Legion of Doom	.12	.30
69	Hulk Hogan	.50	1.25	137	Rockers	.15	.40
70	Ultimate Warrior	.30	.75	138	Earthquake	.10	.25
71	Texas Tornado	.12	.30	139	Superfly Jimmy Snuka	.15	.40
72	Hacksaw Jim Duggan	.12	.30	140	Hulk Hogan	.50	1.25
73	Jake The Snake Roberts	.20	.50	141	The Dragon Ricky Steamboat	.12	.30
74	The Model Rick Martel	.10	.25	142	Sgt. Slaughter	.15	.40
75	Earthquake	.10	.25	143	Texas Tornado	.12	.30
76	Mr. Fuji	.10	.25	144	Million Dollar Man Ted DiBiase	.12	.30
77	Jimmy Hart	.15	.40	145	Earthquake	.10	.25
78	Rockers	.15	.40	146	Legion of Doom	.12	.30
79	Legion of Doom	.12	.30	147	Rockers	.15	.40
80	Tugboat	.10	.25	148	Macho King Randy Savage	.30	.75
81	Paul Roma	.10	.25	149	Earthquake	.10	.25
82	Power & Glory	.10	.25	150	The Model Rick Martel	.10	.25

1994 Coliseum Video WWF Akklaim Strategy Tips

COMPLETE SET (4)		5.00	12.00
NNO	Doink	2.00	5.00
NNO	Luna Vachon	2.00	5.00
NNO	Shawn Michaels	2.50	6.00
NNO	Yokozuna	2.00	5.00

1994 Coliseum Video WWF Bret Hart

COMPLETE SET (5)		2.50	6.00
1	Bret Hitman Hart	.75	2.00
2	Bret Hitman Hart	.75	2.00
3	Bret Hitman Hart	.75	2.00
4	Bret Hitman Hart	.75	2.00
5	Bret Hitman Hart	.75	2.00

1993 Coliseum Video WWF Collectors Cards

COMPLETE SET (9)		10.00	25.00
COLISEUM VIDEO RENTAL EXCLUSIVE			
1	Hulk Hogan/Mr. T	2.50	6.00
2	King Kong Bundy/Hulk Hogan	2.50	6.00
3	Andre The Giant/Hulk Hogan	2.00	5.00
4	Randy Savage/Miss Elizabeth	2.00	5.00
5	Randy Savage/Hulk Hogan	4.00	10.00
6	Ultimate Warrior	1.50	4.00
7	Sgt. Slaughter/Hulk Hogan	2.00	5.00
8	Macho Man Randy Savage	1.50	4.00
9	Wrestlemania IX	1.25	3.00

1993 Coliseum Video WWF Lenticular

COMPLETE SET (5)	
NNO	Bret Hit Man Hart
NNO	Hulk Hogan
NNO	Mr. Perfect
NNO	Tatanka
NNO	The Undertaker

1991 Coliseum Video WWF Superstar Collectors Stamps

COMPLETE SET (12)	
1	Big Boss Man
2	Bret Hit Man Hart
3	Hulk Hogan
4	Kamala
5	Macho Man Randy Savage
6	Mr. Perfect
7	Nasty Boys
8	Razor Ramon
9	Shawn Michaels
10	Steiner Brothers
11	Tatanka
12	Undertaker

1993 Coliseum Video WWF Superstar Postcards

COMPLETE SET (6)	
1	Bret Hit Man Hart
2	Crush
3	Hulk Hogan
4	Macho Man Randy Savage
5	Steiner Brothers
6	Undertaker

2004 Comic Images WWE Raw Deal Armageddon

#			
1	Flying Head Scissors TB C	.12	.25
2	Double Axe Handle TB C	.12	.25
3	Leg Drop TB U	.50	1.00
4	Splash TB U	.50	1.00
5	Flying Clothesline TB R	2.00	4.00
6	Moonsault TB R	2.00	4.00
7	Chump Punch C	.12	.25
8	Slap C	.12	.25
9	Super Punch C	.12	.25
10	Struck by a Kendo Stick TB C	.12	.25
11	Shoulder Thrust U	.50	1.00
12	Solarplex Knife Chop U	.50	1.00
13	Cold-Cocked U	.50	1.00
14	Ensugiri TB U	.50	1.00
15	Knee Lift TB R	2.00	4.00
16	Whirling Backhand R	2.00	4.00
17	European Uppercut R	2.00	4.00
18	Flurry of Strikes R	2.00	4.00
19	Throw C	.12	.25
20	Inverse Atomic Drop TB C	.12	.25
21	Rib Breaker TB C	.12	.25
22	Back Breaker TB C	.12	.25
23	Double Leg Takedown TB U	.50	1.00
24	Fireman's Carry TB U	.50	1.00
25	Toss U	.50	1.00
26	Leg Drag TB U	.50	1.00
27	Brainbuster TB R	2.00	4.00
28	Airplane Spin TB R	2.00	4.00
29	Power Slam TB R	2.00	4.00
30	Atomic Driver R	2.00	4.00
31	Short Arm Hammerlock TB C	.12	.25
32	Cranial Crunch C	.12	.25
33	Chin Lock TB C	.12	.25
34	Go-Behind C	.12	.25
35	Grab U	.50	1.00
36	Head Vise TB U	.50	1.00
37	Chicken Wing TB U	.50	1.00
38	Asphyxiater U	.50	1.00
39	Rest Hold R	2.00	4.00
40	Abdominal Stretch TB R	2.00	4.00
41	STF TB R	2.00	4.00
42	Figure Four Leg Lock TB R	2.00	4.00
43	Anything and Hate It C	.12	.25
44	I Gotta Say, Out of Play U	.50	1.00
45	Raw and Ready R	2.00	4.00
46	Ask Yourself... C	.12	.25
47	I Got That, Too C	.12	.25
48	Hmmmm Don't Think... TB C	.12	.25
49	Back in Style C	.12	.25
50	From the Middle Turnbuckle C	.12	.25
51	Throw Opponent Out... TB C	.12	.25
52	From the Top Rope TB C	.12	.25
53	I'm Desperate C	.12	.25
54	J.R. Style Action U	.50	1.00
55	Volley This U	.50	1.00
56	Flawless Execution U	.50	1.00
57	Great Power Brawl TB U	.50	1.00
58	The Rub U	.50	1.00
59	Egomaniacal U	.50	1.00
60	It's Not Always the Charisma U	.50	1.00
61	Throwback Represent U	.50	1.00
62	Calculated Revenge R	2.00	4.00
63	The Show Must Go On R	2.00	4.00
64	I'm Giving You a Chance R	2.00	4.00
65	Personal Vendetta R	2.00	4.00
66	I Won't Stop R	2.00	4.00

67	Defensive Style TB R	2.00	4.00
68	Take It Back R	2.00	4.00
69	The Switch R	2.00	4.00
70	Like a Bat Out of Hell R	2.00	4.00
71	Boston, Massachusetts C	.12	.25
72	I Want to Play the Game C	.12	.25
73	Old School Antics C	.12	.25
74	San Diego, California C	.12	.25
75	Unbreakable Chain C	.12	.25
76	All Alone in the Night U	.50	1.00
77	Managed by William Regal U	.50	1.00
78	New Orleans, Louisiana U	.50	1.00
79	Buried Alive Match U	.50	1.00
80	Washington, DC U	.50	1.00
81	Little Rock, Arkansas R	2.00	4.00
82	Managed by the Coach R	2.00	4.00
83	Evening Gown Match R	2.00	4.00
84	Singapore City, Singapore R	2.00	4.00
85	Clear the Way C	.12	.25
86	Old-Fashioned Lock-Up C	.12	.25
87	Pop You One C	.12	.25
88	Atomic Bear Hug C	.12	.25
89	Here Comes the Coach C	.12	.25
90	Out of Control U	.50	1.00
91	You'll Really Be Stunned U	.50	1.00
92	The Darkness Before the Dawn U	.50	1.00
93	Goodnight, Everybody U	.50	1.00
94	Sometimes You Need to... U	.50	1.00
95	Here Comes the Headache R	2.00	4.00
96	Suicide Plancha TB R	2.00	4.00
97	I'm Making This Up As I Go Along R	2.00	4.00
98	It's All For My Fans R	2.00	4.00
99	Anybody Can Be King... R	2.00	4.00
100	Babe of the Year EX		
101	Give Me a Little UR	7.50	15.00
102	Time to Catch My Breath UR	7.50	15.00
103	Babe Buster EX		
104	Tyson Interferes EX		
105	Keys to the City EX		
106	John Bradshaw Layfield EX		
107	Ten Gallon Hat UR	7.50	15.00
108	JBL's Limo UR	7.50	15.00
109	Work Harder, Work Smarter EX		
110	You Forgot About Orlando... EX		
111	JBL's Clothesline from Hell EX		
112	The Phenom EX		
113	The Urn UR	7.50	15.00
114	Takin' Care of Business UR	7.50	15.00
115	The Dead Will Rise Again EX		
116	There is No Forgiveness... EX		
117	The Deadman is Alive EX		
118	Randy Orton EX		
119	The Legend Killer UR	7.50	15.00
120	RKO UR	7.50	15.00
121	Youngest Champion in WWE... EX		
122	Third Generation Superstar EX		
123	Overdrive EX		
124	Shane O'Mac EX		
125	Mean Streets of Greenwich, CT UR	7.50	15.00
126	Coast to Coast UR	7.50	15.00
127	Mean Streets Silver Spoon EX		
128	Here's Where the Buck Stops EX		
129	Leap of Faith EX		
130	Shelton Benjamin EX		
131	World's Greatest Upset... UR	7.50	15.00
132	T-Bone Exploder Suplex UR	7.50	15.00
133	Ain't No Stopping Me Now EX		
134	Shelton's Spinning Heel Kick EX		
135	Shelton's Splash EX		
136	Eugene PR		
137	I'm Special UR	7.50	15.00
138	Eugening Up PR		
139	The Jacket's Coming Off PR		
140	The Pride of the Family PR		
141	The Dream Lives On PR		
142	Rene Dupree PR		
143	Rene's Elbow Drop UR	7.50	15.00
144	Managed by Fifi PR		
145	The French Tickler PR		
146	Fifi Interferes PR		
147	The French Neck Breaker PR		
148	Cerebral Spray PR		
149	Pago Pago, American Samoa PR		
150	Out of the Hellfire PR		
151	Don't You Wish You Were Me? PR		
152	For Real PR		
153	El Paso, Texas PR		
154	Angle's Leg Bar PR		
155	Dudleyville, USA PR		
156	You're Just a Puppet PR		
157	Captain Charisma Strikes PR		
158	I Can Slap a Tornado PR		
159	The Hog Log PR		
160	A Less Traveled Road PR		
161	Step Over Heel Kick PR		
162	I Ain't No Minor Leaguer PR		
163	People Like Us Are Just Born... PR		
164	The Best Thing Going Today PR		
165	Double Chop PR		
166	Superhero in Training PR		
167	Crossing Borders PR		
168	The Legend Lives On PR		
169	Throwback PR		
170	Taunt the Crowd PR		
171	Why Can't We Just Dance? UR	7.50	15.00
172	The Inmates Aren't Running... UR	7.50	15.00
173	It's Not a Wig UR	7.50	15.00
174	The Cena Throwback UR	7.50	15.00
175	A Welcome Distraction UR	7.50	15.00
176	Victoria's Secret UR	7.50	15.00
177	Drastic Times... UR	7.50	15.00
178	If You Want to Play... UR	7.50	15.00
179	Master Manipulator UR	7.50	15.00
180	Armageddon is Upon Us UR	7.50	15.00
181	Vinny Mac Attack UR	7.50	15.00

2004 Comic Images WWE Raw Deal Divas Overload

1	Show and Go C	.12	.25
2	Diving Bulldog U	.50	1.00
3	Suicide Dive R	2.00	4.00
4	Girly Punch C	.12	.25
5	Boot Lace C	.12	.25
6	Chop Block C	.12	.25
7	Elbow Smash C	.12	.25
8	Jab U	.50	1.00
9	Forearm Uppercut U	.50	1.00
10	Ax Kick U	.50	1.00
11	Spinning Clothesline U	.50	1.00
12	Chick Kick R	2.00	4.00
13	Double Clothesline Takedown R	2.00	4.00
14	Atomic Lariat R	2.00	4.00
15	Hurricane Clothesline R	2.00	4.00
16	Chest Lock Drop C	.12	.25
17	Wheelbarrow Slam C	.12	.25
18	Running Spinebuster U	.50	1.00
19	Gut Buster On Top Rope U	.50	1.00
20	Top Rope Toss R	2.00	4.00
21	Reverse Fall-away Slam R	2.00	4.00
22	Modified Clutch Onto Opponent C	.12	.25
23	Arm Breaker C	.12	.25
24	Unorthodox Wrist Lock U	.50	1.00
25	Modified Bow and Arrow U	.50	1.00
26	Front Chancery R	2.00	4.00
27	Lady's Grapevine R	2.00	4.00
28	Girl on Girl Action C	.12	.25
29	Some Gals Don't Get Any Action C	.12	.25
30	Overshot Your Mark U	.50	1.00
31	Reach for the Ropes U	.50	1.00
32	Too Many Rules... R	2.00	4.00
33	You Fight Like a Woman R	2.00	4.00
34	Let's Wrestle Already C	.12	.25
35	No Matching Tights C	.12	.25
36	Don't Be Shy C	.12	.25
37	It's Time I Made Some Changes C	.12	.25
38	Lousy Foot Work C	.12	.25
39	Recover Again C	.12	.25
40	Name of the Game... C	.12	.25
41	I've Got a Leg Up On You C	.12	.25
42	I've Got a Nice Bottom U	.50	1.00
43	I'll Take a Shot U	.50	1.00
44	The Hubbub Backstage U	.50	1.00
45	Get a Look at These U	.50	1.00
46	So Solly So Sorey U	.50	1.00
47	Sump'tin' Be Started U	.50	1.00
48	This Diva's Got Claws U	.50	1.00
49	Shake My Hand, Boy U	.50	1.00
50	My New Gimmick R	2.00	4.00
51	Puppy Love R	2.00	4.00
52	What Are You Gawking At? R	2.00	4.00
53	Where's the Payoff? R	2.00	4.00
54	Don't Cross the Boss R	2.00	4.00
55	Twisted Smile R	2.00	4.00
56	Tap Tap Tap, You Sonofa- R	2.00	4.00
57	If You're Not Cheating... R	2.00	4.00
58	Asset Retrieval C	.12	.25
59	Not Today, Cupcake C	.12	.25
60	I'm Always on Top C	.12	.25
61	Distractingly Divalicious C	.12	.25
62	You Should Cover Your Eyes C	.12	.25
63	Old School Psychology C	.12	.25
64	Back to Basics U	.50	1.00
65	Falls Count Anywhere Match U	.50	1.00
66	Skirt vs. Skirt Match U	.50	1.00
67	Dare to Take a Challenge U	.50	1.00
68	Perennial Fan Favorites U	.50	1.00
69	Run the Gauntlet U	.50	1.00
70	Backstage Interview with Terri R	2.00	4.00
71	I've Had More Championships... R	2.00	4.00
72	I'm Gonna Break You R	2.00	4.00
73	Rules Were Meant to be Broken R	2.00	4.00
74	Managed by Miss Jackie R	2.00	4.00
75	Managed by Theodore Long R	2.00	4.00
76	Took That on the Chin C	.12	.25
77	Skirt the Issue C	.12	.25
78	Get the Tables C	.12	.25
79	Teaser Mode C	.12	.25
80	Victory Roll C	.12	.25
81	I'm Trying Not to Lose... U	.50	1.00
82	Panic Assault U	.50	1.00
83	Panic Grab U	.50	1.00
84	Panic Throw U	.50	1.00
85	This Is Going Nowhere Fast U	.50	1.00
86	That's Gonna Leave a Mark R	2.00	4.00
87	It Doesn't Stop R	2.00	4.00
88	Divas Overload R	2.00	4.00
89	It's Over R	2.00	4.00
90	Reverse 180-Degree Chair Shot R	2.00	4.00
91	Goldberg EX		
92	Goooooolllllddddd-berg UR	7.50	15.00
93	Goldberg's Jackhammer UR	7.50	15.00
94	Who's Next? EX		
95	Believe the Hype EX		
96	Goldberg's Spear EX		
97	Stacy Keibler EX		
98	Straddle the Ropes UR	7.50	15.00
99	Superior Leg Work UR	7.50	15.00
100	Test or Freakzilla? EX		
101	Pump Me Up EX		
102	I Know How to Use Them EX		
103	Gail Kim and Molly Holly EX		
104	Change Reality UR	7.50	15.00
105	Gail's Hurricanrana UR	7.50	15.00
106	Wake Up EX		
107	Look Around EX		
108	Molly-Go-Round EX		
109	John Cena EX		
110	Yo Kill da Beat UR	7.50	15.00
111	F-U UR	7.50	15.00
112	You Can't See Me EX		
113	Word Life EX		
114	I'm Gonna Teach You... EX		
115	Sable EX		
116	Sable-licious UR	7.50	15.00
117	And the Men that Come... UR	7.50	15.00
118	APA or A-Train? EX		
119	For the Women that Want... EX		
120	Sable Bomb EX		
121	Torrie Wilson EX		
122	WWE Centerfold of the Year UR	7.50	15.00
123	Torrie's DDT UR	7.50	15.00
124	Does This Look Good on Me? EX		
125	Strike a Pose EX		
126	The Boise Beauty EX		
127	Victoria PR		
128	Widow's Peak UR	7.50	15.00
129	Managed by Stevie Richards PR		
130	All the Things She Said PR		
131	Yes, I've Lost My Mind PR		
132	Stevie Interferes PR		
133	Nidia PR		
134	The Special Kiss UR	7.50	15.00
135	Managed by Jamie Noble PR		
136	Trailer Park Slap PR		
137	Drop Dead Gorgeous PR		
138	Jamie Noble Interferes PR		
139	Do You Want a Hug? PR		
140	You're Gonna Pay PR		
141	The Peep's Champ PR		
142	A Beating You'll Never Forget PR		
143	Unmasked Vengeance PR		
144	Highlight Reel PR		
145	Rikishi's Superkick PR		
146	Wrestling with a Broken... PR		
147	Benoit's German Suplex PR		
148	Gory Special PR		
149	That One Thing PR		
150	Beatings from Dudleyville PR		
151	Side Effect PR		
152	Showdown PR		
153	Mr. Monday Night PR		
154	Houston Hangover PR		

78	Holla If Ya Hear Me UR	7.50	15.00
79	Genetic Freak Push-ups UR	7.50	15.00
80	Freakzilla Says... EX		
81	All I Care About Are My... EX		
82	The Big, Bad Booty Daddy... EX		
83	The Rattlesnake EX		
84	The Bionic Redneck UR	7.50	15.00
85	Gimme a Hell Yeah UR	7.50	15.00
86	Stomp a Mudhole EX		
87	Don't Trust Nobody EX		
88	Walk It Dry EX		
89	Shawn Michaels EX		
90	The Icon, The Showstoppa... UR	7.50	15.00
91	Sweet Chin Music UR	7.50	15.00
92	Don't Hunt What You Can't Kill EX		
93	Top Rope Elbow Drop EX		
94	The Heart Break Kid EX		
95	The Crippler EX		
96	There's No Holding Me Back UR	7.50	15.00
97	Toothless Aggression UR	7.50	15.00
98	Cripple Opponent EX		
99	Rabid Attack in the Corner EX		
100	Surprise Drop Kick EX		
101	Los Guerreros EX		
102	We Lie, We Cheat, We Steal UR	7.50	15.00
103	Chavo's Inverted Powerbomb UR	7.50	15.00
104	Cheat 2 Win EX		
105	Tu Locas, Ese You Crazy, Man EX		
106	Lasso from El Paso EX		
107	Team Angle EX		
108	Collegiate Champions UR	7.50	15.00
109	Leapfrog Stun Gun UR	7.50	15.00
110	Submit EX		
111	It's All About the Benjamins EX		
112	The Haas of Pain EX		
113	Test PR		
114	Test Drive UR	7.50	15.00
115	I Love My Testicles PR		
116	Stacy Keibler, Marketing... PR		
117	Test's Pump Handle Slam PR		
118	Test's Running Boot PR		
119	Rhyno PR		
120	GORE GORE GORE UR	7.50	15.00
121	Extreme Warfare PR		
122	Rhyno's Garbage Can PR		
123	The Manbeast PR		
124	Rhyno Stampede PR		
125	Big Evil - Red Devil PR		
126	Screw the Rules PR		
127	Get Ready... PR		
128	Big Freak'n Powerslam PR		
129	I'm the King of the World PR		
130	Makin' a Difference PR		
131	Dudleyz3 PR		
132	You're a Human Vacuum... PR		
133	I Ain't Not No Sucka Neitha PR		
134	Version 1.0 PR		
135	X-treme Sendoff PR		
136	You Can't Manhandle... PR		
137	Dude Whatever PR		
138	Yo Dawg, Respect... PR		
139	Proper Planning Prevents... PR		
140	I Live for My Hulkamaniacs UR	7.50	15.00
141	You're Going to Space Mountain UR	7.50	15.00
142A	X-treme Hedonism - A Image UR	7.50	15.00
142B	X-treme Hedonism - B Image UR	7.50	15.00
143	No Gimmicks Needed UR	7.50	15.00
144	Double Face Kick UR	7.50	15.00

145	Shining Wizard Kick UR	7.50	15.00
146	Electrifying UR	7.50	15.00
147	Here Comes the Pain UR	7.50	15.00
148	West Coast Bronco Buster UR	7.50	15.00
149	3 Minutes and We're Out UR	7.50	15.00
150	Nidia Interferes UR	7.50	15.00

2006 Comic Images WWE Raw Deal
No Way Out

1	Technical Stomp C	.12	.25
2	Shoot Aerial 360-Degree Kick U	.50	1.00
3	Precision Knee Drop R	2.00	4.00
4	Dynamic Punch C	.12	.25
5	Dynamic Hook C	.12	.25
6	Straight Clothesline C	.12	.25
7	Thrust Kick C	.12	.25
8	Shoot Punch U	.50	1.00
9	Dynamic Forearm U	.50	1.00
10	Technical Clothesline U	.50	1.00
11	Dynamic Knee Lift U	.50	1.00
12	Precision Kick U	.50	1.00
13	Blindside Tornado Strike R	2.00	4.00
14	Whirling Elbow R	2.00	4.00
15	Dynamic Lariat R	2.00	4.00
16	Punch After Punch R	2.00	4.00
17	Snap DDT C	.12	.25
18	Dynamic Throw C	.12	.25
19	Dynamic Drop C	.12	.25
20	Delayed Atomic Drop C	.12	.25
21	Blindside Beal Toss U	.50	1.00
22	Rolling Neck Breaker U	.50	1.00
23	Dynamic Takedown U	.50	1.00
24	Dynamic Slam U	.50	1.00
25	Precision Suplex U	.50	1.00
26	Dynamic Driver R	2.00	4.00
27	Technical Power Bomb R	2.00	4.00
28	Vertical Power Bomb R	2.00	4.00
29	Atomic Power Slam R	2.00	4.00
30	Dynamic Arm Bar C	.12	.25
31	Arm Twist C	.12	.25
32	Dynamic Headlock C	.12	.25
33	Blindside Abdominal Stretch C	.12	.25
34	Arm Wrench U	.50	1.00
35	Vise Lock U	.50	1.00
36	Dynamic Stretch U	.50	1.00
37	Dynamic Bear Hug U	.50	1.00
38	Precision Sleeper U	.50	1.00
39	Technical Crab R	2.00	4.00
40	Fujiwara Arm Bar R	2.00	4.00
41	Dynamic Figure Four R	2.00	4.00
42	Atomic Body Lock R	2.00	4.00
43	It's Great To Be Back Here In... C	.12	.25
44	Just What the Game Needs C	.12	.25
45	The Coach Says... U	.50	1.00
46	Once Again, Kissing Up... R	2.00	4.00
47	You Can't Cheat an Honest Man... R	2.00	4.00
48	Contrary to Popular Opinion C	.12	.25
49	Between the Ropes C	.12	.25
50	Over the Ropes C	.12	.25
51	Painfully Obvious Precision C	.12	.25
52	...And the Crowd Roars U	.50	1.00
53	By Any Means Necessary U	.50	1.00
54	Shoot Action R	2.00	4.00
55	Ashley: Pretty Punk R	2.00	4.00
56	Mickie: Fervent Fanatic R	2.00	4.00
57	Kick Out! R	2.00	4.00
58	Givin' Íem High Fives C	.12	.25
59	In The Interest Of Fairness C	.12	.25

60	Technically Sound & Brutal C	.12	.25
61	I Have A Major Announcement U	.50	1.00
62	You Will Witness History U	.50	1.00
63	There Is No Escape U	.50	1.00
64	Denville, New Jersey R	2.00	4.00
65	WWE Homecoming R	2.00	4.00
66	That's Value! R	2.00	4.00
67	Go For the Cover! C	.12	.25
68	Tormented Tomfoolery C	.12	.25
69	A Punch That'll Take... C	.12	.25
70	Precision Personified U	.50	1.00
71	Shoot Counter U	.50	1.00
72	Blindsided Rage U	.50	1.00
73	A Great Deal Of Confusion R	2.00	4.00
74	Overwhelming Crowd Support R	2.00	4.00
75	Volley Finisher R	2.00	4.00
76	Carlito EX		
77	Carlito's Apple UR	7.50	15.00
78	Carlito's Cabana UR	7.50	15.00
79	I Spit In the Face Of... EX		
80	...People Who Don't Want... EX		
81	Carlito's Way DDT EX		
82	Jake "the Snake" EX		
83	Lucifer UR	7.50	15.00
84	Mind Games EX		
85	The Snake Will Always.... EX		
86	The Snake Bite DDT EX		
87	The Million Dollar Man... EX		
88	The Million Dollar Title Belt UR	7.50	15.00
89	Everybody's Got a Price EX		
90	Everybody's Gonna Pay EX		
91	The Million Dollar Dream EX		
92	The Bookerman EX		
93	Managed by Sharmell UR	7.50	15.00
94	Sharmell Interferes UR	7.50	15.00
95	You Didn't Just Try That... EX		
96	Spinning Straight Elbow EX		
97	Distracted by Sharmell EX		
98	The Largest Athlete... EX		
99	Mine Is Bigger Than Yours UR	7.50	15.00
100	The Biggest Precision... UR	7.50	15.00
101	Colossal Clubbing EX		
102	Big Enough to Eat Somebody EX		
103	The Big & The Small of It EX		
104	X-treme Diva EX		
105	It Just Feels Right UR	7.50	15.00
106	Just the Way I Planned... UR	7.50	15.00
107	Girly Choke EX		
108	Don't Call Me A... EX		
109	Love... Fury... Passion... EX		
110	Chavo Guerrero PR		
111	One for One UR	7.50	15.00
112	My Life For You PR		
113	Guerreros por Siempre! PR		
114	A Family Tradition PR		
115	The Gory Bomb PR		
116	Funaki PR		
117	The Rising Sun UR	7.50	15.00
118	Japanese Flying Bulldog PR		
119	I'll Do Anything For the... PR		
120	...I Do Ask the Tough Questions PR		
121	Springboard Body Block PR		
122	Mexicools PR		
123	Lawn Maintenance... UR	7.50	15.00
124	Forget Your Stereotypes PR		
125	Crazy Moonsault PR		
126	Psychotic Guillotine Leg Drop PR		
127	Mexi-Leg-Lace Powerbomb PR		

128	Viscera PR		
129	The Sex Drive UR	7.50	15.00
130	A Big Man Has A Big... Appetite PR		
131	500 Pound Love Machine PR		
132	Take It Like a Man PR		
133	Flying Somersault Kick PR		
134	STUNNER! PR		
135	Death Waits for No Man PR		
136	Bring the Hammer Down PR		
137	This Is The Rock's Show PR		
138	Journey Into Darkness PR		
139	American By Birth... PR		
140	I'm Driven by Anger PR		
141	Liaison with Lita PR		
142	It's Us vs. Them PR		
143	Nobody Gets Higher PR		
144	Walking a Golden Mile PR		
145	24-inch Pythons PR		
146	Walk That Aisle PR		
147	Trish's Chick Kick PR		
148	Old School Luche Libre... PR		
149	Tuning Up the Band PR		
150	One Issue On My Mind PR		
151	The B!tch Is Back! PR		
152	You Want Some? Come Get Some! PR		
153	Too Hot For TV PR		
154	Is Chloe Your Favorite Puppy? PR		
155	Backed by Torrie & Candice PR		
156	It's Good For Business PR		
157	I Am a Wrestling God UR	7.50	15.00
158	The Ego Cutter UR	7.50	15.00
159	Hold On, Hotshot! UR	7.50	15.00
160	Shelton's Lunging Lariat UR	7.50	15.00
161	Dernier Slam UR	7.50	15.00
162	Unleashed Bomb UR	7.50	15.00
163	The Rowdy Sleeper UR	7.50	15.00
164	Listen Up, Playa! UR	7.50	15.00
165	No Fault Drop UR	7.50	15.00
166	Jillian Hall: The Fixer UR	7.50	15.00
167	The Brain UR	7.50	15.00
168	The Thump UR	7.50	15.00
169	At Ease, Soldier UR	7.50	15.00
170	The Intensity of Ten Cities UR	7.50	15.00
171	Should've Seen This Coming UR	7.50	15.00
172	Pails o' Fun UR	7.50	15.00

2006 Comic Images WWE Raw Deal
Royal Rumble

COMPLETE SET (90)

1	Roundhouse Kick C	.12	.25
2	Big Splash in the Corner U	.50	1.00
3	Technical Tope R	2.00	4.00
4	Handcuffed C	.12	.25
5	Fisticuffs C	.12	.25
6	Armed & Dangerous U	.50	1.00
7	Technical Drop Kick U	.50	1.00
8	Ankle Breaker R	2.00	4.00
9	Running Clothesline R	2.00	4.00
10	Slingshot Into the Ring Post C	.12	.25
11	Slam C	.12	.25
12	Scoop Slam U	.50	1.00
13	Thunder Bulldog U	.50	1.00
14	Fall-away Suplex R	2.00	4.00
15	Technical Slam R	2.00	4.00
16	Hair Pull C	.12	.25
17	Entangle in the Ropes C	.12	.25
18	Key Lock U	.50	1.00
19	Take Your Own Medicine U	.50	1.00

20 Face Stretch R	2.00	4.00	
21 Technical Body Lock R	2.00	4.00	
22 How Many Do You Need? C	.12	.25	
23 Always Have a Plan B U	.30	.75	
24 Once is Enough R	2.00	4.00	
25 Volley Call C	.12	.25	
26 Everyone Wants to Watch... C	.12	.25	
27 Everyone Wants to Watch... C	.12	.25	
28 Chained Aggression C	.12	.25	
29 No Pain, No Chain C	.12	.25	
30 Feel the Fire U	.50	1.00	
31 Sparks of Glory U	.50	1.00	
32 Underestimated Prowess U	.50	1.00	
33 Backed by Eric Bischoff U	.25	.50	
34 Backed by Theodore Long U	.30	.60	
35 Grab the Mic R	2.00	4.00	
36 You Feeling Lucky? R	2.00	4.00	
37 Face the Music R	2.00	4.00	
38 Let the Heeling Begin R	2.00	4.00	
39 I Waited Long Enough R	2.00	4.00	
40 Chain Reaction C	.12	.25	
41 Argue With Tony Chimel C	.15	.30	
42 Product Endorsements C	.12	.25	
43 Unrelenting Assault U	.50	1.00	
44 Restart the Match U	.50	1.00	
45 Sit Right Here and Bide My Time U	.50	1.00	
46 It's Getting Hot in Here R	2.00	4.00	
47 Let's Get It On! R	2.00	4.00	
48 Managed by Lita R	2.00	4.00	
49 A Technical Shoot C	.50	1.00	
50 Quick Poke C	.12	.25	
51 Small Concealed Foreign Object C	.12	.25	
52 USA! USA! USA! C	.12	.25	
53 Chain Barrier U	.50	1.00	
54 Heat Barrier U	.50	1.00	
55 Volley Barrier U	.50	1.00	
56 Too Hot to Handle U	.50	1.00	
57 Future Considerations R	2.00	4.00	
58 The Sex, the Gods... R	2.00	4.00	
59 Ready to Fight R	2.00	4.00	
60 Break It Out, Break You... R	3.00	6.00	
61 Hollywood Hulk Hogan PR	2.00	4.00	
62 Whatcha Gonna Do, Brother? UR	7.50	15.00	
63 When Hulkamania Runs... UR	7.50	15.00	
64 I Live for My Hulkamaniacs... UR	7.50	15.00	
65 Hulkin' Up UR	7.50	15.00	
66 Original <WWE logo> Icon PR			
67 Hollywood's Big Boot PR			
68 Say Your Prayers... PR			
69 Hollywood Leg Drop PR			
70 Sgt. Slaughter PR			
71 Real American Cobra Clutch UR	7.50	15.00	
72 The Motor Pool PR			
73 Boot Camp Match PR			
74 At-Ten-HUT! PR			
75 Gimme Ten, Maggot! PR			
76 The Home Team PR			
77 Because the Fans Demanded It UR	7.50	15.00	
78 Flurry of Finishers UR	7.50	15.00	
79 The Shhhhh Chop PR			
80 Never Back Down - Never Quit PR			
81 I Will Not Die PR			
82 The Whole Dam Show PR			
83 The Heat Seekers PR			
84 On Your Home Turf UR	7.50	15.00	
85 Good Old-Fashioned Mugging UR	7.50	15.00	
86 I Know Cool ... And You're... PR			
87 Kokubetsu PR			
88 The Proper Punch PR			
89 We're Not Mexicans... PR			
90 Violent Vendetta UR	7.50	15.00	

2002 Comic Images WWE Raw Deal SummerSlam

1 Head Butt Drop C	.12	.25
2 Inverted Body Block U	.50	1.00
3 Back Splash R	2.00	4.00
4 Knife-Edge Chop C	.12	.25
5 Spinning Back Fist C	.12	.25
6 Atomic Back Body Drop C	.12	.25
7 Back Rake C	.12	.25
8 Brass Nuks Shot U	.50	1.00
9 Short Arm Clothesline U	.50	1.00
10 Kangaroo Kick U	.50	1.00
11 360-Degree Clothesline R	2.00	4.00
12 Up and At 'em C	.12	.25
13 Double Underhook Back Breaker C	.12	.25
14 Snap Suplex C	.12*	.25
15 Bulldog Lariat C	.12	.25
16 Face-buster Suplex U	.50	1.00
17 Tilt-a-Whirl Powerslam U	.50	1.00
18 Back Breaker Torture Rack R	2.00	4.00
19 Arm Wringer C	.12	.25
20 Nerve Hold C	.12	.25
21 Knee Lock U	.50	1.00
22 Half Crab U	.50	1.00
23 Dragon Sleeper R	2.00	4.00
24 Booby Trap C	.12	.25
25 That's Enough Out of You C	.12	.25
26 There Are Two Things... U	.50	1.00
27 I Change the Questions R	2.00	4.00
28 Grab the Mic C	.12	.25
29 Use 'em or Lose 'em C	.12	.25
30 You Feeling Lucky? C	.12	.25
31 I'm Gonna Try That Again C	.12	.25
32 Battling the Voices C	.12	.25
33 Springboard C	.12	.25
34 Let's Pick Up the Pace C	.12	.25
35 Filthy, Disgusting, Brutal... U	.50	1.00
36 Energy Burst U	.50	1.00
37 Mind Games U	.50	1.00
38 Play the Game U	.50	1.00
39 Give It All I Got U	.50	1.00
40 Beating the Odds R	2.00	4.00
41 Smart Mark R	2.00	4.00
42 Hardcore 'Til the End R	2.00	4.00
43 Simply The Best R	2.00	4.00
44 Pencil-Necked Geek R	2.00	4.00
45 Go For the Cover R	2.00	4.00
46 Don't Hate da Playa, Hate da Game R	2.00	4.00
47 It's Showtime C	.12	.25
48 J.R. Style Clubberin' C	.12	.25
49 Pick Your Spots C	.12	.25
50 Glass Ceiling C	.12	.25
51 In the Interest of Fairness C	.12	.25
52 Do You Know What... U	.50	1.00
53 I'm The Biggest Dog on This Block U	.50	1.00
54 Just Who in the Blue Hell... U	.50	1.00
55 The Game Is Back... U	.50	1.00
56 I'm Better Than You U	.50	1.00
57 Bra and Panties Match R	2.00	4.00
58 Lethal nWo Poison R	2.00	4.00
59 Living Legend R	2.00	4.00
60 Managed by Stephanie... R	2.00	4.00
61 Managed by Torrie Wilson R	2.00	4.00
62 Managed by Stacy Keibler R	2.00	4.00
63 Managed by Terri Runnels R	2.00	4.00
64 I'm Not Outta It Yet C	.12	.25
65 Shove C	.12	.25
66 Business Is About to Pick Up C	.12	.25
67 Get What You're Expectin' C	.12	.25
68 Silent, But Violent C	.12	.25
69 My God He's Broken in Half C	.12	.25
70 Tag Out C	.12	.25
71 It's All in the Teamwork C	.12	.25
72 Save da Drama fo' yo' Mama U	.50	1.00
73 Turn Up the Heat U	.50	1.00
74 Greco-Roman Holiday U	.50	1.00
75 That's a Near Fall U	.50	1.00
76 You Suck You Suck U	.50	1.00
77 Ham-and-Egger U	.50	1.00
78 Not According to the Fine Print R	2.00	4.00
79 Squared Circle is No Place... R	2.00	4.00
80 Been There, Done That R	2.00	4.00
81 Human Highlight Reel R	2.00	4.00
82 To Be the Man... R	2.00	4.00
83 Ring General R	2.00	4.00
84 Hollywood Hogan EX		
85 Whatcha Gonna Do, Brother? UR	7.50	15.00
86 Hulkin' Up UR		
87 Hollywood's Big Boot EX		
88 Say Your Prayers and... EX		
89 Hollywood Leg Drop EX		
90 Ric Flair EX		
91 Stylin', Profilin', Limousine Ridin'... UR	7.50	15.00
92 Wooooooooo UR	7.50	15.00
93 Diamonds are Forever... EX		
94 Now You're Going to School EX		
95 The Dirtiest Player in the Game EX		
96 Hall and Nash EX		
97 Too Sweet UR	7.50	15.00
98 Jack-knife UR		
99 nWo Black and White EX		
100 4 Life EX		
101 Hall's Fall-Away Slam EX		
102 Trish Stratus EX		
103 The T and A Factor UR	7.50	15.00
104 100 Stratusfaction Guaranteed UR		
105 Stratusfaction Bulldog EX		
106 I've Been a Very Naughty Girl EX		
107 Perhaps I Need a Spanking? EX		
108 Billy and Chuck PU		
109 Rico Enters UR	7.50	15.00
110 Oh, Baby, You Look So... PR		
111 Chuck's Jungle Kick PR		
112 Stretching is Good for the Groin PU		
113 I've Had Many Partners... PU		
114 Al Snow PU		
115 Snow Plow UR	7.50	15.00
116 Head PR		
117 What Does Everybody Need? PR		
118 What Does Everybody Want? PU		
119 Snow Slide PU		
120 Tajiri PU		
121 Kick of Death UR		
122 Tarantula PR		
123 Asian Mist PR		
124 Tajiri's Handspring Elbow PU		
125 Japanese Buzzsaw PU		
126 Hurricane PU		
127 Eye of the Hurricane UR		
128 Stand Back There's a... PR		
129 Caped Body Press PR		
130 To the Hurricycle PU		
131 Whassupwitdat??? PU		
132 In the Presence of the Kanenites PR		
133 I'm a Bad Man PR		
134 Do YOU Live By the Three I's? PR		
135 The Mood Is About to Change PR		
136 The Best Technical Wrestler... PR		
137 Whatchoo Talkin' 'bout, Ese? PR		
138 Outsider Distraction PR		
139 Brothers from Another Mother UR		
140 Edge-acution UR		
141 Temper Tantrum UR	7.50	15.00
142 Team X-Treme UR	7.50	15.00
143 Big All Over UR		
144 Lita's Twist of Fate UR		
145 Dude, Nice Hang Time UR		
146 Tell Me You Didn't Just Say That UR	7.50	15.00
147 Damn UR		
148 Giant Killer UR		
149 Listen Up, Sunshine UR		
150 Raven's Shopping Cart UR	7.50	15.00
8/TR cUndisputed Heavyweight Title R	2.00	4.00
9/TR Women's Title Belt R	2.00	4.00

2003 Comic Images WWE Raw Deal Survivor Series 2

1 Spinning Crescent Kick (M) C	.12	.25
2 Knee Smash (S) C	.12	.25
3 Big Splash in the Corner (B) C	.12	.25
4 Inverted Body Block (SS) U	.50	1.00
5 Flying Body Press (PR) U	.50	1.00
6 Flying Tope (M) U	.50	1.00
7 Drive Opponent Thru... (B) U	.50	1.00
8 Back Splash (SS) R	2.00	4.00
9 Superplex (F) R	2.00	4.00
10 Atomic Back Body Drop (SS) C	.12	.25
11 Struck by a Kendo Stick (B) C	.12	.25
12 Gut Punch (M) C	.12	.25
13 Back Rake (SS) C	.12	.25
14 Eye Rake (S) C	.12	.25
15 Shoulder Block (S) U	.50	1.00
16 Kick (S) U	.50	1.00
17 Running Lariat (B) U	.50	1.00
18 Discus Punch (P) U	.50	1.00
19 Garbage Can Lid (B) U	.50	1.00
20 Brass Nuks Shot (SS) U	.50	1.00
21 Pump Kick (M) R	2.00	4.00
22 Superkick (S) R	2.00	4.00
23 European Uppercut (S) R	2.00	4.00
24 360-Degree Clothesline (SS) R	2.00	4.00
25 Running Clothesline (B) R	2.00	4.00
26 Chair Shot (S) R	2.00	4.00
27 Within Your Grasp (M) C	.12	.25
28 Double Underhook... (SS) C	.12	.25
29 Neck Breaker (B) C	.12	.25
30 Headlock Takedown (S) U	.50	1.00
31 Backslide (M) U	.50	1.00
32 German Suplex (F) U	.50	1.00
33 Spine Buster (B) U	.50	1.00
34 Face-buster Suplex (SS) U	.50	1.00
35 Tilt-a-Whirl Powerslam (SS) U	.50	1.00
36 Samoan Drop (S) R	2.00	4.00
37 Fisherman's Suplex (S) R	2.00	4.00
38 DDT (S) R	2.00	4.00
39 Running Bulldog (M) R	2.00	4.00
40 Back Breaker Torture Rack (SS) R	2.00	4.00
41 Clutch onto Opponent (B) C	.12	.25
42 Short Arm Hammerlock (M) C	.12	.25
43 Nerve Hold (SS) C	.12	.25

44	Ankle Lock (S) U	.50	1.00
45	Standing Side Headlock (S) U	.50	1.00
46	Strangle Hold (M) U	.50	1.00
47	Apply Illegal Leverage (B) U	.50	1.00
48	Half Crab (SS) U	.50	1.00
49	Sleeper (S) R	2.00	4.00
50	Boston Crab (S) R	2.00	4.00
51	Claw (S) R	2.00	4.00
52	Sharpshooter (B) R	2.00	4.00
53	Step Aside (S) C	.12	.25
54	Escape Move (S) C	.12	.25
55	Break the Hold (S) C	.12	.25
56	Roll Out of the Way (S) C	.12	.25
57	Clumsy Opponent (B) C	.12	.25
58	No Sell Maneuver (B) C	.12	.25
59	Over Sell Maneuver (B) C	.12	.25
60	All Talk, No Action (M) C	.12	.25
61	Elbow to the Face (S) U	.50	1.00
62	Knee to the Gut (S) U	.50	1.00
63	Rolling Takedown (S) U	.50	1.00
64	There Are Two Things... (SS) U	.50	1.00
65	Clean Break (P) U	.50	1.00
66	Just Bring It (S) U	.50	1.00
67	Hebner Calls It (S) U	.50	1.00
68	Kissing Up to the Stinkin'... (B) U	.50	1.00
69	Partner Interference (S) U	.50	1.00
70	Iron Will (M) R	2.00	4.00
71	Not Today, Pal (M) R	2.00	4.00
72	No Chance in Hell (S) R	2.00	4.00
73	I Change the Questions (SS) R	2.00	4.00
74	Manager Interferes (S) R	2.00	4.00
75	Tag in Partner (S) C	.12	.25
76	You Feeling Lucky? (SS) C	.12	.25
77	Great Technical Knowledge (B) C	.12	.25
78	Jockeying for Position (S) C	.12	.25
79	Turn the Match into a Pier... (B) C	.12	.25
80	Irish Whip (S) C	.12	.25
81	Throw Into the Corner... (S) C	.12	.25
82	From the Top Rope (S) C	.12	.25
83	Little She Devil (M) C	.12	.25
84	Gut Wrench (M) C	.12	.25
85	Amazing Display of Power (B) C	.12	.25
86	Charismatic Style (B) C	.12	.25
87	Cole Calls It Right (M) C	.12	.25
88	Trailer Park Trash (M) C	.12	.25
89	Where the Hell Are We? (PR) U	.50	1.00
90	J.R. Style Slobber-knocker U	.50	1.00
91	Roll Out of the Ring (S) U	.50	1.00
92	Shake It Off (P) U	.50	1.00
93	Defensive Posture (S) U	.50	1.00
94	Energy Burst (SS) U	.50	1.00
95	Table Table Table (FL) U	.50	1.00
96	Backed by Stephanie... (S) U	.50	1.00
97	Offer Handshake (S) U	.50	1.00
98	Who Booked This Match? (F) U	.50	1.00
99	Well Deserved Push (B) U	.50	1.00
100	Get Crowd Support (S) U	.50	1.00
101	Spit at Opponent (S) U	.50	1.00
102	Beating the Odds (SS) R	2.00	4.00
103	Ego Boost (S) R	2.00	4.00
104	Lita to the Xtreme (B) R	2.00	4.00
105	Simply the Best (SS) R	2.00	4.00
106	Maintain Hold (S) R	2.00	4.00
107	Enter the Stratusphere (S) R	2.00	4.00
108	Puppies Puppies (S) R	2.00	4.00
109	Ring Steps (M) R	2.00	4.00
110	Diversion (P) R	2.00	4.00
111	Turn the Tide (S) R	2.00	4.00
112	Don't Hate da Playa... (SS) R	2.00	4.00
113	You're Not in My League (B) R	2.00	4.00
114	Awesome Pyro (B) C	.12	.25
115	It's Showtime (SS) C	.12	.25
116	J.R. Style Clubberin' (SS) C	.12	.25
117	Pick Your Spots (SS) C	.12	.25
118	Glass Ceiling (SS) C	.12	.25
119	Givin' 'em High Fives (B) C	.12	.25
120	Taunt the Fans (B) C	.12	.25
121	Fans Love an Underdog (B) U	.50	1.00
122	Chicago Street Fight (M) U	.50	1.00
123	Trash Talkin' Interview (B) U	.50	1.00
124	Snubbed by the Fans (M) U	.50	1.00
125	Old School Wrestling Match (B) R	2.00	4.00
126	Underrated Superstar (B) R	2.00	4.00
127	Hell in a Cell Match (M) R	2.00	4.00
128	Indian Strap Match (M) R	2.00	4.00
129	Duchess of Queensbury Rules (M) R	2.00	4.00
130	Handicap Match (M) R	2.00	4.00
131	Bra and Panties Match (SS) R	2.00	4.00
132	Managed by Stephanie... (SS) R	2.00	4.00
133	Managed by Torrie Wilson (SS) R	2.00	4.00
134	Managed by Terri Runnels (SS) R	2.00	4.00
135	Backlash (B) C	.12	.25
136	Fortitude Surge (M) C	.12	.25
137	Business Is About to Pick Up (SS) C	.12	.25
138	Silent, But Violent (SS) C	.12	.25
139	Fan Appreciation Day (M) C	.12	.25
140	Dirty Low Blow (B) C	.12	.25
141	Tag Out (SS) C	.12	.25
142	When You Thought You Had... (B) U	.50	1.00
143	Turn Up the Heat (SS) U	.50	1.00
144	Over the Top Rope (M) U	.50	1.00
145	Don't Mess with the Champ (B) R	2.00	4.00
146	Sustained Damage (M) R	2.00	4.00
147	Been There, Done That (SS) R	2.00	4.00
148	Fully Loaded (B) R	2.00	4.00
149	Ring General (SS) R	2.00	4.00
150	No Mercy (B) R	2.00	4.00
151	Dude Love Superstar Card R	2.00	4.00
152	Feel the Love (SS2) R	2.00	4.00
153	Psychedelic Dance Fever (SS2) R	2.00	4.00
154	Tree of Woe (SS2) R	2.00	4.00
156	Split Personalities... (SS2) UR	7.50	15.00
157	Get Softcore (S) UR	7.50	15.00
158	Three Faces of Foley (B) UR	7.50	15.00
159	Foley is Good (M) PR		
160	Chris Jericho Superstar Card (S) R	2.00	4.00
161	Lionsault (S) R	2.00	4.00
162	Y2J (S) R	2.00	4.00
163	Don't You Never Eeeever (S) R	2.00	4.00
164	Walls of Jericho (S) UR	7.50	15.00
165	Ayatollah of Rock 'n' Roll-a (S) UR	7.50	15.00
166	Springboard Drop Kick (S) UR	7.50	15.00
167	Superior Acrobatics (B) UR	7.50	15.00
168	Would You Please Shut... (M) PR		
169	Eddie Guerrero... (F) R	2.00	4.00
170	Snap Senton Splash (F) R	2.00	4.00
171	Study for Your GED (F) R	2.00	4.00
172	Latino Heeeeeeeat (F) R	2.00	4.00
173	Guerrero Frog Splash (F) UR	7.50	15.00
174	Get Your GED (F) UR	7.50	15.00
175	Eddie's Roll Up (B) UR	7.50	15.00
176	Ultimo Rechazo (M) UR	7.50	15.00
177	Whatchoo Talkin' 'bout, Ese (SS) PR		
178	Edge Superstar Card (B) R	2.00	4.00
179	Listen, You Reekazoid (B) R	2.00	4.00
180	Sodas Rule (B) R	2.00	4.00
181	Million Dollar Smile (B) R	2.00	4.00
182	Edge-O-Matic (B) UR	7.50	15.00
183	You Think You Know Me? (M) UR	7.50	15.00
184	Edge-acution (SS) UR	7.50	15.00
185	Big Slide in the Ring (B) PR		
186	Christian Superstar Card (B) R	2.00	4.00
187	This is So Totally Unfair (B) R	2.00	4.00
188	Greetings to Our Fans... (B) R	2.00	4.00
189	Kazoo Theme Songs (B) R	2.00	4.00
190	Unprettier (B) UR	7.50	15.00
191	Temper Tantrum (SS) UR	7.50	15.00
192	Christian's Shades (B) PR		
193	Matt Hardy Superstar Card (B) R	2.00	4.00
194	M.Hardy's Patented Leg Drop (B) R	2.00	4.00
195	Put It All On the Line (B) R	2.00	4.00
196	Matt's Moonsault (B) R	2.00	4.00
197	Twist of Fate (B) UR	7.50	15.00
198	Live for the Moment (M) UR	7.50	15.00
199	Team X-Treme (SS) UR	7.50	15.00
200	Roar For the Fans (B) PR		
201	Jeff Hardy Superstar Card (B) R	2.00	4.00
202	Whisper in the Wind (B) R	2.00	4.00
203	Incite the Fans (B) R	2.00	4.00
204	Ride the Barricade (B) R	2.00	4.00
205	Swanton Bomb (B) UR	7.50	15.00
206	No, Jeff, Don't Do It (B) PR		
207	Big Show Superstar Card (M) R	2.00	4.00
208	Showstopper Chokeslam (M) R	2.00	4.00
209	Big Show Splash (M) R	2.00	4.00
210	500 lbs. of Raw Power (M) R	2.00	4.00
211	Final Cut (M) UR	7.50	15.00
212	Wellllll (M) UR	7.50	15.00
213	Big All Over (SS) UR	7.50	15.00
214	Lita Superstar Card (M) R	2.00	4.00
215	Lita-canrana (M) R	2.00	4.00
216	Lita Drop Kick (M) R	2.00	4.00
217	Crimson Goddess (M) R	2.00	4.00
218	Lita-sault (M) UR	7.50	15.00
219	X-Treme Thong (M) UR	7.50	15.00
220	Lita's Twist of Fate (SS) UR	7.50	15.00
221	Rob Van Dam Superstar Card (M) R	2.00	4.00
222	Five Star Frog Splash (M) R	2.00	4.00
223	Extreme Monkey Flip (M) R	2.00	4.00
224	Rolling Thunder (M) R	2.00	4.00
225	Van Daminator (M) UR	7.50	15.00
226	R-V-D (M) UR	7.50	15.00
227	Dude, Nice Hang Time (SS) UR	7.50	15.00
228	Booker T Superstar Card (M) R	2.00	4.00
229	Can You Dig It, Sucka? (M) R	2.00	4.00
230	Booker's Scissor Kick (M) R	2.00	4.00
231	Spinning T Kick (M) R	2.00	4.00
232	Bookend (M) UR	7.50	15.00
233	Spinnerooni (M) UR	7.50	15.00
234	Tell Me You Didn't Just... (SS) UR	7.50	15.00
235	Trish Stratus... (SS) R	2.00	4.00
236	Stratusfaction Bulldog (SS) R	2.00	4.00
237	I've Been a Very Naughty Girl (SS) R	2.00	4.00
238	Perhaps I Need a Spanking? (SS) R	2.00	4.00
239	The TandA Factor (SS) UR	7.50	15.00
240	100 Stratusfaction... (SS) UR	7.50	15.00
241	Stone Cold Steve Austin... (S) PR		
242	Austin Elbow Smash (S) PR		
243	Double Digits (S) PR		
244	Lou Thesz Press (S) PR		
245	Stone Cold Stunner (S) UR	7.50	15.00
246	Open Up a Can of Whoop-A$ (S) UR	7.50	15.00
247	Patented Austin Kick to the Gut (F) UR	7.50	15.00
248	DTA (B) UR	7.50	15.00
249	What??? (M) PR		
250	Deadman Inc... (S) PR		
251	Bad Ass Chokeslam (S) PR		
252	Old School Clothesline (S) PR		
253	Dead Man Walking (S) PR		
254	The Last Ride (S) UR	7.50	15.00
255	This is My Yard (S) UR	7.50	15.00
256	I'll Make You Famous (S) UR	7.50	15.00
257	Brothers 'til the End (B) UR	7.50	15.00
258	You Will Respect Me (M) PR		
259	Triple H Superstar Card (S) PR		
260	Leaping Knee to the Face (S) PR		
261	Facebuster (S) PR		
262	I Am the Game (S) PR		
263	Pedigree (S) UR	7.50	15.00
264	I've Got Two Words for Ya (F) UR	7.50	15.00
265	Triple H's Reverse Neck... (S) UR	7.50	15.00
266	Sledgehammer Shot (B) UR	7.50	15.00
267	Cerebral Assassin (M) PR		
268	The Rock Superstar Card (S) PR		
269	Take That Move... PR		
270	Rock Bottom (S) PR		
271	Smackdown Hotel (S) PR		
272	The People's Eyebrow (S) UR	7.50	15.00
273	The People's Elbow (S) UR	7.50	15.00
274	Patented Rock Footstomp (F) UR	7.50	15.00
275	The Brahma Bull (B) UR	7.50	15.00
276	Shades of the Great One (M) PR		
277	Kane Superstar Card (S) PR		
278	Kane's Chokeslam (S) PR		
279	Kane's Flying Clothesline (S) PR		
280	Kane's Return (S) PR		
281	Kane's Tombstone...(S) UR	7.50	15.00
282	Hellfire and Brimstone (S) UR	7.50	15.00
283	Masked Vengeance (S) UR	7.50	15.00
284	Born of Hellfire (M) PR		
285	In the Presence of... (SS) PR		
286	Rikishi Superstar Card (F) PR		
287	Drive, Rikishi, Drive (F) PR		
288	Back That A$ Up (F) PR		
289	Stink Face (F) PR		
290	Rikishi Driver (F) UR	7.50	15.00
291	A$ Drop (F) UR	7.50	15.00
292	I Did it for You (B) UR	7.50	15.00
294	I'm a Bad Man (SS) PR		
295	Kurt Angle Superstar Card (S) PR		
296	Intensity (S) PR		
297	Integrity (S) PR		
298	Intelligence (S) PR		
299	Olympic Slam (S) UR	7.50	15.00
300	It's True, It's True (S) UR	7.50	15.00
301	Where Are Your Medals? (B) UR	7.50	15.00
302	Angle Lock (M) UR	7.50	15.00
303	Do YQU Live by... (SS) PR		
304	Tazz (S) PR		
305	T-Bone Tazzplex (S) PR		
306	Head-and-Arms Tazzplex (S) PR		
307	Northern Lights Tazzplex (S) PR		
308	Tazzmission (S) UR	7.50	15.00
309	Thug It - Dead (S) UR	7.50	15.00
310	Just Another Victim (B) UR		
311	Tough Enough (M) UR	7.50	15.00
312	The Mood Is About... (SS) PR		
313	Chris Benoit Superstar Card (S) PR		
314	Kamikaze Headbutt (S) PR		
315	Series of Suplexes (S) PR		
316	Rabid Wolverine (S) PR		
317	Crippler Crossface (S) UR	7.50	15.00

318	Big Stupid Grin (S) UR	7.50	15.00
319	Prove Me Wrong (B) UR	7.50	15.00
320	First to Tap Out Match (M) UR	7.50	15.00
321	The Best Technical... (SS) PR		
322	Dudley Boyz Superstar Card (B) PR		
323	3D (B) UR	7.50	15.00
324	Wazzzzuuup??? (B) PR		
325	Buh-Buh Ray Dudley... (B) UR		
326	Buh-Buh Bomb (B) UR	7.50	15.00
327	Catatonic Stare (B) PR		
328	My Name Is (B) PR		
329	Buh-Buh Drop (B) PR		
330	Buh-Buh Punch (B) PR		
331	D-Von Dudley Superstar Card (B) PR		
332	Testify (B) UR	7.50	15.00
333	Spinning Elbow (B) PR		
334	Doin' the D-Von (B) PR		
335	Thou Shall Not... (B) PR		
336	D-Von Get the Table (B) PR		
337	Greetings from Dudleyville... (M) UR	7.50	15.00
338	Brothers from Another... (SS) UR	7.50	15.00
339	Spike Dudley Superstar Card (M) PR		
340	Dudley Dog (M) UR	7.50	15.00
341	150 lbs. Soaking Wet (M) PR		
342	Good Golly, Miss Molly... (M) PR		
343	Psychotic Bump (M) PR		
344	Brotherly Love (M) PR		
345	Giant Killer (SS) UR	7.50	15.00
346	William Regal... (M) PR		
347	Union Jack (M) PR		
348	I've Been Besmirched (M) PR		
349	Goodwill Ambassador (M) PR		
350	Regal Stretch (M) UR	7.50	15.00
351	Commissioner Regal's... (M) PR		
352	Listen Up, Sunshine (SS) UR	7.50	15.00
353	Hollywood Hulk Hogan... (SS) PR		
354	Hollywood's Big Boot (SS) PR		
355	Say Your Prayers... (SS) PR		
356	Hollywood Leg Drop (SS) PR		
357	Whatcha Gonna Do... (SS) UR	7.50	15.00
358	Hulkin' Up (SS) UR	7.50	15.00
359	Ric Flair Superstar Card (SS) PR		
360	Diamonds are Forever... (SS) PR		
361	Now You're Going... (SS) PR		
362	The Dirtiest Player... (SS) PR		
363	Stylin', Profilin'... (SS) UR	7.50	15.00
364	Wooooooooo (SS) UR	7.50	15.00
365	Rico Enters (SS) UR	7.50	15.00
366	Al Snow Superstar Card (SS) PR		
367	What Does Everybody... (SS) PR		
368	What Does Everybody... (SS) PR		
369	Snow Slide (SS) PR		
370	Snow Plow (SS) UR	7.50	15.00
371	Head (SS) PR		
372	Tajiri Superstar Card (SS) PR		
373	Asian Mist (SS) PR		
374	Tajiri's Handspring Elbow (SS) PR		
375	Japanese Buzzsaw (SS) PR		
376	Kick of Death (SS) UR	7.50	15.00
377	Tarantula (SS) PR		
378	Hurricane Superstar Card (SS) PR		
379	Caped Body Press (SS) PR		
380	To the Hurricycle (SS) PR		
381	Whassupwitdat??? (SS) PR		
382	Eye of the Hurricane (SS) UR	7.50	15.00
383	Stand Back... (SS) PR		
155A	The Love Handle (SS2) UR	7.50	15.00
155B	Sweet Shin Music (SS2) UR	7.50	15.00

293A	Gettin' Cheeky with It - A (M) UR	7.50	15.00
293B	Gettin' Cheeky with It - B (M) UR	7.50	15.00
293C	Gettin' Cheeky with It - C (M) UR	7.50	15.00

2005 Comic Images WWE Raw Deal Survivor Series 3

1	Diving Takedown C	.12	.25
2	Revolving Takedown TB U	.50	1.00
3	Flying Leg Scissors R	2.00	4.00
4	Suicide Dive R	2.00	4.00
5	Superplex TB R	2.00	4.00
6	Girly Punch C	.12	.25
7	Spinning Kick C	.12	.25
8	Right Cross Punch C	.12	.25
9	Left Cross Punch C	.12	.25
10	Atomic Back Body Drop C	.12	.25
11	Kick TB U	.50	1.00
12	Running Lariat U	.50	1.00
13	Lariat U	.50	1.00
14	Garbage Can Lid TB U	.50	1.00
15	Brass Nuks Shot U	.50	1.00
16	Steel Chain Shot TB U	.50	1.00
17	Superkick R	2.00	4.00
18	Lariat Takedown R	2.00	4.00
19	Short Arm Rib Breaker R	2.00	4.00
20	Atomic Lariat R	2.00	4.00
21	Blindside Kick R	2.00	4.00
22	360-Degree Clothesline R	2.00	4.00
23	Chair Shot R	2.00	4.00
24	Double Underhook Back Breaker C	.12	.25
25	Wheelbarrow Slam C	.12	.25
26	Snap Neckbreaker C	.12	.25
27	Face Driver C	.12	.25
28	Neck Breaker C	.12	.25
29	Vertical DDT Drop TB C	.12	.25
30	Shoot Slam U	.50	1.00
31	Judo Takedown U	.50	1.00
32	Quick Snap Body Slam U	.50	1.00
33	Double Underhook Power Bomb U	.50	1.00
34	Tilt-a-Whirl Powerslam U	.50	1.00
35	Blindside Slam U	.50	1.00
36	Suplex R	2.00	4.00
37	Rolling Headlock Vise R	2.00	4.00
38	Reverse Fall-away Slam R	2.00	4.00
39	Military Slam R	2.00	4.00
40	Takedown R	2.00	4.00
41	Death Valley Driver R	2.00	4.00
42	Back Breaker Torture Rack R	2.00	4.00
43	Faceplant TB R	2.00	4.00
44	Clutch onto Opponent C	.12	.25
45	Modified Clutch onto Opponent C	.12	.25
46	Triangle Choke C	.12	.25
47	Arm Breaker TB C	.12	.25
48	Body Lock C	.12	.25
49	Waist Lock TB U	.50	1.00
50	Shoot Headlock U	.50	1.00
51	Judo Choke TB U	.50	1.00
52	Wraparound Wrist Lock U	.50	1.00
53	Headlock U	.50	1.00
54	Strangle Hold TB U	.50	1.00
55	Apply Illegal Leverage U	.50	1.00
56	Front Chancery R	2.00	4.00
57	Apply Legal Leverage TB R	2.00	4.00
58	Blindside Choke R	2.00	4.00
59	Super Hold R	2.00	4.00
60	Inverted Leg Lock R	2.00	4.00
61	Sharpshooter TB R	2.00	4.00
62	Step Aside C	.12	.25

63	Escape Move C	.12	.25
64	No Sell Maneuver C	.12	.25
65	Over Sell Maneuver C	.12	.25
66	Clumsy Opponent C	.12	.25
67	I Already Warned You C	.12	.25
68	Quick Reflexes C	.12	.25
69	Unexpected Turn of Events C	.12	.25
70	Elbow to the Face U	.50	1.00
71	Hold the Phone U	.50	1.00
72	There Are Two Things... U	.50	1.00
73	Blindsided Ego TB U	.50	1.00
74	Overshot Your Mark U	.50	1.00
75	Leave Me Alone U	.50	1.00
76	Blindsided Control U	.50	1.00
77	Just Bring It U	.50	1.00
78	Reach for the Ropes U	.50	1.00
79	Iron Will TB R	2.00	4.00
80	Don't Try This at Home R	2.00	4.00
81	Too Many Rules... R	2.00	4.00
82	Headstrong R	2.00	4.00
83	Sloppy - Very Sloppy R	2.00	4.00
84	Manager Interferes R	2.00	4.00
85	Let's Wrestle Already C	.12	.25
86	Suplex into the Ring TB C	.12	.25
87	Chain Wrestling C	.12	.25
88	When Hell Freezes Over TB C	.12	.25
89	Commission-er Rules C	.12	.25
90	Battling the Voices TB C	.12	.25
91	Irish Whip C	.12	.25
92	Gut Wrench C	.12	.25
93	I've Got a Nice Bottom U	.50	1.00
94	Chained Heat U	.50	1.00
95	Roll Out of the Ring U	.50	1.00
96	Backed by Stephanie McMahon U	.50	1.00
97	Offer Handshake TB U	.50	1.00
98	Spit at Opponent U	.50	1.00
99	Ego Boost R	2.00	4.00
100	I Can't Be Reading This Right R	2.00	4.00
101	Why the Hell are We Back? R	2.00	4.00
102	Escape the Rules R	2.00	4.00
103	That's Broken R	2.00	4.00
104	Twisted Smile R	2.00	4.00
105	The End is Near R	2.00	4.00
106	Don't Hate da Playa... R	2.00	4.00
107	Enough with the Trash Talk TB R	2.00	4.00
108	No Disqualification Match TB C	.12	.25
109	Spontaneous Combustion C	.12	.25
110	This is Gonna Be a Rocket Buster C	.12	.25
111	Old School Psychology C	.12	.25
112	Taunt the Fans C	.12	.25
113	Old School Beating C	.12	.25
114	Chicago Street Fight U	.50	1.00
115	Pay-Per-View Main Event U	.50	1.00
116	Raw or Smackdown... U	.50	1.00
117	Smackdown #1 Announcer... TB U	.50	1.00
118	Calgary, Alberta, Canada U	.50	1.00
119	The Title is on the Line U	.50	1.00
120	You Rang? U	.50	1.00
121	Old School Wrestling Match R	2.00	4.00
122	Underrated Superstar TB R	2.00	4.00
123	Managed by Theodore Long R	2.00	4.00
124	Houston, Texas R	2.00	4.00
125	Philadelphia, Pennsylvania R	2.00	4.00
126	Bitter Rivals R	2.00	4.00
127	Managed by Dawn Marie R	2.00	4.00
128	Backlash C	.12	.25
129	Fortitude Surge C	.12	.25
130	Took That on the Chin C	.12	.25

131	Hardcore Style TB C	.12	.25
132	Skirt the Issue C	.12	.25
133	Check This Out C	.12	.25
134	Really, That's Enough C	.12	.25
135	Fan Appreciation Day C	.12	.25
136	Victory Roll C	.12	.25
137	Dirty Low Blow C	.12	.25
138	Grab the Ref C	.12	.25
139	Turn Up the Heat U	.50	1.00
140	Panic Assault U	.50	1.00
141	Panic Grab U	.50	1.00
142	Panic Throw U	.50	1.00
143	Immune to Pain TB U	.50	1.00
144	You're as Graceful... U	.50	1.00
145	This is Going Nowhere Fast U	.50	1.00
146	Chain Finisher U	.50	1.00
147	Sustained Damage R	2.00	4.00
148	The King Interferes R	2.00	4.00
149	Unscrupulous S.O.B. R	2.00	4.00
150	Reverse 180-Degree Chair Shot R	2.00	4.00
151	Stone Cold Steve Austin RUM		
152	Rattlesnake RUM		
153	Austin Elbow Smash RUM		
154	Double Digits RUM		
155	Lou Thesz Press TB RUM		
156	Stone Cold Stunner UR	7.50	15.00
157	Open Up a Can... UR	7.50	15.00
158	Patented Austin... UR	7.50	15.00
159	Do You Know What... TB RUM		
160	DTA TB UR	7.50	15.00
161	Rattlesnake Rulz RUM		
162	Cause Stone Cold Said So RUM		
163	And That's the Bottom Line RUM		
164	What??? RUM		
165	The Bionic Redneck UR	7.50	15.00
166	Gimme a Hell Yeah UR	7.50.	15.00
167	Stomp a Mudhole RUM		
168	Don't Trust Nobody RUM		
169	Walk it Dry RUM		
170	Do You Want a Hug? RUM		
171	Undertaker RUM		
172	Undertaker's Chokeslam RUM		
173	Undertaker's Flying... TB RUM		
174	Undertaker Sits Up RUM		
175	Undertaker's Tombstone... UR	7.50	15.00
176	Power of Darkness UR	7.50	15.00
177	Rest in Peace UR	7.50	15.00
178	Throttled Within an Inch... RUM		
179	Rollin' - Rollin' - Rollin' RUM		
180	I'm the Biggest Dog... TB RUM		
181	Bad to the Bone RUM		
182	Twelve Years of Terror RUM		
183	Brothers 'til the End UR	7.50	15.00
184	You Will Respect Me RUM		
185	Throwin' Big Ol' Soup... RUM		
186	Big Evil - Red Devil RUM		
187	Your'e Gonna Pay TB RUM		
188	Managed by Paul Bearer RUM		
189	HHH RUM		
190	The Game RUM		
191	Leaping Knee to the Face RUM		
192	Facebuster TB RUM		
193	I Am the Game TB RUM		
194	Ric Flair Interferes UR	7.50	15.00
195	Pedigree UR	7.50	15.00
196	I've Got Two Words for Ya UR	7.50	15.00
197	Triple H's Reverse... UR	7.50	15.00
198	Cause I am That Damn Good RUM		

199	Flip Over the Corner Ringpost RUM		
200	It's Time to Play the Game RUM		
201	Sledgehammer Shot UR	7.50	15.00
202	Cerebral Assassin RUM		
203	The Game is Back... TB RUM		
204	Game Over? UR	7.50	15.00
205	The Game's Sleeper RUM		
206	Lunging Choke Hold RUM		
207	You Don't Want to Play Me RUM		
208	It's All About Control RUM		
209	Screw the Rules RUM		
210	A Beating You'll Never Forget RUM		
211	The Rock RUM		
212	The People's Champion RUM		
213	Take That Move... RUM		
214	Rock Bottom TB RUM		
215	Smackdown Hotel RUM		
216	The People's Eyebrow UR	7.50	15.00
217	The People's Elbow UR	7.50	15.00
218	Patented Rock Footstomp TB UR	7.50	15.00
219	Do You Smell... RUM		
220	Your Brush with... TB RUM		
221	Rock's Spit Punch RUM		
222	The Brahma Bull UR	7.50	15.00
223	Who in the Blue Hell... TB RUM		
224	Shades of the Great One RUM		
225	The People's Kip-Up UR	7.50	15.00
226	Remove the People's... TB RUM		
227	It Doesn't Matter... RUM		
228	You Bring the A$... RUM		
229	The People's DDT RUM		
230	Get Ready... TB RUM		
231	The Peep's Champ RUM		
232	Know Your Role... RUM		
233	Kane RUM		
234	The Big Freak'n Machine RUM		
235	Kane's Chokeslam RUM		
236	Kane's Flying Clothesline TB RUM		
237	Kane's Return RUM		
238	Kane's Tombstone Piledriver UR	7.50	15.00
239	Hellfire and Brimstone UR	7.50	15.00
240	Help's on the Way UR	7.50	15.00
241	Masked Vengeance UR	7.50	15.00
242	Boot to the Face RUM		
243	Chains of Destruction RUM		
244	Born of Hellfire RUM		
245	In the Presence... RUM		
246	Freaks are Cool TB UR	7.50	15.00
247	The Fire Still Burns RUM		
248	Big Freak'n Uppercut RUM		
249	My Path is Chosen RUM		
250	Hellfire Chokeslam TB RUM		
251	Big Freak'n Powerslam RUM		
252	Unmasked Vengeance RUM		
253	Kane's Rage RUM		
254	Chris Jericho RUM		
255	Highlight of the Night TB RUM		
256	Lionsault RUM		
257	Y2J RUM		
258	Don't You Never - Eeeever RUM		
259	Walls of Jericho UR	7.50	15.00
260	Ayatollah of Rock 'n' Roll-a TB UR	7.50	15.00
261	Springboard Drop Kick TB UR	7.50	15.00
262	Jerichoholics TB RUM		
263	Superior Acrobatics UR	7.50	15.00
264	Would You Please... RUM		
265	Happy You're Here... TB RUM		
266	I'm Better Than You TB RUM		
267	The Breakdown RUM		
268	I'm the King of the World RUM		
269	Highlight Reel RUM		
270	You Sanctimonious... UR	7.50	15.00
271	Listen Up, Junior... UR	7.50	15.00
272	My Obscenely Expensive... RUM		
273	Roll the Footage, Monkeys RUM		
274	Jericho's Ensuigri RUM		
275	Kurt Angle TB RUM		
276	Your Freaking Hero RUM		
277	Intensity RUM		
278	Integrity RUM		
279	Intelligence RUM		
280	Olympic Slam UR	7.50	15.00
281	It's True, It's True UR	7.50	15.00
282	I'll Make You Tap RUM		
283	Where Are Your Medals? UR	7.50	15.00
284	Angle Lock UR	7.50	15.00
285	Do YOU Live by... RUM		
286	Just Hold On a Second... RUM		
287	Collegiate Champions UR	7.50	15.00
288	Submit RUM		
289	Wrestling with a... TB RUM		
290	The Straps are Down UR	7.50	15.00
291	Oh, It's True UR	7.50	15.00
292	Angle's German Suplex RUM		
293	Whoo RUM		
294	Angle's Moonsault RUM		
295	Chris Benoit TB RUM		
296	The Crippler RUM		
297	Kamikaze Headbutt RUM		
298	Series of Suplexes RUM		
299	Rabid Wolverine TB RUM		
300	Crippler Crossface UR	7.50	15.00
301	Big Stupid Grin UR	7.50	15.00
302	Prove Me Wrong UR	7.50	15.00
303	First to Tap Out Match TB UR	7.50	15.00
304	Best Technical Wrestler... RUM		
305	A Victim of the Crippler TB RUM		
306	There's No Holding Me Back UR	7.50	15.00
307	Toothless Aggression UR	7.50	15.00
308	Cripple Opponent RUM		
309	Rabid Attack in the Corner TB RUM		
310	Surprise Drop Kick RUM		
311	Benoit's German Suplex RUM		
312	Pain is Inevitable RUM		
313	Eddie Guerrero RUM		
314	Snap Senton Splash RUM		
315	Study for Your GED RUM		
316	Latino Heeeeeeeat RUM		
317	Guerrero Frog Splash UR	7.50	15.00
318	Get Your GED TB UR	7.50	15.00
319	Eddie's Roll Up TB UR	7.50	15.00
320	Ultimo Rechazo UR	7.50	15.00
321	Whatchoo Talkin' 'bout... RUM		
322	Yo, Ese, I Know Your... TB RUM		
323	Lasso from El Paso RUM		
324	Gory Special RUM		
325	Viva La Raza Low Rider TB RUM		
326	Dudley Boyz RUM		
327	3D TB UR	7.50	15.00
328	Wazzzzuuup??? RUM		
329	TLC Match TB UR	7.50	15.00
330	Dudler Tough RUM		
331	Dudleyz3 RUM		
332	Beatings from Dudleyville RUM		
333	Blood is Thicker than Wood RUM		
334	Buh-Buh Ray Dudley TB RUM		
335	Buh-Buh Bomb TB UR	7.50	15.00
336	Catatonic Stare RUM		
337	My Name Is TB RUM		
338	Buh-Buh Drop RUM		
339	Buh-Buh Punch RUM		
340	D-Von Dudley RUM		
341	Testify TB UR	7.50	15.00
342	Spinning Elbow TB RUM		
343	Doin' the D-Von TB RUM		
344	Thou Shall Not... TB RUM		
345	D-Von -- Get the Table RUM		
346	Greetings from Dudleyville... TB UR	7.50	15.00
347	Brothers from Another Mother UR	7.50	15.00
348	Edge RUM		
349	Leader of the Edge... TB RUM		
350	Listen, You Reekazoid RUM		
351	Soda's Rule RUM		
352	Million Dollar Smile RUM		
353	Edge-O-Matic UR	7.50	15.00
354	You Think You Know Me? UR	7.50	15.00
355	Edge's Spear TB RUM		
356	Edge-acution UR	7.50	15.00
357	Big Slide in the Ring RUM		
358	Never Gonna Stop Me RUM		
359	You're a Human Vacuum... RUM		
360	Edgeucation of Adam... UR	7.50	15.00
361	Downward Spiral UR	7.50	15.00
362	Edge Kick RUM		
363	Scream if You Want It RUM		
364	'Cause I Want More RUM		
365	Christian RUM		
366	This is so Totally Unfair RUM		
367	Greetings to Our Fans... RUM		
368	Kazoo Theme Song RUM		
369	Unprettier UR	7.50	15.00
370	Temper Tantrum UR	7.50	15.00
371	Christian's Shades TB RUM		
372	Impaler RUM		
373	I Ain't No Sucka Neitha RUM		
374	To All My Peeps... RUM		
375	Matt Hardy RUM		
376	M.Hardy's Patented Leg Drop RUM		
377	Put It All on the Line TB RUM		
378	Matt's Moonsault TB RUM		
379	Twist of Fate UR	7.50	15.00
380	Live for the Moment UR	7.50	15.00
381	Team X-Treme UR	7.50	15.00
382	Roar for the Fans RUM		
383	Mattitude Adjustment RUM		
384	Version 1.0 TB RUM		
385	Side Effect RUM		
386	Era Mattitude Has Arrived RUM		
387	Big Show RUM		
388	Showstopper Chokeslam RUM		
389	Bog Show Splash RUM		
390	500 lbs. of Raw Power RUM		
391	Final Cut UR		
392	Wellllll UR	7.50	15.00
393	Big All Over UR	7.50	15.00
394	Mountain of a Man UR	7.50	15.00
395	You Can't Manhandle... RUM		
396	Showdown RUM		
397	Lita RUM		
398	Lita-canrana RUM		
399	Lita Drop Kick RUM		
400	Crimson Goddess RUM		
401	Lita-sault UR	7.50	15.00
402	X-Treme Thong UR	7.50	15.00
403	Lita's Twist of Fate UR	7.50	15.00
404	If You've Got It, Flaunt It UR	7.50	15.00
405	X-Treme Hedonism UR	7.50	15.00
406	The Goddess Returns RUM		
407	Lita's DDT TB RUM		
408	Rob Van Dam RUM		
409	Five Star Frog Splash TB RUM		
410	Extreme Monkey Flip TB RUM		
411	Rolling Thunder RUM		
412	Van Daminator UR	7.50	15.00
413	R-V-D UR	7.50	15.00
414	Dude, Nice Hang Time TB UR	7.50	15.00
415	Everything's Cool When... UR	7.50	15.00
416	Dude Whatever RUM		
417	Mr. Monday Night RUM		
418	Van Terminator RUM		
419	Booker T RUM		
420	Can You Dig It, Sucka? RUM		
421	Booker's Scissor Kick TB RUM		
422	Spinning T Kick RUM		
423	Bookend UR	7.50	15.00
424	Spinnerooni UR	7.50	15.00
425	Tell Me You Didn't Just... UR	7.50	15.00
426	Five Time Five Time... UR	7.50	15.00
427	Yo Dawg... RUM		
428	Houston Hangover RUM		
429	How Many Times? RUM		
430	Spike Dudley RUM		
431	Dudley Dog UR	7.50	15.00
432	150 lbs. Soaking Wet RUM		
433	Get Him, Boyz RUM		
434	Psychotic Bump RUM		
435	Brotherly Love RUM		
436	Giant Killer UR	7.50	15.00
437	Pound 4 Pound UR	7.50	15.00
438	William Regal RUM		
439	Union Jack RUM		
440	I've Been Besmirched RUM		
441	Goodwill Ambassador TB RUM		
442	Regal Stretch UR	7.50	15.00
443	Commissioner Regal's... RUM		
444	Listen Up, Sunshine UR	7.50	15.00
445	Regal Upper Class Punch UR	7.50	15.00
446	Proper Planning Prevents... RUM		
447	Keep It Simple, Sir RUM		
448	Ric Flair RUM		
449	Summer of Slam TB RUM		
450	Diamonds are Forever... RUM		
451	Now You're Going to School RUM		
452	The Dirtiest Player... TB RUM		
453	Stylin', Profilin', Limousine Ridin' UR	7.50	15.00
454	Wooooooooo UR	7.50	15.00
455	The Game Interferes TB UR	7.50	15.00
456	You're Going to Space... TB UR	7.50	15.00
457	The Flair Flop RUM		
458	Trish Stratus RUM		
459	Stratusfaction Bulldog TB RUM		
460	I've Been a Very Naughty Girl RUM		
461	Perhaps I Need a Spanking? RUM		
462	The TandA Factor UR	7.50	15.00
463	100 Stratusfaction... UR	7.50	15.00
464	Puppy Power RUM		
465	The StratusFear RUM		
466	Tajiri RUM		
467	Asian Mist TB RUM		
468	Tajiri's Handspring Elbow TB RUM		
469	Japanese Buzzsaw TB RUM		
470	Kick of Death UR	7.50	15.00

471	Tarantula TB RUM		
472	Octopus UR	7.50	15.00
473	Double Face Kick UR	7.50	15.00
474	Series of Kicks RUM		
475	Managed by Kyo Dai TB RUM		
476	Hurricane RUM		
477	Caped Body Press TB RUM		
478	To the Hurricycle TB RUM		
479	Whassupwitdat??? TB RUM		
480	Eye of the Hurricane UR	7.50	15.00
481	Stand Back There's... RUM		
482	Hurrislam UR	7.50	15.00
483	Shining Wizard Kick UR	7.50	15.00
484	Gregory Helms... RUM		
485	I've Got Hurri-Powers RUM		
486	Rey Mysterio RUM		
487	Luche Libre Extravaganza UR	7.50	15.00
488	The West Coast Pop TB UR	7.50	15.00
489	Too Fast For You RUM		
490	The 619 RUM		
491	Rey-Rey's Tope RUM		
492	West Coast Bronco Buster UR	7.50	15.00
493	Flying Body Press UR	7.50	15.00
494	Who's That Jumpin'... TB RUM		
495	Shawn Michaels RUM		
496	The Icon, The Showstoppa... UR	7.50	15.00
497	Sweet Chin Music UR	7.50	15.00
498	Don't Hunt What You... RUM		
499	Top Rope Elbow Drop RUM		
500	The Heart Break Kid RUM		
501	I'm Just a Sexy Boy UR	7.50	15.00
502	All Things are Possible UR	7.50	15.00
503	Rhyno RUM		
504	Gore Gore Gore UR	7.50	15.00
505	Extreme Warfare RUM		
506	Rhyno's Garbage Can RUM		
507	The Manbeast TB RUM		
508	Rhyno Stampede RUM		
509	Unstoppable RUM		
510	Unleash the Beast UR	7.50	15.00
511	Stacy Keibler RUM		
512	Straddle the Ropes UR	7.50	15.00
513	Superior Leg Work TB UR	7.50	15.00
514	Test or Freakzilla? RUM		
515	Pump Me Up RUM		
516	I Know How to Use Them RUM		
517	I Should've Been in that Magazine UR	7.50	15.00
518	Gail Kim and Molly Holly RUM		
519	Change Reality UR	7.50	15.00
520	Gail's Hurricanrana UR	7.50	15.00
521	Wake Up RUM		
522	Look Around RUM		
523	Molly-Go-Round RUM		
524	Control Your World UR	7.50	15.00
525	Bald is Beautiful UR	7.50	15.00
526	John Cena RUM		
527	Yo Kill da Beat UR	7.50	15.00
528	F-U UR		
529	You Can't See Me TB RUM		
530	Word Life TB RUM		
531	I'm Gonna Teach You... RUM		
532	So You Think You're... UR	7.50	15.00
533	Torrie Wilson RUM		
534	WWE Centerfold of the Year UR	7.50	15.00
535	Torrie's DDT UR	7.50	15.00
536	Does This Look Good on Me? RUM		
537	Strike a Pose RUM		
538	The Boise Beauty RUM		
539	Golden Thong Award UR	7.50	15.00
540	Victoria RUM		
541	Widow's Peak UR	7.50	15.00
542	Managed by Stevie Richards RUM		
543	All the Things She Said RUM		
544	Yes, I've Lost My Mind TB RUM		
545	Stevie Interferes RUM		
546	This is Not Enough UR	7.50	15.00
547	Evolution RUM		
548	Evolution is a Mystery UR	7.50	15.00
549	Paid, Laid, and Made UR	7.50	15.00
550	Yesterday is So Long Ago RUM		
551	I See the Line in the Sand RUM		
552	Nothing Ever Stays the Same RUM		
553	Paul Heyman RUM		
554	Let the Bodies Hit the Floor UR	7.50	15.00
555	You're Dangerously Close RUM		
556	Coach, Cole, or Finkel? RUM		
557	Big Boys Club RUM		
558	Do You Know Who... RUM		
559	Raw GM Eric Bischoff RUM		
560	Smackdown GM RUM		
561	Chavo's Inverted Powerbomb UR	7.50	15.00
562	It's All About the Benjamins RUM		
563	Greco Roman Specialists UR	7.50	15.00
564	Stone Cold Steve Austin... RUM		
565	Chris Jericho, Kane... RUM		
566	Rock, Deadman... RUM		
567	Rikishi, Chris Benoit... RUM		
568	APA or A-Train? RUM		
569	RVD or Booker T? UR	7.50	15.00
570	Edge or Big Show? UR	7.50	15.00
571	The People's Champ... RUM		
572	Mankind / Cactus Jack... RUM		
573	Backed by Mr. McMahon TB RUM		
574	Calling You Out RUM		
575	Chain Lashing TB RUM		
576	Managed by Vince... TB RUM		
577	Managed by Paul Heyman RUM		
578	Overhand Chairshot RUM		
579	Suicide Lariat RUM		
580	Atomic Knee Drop RUM		
581	Banned from Ringside RUM		
582	Divas Divas Divas RUM		
583	Vince McMahon Interferes RUM		
584	That Won't Make the Cut RUM		
585	Testicular Fortitude RUM		
586	I'm Hardcore I'm Hardcore RUM		
587	Back to Basics RUM		
588	Arm Bar RUM		
589	Arm Bar Takedown RUM		
590	Arm Drag RUM		
591	Atomic Drop RUM		
592	Belly to Back Suplex RUM		
593	Belly to Belly Suplex RUM		
594	Body Slam RUM		
595	Chop RUM		
596	Clothesline RUM		
597	Collar and Elbow Lockup RUM		
598	Drop Kick RUM		
599	Haymaker RUM		
600	Head Butt RUM		
601	Hip Toss RUM		
602	Press Slam RUM		
603	Punch RUM		
604	Roundhouse Punch RUM		
605	Russian Leg Sweep RUM		
606	Snap Mare RUM		
607	Vertical Suplex RUM		
608	Wrist Lock RUM		
609	Backhand Slap RUM		
610	Drop Toe Hold RUM		
611	Elbow Drop RUM		
612	Foot Stomp RUM		
613	Hammerlock RUM		
614	Comeback TB RUM		
615	Dem Damn Dudleyz TB RUM		
616	Hurricanrana TB RUM		
617	Chop to the Chest TB RUM		
618	Single Arm DDT TB RUM		
619	Ladder in the Ring TB RUM		
620	Drawing Extra Heat TB RUM		
621	Knife-Edge Chop TB RUM		
622	Springboard TB RUM		
623	Gut Punch TB RUM		
624	Spine Buster TB RUM		
625	DDT TB RUM		
626	Ankle Lock TB RUM		
627	No Chance in Hell TB RUM		
628	Great Technical... TB RUM		
629	Throw Into the Corner... RUM		
630	Charismatic Style TB RUM		
631	Table Table Table TB RUM		
632	Who Booked This Match? TB RUM		
633	Maintain Hold TB RUM		
634	Enter the Stratusphere RUM		
635	Puppies Puppies TB RUM		
636	Diversion TB RUM		
637	Hell in a Cell Match RUM		
638	Indian Strap Match RUM		
639	Duchess of Queensbury... RUM		
640	Bulldog Takedown TB RUM		
641	Corkscrew DDT TB RUM		
642	Did I Just Say... TB RUM		
643	Don't Cross the Boss TB RUM		

2005 Comic Images WWE Raw Deal Unforgiven

1	Counter Slash C	.12	.25
2	Corkscrew Elbow C	.12	.25
3	Body Block C	.12	.25
4	Spinning Leg Drop C	.12	.25
5	Missile Dropkick TB U	.50	1.00
6	Shooting Star Press TB U	.50	1.00
7	Girly Slap C	.12	.25
8	Shoulder Block TB C	.12	.25
9	Running Elbow Smash TB C	.12	.25
10	Kidney Punch C	.12	.25
11	Standing Drop Kick TB C	.12	.25
12	Knee Breaker TB U	.50	1.00
13	Back Fist TB U	.50	1.00
14	Back Body Drop TB U	.50	1.00
15	Reverse Clothesline U	.50	1.00
16	Everything and the Kitchen Sink U	.50	1.00
17	Ap Chaki Kick R	2.00	4.00
18	Precision Clothesline R	2.00	4.00
19	Baseball Slide TB R	2.00	4.00
20	Lock, Stock, and Barrel R	2.00	4.00
21	Rolling Hip Toss C	.12	.25
22	Japanese Arm Drag TB C	.12	.25
23	Sidewalk Slam TB C	.12	.25
24	Flip C	.12	.25
25	Running Spinebuster TB C	.12	.25
26	Shoot Suplex C	.12	.25
27	Snap Suplex TB U	.50	1.00
28	Headlock Takedown TB U	.50	1.00
29	Small Package TB U	.50	1.00
30	Swinging Neck Breaker U	.50	1.00
31	Pendulum Back Breaker U	.50	1.00
32	Powerbomb TB U	.50	1.00
33	Full Nelson Slam TB R	2.00	4.00
34	Shoot Russian Leg Sweep R	2.00	4.00
35	German Suplex TB R	2.00	4.00
36	Sit Out Powerbomb TB R	2.00	4.00
37	Tornado DDT TB R	2.00	4.00
38	Workin' on the Knee TB R	2.00	4.00
39	Precision Power Slam R	2.00	4.00
40	Side Headlock C	.12	.25
41	Bear Hug TB C	.12	.25
42	Full Nelson TB C	.12	.25
43	Bow and Arrow TB C	.12	.25
44	Guillotine Stretch TB C	.12	.25
45	Wrist Breaker U	.50	1.00
46	Arm Stretch U	.50	1.00
47	Sleeper TB U	.50	1.00
48	Side Chinlock U	.50	1.00
49	Camel Clutch TB U	.50	1.00
50	Spinning Toe Hold R	2.00	4.00
51	Boston Crab TB R	2.00	4.00
52	Precision Leg Lock R	2.00	4.00
53	Torture Rack TB R	2.00	4.00
54	Choke Hold TB R	2.00	4.00
55	Lift a Boot TB C	.12	.25
56	Spot Adjustment U	.50	1.00
57	A Revolution of the Mind R	2.00	4.00
58	Build Momentum C	.12	.25
59	Viva Las Divas C	.12	.25
60	Shake It Off TB C	.12	.25
61	Listen Loud and Clear C	.12	.25
62	Hardcore Timekeeper's Bell G	.12	.25
63	Not Yet TB C	.12	.25
64	Afterburn U	.50	1.00
65	Stagger TB U	.50	1.00
66	Kickin' It Old School U	.50	1.00
67	That's It U	.50	1.00
68	Marking Out TB U	.50	1.00
69	Grab WWE Timekeeper... U	.50	1.00
70	Sharmell: Sizzling Spouse R	2.00	4.00
71	Maria: Ideal Interviewer R	2.00	4.00
72	Christy: Curvy Cutie R	2.00	4.00
73	Melina: Naughty Manager R	2.00	4.00
74	Lilian: Amazing Announcer R	2.00	4.00
75	Candice: Internet Icon R	2.00	4.00
76	Hello, Ladies C	.12	.25
77	Rochester, New York C	.12	.25
78	Trash Talkin' Interview TB C	.12	.25
79	Who's Cooler... C	.12	.25
80	Blindsided Precision U	.50	1.00
81	Backstage Shenanigans U	.50	1.00
82	Pyrotechnic Volley U	.50	1.00
83	You Can't Spell... U	.50	1.00
84	Fans Love an Underdog R	2.00	4.00
85	Frankie Takes Hollywood R	2.00	4.00
86	Inferno Match TB R	2.00	4.00
87	The Old Switcheroo R	2.00	4.00
88	Not in Front of the Kids C	.12	.25
89	The GM of Stevie Night Heat C	.12	.25
90	This is Just the Beginning C	.12	.25
91	You Knew it Would End This Way C	.12	.25
92	Here I Stand: the Champion U	.50	1.00
93	WWE Divas: the Next Generation U	.50	1.00
94	Eviscerated by Viscera U	.50	1.00
95	WWE Divas Rule U	.50	1.00
96	I'm Just Hitting My Stride R	2.00	4.00

97	In This Ring, I Just Might Be R	2.00	4.00
98	Introduce Your Brain... R	2.00	4.00
99	One More Time... R	2.00	4.00
100	Batista EX		
101	The Destroyer UR	7.50	15.00
102	Batista Bomb UR	7.50	15.00
103	The Animal EX		
104	Physically Dominant Force EX		
105	Batista's Spinebuster EX		
106	Leader of the Peepulation EX		
107	Managed by Tyson Tomko UR	7.50	15.00
108	Just Close Your Eyes UR	7.50	15.00
109	That's How I Roll EX		
110	The Christian Coalition EX		
111	Tomakazi DDT EX		
112	Christy EX		
113	Temecula, California UR	7.50	15.00
114	2004 Diva Search Winner UR	7.50	15.00
115	Ain't It Fair? EX		
116	Christy's Twist EX		
117	Redheaded Sparkplug EX		
118	Immortal One EX		
119	Feathered Boa UR	7.50	15.00
120	I am a Real American UR	7.50	15.00
121	Hogan's Patented... EX		
122	Fight For the Rights... EX		
123	In My Day, a Maneuver... EX		
124	Rowdy Roddy Piper EX		
125	Bagpipe Introduction UR	7.50	15.00
126	Piper's Pit UR	7.50	15.00
127	Over Sell: Hot Rod Style EX		
128	Hot Rod EX		
129	Cowboy Bob Orton Interferes EX		
130	Smackdown GM... EX		
131	Haterade UR	7.50	15.00
132	Holla Holla Holla UR	7.50	15.00
133	Your Freaking Hero... EX		
134	Thuggin' and Buggin' EX		
135	The Mack Militant EX		
136	Heidenreich PR		
137	Disasterpiece UR	7.50	15.00
138	Heidenreich's Elbow Drop PR		
139	Who Wants to be My... PR		
140	A Friendly Boot PR		
141	Running Shoulder Block PR		
142	Gene Snitsky PR		
143	Baby Carriage UR	7.50	15.00
144	You Have Tasty Toes PR		
145	It's Not My Fault PR		
146	No Fault Clothesline PR		
147	No Fault Pump Handle... PR		
148	MNM PR		
149	The Snapshot UR	7.50	15.00
150	Managed by Melina PR		
151	There's Nothing Sweeter PR		
152	A-List Attack PR		
153	Melina Interferes PR		
154	Hurri-Friends PR		
155	The Hurri-Friends Armory UR	7.50	15.00
156	Super Masks... PR		
157	Super Storm Front PR		
158	Greetings, Citizen PR		
159	Stacy's Roundhouse Kick PR		
160	Unleash Hell PR		
161	Nobody's Safe PR		
162	Making the Game PR		
163	Finally The Rock... PR		
164	Another Big Freak'n... PR		
165	Chris Jericho PR		
166	Wolverine's Sharpshooter PR		
167	Addicted to the Heat PR		
168	Kurt Angle Invitational PR		
169	Edge's Running Spear PR		
170	Big Show's F5 PR		
171	When I Get You Alone PR		
172	The Hidden Dragon... PR		
173	Booker's Thrust Kick PR		
174	The Power of the Punch PR		
175	Flair's Chop Block PR		
176	The MaTrish Move PR		
177	Educated Hands PR		
178	Restricted Use in This Area PR		
179	Forever PR		
180	Flying Forearm PR		
181	Uncle Eric's Karate Kick PR		
182	Daddy's Little Girl TB PR		
183	Five Knuckle Shuffle PR		
184	Managed by Stacy Keibler PR		
185	Want to Take My Test? PR		
186	Spider Web Moonsault PR		
187	Girly Grab PR		
188	When You Run... PR		
189	Never Forgive... PR		
190	McMahon-us Interrupt-us UR	7.50	15.00
191	Gentlemen's Establishment UR	7.50	15.00
192	Hardcore Originator of ECW UR	7.50	15.00
193	Orlando Jordan... UR	7.50	15.00
194	Destiny UR	7.50	15.00
195	Here Comes the Money TB UR	7.50	15.00
196	Incredible Athleticism UR	7.50	15.00
197	Hello, My Name is Eugene UR	7.50	15.00
198	Le Bonsoir UR	7.50	15.00

2003 Comic Images WWE Raw Deal Velocity

1	Flying Mare C	.12	.25
2	Diving Takedown C	.12	.25
3	Quick Follow Through U	.50	1.00
4	Shoot Aerial 360-Degree Kick U	.50	1.00
5	Missile Shoulder Block R	2.00	4.00
6	Roll Up R	2.00	4.00
7	Standing Drop Kick C	.12	.25
8	Abdominal Rake C	.12	.25
9	Shoot Punch U	.50	1.00
10	Rapid-Fire Punches U	.50	1.00
11	Lariat Takedown R	2.00	4.00
12	Bionic Elbow R	2.00	4.00
13	Lock-up C	.12	.25
14	Oklahoma Roll C	.12	.25
15	Fall-Away Suplex C	.12	.25
16	Single Leg Takedown U	.50	1.00
17	Shoot Slam U	.50	1.00
18	Corkscrew DDT U	.50	1.00
19	Bulldog Takedown R	2.00	4.00
20	Rolling Headlock Vise R	2.00	4.00
21	Slam Bomb R	2.00	4.00
22	Body Scissors C	.12	.25
23	Breather Hold C	.12	.25
24	Waist Lock U	.50	1.00
25	Shoot Headlock U	.50	1.00
26	Sleeper Bomb R	2.00	4.00
27	Flying Body Lock R	2.00	4.00
28	Cartwheel C	.12	.25
29	Hold the Phone U	.50	1.00
30	Get the F Out R	2.00	4.00
31	He's as Crazy as a Pet Raccoon C	.12	.25
32	I'm Sorry, But You're Boring Me C	.12	.25
33	Measure Him C	.12	.25
34	Not on My Broadcast C	.12	.25
35	Wanna Know What I'm Gonna Do? C	.12	.25
36	Hot Tag [Tag Team Only Symbol] C	.12	.25
37	Back-and-Forth Action U	.50	1.00
38	Fire Extinguisher U	.50	1.00
39	Caught Red-handed U	.50	1.00
40	Gettin' Beat Like a... U	.50	1.00
41	Good Things Sometimes Happen U	.50	1.00
42	It Pays to be Evil U	.50	1.00
43	Here's a Ratings Booster R	2.00	4.00
44	Did I Just Say Three Minutes? R	2.00	4.00
45	One of a Kind R	2.00	4.00
46	Defensive Stance R	2.00	4.00
47	He's Runnin' Like a Scalded Dawg R	2.00	4.00
48	Singapore Cane R	2.00	4.00
49	Don't You Usually Wrestle... C	.12	.25
50	Educated Feet C	.12	.25
51	Ring Psychology: Back C	.12	.25
52	Ring Psychology: Neck C	.12	.25
53	Unorthodox Style of Wrestling C	.12	.25
54	Lumberjack Match U	.50	1.00
55	Pay-Per-View Main Event U	.50	1.00
56	Raw or Smackdown... U	.50	1.00
57	Velocity U	.50	1.00
58	Proper Conditioning U	.50	1.00
59	I Aims ta be Startin' "Sump'tin" R	2.00	4.00
60	Managed by Eric Bischoff R	2.00	4.00
61	Managed by Shane O'Mac R	2.00	4.00
62	I'm the Champ... R	2.00	4.00
63	My Sacrifice R	2.00	4.00
64	You Can't Spell Furniture... C	.12	.25
65	Check This Out C	.12	.25
66	Desire C	.12	.25
67	Dragged to the Center of the Ring C	.12	.25
68	See How It Feels C	.12	.25
69	Reap the Rewards U	.50	1.00
70	The Ref Got in the Way U	.50	1.00
71	Hold On It's Not Time... U	.50	1.00
72	Human Suplex Machine U	.50	1.00
73	Beg For Mercy U	.50	1.00
74	Justice for All R	2.00	4.00
75	The King Interferes R	2.00	4.00
76	That's J.R.'s Animal Hat Trick... R	2.00	4.00
77	Title Belt Clubberin' R	2.00	4.00
78	The Big Freak'n Machine EX		
79	Freaks Are Cool UR	7.50	15.00
80	The Fire Still Burns PR		
81	Big Freak'n Uppercut EX		
82	My Path is Chosen EX		
83	Hellfire Chokeslam EX		
84	The Game EX		
85	Game Over? UR	7.50	15.00
86	The Game's Sleeper PR		
87	Lunging Choke Hold EX		
88	You Don't Want to Play Me EX		
89	It's All About Control EX		
90	Goldust EX		
91	Shattered Dreams Production UR	7.50	15.00
92	Shattered Dreams UR	7.50	15.00
93	<inhale> Goooooooooooldust EX		
94	Butt Bump EX		
95	Director's Cut EX		
96	Brock Lesnar EX		
97	Backstage Warm-up Routine UR	7.50	15.00
98	F-5 UR	7.50	15.00
99	An Irresistible Force... EX		
100	The Next Big Thing EX		
101	Series of Back Breakers EX		
102	The People's Champion EX		
103	The People's Kip-up UR	7.50	15.00
104	Remove the People's... PR		
105	It Doesn't Matter... EX		
106	You Bring the A$... EX		
107	The People's DDT EX		
108	Rey Mysterio EX		
109	Luche Libre Extravaganza UR	7.50	15.00
110	The West Coast Pop UR	7.50	15.00
111	Too Fast For You EX		
112	The 619 EX		
113	Rey-Rey's Tope EX		
114	3 Minute Warning PR		
115	Jamal's Top Rope Splash UR	7.50	15.00
116	Your Three Minutes Are Up PR		
117	Jamal's Atomic Samoan Drop PR		
118	Victim of the Revolving... PR		
119	Double Elbow Drop PR		
120	Jamie Noble PR		
121	The Trailer Hitch UR	7.50	15.00
122	Managed by Nidia PR		
123	Now I'm Gonna Get... PR		
124	I'm Jamie Noble, Boy PR		
125	Go On - Give 'im Some Sugar PR		
126	Throwin' Big Ol' Soup Bones... PR		
127	The Breakdown PR		
128	Raisin' the Roof PR		
129	Just Hold On a Second, Mister PR		
130	Red Hook's Premiere... PR		
131	A Victim of the Crippler PR		
132	Yo, Ese, I Know You, Homes PR		
133	Dudley Tough PR		
134	Never Gonna Stop Me PR		
135	Impaler PR		
136	Mattitude Adjustment PR		
137	That's Suicide PR		
138	Mountain of a Man UR	7.50	15.00
139	If You've Got It, Flaunt It UR	7.50	15.00
140	Everything's Cool When You're UR	7.50	15.00
141	Five Time Five Time... UR	7.50	15.00
142	Pound 4 Pound UR	7.50	15.00
143	Regal Upper Class Punch UR	7.50	15.00
144	Raven's Playground UR	7.50	15.00
145	When Hulkamania Runs... UR	7.50	15.00
146	The Game Interferes UR	7.50	15.00
147	We're Sorry But This Has... UR	7.50	15.00
148	eM pleH UR	7.50	15.00
149	Octopus UR	7.50	15.00
150	Hurrislam UR	7.50	15.00
10/TR	World Heavyweight Title Belt R	2.00	4.00
11/TR	Cruiserweight Title Belt R	2.00	4.00

2004 Comic Images WWE Raw Deal Vengeance

1	Leaping Neck Snap C	.12	.25
2	Revolving Takedown U	.50	1.00
3	Flying Leg Scissors R	2.00	4.00
4	Spinning Kick C	.12	.25
5	Right Cross Punch C	.12	.25
6	Left Cross Punch C	.12	.25
7	Judo Thrust U	.50	1.00
8	Lariat U	.50	1.00
9	Steel Chain Shot U	.50	1.00
10	Short Arm Rib Breaker R	2.00	4.00
11	Blindside Kick R	2.00	4.00
12	Struck by an Unknown... R	2.00	4.00

#	Card	Price 1	Price 2
13	Snap Neckbreaker C	.12	.25
14	Pretzel Jerk C	.12	.25
15	Face Driver C	.12	.25
16	Vertical DDT Drop C	.12	.25
17	Judo Takedown U	.50	1.00
18	Quick Snap Body Slam U	.50	1.00
19	Double Underhook Power Bomb U	.50	1.00
20	Blindside Slam U	.50	1.00
21	Suplex R	2.00	4.00
22	Military Slam R	2.00	4.00
23	Takedown R	2.00	4.00
24	Death Valley Driver R	2.00	4.00
25	Ankle Torque C	.12	.25
26	Triangle Choke C	.12	.25
27	Body Lock C	.12	.25
28	Judo Choke U	.50	1.00
29	Wraparound Wrist Lock U	.50	1.00
30	Headlock U	.50	1.00
31	Apply Legal Leverage R	2.00	4.00
32	Blindside Choke R	2.00	4.00
33	Super Hold R	2.00	4.00
34	I Already Warned You C	.12	.25
35	Quick Reflexes C	.12	.25
36	Unexpected Turn of Events C	.12	.25
37	Blindsided Ego U	.50	1.00
38	Leave Me Alone U	.50	1.00
39	Blindsided Control U	.50	1.00
40	Two R	2.00	4.00
41	Headstrong R	2.00	4.00
42	SloppyVery Sloppy R	2.00	4.00
43	Suplex into the Ring C	.12	.25
44	Chain Wrestling C	.12	.25
45	When Hell Freezes Over C	.12	.25
46	Minute Hold C	.12	.25
47	Throw Into the Ring C	.12	.25
48	J.R. Style Donnybrook C	.12	.25
49	Chained Heat U	.50	1.00
50	Down and Out U	.50	1.00
51	According to the Contract Table U	.50	1.00
52	Last Chance U	.50	1.00
53	J.R. Style Authentic BBQ Sauce U	.50	1.00
54	For the Love of God - Why, King, Why? U	.50	1.00
55	Escape the Rules R	2.00	4.00
56	That's Broken R	2.00	4.00
57	He's Playing Possum? R	2.00	4.00
58	J.R. Style Push R	2.00	4.00
59	Now or Never R	2.00	4.00
60	Enough With the Trash Talk R	2.00	4.00
61	Anaheim, California C	.12	.25
62	Atlanta, Georgia C	.12	.25
63	Newcastle, England C	.12	.25
64	Omaha, Nebraska C	.12	.25
65	Calgary, Alberta, Canada U	.50	1.00
66	Las Vegas, Nevada U	.50	1.00
67	New York, New York U	.50	1.00
68	Saskatoon, Saskatchewan... U	.50	1.00
69	Houston, Texas R	2.00	4.00
70	Philadelphia, Pennsylvania R	2.00	4.00
71	Raleigh, North Carolina R	2.00	4.00
72	Springfield, Illinois R	2.00	4.00
73	A Chorus of Boos C	.12	.25
74	Spontaneous Combustion C	.12	.25
75	This is Gonna Be a Rocket Buster C	.12	.25
76	Old School Beating C	.12	.25
77	First Blood Match U	.50	1.00
78	The Title is on the Line U	.50	1.00
79	You Rang? U	.50	1.00
80	You, Me, and Whoever? U	.50	1.00
81	Bad Blood R	2.00	4.00
82	Bitter Rivals R	2.00	4.00
83	It's All About the Game R	2.00	4.00
84	Managed by Dawn Marie R	2.00	4.00
85	Hardcore Style C	.12	.25
86	Immune to Pain C	.12	.25
87	Number One Contender C	.12	.25
88	The Beautiful People C	.12	.25
89	Grab the Ref C	.12	.25
90	Desperate Tag U	.50	1.00
91	Ringside Assistance U	.50	1.00
92	You're as Graceful... U	.50	1.00
93	Revolutionizing the Business U	.50	1.00
94	Chain Finisher U	.50	1.00
95	All Thatand Nothing? R	2.00	4.00
96	Divas Revealed R	2.00	4.00
97	To the Rescue R	2.00	4.00
98	Unscrupulous S.O.B. R	2.00	4.00
99	Cheap Accolades R	2.00	4.00
100	Evolution EX		
101	Evolution is a Mystery UR	7.50	15.00
102	Paid, Laid, and Made UR	7.50	15.00
103	Yesterday is So Long Ago EX		
104	I See the Line in the Sand EX		
105	Nothing Ever Stays the Same EX		
106	The Highlight of the Night EX		
107	You Sanctimounious... UR	7.50	15.00
108	Listen Up, Junior... UR	7.50	15.00
109	My Obscenely Expensive... EX		
110	Roll the Footage, Monkeys EX		
111	Jericho's Ensugiri EX		
112	The Mystery Wrestler EX		
113	You Don't Want to Go... UR	7.50	15.00
114	Mankind / Cactus Jack... EX		
115	Testicular Fortitude EX		
116	I'm Hardcore I'm Hardcore EX		
117	Leader of the Edge Army EX		
118	Edgeucation of Adam... UR	7.50	15.00
119	Downward Spiral UR	7.50	15.00
120	Edge Kick EX		
121	Scream If You Want It EX		
122	Cause I Want More EX		
123	Paul Heyman EX		
124	Let the Bodies Hit the Floor UR	7.50	15.00
125	You're Dangerously Close PR		
126	Coach, Cole, or Finkel? EX		
127	Big Boys Club EX		
128	Do You Know Who... EX		
129	Your Freaking Hero EX		
130	The Straps are Down UR	7.50	15.00
131	Oh, It's True UR	7.50	15.00
132	Angle's German Suplex EX		
133	Wooooo0 EX		
134	Angle's Moonsault EX		
135	FBI PR		
136	It's a Numbers Game UR	7.50	15.00
137	FBI Hit List PR		
138	The Arrivederci PR		
139	The Whack PR		
140	The Fuhgeddaboutit PR		
141	The A-Train PR		
142	Snot Rocket UR	7.50	15.00
143	Who Do You Think You Are? PR		
144	Chugga-chugga... PR		
145	Derailer PR		
146	Train Wreck PR		
147	Managed by Paul Bearer PR		
148	Know Your Role... PR		
149	Kane's Rage PR		
150	Rikishi's Hip Toss PR		
151	Pain is Inevitable PR		
152	Viva La Raza Low Rider PR		
153	WWE Commentators PR		
154	The Best Surprises... PR		
155	Blood is Thicker Than Wood PR		
156	To All My Peeps... PR		
157	Era of Mattitude Has Arrived PR		
158	Lita's DDT PR		
159	Van Terminator PR		
160	How Many Times? PR		
161	Keep It Simple, Sir PR		
162	The StratusFear PR		
163	Managed by Kyo Dai PR		
164	I've Got Hurri-Powers PR		
165	Who's That Jumpin'... PR		
166	Noble Bomb PR		
167	Didn't I Already Fire You? PR		
168	The People's Champ... PR		
169	Belly-to-Belly Steinerplex UR	7.50	15.00
170	All Things Are Possible UR	7.50	15.00
171	Greco Roman Specialists UR	7.50	15.00
172	Test's Top Rope... UR	7.50	15.00
173	Unleash the Beast UR	7.50	15.00
174	I Should've Been in That Magazine UR	7.50	15.00
175	Control Your World UR	7.50	15.00
176	Bald is Beautiful UR	7.50	15.00
177	So You Think You're... UR	7.50	15.00
178	The Boss's Main Squeeze UR	7.50	15.00
179	Golden Thong Award UR	7.50	15.00
180	This is Not Enough UR	7.50	15.00
181	Nidia's Mink Coat UR	7.50	15.00

2000 Comic Images WWF Raw Deal

#	Card	Price 1	Price 2
1	Chop C	.12	.25
2	Punch C	.12	.25
3	Head Butt C	.12	.25
4	Roundhouse Punch C	.12	.25
5	Haymaker C	.12	.25
6	Back Body Drop C	.12	.25
7	Big Boot C	.12	.25
8	Shoulder Block U	.50	1.00
9	Kick U	.50	1.00
10	Cross Body Block U	.50	1.00
11	Cheap Shot From the Corner U	.50	1.00
12	Ensugiri U	.50	1.00
13	Running Elbow Smash U	.50	1.00
14	Drop Kick U	.50	1.00
15	Discus Punch U	.50	1.00
16	Superkick R	2.00	4.00
17	Spinning Heel Kick R	2.00	4.00
18	Spear R	2.00	4.00
19	Clothesline R	2.00	4.00
20	Chair Shot R	2.00	4.00
21	Hurricanrana R	2.00	4.00
22	Arm Bar Takedown C	.12	.25
23	Hip Toss C	.12	.25
24	Arm Drag C	.12	.25
25	Russian Leg Sweep C	.12	.25
26	Snap Mare C	.12	.25
27	Gut Buster C	.12	.25
28	Body Slam C	.12	.25
29	Back Breaker C	.12	.25
30	Double Leg Takedown U	.50	1.00
31	Fireman's Carry U	.50	1.00
32	Headlock Takedown U	.50	1.00
33	Belly to Belly Suplex U	.50	1.00
34	Atomic Facebuster U	.50	1.00
35	Atomic Drop U	.50	1.00
36	Inverse Atomic Drop U	.50	1.00
37	Vertical Suplex U	.50	1.00
38	Belly to Back Suplex U	.50	1.00
39	Pump Handle Slam U	.50	1.00
40	Reverse DDT U	.50	1.00
41	Samoan Drop R	2.00	4.00
42	Sit Out Powerbomb R	2.00	4.00
43	Bulldog R	2.00	4.00
44	Fisherman's Suplex R	2.00	4.00
45	DDT R	2.00	4.00
46	Power Slam R	2.00	4.00
47	Powerbomb R	2.00	4.00
48	Press Slam R	2.00	4.00
49	Collar and Elbow Lockup C	.12	.25
50	Wrist Lock C	.12	.25
51	Arm Bar C	.12	.25
52	Chin Lock C	.12	.25
53	Bear Hug C	.12	.25
54	Full Nelson C	.12	.25
55	Choke Hold C	.12	.25
56	Step Over Toe Hold C	.12	.25
57	Ankle Lock U	.50	1.00
58	Standing Side Headlock U	.50	1.00
59	Cobra Clutch U	.50	1.00
60	Bow and Arrow U	.50	1.00
61	Chicken Wing U	.50	1.00
62	Sleeper R	2.00	4.00
63	Camel Clutch R	2.00	4.00
64	Boston Crab R	2.00	4.00
65	Guillotine Stretch R	2.00	4.00
66	Abdominal Stretch R	.75	1.50
67	Torture Rack R	2.00	4.00
68	Figure Four Leg Lock R	2.00	4.00
69	Combination Attack R	2.00	4.00
70	Step Aside C	.12	.25
71	Escape Move C	.12	.25
72	Break the Hold C	.12	.25
73	Trip C	.12	.25
74	Rolling Takedown U	.50	1.00
75	Knee to the Gut U	.50	1.00
76	Elbow to the Face U	.50	1.00
77	Clean Break U	.50	1.00
78	Partner Interference R	2.00	4.00
79	Manager Interferes R	2.00	4.00
80	Disqualification R	2.00	4.00
81	No Chance in Hell R	2.00	4.00
82	Hmmm C	.12	.25
83	Don't Think Too Hard C	.12	.25
84	Tag in Partner C	.12	.25
85	Whaddya Got? C	.12	.25
86	Not Yet C	.12	.25
87	Jockeying for Position C	.12	.25
88	Irish Whip C	.12	.25
89	Flash in the Pan C	.12	.25
90	View of Villainy C	.12	.25
91	Shake It Off U	.50	1.00
92	Offer Handshake U	.50	1.00
93	Roll Out of the Ring U	.50	1.00
94	Distract the Ref U	.50	1.00
95	Recovery U	.50	1.00
96	Spit At Opponent U	.50	1.00
97	Double Team U	.50	1.00
98	Get Crowd Support U	.50	1.00
99	Comeback R	2.00	4.00
100	Ego Boost R	2.00	4.00

101	Deluding Yourself R	2.00	4.00
102	Stagger R	2.00	4.00
103	Diversion R	2.00	4.00
104	Marking Out R	2.00	4.00
105	Puppies Puppies R	2.00	4.00
106	Shane O'Mac R	2.00	4.00
107	Maintain Hold R	2.00	4.00
108	Pat and Gerry R	2.00	4.00
109	Stone Cold Stunner UR	7.50	15.00
110	Open Up a Can of Whoop-A$ UR	7.50	15.00
111	Undertaker's Tombstone... UR	7.50	15.00
112	Power of Darkness UR	7.50	15.00
113	Mandible Claw UR	7.50	15.00
114	Mr. Socko UR	7.50	15.00
115	Pedigree UR	7.50	15.00
116	Chyna Interferes UR	7.50	15.00
117	The People's Eyebrow UR	7.50	15.00
118	The People's Elbow UR	7.50	15.00
119	Kane's Tombstone Piledriver UR	7.50	15.00
120	Hellfire and Brimstone UR	7.50	15.00
121	Walls of Jericho UR	7.50	15.00
122	Ayatollah of Rock 'n' Roll-a UR	7.50	15.00
123	STONE COLD STEVE AUSTIN EX		
124	Austin Elbow Smash EX		
125	Lou Thesz Press EX		
126	Double Digits EX		
127	THE UNDERTAKER EX		
128	Undertaker's Chokeslam EX		
129	Undertaker's Flying Clothesline EX		
130	Undertaker Sits Up EX		
131	MANKIND EX		
132	Have a Nice Day EX		
133	Double Arm DDT EX		
134	Tree of Woe EX		
135	HHH EX		
136	Leaping Knee to the Face EX		
137	Facebuster EX		
138	I Am the Game. EX		
139	THE ROCK EX		
140	Smackdown Hotel EX		
141	Take That Move EX		
142	Rock Bottom EX		
143	KANE EX		
144	Kane's Chokeslam EX		
145	Kane's Flying Clothesline EX		
146	Kane's Return EX		
147	CHRIS JERICHO EX		
148	Lionsault EX		
149	Y2J EX		
150	Don't You Never EVER EX		
1TR	WWF Heavyweight Title Belt		
2TR	WWF Intercontinental Title Belt		
3TR	WWF European Title Belt		

2001 Comic Images WWF Raw Deal Backlash

1	Flying Head Scissors C	.12	.25
2	Big Splash in the Corner C	.12	.25
3	Flying Clothesline U	.50	1.00
4	Drive Opponent Thru Announcer's Table U	.50	1.00
5	Crucifix Rollup R	2.00	4.00
6	Chop to the Chest C	.12	.25
7	Slap the Taste out of Your Mouth C	.12	.25
8	Leg Sweep C	.12	.25
9	Struck by a Kendo Stick C	.12	.25
10	Pop the Guy On the Apron U	.50	1.00
11	Running Lariat U	.50	1.00
12	Garbage Can Lid U	.50	1.00
13	Stun Gun R	2.00	4.00
14	Hung Out to Dry R	2.00	4.00
15	Running Clothesline R	2.00	4.00
16	Scoop Slam C	.12	.25
17	Leg Drag C	.12	.25
18	Neck Breaker C	.12	.25
19	Rib Breaker C	.12	.25
20	Tiger Bomb C	.12	.25
21	Single Arm DDT U	.50	1.00
22	Tandem Atomic Drop U	.50	1.00
23	Brainbuster U	.50	1.00
24	Spine Buster U	.50	1.00
25	Workin' on the Knee R	2.00	4.00
26	Half Hour Suplex R	2.00	4.00
27	Clutch onto Opponent C	.12	.25
28	Captive Tag Out C	.12	.25
29	Arm Wrench C	.12	.25
30	Entangle In the Ropes C	.12	.25
31	Apply Illegal Leverage U	.50	1.00
32	Texas Cloverleaf U	.50	1.00
33	Microphone Cord R	2.00	4.00
34	Sharpshooter R	2.00	4.00
35	Clumsy Opponent C	.12	.25
36	No Sell Maneuver C	.12	.25
37	Over Sell Maneuver C	.12	.25
38	Kissing Up to the Stinkin' Fans U	.50	1.00
39	Hey That's Cheap Heat U	.50	1.00
40	Blown Spot R	2.00	4.00
41	Charismatic Style C	.12	.25
42	Set Him Up C	.12	.25
43	Great Technical Knowledge C	.12	.25
44	Turn the Match... C	.12	.25
45	Amazing Display of Power C	.12	.25
46	Adrenaline Rush C	.12	.25
47	Let's Take it Home C	.12	.25
48	Drawing Extra Heat U	.50	1.00
49	Well-Deserved Push U	.50	1.00
50	Propel Partner U	.50	1.00
51	Ladder In the Ring U	.50	1.00
52	Giving Away the Business U	.50	1.00
53	Heel Turn R	2.00	4.00
54	Lita to the Xtreme R	2.00	4.00
55	You're Not in My League R	2.00	4.00
56	Busted Wide Open R	2.00	4.00
57	Seeing Stars R	2.00	4.00
58	Announcer's Table R	2.00	4.00
59	I'm Gonna Put You... R	2.00	4.00
60	Watching My Back R	2.00	4.00
61	Study the Tapes C	.12	.25
62	Student of the Sport C	.12	.25
63	Awesome Pyro C	.12	.25
64	Givin' 'em High Fives C	.12	.25
65	Taunt the Fans C	.12	.25
66	Fans Love an Underdog U	.50	1.00
67	Trash Talkin' Interview U	.50	1.00
68	Jump the Bell U	.50	1.00
69	Old School Wrestling Match R	2.00	4.00
70	Here a Mark, There a Mark... R	2.00	4.00
71	Premiere WWF (logo) Superstar R	2.00	4.00
72	Underrated Superstar R	2.00	4.00
73	Backlash C	.12	.25
74	Dirty Low Blow C	.12	.25
75	Small Concealed Foreign Object C	.12	.25
76	Armageddon (WWF Logo) Style C	.12	.25
77	Per Order of the Chairman U	.50	1.00
78	Spectacular Ring Entrance U	.50	1.00
79	When You Thought You... U	.50	1.00
80	Referee Finally Catches... U	.50	1.00
81	Don't Mess with the Champ R	2.00	4.00
82	Fully Loaded R	2.00	4.00
83	Again With This Crap?? R	2.00	4.00
84	No Mercy R	2.00	4.00
85	Dudley Boyz EX		
86	3D UR	7.50	15.00
87	Wazzzzuuup??? EX		
88	Buh-Buh Ray Dudley U	.50	1.00
89	Buh-Buh Bomb UR	7.50	15.00
90	Catatonic Stare R	2.00	4.00
91	My Name Is U	.50	1.00
92	Buh-Buh Drop EX		
93	Buh-Buh Punch R	2.00	4.00
94	D-Von Dudley U	.50	1.00
95	Testify UR	7.50	15.00
96	Spinning Elbow R	2.00	4.00
97	Doin' the D-Von U	.50	1.00
98	Thou Shall Not ####... EX		
99	D-Von Get the Table R	2.00	4.00
100	Edge and Christian EX		
101	Con-Chair-To UR	7.50	15.00
102	For the Benefit of Those... EX		
103	Edge U	.50	1.00
104	Edge-O-Matic UR	7.50	15.00
105	Million Dollar Smile R	2.00	4.00
106	Big Slide Into the Ring U	.50	1.00
107	Listen, You Reekazoid EX		
108	Sodas Rule R	2.00	4.00
109	Christian U	.50	1.00
110	Unprettier UR	7.50	15.00
111	Kazoo Theme Songs R	2.00	4.00
112	Christian's Shades U	.50	1.00
113	This Is So Totally Unfair EX		
114	Greetings to Our Fans... R	2.00	4.00
115	Hardy Boyz EX		
116	Poetry in Motion UR	7.50	15.00
117	Spin Cycle EX		
118	Matt Hardy U	.50	1.00
119	Twist of Fate UR	7.50	15.00
120	Matt's Moonsault R	2.00	4.00
121	Roar for the Fans U	.50	1.00
122	Matt Hardy's Patented Leg Drop EX		
123	Put It All On the Line R	2.00	4.00
124	Jeff Hardy U	.50	1.00
125	Swanton Bomb UR	7.50	15.00
126	Ride the Barricade R	2.00	4.00
127	No, Jeff, Don't Do It U	.50	1.00
128	Whisper in the Wind EX		
129	Incite the Fans R	2.00	4.00
130	Right to Censor EX		
131	Right to (Censor) Interfere UR	7.50	15.00
132	We're Doing This For... R	2.00	4.00
133	What's Wrong with You People? R	2.00	4.00
134	We're Here to Clean Up... EX		
135	This is Unacceptable Behavior EX		
136	Censored EX		
137	DTA UR	7.50	15.00
138	Brothers 'til the End UR	7.50	15.00
139	Three Faces of Foley UR	7.50	15.00
140	The Brahma Bull UR	7.50	15.00
141	Sledge Hammer Shot UR	7.50	15.00
142	Superior Acrobatics UR	7.50	15.00
143	I Did It For You UR	7.50	15.00
144	Where Are Your Medals? UR	7.50	15.00
145	Ovicular Fortitude UR	7.50	15.00
146	Just Another Victim UR	7.50	15.00
147	Prove Me Wrong UR	7.50	15.00
148	Eddie's Roll Up UR	7.50	15.00
149	Pac's Back UR	7.50	15.00
150	The One Billy Gunn UR	7.50	15.00

2001 Comic Images WWF Raw Deal Fully Loaded

1	Falling Fist C	.12	.25
2	Knee Smash C	.12	.25
3	Elbow Drop C	.12	.25
4	Foot Stomp C	.12	.25
5	Splash U	.50	1.00
6	Leg Drop U	.50	1.00
7	Double Axe Handle U	.50	1.00
8	Shooting Star Press U	.50	1.00
9	Missile Dropkick R	2.00	4.00
10	Suicide Plancha R	2.00	4.00
11	Superplex R	2.00	4.00
12	Moonsault R	2.00	4.00
13	Backhand Slap C	.12	.25
14	Turnbuckle Smash C	.12	.25
15	Eye Rake C	.12	.25
16	Knee Lift U	.50	1.00
17	Baseball Slide U	.50	1.00
18	Surprise Hit U	.50	1.00
19	European Uppercut R	2.00	4.00
20	Trash Can R	2.00	4.00
21	Double Clothesline R	2.00	4.00
22	Jaw Jammer C	.12	.25
23	Japanese Arm Drag C	.12	.25
24	Jackhammer C	.12	.25
25	Drop Toe Hold C	.12	.25
26	Shoulder Breaker C	.12	.25
27	Small Package C	.12	.25
28	Monkey Flip U	.50	1.00
29	Knee Breaker U	.50	1.00
30	Full Nelson Slam U	.50	1.00
31	German Suplex U	.50	1.00
32	Airplane Spin U	.50	1.00
33	Swinging Neck Breaker U	.50	1.00
34	Fall-Away Slam R	2.00	4.00
35	Double Underhook Suplex R	2.00	4.00
36	Sidewalk Slam R	2.00	4.00
37	Giant Swing R	2.00	4.00
38	Northern Lights Suplex R	2.00	4.00
39	Hair Pull C	.12	.25
40	Front Face Lock C	.12	.25
41	Hammerlock C	.12	.25
42	Head Vise U	.50	1.00
43	Surfboard U	.50	1.00
44	Stump Puller U	.50	1.00
45	Claw R	2.00	4.00
46	STF R	2.00	4.00
47	Roll Out of the Way C	.12	.25
48	Borrring Borrring C	.12	.25
49	Shove Off the Top Rope C	.12	.25
50	Tornado DDT C	.12	.25
51	Just Bring It U	.50	1.00
52	Hebner Calls It U	.50	1.00
53	Lift a Boot U	.50	1.00
54	That's Gonna Cost You Reversa		
55	Ref KO'd R	2.00	4.00
56	Attitude Adjustment R	2.00	4.00
57	In This Very Ring C	.12	.25
58	Defensive Cover C	.12	.25
59	Ho Train C	.12	.25
60	Playing With Fire C	.12	.25
61	Stare Down Opponent C	.12	.25
62	Moongoose In the House C	.12	.25
63	Commission-er Rules C	.12	.25

64	McMahon-Helmsley Era C	.12	.25
65	Throw Into the Corner Turnbuckle C	.12	.25
66	From the Top Rope C	.12	.25
67	Hardyz' Ambush C	.12	.25
68	American Bad A$ C	.12	.25
69	Do You Like Pie? C	.12	.25
70	Doing the Job C	.12	.25
71	Go for the Cheap Pop U	.50	1.00
72	Predictable Opponent U	.50	1.00
73	Who Booked This Match? U	.50	1.00
74	JR Style Slobberknocker U	.50	1.00
75	Bait Opponent U	.50	1.00
76	Defensive Posture U	.50	1.00
77	Table Table Table U	.50	1.00
78	Backed by Stephanie McMahon U	.50	1.00
79	Here Kitty, Kitty U	.50	1.00
80	Throw Opponent Out of the Ring U	.50	1.00
81	Quick Count Ref U	.50	1.00
82	Turn the Tide R	2.00	4.00
83	Time Keeper's Bell R	2.00	4.00
84	Inferno Match R	2.00	4.00
85	Call to the Crowd R	2.00	4.00
86	Dem Damn Dudleyz R	2.00	4.00
87	Reeking of Awesomeness Action		
88	Enter the Stratus-phere R	2.00	4.00
89	Kick Out R	2.00	4.00
90	Acolyte Protection Agency R	2.00	4.00
91	Rikishi Driver UR	7.50	15.00
92	A$ Drop UR	7.50	15.00
93	Rikishi EX		
94	Drive, Rikishi, Drive EX		
95	Back That A$ Up EX		
96	Stink Face EX		
97	Olympic Slam UR	7.50	15.00
98	It's True, It's True UR	7.50	15.00
99	Kurt Angle EX		
100	Intensity EX		
101	Integrity EX		
102	Intelligence EX		
103	Chyna's Pedigree UR	7.50	15.00
104	The 9th Wonder of the World UR	7.50	15.00
105	Chyna EX		
106	Handspring Elbow EX		
107	I'd Rather Be In Chyna EX		
108	Chyna's Patented Low Blow EX		
109	Tazzmission UR	7.50	15.00
110	Thug It - Dead UR	7.50	15.00
111	Tazz EX		
112	T-Bone Tazzplex EX		
113	Head-and-Arms Tazzplex EX		
114	Northern Lights Tazzplex EX		
115	Crippler Crossface UR	7.50	15.00
116	Big Stupid Grin UR	7.50	15.00
117	Chris Benoit EX		
118	Kamikaze Headbutt EX		
119	Series of Suplexes EX		
120	Rabid Wolverine EX		
121	Guerrero Frog Splash... UR	7.50	15.00
122	Get Your GED UR	7.50	15.00
123	Eddie Guerrero EX		
124	Snap Senton Splash EX		
125	Study for Your GED EX		
126	Latino Heeeeeeeat EX		
127	Doggy Pump Handle Slam UR	7.50	15.00
128	Road Dogg EX		
129	Kickin' The Shizt-nit... EX		
130	Juke N Jive EX		
131	Let's Make Some Noise EX		

132	X-Factor UR	7.50	15.00
133	X-Pac EX		
134	Leaping Spin Kick EX		
135	Bronco Buster EX		
136	Huge Bump Out of the Ring EX		
137	Fame-A$-er UR	7.50	15.00
138	B. A. Billy Gunn EX		
139	I'm an A$ Man EX		
140	B.A.'s Military Press Slam EX		
141	The Federation's Purest Athlete EX		
142	I've Got Two Words For Ya... UR	7.50	15.00
143	Tori Enters the Fray UR	7.50	15.00
144	Patented Rock Footstomp UR	7.50	15.00
145	Patented Austin Kick... UR	7.50	15.00
146	Rest In Peace UR	7.50	15.00
147	Get Hardcore UR	7.50	15.00
148	Triple H's Reverse... UR	7.50	15.00
149	Masked Vengence UR	7.50	15.00
150	Springboard Drop Kick UR	7.50	15.00

2002 Comic Images WWF Raw Deal Mania

1	Spinning Crescent Kick C	.12	.25
2	Flying Reverse Elbow C	.12	.25
3	Flying TopÈ U	.50	1.00
4	Stackplex U	.50	1.00
5	Asai Moonsault R	2.00	4.00
6	Forearm Shot C	.12	.25
7	Feign Strike C	.12	.25
8	Gut Punch C	.12	.25
9	Step on Opponent's Noggin U	.50	1.00
10	Into the Barricade U	.50	1.00
11	Pump Kick R	2.00	4.00
12	Catapult C	.12	.25
13	Within Your Grasp C	.12	.25
14	Butterfly Suplex C	.12	.25
15	Beal Toss C	.12	.25
16	Backslide U	.50	1.00
17	Tandem Flapjack U	.50	1.00
18	Running Bulldog R	2.00	4.00
19	Short Arm Hammerlock C	.12	.25
20	Knee Bar C	.12	.25
21	Strangle Hold U	.50	1.00
22	Arm Grapevine U	.50	1.00
23	Indian Deathlock R	2.00	4.00
24	All Talk, No Action C	.12	.25
25	Iron Will R	2.00	4.00
26	Not Today, Pal R	2.00	4.00
27	Out Think the Fink C	.12	.25
28	Stratusfied C	.12	.25
29	Got Wood? C	.12	.25
30	Playing by the Rules C	.12	.25
31	Kay-Fabe C	.12	.25
32	Totally Bogus C	.12	.25
33	Little She Devil C	.12	.25
34	Gut Wrench C	.12	.25
35	X-treme Measures C	.12	.25
36	Cole Calls It Right C	.12	.25
37	Trailer Park Trash C	.12	.25
38	Veteran Referee: Tim White U	.50	1.00
39	Daddy's Little Girl U	.50	1.00
40	Messing With the Champ U	.50	1.00
41	Everybody Wants... U	.50	1.00
42	Wooden Palette U	.50	1.00
43	Judgment Day U	.50	1.00
44	Mania U	.50	1.00
45	Torrie Wilson, On It R	2.00	4.00
46	Keibler's Cookies R	2.00	4.00

47	V.K.M.'s Patented Big Gulp R	2.00	4.00
48	Money Talks, BS Walks R	2.00	4.00
49	Ring Rats R	2.00	4.00
50	Billion Dollar Princess R	2.00	4.00
51	Unforgiven R	2.00	4.00
52	Ring Steps R	2.00	4.00
53	No Way Out R	2.00	4.00
54	Superior Training C	.12	.25
55	Slandered Online C	.12	.25
56	Product Endorsements C	.12	.25
57	Backstage Ambush Attempt C	.12	.25
58	No Disqualification Match C	.12	.25
59	Personal Appearance U	.50	1.00
60	Snubbed by the Fans U	.50	1.00
61	Not Done with Any Flair U	.50	1.00
62	Chicago Street Fight U	.50	1.00
63	Four Corners Match U	.50	1.00
64	Hell in a Cell Match R	2.00	4.00
65	Indian Strap Match R	2.00	4.00
66	Duchess of Queensbury Rules R	2.00	4.00
67	Handicap Match R	2.00	4.00
68	Signed Contract with Linda McMahon R	2.00	4.00
69	Fortitude Surge C	.12	.25
70	Fan Appreciation Day C	.12	.25
71	Here Comes the Money C	.12	.25
72	Remove Corner Turnbuckle C	.12	.25
73	Over the Barricade C	.12	.25
74	Touch Turnbuckle #1 U	.50	1.00
75	Touch Turnbuckle #2 U	.50	1.00
76	Touch Turnbuckle #3 U	.50	1.00
77	Touch Turnbuckle #4 U	.50	1.00
78	Over the Top Rope U	.50	1.00
79	Second Wind R	2.00	4.00
80	Sustained Damage R	2.00	4.00
81	Happy You're Here... R	2.00	4.00
82	Test of Strength R	2.00	4.00
83	Debilitating Injury: Concussion R	2.00	4.00
84	Big Show EX		
85	Final Cut UR	7.50	15.00
86	Wellllllllllll UR	7.50	15.00
87	Showstopper Chokeslam EX		
88	Big Show Splash EX		
89	500lbs. of Raw Power EX		
90	Lita EX		
91	Lita-sault UR	7.50	15.00
92	X-treme Thong UR	7.50	15.00
93	Lita-canrana EX		
94	Lita's Drop Kick EX		
95	Crimson Goddess EX		
96	Rob Van Dam EX		
97	Van Daminator UR	7.50	15.00
98	R - V - D UR	7.50	15.00
99	Five Star Frog Splash EX		
100	Extreme Monkey Flip EX		
101	Rolling Thunder EX		
102	Booker T EX		
103	Bookend UR	7.50	15.00
104	Spinnerooni UR	7.50	15.00
105	Can You Dig It, Sucka? EX		
106	Booker's Scissor Kick EX		
107	Spinning T Kick EX		
108	APA PU		
109	Beer, Cards, and More Beer UR	7.50	15.00
110	Dominator PR		
111	Clothesline from Hell PR		
112	Faarooq's Spike Spine Buster PU		
113	Bradshaw's Fall Away Slam PU		
114	Spike Dudley PU		

115	Dudley Dog UR	7.50	15.00
116	150 lbs. Soaking Wet PR		
117	Good Golly, Miss Molly Holly PR		
118	Psychotic Bump PU		
119	Brotherly Love PU		
120	William Regal PU		
121	Regal Stretch UR	7.50	15.00
122	Commissioner Regal's Decree PR		
123	Union Jack PR		
124	I've Been Besmirched PU		
125	Goodwill Ambassador PU		
126	Raven PU		
127	Raven Effect DDT UR	7.50	15.00
128	From the Bowery PR		
129	What About Me? PR		
130	Quoth the Raven Nevermore PU		
131	I Feel Your Pain PU		
132	What??? PR		
133	You Will Respect Me PR		
134	Foley is Good PR		
135	Shades of the Great One PR		
136	Cerebral Assassin PR		
137	Born of Hellfire PR		
138	Would You Please... PR		
139	Gettin' Cheeky with It UR	7.50	15.00
140	Angle Lock UR	7.50	15.00
141	Tough Enough UR	7.50	15.00
142	First to Tap Out Match UR	7.50	15.00
143	/ltimo Rechazo UR	7.50	15.00
144	Pac's Pack UR	7.50	15.00
145	The One and Only UR	7.50	15.00
146	Greetings from Dudleyville... UR	7.50	15.00
147	You Think You Know Me? UR	7.50	15.00
148	Live for the Moment UR	7.50	15.00
149	TLC Match UR	7.50	15.00
150	Censorship Match UR	7.50	15.00
6/TR	WCW Title Belt R	2.00	4.00
7/TR	WWF Light Heavyweight Title R	2.00	4.00

2001 Comic Images WWF Raw Deal Survivor Series 1

COMPLETE SET ()

2a	Punch V1.1
2b	Knee Smash V2.1
3a	Head Butt V1.1
3b	Elbow Drop V2.1
5b	Splash V2.1
8a	Shoulder Block V1.1
9a	Kick V1.1
12b	Moonsault V2.1
13b	Backhand Slap V2.1
15b	Eye Rake V2.1
16a	Superkick V1.1
16b	Superkick V1.2
17a	Spinning Heel Kick V1.1
19b	European Uppercut V2.1
19c	European Uppercut V2.2
20a	Chair Shot V1.1
20b	Trash Can V2.1
21a	Hurricanrana V1.1
22b	Jaw Jammer V2.1
23a	Hip Toss V1.1
24a	Arm Drag V1.1
25b	Drop Toe Hold V2.1
30a	Double Leg Takedown V1.1
32a	Headlock Takedown V1.1
33a	Belly to Belly Suplex V1.1
35b	Double Underhook Suplex V2.1

36b Sidewalk Slam V2.1
37b Giant Swing V2.1
39b Hair Pull V2.1
41a Samoan Drop V1.1
41b Samoan Drop V1.2
42a Sit Out Powerbomb V1.1
43a Bulldog V1.1
44a Fisherman's Suplex V1.1
45a DDT V1.1
45b Claw V2.1
45c Claw V2.2
47b Roll Out of the Way V2.1
48b Boring Boring V2.1
50a Wrist Lock V1.1
51a Arm Bar V1.1
51b Just Bring It V2.1
51c Just Bring It V2.2
52b Hebner Calls It V2.1
53b Lift a Boot V2.1
55a Choke Hold V1.1
56b Attitude Adjustment V2.1
57a Ankle Lock V1.1
58a Standing Side Headlock V1.1
61a Chicken Wing V1.1
62a Sleeper V1.1
63b Commissioner Rules V2.1
64a Boston Crab V1.1
65a Guillotine Stretch V1.1
65b Throw into the Corner... V2.1
66b From the Top Rope V2.1
69a Combination Attack V1.1
70a Step Aside V1.1
71a Escape Move V1.1
71b Go for the Cheap Pop V2.1
72a Break the Hold V1.1
74a Rolling Takedown V1.1
74b JR Style Slobberknocker V2.1
75a Knee to the Gut V1.1
75b Bait Opponent V2.1
76a Elbow to the Face V1.1
76b Elbow to the Face V1.2
76c Defensive Posture V2.1
78a Partner Interference V1.1
78b Backed by Stephanie... V2.1
78c Backed by Stephanie... V2.2
79a Manager Interferes V1.1
79b Manager Interferes V1.2
80a Disqualification V1.1
81a No Chance in Hell V1.1
81b No Chance in Hell V1.2
82b Turn the Tide V2.1
82c Turn the Tide V2.2
84a Tag in Partner V1.1
84b Inferno Match V2.1
87a Jockeying for Position V1.1
88a Irish Whip V1.1
88b Enter the Stratusphere V2.1
92a Offer Handshake V1.1
93a Roll Out of the Ring V1.1
93b Roll Out of the Ring V1.2
95a Recovery V1.1
96a Spit At Opponent V1.1
97b Olympic Slam V2.1
98a Get Crowd Support V1.1
98b It's True, It's True V2.1
99b Kurt Angle V2.1
100a Ego Boost V1.1
100b Intensity V2.1

101b Integrity V2.1
102a Stagger V1.1
102b Intelligence V2.1
104a Marking Out V1.1
105a Puppies Puppies V1.1
105b Puppies Puppies V1.2
107a Maintain Hold V1.1
109a Stone Cold Stunner V1.1
109b Tazzmission V2.1
110a Open a Can of... V1.1
110b Thug It - Dead V2.1
111a The Last Ride V1.1
111b Tazz V2.1
112a This Is My Yard V1.1
112b T-Bone Tazzplex V2.1
113a Cactus's Double Arm DDT V1.1
113b Head-and-Arms Tazzplex V2.1
114a Barbed Wire Baseball Bat V1.1
114b Northern Lights Tazzplex V2.1
115a Pedigree V1.1
115b Crippler Crossface V2.1
116a Stephanie Interferes V1.1
116b Big Stupid Grin V2.1
117a The People's Eyebrow V1.1
117b Chris Benoit V2.1
118a The People's Elbow V1.1
118b Kamikazee Headbutt V2.1
119a Kane's Tombstone... V1.1
119b Series of Suplexes V2.1
120a Hellfire and Brimstone V1.1
120b Rabid Wolverine V2.1
121a Walls of Jericho V1.1
122a Ayatollah of rock'n'Roll-a V1.1
123a Stone Cold Steve Austin V1.1
124a Austin Elbow Smash V1.1
125a Lou Thesz Press V1.1
126a Double Digits V1.1
127a Dead Man Inc. V1.1
128a Bad Ass Chokeslam V1.1
129a Old School Clothesline V1.1
130a Dead Man Walking V1.1
131a Cactus Jack V1.1
132a Bang Bang V1.1
133a Cactus Clothesline V1.1
134a Tree of Woe V1.1
135a Triple H V1.1
136a Leaping Knee to the Face V1.1
137a Facebuster V1.1
138a I Am the Game V1.1
139a The Rock V1.1
140a Smackdown Hotel V1.1
141a Take That Move V1.1
142a Rock Bottom V1.1
143a Kane V1.1
144a Kane's Chokeslam V1.1
145a Kane's Flying Clothesline V1.1
146a Kane's Return V1.1
146b I'll Make You Famous V2.1
147a Chris Jericho V1.1
147b Get Hardcore V2.1
148a Lionsault V1.1
148b Triple H's Reverse... V2.1
149a Y2J V1.1
149b Masked Vengence V2.1
150a Don't You Never Eeeever V1.1
150b Springboard Drop Kick V2.1

2000 Comic Images WWF Axxess Fan Fest

COMPLETE SET (3)		
1 Big Show	4.00	10.00
2 Triple H	6.00	15.00
3 The Rock	10.00	25.00

2000 Comic Images WWF The Divas Promos

COMPLETE SET (8)	12.00	30.00
P1 Chyna	3.00	8.00
P2 Debra	2.50	6.00
P3 Ivory	2.00	5.00
P4 Jacqueline	2.00	5.00
P5 The Kat	2.00	5.00
P6 Terri	3.00	8.00
P7 Tori	2.00	5.00
P8 Trish	4.00	10.00

2000 Comic Images WWF No Mercy

COMPLETE SET (81)	8.00	20.00
UNOPENED BOX (36 PACKS)		
UNOPENED PACK (7 CARDS)		
1 Mankind	.50	1.25
2 Cactus Jack	.50	1.25
3 Stone Cold Steve Austin	.75	2.00
4 Hardcore Holly	.20	.50
5 Al Snow	.20	.50
6 Road Dogg	.12	.30
7 Big Boss Man	.20	.50
8 The Undertaker	.60	1.50
9 Kane	.50	1.25
10 The Rock	.75	2.00
11 Vince McMahon	.50	1.25
12 Shane McMahon	.30	.75
13 Edge/Christian	.50	1.25
14 The Hardy Boyz	.30	.75
15 The Dudley Boyz	.20	.50
16 The Acolytes	.30	.75
17 Faarooq	.12	.30
18 Bradshaw	.30	.75
19 X-Pac	.20	.50
20 The Big Show	.30	.75
21 Viscera	.12	.30
22 Prince Albert	.12	.30
23 Test	.20	.50
24 Mr. Ass	.12	.30
25 Triple H	.75	2.00
26 Chyna	.50	1.25
27 Ken Shamrock	.20	.50
28 Godfather	.12	.30
29 Chris Jericho	.30	.75
30 Tazz	.20	.50
31 Hardcore Belt	.12	.30
32 D-Generation X	.30	.75
33 Gangrel	.12	.30
34 The Headbangers	.12	.30
35 British Bulldog	.20	.50
36 D'Lo Brown	.12	.30
37 Mark Henry	.12	.30
38 Kurt Angle	.50	1.25
39 Mean Street Posse	.12	.30
40 Rikishi Phatu	.20	.50
41 Too Cool	.12	.30
42 Mick Foley	.50	1.25
43 Shawn Michaels	.50	1.25
44 The Undertaker	.60	1.50
45 Stone Cold Steve Austin	.75	2.00
46 Legion Of Doom	.40	1.00
47 Wild Samoans	.20	.50
48 Sgt. Slaughter	.30	.75
49 Mankind/The Rock	.75	2.00
50 Mankind/The Rock	.75	2.00
51 Mankind/The Undertaker	.60	1.50
52 Mankind/Triple H	.75	2.00
53 Mankind/Ken Shamrock	.50	1.25
54 The Rock/Triple H	.75	2.00
55 The Undertaker/Shawn Michaels	.60	1.50
56 The Hardy Boyz/Edge/Christian	.50	1.25
57 The Undertaker/Kane	.60	1.50
58 Undertaker/Kane/Austin	.75	2.00
59 Kane/Vince McMahon/Undertaker	.60	1.50
60 Steve Austin/Kane	.75	2.00
61 Steve Austin/Dude Love	.75	2.00
62 Steve Austin/Undertaker	.75	2.00
63 Steve Austin/Undertaker	.75	2.00
64 Steve Austin/Vince McMahon	.75	2.00
65 Steve Austin/Shane & Vince McMahon	.75	2.00
66 Shane McMahon/Test	.30	.75
67 Al Snow/Big Boss Man	.20	.50
68 Al Snow/Hardcore Holly	.20	.50
69 Al Snow/Minis	.20	.50
70 Ivory/Luna	.50	1.25
71 Ken Shamrock/Steve Blackman	.20	.50
72 Mr. Ass/Hardcore Holly	.20	.50
73 The Acolytes	.30	.75
74 New Age Outlaws/Mankind/Kane	.50	1.25
75 Vince McMahon/Mankind	.50	1.25
76 Sgt. Slaughter/Triple H	.75	2.00
77 Shawn Michaels/The Undertaker	.60	1.50
78 The Rock/Mankind	.75	2.00
79 Triple H/Cactus Jack	.75	2.00
80 The Hardy Boyz/The Dudley Boyz	.30	.75
81 Checklist	.12	.30

2000 Comic Images WWF No Mercy Hardcore Champions Holofoil

COMPLETE SET (8)	3.00	8.00
RANDOMLY INSERTED INTO PACKS		
C1 Mankind	1.25	3.00
C2 Big Bossman	.50	1.25
C3 Road Dogg	.50	1.25
C4 Hardcore Holly	.50	1.25
C5 Al Snow	.50	1.25
C6 Mr. Ass	.50	1.25
C7 British Bulldog	.50	1.25
C8 Test	.50	1.25

2000 Comic Images WWF No Mercy Piece of the Ring Relics

COMPLETE SET (4)	12.00	30.00
RANDOMLY INSERTED INTO PACKS		
P1 Ring Mat	6.00	15.00
P2 Road Dogg Hat	4.00	10.00
P3 Chris Jericho Shirt	8.00	20.00
P4 D-Generation X Shirt	5.00	12.00

2000 Comic Images WWF No Mercy Promos

COMPLETE SET (3)	1.50	4.00
RANDOMLY INSERTED INTO PACKS		
P1 Mankind/The Rock	.75	2.00
P2 The Undertaker/Kane	.75	2.00
P3 Vince McMahon	.75	2.00

2000 Comic Images WWF Rock Solid

COMPLETE SET (72)	10.00	25.00
UNOPENED BOX (36 PACKS)	100.00	150.00
UNOPENED PACK (7 CARDS)	3.00	4.00
1 Title Card	.30	.75
2 Reeling 'Em In	.30	.75
3 Catching Up	.30	.75
4 The People's Threads	.30	.75
5 Sweet Ride	.30	.75
6 The Rock's Roots	.30	.75
7 Shirt Off His Back	.30	.75
8 Electrifying Threads	.30	.75
9 In For A Trim	.30	.75
10 Laying It Down In Miami	.30	.75
11 Electrifying Author	.30	.75
12 The Little People's Champ	.30	.75
13 A Class Act	.30	.75
14 The Fans Bring It	.30	.75
15 They Smell It	.30	.75
16 Another Happy Customer	.30	.75
17 Author, Author	.30	.75
18 Who's The Champ	.15	.75
19 Rocky Rocky Rocky	.30	.75
20 Action, Rock	.30	.75
21 The People's Host	.30	.75
22 Hot, Hot, Hot	.30	.75
23 Getting Cheffy With It	.30	.75
24 The Best-Selling Author	.30	.75
25 The People's Show	.30	.75
26 Check Right In	.30	.75
27 Stretch 'Em Out, Rock	.30	.75
28 Electrifying	.30	.75
29 Rough Landing	.30	.75
30 Goin' Down	.30	.75
31 Off With The Pad	.30	.75
32 Table For One	.30	.75
33 Rock Bottom	.30	.75
34 Over The Top	.30	.75
35 His Own Medicine	.30	.75
36 Not A Friendly Hug	.30	.75
37 Who's The Game	.30	.75
38 The End In Near	.30	.75
39 Say Cheese	.30	.75
40 Respect	.30	.75
41 Taker Takes One	.30	.75
42 Some Pain For Kane	.30	.75
43 Big Blow To The Big Show	.30	.75
44 One Giant Hit For Mankind	.30	.75
45 Crippling The Crippler	.30	.75
46 Take That, Boss	.30	.75
47 Shane Can Smell It	.30	.75
48 Double Trouble	.30	.75
49 Olympic Zero	.30	.75
50 Turn That Camera Sideways And	.30	.75
51 Raw Is Who	.30	.75
52 Rock vs. Brooklyn Brawler	.30	.75
53 Rock vs. Faarooq	.30	.75
54 Rock vs. Triple H	.30	.75
55 Rock vs. Ken Shamrock & Mankind	.30	.75
56 Rock vs. Mr. Ass	.30	.75
57 Rock vs. Steve Austin	.30	.75
58 Rock vs. Mankind	.30	.75
59 Rock vs. Mankind	.30	.75
60 Rock vs. Chris Benoit	.30	.75
61 Rock vs. Triple H	.30	.75
62 Rock vs. Vince McMahon	.30	.75
63 Rock vs. Triple H	.30	.75
64 Rock vs. Mankind	.30	.75
65 Rock 'N' Sock Wins First Title	.30	.75
66 Rock 'N' Sock Wins Third Title	.30	.75
67 CL Rock on runway	.30	.75
68 CL Rock in crowd	.30	.75
69 CL Rock w/Mick Foley	.30	.75
70 CL Rock w/Kane	.30	.75
71 CL Rock w/Steve Austin	.30	.75
72 CL Rock w/Stevie Richards	.30	.75

2000 Comic Images WWF Rock Solid Holofoil

COMPLETE SET (6)	8.00	20.00
STATED ODDS 1:18		
C1 Rock Bottom	2.50	6.00
C2 Lethal Style	2.50	6.00
C3 The People's Champ	2.50	6.00
C4 The People's Elbow	2.50	6.00
C5 Kickin' Back	2.50	6.00
C6 Lights, Camera, Rock	2.50	6.00

2000 Comic Images WWF Rock Solid Promos

P1 Rock w/Sunglasses	1.50	4.00
P2 Rock on Ropes	1.50	4.00
P3 Rock Lounging	1.50	4.00

1999 Comic Images WWF SmackDown

The Chromium set is a partial parallel. Card #29 in the base set is Too Cool while in the Chromium it is Shawn Michaels. The Chromium also contains 18 extra cards (73-90).

COMPLETE SET (72)	6.00	15.00
UNOPENED BOX (36 PACKS)		
UNOPENED PACK (7 CARDS)		
*CHROMIUM: .5X TO 1.2X BASIC CARDS		
1 Title Card	.10	.25
2 Stone Cold Steve Austin	.60	1.50
3 The Rock	.60	1.50
4 The Big Show	.15	.40
5 Mankind	.30	.75
6 The Undertaker	.40	.75
7 X-Pac	.15	.40
8 Triple H	.50	1.25
9 The Road Dogg	.15	.40
10 Mr. Ass	.15	.40
11 Al Snow	.15	.40
12 Big Boss Man	.15	.40
13 Kane	.20	.50
14 D'Lo Brown	.10	.25
15 Droz	.10	.25
16 Edge	.50	1.25
17 Gangrel	.10	.25
18 Christian	.15	.40
19 Godfather	.15	.40
20 Prince Albert	.10	.25
21 Mark Henry	.10	.40
22 Jeff Jarrett	.15	.40
23 Chyna	.50	1.25
24 Mideon	.10	.25
25 Hardcore Holly	.15	.40
26 Test	.10	.25
27 Val Venis	.10	.25
28 Viscera	.10	.25
29 Too Cool	.10	.25
30 The Hardy Boyz	.20	.50
31 Debra	.20	.50
32 Tori	.20	.50
33 P.M.S.	.20	.50
34 Ken Shamrock	.20	.50
35 Jerry The King Lawler	.15	.40
36 Meat	.10	.25
37 Steve Blackman	.10	.25
38 Paul Bearer	.15	.40
39 Ivory	.20	.50
40 Shane McMahon	.15	.40
41 Vince McMahon	.30	.75
42 Stone Cold Steve Austin	.60	1.50
43 The Undertaker	.40	1.00
44 The Big Show	.15	.40
45 The Rock	.60	1.50
46 Mankind	.30	.75
47 Triple H/Chyna	.50	1.25
48 X-Pac	.15	.40
49 Kane	.20	.50
50 Ken Shamrock	.20	.50
51 Mean Street Posse	.10	.25
52 Test	.10	.25
53 Steve Austin/Undertaker	.40	1.00
54 The Rock/Triple H	.40	1.00
55 S.McMahon/The Rock/V.McMahon	.40	1.00
56 The Undertaker/Kane	.30	.75
57 Vince McMahon	.20	.60
58 The Rock/Mick Foley	.40	1.00
59 The Big Show	.15	.40
60 Stone Cold Steve Austin/The Rock	.40	1.00
61 Vince McMahon	.20	.50
62 Mankind/Vince McMahon	.30	.75
63 The Big Show	.20	.50
64 X-Pac/Shane McMahon	.10	.25
65 Mr. Ass	.10	.25
66 Vince McMahon/Shane McMahon	.20	.50
67 Stone Cold Steve Austin	.30	.75
68 The Rock	.40	1.00
69 The Brood	.30	.75
70 X-Pac/Road Dogg	.15	.40
71 Jeff Jarrett/Debra	.15	.40
72 Checklist	.10	.25

1999 Comic Images WWF SmackDown Chromium

COMPLETE SET (90)	6.00	15.00
1 Title Card	.12	.30
2 Stone Cold Steve Austin	.75	2.00
3 The Rock	.75	2.00
4 The Big Show	.20	.50
5 Mankind	.30	.75
6 The Undertaker	.40	1.00
7 X-Pac	.20	.50
8 Triple H	.60	1.50
9 The Road Dogg	.20	.50
10 Mr. Ass	.12	.30
11 Al Snow	.20	.50
12 Big Boss Man	.20	.50
13 Kane	.25	.60
14 D'Lo Brown	.12	.30
15 Droz	.12	.30
16 Edge	.60	1.50
17 Gangrel	.12	.30
18 Christian	.20	.50
19 Godfather	.20	.50
20 Prince Albert	.12	.30
21 Mark Henry	.12	.30
22 Jeff Jarrett	.20	.50
23 Chyna	.25	.60
24 Mideon	.12	.30
25 Hardcore Holly	.20	.50
26 Test	.12	.30
27 Val Venis	.12	.30
28 Viscera	.12	.30
29 Shawn Michaels	.40	1.00
30 The Hardy Boyz	.30	.75
31 Debra	.30	.75
32 Tori	.30	.75
33 P.M.S.	.30	.75
34 Ken Shamrock	.12	.30
35 Jerry The King Lawler	.20	.50
36 Meat	.12	.30
37 Steve Blackman	.12	.30
38 Paul Bearer	.20	.50
39 Ivory	.30	.75
40 Shane McMahon	.20	.50
41 Vince McMahon	.40	1.00
42 Stone Cold Steve Austin	.75	2.00
43 The Undertaker	.40	1.00
44 The Big Show	.20	.50
45 The Rock	.75	2.00
46 Mankind	.30	.75
47 Triple H/Chyna	.60	1.50
48 X-Pac	.20	.50
49 Kane	.25	.60
50 Ken Shamrock	.12	.30
51 Mean Street Posse	.12	.30
52 Test	.12	.30
53 Steve Austin/Undertaker	.50	1.25
54 The Rock/Triple H	.50	1.25
55 S.McMahon/The Rock/V.McMahon	.50	1.25
56 The Undertaker/Kane	.40	1.00
57 Vince McMahon	.30	.75
58 The Rock/Mick Foley	.30	.75
59 The Big Show	.25	.60
60 Stone Cold Steve Austin/The Rock	.50	1.25
61 Vince McMahon	.30	.75
62 Mankind/Vince McMahon	.30	.75
63 The Big Show	.25	.60
64 X-Pac/Shane McMahon	.20	.50
65 Mr. Ass	.12	.30
66 Vince McMahon/Shane McMahon	.25	.60
67 Stone Cold Steve Austin	.50	1.25
68 The Rock	.50	1.25
69 The Brood	.30	.75
70 X-Pac/Road Dogg	.20	.50
71 Jeff Jarrett/Debra	.20	.50
72 The Undertaker/Big Boss Man	.25	.60
73 Four-Way Match	.20	.50
74 Triple Threat Match	.20	.50
75 Shane McMahon/X-Pac	.20	.50
76 Triple H/Kane	.50	1.25
77 Stone Cold Steve Austin	.75	2.00
78 Mr. Ass	.20	.50
79 Road Dogg/Chyna	.20	.50
80 Road Dogg/X-Pac	.20	.50
81 Shane/Vince McMahon	.30	.75
82 Kane/The Big Show	.30	.75
83 X-Pac/Hardcore Holly	.20	.50
84 Triple H/The Rock	.60	1.50
85 Undertaker/Steve Austin	.60	1.50
86 Jeff Jarrett/Edge	.50	1.25
87 D'Lo Brown/Mideon	.12	.30
88 Big Boss Man/Al Snow	.20	.50
89 Acolytes/Hardy Boyz	.30	.75
90 Checklist	.12	.30

1999 Comic Images WWF SmackDown 22KT Gold Signatures

COMPLETE SET (6) 50.00 100.00
STATED ODDS 1:80

1	Stone Cold Steve Austin	12.00	30.00
2	The Undertaker	10.00	25.00
3	The Rock	20.00	50.00
4	Triple H	12.00	30.00
5	The Big Show	12.00	30.00
6	Mankind	8.00	20.00
SE	Stone Cold Steve Austin Special Edition		

1999 Comic Images WWF SmackDown Autographs

COMPLETE SET (8)
STATED ODDS 1:80

NNO	Al Snow	6.00	15.00
NNO	Big Boss Man	15.00	40.00
NNO	D'Lo Brown	6.00	15.00
NNO	Godfather	6.00	15.00
NNO	The Hardy Boyz	15.00	40.00
NNO	Hardcore Holly	6.00	15.00
NNO	Ivory	12.00	30.00
NNO	Tori	6.00	15.00

1999 Comic Images WWF SmackDown Chrome Inserts

COMPLETE SET (6) 5.00 12.00
STATED ODDS 1:18

C1	Stone Cold Steve Austin	1.50	4.00
C2	The Corporate Ministry	1.00	2.50
C3	X-Pac/Kane	.60	1.50
C4	The Brood	1.00	2.50
C5	Mankind	1.00	2.50
C6	The Rock	1.50	4.00

1999 Comic Images WWF SmackDown Promos

P1	Stone Cold Steve Austin	1.50	4.00
	(Non-Sport Update Exclusive)		
P2	The Rock	2.00	5.00
P3	Mankind	1.00	2.50

1999 Comic Images WWF WrestleMania Live 4 X 6

COMPLETE SET (54)
UNOPENED BOX (36 PACKS)
UNOPENED PACK (6 CARDS)

1	Rowdy Roddy Piper/Mr. T
2	Randy Savage/G.Steele
3	Hulk Hogan/K.K. Bundy
4	20 Man Battle Royal
5	Hulk Hogan/Andre the Giant
6	Randy Savage/R.Steamboat
7	Hulk Hogan/Andre the Giant
8	Andre the Giant/J.Roberts
9	Big Boss Man/Akeem
10	Savage/Sherri/D.Rhodes/Sap.
11	Sgt. Slaughter/Hulk Hogan
12	Undertaker/J.Roberts
13	Hulk Hogan/Sid Justice
14	Bret Hit Man Hart/Yokozuna
15	Shawn Michaels/Tatanka
16	S.Michaels/Razor Ramon
17	Owen Hart/Bret Hart
18	Diesel/Shawn Michaels
19	Undertaker/K.K. Bundy
20	Steve Austin/Savio Vega
21	Goldust/Roddy Piper
22	Steve Austin/Bret Hart
23	The Rock/Sultan
24	S.Michaels/Steve Austin
25	Undertaker/Kane
26	Ken Shamrock
27	Undertaker
28	The Rock
29	Jeff Jarrett/Debra
30	The Brood
31	New Age Outlaws
32	Mankind
33	Kane
34	Goldust
35	Stone Cold Steve Austin
36	Val Venis
37	Sable
38	Vince McMahon
39	Shane McMahon
40	D'Lo Brown
41	Mark Henry
42	Owen Hart
43	X-Pac
44	Al Snow
45	J.O.B. Squad
46	Edge
47	Gangrel
48	Christian
49	The Godfather
50	HHH
51	Shawn Michaels
52	Chyna
53	Attendance Record
54	Stone Cold Steve Austin CL

1999 Comic Images WWF WrestleMania Live 4 X 6 Gold Foil

COMPLETE SET (6)

1	Randy Savage
2	Hulk Hogan
3	Yokozuna
4	Shawn Michaels
5	Undertaker
6	Steve Austin

1999 Comic Images WWF WrestleMania Live 4 X 6 Promos

COMPLETE SET (2)

1	WrestleMania XIV
2	WrestleMania V

1982 Cosmos Vending Machine Japanese

COMPLETE SET (6)

NNO	Antonio Inoki
NNO	Hulk Hogan
NNO	Ric Flair
NNO	Tatsumi Fujinami
NNO	Tiger Mask
NNO	Tiger Mask
	(WWF Junior Heavyweight Championship)

2012 CTWE Pro Wrestling Series One

COMPLETE SET (35)

NNO	A.J. Cruise
NNO	Alex Cypher
NNO	Bandido Jr.
NNO	Billy Gunn
NNO	Bobby Ocean
NNO	Brian Anthony
NNO	Brian Fury
NNO	Brian Kendrick
NNO	Bryan Danielson
NNO	Bull Dredd
NNO	Chris Battle
NNO	Colt Cabana
NNO	Dan De Man
NNO	Dace Cole
NNO	Death Proof
NNO	Eddie Edwards
NNO	First Class Vladimir Joseph
NNO	Frankie Arion
NNO	Jimmy Meaz
NNO	JT Dunn
NNO	Julian Starr
NNO	Low Ki
NNO	Lukas Sharp
NNO	The Mac
NNO	Matt Taven w/Kasey Ray
NNO	Mercedes KV
NNO	The Merch Girls
NNO	Mikey Chase
NNO	Monarchy
NNO	Pinkie Sanchez
NNO	Platinum Entourage
NNO	Ricky Reyes
NNO	Ron Zombie
NNO	Slyck Wagner Brown
NNO	Team Tremendous

1999-05 Danbury Mint WWF/WWE 22kt Gold

COMPLETE SET (124) 250.00 500.00

1	Andre The Giant	3.00	8.00
2	Ken Shamrock	2.00	5.00
3	Stone Cold Steve Austin	4.00	10.00
3	Bob Backlund	2.00	5.00
4	The Rock	4.00	10.00
5	B.A. Billy Gunn	1.50	4.00
6	Road Dogg	1.50	4.00
7	Gorilla Monsoon	1.50	4.00
8	Val Venis	1.00	2.50
9	Al Snow	1.25	3.00
10	Kane	2.00	5.00
11	Jesse The Body Ventura	2.50	6.00
12	Undertaker	5.00	12.00
13	Shawn Michaels	6.00	15.00
14	Jerry The King Lawler	4.00	10.00
15	Lita	3.00	8.00
16	Fabulous Moolah	2.50	6.00
17	Rikishi Fatu	1.25	3.00
18	Big Boss Man	1.00	2.50
19	Jim Ross	4.00	10.00
20	The Iron Sheik	1.25	3.00
21	Hardy Boyz	3.00	8.00
22	Trish Stratus	6.00	15.00
23	Chris Jericho	4.00	10.00
24	Sgt. Slaughter	1.50	4.00
25	Triple H	2.50	6.00
26	Stephanie McMahon-Helmsley	2.00	5.00
27	Chris Benoit	8.00	20.00
28	Captain Lou Albano	2.50	6.00
29	George The Animal Steele	2.00	5.00
30	X-Pac	1.25	3.00
31	Vince McMahon	2.00	5.00
32	Shane O Mac	2.50	6.00
33	Stone Cold Steve Austin	3.00	8.00
33	Bob Backlund	2.00	5.00
34	Chyna	3.00	8.00
35	Dudley Boyz	2.50	6.00
36	British Bulldog	2.50	6.00
37	Jimmy Superfly Snuka	1.50	4.00
38	Mankind	4.00	10.00
39	Tazz	2.00	5.00
40	Big Show	1.50	4.00
41	Kurt Angle	2.50	6.00
42	Eddie Guerrero	4.00	10.00
43	Debra	2.00	5.00
44	Mr. Fuji	1.25	3.00
45	The Godfather	2.50	6.00
46	Edge/Christian	2.50	6.00
47	Too Cool	1.25	3.00
48	Test	1.25	3.00
49	The Acolytes	1.50	4.00
50	Steve Blackman	2.50	6.00
51	William Regal	2.00	5.00
52	Ric Flair	5.00	12.00
53	Tajiri	2.00	5.00
54	Rhyno	1.25	3.00
55	Stacy Keibler	6.00	15.00
56	K-Kwik	1.25	3.00
57	Crash Holly	1.25	3.00
58	Molly Holly	1.50	4.00
59	Albert	1.50	4.00
60	Perry Saturn	2.00	5.00
61	Booker T	2.50	6.00
62	Kaientai	1.25	3.00
63	Jacqueline	1.25	3.00
64	Steven Richards	1.25	3.00
65	Raven	1.50	4.00
66	Rob Van Dam	2.00	5.00
67	Earl Hebner	2.50	6.00
68	Spike Dudley	1.25	3.00
69	Hardcore Holly	3.00	8.00
70	Linda McMahon	1.50	4.00
71	Hollywood Hulk Hogan	12.00	30.00
72	Nidia	2.50	6.00
73	Garrison Cade	4.00	10.00
74	Luther Reigns	4.00	10.00
75	Eric Bischoff	3.00	8.00
76	Gail Kim	8.00	20.00
77	Matt Hardy	2.50	6.00
78	Scott Steiner	8.00	20.00
79	Tyson Tomko	6.00	15.00
80	Miss Jackie	3.00	8.00
81	Ivory	4.00	10.00
82	Billy/Chuck	2.00	5.00
83	Chavo Guerrero	3.00	8.00
84	Jamie Noble	2.00	5.00
85	Mark Henry	3.00	8.00
86	Tommy Dreamer	2.50	6.00
87	Diamond Dallas Page	2.00	5.00
88	Mark Jindrak	2.50	6.00
89	Victoria	2.50	6.00
90	Kevin Nash	3.00	8.00
91	Eugene	3.00	8.00
92	John Cena	6.00	15.00
93	Rey Mysterio	4.00	10.00
94	Muhammad Hassan	5.00	12.00
95	The Hurricane	2.00	5.00
96	Matt Morgan	2.50	6.00

#		Low	High
97	Sable	5.00	12.00
98	Rene/Kenzo	2.50	6.00
99	Billy Kidman	2.00	5.00
100	Goldust	2.00	5.00
101	Theodore Long	2.50	6.00
102	JBL	6.00	15.00
103	Lance Storm	2.00	5.00
104	Zach Gowen	3.00	8.00
105	FBI	1.25	3.00
106	Edge	6.00	15.00
107	Randy Orton	2.50	6.00
108	Maven	1.50	4.00
109	La Resistance	2.00	5.00
110	Chavo Guerrero	3.00	8.00
111	Basham Brothers	2.50	6.00
112	Bubba Ray Dudley	2.50	6.00
113	The Coach	4.00	10.00
114	Heidenreich	5.00	12.00
115	Benjamin/Haas	2.50	6.00
116	Jazz	2.50	6.00
117	Batista	2.50	6.00
118	Goldberg	6.00	15.00
119	Torrie Wilson	4.00	10.00
120	Brock Lesnar	3.00	8.00
B1	Mankind Bonus	15.00	40.00
B2	Cactus Jack Bonus	15.00	40.00

1991 Diamond WWF SuperStars Stickers

#		Low	High
COMPLETE SET (150)		12.00	30.00
1	Hulk Hogan	.60	1.50
2	Hulk Hogan (Puzzle)	.60	1.50
3	Hulk Hogan (Puzzle)	.60	1.50
4	Hulk Hogan (Puzzle)	.60	1.50
5	Hulk Hogan (Puzzle)	.60	1.50
6	Nasty Boys	.12	.30
7	Nasty Boys	.12	.30
8	Earthquake	.12	.30
9	Earthquake	.12	.30
10	Earthquake	.12	.30
11	Jimmy Hart	.20	.50
12	Dino Bravo	.12	.30
13	Dino Bravo (Puzzle)	.12	.30
14	Dino Bravo (Puzzle)	.12	.30
15	British Bulldog (Puzzle)	.15	.40
16	British Bulldog (Puzzle)	.15	.40
17	British Bulldog (Puzzle)	.15	.40
18	British Bulldog (Puzzle)	.15	.40
19	British Bulldog	.15	.40
20	British Bulldog	.15	.40
21	Bobby The Brain Heenan	.15	.40
22	Mr. Perfect	.20	.50
23	Mr. Perfect (Puzzle)	.20	.50
24	Mr. Perfect (Puzzle)	.20	.50
25	Texas Tornado	.15	.40
26	Texas Tornado (Puzzle)	.15	.40
27	Texas Tornado (Puzzle)	.15	.40
28	Tugboat	.12	.30
29	Tugboat (Puzzle)	.12	.30
30	Tugboat (Puzzle)	.12	.30
31	Hacksaw Jim Duggan (Puzzle)	.15	.40
32	Hacksaw Jim Duggan (Puzzle)	.15	.40
33	Hacksaw Jim Duggan (Puzzle)	.15	.40
34	Hacksaw Jim Duggan (Puzzle)	.15	.40
35	Hacksaw Jim Duggan	.15	.40
36	Big Boss Man (Puzzle)	.12	.30
37	Big Boss Man (Puzzle)	.12	.30
38	Big Boss Man	.12	.30
39	Big Boss Man	.12	.30
40	Power & Glory (Puzzle)	.12	.30
41	Power & Glory (Puzzle)	.12	.30
42	Power & Glory (Puzzle)	.12	.30
43	Power & Glory (Puzzle)	.12	.30
44	Hercules	.12	.30
45	Paul Roma	.12	.30
46	Slick	.12	.30
47	Ultimate Warrior (Puzzle)	.40	1.00
48	Ultimate Warrior (Puzzle)	.40	1.00
49	Ultimate Warrior (Puzzle)	.40	1.00
50	Ultimate Warrior (Puzzle)	.40	1.00
51	Ultimate Warrior (Puzzle)	.40	1.00
52	Ultimate Warrior (Puzzle)	.40	1.00
53	Ultimate Warrior	.40	1.00
54	Ultimate Warrior (Puzzle)	.40	1.00
55	Ultimate Warrior (Puzzle)	.40	1.00
56	Ultimate Warrior (Puzzle)	.40	1.00
57	Ultimate Warrior (Puzzle)	.40	1.00
58	Rockers (Puzzle)	.20	.50
59	Rockers (Puzzle)	.20	.50
60	Rockers (Puzzle)	.20	.50
61	Rockers (Puzzle)	.20	.50
62	Marty Jannetty	.12	.30
63	Shawn Michaels	.20	.50
64	Rockers	.20	.50
65	Rockers	.20	.50
66	The Model Rick Martel (Puzzle)	.12	.30
67	The Model Rick Martel (Puzzle)	.12	.30
68	The Model Rick Martel (Puzzle)	.12	.30
69	The Model Rick Martel (Puzzle)	.12	.30
70	The Model Rick Martel	.12	.30
71	The Model Rick Martel	.12	.30
72	The Model Rick Martel	.12	.30
73	Hulk Hogan	.60	1.50
74	Hulk Hogan (Puzzle)	.60	1.50
75	Hulk Hogan (Puzzle)	.60	1.50
76	Hulk Hogan (Puzzle)	.60	1.50
77	Hulk Hogan (Puzzle)	.60	1.50
78	Hulk Hogan	.60	1.50
79	Hulk Hogan	.60	1.50
80	Hulk Hogan (Puzzle)	.60	1.50
81	Hulk Hogan (Puzzle)	.60	1.50
82	Hulk Hogan (Puzzle)	.60	1.50
83	Hulk Hogan (Puzzle)	.60	1.50
84	Warlord	.12	.30
85	Warlord	.12	.30
86	Barbarian	.12	.30
87	Barbarian	.12	.30
88	Orient Express	.12	.30
89	Orient Express	.12	.30
90	Mr. Fuji	.12	.30
91	Superfly Jimmy Snuka (Puzzle)	.20	.50
92	Superfly Jimmy Snuka (Puzzle)	.20	.50
93	Superfly Jimmy Snuka	.20	.50
94	Superfly Jimmy Snuka	.20	.50
95	Bushwackers (Puzzle)	.12	.30
96	Bushwackers (Puzzle)	.12	.30
97	Bushwackers (Puzzle)	.12	.30
98	Bushwackers (Puzzle)	.12	.30
99	Bushwackers	.12	.30
100	Macho Man	.40	1.00
101	Macho Man	.40	1.00
102	Macho Man	.40	1.00
103	Macho Man & Queen Sherri	.40	1.00
104	Sensational Queen Sherri	.15	.40
105	Sensational Queen Sherri	.15	.40
106	Million Dollar Man (Puzzle)	.15	.40
107	Million Dollar Man (Puzzle)	.15	.40
108	Million Dollar Man (Puzzle)	.15	.40
109	Million Dollar Man (Puzzle)	.15	.40
110	Million Dollar Man Ted DiBiase	.15	.40
111	Million Dollar Man Ted DiBiase	.15	.40
112	Rowdy Roddy Piper (Puzzle)	.30	.75
113	Rowdy Roddy Piper (Puzzle)	.30	.75
114	Rowdy Roddy Piper	.30	.75
115	Legion of Doom	.20	.50
116	Animal	.20	.50
117	Legion of Doom	.20	.50
118	Legion of Doom	.20	.50
119	Legion of Doom (Puzzle)	.20	.50
120	Legion of Doom (Puzzle)	.20	.50
121	Legion of Doom (Puzzle)	.20	.50
122	Legion of Doom (Puzzle)	.20	.50
123	Haku (Puzzle)	.12	.30
124	Haku (Puzzle)	.12	.30
125	Haku	.12	.30
126	Virgil (Puzzle)	.12	.30
127	Virgil (Puzzle)	.12	.30
128	Sgt. Slaughter (Puzzle)	.20	.50
129	Sgt. Slaughter (Puzzle)	.20	.50
130	Sgt. Slaughter (Puzzle)	.20	.50
131	Sgt. Slaughter (Puzzle)	.20	.50
132	Sgt. Slaughter	.20	.50
133	Sgt. Slaughter (Puzzle)	.20	.50
134	Sgt. Slaughter (Puzzle)	.20	.50
135	Jake The Snake Roberts (Puzzle)	.25	.60
136	Jake The Snake Roberts (Puzzle)	.25	.60
137	Jake The Snake Roberts	.25	.60
138	Jake The Snake Roberts (Puzzle)	.25	.60
139	Jake The Snake Roberts (Puzzle)	.25	.60
140	Jake The Snake Roberts (Puzzle)	.25	.60
141	Jake The Snake Roberts (Puzzle)	.25	.60
142	Koko B. Ware	.12	.30
143	Koko B. Ware	.12	.30
144	The Undertaker (Puzzle)	.50	1.25
145	The Undertaker (Puzzle)	.50	1.25
146	Undertaker/Paul Bearer (Puzzle)	.50	1.25
147	Undertaker/Paul Bearer (Puzzle)	.50	1.25
148	Undertaker/Paul Bearer (Puzzle)	.50	1.25
149	Undertaker/Paul Bearer (Puzzle)	.50	1.25
150	Paul Bearer	.15	.40

1986 Diamond WWF Wrestling Superstars Hulk Hogan's Rock 'n' Wrestling Stickers

COMPLETE SET (225)

1 The Hulkster's pumping iron on the beach
2 Through the rain and wind
3 That storm can do some serious damage
4 Hulk doesn't hesitate.
5 Hold on dude he shouts.
6 The Iron Sheik is refusing Hulk's help!
7 Don't be a dope, Sheik!
8 But the Sheik would rather fight thanÖWHOAH!
9 Suddenly, a giant tidal wave curls over the tiny craft,
10 Where are they now?
11 Not quite.
12 Not quite.
13 Instead of being grateful, Sheik tries to blame Hulk
14 Instead of being grateful, Sheik tries to blame Hulk
15 Who are you kidding, dude?
16 When Hulk tells him they should work together,
17 But he can't seem to decide what they should do first!
18 Sheik says that's just what he was going to say!
19 Hulk leads the way through the jungle.
20 ..because he's going to show Hulk
21 Öand shakes it until he gets them all right
22 After finding some food, it's time to build a shelter.
23 Öthat turns out to be more viper than vine!
24 Thanks to Hulk Hogan,
25 It seems like the best thing for the Sheik
26 Öor worse!
27 Hang on, Sheik!
28 Just as the Sheik is about to go down for the count,
29 Some guys are sore winners!
30 Everything on that side of the stream
31 Hulk Hogan
32 Hulk Hogan
33 Hulk Hogan
34 Hulk Hogan
35 But Sheik doesn't watch where he's walking,
36 Öhe makes a big splash in the stream!
37 Öhe makes a big splash in the stream!
38 Hulk stocks his well-built hut
39 Hulk stocks his well-built hut
40 Sheik would do the same,
41 Seeing Hulk's good work is enough
42 It looks like he's found it with this buzzing beehive.
43 But so could the Sheik,
44 What else would you expect from a Sheik
45 The Sheik turns out to be his own worst enemy,
46 Say one thing for the Sheik
47 This time he's got a gigantic boulder loaded up
48 Sheik's aim misses Hulk's hut,
49 Sheik has seen his own trouble turn back on him
50 Start running, Sheik, 'cause here comes 27 tons of granite trouble!
51 Whew!
52 Or is it?
53 There's that heavy-duty headache!
54 How about getting stuck out in the rain without any shelter?
55 Because the Hulkster is one okay dude!
56 Sheik won't argue with that
57 Help yourself, Sheik!
58 Sack time, after a long hard day of island survival.
59 This could be a rescue ship passing
60 The Sheik spots the ship first but canít figure out what to do.
61 The Sheik spots the ship first but canít figure out what to do.
62 First thing to do is light the signal fire that Hulk built yesterday
63 First thing to do is light the signal fire that Hulk built yesterday
64 Hey Sheik! Maybe you should let Hulk run that flame to the signal fire.
65 Junkyard Dog
66 Junkyard Dog
67 Junkyard Dog
68 Junkyard Dog
69 Övery much luck running!
70 Even though there's no sign of a signal fire,
71 Two wrestler's screaming at each other
72 After the rescue,
73 After the rescue,
74 They can imagine that being stranded on an island
75 They can imagine that being stranded on an island
76 If not for me,
77 The Sheik gets so involved in his story
78 Here you go, Sheik.

79 Hulk Hogan and the Rock-N-Wrestlers fly into India.

80 But where's their guide?

81 That's no problem for Captain Lou.

82 Hey, the food's pretty good around here.

83 YEEEOOW!!! Maybe a lot on the hot side!

84 Whew! I wonder what they've got for dessert in this place.

85 It's Bubar, the Rock-N-Wrestler's faithful guide.

86 On the way, they'll stop in the village of Bangpur

87 They hop in the Rockin' jeep

88 Öand they stop at the local water hole,

89 When Andre overheats,

90 ..they don't want to split up.

91 The wrestlers continue on through the jungle

92 It's a happy reunion when Tito and Raji meet

93 I've been sending you and your family money

94 And I've been sending you farm equipment too.

95 Raji says all they received were letters and photographs.

96 Raji says all they received were letters and photographs.

97 When Hulk finds out who's been ripping off Raji's village,

98 When Hulk finds out who's beèn ripping off Raji's village,

99 Don't worry about a thing, brothers

100 And Hillbilly's got an idea too

101 In the meantime, Captain Lou's got enough grub

102 Iron Sheik

103 Iron Sheik

104 Iron Sheik

105 Iron Sheik

106 They're off!

107 Junkyard's plan brings the gang down to the docks,

108 Hulk puts on a hard hat

109 Hiding inside a crate,

110 Superfly hides away in another crate

111 Tito sent word to the village

112 And now all the Rock-N-Wrestlers have to do is hop

113 Back at the water hole,

114 Poachers!nts! RUN!

115 The little elephant tries his hardest to escape.

116 Now that the poachers have trapped him,

117 Now that the poachers have trapped him,

118 In Bangpur, Hillbilly teaches the villagers

119 In Bangpur, Hillbilly teaches the villagers

120 Öthat spread the seeds all over the farm

121 Captain Lou's fresh veggie burgers!

122 Are you kidding?

123 From a safe distance,

124 We'll get too far behind if we drive behind the falls,

125 When the cargo truck drives straight into town

126 Then the Hulkster checks the back of the truck

127 Before they can think, the truck speeds out of town

128 Let's go dudes!

129 But how did the full gargo truck become suddenly so empty?

130 A hollow cave

131 And guess what the poachers plan on doing

132 That crate is especially heavy for the little elephant

133 He drops the crate and it smashes to pieces.

134 Before they can move,

135 When the bandits lock them in a crate

136 It's a long drop into the hard waters

137 Öthey've got to outlast a rough ride

138 This is no tag-team match.

139 Up on the ridge,

140 Öjust as the Rockin' jeep is in the middle.

141 But they just manage to back off

142 Big John Studd

143 Big John Studd

144 Big John Studd

145 Big John Studd

146 Back in the rapid,

147 So long dudes!

148 But wait!

149 Yes!

150 Yes!

151 On the ridge,

152 On the ridge,

153 But what's that noise?

154 All they have to do now is sneak into the cave

155 Hold it right there, dude!

156 Hillbilly's putting you two guys out

157 Stealing food and supplies from poor villagers

158 Raji's so excited to see Tito that trips on a rope.

159 And here comes a huge elephant,

160 Come on, Amigos!

161 Hulk and Hillbilly do their best to hold back

162 Just in time!

163 But no!

164 The Rock-N-Wrestlers are trapped!

165 Öuntil the Elephant Cavalry comes to the rescue!

166 Now the bandits are caught for good.

167 Now the Rock-N-Wrestlers can help Raji

168 And Tito's not the only one with a foster kid!

169 Watch out, everyone!

170 Watch out, everyone!

171 Not the Sheik.

172 Not the Sheik.

173 Watch out for what?

174 Never mind the rear!

175 This poor woman thinks she's sitting

176 Like a free ride through the roof of the Sheikmobile.

177 She's so confused, she doesn't know who to thank!

178 Canìt she just sit back and enjoy the ride?

179 Nikolai Volkoff

180 Nikolai Volkoff

181 Nikolai Volkoff

182 Nikolai Volkoff

183 Öright through a billboard!

184 Öafter Bobby the Brain gives him a driving lesson.

185 No, no, Sheik!

186 Once the Sheik gets things rolling,

187 Watch out for that alley!

188 Yes sir, Sheik.

189 Bobby can't believe what's happening

190 Öright at a truck loaded with paint!

191 But not before giving Bobby's new car

192 Pull up and stop!

193 What's this in the middle of the street?

194 What's this in the middle of the street?

195 But when he sees the Sheik speeding

196 But when he sees the Sheik speeding

197 Low enough to rip a hole through Bobby's convertible roof!

198 Not until he's taken a shot at some parallel parking.

199 Bobby canìt believe what the Sheik has done.

200 The Sheik tells Bobby that he'll get it

201 The big day: The inspector climbs into the Sheik-mobile

202 No problem says the Sheik.

203 Öwhich are connected directly to Bobby

204 As long as Bobby does the driving,

205 But what's this?

206 Nikolai wants to try it too,

207 Nikolai flies an airplane as well

208 Itìs time for a few tricks.

209 Öthe driving inspector thinks the Sheik is testing

210 Itìs a lot of fun to send a model plane

211 But not so much fun for the Sheik and the driving inspector

212 But not so much fun for the Sheik and the driving inspector

213 Bobby would help the Sheik out if he could,

214 Bobby would help the Sheik out if he could,

215 Time for Nikolai's fun to come to an end

216 Sure says Nikolai.

217 Look at this says Nikolai.

218 But not so smooth for the Sheikmobile.

219 Captain Lou Albano

220 Captain Lou Albano

221 Captain Lou Albano

222 Captain Lou Albano

223 Driver's license?

224 Now the Sheik only wants to know one thing:

225 Simple says Nikolai,

1992 Disney's Limit Comic Stars of the WWF Magazine German

COMPLETE SET (8)

NNO The Big Boss Man

NNO Bret The Hit Man Hart

NNO The British Bulldog

NNO The Mountie

NNO Papa Shango

NNO Randy Macho Man Savage

NNO The Ultimate Warrior

NNO The Undertaker

2002 Doritos WWF Super Stars

Released in Canada.

COMPLETE SET (12)	5.00	12.00
1 The Rock	.75	2.00
2 Stone Cold Steve Austin	.75	2.00
3 Kurt Angle	.50	1.25
4 Booker T	.25	.60
5 Triple H	.75	2.00
6 Edge	.50	1.25
7 Rob Van Dam	.25	.60
8 Chris Jericho	.40	1.00
9 Undertaker	.50	1.25
10 Jeff Hardy	.40	1.00
11 Lita	.75	2.00
12 Trish Stratus	1.25	3.00

1998 DuoCards WWF

Subsets within the set include: RWT = Rookiez Wit Tudes (46-50); FW = Faction Warfare (51-53); DD = Dynamic Duoz (54-61); BBB = Brainz Behind the Brawn (62-68); MTR = Moutz That Roared (69-70)

COMPLETE SET (72)	50.00	100.00
UNOPENED BOX (30 PACKS)		
UNOPENED PACK (7 CARDS)		
1 WWF Attitude	.10	.25
2 Mr. Vince McMahon	.30	.75
3 Commissioner Slaughter	.20	.50
4 Mr. Pat Patterson	.10	.25
5 Mr. Gerald Brisco	.15	.40
6 WWF Champion	.60	1.50
7 WWF Tag Team Champions	.20	.50
8 WWF IC Champ/The Rock	25.00	60.00
9 WWF European Champion	.10	.25
10 WWF Light Heavyweight Champion	.10	.25
11 Stone Cold Steve Austin	.60	1.50
12 Undertaker	1.25	3.00
13 Shawn Michaels	.40	1.00
14 Ken Shamrock	.15	.40
15 The Rock	30.00	75.00
16 Triple H	.20	.50
17 Kane	.20	.50
18 Owen Hart	.30	1.00
19 Mankind	.30	.75
20 Dude Love	.30	.75
21 Cactus Jack	.30	.75
22 Sable	.30	.75
23 X-Pac	.20	.50
24 D'Lo Brown	.10	.25
25 Mark Henry	.10	.25
26 Bradshaw	.20	.50
27 The Godfather	.10	.25
28 Double J	.10	.25
29 Dustin Runnels	.10	.25
30 Marvelous Marc Mero	.10	.25
31 Lethal Weapon Steve Blackman	.10	.25
32 Al Snow and Head	.15	.40
33 Taka Michinoku	.10	.25
34 Badd Ass Billy Gunn	.20	.50
35 Savio Vega	.10	.25
36 Dr. Death Steve Williams	.10	.25
37 Steven Regal	.15	.40
38 Faarooq	.15	.40
39 Scorpio	.10	.25
40 Kurrgan	.10	.25
41 Luna	.10	.25
42 Dan The Beast Severn	.15	.40
43 Golga	.10	.25
44 Giant Silva	.10	.25
45 Road Dog Jesse James	.20	.50
46 Edge RWT	.40	1.00
47 Darren Droz Drozdov RWT	.10	.25
48 Val Venis RWT	.15	.40
49 Papi Chulo RWT	.10	.25
50 Tiger Ali Singh RWT	.15	.40
51 D-Generation X FW	.20	.50
52 The Nation FW	.20	.60
53 Kaientai FW	.10	.25
54 Kane w/Mankind DD	.20	.60
55 New Age Outlaws DD	.20	.50
56 Headbangers DD	.10	.25
57 D.O.A. DD	.10	.25
58 L.O.D. 2000 DD	.15	.40
59 Southern Justice DD	.10	.25
60 Too Much DD	.10	.25
61 Los Boricuas DD	.10	.25
62 Paul Bearer BBB	.10	.25
63 Chyna BBB	.20	.50
64 Jackyl BBB	.10	.25
65 Jim Cornette BBB	.15	.40
66 Yamaguchi-San BBB	.10	.25
67 Jacqueline BBB	.15	.40
68 Paul Ellering BBB	.10	.25
69 Jim Ross MTR	.15	.40

70	Jerry The King Lawler MTR	.20	.50
71	Raw is War	.10	.25
72	Checklist	.10	.25

1998 DuoCards WWF Autographs

COMPLETE SET (13)	250.00	500.00

STATED ODDS 1:100

NNO	Billy Gunn	10.00	25.00
NNO	Chyna	60.00	120.00
NNO	Hawk	50.00	100.00
NNO	Jacqueline	5.00	12.00
NNO	Mankind	15.00	40.00
NNO	Owen Hart	200.00	400.00
NNO	Paul Bearer	20.00	50.00
NNO	Road Dog Jesse James	12.00	30.00
NNO	Sable	15.00	40.00
NNO	Sable - Unsigned	6.00	15.00
NNO	Steve Blackman	5.00	12.00
NNO	The Rock	800.00	1200.00
NNO	Redemption Card	2.00	5.00

1998 DuoCards WWF Stone Cold's Greatest Hitz

COMPLETE SET (8)	15.00	30.00

STATED ODDS 1:20

OMNI1	1996 King of the Ring	2.00	5.00
OMNI2	WM 13 Submission Match	2.00	5.00
OMNI3	1998 Royal Rumble	2.00	5.00
OMNI4	Wrestlemania XIV	2.00	5.00
OMNI5	King of the Ring	2.00	5.00
OMNI6	Raw is War	2.00	5.00
BONUS1	D-X In Your House	2.00	5.00
BONUS2	Arrest That Hyperlink	2.00	5.00

1998 DuoCards WWF Promos

1	Stone Cold Steve Austin	3.00	8.00
2	Sable	1.25	3.00
3	D-Generation X	2.00	5.00
4	Dude Love/Steve Austin	2.00	5.00

2008 DWA Legends Tour

COMPLETE SET (50)

1	Tatanka
2	Bad Bones
3	Sir Robert Lequimez
4	Shaka
5	Bushwhacker Luke
6	Nicky
7	Crazy Johnny Tiger
8	Lu Fisto
9	Cannonball Grizzly
10	Alpha Female
11	Craig BC
12	Sunny
13	Barbara Devil
14	Cleo
15	DNS Evolution
16	Terri Runnels
17	Lazio Fee
18	Bernd Fohr
19	GM2B
20	Chris Raaber Bambikiller
21	Masterpiece Chris Masters
22	Joe Legend
23	Joey Cabray
24	Hate
25	M@d Alexx

26	Michael Knight
27	Miss Mina
28	Rob Raw
29	SigMasta Rappo
30	Mr. Hollywood Dan Reid
31	Karsten Kretschmer
32	Dr. Gangreen
33	Ken Mahler
34	The Monster Marc King
35	Machine
36	Jaxx
37	Marius Devil
38	Evil Rider Martin Nolte
39	Adam Bomb
40	Honky Tonk Man
41	Smash of Demolition
42	Jim Powers
43	Eugene
44	Ax of Demolition
45	Doink the Clown
46	Dink the Clown
47	Repo Man
48	Big Vito
49	Rocker Marty Jannetty
50	Greg Valentine The Hammer

2009 DWA Legends Tour

COMPLETE SET (26)

1	Tatanka
2	Wildcat Robbie Brookside
3	Justin Credible
4	Typhoon
5	The Patriot
6	Aldo Montoya
7	Bushwhacker Luke
8	Terri Runnels
9	Marty Jannetty
10	Tugboat
11	Chimaera
12	Rob Cage
13	Miss Jackie
14	LuFisto
15	Machine
16	Carmel
17	GM2B
18	Mad Alex
19	Rob Raw
20	Hailee Bacardi
21	Johnny Tiger
22	Craig BC
23	Al Snow
24	Ariel
25	Ted DiBiase
26	Virgil

2011 DWA Legends Tour

COMPLETE SET (21)

NNO	Al Snow
NNO	The Conquistadors
NNO	David Steel
NNO	Destructo
NNO	Diane von Hoffman
NNO	DNS Evolution
NNO	Doink
NNO	The Giant Warrior
NNO	Joe Legend
NNO	Legendkiller Martin Nolte

NNO	Logan Storm
NNO	Miss Desiree Peterson
NNO	Nicky
NNO	Powers of Pain
NNO	Preston Steele
NNO	Rob Cage
NNO	Rob Raw
NNO	Robbie Brookside
NNO	Shane Douglas
NNO	Tatanka
NNO	Tony St. Clair

2008 DWA Rock 'N' Wrestling Night

COMPLETE SET (7)

NNO	Angel of S.I.N.
NNO	Chimaera
NNO	Doink the Clown
NNO	Honky Tonk Man
NNO	Jean Pierre Lafitte
NNO	Sunny
NNO	Tatanka

2007 DWA Wrestling

COMPLETE SET (51)

1	Martin Nolte
2	Joey Cabray
4	Mot Van Kunder
5	Nicky
6	Louis Van Eden
7	Violent Tom
8	Jaxx
9	Chris Ramirez
10	Crazy John Tiger
11	Honky Tonk Man
12	Craig BC
13	The Bull Roberto Lequimez
14	James Wallace
15	Machine
16	Destiny
17	Doug Williams
18	Karsten Kretschmer
19	Marius Devil
20	Ken Mahler
21	Shaka
22	The Warlord
23	Justin Dwayne
24	Red Devil
25	Lazio Fee
26	Sensational Sherri Martel
27	Crazy Sexy Mike
28	Wesna
29	Tony St. Clair
30	Ahmed Chaer
31	Homeless Tom
32	Cannonball Grizzly
33	X-Dream
34	Dr. Gangreen
35	Johnny Grunge (Public Enemy)
36	Rocco Rock (Public Enemy)
37	Adrian Serrano
38	Bad Bones John Kay
39	Katie Lea
3A	Joe Legend
3B	Michael Knight
40	Alex Breslin
41	Georgia Mac
42	Mad Cow

43	Candy
44	Red Tiger
45	Diego Latino
46	Tremendous Emil Sitoci
47	T-Bone Thomas Freakz
48	Bruisin Marc Slater
49	Baca Loco
50	Blue Nikita

1999 Eastman Kodak WWF Collectible Motion

COMPLETE SET (6)	15.00	40.00

NNO	Mankind	3.00	8.00
NNO	The Rock	6.00	15.00
NNO	Stone Cold Hell Yeah	6.00	15.00
NNO	Stone Cold Stuns McMahon	6.00	15.00
NNO	The Undertaker	5.00	12.00

2004 Edibas WWE Lamincards

Subsets within the set include: LOGO = Logo Cards (67-100); IA = In Action (101-120)

COMPLETE SET (120)	15.00	40.00

UNOPENED BOX (24 PACKS)

UNOPENED PACK (4 CARDS)

1	Chris Benoit	.75	2.00
2	Randy Orton	.75	2.00
3	Kane	1.25	3.00
4	Chris Jericho	.75	2.00
5	Ric Flair	1.50	4.00
6	Rob Conway	.30	.75
7	Val Venis	.50	1.25
8	Chuck Palumbo	.50	1.25
9	Rosey	.30	.75
10	Tyson Tomko	.50	1.25
11	Shawn Michaels	2.00	5.00
12	The Rock	2.00	5.00
13	Shelton Benjamin	.30	.75
14	Christian	1.00	2.50
15	Mark Henry	.50	1.25
16	Test	.50	1.25
17	A-Train	.30	.75
18	Eric Bischoff	.50	1.25
19	Jonathan Coachman	.30	.75
20	Jerry The King Lawler	.75	2.00
21	Jim Ross	.50	1.25
22	Gail Kim	1.25	3.00
23	Ivory	1.25	3.00
24	Jazz	.75	2.00
25	Lita	2.00	5.00
26	Molly	1.50	4.00
27	Nidia	.75	2.00
28	Stacy Keibler	3.00	8.00
29	Trish Stratus	3.00	8.00
30	Victoria	1.50	4.00
31	Undertaker	1.50	4.00
32	JBL	.75	2.00
33	Eddie Guerrero	1.50	4.00
34	Booker T	1.25	3.00
35	Kurt Angle	1.25	3.00
36	John Cena	2.00	5.00
37	Rob Van Dam	1.25	3.00
38	Rene Dupree	.50	1.25
39	Rey Mysterio	.75	2.00
40	Paul Heyman	.30	.75
41	Hardcore Holly	.50	1.25
42	Paul London	.30	.75
43	Charlie Haas	.30	.75

44	Bubba Ray	.50	1.25
45	Billy Kidman	.30	.75
46	D-Von Dudley	.50	1.25
47	Chavo Guerrero	.50	1.25
48	Nunzio	.30	.75
49	Scotty 2 Hotty	.50	1.25
50	Johnny Stamboli	.30	.75
51	Danny Basham	.30	.75
52	Luther Reigns	.30	.75
53	Orlando Jordan	.30	.75
54	Akio	.30	.75
55	Big Show	1.25	3.00
56	Rico	.30	.75
57	Tazz	.50	1.25
58	Kenzo Suzuki	.30	.75
59	Theodore Long	.30	.75
60	Jon Heidenreich	.30	.75
61	Funaki	.50	1.25
62	Spike Dudley	.50	1.25
63	Hiroko	.30	.75
64	Dawn Marie	.75	2.00
65	Miss Jackie	1.25	3.00
66	Torrie Wilson	3.00	8.00
67	Chris Benoit LOGO	.75	2.00
68	Randy Orton LOGO	.75	2.00
69	Triple H LOGO	2.00	5.00
70	Batista LOGO	1.25	3.00
71	Kane LOGO	1.25	3.00
72	Chris Jericho LOGO	.75	2.00
73	Ric Flair LOGO	1.50	4.00
74	Shawn Michaels LOGO	2.00	5.00
75	Rob Conway LOGO	.30	.75
76	Stacy Keibler LOGO	3.00	8.00
77	Ivory LOGO	1.25	3.00
78	Molly Holly LOGO	1.50	4.00
79	Eddie Guerrero LOGO	1.50	4.00
80	Undertaker LOGO	1.50	4.00
81	Booker T LOGO	1.25	3.00
82	Kurt Angle LOGO	1.25	3.00
83	Rob Van Dam LOGO	1.25	3.00
84	Rey Mysterio LOGO	.75	2.00
85	Hardcore Holly LOGO	.50	1.25
86	Paul London LOGO	.30	.75
87	Billy Kidman LOGO	.30	.75
88	Dawn Marie LOGO	.75	2.00
89	Miss Jackie LOGO	1.25	3.00
90	Torrie Wilson LOGO	3.00	8.00
91	Chavo Guerrero LOGO	.50	1.25
92	Chuck Palumbo LOGO	.50	1.25
93	Mark Henry LOGO	.50	1.25
94	Orlando Jordan LOGO	.30	.75
95	Rico LOGO	.30	.75
96	The Rock LOGO	2.00	5.00
97	Scotty 2 Hotty LOGO	.50	1.25
98	Lita LOGO	2.00	5.00
99	Victoria LOGO	1.50	4.00
100	Gail Kim LOGO	1.25	3.00
101	Benoit vs. Flair IA	1.50	4.00
102	Jericho vs. Michaels IA	2.00	5.00
103	Hurricane vs. The Rock IA	2.00	5.00
104	Orton vs. Benoit IA	.75	2.00
105	Kane vs. Jericho IA	1.25	3.00
106	Test vs. Richards IA	.50	1.25
107	HHH vs. Benoit IA	2.00	5.00
108	Benjamin vs. Orton IA	.75	2.00
109	Conway vs. Hurricane IA	.30	.75
110	Jericho vs. Edge IA	1.25	3.00
111	Guerrero vs. Angle IA	1.50	4.00
112	Orton vs. The Rock IA	2.00	5.00
113	Akio vs. Moore IA	.30	.75
114	Big Show vs. RVD IA	1.25	3.00
115	Dudleys vs. La Resistance IA	.40	1.00
116	Cena vs. Big Show IA	2.00	5.00
117	JBL vs. Mysterio IA	.75	2.00
118	Nunzio vs. Chavo IA	.50	1.25
119	Booker T vs. Guerrero IA	1.50	4.00
120	Undertaker vs. Cena IA	2.00	5.00

2005 Edibas WWE Lamincards

COMPLETE SET (150)		15.00	40.00
UNOPENED BOX (24 PACKS)			
UNOPENED PACK (4 CARDS)			
1	Al Snow	.30	.75
2	Batista	.75	2.00
3	Booker T	.50	1.25
4	Candice	2.00	5.00
5	Chris Benoit	1.25	3.00
6	Christian	1.00	2.50
7	Doug Basham	.30	.75
8	Eddie Guerrero	1.50	4.00
9	Funaki	.30	.75
10	Hardcore Holly	.50	1.25
11	Heidenreich	.30	.75
12	John Bradshaw Layfield	.50	1.25
13	Joey Mercury	.30	.75
14	Johnny Nitro	.30	.75
15	Melina	1.50	4.00
16	Michelle McCool	1.50	4.00
17	Nunzio	.30	.75
18	Orlando Jordan	.30	.75
19	Paul London	.30	.75
20	Randy Orton	.30	.75
21	Rey Mysterio	1.00	2.50
22	Scotty 2 Hotty	.50	1.25
23	Sylvain Grenier	.30	.75
24	Torrie Wilson	3.00	8.00
25	Undertaker	1.50	4.00
26	William Regal	.50	1.25
27	Antonio	.30	.75
28	Big Show	1.25	3.00
29	Carlito	.30	.75
30	Chris Jericho	1.00	2.50
31	Christy Hemme	3.00	8.00
32	Danny Basham	.30	.75
33	Edge	1.00	2.50
34	Eugene	.75	2.00
35	Gene Snitzky	.30	.75
36	Jerry The King Lawler	.75	2.00
37	John Cena	2.00	5.00
38	Kane	1.00	2.50
39	Kerwin White	.30	.75
40	Kurt Angle	1.25	3.00
41	Lita	2.00	5.00
42	Rene Dupree	.30	.75
43	Ric Flair	1.50	4.00
44	Rob Van Dam	1.00	2.50
45	Romeo	.30	.75
46	Rosey	.30	.75
47	Shawn Michaels	1.50	4.00
48	Shelton Benjamin	.30	.75
49	Stacy Keibler	3.00	8.00
50	Tajiri	.30	.75
51	The Hurricane	.30	.75
52	The Rock	2.00	5.00
53	Triple H	1.50	4.00
54	Trish Stratus	3.00	8.00
55	Tyson Tomko	.30	.75
56	Val Venis	.50	1.25
57	Victoria	2.00	5.00
58	Viscera	.30	.75
59	Sicilian Slide	.30	.75
60	The Worm	.50	1.25
61	Clothesline from Hell	.50	1.25
62	Tombstone Piledriver	1.50	4.00
63	Frog Splash	1.50	4.00
64	Crippler Crossface	1.25	3.00
65	ChokeSlam	1.50	4.00
66	Scissors Kick	.50	1.25
67	619	1.50	4.00
68	Flying Headbutt	1.25	3.00
69	Book-End	.50	1.25
70	The Walls of Jericho	1.00	2.50
71	Moonsault	2.00	5.00
72	Gory Bomb	.40	1.00
73	FU	2.00	5.00
74	Rock Bottom	2.00	5.00
75	Super Splash	.30	.75
76	Sweet Chin Music	1.50	4.00
77	Show Stopper	1.25	3.00
78	Ankle Lock	1.25	3.00
79	Twist of Fate	3.00	8.00
80	Chick Kick	3.00	8.00
81	Five Star Frog Splash	1.00	2.50
82	Bear Hug	.30	.75
83	Clothesline	.20	.50
84	Head Lock	.30	.75
85	Boston Crab	1.50	4.00
86	Chinlock	.20	.50
87	Jumping Foot Stomp	.20	.50
88	Shoulder Block	.30	.75
89	Right Hand	.20	.50
90	Hip Toss	2.00	5.00
91	Sleeper Hold	.30	.75
92	Hard Kick	.20	.50
93	Leap Frog	.20	.50
94	Head Lock	1.00	2.50
95	Pescado	1.00	2.50
96	Chinlock	.30	.75
97	Spinebuster	2.00	5.00
98	Chinlock	.20	.50
99	Vertical Suplex	.20	.50
100	Moonsault	1.00	2.50
101	One Leg Boston Crab	1.25	3.00
102	One Leg Boston Crab	.30	.75
103	Rope Walk	1.50	4.00
104	Bulldog	.20	.50
105	Drop Kick	1.00	2.50
106	Clothesline	.30	.75
107	Back Kick	1.00	2.50
108	Clothesline	.30	.75
109	Forearm	1.25	3.00
110	Face Slam	.20	.50
111	Head Lock	.20	.50
112	Belly to Back Suplex	1.50	4.00
113	Shoulder Tackle	2.00	5.00
114	Armbar	1.50	4.00
115	Big Boot	1.50	4.00
116	Armbar	1.50	4.00
117	Sharpshooter	2.00	5.00
118	Gorilla Press Slam	1.25	3.00
119	Double Flying Clothesline	.20	.50
120	Batista	.75	2.00
121	Booker T	.50	1.25
122	Chris Benoit	1.25	3.00
123	Christian	1.00	2.50
124	Eddie Guerrero	1.50	4.00
125	John Bradshaw Layfield	.50	1.25
126	Randy Orton	.30	.75
127	Rey Mysterio	1.00	2.50
128	Undertaker	1.50	4.00
129	Big Show	1.25	3.00
130	Carlito	.30	.75
131	John Cena	2.00	5.00
132	Kane	1.00	2.50
133	Kurt Angle	1.25	3.00
134	Shawn Michaels	1.50	4.00
135	The Hurricane	.30	.75
136	Triple H	1.50	4.00
137	Val Venis	.50	1.25
138	The Rock	2.00	5.00
139	Hulk Hogan	2.00	5.00
140	Sgt. Slaughter	.75	2.00
141	The Iron Sheik	.75	2.00
142	WWE Champion	.20	.50
143	WWE Intercontinental Champion	.20	.50
144	WWE Tag Team Champion	.20	.50
145	WWE Champion	.20	.50
146	WWE Tag Team Champion	.20	.50
147	WWE U.S. Champion	.20	.50
148	WWE Heavyweight Champion	.20	.50
149	WWE Cruiserweight Champion	.20	.50
150	WWE Women's Champion	.20	.50

2008 Edibas WWE Lamincards

COMPLETE SET (162)
UNOPENED BOX (24 PACKS)
UNOPENED PACK (4 CARDS)

1 Batista
2 Big Daddy V
3 Big Show
4 Brian Kendrick
5 Carlito
6 Curt Hawkins
7 DH Smith
8 Domino
9 Edge
10 Festus
11 Funaki
12 Gregory Helms
13 Jeff Hardy
14 Jesse
15 Jimmy Wang Yang
16 Jim Ross
17 Jonathan Coachman
18 Justin Roberts
19 Kenny Dykstra
20 Mick Foley
21 MVP
22 Shannon Moore
23 Shelton Benjamin
24 The Great Khali
25 Trevor Murdock
26 Triple H
27 Umaga
28 Undertaker
29 Vladimir Kozlov
30 Zack Ryder
31 Cherry
32 Eve Torres
33 Maria
34 Maryse
35 Michelle McCool

2014 Edibas WWE Lamincards

132 Kane
Sheamus
133 Drew McIntyre
Darren Young
134 Chris Jericho
Fandango
135 Big Show
Sheamus
136 Bray Wyatt
Daniel Bryan
137 Ryback
Cesaro
138 The Usos
Darren Young
139 Daniel Bryan
Dolph Ziggler
140 New Age Outlaws
The Brotherhood
141 Triple H
Brock Lesnar
142 The Miz
Dolph Ziggler
143 John Cena
Big Show
144 Jack Swagger
Alberto Del Rio
145 Jinder Mahal
Los Matadores
146 Daniel Bryan
The Shield
147 Zack Ryder
Bad News Barrett
148 Fandango
Chris Jericho
149 Big Show
Dean Ambrose
150 The Miz
Christian
151 Camacho
The Usos
152 The Rock
John Cena
153 Booker T
Batista
154 Randy Orton
Heath Slater
155 Sin Cara
Ryback
156 NXT Championship
157 WWE Tag Team Championship
158 Divas Championship
159 WWE World Heavyweight Championship
160 United States Championship

2007 Edibas WWE Lamincards German

COMPLETE SET (162)

1 Batista
2 Brett Major
3 Brian Major
4 Chavo Guerrero
5 Dave Taylor
6 Deuce
7 Domino
8 Edge
9 Finlay
10 Funaki
11 Gregory Helms

12 Hardcore Holly
13 Jamie Noble
14 JBL
15 Jimmy Wang Yang
16 Kane
17 Kenny Dykstra
18 Mark Henry
19 Matt Hardy
20 Michael Cole
21 Montel Vontavious Porter
22 Rey Mysterio
23 Ric Flair
24 Shannon Moore
25 The Great Khali
26 Theodore Long
27 Undertaker
28 Ashley
29 Cherry
30 Maryse
31 Michelle McCool
32 Torrie Wilson
33 Vickie Guerrero
34 Victoria
35 Bobby Lashley
36 Brien Kendrick
37 Carlito
38 Charlie Haas
39 Hacksaw Jim Duggan
40 Jeff Hardy
41 Jerry The King Lawler
42 Jim Ross
43 John Cena
44 Jonathan Coachman
45 Mr. Kennedy
46 Lance Cade
47 Paul London
48 Randy Orton
49 Robbie McAllister
50 Rowdy Roddy Piper
51 Rory McAllister
52 Santino Marella
53 Shawn Michaels
54 Shelton Benjamin
55 Snitsky
56 Stone Cold Steve Austin
57 Super Crazy
58 Todd Grisham
59 Trevor Murdoch
60 Triple H
61 Umaga
62 Val Venis
63 William Regal
64 Candice
65 Jillian
66 Lilian Garcia
67 Maria
68 Melina
69 Mickie James
70 Armando Estrada
71 Balls Mahoney
72 Boogeyman
73 CM Punk
74 Elijah Burke
75 Joey Styles
76 John Morrison
77 Kevin Thorn
78 Matt Striker
79 Mike Knox

80 Nunzio
81 Stevie Richards
82 Tazz
83 The Miz
84 Tommy Dreamer
85 Big Daddy V
86 Kelly Kelly
87 Layla
88 Akeem
89 Bam Bam Bigelow
90 Bobby The Brain Heenan
91 British Bulldog
92 Bushwhackers
93 Chief Jay Strongbow
94 Cowboy Bob Orton
95 Doink The Clown
96 Don Muraco
97 Dusty Rhodes
98 Earthquake
99 Classy Freddie Blassie
100 Gorilla Monsoon
101 Hillbilly Jim
102 Iron Sheik
103 Jake The Snake Roberts
104 Jimmy Hart
105 Jimmy Superfly Snuka
106 Junkyard Dog
107 Kamala
108 Koko B. Ware
109 Mean Gene Okerlund
110 Michael Hayes
111 Million Dollar Man Ted Dibiase
112 Mr. Perfect
113 Mr. Wonderful Paul Orndorff
114 Nikolai Volkoff
115 One Man Gang
116 Papa Shango
117 Paul Bearer
118 Ravishing Rick Rude
119 Sgt. Slaughter
120 Superstar Billy Graham
121 Vader
122 Abdominal Stretch
123 Air Mysterio
124 Back Body Drop
125 Belly-to-Back Suplex
126 Batista Bomb
127 Belly-to-Back Suplex
128 Bodyslam
129 Choke Slam
130 Dropkick
131 Dropkick
132 Elbow Drop
133 Gutbuster
134 Legdrop
135 Legdrop
136 Legdrop
137 Sleeper
138 Stomp
139 Irish Whip
140 Bodyslam
141 Lionsault
142 Back Body Drop
143 Elbow Smash
144 German Suplex
145 Sleeper
146 Beth Phoenix
147 Batista

148 Edge
149 Randy Orton
150 Undertaker
151 Batista
152 MVP
153 Matt Hardy
154 Randy Orton
155 Jeff Hardy
156 Cade & Murdock
157 CM Punk
158 Beth Phoenix
159 WWE Legends
160 SmackDown!
161 Raw
162 ECW

2006 Edigamma WWE Foto Colleziane Stickers

COMPLETE SET (39)

1 John Cena
2 Batista
3 Triple H
4 JBL
5 Undertaker
6 Shawn Michaels
7 Kurt Angle
8 Ken Kennedy
9 Big Show
10 Chris Benoit
11 Matt Hardy
12 Edge
13 Gene Snitsky
14 Trish Stratus
15 Torrie Wilson
16 Victoria
17 Candice Michelle
18 Rey Mysterio
19 Ric Flair
20 Randy Orton
21 Carlito
22 Chris Masters
23 Boogeyman
24 MNM
25 Paul London
26 Chavo Guerrero
27 Orlando Jordan
28 Hardcore Holly
29 Scotty 2 Hotty
30 Gregory Helms
31 Road Warrior Animal
32 Booker T
33 Sharmell
34 Kane
35 Shelton Benjamin
36 Nunzio
37 Rob Van Dam
38 Doug Basham
39 Steven Richards

2007 eTopps WWE

COMPLETE SET W/O AU (6) 50.00 100.00
STATED PRINT RUN 999 SERIAL #'d SETS
WILSON AU STATED PRINT RUN TO 867*

1 Batista	2.00	5.00
2 John Cena	3.00	8.00
3 Shawn Michaels	2.50	6.00
4 The Rock	50.00	100.00

5 Undertaker	10.00	25.00
6 Rowdy Roddy Piper	2.50	6.00
7 Torrie Wilson AU/867	30.00	75.00

1991 Euroflash WWF SuperStars Stickers

COMPLETE SET (150)
UNOPENED BOX (98 PACKS)
UNOPENED PACK (6 STICKERS)

1 Hulk Hogan	.75	2.00
2 Hulk Hogan (Puzzle)	.75	2.00
3 Hulk Hogan (Puzzle)	.75	2.00
4 Hulk Hogan (Puzzle)	.75	2.00
5 Hulk Hogan (Puzzle)	.75	2.00
6 Nasty Boys	.15	.40
7 Nasty Boys	.15	.40
8 Earthquake	.15	.40
9 Earthquake	.15	.40
10 Earthquake	.15	.40
11 Jimmy Hart	.25	.60
12 Dino Bravo	.15	.40
13 Dino Bravo (Puzzle)	.15	.40
14 Dino Bravo (Puzzle)	.15	.40
15 British Bulldog (Puzzle)	.20	.50
16 British Bulldog (Puzzle)	.20	.50
17 British Bulldog (Puzzle)	.20	.50
18 British Bulldog (Puzzle)	.20	.50
19 British Bulldog	.20	.50
20 British Bulldog	.20	.50
21 Bobby The Brain Heenan	.20	.50
22 Mr. Perfect	.25	.60
23 Mr. Perfect (Puzzle)	.25	.60
24 Mr. Perfect (Puzzle)	.25	.60
25 Texas Tornado	.20	.50
26 Texas Tornado (Puzzle)	.20	.50
27 Texas Tornado (Puzzle)	.20	.50
28 Tugboat	.15	.40
29 Tugboat (Puzzle)	.15	.40
30 Tugboat (Puzzle)	.15	.40
31 Hacksaw Jim Duggan (Puzzle)	.20	.50
32 Hacksaw Jim Duggan (Puzzle)	.20	.50
33 Hacksaw Jim Duggan (Puzzle)	.20	.50
34 Hacksaw Jim Duggan (Puzzle)	.20	.50
35 Hacksaw Jim Duggan	.20	.50
36 Big Boss Man (Puzzle)	.15	.40
37 Big Boss Man (Puzzle)	.15	.40
38 Big Boss Man	.15	.40
39 Big Boss Man	.15	.40
40 Power & Glory (Puzzle)	.15	.40
41 Power & Glory (Puzzle)	.15	.40
42 Power & Glory (Puzzle)	.15	.40
43 Power & Glory (Puzzle)	.15	.40
44 Hercules	.15	.40
45 Paul Roma	.15	.40
46 Slick	.15	.40
47 Ultimate Warrior (Puzzle)	.50	1.25
48 Ultimate Warrior (Puzzle)	.50	1.25
49 Ultimate Warrior (Puzzle)	.50	1.25
50 Ultimate Warrior (Puzzle)	.50	1.25
51 Ultimate Warrior (Puzzle)	.50	1.25
52 Ultimate Warrior (Puzzle)	.50	1.25
53 Ultimate Warrior	.50	1.25
54 Ultimate Warrior (Puzzle)	.50	1.25
55 Ultimate Warrior (Puzzle)	.50	1.25
56 Ultimate Warrior (Puzzle)	.50	1.25
57 Ultimate Warrior (Puzzle)	.50	1.25
58 Rockers (Puzzle)	.25	.60
59 Rockers (Puzzle)	.25	.60
60 Rockers (Puzzle)	.25	.60
61 Rockers (Puzzle)	.25	.60
62 Marty Jannetty	.15	.40
63 Shawn Michaels	.25	.60
64 Rockers	.25	.60
65 Rockers	.25	.60
66 The Model Rick Martel (Puzzle)	.15	.40
67 The Model Rick Martel (Puzzle)	.15	.40
68 The Model Rick Martel (Puzzle)	.15	.40
69 The Model Rick Martel (Puzzle)	.15	.40
70 The Model Rick Martel	.15	.40
71 The Model Rick Martel	.15	.40
72 The Model Rick Martel	.15	.40
73 Hulk Hogan	.75	2.00
74 Hulk Hogan (Puzzle)	.75	2.00
75 Hulk Hogan (Puzzle)	.75	2.00
76 Hulk Hogan (Puzzle)	.75	2.00
77 Hulk Hogan (Puzzle)	.75	2.00
78 Hulk Hogan	.75	2.00
79 Hulk Hogan	.75	2.00
80 Hulk Hogan (Puzzle)	.75	2.00
81 Hulk Hogan (Puzzle)	.75	2.00
82 Hulk Hogan (Puzzle)	.75	2.00
83 Hulk Hogan (Puzzle)	.75	2.00
84 Warlord	.15	.40
85 Warlord	.15	.40
86 Barbarian	.15	.40
87 Barbarian	.15	.40
88 Orient Express	.15	.40
89 Orient Express	.15	.40
90 Mr. Fuji	.15	.40
91 Superfly Jimmy Snuka (Puzzle)	.25	.60
92 Superfly Jimmy Snuka (Puzzle)	.25	.60
93 Superfly Jimmy Snuka	.25	.60
94 Superfly Jimmy Snuka	.25	.60
95 Bushwackers (Puzzle)	.15	.40
96 Bushwackers (Puzzle)	.15	.40
97 Bushwackers (Puzzle)	.15	.40
98 Bushwackers (Puzzle)	.15	.40
99 Bushwackers	.15	.40
100 Macho Man	.50	1.25
101 Macho Man (Puzzle)	.50	1.25
102 Macho Man (Puzzle)	.50	1.25
103 Macho Man & Queen Sherri	.50	1.25
104 Sensational Queen Sherri	.20	.50
105 Sensational Queen Sherri	.20	.50
106 Million Dollar Man (Puzzle)	.20	.50
107 Million Dollar Man (Puzzle)	.20	.50
108 Million Dollar Man (Puzzle)	.20	.50
109 Million Dollar Man (Puzzle)	.20	.50
110 Million Dollar Man Ted DiBiase	.20	.50
111 Million Dollar Man Ted DiBiase	.20	.50
112 Rowdy Roddy Piper (Puzzle)	.40	1.00
113 Rowdy Roddy Piper (Puzzle)	.40	1.00
114 Rowdy Roddy Piper	.40	1.00
115 Legion of Doom	.25	.60
116 Animal	.25	.60
117 Legion of Doom	.25	.60
118 Legion of Doom	.25	.60
119 Legion of Doom (Puzzle)	.25	.60
120 Legion of Doom (Puzzle)	.25	.60
121 Legion of Doom (Puzzle)	.25	.60
122 Legion of Doom (Puzzle)	.25	.60
123 Haku (Puzzle)	.15	.40
124 Haku (Puzzle)	.15	.40
125 Haku	.15	.40
126 Virgil (Puzzle)	.15	.40
127 Virgil (Puzzle)	.15	.40
128 Sgt. Slaughter (Puzzle)	.25	.60
129 Sgt. Slaughter (Puzzle)	.25	.60
130 Sgt. Slaughter (Puzzle)	.25	.60
131 Sgt. Slaughter (Puzzle)	.25	.60
132 Sgt. Slaughter	.25	.60
133 Sgt. Slaughter (Puzzle)	.25	.60
134 Sgt. Slaughter (Puzzle)	.25	.60
135 Jake The Snake Roberts (Puzzle)	.30	.75
136 Jake The Snake Roberts (Puzzle)	.30	.75
137 Jake The Snake Roberts	.30	.75
138 Jake The Snake Roberts (Puzzle)	.30	.75
139 Jake The Snake Roberts (Puzzle)	.30	.75
140 Jake The Snake Roberts (Puzzle)	.30	.75
141 Jake The Snake Roberts (Puzzle)	.30	.75
142 Koko B. Ware	.15	.40
143 Koko B. Ware	.15	.40
144 The Undertaker (Puzzle)	.60	1.50
145 The Undertaker (Puzzle)	.60	1.50
146 Undertaker/Paul Bearer (Puzzle)	.60	1.50
147 Undertaker/Paul Bearer (Puzzle)	.60	1.50
148 Undertaker/Paul Bearer (Puzzle)	.60	1.50
149 Undertaker/Paul Bearer (Puzzle)	.60	1.50
150 Paul Bearer	.20	.50

2009 EWA Wrestling

COMPLETE SET (6)

NNO Adam Carelle
NNO Cole Calloway
NNO Link Kory
NNO Nui The Samoan Tsunami
NNO Ryan McBride
NNO Teddy Stigma

1950 Exhibit

COMPLETE SET (34)

NNO Al Williams
NNO Antonio Rocca
NNO Benito Gardini
NNO Bill Brooks
NNO Bill Parks
NNO Billy Goelz
NNO Billy Darnell
NNO Buddy Rogers
NNO Cyclone Anaya
NNO Dave Levin
NNO Don Eagle
NNO Enrique Torres
NNO Farmer Don Marlin
NNO Friedrich Von Schacht
NNO Fritz Schnabel
NNO Gene Stanlee
NNO George Drake
NNO Gorgeous George
NNO Hans Schnabel
NNO Jim Londos
NNO Joe Millich
NNO Joe Savoldi
NNO Lou Thesz
NNO Michael Leone
NNO Pete Bartu
NNO Primo Carnera
NNO Roger MacKay
NNO Rudy Kay
NNO Ruffy Silverstein
NNO The Great Balbo
NNO The Mighty Atlas
NNO Walter Palmer

NNO Zuma (Man of Mars)
NNO Checklist

1960 Exhibit

COMPLETE SET (10)

1 Bob Ortin
2 Hans Herman
3 Hans Schmidt
4 George Macricosta
5 Pat O'Connor
6 Rasputin
7 Roy McClarity
8 Tarzan White
9 Verne Gagne
10 Yukon Eric

1964 Exhibit

COMPLETE SET (16)	50.00	100.00
NNO Andre Drapp	5.00	12.00
NNO Antonio Rocca	3.00	8.00
NNO Bruno Sammartino	15.00	40.00
NNO Buddy Rogers	8.00	20.00
NNO Count Billy Vargo	3.00	8.00
NNO Cowboy Bob Ellis	3.00	8.00
NNO Don Leo Jonathan	3.00	8.00
NNO Enrique Torres	3.00	8.00
NNO Hard Boiled Haggerty	3.00	8.00
NNO Haystacks Calhoun	6.00	15.00
NNO Jerry Graham	3.00	8.00
NNO Lou Thesz	8.00	20.00
NNO Pat O'Connor	3.00	8.00
NNO Pepper Gomez	3.00	8.00
NNO Roy Heffernan	3.00	8.00
NNO Sailor Art Thomas	3.00	8.00

1930 Exhibit W467

COMPLETE SET (39)

NNO Ali Baba
NNO Bill Sledge
NNO Danno O'Mahonney
NNO Dave Levin
NNO Dean Detton
NNO Dick Daviscourt
NNO Dick Shikat
NNO Earl McCready
NNO Ed Don George
NNO Ed Strangler Lewis
NNO Ernie Dusek
NNO Everett Marshall
NNO George Zaharias
NNO Gino Garabaldi
NNO Gus Sonnenberg
NNO Hans Steinke
NNO Henri De Glane
NNO Jack Kennedy
NNO Jim Browning
NNO Jim Londos
NNO Jim McMillan
NNO Joe Savoldi
NNO Joe Stecher
NNO John Pesek
NNO Lin Hale
NNO Little Wolf
NNO Makewicz
NNO Man Mtn Dean
NNO Milo Steinborn
NNO Nick Lutze

NNO	Paul Jones		
NNO	Ray Steel		
NNO	Sammy Stein		
NNO	Sandor Szoba (Szabo)		
NNO	Sixto Escobar		
NNO	Steve Casey		
NNO	Vic Christy		
NNO	Vincent Lopez		
NNO	Wladek Zbyszko		

2010 FCW Summer Slamarama

NNO	Bo Rotunda	12.00	30.00
NNO	Darren Young	10.00	25.00
NNO	Duke Rotunda		
NNO	Heath Slater	8.00	20.00
NNO	Joe Hennig	12.00	30.00
NNO	Justin Angel	8.00	20.00
NNO	Kaval	10.00	25.00
NNO	Naomi Knight	30.00	75.00
NNO	Savannah	10.00	25.00
NNO	Skip Sheffield (Ryback)	8.00	20.00
NNO	Tyler Reks	8.00	20.00
NNO	Wade Barrett	10.00	25.00

2011 FCW Summer Slamarama

Issued during Florida Championship Wrestling's 2011 Summer Slamarama Tour.

NNO	AJ	75.00	150.00
NNO	Aksana	6.00	15.00
NNO	Bo Rotundo	6.00	15.00
NNO	Brad Maddox	4.00	10.00
NNO	Briley Pierce	3.00	8.00
NNO	Brodus Clay	5.00	12.00
NNO	Calvin Raines	2.50	6.00
NNO	Conor O'Brian	2.50	6.00
NNO	Damien Sandow	8.00	20.00
NNO	Dean Ambrose	20.00	50.00
NNO	Hunico	3.00	8.00
NNO	Husky Harris	20.00	50.00
NNO	Jinder Mahal	8.00	20.00
NNO	Kenneth Cameron	2.50	6.00
NNO	Leo Kruger	4.00	10.00
NNO	Mason Ryan	3.00	8.00
NNO	Peter Orlov	2.50	6.00
NNO	Raquel Diaz	3.00	8.00
NNO	Richie Steamboat	6.00	15.00
NNO	Roman Leakee	20.00	50.00
NNO	Seth Rollins	15.00	40.00
NNO	Titus O'Neill	5.00	12.00
NNO	Xavier Woods	6.00	15.00

2012 FCW Summer Slamarama

Issued during Florida Championship Wrestling's 2012 Summer Slamarama Tour.

NNO	Bo Dallas	3.00	8.00
NNO	Brad Maddox	2.00	5.00
NNO	Briley Pierce	2.00	5.00
NNO	Caylee Turner	1.50	4.00
NNO	CJ Parker	1.50	4.00
NNO	Jake Carter	1.50	4.00
NNO	Mike Dalton	6.00	15.00
NNO	Paige	125.00	250.00
NNO	Raquel Diaz	3.00	8.00
NNO	Richie Steamboat	2.00	5.00
NNO	Rick Victor	1.50	4.00
NNO	Sofia Cortez	2.50	6.00
NNO	Summer Rae	30.00	75.00

2020 Finest WWE

COMPLETE SET W/SP (125)

COMPLETE SET W/O SP (100)		25.00	60.00

COMMON SP (101-125)
*REFRACTOR: .5X TO 1.2X BASIC CARDS
*X-FRACTOR: .6X TO 1.5X BASIC CARDS
*BLUE/150: .75X TO 2X BASIC CARDS
*GREEN/99: 1X TO 2.5X BASIC CARDS
*ORANGE/50: 1.2X TO 3X BASIC CARDS
*BLACK/25: UNPRICED DUE TO SCARCITY
*GOLD/10: UNPRICED DUE TO SCARCITY
*RED/5: UNPRICED DUE TO SCARCITY
*SUPERFR/1: UNPRICED DUE TO SCARCITY
SP STATED ODDS (101-125) 1:80

1	Angel Garza	.60	1.50
2	Akam	.60	1.50
3	Aleister Black	1.00	2.50
4	Andrade	.75	2.00
5	Angelo Dawkins	.50	1.25
6	Asuka	1.00	2.50
7	Austin Theory	.75	2.00
8	Becky Lynch	2.00	5.00
9	Bianca Belair	1.25	3.00
10	Bobby Lashley	1.00	2.50
11	Murphy	.60	1.50
12	Charlotte Flair	2.00	5.00
13	Drew McIntyre	1.00	2.50
14	Edge	1.00	2.50
15	Erik	.50	1.25
16	Humberto Carrillo	.75	2.00
17	Ivar	.50	1.25
18	Kairi Sane	1.00	2.50
19	Kevin Owens	.60	1.50
20	Lana	1.25	3.00
21	Liv Morgan	1.25	3.00
22	Montez Ford	.50	1.25
23	Nia Jax	.75	2.00
24	R-Truth	.50	1.25
25	Randy Orton	1.25	3.00
26	Rezar	.50	1.25
27	Ricochet	.75	2.00
28	Riddick Moss	.50	1.25
29	Ruby Riott	.75	2.00
30	Samoa Joe	.75	2.00
31	Seth Rollins	1.00	2.50
32	Shayna Baszler	1.50	4.00
33	Zelina Vega	1.00	2.50
34	AJ Styles	1.50	4.00
35	Alexa Bliss	2.50	6.00
36	Bayley	1.00	2.50
37	Big E	.50	1.25
38	Braun Strowman	1.25	3.00
39	The Fiend Bray Wyatt	1.50	4.00
40	Carmella	1.25	3.00
41	Cesaro	.50	1.25
42	Daniel Bryan	1.50	4.00
43	Dolph Ziggler	.50	1.25
44	Elias	1.00	2.50
45	Jeff Hardy	1.25	3.00
46	Jey Uso	.50	1.25
47	Jimmy Uso	.50	1.25
48	John Morrison	.50	1.25
49	King Corbin	.60	1.50
50	Kofi Kingston	.75	2.00
51	Lacey Evans	1.25	3.00
52	Mandy Rose	2.50	6.00
53	Matt Riddle	1.00	2.50

54	Mojo Rawley	.50	1.25
55	Mustafa Ali	.75	2.00
56	Naomi	1.00	2.50
57	Nikki Cross	1.00	2.50
58	Otis	.50	1.25
59	Robert Roode	.50	1.25
60	Roman Reigns	1.25	3.00
61	Sami Zayn	.60	1.50
62	Sasha Banks	2.00	5.00
63	Sheamus	.60	1.50
64	Shinsuke Nakamura	1.00	2.50
65	Shorty G	.50	1.25
66	Sonya Deville	1.25	3.00
67	Tamina	.60	1.50
68	The Miz	.75	2.00
69	Tucker	.50	1.25
70	Xavier Woods	.50	1.25
71	Adam Cole	1.25	3.00
72	Bobby Fish	.50	1.25
73	Cameron Grimes	.50	1.25
74	Candice LeRae	1.50	4.00
75	Chelsea Green	2.50	6.00
76	Dakota Kai	1.00	2.50
77	Damian Priest	.50	1.25
78	Dominik Dijakovic	.50	1.25
79	Finn Balor	1.25	3.00
80	Io Shirai	.75	2.00
81	Isaiah Swerve Scott	.60	1.50
82	Johnny Gargano	1.00	2.50
83	Kacy Catanzaro	1.00	2.50
84	Karrion Kross	1.00	2.50
85	Keith Lee	.50	1.25
86	Kushida	.60	1.50
87	Kyle O'Reilly	.60	1.50
88	Mia Yim	1.00	2.50
89	Pete Dunne	.50	1.25
90	Rhea Ripley	1.25	3.00
91	Roderick Strong	1.00	2.50
92	Scarlett	2.00	5.00
93	Shotzi Blackheart	1.50	4.00
94	Tegan Nox	1.25	3.00
95	Tommaso Ciampa	1.00	2.50
96	Tyler Breeze	.60	1.50
97	Velveteen Dream	.60	1.50
98	Kay Lee Ray	.75	2.00
99	Toni Storm	1.25	3.00
100	WALTER	1.00	2.50
101	Big Show SP		
102	Jinder Mahal SP		
103	Natalya SP		
104	Ember Moon SP		
105	Dana Brooke SP		
106	Jaxson Ryker SP		
107	Kalisto SP		
108	Kane SP		
109	Aliyah SP		
110	Bronson Reed SP		
111	Robert Stone SP		
112	Santos Escobar SP		
113	Jordan Devlin SP		
114	Mercedes Martinez SP		
115	John Cena SP		
116	Rob Gronkowski SP		
117	Ronda Rousey SP		
118	The Rock SP		
119	Triple H SP		
120	Undertaker SP		
121	Batista SP		

122	Bret Hit Man Hart SP		
123	Goldberg SP		
124	Shawn Michaels SP		
125	Stone Cold Steve Austin SP		

2020 Finest WWE Autographs

*GREEN/99: .6X TO 1.2X BASIC AUTOS
*ORANGE/50 .6X TO 1.5X BASIC AUTOS
*BLACK/25: UNPRICED DUE TO SCARCITY
*GOLD/10: UNPRICED DUE TO SCARCITY
*RED/5: UNPRICED DUE TO SCARCITY
*SUPERFR/1: UNPRICED DUE TO SCARCITY
STATED ODDS 1:17

AAB	Aleister Black	8.00	20.00
AAC	Adam Cole	10.00	25.00
AAD	Angelo Dawkins	5.00	12.00
AAG	Angel Garza	12.00	30.00
AAJ	AJ Styles	15.00	40.00
AAN	Andrade	5.00	12.00
AAS	Asuka	30.00	75.00
ABA	Bayley	25.00	60.00
ABB	Bianca Belair	10.00	25.00
ABD	Roman Reigns	15.00	40.00
ABE	Big E	6.00	15.00
ABM	Murphy	5.00	12.00
ABO	Bobby Lashley	8.00	20.00
ABW	The Fiend Bray Wyatt	30.00	75.00
ACG	Cameron Grimes	10.00	25.00
ACS	Cesaro	6.00	15.00
ADD	Dominik Dijakovic	5.00	12.00
ADK	Dakota Kai	20.00	50.00
ADM	Drew McIntyre	15.00	40.00
ADZ	Dolph Ziggler	6.00	15.00
AEK	Erik	5.00	12.00
AFB	Finn Balor	10.00	25.00
AIO	Io Shirai	30.00	75.00
AIS	Isaiah Swerve Scott	8.00	20.00
AJE	Jey Uso	6.00	15.00
AJG	Johnny Gargano	5.00	12.00
AJH	Jeff Hardy	12.00	30.00
AKC	King Corbin	6.00	15.00
AKL	Keith Lee	10.00	25.00
AKU	Kushida	5.00	12.00
ALM	Liv Morgan	20.00	50.00
AMA	Mandy Rose	25.00	60.00
AMF	Montez Ford	6.00	15.00
AMY	Mia Yim	10.00	25.00
ANC	Nikki Cross	10.00	25.00
AOT	Otis	8.00	20.00
AQS	Shayna Baszler	10.00	25.00
ARC	Ricochet	10.00	25.00
ARH	Rhea Ripley	50.00	100.00
ARR	Ruby Riott	15.00	40.00
ART	R-Truth	8.00	20.00
ASB	Sasha Banks	50.00	100.00
ASG	Shorty G	5.00	12.00
ASH	Sheamus	6.00	15.00
ASJ	Samoa Joe	5.00	12.00
ASN	Shinsuke Nakamura	8.00	20.00
ASR	Seth Rollins	10.00	25.00
ATB	Tyler Breeze	5.00	12.00
ATC	Tucker	6.00	15.00
ATN	Tegan Nox	30.00	75.00
ATO	Tommaso Ciampa	10.00	25.00
AVD	Velveteen Dream	5.00	12.00
AZV	Zelina Vega	15.00	40.00

2020 Finest WWE Decade's Finest Debuts

COMPLETE SET (9)		6.00	15.00
*GOLD/50: .6X TO 1.5X BASIC CARDS			
*RED/5: UNPRICED DUE TO SCARCITY			
*SUPERFR/1: UNPRICED DUE TO SCARCITY			
STATED ODDS 1:11			
D1	Daniel Bryan	2.00	5.00
D2	Roman Reigns	1.50	4.00
D3	Seth Rollins	1.25	3.00
D4	Kevin Owens	.75	2.00
D5	Samoa Joe	1.00	2.50
D6	Braun Strowman	1.50	4.00
D7	AJ Styles	2.00	5.00
D8	Shinsuke Nakamura	1.25	3.00
D9	Adam Cole	1.50	4.00

2020 Finest WWE Decade's Finest Debuts Autographs

*GOLD/50: .5X TO 1.2X BASIC AUTOS			
*RED/5: UNPRICED DUE TO SCARCITY			
*SUPERFR/1: UNPRICED DUE TO SCARCITY			
STATED ODDS 1:124			
DAC	Adam Cole	12.00	30.00
DAJ	AJ Styles	12.00	30.00
DKO	Kevin Owens	6.00	15.00
DSJ	Samoa Joe	6.00	15.00
DSN	Shinsuke Nakamura	8.00	20.00

2020 Finest WWE Decade's Finest Returns

COMPLETE SET (17)		12.00	30.00
*GOLD/50: .6X TO 1.5X BASIC CARDS			
*RED/5: UNPRICED DUE TO SCARCITY			
*SUPERFR/1: UNPRICED DUE TO SCARCITY			
STATED ODDS 1:7			
R1	Bret Hit Man Hart	1.50	4.00
R2	Booker T	1.25	3.00
R3	Diesel	1.00	2.50
R4	The Rock	3.00	8.00
R5	Kane	.75	2.00
R6	Undertaker	2.50	6.00
R7	Ultimate Warrior	1.50	4.00
R8	Shane McMahon	1.00	2.50
R9	Seth Rollins	1.25	3.00
R10	Goldberg	2.50	6.00
R11	Paige	1.50	4.00
R12	Daniel Bryan	2.00	5.00
R13	Bobby Lashley	1.25	3.00
R14	Roman Reigns	1.50	4.00
R15	Trish Stratus	3.00	8.00
R16	Batista	1.00	2.50
R17	Sasha Banks	2.50	6.00

2020 Finest WWE Decade's Finest Returns Autographs

*GOLD/50: .5X TO 1.2X BASIC AUTOS			
*RED/5: UNPRICED DUE TO SCARCITY			
*SUPERFR/1: UNPRICED DUE TO SCARCITY			
STATED ODDS 1:106			
RBL	Bobby Lashley	8.00	20.00
RRR	Roman Reigns	20.00	50.00
RSB	Sasha Banks	50.00	100.00
RSR	Seth Rollins	8.00	20.00

2020 Finest WWE Decade's Finest Superstars

COMPLETE SET (10)		10.00	25.00
*GOLD/50: .6X TO 1.5X BASIC CARDS			
*RED/5: UNPRICED DUE TO SCARCITY			
*SUPERFR/1: UNPRICED DUE TO SCARCITY			
STATED ODDS 1:11			
S1	Becky Lynch	2.50	6.00
S2	Charlotte Flair	2.50	6.00
S3	Daniel Bryan	2.00	5.00
S4	John Cena	2.50	6.00
S5	Kofi Kingston	1.00	2.50
S6	Randy Orton	1.50	4.00
S7	Roman Reigns	1.50	4.00
S8	Seth Rollins	1.25	3.00
S9	Sheamus	.75	2.00
S10	The Miz	1.00	2.50

2020 Finest WWE Decade's Finest Superstars Autographs

*GOLD/50: .5X TO 1.2X BASIC AUTOS			
*RED/5: UNPRICED DUE TO SCARCITY			
*SUPERFR/1: UNPRICED DUE TO SCARCITY			
STATED ODDS 1:123			
SKK	Kofi Kingston	.6.00	15.00
SRR	Roman Reigns	15.00	40.00
SSR	Seth Rollins	12.00	30.00

2020 Finest WWE Finest Careers Die-Cuts

COMPLETE SET (10)		30.00	75.00
*GOLD/50: .6X TO 1.5X BASIC CARDS			
*RED/5: UNPRICED DUE TO SCARCITY			
*SUPERFR/1: UNPRICED DUE TO SCARCITY			
STATED ODDS 1:48			
C1	Austin 3:16 Is Born	6.00	15.00
C2	Stunner Heard Around World	6.00	15.00
C3	First WWE Championship	6.00	15.00
C4	Zamboni Mayhem	6.00	15.00
C5	Cementing the Boss' Car	6.00	15.00
C6	Raining on Corporation's Parade	6.00	15.00
C7	Stone Cold's Final Match	6.00	15.00
C8	Chasing Down Mr. McMahon	6.00	15.00
C9	Mr. McMahon Inducts Austin	6.00	15.00
C10	Celebrating Raw's 25th Anniversary	6.00	15.00

2020 Finest WWE Finest Tag Teams

COMPLETE SET (17)		12.00	30.00
*GOLD/50: .6X TO 1.5X BASIC CARDS			
*RED/5: UNPRICED DUE TO SCARCITY			
*SUPERFR/1: UNPRICED DUE TO SCARCITY			
STATED ODDS 1:7			
TT1	Akam/Rezar	1.00	2.50
TT2	Montez Ford/Angelo Dawkins	.75	2.00
TT3	Kairi Sane/Asuka	1.50	4.00
TT4	Billie Kay/Peyton Royce	1.50	4.00
TT5	Ivar/Erik	.75	2.00
TT6	Alexa Bliss/Nikki Cross	4.00	10.00
TT7	Sasha Banks/Bayley	3.00	8.00
TT8	Big E/Kofi Kingston	1.25	3.00
TT9	John Morrison/The Miz	1.25	3.00
TT10	Jimmy Uso/Jey Uso	.75	2.00
TT11	Tucker/Otis	.75	2.00
TT12	Bobby Fish/Kyle OiReilly	1.00	2.50
TT13	Pete Dunne/Matt Riddle	1.50	4.00
TT14	Wesley Blake/Steve Cutler	1.00	2.50
TT15	Wolfgang/Mark Coffey	1.00	2.50
TT16	James Drake/Zack Gibson	1.00	2.50
TT17	Marcel Barthel/Fabian Aichner	.75	2.00

2020 Finest WWE Finest Tag Teams Autographs

*GOLD REF/25: UNPRICED DUE TO SCARCITY			
*RED REF/5: UNPRICED DUE TO SCARCITY			
*SUPERFR/1: UNPRICED DUE TO SCARCITY			
STATED ODDS 1:74			
TTBC	Alexa Bliss/Nikki Cross	75.00	150.00
TTBH	Sasha Banks/Bayley	100.00	200.00
TTHM	Tucker/Otis	20.00	50.00
TTII	Billie Kay/Peyton Royce	60.00	120.00
TTIM	Marcel Barthel/Fabian Aichner	10.00	25.00
TTMM	John Morrison/The Miz	30.00	75.00
TTSP	Angelo Dawkins/Montez Ford	15.00	40.00
TTUE	Bobby Fish/Kyle OiReilly	15.00	40.00
TTVR	Ivar/Erik	10.00	25.00

2002 Fleer WWE Absolute Divas

Trish Stratus, Lita, and all the women of the WWE shine in this set. The card fronts feature photos of them in various outfits and poses while the card backs contain information about them. Subsets within the set include: PS = Partnerships (46-65); DM = Diva Moments (66-80); GOF = Girls on Film (81-100). Also, thirty different mini-posters were produced and inserted into every pack.

COMPLETE SET (100)		10.00	25.00
UNOPENED BOX (24 PACKS)			
UNOPENED PACK (8 CARDS)			
*DIVA GEM: 1X TO 2.5X BASIC CARDS			
1	Trish Stratus	.60	1.50
2	Terri	.30	.75
3	Ivory	.25	.60
4	Lita	.40	1.00
5	Jackie	.25	.60
6	Stacy Keibler	.60	1.50
7	Torrie Wilson	.60	1.50
8	Jacqueline	.15	.40
9	Molly	.15	.40
10	Jazz	.15	.40
11	Stephanie McMahon	.30	.75
12	Nidia	.15	.40
13	Dawn Marie	.15	.40
14	Victoria	.30	.75
15	Linda	.15	.40
16	Trish Stratus	.60	1.50
17	Terri	.30	.75
18	Ivory	.25	.60
19	Lita	.40	1.00
20	Jazz	.15	.40
21	Stacy Keibler	.60	1.50
22	Torrie Wilson	.60	1.50
23	Jacqueline	.15	.40
24	Molly	.15	.40
25	Stephanie McMahon	.30	.75
26	Trish Stratus	.60	1.50
27	Terri	.30	.75
28	Ivory	.25	.60
29	Lita	.40	1.00
30	Jackie	.25	.60
31	Stacy Keibler	.60	1.50
32	Torrie Wilson	.60	1.50
33	Jacqueline	.15	.40
34	Molly	.15	.40
35	Jazz	.15	.40
36	Trish Stratus	.60	1.50
37	Terri	.30	.75
38	Ivory	.25	.60
39	Lita	.40	1.00
40	Stacy Keibler	.60	1.50
41	Torrie Wilson	.60	1.50
42	Jacqueline	.15	.40
43	Molly	.15	.40
44	Jazz	.15	.40
45	Lita PS	.40	1.00
46	Bubba Ray PS	.10	.25
47	Jamie Noble PS	.10	.25
48	Matt Hardy PS	.15	.40
49	Brock Lesnar with Paul Heyman PS	.60	1.50
50	William Regal PS	.10	.25
51	Triple H PS	.40	1.00
52	Vince McMahon PS	.25	.60
53	Booker T PS	.25	.60
54	Tajiri PS	.10	.25
55	Steven Richards PS	.10	.25
56	Chris Jericho PS	.15	.40
57	D-Von Dudley PS	.10	.25
58	Rob Van Dam PS	.25	.60
59	The Rock PS	.40	1.00
60	Ric Flair PS	.30	.75
61	Bradshaw PS	.15	.40
62	Hollywood Hulk Hogan PS	.60	1.50
63	Hurricane PS	.05	.15
64	Jeff Hardy PS	.15	.40
65	Kurt Angle PS	.25	.60
66	Jazz DM	.15	.40
67	Trish Stratus DM	.60	1.50
68	Molly DM	.15	.40
69	Lita DM	.40	1.00
70	Stacy Keibler DM	.60	1.50
71	Torrie Wilson DM	.60	1.50
72	Trish Stratus DM	.60	1.50
73	Jacqueline DM	.15	.40
74	Ivory DM	.25	.60
75	Trish Stratus DM	.60	1.50
76	Lita DM	.40	1.00
77	Terri DM	.30	.75
78	Jacqueline DM	.15	.40
79	Molly DM	.15	.40
80	Dawn Marie DM	.15	.40
81	Lita GOF	.40	1.00
82	Jacqueline GOF	.15	.40
83	Molly GOF	.15	.40
84	Stacy Keibler GOF	.60	1.50
85	Ivory GOF	.25	.60
86	Trish Stratus GOF	.60	1.50
87	Torrie Wilson GOF	.60	1.50
88	Terri GOF	.30	.75
89	Victoria GOF	.30	.75
90	Jazz GOF	.15	.40
91	Trish Stratus GOF	.60	1.50
92	Torrie Wilson GOF	.60	1.50
93	Ivory GOF	.25	.60
94	Lita GOF	.40	1.00
95	Dawn Marie GOF	.15	.40
96	Terri GOF	.30	.75
97	Linda GOF	.15	.40
98	Stacy Keibler GOF	.60	1.50
99	Molly GOF	.15	.40
100	Jackie GOF	.25	.60

2002 Fleer WWE Absolute Divas Cover Shots

COMPLETE SET (10)	15.00	40.00
STATED ODDS 1:12 HOBBY		
1 Ivory	1.25	3.00
2 Jacqueline	.75	2.00
3 Lita	2.50	6.00
4 Dawn Marie	.75	2.00
5 Stacy Keibler (w/Dudley Boyz)	5.00	12.00
6 Terri	1.50	4.00
7 Torrie Wilson	3.00	8.00
8 Trish Stratus	3.00	8.00
9 Stephanie McMahon	1.50	4.00
10 Stacy & Torrie	4.00	10.00

2002 Fleer WWE Absolute Divas Diva Ink

STATED ODDS 1:198 HOBBY		
CARDS AVAILABLE BY EXCH ONLY		
NNO Dawn Marie	6.00	15.00
NNO Jackie	8.00	20.00
NNO Linda	5.00	12.00
NNO Stacy Keibler	15.00	40.00
NNO Torrie Wilson	20.00	50.00

2002 Fleer WWE Absolute Divas Diva Ink Redemption

COMPLETE SET (5)	
RANDOMLY INSERTED INTO PACKS	
NNO Dawn Marie	
NNO Jackie	
NNO Linda	
NNO Stacy Keibler	
NNO Torrie Wilson	

2002 Fleer WWE Absolute Divas Inter-Actions

COMPLETE SET (20)	10.00	25.00
STATED ODDS 1:6 HOBBY		
1 Swimsuit Competition	1.50	4.00
2 Terri Wins The Hardcore Championship	.75	2.00
3 Six-Person Intergender Match	1.50	4.00
4 Bra And Panties Paddle On A Pole Match	.75	2.00
5 Mixed Tag Team Match	1.50	4.00
6 Tag Team	1.50	4.00
7 Bikini Match	1.50	4.00
8 Table Match	.40	1.00
9 Mixed Tag Team Match	1.50	4.00
10 Tag Team Hardcore Women's Title Match	1.50	4.00
11 Tag Team	1.50	4.00
12 Judgment Day Match	1.50	4.00
13 Gravy Bowl Match	1.50	4.00
14 Tag Team Match	1.50	4.00
15 Wrestlemania X-8 Triple Threat	1.00	2.50
16 Tag Team	.40	1.00
17 Swimsuit Competition	.40	1.00
18 Women's Title Match-KOTR	1.50	4.00
19 Bra And Panties Match (Women's Title)	1.50	4.00
20 Lingerie Match	1.50	4.00

2002 Fleer WWE Absolute Divas Lip Service

STATED PRINT RUN 50 SER. #'d SETS		
CARDS AVAILABLE BY EXCH ONLY		
NNO Dawn Marie	15.00	40.00
NNO Jackie	12.00	30.00
NNO Linda	10.00	25.00
NNO Stacy Keibler	50.00	100.00
NNO Torrie Wilson	50.00	100.00

2002 Fleer WWE Absolute Divas Lip Service Redemption

COMPLETE SET (5)	
RANDOMLY INSERTED INTO PACKS	
NNO Dawn Marie	
NNO Jackie	
NNO Linda	
NNO Stacy Keibler	
NNO Torrie Wilson	

2002 Fleer WWE Absolute Divas Material Girls

STATED ODDS 1:36 HOBBY		
NNO Dawn Marie Skirt	4.00	10.00
NNO Ivory Mat	2.00	5.00
NNO Jazz Mat	2.00	5.00
NNO Lita Mat	3.00	8.00
NNO Lita Top	6.00	15.00
NNO Molly Top	4.00	10.00
NNO Nidia Shorts	4.00	10.00
NNO Stacy Keibler Top	8.00	20.00
NNO Stacy Keibler T-Shirt	8.00	20.00
NNO Terri Outfit	6.00	15.00
NNO Torrie Wilson Bikini	8.00	20.00
NNO Trish Stratus Mat	4.00	10.00
NNO Trish Stratus Top	8.00	20.00
NNO Victoria Shorts	6.00	15.00

2002 Fleer WWE Absolute Divas Mini-Posters

COMPLETE SET (30)	8.00	20.00
STATED ODDS 1:1 HOBBY		
NNO Booker T	.40	1.00
NNO Brock Lesnar/Paul Heyman	1.00	2.50
NNO Chris Jericho	.25	.60
NNO Dawn Marie	.25	.60
NNO Hollywood Hulk Hogan	1.00	2.50
NNO Ivory	.40	1.00
NNO Jackie (orange border)	.40	1.00
NNO Jackie (yellow border)	.40	1.00
NNO Jacqueline	.25	.60
NNO Jazz	.25	.60
NNO Jeff Hardy	.25	.60
NNO Kurt Angle	.40	1.00
NNO Lita (blue border)	.60	1.50
NNO Lita (purple border)	.60	1.50
NNO Matt Hardy	.25	.60
NNO Molly	.25	.60
NNO Nidia	.25	.60

NNO Rob Van Dam	.40	1.00
NNO The Rock	.60	1.50
NNO Stacy Keibler (purple border)	1.00	2.50
NNO Stacy Keibler (red border)	1.00	2.50
NNO Stephanie McMahon	.50	1.25
NNO Terri (orange border)	.50	1.25
NNO Terri (purple border)	.50	1.25
NNO Torrie Wilson (black outfit)	1.00	2.50
NNO Torrie Wilson (blue outfit)	1.00	2.50
NNO Triple H	.60	1.50
NNO Trish Stratus (red border)	1.00	2.50
NNO Trish Stratus (yellow border)	1.00	2.50
NNO Victoria	.50	1.25

2002 Fleer WWE Absolute Divas Signed with a Kiss

STATED PRINT RUN 50 SER. #'d SETS		
AVAILABLE BY EXCH ONLY		
NNO Dawn Marie	20.00	50.00
NNO Ivory	20.00	50.00
NNO Jackie	30.00	75.00
NNO Linda	12.00	30.00
NNO Lita	50.00	100.00
NNO Stacy Keibler	100.00	200.00
NNO Torrie Wilson	100.00	200.00

2002 Fleer WWE Absolute Divas Signed with a Kiss Redemption

COMPLETE SET (7)	
RANDOMLY INSERTED INTO PACKS	
NNO Dawn Marie	
NNO Ivory	
NNO Jackie	
NNO Linda	
NNO Lita	
NNO Stacy Keibler	
NNO Torrie Wilson	

2002 Fleer WWE Absolute Divas Tropical Pleasures

COMPLETE SET (10)	12.00	30.00
STATED ODDS 1:12 HOBBY		
1 Ivory	1.25	3.00
2 Trish Stratus	3.00	8.00
3 Lita	2.00	5.00
4 Lita and Trish Stratus	3.00	8.00
5 Stacy Keibler	3.00	8.00
6 Terri	1.50	4.00
7 Torrie Wilson	3.00	8.00
8 Jacqueline	.75	2.00
9 Molly Holly	.75	2.00
10 Victoria	1.50	4.00

2002 Fleer WWE Absolute Divas Wardrobe Closet

STATED ODDS 1:23 HOBBY		
NNO Lita Jacket	6.00	15.00
NNO Molly Top	4.00	10.00
NNO Nidia Shorts	3.00	8.00
NNO Stacy Keibler T-Shirt	8.00	20.00
NNO Torrie Wilson Pants	8.00	20.00
NNO Torrie Wilson	8.00	20.00

Top		
NNO Trish Stratus	12.00	30.00
Top		
NNO Victoria	3.00	8.00
Top		

2003 Fleer WWE Aggression

Subset within the set includes: DL = DivaLicious (79-89)

COMPLETE SET (89)	10.00	25.00
UNOPENED BOX (24 PACKS)		
UNOPENED PACK (5 CARDS)		
1 Goldberg	.75	2.00
2 Batista	.50	1.25
3 Booker T	.50	1.25
4 Bradshaw	.30	.75
5 Bubba Ray Dudley	.20	.50
6 Chief Morley	.20	.50
7 Chris Jericho	.30	.75
8 Chris Nowinski	.12	.30
9 Christian	.30	.75
10 D-Von Dudley	.20	.50
11 Eric Bischoff	.20	.50
12 Goldust	.12	.30
13 Ivory	.50	1.25
14 Jacqueline	.30	.75
15 Jazz	.20	.50
16 Jamal	.20	.50
17 Charlie Haas	.12	.30
18 Kane	.50	1.25
19 Kevin Nash	.60	1.50
20 Lance Storm	.12	.30
21 Al Snow	.12	.30
22 Lita	.75	2.00
23 Maven	.12	.30
24 Molly	.60	1.50
25 Randy Orton	.30	.75
26 Ric Flair	.60	1.50
27 Rico	.12	.30
28 Rob Van Dam	.50	1.25
29 Rosey	.12	.30
30 Scott Steiner	.60	1.50
31 Shawn Michaels	.75	2.00
32 Spike Dudley	.20	.50
33 Stacy Keibler	1.25	3.00
34 Steven Richards	.20	.50
35 Stone Cold Steve Austin	.75	2.00
36 Terri	.60	1.50
37 Test	.20	.50
38 The Hurricane	.12	.30
39 Tommy Dreamer	.12	.30
40 Trish Stratus	1.25	3.00
41 Triple H	.75	2.00
42 Victoria	.60	1.50
43 William Regal	.30	.75
44 Big Show	.50	1.25
45 Bill DeMott	.12	.30
46 Billy Kidman	.12	.30
47 Brock Lesnar	1.25	3.00
48 Chavo Guerrero	.20	.50
49 Chuck Palumbo	.20	.50
50 Chris Benoit	.30	.75
51 Crash	.12	.30
52 Dawn Marie	.60	1.50
53 Edge	.50	1.25
54 Eddie Guerrero	.60	1.50
55 Funaki	.20	.50
56 Sable	.75	2.00

57 Hulk Hogan	.75	2.00
58 Jamie Noble	.12	.30
59 John Cena	.75	2.00
60 Johnny Stamboli	.12	.30
61 Kurt Angle	.50	1.25
62 Mark Henry	.20	.50
63 Matt Hardy	.30	.75
64 Nathan Jones	.12	.30
65 Nidia	.30	.75
66 Nunzio	.12	.30
67 Rey Mysterio	.30	.75
68 Rhyno	.50	1.25
69 Rikishi	.30	.75
70 Shannon Moore	.12	.30
71 The Rock	.75	2.00
72 Tajiri	.12	.30
73 Torrie Wilson	1.25	3.00
74 Tazz	.20	.50
75 Undertaker	.60	1.50
76 A-Train	.12	.30
77 Paul Heyman	.12	.30
78 Brian Kendrick	.20	.50
79 Torrie Wilson DL	1.25	3.00
80 Sable DL	.75	2.00
81 Lita DL	.75	2.00
82 Ivory DL	.50	1.25
83 Jacqueline DL	.30	.75
84 Jazz DL	.20	.50
85 Molly DL	.60	1.50
86 Stacy Keibler DL	1.25	3.00
87 Terri DL	.60	1.50
88 Trish Stratus DL	1.25	3.00
89 Nidia DL	.30	.75

2003 Fleer WWE Aggression Matitude

COMPLETE SET (10)	10.00	25.00
STATED ODDS 1:12 HOBBY		
1 Triple H	2.00	5.00
2 The Rock	2.00	5.00
3 Brock Lesnar	3.00	8.00
4 Stone Cold Steve Austin	2.00	5.00
5 Kurt Angle	1.25	3.00
6 Chris Jericho	.75	2.00
7 Hulk Hogan	2.00	5.00
8 Scott Steiner	1.50	4.00
9 Rob Van Dam	1.25	3.00
10 Undertaker	1.50	4.00

2003 Fleer WWE Aggression Matitude Event Used

MR The Rock	4.00	10.00
MU Undertaker	3.00	8.00
MBL Brock Lesnar	3.00	8.00
MCJ Chris Jericho	2.50	6.00
MHH Hollywood Hulk Hogan	6.00	15.00
MKA Kurt Angle	4.00	10.00
MSA Stone Cold Steve Austin	3.00	8.00
MSS Scott Steiner	2.00	5.00
MTR Triple H	3.00	8.00
MRVD Rob Van Dam	2.00	5.00

2003 Fleer WWE Aggression Matitude Event Used Jumbo Images

STATED PRINT RUN 50 SER.#'d SETS		
MR The Rock	15.00	40.00
MU Undertaker	15.00	40.00

MBL Brock Lesnar	20.00	50.00
MCJ Chris Jericho	10.00	25.00
MHH Hollywood Hulk Hogan	25.00	60.00
MKA Kurt Angle	12.00	30.00
MSA Stone Cold Steve Austin	15.00	40.00
MSS Scott Steiner	12.00	30.00
MTH Triple H	15.00	40.00
MRVD Rob Van Dam	10.00	25.00

2003 Fleer WWE Aggression Queens of the Ring

COMPLETE SET (10)	12.00	30.00
STATED ODDS 1:8 HOBBY		
1 Lita	1.50	4.00
2 Ivory	1.00	2.50
3 Jacqueline	.60	1.50
4 Jazz	.40	1.00
5 Molly	1.25	3.00
6 Stacy Keibler	2.50	6.00
7 Terri	1.25	3.00
8 Trish Stratus	2.50	6.00
9 Nidia	.60	1.50
10 Torrie Wilson	2.50	6.00

2003 Fleer WWE Aggression Queens of the Ring Autographs

STATED PRINT RUN 50 SER.#'d SETS		
SK AVAILABLE AT NATIONAL ONLY		
SK STATED PRINT RUN 1500 CARDS		
NNO Ivory/50	30.00	75.00
NNO Molly Holly/50	50.00	100.00
NNO Stacy Keibler/50	75.00	150.00
NNO Stacy Keibler NSCC	20.00	50.00
NNO Terri/50	60.00	125.00
NNO Trish Stratus/50	75.00	150.00

2003 Fleer WWE Aggression Queens of the Ring Event Used

STATED ODDS 1:115 HOBBY		
QRI Ivory	10.00	25.00
QRJ Jacqueline	8.00	20.00
QRL Lita	12.00	30.00
QRN Nidia	8.00	20.00
QRT Terri	12.00	30.00
QRJA Jazz	8.00	20.00
QRMH Molly Holly	8.00	20.00
QRSK Stacy Keibler	20.00	50.00
QRTS Trish Stratus	15.00	40.00
QRTW Torrie Wilson	20.00	50.00

2003 Fleer WWE Aggression Ring Leaders

COMPLETE SET (15)	8.00	20.00
STATED ODDS 1:4 HOBBY		
1 Triple H	1.25	3.00
2 The Rock	1.25	3.00
3 Brock Lesnar	2.00	5.00
4 Stone Cold Steve Austin	1.25	3.00
5 The Hurricane	.20	.50
6 Undertaker	1.00	2.50
7 Kane	.75	2.00
8 Chris Jericho	.50	1.25
9 Hulk Hogan	1.25	3.00
10 Scott Steiner	1.00	2.50
11 Rob Van Dam	.75	2.00
12 Shawn Michaels	1.25	3.00
13 Chris Benoit	.50	1.25

14 Edge	.75	2.00
15 Booker T	.75	2.00

2003 Fleer WWE Aggression Ring Leaders Event Used

STATED ODDS 1:29 HOBBY		
RLE Edge	6.00	15.00
RLH The Hurricane	3.00	8.00
RLK Kane	4.00	10.00
RLR The Rock	8.00	20.00
RLU Undertaker	6.00	15.00
RLBL Brock Lesnar	8.00	20.00
RLBT Booker T	3.00	8.00
RLCB Chris Benoit	4.00	10.00
RLCJ Chris Jericho	4.00	10.00
RLHH Hollywood Hulk Hogan	8.00	20.00
RLSA Stone Cold Steve Austin	8.00	20.00
RLSM Shawn Michaels	4.00	10.00
RLSS Scott Steiner	4.00	10.00
RLTH Triple H	6.00	15.00
RLRVD Rob Van Dam	4.00	10.00

2004 Fleer WWE Chaos

Subsets within the set include: SI = Simply Irresistible (70-85); PI = Pumping Iron (86-95)

COMPLETE SET (95)	10.00	25.00
UNOPENED BOX (24 PACKS)		
UNOPENED PACK (5 CARDS)		
*GOLD: 1X TO 2.5X BASIC CARDS		
1 Stone Cold Steve Austin	1.25	3.00
2 Test	.30	.75
3 Jazz	.50	1.25
4 Kurt Angle	.75	2.00
5 Batista	.75	2.00
6 The Hurricane		
7 Rey Mysterio	.50	1.25
8 Steven Richards	.30	.75
9 Goldberg	1.50	4.00
10 Chris Benoit	.50	1.25
11 Doug Basham	.20	.50
12 Torrie Wilson	2.00	5.00
13 Booker T	.75	2.00
14 Lance Storm	.20	.50
15 Rhyno	.75	2.00
16 Matt Hardy	.50	1.25
17 Maven	.20	.50
18 Rico	.20	.50
19 Rodney Mack	.20	.50
20 Jacqueline	.60	1.50
21 Rosey	.20	.50
22 Rikishi	.50	1.25
23 Scotty 2 Hotty	.30	.75
24 Mark Jindrak	.20	.50
25 Spike Dudley	.30	.75
26 Shawn Michaels	1.25	3.00
27 Paul Heyman	.20	.50
28 Val Venis	.30	.75
29 Shannon Moore	.20	.50
30 Triple H	1.25	3.00
31 Rob Conway	.20	.50
32 Edge	.75	2.00
33 A-Train	.20	.50
34 Big Show	.75	2.00
35 Theodore Long	.20	.50
36 Shelton Benjamin	.20	.50
37 Billy Gunn	.25	.60
38 Billy Kidman	.20	.50

39 Bradshaw	.50	1.25
40 Kane	.75	2.00
41 Charlie Haas	.20	.50
42 Chavo Guerrero	.30	.75
43 The Rock	1.25	3.00
44 Danny Basham	.20	.50
45 Chuck Palumbo	.30	.75
46 D-Von Dudley	.30	.75
47 Eddie Guerrero	1.00	2.50
48 Rene Dupree	.30	.75
49 Tajiri	.20	.50
50 Undertaker	1.00	2.50
51 Rob Van Dam	.75	2.00
52 Ric Flair	1.00	2.50
53 Matt Morgan	.25	.60
54 Eric Bischoff	.30	.75
55 Garrison Cade	.20	.50
56 Funaki	.30	.75
57 Brock Lesnar	2.00	5.00
58 Chris Jericho	.50	1.25
59 Hardcore Holly	.30	.75
60 Ultimo Dragon	.20	.50
61 Jamie Noble	.20	.50
62 Scott Steiner	1.00	2.50
63 John Cena	1.25	3.00
64 Randy Orton	.50	1.25
65 Johnny Stamboli	.20	.50
66 Nunzio	.20	.50
67 Bubba Ray Dudley	.30	.75
68 Mark Henry	.30	.75
69 Christian	.60	1.50
70 Jazz SI	.50	1.25
71 Torrie Wilson SI	2.00	5.00
72 Trish Stratus SI	2.00	5.00
73 Dawn Marie SI	.50	1.25
74 Stacy Keibler SI	2.00	5.00
75 Nidia SI	.50	1.25
76 Shaniqua SI	.50	1.25
77 Lita SI	1.25	3.00
78 Jacqueline SI	.60	1.50
79 Victoria SI	1.00	2.50
80 Terri SI	1.00	2.50
81 Ivory SI	.75	2.00
82 Gail Kim SI	.75	2.00
83 Miss Jackie SI	.75	2.00
84 Molly SI	1.00	2.50
85 Sable SI	1.25	3.00
86 Brock Lesnar PI	2.00	5.00
87 Triple H PI	1.25	3.00
88 Kurt Angle PI	.75	2.00
89 Batista PI	.75	2.00
90 Test PI	.30	.75
91 Randy Orton PI	.50	1.25
92 Scott Steiner PI	1.00	2.50
93 Booker T PI	.75	2.00
94 The Rock PI	1.25	3.00
95 Goldberg PI	1.50	4.00

2004 Fleer WWE Chaos Controlled Chaos

COMPLETE SET (15)	8.00	20.00
STATED ODDS 1:6 HOBBY AND RETAIL		
1 Brock Lesnar	2.00	5.00
2 Chris Benoit	.50	1.25
3 Triple H	1.25	3.00
4 Kurt Angle	.75	2.00
5 Kane	.75	2.00
6 Shawn Michaels	1.25	3.00

7 Edge		.75	2.00
8 Chris Jericho		.50	1.25
9 Stone Cold		1.25	3.00
10 Big Poppa Pump		1.00	2.50
11 Undertaker		1.00	2.50
12 Rob Van Dam		.75	2.00
13 Ric Flair		1.00	2.50
14 The Rock		1.25	3.00
15 Goldberg		1.50	4.00

2004 Fleer WWE Chaos Showing Off

COMPLETE SET (16)	12.50	30.00
STATED ODDS 1:4 HOBBY AND RETAIL		
1 Lita	1.50	4.00
2 Jacqueline	.75	2.00
3 Ivory	1.00	2.50
4 Dawn Marie	.60	1.50
5 Stacy Keibler	2.50	6.00
6 Nidia	.60	1.50
7 Molly Holly	1.25	3.00
8 Jazz	.60	1.50
9 Torrie Wilson	2.50	6.00
10 Victoria	1.25	3.00
11 Terri	1.25	3.00
12 Trish Stratus	2.50	6.00
13 Sable	1.50	4.00
14 Miss Jackie	1.00	2.50
15 Shaniqua	.60	1.50
16 Gail Kim	1.00	2.50

2004 Fleer WWE Chaos Showing Off Autographs

STATED PRINT RUN 25 SER.#'d SETS		
NNO Dawn Marie	50.00	100.00
NNO Gail Kim	60.00	125.00
NNO Ivory	60.00	125.00
NNO Jacqueline	30.00	75.00
NNO Jazz	50.00	100.00
NNO Lita	75.00	150.00
NNO Molly	50.00	100.00
NNO Miss Jackie	60.00	125.00
NNO Nidia	30.00	75.00
NNO Sable	75.00	150.00
NNO Shaniqua	30.00	75.00
NNO Stacy Keibler	100.00	200.00
NNO Terri	100.00	200.00
NNO Torrie Wilson	100.00	200.00
NNO Trish Stratus	125.00	250.00
NNO Victoria	30.00	75.00

2004 Fleer WWE Chaos Showing Off Memorabilia

STATED ODDS 1:36 HOBBY; 1:72 RETAIL		
SOI Ivory	5.00	12.00
SOJ Jacqueline	4.00	10.00
SOJ Jazz	4.00	10.00
SOL Lita	6.00	15.00
SOM Molly	5.00	12.00
SON Nidia	4.00	10.00
SOS Sable	6.00	15.00
SOS Shaniqua	4.00	10.00
SOT Terri	6.00	15.00
SOV Victoria	5.00	12.00
SODM Dawn Marie	5.00	12.00
SOGK Gail Kim	6.00	15.00
SOMJ Miss Jackie	6.00	15.00
SOSK Stacy Keibler	10.00	25.00

SOTS Trish Stratus	10.00	25.00
SOTW Torrie Wilson	10.00	25.00

2004 Fleer WWE Chaos Tuff Guys

COMPLETE SET (12)	12.00	30.00
STATED ODDS 1:12 HOBBY AND RETAIL		
1 The Rock	2.50	6.00
2 Eddie Guerrero	2.00	5.00
3 Triple H	2.50	6.00
4 Kurt Angle	1.50	4.00
5 Undertaker	2.00	5.00
6 Shawn Michaels	2.50	6.00
7 Rob Van Dam	1.50	4.00
8 Stone Cold Steve Austin	2.50	6.00
9 Chris Benoit	1.00	2.50
10 Brock Lesnar	4.00	10.00
11 Chris Jericho	1.00	2.50
12 Kane	1.50	4.00

2004 Fleer WWE Chaos Tuff Guys Event Used Mat

STATED ODDS 1:8 RETAIL		
TGK Kane	2.00	5.00
TGU Undertaker	2.50	6.00
TGBL Brock Lesnar	6.00	15.00
TGCB Chris Benoit	1.50	4.00
TGCJ Chris Jericho	1.50	4.00
TGEG Eddie Guerrero	1.50	4.00
TGKA Kurt Angle	2.00	5.00
TGRV Rob Van Dam	1.50	4.00
TGSA Stone Cold Steve Austin	3.00	8.00
TGSM Shawn Michaels	2.50	6.00
TGTH Triple H	2.50	6.00
TGTR The Rock	3.00	8.00

2004 Fleer WWE Chaos Tuff Guys Event Worn Memorabilia

STATED ODDS 1:12 HOBBY EXCLUSIVE		
TGK Kane	3.00	8.00
TGU Undertaker	4.00	10.00
TGBL Brock Lesnar	5.00	12.00
TGCB Chris Benoit	5.00	15.00
TGCJ Chris Jericho	2.50	6.00
TGEG Eddie Guerrero	3.00	10.00
TGKA Kurt Angle	4.00	10.00
TGRV Rob Van Dam	2.50	6.00
TGSA Stone Cold Steve Austin	5.00	12.00
TGSM Shawn Michaels	3.00	8.00
TGTH Triple H	4.00	10.00
TGTR The Rock	5.00	12.00

2003 Fleer WWE Divine Divas

Subset within the set includes: DT = Double Trouble (79-90)

COMPLETE SET (90)	10.00	25.00
UNOPENED BOX (24 PACKS)		
UNOPENED PACK (5 CARDS)		
1 Lita	.60	1.50
2 Jacqueline	.25	.60
3 Ivory	.40	1.00
4 Dawn Marie	.50	1.25
5 Stacy Keibler	1.00	2.50
6 Nidia	.25	.60
7 Molly	.50	1.25
8 Jazz	.15	.40
9 Torrie Wilson	1.00	2.50
10 Victoria	.50	1.25

11 Terri	.50	1.25
12 Trish Stratus	1.00	2.50
13 Sable	.60	1.50
14 Lita	.60	1.50
15 Jacqueline	.25	.60
16 Ivory	.40	1.00
17 Dawn Marie	.50	1.25
18 Stacy Keibler	1.00	2.50
19 Nidia	.25	.60
20 Molly	.50	1.25
21 Jazz	.15	.40
22 Torrie Wilson	1.00	2.50
23 Victoria	.50	1.25
24 Terri	.50	1.25
25 Trish Stratus	1.00	2.50
26 Sable	.60	1.50
27 Lita	.60	1.50
28 Jacqueline	.25	.60
29 Ivory	.40	1.00
30 Dawn Marie	.50	1.25
31 Stacy Keibler	1.00	2.50
32 Nidia	.25	.60
33 Molly	.50	1.25
34 Jazz	.15	.40
35 Torrie Wilson	1.00	2.50
36 Victoria	.50	1.25
37 Terri	.50	1.25
38 Trish Stratus	1.00	2.50
39 Sable	.60	1.50
40 Lita	.60	1.50
41 Jacqueline	.25	.60
42 Ivory	.40	1.00
43 Dawn Marie	.50	1.25
44 Stacy Keibler	1.00	2.50
45 Nidia	.25	.60
46 Molly	.50	1.25
47 Jazz	.15	.40
48 Torrie Wilson	1.00	2.50
49 Victoria	.50	1.25
50 Terri	.50	1.25
51 Trish Stratus	1.00	2.50
52 Sable	.60	1.50
53 Lita	.60	1.50
54 Jacqueline	.25	.60
55 Ivory	.40	1.00
56 Dawn Marie	.50	1.25
57 Stacy Keibler	1.00	2.50
58 Nidia	.25	.60
59 Molly	.50	1.25
60 Jazz	.15	.40
61 Torrie Wilson	1.00	2.50
62 Victoria	.50	1.25
63 Terri	.50	1.25
64 Trish Stratus	1.00	2.50
65 Sable	.60	1.50
66 Lita	.60	1.50
67 Jacqueline	.25	.60
68 Ivory	.40	1.00
69 Dawn Marie	.50	1.25
70 Stacy Keibler	1.00	2.50
71 Nidia	.25	.60
72 Molly	.50	1.25
73 Jazz	.15	.40
74 Torrie Wilson	1.00	2.50
75 Victoria	.50	1.25
76 Terri	.50	1.25
77 Trish Stratus	1.00	2.50
78 Sable	.60	1.50

79 Triple H/Victoria DT	.60	1.50
80 Trish Stratus/The Rock DT	1.00	2.50
81 Sable/Brock Lesnar DT	1.00	2.50
82 Lita/Edge DT	.60	1.50
83 Stacy Keibler/Scott Steiner DT	1.00	2.50
84 Terri/Stone Cold Steve Austin DT	.60	1.50
85 Chris Jericho/Ivory DT	.25	.60
86 Kurt Angle/Torrie Wilson DT	1.00	2.50
87 Booker T/Jazz DT	.40	1.00
88 Gail Kim/Kane DT	.40	1.00
89 Nidia/Jamie Noble DT	.25	.60
90 Zach Gowen/Stephanie DT	.50	1.25

2003 Fleer WWE Divine Divas Dress Code Memorabilia

STATED ODDS 1:288 HOBBY		
NNO Dawn Marie	10.00	25.00
NNO Ivory	20.00	50.00
NNO Molly	12.00	30.00
NNO Nidia	12.00	30.00
NNO Sable	30.00	80.00
NNO Stacy Keibler	50.00	100.00
NNO Trish Stratus	50.00	100.00
NNO Victoria	15.00	40.00

2003 Fleer WWE Divine Divas Hugs and Kisses

COMPLETE SET (14)	15.00	40.00
STATED ODDS 1:8		
NNO Dawn Marie	1.50	4.00
NNO Gail Kim	1.25	3.00
NNO Ivory	1.25	3.00
NNO Lita	2.00	5.00
NNO Miss Jackie	1.25	3.00
NNO Molly	1.50	4.00
NNO Nidia	.75	2.00
NNO Sable	2.00	5.00
NNO Shaniqua	.75	2.00
NNO Stacy Keibler	3.00	8.00
NNO Terri	1.50	4.00
NNO Torrie Wilson	3.00	8.00
NNO Trish Stratus	3.00	8.00
NNO Victoria	1.50	4.00

2003 Fleer WWE Divine Divas Hugs and Kisses Autographs

STATED PRINT RUN 25 SER #'d SETS		
NNO Dawn Marie	50.00	100.00
NNO Gail Kim	60.00	125.00
NNO Ivory	30.00	75.00
NNO Jazz	30.00	75.00
NNO Miss Jackie	60.00	125.00
NNO Lita	75.00	150.00
NNO Molly	50.00	100.00
NNO Nidia	30.00	75.00
NNO Sable EXCH	75.00	150.00
NNO Shaniqua	30.00	75.00
NNO Stacy Keibler	200.00	350.00
NNO Terri	100.00	200.00
NNO Trish Stratus	125.00	250.00
NNO Victoria	60.00	125.00
NNO Torrie Wilson	200.00	350.00

2003 Fleer WWE Divine Divas On Location

COMPLETE SET (16)	20.00	50.00
STATED ODDS 1:12 HOBBY AND RETAIL		

1	Jacqueline	1.00	2.50
2	Jazz	.60	1.50
3	Nidia	1.00	2.50
4	Dawn Marie	2.00	5.00
5	Torrie Wilson	4.00	10.00
6	Lita	2.50	6.00
7	Sable	2.50	6.00
8	Ivory	1.50	4.00
9	Stacy Keibler	4.00	10.00
10	Trish Stratus	4.00	10.00
11	Terri	2.00	5.00
12	Victoria	2.00	5.00
13	Molly	2.00	5.00
14	Miss Jackie	1.50	4.00
15	Shaniqua	1.00	2.50
16	Gail Kim	1.50	4.00

2003 Fleer WWE Divine Divas On Location Memorabilia

STATED ODDS 1:24 HOBBY: 1:96 RETAIL

NNO	Dawn Marie	5.00	12.00
NNO	Ivory	6.00	15.00
NNO	Miss Jackie	6.00	15.00
NNO	Molly	5.00	12.00
NNO	Nidia	4.00	10.00
NNO	Sable	8.00	20.00
NNO	Shaniqua	4.00	10.00
NNO	Victoria	6.00	15.00

2003 Fleer WWE Divine Divas With Love

1	Lita	1.25	3.00
2	Jacqueline	.50	1.25
3	Ivory	.75	2.00
4	Dawn Marie	1.00	2.50
5	Stacy Keibler	2.00	5.00
6	Nidia	.50	1.25
7	Molly	1.00	2.50
8	Jazz	.30	.75
9	Torrie Wilson	2.00	5.00
10	Victoria	1.00	2.50
11	Terri	1.00	2.50
12	Trish Stratus	2.00	5.00
13	Sable	1.25	3.00
14	Shaniqua	.50	1.25
15	Gail Kim	.75	2.00
16	Miss Jackie	.75	2.00

2003 Fleer WWE Divine Divas With Love Autographs

STATED PRINT RUN 100 SER.#'d SETS

NNO	Dawn Marie	12.00	30.00
NNO	Gail Kim	15.00	40.00
NNO	Ivory	20.00	50.00
NNO	Jacqueline	12.00	30.00
NNO	Jazz	12.00	30.00
NNO	Miss Jackie	15.00	40.00
NNO	Molly	15.00	40.00
NNO	Nidia	12.00	30.00
NNO	Sable EXCH	20.00	50.00
NNO	Shaniqua	12.00	30.00
NNO	Stacy Keibler	30.00	75.00
NNO	Trish Stratus	50.00	100.00
NNO	Victoria	15.00	40.00

2003 Fleer WWE Divine Divas With Love Memorabilia

NNO	Dawn Marie	4.00	10.00
NNO	Gail Kim	6.00	15.00
NNO	Ivory	6.00	15.00
NNO	Jacqueline	3.00	8.00
NNO	Miss Jackie	5.00	12.00
NNO	Molly	4.00	10.00
NNO	Nidia	3.00	8.00
NNO	Sable	6.00	15.00
NNO	Shaniqua	3.00	8.00
NNO	Stacy Keibler	8.00	20.00
NNO	Trish Stratus	8.00	20.00
NNO	Victoria	4.00	10.00

2003 Fleer WWE Divine Divas Promo

5	Stacy Keibler	1.50	4.00

2004 Fleer WWE Divine Divas 2005

Subsets within the set include: CF = Catfights (53-65); OS = Opposite Sex (66-79)

COMPLETE SET (80) 10.00 25.00
UNOPENED BOX
UNOPENED PACK

1	Lita	.50	1.25
2	Ivory	.30	.75
3	Dawn Marie	.20	.50
4	Stacy Keibler	.75	2.00
5	Nidia	.20	.50
6	Molly Holly	.40	1.00
7	Jazz	.20	.50
8	Torrie Wilson	.75	2.00
9	Victoria	.40	1.00
10	Trish Stratus	.75	2.00
11	Sable	.50	1.25
12	Miss Jackie	.30	.75
13	Gail Kim	.30	.75
14	Lita	.50	1.25
15	Ivory	.30	.75
16	Dawn Marie	.20	.50
17	Stacy Keibler	.75	2.00
18	Nidia	.20	.50
19	Molly Holly	.40	1.00
20	Jazz	.20	.50
21	Torrie Wilson	.75	2.00
22	Victoria	.40	1.00
23	Trish Stratus	.75	2.00
24	Sable	.50	1.25
25	Miss Jackie	.30	.75
26	Gail Kim	.30	.75
27	Lita	.50	1.25
28	Ivory	.30	.75
29	Dawn Marie	.20	.50
30	Stacy Keibler	.75	2.00
31	Torrie Wilson	.20	.50
32	Molly Holly	.40	1.00
33	Jazz	.20	.50
34	Torrie Wilson	.75	2.00
35	Victoria	.40	1.00
36	Trish Stratus	.75	2.00
37	Sable	.50	1.25
38	Miss Jackie	.30	.75
39	Gail Kim	.30	.75
40	Lita	.50	1.25
41	Ivory	.30	.75
42	Dawn Marie	.20	.50
43	Stacy Keibler	.75	2.00

44	Stacy Keibler	.75	2.00
45	Molly Holly	.40	1.00
46	Jazz	.20	.50
47	Torrie Wilson	.75	2.00
48	Victoria	.40	1.00
49	Trish Stratus	.75	2.00
50	Sable	.50	1.25
51	Miss Jackie	.30	.75
52	Gail Kim	.30	.75
53	Trish/Victoria CF	.75	2.00
54	Jazz & Gail Kim CF	.30	.75
55	Victoria & Molly Holly CF	.40	1.00
56	Sable/Torri/Stacy/Jackie CF	.75	2.00
57	Gail Kim & Lita CF	.50	1.25
58	Molly Holly & Gail Kim CF	.40	1.00
59	Jazz & Trish Stratus CF	.75	2.00
60	Lita & Trish Stratus CF	.75	2.00
61	Stacy Keibler & Miss Jackie CF	.75	2.00
62	Victoria & Gail Kim CF	.40	1.00
63	Molly Holly & Trish Stratus CF	.75	2.00
64	Sable & Torrie Wilson CF	.75	2.00
65	Victoria & Jazz CF	.40	1.00
66	Triple H OS	.50	1.25
67	Chris Jericho OS	.20	.50
68	Kurt Angle OS	.30	.75
69	Christian OS	.25	.60
70	Eric Bischoff OS	.12	.30
71	Shawn Michaels OS	.50	1.25
72	Eddie Guerrero OS	.40	1.00
73	Undertaker OS	.40	1.00
74	Booker T OS	.30	.75
75	Tyson Tomko OS	.12	.30
76	Chris Benoit OS	.20	.50
77	Eugene OS	.12	.30
78	Randy Orton OS	.20	.50
79	Edge OS	.30	.75
80	Babe of the Year Trish Stratus	.75	2.00

2004 Fleer WWE Divine Divas 2005 Body and Soul

COMPLETE SET (10) 8.00 20.00
STATED ODDS 1:8 HOBBY

1	Dawn Marie	.60	1.50
2	Stacy Keibler	2.50	6.00
3	Torrie Wilson	2.50	6.00
4	Trish Stratus	2.50	6.00
5	Victoria	1.25	3.00
6	Miss Jackie	1.00	2.50
7	Lita	1.50	4.00
8	Ivory	1.00	2.50
9	Nidia	.60	1.50
10	Sable	1.50	4.00

2004 Fleer WWE Divine Divas 2005 Body and Soul Memorabilia

STATED ODDS 1:288 HOBBY

BSDM	Dawn Marie	4.00	10.00
BSIV	Ivory	6.00	15.00
BSLI	Lita	8.00	20.00
BSMJ	Miss Jackie	5.00	12.00
BSNI	Nidia	4.00	10.00
BSSA	Sable	8.00	20.00
BSSK	Stacy Keibler	10.00	25.00
BSTS	Trish Stratus	10.00	25.00
BSTW	Torrie Wilson	8.00	20.00
BSVI	Victoria	6.00	15.00

2004 Fleer WWE Divine Divas 2005 Divas Uncensored

COMPLETE SET (13) 15.00 40.00
STATED ODDS 1:12 HOBBY

1	Dawn Marie	1.25	3.00
2	Jazz	1.25	3.00
3	Sable	3.00	8.00
4	Nidia	1.25	3.00
5	Victoria	2.50	6.00
6	Gail Kim	2.00	5.00
7	Ivory	2.00	5.00
8	Molly Holly	2.50	6.00
9	Trish Stratus	5.00	12.00
10	Lita	3.00	8.00
11	Stacy Keibler	5.00	12.00
12	Torrie Wilson	5.00	12.00
13	Miss Jackie	2.00	5.00

2004 Fleer WWE Divine Divas 2005 Divas Uncensored Memorabilia

STATED ODDS 1:24 HOBBY

DUL	Lita	6.00	15.00
DUDM	Dawn Marie	4.00	10.00
DUGK	Gail Kim	4.00	10.00
DUIV	Ivory	5.00	12.00
DUJA	Jazz	3.00	8.00
DUMH	Molly Holly	4.00	10.00
DUMJ	Miss Jackie	5.00	12.00
DUNI	Nidia	3.00	8.00
DUSA	Sable	6.00	15.00
DUSK	Stacy Keibler	12.00	30.00
DUTS	Trish Stratus	8.00	20.00
DUTW	Torrie Wilson	12.00	30.00
DUVI	Victoria	4.00	10.00

2004 Fleer WWE Divine Divas 2005 Femme Physique

COMPLETE SET (13) 8.00 20.00
STATED ODDS 1:4 HOBBY

1	Lita	1.25	3.00
2	Ivory	.75	2.00
3	Dawn Marie	.50	1.25
4	Stacy Keibler	2.00	5.00
5	Nidia	.50	1.25
6	Molly Holly	1.00	2.50
7	Jazz	.50	1.25
8	Torrie Wilson	2.00	5.00
9	Victoria	1.00	2.50
10	Trish Stratus	2.00	5.00
11	Sable	1.25	3.00
12	Miss Jackie	.75	2.00
13	Gail Kim	.75	2.00

2004 Fleer WWE Divine Divas 2005 Femme Physique Memorabilia

STATED ODDS 1:28 HOBBY

FPL	Lita	6.00	15.00
FPDM	Dawn Marie	3.00	8.00
FPGK	Gail Kim	3.00	8.00
FPIV	Ivory	4.00	10.00
FPJA	Jazz	3.00	8.00
FPMH	Molly Holly	4.00	10.00
FPMJ	Miss Jackie	5.00	12.00
FPNI	Nidia	3.00	8.00
FPSA	Sable	6.00	15.00
FPSK	Stacy Keibler	8.00	20.00

FPTS Trish Stratus 8.00 20.00
FPTW Torrie Wilson 8.00 20.00
FPVI Victoria 4.00 10.00

2004 Fleer WWE Divine Divas 2005 Hugs and Kisses Autographs

STATED PRINT RUN 15 SER.#'d SETS

HKDM Dawn Marie 50.00 100.00
HKIV Ivory 60.00 125.00
HKLI Lita 75.00 150.00
HKMJ Miss Jackie 60.00 125.00
HKNI Nidia 50.00 100.00
HKSA Sable 75.00 150.00
HKSK Stacy Keibler 175.00 300.00
HKTM Torrie Wilson 175.00 300.00
HKTS Trish Stratus 150.00 250.00
HKVI Victoria 60.00 125.00

2004 Fleer WWE Divine Divas 2005 With Love Wardrobe Autographs

WLDM Dawn Marie
WLIV Ivory
WLLI Lita
WLMJ Miss Jackie
WLNI Nidia
WLSA Sable
WLSK Stacy Keibler
WLTS Trish Stratus
WLTW Torrie Wilson
WLVI Victoria

2002 Fleer WWE KB Toys SmackDown! Shut Your Mouth

1 Kurt Angle 2.00 5.00
2 The Rock 5.00 12.00
3 Undertaker 2.50 6.00
4 Trish Stratus 4.00 10.00
5 Stacy Keibler 4.00 10.00
6 Triple H 2.50 6.00
7 Chris Jericho 2.00 5.00
8 Booker T 1.25 3.00
9 Rob Van Dam 1.25 3.00
10 Hollywood Hulk Hogan 4.00 10.00

2002 Fleer WWE Raw vs. SmackDown

Subsets within the set include: QR = Queens of the Ring (66-75); RVS = Raw vs. Smackdown (76-90)

COMPLETE SET (90) 8.00 20.00
UNOPENED BOX (24 PACKS)
UNOPENED PACK (8 CARDS)
1 The Rock .75 2.00
2 Undertaker .60 1.50
3 Kurt Angle .50 1.25
4 Kevin Nash .60 1.50
5 Jim Ross .20 .50
6 X-Pac .20 .50
7 Chris Benoit .30 .75
8 Kane .50 1.25
9 Hollywood Hulk Hogan 1.25 3.00
10 Rob Van Dam .50 1.25
11 Billy Gunn .20 .50
12 Chuck Palumbo .20 .50
13 Booker T .50 1.25
14 Edge .50 1.25
15 Big Show .50 1.25
16 Rikishi .30 .75

17 Bubba Ray Dudley .20 .50
18 D-Von Dudley .20 .50
19 Brock Lesnar 1.25 3.00
20 Mark Henry .20 .50
21 William Regal .20 .50
22 Maven .12 .30
23 Lita .75 2.00
24 Billy Kidman .12 .30
25 Bradshaw .30 .75
26 Tajiri .20 .50
27 Steven Richards .20 .50
28 Chris Jericho .30 .75
29 Matt Hardy .30 .75
30 Ivory .50 1.25
31 Raven .20 .50
32 Albert .12 .30
33 Jeff Hardy .30 .75
34 The Hurricane .12 .30
35 Jerry Lawler .30 .75
36 Al Snow .20 .50
37 D'Lo Brown .12 .30
38 Diamond Dallas Page .20 .50
39 Shawn Stasiak .12 .30
40 Torrie Wilson 1.25 3.00
41 Terri .60 1.50
42 Scotty 2 Hotty .20 .50
43 Jacqueline .30 .75
44 Stacy Keibler 1.25 3.00
45 Goldust .12 .30
46 Christian .30 .75
47 Trish Stratus 1.25 3.00
48 Test .20 .50
49 Justin Credible .12 .30
50 Faarooq .12 .30
51 Boss Man .12 .30
52 Tazz .20 .50
53 Tommy Dreamer .12 .30
54 Hardcore Holly .20 .50
55 Crash .12 .30
56 The Big Valbowski .20 .50
57 Molly Holly .30 .75
58 Perry Saturn .12 .30
59 Spike Dudley .20 .50
60 Lance Storm .12 .30
61 Triple H .75 2.00
62 Vince McMahon .50 1.25
63 Ric Flair .60 1.50
64 nWo .20 .50
65 Rico .12 .30
66 Debra QR .30 .75
67 Jazz QR .30 .75
68 Lita QR .75 2.00
69 Ivory QR .50 1.25
70 Terri QR .60 1.50
71 Torrie Wilson QR 1.25 3.00
72 Jacqueline QR .30 .75
73 Stacy Keibler QR 1.25 3.00
74 Trish Stratus QR 1.25 3.00
75 Molly Holly QR .30 .75
76 Rob Van Dam/Kurt Angle RVS .50 1.25
77 Big Show/Rikishi RVS .50 1.25
78 Undertaker/DDP RVS .60 1.50
79 Stone Cold/The Rock RVS .75 2.00
80 William Regal/Chris Jericho RVS .20 .50
81 Bubba Ray Dudley/D-Von Dudley RVS .20 .50
82 Trish Stratus/Torrie Wilson RVS 1.25 3.00
83 Lita/Stacy Keibler RVS 1.25 3.00
84 Jacqueline/Ivory RVS .50 1.25

85 Raven/Tajiri RVS .20 .50
86 Brock Lesnar/The Rock RVS 1.25 3.00
87 Booker T/Edge RVS .50 1.25
88 Goldust/The Hurricane RVS .12 .30
89 Bradshaw/Faarooq RVS .30 .75
90 Kane/Hulk Hogan RVS 1.25 3.00

2002 Fleer WWE Raw vs. SmackDown Catch Phrases

COMPLETE SET (15) 6.00 15.00
STATED ODDS 1:4 HOBBY

CP1 The Rock 1.25 3.00
CP2 Ric Flair 1.00 2.50
CP3 Kurt Angle .75 2.00
CP4 Stone Cold Steve Austin 1.25 3.00
CP5 Tazz .30 .75
CP6 Raven .30 .75
CP7 Trish Stratus 2.00 5.00
CP8 Triple H 1.25 3.00
CP9 The Big Valbowski .30 .75
CP10 Booker T .75 2.00
CP11 Chris Jericho .50 1.25
CP12 Hollywood Hulk Hogan 2.00 5.00
CP13 nWo .30 .75
CP14 Jim Ross .30 .75
CP15 Chris Benoit .50 1.25

2002 Fleer WWE Raw vs. SmackDown Exposure

COMPLETE SET (10) 8.00 20.00
STATED ODDS 1:8 HOBBY

XP1 Debra .60 1.50
XP2 Ivory 1.00 2.50
XP3 Jacqueline .60 1.50
XP4 Jazz .60 1.50
XP5 Lita 1.50 4.00
XP6 Molly Holly .60 1.50
XP7 Stacy Keibler 2.50 6.00
XP8 Terri 1.25 3.00
XP9 Torrie Wilson 2.50 6.00
XP10 Trish Stratus 2.50 6.00

2002 Fleer WWE Raw vs. SmackDown Pay-Per-View Relics

COMPLETE SET (5) 10.00 25.00
STATED ODDS 1:33 HOBBY

NNO Kurt Angle/Kane 3.00 8.00
NNO Ric Flair/Undertaker 3.00 8.00
NNO The Rock/Hulk Hogan 4.00 10.00
NNO Scott Hall/Steve Austin 3.00 8.00
NNO William Regal/Rob Van Dam 2.00 5.00

2002 Fleer WWE Raw vs. SmackDown Pop-Ups

COMPLETE SET (10) 20.00 50.00
STATED ODDS 1:HOBBY BOX

NNO Chris Jericho 1.25 3.00
NNO Hollywood Hulk Hogan 5.00 12.00
NNO Kurt Angle 2.00 5.00
NNO Lita 3.00 8.00
NNO The Rock 3.00 8.00
NNO Stacy Keibler 5.00 12.00
NNO Stone Cold Steve Austin 3.00 8.00
NNO Triple H 3.00 8.00
NNO Trish Stratus 5.00 12.00
NNO Undertaker 2.50 6.00

2002 Fleer WWE Raw vs. SmackDown Raw Certified

All swatches come from a shirt.
STATED ODDS 1:72

NNO Kevin Nash 10.00 25.00
NNO Rob Van Dam 8.00 20.00
NNO Spike Dudley 8.00 20.00
NNO William Regal 8.00 20.00
NNO X-Pac 8.00 20.00

2002 Fleer WWE Raw vs. SmackDown SmackDown Authentics

STATED ODDS 1:36 HOBBY

NNO Billy Gunn 4.00 10.00
Headband
NNO Chuck Palumbo 4.00 10.00
Headband
NNO DDP 5.00 12.00
Pants
NNO Edge 6.00 15.00
Shirt
NNO Hollywood Hulk Hogan 8.00 20.00
Shirt
NNO Triple H 6.00 15.00
Shirt
NNO Undertaker 6.00 15.00
Shirt

2002 Fleer WWE Raw vs. SmackDown Triple Exposure

NNO Lita/Debra/Molly 25.00 60.00
NNO Molly/Stacy Keibler/Debra 30.00 75.00
NNO Terri/Torrie/Stacy 75.00 150.00

2002 Fleer WWE Raw vs. SmackDown Ultimate Exposure

STATED ODDS 1:96 HOBBY

NNO Debra 8.00 20.00
Jacket
NNO Lita 10.00 25.00
Top
NNO Molly Holly 6.00 15.00
Swimsuit
NNO Molly Holly 6.00 15.00
Top
NNO Stacy Keibler 12.00 30.00
Shirt
NNO Terri 10.00 25.00
Dress
NNO Torrie Wilson 12.00 30.00
Stocking

2002 Fleer WWE Royal Rumble

Subset within the set includes: AKA (76-90)

COMPLETE SET W/CENA (90) 150.00 300.00
COMPLETE SET W/O CENA (89) 30.00 75.00
UNOPENED PACK (8 CARDS)
UNOPENED BOX (24 PACKS)
1 Big Show .50 1.25
2 Booker T .50 1.25
3 Bradshaw .30 .75
4 Brock Lesnar 6.00 15.00
5 Bubba Ray Dudley .20 .50
6 Chris Nowinski .12 .30
7 John Cena 125.00 250.00
8 D'Lo Brown .12 .30

9 Eddie Guerrero | .60 | 1.50
10 Goldust | .12 | .30
11 Jacqueline | .30 | .75
12 Jazz | .30 | .75
13 Jeff Hardy | .30 | .75
14 Randy Orton | 10.00 | 25.00
15 Kane | .50 | 1.25
16 Kevin Nash | .60 | 1.50
17 Lita | .75 | 2.00
18 Mark Henry | .20 | .50
19 Matt Hardy | .30 | .75
20 Molly | .30 | .75
21 Rob Van Dam | .50 | 1.25
22 Raven | .20 | .50
23 Shawn Michaels | .75 | 2.00
24 Shawn Stasiak | .12 | .30
25 Spike Dudley | .20 | .50
26 Steven Richards | .20 | .50
27 Terri | .60 | 1.50
28 Ric Flair | .60 | 1.50
29 William Regal | .20 | .50
30 X-Pac | .20 | .50
31 Al Snow | .20 | .50
32 Billy | .20 | .50
33 Billy Kidman | .12 | .30
34 Chris Benoit | .30 | .75
35 Christian | .30 | .75
36 Chuck | .20 | .50
37 D-Von | .20 | .50
38 Paul Heyman | .12 | .30
39 Edge | .50 | 1.25
40 Faarooq | .12 | .30
41 Funaki | .20 | .50
42 Chris Jericho | .30 | .75
43 Hollywood Hulk Hogan | 1.25 | 3.00
44 The Hurricane | |
45 Ivory | .50 | 1.25
46 Kurt Angle | .50 | 1.25
47 Maven | .12 | .30
48 Nidia | .30 | .75
49 Rico | .12 | .30
50 The Rock | .75 | 2.00
51 Tajiri | .20 | .50
52 Torrie Wilson | 1.25 | 3.00
53 Triple H | .75 | 2.00
54 Scotty 2 Hotty | .20 | .50
55 Stacy Keibler | 1.25 | 3.00
56 Lance Storm | .12 | .30
57 Tazz | .20 | .50
58 Test | .20 | .50
59 Eric Bischoff | .12 | .30
60 Jackie | .50 | 1.25
61 Victoria | .60 | 1.50
62 Stephanie | .60 | 1.50
63 Vince McMahon | .50 | 1.25
64 Rikishi | .30 | .75
65 Jerry Lawler | .30 | .75
66 Jim Ross | .20 | .50
67 Deacon Batista | 15.00 | 40.00
68 Shane McMahon | .30 | .75
69 Albert | .12 | .30
70 Trish Stratus | 1.25 | 3.00
71 Undertaker | .60 | 1.50
72 Dawn Marie | .30 | .75
73 Chavo Guerrero | .20 | .50
74 Rey Mysterio | .30 | .75
75 Tommy Dreamer | .12 | .30
76 Eddie Guerrero AKA | .60 | 1.50

77 Brock Lesnar AKA | 4.00 | 10.00
78 Chris Benoit AKA | .30 | .75
79 Triple H AKA | .75 | 2.00
80 Undertaker AKA | .60 | 1.50
81 The Rock AKA | .75 | 2.00
82 Jim Ross AKA | .20 | .50
83 Jerry Lawler AKA | .30 | .75
84 Ric Flair AKA | .60 | 1.50
85 Shawn Stasiak AKA | .12 | .30
86 Kurt Angle AKA | .50 | 1.25
87 Shawn Michaels AKA | .75 | 2.00
88 Hulk Hogan AKA | 1.25 | 3.00
89 Rob Van Dam AKA | .50 | 1.25
90 J.Hardy/M.Hardy/Lita AKA | .75 | 2.00

2002 Fleer WWE Royal Rumble AKA Memorabilia

STATED ODDS 1:24 HOBBY

NNO Triple H Ring Mat | 4.00 | 10.00
NNO Undertaker Ring Mat | 4.00 | 10.00

2002 Fleer WWE Royal Rumble Divastating

COMPLETE SET (15) | 10.00 | 25.00
STATED ODDS 1:8 HOBBY

D1 Ivory | 1.00 | 2.50
D2 Torrie Wilson | 2.50 | 6.00
D3 Terri | 1.25 | 3.00
D4 Stacy Keibler | 2.50 | 6.00
D5 Trish Stratus | 2.50 | 6.00
D6 Molly | .60 | 1.50
D7 Stephanie McMahon | 1.25 | 3.00
D8 Jazz | .60 | 1.50
D9 Jacqueline | .60 | 1.50
D10 Lita | 1.50 | 4.00
D11 Dawn Marie | .60 | 1.50
D12 Nidia | .60 | 1.50
D13 Linda | .60 | 1.50
D14 Jackie | 1.00 | 2.50
D15 Victoria | 1.25 | 3.00

2002 Fleer WWE Royal Rumble Divastating Autographs

PRINT RUN 100 SER. #'d SETS

NNO Lita | 50.00 | 100.00
NNO Stacy Keibler | 75.00 | 150.00
NNO Terri | 25.00 | 60.00
NNO Torrie Wilson | 60.00 | 120.00

2002 Fleer WWE Royal Rumble Divastating Memorabilia

STATED ODDS 1:48 HOBBY

NNO Dawn Marie Dress | 4.00 | 10.00
NNO Ivory Undergarment | 6.00 | 15.00
NNO Jazz Ring Mat | 4.00 | 10.00
NNO Stacy Keibler Shirt | 10.00 | 25.00
NNO Torrie Wilson Skirt | 10.00 | 25.00
NNO Trish Stratus Pants | 8.00 | 20.00

2002 Fleer WWE Royal Rumble Factions

COMPLETE SET (5) | 20.00 | 50.00
STATED ODDS 1:120

F1 The Nation of Domination | 6.00 | 15.00
F2 The Corporation | 6.00 | 15.00
F3 The Radicalz | 6.00 | 15.00
F4 D-Generation X | 6.00 | 15.00
F5 New World Order | 6.00 | 15.00

2002 Fleer WWE Royal Rumble Factions Memorabilia

STATED ODDS 1:48 HOBBY

NNO The Rock Shirt | 8.00 | 20.00
NNO Shawn Michaels D-X Shirt | 6.00 | 15.00
NNO Shawn Michaels nWo Shirt | 6.00 | 15.00
NNO X-Pac Shirt | 4.00 | 10.00

2002 Fleer WWE Royal Rumble Gimmick Matches

COMPLETE SET (10) | 6.00 | 15.00
STATED ODDS 1:4 HOBBY

GM1 Triple H/Chris Jericho | 1.25 | 3.00
GM2 Undertaker/Jeff Hardy | 1.00 | 2.50
GM3 Rob Van Dam/Eddie Guerrero | 1.00 | 2.50
GM4 Kurt Angle/Edge | .75 | 2.00
GM5 Rob Van Dam/Jeff Hardy | .75 | 2.00
GM6 Stacy Keibler/Trish Stratus | 2.00 | 5.00
GM7 The Rock/Trish Stratus | 2.00 | 5.00
GM8 Kurt Angle/Shane McMahon | .75 | 2.00
GM9 Chris Jericho/Kane | .75 | 2.00
GM10 Kurt Angle/Edge | .75 | 2.00

2002 Fleer WWE Royal Rumble Gimmick Matches Dual Memorabilia

STATED PRINT RUN 25 SER. #'d SETS

NNO The Rock/Trish Stratus | 30.00 | 75.00
NNO Stacy Keibler/Trish Stratus | 50.00 | 100.00
NNO Triple H/Chris Jericho | 20.00 | 50.00
NNO Undertaker/Jeff Hardy | 30.00 | 75.00

2002 Fleer WWE Royal Rumble Gimmick Matches Memorabilia

STATED ODDS 1:24 HOBBY

NNO Chris Jericho Shirt (Hell in a Cell) | 6.00 | 15.00
NNO Chris Jericho Shirt (Last Man Standing) | 6.00 | 15.00
NNO Edge Shirt (Cage Match) | 8.00 | 20.00
NNO Edge Shirt (Hair vs Hair) | 8.00 | 20.00
NNO Jeff Hardy Shirt (Ladder Match) | 8.00 | 20.00
NNO Jeff Hardy Tank Top (Hardcore Match) | 8.00 | 20.00
NNO Stacy Keibler Shirt (Gravy Bowl Match) | 10.00 | 25.00
NNO Triple H Shirt (Hell in a Cell) | 8.00 | 20.00
NNO Trish Stratus Pants (Gender Match) | 10.00 | 25.00
NNO Trish Stratus Shirt (Gender Match) | 10.00 | 25.00
NNO Trish Stratus Shirt (Gravy Bowl Match) | 10.00 | 25.00
NNO Undertaker Shirt (Ladder Match) | 8.00 | 20.00

2002 Fleer WWE Royal Rumble Memorabilia

STATED ODDS 1:24 HOBBY

NNO Brock Lesnar Shirt | 8.00 | 20.00
NNO Chris Benoit Ring Skirt | 5.00 | 12.00
NNO Edge Ring Mat | 6.00 | 15.00
NNO Funaki Shirt | 3.00 | 8.00
NNO Hollywood Hulk Hogan T-Shirt | 8.00 | 20.00
NNO The Hurricane Ring Mat | 3.00 | 8.00
NNO Kane Ring Mat | 5.00 | 12.00
NNO Kurt Angle Ring Mat | 5.00 | 12.00
NNO Maven T-Shirt | 3.00 | 8.00
NNO Rey Mysterio Shirt | 4.00 | 10.00
NNO Rob Van Dam Ring Mat | 4.00 | 10.00
NNO The Rock Ring Mat | 8.00 | 20.00
NNO Scotty 2 Hotty Jeans | 4.00 | 10.00
NNO Shawn Michaels Shirt | 5.00 | 12.00
NNO Tazz Sweat Pants | 3.00 | 8.00

2002 Fleer WWE Royal Rumble Recap

COMPLETE SET (10) | 15.00 | 40.00
STATED ODDS 1:24 HOBBY

RR1 Kane | 1.50 | 4.00
RR2 Kane vs The Undertaker | 2.00 | 5.00
RR3 Triple H vs Cactus Jack | 2.50 | 6.00
RR4 Vince McMahon | 1.50 | 4.00
RR5 Stone Cold | 2.50 | 6.00
RR6 Hollywood Hulk Hogan | 4.00 | 10.00
RR7 Ric Flair | 2.00 | 5.00
RR8 The Rock vs Mankind | 2.50 | 6.00
RR9 Shawn Michaels | 2.50 | 6.00
RR10 Mae Young | 1.00 | 2.50

2003 Fleer WWE WrestleMania XIX

Subset within the set includes: MM = Multiple Mania (76-90)

COMPLETE SET (90) | 12.50 | 30.00
UNOPENED BOX (24 PACKS) | |
UNOPENED PACK (5 CARDS) | |

1 Scott Steiner | .60 | 1.50
2 Scotty 2 Hotty | .20 | .50
3 Albert | .12 | .30
4 Kurt Angle | .50 | 1.25
5 Batista | .50 | 1.25

6	Chris Benoit	.30	.75
7	Big Show	.50	1.25
8	Billy	.20	.50
9	Eric Bischoff	.20	.50
10	Bradshaw	.30	.75
11	D'Lo Brown	.20	.50
12	John Cena	.75	2.00
13	Christian	.30	.75
14	Chuck	.20	.50
15	Tommy Dreamer	.12	.30
16	Bubba Ray Dudley	.20	.50
17	Spike Dudley	.20	.50
18	D-Von	.20	.50
19	Edge	.50	1.25
20	Ron Simmons	.20	.50
21	Ric Flair	.60	1.50
22	Funaki	.20	.50
23	Goldust	.12	.30
24	Crash	.12	.30
25	Eddie Guerrero	.60	1.50
26	Triple H	.75	2.00
27	Jeff Hardy	.30	.75
28	Matt Hardy	.30	.75
29	Hollywood Hulk Hogan	.75	2.00
30	The Hurricane	.12	.30
31	Chris Jericho	.30	.75
32	Kane	.50	1.25
33	Billy Kidman	.12	.30
34	Jerry Lawler	.30	.75
35	Brock Lesnar	1.25	3.00
36	Mark Henry	.20	.50
37	Maven	.12	.30
38	Godfather	.12	.30
39	Johnny Stamboli	.12	.30
40	Shawn Michaels	.75	2.00
41	Rey Mysterio	.30	.75
42	Kevin Nash	.60	1.50
43	Chris Nowinski	.12	.30
44	Randy Orton	.30	.75
45	Raven	.30	.75
46	William Regal	.30	.75
47	Steven Richards	.20	.50
48	Rico	.12	.30
49	Rikishi	.30	.75
50	The Rock	.75	2.00
51	Jim Ross	.20	.50
52	Al Snow	.12	.30
53	Jamie Noble	.12	.30
54	Lance Storm	.12	.30
55	Booker T	.50	1.25
56	Tajiri	.12	.30
57	Tazz	.20	.50
58	Test	.20	.50
59	Undertaker	.60	1.50
60	Rob Van Dam	.50	1.25
61	Lilian Garcia	1.00	2.50
62	Dawn Marie	.60	1.50
63	Trish Stratus	1.25	3.00
64	Jackie	.50	1.25
65	Victoria	.60	1.50
66	Stephanie	.60	1.50
67	Torrie Wilson	1.25	3.00
68	Stacy Keibler	1.25	3.00
69	Nidia	.30	.75
70	Ivory	.50	1.25
71	Terri	.60	1.50
72	Jacqueline	.30	.75
73	Jazz	.20	.50

74	Lita	.75	2.00
75	Molly	.60	1.50
76	Undertaker MM	.60	1.50
77	Kane MM	.50	1.25
78	Hollywood Hulk Hogan MM	.75	2.00
79	The Rock MM	.75	2.00
80	Triple H MM	.75	2.00
81	Kurt Angle MM	.50	1.25
82	Chris Jericho MM	.30	.75
83	Trish Stratus MM	1.25	3.00
84	Shawn Michaels MM	.75	2.00
85	Ivory MM	.50	1.25
86	Lita MM	.75	2.00
87	Jeff Hardy MM	.30	.75
88	Ric Flair MM	.60	1.50
89	Rikishi MM	.30	.75
90	Stone Cold Steve Austin MM	.75	2.00

2003 Fleer WWE WrestleMania XIX Diva Las Vegas

COMPLETE SET (2)		
NNO Dawn Marie/1350	8.00	20.00
NNO Torrie Wilson/150	20.00	50.00

2003 Fleer WWE WrestleMania XIX Flashbacks

COMPLETE SET (6)	30.00	60.00
STATED ODDS 1:48 HOBBY		
NNO Chris Jericho	4.00	10.00
NNO Hollywood Hulk Hogan	12.00	30.00
NNO Kurt Angle	6.00	15.00
NNO Stone Cold Steve Austin	6.00	15.00
NNO Triple H	10.00	25.00
NNO Undertaker	10.00	25.00

2003 Fleer WWE WrestleMania XIX Mat Finish

COMPLETE SET (10)	40.00	80.00
STATED ODDS 1:24 HOBBY		
NNO Brock Lesnar	6.00	15.00
NNO Edge	5.00	12.00
NNO The Hurricane	4.00	10.00
NNO Kurt Angle	5.00	12.00
NNO Rob Van Dam	4.00	10.00
NNO The Rock	6.00	15.00
NNO Stone Cold Steve Austin	6.00	15.00
NNO Triple H	5.00	12.00
NNO Trish Stratus	6.00	15.00
NNO Undertaker	5.00	12.00

2003 Fleer WWE WrestleMania XIX Title Shots

COMPLETE SET (7)	50.00	100.00
STATED ODDS 1:48 HOBBY		
NNO Brock Lesnar	10.00	25.00
NNO Kane	6.00	15.00
NNO Kurt Angle	8.00	20.00
NNO Rob Van Dam	6.00	15.00
NNO The Rock	12.00	30.00
NNO Triple H	8.00	20.00
NNO Undertaker	8.00	20.00

2004 Fleer WWE WrestleMania XX

Subsets within the set include: RD = Ring Divas (59-74); MM = Mania Memories (75-84)

COMPLETE SET (84)	10.00	25.00
UNOPENED BOX (24 PACKS)		

UNOPENED PACK (5 CARDS)		
*GOLD: .75X TO 2X BASIC CARDS		
1	Batista	.50	1.25
2	A-Train	.12	.30
3	Chris Jericho	.30	.75
4	Bill DeMott	.12	.30
5	Goldberg	1.00	2.50
6	Undertaker	.60	1.50
7	Kevin Nash	.60	1.50
8	Eddie Guerrero	.60	1.50
9	Mark Henry	.20	.50
10	John Cena	.75	2.00
11	Ric Flair	.60	1.50
12	Shannon Moore	.12	.30
13	Scott Steiner	.60	1.50
14	Brock Lesnar	1.25	3.00
15	Shawn Michaels	.75	2.00
16	Basham Brothers	.12	.30
17	Mark Jindrak & Garrison Cade	.12	.30
18	Chavo Guerrero	.20	.50
19	Eric Bischoff	.20	.50
20	Ultimo Dragon	.12	.30
21	Triple H	.75	2.00
22	The World's Greatest Tag Team	.12	.30
23	La Resistance	.12	.30
24	Rhyno	.50	1.25
25	Rico	.12	.30
26	Edge	.50	1.25
27	Steven Richards	.20	.50
28	Jerry The King Lawler	.30	.75
29	Vince McMahon	.50	1.25
30	Linda McMahon	.20	.50
31	Stephanie McMahon	.60	1.50
32	Shane McMahon	.30	.75
33	Jim Ross	.20	.50
34	Chris Nowinski	.12	.30
35	Tazz	.20	.50
36	Maven	.12	.30
37	Sean O'Haire	.12	.30
38	Dudley Boyz	.20	.50
39	The Hurricane		
40	Rey Mysterio	.30	.75
41	Test	.20	.50
42	Tajiri	.12	.30
43	Stone Cold Steve Austin	.75	2.00
44	Chris Benoit	.30	.75
45	The Rock	.75	2.00
46	APA	.30	.75
47	Rosey	.12	.30
48	Rodney Mack	.12	.30
49	Matt Hardy	.30	.75
50	Randy Orton	.30	.75
51	Kurt Angle	.50	1.25
52	Lance Storm	.12	.30
53	FBI		
54	Kane	.50	1.25
55	Billy Kidman	.12	.30
56	Christian	.40	1.00
57	Big Show	.50	1.25
58	Booker T	.50	1.25
59	Sable RD	.75	2.00
60	Lita RD	.75	2.00
61	Ivory RD	.50	1.25
62	Stacy Keibler RD	1.25	3.00
63	Molly RD	.60	1.50
64	Torrie Wilson RD	1.25	3.00
65	Terri RD	.60	1.50
66	Shaniqua RD	.30	.75

67	Gail Kim	.50	1.25
68	Miss Jackie RD	.50	1.25
69	Victoria RD	.60	1.50
70	Jazz RD	.30	.75
71	Nidia RD	.30	.75
72	Dawn Marie RD	.30	.75
73	Jacqueline RD	.40	1.00
74	Trish Stratus RD	1.25	3.00
75	Ric Flair MM	.60	1.50
76	Shawn Michaels MM	.75	2.00
77	Shawn Michaels MM	.75	2.00
78	Undertaker MM	.60	1.50
79	Stone Cold Steve Austin MM	.75	2.00
80	The Rock MM	.75	2.00
81	Triple H MM	.75	2.00
82	Steve Austin & The Rock MM	.75	2.00
83	Triple H MM	.75	2.00
84	Brock Lesnar MM	1.25	3.00

2004 Fleer WWE WrestleMania XX Champions and Contenders

COMPLETE SET (17)	8.00	20.00
STATED ODDS 1:4 HOBBY AND RETAIL		
1 Kurt Angle	1.50	4.00
Brock Lesnar		
2 Steve Austin	2.00	5.00
The Rock		
3 Trish Stratus	1.50	4.00
Jazz		
4 Triple H	1.00	2.50
Booker T		
5 Kane	.60	1.50
Big Show		
6 Eddie Guerrero	.75	2.00
Test		
7 Undertaker	.75	2.00
Ric Flair		
8 Edge & Christian	.60	1.50
Dudley Boyz		
9 Jazz	1.00	2.50
Lita		
10 Triple H	1.00	2.50
The Rock		
11 Shane McMahon	.60	1.50
Vince McMahon		
12 Chris Benoit	.40	1.00
Chris Jericho		
13 Rob Van Dam	.60	1.50
William Regal		
14 Trish Stratus	1.50	4.00
Victoria		
15 Matt Hardy	.40	1.00
Rey Mysterio		
16 Steve Austin	1.00	2.50
Shawn Michaels		
17 Triple H	1.00	2.50
Chris Jericho		

2004 Fleer WWE WrestleMania XX Champions and Contenders Dual Memorabilia

STATED ODDS 1:144 HOBBY		
CCDJ/L Jazz	6.00	12.00
Lita		
CCDK/BS Kane	6.00	12.00
Big Show		
CCDSA/R Steve Austin	10.00	20.00

The Rock

CCDTS/J	Trish Stratus Jazz	10.00	20.00
CCDCB/CJ	Chris Benoit Chris Jericho	5.00	10.00
CCDKA/BL	Kurt Angle Brock Lesnar	7.50	15.00
CCDMH/RM	Matt Hardy Rey Mysterio	6.00	12.00
CCDSA/SM	Steve Austin Shawn Michaels	7.50	15.00
CCDTH/BT	Triple H Booker T	6.00	12.00
CCDTH/CJ	Triple H Chris Jericho	6.00	12.00

2004 Fleer WWE WrestleMania XX Champions and Contenders Memorabilia

STATED ODDS 1:18 HOBBY

CCSJ	Jazz	3.00	8.00
CCSK	Kane	4.00	10.00
CCSL	Lita	5.00	12.00
CCSR	The Rock	6.00	15.00
CCST	Test	3.00	8.00
CCSU	Undertaker	5.00	12.00
CCSBL	Brock Lesnar	6.00	15.00
CCSBT	Booker T	3.00	8.00
CCSCB	Chris Benoit	3.00	8.00
CCSCJ	Chris Jericho	3.00	8.00
CCSKA	Kurt Angle	4.00	10.00
CCSMH	Matt Hardy	5.00	12.00
CCSSA	Stone Cold Steve Austin	6.00	15.00
CCSSM	Shawn Michaels	5.00	12.00
CCSTH	Triple H	5.00	12.00
CCSTS	Trish Stratus	6.00	15.00
CCSRVD	Rob Van Dam	3.00	8.00

2004 Fleer WWE WrestleMania XX Road to WrestleMania

COMPLETE SET (10) 20.00 50.00
STATED ODDS 1:24 HOBBY AND RETAIL

1	Shawn Michaels	3.00	8.00
2	Trish Stratus	5.00	12.00
3	Brock Lesnar	5.00	12.00
4	Stone Cold Steve Austin	3.00	8.00
5	Undertaker	2.50	6.00
6	Scott Steiner	2.50	6.00
7	Lita	3.00	8.00
8	Triple H	3.00	8.00
9	The Rock	3.00	8.00
10	Kurt Angle	2.00	5.00

2004 Fleer WWE WrestleMania XX To the Mat Memorabilia

STATED ODDS 1:48 HOBBY

1	Lita	6.00	15.00
2	Stacy Keibler	8.00	20.00
3	Molly	4.00	10.00
4	Torrie Wilson	8.00	20.00
5	Gail Kim	4.00	10.00
6	Victoria	5.00	12.00
7	Miss Jackie	5.00	12.00
8	Trish Stratus	8.00	20.00
9	Sable	6.00	15.00
10	Ivory	5.00	12.00

2004 Fleer WWE WrestleMania XX To the Mat Memorabilia Autographs

STATED PRINT RUN 50 SER.#'d SETS

TTML	Lita	50.00	100.00
TTMS	Sable	30.00	75.00
TTMSK	Stacy Keibler	60.00	120.00
TTMTS	Trish Stratus	75.00	150.00
TTMTW	Torrie Wilson	30.00	75.00

2002 Fleer WWF All Access

Subsets within the set include: OTM = Off the Mat (51-80); RR = Road to the Ring (81-100)

COMPLETE SET (100) 8.00 20.00
UNOPENED BOX (24 PACKS)
UNOPENED PACK (8 CARDS)

1	Justin Credible	.12	.30
2	Shane McMahon	.30	.75
3	Tajiri	.20	.50
4	Jerry Lynn	.12	.30
5	Christian	.30	.75
6	Haku	.12	.30
7	Kurt Angle	.50	1.25
8	Albert	.12	.30
9	Chris Jericho	.30	.75
10	Jeff Hardy	.30	.75
11	Triple H	.75	2.00
12	The One Billy Gunn	.20	.50
13	Booker T	.50	1.25
14	Funaki	.20	.50
15	Chris Benoit	.30	.75
16	The Rock	.75	2.00
17	Bradshaw	.30	.75
18	Stephanie McMahon-Helmsley	.60	1.50
19	Crash Holly	.12	.30
20	Rhyno	.30	.75
21	Faarooq	.12	.30
22	Al Snow	.20	.50
23	Hardcore Holly	.20	.50
24	Rikishi	.30	.75
25	Rob Van Dam	.50	1.25
26	X-Pac	.20	.50
27	D-Von Dudley	.20	.50
28	Kane	.50	1.25
29	Spike Dudley	.20	.50
30	William Regal	.20	.50
31	Taka Michinoku	.12	.30
32	Mick Foley	.50	1.25
33	Undertaker	.60	1.50
34	Edge	.50	1.25
35	Stone Cold Steve Austin	.75	2.00
36	Jim Ross	.20	.50
37	Bubba Ray Dudley	.20	.50
38	Steve Blackman	.12	.30
39	Test	.20	.50
40	Molly Holly	.30	.75
41	Vince Mcmahon	.50	1.25
42	Stacy Keibler	1.25	3.00
43	Torrie Wilson	1.25	3.00
44	Perry Saturn	.12	.30
45	Raven	.20	.50
46	Scotty 2 Hotty	.20	.50
47	Big Show	.50	1.25
48	Matt Hardy	.30	.75
49	Tazz	.20	.50
50	The Hurricane	.12	.30
51	Kane OTM	.50	1.25
52	Mick Foley OTM	.50	1.25
53	Lita OTM	.75	2.00
54	Justin Credible OTM	.12	.30
55	Big Show OTM	.50	1.25
56	Chris Benoit OTM	.30	.75
57	Stone Cold OTM	.75	2.00
58	Edge OTM	.50	1.25
59	Trish Stratus OTM	1.25	3.00
60	Faarooq OTM	.12	.30
61	Linda McMahon OTM	.20	.50
62	Matt Hardy OTM	.30	.75
63	Diamond Dallas Page OTM	.20	.50
64	The Hurricane OTM	.12	.30
65	Kurt Angle OTM	.50	1.25
66	Ric Flair OTM	.60	1.50
67	Undertaker OTM	.60	1.50
68	Tajiri OTM	.20	.50
69	Vince McMahon OTM	.50	1.25
70	Chris Jericho OTM	.30	.75
71	Triple H OTM	.75	2.00
72	Tazz OTM	.20	.50
73	Rob Van Dam OTM	.50	1.25
74	Sgt. Slaughter OTM	.30	.75
75	The Rock OTM	.75	2.00
76	Jim Ross OTM	.20	.50
77	Bradshaw OTM	.30	.75
78	Matt Hardy OTM	.30	.75
79	Perry Saturn OTM	.12	.30
80	X-Pac OTM	.20	.50
81	Maven RR	.12	.30
82	Molly Holly RR	.30	.75
83	Big Show RR	.50	1.25
84	Edge RR	.50	1.25
85	Stone Cold Steve Austin RR	.75	2.00
86	Vince McMahon RR	.50	1.25
87	Jeff Hardy RR	.30	.75
88	Kane RR	.50	1.25
89	Lita RR	.75	2.00
90	Ivory RR	.50	1.25
91	Kurt Angle RR	.50	1.25
92	Triple H RR	.75	2.00
93	Rob Van Dam RR	.50	1.25
94	Trish Stratus RR	1.25	3.00
95	Nidia RR	.30	.75
96	Matt Hardy RR	.30	.75
97	Christian RR	.30	.75
98	Mick Foley RR	.50	1.25
99	The Rock RR	.75	2.00
100	Undertaker RR	.60	1.50

2002 Fleer WWF All Access All Access Memorabilia

STATED ODDS 1:15

AAMF	Funaki	3.00	8.00
AAMH	The Hurricane SP		
AAMK	Kane	5.00	12.00
AAMU	Undertaker	6.00	15.00
AAMA	Stone Cold Steve Austin	8.00	20.00
AAMJH	Jeff Hardy	5.00	12.00
AAMKA	Kurt Angle		
AAMMH	Molly Holly	5.00	12.00
AAMSH	Scotty 2 Hotty	4.00	10.00
AAMSK	Stacy Keibler	8.00	20.00
AAMT1	Tajiri	3.00	8.00
AAMT2	Tazz	3.00	8.00
AAMTH	Triple H	6.00	15.00
AAMTW	Torrie Wilson	8.00	20.00
AAMDVD	D-Von Dudley	5.00	12.00
AAMRVD	Rob Van Dam	4.00	10.00

2002 Fleer WWF All Access Famous Rides

COMPLETE SET (12) 5.00 12.00
STATED ODDS 1:6

FR1	Diamond Dallas Page's Pink Cadillac	.30	.75
FR2	Stone Cold's Truck	1.25	3.00
FR3	The Rock's Limo	1.25	3.00
FR4	D-Generation X's Tank Jeep	.30	.75
FR5	Stone Cold Destroys Vince's Vette	1.25	3.00
FR6	Vince McMahon's Jet	.75	2.00
FR7	Big Show's Purple Car	.75	2.00
FR8	Kurt Angle's Scooter	.75	2.00
FR9	Jeff Hardy's Motorcycle	.50	1.25
FR10	Stone Cold's 18-Wheeler	1.25	3.00
FR11	D-Generation X's Bus	.30	.75
FR12	Al Snow's Lil' Racecar	.30	.75

2002 Fleer WWF All Access Match Makers

COMPLETE SET (15) 6.00 15.00
STATED ODDS 1:6

MM1	Triple H & Stephanie	1.00	2.50
MM2	Kane & Undertaker	.75	2.00
MM3	Debra & Stone Cold	1.00	2.50
MM4	Dudley Boyz	.25	.60
MM5	The Rock & Mick Foley	1.00	2.50
MM6	Edge & Christian	.60	1.50
MM7	Stephanie & Chris Jericho	.75	2.00
MM8	Kurt Angle & Triple H	1.00	2.50
MM9	The Rock & Stone Cold	1.00	2.50
MM10	Kaientai	.25	.60
MM11	Benoit & Jericho	.40	1.00
MM12	Stone Cold & Undertaker	1.00	2.50
MM13	Kurt Angle & The Rock	1.00	2.50
MM14	Matt Hardy, Lita & Jeff Hardy	1.00	2.50
MM15	Mr. McMahon & Stone Cold	1.00	2.50

2002 Fleer WWF All Access Match Makers Memorabilia

STATED ODDS 1:95

MMDB	Dudley Boyz	8.00	20.00
MMEC	Edge & Christian	8.00	20.00
MMKU	Kane & Undertaker	10.00	25.00
MMRKA	Kurt Angle & The Rock	12.00	30.00
MMRMF	The Rock & Mick Foley	12.00	30.00
MMRSA	The Rock & Stone Cold	15.00	40.00
MMSAU	Stone Cold & Undertaker	12.00	30.00

2002 Fleer WWF All Access Off The Mat Autographs

The Maven autograph card was never produced. Collectors submitting the Maven Exchange card were compensated with an alternate autographed card.
RANDOMLY INSERTED INTO PACKS

NNO	The Hurricane	12.00	30.00
NNO	Jim Ross	20.00	50.00
NNO	Lita	25.00	60.00
NNO	Rob Van Dam	25.00	60.00
NNO	Stacy Keibler	50.00	100.00
NNO	Torrie Wilson	30.00	80.00
NNO	Triple H	175.00	300.00
NNO	Trish Stratus	60.00	120.00

2002 Fleer WWF All Access Pay-Per-View Posters

COMPLETE SET (8) 15.00 40.00

STATED ODDS 1:33

PPV1 Backlash	3.00	8.00
PPV2 Invasion	2.00	5.00
PPV3 Judgment Day	3.00	8.00
PPV4 No Mercy	2.00	5.00
PPV5 No Way Out	2.00	5.00
PPV6 SummerSlam	3.00	8.00
PPV7 Unforgiven	3.00	8.00
PPV8 Vengeance	3.00	8.00
PPV9 WrestleMania X-7	3.00	8.00
PPV10 Survivor Series	5.00	12.00

2001 Fleer WWF Championship Clash

Subset within the set includes: PC = Profile of a Champion (41-80)

COMPLETE SET (80)	8.00	20.00
UNOPENED BOX (24 PACKS)		
UNOPENED PACK (5 CARDS)		

1 The Rock	.75	2.00
2 K-Kwik	.12	.30
3 Steve Blackman	.12	.30
4 Eddie Guerrero	.50	1.25
5 Jerry Lynn	.12	.30
6 Christian	.30	.75
7 Kane	.50	1.25
8 Tazz	.20	.50
9 Stone Cold Steve Austin	.75	2.00
10 Crash Holly	.12	.30
11 Matt Hardy	.30	.75
12 Undertaker	.60	1.50
13 Al Snow	.20	.50
14 Tajiri	.12	.30
15 Scotty 2 Hotty	.20	.50
16 Dean Malenko	.20	.50
17 Raven	.12	.30
18 Big Show	.50	1.25
19 Jeff Hardy	.30	.75
20 Spike Dudley	.20	.50
21 Chris Jericho	.30	.75
22 Kurt Angle	.50	1.25
23 Test	.20	.50
24 Chris Benoit	.30	.75
25 William Regal	.20	.50
26 Rikishi	.20	.50
27 D-Von Dudley	.20	.50
28 Mick Foley	.50	1.25
29 Triple H	.75	2.00
30 Albert	.12	.30
31 Haku	.12	.30
32 Perry Saturn	.12	.30
33 The One Billy Gunn	.12	.30
34 Hardcore Holly	.20	.50
35 Shane McMahon	.30	.75
36 Edge	.50	1.25
37 Rhyno	.20	.50
38 Bubba Ray Dudley	.20	.50
39 Justin Credible	.12	.30
40 X-Pac	.20	.50
41 The Rock PC	.75	2.00
42 K-Kwik PC	.12	.30
43 Steve Blackman PC	.12	.30
44 Eddie Guerrero PC	.50	1.25
45 Jerry Lynn PC	.12	.30
46 Christian PC	.30	.75
47 Kane PC	.50	1.25
48 Tazz PC	.20	.50

49 Stone Cold Steve Austin PC	.75	2.00
50 Crash Holly PC	.12	.30
51 Matt Hardy PC	.30	.75
52 Undertaker PC	.60	1.50
53 Al Snow PC	.20	.50
54 Tajiri PC	.12	.30
55 Scotty 2 Hotty PC	.20	.50
56 Dean Malenko PC	.20	.50
57 Raven PC	.12	.30
58 Big Show PC	.50	1.25
59 Jeff Hardy PC	.30	.75
60 Spike Dudley PC	.20	.50
61 Chris Jericho PC	.30	.75
62 Kurt Angle PC	.50	1.25
63 Test PC	.20	.50
64 Chris Benoit PC	.30	.75
65 William Regal PC	.20	.50
66 Rikishi PC	.20	.50
67 D-Von Dudley PC	.20	.50
68 Mick Foley PC	.50	1.25
69 Triple H PC	.75	2.00
70 Albert PC	.12	.30
71 Haku PC	.12	.30
72 Perry Saturn PC	.12	.30
73 The One Billy Gunn PC	.12	.30
74 Hardcore Holly PC	.20	.50
75 Shane McMahon PC	.30	.75
76 Edge PC	.50	1.25
77 Rhyno PC	.20	.50
78 Bubba Ray Dudley PC	.20	.50
79 Justin Credible PC	.12	.30
80 X-Pac PC	.20	.50

2001 Fleer WWF Championship Clash Divas Private Collection

STATED ODDS 1:30 HOBBY; 1:576 RETAIL

DPDE Debra Skirt	6.00	12.00
DPTO Tori Skirt/Tights	6.00	12.00
DPCIV Ivory Scarf	7.50	15.00
DPCMH Molly Holly Halter Top	4.00	10.00
DPCTE Terri Dress	7.50	15.00
DPCLBT Lita Bikini Top	25.00	50.00
DPCLTS Lita T-Shirt	7.50	15.00

2001 Fleer WWF Championship Clash Divas Private Signing

COMPLETE SET (8)	175.00	350.00
STATED ODDS 1:120		
CARDS 1-4 AVAIL.IN CHAMP.CLASH		
CARDS 5-8 AVAIL.IN ULT DIVA COL.		
HOBBY EXCLUSIVE		

DPSD Debra	20.00	40.00
DPSI Ivory	12.00	30.00
DPSJ Jacqueline	20.00	40.00
DPSL Lita	25.00	50.00
DPSMH Molly Holly	20.00	30.00
DPSSM Stephanie McMahon-Helmsley	100.00	200.00
DPSTE Terri	25.00	50.00
DPSTS Trish Stratus	60.00	120.00

2001 Fleer WWF Championship Clash Females

COMPLETE SET (9)	6.00	15.00
STATED ODDS 1:4 HOBBY; 1:7 RETAIL		
WF1 Ivory	.75	2.00
WF2 Trish Stratus	2.00	5.00
WF3 Lita	1.25	3.00
WF4 Molly Holly	.75	2.00
WF5 Debra	1.00	2.50
WF6 Stephanie McMahon	1.00	2.50
WF7 Terri	1.00	2.50
WF8 Jacqueline	.75	2.00
WF9 Tori	1.00	2.50

2001 Fleer WWF Championship Clash Main Event Memorabilia

COMPLETE SET (9)	20.00	40.00
STATED ODDS 1:24 HOBBY; 1:144 RETAIL		
SA Steve Austin Ring Skirt	5.00	12.00
BKR Big Show vs. Kane vs. Raven Ring Mat	3.00	8.00
EGT Test vs. Eddie Guerrero Ring Mat	2.50	6.00
CBCJ Chris Benoit vs. Chris Jericho Ring Skirt	2.50	6.00
CJWR William Regal vs. Chris Jericho Ring Mat	2.50	6.00
KATH Triple H vs. Kurt Angle Ring Skirt	4.00	10.00
SATR Steve Austin vs. The Rock Ring Mat	5.00	12.00
SMKA Shane McMahon vs. Kurt Angle Garbage Can SP	3.00	8.00
SAKACJ Kurt Angle vs. Chris Jericho vs. Steve Austin Steel Chair SP	4.00	10.00

2001 Fleer WWF Championship Clash Piece of the Champion

STATED ODDS 1:24 HOBBY; 1:576 RETAIL

PCB Bradshaw T-Shirt	10.00	20.00
PCCJ Chris Jericho T-Shirt	10.00	20.00
PCER Essa Rios Pants	6.00	12.00
PCFA Faarooq (spelled Faaroog) Knee Brace UER SP		
PCFN Funaki T-Shirt	6.00	12.00
PCJH Jeff Hardy T-Shirt	15.00	30.00
PCKA K. Angle Gold Medal Strap SP	125.00	250.00
PCKA2 Kurt Angle T-Shirt	15.00	30.00
PCMH Matt Hardy T-Shirt	15.00	30.00
PCSA Steve Austin T-Shirt	15.00	30.00
PCSH Scotty 2 Hotty Pants	7.50	15.00
PCTM Taka Michinoku T-Shirt	6.00	12.00
PCXP X- Pac Bandana	10.00	20.00

2001 Fleer WWF Diva Magazine Set 1

1 Chyna
2 Chyna
3 Chyna
4 Jacqueline
5 Jacqueline
6 Jacqueline
7 The Kat
8 The Kat
9 The Kat

2001 Fleer WWF Diva Magazine Set 2

1 Lita
2 Lita
3 Lita
4 Terri
5 Terri
6 Terri
7 Tori
8 Tori
9 Tori

2001 Fleer WWF Diva Magazine Set 3

1 Trish Stratus
2 Trish Stratus
3 Trish Stratus
4 Debra
5 Debra
6 Debra
7 Molly Holly
8 Molly Holly
9 Molly Holly

2002 Fleer WWF Divas Magazine Series 1

1 Lita	.40	1.00
2 Lita	.40	1.00
3 Lita	.40	1.00
4 Jacqueline	.20	.50
5 Jacqueline	.20	.50
6 Jacqueline	.20	.50
7 Torrie	.60	1.50
8 Torrie	.60	1.50
9 Torrie	.60	1.50

2002 Fleer WWF Divas Magazine Series 2

1 Trish	.60	1.50
2 Trish	.60	1.50
3 Trish	.60	1.50
4 Ivory	.20	.50
5 Ivory	.20	.50
6 Ivory	.20	.50
7 Terri	.30	.75
8 Terri	.30	.75
9 Terri	.30	.75

2002 Fleer WWF Divas Magazine Series 3

1 Stacy	.60	1.50
2 Stacy	.60	1.50
3 Stacy	.60	1.50
4 Sharmell	.20	.50
5 Sharmell	.20	.50

#			
6 Sharmell		.20	.50
7 Molly		.20	.50
8 Molly		.20	.50
9 Molly		.20	.50

2001 Fleer WWF KB Toys Get Real

COMPLETE SET (18)		12.00	30.00
UNOPENED PACK (3 CARDS)		1.50	2.00
1 The Rock		2.50	6.00
2 Undertaker		2.50	6.00
3 Kane		1.25	3.00
4 Stone Cold Steve Austin		2.00	5.00
5 Kurt Angle		.75	2.00
6 Triple H		.75	2.00
7 Albert		.50	1.25
8 The Dudley Boyz		1.25	3.00
9 The Hardy Boyz		1.50	4.00
10 Lita		3.00	8.00
11 Edge		1.50	4.00
12 Christian		.60	1.50
13 Tazz		.50	1.25
14 Raven		.75	2.00
15 Chris Jericho		2.00	5.00
16 Jacqueline		.75	2.00
17 Ivory		.75	2.00
18 Trish Stratus		2.50	6.00

2001 Fleer WWF Raw Is War

Subsets within the set include: WZ = War Zone (50-84); SE = Show Enders (85-100)

COMPLETE SET (100)		8.00	20.00
UNOPENED BOX (24 PACKS)			
UNOPENED PACK (8 CARDS)			
1 Stone Cold Steve Austin		.75	2.00
2 Triple H		.75	2.00
3 Mick Foley		.50	1.25
4 Dean Malenko		.20	.50
5 Chris Jericho		.30	.75
6 Lita		.75	2.00
7 Bubba Ray Dudley		.20	.50
8 JR		.20	.50
9 Bull Buchanan		.12	.30
10 Kane		.50	1.25
11 Gerald Brisco		.20	.50
12 The Goodfather		.20	.50
13 Matt Hardy		.30	.75
14 Rikishi		.20	.50
15 Vince McMahon		.50	1.25
16 Ivory		.50	1.25
17 Trish Stratus		1.25	3.00
18 Test		.20	.50
19 Raven		.12	.30
20 Albert		.12	.30
21 Val Venis		.20	.50
22 Tazz		.20	.50
23 Chyna		.50	1.25
24 Molly Holly		.50	1.25
25 Christian		.30	.75
26 Edge		.50	1.25
27 William Regal		.20	.50
28 Crash Holly		.12	.30
29 Jeff Hardy		.30	.75
30 Kurt Angle		.50	1.25
31 K-Kwik		.12	.30
32 Bradshaw		.30	.75
33 Terri		.60	1.50
34 Bob Hardcore Holly		.20	.50

35 Grandmaster Sexay			
36 Perry Saturn		.12	.30
37 D-Von Dudley		.20	.50
38 The One Billy Gunn		.12	.30
39 The Rock		.75	2.00
40 Eddie Guererro		.50	1.25
41 Steven Richards		.20	.50
42 Pat Patterson		.20	.50
43 Chris Benoit		.30	.75
44 Big Show		.50	1.25
45 Faarooq		.12	.30
46 Steve Blackman		.12	.30
47 Undertaker		.60	1.50
48 Jacqueline		.50	1.25
49 Scotty Too Hotty		.20	.50
50 Chris Jericho WZ		.30	.75
51 APA WZ		.30	.75
52 Billy Gunn vs. Val Venis WZ		.20	.50
53 Taka Michinoku WZ		.12	.30
54 Triple H vs.The Rock WZ		.75	2.00
55 Edge & Christian WZ		.50	1.25
56 Big Show WZ		.50	1.25
57 Hardy Boyz vs. Edge & Christian WZ	.50		1.25
58 Debra WZ		.60	1.50
59 Kurt Angle WZ		.50	1.25
60 Kaientai WZ		.12	.30
61 Rock & Undertaker vs. Edge & Christian WZ		.75	2.00
62 Right to Censor WZ		.12	.30
63 Undertaker WZ		.60	1.50
64 Billy Gunn with Chyna WZ		.50	1.25
65 Dudleyz vs. Edge & Christian WZ		.50	1.25
66 Lita vs. Trish Stratus WZ		1.25	3.00
67 The Rock WZ		.75	2.00
68 Stephanie McMahon-Helmsley WZ		.60	1.50
69 Dudley Boyz WZ		.20	.50
70 Triple H WZ		.75	2.00
71 Steve Austin vs. Vince McMahon WZ	.75		2.00
72 Shane McMahon WZ		.30	.75
73 Perry Saturn with Terri WZ		.60	1.50
74 Too Cool WZ		.12	.30
75 Triple H WZ		.50	1.25
76 Hardy Boyz WZ		.30	.75
77 Stone Cold Steve Austin WZ		.75	2.00
78 Undertaker vs. Kane WZ		.60	1.50
79 Hardcore/Molly/Crash Holly WZ		.50	1.25
80 William Regal WZ		.20	.50
81 Steve Austin vs. Kurt Angle WZ		.75	2.00
82 Vince McMahon WZ		.50	1.25
83 Right to Censor vs. Hardy Boyz WZ		.30	.75
84 Kane WZ		.50	1.25
85 The Rock vs. Undertaker SE		.60	1.50
86 Steve Austin vs. William Regal SE		.60	1.50
87 Steve Austin vs. Chris Benoit SE		.60	1.50
88 Steve Austin vs. Rikishi vs. Angle SE		.60	1.50
89 Chris Jericho vs. The Rock SE		.60	1.50
90 Steve Austin vs. Kurt Angle SE		.60	1.50
91 Steve Austin vs. Edge & Christian & Angle SE		.60	1.50
92 Triple H vs. Kurt Angle SE		.60	1.50
93 Undertaker vs. The Rock SE		.60	1.50
94 Chris Jericho vs. Benoit SE		.30	.75
95 Rock vs. HHH vs. Kurt Angle SE		.60	1.50
96 Shane McMahon vs. The Rock SE		.60	1.50
97 Triple H vs. The Rock SE		.60	1.50
98 The Rock vs. Kane SE		.60	1.50
99 Lita vs. Stephanie SE		.60	1.50
100 The Rock vs. Benoit SE		.60	1.50

2001 Fleer WWF Raw Is War Booty

STATED ODDS 1:26 HOBBY; 1:134 RETAIL

NNO Chris Benoit Ring Skirt		10.00	25.00
NNO Chris Jericho Ring Skirt		10.00	25.00
NNO Dudley Boyz Ring Skirt		8.00	20.00
NNO Edge & Christian Ring Skirt		10.00	25.00
NNO Hardy Boyz Ring Mat		10.00	25.00
NNO Kane Ring Skirt		6.00	15.00
NNO Kurt Angle T-Shirt		12.00	30.00
NNO Mick Foley Ring Mat		10.00	25.00
NNO The One Billy Gunn Ring Trunks		12.00	30.00
NNO The Rock Ring Mat		20.00	50.00
NNO Stone Cold Steve Austin Ring Mat		20.00	50.00
NNO Triple H Ring Mat		10.00	25.00
NNO Undertaker Ring Mat		10.00	25.00
NNO Vince McMahon Ring Mat		8.00	20.00
NNO William Regal Ring Skirt		6.00	15.00

2001 Fleer WWF Raw Is War Booty Autographs

STATED ODDS 1:354
EXCH.EXPIRATION: 07/01/2002

NNO Christian		20.00	50.00
NNO Edge		30.00	75.00
NNO Triple H			
NNO Undertaker		200.00	400.00

2001 Fleer WWF Raw Is War Famous Nicknames

COMPLETE SET (14)		25.00	60.00
STATED ODDS 1:15 HOBBY; 1:20 RETAIL			
FN1 Chyna		3.00	8.00
FN2 Steve Austin		4.00	10.00
FN3 Kurt Angle		3.00	8.00
FN4 Billy Gunn		1.50	4.00
FN5 Triple H		3.00	8.00
FN6 Lita		5.00	12.00
FN7 Steve Blackman		1.50	4.00
FN8 The Rock		4.00	10.00
FN9 Shawn Michaels		3.00	8.00
FN10 Chris Jericho		3.00	8.00
FN11 Chris Benoit		2.50	6.00
FN12 Undertaker		3.00	8.00
FN13 Jim Ross		1.25	3.00
FN14 Eddie Guerrero		1.50	4.00

2001 Fleer WWF Raw Is War Femme Fatale

COMPLETE SET (20)		7.50	15.00
STATED ODDS 1:2 HOBBY AND RETAIL			
FF1 Trish Stratus		.60	1.50

FF2 Molly Holly		.25	.60
FF3 Terri		.40	1.00
FF4 Lita		.75	2.00
FF5 Tori		.30	.75
FF6 Trish Stratus		.60	1.50
FF7 Molly Holly		.25	.60
FF8 Terri		.40	1.00
FF9 Lita		.75	2.00
FF10 Tori		.30	.75
FF11 Trish Stratus		.60	1.50
FF12 Molly Holly		.25	.60
FF13 Terri		.40	1.00
FF14 Lita		.75	2.00
FF15 Tori		.30	.75
FF16 Trish Stratus		.60	1.50
FF17 Molly Holly		.25	.60
FF18 Terri		.40	1.00
FF19 Lita		.75	2.00
FF20 Tori		.30	.75

2001 Fleer WWF Raw Is War Raw Is Jericho

COMPLETE SET (15)		4.00	10.00
STATED ODDS 1:2 HOBBY AND RETAIL			
RJ1 The Rock		.40	1.00
RJ2 Stone Cold Steve Austin		.40	1.00
RJ3 Chris Benoit		.40	1.00
RJ4 Kurt Angle		.40	1.00
RJ5 Edge and Christian		.40	1.00
RJ6 Kane		.40	1.00
RJ7 Undertaker		.40	1.00
RJ8 Chyna		.40	1.00
RJ9 Triple H		.40	1.00
RJ10 McMahon Family		.40	1.00
RJ11 Dudley Boyz		.40	1.00
RJ12 Hardy Boyz		.40	1.00
RJ13 Divas		.40	1.00
RJ14 Mick Foley		.40	1.00
RJ15 Chris Jericho		.40	1.00

2001 Fleer WWF Raw Is War TLC

COMPLETE SET (15)		10.00	25.00
STATED ODDS 1:5 HOBBY; 1:10 RETAIL			
TLC1 Hardy Boyz vs. Dudley Boyz vs. Edge & Christian		.60	1.50
TLC2 Hardy Boyz		1.25	3.00
TLC3 Dudley Boyz		1.25	3.00
TLC4 Edge & Christian		1.25	3.00
TLC5 Rock/Dudleyz vs. Angle Edge/Christian		.60	1.50
TLC6 Jericho/Dudleyz vs. Angle Edge/Christian		.60	1.50
TLC7 Bob Holly vs. Steve Blackman		.60	1.50
TLC8 Triple H		1.25	3.00
TLC9 Stone Cold Steve Austin		1.50	4.00
TLC10 Kane		1.00	2.50
TLC11 Chris Jericho		1.25	3.00
TLC12 Kurt Angle		1.25	3.00
TLC13 Big Show		1.00	2.50
TLC14 Undertaker		1.25	3.00
TLC15 The Rock		1.50	4.00

2001 Fleer WWF The Ultimate Diva Collection

Subsets within the set include: RP = Ring Presence (56-65); ITR = In the Ring (66-85)

COMPLETE SET (100)		20.00	45.00

COMPLETE SET W/O SP (85)	12.50	25.00
UNOPENED BOX (24 PACKS)		
UNOPENED PACK (8 CARDS)		
*GOLD (1-85): 1X TO 2.5X BASIC CARDS		
*GOLD SP (86-100): 2X TO 5X BASIC CARDS		
HEDONISM STATED ODDS 1:4		
1 Trish Stratus	.60	1.50
2 Debra	.30	.75
3 Ivory	.25	.60
4 Jacqueline	.25	.60
5 Lita	.40	1.00
6 Molly Holly	.25	.60
7 Terri	.30	.75
8 Trish Stratus	.60	1.50
9 Debra	.30	.75
10 Ivory	.25	.60
11 Jacqueline	.25	.60
12 Lita	.40	1.00
13 Molly Holly	.25	.60
14 Debra	.30	.75
15 Trish Stratus	.60	1.50
16 Debra	.30	.75
17 Ivory	.25	.60
18 Jacqueline	.25	.60
19 Lita	.40	1.00
20 Molly Holly	.25	.60
21 Terri	.30	.75
22 Trish Stratus	.60	1.50
23 Debra	.30	.75
24 Ivory	.25	.60
25 Jacqueline	.25	.60
26 Lita	.40	1.00
27 Molly Holly	.25	.60
28 Terri	.30	.75
29 Trish Stratus	.60	1.50
30 Debra	.30	.75
31 Ivory	.25	.60
32 Jacqueline	.25	.60
33 Lita	.40	1.00
34 Molly Holly	.25	.60
35 Terri	.30	.75
36 Trish Stratus	.60	1.50
37 Debra	.30	.75
38 Ivory	.25	.60
39 Jacqueline	.25	.60
40 Lita	.40	1.00
41 Molly Holly	.25	.60
42 Terri	.30	.75
43 Trish Stratus	.60	1.50
44 Debra	.30	.75
45 Ivory	.25	.60
46 Jacqueline	.25	.60
47 Lita	.40	1.00
48 Molly Holly	.25	.60
49 Terri	.30	.75
50 Trish Stratus	.60	1.50
51 Debra	.30	.75
52 Ivory	.25	.60
53 Jacqueline	.25	.60
54 Lita	.40	1.00
55 Molly Holly	.25	.60
56 The Rock RP	.60	1.50
57 Stone Cold Steve Austin RP	.60	1.50
58 Triple H RP	.60	1.50
59 Undertaker RP	.50	1.25
60 APA RP	.15	.40
61 The Hardy Boyz RP	.25	.60
62 Dudley Boyz RP	.15	.40

63 Chris Jericho RP	.25	.60
64 Kurt Angle RP	.40	1.00
65 Kane RP	.40	1.00
66 Debra ITR	.30	.75
67 Jacqueline ITR	.25	.60
68 Lita ITR	.40	1.00
69 Trish Stratus ITR	.60	1.50
70 Lita ITR	.40	1.00
71 Molly Holly ITR	.25	.60
72 Jacqueline ITR	.25	.60
73 Terri ITR	.30	.75
74 Ivory ITR	.25	.60
75 Debra ITR	.30	.75
76 Molly Holly ITR	.25	.60
77 Lita ITR	.40	1.00
78 Ivory ITR	.25	.60
79 Terri ITR	.30	.75
80 Trish Stratus ITR	.60	1.50
81 M.Holly/T.Stratus ITR	.60	1.50
82 M.Holly/Jacqueline ITR	.25	.60
83 Lita/T.Stratus ITR	.60	1.50
84 M.Holly/Lita ITR	.40	1.00
85 Terri/T.Stratus ITR	.60	1.50
86 Debra HED SP	.75	2.00
87 Terri HED SP	.75	2.00
88 Lita HED SP	1.00	2.50
89 Trish Stratus HED SP	1.50	4.00
90 Jacqueline HED SP	.60	1.50
91 Debra HED SP	.75	2.00
92 Terri HED SP	.75	2.00
93 Lita HED SP	1.00	2.50
94 Trish Stratus HED SP	1.50	4.00
95 Jacqueline HED SP	.60	1.50
96 Debra HED SP	.75	2.00
97 Terri HED SP	.75	2.00
98 Lita HED SP	1.00	2.50
99 Trish Stratus HED SP	1.50	4.00
100 Jacqueline HED SP	.60	1.50

2001 Fleer WWF The Ultimate Diva Collection The Bad and The Beautiful

COMPLETE SET (15)	10.00	20.00
STATED ODDS 1:4 HOBBY; 1:8 RETAIL		
1 Trish Stratus	1.25	3.00
2 Jacqueline	.50	1.25
3 Ivory	.50	1.25
4 Molly Holly	.50	1.25
5 Lita	.75	2.00
6 Terri	.60	1.50
7 Trish Stratus	1.25	3.00
8 Jacqueline	.50	1.25
9 Debra	.60	1.50
10 Ivory	.50	1.25
11 Molly Holly	.50	1.25
12 Debra	.60	1.50
13 Terri	.60	1.50
14 Lita	.75	2.00
15 Trish Stratus	1.25	3.00

2001 Fleer WWF The Ultimate Diva Collection Diva Ink

COMPLETE SET (2)	150.00	300.00
STATED ODDS 1:104 HOBBY; 1:1,787 RETAIL		
EXCH.EXPIRATION: 1/1/2003		
NNO Debra	20.00	40.00
NNO Ivory	30.00	60.00
NNO Jacqueline	20.00	40.00

NNO Lita	30.00	60.00
NNO Molly Holly	20.00	40.00
NNO Terri	30.00	60.00
NNO Trish Stratus	40.00	80.00

2001 Fleer WWF The Ultimate Diva Collection Kiss and Tell

COMPLETE SET (12)	15.00	30.00
STATED ODDS 1:12 HOBBY; 1:20 RETAIL		
1 Vince McMahon	3.00	8.00
Trish Stratus		
2 Kurt Angle	1.50	4.00
Stephanie McMahon-Helmsley		
3 Chris Jericho	1.50	4.00
Terri		
4 Stone Cold Steve Austin	2.00	5.00
Debra		
5 Triple H	2.00	5.00
Stephanie McMahon-Helmsley		
6 APA	1.25	3.00
Jacqueline		
7 Perry Saturn	1.50	4.00
Terri		
8 Undertaker	1.50	4.00
Ivory		
9 The Hardy Boyz	2.00	5.00
Lita		
10 The Rock	3.00	8.00
Trish Stratus		
11 Dudley Boyz	1.25	3.00
Molly Holly		
12 Kane	1.25	3.00
Ivory		

2001 Fleer WWF The Ultimate Diva Collection Matching Set

COMPLETE SET (8)	40.00	80.00
COMMON CARD (1-8)	6.00	12.00
SEMISTARS		
UNLISTED STARS		
NNO Debra/Stone Cold	10.00	20.00
NNO Jacqueline/APA	6.00	12.00
NNO Jacqueline/Bradshaw	6.00	12.00
NNO Lita/Jeff Hardy	7.50	15.00
NNO Lita/Matt Hardy	7.50	15.00
NNO Molly Holly/Spike Dudley	6.00	12.00
NNO Terri/Perry Saturn	7.50	15.00
NNO Trish Stratus/Big Show	7.50	15.00

2001 Fleer WWF The Ultimate Diva Collection National Assets

COMPLETE SET (15)	15.00	30.00
STATED ODDS 1:12 HOBBY; 1:20 RETAIL		
1 Lita	1.50	4.00
2 Debra	1.25	3.00
3 Ivory	1.00	2.50
4 Terri	1.25	3.00
5 Trish Stratus	2.50	6.00
6 Terri	1.25	3.00
7 Molly Holly	1.00	2.50
8 Jacqueline	1.00	2.50
9 Debra	1.25	3.00
10 Molly Holly	1.00	2.50
11 Trish Stratus	2.50	6.00
12 Terri	1.25	3.00
13 Ivory	1.00	2.50

NNO Lita	30.00	60.00
NNO Molly Holly	20.00	40.00
NNO Terri	30.00	60.00
NNO Trish Stratus	40.00	80.00

2001 Fleer WWF The Ultimate Diva Collection Ring Accessories

COMPLETE SET (7)	30.00	60.00
COMMON CARD (1-7)	4.00	8.00
SEMISTARS	4.00	10.00
UNLISTED STARS	5.00	12.00
NNO Debra	4.00	8.00
NNO Ivory	5.00	12.00
NNO Jacqueline	4.00	8.00
NNO Lita	7.50	15.00
NNO Molly Holly	5.00	10.00
NNO Terri	5.00	12.00
NNO Trish Stratus	10.00	20.00

2001 Fleer WWF The Ultimate Diva Collection Signed with a Kiss

RANDOMLY INSERTED INTO PACKS
STATED PRINT RUN 50 SERIAL #'d SETS
EXCH.EXPIRATION: 1/1/2003

NNO Debra	20.00	50.00
NNO Ivory	20.00	50.00
NNO Jacqueline	15.00	40.00
NNO Lita	75.00	150.00
NNO Molly Holly	25.00	60.00
NNO Terri Runnels	15.00	40.00
NNO Trish Stratus	100.00	200.00

2001 Fleer WWF WrestleMania

Subsets within the set include: DIVAS = WWF Divas (61-70); TT = Tag Teams (71-80); WR = Wrestlemania Rewind (81-100)

COMPLETE SET (100)	8.00	20.00
UNOPENED BOX (28 PACKS)		
UNOPENED PACK (7 CARDS)		
*CH GOLD: 1.2X TO 3X BASIC CARDS		
1 The Rock	.75	2.00
2 D-Von Dudley	.20	.50
3 Matt Hardy	.30	.75
4 Test	.20	.50
5 Raven	.12	.30
6 Chris Benoit	.30	.75
7 Jeff Hardy	.30	.75
8 Shane McMahon	.30	.75
9 Brooklyn Brawler	.12	.30
10 Gerald Brisco	.20	.50
11 Linda McMahon	.20	.50
12 Albert	.12	.30
13 Eddie Guerrero	.50	1.25
14 Mick Foley	.50	1.25
15 The Goodfather	.20	.50
16 Buh-Buh Ray Dudley	.20	.50
17 Grandmaster Sexay	.20	.50
18 Scotty 2 Hotty	.20	.50
19 William Regal	.20	.50
20 Big Boss Man	.20	.50
21 Edge	.50	1.25
22 Mideon	.12	.30
23 Al Snow	.20	.50
24 Stephanie McMahon-Helmsley	.60	1.50
25 Dean Malenko	.20	.50
26 Tazz	.20	.50
27 Bull Buchanan	.12	.30
28 Hardcore Holly	.20	.50
29 Sgt. Slaughter	.30	.75

Top of third column (above Kiss and Tell):

NNO Lita	30.00	60.00
NNO Molly Holly	20.00	40.00
NNO Terri	30.00	60.00
NNO Trish Stratus	40.00	80.00

Top of fourth column:

14 Jacqueline	1.00	2.50
15 Lita	1.50	4.00

30	X-Pac	.20	.50
31	Christian	.30	.75
32	Jim JR Ross	.20	.50
33	Steve Blackman	.12	.30
34	Fabulous Moolah	.20	.50
35	Gangrel	.12	.30
36	Rikishi	.20	.50
37	Vince McMahon	.50	1.25
38	Essa Rios	.12	.30
39	Pat Patterson	.20	.50
40	Triple H	.75	2.00
41	K-Kwik	.12	.30
42	Crash Holly	.12	.30
43	Kane	.50	1.25
44	Steven Richards	.20	.50
45	Joey Abs	.12	.30
46	The One Billy Gunn	.12	.30
47	Faarooq	.12	.30
48	Undertaker	.60	1.50
49	Tiger Ali Singh	.12	.30
50	D'Lo Brown	.12	.30
51	Kurt Angle	.50	1.25
52	Stone Cold Steve Austin	.75	2.00
53	Chaz	.12	.30
54	Chris Jericho	.30	.75
55	Jerry The King Lawler	.20	.50
56	Mae Young	.20	.50
57	Bradshaw	.30	.75
58	Funaki	.12	.30
59	Perry Saturn	.12	.30
60	Val Venis	.20	.50
61	Tori DIVAS	.60	1.50
62	Debra DIVAS	.60	1.50
63	Chyna DIVAS	.50	1.25
64	Ivory DIVAS	.50	1.25
65	Jacqueline DIVAS	.50	1.25
66	The Kat DIVAS	.15	.40
67	Lita DIVAS	.75	2.00
68	Trish Stratus DIVAS	1.25	3.00
69	Molly Holly DIVAS	.50	1.25
70	Terri DIVAS	.60	1.50
71	Edge & Christian TT	.50	1.25
72	Hardy Boyz TT	.30	.75
73	Dudley Boyz TT	.20	.50
74	T & A TT	.20	.50
75	Right to Censor TT	.20	.50
76	The Radicalz TT	.50	1.25
77	The Hollys TT	.20	.50
78	K-Kwik & Road Dogg TT	.12	.30
79	Lo Down TT	.12	.30
80	Too Cool TT	.20	.50
81	I Pity the Fool WR	.20	.50
82	Hulkamania Runs Wild WR	.60	1.50
83	Rage in the Cage WR	.60	1.50
84	A New Attendance Record WR	.12	.30
85	The Proud Chairman WR	.50	1.25
86	Brain Awakens Sleeping Giant WR	.40	1.00
87	Stars and Stripes Challenge WR	.12	.30
88	Don't Do It, Roddy WR	.30	.75
89	When in Rome WR	.20	.50
90	Megabucks vs. Megamaniacs WR	.60	1.50
91	Good Friends, Better Enemies WR	.15	.40
92	Enter the Rattlesnake WR	.75	2.00
93	Dark Days Cometh WR	.60	1.50
94	Rock/Rikishi Early Years WR	.75	2.00
95	Hardcore Highlight WR	.12	.30
96	Rough Night for Charlie Hustle WR	.12	.30
97	The Stone Cold Age Begins WR	.75	2.00
98	Strike Two for the Hit King WR	.20	.50
99	The Rattlesnake Reigns Supreme WR	.75	2.00
100	Tag Team Daredevils WR	.12	.30

2001 Fleer WWF WrestleMania Foreign Objects

COMPLETE SET (9)		150.00	300.00
UNLISTED STARS		20.00	50.00
STATED ODDS 1:63 HOBBY EXCLUSIVE			
NNO	Chris Jericho Jersey	10.00	25.00
NNO	Dudley Boyz Table SP	100.00	175.00
NNO	The Rock T-Shirt	15.00	40.00
NNO	Stone Cold Steve Austin T-Shirt	10.00	25.00
NNO	Triple H Jeans	10.00	25.00
NNO	Triple H T-Shirt	10.00	25.00
NNO	Trish Stratus Shirt	20.00	50.00
NNO	Trish Stratus Skirt	20.00	50.00
NNO	Undertaker T-Shirt	10.00	25.00

2001 Fleer WWF WrestleMania Lip Service

Randomly inserted in packs, This 8 card set features the most well known WWF divas such as Chyna and Trish Stratus. Cards feature an all color photo on card front along with an actual Lipstick impression. Card back has congratulations statement from Fleer CEO. Please note that all cards were originally issued as trade cards.
STATED PRINT RUN 50 SERIAL #'d SETS
EXCH.EXPIRATION: 04/01/2002
HOBBY EXCLUSIVE

NNO	Chyna	50.00	100.00
NNO	Ivory	40.00	80.00
NNO	Jacqueline	40.00	80.00
NNO	Lita	75.00	150.00
NNO	Molly Holly	40.00	80.00
NNO	Terri	40.00	80.00
NNO	Tori	40.00	80.00
NNO	Trish Stratus	150.00	250.00

2001 Fleer WWF WrestleMania The People's Champion

COMPLETE SET (15)		2.00	5.00
STATED ODDS 1:2			
PC1	The People's Elbow	.20	.50
PC2	The Rock on the Mic	.20	.50
PC3	The People's Eyebrow	.20	.50
PC4	Blood From a Rock	.20	.50
PC5	Football Career	.20	.50
PC6	The Rock, The Author	.20	.50
PC7	The Great One	.20	.50
PC8	The Brahma Bull	.20	.50
PC9	Layeth the Smackdown	.20	.50
PC10	The Rock Bottom	.20	.50
PC11	Can You Smell?	.20	.50
PC12	Just Bring It Jabroni	.20	.50
PC13	Five-Time WWF Champion	.20	.50
PC14	The Millions And Millions	.20	.50
PC15	Not Just a WWF Superstar	.20	.50

2001 Fleer WWF WrestleMania Signature Moves

COMPLETE SET (15)		40.00	80.00
STATED ODDS 1:24 HOBBY EXCLUSIVE			
SM1	The Rock	6.00	12.00
SM2	Stone Cold Steve Austin	6.00	12.00
SM3	Kurt Angle	5.00	10.00
SM4	Triple H	5.00	10.00
SM5	Chris Jericho	5.00	10.00
SM6	Chris Benoit	4.00	8.00
SM7	Undertaker	5.00	10.00
SM8	Kane	4.00	8.00
SM9	Too Cool	4.00	8.00
SM10	Hardy Boyz	5.00	10.00
SM11	Dudley Boyz	5.00	10.00
SM12	Tazz	5.00	10.00
SM13	Eddie Guerrero	2.00	5.00
SM14	The One Billy Gunn	2.00	5.00
SM15	Lita	7.50	15.00

2001 Fleer WWF WrestleMania Signature Moves Autographs

Randomly inserted in packs, this 5 card set features some of the top WWF superstars along with an authentic autograph on card front along with a congratulatory message on the back from Fleer's CEO. Cards were hand numbered on card back to 500 of each signed.

COMPLETE SET (4)		75.00	150.00
RANDOM INSERTS IN PACKS			
STATED PRINT RUN 500 SERIAL #'d SETS			
STRATUS PROMO ONLY AVAILABLE AT '01 NSCC			
NNO	Bubba Ray Dudley	10.00	20.00
NNO	D-Von Dudley	10.00	20.00
NNO	Kurt Angle	25.00	60.00
NNO	Stone Cold Steve Austin	120.00	250.00
NNO	Trish Stratus (NSCC Exclusive)	75.00	150.00

2001 Fleer WWF WrestleMania Stone Cold Said So

COMPLETE SET (15)		5.00	12.00
STATED ODDS 1:2			
SC1	The Rock	.60	1.50
SC2	Kurt Angle	.50	1.25
SC3	Rikishi	.30	.75
SC4	Chris Benoit	.40	1.00
SC5	Chris Jericho	.50	1.25
SC6	Triple H	.50	1.25
SC7	Vince McMahon	.40	1.00
SC8	Undertaker	.50	1.25
SC9	Kane	.40	1.00
SC10	Stephanie McMahon-Helmsley	.40	1.00
SC11	X-Pac	.30	.75
SC12	Mick Foley	.50	1.25
SC13	Tazz	.50	1.25
SC14	Shane McMahon	.40	1.00
SC15	The One Billy Gunn	.30	.75

2015 Frame By Frame WWE Flip Madness Collection

COMPLETE SET W/SP (36)			
COMPLETE SET W/O SP (20)			
UNOPENED BOX (24 PACKS)			
UNOPENED PACK (1 FLIPBOOK)			
COMMON GOLD SP (21-30)		1.25	3.00
COMMON TITANIUM SP (31-36)		2.00	5.00
1	Batista	1.50	4.00
2	Big Show	1.50	4.00
3	Brock Lesnar	2.50	6.00
4	Cesaro	.60	1.50
5	Roman Reigns	1.50	4.00
6	Daniel Bryan	2.50	6.00
7	Dean Ambrose	1.50	4.00
8	Dolph Ziggler	1.00	2.50
9	Goldust	.60	1.50
10	John Cena	3.00	8.00
11	Kofi Kingston	.60	1.50
12	Mark Henry	1.00	2.50
13	Randy Orton	2.50	6.00
14	Ryback	.60	1.50
15	Seth Rollins	1.00	2.50
16	Sheamus	1.50	4.00
17	The Miz	1.00	2.50
18	King Barrett	.60	1.50
19	Triple H	2.50	6.00
20	Undertaker	2.50	6.00
21	Big Show SP	3.00	8.00
22	Brock Lesnar SP	5.00	12.00
23	Cesaro SP	1.25	3.00
24	Dolph Ziggler SP	2.00	5.00
25	Goldust SP	1.25	3.00
26	Roman Reigns SP	3.00	8.00
27	Ryback SP	1.25	3.00
28	Sheamus SP	3.00	8.00
29	Triple H SP	5.00	12.00
30	Undertaker SP	5.00	12.00
31	Daniel Bryan SP	8.00	20.00
32	Dean Ambrose SP	5.00	12.00
33	John Cena SP	10.00	25.00
34	Randy Orton SP	8.00	20.00
35	Seth Rollins SP	3.00	8.00
36	King Barrett SP	2.00	5.00

2011 Future Stars of Wrestling Volume One

COMPLETE SET (21)
NNO 702 Wrekking Crew
NNO Beast
NNO Big Unit & Rocky T
NNO Bryce Harrison
NNO Dino Dinelli
NNO Dylon Klein
NNO Franco D'Angelo
NNO Funny Bone
NNO Joe Defalco & Jack Slammy
NNO Kenny King
NNO Kid Vegas
NNO Legacy
NNO Leon Hater
NNO Michael Modest
NNO Mike Dalite
NNO Remy Marcel
NNO Rush
NNO Sinn
NNO Suburban Commandos
NNO Sugar Brown
NNO Von Dooms (Cyanide & Vintage Dragon)

2010 WWE Magazine Future WWE Hall of Famers

COMPLETE SET (18)
1 Rey Mysterio
2 Undertaker

3 Shawn Michaels
4 John Cena
5 Randy Orton
6 Triple H
7 Edge
8 Sheamus
9 Jack Swagger
10 Big Show
11 Chris Jericho
12 The Miz
13 Ted DiBiase
14 Kane
15 Beth Phoenix
16 CM Punk
17 Kofi Kingston
18 Wade Barrett

1973 GC London Wrestling Annual

COMPLETE SET (36)

NNO Andre the Giant Jean Ferre
NNO Bill Robinson
NNO Bobo Brazil
NNO Bruiser
NNO Bull Bullinski
NNO Chief Jay Strongbow
NNO Chief Wahoo McDaniel
NNO Cowboy Bob Ellis
NNO Crusher
NNO Dom Denucci
NNO Don Leo Jonathan
NNO Dory Funk Jr.
NNO Edouard Carpentier
NNO Ernie Ladd
NNO Fred Curry
NNO Haystacks Calhoun
NNO Jack Brisco
NNO Joe Leduc
NNO Killer Kowalski
NNO Lars Anderson
NNO Manny Soto
NNO Mighty Igor
NNO Mil Mascaras
NNO Pampero Firpo
NNO Paul Jones
NNO Pedro Morales
NNO Ray Stevens
NNO Raymond Rougeau
NNO Red Bastien
NNO Rene Goulet
NNO Ricky Romero
NNO The Destroyer
NNO The Great Mephisto
NNO The Sheik
NNO Verne Gagne
NNO Victor Rivera

1978 GC London Wrestling Annual

COMPLETE SET (32)

NNO Andre the Giant
NNO Bob Backlund
NNO Bruno Sammartino
NNO Chief Jay Strongbow
NNO Chavo Guerrero
NNO Dick Slater
NNO Dory Funk Jr.
NNO Dusty Rhodes
NNO Ernie Ladd

NNO Greg Gagne
NNO Greg Valentine
NNO Harley Race
NNO Ivan Koloff
NNO Ivan Putski
NNO Jack Brisco
NNO Jim Brunzell
NNO Ken Patera
NNO Lars Anderson
NNO Mil Mascaras
NNO Mr. Wrestling II
NNO Nick Bockwinkle UER
NNO Paul Jones
NNO Pedro Morales
NNO Peter Maivia
NNO Ray Stevens
NNO Ric Flair
NNO Rick Steamboat
NNO Rocky Johnson
NNO Superstar Graham
NNO Terry Funk
NNO Verne Gagne
NNO Wahoo McDaniel

1981 GC London Wrestling Super Stars

COMPLETE SET (44)

NNO Abdullah The Butcher
NNO Andre The Giant
NNO Baron Von Raschke
NNO Bob Backlund
NNO Bruno Sammartino
NNO Dick Murdoch
NNO Dick Slater
NNO Dino Bravo
NNO Dory Funk Jr.
NNO Dusty Rhodes
NNO Ernie Ladd
NNO Fred Blassie
NNO Gary Hart
NNO Greg Valentine
NNO Harley Race
NNO Hulk Hogan
NNO Hussein Arab
NNO Ivan Koloff
NNO Ivan Putski
NNO Jack Brisco
NNO Jimmy Snuka
NNO John Studd
NNO Ken Patera
NNO Kerry Von Erich
NNO Killer Khan
NNO Larry Zbyszko
NNO Lou Albano
NNO Masked Grappler
NNO Mil Mascaras
NNO Mr. Wrestling II
NNO Nick Bockwinkel
NNO Pat Patterson
NNO Pedro Morales
NNO Ray Stevens
NNO Ric Flair
NNO Rick Steamboat
NNO Ted Dibiase
NNO Terry Funk
NNO The Grand Wizard
NNO The Samoans
NNO Tommy Rich

NNO Tony Atlas
NNO Verne Gagne
NNO Wahoo McDaniel

2019 GCW Deathmatch All-Stars Volume One

COMPLETE SET (28)

1 Nick Gace
2 Wifebeater
3 Zandig
4 Sick Nick Mondo
5 Conor Claxton
6 Nate Hatred
7 Isami Kodaka
8 Danny Havoc
9 Mad Man Pondo
10 Ciclope
11 Necro Butcher
12 G-Raver
13 Jun Kasai
14 Mashashi Taked
15 Alex Colon
16 Jimmy Lloyd
17 Shlak
18 Masada
19 Eric Ryan
20 Orin Veidt
21 Matt Tremont
22 JWM
23 Reed Bentley
24 Low Life Louie
25 Markus Crane
26 Miedo Extremo
27 JC Bailey
28 Brain Damage
29 Great Sasuke
30 Toshiyuki Sakuda

2019 GCW Joey Janela's Spring Break 3 Part One

COMPLETE SET (28)

1 Joey Janela
2 Marko Stunt
3 Shinjiro Otani
4 Jungle Boy
5 Slim J
6 Invisible Stan
7 Australian Suicide
8 Tony Deppen
9 Nick Gage
10 A-Kid
11 Masashi Takeda
12 Jimmy Lloyd
13 Atsushi Onita
14 Penelope Ford
15 Orange Cassidy
16 The Invisible Man
17 The Invisible Man - In Memoriam
18 Giancarlo Dittamo
19 Walter vs. PCO
20 Marty Jannetty
21 Jake Atlas
22 Shane Mercer
23 Elmo Boudreaux
24 Great Sasuke
25 Glacier vs. Dink
26 Alabama Doink

27 Severn vs. Riddle
28 Pat (Jimmy's Mom)

2019 GCW Joey Janela's Spring Break 3 Part Two

COMPLETE SET (28)

1 La Park
2 Masato Tanaka
3 Ethan Page
4 Necro Butcher
5 Shlak
6 Rock 'N' Roll Express
7 LAX (Ortiz & Santana)
8 Mantaur
9 Allie Kat
10 nWo Sting
11 Kikutaro
12 Shazza McKenzie
13 Teddy Hart
14 Arik Cannon
15 Georgie "Boy" Gatton
16 MJF
17 Effy
18 Logan Stunt
19 Matt Tremont
20 Essa Rios
21 Homicide
22 G-Raver
23 Solo Darling
24 KTB
25 Virgil
26 Nate Webb
27 Parrow
28 Crowbar

1999 Gladiadores de la WCW/nWo

COMPLETE SET (108)

1 Hollywood Hogan
2 Rowdy Roddy Piper
3 Randy Savage
4 Ric Flair
5 Arn Anderson
6 Dean Malenko
7 Chris Benoit
8 Steve McMichael
9 Kimberly Page
10 A.C. Jazz
11 Fyre
12 Spice
13 Chae
14 Tygress
15 Whisper
16 Scott Hall MET
17 Kevin Nash
18 Scott Steiner
19 Lex Luger
20 Disco Inferno
21 Hollywood Hogan
22 Sting
23 Stevie Ray
24 Vincent
25 Brian Adams
26 Horace Hogan
27 Scott Norton
28 The Disciple
29 Eric Bischoff
30 Curt Henning UER

31 Buff Bagwell
32 Miss Elizabeth
33 Rick Rude
34 Goldberg (metal)
35 Kevin Nash
36 Kidman
37 Bret Hart
38 Chris Jericho
39 Rowdy Roddy Piper
40 Eddy Guerrero MET UER
41 Chavo Guerrero Jr.
42 Rey Mysterio Jr.
43 Juventud Guerrera
44 Ultimo Dragon
45 Psychosis
46 Hollywood Hogan
47 Goldberg
48 DDP
49 Kevin Nash MET
50 Randy Savage
51 Bret Hart
52 Konnan
53 Raven
54 British Bulldog
55 Booker T
56 Lex Luger
57 Chris Jericho
58 Wrath MET
59 Kevin Nash
60 Jim Neidhart
61 Lodi
62 Riggs
63 Rick Steiner
64 Hugh Morrus
65 Ernest Miller (The Cat)
66 Kanyon
67 Kaz Hayashi
68 Alex Wright
69 Saturn
70 Fit Finley UER
71 Sick Boy
72 Jimmy Hart
73 Meng
74 Gene Okerlund
75 Big Poppa Pump MET
76 DDP
77 Kidman
78 Buff Bagwell
79 Konnan
80 Fyre
81 Kimberly Page
82 Chae
83 Fyre
84 Konnan
85 Ric Flair MET
86 Steve McMichael
87 Dean Malenko
88 Goldberg
89 Bam Bam Bigelow
90 Eddy Guerrero UER
91 Bret Hart
92 British Bulldog
93 Chris Benoit
94 Saturn
95 Sting
96 Kevin Nash
97 Jim Neidhart
98 Buff Bagwell

99 Goldberg
100 DDP (metal)
101 Rick Steiner
102 Cyborg/Montana/Hogan
103 Macho Man Randy Savage
104 Rowdy Roddy Piper
105 Rick Hogan
106 Cyborg
107 Montana
108 Rowdy Roddy Piper

1988 Gold Bond WWF

COMPLETE SET (12)		15.00	40.00
NNO Andre The Giant		5.00	12.00
NNO Bobby The Brain Heenan		4.00	10.00
NNO Elizabeth		3.00	8.00
NNO George The Animal Steele		2.50	6.00
NNO Hillbilly Jim		2.00	5.00
NNO Honky Tonk Man		2.00	5.00
NNO Hulk Hogan		5.00	12.00
NNO Koko B. Ware		1.50	4.00
NNO The Million Dollar Man Ted DiBiase	3.00	8.00
NNO Randy Macho Man Savage		3.00	8.00
NNO Ricky The Dragon Steamboat		1.50	4.00
NNO Strike Force		1.50	4.00

1989 Gold Bond WWF

COMPLETE SET (12)			
NNO Andre the Giant		3.00	8.00
NNO Bobby The Brain Heenan			
NNO Brutus The Barber Beefcake		1.50	4.00
NNO Demolition (Ax & Smash)			
NNO Hacksaw Jim Duggan		2.50	6.00
NNO Hercules			
NNO Hulk Hogan		6.00	15.00
NNO Jake The Snake Roberts		3.00	8.00
NNO Macho Man Randy Savage		4.00	10.00
NNO Million Dollar Man Ted DiBiase		1.50	4.00
NNO Miss Elizabeth		3.00	8.00
NNO Ultimate Warrior			

1990 Gold Bond WWF

COMPLETE SET (12)		12.00	30.00
NNO Andre the Giant		2.50	6.00
NNO Bobby The Brain Heenan		2.00	5.00
NNO Brutus The Barber Beefcake		1.50	4.00
NNO Demolition		1.50	4.00
NNO Hulk Hogan		3.00	8.00
NNO Hulk Hogan		4.00	10.00
No Holds Barred			
NNO Macho Man Randy Savage		3.00	8.00
NNO Million Dollar Man Ted Dibiase		1.50	4.00
NNO Ravishing Rick Rude		1.50	4.00
NNO Rowdy Roddy Piper		3.00	8.00
NNO Ultimate Warrior		3.00	8.00
NNO Wrestlemania III		1.00	2.50

1991 Gold Bond WWF

COMPLETE SET (12)			
NNO Big Boss Man			
NNO Honky Tonk Man			
NNO Hulk Hogan		3.00	8.00
NNO Jake The Snake Roberts		2.00	5.00
NNO Macho King Randy Savage		3.00	8.00
NNO Million Dollar Man Ted Dibiase		5.00	12.00
NNO Mr. Perfect		4.00	10.00
NNO Rowdy Roddy Piper		3.00	8.00

NNO Sensational Queen Sherri	10.00	25.00
NNO Sgt. Slaughter	2.50	6.00
NNO Superfly Jimmy Snuka		
NNO Ultimate Warrior		

1985 Golden Hulk Hogan's Rock 'n' Wrestling Card Game

NNO Andre the Giant
NNO Big John Studd
NNO Fabulous Moolah
NNO Hillbilly Jim
NNO Hulk Hogan
NNO Hulk Hogan/Iron Sheik Flip Card
NNO Iron Sheik
NNO Jimmy "Superfly" Snuka
NNO Junkyard Dog
NNO Mr. Fuji
NNO Nikolai Volkoff
NNO Rowdy Roddy Piper
NNO Tito Santana
NNO Wendi Richter

2004 Good Humor WWE

COMPLETE SET (8)
NNO Big Show
NNO Chris Jericho
NNO Eddie Guerrero
NNO John Cena
NNO Kane
NNO Randy Orton
NNO Rey Mysterio
NNO Triple H

1992 Good Humor WWF

COMPLETE SET (12)			
NNO Big Boss Man			
NNO Bret Hit Man Hart		6.00	15.00
NNO Elizabeth		3.00	8.00
NNO Hulk Hogan		12.00	30.00
NNO Legion of Doom			
NNO Macho Man Randy Savage		5.00	12.00
NNO Million Dollar Man Ted Dibiase	3.00	8.00
NNO Mr. Perfect			
NNO Rowdy Roddy Piper		5.00	12.00
NNO Sid Justice			
NNO The Nasty Boys			
NNO The Undertaker		6.00	15.00

1993 Good Humor WWF

COMPLETE SET (12)
NNO Big Boss Man
NNO Bret Hit Man Hart
NNO Hacksaw Jim Duggan
NNO Hulk Hogan
NNO Macho Man Randy Savage
NNO Million Dollar Man Ted DiBiase
NNO Mr. Perfect
NNO Razor Ramon
NNO Ric Flair
NNO Shawn Michaels
NNO Tatanka
NNO The Undertaker

1994 Good Humor WWF

COMPLETE SET (12)
NNO Bret Hart
NNO Bam Bam Bigelow

NNO Crush
NNO Doink
NNO IRS
NNO Lex Luger
NNO Mr. Perfect
NNO Randy Savage
NNO Razor Ramon
NNO Tatanka
NNO Undertaker
NNO Yokozuna

1995 Good Humor WWF

COMPLETE SET (13)
NNO 1-2-3 Kid
NNO Alundra Blayze
NNO Bam Bam Bigelow
NNO Bret Hit Man Hart
NNO Diesel
NNO Paul Bearer
NNO Razor Ramon
NNO Shawn Michaels
NNO Smoking Gunns (back-to-back)
NNO Smoking Gunns (w/jackets)
NNO Smoking Gunns 3 (w/o jackets)
NNO Undertaker
NNO Yokozuna

1997 Good Humor WWF

COMPLETE SET (12)
NNO Ahmed Johnson
NNO Bret Hit Man Hart
NNO British Bulldog
NNO Goldust
NNO Owen Hart
NNO Shawn Michaels
NNO Sunny
NNO Sycho Sid
NNO Undertaker
NNO Vader
NNO Wildman Marc Mero
NNO Yokozuna

1998 Good Humor WWF

COMPLETE SET (12)
NNO Ahmed Johnson
NNO The British Bulldog
NNO Faarooq
NNO Goldust
NNO Kane
NNO Ken Shamrock
NNO Legion of Doom
NNO Mankind
NNO Shawn Michaels
NNO Stone Cold Steve Austin
NNO The Undertaker
NNO Vader

1999 Good Humor WWF

COMPLETE SET (12)
NNO Cactus Jack
NNO Chyna
NNO Edge
NNO Gangrel
NNO Hunter Hearst Helmsley
NNO Jeff Jarrett
NNO Kane
NNO Ken Shamrock

NNO The Rock
NNO Sable
NNO Stone Cold Steve Austin
NNO The Undertaker

2000 Good Humor WWF

COMPLETE SET (10)

NNO Big Show
NNO Chris Jericho
NNO Edge
NNO Hunter Hearst Hemsley
NNO Kane
NNO Mankind
NNO Road Dogg Jesse James
NNO The Rock
NNO Stone Cold Steve Austin #1
NNO The Undertaker

2002 Good Humor WWF

COMPLETE SET (10)	15.00	40.00
NNO Chris Jericho	1.50	4.00
NNO Dudley Boyz	1.50	4.00
NNO Edge & Christian	2.50	6.00
NNO Hardy Boyz	1.50	4.00
NNO Kane	2.50	6.00
NNO Kurt Angle	2.50	6.00
NNO The Rock	4.00	10.00
NNO Stone Cold Steve Austin	4.00	10.00
NNO Triple H	4.00	10.00
NNO The Undertaker	3.00	8.00

1999 Hallmark WCW Valentine's Day Cards

NNO Bret "Hit Man" Hart
You're a Hit with Me, Valentine!
NNO DDP
Hope Your Valentine's Day Is a Bang!
NNO Goldberg
You're Next, Valentine!
NNO Hollywood Hogan
Be Mine 4 Life!
NNO Kevin Nash
You're Too Sweet, Valentine!
NNO Konnan
Have a "Rowdy Rowdy" and "Bout-It Bout-It" Valentine's Day!
NNO Ric Flair
Hope Your Valentine's Day Is "WOOOO!"
NNO Sting
Just Dropped in to Wish You a Happy Valentine's Day!
NNO A Valentine for My TeacherÖ
Hogan/Sting/Goldberg/DDP

1990 Hasbro WWF Flips Trading Cards

COMPLETE SET (10)

NNO Big Boss Man	1.25	3.00
NNO Brutus The Barber Beefcake	1.50	4.00
NNO The Bushwhackers		
NNO Hacksaw Jim Duggan	4.00	10.00
NNO Hulk Hogan	6.00	15.00
NNO Jake The Snake Roberts		
NNO Macho King Randy Savage	5.00	12.00
NNO Million Dollar Man Ted Dibiase		
NNO The Rockers		
NNO Ultimate Warrior		

1988 Hostess WWF WrestleMania IV Stickers

COMPLETE SET (34)

1 Jake The Snake Roberts		
2 Billy Jack Haynes		
3 Brutus The Barber Beefcake	.40	1.00
4 Randy Macho Man Savage and Elizabeth		
5 Koko B. Ware	.40	1.00
6 George The Animal Steele		
7 Hulk Hogan	4.00	10.00
8 Junkyard Dog		
9 Magnificent Muraco	.40	1.00
10 Bam Bam Bigelow	.75	2.00
11 Elizabeth		
12 The Honky Tonk Man	.75	2.00
13 Ted DiBiase	.40	1.00
14 The Natural Butch Reed	.40	1.00
15 Ravishing Rick Rude		
16 Killer Khan		
17 Bobby The Brain Heenan		
18 Jimmy Hart		
19 Slick The Doctor of Style		
20 Hulk Hogan	8.00	20.00
21 Mr. Fuji		
22 Oliver Humperdink		
23 Strike Force		
24 The British Bulldogs		
25 The Killer Bees		
26 Demolition Ax and Smash		
27 The Islanders		
28 Ken Patera		
29 The Rougeau Brothers		
30 The Hart Foundation		
31 Strike Force		
32 Jesse The Body Ventura		
33 Hillbilly Jim		
34 Randy Macho Man Savage		

1987 Hostess Munchies WWF Stickers

COMPLETE SET (20)	10.00	20.00
NNO British Bulldogs	.20	.50
NNO Don Muraco	.15	.40
NNO George The Animal Steele	.40	1.00
NNO Hillbilly Jim	.20	.50
NNO Honky Tonk Man	.20	.50
NNO Hulk Hogan	3.00	8.00
NNO Hulk Hogan	3.00	8.00
NNO Iron Sheik and Nikoli Volkoff	.25	.60
NNO Jake The Snake Roberts	.50	1.25
NNO Junkyard Dog	.20	.50
NNO Kamala	.15	.40
NNO King Kong Bundy	.20	.50
NNO Koko B. Ware	.15	.40
NNO Outback Jack	.15	.40
NNO Paul Mr. Wonderful Orndorff	.20	.50
NNO Randy Savage and Elizabeth	1.50	4.00
NNO Ricky The Dragon Steamboat	.20	.50
NNO Rowdy Roddy Piper	1.25	3.00
NNO Sika	.40	1.00
NNO Tito Santana	.15	.40

1999 Hot Shots WWF Stickers

COMPLETE SET (212)	12.00	30.00
1 Stone Cold Steve Austin	.75	2.00
2 Stone Cold Steve Austin	.75	2.00
3 Stone Cold Steve Austin	.75	2.00
4 Stone Cold Steve Austin	.75	2.00
5 Stone Cold Steve Austin	.75	2.00
6 Stone Cold Steve Austin	.75	2.00
7 Stone Cold Steve Austin	.75	2.00
8 Stone Cold Steve Austin	.75	2.00
9 Stone Cold Steve Austin	.75	2.00
10 Stone Cold Steve Austin	.75	2.00
11 Stone Cold Steve Austin	.75	2.00
12 Stone Cold Steve Austin	.75	2.00
13 Stone Cold Steve Austin	.75	2.00
14 Stone Cold Steve Austin	.75	2.00
15 Stone Cold Steve Austin	.75	2.00
16 Stone Cold Steve Austin	.75	2.00
17 Stone Cold Steve Austin	.75	2.00
18 Stone Cold Steve Austin	.75	2.00
19 The Rock	.75	2.00
20 The Rock	.75	2.00
21 The Rock	.75	2.00
22 The Rock	.75	2.00
23 The Rock	.75	2.00
24 The Rock	.75	2.00
25 The Rock	.75	2.00
26 The Rock	.75	2.00
27 The Rock	.75	2.00
28 The Rock	.75	2.00
29 The Rock	.75	2.00
30 The Rock	.75	2.00
31 The Rock	.75	2.00
32 The Rock	.75	2.00
33 The Rock	.75	2.00
34 The Rock	.75	2.00
35 The Rock	.75	2.00
36 The Rock	.75	2.00
37 Big Show	.25	.60
38 Big Show	.25	.60
39 Big Show	.25	.60
40 Big Show	.25	.60
41 Big Show	.25	.60
42 Big Show	.25	.60
43 Undertaker	.60	1.50
44 Undertaker	.60	1.50
45 Undertaker	.60	1.50
46 Undertaker	.60	1.50
47 Undertaker	.60	1.50
48 Undertaker	.60	1.50
49 Undertaker	.60	1.50
50 Undertaker	.60	1.50
51 Undertaker	.60	1.50
52 Undertaker	.60	1.50
53 Undertaker	.60	1.50
54 Undertaker	.60	1.50
55 Undertaker	.60	1.50
56 Undertaker	.60	1.50
57 Undertaker	.60	1.50
58 Undertaker	.60	1.50
59 Undertaker	.60	1.50
60 Undertaker	.60	1.50
61 Acolytes	.12	.30
62 Corporate Ministry	.12	.30
63 Viscera	.12	.30
64 Chyna	.20	.50
65 Chyna	.20	.50
66 Big Boss Man	.12	.30
67 Big Boss Man	.12	.30
68 Viscera	.12	.30
69 Corporate Ministry	.12	.30
70 Big Boss Man	.12	.30
71 Acolytes	.12	.30
72 Paul Bearer	.15	.40
73 Ken Shamrock	.15	.40
74 Ken Shamrock	.15	.40
75 Ken Shamrock	.15	.40
76 Ken Shamrock	.15	.40
77 Ken Shamrock	.15	.40
78 Ken Shamrock	.15	.40
79 Mankind	.30	.75
80 Mankind	.30	.75
81 Mankind	.30	.75
82 Mankind	.30	.75
83 Mankind	.30	.75
84 Mankind	.30	.75
85 Mankind	.30	.75
86 Mankind	.30	.75
87 Mankind	.30	.75
88 Mankind	.30	.75
89 Mankind	.30	.75
90 Mankind	.30	.75
91 Vince McMahon	.20	.50
92 Vince McMahon	.20	.50
93 Vince McMahon	.20	.50
94 Vince McMahon	.20	.50
95 Vince McMahon	.20	.50
96 Vince McMahon	.20	.50
97 Shane McMahon	.20	.50
98 Shane McMahon	.20	.50
99 Shane McMahon	.20	.50
100 Shane McMahon	.20	.50
101 Shane McMahon	.20	.50
102 Shane McMahon	.20	.50
103 Triple H	.30	.75
104 Triple H	.30	.75
105 Triple H	.30	.75
106 Triple H	.30	.75
107 Triple H	.30	.75
108 Triple H	.30	.75
109 Jeff Jarrett	.25	.60
110 Jeff Jarrett	.25	.60
111 Jeff Jarrett	.25	.60
112 Jeff Jarrett	.25	.60
113 Jeff Jarrett	.25	.60
114 Jeff Jarrett	.25	.60
115 Debra	.30	.75
116 Debra	.30	.75
117 Debra	.30	.75
118 Debra	.30	.75
119 Debra	.30	.75
120 Debra	.30	.75
121 Kane	.25	.60
122 Kane	.25	.60
123 Kane	.25	.60
124 Kane	.25	.60
125 Kane	.25	.60
126 Kane	.25	.60
127 Kane	.25	.60
128 Kane	.25	.60
129 Kane	.25	.60
130 Kane	.25	.60
131 Kane	.25	.60
132 Kane	.25	.60
133 X-Pac	.25	.60
134 X-Pac	.25	.60
135 X-Pac	.25	.60
136 X-Pac	.25	.60
137 X-Pac	.25	.60
138 X-Pac	.25	.60
139 Road Dogg	.25	.60

140	Road Dogg	.25	.60
141	Road Dogg	.25	.60
142	Road Dogg	.25	.60
143	Road Dogg	.25	.60
144	Road Dogg	.25	.60
145	Billy Gunn	.25	.60
146	Billy Gunn	.25	.60
147	Billy Gunn	.25	.60
148	Billy Gunn	.25	.60
149	Billy Gunn	.25	.60
150	Billy Gunn	.25	.60
151	Al Snow	.15	.40
152	Al Snow	.15	.40
153	Al Snow	.15	.40
154	Al Snow	.15	.40
155	Al Snow	.15	.40
156	Al Snow	.15	.40
157	Val Venis	.15	.40
158	Val Venis	.15	.40
159	Val Venis	.15	.40
160	Val Venis	.15	.40
161	Val Venis	.15	.40
162	Val Venis	.15	.40
163	The Brood	.30	.75
164	Edge	.30	.75
165	The Brood	.30	.75
166	Christian	.25	.60
167	Edge	.30	.75
168	Christian	.25	.60
169	Gangrel	.12	.30
170	Gangrel	.12	.30
171	Gangrel	.12	.30
172	Gangrel	.12	.30
173	Gangrel	.12	.30
174	Gangrel	.12	.30
175	D-Lo Brown	.12	.30
176	D-Lo Brown	.12	.30
177	D-Lo Brown	.12	.30
178	D-Lo Brown	.12	.30
179	Mark Henry	.15	.40
180	Mark Henry	.15	.40
181	Goldust	.25	.60
182	Goldust	.25	.60
183	Goldust	.25	.60
184	Goldust	.25	.60
185	Goldust	.25	.60
186	Goldust	.25	.60
187	Godfather	.20	.50
188	Godfather	.20	.50
189	Godfather	.20	.50
190	Godfather	.20	.50
191	Godfather	.20	.50
192	Godfather	.20	.50
193	PMS	.15	.40
194	PMS	.15	.40
195	PMS	.15	.40
196	PMS	.15	.40
197	PMS	.15	.40
198	PMS	.15	.40
199	Nicole Bass	.12	.30
200	Droz	.12	.30
201	Shawn Michaels	.40	1.00
202	Ivory	.20	.50
203	Droz	.12	.30
204	Hardcore Holly	.12	.30
205	Test	.12	.30
206	Tiger Ali Singh	.12	.30
207	Tiger Ali Singh	.12	.30

208	Kurrgan	.12	.30
209	Test	.12	.30
210	Shawn Michaels	.40	1.00
211	Test	.12	.30
212	Raw Is War	.12	.30

2018 Ignite Wrestling

1	Aaron Epic
2	Alex Cruz
3	Amber Nova
4	Amy Rose
5	Andrew Merlin
6	Angel Rose
7	Ari Alvarado
8	Aspyn Rose
9	Beastly Brody
10	Calvin Tankman
11	Carlos Gabriel
12	Chico Adams
13	Chip Day
14	Chuckles the Clown
15	Critical Mayhem
16	Chasyn Rance
17	CT Brown
18	Dave Crist
19	Dezmond Xavier
20	Gary Jav
21	Gym Nasty Boys
22	Jake Parnell
23	Jesus Rodriguez
24	Joey Ozbourne
25	Johnathan Wolf
26	Kaci Lennox
27	Matt Kenway
28	Lacey Lane
29	Martin Stone
30	Maxx Stardom
31	Mr. Haystack
32	Nick Nero
33	Ophidian the Cobra
34	Rex Bacchus
35	Rey Fury
36	Santana Garrett
37	Serpentico
38	Shawn Kemp
39	Slade Porter
40	Sofia Castillo
41	Stevie Fierce
42	Tech
43	The Ugly Ducklings
44	TNT
45	Tony Stabile

2019 Ignite Wrestling

1	Aaron Epic
2	Alex Cruz
3	Amber Nova
4	Amy Rose
5	Andrew Merlin
6	Angel Rose
7	Avery Taylor
8	Beastly
9	Carlos Gabriel
10	Chip Day
11	Chuckles
12	Critical Mayhem
13	Daniel Max Shaw
14	Dream Girl Ellie

15	Ethan Case
16	Fred Yehi
17	Gabriel Lacey
18	Gary Jay
19	Gym Nasty Boys
20	Hunter Law
21	Jake Parnell
22	Jarett Diaz
23	Jason Cade
24	Jay Sky
25	Kaci Lennox
26	Kai Fayden
27	Katalina Perez
28	Kilynn King
29	Leon Scott
30	Marina Tucker
31	Ref Tony Stabile
32	Ref Julie Dilbert
33	Rey Fury
34	Romeo Quevedo
35	Serpentico
36	Skyler Moore
37	Sofia Castillo
38	Snoop Strikes
39	Tech
40	That Klassic Tag Team
41	The Bomb Shelter
42	The Rapture
43	The Ugly Ducklings
44	Tripp Cassidy
45	Troy Hollywood
46	Victor Vences
47	Young Professor
48	Zachary Cooper

1991 Imagine Wrestling Legends

	COMPLETE SET (60)	25.00	60.00
1	Bruno Sammartino	1.25	3.00
2	Buddy Rogers	.75	2.00
3	Ivan Koloff	.75	2.00
4	Lou Albano	.40	1.00
5	Billy Graham	1.00	2.50
6	Killer Kowalski	1.00	2.50
7	Lou Thesz	1.25	3.00
8	Domenic DeNucci	.40	1.00
9	Bruno Sammartino	1.25	3.00
10	Buddy Rogers	.75	2.00
11	Ivan Koloff	.75	2.00
12	Lou Albano	.40	1.00
13	Billy Graham	1.00	2.50
14	Killer Kowalski	1.00	2.50
15	Lou Thesz	1.25	3.00
16	Bill Miller	.40	1.00
17	Domenic DeNucci	.40	1.00
18	Bruno Sammartino	1.25	3.00
19	Antonio Rocca	.40	1.00
20	Buddy Rogers	.75	2.00
21	Ivan Koloff	.75	2.00
22	Primo Carnerra	.75	2.00
23	Lou Albano	.40	1.00
24	Bruno Sammartino	1.25	3.00
25	Crusher Lisowski	.75	2.00
26	Billy Graham	1.00	2.50
27	Killer Kowalski	1.00	2.50
28	Domenic DeNucci	.40	1.00
29	Rocca & Perez	.75	2.00
30	Bill Watts	.40	1.00
31	BoBo Brazil	.75	2.00

32	Lou Thesz	1.25	3.00
33	Pedro Morales	1.00	2.50
34	Johnny Valentine	.75	2.00
35	Argentine Apollo	.40	1.00
36	Billy Graham	1.00	2.50
37	Haystacks Calhoun	.40	1.00
38	Bruno Sammartino	1.25	3.00
39	The Destroyer	.75	2.00
40	Buddy Rogers	.75	2.00
41	Ray Stevens	.75	2.00
42	Lou Albano	.40	1.00
43	Edouard Carpentier	.40	1.00
44	Killer Kowalski	1.00	2.50
45	Bob Backlund	1.00	2.50
46	Killer Kowalski	1.00	2.50
47	Mil Mascaras	1.00	2.50
48	Domenic DeNucci	.40	1.00
49	Smasher Sloan	.40	1.00
50	Ivan Koloff	.75	2.00
51	Lou Albano	.40	1.00
52	Lou Thesz	1.25	3.00
53	Harly Race UER	1.25	3.00
54	Billy Graham	1.00	2.50
55	Domenic DeNucci	.40	1.00
56	Hawk & Hansen	.75	2.00
57	Lou Thesz	1.25	3.00
58	Ivan Koloff	.75	2.00
59	Buddy Rogers	.75	2.00
60	Bruno Sammartino	1.25	3.00
61	Bruno Sammartino AU	50.00	100.00
62	Buddy Rogers AU	25.00	60.00
63	Lou Thesz AU	25.00	60.00
64	Billy Graham AU	15.00	40.00
65	Ivan Koloff AU	15.00	40.00
66	Killer Kowalski AU	30.00	75.00
67	Lou Albano AU	20.00	50.00
68	Domenic DeNucci AU	12.00	30.00

1991 Impel WCW

	COMPLETE SET (162)	6.00	15.00
	UNOPENED BOX (36 PACKS)		
	UNOPENED PACK (12 CARDS)		
1	Sting	.20	.50
2	Sting	.20	.50
3	Sting	.20	.50
4	Sting	.20	.50
5	Sting	.20	.50
6	Sting	.20	.50
7	Sting	.20	.50
8	Sting	.20	.50
9	Sting	.20	.50
10	Sting	.20	.50
11	Sting	.20	.50
12	Sting	.20	.50
13	Sting	.20	.50
14	Lex Luger	.10	.25
15	Lex Luger	.10	.25
16	Lex Luger	.10	.25
17	Lex Luger	.10	.25
18	Lex Luger	.10	.25
19	Lex Luger	.10	.25
20	Lex Luger	.10	.25
21	Lex Luger	.10	.25
22	Lex Luger	.10	.25
23	Lex Luger	.10	.25
24	Sid Vicious	.07	.20
25	Sid Vicious	.07	.20
26	Sid Vicious	.07	.20

27	Sid Vicious	.07	.20
28	Sid Vicious	.07	.20
29	Sid Vicious	.07	.20
30	Sid Vicious	.07	.20
31	Sid Vicious	.07	.20
32	Sid Vicious	.07	.20
33	Sid Vicious	.07	.20
34	Sid Vicious	.07	.20
35	Sid Vicious	.07	.20
36	Ric Flair	.30	.75
37	Ric Flair	.30	.75
38	Ric Flair	.30	.75
39	Ric Flair	.30	.75
40	Ric Flair	.30	.75
41	Ric Flair	.30	.75
42	Ric Flair	.30	.75
43	Ric Flair	.30	.75
44	Ric Flair	.30	.75
45	Ric Flair	.30	.75
46	Ric Flair	.30	.75
47	Ric Flair	.30	.75
48	Arn Anderson	.10	.25
49	Arn Anderson	.10	.25
50	Arn Anderson	.10	.25
51	Arn Anderson	.10	.25
52	Arn Anderson	.10	.25
53	Arn Anderson	.10	.25
54	Arn Anderson	.10	.25
55	Flyin Brian	.07	.20
56	Flyin Brian	.07	.20
57	Flyin Brian	.07	.20
58	Flyin Brian	.07	.20
59	Flyin Brian	.07	.20
60	Flyin Brian	.07	.20
61	Flyin Brian	.07	.20
62	Flyin Brian	.07	.20
63	Flyin Brian	.07	.20
64	Flyin Brian	.07	.20
65	Z-Man	.07	.20
66	Z-Man	.07	.20
67	Z-Man	.07	.20
68	Terry Taylor	.07	.20
69	Terry Taylor	.07	.20
70	Terry Taylor	.07	.20
71	Terry Taylor	.07	.20
72	Terry Taylor	.07	.20
73	Terry Taylor	.07	.20
74	Terry Taylor	.07	.20
75	Terry Taylor	.07	.20
76	Dutch Mantell	.10	.25
77	Dutch Mantell	.10	.25
78	Dutch Mantell	.10	.25
79	Dutch Mantell	.10	.25
80	Dutch Mantell	.10	.25
81	Dutch Mantell	.10	.25
82	Mr. Wall Street	.07	.20
83	Mr. Wall Street	.07	.20
84	Mr. Wall Street	.07	.20
85	El Gigante	.07	.20
86	El Gigante	.07	.20
87	El Gigante	.07	.20
88	El Gigante	.07	.20
89	El Gigante	.07	.20
90	El Gigante	.07	.20
91	El Gigante	.07	.20
92	El Gigante	.07	.20
93	Tommy Rich	.07	.20
94	Tommy Rich	.07	.20

95	Tommy Rich	.07	.20
96	Tommy Rich	.07	.20
97	Ricky Morton	.07	.20
98	Ricky Morton	.07	.20
99	Ricky Morton	.07	.20
100	Ricky Morton	.07	.20
101	Ricky Morton	.07	.20
102	Ricky Morton	.07	.20
103	Steiner Brothers	.10	.25
104	Steiner Brothers	.10	.25
105	Steiner Brothers	.10	.25
106	Steiner Brothers	.10	.25
107	Steiner Brothers	.10	.25
108	Steiner Brothers	.10	.25
109	Steiner Brothers	.10	.25
110	Steiner Brothers	.10	.25
111	Steiner Brothers	.10	.25
112	Steiner Brothers	.10	.25
113	Steiner Brothers	.10	.25
114	Steiner Brothers	.10	.25
115	Steiner Brothers	.10	.25
116	Steiner Brothers	.10	.25
117	Fabulous Freebirds	.10	.25
118	Fabulous Freebirds	.10	.25
119	Fabulous Freebirds	.10	.25
120	Fabulous Freebirds	.10	.25
121	Fabulous Freebirds	.10	.25
122	Fabulous Freebirds	.10	.25
123	Fabulous Freebirds	.10	.25
124	Fabulous Freebirds	.10	.25
125	Fabulous Freebirds	.10	.25
126	Fabulous Freebirds	.10	.25
127	Fabulous Freebirds	.10	.25
128	Fabulous Freebirds	.10	.25
129	Southern Boys	.07	.20
130	Southern Boys	.07	.20
131	Southern Boys	.07	.20
132	Southern Boys	.07	.20
133	Southern Boys	.07	.20
134	Southern Boys	.07	.20
135	Southern Boys	.07	.20
136	Southern Boys	.07	.20
137	Southern Boys	.07	.20
138	Southern Boys	.07	.20
139	Doom	.10	.25
140	Doom	.10	.25
141	Doom	.10	.25
142	Doom	.10	.25
143	Doom	.10	.25
144	Doom	.10	.25
145	Doom	.10	.25
146	Doom	.10	.25
147	Doom	.10	.25
148	Doom	.10	.25
149	Doom	.10	.25
150	Doom	.10	.25
151	Teddy Long	.07	.20
152	Teddy Long	.07	.20
153	Teddy Long	.07	.20
154	Jim Ross	.07	.20
155	Jim Ross	.07	.20
156	Jim Ross	.07	.20
157	Missy Hyatt	.10	.25
158	Missy Hyatt	.10	.25
159	Missy Hyatt	.10	.25
160	Missy Hyatt	.10	.25
161	Checklist	.07	.20

162	Checklist	.07	.20
NNO	Sting HOLO	4.00	10.00

1990 International Games WCW Slam-A-Rama Wrestling Card Game

COMPLETE SET (49)

1	Arn Anderson (body slam)		
2	Arn Anderson (drop kick)		
3	Arn Anderson (pin)		
4	Arn Anderson (press)		
5	Barry Windham (body slam)		
6	Barry Windham (drop kick)		
7	Barry Windham (pin)		
8	Barry Windham (press)		
9	Brian Pillman (body slam)		
10	Brian Pillman (drop kick)		
11	Brian Pillman (pin)		
12	Brian Pillman (press)		
13	Butch Reed (body slam)		
14	Butch Reed (drop kick)		
15	Butch Reed (pin)		
16	Butch Reed (press)		
17	Lex Luger (body slam)		
18	Lex Luger (drop kick)		
19	Lex Luger (pin)		
20	Lex Luger (press)		
21	Ric Flair (body slam)		
22	Ric Flair (drop kick)		
23	Ric Flair (pin)		
24	Ric Flair (press)		
25	Rick Steiner (body slam)		
26	Rick Steiner (drop kick)		
27	Rick Steiner (pin)		
28	Rick Steiner (press)		
29	Ron Simmons (body slam)		
30	Ron Simmons (drop kick)		
31	Ron Simmons (pin)		
32	Ron Simmons (press)		
33	Scott Steiner (body slam)		
34	Scott Steiner (drop kick)		
35	Scott Steiner (pin)		
36	Scott Steiner (press)		
37	Sid Vicious (body slam)		
38	Sid Vicious (drop kick)		
39	Sid Vicious (pin)		
40	Sid Vicious (press)		
41	Sting (body slam)		
42	Sting (drop kick)		
43	Sting (pin)		
44	Sting (press)		
45	Tag Team (header)		
46	Tom Zenk (body slam)		
47	Tom Zenk (drop kick)		
48	Tom Zenk (pin)		
49	Tom Zenk (press)		

1997 IPC WCW/nWo Limited Edition Pin Card Pins

COMPLETE SET (6)

NNO The Giant
NNO Hollywood Hogan
NNO Lex Luger
NNO Macho Man
NNO Ric Flair
NNO Sting

1997 IPC WCW/nWo Limited Edition Pin Cards

COMPLETE SET (6)

NNO The Giant
NNO Hollywood Hogan
NNO Lex Luger
NNO Macho Man
NNO Ric Flair
NNO Sting

2015 IPW Wrestling

1 Ach
2 Adam Cole
3 Adam Thornstone
4 AJ Styles
5 AR Fox
6 Biff Busick
7 Boyce Legrande
8 Brian Cage
9 Brian Myers
10 Candice LeRae
11 Cedric Alexander
12 Chris Hero
13 Christina Von Eeric
14 Christopher Daniels
15 Chuck Taylor
16 Daniel Torch
17 Dave Dutra
18 Drake Younger
19 Drew Gulak
20 Dylan Drake
21 El Chupacabro
22 El Generico
23 Excaliber
24 Human Tornado
25 Jay Briscoe
26 Jeckles the Jester
27 Jeff Cobb
28 Jody Kristofferson
29 Joe DeSoul
30 Joey Ryan
31 Johnny Gargano
32 JR Kratos
33 Kenny Omega
34 Kevin Steen
35 Kyle O'Reilly
36 Mark Briscoe
37 Matt Carlos
38 Matt Sydal
39 Michael Eglin
40 Mount Rushmore
41 Rich Swann
42 Rick Knox
43 Ricochet
44 Rik Luxury
45 Rocknes Monsters
46 Roderick Strong
47 Ryan McQueen
48 Sir Samurai
49 Sparkey Ballard
50 Super Dragon
51 Super Smash Brothers
52 Timothy Thatcher
53 Tommaso Ciampa
54 Trent?
55 Trevor Lee
56 Uhaa Nation

57	Vinnie Massaro		
58	Virgil Flynn		
59	Willie Mack		
60	The Young Bucks		
NNO	Series I Header		
NNO	Series II Header		

2000 Jakks WWF Computer and Video Games Magazine UK

COMPLETE SET (20)

1	Matt Hardy	
2	Chris Jericho	
3	Chyna	
4	Dean Malenko	
5	Mick Foley/Mankind	
6	Jeff Hardy	
7	Kane	
8	Kurt Angle	
9	Perry Saturn	
10	Rikishi	
11	Road Dogg	
12	Scotty Too Hotty	
13	Shane McMahon	
14	Tazz	
15	Test	
16	The Rock	
17	The Undertaker	
18	Triple H	
19	Val Venis	
20	Vince McMahon	

1973-74 Jalart House All-Star Wrestling

COMPLETE SET (4)

1	Ron Pritchard
2	Norman Charles Frederick III of the Royal Kangaroos
3	Paul Jones
4	The Sheik

1988 Jay's Potato Chips WWF Tag Teams of the Year

COMPLETE SET (12)

NNO	Billy Jack Haynes		
NNO	The British Bulldogs		
NNO	George The Animal Steele		
NNO	The Honky Tonk Man		
NNO	Hulk Hogan	2.50	6.00
NNO	Jake The Snake Roberts		
NNO	Ken Patera		
NNO	The Killer Bees		
NNO	Randy Savage and Elizabeth		
NNO	Slick		
NNO	Smash and Ax - Demolition		
NNO	Strike Force		

2008 KOCH Vision ROH Limited Edition

COMPLETE SET (6)

NNO	Austin Aries
NNO	Bryan Danielson
NNO	Chris Hero
NNO	Mark and Jay Briscoe
NNO	Nigel McGuinness
NNO	Roderick Strong

2018 Leaf Legends of Wrestling Autographs

UNOPENED BOX (8 CARDS)
*SILVER/25: X TO X BASIC AUTOS
*GREEN/15: UNPRICED DUE TO SCARCITY
*GOLD/10: UNPRICED DUE TO SCARCITY
*PURPLE/5: UNPRICED DUE TO SCARCITY
*RED/1: UNPRICED DUE TO SCARCITY

LWC1	Christian	5.00	12.00
LWE1	Edge	8.00	20.00
LWK1	Konnan	4.00	10.00
LWR1	Ricochet	15.00	40.00
LWS1	Slick	5.00	12.00
LW2CS	2 Cold Scorpio	4.00	10.00
LWAS1	Alexis Smirnoff	12.00	30.00
LWBF1	Bad Luck Fale	6.00	15.00
LWBH1	Bret Hart	8.00	20.00
LWBL1	Bobby Lashley	6.00	15.00
LWBVR	Baron Von Raschke	10.00	25.00
LWBW1	Barry Windham	5.00	12.00
LWCJ1	Chris Jericho	8.00	20.00
LWCK1	Corporal Kirchner	5.00	12.00
LWCR1	Cody Rhodes	15.00	40.00
LWDK1	Dynamite Kid	12.00	30.00
LWGS1	The Great Sasuke	6.00	15.00
LWGV1	Greg Valentine	5.00	12.00
LWHT1	Hiroshi Tanahashi	6.00	15.00
LWJB1	Jim Brunzell	4.00	10.00
LWJH1	Jimmy Hart	5.00	12.00
LWJR1	Jacques Rougeau	4.00	10.00
LWJR2	Jake Roberts	6.00	15.00
LWJR3	Jim Ross	6.00	15.00
LWJV1	Jesse Ventura	20.00	50.00
LWJV2	Jesse Ventura	20.00	50.00
LWKF1	Kazuyuki Fujita	8.00	20.00
LWKI1	Kota Ibushi	10.00	25.00
LWKK1	Kendo Kashin	4.00	10.00
LWKN1	Kevin Nash	6.00	15.00
LWKO1	Kazuchika Okada	12.00	30.00
LWKO2	Kenny Omega	25.00	60.00
LWKS1	Katsuyori Shibata	8.00	20.00
LWLH1	Larry Hennig	12.00	30.00
LWMS1	Minoru Suzuki	8.00	20.00
LWMW1	Mikey Whipwreck	4.00	10.00
LWPE1	Penta El Zero M	10.00	25.00
LWPO1	Pierre Ouellet	6.00	15.00
LWRF1	Ric Flair	15.00	40.00
LWRR1	Rocky Romero	4.00	10.00
LWSD1	Shane Douglas	4.00	10.00
LWSH1	Sam Houston	5.00	12.00
LWTI1	Tomohiro Ishii	12.00	30.00
LWTL1	Tanga Loa	12.00	30.00
LWTN1	Tetsuya Naito	12.00	30.00
LWTT1	Tama Tonga	10.00	25.00
LWWO1	Will Ospreay	12.00	30.00

2018 Leaf Legends of Wrestling Dual Autographs

STATED ODDS

LWD1	Edge /Christian	12.00	30.00
LWD2	C.Jericho/Christian	10.00	25.00
LWD3	K.Ibushi/B.L.Fale	8.00	20.00
LWD4	B.Hart/K.Nash		
LWD5	K.Nash/Konnan	10.00	25.00
LWD6	Konnan/S.Douglas		
LWD7	S.Douglas/2 Cold Scorpio	8.00	20.00
LWD8	J.Rougeau/P.Ouellet		
LWD9	2 Cold Scorpio/M.Whipwreck		
LWD10	B.L.Fale/T.Loa	12.00	30.00
LWD11	B.Windham/2 Cold Scorpio	8.00	20.00
LWD12	C.Rhodes/Christian		
LWD13	G.Valentine/J.Roberts	8.00	20.00
LWD14	L.Hennig/B.Von Raschke		
LWD15	Minoru Suzuki	15.00	40.00
	Tomohiro Ishii		

2018 Leaf Legends of Wrestling Originals Update Autographs

STATED ODDS

E1	Edge (2014)	6.00	15.00
S3	Sunny (2014)	8.00	20.00
BW1	The Bushwackers (2014)	15.00	40.00
DB1	Dick Beyer (2017)	8.00	20.00
FE1	Fedor Emelianenko (2016)	12.00	30.00
JB1	Jim Brunzell (2017)	6.00	15.00
KS1	Kazuski Sakuraba (2016)	8.00	20.00
MTA	Magnum T.A. (2017)	6.00	15.00
PP1	Pat Patterson (2014)	6.00	15.00
PVZ	Paige VanZant (2016)	10.00	25.00
RG1	Royce Gracie (2016)	12.00	30.00
RMJ	Rey Mysterio Jr. (2017)	10.00	25.00
RS1	Ricky Steamboat (2017)	8.00	20.00
RS2	Ryan Shamrock (2017)	5.00	12.00
SL1	Stan Lane (2014)	5.00	12.00
SR2	Stevie Richards (2014)	5.00	12.00

2012 Leaf Originals Wrestling

UNOPENED BOX (5 CARDS)
*YELLOW/99: .5X TO 1.2X BASIC AUTOS
*BLUE/25: .6X TO 1.5X BASIC AUTOS
*RED/10: UNPRICED DUE TO SCARCITY
*BLACK/1: UNPRICED DUE TO SCARCITY
*P.P.BLACK/1: UNPRICED DUE TO SCARCITY
*P.P.CYAN/1: UNPRICED DUE TO SCARCITY
*P.P.MAGENTA/1: UNPRICED DUE TO SCARCITY
*P.P.YELLOW/1: UNPRICED DUE TO SCARCITY
*A.A.: SAME VALUE AS BASIC AUTOS
*A.A.YELLOW/25: .6X TO 1.5X BASIC AUTOS
*A.A.BLUE/10: UNPRICED DUE TO SCARCITY
*A.A.RED/5: UNPRICED DUE TO SCARCITY
*A.A.BLACK/1: UNPRICED DUE TO SCARCITY
*A.A.P.P.BLACK/1: UNPRICED DUE TO SCARCITY
*A.A.P.P.CYAN/1: UNPRICED DUE TO SCARCITY
*A.A.P.P.MAGENTA/1: UNPRICED DUE TO SCARCITY
*A.A.P.P.YELLOW/1: UNPRICED DUE TO SCARCITY

ATB	Abdullah the Butcher	10.00	25.00
BB1	Bob Backlund	10.00	25.00
BB2	Brutus Beefcake	8.00	20.00
BB3	Buff Bagwell	8.00	20.00
BH1	Bobby Heenan	12.00	30.00
BH2	Bret Hart	40.00	80.00
BO1	Cowboy Bob Orton Jr.	8.00	20.00
BS1	Bruno Sammartino	15.00	40.00
DDP	Diamond Dallas Page	8.00	20.00
DS1	Dan Severn	6.00	15.00
GJG	Jimmy Garvin	6.00	15.00
GS1	George Steele	10.00	25.00
GV1	Greg Valentine	8.00	20.00
HH1	Hulk Hogan	60.00	120.00
HJ1	Hillbilly Jim	10.00	25.00
HTM	The Honky Tonk Man	10.00	25.00
IK1	Ivan Koloff	8.00	20.00
JP1	The Polish Hammer Ivan Putski	8.00	20.00
JD1	Hacksaw Jim Duggan	12.00	30.00

JH1	Jimmy Hart	10.00	25.00
JN1	Jim Neidhart	8.00	20.00
JR1	Jake Roberts	12.00	30.00
KA1	Kamala	8.00	20.00
KBW	Koko B. Ware	8.00	20.00
KN1	Kevin Nash	15.00	40.00
KS1	Ken Shamrock	8.00	20.00
LL1	Lex Luger	10.00	25.00
LP1	Lanny Poffo	6.00	15.00
LZ1	Larry Zbyszko	6.00	15.00
MH1	Missy Hyatt	6.00	15.00
MJ1	Marty Jannetty	6.00	15.00
NK1	Nikita Koloff	8.00	20.00
NV1	Nikolai Volkoff	8.00	20.00
OMG	One Man Gang	8.00	20.00
PO1	Paul Orndorff	10.00	25.00
PR1	Pete Rose	12.00	30.00
RM1	Rick Martel	6.00	15.00
RRP	Rowdy Roddy Piper	50.00	100.00
RS1	Rick Steiner	6.00	15.00
SBG	Billy Graham	25.00	50.00
SH1	Scott Hall	12.00	30.00
SID	Sid	8.00	20.00
SS1	Scott Steiner	8.00	20.00
TA1	Tony Atlas	6.00	15.00
TAT	Tatanka	8.00	20.00
TDB	Ted DiBiase	10.00	25.00
TIS	The Iron Sheik	10.00	25.00
TNB	Ric Flair	30.00	75.00
TS1	Tito Santana	8.00	20.00
VAD	Vader	10.00	25.00
WR1	Wendi Richter	8.00	20.00
PARWA	Road Warrior Animal LOS	30.00	75.00

2014 Leaf Originals Wrestling

UNOPENED BOX (5 CARDS)
*YELLOW/99: SAME VALUE AS BASIC AUTOS
*BLUE/25: .5X TO 1.2X BASIC AUTOS
*RED/10: UNPRICED DUE TO SCARCITY
*BLACK/1: UNPRICED DUE TO SCARCITY
*P.P.BLACK/1: UNPRICED DUE TO SCARCITY
*P.P.CYAN/1: UNPRICED DUE TO SCARCITY
*P.P.MAGENTA/1: UNPRICED DUE TO SCARCITY
*P.P.YELLOW/1: UNPRICED DUE TO SCARCITY
*ALT.ART./ .5X TO 1.2X BASIC AUTOS
*A.A.YELLOW/25: .6X TO 1.5X BASIC AUTOS
*A.A.BLUE/10: UNPRICED DUE TO SCARCITY
*A.A.RED/5: UNPRICED DUE TO SCARCITY
*A.A.BLACK/1: UNPRICED DUE TO SCARCITY
*A.A.P.P.BLACK/1: UNPRICED DUE TO SCARCITY
*A.A.P.P.CYAN/1: UNPRICED DUE TO SCARCITY
*A.A.P.P.MAGENTA/1: UNPRICED DUE TO SCARCITY
*A.A.P.P.YELLOW/1: UNPRICED DUE TO SCARCITY

AF1	Francine	5.00	12.00
AG1	Gangrel SP	6.00	15.00
AG2	Godfather	5.00	12.00
AG3	Goldberg	25.00	60.00
AM1	Maryse	6.00	15.00
AR1	Raven	5.00	12.00
AS1	Sabu	5.00	12.00
AS2	Samu	6.00	15.00
AS2	Sting	25.00	60.00
AS3	Sandman	5.00	12.00
AW1	Warlord	5.00	12.00
AZ1	Zeus	5.00	12.00
A2CS	2 Cold Scorpio SP	5.00	12.00
AAB1	Adam Bomb	5.00	12.00
AAS1	Al Snow	5.00	12.00

ABH1	Bob Holly	5.00	12.00
ABH1	Bobby Heenan SP	12.00	30.00
ABM1	Balls Mahoney	5.00	12.00
ABM1	Blue Meanie	5.00	12.00
ACM1	Candice Michelle SP	10.00	25.00
ADA1	Demolition Ax	5.00	12.00
ADK1	Dynamite Kid SP	12.00	30.00
ADM1	Don Muraco	5.00	12.00
ADR1	Dennis Rodman SP	15.00	40.00
ADS1	Demolition Smash	5.00	12.00
AGB1	Gerald Brisco	5.00	12.00
AHH1	Hulk Hogan SP	25.00	60.00
AIS1	Iron Sheik	6.00	15.00
AJD1	J.J. Dillon	5.00	12.00
AJH1	Jeff Hardy SP	10.00	25.00
AJR2	Jake Roberts SP	10.00	25.00
AKK1	Kelly Kelly	6.00	15.00
AKKB	King Kong Bundy	6.00	15.00
AKN1	Kevin Nash	8.00	20.00
AKP1	Ken Patera	5.00	12.00
AKVE	Kevin Von Erich	6.00	15.00
ALS1	Lance Storm	5.00	12.00
AMK1	Maria Kanellis	6.00	15.00
AMT1	Mike Tyson SP	80.00	150.00
AOA1	Ole Anderson	5.00	12.00
ARF1	Ric Flair SP	25.00	60.00
ARF2	Rikishi Fatu	10.00	25.00
ARG1	Robert Gibson	5.00	12.00
ARM1	Ricky Morton	5.00	12.00
ARP1	Roddy Piper SP	15.00	40.00
ARS1	Ron Simmons	6.00	15.00
ASH1	Scott Hall	15.00	40.00
ASR1	Stevie Ray SP	6.00	15.00
ATB1	The Barbarian	5.00	12.00
ATD1	Tommy Dreamer	5.00	12.00
ATF1	Terry Funk	8.00	20.00
ATNB	The Nasty Boys	8.00	20.00
ATS1	Trish Stratus	12.00	30.00
AVV1	Val Venis	5.00	12.00

2014 Leaf Originals Wrestling Flair's Epic Battles

*YELLOW/25: X TO X BASIC AUTO
*BLUE/10: UNPRICED DUE TO SCARCITY
*RED/5: UNPRICED DUE TO SCARCITY
*BLACK/1: UNPRICED DUE TO SCARCITY
*P.P.BLACK/1: UNPRICED DUE TO SCARCITY
*P.P.CYAN/1: UNPRICED DUE TO SCARCITY
*P.P.MAGENTA/1: UNPRICED DUE TO SCARCITY
*P.P.YELLOW/1: UNPRICED DUE TO SCARCITY

RFBH1	Ric Flair	80.00	150.00
	Bret Hart		
RFHH1	Ric Flair/Hulk Hogan	120.00	250.00
RFRM1	Ric Flair/Ricky Morton	20.00	50.00
RFRP1	Ric Flair/Roddy Piper	80.00	150.00

2017 Leaf Originals Wrestling Autographs

COMPLETE SET (17)
UNOPENED BOX (5 CARDS)
*YELLOW/99: .6X TO 1.5X BASIC AUTOS
*BLUE/25: .75X TO 2X BASIC AUTOS
*RED/10: 1X TO 2.5X BASIC CARDS
*BLACK/1: UNPRICED DUE TO SCARCITY
*ALT.ART: SAME VALUE AS BASIC AUTOS
*ALT.YELLOW/25: .75X TO 2X BASIC AUTOS
*ALT.BLUE/10: 1X TO 2.5X BASIC AUTOS
*ALT.RED/5: UNPRICED DUE TO SCARCITY
*ALT.BLACK/1: UNPRICED DUE TO SCARCITY

K1	Konnan	8.00	20.00
V2	Victoria	5.00	12.00
BB1	B. Brian Blair	5.00	12.00
BL1	Bobby Lashley	5.00	12.00
BW1	Barry Windham	6.00	15.00
DFJ	Dory Funk Jr.	6.00	15.00
DLB	D'Lo Brown	5.00	12.00
DM2	Dutch Mantel	5.00	12.00
JR1	Jacques Rougeau	5.00	12.00
JR2	Jim Ross	8.00	20.00
LK1	Leilani Kai	5.00	12.00
MF1	Manny Fernandez	5.00	12.00
MM1	Marc Mero	5.00	12.00
MVP	MVP	6.00	15.00
SB1	Shelton Benjamin	6.00	15.00
SD1	Shane Douglas	5.00	12.00
TW1	Torrie Wilson	8.00	20.00

2017 Leaf Originals Wrestling '14 Design Autographs

*YELLOW/50-99: .6X TO 1.5X BASIC AUTOS
*BLUE/25: .75X TO 2X BASIC AUTOS
*RED/10: 1X TO 2.5X BASIC AUTOS
*BLACK/1: UNPRICED DUE TO SCARCITY
*P.P.BLACK/1: UNPRICED DUE TO SCARCITY
*P.P.CYAN/1: UNPRICED DUE TO SCARCITY
*P.P.MAGENTA/1: UNPRICED DUE TO SCARCITY
*P.P.YELLOW/1: UNPRICED DUE TO SCARCITY
*ALT.ART: SAME VALUE AS BASIC AUTOS
*ALT.YELLOW/25: .75X TO 2X BASIC AUTOS
*ALT.BLUE/10: 1X TO 2.5X BASIC AUTOS
*ALT.RED/5: UNPRICED DUE TO SCARCITY
*ALT.BLACK/1: UNPRICED DUE TO SCARCITY
*ALT.P.P.BLACK/1: UNPRICED DUE TO SCARCITY
*ALT.P.P.CYAN/1: UNPRICED DUE TO SCARCITY
*ALT.P.P.MAGENTA/1: UNPRICED DUE TO SCARCITY
*ALT.P.P.YELLOW/1: UNPRICED DUE TO SCARCITY

C1	Chyna	20.00	50.00
H1	Haku	6.00	15.00
S1	Slick	5.00	12.00
BE1	Bobby Eaton	5.00	12.00
BG1	Billy Gunn	5.00	12.00
BH2	Bret Hart	15.00	40.00
BR1	Butch Reed	5.00	12.00
BT1	Booker T	8.00	20.00
CH1	Christy Hemme	6.00	15.00
CJ1	Chris Jericho	8.00	20.00
DC1	Dennis Condrey	5.00	12.00
DH1	Danny Hodge	6.00	15.00
EB1	Eric Bischoff	5.00	12.00
JC1	Jim Cornette	6.00	15.00
JJ1	Jeff Jarrett	6.00	15.00
JL1	Jushin Liger	8.00	20.00
KS1	Kevin Sullivan	5.00	12.00
MF1	Mick Foley	8.00	20.00
MH1	Matt Hardy	5.00	12.00
RVD	Rob Van Dam	5.00	12.00
TB1	Tully Blanchard	5.00	12.00
TR1	Terri Runnels	6.00	15.00
WS1	Wild Samoans	8.00	20.00
XP1	X-Pac	6.00	15.00

2017 Leaf Originals Wrestling '16 Design Autographs

COMPLETE SET (2)

*YELLOW/50: .6X TO 1.5X BASIC AUTOS
*BLUE/25: .75X TO 2X BASIC AUTOS
*RED/10: 1X TO 2.5X BASIC AUTOS
*BLACK/1: UNPRICED DUE TO SCARCITY
*ALT.ART: SAME VALUE AS BASIC AUTOS
*ALT.YELLOW/25: .75X TO 2X BASIC AUTOS
*ALT.BLUE/10: 1X TO 2.5X BASIC AUTOS
*ALT.RED/5: UNPRICED DUE TO SCARCITY
*ALT.BLACK/1: UNPRICED DUE TO SCARCITY

| HH1 | Hulk Hogan | 20.00 | 50.00 |
| KS1 | Kazushi Sakuraba | 12.00 | 30.00 |

2016 Leaf Signature Series Wrestling

UNOPENED BOX (8 CARDS)
*BLUE/7-50: UNPRICED DUE TO SCARCITY
*GREEN/5-25: UNPRICED DUE TO SCARCITY
*RED/3-10: UNPRICED DUE TO SCARCITY
*BLACK/2-5: UNPRICED DUE TO SCARCITY
*PURPLE/1: UNPRICED DUE TO SCARCITY
*P.P.BLACK/1: UNPRICED DUE TO SCARCITY
*P.P.CYAN/1: UNPRICED DUE TO SCARCITY
*P.P.MAGENTA/1: UNPRICED DUE TO SCARCITY
*P.P.BLACK/1: UNPRICED DUE TO SCARCITY

1	6-Pac	8.00	20.00
2	Adam Bomb	8.00	20.00
3	Adam Pearce	8.00	20.00
4	Al Snow	6.00	15.00
5	Balls Mahoney	10.00	25.00
6	The Barbarian	8.00	20.00
7	Barry Windham	10.00	25.00
8	Goldberg	25.00	60.00
9	Blue Meanie	8.00	20.00
10	Bob Holly	6.00	15.00
11	Bobby Heenan	30.00	75.00
12	Bolo Mongol	10.00	25.00
	Demolition Ax		
13	Brutus Beefcake	8.00	20.00
14	Bushwacker Luke	8.00	20.00
15	Carlito	6.00	15.00
16	Carlos Colon	10.00	25.00
17	Chris Masters	6.00	15.00
18	Christopher Daniels	6.00	15.00
19	Christy Hemme	12.00	30.00
20	Debra McMichael	10.00	25.00
21	Dennis Condrey	6.00	15.00
22	Dennis Rodman	15.00	40.00
23	Dynamite Kid	10.00	25.00
24	Ezekiel Jackson	6.00	15.00
25	Fifi the Maid	10.00	25.00
	Wendy Barlow		
26	Francine	10.00	25.00
27	Frankie Kazarian	6.00	15.00
28	Gangrel	6.00	15.00
29	Greg Valentine	10.00	25.00
30	Harley Race	12.00	30.00
31	Headshrinker Fatu	8.00	20.00
32	Hulk Hogan	30.00	80.00
33	Jeff Jarrett	10.00	25.00
34	Gerald Brisco	6.00	15.00
35	Jesus	6.00	15.00
36	Jimmy Garvin	6.00	15.00
37	Jimmy Hart	8.00	20.00
38	J.J. Dillon	8.00	20.00
39	Jushin Liger	15.00	40.00
40	Kama	6.00	15.00
	Kama Mustafa		

41	Kamala	8.00	20.00
42	Kelly Kelly	15.00	40.00
43	Ken Patera	8.00	20.00
44	Kevin Nash	10.00	25.00
45	Kevin Sullivan	10.00	25.00
46	King Kong Bundy	10.00	25.00
47	King Mo	6.00	15.00
48	Lanny Poffo	6.00	15.00
49	Larry Zbyszko	8.00	20.00
50	Lita	15.00	40.00
51	Maria Kanellis	10.00	25.00
52	Marlena	12.00	30.00
53	Masato Tanaka	8.00	20.00
54	Matt Hardy	8.00	20.00
55	Matt Striker	6.00	15.00
56	Mike Tyson	50.00	100.00
57	Mil Mascaras	30.00	80.00
58	Nick Bockwinkel	30.00	75.00
59	Nikita Koloff	8.00	20.00
60	Nikolai Volkoff	8.00	20.00
61	Ole Anderson	10.00	25.00
62	Papa Shango	8.00	20.00
63	Pat Tanaka	6.00	15.00
64	Pete Rose	15.00	40.00
65	Reby Sky	8.00	20.00
66	Repo Man	12.00	30.00
67	Ric Flair	20.00	50.00
68	Rick Steiner	10.00	25.00
69	Ricky Morton	8.00	20.00
70	Robert Gibson	8.00	20.00
71	Ron Simmons	8.00	20.00
72	Sabu	8.00	20.00
73	Samu	6.00	15.00
74	Scott Hall	15.00	40.00
75	Scott Norton	6.00	15.00
76	Sid Vicious	10.00	25.00
77	Steve Corino	6.00	15.00
78	Stevie Ray	8.00	20.00
79	Sunny	12.00	30.00
80	Terri Runnels	10.00	25.00
81	The Godfather	6.00	15.00
82	Iron Sheik	12.00	30.00
83	Tito Santana	10.00	25.00
84	Tommy Dreamer	8.00	20.00
85	Tully Blanchard	10.00	25.00
86	Val Venis	6.00	15.00
87	Warlord	6.00	15.00
88	Wendi Richter	15.00	40.00
89	Wrath	8.00	20.00
90	X-Pac	8.00	20.00
91	Zeus	12.00	30.00
92	Zodiac	8.00	20.00

2016 Leaf Signature Series Wrestling Adversaries

*BLUE/15-25: UNPRICED DUE TO SCARCITY
*GREEN/10: UNPRICED DUE TO SCARCITY
*RED/5: UNPRICED DUE TO SCARCITY
*BLACK/3: UNPRICED DUE TO SCARCITY
*PURPLE/1: UNPRICED DUE TO SCARCITY
*P.P.BLACK/1: UNPRICED DUE TO SCARCITY
*P.P.CYAN/1: UNPRICED DUE TO SCARCITY
*P.P.MAGENTA/1: UNPRICED DUE TO SCARCITY
*P.P.YELLOW/1: UNPRICED DUE TO SCARCITY
RANDOMLY INSERTED INTO PACKS

ADV01	S.Corino/T.Funk	15.00	40.00
ADV02	R.Flair/J.Garvin	20.00	50.00
ADV03	123 Kid/S.Hall	12.00	30.00

ADV05	B.Windham/B.Beefcake	12.00	30.00
ADV06	B.Eaton/R.Morton	12.00	30.00
ADV07	Carlito/Sabu	10.00	25.00
ADV09	S.Douglas/C.Daniels	10.00	25.00
ADV10	C.Hemme/V.Sky	20.00	50.00
ADV11	T.Dreamer/Francine	15.00	40.00
ADV12	Raven /F.Kazarian	10.00	25.00
ADV13	Animal/K.Sullivan	12.00	30.00
ADV14	Sandman/M.Striker	10.00	25.00
ADV15	Bushwacker Luke/P.Tanaka	12.00	30.00
ADV16	T.Dreamer/Sabu	15.00	40.00
ADV17	Zeus/H.Hogan	60.00	120.00

2016 Leaf Signature Series Wrestling Hall of Fame

*BLUE/15-50: UNPRICED DUE TO SCARCITY
*GREEN/10-25: UNPRICED DUE TO SCARCITY
*RED/5-10: UNPRICED DUE TO SCARCITY
*BLACK/3-5: UNPRICED DUE TO SCARCITY
*PURPLE/1: UNPRICED DUE TO SCARCITY
*P.P.BLACK/1: UNPRICED DUE TO SCARCITY
*P.P.CYAN/1: UNPRICED DUE TO SCARCITY
*P.P.MAGENTA/1: UNPRICED DUE TO SCARCITY
*P.P.YELLOW/1: UNPRICED DUE TO SCARCITY
RANDOMLY INSERTED INTO PACKS

HOF01	Bobby Heenan	20.00	50.00
HOF02	Carlos Colon	10.00	25.00
HOF03	Iron Sheik	10.00	25.00
HOF04	Wendi Richter	10.00	25.00
HOF05	Ron Simmons	10.00	25.00
HOF06	Nick Bockwinkel	50.00	100.00
HOF07	Ric Flair	25.00	60.00
HOF08	Mil Mascaras	30.00	80.00
HOF09	Harley Race	12.00	30.00
HOF10	Pete Rose	15.00	40.00
HOF11	Mike Tyson	50.00	100.00

2016 Leaf Signature Series Wrestling Ring Showdowns

*BLUE/7-50: UNPRICED DUE TO SCARCITY
*GREEN/5-10: UNPRICED DUE TO SCARCITY
*RED/3-5: UNPRICED DUE TO SCARCITY
*BLACK/2-3: UNPRICED DUE TO SCARCITY
*PURPLE/1: UNPRICED DUE TO SCARCITY
*P.P.BLACK/1: UNPRICED DUE TO SCARCITY
*P.P.CYAN/1: UNPRICED DUE TO SCARCITY
*P.P.MAGENTA/1: UNPRICED DUE TO SCARCITY
*P.P.YELLOW/1: UNPRICED DUE TO SCARCITY
RANDOMLY INSERTED INTO PACKS

RS201	Steve Corino/Greg Valentine	12.00	30.00
RS202	B.Bagwell/S.Norton	10.00	25.00
RS203	X-Pac /V.Venis	10.00	25.00
RS204	123 Kid/P.Tanaka	10.00	25.00
RS206	A.Bomb/Virgil	8.00	20.00
RS207	A.Snow/Raven	10.00	25.00
RS208	B.Mahoney/Sabu	15.00	40.00
RS209	Gangrel/Blue Meanie	10.00	25.00
RS210	H.Hogan/B.Beefcake	25.00	60.00
RS211	B.Beefcake/Masked Superstar	20.00	50.00
RS213	X-Pac /Gangrel	8.00	20.00
RS214	Gangrel /Godfather	8.00	20.00
RS215	K.Patera/T.Atlas	12.00	30.00
RS216	M.Bennett/S.Richards	8.00	20.00
RS217	M.Hardy/M.Bennett	12.00	30.00
RS218	R.Steiner/Vincent	8.00	20.00
RS219	K.Nash/R.Steiner	15.00	40.00
RS220	K.Nash/S.Vicious	15.00	40.00

RS222	T.Runnels/S.Richards	10.00	25.00
RS224	H.Hogan/D.Rodman	50.00	100.00

2016 Leaf Signature Series Wrestling Team Effort

*BLUE/7-50: UNPRICED DUE TO SCARCITY
*GREEN/5-25: UNPRICED DUE TO SCARCITY
*RED/3-10: UNPRICED DUE TO SCARCITY
*BLACK/2-5: UNPRICED DUE TO SCARCITY
*PURPLE/1: UNPRICED DUE TO SCARCITY
*P.P.BLACK/1: UNPRICED DUE TO SCARCITY
*P.P.CYAN/1: UNPRICED DUE TO SCARCITY
*P.P.MAGENTA/1: UNPRICED DUE TO SCARCITY
*P.P.YELLOW/1: UNPRICED DUE TO SCARCITY
RANDOMLY INSERTED INTO PACKS

TE01	S.Corino/A.Pearce	12.00	30.00
TE02	K.Patera/S.Norton	10.00	25.00
TE03	Konnan/S.Norton	20.00	50.00
TE05	J.Garvin/Precious	15.00	40.00
TE06	Ax/Smash	20.00	50.00
TE08	B.Eaton/D.Condrey	12.00	30.00
TE09	S.Lane/B.Eaton	12.00	30.00
TE10	S.Too Hotty/B.Christopher	15.00	40.00
TE11	B.Knobbs/J.Sags	12.00	30.00
TE13	J.Cornette/D.Condrey	10.00	25.00
TE14	Kama/Tatanka	10.00	25.00
TE15	C.Michelle/K.Kelly	12.00	30.00
TE16	N.Koloff/K.Kruschev	15.00	40.00
TE18	T.Runnels/V.Venis	15.00	40.00
TE19	N.Jackson/M.Jackson	8.00	20.00
TE20	M.Kanellis/M.Bennett	15.00	40.00
TE21	R.Steiner/S.Steiner	20.00	50.00
TE22	R.Morton/R.Gibson	12.00	30.00
TE23	Rikishi Fatu Samu	8.00	20.00
TE24	Tori/X-Pac	12.00	30.00

2020 Leaf Ultimate Wrestling Ultimate Stars Autographs

*PURPLE/45>: X TO X BASIC AUTOS
*PLATINUM/25>: UNPRICED DUE TO SCARCITY
*RED/10>: UNPRICED DUE TO SCARCITY
*EMERALD/5>: UNPRICED DUE TO SCARCITY
*SILVER/3>: UNPRICED DUE TO SCARCITY
*GOLD/1: UNPRICED DUE TO SCARCITY
*P.P.BLACK/1: UNPRICED DUE TO SCARCITY
*P.P.CYAN/1: UNPRICED DUE TO SCARCITY
*P.P.MAGENTA/1: UNPRICED DUE TO SCARCITY
*P.P.YELLOW/1: UNPRICED DUE TO SCARCITY

USE1	Edge	12.00	30.00
USG1	Goldberg	25.00	60.00
USK1	Kamala	10.00	25.00
UST1	Tugboat/Typhoon/Shockmaster	20.00	50.00
USW1	Warlord	8.00	20.00
USAA1	Arn Anderson	12.00	30.00
USAP1	Adam Page	15.00	40.00
USBB1	Britt Baker	12.00	30.00
USBB1	Brutus Beefcake	6.00	15.00
USBH1	Bret Hart	15.00	40.00
USBL1	Brother Love	8.00	20.00
USBOJ	Bob Orton Jr.	6.00	15.00
USBP1	Brian Pillman Jr.	6.00	15.00
USBV1	Baron Von Raschke	10.00	25.00
USBW1	Barry Windham	10.00	25.00
USCC1	Colt Cabana	6.00	15.00
USCM1	Cima	5.00	12.00
USCR1	Cody Rhodes	15.00	40.00

USDA1	Demolition Ax	8.00	20.00
USDF1	Don Frye	6.00	15.00
USDS1	Demolition Smash	12.00	30.00
USEB1	Eric Bischoff	10.00	25.00
USED1	El Hijo del Fantasma	6.00	15.00
USFG1	Flip Gordon	5.00	12.00
USFL1	Flamita	5.00	12.00
USFU1	Funaki	6.00	15.00
USGM1	The Great Muta	15.00	40.00
USHH1	Hulk Hogan	60.00	120.00
USHT1	Hiroshi Tanahashi	8.00	20.00
USHTM	The Honky Tonk Man	10.00	25.00
USJB1	Josh Barnett	10.00	25.00
USJH1	Jimmy Hart	8.00	20.00
USJL1	Jushin Liger	15.00	40.00
USKBW	Koko B. Ware	10.00	25.00
USKI1	Kota Ibushi	15.00	40.00
USKO1	Kenny Omega	15.00	40.00
USKS1	Ken Shamrock	15.00	40.00
USLH1	Larry Hennig	10.00	25.00
USMF1	Manny Fernandez	6.00	15.00
USMF1	Mick Foley	15.00	40.00
USMS1	Minoru Suzuki	10.00	25.00
USPE1	Penta El Zero M	10.00	25.00
USPF1	Penelope Ford	10.00	25.00
USPS1	Perry Saturn	5.00	12.00
USRF1	Ric Flair	25.00	60.00
USRS1	Ricky Steamboat	10.00	25.00
USSS1	Sumie Sakai	5.00	12.00
USSV1	Sid Vicious	6.00	15.00
USTA1	Tony Atlas	6.00	15.00
USTB1	The Barbarian	6.00	15.00
USTB1	Tully Blanchard	10.00	25.00
USTD1	Ted DiBiase	10.00	25.00
USTF1	Terry Funk	15.00	40.00
USTS1	Tito Santana	8.00	20.00
USTZ1	Tazz	8.00	20.00
USVP1	Vampiro	8.00	20.00
USYH1	Yoshi-Hashi	6.00	15.00

2020 Leaf Ultimate Wrestling Clearly Dominant Autographs

COMPLETE SET (14)
*PINK/10-15: UNPRICED DUE TO SCARCITY
*PLATINUM/10: UNPRICED DUE TO SCARCITY
*GREEN/4-6: UNPRICED DUE TO SCARCITY
*RED/3-5: UNPRICED DUE TO SCARCITY
*SILVER/2-3: UNPRICED DUE TO SCARCITY
*GOLD/1: UNPRICED DUE TO SCARCITY
STATED PRINT RUN 25 SER.#'d SETS

CDG1	Goldberg	20.00	50.00
CDAA1	Arn Anderson	15.00	40.00
CDBH1	Bret Hart	20.00	50.00
CDCJ1	Chris Jericho	15.00	40.00
CDGM1	The Great Muta	30.00	75.00
CDHH1	Hulk Hogan	75.00	150.00
CDHT1	Hiroshi Tanahashi	12.00	30.00
CDJL1	Jushin Liger	20.00	50.00
CDJV1	Jesse Ventura		
CDKK1	Kenta Kobashi	25.00	60.00
CDKN1	Kevin Nash	12.00	30.00
CDKO1	Kenny Omega	25.00	60.00
CDMF1	Mick Foley	15.00	40.00
CDRF1	Ric Flair	50.00	100.00

2020 Leaf Ultimate Wrestling Enshrined Autographs

COMPLETE SET (9)
*PURPLE/35>: UNPRICED DUE TO SCARCITY
*PLATINUM/10-15: UNPRICED DUE TO SCARCITY
*RED/7-10: UNPRICED DUE TO SCARCITY
*EMERALD/5: UNPRICED DUE TO SCARCITY
*SILVER/3: UNPRICED DUE TO SCARCITY
*GOLD/1: UNPRICED DUE TO SCARCITY
*P.P.BLACK/1: UNPRICED DUE TO SCARCITY
*P.P.CYAN/1: UNPRICED DUE TO SCARCITY
*P.P.MAGENTA/1: UNPRICED DUE TO SCARCITY
*P.P.YELLOW/1: UNPRICED DUE TO SCARCITY
RANDOMLY INSERTED INTO PACKS

EBB1	Brutus Beefcake	6.00	15.00
EBH1	Bret Hart	15.00	40.00
EBOJ	Bob Orton Jr.	8.00	20.00
EHH1	Hulk Hogan	50.00	100.00
EJH1	Jimmy Hart	6.00	15.00
EKBW	Koko B. Ware	6.00	15.00
EKN1	Kevin Nash	10.00	25.00
ERS1	Ricky Steamboat	12.00	30.00
ETA1	Tony Atlas	6.00	15.00

2020 Leaf Ultimate Wrestling Ultimate Ring Queens Autographs

COMPLETE SET (9)
*PURPLE/6-25: UNPRICED DUE TO SCARCITY
*PLATINUM/5-10: UNPRICED DUE TO SCARCITY
*RED/4-7: UNPRICED DUE TO SCARCITY
*EMERALD/3-5: UNPRICED DUE TO SCARCITY
*SILVER/2-3: UNPRICED DUE TO SCARCITY
*GOLD/1: UNPRICED DUE TO SCARCITY
*P.P.BLACK/1: UNPRICED DUE TO SCARCITY
*P.P.CYAN/1: UNPRICED DUE TO SCARCITY
*P.P.MAGENTA/1: UNPRICED DUE TO SCARCITY
*P.P.YELLOW/1: UNPRICED DUE TO SCARCITY
RANDOMLY INSERTED INTO PACKS

RQBB1	Britt Baker	12.00	40.00
RQBR1	Brandi Rhodes	15.00	40.00
RQIV1	Ivelisse	8.00	20.00
RQJH1	Jackie Haas	8.00	20.00
RQPF1	Penelope Ford	12.00	30.00
RQRS1	Ryan Shamrock		
RQSB1	Scarlett Bordeaux	25.00	60.00
RQTB1	Tessa Blanchard	15.00	40.00
RQVI1	Victoria	6.00	15.00

2020 Leaf Ultimate Wrestling Ultimate Signatures 2

COMPLETE SET (21)
*PURPLE/40>: X TO X BASIC AUTOS
*PLATINUM/25>: UNPRICED DUE TO SCARCITY
*RED/15>: UNPRICED DUE TO SCARCITY
*EMERALD/5>: UNPRICED DUE TO SCARCITY
*SILVER/2-3: UNPRICED DUE TO SCARCITY
*GOLD/1: UNPRICED DUE TO SCARCITY
*P.P.BLACK/1: UNPRICED DUE TO SCARCITY
*P.P.CYAN/1: UNPRICED DUE TO SCARCITY
*P.P.MAGENTA/1: UNPRICED DUE TO SCARCITY
*P.P.YELLOW/1: UNPRICED DUE TO SCARCITY
RANDOMLY INSERTED INTO PACKS

US201	Ax/Smash	20.00	50.00
US202	Barbarian/Warlord	15.00	40.00
US203	B.Baker/P.Ford	25.00	60.00
US204	B.Beefcake/H.Hogan	60.00	120.00
US205	C.Cabana/T.Yano	15.00	40.00

US206	K.Omega/Cima	20.00	50.00
US207	E.Bischoff/T.Funk	20.00	50.00
US208	Honky Tonk Man/J.B. Badd	10.00	25.00
US209	T.DiBiase/J.Hart	12:00	30.00
US210	K.B. Ware/Bushwacker Luke	12.00	30.00
US211	S.Vicious/Vampiro	12.00	30.00
US212	Tazz/Funaki	12.00	30.00
US213	Tully & Tessa Blanchard	25.00	60.00
US214	T.Santana/T.DiBiase	15.00	40.00
US215	K.B. Ware/Warlord	10.00	25.00
US216	M.Foley/Edge	20.00	50.00
US217	Kat/Victoria	10.00	25.00
US218	Victoria/B.Reed	10.00	25.00
US219	T.Tonga/T.Loa	12.00	30.00
US220	A.Page/Y.Takahashi	15.00	40.00
US221	H.Hogan/D.Rodman	100.00	200.00

2020 Leaf Ultimate Wrestling Ultimate Signatures 4

COMPLETE SET (2)
*PURPLE/10-25: UNPRICED DUE TO SCARCITY
*PLATINUM/7-10: UNPRICED DUE TO SCARCITY
*RED/6-7: UNPRICED DUE TO SCARCITY
*EMERALD/4-5: UNPRICED DUE TO SCARCITY
*SILVER/3: UNPRICED DUE TO SCARCITY
*GOLD/1: UNPRICED DUE TO SCARCITY
*P.P.BLACK/1: UNPRICED DUE TO SCARCITY
*P.P.CYAN/1: UNPRICED DUE TO SCARCITY
*P.P.MAGENTA/1: UNPRICED DUE TO SCARCITY
*P.P.YELLOW/1: UNPRICED DUE TO SCARCITY
RANDOMLY INSERTED INTO PACKS

US401	Anderson/Blanchard/Flair/Windham		
US402	Barbarian/Warlord/Ax/Smash	60.00	120.00

1999 Little Caesar's WCW/nWo Lenticular

COMPLETE SET (4)		3.00	8.00
NNO	Diamond Dallas Page	1.25	3.00
NNO	Goldberg	2.50	6.00
NNO	Hollywood Hogan	2.00	5.00
NNO	Sting	2.50	6.00

2009 Mad Butcher WWE Slam Series

COMPLETE SET (36)
1 Finlay
2 Triple H
3 Big Show
4 Edge
5 Carlito
6 Primo Colon
7 Umaga
8 Brian Kendrick
9 Mr. Kennedy
10 Shelton Benjamin
11 Undertaker
12 Michelle McCool
13 Eve
14 Maria
15 John Morrison
16 Matt Hardy
17 John Cena
18 William Regal
19 Batista
20 Rey Mysterio
21 Santino
22 Shawn Michaels
23 Chris Jericho
24 Randy Orton
25 Kane
26 Kofi Kingston
27 CM Punk
28 Mickie James
29 Candice Michelle
30 Beth Phoenix
31 Undertaker
32 Triple H
33 Shelton Benjamin
34 Rey Mysterio
35 John Cena
36 Batista

1989 Market-Scene WWF Bubblegum Super Stars of Wrestling Series 1

COMPLETE SET (21)
1 Bret The Hitman Hart
2 Andre The Giant
3 Jake The Snake
4 Big Boss Man
5 Bad News Brown
6 Barbarian
7 Demolition
8 Bush Wackers
9 Rockers
10 Miss Elizabeth
11 Bobby The Brain Heenan
12 Sensational Sherri
13 Akeem
14 Virgil
15 Brutus The Barber Beefcake
16 Jimmy Hart
17 Honky Tonk Man
18 Brother Love
19 Hercules
20 Rougeau Brothers
NNO Series One Directory (Checklist)

1989 Market-Scene WWF Bubblegum Super Stars of Wrestling Series 2

COMPLETE SET (21)
1 Hulk Hogan
2 Brain Busters
3 Jim The Anvil Neidhart
4 Haku
5 The Million Dollar Man Ted DiBiase
6 Tito Santana
7 Slickster (Slick)
8 Ravishing Rick Rude
9 Dino Bravo
10 Greg The Hammer Valentine
11 Mr. Perfect
12 Koko B. Ware
13 King Duggan (Hacksaw)
14 Jim Powers
15 Brooklyn Brawler
16 Superfly Snuka
17 Paul Roma
18 Red Rooster
19 Rugged Ronnie Garvin
20 Hillbilly Jim
NNO Series Two Directory (Checklist)

1989-90 Market-Scene WWF Bubblegum Super Stars of Wrestling Series 3 Version 1

COMPLETE SET (21)
1 Warlord
2 Zeus
3 Sean Mooney
4 Hulk Hogan Starring as RIP
5 Macho King Randy Savage
6 Dusty Rhodes
7 The Powers of Pain
8 The Hart Foundation
9 Mr. Fuji
10 Rowdy Roddy Piper
11 The Ultimate Warrior
12 Rick The Model Martel
13 The Widow Maker
14 Twin Towers
15 The Genius
16 Danny Davis
17 Mean Gene Okerland
18 Gorilla Monsoon
19 Barry Horowitz
20 Jack Tunney
NNO Series Three Directory (Checklist)

1990 Market-Scene WWF Bubblegum Super Stars of Wrestling Series 3 Version 2

COMPLETE SET (21)
1 Demolition
2 Earthquake
3 Sean Mooney
4 Hulk Hogan Starring as RIP
5 Macho King Randy Savage
6 Dusty Rhodes
7 Andre The Giant
8 The Hart Foundation
9 Mr. Fuji
10 Rowdy Roddy Piper
11 The Ultimate Warrior
12 Widow Maker
13 Rick The Model Martel
14 Akeem
15 The Genius
16 Danny Davis
17 Gene Okerland
18 Gorilla Monsoon
19 Barry Horowitz
20 Jack Tunney
NNO Series Three Directory (Checklist)

1989 Market-Scene Superstars of Wrestling Postcards

COMPLETE SET (10)
NNO Brutus The Barber Beefcake
NNO Bushwhackers
NNO Dusty Rhodes
NNO Hacksaw Jim Duggan
NNO Hulk Hogan
NNO Jake the Snake
NNO Macho Man Randy Savage
NNO Ravishing Rick Rude
NNO Rockers
NNO Ultimate Warrior

1991 Mello Smello WWF Stickers

COMPLETE SET (6)		15.00	40.00
1	Hulk Hogan	10.00	25.00
2	The Bushwhackers	3.00	8.00
3	Big Boss Man	3.00	8.00
4	The Ultimate Warrior	6.00	15.00
5	The Legion of Doom	6.00	15.00
6	Jake The Snake Roberts	4.00	10.00

2006 Merlin WWE Champions Stickers

COMPLETE SET (250)
1 WWE Logo (lg)
2 Raw Logo (Foil)
3 SmackDown! Logo (Foil)
4 Spirit Squad
5 Mickie James
6 Shelton Benjamin
7 Triple H
8 Big Show
9 John Cena (lg)
10 Kane (Foil)
11 Ric Flair
12 Jim Ross
13 Stone Cold Steve Austin
14 Hulk Hogan
15 Edge
16 Batista
17 Lita
18 JBL
19 Gregory Helms
20 Paul London
21 Brian Kendrick
22 Rey Mysterio (lg)
23 Undertaker
24 Chris Benoit (Foil)
25 Kurt Angle
26 Randy Orton
27 Booker T
28 Boogeyman
29 Paul Burchill
30 Judgment Day Logo (Foil)
31 John Cena
32 JBL
33 John Cena
34 Eddie Guerrero
35 Rey Mysterio (lg)
36 Eddie Guerrero
37 Rey Mysterio
38 Booker T (lg)
39 Kurt Angle
40 Chavo Guerrero
41 Chavo Guerrero
42 Paul London
43 ECW One Night Stand (Foil)
44 Eddie Guerrero
45 Chris Benoit
46 Eddie Guerrero
47 Rey Mysterio
48 Psicosis (lg)
49 Nunzio
50 Super Crazy
51 Nunzio (lg)
52 Tajiri
53 RVD
54 RVD
55 Paul Heyman

56 Vengeance Logo (Foil)
57 Batista
58 Triple H
59 Batista (Ig)
60 Triple H
61 Carlito
62 Shelton Benjamin
63 Carlito
64 Shawn Michaels (Ig)
65 Kurt Angle
66 Kane
67 Edge (Foil)
68 Kane
69 Great American Bash Logo (Foil)
70 JBL
71 Batista
72 Batista
73 JBL
74 JBL (Ig)
75 JBL
76 Melina
77 Torrie Wilson (Ig)
78 Melina
79 Torrie Wilson
80 Melina
81 Torrie Wilson
82 SummerSlam Logo (Foil)
83 Shawn Michaels
84 Hulk Hogan
85 Hulk Hogan
86 Randy Orton (Foil)
87 Undertaker (Ig)
88 Randy Orton
89 Kurt Angle
90 Eugene (Ig)
91 Edge
92 Matt Hardy
93 Edge
94 Matt Hardy
95 Unforgiven Logo (Foil)
96 John Cena
97 Kurt Angle
98 John Cena
99 Carlito (Ig)
100 Ric Flair (Foil)
101 Ric Flair
102 Big Show (Ig)
103 Snitsky
104 Trish & Ashley
105 Victoria, Torrie, & Candice
106 Torrie Wilson
107 No Mercy Logo (Foil)
108 Batista
109 Eddie Guerrero
110 Batista
111 Eddie Guerrero
112 Randy Orton (Ig)
113 Undertaker
114 Randy Orton
115 Undertaker (Ig)
116 Bobby Lashley
117 Simon Dean
118 Simon Dean
119 Bobby Lashley
120 John Cena (Ig)
121 Rey Mysterio (Ig)
122 Batista (Foil)
123 Triple H

124 Kurt Angle (Foil)
125 Ric Flair
126 RVD
127 Chris Benoit
128 Big Show & Kane
129 MNM
130 Trish Stratus
131 Nunzio
132 Gregory Helms
133 Taboo Tuesday Logo (Foil)
134 John Cena
135 Kurt Angle
136 Kurt Angle
137 Ric Flair
138 Triple H
139 Ric Flair
140 Triple H
141 Mick Foley
142 Carlito
143 Divas Battle Royal
144 Divas Battle Royal (Ig)
145 Survivor Series Logo (Foil)
146 Shawn Michaels
147 Kane
148 Big Show (Foil)
149 Carlito
150 Chris Masters
151 Batista
152 Randy Orton
153 JBL (Ig)
154 Rey Mysterio (Foil)
155 Bobby Lashley
156 Shawn Michaels
157 Team Raw vs Team SmackDown!
158 Armageddon Logo (Foil)
159 Undertaker
160 Randy Orton
161 Undertaker
162 Randy Orton
163 Rey Mysterio & Batista (Ig)
164 Kane and Big Show
165 Kane
166 Chris Benoit
167 Booker T
168 Chris Benoit
169 Matt Hardy
170 JBL (Ig)
171 Revolution Logo (Foil)
172 John Cena
173 Shawn Michaels
174 Kurt Angle
175 Chris Masters
176 Carlito (Ig)
177 Kane
178 John Cena
179 John Cena
180 Edge
181 Big Show
182 Triple H
183 Big Show (Ig)
184 Royal Rumble Logo (Foil)
185 Joey Mercury
186 Chris Benoit
187 Chris Masters
188 Viscera
189 Rey Mysterio (Ig)
190 Shawn Michaels
191 Viscera

192 RVD
193 Big Show
194 Jonathan Coachman
195 Rey Mysterio
196 Rey Mysterio (Ig)
197 No Way Out Logo (Foil)
198 Kurt Angle
199 Undertaker
200 Kurt Angle
201 Randy Orton
202 Rey Mysterio
203 Randy Orton
204 Tatanka & Matt Hardy
205 Nitro & Mercury (Ig)
206 Tatanka
207 JBL
208 Bobby Lashley
209 JBL (Ig)
210 WrestleMania 22 Logo (Foil)
211 John Cena
212 Triple H (Foil)
213 John Cena
214 Rey Mysterio
215 Randy Orton (Ig)
216 Kurt Angle
217 Rey Mysterio
218 Booker T (Foil)
219 Boogeyman
220 Boogeyman
221 Booker T
222 Boogeyman (Ig)
223 Judgment Day Logo (Foil)
224 Rey Mysterio
225 JBL
226 Rey Mysterio
227 JBL
228 MNM (Ig)
229 Johnny Nitro
230 London & Kendrick
231 Bobby Lashley
232 Booker T
233 Booker T
234 Bobby Lashley (Ig)
235 ECW Logo (Foil)
236 RVD
237 John Cena
238 RVD
239 RVD
240 Sabu (Ig)
241 Rey Mysterio
242 Rey Mysterio
243 Sabu
244 Tazz
245 Jerry Lawler (Foil)
246 Tazz (Ig)
247 Rey Mysterio
248 Randy Orton
249 Kurt Angle
250 Rey Mysterio (Ig)

2006 Merlin WWE Champions Stickers Rey Mysterio

COMPLETE SET (10)
RANDOMLY INSERTED INTO PACKS

R1 Mysterio vs Angle (Ig)
R2 Mysterio vs Angle (Ig)
R3 Mysterio vs Angle (Ig)
R4 Mysterio vs Khali (Ig)

R5 Mysterio vs Henry
R6 Rey Mysterio
R7 Mysterio vs Kane
R8 Mysterio Posing
R9 Mysterio vs Finlay
R10 Mysterio vs. JBL

2008 Merlin WWE Heroes Stickers

	COMPLETE SET (230)	50.00	100.00
1	RAW Logo	.15	.40
2	SmackDown Logo	.15	.40
3	ECW Logo	.15	.40
4	Randy Orton	.40	1.00
5	Randy Orton	.40	1.00
6	Randy Orton	.40	1.00
7	Randy Orton	.40	1.00
8	Randy Orton	.40	1.00
9	Randy Orton	.40	1.00
10	Randy Orton	.40	1.00
11	Randy Orton	.40	1.00
12	Randy Orton	.40	1.00
13	Randy Orton	.40	1.00
14	Randy Orton	.40	1.00
15	Undertaker	.75	2.00
16	Undertaker	.75	2.00
17	Undertaker	.75	2.00
18	Undertaker	.75	2.00
19	Undertaker	.75	2.00
20	Undertaker	.75	2.00
21	Undertaker	.75	2.00
22	Undertaker	.75	2.00
23	Undertaker	.75	2.00
24	Undertaker	.75	2.00
25	Undertaker	.75	2.00
26	Shawn Michaels	1.00	2.50
27	Shawn Michaels	1.00	2.50
28	Shawn Michaels	1.00	2.50
29	Shawn Michaels	1.00	2.50
30	Shawn Michaels	1.00	2.50
31	Shawn Michaels	1.00	2.50
32	Shawn Michaels	1.00	2.50
33	Shawn Michaels	1.00	2.50
34	Shawn Michaels	1.00	2.50
35	Shawn Michaels	1.00	2.50
36	Shawn Michaels	1.00	2.50
37	MVP	.25	.60
38	MVP	.25	.60
39	MVP	.25	.60
40	MVP	.25	.60
41	MVP	.25	.60
42	MVP	.25	.60
43	Michelle McCool	.75	2.00
44	Michelle McCool	.75	2.00
45	Michelle McCool	.75	2.00
46	Michelle McCool	.75	2.00
47	Michelle McCool	.75	2.00
48	Triple H	1.00	2.50
49	Triple H	1.00	2.50
50	Triple H	1.00	2.50
51	Triple H	1.00	2.50
52	Triple H	1.00	2.50
53	Triple H	1.00	2.50
54	Triple H	1.00	2.50
55	Triple H	1.00	2.50
56	Triple H	1.00	2.50
57	Triple H	1.00	2.50
58	Triple H	1.00	2.50
59	Batista	.60	1.50

#	Name			#	Name			#	Name			#	Name
60	Batista	.60	1.50	128	Kane	.60	1.50	196	Edge	.60	1.50	31	Edge
61	Batista	.60	1.50	129	Kane	.60	1.50	197	Edge	.60	1.50	32	Edge (lg)
62	Batista	.60	1.50	130	Kane	.60	1.50	198	Edge	.60	1.50	33	Edge
63	Batista	.60	1.50	131	Kane	.60	1.50	199	Edge	.60	1.50	34	Edge
64	Batista	.60	1.50	132	Kane	.60	1.50	200	Edge	.60	1.50	35	Edge
65	Batista	.60	1.50	133	Kane	.60	1.50	201	Edge	.60	1.50	36	Edge
66	Batista	.60	1.50	134	Kane	.60	1.50	202	Jeff Hardy	.60	1.50	37	Matt Hardy
67	Batista	.60	1.50	135	Kane	.60	1.50	203	Jeff Hardy	.60	1.50	38	Matt Hardy
68	Batista	.60	1.50	136	John Cena	1.00	2.50	204	Jeff Hardy	.60	1.50	39	Jeff Hardy (lg)
69	Batista	.60	1.50	137	John Cena	1.00	2.50	205	Jeff Hardy	.60	1.50	40	Matt Hardy
70	Umaga	.25	.60	138	John Cena	1.00	2.50	206	Jeff Hardy	.60	1.50	41	Matt Hardy
71	Umaga	.25	.60	139	John Cena	1.00	2.50	207	Jeff Hardy	.60	1.50	42	Matt Hardy
72	Umaga	.25	.60	140	John Cena	1.00	2.50	208	Jeff Hardy	.60	1.50	43	Matt Hardy (lg)
73	Umaga	.25	.60	141	John Cena	1.00	2.50	209	Jeff Hardy	.60	1.50	44	Matt Hardy
74	Umaga	.25	.60	142	John Cena	1.00	2.50	210	Jeff Hardy	.60	1.50	45	Jeff Hardy
75	Umaga	.25	.60	143	John Cena	1.00	2.50	211	Jeff Hardy	.60	1.50	46	Matt Hardy
76	Hornswoggle	.25	.60	144	John Cena	1.00	2.50	212	Jeff Hardy	.60	1.50	47	Matt Hardy
77	Hornswoggle	.25	.60	145	John Cena	1.00	2.50	213	Undertaker/Mark Henry	.75	2.00	48	MVP (Foil)
78	Hornswoggle	.25	.60	146	John Cena	1.00	2.50	214	CM Punk/Miz	.25	.60	49	MVP
79	Hornswoggle	.25	.60	147	Rey Mysterio	.40	1.00	215	Carlito/Mr. Anderson	.40	1.00	50	MVP
80	Hornswoggle	.25	.60	148	Rey Mysterio	.40	1.00	P1	Undertaker	.75	2.00	51	MVP
81	Matt Hardy	.60	1.50	149	Rey Mysterio	.40	1.00	P2	World Title	.15	.40	52	MVP
82	Matt Hardy	.60	1.50	150	Rey Mysterio	.40	1.00	P3	Randy Orton	.40	1.00	53	The Great Khali
83	Matt Hardy	.60	1.50	151	Rey Mysterio	.40	1.00	P4	Batista	.60	1.50	54	The Great Khali (lg)
84	Matt Hardy	.60	1.50	152	Rey Mysterio	.40	1.00	P5	Rey Mysterio	.40	1.00	55	The Great Khali
85	Matt Hardy	.60	1.50	153	Rey Mysterio	.40	1.00	P6	Triple H	1.00	2.50	56	The Great Khali
86	Matt Hardy	.60	1.50	154	Rey Mysterio	.40	1.00	P7	WWE Title	.15	.40	57	The Great Khali
87	Matt Hardy	.60	1.50	155	Rey Mysterio	.40	1.00	P8	John Cena	1.00	2.50	58	The Great Khali
88	Matt Hardy	.60	1.50	156	Rey Mysterio	.40	1.00	P9	Randy Orton	.40	1.00	59	D-Generation X (Foil)
89	Matt Hardy	.60	1.50	157	Rey Mysterio	.40	1.00	P10	Edge	.60	1.50	60	Triple H
90	Matt Hardy	.60	1.50	158	Chris Jericho	.40	1.00	P11	JBL	.15	.40	61	Triple H (lg)
91	Matt Hardy	.60	1.50	159	Chris Jericho	.40	1.00	P12	Beth Phoenix	.75	2.00	62	Shawn Michaels
92	CM Punk	.15	.40	160	Chris Jericho	.40	1.00	P13	WWE Women's Title	.15	.40	63	Triple H
93	CM Punk	.15	.40	161	Chris Jericho	.40	1.00	P14	Melina	.60	1.50	64	Shawn Michaels
94	CM Punk	.15	.40	162	Chris Jericho	.40	1.00	P15	Mickie James	1.00	2.50	65	Shawn Michaels (lg)
95	CM Punk	.15	.40	163	Chris Jericho	.40	1.00					66	Triple H
96	CM Punk	.15	.40	164	Beth Phoenix	.75	2.00	**2007 Merlin WWE Superstar Stickers**				67	Triple H
97	CM Punk	.15	.40	165	Beth Phoenix	.75	2.00	COMPLETE SET (218)				68	Shawn Michaels
98	The Miz	.25	.60	166	Beth Phoenix	.75	2.00	1 Raw Logo				69	Shawn Michaels
99	The Miz	.25	.60	167	Beth Phoenix	.75	2.00	2 SmackDown! Logo				70	Batista (Foil)
100	The Miz	.25	.60	168	Beth Phoenix	.75	2.00	3 ECW Logo				71	Batista
101	The Miz	.25	.60	169	Chavo Guerrero	.25	.60	4 Undertaker (Foil)				72	Batista (lg)
102	The Miz	.25	.60	170	Chavo Guerrero	.25	.60	5 Undertaker				73	Batista
103	Ken Kennedy	.40	1.00	171	Chavo Guerrero	.25	.60	6 Undertaker (lg)				74	Batista
104	Ken Kennedy	.40	1.00	172	Chavo Guerrero	.25	.60	7 Undertaker				75	Batista
105	Ken Kennedy	.40	1.00	173	Chavo Guerrero	.25	.60	8 Undertaker				76	Batista (lg)
106	Ken Kennedy	.40	1.00	174	The Great Khali	.15	.40	9 Undertaker				77	Batista
107	Ken Kennedy	.40	1.00	175	The Great Khali	.15	.40	10 Undertaker				78	Batista
108	Ken Kennedy	.40	1.00	176	The Great Khali	.15	.40	11 Undertaker (lg)				79	Batista
109	Melina	.60	1.50	177	The Great Khali	.15	.40	12 Undertaker				80	Batista
110	Melina	.60	1.50	178	The Great Khali	.15	.40	13 Undertaker				81	Randy Orton (Foil)
111	Melina	.60	1.50	179	The Great Khali	.15	.40	14 Undertaker				82	Randy Orton
112	Melina	.60	1.50	180	Shelton Benjamin	.15	.40	15 John Cena (Foil)				83	Randy Orton
113	Melina	.60	1.50	181	Shelton Benjamin	.15	.40	16 John Cena				84	Randy Orton (lg)
114	John Morrison	.15	.40	182	Shelton Benjamin	.15	.40	17 John Cena (lg)				85	Randy Orton
115	John Morrison	.15	.40	183	Shelton Benjamin	.15	.40	18 John Cena				86	Umaga
116	John Morrison	.15	.40	184	Shelton Benjamin	.15	.40	19 John Cena				87	Umaga (lg)
117	John Morrison	.15	.40	185	Boogeyman	.25	.60	20 John Cena				88	Umaga
118	John Morrison	.15	.40	186	Boogeyman	.25	.60	21 John Cena (lg)				89	Umaga
119	Elijah Burke	.15	.40	187	Boogeyman	.25	.60	22 John Cena				90	Umaga
120	Elijah Burke	.15	.40	188	Boogeyman	.25	.60	23 John Cena				91	Umaga
121	Elijah Burke	.15	.40	189	Boogeyman	.25	.60	24 John Cena				92	Melina (Foil)
122	Elijah Burke	.15	.40	190	Boogeyman	.25	.60	25 John Cena				93	Melina
123	Elijah Burke	.15	.40	191	Edge	.60	1.50	26 Edge (Foil)				94	Candice
124	Elijah Burke	.15	.40	192	Edge	.60	1.50	27 Edge				95	Torrie Wilson
125	Kane	.60	1.50	193	Edge	.60	1.50	28 Edge (lg)				96	Mickie James
126	Kane	.60	1.50	194	Edge	.60	1.50	29 Edge				97	Ashley
127	Kane	.60	1.50	195	Edge	.60	1.50	30 Edge				98	Ashley (Foil)

99   Victoria
100 Cherry
101 Kelly Kelly
102 Layla
103 Rowdy Roddy Piper
104 Don Muraco
105 Dusty Rhodes
106 Jimmy Snuka
107 Sgt. Slaughter
108 Bobby Heenan
109 Mr. Perfect
110 Nikolai Volkoff
111 The Samoans
112 Superstar Billy Graham
113 Junkyard Dog
114 Rey Mysterio (Foil)
115 Rey Mysterio
116 Rey Mysterio (Ig)
117 Rey Mysterio
118 Rey Mysterio
119 Rey Mysterio
120 Rey Mysterio (Ig)
121 Rey Mysterio
122 Rey Mysterio
123 Rey Mysterio
124 John Morrison
125 John Morrison
126 John Morrison
127 John Morrison (Foil)
128 John Morrison
129 John Morrison
130 Boogeyman
131 Boogeyman
132 Boogeyman (Foil)
133 Boogeyman
134 Boogeyman
135 Boogeyman
136 Cryme Tyme (Foil)
137 Cryme Tyme
138 JTG (Ig)
139 JTG
140 Shad
141 Shad
142 Shad (Ig)
143 JTG
144 JTG
145 JTG
146 Shad
147 Elijah Burke
148 Elijah Burke
149 Elijah Burke
150 Elijah Burke (Ig)
151 Elijah Burke
152 Tommy Dreamer (Foil)
153 Tommy Dreamer (Ig)
154 Tommy Dreamer
155 Tommy Dreamer
156 Tommy Dreamer
157 Tommy Dreamer
158 Deuce & Domino
159 Deuce
160 Deuce (Ig)
161 Domino
162 Domino
163 Deuce
164 Domino (Ig)
165 Deuce
166 Deuce & Domino

167 Deuce
168 Deuce
169 Marcus Cor Von (Foil)
170 Marcus Cor Von
171 Marcus Cor Von
172 Marcus Cor Von (Ig)
173 Marcus Cor Von
174 Marcus Cor Von
175 CM Punk
176 CM Punk (Ig)
177 CM Punk
178 CM Punk
179 CM Punk
180 King Booker (Foil)
181 King Booker
182 King Booker (Ig)
183 King Booker
184 King Booker
185 King Booker
186 Queen Sharmell (Ig)
187 Queen Sharmell
188 King Booker
189 Queen Sharmell
190 King Booker
191 Kane (Foil)
192 Kane
193 Kane
194 Kane (Ig)
195 Kane
196 Chavo Guerrero (Foil)
197 Chavo Guerrero (Ig)
198 Chavo Guerrero
199 Chavo Guerrero
200 Chavo Guerrero
201 Chavo Guerrero
202 Bobby Lashley (Foil)
203 Bobby Lashley
204 Bobby Lashley
205 Bobby Lashley (Ig)
206 Bobby Lashley
207 Bobby Lashley
208 Snitsky
209 Snitsky (Ig)
210 Snitsky
211 Snitsky
212 Snitsky
213 King Booker
214 Rey Mysterio
215 Undertaker
216 Edge
217 CM Punk
218 Shawn Michaels

2007 Merlin WWE Superstar Stickers
Superstar Inserts

COMPLETE SET (14)
RANDOMLY INSERTED INTO PACKS

P1   John Cena
P2   King Booker
P3   John Cena
P4   Rey Mysterio vs Mark Henry
P5   CM Punk vs Ken Kennedy
P6   Edge
P7   Ric Flair
P8   Kane
P9   Chavo Guerrero
P10 Triple H
P11 Ken Kennedy

P12 Bobby Lashley
P13 Batista
P14 Gregory Helms

1990 Merlin WWF Stickers

COMPLETE SET (216)

1   Hulk Hogan Logo
2   Hulk Hogan Puzzle
3   Hulk Hogan Puzzle
4   Hulk Hogan Puzzle
5   Hulk Hogan Puzzle
6   Hulk Hogan Puzzle
7   Hulk Hogan Puzzle
8   Earthquake
9   Earthquake Logo
10 Earthquake
11 Dino Bravo Logo
12 Dino Bravo Puzzle
13 Dino Bravo Puzzle
14 Tugboat Puzzle
15 Tugboat Puzzle
16 Tugboat Puzzle
17 Tugboat Puzzle
18 Tugboat Puzzle
19 Tugboat Puzzle
20 The Colonel Jimmy Hart
21 Jimmy Hart Logo
22 The Colonel Jimmy Hart
23 Ravishing Rick Rude Puzzle
24 Ravishing Rick Rude Puzzle
25 Ravishing Rick Rude Puzzle
26 Ravishing Rick Rude Puzzle
27 Ravishing Rick Rude Puzzle
28 Ravishing Rick Rude Puzzle
29 Bobby The Brain Heenan
30 Ravishing Rick Rude
31 Ravishing Rick Rude Logo
32 Bobby The Brain Heenan Puzzle
33 Bobby The Brain Heenan Puzzle
34 Bobby Heenan Logo
35 Mr. Perfect Puzzle
36 Mr. Perfect Puzzle
37 Mr. Perfect Logo
38 Mr. Perfect
39 The Texas Tornado Puzzle
40 The Texas Tornado Puzzle
41 WWF Superstars Logo
42 The Texas Tornado Puzzle
43 The Texas Tornado Puzzle
44 The Texas Tornado Puzzle
45 The Texas Tornado Puzzle
46 Big Boss Man Logo
47 Big Boss Man Puzzle
48 Big Boss Man Puzzle
49 Big Boss Man Puzzle
50 Big Boss Man Puzzle
51 Big Boss Man Puzzle
52 Big Boss Man Puzzle
53 Hacksaw Jim Duggan Puzzle
54 Hacksaw Jim Duggan Puzzle
55 Hacksaw Jim Duggan Puzzle
56 Hacksaw Jim Duggan Puzzle
57 Hacksaw Jim Duggan Logo
58 Nikolai Volkoff Puzzle
59 Nikolai Volkoff Puzzle
60 The Hart Foundation Puzzle
61 The Hart Foundation Puzzle
62 The Hart Foundation Puzzle

63   The Hart Foundation Puzzle
64   Jim The Anvil Neidhart
65   Bret Hitman Hart
66   Tito Santana Puzzle
67   Tito Santana Puzzle
68   Tito Santana Logo
69   Brother Love Puzzle
70   Brother Love Puzzle
71   Brother Love Logo
72   Ax
73   Smash
74   Crush
75   Demolition Logo
76   Demolition Puzzle
77   Demolition Puzzle
78   Demolition Puzzle
79   Demolition Puzzle
80   Demolition Puzzle
81   Demolition Puzzle
82   Power and Glory Puzzle
83   Power and Glory Puzzle
84   The Rockers Logo
85   Slick Puzzle
86   Slick Puzzle
87   Slick Logo
88   The Rockers Puzzle
89   The Rockers Puzzle
90   The Rockers Puzzle
91   The Rockers Puzzle
92   The Rockers
93   Marty Jannetty
94   Shawn Michaels
95   Marty Jannetty
96   Rhythm & Blues Puzzle
97   Rhythm & Blues Puzzle
98   Rhythm & Blues Puzzle
99   Rhythm & Blues Puzzle
100 Rhythm & Blues Logo
101 Honky Tonk Man
102 Rhythm & Blues
103 Greg The Hammer Valentine
104 The Model Logo
105 The Model Rick Martel Puzzle
106 The Model Rick Martel Puzzle
107 The Model Rick Martel
108 The Model Rick Martel
109 The Model Rick Martel
110 WWF Logo
111 Ultimate Warrior Logo
112 Ultimate Warrior Puzzle
113 Ultimate Warrior Puzzle
114 Ultimate Warrior Puzzle
115 Ultimate Warrior Puzzle
116 Ultimate Warrior Puzzle
117 Ultimate Warrior Puzzle
118 Ultimate Warrior Puzzle
119 Ultimate Warrior Puzzle
120 Ultimate Warrior
121 Ultimate Warrior
122 Superfly Jimmy Snuka
123 Warlord Puzzle
124 Warlord Puzzle
125 Jimmy The Superfly Snuka Logo
126 Superfly Jimmy Snuka Puzzle
127 Superfly Jimmy Snuka Puzzle
128 Superfly Jimmy Snuka Puzzle
129 Superfly Jimmy Snuka Puzzle
130 Barbarian Puzzle

131 Barbarian Puzzle
132 Barbarian Puzzle
133 Barbarian Puzzle
134 Barbarian Logo
135 Barbarian
136 Barbarian
137 Mr. Fuji
138 Mr. Fuji Logo
139 Orient Express Puzzle
140 Orient Express Puzzle
141 The Bushwhackers
142 The Bushwhackers
143 The Bushwhackers
144 The Bushwhackers Logo
145 The Bushwhackers Puzzle
146 The Bushwhackers Puzzle
147 The Bushwhackers Puzzle
148 The Bushwhackers Puzzle
149 Macho King Randy Savage Puzzle
150 Macho King Randy Savage Puzzle
151 Macho King Randy Savage Logo
152 Sensational Queen Sherri Logo
153 Macho King Randy Savage
154 Sensational Queen Sherri
155 Sensational Queen Sherri
156 Sensational Queen Sherri
157 Dusty Rhodes Puzzle
158 Dusty Rhodes Puzzle
159 Dusty Rhodes Puzzle
160 Dusty Rhodes Puzzle
161 Dusty Rhodes Puzzle
162 Dusty Rhodes Puzzle
163 Dusty Rhodes
164 Dusty Rhodes
165 Dusty Rhodes Logo
166 Haku Puzzle
167 Haku Puzzle
168 Haku Logo
169 Rowdy Roddy Piper
170 Rowdy Roddy Piper
171 Legion of Doom Puzzle
172 Legion of Doom Puzzle
173 Legion of Doom Puzzle
174 Legion of Doom Puzzle
175 Legion of Doom Puzzle
176 Legion of Doom Puzzle
177 Legion of Doom Puzzle
178 Legion of Doom Puzzle
179 Million Dollar Man Ted DiBiase Puzzle
180 Million Dollar Man Ted DiBiase Puzzle
181 Million Dollar Man Ted DiBiase Puzzle
182 Million Dollar Man Ted DiBiase Puzzle
183 Million Dollar Man Ted DiBiase Logo
184 Ted DiBiase
185 Virgil Logo
186 Virgil
187 Jake The Snake Roberts Puzzle
188 Jake The Snake Roberts Puzzle
189 Jake The Snake Logo
190 Jake The Snake Roberts
191 Jake The Snake Roberts Puzzle
192 Jake The Snake Roberts Puzzle
193 Jake The Snake Roberts Puzzle
194 Jake The Snake Roberts Puzzle
195 Akeem Puzzle
196 Akeem Puzzle
197 Akeem Logo
198 Sergeant Slaughter

199 Sergeant Slaughter Puzzle
200 Sergeant Slaughter Puzzle
201 Sergeant Slaughter Puzzle
202 Sergeant Slaughter Puzzle
203 Rugged Ronnie Garvin Logo
204 Rugged Ronnie Garvin
205 Rugged Ronnie Garvin
206 Koko B. Ware
207 Koko B. Ware
208 Koko B. Ware Logo
209 Boris Zhukov
210 Hillbilly Jim Logo
211 Hillbilly Jim Puzzle
212 Hillbilly Jim Puzzle
213 Andre The Giant
214 Andre The Giant Logo
215 Brooklyn Brawler Logo
216 Brooklyn Brawler

1991 Merlin WWF

COMPLETE SET (150)
UNOPENED BOX
UNOPENED PACK (8 CARDS)
*GERMAN: X TO X BASIC CARDS
*ITALIAN: X TO X BASIC CARDS

1 Hulk Hogan CL
2 The Nasty Boys
3 Sid Justice
4 Big Bully Busick/Harvey Wippleman
5 Natural Disasters
6 The Nasty Boys with Jimmy Hart
7 Jake The Snake Roberts
8 Randy Savage and Elizabeth CL
9 Luke of the Bushwhackers
10 Rowdy Roddy Piper
11 Sgt. Slaughter
12 The Genius
13 Texas Tornado
14 Sid Justice
15 Warlord
16 Greg The Hammer Valentine
17 Randy Savage and Elizabeth
18 Macho Man Randy Savage
19 Legion of Doom
20 Ted DiBiase and Sensational Sherri
21 Marty Jannetty
22 Jim The Anvil Neidhart
23 British Bulldog
24 Hulk Hogan
25 Ted DiBiase
26 Beverly Brothers
27 Mr. Perfect
28 The Mountie
29 Macho Man Randy Savage
30 The Undertaker CL
31 Brutus The Barber Beefcake
32 Bret Hitman Hart
33 El Matador
34 Bobby Heenan
35 Andre the Giant
36 Hulk Hogan
37 Sid Justice Face to Face with The Undertaker CL
38 Sgt. Slaughter
39 Hacksaw Jim Duggan
40 The Undertaker
41 Irwin R. Schyster
42 Jake The Snake Roberts
43 Brian Knobbs of the Nasty Boys

44 Beverly Brothers
45 Superfly Jimmy Snuka
46 Sensational Sherri
47 Jake The Snake Roberts
48 Skinner
49 Harvey Wippleman
50 Mr. Perfect
51 Irwin R. Schyster
52 The Bushwhackers
53 Big Boss Man
54 Slick
55 Sid Justice
56 Texas Tornado
57 Greg The Hammer Valentine
58 Mr. Perfect
59 Skinner
60 British Bulldog CL
61 Hulk Hogan
62 Sensational Sherri
63 Superfly Jimmy Snuka
64 The Mountie
65 El Matador
66 Butch of the Bushwhackers
67 Texas Tornado
68 Sgt. Slaughter
69 Rowdy Roddy Piper
70 Jimmy Hart
71 Sid Justice CL
72 Virgil
73 Virgil
74 The Mountie
75 Legion of Doom
76 Sensational Sherri
77 El Matador
78 Natural Disasters
79 Legion of Doom
80 Beverly Brothers
81 Jerry Sags of the Nasty Boys
82 Jake The Snake Roberts CL
83 Hacksaw Jim Duggan
84 Jim The Anvil Neidhart
85 Elizabeth
86 Bret Hitman Hart
87 Big Boss Man
88 Bret Hitman Hart
89 The Bushwhackers
90 Macho Man Randy Savage
91 Ted DiBiase
92 Hulk Hogan
93 Jim The Anvil Neidhart
94 Skinner
95 Harvey Wippleman CL
96 Superfly Jimmy Snuka
97 Mr. Perfect
98 The Berzerker
99 Warlord
100 Brutus The Barber Beefcake
101 Sgt. Slaughter
102 Big Boss Man
103 The Undertaker
104 The Undertaker
105 Sgt. Slaughter
106 The Berzerker with Mr. Fuji
107 Big Bully Busick
108 Beverly Brothers
109 Ted DiBiase
110 Hulk Hogan
111 British Bulldog

112 Legion of Doom
113 The Nasty Boys
114 Jim The Anvil Neidhart
115 Macho Man Randy Savage
116 The Mountie
117 Hacksaw Jim Duggan
118 The Undertaker
119 Butch of the Bushwhackers
120 The Undertaker with Paul Bearer
121 Andre the Giant
122 Bret Hitman Hart
123 Bobby Heenan
124 Virgil
125 Sgt. Slaughter
126 The Bushwhackers
127 Hacksaw Jim Duggan
128 Sid Justice
129 Hulk Hogan
130 Koko B. Ware
131 Superfly Jimmy Snuka CL
132 British Bulldog
133 Sensational Sherri
134 Macho Man Randy Savage
135 The Berzerker with Mr. Fuji
136 The Undertaker with Paul Bearer
137 Sid Justice
138 Skinner
139 Big Boss Man
140 Rowdy Roddy Piper
141 Paul Bearer
142 Luke of the Bushwhackers CL
143 Jake The Snake Roberts
144 El Matador
145 Skinner
146 Natural Disasters
147 Koko B. Ware
148 Superfly Jimmy Snuka
149 Natural Disasters
150 Virgil

1993 Merlin WWF German

COMPLETE SET (198)

1 World Wrestling Federation Title
2 Intercontinental Title
3 Tag Team Championship
4 Bret Hit Man Hart
5 The Undertaker
6 Razor Ramon
7 Macho Man Randy Savage
8 Hulk Hogan
9 Tatanka
10 Yokozuna
11 Kamala
12 Crush
13 Hacksaw Jim Duggan
14 Bam Bam Bigelow
15 Bob Backlund
16 Mr. Perfect
17 Brutus The Barber Beefcake
18 Papa Shango
19 Shawn Michaels
20 Damian Demento
21 Repo Man
22 The Narcissist Lex Luger
23 Doink the Clown
24 The Model Rick Martel
25 Virgil
26 Skinner

27 The Berzerker
28 Bobby The Brain Heenan
29 Brooklyn Brawler
30 Giant Gonzalez
31 Money Inc.
32 Steiner Brothers
33 The Beverly Brothers
34 The Head Shrinkers
35 High Energy
36 The Nasty Boys
37 Macho Man Randy Savage
38 The Undertaker
39 Paul Bearer
40 Razor Ramon
41 Mr. Perfect
42 Shawn Michaels
43A Kamala (w/mask)
43B Kamala (no mask)
44 Reverend Slick
45 Kimchee
46 Crush
47A Bam Bam Bigelow (facing forward)
47B Bam Bam Bigelow (facing left)
48 Bret Hit Man Hart
49 Tatanka
50 Bob Backlund
51 Damian Demento
52 Yokozuna
53 Yokozuna and Mr. Fuji
54 Papa Shango
55 Hacksaw Jim Duggan
56 Skinner
57 Doink the Clown
58 The Narcissist Lex Luger
59 Brooklyn Brawler
60 Virgil
61 Sensational Sherri
62 The Model Rick Martel
63 The Berzerker
64 Repo Man
65 Giant Gonzalez
66 The Mega-Maniacs/Jimmy Hart
67 Hulk Hogan
68 Brutus The Barber Beefcake
69 Jimmy Hart
70 Yokozuna
71 The Berzerker
72 Rick of the Steiner Brothers
73A Scott of the Steiner Brothers (raising left arm)
73B Scott of the Steiner Brothers (in Boston crab)
74 Money Inc.
75 Irwin R. Schyster of Money Inc.
76 Ted DiBiase of Money Inc.
77 Samu of the Head Shrinkers
78 Fatu of the Head Shrinkers
79 Afa
80 The Nasty Boys
81 Jerry Sags of the Nasty Boys
82 Brian Knobbs of the Nasty Boys
83 High Energy
84 Koko B. Ware of High Energy
85 The Rocket Owen Hart of High Energy
86 Beverly Brothers
87A Beau of the Beverly Brothers (w/cape)
87B Beau of the Beverly Brothers (no cape)
88 Blake of the Beverly Brothers
89 WWF Logo
90 WrestleMania IX

91 SummerSlam
92 Survivor Series
93 Royal Rumble
94 Yokozuna
95 Bret Hit Man Hart
96 The Undertaker
97 Giant Gonzalez/Harvey Wippleman
98 Razor Ramon
99 Mr. Perfect
100 The Narcissist Lex Luger
101 Shawn Michaels
102 Tatanka
103 Crush
104 Doink the Clown
105 Macho Man Randy Savage
106 Bob Backlund
107 Bam Bam Bigelow
108 Damian Demento
109 Repo Man
110 Kamala
111 Virgil
112 The Model Rick Martel
113 Hacksaw Jim Duggan
114 Skinner
115 Papa Shango
116 Brooklyn Brawler
117 Paul Bearer
118 Afa
119 Reverend Slick
120 Kimchee
121 Sensational Sherri
122 Yokozuna and Mr. Fuji
123 Jimmy Hart
124 Vince McMahon and Bobby Heenan
125 Hulk Hogan
126 Steiner Brothers
127 The Nasty Boys
128 High Energy
129 Beverly Brothers
130 Money Inc.
131 Irwin R. Schyster of Money Inc.
132 Ted DiBiase of Money Inc.
133 Tatanka
134 Kamala and Reverend Slick
135 The Model Rick Martel
136 Crush
137 Hacksaw Jim Duggan
138 Virgil
139 Skinner
140 The Berzerker
141 Bam Bam Bigelow
142 Yokozuna
143 Bob Backlund
144 Damian Demento
145 The Undertaker
146 Macho Man Randy Savage
147 Hulk Hogan
148 Bret Hit Man Hart
149 Mr. Perfect
150 Papa Shango
151 Repo Man
152 Shawn Michaels
153 Razor Ramon
154 Giant Gonzalez
155 Brooklyn Brawler
156 The Narcissist Lex Luger
157 High Energy
158 Koko B. Ware of High Energy

159 The Rocket Owen Hart of High Energy
160 The Nasty Boys
161 Jerry Sags of the Nasty Boys
162 Brian Knobbs of the Nasty Boys
163 The Head Shrinkers and Afa
164 Samu of he Head Shrinkers
165 Scott of the Steiner Brothers
166 Rick of the Steiner Brothers
167 Irwin R. Schyster of Money Inc.
168 Ted Dibiase of Money Inc.
169 Virgil
170 Bret Hit Man Hart
171 Hulk Hogan
172 Brutus The Barber Beefcake
173 Razor Ramon
174 The Undertaker
175 Bam Bam Bigelow
176 Crush
177 Macho Man Randy Savage
178 Mr. Perfect
179 Tatanka
180A Kamala (profile)
180B Kamala (in the ring)
181 Papa Shango
182 Shawn Michaels
183 Repo Man
184 Damian Demento
185 The Narcissist Lex Luger
186 Bob Backlund
187 Doink the Clown
188 Giant Gonzalez and the Undertaker
189A The Model Rick Martel (in the ring)
189B The Model Rick Martel (profile)
190 Bret Hit Man Hart
191 Macho Man Randy Savage
192 Paul Bearer and The Undertaker
NNO Undertaker Header Ad Card
(Hasbro Power Catcher Exclusive)

1992 Merlin WWF Gold Series 1

COMPLETE SET (96)

1 Wembley Stadium
2 Macho Man Randy Savage vs. Ultimate Warrior
3 Bret Hitman Hart vs. British Bulldog
4 The Undertaker vs. Kamala
5 Money Inc. vs. Legion of Doom
6 Hawk of the Legion of Doom vs. Jerry Sags of the Nasty Boys
7 Texas Tornado vs. Mr. Perfect
8 Meadowlands Arena
9 Hulk Hogan vs. Ted DiBiase
10 Hulk Hogan
11 Ultimate Warrior
12 The Undertaker
13 Ric Flair
14 Macho Man Randy Savage
15 Papa Shango
16 British Bulldog
17 Kamala
18 Big Boss Man
19 Tatanka
20 El Matador
21 Shawn Michaels
22 Hacksaw Jim Duggan
23 The Model Rick Martel
24 Sgt. Slaughter
25 Crush
26 The Mountie

27 Repo Man
28 Hacksaw Jim Duggan
29 Sensational Sherri .
30 Money Inc.
31 Ted DiBiase of Money Inc.
32 Irwin R. Schyster of Money Inc.
33 Legion of Doom
34 Animal of the Legion of Doom
35 Hawk of the Legion of Doom
36 High Energy
37 The Rocket Owen Hart of High Energy
38 Koko B. Ware of High Energy
39 Crush
40 Nailz
41 The Berzerker
42 Bret Hitman Hart
43 Virgil
44 Rowdy Roddy Piper
45 Skinner
46 Texas Tornado
47 Bobby Heenan
48 The Bushwhackers
49 Luke of the Bushwhackers
50 Butch of the Bushwhackers
51 Natural Disasters
52 Earthquake of Natural Disasters
53 Typhoon of Natural Disasters
54 The Nasty Boys
55 Brian Knobbs of the Nasty Boys
56 Jerry Sags of the Nasty Boys
57 Beverly Brothers with The Genius
58 Beau of the Beverly Brothers
59 Blake of the Beverly Brothers
60 The Undertaker
61 Paul Bearer
62 Bret Hitman Hart
63 Hulk Hogan
64 British Bulldog
65 Papa Shango
66 Ultimate Warrior
67 Kamala
68 Macho Man Randy Savage
69 Ric Flair
70 Legion of Doom
71 Tatanka
72 The Mountie
73 Big Boss Man
74 Money Inc.
75 The Berzerker
76 El Matador
77 Sgt. Slaughter
78 Beverly Brothers with The Genius
79 Natural Disasters
80 Sensational Sherri with Shawn Michaels
81 Rowdy Roddy Piper
82 The Bushwhackers
83 The Model Rick Martel
84 Repo Man
85 Mr. Perfect
86 British Bulldog
87 Hulk Hogan
88 Ultimate Warrior
89 Macho Man Randy Savage
90 Bret Hitman Hart
91 Paul Bearer and the Undertaker
92 Virgil
93 Papa Shango
94 Kamala

95 Tatanka
96 Big Boss Man

1992 Merlin WWF Gold Series 2

COMPLETE SET (96)
UNOPENED BOX
UNOPENED PACK (8 CARDS)
1 Tatanka with Two Young Fans
2 Wembley Stadium
3 Macho Man Randy Savage vs. Ultimate Warrior
4 Macho Man Randy Savage vs. Ultimate Warrior
5 Macho Man Randy Savage
6 Flair/Warrior/Perfect/Savage
7 British Bulldog vs. Bret Hitman Hart
8 British Bulldog vs. Bret Hitman Hart
9 Rowdy Roddy Piper
10 Natural Disasters
11 Kamala vs. The Undertaker
12 The Model Rick Martel
13 The Model Rick Martel vs. Shawn Michaels
14 Crush vs. Repo Man
15 Crush vs. Repo Man
16 Virgil vs. Nailz
17 The Undertaker
18 Macho Man Randy Savage
19 Ultimate Warrior
20 Hulk Hogan
21 Shawn Michaels
22 Natural Disasters
23 British Bulldog
24 Bret Hitman Hart
25 Tatanka
26 Ric Flair
27 Mr. Perfect
28 Money Inc.
29 The Bushwhackers
30 Papa Shango
31 Big Boss Man
32 Repo Man
33 Shawn Michaels
34 The Nasty Boys
35 High Energy
36 Razor Ramon
37 Kamala
38 The Model Rick Martel
39 Sgt. Slaughter
40 The Beverly Brothers
41 The Genius
42 El Matador
43 Crush
44 Nailz
45 The Mountie
46 Hacksaw Jim Duggan
47 Virgil
48 Skinner
49 The Berzerker
50 Bobby Heenan
51 Rowdy Roddy Piper
52 Sensational Sherri
53 Hulk Hogan
54 Tatanka
55 Ultimate Warrior
56 Macho Man Randy Savage
57 British Bulldog
58 Earthquake of Natural Disasters
59 Typhoon of Natural Disasters
60 British Bulldog
61 Virgil

62 The Undertaker
63 Papa Shango
64 Bret Hitman Hart
65 Shawn Michaels
66 Irwin R. Schyster of Money Inc.
67 Ted DiBiase of Money Inc.
68 Jerry Sags of the Nasty Boys
69 Brian Knobbs of the Nasty Boys
70 Ric Flair
71 Razor Ramon
72 Kamala
73 Big Boss Man
74 The Rocket Owen Hart of High Energy
75 Koko B. Ware of High Energy
76 Luke of the Bushwhackers
77 Butch of the Bushwhackers
78 Repo Man
79 Virgil (w/Shawn Michaels)
80 El Matador
81 The Model Rick Martel
82 Sgt. Slaughter
83 The Mountie
84 The Berzerker
85 Tatanka
86 Hulk Hogan
87 Nailz
88 Crush
89 Skinner
90 Hacksaw Jim Duggan
91 Paul Bearer
92 Macho Man Randy Savage
93 The Undertaker
94 Ultimate Warrior
95 Check List Part 1
96 Check List Part 2

2001 Merlin WWF Mega Stickers

MG = Mega Glitter
COMPLETE SET (48)
UNOPENED BOX
UNOPENED PACK (8 STICKERS)
MEGA GLITTER ODDS 2:1
1 Vince McMahon
2 The Rock MG
3 The Rock
4 The Rock
5 Stone Cold Steve Austin MG
6 Stone Cold Steve Austin
7 Stone Cold Steve Austin
8 Triple H MG
9 Triple H
10 Triple H
11 Kurt Angle MG
12 Kurt Angle
13 Kurt Angle
14 Undertaker MG
15 Undertaker
16 Undertaker
17 Kane MG
18 Kane
19 Rikishi MG
20 Rikishi
21 Chris Jericho MG
22 Chris Jericho
23 William Regal
24 Raven
25 Chris Benoit
26 Perry Saturn

27 X-Pac
28 Stephanie McMahon MG
29 Stephanie McMahon
30 Chyna MG
31 Chyna
32 Lita MG
33 Lita
34 Trish Stratus MG
35 Trish Stratus
36 Debra
37 Ivory
38 Kat
39 Terri
40 Tori
41 Jacqueline
42 Molly Holly
43 APA
44 Edge & Christian
45 Hardy Boyz
46 Dudley Boyz
47 Right To Censor
48 Too Cool

1993 Merlin WWF SuperStars Stickers

COMPLETE SET (300)			
1 WWF Logo FOIL	.10	.25	
2 Battle Royal (Puzzle)	.10	.25	
3 Battle Royal (Puzzle)	.10	.25	
4 Battle Royal (Puzzle)	.10	.25	
5 Lex Luger Logo FOIL	.10	.25	
6 Lex Luger	.10	.25	
7 Lex Luger	.10	.25	
8 Lex Luger (Puzzle)	.10	.25	
9 Lex Luger (Puzzle)	.10	.25	
10 Lex Luger	.10	.25	
11 Lex Luger (Puzzle)	.10	.25	
12 Lex Luger (Puzzle)	.10	.25	
13 Lex Luger FOIL	.10	.25	
14 Lex Luger	.10	.25	
15 Bob Backlund	.10	.25	
16 Bob Backlund Logo FOIL	.10	.25	
17 Bob Backlund	.10	.25	
18 Bob Backlund	.10	.25	
19 Bob Backlund FOIL	.10	.25	
20 Bob Backlund (Puzzle)	.10	.25	
21 Bob Backlund (Puzzle)	.10	.25	
22 Bob Backlund	.10	.25	
23 The Undertaker Logo FOIL	.10	.25	
24 The Undertaker	.10	.25	
25 The Undertaker	.10	.25	
26 The Undertaker	.10	.25	
27 The Undertaker FOIL	.10	.25	
28 The Undertaker	.10	.25	
29 The Undertaker (Puzzle)	.10	.25	
30 The Undertaker (Puzzle)	.10	.25	
31 The Undertaker (Puzzle)	.10	.25	
32 The Undertaker (Puzzle)	.10	.25	
33 Paul Bearer (Puzzle)	.10	.25	
34 Paul Bearer (Puzzle)	.10	.25	
35 Paul Bearer	.10	.25	
36 Paul Bearer (Puzzle)	.10	.25	
37 Paul Bearer (Puzzle)	.10	.25	
38 The Model Rick Martel Logo FOIL	.10	.25	
39 The Model Rick Martel (Puzzle)	.10	.25	
40 The Model Rick Martel (Puzzle)	.10	.25	
41 The Model Rick Martel (Puzzle)	.10	.25	
42 The Model Rick Martel (Puzzle)	.10	.25	

43 Bret Hit Man Hart Logo FOIL	.10	.25	
44 Bret Hit Man Hart	.10	.25	
45 Bret Hit Man Hart	.10	.25	
46 Bret Hit Man Hart (Puzzle)	.10	.25	
47 Bret Hit Man Hart (Puzzle)	.10	.25	
48 Bret Hit Man Hart	.10	.25	
49 Bret Hit Man Hart	.10	.25	
50 Bret Hit Man Hart (Puzzle)	.10	.25	
51 Bret Hit Man Hart (Puzzle)	.10	.25	
52 Bret Hit Man Hart	.10	.25	
53 Diesel (Puzzle)	.10	.25	
54 Diesel (Puzzle)	.10	.25	
55 Diesel	.10	.25	
56 Diesel (Puzzle)	.10	.25	
57 Diesel (Puzzle)	.10	.25	
58 Diesel (Puzzle)	.10	.25	
59 Diesel (Puzzle)	.10	.25	
60 Diesel	.10	.25	
61 Hulk Hogan Logo FOIL	.10	.25	
62 Hulk Hogan (Puzzle)	.10	.25	
63 Hulk Hogan (Puzzle)	.10	.25	
64 Hulk Hogan	.10	.25	
65 Hulk Hogan FOIL	.10	.25	
66 Hulk Hogan	.10	.25	
67 Hulk Hogan	.10	.25	
68 Hulk Hogan	.10	.25	
69 Hulk Hogan (Puzzle)	.10	.25	
70 Hulk Hogan (Puzzle)	.10	.25	
71 Irwin R. Schyster	.10	.25	
72 Irwin R. Schyster Logo FOIL	.10	.25	
73 Irwin R. Schyster	.10	.25	
74 Irwin R. Schyster (Puzzle)	.10	.25	
75 Irwin R. Schyster (Puzzle)	.10	.25	
76 Irwin R. Schyster	.10	.25	
77 Irwin R. Schyster	.10	.25	
78 Irwin R. Schyster FOIL	.10	.25	
79 Irwin R. Schyster	.10	.25	
80 Yokozuna Logo FOIL	.10	.25	
81 Yokozuna (Puzzle)	.10	.25	
82 Yokozuna (Puzzle)	.10	.25	
83 Yokozuna	.10	.25	
84 Yokozuna FOIL	.10	.25	
85 Yokozuna	.10	.25	
86 Yokozuna (Puzzle)	.10	.25	
87 Yokozuna (Puzzle)	.10	.25	
88 Yokozuna	.10	.25	
89 Yokozuna	.10	.25	
90 Mr. Fuji	.10	.25	
91 Mr. Fuji FOIL	.10	.25	
92 Mr. Fuji	.10	.25	
93 Mr. Fuji (Puzzle)	.10	.25	
94 Mr. Fuji (Puzzle)	.10	.25	
95 Shawn Michaels Logo FOIL	.10	.25	
96 Shawn Michaels (Puzzle)	.10	.25	
97 Shawn Michaels (Puzzle)	.10	.25	
98 Shawn Michaels	.10	.25	
99 Shawn Michaels	.10	.25	
100 Adam Bomb FOIL	.10	.25	
101 Adam Bomb	.10	.25	
102 Adam Bomb	.10	.25	
103 Adam Bomb (Puzzle)	.10	.25	
104 Adam Bomb (Puzzle)	.10	.25	
105 Adam Bomb (Puzzle)	.10	.25	
106 Adam Bomb (Puzzle)	.10	.25	
107 Adam Bomb (Puzzle)	.10	.25	
108 Adam Bomb (Puzzle)	.10	.25	
109 Adam Bomb FOIL	.10	.25	
110 Randy Savage Logo FOIL	.10	.25	

111 Randy Savage (Puzzle)	.10	.25	
112 Randy Savage (Puzzle)	.10	.25	
113 Randy Savage	.10	.25	
114 Randy Savage	.10	.25	
115 Randy Savage (Puzzle)	.10	.25	
116 Randy Savage (Puzzle)	.10	.25	
117 Randy Savage	.10	.25	
118 Randy Savage	.10	.25	
119 Randy Savage FOIL	.10	.25	
120 Marty Jannetty	.10	.25	
121 Marty Jannetty	.10	.25	
122 Marty Jannetty (Puzzle)	.10	.25	
123 Marty Jannetty (Puzzle)	.10	.25	
124 Marty Jannetty Logo FOIL	.10	.25	
125 Marty Jannetty (Puzzle)	.10	.25	
126 Marty Jannetty (Puzzle)	.10	.25	
127 Marty Jannetty (Puzzle)	.10	.25	
128 Marty Jannetty (Puzzle)	.10	.25	
129 Tatanka Logo FOIL	.10	.25	
130 Tatanka (Puzzle)	.10	.25	
131 Tatanka (Puzzle)	.10	.25	
132 Tatanka FOIL	.10	.25	
133 Tatanka (Puzzle)	.10	.25	
134 Tatanka (Puzzle)	.10	.25	
135 Tatanka	.10	.25	
136 Tatanka (Puzzle)	.10	.25	
137 Tatanka (Puzzle)	.10	.25	
138 Tatanka	.10	.25	
139 Ludvig Borga Logo FOIL	.10	.25	
140 Ludvig Borga (Puzzle)	.10	.25	
141 Ludvig Borga (Puzzle)	.10	.25	
142 Ludvig Borga	.10	.25	
143 Ludvig Borga (Puzzle)	.10	.25	
144 Ludvig Borga (Puzzle)	.10	.25	
145 Ludvig Borga FOIL	.10	.25	
146 Ludvig Borga	.10	.25	
147 Ludvig Borga	.10	.25	
148 King of the Ring Logo FOIL	.10	.25	
149 Summer Slam Logo FOIL	.10	.25	
150 Survivor Series Logo FOIL	.10	.25	
151 Royal Rumble Logo FOIL	.10	.25	
152 WrestleMania Logo FOIL	.10	.25	
153 123 Kid Logo FOIL	.10	.25	
154 123 Kid (Puzzle)	.10	.25	
155 123 Kid (Puzzle)	.10	.25	
156 123 Kid	.10	.25	
157 123 Kid	.10	.25	
158 123 Kid	.10	.25	
159 123 Kid (Puzzle)	.10	.25	
160 123 Kid (Puzzle)	.10	.25	
161 123 Kid (Puzzle)	.10	.25	
162 123 Kid (Puzzle)	.10	.25	
163 Razor Ramon Logo FOIL	.10	.25	
164 Razor Ramon	.10	.25	
165 Razor Ramon	.10	.25	
166 Razor Ramon (Puzzle)	.10	.25	
167 Razor Ramon (Puzzle)	.10	.25	
168 Razor Ramon (Puzzle)	.10	.25	
169 Razor Ramon (Puzzle)	.10	.25	
170 Razor Ramon FOIL	.10	.25	
171 Razor Ramon (Puzzle)	.10	.25	
172 Razor Ramon (Puzzle)	.10	.25	
173 Bam Bam Bigelow Logo FOIL	.10	.25	
174 Bam Bam Bigelow	.10	.25	
175 Bam Bam Bigelow	.10	.25	
176 Bam Bam Bigelow (Puzzle)	.10	.25	
177 Bam Bam Bigelow (Puzzle)	.10	.25	
178 Bam Bam Bigelow (Puzzle)	.10	.25	
179 Bam Bam Bigelow (Puzzle)	.10	.25	
180 Bam Bam Bigelow	.10	.25	
181 Bam Bam Bigelow FOIL	.10	.25	
182 Bam Bam Bigelow	.10	.25	
183 Luna Vachon	.10	.25	
184 Luna Vachon Logo FOIL	.10	.25	
185 Luna Vachon	.10	.25	
186 Luna Vachon	.10	.25	
187 Luna Vachon	.10	.25	
188 Luna Vachon	.10	.25	
189 Luna Vachon FOIL	.10	.25	
190 Luna Vachon (Puzzle)	.10	.25	
191 Luna Vachon (Puzzle)	.10	.25	
192 Bastion Booger (Puzzle)	.10	.25	
193 Bastion Booger (Puzzle)	.10	.25	
194 Bastion Booger	.10	.25	
195 Bastion Booger	.10	.25	
196 Bastion Booger (Puzzle)	.10	.25	
197 Bastion Booger (Puzzle)	.10	.25	
198 Bastion Booger	.10	.25	
199 Bastion Booger (Puzzle)	.10	.25	
200 Bastion Booger (Puzzle)	.10	.25	
201 Crush FOIL	.10	.25	
202 Crush (Puzzle)	.10	.25	
203 Crush (Puzzle)	.10	.25	
204 Crush Logo FOIL	.10	.25	
205 Crush	.10	.25	
206 MVP	.10	.25	
207 MVP (Puzzle)	.10	.25	
208 MVP (Puzzle)	.10	.25	
209 MVP (Puzzle)	.10	.25	
210 MVP (Puzzle)	.10	.25	
211 Harvey Wippleman	.10	.25	
212 Harvey Wippleman	.10	.25	
213 Harvey Wippleman (Puzzle)	.10	.25	
214 Harvey Wippleman (Puzzle)	.10	.25	
215 Bobby Heenan (Puzzle)	.10	.25	
216 Bobby Heenan (Puzzle)	.10	.25	
217 Bobby Heenan Logo FOIL	.10	.25	
218 Doink Logo FOIL	.10	.25	
219 Doink	.10	.25	
220 Doink (Puzzle)	.10	.25	
221 Doink (Puzzle)	.10	.25	
222 Doink	.10	.25	
223 Doink FOIL	.10	.25	
224 Doink	.10	.25	
225 Doink (Puzzle)	.10	.25	
226 Doink (Puzzle)	.10	.25	
227 Doink	.10	.25	
228 Rick of the Steiner Brother	.10	.25	
229 The Steiner Brothers FOIL	.10	.25	
230 The Steiner Brothers (Puzzle)	.10	.25	
231 The Steiner Brothers (Puzzle)	.10	.25	
232 Scott of the Steiner Brother	.10	.25	
233 The Steiner Brothers (Puzzle)	.10	.25	
234 The Steiner Brothers (Puzzle)	.10	.25	
235 The Steiner Brothers Logo FOIL	.10	.25	
236 The Steiner Brothers (Puzzle)	.10	.25	
237 The Steiner Brothers (Puzzle)	.10	.25	
238 Men On A Mission (Puzzle)	.10	.25	
239 Men On A Mission (Puzzle)	.10	.25	
240 Men On A Mission FOIL	.10	.25	
241 Mabel of Men On A Mission	.10	.25	
242 Men On A Mission (Puzzle)	.10	.25	
243 Men On A Mission (Puzzle)	.10	.25	
244 Mo of Men On A Mission	.10	.25	
245 Men On A Mission Logo FOIL	.10	.25	
246 Men On A Mission (Puzzle)	.10	.25	
247 Men On A Mission (Puzzle)	.10	.25	
248 Well Dunn Logo FOIL	.10	.25	
249 Well Dunn (Puzzle)	.10	.25	
250 Well Dunn (Puzzle)	.10	.25	
251 Well Dunn (Puzzle)	.10	.25	
252 Well Dunn (Puzzle)	.10	.25	
253 Quebecers (Puzzle)	.10	.25	
254 Quebecers (Puzzle)	.10	.25	
255 Quebecers	.10	.25	
256 Quebecers Logo FOIL	.10	.25	
257 Jacques of the Quebecers	.10	.25	
258 Head Shrinkers Logo FOIL	.10	.25	
259 Head Shrinkers	.10	.25	
260 Head Shrinkers (Puzzle)	.10	.25	
261 Head Shrinkers (Puzzle)	.10	.25	
262 Fatu of the Head Shrinkers	.10	.25	
263 Head Shrinkers (Puzzle)	.10	.25	
264 Head Shrinkers (Puzzle)	.10	.25	
265 Head Shrinkers	.10	.25	
266 Head Shrinkers and Afa (Puzzle)	.10	.25	
267 Head Shrinkers and Afa (Puzzle)	.10	.25	
268 Tom Prichard of Heavenly Bodies	.10	.25	
269 Heavenly Bodies (Puzzle)	.10	.25	
270 Heavenly Bodies (Puzzle)	.10	.25	
271 Jimmy Del Ray of Heavenly Bodies	.10	.25	
272 Heavenly Bodies/J.Cornette (Puzzle)	.10	.25	
273 Heavenly Bodies/J.Cornette (Puzzle)	.10	.25	
274 Jim Cornette	.10	.25	
275 Heavenly Bodies/J.Cornette (Puzzle)	.10	.25	
276 Heavenly Bodies/J.Cornette (Puzzle)	.10	.25	
277 Jim Cornette		.10	.25
278 Smoking Gunns Logo FOIL		.10	.25
279 Smoking Gunns (Puzzle)		.10	.25
280 Smoking Gunns (Puzzle)		.10	.25
281 Bart of Smoking Gunns		.10	.25
282 Billy of Smoking Gunns		.10	.25
283 Smoking Gunns (Puzzle)		.10	.25
284 Smoking Gunns (Puzzle)		.10	.25
285 Smoking Gunns FOIL		.10	.25
286 Smoking Gunns (Puzzle)		.10	.25
287 Smoking Gunns (Puzzle)		.10	.25
288 The Bushwhackers Logo FOIL		.10	.25
289 The Bushwhackers (Puzzle)		.10	.25
290 The Bushwhackers (Puzzle)		.10	.25
291 Luke of The Bushwhackers		.10	.25
292 The Bushwhackers (Puzzle)		.10	.25
293 The Bushwhackers (Puzzle)		.10	.25
294 Butch of The Bushwhackers		.10	.25
295 The Bushwhackers FOIL		.10	.25
296 The Bushwhackers (Puzzle)		.10	.25
297 The Bushwhackers (Puzzle)		.10	.25
298 WWF Title Belt FOIL		.10	.25
299 WWF Intercontinental Belt FOIL		.10	.25
300 WWF Tag Team Title Belt FOIL		.10	.25

1995 Merlin WWF

COMPLETE SET (196)

1 Bret Hit Man Hart
2 IRS
3 Tatanka
4 Bull Nakano
5 Abe Schwartz
6 Shawn Michaels
7 British Bulldog
8 123 Kid
9 Jim Neidhart
10 Adam Bomb
11 Luna Vachon
12 Smoking Gunns
13 Pierre
14 Ted DiBiase
15 Diesel
16 Duke Droese
17 King Kong Bundy
18 Nikolai Volkoff
19 Mr. Fuji
20 Yokozuna
21 The Bushwhackers
22 Bob Backlund
23 Jeff Jarrett
24 Bam Bam Bigelow
25 Bob Spark Plugg Holly
26 Mabel
27 Jim Cornette
28 The Undertaker
29 Heavenly Bodies
30 Alundra Blayze
31 Lex Luger
32 Jerry Lawler
33 Paul Bearer
34 Well Dunn
35 Razor Ramon
36 Doink
37 Dink
38 Head Shrinkers
39 Lou Albano
40 Afa
41 Kwang
42 Harvey Wippleman
43 Intercontinental Title
44 World Wrestling Federation Title
45 Tag Team Championship
46 Bret Hit Man Hart
47 IRS
48 Tatanka
49 Bull Nakano
50 Abe Schwartz
51 Shawn Michaels
52 British Bulldog
53 123 Kid
54 Jim Neidhart
55 Adam Bomb
56 Luna Vachon
57 Smoking Gunns
58 Pierre
59 Ted DiBiase
60 Diesel
61 Duke Droese
62 King Kong Bundy
63 Nikolai Volkoff
64 Mr. Fuji
65 Yokozuna
66 The Bushwhackers
67 Bob Backlund
68 Jeff Jarrett
69 Bam Bam Bigelow
70 Bob Spark Plugg Holly
71 Mabel
72 Jim Cornette
73 The Undertaker
74 Alundra Blayze
75 Lex Luger
76 Jerry Lawler
77 Paul Bearer
78 Well Dunn
79 Razor Ramon

2010-13 Missouri Wrestling Revival

COMPLETE SET (100)

1986 Monty Gum Wrestling

COMPLETE SET (100)	75.00	150.00
UNOPENED BOX (50 PACKS)		
UNOPENED PACK		
1 Rip Rogers	.40	1.00
2 Chris Adams	.25	.75
3 Black Bart	.20	.50
4 Steve Regal	.60	1.50
5 Gino Hernandez	.40	1.00
6 Ricky Steamboat	.75	2.00
7 The Road Warriors	1.00	2.50
8 Joe LeDuc	.60	1.50
9 Fritz Von Erich	.60	1.50
10 Kevin Von Erich	.60	1.50
11 Kerry Von Erich	.60	1.50
12 Baron Von Raschke UER	.20	.50
13 Sgt. Slaughter	.75	2.00
14 Magnificent Don Muraco	.40	1.00
15 Bobby Jaggers	.20	.50
16 Wahoo McDaniel	2.00	5.00
17 The Great Kabuki & Sunshine	1.00	2.50
18 The Iron Sheik	.30	.75
19 Greg Valentine	.50	1.25
20 Rick Martel	.40	1.00
21 The Road Warriors	1.00	2.50
22 Hulk Hogan	4.00	10.00
23 Kerry Von Erich	1.00	2.50
24 David Schultz	1.25	3.00
25 The Road Warriors	1.25	3.00
26 Nikita Koloff	.25	.60
27 Baron Von Raschke	.20	.50
28 Hercules Hernandez	.50	1.25
29 The RPM's	.30	.75
30 Buzz Sawyer	1.00	2.50
31 Junkyard Dog UER	.40	1.00
32 Nikita Koloff	.40	1.00
33 Krusher Khruschev & Ivan Koloff	.20	.50
34 Kevin Von Erich (Ric Flair) UER	.75	2.00
35 Kerry Von Erich	.75	2.00
36 Bobby Fulton & Tommy Rogers	.75	2.00
37 Magnificent Don Muraco	.20	.50
38 Rick Martel	.40	1.00
39 Rick Martel	.20	.50
40 Rick Martel	.75	2.00
41 Gino Hernandez	.20	.50
42 Terry Taylor	.50	1.25
43 Rock 'N Roll Express	.75	2.00
44 Billy Jack Haynes & Rick Rude	.50	1.25
45 Billy Jack Haynes & Rick Rude	.50	1.25
46 Arn Anderson & Brett Sawyer	.40	1.00
47 Kerry Von Erich	.75	2.00

48	Rick Martel & Nick Bockwinkel	.20	.50
49	Hulk Hogan (w/Joan Rivers)	8.00	20.00
50	Hulk Hogan & Cyndi Lauper	4.00	10.00
51	Hulk Hogan & Muhammed Ali	8.00	20.00
52	Hulk Hogan & M.Ali (Stallone) UER	4.00	10.00
53	Tully Blanchard	1.25	3.00
54	Bruno Sammartino/Nikolai Volkoff	.75	2.00
55	Bruno Sammartino	1.25	3.00
56	B.Sammartino & Killer Kowalski	.50	1.25
57	B.Sammartino & Johnny Valentine	.75	2.00
58	Ric Flair & Kerry Von Erich	1.00	2.50
59	Ric Flair	5.00	12.00
60	Ric Flair & Dusty Rhodes	4.00	10.00
61	Hulk Hogan & Nick Bockwinkel	5.00	12.00
62	Hulk Hogan	8.00	20.00
63	Hulk Hogan & Ken Patera	3.00	8.00
64	Dusty Rhodes & Manny Fernandez	.30	.75
65	Dusty Rhodes	3.00	8.00
66	Dusty Rhodes & King Curtis	.75	2.00
67	The Missing Link	.75	2.00
68	The Road Warriors	1.00	2.50
69	Precious Paul Ellering	.20	.50
70	Fabulous Free-Birds: Terry Gordy	.75	2.00
71	Fabulous Freebirds: Michael Hayes	1.25	3.00
72	Jim Cornette UER	.75	2.00
73	Jesse Barr	.25	.60
74	Rip Rogers & Bugsy McGraw	.30	.75
75	Konga, the Barbarian	.40	1.00
76	Eric Embry	.20	.50
77	Magnum T.A. Terry Allen	1.50	4.00
78	Magnum T.A. Terry Allen	1.25	3.00
79	Greg Allen (Valentine) UER	.30	.75
80	Tully Blanchard	.40	1.00
81	The Sheepherders	.75	2.00
82	Tito Santana	.40	1.00
83	The One Man Gang	.75	2.00
84	Gary Hart	.20	.50
85	Brett Sawyer	.20	.50
86	Ron Bass	.20	.50
87	Hulk Hogan	6.00	15.00
88	Rick Flair UER	2.00	5.00
89	Rick Flair & Sgt. Slaughter UER	1.50	4.00
90	Rick Flair UER	6.00	15.00
91	Sgt. Slaughter	.75	2.00
92	Rick Steamboat	1.25	3.00
93	King Kong Brody	.50	1.25
94	Randy Savage	12.00	30.00
95	Dusty Rhodes	1.00	2.50
96	King Kong Bundy	.50	1.25
97	Nikita Koloff	.75	2.00
98	Nikita Koloff & Dusty Rhodes	.50	1.25
99	Butch Reed	.40	1.00
100	Konga, the Barbarian	.75	2.00

1989 MSL Greeting Cards WWF

COMPLETE SET (5)

1	Bushwhackers
2	Hulk Hogan
3	Macho Man Randy Savage
4	Miss Elizabeth
5	The Ultimate Warrior

1989 MSL Superstars of Wrestling Postcards WWF

COMPLETE SET (10)

1	Brutus The Barber Beefcake
2	Bushwhackers
3	Dusty Rhodes
4	Hacksaw Jim Duggan
5	Hulk Hogan
6	Jake The Snake Roberts
7	Macho Man Randy Savage
8	Ravishing Rick Rude
9	The Rockers
10	The Ultimate Warrior

2005 NBC Universal WWE RAW Ringside Sweepstakes

COMPLETE SET (4)		4.00	10.00
NNO	Carlito	1.25	3.00
NNO	John Cena	2.00	5.00
NNO	Torrie Wilson	1.50	4.00
NNO	Triple H	1.25	3.00

1985 O'Quinn Wrestling All-Stars

COMPLETE SET (54)   30.00   75.00
ONLY AVAILABLE IN WRESTLING ALL STARS MAGAZINE

1	Hulk Hogan	10.00	30.00
2	Ric Flair	8.00	20.00
3	Rick Martel	.40	1.00
4	Sergeant Slaughter	2.00	5.00
5	The Iron Sheik	.60	1.50
6	Kamala	.50	1.25
7	Dusty Rhodes	.50	1.25
8	Paul Orndorff	.60	1.50
9	The Fabulous Freebirds	.50	1.25
10	Big John Studd	.40	1.00
11	Kerry Von Erich	.50	1.25
12	Jimmy Valiant	.40	1.00
13	Baron Von Raschke	.40	1.00
14	Missing Link	.40	1.00
15	Roddy Piper	2.00	5.00
16	Terry Taylor	.40	1.00
17	Superstar Billy Graham	.50	1.25
18	Carlos Colon	.40	1.00
19	Kevin Sullivan	.40	1.00
20	Tommy Rich	.40	1.00
21	(Jesse) The Body Ventura	3.00	8.00
22	Kevin Von Erich	.60	1.50
23	King Kong Bundy	.50	1.25
24	Wahoo McDaniel	.40	1.00
25	Greg Valentine	.50	1.25
26	Ken Patera	.40	1.00
27	Terry Allen	.40	1.00
28	Rock n Roll Express	.40	1.00
29	Jerry Lawler	.60	1.50
30	Junkyard Dog	.60	1.50
31	Barry Windham	.40	1.00
32	The Youngbloods	.40	1.00
33	Ricky Steamboat	.60	1.50
34	Superfly Snuka	.60	1.50
35	The Road Warriors	.50	1.25
36	Bob Orton	.50	1.25
37	Mil Mascaras	.40	1.00
38	Ivan Putski	.40	1.00
39	Jimmy Garvin	.40	1.00
40	Mike Von Erich	.40	1.00
41	Chris Adams	.40	1.00
42	Brad Armstrong	.40	1.00
43	Gino Hernandez	.40	1.00
44	Tully Blanchard	.40	1.00
45	The Sheepherders	.40	1.00
46	Andre The Giant	6.00	15.00

1985 O-Pee-Chee WWF

COMPLETE SET W/HOGAN (66)		200.00	400.00
COMPLETE SET W/O HOGAN (60)		30.00	75.00
UNOPENED BOX (36 PACKS)			
UNOPENED PACK (9 CARDS+1 STICKER)			
RINGSIDE ACTION (22-56)			
SUPERSTARS SPEAK (57-66)			

1	Hulk Hogan	75.00	150.00
2	The Iron Sheik	1.00	2.50
3	Captain Lou Albano	.75	2.00
4	Junk Yard Dog	1.00	2.50
5	Paul Mr. Wonderful Orndorff	.60	1.50
6	Jimmy Superfly Snuka	.60	1.50
7	Rowdy Roddy Piper	6.00	15.00
8	Wendi Richter	.75	2.00
9	Greg The Hammer Valentine	1.00	2.50
10	Brutus Beefcake	1.00	2.50
11	Jesse The Body Ventura	3.00	8.00
12	Big John Studd	.60	1.50
13	Fabulous Moolah	1.25	3.00
14	Tito Santana	1.25	3.00
15	Hillbilly Jim	1.00	2.50
16	Hulk Hogan	100.00	200.00
17	Mr. Fuji	.75	2.00
18	Rotundo & Windham	.75	2.00
19	Moondog Spot	.50	1.25
20	Chief Jay Strongbow	.50	1.25
21	George The Animal Steele	1.25	3.00
22	Let Go of My Toe! RA	.50	1.25
23	Lock 'Em Up! RA	.50	1.25
24	Scalp 'Em! RA	.50	1.25
25	Going for the Midsection! RA	.75	2.00
26	Up in the Air! RA	.60	1.50
27	All Tied Up! RA	1.50	4.00
28	Here She Comes! RA	.50	1.25
29	Stretched to the Limit! RA	3.00	8.00
30	Over He Goes! RA	1.00	2.50
31	An Appetite for Mayhem! RA	.60	1.50
32	Putting on Pressure! RA	.50	1.25
33	Smashed on a Knee! RA	.75	2.00
34	A Fist Comes Flying! RA	.50	1.25
35	Lemme' Out of This! RA	.50	1.25
36	No Fair Chokin'! RA	.50	1.25
37	Attacked by an Animal! RA	.50	1.25
38	One Angry Man! RA	1.25	3.00
39	Someone's Going Down! RA	1.25	3.00
40	Strangle Hold! RA	2.00	5.00
41	Bending an Arm! RA	.50	1.25
42	Ready for a Pile Driver! RA	.75	2.00
43	Face to the Canvas! RA	.50	1.25
44	Paul Wants It All! RA	.75	2.00
45	Kick to the Face! RA	3.00	8.00
46	Ready for Action! RA	.50	1.25
47	Putting on the Squeeze! RA	.60	1.50
48	Giants in Action! RA	1.50	4.00
49	Camel Clutch! RA	.60	1.50
50	Pile Up! RA	2.00	5.00
51	Can't Get Away! RA	.60	1.50
52	Going for the Pin! RA	.50	1.25
47	The Fabulous Ones	.40	1.00
48	The Tonga Kid	.40	1.00
49	Masked Superstar	.40	1.00
50	Billy Haynes	.40	1.00
51	Adrian Street	.40	1.00
52	Pedro Morales	.40	1.00
53	David Sammartino	.40	1.00
54	Bruno Sammartino	.50	1.25
53	Ready to Fly! RA	2.00	5.00
54	Crusher in a Crusher! RA	.50	1.25
55	Fury of the Animal! RA	.75	2.00
56	Wrong Kind of Music! RA	6.00	15.00
57	Who's your next challenger? SS	2.50	6.00
58	This dog has got a mean bite! SS	.75	2.00
59	I don't think I'll ask... SS	1.25	3.00
60	You Hulkster fans... SS	8.00	20.00
61	This ain't my idea... SS	1.00	2.50
62	You mean Freddie Blassie... SS	1.25	3.00
63	Mppgh Ecch Oong. SS	1.00	2.50
64	Rock n' wrestling connection SS	.75	2.00
65	Arrrgggghhhh! SS	.60	1.50
66	They took my reindeer! SS	.60	1.50

1985 O-Pee-Chee WWF Stickers

COMPLETE SET W/HOGAN (22)		50.00	100.00
COMPLETE SET W/O HOGAN (17)		12.00	30.00
STATED ODDS 1:1			

1	Hulk Hogan	15.00	40.00
2	Captain Lou Albano	.75	2.00
3	Brutus Beefcake	1.25	3.00
4	Jesse Ventura	2.00	5.00
5	The Iron Sheik	1.50	4.00
6	Wendi Richter	1.25	3.00
7	Jimmy Snuka	.75	2.00
8	Ivan Putski	1.00	2.50
9	Hulk Hogan	4.00	10.00
10	Junk Yard Dog	1.25	3.00
11	Hulk Hogan	6.00	15.00
12	Captain Lou Albano	.75	2.00
13	Captain Lou Albano	.75	2.00
14	Freddy Blassie & Iron Sheik	.75	2.00
15	Jimmy Snuka	.75	2.00
16	Hulk Hogan	10.00	25.00
17	Iron Sheik	1.50	4.00
18	Rene Goulet & S.D. Jones	1.25	3.00
19	Junk Yard Dog	.75	2.00
20	Wendi Richter	1.25	3.00
21	Le gÈant FerrÈ	3.00	8.00
22	Hulk Hogan	8.00	20.00

1985-86 O-Pee-Chee WWF Series 2

While many collectors have recognized this as a 1985 release (as the copyright date on all the cards indicate), there are indeed cards that depict highlights from WrestleMania II which took place on April 7, 1986. Therefore, this release is aptly titled 1985-86 O-Pee-Chee WWF.

COMPLETE SET (75)		60.00	120.00
UNOPENED BOX (36 PACKS)			
UNOPENED PACK (10 CARDS)			

1	Nikolai Volkoff	4.00	10.00
2	The Magnificent Muraco	1.25	3.00
3	Tony Atlas	.40	1.00
4	Jim The Anvil Neidhart	.40	1.00
5	Ricky Steamboat	.75	2.00
6	The British Bulldogs	1.50	4.00
7	King Kong Bundy	3.00	8.00
8	Bobby The Brain Heenan	1.25	3.00
9	Lei Lani Kai	.40	1.00
10	Snaky Squeeze!	.75	2.00
11	Savage Attack!	15.00	40.00
12	Cowboy Bob Orton	.50	1.25
13	Showing the Flag	1.25	3.00
14	Showboating!	1.50	4.00
15	Terry Funk	1.25	3.00

No.	Card	Lo	Hi
16	Martial Artist!	1.25	3.00
17	Don't Call Me Beach Bum	.75	2.00
18	Up and Over!	.30	1.00
19	Brewing Up Trouble!	.40	1.00
20	A Leg Up!	.75	2.00
21	About To Explode	.40	1.00
22	Twister!	.50	1.25
23	Headed For the Turnbuckle	5.00	12.00
24	Hercules Hernandez	2.50	6.00
25	Leggo' My Head!	.40	1.00
26	The Dragon Has Struck!	.40	1.00
27	Top Dog	1.00	2.50
28	Watch Out For Me	1.25	3.00
29	It's Time For A Little Road Work!	.60	1.50
30	Karate Chop!	.60	1.50
31	Crafty Fuji	.75	2.00
32	Bulldog Grip!	.60	1.50
33	Jake The Snake	4.00	10.00
34	Siva Afi	.60	1.50
35	This Is Gonna' Hurt!	1.25	3.00
36	Military Press!	.60	1.50
37	Tower Of Strength!	.40	1.00
38	Bulldog Grip!	.40	1.00
39	Piggyback!	2.00	5.00
40	Shove Off!	.40	1.00
41	Jimmy Mouth of the South Hart	1.25	3.00
42	Fliperoo!	.50	1.25
43	Ring Toss!	.50	1.25
44	Uncle Elmer	.50	1.25
45	Iran and Russia - Number One?	1.25	3.00
46	The Killer Bees	.50	1.25
47	Secret Plans	.50	1.25
48	Davey Boy Smith	1.50	4.00
49	Aerial Escape!	.40	1.00
50	Caught by Kong!	.60	1.50
51	Banging Away!	1.50	4.00
52	All American Boy!	.40	1.00
53	Fiji Fury!	.40	1.00
54	What d'ya mean...	1.00	2.50
55	Do you know any way...	.40	1.00
56	Those are the biggest feet...	.40	1.00
57	I make sukiyaki...	1.25	3.00
58	This guy really looks sick.	.40	1.00
59	Nikolai, he sings...	.40	1.00
60	The Animal In Love!	.40	1.00
61	Hoss Funk	.75	2.00
62	Can I autograph your cast?	.60	1.50
63	Randy Savage & Elizabeth	12.00	30.00
64	I don't know...	.40	1.00
65	If anybody calls you...	.40	1.00
66	It's rock and wrestling - forever!	2.00	5.00
67	Wrestlers vs. Football Greats	1.25	3.00
68	Big Men Battle	.50	1.25
69	Help Coming	.40	1.00
70	The Body Struts His Stuff	.40	1.00
71	In the Corner	1.25	3.00
72	Plenty of Beef	.75	2.00
73	Battle Royal Winner	.50	1.25
74	Working for a Position	.40	1.00
75	Ready for a War!	1.50	4.00

1987 O-Pee-Chee WWF

No.	Card	Lo	Hi
	COMPLETE SET (75)	60.00	120.00
	UNOPENED BOX (36 PACKS)		
	UNOPENED PACK (10 CARDS)		
1	Bret "Hit Man" Hart	25.00	60.00
2	Andre the Giant	6.00	15.00
3	Hulk Hogan	5.00	12.00
4	Frankie	.75	2.00
5	Koko B. Ware	.75	2.00
6	Tito Santana	.60	1.50
7	Randy Savage & Elizabeth	10.00	25.00
8	Billy Jack Haynes	.40	1.00
9	Hercules & Bobby Heenan	.40	1.00
10	King Harley Race	.60	1.50
11	Kimchee & Kamala	.40	1.00
12	Bravo/Johnny V/Valentine	.50	1.25
13	Honky Tonk Man	1.00	2.50
14	Outback Jack	.40	1.00
15	King Kong Bundy	1.25	3.00
16	The Magnificent Muraco	.40	1.00
17	Mr. Fuji and Killer Khan	.75	2.00
18	The Natural Butch Reed	.60	1.50
19	Davey Boy Smith	.75	2.00
20	The Dynamite Kid	.40	1.00
21	Ricky The Dragon Steamboat	1.50	4.00
22	Two-Man Clothesline RA	.40	1.00
23	Ref Turned Wrestler RA	.75	2.00
24	Ready to Strike RA	.60	1.50
25	In the Outback RA	.40	1.00
26	The Hulkster Explodes RA	2.00	5.00
27	Double Whammy RA	.40	1.00
28	Spoiling for a Fight RA	.40	1.00
29	Flip Flop RA	.40	1.00
30	Islanders Attack RA	.40	1.00
31	King Harley Parades RA	.40	1.00
32	Backbreaker RA	.40	1.00
33	Double Dropkick RA	.40	1.00
34	The Loser Must Bow RA	.40	1.00
35	American-Made RA	2.50	6.00
36	A Challenge Answered RA	2.00	5.00
37	Champ in the Ring RA	4.00	10.00
38	Listening to Hulkamania RA	2.00	5.00
39	Heading for the Ring RA	.40	1.00
40	Out to Destroy RA	.40	1.00
41	Tama Takes a Beating RA	.40	1.00
42	Bundy in Mid-Air RA	.40	1.00
43	Karate Stance RA	.40	1.00
44	Her Eyes on Randy RA	2.50	6.00
45	The Olympian Returns RA	.40	1.00
46	Reed Is Riled RA	.40	1.00
47	Flying Bodypress RA	.40	1.00
48	Hooking the Leg RA	.40	1.00
49	A Belly Buster WMIII	.40	1.00
50	Revenge on Randy WMIII	.75	2.00
51	Fighting the Full Nelson WMIII	.40	1.00
52	Honky Tonk Goes Down WMIII	.40	1.00
53	Over the Top WMIII	.40	1.00
54	The Giant Is Slammed WMIII	1.25	3.00
55	Out of the Ring WMIII	.75	2.00
56	And Still Champion WMIII	1.50	4.00
57	Harts Hit Concrete WMIII	.40	1.00
58	The Challenge RA	1.25	3.00
59	Bearhug RA	.40	1.00
60	Fantastic Bodypress RA	.40	1.00
61	Aerial Maneuvers RA	.40	1.00
62	Ready to Sting! RA	.40	1.00
63	Showing Off RA -	.40	1.00
64	Scare Tactics RA	.40	1.00
65	Taking a Bow RA	.60	1.50
66	Out to Eat a Turnbuckle RA	.40	1.00
67	Nice guys finish last! SS	.40	1.00
68	Here's how we keep... SS	.40	1.00
69	Urrggh. Nice! SS	.40	1.00
70	No Kamala...him not dinner! SS	.40	1.00
71	We are the original destroyers. SS	.40	1.00
72	I think the fans are mad at me. SS	.40	1.00
73	You ain't nothin'... SS	.40	1.00
74	I'm gonna take a big bit... SS	.40	1.00
75	Good! SS	.40	1.00

1991 Omnipress Wrestling

COMPLETE SET (29)

NNO Barry Windham
NNO Bruiser Brody
NNO Cactus Jack
NNO Cactus Jack
NNO Cactus Jack
NNO Cactus Jack
NNO Cactus Jack
NNO Cactus Jack
(Omnipress Wrestler of the Year)
NNO Eddie Gilbert
NNO Eddie Gilbert
NNO Eddie Gilbert
NNO Eddie Gilbert/Cactus Jack
NNO Eric Embry
NNO Jerry Lawler
NNO Jerry Lawler
NNO Ric Flair
NNO Ric Flair
NNO Ric Flair
NNO Stan Hansen
NNO Superclash Controversy, Jerry Lawler
NNO Superclash Controversy, Kerry Von Erich
NNO Terry Funk
NNO Terry Funk
NNO Terry Funk
NNO Terry Funk
NNO Terry Funk
NNO Terry Funk
NNO Terry Funk
NNO Tom Prichard

2012 OVW Series One

COMPLETE SET (9)

NNO Danny Davis
NNO Dean Hill
NNO Jason Wayne
NNO Johnny Spade
NNO Michael Hayes
NNO Paredyse
NNO Randy Terrez
NNO Taeler Hendrix
NNO Trailer Park Trash

2004 Pacific TNA

No.	Card	Lo	Hi
	COMPLETE SET (75)	10.00	25.00
	UNOPENED BOX (24 PACKS)	85.00	100.00
	UNOPENED PACK (5 CARDS)	4.00	5.00
	*RED: .6X TO 1.5X BASIC CARDS		
1	April	.20	.50
2	Chelsea	.12	.30
3	Goldylocks	.75	2.00
4	Lollipop	.30	.75
5	Athena	.20	.50
6	Abyss	.30	.75
7	Jeremy Borash	.12	.30
8	Traci	.50	1.25
9	D'Lo Brown	.20	.50
10	Christopher Daniels	.12	.30
11	Delirious	.12	.30
12	Simon Diamond	.12	.30
13	Julio Dinero	.12	.30
14	Shane Douglas	.12	.30
15	Sonjay Dutt	.12	.30
16	Ekmo Fatu	.20	.50
17	Glenn Gilberti	.12	.30
18	Juventud Guerrera	.12	.30
19	Chris Harris	.12	.30
20	Don Harris	.12	.30
21	Ron Harris	.12	.30
22	Chris Hero	.12	.30
23	BG James	.20	.50
24	Jeff Jarrett	.60	1.50
25	Kid Kash	.12	.30
26	Frankie Kazarian	.12	.30
27	Ron Killings	.20	.50
28	Konnan	.12	.30
29	Lazz	.12	.30
30	Jerry Lynn	.12	.30
31	Father James Mitchell	.12	.30
32	Kevin Northcutt	.12	.30
33	Nosawa	.12	.30
34	CM Punk	5.00	12.00
35	Raven	.50	1.25
36	Dusty Rhodes	.30	.75
37	Vince Russo	.12	.30
38	Chris Sabin	.12	.30
39	Sandman	.20	.50
40	Rick Santel	.12	.30
41	Michael Shane	.12	.30
42	Shark Boy	.12	.30
43	Sonny Siaki	.12	.30
44	Sinn	.12	.30
45	Slash	.12	.30
46	James Storm	.20	.50
47	AJ Styles	3.00	8.00
48	Johnny Swinger	.12	.30
49	Terry Taylor	.12	.30
50	Trinity	.20	.50
51	Chris Vaughn	.12	.30
52	Ryan Wilson	.12	.30
53	David Young	.12	.30
54	Scott Hudson	.12	.30
55	Mike Tenay	.12	.30
56	Don West	.12	.30
57	Don Callis	.12	.30
58	Erik Watts	.12	.30
59	Rudy Charles	.12	.30
60	Mike Posey	.12	.30
61	Andrew Thomas	.12	.30
62	3Live Kru	.20	.50
63	America's Most Wanted	.20	.50
64	D'Lo Brown	.20	.50
65	Simon Diamond	.12	.30
66	Jeff Jarrett	.60	1.50
67	Raven	.50	1.25
68	Dusty Rhodes	.30	.75
69	Chris Sabin	.12	.30
70	Sonny Siaki	.12	.30
71	AJ Styles	2.50	6.00
72	Chris Vaughn	.12	.30
73	Trinity	.20	.50
74	Goldylocks	.75	2.00
75	Lollipop	.30	.75

2004 Pacific TNA Event-Used

STATED PRINT RUN 1,525 SER.#'d SETS

No.	Card	Lo	Hi
1	America's Most Wanted	4.00	8.00
2	AJ Styles	5.00	10.00

3	D'Lo Brown	4.00	8.00
4	Raven	4.00	8.00
5	BG James	4.00	8.00

2004 Pacific TNA Event-Used Limited Edition

NOT AVAILABLE IN PACKS

1	TNA Babes	15.00	40.00
2	America's Most Wanted	15.00	40.00

2004 Pacific TNA Legends And Superstars Autographs

COMPLETE SET (6) 30.00 75.00
STATED ODDS 1:24 HOBBY

1	Rowdy Roddy Piper	50.00	100.00
3	Jeff Jarrett	8.00	20.00
4	Terry Taylor	5.00	12.00
5	Dusty Rhodes	60.00	120.00
6	Harley Race	12.00	30.00
7	Raven	5.00	12.00

2004 Pacific TNA Main Event Autographs

STATED ODDS 1:24 HOBBY

NNO	AJ Styles Red Border SP	15.00	40.00
NNO	AJ Styles Gold Border SP	15.00	40.00
NNO	AMW DUAL AU	6.00	15.00
NNO	April	4.00	10.00
NNO	Goldylocks	4.00	10.00
NNO	Lollipop	5.00	12.00
NNO	Chris Vaughn	4.00	10.00
NNO	Trinity	4.00	10.00

2004 Pacific TNA Tag Teams

COMPLETE SET (8) 2.00 5.00
STATED ODDS 1:5 HOBBY

1	Diamond/Swinger	.30	.75
2	The Naturals	.30	.75
3	3Live Kru	.50	1.25
4	The Gathering	2.00	5.00
5	Red Shirt Security	.30	.75
6	Black Shirt Security	.30	.75
7	Gilberti/Young	.30	.75
8	America's Most Wanted	.50	1.25

2004 Pacific TNA Tattoos

COMPLETE SET (28) 3.00 8.00
STATED ODDS 1:1 HOBBY

1	TNA Logo 1	.12	.30
2	TNA Logo 2	.12	.30
3	TNA Logo 3	.12	.30
4	Total Non-Stop Action	.12	.30
5	PTC Logo 1	.12	.30
6	PTC Logo 2	.12	.30
7	PTC Logo 3	.12	.30
8	Raven	.50	1.25
9	AJ Styles	.30	.75
10	Jeff Jarrett	.60	1.50
11	D'Lo Brown	.20	.50
12	Chris Harris	.12	.30
13	James Storm	.20	.50
14	Shark Boy	.12	.30
15	Ron Killings	.20	.50
16	Konnan	.12	.30
17	BG James	.20	.50
18	Chris Sabin	.12	.30
19	Michael Shane	.12	.30
20	Sonny Siaki	.12	.30
21	Chris Vaughn	.12	.30
22	Trinity	.20	.50
23	America's Most Wanted	.20	.50
24	3Live Kru	.20	.50
25	Red Shirt Security	.12	.30
26	Black Shirt Security	.12	.30
27	Lollipop	.30	.75
28	Goldylocks	.75	2.00

1998 Panini WCW/nWo Photocards

COMPLETE SET (108) 15.00 40.00
UNOPENED BOX (24 PACKS)
UNOPENED PACK (6 CARDS)

1	Goldberg	.50	1.25
2	Goldberg	.50	1.25
3	Goldberg	.50	1.25
4	Goldberg	.50	1.25
5	Goldberg	.50	1.25
6	Goldberg	.50	1.25
7	Goldberg	.50	1.25
8	Goldberg	.50	1.25
9	Goldberg	.50	1.25
10	Goldberg	.50	1.25
11	Goldberg Logo	.50	1.25
12	Goldberg	.50	1.25
13	Goldberg	.50	1.25
14	Goldberg	.50	1.25
15	Goldberg vs. Konnan	.50	1.25
16	Disco Inferno	.12	.30
17	Sting	.50	1.25
18	Sting	.50	1.25
19	Sting	.50	1.25
20	Sting	.50	1.25
21	Sting	.50	1.25
22	Sting Logo	.75	2.00
23	Sting	.50	1.25
24	Sting	.50	1.25
25	Hollywood Hogan	.60	1.50
26	Hollywood Hogan	.60	1.50
27	Hollywood Hogan	.60	1.50
28	Hollywood Hogan Logo	.60	1.50
29	Hollywood Hogan	.60	1.50
30	Hogan vs. Luger	.60	1.50
31	Hollywood Hogan	.60	1.50
32	Ric Flair	.40	1.00
33	Diamond Dallas Page	.30	.75
34	Diamond Dallas Page	.30	.75
35	Dallas Page Logo	.30	.75
36	Diamond Dallas Page	.30	.75
37	Scott Hall	.30	.75
38	Hall vs. Piper	.30	.75
39	Scott Hall	.30	.75
40	Scott Hall	.30	.75
41	Kevin Nash	.25	.60
42	Kevin Nash	.25	.60
43	Kevin Nash Logo	.25	.60
44	Kevin Nash	.25	.60
45	Macho Man	.40	1.00
46	Macho Man Logo	.40	1.00
47	Macho Man	.40	1.00
48	Macho Man vs. Hart	.40	1.00
49	Public Enemy	.12	.30
50	Public Enemy	.12	.30
51	Lex Luger	.20	.50
52	Lex Luger	.20	.50
53	Luger vs. Hogan	.30	.75
54	Lex Luger	.20	.50
55	Lex Luger Logo	.20	.50
56	Lex Luger	.20	.50
57	Buff Bagwell	.12	.30
58	Bagwell vs. Booker T	.15	.40
59	Buff Bagwell	.12	.30
60	Anvil	.15	.40
61	Rick Steiner	.15	.40
62	Rick Steiner	.15	.40
63	Scott Steiner	.15	.40
64	Scott Steiner	.15	.40
65	Raven	.15	.40
66	Raven Logo	.15	.40
67	Raven	.15	.40
68	Glacier	.12	.30
69	Roddy Piper	.40	1.00
70	Piper vs. Hogan	.50	1.25
71	Roddy Piper	.40	1.00
72	Scott Norton	.12	.30
73	Rey Mysterio	.30	.75
74	Rey Mysterio Logo	.30	.75
75	Chris Benoit	.25	.60
76	Benoit vs. Malenko	.25	.60
77	Alex Wright	.12	.30
78	Alex Wright	.12	.30
79	Brian Adams	.12	.30
80	Brian Adams	.12	.30
81	Guerrero vs Konnan	.12	.30
82	Eddie Guerrero	.40	1.00
83	Guerrero vs Malenko	.40	1.00
84	Wrath	.15	.40
85	Chris Jericho	.40	1.00
86	Chris Jericho	.40	1.00
87	Jericho vs. Wright	.40	1.00
88	Chris Jericho	.40	1.00
89	Dean Malenko	.15	.40
90	Malenko vs. Benoit	.15	.40
91	Dean Malenko Logo	.15	.40
92	Dean Malenko	.15	.40
93	Dragon vs Wright	.15	.40
94	Dragon vs Mysterio	.25	.60
95	Konnan	.20	.50
96	Konnan	.20	.50
97	Bret Hart	.40	1.00
98	Bret Hart	.40	1.00
99	Bret Hart	.40	1.00
100	British Bulldog	.30	.75
101	Juventud vs Kidman	.15	.40
102	Juventud vs Kidman	.15	.40
103	Juventud vs Kidman	.15	.40
104	Curt Hennig	.25	.60
105	Saturn	.12	.30
106	Saturn	.12	.30
107	Saturn	.12	.30
108	Nitro Girls	.75	2.00

1999 Panini WCW/nWo Stickers

COMPLETE SET (120) 20.00 50.00
UNOPENED BOX (100 PACKS)
UNOPENED PACK

1	Bill Goldberg	.60	1.50
2	Kevin Nash	.30	.75
3	Diamond Dallas Page	.30	.75
4	Hollywood Hogan	.60	1.50
5	Ric Flair	.50	1.25
6	Nash & Luger Rule!	.30	.75
7	Kevin Nash	.30	.75
8	Kevin Nash	.30	.75
9	Goldberg-Nash Bash!!!	.75	2.00
10	Kevin Nash	.30	.75
11	Kevin Nash	.25	.60
12	Kevin Nash	.30	.75
13	Kevin Nash	.30	.75
14	Kevin Nash	.30	.75
15	Red & Black Attack	.25	.60
16	Who's Next?	.40	1.00
17	Bill Goldberg	.60	1.50
18	Bill Goldberg	.60	1.50
19	Bill Goldberg	.60	1.50
20	Raven's Wings Are Clipped!	.40	1.00
21	A Crushing Headlock On Konnan	.40	1.00
22	Goldberg Tattoo	.75	2.00
23	Bill Goldberg	.60	1.50
24	Bill Goldberg	.60	1.50
25	Bill Goldberg	.60	1.50
26	Hogan Hands Out A Beating!	.60	1.50
27	Hollywood Hogan	.60	1.50
28	Hollywood Hogan	.60	1.50
29	Hollywood Hogan	.60	1.50
30	Hollywood Hogan	.60	1.50
31	Hogan And His Buddy Bischoff!	.60	1.50
32	No Mercy!	.25	.60
33	Hollywood Hogan	.60	1.50
34	Hollywood Hogan	.60	1.50
35	Hollywood Hogan	.60	1.50
36	Ric Flair Struts His Stuff!	.50	1.25
37	Horsemen/Arn Anderson	.40	1.00
38	Chris Benoit	.25	.60
39	Dean Makenko	.15	.40
40	Steve McMichael	.12	.30
41	Malenko Mauls Benoit!	.20	.50
42	Ric Flair Tells It Like It Is...	.60	1.50
43	WOOOOOOOOO!!!	.50	1.25
44	Ric Flair In Action...	.40	1.00
45	Four Horsemen	.25	.60
46	Eddie Guerrero	.40	1.00
47	Juventud Guerrera	.15	.40
48	Rey Mysterio	.40	1.00
49	Juventud Jumps Kidman!	.15	.40
50	Guerrero Airborne!	.40	1.00
51	Eddie Guerrero	.40	1.00
52	Hector Garza	.12	.30
53	La Parka	.12	.30
54	Damian	.12	.30
55	Psychosis	.12	.30
56	Che, Fyre, and Spice	.40	1.00
57	Tigress	.40	1.00
58	The Happy Loving Couple...	.60	1.50
59	AC Jazz	.40	1.00
60	Whisper	.40	1.00
61	Alex Wright...	.12	.30
62	Kidman Gets Drop...	.15	.40
63	Kidman	.15	.40
64	Wrath's Guillotine Drop!	.12	.30
65	Kidman Hangs Tough!	.15	.40
66	Konnan Krushes Eddie Guerrero!	.30	.75
67	Konnan	.20	.50
68	Whisper	.40	1.00
69	British Bulldog	.30	.75
70	Disco Inferno	.12	.30
71	Van Hammer Slams Alex Wright!	.12	.30
72	Booker T.	.25	.60
73	Saturn	.12	.30
74	Ernest Miller Wrestling...	.15	.40
75	Chavo and Pepe	.15	.40
76	Diamond Dallas Page	.30	.75

#			
77 Diamond Dallas Page	.30	.75
78 DDP Has Hart!	.40	1.00
79 DDP Gets The Drop On Sting!	.40	1.00
80 Diamond Dallas Page	.30	.75
81 Bret Hart	.40	1.00
82 Hart Gets A Leg up!	.40	1.00
83 Hart Puts The Hurt On DDP!	.40	1.00
84 DDP Gets Hit By The Hitman!	.40	1.00
85 Your Seat Is Ready!	.40	1.00
86 Scott Hall	.30	.75
87 The Pac In The House!	.30	.75
88 Scott Hall	.30	.75
89 Scott Hall	.30	.75
90 Scott Hall	.30	.75
91 Luger Lights It Up!	.20	.50
92 Luger's Got A Flair For Winning!	.20	.50
93 Lex Luger	.20	.50
94 Lex Luger	.20	.50
95 Lex Luger	.20	.50
96 Big Poppa Pump Pumps It Up!	.15	.40
97 Big Poppa Pump Pummels XXX!	.15	.40
98 NWO Bad Boy Buff Bagwell!	.12	.30
99 Big Poppa Pump Makes His Point!	.15	.40
100 Steiner's Super Bod!	.15	.40
101 Hollywood Hogan Gets Stung!	.40	1.00
102 Sting	.50	1.25
103 Scorpion	.50	1.25
104 Sting	.50	1.25
105 Sting	.50	1.25
106 Alex Wright	.12	.30
107 Chris Jericho	.40	1.00
108 Eric Bischoff	.25	.60
109 Scott Norton	.12	.30
110 Glacier	.12	.30
111 Rick Steiner	.15	.40
112 Public Enemy	.12	.30
113 Brian Adams	.12	.30
114 Bagwell Bags Rick Steiner!	.15	.40
115 The Announcers	.12	.30
116 Kendall Windham Slam...	.12	.30
117 Where The Big Boys Play!	.25	.60
118 Raven At Rest!	.15	.40
119 Wright Or Wrong?	.12	.30
120 Anvil!!! (Bam Bam Bigelow)	.20	.50

1995 Panini WWF

1 Bret "Hit Man" Hart
2 Diesel
3 Shawn Michaels
4 Razor Ramon
5 The Undertaker
6 Bam Bam Bigelow
7 British Bulldog
8 Smoking Gunns
9 King Mabel & Sir Mo
10 Yokozuna
11 Body Donnas
12 Savio Vega
13 1-2-3 Kid
14 Bertha Faye
15 Bob "Spark Plugg" Holly
16 Goldust
17 King Kong Bundy
18 Isaac Yankem
19 Sid
20 Waylon Mercy
21 Dean Douglas
22 Owen Hart

23 Hakushi
24 Henry "Hog" Godwinn
25 Hunter Hearst-Helmsley
26 Bret "Hit Man" Hart
27 Diesel
28 Shawn Michaels
29 Razor Ramon
30 The Undertaker
31 Bam Bam Bigelow
32 British Bulldog
33 Smoking Gunns
34 King Mabel & Sir Mo
35 Yokozuna
36 Body Donnas
37 Savio Vega
38 1-2-3 Kid
39 Bertha Faye
40 Bob "Spark Plugg" Holly
41 Goldust
42 King Kong Bundy
43 Isaac Yankem
44 Sid
45 Waylon Mercy
46 Dean Douglas
47 Owen Hart
48 Hakushi
49 Henry "Hog" Godwinn
50 Hunter Hearst-Helmsley
51 Bret "Hit Man" Hart
52 Diesel
53 Shawn Michaels
54 Razor Ramon
55 The Undertaker
56 Bam Bam Bigelow
57 British Bulldog
58 Smoking Gunns
59 King Mabel & Sir Mo
60 Yokozuna
61 Body Donnas
62 Savio Vega
63 1-2-3 Kid
64 Bertha Faye
65 Bob "Spark Plugg" Holly
66 Goldust
67 King Kong Bundy
68 Isaac Yankem
69 Sid
70 Waylon Mercy
71 Dean Douglas
72 Owen Hart
73 Hakushi
74 Henry "Hog" Godwinn
75 Hunter Hearst-Helmsley
76 Bret "Hit Man" Hart
77 Diesel
78 Shawn Michaels
79 Razor Ramon
80 The Undertaker
81 Bam Bam Bigelow
82 British Bulldog
83 Smoking Gunns
84 King Mabel & Sir Mo
85 Yokozuna
86 Body Donnas
87 Savio Vega
88 1-2-3 Kid
89 Bertha Faye
90 Bob "Spark Plugg" Holly

91 Goldust
92 King Kong Bundy
93 Isaac Yankem
94 Sid
95 Waylon Mercy
96 Dean Douglas
97 Owen Hart
98 Hakushi
99 Henry "Hog" Godwinn
100 Hunter Hearst-Helmsley

1997 Panini WWF

COMPLETE SET (180)
UNOPENED BOX (50 PACKS)
UNOPENED PACK

1 In Your House
2 WrestleMania XII
3 SummerSlam
4 Monday Night RAW
5 Undertaker
6 Undertaker
7 Undertaker
8 Undertaker
9 Undertaker
10 Undertaker
11 Undertaker
12 Undertaker
13 Undertaker
14 Undertaker
15 Undertaker
16 Undertaker
17 Shawn Michaels
18 Shawn Michaels
19 Shawn Michaels
20 Shawn Michaels
21 Shawn Michaels
22 Shawn Michaels
23 Shawn Michaels
24 Shawn Michaels
25 Shawn Michaels
26 Shawn Michaels
27 Shawn Michaels
28 Shawn Michaels
29 Sycho Sid
30 Sycho Sid
31 Sycho Sid
32 Sycho Sid
33 Sycho Sid
34 Sycho Sid
35 Sycho Sid
36 Sycho Sid
37 Sycho Sid
38 Sycho Sid
39 Sycho Sid
40 Sycho Sid
41 Stone Cold Steve Austin
42 Stone Cold Steve Austin
43 Stone Cold Steve Austin
44 Stone Cold Steve Austin
45 Stone Cold Steve Austin
46 Stone Cold Steve Austin
47 Stone Cold Steve Austin
48 Stone Cold Steve Austin
49 Stone Cold Steve Austin
50 Stone Cold Steve Austin
51 Stone Cold Steve Austin
52 Stone Cold Steve Austin
53 Goldust

54 Goldust
55 Goldust
56 Goldust
57 Goldust
58 Goldust
59 Goldust
60 Goldust
61 Goldust
62 Goldust
63 Goldust
64 Marlena
65 Bret "Hit Man" Hart
66 Bret "Hit Man" Hart
67 Bret "Hit Man" Hart
68 Bret "Hit Man" Hart
69 Bret "Hit Man" Hart
70 Bret "Hit Man" Hart
71 Bret "Hit Man" Hart
72 Bret "Hit Man" Hart
73 Bret "Hit Man" Hart
74 Bret "Hit Man" Hart
75 Bret "Hit Man" Hart
76 Bret "Hit Man" Hart
77 Mankind
78 Mankind
79 Mankind
80 Mankind
81 Mankind
82 Mankind
83 Mankind
84 Mankind
85 Mankind
86 Mankind
87 Mankind
88 Mankind
89 The British Bulldog
90 The British Bulldog
91 The British Bulldog
92 The British Bulldog
93 The British Bulldog
94 The British Bulldog
95 The British Bulldog
96 The British Bulldog
97 The British Bulldog
98 The British Bulldog
99 The British Bulldog
100 The British Bulldog
101 Ahmed Johnson
102 Ahmed Johnson
103 Ahmed Johnson
104 Ahmed Johnson
105 Ahmed Johnson
106 Ahmed Johnson
107 Ahmed Johnson
108 Ahmed Johnson
109 Ahmed Johnson
110 Ahmed Johnson
111 Ahmed Johnson
112 Ahmed Johnson
113 Rocky Maivia
114 Rocky Maivia
115 Rocky Maivia
116 Rocky Maivia
117 Rocky Maivia
118 Rocky Maivia
119 Rocky Maivia
120 Rocky Maivia
121 Rocky Maivia

122 Rocky Maivia
123 Rocky Maivia
124 Rocky Maivia
125 The Godwinns
126 The Godwinns
127 The Headbangers
128 The Headbangers
129 The Headbangers
130 The Godwinns
131 The Godwinns
132 Bart Gunn
133 Bart Gunn
134 Honky Tonk Man
135 Honky Tonk Man
136 Owen Hart
137 Owen Hart
138 Owen Hart
139 Owen Hart
140 Owen Hart
141 The Legion of Doom
142 The Legion of Doom
143 The Legion of Doom
144 The Legion of Doom
145 The Legion of Doom
146 Marc Mero
147 Marc Mero
148 Sable
149 Marc Mero
150 Marc Mero
151 Triple H
152 Triple H
153 Triple H
154 Triple H
155 Chyna
156 Flash Funk
157 Flash Funk
158 Flash Funk
159 Flash Funk
160 Flash Funk
161 Faarooq
162 Faarooq
163 Faarooq
164 Faarooq
165 Faarooq
166 Crush
167 Crush
168 Crush
169 Crush
170 Crush
171 Savio Vega
172 Savio Vega
173 Savio Vega
174 Savio Vega
175 Savio Vega
176 Vader
177 Vader
178 Vader
179 Vader
180 Vader

1999 Paper Magic nWo Valentine's Day Cards

NNO Buff Bagwell
NNO Disco Inferno
NNO Hollywood Hogan
NNO Kevin Nash
NNO Lex Luger
NNO nWo Happy Valentine's Day

Hogan/Hall/Luger
NNO Scott Hall
NNO Scott Steiner

1998 Paper Magic WCW-nWo Valentine's Day Cards

NNO Macho Man Randy Savage
NNO Bret "Hit Man" Hart
NNO Curt Hennig
NNO DDP
NNO The Giant
NNO Goldberg
NNO Hollywood Hogan
NNO Kevin Nash
NNO Lex Luger
NNO Sting

2013 Paper Magic WWE Valentine's Day 3-D Lenticular Cards

NNO Alberto Del Rio
NNO CM Punk
NNO John Cena
NNO Kofi Kingston
NNO Randy Orton
NNO Rey Mysterio
NNO The Rock
NNO Sheamus
NNO Undertaker

2017 Paper Magic WWE Valentine's Day 3-D Lenticular Cards

NNO AJ Styles
NNO Dean Ambrose
NNO The Demon Finn Balor
NNO Goldberg
NNO John Cena
NNO The New Day
NNO Roman Reigns
NNO Seth Rollins

2019 Paper Magic WWE Valentine's Day 3-D Lenticular Cards

NNO AJ Styles
You Are a Superstar, Valentine!
NNO Alexa Bliss
You Are Amazing, Valentine!
NNO John Cena
Never Give Up, Valentine!
NNO Naomi
You Are a Sensation, Valentine!
NNO Roman Reigns
You Reign, Valentine!
NNO Sasha Banks
Happy Valentine's Day to You!
NNO Seth Rollins
Have a Fantastic Valentine's Day!
NNO Shinsuke Nakamura
I Hope You Have an Exciting Valentine's Day!

2012 Paper Magic WWE Valentine's Day Cards

NNO John Cena
Happy Valentine's Day to You Friend!
NNO Kofi Kingston
I Hope Your Valentine's Day Is Great!
NNO The Miz
I Hope Your Valentine's Day Is Awesome!

NNO The Rock
Hope Your Valentine's Day Rocks!
NNO The Rock/John Cena
You're the Best Valentine!
NNO Sin Cara
Have a High-Flying Valentine's Day!
NNO Triple H
You Are a Winner Valentine!
NNO Undertaker
Have a Fantastic Valentine's Day!

2012 Paper Magic WWE Valentine's Day Cards Poster

NNO John Cena vs. The Rock

2013 Paper Magic WWE Valentine's Day Cards

NNO Alberto Del Rio
You Are the Best, Valentine!
NNO CM Punk
Go for It, Valentine!
NNO John Cena
Happy Valentine's Day to You!
NNO Kofi Kingston
Have a Great Valentine's Day!
NNO Randy Orton
I Hope Your Valentine's Day Is Awesome!
NNO Rey Mysterio
NNO The Rock
Hope Your Valentine's Day Rocks!
NNO Sheamus
You Are a Winner, Valentine!
NNO Undertaker
Have a Fantastic Valentine's Day

2014 Paper Magic WWE Valentine's Day Cards

NNO Daniel Bryan
Be the Best, Valentine!
NNO HHH/Cena/Orton
Hope Your Valentine's Day Is Full of Excitement!
NNO John Cena
You Are Amazing!
NNO Kofi Kingston
Hope You Have a Dynamic Valentine's Day!
NNO Randy Orton
Have an Intense Valentine's Day!
NNO The Rock
Valentine, You Rock!
NNO Sheamus
Have a Fantastic Valentine's Day!
NNO Triple H
Valentine, You're a Winner!

2014 Paper Magic WWE Valentine's Day Cards Sheet Inserts

NNO Stickers
NNO Tattoos

2015 Paper Magic WWE Valentine's Day Cards

NNO Bray Wyatt
NNO Daniel Bryan
NNO Dean Ambrose
NNO John Cena
NNO Kofi Kingston
NNO The Rock

NNO Roman Reigns
NNO Seth Rollins
NNO Undertaker

2016 Paper Magic WWE Valentine's Day Cards

NNO Dean Ambrose
Happy Valentine's Day to You!
NNO John Cena
Never Give Up, Valentine!
NNO Kalisto & Sin Cara
Hope You Have an Exciting Valentine's Day!
NNO The New Day
Have a Fantastic Valentine's Day!
NNO Randy Orton
You Are a Legend, Valentine!
NNO The Rock
You Rock Valentine!
NNO Roman Reigns
You Reign Valentine!
NNO Seth Rollins
You Are a Sensation, Valentine!

2017 Paper Magic WWE Valentine's Day Cards

NNO Dean Ambrose
Happy Valentine's Day to You!
NNO The Demon Finn Balor
You Are the Best Valentine!
NNO Goldberg
You Are a Legend, Valentine!
NNO John Cena
You Are a Champ, Valentine!
NNO The New Day
Have a Fantastic Valentine's Day!
NNO Roman Reigns
You Reign, Valentine!
NNO Sasha Banks
You Are the Boss, Valentine!
NNO Seth Rollins
You Are a Winner, Valentine!

2018 Paper Magic WWE Valentine's Day Cards

NNO AJ Styles
You Are a Superstar Valentine!
NNO Bayley
You Are Amazing, Valentine!
NNO John Cena
Never Give Up, Valentine!
NNO Naomi
You Are a Sensation, Valentine!
NNO Roman Reigns
You Reign Valentine!
NNO Sasha Banks
Happy Valentine's Day to You!
NNO Seth Rollins
Have a Fantastic Valentine's Day!
NNO Shinsuke Nakamura
Hope You Have an Exciting Valentine's Day!

2019 Paper Magic WWE Valentine's Day Cards

NNO AJ Styles
NNO Alexa Bliss
NNO John Cena
NNO Naomi

NNO Roman Reigns
NNO Sasha Banks
NNO Seth Rollins
NNO Shinsuke Nakamura

2017 Paper Magic WWE Valentine's Day Scratch-Off Cards

NNO Dean Ambrose
Valentine, You Are Unstoppable!
NNO John Cena
Never Give Up, Valentine!
NNO The New Day
Have an Amazing Valentine's Day!
NNO Roman Reigns
You Reign, Valentine!

1991 Paper Magic WWF Valentine's Day Cards

NNO Big Boss Man
Get Ready for Some Heart Time!
NNO Hulk Hogan
Be Mine!
NNO Hulk Hogan
Hulkamania's Runnin' Wild on Valentine's Day!
NNO Hulk Hogan
You're My #1 Hulkamaniac Valentine!
NNO Jake "The Snake" Roberts
Here's Looking at You, Valentine!
NNO Jake "The Snake" Roberts
Would You Be My S-S-Sweetheart!
NNO Legion of Doom
What a Rush, Valentine!
NNO Macho Man Randy Savage
Oh Yeah, I Want to Be Your Valentine!
NNO The Million Dollar Man Ted DiBiase
You're My Million Dollar Valentine!
NNO Mr. Perfect
You're the Perfect Valentine for Me!
NNO The Rockers
Have a Rock'n Valentine's Day!
NNO Texas Tornado
February 14th Is the Main Event!
NNO Ultimate Warrior
Wishing You the "Ultimate" Valentine's Day!

1954-55 Parkhurst Wrestling

COMPLETE SET (75)	350.00	600.00
*PREMIUM BACKS: SAME VALUE		
1 Lou Thesz	10.00	25.00
2 Sky Hi Lee	4.00	10.00
3 Whipper Billy Watson	4.00	10.00
4 Johnny Barend	4.00	10.00
5 Antonio Argentina Rocca	6.00	15.00
6 Dirty Dick Raines	4.00	10.00
7 Frank Valois	4.00	10.00
8 Hombre Montana	4.00	10.00
9 Lou Plummer	4.00	10.00
10 Chief Big Heart	4.00	10.00
11 Man Mountain Dean Jr.	4.00	10.00
12 Primo Carnera	10.00	25.00
13 Paul Baillargeon	4.00	10.00
14 Nick Roberts	4.00	10.00
15 Tim Geohagen	4.00	10.00
16 The Togo Brothers	4.00	10.00
17 Verne Gagne	12.00	30.00
18 Maurice Tillet	4.00	10.00
19 Yukon Eric	4.00	10.00
20 Toar Morgan	4.00	10.00
21 Mighty Schultz	4.00	10.00
22 Bill Stack	4.00	10.00
23 Argentina Rocca	6.00	15.00
24 Big Ben Morgan	4.00	10.00
25 Lou Pitoscia	4.00	10.00
26 Earl McCready & Billy Watson	4.00	10.00
27 Hans Schmidt	4.00	10.00
28 Lu Kim	4.00	10.00
29 Roy McLarity	4.00	10.00
30 Lord Jan Blears	4.00	10.00
31 Lee Henning & Fred Atkins	4.00	10.00
32 Jim Goon Henry	4.00	10.00
33 Wee Willie Davis	4.00	10.00
34 Yvon Robert	4.00	10.00
35 Joe Killer Christie	4.00	10.00
36 Bo Bo Brazil	8.00	20.00
37 The Sharpe Brothers	4.00	10.00
38 Larry Moquin	4.00	10.00
39 Nanjo Singh	4.00	10.00
40 Wladek Kowalski	10.00	25.00
41 Frank Sexton	4.00	10.00
42 George Bollas	4.00	10.00
43 Ray Villmer	4.00	10.00
44 Steve Stanlee	4.00	10.00
45 Tuffy McCrae & Little Beaver	4.00	10.00
46 Johnny Rougeau	4.00	10.00
47 Harry Lewis	4.00	10.00
48 Pat Flanagan	4.00	10.00
49 Ovila Asselin	4.00	10.00
50 Sammy Berg	4.00	10.00
51 The Mighty Ursus	4.00	10.00
52 Lou Newman	4.00	10.00
53 George Scott	4.00	10.00
54 Hans Hermann	4.00	10.00
55 Bob Wagner	4.00	10.00
56 Little Beaver/Salassi	4.00	10.00
57 Sandor Kovacs	4.00	10.00
58 The Mills Brothers	4.00	10.00
59 Roberto Pico	4.00	10.00
60 Fred Atkins	4.00	10.00
61 Wild Bill Longson	4.00	10.00
62 Bobby Managoff	4.00	10.00
63 Athol Layton	4.00	10.00
64 Warren Bockwinkle	4.00	10.00
65 The Mighty Atlas	4.00	10.00
66 Mike Sharpe	4.00	10.00
67 Ernie Dusek	4.00	10.00
68 Danno O'Shocker	4.00	10.00
69 Gorgeous George	20.00	50.00
70 The Great Togo	4.00	10.00
71 Bob Langevin	4.00	10.00
72 Emil Dusek	4.00	10.00
73 Chief Sunni War Cloud	4.00	10.00
74 Pat O'Connor	4.00	10.00
75 Baron Leone	5.00	12.00

1955-56 Parkhurst Wrestling

COMPLETE SET (121)	450.00	800.00
1 Frank Valois	6.00	15.00
2 Johnny Barend	4.00	10.00
3 Sky Hi Lee	4.00	10.00
4 Hans Schmidt	4.00	10.00
5 Hans Hermann	4.00	10.00
6 Bo Bo Brazil	8.00	20.00
7 Chief Sunni War Cloud	4.00	10.00
8 The Mills Brothers	4.00	10.00
9 Roy McLarity	4.00	10.00
10 Danno O'Shocker	4.00	10.00
11 Chief Big Heart	4.00	10.00
12 Bob Wagner	4.00	10.00
13 Lou Pitoscia	4.00	10.00
14 Ernie Dusek	4.00	10.00
15 Whipper Watson	4.00	10.00
16 Johnny Rougeau	4.00	10.00
17 Ovila Asselin	4.00	10.00
18 Bill Stack	4.00	10.00
19 Ken Kenneth	4.00	10.00
20 Lou Newman	4.00	10.00
21 Warren Bockwinkle	4.00	10.00
22 The Sharpe Brothers	4.00	10.00
23 Bobby Managoff	4.00	10.00
24 Nick Roberts	4.00	10.00
25 Lee Henning	4.00	10.00
26 Joe Christie	4.00	10.00
27 Larry Moquin	4.00	10.00
28 Jim Goon Henry	4.00	10.00
29 Bob Langevin	4.00	10.00
30 Roberto Pico	4.00	10.00
31 Sammy Berg	4.00	10.00
32 Mighty Atlas	4.00	10.00
33 Baron Leone	4.00	10.00
34 Hassen Bay	4.00	10.00
35 Allen Garfield	4.00	10.00
36 Don Evans	4.00	10.00
37 Dory Funk	8.00	20.00
38 Art Neilson	4.00	10.00
39 Don Lee Jonathan	4.00	10.00
40 Argentina Rocca	6.00	15.00
41 Tex McKenzie	4.00	10.00
42 Pat Flanagan	4.00	10.00
43 Verne Gagne	8.00	20.00
44 Selassi & Little Beaver	4.00	10.00
45 Steve Stanlee	4.00	10.00
46 Frank Sexton	4.00	10.00
47 Pat O'Connor	4.00	10.00
48 Nanjo Singh	4.00	10.00
49 Toar Morgan	4.00	10.00
50 Harry Lewis	4.00	10.00
51 Doug Hepburn	4.00	10.00
52 Reggie Lisowski	4.00	10.00
53 Kenny Ackles	4.00	10.00
54 Argentina Rocca	6.00	15.00
55 Herb Parks	4.00	10.00
56 Bearcat Wright	4.00	10.00
57 Yvon Robert	4.00	10.00
58 Waldo Von Sieber	4.00	10.00
59 Harold Nelson	4.00	10.00
60 Sumo Wrestlers	4.00	10.00
61 Golden Hawk	4.00	10.00
62 Wee Willie Davis	4.00	10.00
63 Mike Sharpe	4.00	10.00
64 Sandor Kovacs	4.00	10.00
65 Lord Blears	4.00	10.00
66 Tim Goehagen	4.00	10.00
67 Jack Laskin	4.00	10.00
68 Emil Dusek	4.00	10.00
69 Ben Morgan	4.00	10.00
70 Lu Kim	4.00	10.00
71 Frank Marconi	4.00	10.00
72 Prince Maiava	4.00	10.00
73 Larry Kasaboski	4.00	10.00
74 Frank Thompson	4.00	10.00
75 Yukon Eric	4.00	10.00
76 Lou Thesz	6.00	15.00
77 Bill Longson	4.00	10.00
78 Fred Atkins	4.00	10.00
79 Lord Layton	4.00	10.00
80 Dusek Brothers	4.00	10.00
81 Zorra	4.00	10.00
82 Lou Thesz	10.00	25.00
83 Luther Lindsey	4.00	10.00
84 Jack Bence	4.00	10.00
85 Primo Carnera	8.00	20.00
86 Kalmikoff Brothers	4.00	10.00
87 The Great Togo	4.00	10.00
88 Lou Plummer	4.00	10.00
89 Bates Ford	4.00	10.00
90 Ursus and Montana	4.00	10.00
91 Paul Baillargeon	4.00	10.00
92 Bill McDaniels	4.00	10.00
93 Ray Villmer	4.00	10.00
94 Yvon Robert	4.00	10.00
95 Gorgeous George	15.00	40.00
96 Scott Brothers	4.00	10.00
97 Bronko Nagurski	50.00	100.00
98 Pete Managoff	4.00	10.00
99 The Togo Brothers	4.00	10.00
100 Don Lee	4.00	10.00
101 Steve Patrick	4.00	10.00
102 George Gordienko	4.00	10.00
103 Vic Holbrook	4.00	10.00
104 Gil Mains	4.00	10.00
105 Firpo Zbyszko	4.00	10.00
106 Mike Paidousis	4.00	10.00
107 Al Oeming	4.00	10.00
108 Matt Murphy	4.00	10.00
109 Martin Hutzler	4.00	10.00
110 Tommy O'Toole	4.00	10.00
111 Steve Gob	4.00	10.00
112 Riot Call Wright	4.00	10.00
113 Leo Newman	4.00	10.00
114 Frank Hurley	4.00	10.00
115 Jack Claybourne	4.00	10.00
116 Ken Colley	4.00	10.00
117 Whipper Watson	4.00	10.00
118 Steve McGill	4.00	10.00
119 Buddy Rogers	4.00	10.00
120 Gino Garibaldi	4.00	10.00
121 Ed Gardenia	5.00	12.00

2006 Popeye's WWE Mania Moments

COMPLETE SET (21)	15.00	40.00
1 Andre the Giant	1.50	4.00
2 Rowdy Roddy Piper	1.50	4.00
3 Hulk Hogan	2.00	5.00
4 Ted Dibiase	1.25	3.00
5 Jake The Snake Roberts	1.50	4.00
6 Skydome	.60	1.50
7 Sgt. Slaughter	2.00	5.00
8 Ric Flair	1.50	4.00
9 Bobby Heenan	.75	2.00
10 Mr. Perfect	1.00	2.50
11 Bam Bam Bigelow	1.00	2.50
12 Shawn Michaels	2.00	5.00
13 Undertaker	1.50	4.00
14 Stone Cold Steve Austin	2.00	5.00
15 The Rock	2.00	5.00
16 Mick Foley	1.00	2.50
17 Kurt Angle	1.25	3.00
18 Triple H	2.00	5.00
19 Rey Mysterio	1.25	3.00
20 Chris Benoit	1.25	3.00
21 Batista / John Cena	2.00	5.00

1997 Prima WCW vs. nWo World Tour Strategy

COMPLETE SET (9)

NNO Buff Bagwell
NNO Giant
NNO Hulk Hogan
NNO Kevin Nash
NNO Lex Luger
NNO Sting
NNO Syxx
NNO Ultimo Dragon
NNO WCW vs. nWo World Tour Title Ad

1998 PrimeTime Industries WCW/nWo Talking Portrait Promos

Exclusive to the 19th National Sports Collectors Convention (NSCC).

NNO Brett Hitman Hart UER
NNO Diamond Dallas Page
NNO The Giant
NNO Hollywood Hogan
NNO Randy Macho Man Savage
NNO Sting

2005 Prominter WWE Smackdown!/RAW Animotion Italian

COMPLETE SET (192)
UNOPENED BOX (24 PACKS)
UNOPENED PACK (4 CARDS)

1 Booker T
2 Doug Basham
3 Basham Brothers
4 Batista
5 Batista
6 Batista
7 Big Show
8 Carlito
9 Carlito
10 Charlie Haas
11 Chris Benoit
12 Chris Benoit
13 Chris Jericho
14 Christopher Nowinski
15 Christy Hemme
16 Christian
17 Christian
18 Christian
19 Dawn Marie
20 Danny Basham
21 Dudley Boyz
22 Eddie Guerrero
23 Edge
24 Edge
25 Eugene
26 Eugene
27 Eugene
28 Eugene
29 Garrison Cade
30 Gene Snitsky
31 Hardcore Holly
32 Heidenreich
33 Heidenreich
34 The Hurricane
35 Jerry The King Lawler
36 Jim Ross
37 John Bradshaw Layfield
38 John Cena
39 John Cena
40 John Cena
41 Kane
42 Kane
43 Kane
44 Kurt Angle
45 Lita
46 Los Guerreros vs. Basham Brothers
47 Luther Reigns
48 Mark Henry
49 Matt Hardy
50 Mark Jindrak
51 Matt Morgan
52 Maven
53 Mick Foley
54 Miss Jackie
55 Molly Holly
56 Nunzio
57 Nunzio
58 Orlando Jordan
59 Paul London
60 Paul Heyman
61 Rob Van Dam
62 Rob Van Dam
63 Randy Orton
64 Rene Dupree
65 Rey Mysterio
66 Rey Mysterio
67 Rhyno
68 Ric Flair
69 Rob Conway
70 The Rock
71 The Rock
72 Rosey
73 Rosey
74 Scotty 2 Hotty
75 Shawn Michaels
76 Shawn Michaels
77 Shane McMahon
78 Shannon Moore
79 Shelton Benjamin
80 Stacy Keibler
81 Stacy Keibler
82 Stacy Keibler
83 Stevie Richards
84 Tajiri
85 Tajiri
86 Theodore Long
87 Chavo Guerrero
88 Torrie Wilson
89 Trish Stratus
90 Trish Stratus
91 Trish Stratus
92 Ultimo Dragon
93 Undertaker
94 Victoria
95 Vince McMahon
96 William Regal
97 Al Snow
98 Akio
99 Akio
100 Hugh Morrus
101 The Coach
102 Ivory
103 Kenzo Suzuki
104 Kenzo Suzuki
105 Sylvain Grenier
106 Stephanie McMahon
107 Tazz
108 Val Venis
109 Tyson Tomko
110 Christian
111 Big Show
112 Kurt Angle
113 Kurt Angle
114 Rene Dupree
115 Triple H
116 Triple H
117 Tajiri
118 John Cena
119 John Cena
120 Eric Bischoff
121 Muhammad Hassan
122 Eric Bischoff
123 Funaki
124 Hiroko
125 Simon Dean
126 Booker T
127 Bubba Rey Dudley
128 Bubba Rey Dudley
129 D-Von Dudley
130 John Bradshaw Layfield
131 Batista
132 Kane
133 Gene Snitsky
134 Rob Van Dam
135 Undertaker
136 Undertaker
137 Undertaker
138 The Hurricane
139 The Hurricane
140 Molly Holly
141 Shawn Michaels
142 Edge
143 Trish Stratus
144 Victoria
145 Victoria vs. Trish Stratus
146 Batista vs. Randy Orton
147 Big Show vs. Kurt Angle
148 Big Show vs. Tutti
149 Billy Kidman vs. Matt Morgan
150 Victoria vs. Molly Holly
151 Batista vs. Gene Snitsky
152 Big Show vs. Danny Basham
153 Big Show vs. Danny Basham
154 Gene Snitsky vs. Kane
155 Edge vs. Randy Orton
156 Christian vs. Shelton Benjamin
157 Batista vs. Rene Dupree
158 Kane vs. Gene Snitsky
159 Kane vs. Shelton Benjamin
160 Edge vs. Gene Snitsky
161 Lita vs. Victoria
162 Lita vs. Molly Holly
163 JBL vs. Kurt Angle
164 JBL
165 John Cena vs. Doug Basham
166 Eugene vs. Sylvain Grenier
167 Eugene vs. Sylvain Grenier
168 Trish Stratus vs. Lita
169 Kane vs. Maven
170 Shelton Benjamin vs. Christian
171 Molly Holly vs. Trish Stratus
172 Randy Orton vs. Edge
173 Randy Orton vs. Christian
174 Randy Orton vs. Christian
175 Kane vs. Chris Jericho
176 Kenzo Suzuki vs. Rob Van Dam
177 Kenzo Suzuki vs. Scotty 2 Hotty
178 John Cena vs. Danny Basham
179 John Cena vs. Danny Basham
180 Kurt Angle vs. Eddie Guerrero
181 Rosey & Hurricane
182 Big Show vs. Kurt Angle
183 Eddie Guerrero vs. Rey Mysterio
184 Booker T vs. Rene Dupree
185 Eddie Guerrero vs. Luther Reigns
186 Eddie Guerrero vs. Rey Mysterio
187 John Cena vs. Booker T
188 Triple H vs. Chris Benoit
189 John Cena vs. Chavo Guerrero
190 John Cena
191 Kurt Angle
192 Triple H

1982 PWE Wrestling All-Stars Series A

COMPLETE SET (36)		650.00	1300.00
CARDS PRICED IN NR-MT CONDITION			
1	Andre the Giant	200.00	400.00
2	Hulk Hogan	300.00	600.00
3	Mil Mascaras	20.00	50.00
4	Ted DiBiase	30.00	75.00
5	The Junkyard Dog	20.00	50.00
6	Dusty Rhodes	50.00	100.00
7	Jack Brisco	8.00	20.00
8	Harley Race	15.00	40.00
9	Dory Funk Jr.	5.00	12.00
10	Terry Funk	30.00	75.00
11	Nick Bockwinkel	12.00	30.00
12	Bob Backlund	15.00	40.00
13	Bruno Sammartino	20.00	50.00
14	Pedro Morales	5.00	12.00
15	Don Muraco	8.00	20.00
16	Bill Dundee	5.00	12.00
17	Steve Olsonoski	5.00	12.00
18	Tommy Rich	10.00	25.00
19	Angelo Mosca	5.00	12.00
20	Bruiser Brody	75.00	150.00
21	The Fabulous Moolah	15.00	40.00
22	Wahoo McDaniel	12.00	30.00
23	Billy Robinson	6.00	15.00
24	Ivan Koloff	8.00	20.00
25	Tony Atlas	10.00	25.00
26	Pat Patterson	15.00	40.00
27	Ric Flair	250.00	500.00
28	Ivan Putski	10.00	25.00
29	Dick Murdoch	5.00	12.00
30	The Crusher	8.00	20.00
31	Ken Patera	8.00	20.00
32	Ernie Ladd	8.00	20.00
33	Dick the Bruiser	8.00	20.00
34	Jerry Lawler	30.00	75.00
35	Cowboy Bill Watts	5.00	12.00
36	The Destroyer	5.00	12.00

1983 PWE Wrestling All-Stars Series A

COMPLETE SET (36)		200.00	400.00
CARDS PRICED IN NR-MT CONDITION			
1	Superstar (Billy) Graham	8.00	20.00
2	Tiger Mask	3.00	8.00
3	Sheik El Kaissey	2.00	5.00

4	Sgt. Jacque Goulet	2.00	5.00
5	Curt Hennig	25.00	60.00
6	Tully Blanchard	10.00	25.00
7	Jimmy Superfly Snuka	15.00	40.00
8	Gino Hernandez	2.00	5.00
9	Lou Thesz	6.00	15.00
10	Hacksaw (Jim) Duggan	20.00	50.00
11	Mr. Olympia	2.00	5.00
12	Iron Mike Sharpe	3.00	8.00
13	Jimmy Hart	6.00	15.00
14	Spike Huber	2.00	5.00
15	Steve Regal	3.00	8.00
16	Buddy Rogers	6.00	15.00
17	Jules Strongbow	6.00	15.00
18	Salvatore Bellomo	2.50	6.00
19	Bob Sweetan	2.00	5.00
20	Scott Casey	2.00	5.00
21	The Grappler	5.00	12.00
22	Big John Studd	10.00	25.00
23	Buddy Rose	5.00	12.00
24	Rocky Johnson	25.00	60.00
25	Jake Roberts	50.00	100.00
26	The Super Destroyer	3.00	8.00
27	Antonio Inoki	10.00	25.00
28	Dick Slater	3.00	8.00
29	Ken Lucas	2.00	5.00
30	Ricky Morton	8.00	20.00
31	Fred Blassie	12.00	30.00
32	Lou Albano	12.00	30.00
33	The Grand Wizard	4.00	10.00
34	Candi Divine	5.00	12.00
35	Austin Idol	4.00	10.00
36	Matt Borne	3.00	8.00

1982 PWE Wrestling All-Stars Series B

COMPLETE SET (36)   300.00 600.00
CARDS PRICED IN NR-MT CONDITION

1	Rick Martel	10.00	25.00
2	Tony Garea	8.00	20.00
3	Bob Roop	8.00	20.00
4	Greg Gagne	12.00	30.00
5	Jim Brunzell	6.00	15.00
6	Jay Strongbow	10.00	25.00
7	Kerry Von Erich	60.00	120.00
8	S.D. Jones	6.00	15.00
9	Brad Rheingans	6.00	15.00
10	Killer Khan	15.00	40.00
11	Ricky Steamboat	30.00	75.00
12	Paul Orndorff	15.00	40.00
13	Tito Santana	15.00	40.00
14	Sergeant Slaughter	25.00	60.00
15	Verne Gagne	10.00	25.00
16	Bobby Heenan	15.00	40.00
17	Jerry Blackwell	8.00	20.00
18	Les Thornton	4.00	10.00
19	Adrian Adonis	10.00	25.00
20	Jesse Ventura	30.00	75.00
21	Buck Zum Hofe	4.00	10.00
22	Jimmy Valiant	8.00	20.00
23	Steve Keirn	5.00	12.00
24	Ray Stevens	6.00	15.00
25	The Iron Sheik	50.00	100.00
26	Mr. Wrestling II	12.00	30.00
27	Col. Buck Robley	4.00	10.00
28	Bobby Duncum	5.00	12.00
29	Mike George	4.00	10.00
30	Dino Bravo	6.00	15.00

31	Baron Von Raschke	12.00	30.00
32	Bobo Brazil	6.00	15.00
33	Greg Valentine	10.00	25.00
34	Joyce Grable	6.00	15.00
35	Sweet Brown Sugar	4.00	10.00
36	Dutch Mantell	10.00	25.00

2005-06 PWMA First Edition

COMPLETE SET (26)
STATED PRINT RUN 500 SETS

1 The Russian Bear Ivan Koloff
2 Simply Perfect Preston Quinn
3 Mr. USA Tony Atlas
4 Old School Empire Damien Wayne & Mike Booth
5 Jimmy Superfly Snuka
6 Shane Falco
7 Rock N Roll Robert Gibson
8 Prince Malik
9 The Hands of Stone Ronnie Garvin
10 The Chincoteague Kid Dustin Tarr
11 Beautiful Bobby Eaton
12 Brad Thomas
13 High Flying Chris Hamrick
14 Eric Stace
15 Rock N Roll Ricky Morton
16 Brett Smalls
17 Greg The Hammer Valentine
18 The Living Legend Larry Zbyszko
19 Generation Next David Flair
20 Quickstyle
21 The Natural Mark Fleming
22 Sensational Alexx Sage
23 The 10th Inning Don & Carolynn Harrison
24 Stardust Marc Anthony
25 Mike Valentine Old School Ref
26 Logo/Checklist/Credits

2005 PWX

COMPLETE SET (22)

1 Maddog
2 Kaos
3 Cody Steele
4 Eddie Osbourne
5 Jessy Jones
6 Jacqui Jones
7 Phil Latio
8 Dark Soul
9 Freak Show
10 CK Sexx
11 Predator
12 Jayson Chambers
13 PD Skillz
14 Jeff Black
15 Latino Pete
16 Dragon X
17 Quinson Valentino
18 Evan Storm
19 Aurora
20 AJ Parr
21 21st Century Fox
22 Potbox Hero

2006 PWX

COMPLETE SET (22)

1 Jacqui Jones
2 Jessy Jones
3 Derek Wylde

4	Dragon X
5	Freak Show
6	Cherry Bomb
7	Danyah
8	Canadian Gold'N Boyz
9	Jayson Chambers
10	Buck 10 with Sam Allen
11	Michael Elgin
12	Wildthing Willy Allen
13	Reck
14	Cody Deaner
15	Krystal Banks
16	Independant Soldier
17	The One and Only Jamie D
18	Hickster
19	Flesh
420	PD Skillz
21	Phil Atlas
22	Ty Prattis

2007 PWX

COMPLETE SET (18)

1 Jen Blake
2 Cody Deaner
3 Derek Wylde
4 Freak Show
5 Tyson Dux
6 Kobra Kai
7 Reck
8 Michael Elgin
9 Angela Davis
10 Haley Rogers
11 Hayden Avery
12 Tiana Ringer
13 Daemon Reznor
14 Matt Burns
15 Goldeni Boyz
16 Ash
17 Phil Atlas
18 AJ Parr/JC3

2007 PWX Special Appearances

COMPLETE SET (16)

SP1 Scott Steiner
SP2 Al Snow
SP3 Bobcat
SP420 PD Skillz
SP5 50/50 Girl
SP6 Billy Gunn
SP7 Annie Social
SP8 Brutus Beefcake
SP9 Johnny Trackpants
SP10 April Hunter
SP11 Zach Gowen
SP12 Scotty 2 Hotty
SP13 Gangrel
SP14 Big H
SP15 Shelly Martinez
SP16 Rhyno

1988 Quaker Dipps WWF Canadian

COMPLETE SET (18)

1 Hulk Hogan
2 Randy Macho Man Savage and Elizabeth
3 The Million Dollar Man Ted DiBiase
4 Honky Tonk Man
5 Andre the Giant

6	Hacksaw Jim Duggan
7	The Ultimate Warrior
8	One Man Gang
9	Greg The Hammer Valentine
10	Brutus The Barber Beefcake
11	Bam Bam Bigelow
12	Jake The Snake Roberts
13	Koko B. Ware
14	Hercules
15	Demolition
16	The Killer Bees
17	The Young Stallions
18	The British Bulldogs

1989 Quaker Dipps WWF Canadian

COMPLETE SET (18)

NNO Andre the Giant
NNO Bobby The Brain Heenan
NNO Bret Hit Man Hart
NNO Brutus The Barber Beefcake
NNO The Bushwackers
NNO Demolition
NNO Hacksaw Jim Duggan
NNO Hillbilly Jim
NNO Hulk Hogan
NNO Jake The Snake Roberts
NNO Jimmy Superfly Snuka
NNO Macho Man Randy Savage
NNO Million Dollar Man Ted DiBiase
NNO Mouth of the South Jimmy Hart
NNO Ravishing Rick Rude
NNO The Rockers
NNO Tito Santana
NNO Ultimate Warrior

1999 Racing Champions WCW Nitro Streetrods Limited Edition nWo Black and White

COMPLETE SET (6)

NNO Booker T & Bret Hart
NNO Chris Jericho & Scott Steiner
NNO Diamond Dallas Page & Kevin Nash
NNO Disco Inferno & Brian Adams
NNO Giant & Konnan
NNO Goldberg & Hogan

1999 Racing Champions WCW Nitro Streetrods Limited Edition nWo Wolf Pack

COMPLETE SET (5)

NNO Bam Bam Bigelow & Ric Flair
NNO Billy Kidman & Psychosis
NNO Diamond Dallas Page & Kevin Nash
NNO Juventud Guerrera & Buff Bagwell
NNO Raven & Lex Luger

1979 Rax Roast Beef Gulas NWA Mid America Championship Wrestling

This may very well be the rarest set of professional wrestling cards ever created. This set was offered at the Gulas Pro Wrestling Thanksgiving Spectacular in Nashville, Tennessee on November 21, 1979. The set contains early cards of Bobby Eaton, Robert Gibson and Haku aka Prince Tonga.

NNO Cover Card
NNO Bobby Eaton
NNO Chief Thundercloud

NNO David Shultz
NNO Dennis Condry
NNO Donna Bower
NNO George Gulas
NNO Hans Shroeder
NNO Jerry Barber
NNO Ken Lucas
NNO Len Rossi
NNO Mike St. John
NNO Nick Gulas
NNO Pat Smith
NNO Prince Tonga
NNO The Red Terror
NNO Ricky Gibson
NNO Robert Gibson
NNO Tojo Yamamoto
NNO Tom Renesto, Jr.
NNO Tom Renesto, Sr.
NNO Tommy Kerkeles
NNO Tommy Sloan

2014 Resurrection British Wrestling Magazine

1 Dean Allmark
2 Mark Andrews
3 Mike Bird
4 The Blossom Twins
5 Josh Bodom
6 Chris Brookes
7 Rampage Brown
8 Bubblegum
9 Xander Cooper
10 Jervis Cottonbelly
11 Nathan Cruz
12 Cyanide
13 Noam Dar
14 Eddie Dennis
15 Kid Fite
16 Zack Gibson
17 Jimmy Havoc
18 Danny Hope
19 Hunter Brothers
20 Marty Jones
21 Klondyke Kate
22 Colossus Kennedy
23 Martin Kirby
24 Saraya Knight
25 Lionheart
26 Dave Mastiff
27 Nigel McGuinness
28 Keith Myatt
29 Damian O'Connor
30 Will Ospreay
31 Kay Lee Ray
32 Joel Redman
33 Zack Sabre
34 Marty Scurll
35 RJ Singh
36 Skarlett
37 Frankie Sloan
38 Stixx
39 Martin Stone
40 Adrian Street
41 Dave Taylor
42 Kris Travis
43 Flash Morgan Webster
44 Wild Boar
45 Doug Williams

2017 Resurrection British Wrestling Magazine

1 Nathan Cruz
2 Robbie Dynamite
3 Savvy Sid Scala
4 Dean Allmark
5 Donovan Dijak
6 Hustle Malone
7 Jeff Cobb
8 Bubblegum
9 Ashley Dunn
10 John Hennigan
11 Lewis Girvan
12 Mr. Williams
13 Ashleigh Stark
14 Santana Garrett
15 Xia Brookside
16 Kazza G
17 Solo Darling
18 Lucy Cole
19 Little Miss Roxxy
20 Session Moth Martina
21 Deonna Purrazzo
22 Chakara
23 Scary Su
24 Pikasu

2008 Riot Act Wrestling

COMPLETE SET (8)
1 Nancy Boi Nathaniel Grimm
2 The Red Haired Loon
3 Psycho Steve
4 Jordan E
5 E-Train Edgar Stryfe
6 Tiger Kid
7 The Magic Circle
8 The Brutal Bad Boy Boo Lemont
0 Omer Ibrahim SP

2019 Sabotage Wrestling Series 1

1 Title Card
2 Delilah Doom
3 Jenna Lynn
4 Fun & Sexy
Baby D & Phoebe
5 Rok-C
6 Fun & Sexy
Phoebe & Baby D
7 Shotzi Blackheart
8 Delilah Doom
9 Sea Stars
Ashley & Delmi
10 Shotzi Blackheart
11 Thunder Rosa
NNO Delilah Doom
NNO Delilah Doom Becomes the First Ever Champion at Sabotage
NNO Fun & Sexy
NNO Fun & Sexy Become Tag Partners & Sabotage Tag Champions
NNO Jenna Lynn
NNO Rok-C
NNO Sea Stars
NNO Shotzi Blackheart
NNO Shotzi Blackheart Becomes the First Ever War of the Genders Champion
NNO Thunder Rosa

2019 Sabotage Wrestling Series 2

1 Title Card
2 Sea Stars
3 Hyan
4 Fuego Del Sol
5 The Renaissance
6 Leyla Hirsch
7 Kiki Vibez
8 Ricky Starks
9 GPA
10 Erica Torres
11 Hyan
NNO Erica Torres
NNO Fuego Del Sol
NNO Fuego Del Sol Becomes Sabotage Champion
NNO GPA
NNO Hyan
NNO Hyan Becomes Longest Reigning Sabotage Champion
NNO Kiki Vibez
NNO Renaissance
NNO Sea Stars Dethrone Fun & Sexy and Become Sabotage Tag Team Champions

2019 Sabotage Wrestling Series 3

1 Title Card
2 Joey Ryan
3 Alex Gracia
4 Roxy Castillo
5 Raychell Rose
6 Kelly Klein
7 Delilah Doom
8 GPA
9 Chris Cruz
10 Ali Bama
11 Erica Torres
NNO Alex Gracia
NNO Ali Bama
NNO Chris Cruz
NNO Delilah Doom
NNO Erica Torres Becomes Sabotage Champion
NNO GPA Dethrones Shotzi to Become WOTG Champion
NNO Joey Ryan
NNO Kelly Klein
NNO Raychell Rose
NNO Roxy Castillo Becomes GM

2020 Sabotage Wrestling Series 4

NNO Alex Gracia
NNO ASF
NNO Baby D
NNO Chris Cruz
NNO Fuego Del Sol
NNO GPA
NNO Heather Monroe
NNO Hyan
NNO Jazzy J Serious
NNO Kylie Rae

2020 Sabotage Wrestling Series 5

NNO Alex Gracia
NNO Danni Bee
NNO Delilah Doom Defining Moment
NNO Kiefer Bartek Defining Moment
NNO Nastico
NNO Promise Braxton

NNO Rok-C
NNO Seas Stars Defining Moments
NNO Vertvixen
NNO Viva Van

2010 Sabritas Cheetos WWE

COMPLETE SET (10)
NNO Batista
NNO Big Show
NNO Chavo Guerrero
NNO CM Punk
NNO John Cena
NNO John Morrison
NNO Kane
NNO Rey Mysterio
NNO Triple H
NNO Undertaker

2000 Safarir Magazine WWF Trading Cards

COMPLETE SET (11)
NNO Al Snow
NNO Big Boss Man
NNO Chyna
NNO Kane
NNO The Cat/Miss Kitty
NNO Mankind
NNO The Rock
NNO Sexual Chocolate
NNO Stone Cold Steve Austin
NNO Triple H
NNO The Undertaker

2011 Sassy Stephie Official Series One

COMPLETE SET (8)
NNO Sassy Stephie
(belt on waist)
NNO Sassy Stephie
(blue top close-up)
NNO Sassy Stephie
(dropping elbow)
NNO Sassy Stephie
(pulling opponents hair)
NNO Sassy Stephie
(reverse bulldog)
NNO Sassy Stephie
(right hand on head/posing)
NNO Sassy Stephie
(spirit on belt)
NNO Sassy Stephie
(walking to the ring)

1986 Scanlens WWF Australian

COMPLETE SET (66)	20.00	50.00
UNOPENED BOX		
UNOPENED PACK		
RINGSIDE ACTION (22-56)		
SUPERSTARS SPEAK (57-66)		
1 Hulk Hogan	100.00	200.00
2 The Iron Sheik	.20	.50
3 Captain Lou Albano	.20	.50
4 Junk Yard Dog	.20	.50
5 Paul Mr. Wonderful Orndorff	.15	.40
6 Jimmy Superfly Snuka	.15	.40
7 Rowdy Roddy Piper	2.00	5.00
8 Wendi Richter	.20	.50

9 Greg The Hammer Valentine	.15	.40
10 Brutus Beefcake	.12	.30
11 Jesse The Body Ventura	1.50	4.00
12 Big John Studd	.15	.40
13 Fabulous Moolah	.15	.40
14 Tito Santana	.12	.30
15 Hillbilly Jim	.15	.40
16 Hulk Hogan	125.00	250.00
17 Mr. Fuji	.12	.30
18 Rotundo & Windham	.12	.30
19 Moondog Spot	.12	.30
20 Chief Jay Strongbow	.12	.30
21 George "The Animal" Steele	.15	.40
22 Let Go of My Toe! RA	.15	.40
23 Lock 'Em Up! RA	.15	.40
24 Scalp 'Em! RA	.20	.50
25 Going for the Midsection! RA	.20	.50
26 Up in the Air! RA	.12	.30
27 All Tied Up! RA	.40	1.00
28 Here She Comes! RA	.12	.30
29 Stretched to the Limit! RA	2.00	5.00
30 Over He Goes! RA	.15	.40
31 An Appetite for Mayhem! RA	.15	.40
32 Putting on Pressure! RA	.20	.50
33 Smashed on a Knee! RA	.15	.40
34 A Fist Comes Flying! RA	.12	.30
35 Lemme' Out of This! RA	.12	.30
36 No Fair Chokin'! RA	.15	.40
37 Attacked by an Animal! RA	.15	.40
38 One Angry Man! RA	.40	1.00
39 Someone's Going Down! RA	.40	1.00
40 Strangle Hold! RA	.40	1.00
41 Bending an Arm! RA	.12	.30
42 Ready for a Pile Driver! RA	.15	.40
43 Face to the Canvas! RA	.12	.30
44 Paul Wants It All! RA	.15	.40
45 Kick to the Face! RA	.75	2.00
46 Ready for Action! RA	.12	.30
47 Putting on the Squeeze! RA	.20	.50
48 Giants in Action! RA	.40	1.00
49 Camel Clutch! RA	.20	.50
50 Pile Up! RA	.75	2.00
51 Can't Get Away! RA	.20	.50
52 Going for the Pin! RA	.12	.30
53 Ready to Fly! RA	.40	1.00
54 Crusher in a Crusher! RA	.20	.50
55 Fury of the Animal! RA	.15	.40
56 Wrong Kind of Music! RA	2.00	5.00
57 Who's your next challenger? SS	2.00	5.00
58 This dog has got a mean bite! SS	.20	.50
59 I don't think I'll ask... SS	.40	1.00
60 You Hulkster fans... SS	2.00	5.00
61 This ain't my idea... SS	.40	1.00
62 You mean Freddie Blassie... SS	.40	1.00
63 Mppgh Ecch Oong. SS	.20	.50
64 Rock n' wrestling... SS	.20	.50
65 Arrrggghhhh! SS	.15	.40
66 They took my reindeer! SS	.20	.50

2010 SCWA JT Smooth Series One

COMPLETE SET (9)

NNO JT Smooth Cell 3E Edition
NNO JT Smooth Evolution Fire Edition
NNO JT Smooth Special Hardcore Edition Picture
NNO Smooth Gel Bubbles Edition
NNO Smooth Gel Ultimate Fire Edition
NNO Smooth Metallic Gel Edition
NNO The Under Armour Warrior

NNO Ultimate 3E Transformation Edition
NNO Ultimate Destruction Chaos Edition

2006 7-11 WWE Slam Philippines

COMPLETE SET (36)	20.00	50.00
1 Finlay	.75	2.00
2 William Regal	.75	2.00
3 Batista	1.25	3.00
4 Matt Hardy	.75	2.00
5 Lashley	.75	2.00
6 Rey Mysterio	1.25	3.00
7 Brian Kendrick	.30	.75
8 Paul London	.30	.75
9 Vito	.30	.75
10 Michelle McCool	1.50	4.00
11 Mr. Kennedy	.75	2.00
12 Booker T	.75	2.00
13 Undertaker	1.50	4.00
14 Ashley	1.25	3.00
15 Big Show	1.25	3.00
16 Rob Van Dam	.75	2.00
17 Nitro	.50	1.25
18 Hulk Hogan	2.00	5.00
19 Edge	1.25	3.00
20 Ric Flair	1.50	4.00
21 Carlito	1.25	3.00
22 Umaga	.50	1.25
23 Torrie Wilson	3.00	8.00
24 John Cena	2.00	5.00
25 Randy Orton	.75	2.00
26 Kane	1.25	3.00
27 Candice Michelle	2.00	5.00
28 Mickie James	2.00	5.00
29 Triple H	2.00	5.00
30 Shawn Michaels	2.00	5.00
31 Undertaker	1.50	4.00
32 Rey Mysterio	1.25	3.00
33 Batista	1.25	3.00
34 Triple H	2.00	5.00
35 John Cena	2.00	5.00
36 Shawn Michaels	2.00	5.00

2011 SoCal Pro Wrestling Series One

COMPLETE SET (36)

1 SoCal Crazy
2 Mr. Mega Star Tommy Wilson
3 Kid Caramba
4 Hector Canales
5 Nick Lovin
6 Duke
7 Shannon Ballard
8 Jason Redondo
9 Adam Pearce
10 Johnny Yuma
11 Peter Avalon
12 David E. Jones
13 Ricky Mandel
14 Eddie Randle
15 Shane Ballard
16 Destro
17 Ryan Kidd
18 Johnny Paradise
19 Johnny Goodtime
20 Todd Chandler
21 Brandon Parker
22 Angel Santos
23 Ryan Stone

24 Ric Ellis
25 TNT
26 Slymm
27 James MacFarlane
28 C. Edward Vanderpyle
29 Chimaera
30 Al Katrazz
31 Scott Lost
32 Officials
33 Troy Stone & Jeff Resnick
34 Dynamic Brothers
35 SoCal Pro Staff
NNO Checklist

2011 SoCal Pro Wrestling Series One Autographs

COMPLETE SET (12)

AUTO1 Adam Pearce
AUTO2 Tommy Wilson
AUTO3 SoCal Crazy
AUTO4 Ricky Mandel
AUTO5 Jason Redondo
AUTO6 Hector Canales
AUTO7 Kid Caramba
AUTO8 Todd Chandler
AUTO9 Rocknes Monsters
AUTO10 2 Skinny White Guys
AUTO11 Damage Control
AUTO12 Frosted Tip Warriors

2012 SoCal Pro Wrestling Series Two

COMPLETE SET (32)

1 SoCal Crazy
2 Nick Lovin
3 Jason Redondo
4 Pulpo Dorado
5 Tommy Wilson
6 Duke
7 Ricky Mandel
8 Kid Caramba
9 Ryan Kidd
10 Joey Barone
11 Peter Avalon
12 Eddie Randel
13 Adam Pierce
14 Destro
15 Nick Madrid
16 Todd Chandler
17 Johnny Paradise
18 Nightmare Azteca
19 Johnny Yuma
20 JRW
21 Ryan Stone
22 Ric Ellis
23 Andre Machievski
24 Johnny Goodtime
25 Brandon Parker
26 David E. Jones
27 B-Boy
28 Tag Team Titles
29 Heavyweight Title
32 Checklist

2012 SoCal Pro Wrestling Series Two Autographs

1 Nick Lovin
2 David E. Jones & Ryan Stone

3 Tommy Wilson
4 Kid Caramba
5 SoCal Crazy
6 Johnny Yuma

2000 Solluna AAA Wrestling

COMPLETE SET (9)

1 Abismo Negro & Electro Shock
2 El Oriental
3 Cibernetico
4 Alebrije with Cuije
5 Heavy Metal
6 Charly Manson
7 Los Viders (Psicosis / Histeria / Maniaco)
8 Pentagon
9 Octagon

2009 SPW Complete Series

COMPLETE SET (146)
COMPLETE VOLUME ONE SET (88)
COMPLETE VOLUME TWO SET (58)

1 Marius
2 Beautiful Bobby Jay
3 Matt Faitlane
4 Big Brian Rich
5 Ainsley Mosienko
6 AJ Sanchez
7 Bobby Fox
8 Chris Cannon
9 Dean Devlin
10 Duke Delinquent
11 The Epic
12 Jay Lanza
13 JJ Sanchez
14 LA Sombra
15 Lynn Adams
16 Rick Matthews
17 Shadow Extreme
18 Mentallo
19 The Barn Owl
20 Big Jess
21 Bobby Sharp
22 Drezden
23 Rick Martel
24 Ike Idol
25 Gibby Guerrero
26 Billy Braze
27 Kevy Chevy
28 Austin Aries
29 Doom
30 Pepito
31 PJ Tyler
32 Chris Dion
33 Camikaz
34 Jon Cutler
35 Ernie Todd
36 Mikey Miracle
37 Scotty Raver
38 TJ Bratt
39 TK Beoffra
40 Buddy Body
41 Pyro
42 Jimmy Jordan
43 Wayne Stanton
44 Mr. Insane
45 Zack Mercury
46 Mystique

47 Josh Maxwell
48 Danny Duggan
49 Louie
50 Rob Stardom
51 Mike Arnott
52 Mike the Hammer
53 Scotty Valentine
54 Sampson
55 Jake O'Reilly
56 Kyle Sebastion
57 Vance Nevada
58 Nacho Slurpee
59 Mitch Nightmare
60 Psyinide
61 Scotty Putty
62 Tom Steel
63 Pierre North
64 Tyler Perry
65 Steve Cox
66 Matt Burns
67 Moose
68 Eclipse
69 Heavy Metal
70 Andrew Hawk
71 Mr. Nasty
72 Bo Nanas
73 Crasher
74 Big Daddy Kash
75 Headmaster Joe
76 Beautiful Bruce
77 Rocky
78 AJ Sign
79 Jonathan Sayers
80 Jenine
81 Sydney Manson
82 Submission Squad
83 Annabelle
84 Marty Mackeral
85 Jerin Rose
86 Julio Gonzalez
87 Carol Stanton
88 El Bano
89 Chi Chi Cruz
90 Claudio Castagnoli
91 Alexis Anderson
92 Kenny Rogers
93 Braeden Finbogasson
94 Dirty Doug Irwin
95 Aaron Everhard
96 The Hitman Brett Caruthers
97 The Hood
98 The Hoodlum
99 Heavenly Juggs
100 Super Big Gulp
101 Shannon
102 Chris Raine
103 Pete Chee
104 Bad Boy Brian Jewel
105 Justin Noreaga
106 Kory Kincaid
107 Andrew Spoljar
108 Mark Merric
109 Mike Davidson
110 Corey Diamond
111 Big Cliff Corleone
112 Jumping Jason Jeeter
113 Double Impact
114 Terrible Timm Larson

115 TB Hump
116 Alex Shaver
117 Kid Thunder
118 Kenny K
119 Reggie Gallagher
120 Alex Plexis
121 The Rebel Bobby Collins
122 The Red Dragon
123 Lucky O'Shea
124 Ravenous Randy Myers
125 Ronnie Angels
126 Superfly Dan Myers
127 Tenille Tayla
128 Britany McLeod
129 CJ Witkowski
130 Shawn Coates
131 Ian Calliou
132 Wildman Firpo
133 The Machine
134 Syko
135 Sashka
136 Chip the Kid Fletcher
137 Chris Forigno
138 Young Gun Kid
139 Lyle Lovelace
140 Steve Denton
141 Tyler Trooper
142 Tyson McHauchlan
143 Lenny Travis
144 Baroness
145 Rocky Brunzell
146 Gunner Clash

2017 Staten Island Yankees Global Force Wrestling Impact Live

1 Allie
2 EC3
3 James Storm
4 LAX - Santana & Ortiz
5 Lashley

2005 The Star WWE UK Event Promos

COMPLETE SET (11)

1 John Cena
2 Kurt Angle
3 Shawn Michaels
4 Big Show
5 Torrie Wilson
6 WWE
7 Batista
8 Undertaker
9 Rey Mysterio
10 Chris Benoit
11 Stacy Keibler

1997 Stridex WWF

COMPLETE SET (7)		8.00	20.00
NNO Header Card		.75	2.00
NNO Ahmed Johnson		.75	2.00
NNO Bret Hit Man Hart		2.00	5.00
NNO Shawn Michaels		2.00	5.00
NNO Stone Cold Steve Austin		3.00	8.00
NNO Sycho Sid		1.25	3.00
NNO Undertaker		3.00	8.00

1987 Stuart WWF Canadian

COMPLETE SET (16)		15.00	40.00
*CUT: X TO X BASIC CARDS			
1 Brutus The Barber Beefcake		1.25	3.00
2 Les Freres Rougeau Brothers		1.00	2.50
3 Strike Force		1.25	3.00
4 The Honky Tonk Man		1.25	3.00
5 Randy Savage with Elizabeth		4.00	10.00
6 Hulk Hogan		6.00	15.00
7 Demolition		1.25	3.00
8 Koko B. Ware		1.00	2.50
9 Ted DiBiase UER		1.50	4.00
10 Slick The Doctor of Style		1.25	3.00
11 British Bulldogs		1.25	3.00
12 Bobby The Brain Heenan		1.50	4.00
13 Jimmy Hart		1.25	3.00
14 George The Animal Steele		1.50	4.00
15 Jake The Snake Roberts		2.00	5.00
16 The Junk Yard Dog		1.25	3.00

1991 Swanson WWF Wrestling Canadian

COMPLETE SET (12)		30.00	75.00
NNO Big Boss Man		4.00	10.00
NNO Bret Hitman Hart		5.00	12.00
NNO The Bushwhackers		4.00	10.00
NNO Hulk Hogan		10.00	25.00
NNO Jake The Snake Roberts		3.00	8.00
NNO Legion of Doom		5.00	12.00
NNO Macho Man Randy Savage		6.00	15.00
NNO Million Dollar Man Ted DiBiase		3.00	8.00
NNO The Mountie		2.50	6.00
NNO Rockers Marty and Shawn		4.00	10.00
NNO Texas Tornado		2.50	6.00
NNO Ultimate Warrior		5.00	12.00

2016 Take Two Interactive WWE Supercard Supertoken Cards

NNO Brock Lesnar
NNO Daniel Bryan
NNO Dean Ambrose
NNO John Cena
NNO Paige
NNO Roman Reigns
NNO Seth Rollins
NNO Sting
NNO Undertaker

2016 Take Two Interactive WWE Supercard Supertoken Tokens

NNO Brock Lesnar
NNO Daniel Bryan
NNO Dean Ambrose
NNO John Cena
NNO Paige
NNO Roman Reigns
NNO Seth Rollins
NNO Sting
NNO Undertaker

1991 Titan Sports WWF Playing Cards

COMPLETE SET (56)

1C Hulk Hogan
1D Hulk Hogan
1H Hulk Hogan
1S Hulk Hogan

2C British Bulldog
2D British Bulldog
2H British Bulldog
2S British Bulldog
3C Hacksaw Jim Duggan
3D Hacksaw Jim Duggan
3H Hacksaw Jim Duggan
3S Hacksaw Jim Duggan
4C Million Dollar Man Ted DiBiase
4D Million Dollar Man Ted DiBiase
4H Million Dollar Man Ted DiBiase
4S Million Dollar Man Ted DiBiase
5C Warlord
5D Warlord
5H Warlord
5S Warlord
6C Ricky The Dragon Steamboat
6D Ricky The Dragon Steamboat
6H Ricky The Dragon Steamboat
6S Ricky The Dragon Steamboat
7C Mr. Perfect
7D Mr. Perfect
7H Mr. Perfect
7S Mr. Perfect
8C Big Boss Man
8D Big Boss Man
8H Big Boss Man
8S Big Boss Man
9C Undertaker
9D Undertaker
9H Undertaker
9S Undertaker
10C Legion of Doom
10D Legion of Doom
10H Legion of Doom
10S Legion of Doom
11C The Ultimate Warrior
11D The Ultimate Warrior
11H The Ultimate Warrior
11S The Ultimate Warrior
12C Miss Elizabeth
12D Miss Elizabeth
12H Miss Elizabeth
12S Miss Elizabeth
13C Macho Man Randy Savage
13D Macho Man Randy Savage
13H Macho Man Randy Savage
13S Macho Man Randy Savage
JOK1 Hotrod
JOK1 Hotrod
JOK2 Hotrod
JOK2 Hotrod

1994 Titan Sports WWF Vending Hologram Stickers

COMPLETE SET (10)		8.00	20.00
NNO Adam Bomb		1.00	2.50
NNO Bret Hitman Hart		2.00	5.00
NNO Doink		1.00	2.50
NNO Lex Luger		1.50	4.00
NNO Ludvig Borga		1.00	2.50
NNO Macho Man Randy Savage		2.00	5.00
NNO Razor Ramon		1.25	3.00
NNO Tatanka		1.00	2.50
NNO Undertaker		3.00	8.00
NNO Yokozuna		1.25	3.00

1985 Titan Sports WWF Wrestling Stars Game

COMPLETE SET (12)

1 Andre the Giant
2 Big John Studd
3 Hillbilly Jim
4 Hulk Hogan
5 Iron Sheik
6 Junkyard Dog
7 Magnificent Muraco
8 Nikolai Volkoff
9 Paul Mr. Wonderful Orndorff
10 Ricky The Dragon Steamboat
11 Rowdy Roddy Piper
12 Tito Santana

2006 TNA Spike TV Wizard World LA

COMPLETE SET (5)

NNO Christian Cage
NNO Jeff Jarrett
NNO Raven
NNO AJ Styles
NNO Abyss

2006 TNA Spike TV Wizard World Philadelphia

COMPLETE SET (6)

NNO Brother Devon
NNO Brother Ray
NNO Jackie
NNO Jeff Jarrett
NNO Traci
NNO Raven

2006 TNA Spike TV Wizard World Texas

COMPLETE SET (5)

NNO Jeff Jarrett
NNO Gail Kim
NNO Konnan
NNO Tracy
NNO The Naturals

2011 Top Trumps Specials WWE All-Time Greats

COMPLETE SET (31)

NNO Title Card
NNO Akeem
NNO Big Boss Man
NNO Bobby The Brain Heenan
NNO British Bulldog
NNO Cowboy Bob Orton
NNO Doink the Clown
NNO Dusty Rhodes
NNO Gorilla Monsoon
NNO Greg The Hammer Valentine
NNO Hacksaw Jim Duggan
NNO Harley Race
NNO Hillbilly Jim
NNO Jake "The Snake" Roberts
NNO Jimmy Superfly Snuka
NNO Junkyard Dog
NNO Koko B. Ware
NNO Mean Gene Okerlund
NNO Million Dollar Man Ted DiBiase
NNO Mr. Perfect Curt Hennig

NNO Papa Shango
NNO Paul Bearer
NNO Paul Orndorff
NNO Ravishing Rick Rude
NNO Ricky The Dragon Steamboat
NNO Rowdy Roddy Piper
NNO Sgt. Slaughter
NNO Shawn Michaels
NNO The Bushwhackers
NNO Tito Santana
NNO Yokozuna

2005 Top Trumps Specials WWE Superstars 1

COMPLETE SET (31)

NNO Title Card
NNO Batista
NNO Big Show
NNO Booker T
NNO Carlito
NNO Chavo Guerrero
NNO Christy Hemme
NNO Eddie Guerrero
NNO Edge
NNO Eric Bischoff
NNO Eugene
NNO Heidenreich
NNO Hulk Hogan
NNO JBL
NNO John Cena
NNO Kane
NNO Kurt Angle
NNO Orlando Jordan
NNO Rey Mysterio
NNO Ric Flair
NNO Rob Van Dam
NNO Shawn Michaels
NNO Shelton Benjamin
NNO Snitsky
NNO Stacy Keibler
NNO Tajiri
NNO Torrie Wilson
NNO Triple H
NNO Trish Stratus
NNO Undertaker
NNO William Regal

2006 Top Trumps Specials WWE Superstars 2

COMPLETE SET (31)

NNO Title Card
NNO Ashley
NNO Charlie Haas
NNO Chris Masters
NNO Finlay
NNO The Great Khali
NNO Gregory Helms
NNO Hardcore Holly
NNO Jake "The Snake" Roberts
NNO Jamie Noble
NNO Jerry "The King" Lawler
NNO Johnny Nitro
NNO Lance Cade
NNO Lashley
NNO Lita
NNO Mark Henry
NNO Matt Hardy

NNO Michelle McCool
NNO Mick Foley
NNO Mickie James
NNO Paul Burchill
NNO Rene Dupree
NNO The Rock
NNO Roddy Piper
NNO Sgt. Slaughter
NNO Spirit Squad
NNO Stone Cold Steve Austin
NNO Tatanka
NNO Umaga
NNO Victoria
NNO Viscera

2013 Topps Best of WWE

COMPLETE SET (110)	8.00	20.00
UNOPENED BOX (24 PACKS)		
UNOPENED PACK (7 CARDS)		
*BLUE: .6X TO 1.5X BASIC CARDS		
*BRONZE: .6X TO 1.5X BASIC CARDS		
*SILVER: 2.5X TO 6X BASIC CARDS		
*GOLD/10: 5X TO 12X BASIC CARDS		
*P.P.BLACK/1: UNPRICED DUE TO SCARCITY		
*P.P.CYAN/1: UNPRICED DUE TO SCARCITY		
*P.P.MAGENTA/1: UNPRICED DUE TO SCARCITY		
*P.P.YELLOW/1: UNPRICED DUE TO SCARCITY		
1 The Rock	.75	2.00
2 Brock Lesnar/John Cena	.75	2.00
3 Daniel Bryan/AJ Lee	.75	2.00
4 Dusty Rhodes/Cody Rhodes	.25	.60
5 AJ Lee/Kaitlyn	.75	2.00
6 Layla/Nikki Bella	.30	.75
7 Cody Rhodes	.15	.40
8 CM Punk/Chris Jericho	.60	1.50
9 John Cena/Brock Lesnar	.75	2.00
10 Brock Lesnar/Triple H	.60	1.50
11 Kofi Kingston/R-Truth	.15	.40
12 Damien Sandow	.15	.40
13 John Laurinaitis/Big Show	.30	.75
14 Christian/Cody Rhodes	.15	.40
15 John Laurinaitis/John Cena	.75	2.00
16 AJ Lee/Kane	.75	2.00
17 Big Show/Mr. McMahon	.30	.75
18 CM Punk/Kane	.60	1.50
19 John Cena/John Laurinaitis	.75	2.00
20 Dolph Ziggler/Jack Swagger	.25	.60
21 AJ Lee	.75	2.00
22 Zack Ryder	.15	.40
23 AJ Lee/CM Punk	.75	2.00
24 Dolph Ziggler	.25	.60
25 John Cena	.75	2.00
26 AJ Lee/Daniel Bryan	.75	2.00
27 D-Generation X	.60	1.50
28 Dude Love/Brodus Clay	.60	1.50
29 Trish Stratus/Triple H	.75	2.00
30 AJ Lee/Daniel Bryan	.75	2.00
31 The Miz/Christian	.25	.60
32 APA/Heath Slater	.15	.40
33 Undertaker/Kane	.60	1.50
34 John Cena/Big Show	.75	2.00
35 CM Punk/The Rock	.75	2.00
36 Daniel Bryan	.40	1.00
37 Mr.McMahon/Booker T	.25	.60
38 Daniel Bryan	.40	1.00
39 Brock Lesnar/Shawn Michaels	.60	1.50
40 Antonio Cesaro/Santino Marella	.15	.40
41 Daniel Bryan/Kane	.40	1.00

42 Brock Lesnar/Triple H	.60	1.50
43 Dolph Ziggler/Chris Jericho	.60	1.50
44 Daniel Bryan/Kane	.40	1.00
45 CM Punk/Jerry Lawler	.60	1.50
46 Kane/Daniel Bryan	.40	1.00
47 CM Punk/Paul Heyman	.60	1.50
48 Kaitlyn	.30	.75
49 Kane/Bryan/Truth	.40	1.00
50 Eve	.60	1.50
51 CM Punk/John Cena	.75	2.00
52 CM Punk/Mr. McMahon	.60	1.50
53 Kofi Kingston/The Miz	.25	.60
54 AJ Lee/Vickie Guerrero	.75	2.00
55 Big Show/Sheamus	.30	.75
56 Brad Maddox/Ryback	.15	.40
57 Vickie Guerrero/John Cena	.75	2.00
58 Big Show/Sheamus	.30	.75
59 Randy Orton/Alberto Del Rio	.50	1.25
60 CM Punk/Jerry Lawler	.60	1.50
61 Ryback/Brad Maddox	.15	.40
62 Team Ziggler/Team Foley	.25	.60
63 Shield/Cena/Ryback	.75	2.00
64 John Cena/AJ Lee	.75	2.00
65 John Cena/Dolph Ziggler	.75	2.00
66 Vicki/AJ Lee/Maddox	.75	2.00
67 Cody Rhodes	.15	.40
68 Reigns/Bryan/Ambrose	.40	1.00
69 AJ Lee/Cena/Ziggler	.75	2.00
70 Big E Langston/John Cena	.75	2.00
71 8 Divas	.60	1.50
72 John Cena/Alberto Del Rio	.75	2.00
73 Great Khali	.15	.40
74 Wade Barrett/Kofi Kingston	.15	.40
75 Dolph Ziggler/AJ Lee	.75	2.00
76 Antonio Cesaro/Great Khali	.15	.40
77 CM Punk/Ryback	.60	1.50
78 The Rock/CM Punk	.75	2.00
79 Alberto Del Rio/Big Show	.30	.75
80 Kaitlyn/Eve	.60	1.50
81 Kane/Daniel Bryan	.40	1.00
82 Chris Jericho	.60	1.50
83 Bo Dallas	.15	.40
84 John Cena	.75	2.00
85 The Rock/CM Punk	.75	2.00
86 Brock Lesnar/Mr. McMahon	.60	1.50
87 Jack Swagger	.25	.60
88 Roman Reigns/Ryback	.25	.60
89 The Rock/CM Punk	.75	2.00
90 Vickie Guerrero/Brad Maddox	.25	.60
91 The Rock	.75	2.00
92 Heyman/McMahon/Brock/HHH	.60	1.50
93 John Cena/CM Punk	.75	2.00
94 The Deadman	.60	1.50
95 Ted Dibiase	.25	.60
96 Outlaws/Primo/Epico	.15	.40
97 CM Punk/Randy Orton	.60	1.50
98 Undertaker	.60	1.50
99 Brie Bella/Nikki Bella	.60	1.50
100 CM Punk/Undertaker	.60	1.50
101 Mick Foley/Chris Jericho	.60	1.50
102 Trish Stratus	.75	2.00
103 Booker T	.25	.60
104 Bob Backlund	.40	1.00
105 Bruno Sammartino	.40	1.00
106 The Miz/Wade Barrett	.25	.60
107 Fandango/Chris Jericho	.60	1.50
108 Undertaker/CM Punk	.60	1.50

109 Triple H/Brock Lesnar	.60	1.50
110 John Cena/The Rock	.75	2.00

2013 Topps Best of WWE Autographs

STATED ODDS 1:48 HOBBY AND RETAIL

NNO American Dream Dusty Rhodes	75.00	150.00
NNO Big E Langston	8.00	20.00
NNO Bob Backlund	15.00	40.00
NNO Brie Bella	15.00	40.00
NNO Bruno Sammartino	20.00	50.00
NNO Cactus Jack	15.00	40.00
NNO Damien Sandow	8.00	20.00
NNO Dean Ambrose	15.00	40.00
NNO Dude Love	15.00	40.00
NNO JBL	10.00	25.00
NNO Lilian Garcia	12.00	30.00
NNO Mankind	15.00	40.00
NNO Mick Foley	20.00	50.00
NNO Nikki Bella	15.00	40.00
NNO Paul Heyman	30.00	75.00
NNO Roman Reigns	20.00	50.00
NNO Seth Rollins	15.00	40.00
NNO Trish Stratus	20.00	50.00
NNO Vickie Guerrero	15.00	20.00

2013 Topps Best of WWE Dual Autographs

STATED PRINT RUN 10 SER. #'d SETS

NNO Brie Bella/Nikki Bella	75.00	150.00
NNO B.Sammartino/B.Backlund		
NNO D.Sandow/Big E	25.00	60.00
NNO D.Ambrose/P.Heyman	60.00	120.00
NNO J.Swagger/V.Guerrero	25.00	60.00
NNO JBL/L.Garcia	50.00	100.00
NNO M.Foley/T.Stratus	50.00	100.00
NNO R.Dogg/B.Gunn	75.00	150.00
NNO S.Rollins/R.Reigns	75.00	150.00
NNO S.Michaels/X-Pac	100.00	200.00

2013 Topps Best of WWE Jerry Lawler Portraits

COMPLETE SET (10)	30.00	80.00
*P.P.BLACK/1: UNPRICED DUE TO SCARCITY		
*P.P.CYAN/1: UNPRICED DUE TO SCARCITY		
*P.P.MAGENTA/1: UNPRICED DUE TO SCARCITY		
*P.P.YELLOW/1: UNPRICED DUE TO SCARCITY		
RANDOMLY INSERTED INTO RETAIL PACKS		
1 CM Punk	6.00	15.00
2 R-Truth	1.50	4.00
3 Undertaker	6.00	15.00
4 Kane	3.00	8.00
5 Paul Bearer	2.50	6.00
6 Vickie Guerrero	2.50	6.00
7 Stone Cold Steve Austin	6.00	15.00
8 Sgt. Slaughter	2.50	6.00
9 Vader	1.50	4.00
10 Doink the Clown	1.50	4.00

2013 Topps Best of WWE Swatch Relics

STATED ODDS 1:24 HOBBY EXCLUSIVE

NNO AJ Lee/Shirt	20.00	50.00
NNO AJ Lee/Teddy Bear	60.00	120.00
NNO Brodus Clay/Shirt	4.00	10.00
NNO CM Punk/Shirt	6.00	15.00
NNO Damien Sandow Shirt	4.00	10.00

NNO Daniel Bryan/Shirt	5.00	12.00
NNO Dean Ambrose/Shirt	5.00	12.00
NNO Dolph Ziggler/Shirt	5.00	12.00
NNO Great Khali/Referee Shirt	4.00	10.00
NNO John Cena/Hat	40.00	80.00
NNO John Cena/Headband		
NNO John Cena/Shirt	6.00	15.00
NNO John Cena/Wristband	40.00	80.00
NNO Miz/Shirt	4.00	10.00
NNO Randy Orton/Shirt	5.00	12.00
NNO Roman Reigns/Shirt	5.00	12.00
NNO Ryback/Shirt	4.00	10.00
NNO Seth Rollins/Shirt	6.00	15.00
NNO Sheamus/Shirt	4.00	10.00
NNO Wade Barrett/Shirt	4.00	10.00

2013 Topps Best of WWE Top 10 Catchphrases

COMPLETE SET (10)	4.00	10.00
*P.P.BLACK/1: UNPRICED DUE TO SCARCITY		
*P.P.CYAN/1: UNPRICED DUE TO SCARCITY		
*P.P.MAGENTA/1: UNPRICED DUE TO SCARCITY		
*P.P.YELLOW/1: UNPRICED DUE TO SCARCITY		
STATED ODDS OVERALL 3:1 HOBBY AND RETAIL		
1 The Rock/If Ya Smell	3.00	8.00
2 Undertaker/Rest in Peace	1.50	4.00
3 John Cena/You Can't See Me!	1.25	3.00
4 Booker T/Can You Dig It, Sucka?	.30	.75
5 The Miz/Because I'm the Miz...	.30	.75
6 Daniel Bryan/Yes!	.50	1.25
7 CM Punk/Best in the World	.75	2.00
8 Zack Ryder/Woo Woo Woo	.20	.50
9 Damien Sandow/You're Welcome!	.20	.50
10 Vickie Guerrero/Excuse Me!	.30	.75

2013 Topps Best of WWE Top 10 Finishers

COMPLETE SET (10)	5.00	12.00
*P.P.BLACK/1: UNPRICED DUE TO SCARCITY		
*P.P.CYAN/1: UNPRICED DUE TO SCARCITY		
*P.P.MAGENTA/1: UNPRICED DUE TO SCARCITY		
*P.P.YELLOW/1: UNPRICED DUE TO SCARCITY		
STATED ODDS OVERALL 3:1 HOBBY AND RETAIL		
1 Undertaker/Tombstone	2.50	6.00
2 Stone Cold Steve Austin/Stunner	1.50	4.00
3 Randy Orton/RKO	.75	2.00
4 Shawn Michaels/Sweet Chin Music	.75	2.00
5 Triple H/Pedigree	.75	2.00
6 The Rock/Rock Bottom	1.00	2.50
7 John Cena/Attitude Adjustment	1.00	2.50
8 CM Punk/GTS	.75	2.00
9 Rey Mysterio/619	.50	1.25
10 Eddie Guerrero/Frog Splash	.20	.50

2013 Topps Best of WWE Top 10 Greatest WWE Moments

COMPLETE SET (10)	5.00	12.00
*P.P.BLACK/1: UNPRICED DUE TO SCARCITY		
*P.P.CYAN/1: UNPRICED DUE TO SCARCITY		
*P.P.MAGENTA/1: UNPRICED DUE TO SCARCITY		
*P.P.YELLOW/1: UNPRICED DUE TO SCARCITY		
STATED ODDS OVERALL 3:1 HOBBY AND RETAIL		
1 Undertaker/Shawn Michaels	2.50	6.00
2 Triple H	1.50	4.00
3 John Cena	1.25	3.00
4 The Rock/John Cena	1.00	2.50
5 Eddie Guerrero/Brock Lesnar	.75	2.00

6 The Rock/Hollywood Hogan	1.00	2.50
7 John Cena/JBL	1.00	2.50
8 CM Punk	.75	2.00
9 CM Punk/John Cena	1.00	2.50
10 Mr. McMahon	.20	.50

2013 Topps Best of WWE Top 10 Intercontinental Champions

COMPLETE SET (10)	3.00	8.00
*P.P.BLACK/1: UNPRICED DUE TO SCARCITY		
*P.P.CYAN/1: UNPRICED DUE TO SCARCITY		
*P.P.MAGENTA/1: UNPRICED DUE TO SCARCITY		
*P.P.YELLOW/1: UNPRICED DUE TO SCARCITY		
STATED ODDS OVERALL 3:1 HOBBY AND RETAIL		
1 Randy Orton	2.00	5.00
2 Rey Mysterio	1.00	2.50
3 Christian	.25	.60
4 Kofi Kingston	.20	.50
5 Cody Rhodes	.20	.50
6 Wade Barrett	.20	.50
7 Dolph Ziggler	.30	.75
8 William Regal	.25	.60
9 Santino Marella	.20	.50
10 Ezekiel Jackson	.20	.50

2013 Topps Best of WWE Top 10 Rivalries

COMPLETE SET (10)	5.00	12.00
*P.P.BLACK/1: UNPRICED DUE TO SCARCITY		
*P.P.CYAN/1: UNPRICED DUE TO SCARCITY		
*P.P.MAGENTA/1: UNPRICED DUE TO SCARCITY		
*P.P.YELLOW/1: UNPRICED DUE TO SCARCITY		
STATED ODDS OVERALL 3:1 HOBBY AND RETAIL		
1 Shawn Michaels/Undertaker	2.50	6.00
2 Undertaker/Triple H	1.50	4.00
3 John Cena/The Rock	1.25	3.00
4 Undertaker/Kane	.75	2.00
5 CM Punk/John Cena	1.00	2.50
6 Triple H/Shawn Michaels	.75	2.00
7 Triple H/Randy Orton	.75	2.00
8 John Cena/Brock Lesnar	1.00	2.50
9 Triple H/Batista	.75	2.00
10 Rey Mysterio/Eddie Guerrero	.50	1.25

2013 Topps Best of WWE Top 10 Trash Talkers

COMPLETE SET (10)	5.00	12.00
*P.P.BLACK/1: UNPRICED DUE TO SCARCITY		
*P.P.CYAN/1: UNPRICED DUE TO SCARCITY		
*P.P.MAGENTA/1: UNPRICED DUE TO SCARCITY		
*P.P.YELLOW/1: UNPRICED DUE TO SCARCITY		
STATED ODDS OVERALL 3:1 HOBBY AND RETAIL		
1 Stone Cold Steve Austin	2.50	6.00
2 The Rock	2.00	5.00
3 CM Punk	1.00	2.50
4 Triple H	.75	2.00
5 Rowdy Roddy Piper	.50	1.25
6 John Cena	1.00	2.50
7 The Miz	.30	.75
8 Shawn Michaels	.75	2.00
9 Paul Heyman	.20	.50
10 AJ Lee	1.00	2.50

2013 Topps Best of WWE Top 10 2K14

COMPLETE SET (10)	60.00	120.00
RANDOMLY INSERTED INTO PACKS		

1 John Cena	15.00	40.00
2 Triple H	8.00	20.00
3 The Rock	20.00	50.00
4 Undertaker	10.00	25.00
5 CM Punk		
6 Sheamus		
7 Brock Lesnar	8.00	20.00
8 Eddie Guerrero	8.00	20.00
9 The Miz	6.00	15.00
10 JBL	6.00	15.00

2013 Topps Best of WWE Top 10 Undertaker Matches

COMPLETE SET (10)	5.00	12.00
*P.P.BLACK/1: UNPRICED DUE TO SCARCITY		
*P.P.CYAN/1: UNPRICED DUE TO SCARCITY		
*P.P.MAGENTA/1: UNPRICED DUE TO SCARCITY		
*P.P.YELLOW/1: UNPRICED DUE TO SCARCITY		
STATED ODDS OVERALL 3:1 HOBBY AND RETAIL		
1 Vs. Triple H	2.50	6.00
2 Vs. Shawn Michaels	1.50	4.00
3 Vs. Shawn Michaels	1.00	2.50
4 Vs. Triple H	.75	2.00
5 Vs. Stone Cold Steve Austin	.75	2.00
6 Wins Royal Rumble	.75	2.00
7 Vs. Batista	.75	2.00
8 Vs. Kane	.75	2.00
9 Vs. Randy Orton	.75	2.00
10 Vs. CM Punk	.75	2.00

2013 Topps Best of WWE Top 10 World Heavyweight Champions

COMPLETE SET (10)	4.00	10.00
*P.P.BLACK/1: UNPRICED DUE TO SCARCITY		
*P.P.CYAN/1: UNPRICED DUE TO SCARCITY		
*P.P.MAGENTA/1: UNPRICED DUE TO SCARCITY		
*P.P.YELLOW/1: UNPRICED DUE TO SCARCITY		
STATED ODDS OVERALL 3:1 HOBBY AND RETAIL		
1 Undertaker	2.50	6.00
2 Triple H	1.50	4.00
3 Randy Orton	.75	2.00
4 Batista	.50	1.25
5 Sheamus	.40	1.00
6 Rey Mysterio	.50	1.25
7 Kane	.40	1.00
8 CM Punk	.75	2.00
9 Booker T	.30	.75
10 Daniel Bryan	.50	1.25

2013 Topps Best of WWE Top 10 WWE Champions

COMPLETE SET (10)	5.00	12.00
*P.P.BLACK/1: UNPRICED DUE TO SCARCITY		
*P.P.CYAN/1: UNPRICED DUE TO SCARCITY		
*P.P.MAGENTA/1: UNPRICED DUE TO SCARCITY		
*P.P.YELLOW/1: UNPRICED DUE TO SCARCITY		
STATED ODDS OVERALL 3:1 HOBBY AND RETAIL		
1 John Cena	3.00	8.00
2 Triple H	1.50	4.00
3 The Rock	1.25	3.00
4 Undertaker	.75	2.00
5 CM Punk	.75	2.00
6 Sheamus	.40	1.00
7 Brock Lesnar	.75	2.00
8 Eddie Guerrero	.20	.50
9 The Miz	.30	.75
10 JBL	.30	.75

2013 Topps Best of WWE Top 10 WWE Tag Team Champions

COMPLETE SET (10)		3.00	8.00

*P.P.BLACK/1: UNPRICED DUE TO SCARCITY
*P.P.CYAN/1: UNPRICED DUE TO SCARCITY
*P.P.MAGENTA/1: UNPRICED DUE TO SCARCITY
*P.P.YELLOW/1: UNPRICED DUE TO SCARCITY
STATED ODDS OVERALL 3:1 HOBBY AND RETAIL

1	D-Generation X	2.50	6.00
2	Team Hell No	1.00	2.50
3	Rey Mysterio/Eddie Guerrero	.60	1.50
4	Big Show/Kane	.40	1.00
5	Kofi Kingston/R-Truth	.20	.50
6	Air Boom	.20	.50
7	ShoMiz	.40	1.00
8	Ted DiBiase/Cody Rhodes	.25	.60
9	Curt Hawkins/Zack Ryder	.20	.50
10	Primo & Epico	.20	.50

2013 Topps Best of WWE WrestleMania 29 Mat Relics

STATED ODDS 1:48 HOBBY AND RETAIL

NNO	Alberto Del Rio	4.00	10.00
NNO	Big E Langston	4.00	10.00
NNO	Big Show	4.00	10.00
NNO	Brock Lesnar	5.00	12.00
NNO	Chris Jericho	5.00	12.00
NNO	CM Punk	6.00	15.00
NNO	Daniel Bryan	5.00	12.00
NNO	Dolph Ziggler	4.00	10.00
NNO	Fandango	6.00	15.00
NNO	Jack Swagger	4.00	10.00
NNO	John Cena	6.00	20.00
NNO	Kane	5.00	12.00
NNO	Mark Henry	4.00	10.00
NNO	Randy Orton	6.00	15.00
NNO	Ryback	5.00	12.00
NNO	Sheamus	4.00	10.00
NNO	The Shield	6.00	15.00
NNO	Triple H	5.00	12.00
NNO	Undertaker	5.00	12.00
NNO	The Rock	8.00	20.00

2014 Topps Chrome WWE

Subset includes: L = Legends (96-110)

COMPLETE SET (110)		8.00	20.00
UNOPENED BOX (24 PACKS)			
UNOPENED PACK (4 CARDS)			

*REF.: .4X TO 1.2X BASIC CARDS
*ATOMIC REF.: .6X TO 1.5X BASIC CARDS
*XFRACTOR: .6X TO 1.5X BASIC CARDS
*GOLD REF./50: 2X TO 5X BASIC CARDS
*SUPERFR./1: UNPRICED DUE TO SCARCITY
*P.P.BLACK/1: UNPRICE DUE TO SCARCITY
*P.P.CYAN/1: UNPRICE DUE TO SCARCITY
*P.P.MAGENTA/1: UNPRICE DUE TO SCARCITY
*P.P.YELLOW/1: UNPRICE DUE TO SCARCITY

1	AJ Lee	1.50	4.00
2	Alex Riley	.30	.75
3	Big E Langston	.30	.75
4	Bo Dallas	.30	.75
5	Brad Maddox	.30	.75
6	Bray Wyatt	.75	2.00
7	Brie Bella	1.00	2.50
8	Brock Lesnar	1.25	3.00
9	Brodus Clay	.30	.75
10	Cameron	.50	1.25
11	Chris Jericho	.75	2.00
12	CM Punk	1.25	3.00
13	Curtis Axel	.30	.75
14	Daniel Bryan	.50	1.25
15	David Otunga	.30	.75
16	Dean Ambrose	.75	2.00
17	Diego	.30	.75
18	Dolph Ziggler	.50	1.25
19	Erick Rowan	.50	1.25
20	Eva Marie	1.25	3.00
21	Fandango	.50	1.25
22	Fernando	.30	.75
23	Jack Swagger	.50	1.25
24	Jerry The King Lawler	.75	2.00
25	John Cena	1.50	4.00
26	JoJo	.50	1.25
27	Justin Roberts	.30	.75
28	Kane	.75	2.00
29	Kofi Kingston	.30	.75
30	Luke Harper	.50	1.25
31	El Torito	.30	.75
32	Michael Cole	.30	.75
33	The Miz	.50	1.25
34	Naomi	.50	1.25
35	Nikki Bella	1.00	2.50
36	Paul Heyman	.30	.75
37	R-Truth	.30	.75
38	Randy Orton	1.25	3.00
39	Rey Mysterio	.75	2.00
40	The Rock	1.50	4.00
41	Rob Van Dam	.75	2.00
42	Roman Reigns	.75	2.00
43	Ryback	.30	.75
44	Santino Marella	.50	1.25
45	Scott Stanford	.30	.75
46	Seth Rollins	.30	.75
47	Stephanie McMahon	.50	1.25
48	Summer Rae	1.25	3.00
49	Tamina Snuka	.50	1.25
50	Tensai	.30	.75
51	Triple H	1.25	3.00
52	Zack Ryder	.30	.75
53	Zeb Colter	.50	1.25
54	Aksana	.75	2.00
55	Alberto Del Rio	.75	2.00
56	Alicia Fox	.50	1.25
57	Antonio Cesaro	.30	.75
58	Big Show	.75	2.00
59	Booker T	.50	1.25
60	Camacho	.30	.75
61	Christian	.30	.75
62	Cody Rhodes	.30	.75
63	Curt Hawkins	.30	.75
64	Damien Sandow	.30	.75
65	Darren Young	.30	.75
66	Drew McIntyre	.30	.75
67	Ezekiel Jackson	.50	1.25
68	The Great Khali	.30	.75
69	Heath Slater	.30	.75
70	Hornswoggle	.50	1.25
71	Hunico	.30	.75
72	JBL	.50	1.25
73	Jey Uso	.30	.75
74	Jimmy Uso	.30	.75
75	Jinder Mahal	.30	.75
76	Josh Mathews	.30	.75
77	Justin Gabriel	.30	.75
78	Goldust	.30	.75
79	Layla	.75	2.00
80	Lilian Garcia	.75	2.00
81	Mark Henry	.50	1.25
82	Natalya	1.00	2.50
83	Renee Young	1.25	3.00
84	Ricardo Rodriguez	.30	.75
85	Rosa Mendes	.50	1.25
86	Sheamus	.75	2.00
87	Sin Cara	.75	2.00
88	Theodore Long	.30	.75
89	Titus O'Neil	.30	.75
90	Tony Chimel	.30	.75
91	Tyson Kidd	.30	.75
92	Undertaker	1.25	3.00
93	Vickie Guerrero	.50	1.25
94	Bad News Barrett	.30	.75
95	William Regal	.50	1.25
96	Andre the Giant L	1.25	3.00
97	Billy Gunn L	.50	1.25
98	Bob Backlund L	.50	1.25
99	Diamond Dallas Page L	.50	1.25
100	Eddie Guerrero L	.50	1.25
101	Honky Tonk Man L	.50	1.25
102	Jim Ross L	.50	1.25
103	Junkyard Dog L	.50	1.25
104	Kevin Nash L	.75	2.00
105	Larry Zbyszko L	.50	1.25
106	Mick Foley L	.75	2.00
107	Paul Bearer L	.50	1.25
108	Road Dogg L	.50	1.25
109	Shawn Michaels L	1.25	3.00
110	X-Pac L	.30	.75

2014 Topps Chrome WWE Autographs

*REFRACTOR/50: .5X TO 1.2X BASIC AUTOS
*RED REF./25: .75X TO 2X BASIC AUTOS
*GOLD REF./10: UNPRICED DUE TO SCARCITY
*SUPERFR./1: UNPRICE DUE TO SCARCITY

NNO	Aksana	10.00	25.00
NNO	Alicia Fox	5.00	12.00
NNO	Diamond Dallas Page	12.00	30.00
NNO	Dolph Ziggler	10.00	25.00
NNO	Fandango	6.00	15.00
NNO	Honky Tonk Man	8.00	20.00
NNO	Kane	12.00	30.00
NNO	Natalya	12.00	30.00
NNO	Roman Reigns	12.00	30.00
NNO	Sin Cara	5.00	12.00

2014 Topps Chrome WWE Championship Plates

*SUPERFR./1: UNPRICED DUE TO SCARCITY.
SP CARDS ARE SER.#'d TO 25

NNO	AJ Lee SP	75.00	150.00
NNO	Alicia Fox	12.00	30.00
NNO	Batista	15.00	40.00
NNO	Brie Bella	15.00	40.00
NNO	Chris Jericho SP	20.00	50.00
NNO	Cody Rhodes	8.00	20.00
NNO	Cody Rhodes and Goldust	8.00	20.00
NNO	Daniel Bryan	12.00	30.00
World Title			
NNO	Daniel Bryan	12.00	30.00
WWE Title			
NNO	Dolph Ziggler	12.00	30.00
NNO	Edge and Christian	15.00	40.00
NNO	Greg The Hammer Valentine	8.00	20.00
NNO	Honky Tonk Man	12.00	30.00
NNO	John Cena SP	20.00	50.00
NNO	Natalya	15.00	40.00
NNO	Nikki Bella	15.00	40.00
NNO	Randy Orton	20.00	50.00
NNO	Ravishing Rick Rude	8.00	20.00
NNO	Rey Mysterio	12.00	30.00
NNO	Ricky The Dragon Steamboat	8.00	20.00
NNO	RVD and Rey Mysterio	12.00	30.00
NNO	Sgt. Slaughter	25.00	60.00
NNO	Shawn Michaels	20.00	50.00
World Title			
NNO	Shawn Michaels	20.00	50.00
WWE Title			
NNO	Sheamus	12.00	30.00
NNO	The Shield SP	120.00	200.00
NNO	ShoMiz	12.00	30.00
NNO	Stone Cold Steve Austin SP	25.00	60.00
NNO	Triple H	20.00	50.00
NNO	Undertaker SP	25.00	60.00

2014 Topps Chrome WWE Champions Tribute Batista

COMPLETE SET (5)		5.00	12.00

*P.P.BLACK/1: UNPRICED DUE TO SCARCITY
*P.P.CYAN/1: UNPRICED DUE TO SCARCITY
*P.P.MAGENTA/1: UNPRICED DUE TO SCARCITY
*P.P.YELLOW/1: UNPRICED DUE TO SCARCITY
STATED OVERALL ODDS 1:6

1	Batista	1.50	4.00
2	Batista	1.50	4.00
3	Batista	1.50	4.00
4	Batista	1.50	4.00
5	Batista	1.50	4.00

2014 Topps Chrome WWE Champions Tribute Eddie Guerrero

COMPLETE SET (5)		2.50	6.00

*P.P.BLACK/1: UNPRICED DUE TO SCARCITY
*P.P.CYAN/1: UNPRICED DUE TO SCARCITY
*P.P.MAGENTA/1: UNPRICED DUE TO SCARCITY
*P.P.YELLOW/1: UNPRICED DUE TO SCARCITY
STATED OVERALL ODDS 1:6

1	Eddie Guerrero	.75	2.00
2	Eddie Guerrero	.75	2.00
3	Eddie Guerrero	.75	2.00
4	Eddie Guerrero	.75	2.00
5	Eddie Guerrero	.75	2.00

2014 Topps Chrome WWE Champions Tribute Edge

COMPLETE SET (5)		4.00	10.00

*P.P.BLACK/1: UNPRICED DUE TO SCARCITY
*P.P.CYAN/1: UNPRICED DUE TO SCARCITY
*P.P.MAGENTA/1: UNPRICED DUE TO SCARCITY
*P.P.YELLOW/1: UNPRICED DUE TO SCARCITY
STATED OVERALL ODDS 1:6

1	Edge	1.25	3.00
2	Edge	1.25	3.00
3	Edge	1.25	3.00
4	Edge	1.25	3.00
5	Edge	1.25	3.00

2014 Topps Chrome WWE Champions Tribute Iron Sheik

COMPLETE SET (5)	

*P.P.CYAN/1: UNPRICED DUE TO SCARCITY
*P.P.MAGENTA/1: UNPRICED DUE TO SCARCITY
*P.P.YELLOW/1: UNPRICED DUE TO SCARCITY
STATED OVERALL ODDS 1:6

1 Iron Sheik	.75	2.00
2 Iron Sheik	.75	2.00
3 Iron Sheik	.75	2.00
4 Iron Sheik	.75	2.00
5 Iron Sheik	.75	2.00

2014 Topps Chrome WWE Champions Tribute JBL

COMPLETE SET (5)	2.50	6.00

*P.P.BLACK/1: UNPRICED DUE TO SCARCITY
*P.P.CYAN/1: UNPRICED DUE TO SCARCITY
*P.P.MAGENTA/1: UNPRICED DUE TO SCARCITY
*P.P.YELLOW/1: UNPRICED DUE TO SCARCITY
STATED OVERALL ODDS 1:6

1 JBL	.75	2.00
2 JBL	.75	2.00
3 JBL	.75	2.00
4 JBL	.75	2.00
5 JBL	.75	2.00

2014 Topps Chrome WWE Champions Tribute Kevin Nash

COMPLETE SET (5)	4.00	10.00

*P.P.BLACK/1: UNPRICED DUE TO SCARCITY
*P.P.CYAN/1: UNPRICED DUE TO SCARCITY
*P.P.MAGENTA/1: UNPRICED DUE TO SCARCITY
*P.P.YELLOW/1: UNPRICED DUE TO SCARCITY
STATED OVERALL ODDS 1:6

1 Kevin Nash	1.25	3.00
2 Kevin Nash	1.25	3.00
3 Kevin Nash	1.25	3.00
4 Kevin Nash	1.25	3.00
5 Kevin Nash	1.25	3.00

2014 Topps Chrome WWE Champions Tribute Mick Foley

COMPLETE SET (5)	4.00	10.00

*P.P.BLACK/1: UNPRICED DUE TO SCARCITY
*P.P.CYAN/1: UNPRICED DUE TO SCARCITY
*P.P.MAGENTA/1: UNPRICED DUE TO SCARCITY
*P.P.YELLOW/1: UNPRICED DUE TO SCARCITY
STATED OVERALL ODDS 1:6

1 Mick Foley	1.25	3.00
2 Mick Foley	1.25	3.00
3 Mick Foley	1.25	3.00
4 Mick Foley	1.25	3.00
5 Mick Foley	1.25	3.00

2014 Topps Chrome WWE Champions Tribute Sgt. Slaughter

COMPLETE SET (5)	4.00	10.00

*P.P.BLACK/1: UNPRICED DUE TO SCARCITY
*P.P.CYAN/1: UNPRICED DUE TO SCARCITY
*P.P.MAGENTA/1: UNPRICED DUE TO SCARCITY
*P.P.YELLOW/1: UNPRICED DUE TO SCARCITY
STATED OVERALL ODDS 1:6

1 Sgt. Slaughter	1.25	3.00
2 Sgt. Slaughter	1.25	3.00
3 Sgt. Slaughter	1.25	3.00
4 Sgt. Slaughter	1.25	3.00
5 Sgt. Slaughter	1.25	3.00

2014 Topps Chrome WWE Champions Tribute Shawn Michaels

COMPLETE SET (5)	6.00	15.00

*P.P.BLACK/1: UNPRICED DUE TO SCARCITY
*P.P.CYAN/1: UNPRICED DUE TO SCARCITY
*P.P.MAGENTA/1: UNPRICED DUE TO SCARCITY
*P.P.YELLOW/1: UNPRICED DUE TO SCARCITY
STATED OVERALL ODDS 1:6

1 Shawn Michaels	2.00	5.00
2 Shawn Michaels	2.00	5.00
3 Shawn Michaels	2.00	5.00
4 Shawn Michaels	2.00	5.00
5 Shawn Michaels	2.00	5.00

2014 Topps Chrome WWE Champions Tribute Yokozuna

COMPLETE SET (5)	2.50	6.00

*P.P.BLACK/1: UNPRICED DUE TO SCARCITY
*P.P.CYAN/1: UNPRICED DUE TO SCARCITY
*P.P.MAGENTA/1: UNPRICED DUE TO SCARCITY
*P.P.YELLOW/1: UNPRICED DUE TO SCARCITY
STATED OVERALL ODDS 1:6

1 Yokozuna	.75	2.00
2 Yokozuna	.75	2.00
3 Yokozuna	.75	2.00
4 Yokozuna	.75	2.00
5 Yokozuna	.75	2.00

2014 Topps Chrome WWE Dual Autographs

STATED PRINT RUN 5 SER.#'d SETS

NNO D.Bryan/B.Wyatt	150.00	300.00
NNO D.Rhodes/J.Swagger	100.00	200.00
NNO J.Cena/R.Orton	150.00	300.00
NNO L.Harper/E.Rowan	100.00	200.00

2014 Topps Chrome WWE Jerry Lawler's Tributes

COMPLETE SET (10)	10.00	25.00

*P.P.BLACK/1: UNPRICED DUE TO SCARCITY
*P.P.CYAN/1: UNPRICED DUE TO SCARCITY
*P.P.MAGENTA/1: UNPRICED DUE TO SCARCITY
*P.P.YELLOW/1: UNPRICED DUE TO SCARCITY
STATED ODDS 1:12 HOBBY AND RETAIL

1 The Iron Sheik	1.00	2.50
2 Sgt. Slaughter	1.50	4.00
3 Yokozuna	1.00	2.50
4 Kevin Nash	1.50	4.00
5 Shawn Michaels	2.50	6.00
6 Mick Foley	1.50	4.00
7 Eddie Guerrero	1.00	2.50
8 JBL	1.00	2.50
9 Batista	2.00	5.00
10 Edge	1.50	4.00

2014 Topps Chrome WWE Kiss

NNO AJ Lee	50.00	100.00
NNO Aksana	20.00	50.00
NNO Alicia Fox	20.00	50.00
NNO Cameron	30.00	60.00
NNO Eva Marie	30.00	80.00
NNO Naomi	30.00	60.00
NNO Tamina Snuka	12.00	30.00
NNO Vickie Guerrero	12.00	30.00

2014 Topps Chrome WWE Kiss Autographs

NNO AJ Lee	200.00	350.00
NNO Aksana	30.00	75.00
NNO Cameron	30.00	75.00
NNO Tamina Snuka	30.00	75.00
NNO Vickie Guerrero	60.00	120.00

2014 Topps Chrome WWE NXT Prospects

COMPLETE SET (20)	30.00	75.00

*P.P.BLACK/1: UNPRICED DUE TO SCARCITY
*P.P.CYAN/1: UNPRICED DUE TO SCARCITY
*P.P.MAGENTA/1: UNPRICED DUE TO SCARCITY
*P.P.YELLOW/1: UNPRICED DUE TO SCARCITY
STATED ODDS 1:3 HOBBY AND RETAIL

1 Adrian Neville	1.25	3.00
2 Alexander Rusev	1.50	4.00
3 Baron Corbin	.60	1.50
4 Bayley	5.00	12.00
5 Charlotte	12.00	30.00
6 CJ Parker	.60	1.50
7 Konnor O'Brian	.60	1.50
8 Corey Graves	.60	1.50
9 Emma	2.00	5.00
10 Enzo Amore	1.25	3.00
11 Jason Jordan	.60	1.50
12 Leo Kruger	.60	1.50
13 Mojo Rawley	.60	1.50
14 Paige	8.00	20.00
15 Rick Viktor	.60	1.50
16 Sami Zayn	1.25	3.00
17 Sasha Banks	10.00	25.00
18 Sylvester Lefort	.60	1.50
19 Tyler Breeze	.60	1.50
20 Xavier Woods	.60	1.50

2014 Topps Chrome WWE Royal Rumble Mat Relics

*SUPERFR./1: UNPRICED DUE TO SCARCITY
STATED ODDS

NNO Alberto Del Rio	4.00	10.00
NNO Alexander Rusev	6.00	15.00
NNO Batista	10.00	25.00
NNO Big E	3.00	8.00
NNO Billy Gunn	5.00	12.00
NNO Bray Wyatt	8.00	20.00
NNO Brock Lesnar	8.00	20.00
NNO Cody Rhodes	3.00	8.00
NNO Daniel Bryan	8.00	20.00
NNO El Torito	3.00	8.00
NNO Goldust	3.00	8.00
NNO JBL	5.00	12.00
NNO John Cena	10.00	25.00
NNO Kane	6.00	15.00
NNO Kevin Nash	8.00	20.00
NNO Randy Orton	8.00	20.00
NNO Rey Mysterio	8.00	20.00
NNO Road Dogg	5.00	12.00
NNO Roman Reigns	10.00	25.00
NNO Sheamus	6.00	15.00

2014 Topps Chrome WWE Swatch Relics

NNO Alberto Del Rio	6.00	15.00
NNO Bray Wyatt	12.00	30.00
NNO Curtis Axel	3.00	8.00

NNO Damien Sandow	3.00	8.00
NNO Daniel Bryan	8.00	20.00
NNO Diego	3.00	8.00
NNO Dolph Ziggler	5.00	12.00
NNO Fernando	3.00	8.00
NNO Goldust	3.00	8.00
NNO Jack Swagger	6.00	15.00
NNO John Cena	12.00	30.00
NNO Kofi Kingston	3.00	8.00
NNO Mark Henry	5.00	12.00
NNO The Miz	5.00	12.00
NNO Rey Mysterio	5.00	12.00
NNO Undertaker	15.00	40.00

2014 Topps Chrome WWE WrestleMania DVD Promo

P1 John Cena

2015 Topps Chrome WWE

Subsets include NXT (91-100)

COMPLETE SET (100)	8.00	20.00
UNOPENED BOX (24 PACKS)	60.00	80.00
UNOPENED PACK (4 CARDS)	3.50	4.00

*REF.: .4X TO 1.2X BASIC CARDS
*ATOMIC: .6X TO 1.5X BASIC CARDS
*XFRACTOR: .6X TO 1.5X BASIC CARDS
*PULSAR/75: 1.5X TO 4X BASIC CARDS
*GOLD/50: 2X TO 5X BASIC CARDS
*SILVER WAVE/20: 3X TO 8X BASIC CARDS
*SHIMMER/10: 5X TO 12X BASIC CARDS
*RED/5: UNPRICED DUE TO SCARCITY
*SUPERFR./1: UNPRICED DUE TO SCARCITY
*P.P.BLACK/1: UNPRICED DUE TO SCARCITY
*P.P.CYAN/1: UNPRICED DUE TO SCARCITY
*P.P.MAGENTA/1: UNPRICED DUE TO SCARCITY
*P.P.YELLOW/1: UNPRICED DUE TO SCARCITY

1 Adam Rose	.30	.75
2 AJ Lee	1.25	3.00
3 Alicia Fox	.50	1.25
4 Bad News Barrett	.25	.60
5 Batista	.60	1.50
6 Big E	.40	1.00
7 Big Show	.60	1.50
8 Bo Dallas	.25	.60
9 Booker T	.40	1.00
10 Bray Wyatt	1.00	2.50
11 Brie Bella	.75	2.00
12 Brock Lesnar	1.00	2.50
13 Cameron	.40	1.00
14 Cesaro	.25	.60
15 Chris Jericho	.60	1.50
16 Christian	.25	.60
17 Curtis Axel	.25	.60
18 Damien Mizdow	.40	1.00
19 Daniel Bryan	1.00	2.50
20 Darren Young	.25	.60
21 David Otunga	.25	.60
22 Dean Ambrose	.60	1.50
23 Diego	.25	.60
24 Dolph Ziggler	.40	1.00
25 Eden	.40	1.00
26 Emma	.40	1.00
27 Erick Rowan	.40	1.00
28 Eva Marie	1.00	2.50
29 Fandango	.25	.60
30 Fernando	.25	.60
31 Goldust	.25	.60
32 Heath Slater	.25	.60

33	Hornswoggle	.40	1.00
34	Jack Swagger	.40	1.00
35	Jerry The King Lawler	.40	1.00
36	Jey Uso	.25	.60
37	Jimmy Uso	.25	.60
38	John Cena	1.25	3.00
39	Justin Gabriel	.25	.60
40	Kane	.60	1.50
41	Kofi Kingston	.25	.60
42	Lana	1.00	2.50
43	Layla	.60	1.50
44	Lilian Garcia	.60	1.50
45	Luke Harper	.40	1.00
46	Mark Henry	.40	1.00
47	The Miz	.40	1.00
48	Naomi	.40	1.00
49	Natalya	.75	2.00
50	Nikki Bella	.75	2.00
51	Paige	1.25	3.00
52	Paul Heyman	.25	.60
53	R-Truth	.25	.60
54	Randy Orton	2.00	5.00
55	Renee Young	1.00	2.50
56	Rey Mysterio	.60	1.50
57	The Rock	1.25	3.00
58	Rob Van Dam	.60	1.50
59	Roman Reigns	.60	1.50
60	Rosa Mendes	.40	1.00
61	Rusev	.60	1.50
62	Ryback	.25	.60
63	Seth Rollins	.40	1.00
64	Sheamus	.60	1.50
65	Sin Cara	.40	1.00
66	Stardust	.25	.60
67	Stephanie McMahon	.40	1.00
68	Summer Rae	1.00	2.50
69	Tamina Snuka	.40	1.00
70	Titus O'Neil	.25	.60
71	El Torito	.25	.60
72	Triple H	1.00	2.50
73	Tyson Kidd	.25	.60
74	Undertaker	1.00	2.50
75	William Regal	.40	1.00
76	Xavier Woods	.40	1.00
77	Zack Ryder	.25	.60
78	Zeb Colter	.40	1.00
79	Bret Hit Man Hart	.75	2.00
80	Bruno Sammartino	.60	1.50
81	George The Animal Steele	.30	.75
82	Gerald Brisco	.40	1.00
83	Hulk Hogan	1.25	3.00
84	Larry Zbyszko	.40	1.00
85	Mouth of the South Jimmy Hart	.30	.75
86	Pat Patterson	.25	.60
87	Ric Flair	1.25	3.00
88	Rowdy Roddy Piper	.75	2.00
89	Sting	.60	1.50
90	Ultimate Warrior	.75	2.00
91	Aiden English NXT	.30	.75
92	Alexa Bliss NXT	8.00	20.00
93	Angelo Dawkins NXT	.30	.75
94	Bull Dempsey NXT	.40	1.00
95	Colin Cassady NXT	.40	1.00
96	Hideo Itami NXT	.25	.60
97	Kalisto NXT	.40	1.00
98	Marcus Louis NXT	.40	1.00
99	Sawyer Fulton NXT	.40	1.00
100	Tye Dillinger NXT	.40	1.00

2015 Topps Chrome WWE Autographs

*PULSAR/75: .5X TO 1.2X BASIC AUTOS
*GOLD/10: 1X TO 2.5X BASIC AUTOS
*RED/5: UNPRICED DUE TO SCARCITY

NNO	Adam Rose	6.00	15.00
NNO	Brie Bella	10.00	25.00
NNO	Bruno Sammartino	15.00	40.00
NNO	Eva Marie	20.00	50.00
NNO	Hulk Hogan	200.00	400.00
NNO	Lana	25.00	60.00
NNO	Lita	10.00	25.00
NNO	Nikki Bella	12.00	30.00
NNO	Renee Young	12.00	30.00
NNO	Roman Reigns	15.00	40.00

2015 Topps Chrome WWE Commemorative Championship Plates

*PULSAR/75: .6X TO 1.5X BASIC PLATES
*RED/5: UNPRICED DUE TO SCARCITY

NNO	Adrian Neville	6.00	15.00
	NXT Champion		
NNO	Adrian Neville	6.00	15.00
	NXT Tag Champion		
NNO	Big E	5.00	12.00
NNO	Bo Dallas	3.00	8.00
NNO	Charlotte	10.00	25.00
NNO	Corey Graves	6.00	15.00
NNO	Erick Rowan	5.00	12.00
NNO	Kalisto	5.00	12.00
NNO	Konnor	8.00	20.00
NNO	Luke Harper	5.00	12.00
NNO	Paige	15.00	40.00
NNO	Seth Rollins	6.00	15.00
NNO	Sin Cara	5.00	12.00
NNO	Viktor	8.00	20.00

2015 Topps Chrome WWE Diva Kiss

RANDOMLY INSERTED INTO PACKS

NNO	Brie Bella	20.00	50.00
NNO	Cameron	10.00	25.00
NNO	Eden	10.00	25.00
NNO	Emma	30.00	60.00
NNO	Naomi	20.00	40.00
NNO	Natalya	20.00	50.00
NNO	Nikki Bella	40.00	80.00
NNO	Renee Young	25.00	60.00
NNO	Summer Rae	25.00	60.00
NNO	Tamina Snuka	10.00	25.00

2015 Topps Chrome WWE Diva Kiss Autographs

*RED REF./5: UNPRICED DUE TO SCARCITY
*SUPERFR./1: UNPRICED DUE TO SCARCITY
STATED PRINT RUN 25 SER.#'d SETS

NNO	Brie Bella	50.00	100.00
NNO	Cameron	12.00	30.00
NNO	Eden	15.00	40.00
NNO	Emma	25.00	60.00
NNO	Naomi	15.00	50.00
NNO	Natalya	20.00	50.00
NNO	Nikki Bella	50.00	100.00
NNO	Renee Young	20.00	50.00
NNO	Summer Rae	30.00	75.00
NNO	Tamina Snuka	15.00	40.00

2015 Topps Chrome WWE Dual Autographs

STATED PRINT RUN 5 SER. #'d SETS
UNPRICED DUE TO SCARCITY

1	AJ Lee/Paige	
2	D.Ambrose/S.Rollins	
3	Emma/Eden	
4	J.Cena/B.Wyatt	

2015 Topps Chrome WWE King of the Ring Sign Relics

*RED/5: UNPRICED DUE TO SCARCITY
*SUPERFR./1: UNPRICED DUE TO SCARCITY
STATED ODDS 1:1,156 HOBBY

NNO	Billy Gunn	5.00	12.00
NNO	Bret Hit Man Hart	12.00	30.00
NNO	Brock Lesnar	15.00	40.00
NNO	Don Muraco	5.00	12.00
NNO	Edge	8.00	20.00
NNO	Harley Race	5.00	12.00
NNO	King Booker	5.00	12.00
NNO	Million Dollar Man Ted DiBiase	5.00	12.00
NNO	Sheamus	8.00	20.00
NNO	Stone Cold Steve Austin	10.00	25.00
NNO	Tito Santana	5.00	12.00
NNO	Triple H	8.00	20.00
NNO	William Regal	5.00	12.00

2015 Topps Chrome WWE Night of Champions Mat Relics

RANDOMLY INSERTED INTO PACKS
*PULSAR/75: .6X TO 1.5X BASIC RELICS

1	AJ Lee	12.00	30.00
2	Brock Lesnar	10.00	25.00
3	Cesaro	2.50	6.00
4	Chris Jericho	6.00	15.00
5	Dean Ambrose	6.00	15.00
6	Dolph Ziggler	4.00	10.00
7	John Cena	12.00	30.00
8	Mark Henry	4.00	10.00
9	The Miz	4.00	10.00
10	Nikki Bella	8.00	20.00
11	Paige	12.00	30.00
12	Randy Orton	10.00	25.00
13	Rusev	6.00	15.00
14	Seth Rollins	4.00	10.00
15	Sheamus	6.00	15.00

2015 Topps Chrome WWE Night of Champions Turnbuckle Relics

*SUPERFR./1: UNPRICED DUE TO SCARCITY
STATED PRINT RUN 33 SER.#'d SETS

NNO	AJ Lee	80.00	150.00
NNO	Brock Lesnar	15.00	40.00
NNO	Chris Jericho	12.00	30.00
NNO	Dean Ambrose	25.00	50.00
NNO	John Cena	25.00	60.00
NNO	Nikki Bella	15.00	40.00
NNO	Paige	25.00	60.00
NNO	Randy Orton	15.00	40.00
NNO	Seth Rollins	8.00	20.00

2015 Topps Chrome WWE NXT Autographs

*GOLD/10: .75X TO 2X BASIC AUTOS
*ATOMIC/5: UNPRICED DUE TO SCARCITY

*RED/5: UNPRICED DUE TO SCARCITY
*SUPERFR./1: UNPRICED DUE TO SCARCITY
RANDOMLY INSERTED INTO PACKS

NNO	Aiden English	6.00	15.00
NNO	Alexa Bliss	200.00	350.00
NNO	Charlotte	30.00	80.00
NNO	Colin Cassady	12.00	30.00
NNO	Sawyer Fulton	5.00	12.00

2015 Topps Chrome WWE Swatch Relics

RANDOMLY INSERTED INTO PACKS
*PULSAR/75: .1X TO 2.5X BASIC RELICS

NNO	Cesaro	1.50	4.00
NNO	Curtis Axel	1.50	4.00
NNO	Damien Mizdow	2.50	6.00
NNO	Daniel Bryan	6.00	15.00
NNO	Darren Young	1.50	4.00
NNO	Diego	1.50	4.00
NNO	Jack Swagger	2.50	6.00
NNO	Jerry The King Lawler	2.50	6.00
NNO	Jimmy Uso	1.50	4.00
NNO	John Cena	8.00	20.00
NNO	Kofi Kingston	1.50	4.00
NNO	Mark Henry	2.50	6.00
NNO	Paige	8.00	20.00
NNO	Randy Orton	6.00	15.00
NNO	Sheamus	4.00	10.00
NNO	Titus O'Neil	1.50	4.00
NNO	Tyson Kidd	1.50	4.00
NNO	Zack Ryder	1.50	4.00

2015 Topps Chrome WWE Ultimate Warrior Commemorative Face Paint Plate

*PULSAR REF/75: 1.2X TO 3X BASIC MEM
RANDOMLY INSERTED INTO PACKS

NNO	Ultimate Warrior	5.00	12.00

2020 Topps Chrome WWE

COMPLETE SET (100)   15.00   40.00
*REF: .5X TO 1.2X BASIC CARDS
*XFRAC: .6X TO 1.5X BASIC CARDS
*GREEN/99: 1.2X TO 3X BASIC CARDS
*GOLD/50: 2X TO 5X BASIC CARDS
*ORANGE/25: UNPRICED DUE TO SCARCITY
*BLACK/10: UNPRICED DUE TO SCARCITY
*RED/5: UNPRICED DUE TO SCARCITY
*SUPER/1: UNPRICED DUE TO SCARCITY

1	AJ Styles	1.25	3.00
2	Aleister Black	.75	2.00
3	Alexa Bliss	2.00	5.00
4	Mustafa Ali	.60	1.50
5	Andrade	.60	1.50
6	Asuka	.75	2.00
7	King Corbin	.50	1.25
8	Bayley	.75	2.00
9	Becky Lynch	1.50	4.00
10	Big E	.40	1.00
11	Big Show	.50	1.25
12	Billie Kay	.75	2.00
13	Bobby Lashley	.75	2.00
14	Braun Strowman	1.00	2.50
15	The Fiend Bray Wyatt	1.25	3.00
16	Brock Lesnar	1.50	4.00
17	Murphy	.50	1.25
18	Carmella	1.00	2.50

19	Cesaro	.40	1.00
20	Charlotte Flair	1.50	4.00
21	Daniel Bryan	1.25	3.00
22	Drake Maverick	.40	1.00
23	Drew McIntyre	.75	2.00
24	Elias	.40	1.00
25	Erik	.40	1.00
26	Ember Moon	.75	2.00
27	Finn Balor	1.00	2.50
28	Humberto Carrillo	.60	1.50
29	Ivar	.40	1.00
30	Jeff Hardy	1.00	2.50
31	Jey Uso	.40	1.00
32	Jimmy Uso	.40	1.00
33	John Cena	1.50	4.00
34	Kairi Sane	.75	2.00
35	Kane	.50	1.25
36	Karl Anderson	.40	1.00
37	Kevin Owens	.50	1.25
38	Kofi Kingston	.60	1.50
39	Lana	1.00	2.50
40	Lacey Evans	1.00	2.50
41	Luke Gallows	.40	1.00
42	Mandy Rose	2.00	5.00
43	Naomi	.75	2.00
44	Natalya	.60	1.50
45	Nia Jax	.60	1.50
46	Nikki Cross	.75	2.00
47	Peyton Royce	.75	2.00
48	Randy Orton	1.00	2.50
49	Ricochet	.60	1.50
50	Roman Reigns	1.00	2.50
51	Ronda Rousey	2.00	5.00
52	R-Truth	.40	1.00
53	Ruby Riott	.60	1.50
54	Rusev	.50	1.25
55	Sami Zayn	.50	1.25
56	Samoa Joe	.60	1.50
57	Sasha Banks	1.50	4.00
58	Seth Rollins	.75	2.00
59	Sheamus	.50	1.25
60	Shinsuke Nakamura	.75	2.00
61	Shorty G	.40	1.00
62	Sonya Deville	1.00	2.50
63	The Miz	.60	1.50
64	The Rock	2.00	5.00
65	Triple H	1.00	2.50
66	Undertaker	1.50	4.00
67	Xavier Woods	.40	1.00
68	Zelina Vega	.75	2.00
69	Adam Cole	1.00	2.50
70	Angel Garza	.50	1.25
71	Angelo Dawkins	.40	1.00
72	Bianca Belair	1.00	2.50
73	Boa	.40	1.00
74	Bobby Fish	.40	1.00
75	Bronson Reed	.40	1.00
76	Cameron Grimes	.40	1.00
77	Candice LeRae	1.25	3.00
78	Damian Priest	.40	1.00
79	Dexter Lumis	.40	1.00
80	Io Shirai	.60	1.50
81	Isaiah Swerve Scott	.50	1.25
82	Joaquin Wilde	.40	1.00
83	Johnny Gargano	.75	2.00
84	Kushida	.50	1.25
85	Kyle O'Reilly	.50	1.25
86	Lio Rush	.40	1.00
87	Matt Riddle	.75	2.00
88	Mia Yim	.75	2.00
89	Montez Ford	.40	1.00
90	Roderick Strong	.75	2.00
91	Shayna Baszler	1.25	3.00
92	Velveteen Dream	.50	1.25
93	Alexander Wolfe	.40	1.00
94	Fabian Aichner	.40	1.00
95	Marcel Barthel	.40	1.00
96	Pete Dunne	.40	1.00
97	Rhea Ripley	1.00	2.50
98	Toni Storm	1.00	2.50
99	Travis Banks	.40	1.00
100	Walter	.75	2.00

2020 Topps Chrome WWE Autographs

*GREEN/99: .5X TO 1.2X BASIC AUTOS
*GOLD/50: .6X TO 1.5X BASIC AUTOS
*ORANGE/25: UNPRICED DUE TO SCARCITY
*BLACK/10: UNPRICED DUE TO SCARCITY
*RED/5: UNPRICED DUE TO SCARCITY
*SUPER/1: UNPRICED DUE TO SCARCITY
RANDOMLY INSERTED INTO PACKS

AAB	Aleister Black	8.00	20.00
AAC	Adam Cole	10.00	25.00
AAL	Alexa Bliss	60.00	120.00
AAN	Andrade	8.00	20.00
AAS	AJ Styles	12.00	30.00
ABY	Bayley	20.00	50.00
ACF	Charlotte Flair	20.00	50.00
ADB	Daniel Bryan	8.00	20.00
ADM	Drew McIntyre	12.00	30.00
AFB	Finn Balor	12.00	30.00
AHC	Humberto Carrillo	6.00	15.00
AIS	Io Shirai	30.00	75.00
AKC	King Corbin	6.00	15.00
AKK	Kofi Kingston	6.00	15.00
AKU	Kushida	8.00	20.00
ALE	Lacey Evans	15.00	40.00
AMA	Mustafa Ali	8.00	20.00
ARH	Rhea Ripley	30.00	75.00
ASB	Shayna Baszler	10.00	25.00
ASD	Johnny Gargano	6.00	15.00
ASJ	Samoa Joe	6.00	15.00
ASN	Shinsuke Nakamura	12.00	30.00
ASR	Seth Rollins	8.00	20.00
ATM	The Miz	8.00	20.00

2020 Topps Chrome WWE Big Legends

COMPLETE SET (25) 12.00 30.00
*GREEN/99: .75X TO 2X BASIC CARDS
*GOLD/50: 1.2X TO 3X BASIC CARDS
*ORANGE/25: UNPRICED DUE TO SCARCITY
*BLACK/10: UNPRICED DUE TO SCARCITY
*RED/5: UNPRICED DUE TO SCARCITY
*SUPER/1: UNPRICED DUE TO SCARCITY
RANDOMLY INSERTED INTO PACKS

BL1	Alundra Blayze	1.00	2.50
BL2	Boogeyman	.60	1.50
BL3	Booker T	1.25	3.00
BL4	Brutus The Barber Beefcake	.60	1.50
BL5	Christian	.75	2.00
BL6	Eve	1.25	3.00
BL7	Gerald Brisco	.60	1.50
BL8	The Godfather	.60	1.50
BL9	The Hurricane	.60	1.50
BL10	Jerry The King Lawler	1.50	4.00
BL11	Kerry Von Erich	1.00	2.50
BL12	Kevin Nash	1.00	2.50
BL13	Kurt Angle	1.50	4.00
BL14	Mick Foley	1.25	3.00
BL15	Molly Holly	.75	2.00
BL16	Pat Patterson	.60	1.50
BL17	Razor Ramon	1.00	2.50
BL18	Ric Flair	2.50	6.00
BL19	Rikishi	.60	1.50
BL20	Road Dogg Jesse James	.75	2.00
BL21	Ron Simmons	1.00	2.50
BL22	Sgt. Slaughter	1.25	3.00
BL23	The Million Dollar Man Ted DiBiase	1.25	3.00
BL24	Wendi Richter	.75	2.00
BL25	X-Pac	.60	1.50

2020 Topps Chrome WWE Big Legends Autographs

*GREEN/99: .5X TO 1.2X BASIC CARDS
*GOLD/50: .6X TO 1.5X BASIC CARDS
*ORANGE/25: UNPRICED DUE TO SCARCITY
*BLACK/10: UNPRICED DUE TO SCARCITY
*RED/5: UNPRICED DUE TO SCARCITY
*SUPER/1: UNPRICED DUE TO SCARCITY
RANDOMLY INSERTED INTO PACKS

BLJJ	Road Dogg Jesse James	10.00	25.00
BLJL	Jerry The King Lawler	12.00	30.00
BLHBK	Shawn Michaels		

2020 Topps Chrome WWE Fantasy Matches

COMPLETE SET (22) 15.00 40.00
*GREEN/99: .6X TO 1.5X BASIC CARDS
*GOLD/50: .75X TO 2X BASIC CARDS
*ORANGE/25: UNPRICED DUE TO SCARCITY
*BLACK/10: UNPRICED DUE TO SCARCITY
*RED/5: UNPRICED DUE TO SCARCITY
*SUPER/1: UNPRICED DUE TO SCARCITY
RANDOMLY INSERTED INTO PACKS

FM1	Samoa Joe/John Cena	2.50	6.00
FM2	Beth Phoenix/Chyna	1.50	4.00
FM3	Batista/Ultimate Warrior	1.50	4.00
FM4	AJ Styles/Mr. Perfect	2.00	5.00
FM5	Drew McIntyre/Booker T	1.25	3.00
FM6	The Miz/Rowdy Roddy Piper	1.50	4.00
FM7	Roman Reigns/The Rock	3.00	8.00
FM8	Randy Orton/DDP	1.50	4.00
FM9	Bret Hit Man Hart/Daniel Bryan	2.00	5.00
FM10	Alexa Bliss/Trish Stratus	3.00	8.00
FM11	Charlotte Flair/Lita	2.50	6.00
FM12	The Fiend/Jake The Snake Roberts	2.00	5.00
FM13	Seth Rollins/Shawn Michaels	1.50	4.00
FM14	Kurt Angle/Ken Shamrock	1.50	4.00
FM15	Mankind/Jeff Hardy	1.50	4.00
FM16	Braun Strowman/Goldberg	2.50	6.00
FM17	Finn Balor/Undertaker	2.50	6.00
FM18	Rick Rude/Robert Roode	.75	2.00
FM19	KO/Stone Cold Steve Austin	3.00	8.00
FM20	Big Show/Vader	1.00	2.50
FM21	Randy Savage/Kofi Kingston	2.00	5.00
FM22	Andrade/Eddie Guerrero	1.50	4.00

2020 Topps Chrome WWE Fantasy Matches Autographs

*BLACK/10: UNPRICED DUE TO SCARCITY
*RED/5: UNPRICED DUE TO SCARCITY
*SUPER/1: UNPRICED DUE TO SCARCITY
STATED PRINT RUN 25 SER.#'d SETS

FMKK	Jeff Hardy/Mankind	75.00	150.00
FMLC	Charlotte Flair/Lita	125.00	250.00
FMSA	Seth Rollins/Shawn Michaels	75.00	150.00
FMTA	Alexa Bliss/Trish Stratus	250.00	500.00

2020 Topps Chrome WWE Image Variations

COMPLETE SET (25)
*GREEN/99: .5X TO 1.2X BASIC CARDS
*GOLD/50: .6X TO 1.5X BASIC CARDS
*ORANGE/25: UNPRICED DUE TO SCARCITY
*BLACK/10: UNPRICED DUE TO SCARCITY
*RED/5: UNPRICED DUE TO SCARCITY
*SUPER/1: UNPRICED DUE TO SCARCITY
RANDOMLY INSERTED INTO PACKS

IV1	AJ Styles	2.00	5.00
IV2	Alexa Bliss	5.00	12.00
IV3	Mustafa Ali	1.50	4.00
IV4	Asuka	3.00	8.00
IV5	Bayley	1.50	4.00
IV6	Becky Lynch	6.00	15.00
IV7	Bianca Belair	2.50	6.00
IV8	The Fiend Bray Wyatt	4.00	10.00
IV9	Carmella	4.00	10.00
IV10	Charlotte Flair	5.00	12.00
IV11	Ember Moon	1.50	4.00
IV12	Finn Balor	2.00	5.00
IV13	Jeff Hardy	2.50	6.00
IV14	Kairi Sane	3.00	8.00
IV15	Kofi Kingston	1.50	4.00
IV16	Lacey Evans	3.00	8.00
IV17	Matt Riddle	2.50	6.00
IV18	Naomi	2.50	6.00
IV19	Nikki Cross	3.00	8.00
IV20	Ricochet	2.00	5.00
IV21	Samoa Joe	2.00	5.00
IV22	Seth Rollins	2.00	5.00
IV23	Sonya Deville	2.50	6.00
IV24	Velveteen Dream	2.00	5.00
IV25	King Corbin	1.50	4.00

2020 Topps Chrome WWE Shocking Wins

COMPLETE SET (25) 12.00 30.00
*GREEN/99: .5X TO 1.2X BASIC CARDS
*GOLD/50: .6X TO 1.5X BASIC CARDS
*ORANGE/25: UNPRICED DUE TO SCARCITY
*BLACK/10: UNPRICED DUE TO SCARCITY
*RED/5: UNPRICED DUE TO SCARCITY
*SUPER/1: UNPRICED DUE TO SCARCITY
RANDOMLY INSERTED INTO PACKS

SW1	Ron Simmons	1.00	2.50
SW2	The 1-2-3 Kid	.60	1.50
SW3	Yokozuna	1.00	2.50
SW4	Shawn Michaels	1.50	4.00
SW5	Kevin Nash	1.00	2.50
SW6	Mankind	1.25	3.00
SW7	Jeff Hardy	1.50	4.00
SW8	Brock Lesnar	2.50	6.00
SW9	The Hurricane	.60	1.50
SW10	Eddie Guerrero	1.50	4.00
SW11	Shelton Benjamin	.75	2.00
SW12	Bobby Lashley	1.25	3.00
SW13	Sheamus	.75	2.00

SW14	The Miz	1.00	2.50
SW15	Sheamus	.75	2.00
SW16	Lord Tensai	.60	1.50
SW17	Bo Dallas	.60	1.50
SW18	Fandango	.60	1.50
SW19	Brock Lesnar	2.50	6.00
SW20	Paige	1.50	4.00
SW21	Charlotte Flair	2.50	6.00
SW22	Heath Slater	.60	1.50
SW23	Kevin Owens	.75	2.00
SW24	Finn Balor	1.50	4.00
SW25	Jinder Mahal	.60	1.50

2020 Topps Chrome WWE Shocking Wins Autographs

*GREEN/99: .5X TO 1.2X BASIC AUTOS
*GOLD/50: .6X TO 1.5X BASIC AUTOS
*ORANGE/25: UNPRICED DUE TO SCARCITY
*BLACK/10: UNPRICED DUE TO SCARCITY
*RED/5: UNPRICED DUE TO SCARCITY
*SUPER/1: UNPRICED DUE TO SCARCITY
RANDOMLY INSERTED INTO PACKS

SWABD	Bo Dallas	5.00	12.00
SWACF	Charlotte Flair	15.00	40.00
SWAFB	Finn Balor	12.00	30.00
SWAJH	Jeff Hardy	10.00	25.00
SWAJL	Jerry The King Lawler		
SWAJM	Jinder Mahal		
SWAKO	Kevin Owens	6.00	15.00
SWALA	Bobby Lashley	5.00	12.00
SWALT	Lord Tensai	5.00	12.00
SWAMA	Mustafa Ali	5.00	12.00
SWAMK	Mankind		
SWASB	Shelton Benjamin	6.00	15.00
SWASH	Sheamus		
SWASM	Sheamus	8.00	20.00
SWATM	The Miz	8.00	20.00
SWAZR	Zack Ryder		

1993 Topps CMLL Wrestling

COMPLETE SET (66)

1	Aguila Solitaria	
2	Aguilita Solitaria	
3	Arkangel	
4	Atlantis	
5	Aestia Salvaje	
6	Black Magic (Norman Smiley)	
7	Blue Demon Jr.	
8	Brazo de Oro	
9	Brazo de Plata	
10	Bronce	
11	Broncito	
12	Cachorro Mendoza	
13	Ciclon Ramirez	
14	Cicloncito Ramirez	
15	Cintya Moreno	
16	Corazon de Leon	
17	Dr. Wagner Jr.	
18	Damian el Guerrero	
19	El Brazo	
20	El Dandy	
21	Emilio Charles Jr.	
22	Felino	
23	Gran Markus Jr.	
24	Guerrero del Futuro	
25	Guerrero de la Muerte	
26	Guerrero Maya	
27	Guerrero Samuray	
28	Hijo del Gladiador	
29	Jaque Mate	
30	Kato Jr.	
31	La Fiera	
32	Lady Apache	
33	Lynx	
34	Mano Negra	
35	Mazakre	
36	Mazakrito	
37	Mascara Magica	
38	Mascarita Magica	
39	Metalico	
40	Mogur	
41	Negro Casas	
42	Orito	
43	Oro	
44	Pantera	
45	Pegasso II	
46	Pequeno Felino	
47	Pequeno Jaque Mate	
48	Pequeno Ultratumbita	
49	Pierroth Jr.	
50	Pirata Morgan	
51	Piratita Morgan	
52	Plata	
53	Popitekus	
54	Ringo Mendoza	
55	Sangre Chicana	
56	Talisman	
57	Titan	
58	Triton	
59	Tritoncito	
60	Trueno	
61	Ultimo Dragon	
62	Ultimo Dragoncito	
63	Vampiro Casanova	
64	Xavier Cruz	
65	Xochitl Hamada	
66	Lista de Verificacion	

2006 Topps Heritage Chrome WWE

Subsets include: DV = Divas (58-70); L = Legends (71-89)

COMPLETE SET (90)		10.00	25.00
UNOPENED BOX (24 PACKS)			
UNOPENED PACK (5 CARDS)			

*REFRACTORS: .75X TO 2X BASIC CARDS
*X-FRACTORS: 1.5X TO 4X BASIC CARDS
*SUPERFR./25: 10X TO 25X BASIC CARDS

1	John Cena	1.25	3.00
2	Batista	.75	2.00
3	Carlito	.75	2.00
4	Orlando Jordan	.20	.50
5	Paul London	.20	.50
6	Johnny Nitro	.30	.75
7	Joey Mercury	.20	.50
8	The Hurricane	.20	.50
9	Rosey	.20	.50
10	The Rock	1.25	3.00
11	Stone Cold Steve Austin	1.25	3.00
12	Hulk Hogan	1.25	3.00
13	Big Show	.75	2.00
14	The Boogeyman	.30	.75
15	Danny Basham	.20	.50
16	Edge	.75	2.00
17	Finlay	.50	1.25
18	Eugene	.20	.50
19	Joey Styles	.20	.50
20	Jonathan Coachman	.20	.50
21	Kane	.75	2.00
22	Kid Kash	.20	.50
23	Kurt Angle	.75	2.00
24	Rene Dupree	.30	.75
25	Ric Flair	1.00	2.50
26	Rob Van Dam	.50	1.25
27	Shawn Michaels	1.25	3.00
28	Triple H	1.25	3.00
29	Chavo Guerrero	.30	.75
30	Val Venis	.30	.75
31	Viscera	.30	.75
32	Steven Richards	.30	.75
33	Booker T	.50	1.25
34	Chris Benoit	.75	2.00
35	Ken Kennedy	.50	1.25
36	Doug Basham	.30	.75
37	Lashley	.50	1.25
38	Funaki	.30	.75
39	Hardcore Holly	.30	.75
40	JBL	.50	1.25
41	Paul Burchill	.20	.50
42	Psicosis	.20	.50
43	Super Crazy	.30	.75
44	Shelton Benjamin	.20	.50
45	Chris Masters	.30	.75
46	Nunzio	.20	.50
47	Randy Orton	.50	1.25
48	Rey Mysterio	.75	2.00
49	Scotty 2 Hotty	.30	.75
50	Tazz	.30	.75
51	Theodore Long	.20	.50
52	Undertaker	1.00	2.50
53	William Regal	.50	1.25
54	Antonio	.20	.50
55	Romeo	.20	.50
56	Snitsky	.30	.75
57	Robert Conway	.30	.75
58	Mickie James DV	1.25	3.00
59	Sharmell DV	.75	2.00
60	Trish Stratus DV	2.00	5.00
61	Torrie Wilson DV	2.00	5.00
62	Ashley DV	.75	2.00
63	Lita DV	1.25	3.00
64	Lilian Garcia DV	1.00	2.50
65	Maria DV	.75	2.00
66	Stacy Keibler DV	2.00	5.00
67	Victoria DV	1.25	3.00
68	Candice Michelle DV	1.25	3.00
69	Michelle McCool DV	1.00	2.50
70	Melina DV	.75	2.00
71	The British Bulldog L	.75	2.00
72	Chief Jay Strongbow L	.30	.75
73	Classy Freddie Blassie L	.30	.75
74	Cowboy Bob Orton L	.50	1.25
75	Bobby The Brain Heenan L	.50	1.25
76	Gorilla Monsoon L	.30	.75
77	Hillbilly Jim L	.30	.75
78	Iron Sheik L	.75	2.00
79	Jake The Snake Roberts L	.60	1.50
80	Jerry The King Lawler L	.60	1.50
81	Junkyard Dog L	.60	1.50
82	Mouth of the South Jimmy Hart L	.75	2.00
83	Mr. Wonderful Paul Orndorff L	.75	2.00
84	Nikolai Volkoff L	.50	1.25
85	Rowdy Roddy Piper L	1.00	2.50
86	Sgt. Slaughter L	.75	2.00
87	Superstar Billy Graham L	.30	.75
88	Million-Dollar Man Ted DiBiase L	.75	2.00
89	Godfather L	.30	.75
90	Checklist	.20	.50

2006 Topps Heritage Chrome WWE Autographs

GROUP A ODDS: 1:404 HOBBY
GROUP B ODDS: 1:719 HOBBY
GROUP C ODDS: 1:167 HOBBY
GROUP D ODDS: 1:31 HOBBY

NNO	Ashley D	8.00	20.00
NNO	Big Show D	15.00	40.00
NNO	Bobby The Brain Heenan D	50.00	100.00
NNO	Boogeyman D	10.00	25.00
NNO	Booker T A	8.00	20.00
NNO	Carlito C	6.00	15.00
NNO	Chavo Guerrero D	6.00	15.00
NNO	Chief Jay Strongbow D	12.00	30.00
NNO	Chris Benoit D	250.00	400.00
NNO	Hillbilly Jim D	20.00	50.00
NNO	JBL A	25.00	60.00
NNO	Jerry The King Lawler D	15.00	40.00
NNO	John Cena D	20.00	50.00
NNO	Kane B	12.00	30.00
NNO	Ken Kennedy D	6.00	15.00
NNO	Kurt Angle C	10.00	25.00
NNO	Lashley D	6.00	15.00
NNO	Lilian Garcia D	12.00	30.00
NNO	Lita D	15.00	40.00
NNO	Mickie James D	15.00	40.00
NNO	Rey Mysterio D	20.00	50.00
NNO	Sgt. Slaughter D	12.00	30.00
NNO	Shawn Michaels D	30.00	80.00
NNO	Tazz C	6.00	15.00
NNO	Torrie Wilson D	12.00	30.00
NNO	Trish Stratus C	20.00	50.00
NNO	Victoria D	12.00	30.00

2006 Topps Heritage Chrome WWE Ringside Relics

COMPLETE SET (2)		10.00	25.00
RETAIL EXCLUSIVE			
NNO	JBL/Batista	6.00	15.00
NNO	Melina/T.Wilson	8.00	20.00

2007 Topps Heritage II Chrome WWE

Subsets include: DV = Divas (58-69); L = Legends (70-89); TR = Turkey Red (90-99)

COMPLETE SET (100)		10.00	25.00
UNOPENED BOX (24 PACKS)			
UNOPENED PACK (5 CARDS)			

*REFRACTORS: .8X TO 2X BASIC CARDS
*X-FRACTORS: 1.5X TO 4X BASIC CARDS
*SUPERFR/25: 10X TO 25X BASIC CARDS

1	John Cena	1.25	3.00
2	Batista	.75	2.00
3	Carlito	.75	2.00
4	Tatanka	.20	.50
5	Highlanders	.30	.75
6	Johnny Nitro	.30	.75
7	The Great Khali	.30	.75
8	Gregory Helms	.20	.50
9	Jeff Hardy	.50	1.25
10	The Rock	1.50	4.00
11	Stone Cold Steve Austin	1.25	3.00
12	Matt Striker	.20	.50

#	Name		
13	Montel Vontavious Porter	.30	.75
14	The Boogeyman	.30	.75
15	Mark Henry	.30	.75
16	Edge	.75	2.00
17	Finlay	.50	1.25
18	Eugene	.20	.50
19	Sandman	.30	.75
20	Sabu	.20	.50
21	Kane	.75	2.00
22	Brian Kendrick/Paul London	.50	1.25
23	Rene Dupree	.30	.75
24	Ric Flair	.75	2.00
25	Rob Van Dam	.75	2.00
26	Shawn Michaels	1.25	3.00
27	Triple H	1.25	3.00
28	Chavo Guerrero	.30	.75
29	Vito	.20	.50
30	Viscera	.50	1.25
31	King Booker	.75	2.00
32	Chris Benoit	.50	1.25
33	Ken Kennedy	.50	1.25
34	Bobby Lashley	.75	2.00
35	Funaki	.30	.75
36	Matt Hardy	.50	1.25
37	JBL	.50	1.25
38	Paul Burchill	.20	.50
39	CM Punk	.30	.75
40	Super Crazy	.30	.75
41	Shelton Benjamin	.20	.50
42	Chris Masters	.75	2.00
43	Little Guido Maritato	.20	.50
44	Randy Orton	.75	2.00
45	Rey Mysterio	.50	1.25
46	Scotty 2 Hotty	.30	.75
47	Kenny Dykstra	.30	.75
48	Undertaker	1.00	2.50
49	William Regal	.50	1.25
50	Charlie Haas	.20	.50
51	Umaga	.30	.75
52	Snitsky	.30	.75
53	Rob Conway	.20	.50
54	Mr. McMahon	.75	2.00
55	Shane McMahon	.50	1.25
56	Stephanie McMahon	1.00	2.50
57	Linda McMahon	.30	.75
58	Mickie James DV	1.00	2.50
59	Sharmell DV	.50	1.25
60	Torrie Wilson DV	1.50	4.00
61	Ashley DV	.75	2.00
62	Michelle McCool DV	1.00	2.50
63	Layla DV	.75	2.00
64	Maria DV	.75	2.00
65	Kristal DV	.75	2.00
66	Victoria DV	1.00	2.50
67	Candice Michelle DV	1.00	2.50
68	Jillian Hall DV	1.00	2.50
69	Melina DV	.75	2.00
70	Mean Gene Okerlund L	.50	1.25
71	Don Muraco L	.30	.75
72	Paul Bearer L	.30	.75
73	One Man Gang L	.30	.75
74	Dusty Rhodes L	.50	1.25
75	Bushwhackers L	.20	.50
76	The Wild Samoans L	.30	.75
77	Bam Bam Bigelow L	.50	1.25
78	Mr. Perfect Curt Hennig L	.50	1.25
79	The British Bulldog L	.75	2.00
80	Earthquake L	.30	.75
81	Rocky Johnson L	.30	.75
82	Papa Shango L	.25	.60
83	Jerry The King Lawler L	.50	1.25
84	High Chief Peter Maivia L	.20	.50
85	Arn Anderson L	.20	.50
86	Mick Foley L	.75	2.00
87	Ravishing Rick Rude L	.50	1.25
88	Doink L	.20	.50
89	Andre The Giant L	.75	2.00
90	Batista TR	.75	2.00
91	Triple H TR	1.25	3.00
92	Carlito TR	.75	2.00
93	John Cena TR	1.25	3.00
94	Rey Mysterio TR	.50	1.25
95	Andre The Giant TR	.75	2.00
96	Iron Sheik TR	.75	2.00
97	Jerry The King Lawler TR	.50	1.25
98	Rowdy Roddy Piper TR	.75	2.00
99	Superstar Billy Graham TR	.30	.75
100	Cena/Booker/Ashley/Mysterio CL	1.25	3.00

2007 Topps Heritage II Chrome WWE Autographs

STATED ODDS 1:24 HOBBY EXCLUSIVE

NNO	Ashley	12.00	30.00
NNO	Jeff Hardy	15.00	40.00
NNO	John Cena	25.00	60.00
NNO	Ken Kennedy	8.00	20.00
NNO	Layla	10.00	25.00
NNO	Melina	10.00	25.00
NNO	Michelle McCool	10.00	25.00
NNO	Mickie James	15.00	40.00
NNO	Sabu	10.00	25.00
NNO	Sandman	15.00	40.00
NNO	Sharmell	6.00	15.00
NNO	Torrie Wilson	15.00	40.00
NNO	William Regal	10.00	25.00

2007 Topps Heritage II Chrome WWE Mini

COMPLETE SET (5)
1 John Cena
2 Rey Mysterio
3 Andre The Giant
4 Hulk Hogan
5 Batista

2007 Topps Heritage II Chrome WWE Ringside Relics

STATED ODDS 1:24 RETAIL EXCLUSIVE

NNO	Jeff Hardy/Carlito	4.00	10.00
NNO	Kane/Umaga	4.00	10.00
NNO	Lita/Mickie James	6.00	15.00

2008 Topps Heritage III Chrome WWE

Subsets include: DV = Divas (58-69); L = Legends (70-89)

COMPLETE SET (90) 8.00 20.00
UNOPENED BOX (24 PACKS)
UNOPEND PACK (5 CARDS)
*REFRACTORS: .8X TO 2X BASIC CARDS
*X-FRACTORS: 1.5X TO 4X BASIC CARDS
*SUPERFR./25: 10X TO 25X BASIC CARDS

#	Name		
1	John Cena	1.25	3.00
2	Batista	.75	2.00
3	Rey Mysterio	.50	1.25
4	Stone Cold	1.25	3.00
5	The Great Khali	.20	.50
6	Chris Jericho	.50	1.25
7	Edge	.75	2.00
8	Hard Core Holly	.30	.75
9	Umaga	.30	.75
10	Montel Vontavious Porter	.30	.75
11	Stevie Richards	.30	.75
12	Deuce	.20	.50
13	Lance Cade	.20	.50
14	Super Crazy	.30	.75
15	Chuck Palumbo	.30	.75
16	Domino	.20	.50
17	Trevor Murdoch	.20	.50
18	Zack Ryder	.20	.50
19	Festus	.20	.50
20	Mark Henry	.30	.75
21	Boogeyman	.30	.75
22	Brian Kendrick	.30	.75
23	Tommy Dreamer	.20	.50
24	Charlie Haas	.20	.50
25	JBL	.20	.50
26	Armando Estrada	.20	.50
27	CM Punk	.20	.50
28	Triple H	1.25	3.00
29	Shannon Moore	.20	.50
30	Hacksaw Jim Duggan	.50	1.25
31	Jeff Hardy	.75	2.00
32	Kane	.75	2.00
33	Ron Simmons	.20	.50
34	Finlay	.30	.75
35	The Miz	.30	.75
36	Kenny Dykstra	.30	.75
37	Snitsky	.30	.75
38	Jesse	.20	.50
39	Santino Marella	.20	.50
40	Cody Rhodes	.20	.50
41	Shelton Benjamin	.20	.50
42	Hornswoggle	.30	.75
43	Big Daddy V	.30	.75
44	Matt Striker	.20	.50
45	Curt Hawkins	.20	.50
46	William Regal	.50	1.25
47	Jimmy Wang Yang	.20	.50
48	Elijah Burke	.20	.50
49	Chavo Guerrero	.30	.75
50	Paul London	.20	.50
51	Mr. Kennedy	.50	1.25
52	John Morrison	.20	.50
53	Matt Hardy	.75	2.00
54	Shawn Michaels	1.25	3.00
55	Randy Orton	.50	1.25
56	Ric Flair	.75	2.00
57	Undertaker	1.00	2.50
58	Torrie Wilson DV	1.50	4.00
59	Candice DV	1.00	2.50
60	Michelle McCool DV	1.00	2.50
61	Melina DV	.75	2.00
62	Cherry DV	.75	2.00
63	Jillian DV	.75	2.00
64	Ashley DV	.75	2.00
65	Maria DV	.75	2.00
66	Kelly Kelly DV	.75	2.00
67	Mickie James DV	1.25	3.00
68	Maryse DV	.75	2.00
69	Victoria DV	1.00	2.50
70	Anderson/Blanchard L	.30	.75
71	Brian Pillman L	.30	.75
72	Dean Malenko L	.50	1.25
73	Funk Brothers L	.30	.75
74	Dusty Rhodes L	.50	1.25
75	The Freebirds L	.30	.75
76	Jimmy Superfly Snuka L	.50	1.25
77	Jimmy Garvin L	.30	.75
78	Papa Shango L	.20	.50
79	Pat Patterson L	.20	.50
80	Bam Bam Bigelow L	.50	1.25
81	Gorilla Monsoon L	.50	1.25
82	Ted Dibiase L	.50	1.25
83	Rocky Johnson L	.30	.75
84	Bruiser Brody L	.30	.75
85	Kamala L	.30	.75
86	Earthquake L	.30	.75
87	Vader L	.30	.75
88	Jack and Gerry Brisco L	.30	.75
89	Cowboy Bob Orton L	.50	1.25
100	Checklist	.20	.50

2008 Topps Heritage III Chrome WWE Allen and Ginter Superstars

COMPLETE SET (10) 6.00 15.00
*REFRACTORS: .8X TO 2X BASIC CARDS
*X-FRACTORS: 1.5X TO 4X BASIC CARDS
*SUPERFR/25: 10X TO 25X BASIC CARDS

#	Name		
1	John Cena	1.25	3.00
2	Batista	.75	2.00
3	Rey Mysterio	.50	1.25
4	Triple H	1.25	3.00
5	Shawn Michaels	1.25	3.00
6	Undertaker	1.00	2.50
7	Rowdy Roddy Piper	.75	2.00
8	Chief Jay Strongbow	.50	1.25
9	Sgt. Slaughter	.50	1.25
10	Iron Sheik	.75	2.00

2008 Topps Heritage III Chrome WWE Autographs

STATED ODDS 1:24 HOBBY EXCLUSIVE

NNO	Ashley	10.00	25.00
NNO	Carlito	6.00	15.00
NNO	Cherry	8.00	20.00
NNO	Chuck Palumbo	6.00	15.00
NNO	Festus	6.00	15.00
NNO	Jeff Hardy	15.00	40.00
NNO	Jesse	8.00	20.00
NNO	Kane	12.00	30.00
NNO	Layla	8.00	20.00
NNO	Montel Vontavious Porter	6.00	15.00
NNO	Tommy Dreamer	6.00	15.00
NNO	Trevor Murdoch	6.00	15.00

2008 Topps Heritage III Chrome WWE Mini-Cards

COMPLETE SET (5)
1 Stone Cold Steve Austin
2 John Cena
3 Edge
4 Umaga
5 The Great Khali

2008 Topps Heritage III Chrome WWE Ringside Relics

STATED ODDS 1:24 RETAIL EXCLUSIVE

NNO	Hardcore Holly vs. Carlito	4.00	10.00
NNO	Mickie James vs. Beth Phoenix	4.00	10.00
NNO	Mr. Kennedy vs. Shawn Michaels	5.00	12.00

2006 Topps Heritage II WWE

Subsets include: DV = Divas (58-69); L = Legends (70-89)

COMPLETE SET (90)	8.00	20.00
UNOPENED BOX (24 PACKS)		
UNOPENED PACK (5 CARDS)		

1	John Cena	.75	2.00
2	Batista	.40	1.00
3	Carlito	.30	.75
4	Tatanka	.12	.30
5	Paul London/Brian Kendrick	.30	.75
6	Johnny Nitro	.12	.30
7	The Great Khali	.12	.30
8	Gregory Helms	.12	.30
9	Gunnar Scott	.30	.75
10	The Rock	.75	2.00
11	Stone Cold Steve Austin	.75	2.00
12	Hulk Hogan	.75	2.00
13	Big Show	.40	1.00
14	The Boogeyman	.20	.50
15	Mark Henry	.30	.75
16	Edge	.40	1.00
17	Finlay	.30	.75
18	Eugene	.12	.30
19	Matt Striker	.12	.30
20	Jake and Jesse Gymini	.20	.50
21	Kane	.50	1.25
22	Kid Kash	.20	.50
23	Kurt Angle	.75	2.00
24	Rene Dupree	.12	.30
25	Ric Flair	.60	1.50
26	Rob Van Dam	.50	1.25
27	Shawn Michaels	.60	1.50
28	Triple H	.75	2.00
29	Chavo Guerrero	.30	.75
30	Vito	.12	.30
31	Viscera	.20	.50
32	Steven Richards	.20	.50
33	Booker T	.30	.75
34	Chris Benoit	.30	.75
35	Ken Kennedy	.30	.75
36	Goldust	.30	.75
37	Bobby Lashley	.30	.75
38	Funaki	.20	.50
39	Matt Hardy	.20	.50
40	JBL	.40	1.00
41	Paul Burchill	.12	.30
42	Psicosis	.12	.30
43	Super Crazy	.20	.50
44	Shelton Benjamin	.12	.30
45	Chris Masters	.40	1.00
46	Little Guido Maritato	.12	.30
47	Randy Orton	.40	1.00
48	Rey Mysterio	.30	.75
49	Scotty 2 Hotty	.20	.50
50	Tazz	.20	.50
51	Spirit Squad	.20	.50
52	Undertaker	.60	1.50
53	William Regal	.30	.75
54	Charlie Haas	.12	.30
55	Umaga	.20	.50
56	Snitsky	.20	.50
57	Rob Conway	.12	.30
58	Mickie James DV	.75	2.00
59	Sharmell DV	.40	1.00
60	Torrie Wilson DV	.75	2.00
61	Ashley DV	.40	1.00
62	Lita DV	.60	1.50
63	Beth Phoenix DV	.40	1.00
64	Maria DV	.50	1.25
65	Kristal DV	.40	1.00
66	Victoria DV	.60	1.50
67	Candice Michelle DV	.60	1.50
68	Jillian Hall DV	.50	1.25
69	Melina DV	.50	1.25
70	Mean Gene Okerlund L	.30	.75
71	Don Muraco L	.20	.50
72	Paul Bearer L	.20	.50
73	One Man Gang L	.20	.50
74	Dusty Rhodes L	.30	.75
75	Bushwhackers L	.20	.50
76	The Wild Samoans L	.30	.75
77	Bam Bam Bigelow L	.20	.50
78	Mr. Perfect Curt Hennig L	.30	.75
79	The British Bulldog L	.50	1.25
80	Earthquake L	.20	.50
81	Kamala L	.30	.75
82	Koko B Ware L	.20	.50
83	Jerry The King Lawler L	.30	.75
84	High Chief Peter Maivia L	.12	.30
85	Arn Anderson L	.12	.30
86	Mick Foley L	.50	1.25
87	Ravishing Rick Rude L	.30	.75
88	Vader L	.30	.75
89	Andre The Giant L	.50	1.25
90	Checklist	.12	.30

2006 Topps Heritage II WWE Autographs

SEMISTARS	8.00	20.00
UNLISTED STARS	10.00	25.00
STATED ODDS 1:24 HOBBY EXCLUSIVE		

NNO	Ashley	10.00	25.00
NNO	Bobby Lashley	8.00	20.00
NNO	Booker T	10.00	25.00
NNO	Brian Kendrick	8.00	20.00
NNO	Carlito	8.00	20.00
NNO	Charlie Haas	6.00	15.00
NNO	Chavo Guerrero	6.00	15.00
NNO	Edge	20.00	50.00
NNO	Gene Snitsky	6.00	15.00
NNO	Jamie Noble	6.00	15.00
NNO	Jillian Hall	10.00	25.00
NNO	John Cena	20.00	50.00
NNO	Johnny Nitro	8.00	20.00
NNO	Kane	12.00	30.00
NNO	Ken Kennedy	8.00	20.00
NNO	Kurt Angle	12.00	30.00
NNO	Melina	10.00	25.00
NNO	Michelle McCool	15.00	40.00
NNO	Mickie James	12.00	30.00
NNO	The Miz	8.00	20.00
NNO	Paul London	6.00	15.00
NNO	Randy Orton	20.00	50.00
NNO	Sharmell	8.00	20.00
NNO	Shawn Michaels	30.00	80.00
NNO	Umaga	15.00	40.00
NNO	Vito	6.00	15.00

2006 Topps Heritage II WWE Magazine Promos

COMPLETE SET (9)	4.00	10.00
WWE MAGAZINE EXCLUSIVE		

W1	John Cena	1.00	2.50
W2	Triple H	1.00	2.50
W3	Edge	.75	2.00
W4	Batista	.60	1.50
W5	Undertaker	.60	1.50
W6	Rey Mysterio	.60	1.50
W7	Hulk Hogan	1.00	2.50
W8	Rowdy Roddy Piper	.75	2.00
W9	Sgt. Slaughter	.75	2.00

2006 Topps Heritage II WWE Magnets

COMPLETE SET (9)	6.00	15.00
STATED ODDS 1:4 RETAIL EXCLUSIVE		

1	John Cena	1.50	4.00
2	Batista	1.00	2.50
3	Carlito	.60	1.50
4	Shawn Michaels	1.50	4.00
5	Triple H	1.50	4.00
6	Rey Mysterio	.60	1.50
7	Edge	1.00	2.50
8	Hulk Hogan	1.50	4.00
9	Torrie Wilson	2.00	5.00

2006 Topps Heritage II WWE Raw vs. Smackdown

COMPLETE SET (2)	.75	2.00

V1	John Cena	.60	1.50
V2	Rey Mysterio	.40	1.00

2006 Topps Heritage II WWE Ringside Relics

COMPLETE SET (8)		
STATED ODDS 1:24 HOBBY		

NNO	Big Show	8.00	20.00
NNO	Carlito	5.00	12.00
NNO	Hulk Hogan	10.00	25.00
NNO	John Cena Hat	30.00	75.00
NNO	John Cena Shirt	10.00	25.00
NNO	Psicosis	5.00	12.00
NNO	Shawn Michaels	12.00	30.00
NNO	Triple H	8.00	20.00

2006 Topps Heritage II WWE Ringside Relics Doubles

NNO	Gregory Helms Super Crazy	5.00	12.00
NNO	Ken Kennedy Gunner Scott	5.00	12.00
NNO	Bobby Lashley King Booker	5.00	12.00

2006 Topps Heritage II WWE Tin Inserts

COMPLETE SET (6)	6.00	15.00
STATED ODDS 1:RETAIL TIN		

TLB1	John Cena	2.50	6.00
TLB2	Hulk Hogan	2.00	5.00
TLB3	Edge	1.50	4.00
TLB4	Triple H	2.00	5.00
TLB5	Rey Mysterio	1.00	2.50
TLB6	Andre The Giant	1.50	4.00

2006 Topps Heritage II WWE Toppers

COMPLETE SET (12)	4.00	10.00
B1-B3 STATED ODDS 1:HOBBY BOX		
B4-B9 STATED ODDS 1:RETAIL TIN		
B10-B12 STATED ODDS 1:2 RETAIL BLISTER		

B1	D-Generation X	1.00	2.50
B2	Edge & Lita	.75	2.00
B3	Armando Alejandro Estrada/Umaga	.30	.75
B4	Booker T & Sharmell	.60	1.50
B5	Johnny Nitro & Melina	.60	1.50
B6	Spirit Squad	.30	.75
B7	D-Generation X	1.00	2.50
B8	Edge & Lita	.75	2.00
B9	Armando Alejandro Estrada/Umaga	.30	.75
B10	The Great Khali/Daivari	.30	.75
B11	Highlanders	.30	.75
B12	Brian Kendrick/Paul London	.60	1.50

2006 Topps Heritage II WWE Turkey Red Legends

COMPLETE SET (12)	6.00	15.00
STATED ODDS 1:6 HOBBY EXCLUSIVE		

1	Rowdy Roddy Piper	1.00	2.50
2	Jake The Snake Roberts	.60	1.50
3	Sgt. Slaughter	.75	2.00
4	Chief Jay Strongbow	.30	.75
5	Jerry The King Lawler	.60	1.50
6	Gorilla Monsoon	.30	.75
7	Iron Sheik	.75	2.00
8	Junkyard Dog	.75	2.00
9	Superstar Billy Graham	.30	.75
10	Classy Freddie Blassie	.30	.75
11	Bobby The Brain Heenan	.50	1.25
12	Andre The Giant	1.00	2.50

2006 Topps Heritage II WWE Turkey Red Superstars

COMPLETE SET (12)	10.00	20.00
STATED ODDS 1:6 RETAIL EXCLUSIVE		

1	John Cena	1.50	4.00
2	Batista	1.00	2.50
3	Carlito	.60	1.50
4	Big Show	1.00	2.50
5	Shawn Michaels	1.50	4.00
6	Rey Mysterio	.60	1.50
7	Kurt Angle	1.00	2.50
8	Edge	1.00	2.50
9	Rob Van Dam	.60	1.50
10	Triple H	1.50	4.00
11	Hulk Hogan	1.50	4.00
12	Ric Flair	1.25	3.00

2007 Topps Heritage III WWE

Subsets include: DV = Divas (58-69); L = Legends (70-89)

COMPLETE SET (90)	8.00	20.00
UNOPENED BOX (24 PACKS)		
UNOPENED PACK (5 CARDS)		

1	John Cena	1.00	2.50
2	Batista	.60	1.50
3	Rey Mysterio	.40	1.00
4	Stone Cold Steve Austin	1.00	2.50
5	The Great Khali	.25	.60
6	Carlito	.60	1.50
7	Edge	.60	1.50
8	Hardcore Holly	.40	1.00
9	Umaga	.25	.60
10	Montel Vontavious Porter	.25	.60
11	Stevie Richards	.25	.60
12	Deuce	.15	.40

13	Lance Cade	.15	.40
14	Super Crazy	.25	.60
15	Chuck Palumbo	.15	.40
16	Domino	.15	.40
17	Trevor Murdoch	.15	.40
18	Val Venis	.40	1.00
19	Bobby Lashley	.60	1.50
20	Mark Henry	.25	.60
21	Boogeyman	.25	.60
22	Brian Kendrick	.25	.60
23	Tommy Dreamer	.20	.50
24	Charlie Haas	.15	.40
25	JBL	.40	1.00
26	Armando Estrada	.15	.40
27	CM Punk	.25	.60
28	Triple H	1.00	2.50
29	Shannon Moore	.15	.40
30	Hacksaw Jim Duggan	.25	.60
31	Jeff Hardy	.40	1.00
32	Kane	.60	1.50
33	Ron Simmons	.25	.60
34	Finlay	.40	1.00
35	The Miz	.30	.75
36	Kenny Dykstra	.25	.60
37	Snitsky	.25	.60
38	Chris Masters	.60	1.50
39	Santino Marella	.20	.50
40	Cody Rhodes	.25	.60
41	Shelton Benjamin	.15	.40
42	Hornswoggle	.20	.50
43	Big Daddy V	.40	1.00
44	Matt Striker	.15	.40
45	Jamie Noble	.15	.40
46	William Regal	.40	1.00
47	Jimmy Wang Yang	.15	.40
48	Elijah Burke	.15	.40
49	Chavo Guerrero	.25	.60
50	Paul London	.40	1.00
51	Mr. Kennedy	.40	1.00
52	John Morrison	.25	.60
53	Matt Hardy	.40	1.00
54	Shawn Michaels	1.00	2.50
55	Randy Orton	.60	1.50
56	Ric Flair	.60	1.50
57	Undertaker	.75	2.00
58	Torrie Wilson DV	1.25	3.00
59	Candice DV	.75	2.00
60	Michelle McCool DV	.75	2.00
61	Melina DV	.60	1.50
62	Cherry DV	.15	.40
63	Jillian DV	.75	2.00
64	Ashley DV	.60	1.50
65	Maria DV	.60	1.50
66	Kelly Kelly DV	.40	1.00
67	Mickie James DV	.75	2.00
68	Maryse DV	.30	.75
69	Victoria DV	.75	2.00
70	Anderson/Blanchard L	.15	.40
71	Brian Pillman L	.15	.40
72	Dean Malenko L	.15	.40
73	Funk Brothers Dory & Terry L	.15	.40
74	Dusty Rhodes L	.40	1.00
75	The Freebirds L	.15	.40
76	Jimmy Superfly Snuka L	.25	.60
77	Jimmy Garvin L	.15	.40
78	Papa Shango L	.20	.50
79	Pat Patterson L	.15	.40
80	Bam Bam Bigelow L	.40	1.00

81	Gorilla Monsoon L	.30	.75
82	Ted DiBiase L	.30	.75
83	Rocky Johson L	.25	.60
84	Bruiser Brody L	.15	.40
85	Kamala L	.20	.50
86	Earthquake L	.25	.60
87	Vader L	.25	.60
88	Jack and Gerry Brisco L	.15	.40
89	Cowboy Bob Orton L	.20	.50
90	John Cena CL	1.00	2.50

2007 Topps Heritage III WWE Allen and Ginter Legends

COMPLETE SET (12) — 6.00 — 15.00
STATED ODDS 1:6 HOBBY EXCLUSIVE

1	Rowdy Roddy Piper	1.00	2.50
2	Chief Jay Strongbow	.30	.75
3	Sgt. Slaughter	.60	1.50
4	Iron Sheik	.60	1.50
5	Don Muraco	.20	.50
6	Ravishing Rick Rude	.60	1.50
7	Classy Freddie Blassie	.30	.75
8	Bobby The Brain Heenan	.60	1.50
9	The British Bulldog	.60	1.50
10	Jake The Snake Roberts	.60	1.50
11	Nikolai Volkoff	.60	1.50
12	Junkyard Dog	1.00	2.50

2007 Topps Heritage III WWE Allen and Ginter Superstars

COMPLETE SET (12) — 10.00 — 25.00
STATED ODDS 1:6 RETAIL EXCLUSIVE

1	John Cena	1.50	4.00
2	Batista	.75	2.00
3	Rey Mysterio	.60	1.50
4	Carlito	.60	1.50
5	Edge	.75	2.00
6	Bobby Lashley	.60	1.50
7	Mr. Kennedy	.75	2.00
8	Triple H	1.50	4.00
9	Shawn Michaels	1.25	3.00
10	Undertaker	1.25	3.00
11	Ric Flair	1.25	3.00
12	Booker T	.75	2.00

2007 Topps Heritage III WWE Allen and Ginter Tin Inserts

COMPLETE SET (6)
STATED ODDS 1:1 TIN EXCLUSIVES

1	John Cena
2	Batista
3	Ric Flair
4	Undertaker
5	Edge
6	Shawn Michaels

2007 Topps Heritage III WWE Autographs

STATED ODDS 1:24 HOBBY EXCLUSIVE

NNO	Candice	8.00	20.00
NNO	Carlito	6.00	15.00
NNO	Cherry	6.00	15.00
NNO	Chuck Palumbo	6.00	15.00
NNO	CM Punk	25.00	60.00
NNO	Deuce	6.00	15.00
NNO	Domino	6.00	15.00
NNO	Hacksaw Jim Duggan	8.00	20.00

NNO	Jeff Hardy	20.00	50.00
NNO	John Cena	25.00	60.00
NNO	Kane	12.00	30.00
NNO	Kelly Kelly	20.00	50.00
NNO	Lance Cade	6.00	15.00
NNO	Maria	12.00	30.00
NNO	Miz	12.00	30.00
NNO	Montel Vontavious Porter	8.00	20.00
NNO	Randy Orton	25.00	60.00
NNO	Stevie Richards	6.00	15.00
NNO	Super Crazy	6.00	15.00
NNO	Torrie Wilson	10.00	25.00
NNO	Trevor Murdoch	6.00	15.00
NNO	Victoria	12.00	30.00

2007 Topps Heritage III WWE Event-Used Mat Ringside Relics

STATED ODDS 1:24 RETAIL EXCLUSIVE

NNO	John Cena/Randy Orton	4.00	10.00
NNO	Rey Mysterio/Chavo Guerrero	3.00	8.00
NNO	Triple H/King Booker	4.00	10.00

2007 Topps Heritage III WWE Ringside Relics

STATED ODDS 1:24 HOBBY EXCLUSIVE

NNO	Bobby Lashley	5.00	10.00
NNO	Carlito	5.00	10.00
NNO	John Cena	6.00	12.00
NNO	Matt Hardy	5.00	10.00
NNO	Mr. Kennedy	5.00	10.00

2007 Topps Heritage III WWE Magnets

COMPLETE SET (9) — 6.00 — 15.00
STATED ODDS 1:4 RETAIL

1	John Cena	1.50	4.00
2	Batista	1.00	2.50
3	Rey Mysterio	.60	1.50
4	Carlito	1.00	2.50
5	Edge	1.00	2.50
6	Bobby Lashley	1.00	2.50
7	Mr. Kennedy	.60	1.50
8	Triple H	1.50	4.00
9	Ric Flair	1.00	2.50

2007 Topps Heritage III WWE Ringside Bonus

COMPLETE SET (16) — 25.00 — 60.00
STATED ODDS 4:1 WAL-MART BLASTER

R1	John Cena	5.00	12.00
R2	Carlito	2.50	6.00
R3	CM Punk	2.50	6.00
R4	Randy Orton	4.00	10.00
R5	Hornswoggle	1.50	4.00
R6	Jamie Noble	1.50	4.00
R7	Super Crazy	1.50	4.00
R8	Great Khali	2.50	6.00
R9	Jeff Hardy	3.00	8.00
R10	Matt Hardy	3.00	8.00
R11	Chavo Guerrero	1.50	4.00
R12	Finlay	1.50	4.00
R13	Kane	3.00	8.00
R14	Hardcore Holly	2.50	6.00
R15	Rey Mysterio	3.00	8.00
R16	Jimmy Wang Yang	1.50	4.00

2007 Topps Heritage III WWE Ringside Rookie Bonus

COMPLETE SET (4) — 10.00 — 25.00
STATED ODDS 1:1 WAL-MART BLASTER

RK1	Cody Rhodes	4.00	10.00
RK2	Santino Marella	4.00	10.00
RK3	Deuce	3.00	8.00
RK4	Domino	3.00	8.00

2007 Topps Heritage III WWE Superstar Team

1	Brian Kendrick/Paul London	.20	.50
2	C.Haas/S.Benjamin	.12	.30
3	Lance Cade/Trevor Murdoch	.12	.30

2007 Topps Heritage III WWE Superstar Team Oversized

COMPLETE SET (3)
STATED ODDS 1:1 HOBBY EXCLUSIVES

1	Brian Kendrick/Paul London
2	Charlie Haas/Shelton Benjamin
3	Lance Cade/Trevor Murdoch

2007 Topps Heritage III WWE Tin Inserts

COMPLETE SET (6)
STATED ODDS 1:1 TIN EXCLUSIVES

B1	John Cena
B2	Batista
B3	Ric Flair
B4	Undertaker
B5	Edge
B6	Shawn Michaels

2008 Topps Heritage IV WWE

Subsets include: DV = Divas (56-71); A = Announcers (72-74); L = Legends (75-89)
COMPLETE SET (90) — 8.00 — 20.00
UNOPENED BOX (24 PACKS)
UNOPENED PACK (5 CARDS)

1	Armando Estrada	.12	.30
2	Ricky Ortiz	.12	.30
3	Bam Neely	.12	.30
4	Batista	.50	1.25
5	Big Show	.30	.75
6	Brian Kendrick	.20	.50
7	Carlito	.30	.75
8	Chavo Guerrero	.20	.50
9	Chris Jericho	.30	.75
10	CM Punk	.12	.30
11	Cody Rhodes	.12	.30
12	Undertaker	.60	1.50
13	Curt Hawkins	.12	.30
14	D-Lo Brown	.20	.50
15	Edge	.50	1.25
16	Evan Bourne	.12	.30
17	Ezekiel	.20	.50
18	Festus	.12	.30
19	Finlay	.20	.50
20	The Great Khali	.12	.30
21	Hardcore Holly	.20	.50
22	Hornswoggle	.20	.50
23	Jamie Noble	.12	.30
24	John Bradshaw Layfield	.12	.30
25	Jeff Hardy	.50	1.25
26	Jesse	.12	.30
27	John Cena	.75	2.00

28	John Morrison	.12	.30
29	JTG	.12	.30
30	Kane	.50	1.25
31	Kofi Kingston	.20	.50
32	Lance Cade	.12	.30
33	Mark Henry	.20	.50
34	Matt Hardy	.50	1.25
35	Primo Colon	.12	.30
36	Mike Knox	.12	.30
37	The Miz	.20	.50
38	Mr. Kennedy	.30	.75
39	MVP	.20	.50
40	Paul Burchill	.12	.30
41	Randy Orton	.30	.75
42	Rey Mysterio	.30	.75
43	Santino Marella	.12	.30
44	Shad	.12	.30
45	Shawn Michaels	.75	2.00
46	Shelton Benjamin	.12	.30
47	Snitsky	.20	.50
48	Super Crazy	.20	.50
49	Ted DiBiase Jr.	.30	.75
50	Tommy Dreamer	.12	.30
51	Tony Atlas	.12	.30
52	Triple H	.75	2.00
53	Umaga	.20	.50
54	Vladimir Kozlov	.20	.50
55	Zack Ryder	.12	.30
56	Tiffany DV	.60	1.50
57	Beth Phoenix DV	.60	1.50
58	Candice DV	.60	1.50
59	Eve DV	.50	1.25
60	Jillian DV	.50	1.25
61	Katie Lea Burchill DV	.50	1.25
62	Kelly Kelly DV	.50	1.25
63	Layla DV	.50	1.25
64	Lilian Garcia DV	.50	1.25
65	Maria DV	.50	1.25
66	Maryse DV	.50	1.25
67	Melina DV	.50	1.25
68	Michelle McCool DV	.60	1.50
69	Mickie James DV	.75	2.00
70	Natalya DV	.50	1.25
71	Victoria DV	.60	1.50
72	Tazz/Jim Ross A	.12	.30
73	Jerry Lawler/Michael Cole A	.12	.30
74	Matt Striker/Todd Grisham A	.12	.30
75	Bobby The Brain Heenan	.50	1.25
76	Brian Pillman L	.20	.50
77	Gerald Brisco L	.20	.50
78	Jack Brisco L	.20	.50
79	Mr. Perfect Curt Hennig	.30	.75
80	Mr. Wonderful Paul Orndorff	.30	.75
81	Rowdy Roddy Piper	.50	1.25
82	Superfly Jimmy Snuka	.30	.75
83	British Bulldog L	.30	.75
84	Hillbilly Jim L	.30	.75
85	Junkyard Dog L	.30	.75
86	Mean Gene Okerlund	.30	.75
87	Million-Dollar Man Ted DiBiase	.30	.75
88	Tully Blanchard L	.20	.50
89	Dusty Rhodes L	.30	.75
90	Checklist	.12	.30

2008 Topps Heritage IV WWE Allen and Ginter Legends

COMPLETE SET (12) 6.00 15.00
STATED ODDS 1:6 HOBBY

1	Bobby The Brain Heenan	.60	1.50
2	Junkyard Dog	1.00	2.50
3	Hillbilly Jim	.60	1.50
4	British Bulldog	.60	1.50
5	Mean Gene Okerlund	.60	1.50
6	Mr. Perfect Curt Hennig	.40	1.00
7	Rowdy Roddy Piper	1.00	2.50
8	Jimmy Superfly Snuka	.60	1.50
9	Mr. Wonderful Paul Orndorff	.40	1.00
10	Million-Dollar Man Ted DiBiase	.60	1.50
11	Tully Blanchard	.40	1.00
12	Brian Pillman	.40	1.00

2008 Topps Heritage IV WWE Allen and Ginter Superstars

COMPLETE SET (12) 10.00 25.00
STATED ODDS 1:6 RETAIL EXCLUSIVE

1	Batista	2.00	5.00
2	John Cena	3.00	8.00
3	Chavo Guerrero	1.25	3.00
4	Chris Jericho	1.25	3.00
5	Edge	2.00	5.00
6	Triple H	3.00	8.00
7	Jeff Hardy	2.00	5.00
8	Matt Hardy	2.00	5.00
9	Mr. Kennedy	1.25	3.00
10	CM Punk	1.25	3.00
11	Rey Mysterio	1.25	3.00
12	Undertaker	2.50	6.00

2008 Topps Heritage IV WWE Autographs

Target Gravity Feed Exclusives include: Carlito, and Layla; Walmart Gravity Feed Exclusives include: John Cena, and Mickie James
RANDOM INSERTS IN PACKS
STATED ODDS 1:24 HOBBY/TARGET/WALMART

NNO	Beth Phoenix	12.00	30.00
NNO	Carlito	25.00	60.00
NNO	Chavo Guerrero	8.00	20.00
NNO	Cody Rhodes	15.00	40.00
NNO	Deuce	6.00	15.00
NNO	John Cena	75.00	150.00
NNO	Kofi Kingston	12.00	30.00
NNO	Layla	15.00	40.00
NNO	Matt Hardy	12.00	30.00
NNO	Mickie James	75.00	150.00
NNO	Natalya	12.00	30.00
NNO	Tazz	6.00	15.00
NNO	Ted DiBiase Jr.	12.00	30.00

2008 Topps Heritage IV WWE Blister Bonus

COMPLETE SET (3)
RANDOMLY INSERTED INTO PACKS
RETAIL EXCLUSIVE

1 Edge
2 John Cena
3 Matt Hardy

2008 Topps Heritage IV WWE Magnets

COMPLETE SET (9) 12.00 30.00
STATED ODDS 1:4 RETAIL EXCLUSIVE

1	John Cena	3.00	8.00
2	Mr. Kennedy	1.25	3.00
3	CM Punk	2.50	6.00
4	Chris Jericho	1.25	3.00
5	Batista	2.00	5.00
6	Triple H	3.00	8.00
7	Edge	2.00	5.00
8	Mickie James	3.00	8.00
9	Melina	2.00	5.00

2008 Topps Heritage IV WWE Mat Relics

STATED ODDS 1:24 RETAIL EXCLUSIVES

NNO	Batista vs. Paul Burchill	3.00	8.00
NNO	John Cena vs. Cody Rhodes	5.00	12.00
NNO	John Cena vs. Ted DiBiase	5.00	12.00

2008 Topps Heritage IV WWE Ringside Rookies

COMPLETE SET (4) 15.00 40.00
STATED ODDS 1:WALMART BLASTER

RK1	Ted DiBiase Jr.	8.00	20.00
RK2	Vladimir Kozlov	4.00	10.00
RK3	Evan Bourne	5.00	12.00
RK4	Natalya	8.00	20.00

2008 Topps Heritage IV WWE Ringside Superstars

COMPLETE SET (16) 30.00 80.00
STATED ODDS 4:1 WALMART BLASTER

R1	John Cena	6.00	15.00
R2	Batista	4.00	10.00
R3	CM Punk	2.00	5.00
R4	Rey Mysterio	2.50	6.00
R5	Triple H	6.00	15.00
R6	Undertaker	5.00	12.00
R7	MVP	2.00	5.00
R8	Jeff Hardy	4.00	10.00
R9	Matt Hardy	4.00	10.00
R10	Tommy Dreamer	2.00	5.00
R11	Mark Henry	2.00	5.00
R12	John Morrison	2.00	5.00
R13	Mickie James	6.00	15.00
R14	Beth Phoenix	5.00	12.00
R15	Candice	5.00	12.00
R16	Michelle McCool	5.00	12.00

2008 Topps Heritage IV WWE Shirt Relics

STATED ODDS

NNO	Jeff Hardy	7.50	15.00
NNO	MVP	6.00	12.00
NNO	Rey Mysterio	6.00	12.00

2008 Topps Heritage IV WWE Tin Inserts

COMPLETE SET (6) 12.00 30.00
STATED ODDS 1:TIN RETAIL EXCLUSIVE

1	John Cena	4.00	10.00
2	Rey Mysterio	2.50	6.00
3	Shawn Michaels	4.00	10.00
4	Edge	2.50	6.00
5	Randy Orton	2.50	6.00
6	Triple H	4.00	10.00

2005 Topps Heritage WWE

Subsets include: DV = Divas (59-70); L = Legends (71-89)
COMPLETE SET (90) 8.00 20.00
UNOPENED BOX (24 PACKS)
UNOPENED PACK (5 CARDS)

1	John Cena	1.25	3.00
2	Batista	.50	1.25
3	Carlito	.20	.50
4	Orlando Jordan	.20	.50
5	Paul London	.20	.50
6	Johnny Nitro	.20	.50
7	Joey Mercury	.20	.50
8	Hurricane	.20	.50
9	Rosey	.20	.50
10	The Rock	1.25	3.00
11	Stone Cold Steve Austin	1.25	3.00
12	Hulk Hogan	1.25	3.00
13	Big Show	.75	2.00
14	Chris Jericho	.60	1.50
15	Danny Basham	.20	.50
16	Edge	.60	1.50
17	Eric Bischoff	.30	.75
18	Eugene	.50	1.25
19	Jim Ross	.30	.75
20	Jonathan Coachman	.20	.50
21	Kane	.60	1.50
22	Heidenreich	.20	.50
23	Kurt Angle	.75	2.00
24	Rene Dupree	.20	.50
25	Ric Flair	1.00	2.50
26	Rob Van Dam	.60	1.50
27	Shawn Michaels	1.00	2.50
28	Tajiri	.20	.50
29	Triple H	1.00	2.50
30	Kerwin White	.20	.50
31	Val Venis	.30	.75
32	Viscera	.20	.50
33	Steven Richards	.20	.50
34	Booker T	.30	.75
35	Chris Benoit	.75	2.00
36	Christian	.60	1.50
37	Doug Basham	.20	.50
38	Eddie Guerrero	1.00	2.50
39	Funaki	.20	.50
40	Hardcore Holly	.30	.75
41	JBL	.30	.75
42	Juventud	.20	.50
43	Psicosis	.20	.50
44	Super Crazy	.20	.50
45	Shelton Benjamin	.20	.50
46	Chris Masters	.20	.50
47	Nunzio	.20	.50
48	Randy Orton	.20	.50
49	Rey Mysterio	.60	1.50
50	Scotty 2 Hotty	.30	.75
51	Tazz	.20	.50
52	Theodore Long	.20	.50
53	Undertaker	1.00	2.50
54	William Regal	.30	.75
55	Antonio	.20	.50
56	Romeo	.20	.50
57	Snitsky	.20	.50
58	Robert Conway	.20	.50
59	Sharmell DV	1.00	2.50
60	Trish Stratus DV	2.00	5.00
61	Torrie Wilson DV	2.00	5.00
62	Christy Hemme DV	2.00	5.00
63	Lita DV	1.25	3.00
64	Lilian Garcia DV	1.00	2.50
65	Maria DV	1.25	3.00
66	Stacy Keibler DV	2.00	5.00
67	Victoria DV	1.25	3.00

68	Candice Michelle DV	1.25	3.00
69	Michelle McCool DV	1.00	2.50
70	Melina DV	1.00	2.50
71	The British Bulldog L	.30	.75
72	Chief Jay Strongbow L	.20	.50
73	Classy Freddie Blassie L	.20	.50
74	Cowboy Bob Orton L	.30	.75
75	Bobby The Brain Heenan L	.30	.75
76	Gorilla Monsoon L	.20	.50
77	Hillbilly Jim L	.30	.75
78	Iron Sheik L	.50	1.25
79	Jake The Snake Roberts L	.50	1.25
80	Jerry The King Lawler L	.50	1.25
81	Junkyard Dog L	.50	1.25
82	Mouth of the South Jimmy Hart L	.60	1.50
83	Mr. Wonderful Paul Orndorff L	.60	1.50
84	Nikolai Volkoff L	.30	.75
85	Rowdy Roddy Piper L	1.00	2.50
86	Sgt. Slaughter L	.50	1.25
87	Superstar Billy Graham L	.30	.75
88	The Million Dollar Man Ted DiBiase L	.60	1.50
89	Godfather L	.20	.50
90	Hogan/Cena/Batista CL	1.25	3.00

2005 Topps Heritage WWE Autographs

The following cards, originally scheduled to appear in the set, have yet to surface on the secondary market: Batista, JBL, Jake the Snake Roberts, Ric Flair, Stone Cold Steve Austin, Triple H, and Undertaker.
OVERALL STATED ODDS 1:36
HEMME ODDS 1:1574 H
ANGLE, HOGAN, SHIEK ODDS 1:530 H
MICHAELS, SLAUGHTER, WILSON ODDS 1:520 H
CENA, KANE, KIEBLER, LAWLER, PIPER, STRATUS, STRONBOW ODDS 1:510
HILLBILLY, HEENAN ODDS 1:473 RETAIL

NNO	Bobby The Brain Heenan RET	60.00	120.00
NNO	Chief Jay Strongbow	20.00	50.00
NNO	Christy Hemme	50.00	100.00
NNO	Hillbilly Jim RET	25.00	60.00
NNO	Hulk Hogan	150.00	300.00
NNO	Iron Sheik	15.00	40.00
NNO	Jerry The King Lawler	15.00	40.00
NNO	John Cena	125.00	250.00
NNO	Kane	15.00	40.00
NNO	Kurt Angle	15.00	40.00
NNO	Lita	20.00	50.00
NNO	Rowdy Roddy Piper	20.00	50.00
NNO	Sgt. Slaughter	15.00	40.00
NNO	Shawn Michaels	50.00	100.00
NNO	Stacy Keibler	25.00	60.00
NNO	Torrie Wilson	20.00	50.00
NNO	Trish Stratus	25.00	60.00

2005 Topps Heritage WWE Event-Used Mat Ringside Relics

STATED ODDS 1:12 RETAIL EXCLUSIVES

NNO	Booker T/Christian		
NNO	Rey Mysterio/Eddie Guerrero		
NNO	JBL/Batista		

2005 Topps Heritage WWE Event-Worn Ringside Relics

OVERALL STATED ODDS 1:17
EUGENE ODDS 1:214
MICHAELS ODDS 1:196

ANGLE ODDS 1:185
JERICHO ODDS 1:158
TRIPLE H ODDS 1:104
CENA ODDS 1:89
HOGAN ODDS 1:70

NNO	Chris Jericho	6.00	15.00
NNO	Eugene	8.00	20.00
NNO	Hulk Hogan	10.00	25.00
NNO	John Cena	10.00	30.00
NNO	Kurt Angle	8.00	20.00
NNO	Shawn Michaels	10.00	25.00
NNO	Triple H	10.00	25.00

2005 Topps Heritage WWE Stickers

COMPLETE SET (10) — 12.50 / 30.00
STATED ODDS 1:4 HOBBY

#			
1	Hulk Hogan	2.00	5.00
2	The Rock	2.00	5.00
3	Batista	.75	2.00
4	Shawn Michaels	1.50	4.00
5	Carlito	.30	.75
6	Kurt Angle	1.25	3.00
7	Triple H	1.50	4.00
8	John Cena	2.00	5.00
9	Torrie Wilson	3.00	8.00
10	Christy Hemme	3.00	8.00

2005 Topps Heritage WWE World's Greatest Wrestling Managers DVD Promos

COMPLETE SET (4) — 3.00 / 8.00
STATED ODDS 1:SET PER DVD

V1	Bobby The Brain Heenan	1.25	3.00
V2	Classy Freddie Blassie	.60	1.50
V3	Mouth of the South Jimmy Hart	.75	2.00
V4	Paul Bearer	1.25	3.00

2005 Topps Heritage WWE Promo

NNO	John Cena	1.50	4.00

2012 Topps Heritage WWE

COMPLETE SET (110) — 10.00 / 25.00
UNOPENED BOX (24 PACKS)
UNOPENED PACK (9 CARDS)
*RED: X TO X BASIC CARDS
*SILVER: .75X TO 2X BASIC CARDS
*BLACK: 5X TO 12X BASIC CARDS
*GOLD/10: UNPRICED DUE TO SCARCITY

#			
1	AJ Lee	.75	2.00
2	Aksana	.40	1.00
3	Alberto Del Rio	.40	1.00
4	Alicia Fox	.25	.60
5	Beth Phoenix	.40	1.00
6	Big Show	.40	1.00
7	Brock Lesnar	.60	1.50
8	Brodus Clay	.15	.40
9	Cameron	.25	.60
10	Chris Jericho	.60	1.50
11	Christian	.15	.40
12	CM Punk	.60	1.50
13	Cody Rhodes	.15	.40
14	Damien Sandow	.15	.40
15	Daniel Bryan	.15	.40
16	Dolph Ziggler	.25	.60
17	Eve	.60	1.50
18	Jack Swagger	.25	.60
19	John Cena	.75	2.00
20	Kaitlyn	.40	1.00
21	Kane	.40	1.00
22	Ryback	.15	.40
23	Kofi Kingston	.15	.40
24	Layla	.40	1.00
25	Lilian Garcia	.40	1.00
26	Mark Henry	.25	.60
27	The Miz	.25	.60
28	Naomi	.25	.60
29	Natalya	.60	1.50
30	R-Truth	.15	.40
31	Randy Orton	.60	1.50
32	Rey Mysterio	.40	1.00
33	The Rock	.75	2.00
34	Rosa Mendes	.25	.60
35	Santino Marella	.25	.60
36	Sheamus	.40	1.00
37	Kama Mustafa	.15	.40
38	Tamina Snuka	.25	.60
39	Tensai	.15	.40
40	Triple H	.60	1.50
41	Tyson Kidd	.15	.40
42	Undertaker	.60	1.50
43	Zack Ryder	.15	.40
44	Batista	.25	.60
45	Booker T	.25	.60
46	Cactus Jack	.60	1.50
47	Dude Love	.60	1.50
48	Jerry The King Lawler	.40	1.00
49	Jim Ross	.15	.40
50	Kevin Nash	.25	.60
51	Mankind	.60	1.50
52	Mick Foley	.60	1.50
53	Shawn Michaels	.60	1.50
54	Stone Cold Steve Austin	.75	2.00
55	Trish Stratus	.75	2.00
56	Akeem	.15	.40
57	The American Dream Dusty Rhodes	.25	.60
58	Andre The Giant	.75	2.00
59	Arn Anderson	.25	.60
60	Barry Windham	.25	.60
61	Big Boss Man	.15	.40
62	Big John Studd	.25	.60
63	Bobby The Brain Heenan	.25	.60
64	Brian Pillman	.25	.60
65	The British Bulldog	.25	.60
66	Bushwhacker Butch	.15	.40
67	Bushwhacker Luke	.15	.40
68	Chief Jay Strongbow	.25	.60
69	Classy Freddie Blassie	.25	.60
70	Cowboy Bob Orton	.25	.60
71	Dean Malenko	.25	.60
72	Doink The Clown	.25	.60
73	Don Muraco	.25	.60
74	The Godfather	.15	.40
75	Gorilla Monsoon	.25	.60
76	Greg The Hammer Valentine	.25	.60
77	Hacksaw Jim Duggan	.25	.60
78	Harley Race	.25	.60
79	Hillbilly Jim	.25	.60
80	Howard Finkel	.25	.60
81	The Iron Sheik	.25	.60
82	Irwin R. Schyster	.15	.40
83	Jake The Snake Roberts	.25	.60
84	Jimmy Superfly Snuka	.25	.60
85	Junkyard Dog	.25	.60
86	Sin Cara	.40	1.00
87	Kamala	.25	.60
88	Koko B. Ware	.25	.60
89	Mean Gene Okerlund	.25	.60
90	Michael PS Hayes	.15	.40
91	Million Dollar Man Ted DiBiase	.25	.60
92	Mr. Perfect	.25	.60
93	Mr. Wonderful Paul Orndorff	.25	.60
94	Nikolai Volkoff	.25	.60
95	One Man Gang	.15	.40
96	Papa Shango	.15	.40
97	Paul Bearer	.15	.40
98	Ravishing Rick Rude	.25	.60
99	Ricky The Dragon Steamboat	.25	.60
100	Road Warrior Animal	.25	.60
101	Road Warrior Hawk	.25	.60
102	Rocky Johnson	.25	.60
103	Rowdy Roddy Piper	.40	1.00
104	Sgt. Slaughter	.25	.60
105	Terry Funk	.25	.60
106	Tito Santana	.25	.60
107	Tom Prichard	.15	.40
108	Tully Blanchard	.25	.60
109	Vader	.25	.60
110	Yokozuna	.25	.60

2012 Topps Heritage WWE Allen and Ginter

COMPLETE SET (30) — 30.00 / .75.00
STATED ODDS 1:6 HOBBY AND RETAIL

#			
1	Brock Lesnar	3.00	8.00
2	Christian	.75	2.00
3	CM Punk	3.00	8.00
4	Daniel Bryan	.75	2.00
5	John Cena	4.00	10.00
6	Kelly Kelly	3.00	8.00
7	Kofi Kingston	.75	2.00
8	Layla	2.00	5.00
9	Randy Orton	3.00	8.00
10	Sheamus	2.00	5.00
11	Booker T	1.25	3.00
12	Diesel	1.25	3.00
13	Mankind	3.00	8.00
14	Stone Cold Steve Austin	4.00	10.00
15	Trish Stratus	4.00	10.00
16	The American Dream Dusty Rhodes	1.25	3.00
17	Andre The Giant	4.00	10.00
18	Big Boss Man	.75	2.00
19	Big John Studd	1.25	3.00
20	Cowboy Bob Orton	1.25	3.00
21	Doink The Clown	1.25	3.00
22	Hacksaw Jim Duggan	1.25	3.00
23	Kamala	1.25	3.00
24	Koko B. Ware	1.25	3.00
25	Papa Shango	.75	2.00
26	Paul Bearer	.75	2.00
27	Ricky The Dragon Steamboat	1.25	3.00
28	Terry Funk	1.25	3.00
29	Vader	1.25	3.00
30	Yokozuna	1.25	3.00

2012 Topps Heritage WWE Andre the Giant Tribute

COMPLETE SET (10) — 8.00 / 20.00
*SILVER/85: 1X TO 2.5X BASIC CARDS
*GOLD/10: UNPRICED DUE TO SCARCITY
STATED ODDS 1:8 HOBBY AND RETAIL

#			
1	Andre the Giant	1.25	3.00
2	Andre the Giant	1.25	3.00

3	Andre the Giant	1.25	3.00
4	Andre the Giant	1.25	3.00
5	Andre the Giant	1.25	3.00
6	Andre the Giant	1.25	3.00
7	Andre the Giant	1.25	3.00
8	Andre the Giant	1.25	3.00
9	Andre the Giant	1.25	3.00
10	Andre the Giant	1.25	3.00

2012 Topps Heritage WWE Autographs

STATED ODDS HOBBY EXCLUSIVE 1:44
STATED ODDS RETAIL EXCLUSIVE 1:120

NNO	Akeem	25.00	60.00
NNO	Cameron	15.00	40.00
NNO	CM Punk	50.00	100.00
NNO	Doink The Clown	20.00	50.00
NNO	The Godfather	25.00	60.00
NNO	Howard Finkel	20.00	50.00
NNO	Irwin R. Schyster	25.00	60.00
NNO	Jake The Snake Roberts	20.00	50.00
NNO	John Cena	25.00	60.00
NNO	Kama Mustafa	20.00	50.00
NNO	Kamala	15.00	40.00
NNO	Layla	15.00	40.00
NNO	Mean Gene Okerlund	15.00	40.00
NNO	Michael PS Hayes	20.00	50.00
NNO	Naomi	15.00	40.00
NNO	Natalya	15.00	40.00
NNO	One Man Gang	25.00	60.00
NNO	Papa Shango	20.00	50.00
NNO	Paul Bearer	15.00	40.00
NNO	Vader	30.00	75.00

2012 Topps Heritage WWE Fabled Tag Teams

COMPLETE SET (10)   6.00   15.00
STATED ODDS 1:12 HOBBY AND RETAIL

1	Nikolai Volkoff/Iron Sheik	.75	2.00
2	The Brain Busters	.75	2.00
3	Big Boss Man/Akeem	.50	1.25
4	The Road Warriors	.75	2.00
5	The Bushwhackers	.50	1.25
6	Money Inc	.75	2.00
7	The Rock N Sock Connection	2.50	6.00
8	The Brothers of Destruction	2.00	5.00
9	The Two-Man Power Trip	2.50	6.00
10	D-Generation X	2.00	5.00

2012 Topps Heritage WWE Family History

COMPLETE SET (10)   6.00   15.00
STATED ODDS 1:8 HOBBY AND RETAIL

1	B.Orton/R.Orton	2.00	5.00
2	T.DiBiase Sr./T.DiBiase Jr.	.75	2.00
3	J.Snuka/T.Snuka	.75	2.00
4	R.Johnson/The Rock	2.50	6.00
5	Yokozuna	.75	2.00
	The Usos		
6	B.Bulldog/Natalya	2.00	5.00
7	D.Rhodes/C.Rhodes	.75	2.00
8	Animal/J.Laurinaitis	.50	1.25
9	Mr. Perfect/M.McGillicutty	.75	2.00
10	P.Bearer/Kane	1.25	3.00

2012 Topps Heritage WWE Jerry the King Lawler Portraits

COMPLETE SET (10)   12.00   30.00
STATED ODDS 1:24 HOBBY AND RETAIL

1	Big Show	2.50	6.00
2	Brodus Clay	1.00	2.50
3	CM Punk	4.00	10.00
4	Hornswoggle	1.50	4.00
5	Kelly Kelly	4.00	10.00
6	Rey Mysterio	2.50	6.00
7	Santino Marella	1.50	4.00
8	Sheamus	2.50	6.00
9	The Miz	1.50	4.00
10	Undertaker	4.00	10.00

2012 Topps Heritage WWE Ringside Action

COMPLETE SET (55)   10.00   25.00
STATED ODDS 1:1 HOBBY AND RETAIL

1	Superfly Splash	.60	1.50
	Jimmy Superfly Snuka		
2	Double A Spinebuster	.60	1.50
3	Stone Cold Stunner	2.00	5.00
4	Perfect-Plex	.60	1.50
5	Cobra Clutch	.60	1.50
6	DDT	.60	1.50
7	Flying Fist Drop	1.00	2.50
8	Figure Four Leglock	.60	1.50
9	Mandible Claw	1.50	4.00
10	Jackknife Powerbomb	.60	1.50
11	Superplex	.60	1.50
12	Running Powerslam	.60	1.50
13	Doomsday Device	.60	1.50
14	Bionic Elbow	.60	1.50
15	Camel Clutch	.60	1.50
16	Flying Cross-body Press	.60	1.50
17	Three Point Stance Clothesline	.60	1.50
18	Scissor Kick	.60	1.50
19	Rude Awakening	.60	1.50
20	Chokeslam	1.00	2.50
21	Lariat	.60	1.50
22	Texas Cloverleaf	.60	1.50
23	Flying Splash	.60	1.50
24	Million Dollar Dream	.60	1.50
25	Rock Bottom	2.00	5.00
26	F-5	1.50	4.00
27	Battering Ram	.40	1.00
28	The Write-Off	.40	1.00
29	Killswitch	.40	1.00
30	Sidewalk Slam	.40	1.00
31	Flying Forearm	.60	1.50
32	Pimp Drop	.40	1.00
	The Godfather		
33	The Whoopie Cushion		
34	Diving Headbutt	.60	1.50
35	STF	.40	1.00
36	619	1.00	2.50
37	Battering Ram		
38	G.T.S. (Go to Sleep)	1.50	4.00
39	World's Strongest Slam	.60	1.50
40	RKO	1.50	4.00
41	Moonsault Side Slam	1.00	2.50
42	Vader Bomb	.60	1.50
43	Air Pillman	.60	1.50
44	The Claw	.40	1.00
45	Banzai Drop	.60	1.50
46	Wasteland	.40	1.00
47	Brogue Kick	1.00	2.50
48	Attitude Adjustment	2.00	5.00
49	Reverse Piledriver	.60	1.50
50	Knockout Punch	.60	1.50
51	The Walls of Jericho	1.50	4.00
52	Sweet Chin Music	1.50	4.00
53	Batista Bomb	.60	1.50
54	Pedigree	1.50	4.00
55	Yes! Lock	.40	1.00
86	Dream Street	.60	1.50

2012 Topps Heritage WWE Shirt Relics

TWO AUTO OR MEM PER HOBBY BOX
STATED ODDS 1:97 RETAIL

NNO	Alberto Del Rio/Scarf	6.00	15.00
NNO	Batista	6.00	15.00
NNO	CM Punk	6.00	15.00
NNO	Cody Rhodes	5.00	12.00
NNO	Daniel Bryan	5.00	12.00
NNO	Dolph Ziggler	6.00	15.00
NNO	John Cena	8.00	20.00
NNO	Kofi Kingston	5.00	12.00
NNO	Mark Henry	5.00	12.00
NNO	The Miz	5.00	12.00
NNO	Randy Orton	6.00	15.00
NNO	Rey Mysterio	6.00	15.00
NNO	R-Truth	5.00	12.00
NNO	Santino Marella	5.00	12.00
NNO	Sheamus	5.00	12.00
NNO	Stone Cold Steve Austin	8.00	20.00
NNO	Wade Barrett	5.00	12.00
NNO	Zack Ryder	5.00	12.00

2012 Topps Heritage WWE Stickers

COMPLETE SET (18)   10.00   25.00
STATED ODDS 1:4 HOBBY AND RETAIL

1	Ricky The Dragon Steamboat	.75	2.00
2	Rey Mysterio	1.25	3.00
3	Trish Stratus	2.50	6.00
4	Undertaker	2.00	5.00
5	Mankind	2.00	5.00
6	Ravishing Rick Rude	.75	2.00
7	Sin Cara	1.25	3.00
8	Vader	.75	2.00
9	Dude Love	2.00	5.00
10	Jake The Snake Roberts	.75	2.00
11	Gorilla Monsoon	.75	2.00
12	Greg The Hammer Valentine	.75	2.00
13	Rowdy Roddy Piper	1.25	3.00
14	Doink The Clown	.75	2.00
15	Booker T	.75	2.00
16	Koko B. Ware	.75	2.00
17	Kamala	.75	2.00
18	Kane	1.25	3.00

2012 Topps Heritage WWE The Superstars Speak

COMPLETE SET (20)   8.00   20.00
STATED ODDS 1:4 HOBBY AND RETAIL

1	Stone Cold Steve Austin	2.00	5.00
2	Cactus Jack	1.50	4.00
3	Booker T	.60	1.50
4	Road Warrior Hawk	.60	1.50
5	Gorilla Monsoon	.60	1.50
6	Rowdy Roddy Piper	1.00	2.50
7	The American Dream Dusty Rhodes	.60	1.50
8	Classy Freddie Blassie	.60	1.50

9	The Iron Sheik	.60	1.50
10	Trish Stratus	2.00	5.00
11	The Rock	2.00	5.00
12	Mr. Perfect	.60	1.50
13	Kevin Nash	.60	1.50
14	Mankind	1.50	4.00
15	Hacksaw Jim Duggan	.60	1.50
16	Jim Ross	.40	1.00
17	Vader	.60	1.50
18	Million Dollar Man Ted DiBiase	.60	1.50
19	Yokozuna	.40	1.00
20	Sgt. Slaughter	.60	1.50

2012 Topps Heritage WWE Wrestlemania XXVII Mat Relics

TWO AUTO OR MEM PER HOBBY BOX
STATED ODDS 1:97 RETAIL

NNO	Alberto Del Rio	6.00	15.00
NNO	Big Show	6.00	15.00
NNO	Booker T	4.00	10.00
NNO	Christian	4.00	10.00
NNO	CM Punk	6.00	15.00
NNO	Cody Rhodes	5.00	12.00
NNO	Dolph Ziggler	4.00	10.00
NNO	Ezekiel Jackson	4.00	10.00
NNO	Heath Slater	4.00	10.00
NNO	Jerry The King Lawler	5.00	12.00
NNO	John Cena	6.00	15.00
NNO	Justin Gabriel	5.00	12.00
NNO	Kane	5.00	12.00
NNO	Kofi Kingston	5.00	12.00
NNO	Layla	6.00	15.00
NNO	Michael Cole	4.00	10.00
NNO	The Miz	4.00	10.00
NNO	Randy Orton	6.00	15.00
NNO	The Rock	8.00	20.00
NNO	Santino Marella	5.00	12.00
NNO	Stone Cold Steve Austin	8.00	20.00
NNO	Triple H	6.00	15.00
NNO	Trish Stratus	8.00	20.00
NNO	Undertaker	6.00	15.00
NNO	Wade Barrett	5.00	12.00

2015 Topps Heritage WWE

COMPLETE SET (110)   12.00   30.00
UNOPENED BOX (24 PACKS)
UNOPENED PACK (9 CARDS)
*BLACK: .75X TO 2X BASIC CARDS
*SILVER: 5X TO 12X BASIC CARDS
*GOLD/10: 8X TO 20X BASIC CARDS
*RED/1: UNPRICED DUE TO SCARCITY
*P.P.BLACK/1: UNPRICED DUE TO SCARCITY
*P.P.CYAN/1: UNPRICED DUE TO SCARCITY
*P.P.MAGENTA/1: UNPRICED DUE TO SCARCITY
*P.P.YELLOW/1: UNPRICED DUE TO SCARCITY

1	The American Dream Dusty Rhodes	.25	.60
2	The Acolytes	.25	.60
3	Bob Backlund	.15	.40
4	Bam Bam Bigelow	.20	.50
5	Booker T	.25	.60
6	Bret Hit Man Hart	.50	1.25
7	The British Bulldog	.25	.60
8	Bruno Sammartino	.40	1.00
9	The Bushwhackers	.15	.40
10	Cowboy Bob Orton	.15	.40
11	D-Generation X	.60	1.50
12	Diamond Dallas Page	.30	.75

#	Card	Lo	Hi
13	Doink the Clown	.15	.40
14	Earthquake	.15	.40
15	Edge	.40	1.00
16	The Foreign Legion	.25	.60
17	The Four Horsemen	.50	1.25
18	The Funks	.20	.50
19	Eddie Guerrero	.40	1.00
20	George The Animal Steele	.20	.50
21	Papa Shango	.15	.40
22	Hacksaw Jim Duggan	.25	.60
23	Hillbilly Jim	.25	.60
24	Rob Van Dam	.40	1.00
25	Jake The Snake Roberts	.25	.60
26	Jerry The King Lawler	.25	.60
27	Jim Ross	.25	.60
28	Junkyard Dog	.20	.50
29	Kamala	.20	.50
30	The King Harley Race	.25	.60
31	Koko B. Ware	.20	.50
32	Money Inc.	.25	.60
33	Mr. Perfect Curt Hennig	.25	.60
34	Mr. Wonderful Paul Orndorff	.25	.60
35	The Nasty Boys	.25	.60
36	The Outsiders	.40	1.00
37	Ravishing Rick Rude	.25	.60
38	Ricky The Dragon Steamboat	.25	.60
39	Rocky Johnson	.25	.60
40	Rowdy Roddy Piper	.50	1.25
41	Rhythm & Blues	.25	.60
42	Sgt. Slaughter	.25	.60
43	Lex Luger & Sting	.40	1.00
44	Stone Cold Steve Austin	.75	2.00
45	Tito Santana	.25	.60
46	The Twin Towers	.20	.50
47	Ultimate Warrior	.50	1.25
48	Vader	.20	.50
49	Virgil	.15	.40
50	Yokozuna	.25	.60
51	Eve	.30	.75
52	Lita	.60	1.50
53	Trish Stratus	.75	2.00
54	Alicia Fox	.30	.75
55	The Bella Twins	.50	1.25
56	Emma	.25	.60
57	Lana	.60	1.50
58	Naomi	.25	.60
59	Natalya	.50	1.25
60	Paige	.75	2.00
61	King Barrett	.15	.40
62	Batista	.40	1.00
63	Big Show	.40	1.00
64	Bo Dallas	.15	.40
65	Bray Wyatt	.60	1.50
66	Brock Lesnar	.60	1.50
67	Chris Jericho	.40	1.00
68	Christian	.15	.40
69	Damien Sandow	.15	.40
70	Daniel Bryan	.60	1.50
71	Dean Ambrose	.40	1.00
72	Dolph Ziggler	.25	.60
73	Goldust	.15	.40
74	J & J Security	.15	.40
75	John Cena	.75	2.00
76	Kalisto	.25	.60
77	Kane	.40	1.00
78	Luke Harper	.25	.60
79	Mark Henry	.25	.60
80	The Miz	.25	.60
81	Neville	.30	.75
82	The New Day	.25	.60
83	The Prime Time Players	.15	.40
84	R-Truth	.15	.40
85	Randy Orton	.60	1.50
86	The Rock	.75	2.00
87	Fandango	.15	.40
88	Roman Reigns	.40	1.00
89	Rusev	.40	1.00
90	Ryback	.15	.40
91	Santino Marella	.15	.40
92	Seth Rollins	.25	.60
93	Sheamus	.40	1.00
94	Sin Cara	.25	.60
95	Stardust	.15	.40
96	Cesaro	.15	.40
97	Undertaker	.60	1.50
98	The Usos	.15	.40
99	William Regal	.25	.60
100	Zack Ryder	.15	.40
101	Alexa Bliss	4.00	10.00
102	Baron Corbin	.25	.60
103	Bull Dempsey	.25	.60
104	Charlotte	.50	1.25
105	Finn Balor	.50	1.25
106	Hideo Itami	.15	.40
107	Kevin Owens	.50	1.25
108	Sami Zayn	.25	.60
109	Sasha Banks	.30	.75
110	Tyler Breeze	.15	.40
111	Steve Austin 2K16 SP		
111B	Steve Austin 2K16 SP Black		
111C	Steve Austin 2K16 SP Blue		
111D	Steve Austin 2K16 SP Yellow		

2015 Topps Heritage WWE 2K16

COMPLETE SET (8) 10.00 25.00
*BLACK/50: 1.2X TO 3X BASIC CARDS
*P.P.BLACK/1: UNPRICED DUE TO SCARCITY
*P.P.CYAN/1: UNPRICED DUE TO SCARCITY
*P.P.MAGENTA/1: UNPRICED DUE TO SCARCITY
*P.P.YELLOW/1: UNPRICED DUE TO SCARCITY

#	Card	Lo	Hi
1	Stone Cold Steve Austin	4.00	10.00
2	Daniel Bryan	3.00	8.00
3	Finn Balor	2.50	6.00
4	King Barrett	.75	2.00
5	Paige	4.00	10.00
6	Paul Heyman	.75	2.00
7	Seth Rollins	1.25	3.00
8	Stone Cold Steve Austin	4.00	10.00

2015 Topps Heritage WWE Autographs

*BLACK/50: .5X TO 1.2X BASIC AUTOS
*SILVER/25: .75X TO 2X BASIC AUTOS
*GOLD/10: UNPRICED DUE TO SCARCITY
*RED/1: UNPRICED DUE TO SCARCITY

Card	Lo	Hi
NNO Alundra Blayze	12.00	30.00
NNO Daniel Bryan	15.00	40.00
NNO Dean Ambrose	15.00	40.00
NNO Dolph Ziggler	10.00	25.00
NNO Eva Marie	10.00	25.00
NNO Finn Balor	20.00	50.00
NNO Hideo Itami	10.00	25.00
NNO John Cena	20.00	50.00
NNO Neville	10.00	25.00
NNO Pat Patterson	10.00	25.00
NNO Roman Reigns	15.00	40.00
NNO Sasha Banks	15.00	40.00
NNO Seth Rollins	15.00	40.00

2015 Topps Heritage WWE Money in the Bank Relics

*BLACK/50: .5X TO 1.2X BASIC MEM
*SILVER/25: .75X TO 2X BASIC MEM
*GOLD/10: UNPRICED DUE TO SCARCITY
*RED/1: UNPRICED DUE TO SCARCITY

Card	Lo	Hi
NNO Big E	3.00	8.00
NNO Big Show	5.00	12.00
NNO Darren Young	2.00	5.00
NNO Dean Ambrose	5.00	12.00
NNO Dolph Ziggler	3.00	8.00
NNO John Cena	10.00	25.00
NNO Kane	5.00	12.00
NNO Kevin Owens	6.00	15.00
NNO King Barrett	2.00	5.00
NNO Kofi Kingston	2.00	5.00
NNO Neville	4.00	10.00
NNO Nikki Bella	6.00	15.00
NNO Paige	10.00	25.00
NNO Randy Orton	8.00	20.00
NNO Roman Reigns	5.00	12.00
NNO R-Truth	2.00	5.00
NNO Ryback	2.00	5.00
NNO Seth Rollins	3.00	8.00
NNO Sheamus	5.00	12.00
NNO Titus O'Neil	2.00	5.00
NNO Xavier Woods	3.00	8.00

2015 Topps Heritage WWE nWo Autographs

RANDOMLY INSERTED INTO PACKS

Card	Lo	Hi
NNO Big Show	20.00	50.00
NNO Booker T	12.00	30.00
NNO Bret Hit Man Hart	25.00	60.00
NNO Kevin Nash	20.00	50.00
NNO Lex Luger	12.00	30.00
NNO Shawn Michaels	60.00	120.00
NNO X-Pac	15.00	40.00

2015 Topps Heritage WWE nWo Tribute

COMPLETE SET (10) 10.00 25.00
RANDOMLY INSERTED INTO PACKS

#	Card	Lo	Hi
31	Scott Hall	2.50	6.00
32	Kevin Nash	2.50	6.00
33	The Giant	2.50	6.00
34	Syxx	2.00	5.00
35	Miss Elizabeth	2.00	5.00
36	Mr. Wallstreet	1.00	2.50
37	Big Bubba Rogers	1.00	2.50
38	Curt Hennig	1.50	4.00
39	Bret Hit Man Hart	3.00	8.00
40	Stevie Ray	1.00	2.50

2015 Topps Heritage WWE NXT Called Up

COMPLETE SET (30) 8.00 20.00
*P.P.BLACK/1: UNPRICED DUE TO SCARCITY
*P.P.CYAN/1: UNPRICED DUE TO SCARCITY
*P.P.MAGENTA/1: UNPRICED DUE TO SCARCITY
*P.P.YELLOW/1: UNPRICED DUE TO SCARCITY
STATED ODDS 1:1

#	Card	Lo	Hi
1	Bad News Barrett	.30	.75
2	David Otunga	.30	.75
3	Heath Slater	.30	.75
4	Darren Young	.30	.75
5	Daniel Bryan	1.25	3.00
6	Ryback	.30	.75
7	Alex Riley	.30	.75
8	Curtis Axel	.30	.75
9	Naomi	.50	1.25
10	Titus OfNeil	.30	.75
11	Dean Ambrose	.75	2.00
12	Roman Reigns	.75	2.00
13	Seth Rollins	.50	1.25
14	Big E	.50	1.25
15	Bo Dallas	.30	.75
16	Bray Wyatt	1.25	3.00
17	Luke Harper	.50	1.25
18	Erick Rowan	.50	1.25
19	Adam Rose	.40	1.00
20	Summer Rae	1.25	3.00
21	Xavier Woods	.50	1.25
22	Emma	.50	1.25
23	Byron Saxton	.30	.75
24	Rusev	.75	2.00
25	Lana	1.25	3.00
26	Paige	1.50	4.00
27	Konnor	.40	1.00
28	Viktor	.30	.75
29	Kalisto	.50	1.25
30	Neville	.60	1.50

2015 Topps Heritage WWE Rookie of the Year

COMPLETE SET (30) 10.00 25.00
*P.P.BLACK/1: UNPRICED DUE TO SCARCITY
*P.P.CYAN/1: UNPRICED DUE TO SCARCITY
*P.P.MAGENTA/1: UNPRICED DUE TO SCARCITY
*P.P.YELLOW/1: UNPRICED DUE TO SCARCITY
STATED ODDS 1:1

#	Card	Lo	Hi
1	Mr. Wonderful Paul Orndorff	.50	1.25
2	Rowdy Roddy Piper	1.00	2.50
3	Davey Boy Smith	.50	1.25
4	Jake The Snake Roberts	.50	1.25
5	Ultimate Warrior	1.00	2.50
6	Shawn Michaels	1.25	3.00
7	Earthquake	.30	.75
8	Undertaker	1.25	3.00
9	I.R.S.	.30	.75
10	Razor Ramon	.75	2.00
11	Diesel	.75	2.00
12	Kama	.30	.75
13	Hunter Hearst Helmsley	1.25	3.00
14	Mark Henry	.50	1.25
15	Kane	.75	2.00
16	Edge	.75	2.00
17	Chris Jericho	.75	2.00
18	Lita	1.25	3.00
19	Brock Lesnar	1.25	3.00
20	Joey Mercury	.30	.75
21	The Miz	.50	1.25
22	Santino Marella	.30	.75
23	Dolph Ziggler	.50	1.25
24	Sheamus	.75	2.00
25	Daniel Bryan	1.25	3.00
26	Sin Cara	.50	1.25
27	Dean Ambrose	.75	2.00
28	Bray Wyatt	1.25	3.00
29	Rusev	.75	2.00
30	Neville	.60	1.50

2015 Topps Heritage WWE Swatch Relics

*BLACK/50: .5X TO 1.2 BASIC MEM
*GOLD/10: UNPRICED DUE TO SCARCITY
*RED/1: UNPRICED DUE TO SCARCITY

NNO	Aiden English	3.00	8.00
NNO	Baron Corbin	4.00	10.00
NNO	Bayley	5.00	12.00
NNO	Becky Lynch	5.00	12.00
NNO	Big E	4.00	10.00
NNO	Big Show	6.00	15.00
NNO	Bo Dallas	2.50	6.00
NNO	Bray Wyatt	10.00	25.00
NNO	Cesaro	2.50	6.00
NNO	Charlotte	8.00	20.00
NNO	Colin Cassady	4.00	10.00
NNO	Curtis Axel	2.50	6.00
NNO	Damien Sandow	2.50	6.00
NNO	Daniel Bryan	10.00	25.00
NNO	Darren Young	2.50	6.00
NNO	Dean Ambrose	6.00	15.00
NNO	Dolph Ziggler	4.00	10.00
NNO	Enzo Amore	2.50	6.00
NNO	Finn Balor	8.00	20.00
NNO	Goldust	2.50	6.00
NNO	Jack Swagger	4.00	10.00
NNO	Jimmy Uso	2.50	6.00
NNO	John Cena	12.00	30.00
NNO	Kalisto	4.00	10.00
NNO	Kevin Owens	8.00	20.00
NNO	King Barrett	2.50	6.00
NNO	Kofi Kingston	2.50	6.00
NNO	Konnor	3.00	8.00
NNO	Luke Harper	4.00	10.00
NNO	Luke Harper	4.00	10.00
NNO	Mojo Rawley	2.50	6.00
NNO	Natalya	8.00	20.00
NNO	Neville	5.00	12.00
NNO	Randy Orton	10.00	25.00
NNO	Roman Reigns	6.00	15.00
NNO	Rusev	6.00	15.00
NNO	Ryback	2.50	6.00
NNO	Samoa Joe	6.00	15.00
NNO	Sasha Banks	5.00	12.00
NNO	Seth Rollins	4.00	10.00
NNO	Sheamus	6.00	15.00
NNO	Simon Gotch	2.50	6.00
NNO	Sin Cara	4.00	10.00
NNO	Tamina	4.00	10.00
NNO	The Miz	4.00	10.00
NNO	Titus O'Neil	2.50	6.00
NNO	Tyler Breeze	2.50	6.00
NNO	Viktor	2.50	6.00
NNO	Xavier Woods	4.00	10.00
NNO	Zack Ryder	2.50	6.00

2015 Topps Heritage WWE Then and Now

COMPLETE SET (30)		10.00	25.00

*P.P.BLACK/1: UNPRICED DUE TO SCARCITY
*P.P.CYAN/1: UNPRICED DUE TO SCARCITY
*P.P.MAGENTA/1: UNPRICED DUE TO SCARCITY
*P.P.YELLOW/1: UNPRICED DUE TO SCARCITY
STATED ODDS 1:1

1	Batista	.75	2.00
2	Big Show	.75	2.00
3	Booker T	.50	1.25
4	Brock Lesnar	1.25	3.00
5	Chris Jericho	.75	2.00
6	Christian	.30	.75
7	Daniel Bryan	1.25	3.00
8	Damien Sandow	.30	.75
9	Darren Young	.30	.75
10	Dean Ambrose	.75	2.00
11	Edge	.75	2.00
12	Goldust	.30	.75
13	Hornswoggle	.50	1.25
14	Jamie Noble	.30	.75
15	JBL	.30	.75
16	Joey Mercury	.30	.75
17	John Cena	1.50	4.00
18	Kane	.75	2.00
19	Mark Henry	.50	1.25
20	The Miz	.50	1.25
21	Randy Orton	1.25	3.00
22	Ryback	.30	.75
23	Seth Rollins	.50	1.25
24	Sting	.75	2.00
25	Stone Cold Steve Austin	1.50	4.00
26	Triple H	1.25	3.00
27	Trish Stratus	1.50	4.00
28	Undertaker	1.25	3.00
29	William Regal	.50	1.25
30	Zack Ryder	.30	.75

2016 Topps Heritage WWE

Subset includes: L = Legends (71-110)

COMPLETE SET (110)		10.00	25.00
UNOPENED BOX (24 PACKS)			
UNOPENED PACKS (9 CARDS)			

*BRONZE/99: 1.2X TO 3X BASIC CARDS
*SILVER/50: 2.5X TO 6X BASIC CARDS
*BLUE/25: 4X TO 10X BASIC CARDS
*GOLD/10: 8X TO 20X BASIC CARDS
*RED/1: UNPRICED DUE TO SCARCITY
*P.P.BLACK/1: UNPRICED DUE TO SCARCITY
*P.P.CYAN/1: UNPRICED DUE TO SCARCITY
*P.P.MAGENTA/1: UNPRICED DUE TO SCARCITY
*P.P.YELLOW/1: UNPRICED DUE TO SCARCITY

1	AJ Styles	1.00	2.50
2	Alberto Del Rio	.40	1.00
3	Big E	.25	.60
4	Big Show	.50	1.25
5	Braun Strowman	.30	.75
6	Bray Wyatt	1.00	2.50
7	Brock Lesnar	1.25	3.00
8	Bubba Ray Dudley	.50	1.25
9	Cesaro	.50	1.25
10	Chris Jericho	.60	1.50
11	D-Von Dudley	.40	1.00
12	Dean Ambrose	.75	2.00
13	Dolph Ziggler	.30	.75
14	Erick Rowan	.25	.60
15	Goldust	.40	1.00
16	Jack Swagger	.25	.60
17	Jey Uso	.25	.60
18	Jimmy Uso	.25	.60
19	John Cena	1.25	3.00
20	Kalisto	.60	1.50
21	Kane	.40	1.00
22	Kevin Owens	.60	1.50
23	Karl Anderson	.25	.60
24	Kofi Kingston	.25	.60
25	Luke Harper	.25	.60
26	Neville	.60	1.50
27	Randy Orton	.60	1.50
28	The Rock	1.25	3.00
29	Roman Reigns	.75	2.00
30	Rusev	.60	1.50
31	Luke Gallows	.30	.75
32	Seth Rollins	.40	1.00
33	Sheamus	.60	1.50
34	Sin Cara	.30	.75
35	Zack Ryder	.25	.60
36	Sting	.60	1.50
37	Triple H	1.00	2.50
38	Tyson Kidd	.25	.60
39	Undertaker	1.00	2.50
40	Xavier Woods	.25	.60
41	Alicia Fox	.40	1.00
42	Becky Lynch	.75	2.00
43	Brie Bella	.50	1.25
44	Charlotte	.75	2.00
45	Eva Marie	.50	1.25
46	Lana	1.00	2.50
47	Mandy Rose	.60	1.50
48	Naomi	.40	1.00
49	Natalya	.40	1.00
50	Nikki Bella	.75	2.00
51	Paige	.75	2.00
52	Rosa Mendes	.25	.60
53	Sasha Banks	.75	2.00
54	Summer Rae	.60	1.50
55	Tamina	.30	.75
56	Aiden English	.25	.60
57	Angelo Dawkins	.25	.60
58	Apollo Crews	.25	.60
59	Asuka	1.00	2.50
60	Bayley	.60	1.50
61	Baron Corbin	.30	.75
62	Carmella	.60	1.50
63	Colin Cassady	.50	1.25
64	Enzo Amore	.50	1.25
65	Finn Balor	.75	2.00
66	Hideo Itami	.30	.75
67	Nia Jax	.40	1.00
68	Sami Zayn	.40	1.00
69	Samoa Joe	.60	1.50
70	Simon Gotch	.40	1.00
71	Alundra Blayze L	.40	1.00
72	American Dream Dusty Rhodes L	.25	.60
73	Andre The Giant L	.75	2.00
74	Bam Bam Bigelow L	.30	.75
75	Bret Hit Man Hart L	.60	1.50
76	The British Bulldog L	.30	.75
77	Bruno Sammartino L	.30	.75
78	Daniel Bryan L	1.00	2.50
79	Diamond Dallas Page L	.40	1.00
80	Eddie Guerrero L	.60	1.50
81	Edge L	.60	1.50
82	Eve L	.50	1.25
83	The Honky Tonk Man L	.25	.60
84	Irwin R. Schyster L	.25	.60
85	Jake The Snake Roberts L	.50	1.25
86	Jim The Anvil Neidhart L	.25	.60
87	Kevin Nash L	.60	1.50
88	Lex Luger L	.40	1.00
89	Lita L	.75	2.00
90	Macho Man Randy Savage L	.60	1.50
91	Million Dollar Man Ted DiBiase L	.30	.75
92	Miss Elizabeth L	.25	.60
93	Mr. Perfect Curt Hennig L	.60	1.50
94	Ravishing Rick Rude L	.40	1.00
95	Ric Flair L	1.00	2.50
96	Ricky The Dragon Steamboat L	.30	.75
97	Rikishi L	.30	.75
98	Road Dogg L	.40	1.00
99	Rob Van Dam L	.50	1.25
100	Ron Simmons L	.60	1.50
101	Rowdy Roddy Piper L	.75	2.00
102	Scott Hall L	.60	1.50
103	Sensational Sherri L	.40	1.00
104	Shawn Michaels L	1.00	2.50
105	The Iron Sheik L	.25	.60
106	Stone Cold Steve Austin L	1.25	3.00
107	Tatanka L	.25	.60
108	Trish Stratus L	1.25	3.00
109	Ultimate Warrior L	.60	1.50
110	X-Pac L	.40	1.00
113	Macho Man Randy Savage SP		

2016 Topps Heritage WWE All-Star Patches

*BRONZE/99: .5X TO 2X BASIC MEM
*SILVER/50: .6X TO 1.5X BASIC MEM
*BLUE/25: .75X TO 2X BASIC MEM
*GOLD/10: UNPRICED DUE TO SCARCITY
*P.P.BLACK/1: UNPRICED DUE TO SCARCITY
*P.P.CYAN/1: UNPRICED DUE TO SCARCITY
*P.P.MAGENTA/1: UNPRICED DUE TO SCARCITY
*P.P.YELLOW/1: UNPRICED DUE TO SCARCITY
RANDOMLY INSERTED INTO PACKS

NNO	Andre the Giant	6.00	15.00
NNO	Bam Bam Bigelow	2.50	6.00
NNO	Bayley	5.00	12.00
NNO	Big Van Vader	4.00	10.00
NNO	Booker T	4.00	10.00
NNO	Bret Hit Man Hart	5.00	12.00
NNO	Brock Lesnar	10.00	25.00
NNO	Bubba Ray Dudley	4.00	10.00
NNO	Curt Hennig	5.00	12.00
NNO	D-Von Dudley	3.00	8.00
NNO	Finn Balor	6.00	15.00
NNO	The Giant	4.00	10.00
NNO	Hideo Itami	2.50	6.00
NNO	John Cena	10.00	25.00
NNO	Kevin Nash	5.00	12.00
NNO	Lex Luger	3.00	8.00
NNO	Macho Man Randy Savage	5.00	12.00
NNO	Ric Flair	8.00	20.00
NNO	Rob Van Dam	4.00	10.00
NNO	The Rock	10.00	25.00
NNO	Sami Zayn	3.00	8.00
NNO	Samoa Joe	5.00	12.00
NNO	Scott Hall	5.00	12.00
NNO	Sting	5.00	12.00
NNO	Stone Cold Steve Austin	10.00	25.00
NNO	Syxx	3.00	8.00
NNO	Terry Funk	2.00	5.00
NNO	Triple H	8.00	20.00
NNO	Ultimate Warrior	5.00	12.00
NNO	Undertaker	8.00	20.00

2016 Topps Heritage WWE Autographs

*SILVER/50: .5X TO 1.2X BASIC AUTOS
*BLUE/25: .6X TO 1.5X BASIC AUTOS
*GOLD/10: 1X TO 2.5X BASIC AUTOS
*P.P.BLACK/1: UNPRICED DUE TO SCARCITY
*P.P.CYAN/1: UNPRICED DUE TO SCARCITY

*P.P.MAGENTA/1: UNPRICED DUE TO SCARCITY
*P.P.YELLOW/1: UNPRICED DUE TO SCARCITY
RANDOMLY INSERTED INTO PACKS

NNO Asuka	12.00	30.00
NNO Bayley	15.00	40.00
NNO Becky Lynch	12.00	30.00
NNO Big E	6.00	15.00
NNO Brian Knobbs	6.00	15.00
NNO Brie Bella	10.00	25.00
NNO Brock Lesnar	60.00	120.00
NNO Dean Ambrose	12.00	30.00
NNO Finn Balor	15.00	40.00
NNO Hideo Itami	10.00	25.00
NNO Jake The Snake Roberts	15.00	40.00
NNO Jerry Sags	6.00	15.00
NNO Jim The Anvil Neidhart	5.00	12.00
NNO John Cena	20.00	50.00
NNO Kevin Owens	15.00	40.00
NNO Kofi Kingston	6.00	15.00
NNO Nia Jax	8.00	20.00
NNO Nikki Bella	10.00	25.00
NNO Roman Reigns	12.00	30.00
NNO Sami Zayn	10.00	25.00
NNO Samoa Joe	12.00	30.00
NNO Sasha Banks	25.00	60.00
NNO Sting	25.00	60.00
NNO Tatanka	5.00	12.00
NNO Tyler Breeze	6.00	15.00
NNO Typhoon	5.00	12.00
NNO Xavier Woods	6.00	15.00

2016 Topps Heritage WWE Diva Kiss

GOLD/10: UNPRICED DUE TO SCARCITY
RANDOMLY INSERTED INTO PACKS

NNO Asuka	25.00	60.00
NNO Billie Kay	20.00	50.00
NNO Charlotte	25.00	60.00
NNO Dasha Fuentes	15.00	40.00
NNO Mandy Rose	25.00	60.00
NNO Naomi	12.00	30.00
NNO Nia Jax	20.00	50.00
NNO Peyton Royce	15.00	40.00

2016 Topps Heritage WWE Diva Kiss Autographs

*GOLD/10: UNPRICED DUE TO SCARCITY
*P.P.BLACK/1: UNPRICED DUE TO SCARCITY
*P.P.CYAN/1: UNPRICED DUE TO SCARCITY
*P.P.MAGENTA/1: UNPRICED DUE TO SCARCITY
*P.P.YELLOW/1: UNPRICED DUE TO SCARCITY
RANDOMLY INSERTED INTO PACKS

NNO Asuka	50.00	100.00
NNO Billie Kay	50.00	100.00
NNO Charlotte	60.00	120.00
NNO Dasha Fuentes	30.00	80.00
NNO Mandy Rose	50.00	100.00
NNO Naomi	20.00	50.00
NNO Nia Jax	60.00	120.00
NNO Peyton Royce	80.00	150.00

2016 Topps Heritage WWE Dual Autographs

STATED PRINT RUN 11 SER.#'d SETS

NNO Asuka/N.Jax	50.00	100.00
NNO B.Knobbs/J.Sags	25.00	60.00
NNO Charlotte/B.Lynch	125.00	250.00
NNO F.Balor/S.Joe	80.00	150.00

NNO J.Roberts/J.Neidhart	50.00	100.00
NNO J.Cena/Sting	100.00	200.00
NNO K.Owens/D.Ziggler	60.00	120.00
NNO N.Bella/B.Bella	60.00	120.00
NNO R.Reigns/D.Ambrose	50.00	100.00
NNO S.Zayn/H.Itami	25.00	60.00
NNO S.Banks/Bayley	125.00	250.00
NNO Tatanka	25.00	60.00
Typhoon		

2016 Topps Heritage WWE NXT University of Central Florida Mat Relics

*BRONZE/99: .5X TO 1.2X BASIC MEM
GOLD/10: UNPRICED DUE TO SCARCITY
STATED PRINT RUN 99 SER.#'d SETS

NNO Alex Riley	2.50	6.00
NNO Asuka	10.00	25.00
NNO Bayley	6.00	15.00
NNO Carmella	6.00	15.00
NNO Colin Cassady	5.00	12.00
NNO Enzo Amore	5.00	12.00
NNO Nia Jax	4.00	10.00
NNO Sami Zayn	4.00	10.00
NNO Samoa Joe	6.00	15.00
NNO Tye Dillinger	3.00	8.00

2016 Topps Heritage WWE Record Breakers

COMPLETE SET (30)	12.00	30.00

*P.P.BLACK/1: UNPRICED DUE TO SCARCITY
*P.P.CYAN/1: UNPRICED DUE TO SCARCITY
*P.P.MAGENTA/1: UNPRICED DUE TO SCARCITY
*P.P.YELLOW/1: UNPRICED DUE TO SCARCITY

1 Bruno Sammartino	.40	1.00
2 John Cena	1.50	4.00
3 Brock Lesnar	1.50	4.00
4 Andre the Giant	1.00	2.50
5 Ric Flair	1.25	3.00
6 Triple H	1.25	3.00
7 Randy Orton	1.00	2.50
8 Edge	1.00	2.50
9 Honky Tonk Man	.40	1.00
10 Chris Jericho	1.00	2.50
11 Lex Luger	.60	1.50
12 Ric Flair	1.50	4.00
13 Nikki Bella	1.25	3.00
14 Eve Torres	.75	2.00
15 The Dudley Boyz	.75	2.00
16 Edge	1.00	2.50
17 Finn Balor	1.25	3.00
18 Paige	1.25	3.00
19 The Ascension	.40	1.00
20 Neville	1.00	2.50
21 The British Bulldog	.50	1.25
22 Big Boss Man	.60	1.50
23 Harlem Heat	.75	2.00
24 Undertaker	1.50	4.00
25 Stone Cold Steve Austin	2.00	5.00
26 Roman Reigns	1.25	3.00
27 Kane	.60	1.50
28 Triple H	1.50	4.00
29 Kane	.60	1.50
30 Bret Hit Man Hart	1.00	2.50

2016 Topps Heritage WWE Survivor Series 2015 Mat Relics

*BRONZE/99: SAME VALUE AS BASIC MEM
*SILVER/50: .5X TO 1.2X BASIC MEM
*BLUE/25: .6X TO 1.5X BASIC MEM
*GOLD/10: UNPRICED DUE TO SCARCITY
*P.P.BLACK/1: UNPRICED DUE TO SCARCITY
*P.P.CYAN/1: UNPRICED DUE TO SCARCITY
*P.P.MAGENTA/1: UNPRICED DUE TO SCARCITY
*P.P.YELLOW/1: UNPRICED DUE TO SCARCITY
RANDOMLY INSERTED INTO PACKS

NNO Alberto Del Rio	4.00	10.00
NNO Bray Wyatt	10.00	25.00
NNO Bubba Ray Dudley	5.00	12.00
NNO Charlotte	8.00	20.00
NNO D-Von Dudley	4.00	10.00
NNO Dean Ambrose	8.00	20.00
NNO Dolph Ziggler	3.00	8.00
NNO Goldust	4.00	10.00
NNO Jey Uso	2.50	6.00
NNO Jimmy Uso	2.50	6.00
NNO Kalisto	6.00	15.00
NNO Kane	4.00	10.00
NNO Kevin Owens	6.00	15.00
NNO Luke Harper	2.50	6.00
NNO Paige	8.00	20.00
NNO Roman Reigns	8.00	20.00
NNO Sheamus	6.00	15.00
NNO Titus O'Neil	2.50	6.00
NNO Tyler Breeze	2.50	6.00
NNO Undertaker	10.00	25.00

2016 Topps Heritage WWE Swatch Relics

*BRONZE/150: SAME VALUE AS BASIC MEM
*SILVER/50: .5X TO 1.2X BASIC MEM
*BLUE/25: .6X TO 1.5X BASIC MEM
*GOLD/10: UNPRICED DUE TO SCARCITY
*P.P.BLACK/1: UNPRICED DUE TO SCARCITY
*P.P.CYAN/1: UNPRICED DUE TO SCARCITY
*P.P.MAGENTA/1: UNPRICED DUE TO SCARCITY
*P.P.YELLOW/1: UNPRICED DUE TO SCARCITY
RANDOMLY INSERTED INTO PACKS

1 Aiden English	2.50	6.00
2 Alberto Del Rio	4.00	10.00
3 Asuka	10.00	25.00
4 Bayley	6.00	15.00
5 Big E	2.50	6.00
6 Bray Wyatt	10.00	25.00
7 Brock Lesnar	12.00	30.00
8 Bubba Ray Dudley	5.00	12.00
9 Cesaro	5.00	12.00
10 Charlotte	8.00	20.00
11 D-Von Dudley	4.00	10.00
12 Dean Ambrose	8.00	20.00
13 Dolph Ziggler	3.00	8.00
14 Finn Balor	8.00	20.00
15 Jey Uso	2.50	6.00
16 Jimmy Uso	2.50	6.00
17 John Cena	12.00	30.00
18 Kevin Owens	6.00	15.00
19 Kofi Kingston	2.50	6.00
20 Paige	8.00	20.00
21 Roman Reigns	8.00	20.00
22 Samoa Joe	6.00	15.00
23 Sheamus	6.00	15.00
24 Simon Gotch	4.00	10.00

25 Xavier Woods	2.50	6.00
26 Zack Ryder	2.50	6.00

2016 Topps Heritage WWE Turn Back the Clock

COMPLETE SET (15)	10.00	25.00

*P.P.BLACK/1: UNPRICED DUE TO SCARCITY
*P.P.CYAN/1: UNPRICED DUE TO SCARCITY
*P.P.MAGENTA/1: UNPRICED DUE TO SCARCITY
*P.P.YELLOW/1: UNPRICED DUE TO SCARCITY
RANDOMLY INSERTED INTO PACKS

1 The Iron Sheik	.50	1.25
2 Andre the Giant	1.50	4.00
3 Ricky The Dragon Steamboat	.60	1.50
4 Jake The Snake Roberts	1.00	2.50
5 Texas Tornado	.75	2.00
6 Big Boss Man	.75	2.00
7 Hacksaw Jim Duggan	.50	1.25
8 Rowdy Roddy Piper	1.50	4.00
9 Tatanka	.50	1.25
10 Undertaker	2.00	5.00
11 Macho Man Randy Savage	1.25	3.00
12 Sgt. Slaughter	.60	1.50
13 Shawn Michaels	2.00	5.00
14 Bret Hit Man Hart	1.25	3.00
15 The British Bulldog	.60	1.50

2016 Topps Heritage WWE WCW/nWo All-Stars

COMPLETE SET (40)	20.00	50.00

*P.P.BLACK/1: UNPRICED DUE TO SCARCITY
*P.P.CYAN/1: UNPRICED DUE TO SCARCITY
*P.P.MAGENTA/1: UNPRICED DUE TO SCARCITY
*P.P.YELLOW/1: UNPRICED DUE TO SCARCITY

1 Scott Hall	1.50	4.00
2 Kevin Nash	1.50	4.00
3 Trillionaire Ted DiBiase	.75	2.00
4 The Giant	1.25	3.00
5 Syxx	1.00	2.50
6 Vincent	.60	1.50
7 Miss Elizabeth	.60	1.50
8 Mr. Wallstreet	.60	1.50
9 Big Bubba Rogers	1.00	2.50
10 Macho Man Randy Savage	1.50	4.00
11 Curt Hennig	1.50	4.00
12 Rick Rude	1.00	2.50
13 Dusty Rhodes	.60	1.50
14 Bret Hit Man Hart	1.50	4.00
15 Stevie Ray	.60	1.50
16 Lex Luger	1.00	2.50
17 Sting	1.50	4.00
18 Shawn Michaels	2.50	6.00
19 Booker T	1.25	3.00
20 Ric Flair	2.50	6.00
21 Arn Anderson	.60	1.50
22 Diamond Dallas Page	1.00	2.50
23 Rowdy Roddy Piper	2.00	5.00
24 Ultimate Warrior	1.50	4.00
25 The British Bulldog	.75	2.00
26 Jim The Anvil Neidhart	.60	1.50
27 Hacksaw Jim Duggan	.60	1.50
28 Chris Jericho	1.50	4.00
29 Eddie Guerrero	1.50	4.00
30 Dean Malenko	.60	1.50
31 Mr. Wonderful Paul Orndorff	.60	1.50
32 Terry Funk	.60	1.50
33 Larry Zbyszko	.60	1.50

34	John Tenta	.60	1.50
35	Bam Bam Bigelow	.75	2.00
36	Brian Pillman	.75	2.00
37	Steven Regal	.60	1.50
38	Brian Knobbs	.60	1.50
39	Jerry Sags	.75	2.00
40	Madusa	.75	2.00

2017 Topps Heritage WWE

Subset included: L = Legends (68-100)

COMPLETE SET (100) 10.00 25.00
UNOPENED BOX (24 PACKS)
UNOPENED PACK (9 CARDS)
*BRONZE: .5X TO 1.2X BASIC CARDS
*BLUE/99: .75X TO 2X BASIC CARDS
*SILVER/25: 1.2X TO 3X BASIC CARDS
*GOLD/10: 2X TO 5X BASIC CARDS
*RED/1: UNPRICED DUE TO SCARCITY
*P.P.BLACK/1: UNPRICED DUE TO SCARCITY
*P.P.CYAN/1: UNPRICED DUE TO SCARCITY
*P.P.MAGENTA/1: UNPRICED DUE TO SCARCITY
*P.P.YELLOW/1: UNPRICED DUE TO SCARCITY

1	Asuka	1.25	3.00
2	Bobby Roode	1.00	2.50
3	Ember Moon	1.00	2.50
4	Eric Young	.75	2.00
5	Hideo Itami	.60	1.50
6	Johnny Gargano	.40	1.00
7	Liv Morgan	.60	1.50
8	Tommaso Ciampa	.40	1.00
9	The Rock	2.00	5.00
10	Alicia Fox	.60	1.50
11	Austin Aries	.75	2.00
12	Bayley	1.25	3.00
13	Big Cass	.50	1.25
14	Big E	.50	1.25
15	Bob Backlund	.40	1.00
16	The Brian Kendrick	.40	1.00
17	Brock Lesnar	2.00	5.00
18	Cesaro	.75	2.00
19	Charlotte Flair	1.50	4.00
20	Chris Jericho	1.00	2.50
21	Enzo Amore	1.25	3.00
22	Finn Balor	1.50	4.00
23	Goldberg	1.50	4.00
24	Karl Anderson	.40	1.00
25	Kevin Owens	1.00	2.50
26	Kofi Kingston	.50	1.25
27	Lana	1.25	3.00
28	Luke Gallows	.60	1.50
29	Mick Foley	1.00	2.50
30	Roman Reigns	1.25	3.00
31	Rusev	.75	2.00
32	Sami Zayn	.50	1.25
33	Samoa Joe	1.25	3.00
34	Sasha Banks	1.25	3.00
35	Seth Rollins	1.25	3.00
36	Sheamus	.75	2.00
37	Triple H	1.00	2.50
38	Xavier Woods	.50	1.25
39	AJ Styles	2.00	5.00
40	Alexa Bliss	2.00	5.00
41	Baron Corbin	.60	1.50
42	Becky Lynch	1.25	3.00
43	Bray Wyatt	1.00	2.50
44	Carmella	1.00	2.50
45	Chad Gable	.50	1.25
46	Daniel Bryan	1.50	4.00
47	Dean Ambrose	1.25	3.00
48	Dolph Ziggler	.60	1.50
49	Heath Slater	.40	1.00
50	Jason Jordan	.50	1.25
51	Jey Uso	.50	1.25
52	Jimmy Uso	.50	1.25
53	John Cena	2.00	5.00
54	Kalisto	.60	1.50
55	Kane	.50	1.25
56	Luke Harper	.40	1.00
57	Maryse	.75	2.00
58	The Miz	.75	2.00
59	Mojo Rawley	.50	1.25
60	Naomi	.75	2.00
61	Natalya	.75	2.00
62	Nikki Bella	1.00	2.50
63	Randy Orton	1.00	2.50
64	Rhyno	.40	1.00
65	Shinsuke Nakamura	1.00	2.50
66	Undertaker	1.50	4.00
67	Zack Ryder	.40	1.00
68	Alundra Blayze L	.50	1.25
69	Andre the Giant L	.75	2.00
70	Batista L	.75	2.00
71	Bret Hit Man Hart L	.75	2.00
72	British Bulldog L	.40	1.00
73	Brutus The Barber Beefcake L	.40	1.00
74	Diamond Dallas Page L	.50	1.25
75	Dusty Rhodes L	.50	1.25
76	Edge L	1.00	2.50
77	Fit Finlay L	.40	1.00
78	Jake The Snake Roberts L	.50	1.25
79	Jim The Anvil Neidhart L	.40	1.00
80	Ken Shamrock L	.40	1.00
81	Kevin Nash L	.60	1.50
82	Lex Luger L	.50	1.25
83	Terri Runnels L	.40	1.00
84	Macho Man Randy Savage L	.75	2.00
85	Million Dollar Man Ted DiBiase L	.50	1.25
86	Mr. Perfect L	.75	2.00
87	Ravishing Rick Rude L	.60	1.50
88	Ric Flair L	1.00	2.50
89	Rob Van Dam L	.75	2.00
90	Ron Simmons L	.50	1.25
91	Rowdy Roddy Piper L	.75	2.00
92	Scott Hall L	.50	1.25
93	Sgt. Slaughter L	.50	1.25
94	Shawn Michaels L	1.00	2.50
95	Sid Vicious L	.50	1.25
96	Sting L	1.25	3.00
97	Stone Cold Steve Austin L	1.50	4.00
98	Trish Stratus L	1.50	4.00
99	Ultimate Warrior L	.75	2.00
100	Wendi Richter L	.50	1.25

2017 Topps Heritage WWE Thirty Years of SummerSlam

COMPLETE SET (50) 5.00 12.00
*P.P.BLACK/1: UNPRICED DUE TO SCARCITY
*P.P.CYAN/1: UNPRICED DUE TO SCARCITY
*P.P.MAGENTA/1: UNPRICED DUE TO SCARCITY
*P.P.YELLOW/1: UNPRICED DUE TO SCARCITY
STATED ODDS 2:1

1	Ultimate Warrior	.50	1.25
2	The Mega Powers	.50	1.25
3	Ultimate Warrior	.50	1.25
4	Texas Tornado	.25	.60
5	Hart Foundation	.50	1.25
6	Ultimate Warrior	.50	1.25
7	Bret Hit Man Hart	.50	1.25
8	Virgil	.25	.60
9	Ultimate Warrior	.50	1.25
10	British Bulldog	.25	.60
11	Lex Luger	.30	.75
12	Alundra Blayze	.30	.75
13	Razor Ramon	.30	.75
14	Shawn Michaels	.60	1.50
15	Diesel	.40	1.00
16	Mankind	.60	1.50
17	Shawn Michaels	.60	1.50
18	Mankind	.60	1.50
19	Bret Hit Man Hart	.50	1.25
20	Triple H	.60	1.50
21	Stone Cold Steve Austin	1.00	2.50
22	Unholy Alliance	1.00	2.50
23	Mankind	.60	1.50
24	X-Pac	.25	.60
25	X-Pac	.25	.60
26	The Rock	1.25	3.00
27	Shawn Michaels	.60	1.50
28	Brock Lesnar	1.25	3.00
29	Kane	.30	.75
30	Kurt Angle	.50	1.25
31	JBL	.30	.75
32	John Cena	1.25	3.00
33	Edge	.60	1.50
34	John Cena	1.25	3.00
35	Undertaker	1.00	2.50
36	Randy Orton	.60	1.50
37	Randy Orton	.60	1.50
38	Team WWE	1.00	2.50
39	Randy Orton	.60	1.50
40	Brock Lesnar	1.25	3.00
41	Daniel Bryan	1.00	2.50
42	Randy Orton	.60	1.50
43	Roman Reigns	.75	2.00
44	Brock Lesnar	1.25	3.00
45	Seth Rollins	.75	2.00
46	Undertaker	1.00	2.50
47	Charlotte	1.00	2.50
48	AJ Styles	1.25	3.00
49	Finn Balor	1.00	2.50
50	Brock Lesnar	1.25	3.00

2017 Topps Heritage WWE Autographed NXT TakeOver Toronto 2016 Mat Relics

STATED ODDS 1:9,056
STATED PRINT RUN 10 SER. #'d SETS
UNPRICED DUE TO SCARCITY

NNO Asuka
NNO Booby Roode
NNO Johnny Gargano
NNO Mickie James
NNO Samoa Joe
NNO Shinsuke Nakamura
NNO Tommaso Ciampa

2017 Topps Heritage WWE Autographed Survivor Series 2016 Mat Relics

STATED ODDS 1:3,544
STATED PRINT RUN 10 SER. #'d SETS
UNPRICED DUE TO SCARCITY

NNO AJ Styles

NNO Alexa Bliss
NNO Alicia Fox
NNO Bayley
NNO Becky Lynch
NNO Braun Strowman
NNO Bray Wyatt
NNO Brock Lesnar
NNO Carmella
NNO Charlotte Flair
NNO Chris Jericho
NNO Goldberg
NNO Kevin Owens
NNO Natalya
NNO Randy Orton
NNO Roman Reigns
NNO Sasha Banks
NNO Seth Rollins

2017 Topps Heritage WWE Autographs

*BLUE/50: .5X TO 1.2X BASIC AUTOS
*SILVER/25: .6X TO 1.5X BASIC AUTOS
*GOLD/10: UNPRICED DUE TO SCARCITY
*RED/1: UNPRICED DUE TO SCARCITY
*P.P.BLACK/1: UNPRICED DUE TO SCARCITY
*P.P.CYAN/1: UNPRICED DUE TO SCARCITY
*P.P.MAGENTA/1: UNPRICED DUE TO SCARCITY
*P.P.YELLOW/1: UNPRICED DUE TO SCARCITY
STATED ODDS 1:24

NNO	AJ Styles	15.00	40.00
NNO	Alexa Bliss	60.00	120.00
NNO	Asuka	12.00	30.00
NNO	Bayley	15.00	40.00
NNO	Becky Lynch	15.00	40.00
NNO	Bobby Roode	12.00	30.00
NNO	Bray Wyatt	12.00	30.00
NNO	Bret Hit Man Hart	20.00	50.00
NNO	Brutus The Barber Beefcake	12.00	30.00
NNO	Charlotte Flair	15.00	40.00
NNO	Chris Jericho	10.00	25.00
NNO	Dean Ambrose	8.00	20.00
NNO	Ember Moon	6.00	15.00
NNO	Eric Young	6.00	15.00
NNO	Finn Balor	15.00	40.00
NNO	Fit Finlay	10.00	25.00
NNO	Goldberg	30.00	80.00
NNO	Kevin Owens	8.00	20.00
NNO	Sasha Banks	20.00	50.00
NNO	Shinsuke Nakamura	15.00	40.00
NNO	Sting	15.00	40.00

2017 Topps Heritage WWE Autographs Blue

STATED ODDS 1:93
STATED PRINT RUN 50 SER.#'d SETS

NNO	Undertaker	120.00	250.00

2017 Topps Heritage WWE Autographs Silver

NNO	Brock Lesnar	30.00	75.00

2017 Topps Heritage WWE Bizarre SummerSlam Matches

COMPLETE SET (10) 3.00 8.00
*P.P.BLACK/1: UNPRICED DUE TO SCARCITY
*P.P.CYAN/1: UNPRICED DUE TO SCARCITY
*P.P.MAGENTA/1: UNPRICED DUE TO SCARCITY

*P.P.YELLOW/1: UNPRICED DUE TO SCARCITY
STATED ODDS 1:3

1	Big Boss Man	.40	1.00
2	Undertaker	1.25	3.00
3	Mankind	.75	2.00
4	British Bulldog	.30	.75
5	X-Pac	.30	.75
6	Ken Shamrock	.30	.75
7	Kane	.40	1.00
8	Ric Flair	.75	2.00
9	Bray Wyatt	.75	2.00
10	Rusev	.60	1.50

2017 Topps Heritage WWE Commemorative Patches

*BRONZE/99: .5X TO 1.2X BASIC MEM
*BLUE/50: .6X TO 1.5X BASIC MEM
*SILVER/25: .75X TO 2X BASIC MEM
*GOLD/10: UNPRICED DUE TO SCARCITY
*RED/1: UNPRICED DUE TO SCARCITY
*P.P.BLACK/1: UNPRICED DUE TO SCARCITY
*P.P.CYAN/1: UNPRICED DUE TO SCARCITY
*P.P.MAGENTA/1: UNPRICED DUE TO SCARCITY
*P.P.YELLOW/1: UNPRICED DUE TO SCARCITY
STATED ODDS 1:115

NNO	AJ Styles	6.00	15.00
NNO	Asuka	4.00	10.00
NNO	Bobby Roode	3.00	8.00
NNO	Charlotte Flair	5.00	12.00
NNO	Chris Jericho	3.00	8.00
NNO	Dean Ambrose	4.00	10.00
NNO	Dolph Ziggler	2.00	5.00
NNO	Ember Moon	3.00	8.00
NNO	Eric Young	2.50	6.00
NNO	Hideo Itami	2.00	5.00
NNO	John Cena	6.00	15.00
NNO	Kevin Owens	3.00	8.00
NNO	The Miz	2.50	6.00
NNO	Ric Flair	3.00	8.00
NNO	Roman Reigns	4.00	10.00
NNO	Rowdy Roddy Piper	2.50	6.00
NNO	Seth Rollins	4.00	10.00
NNO	Shawn Michaels	3.00	8.00
NNO	Sting	4.00	10.00
NNO	Trish Stratus	5.00	12.00

2017 Topps Heritage WWE Dual Autographs

STATED ODDS 1:2,264
STATED PRINT RUN 10 SER.#'d SETS
RANDOMLY INSERTED INTO PACKS

NNO	Big E/K.Kingston/10	30.00	75.00
NNO	B.Sammartino/L.Zbyszko/9	100.00	200.00
NNO	J.Lawler/M.Cole/10	50.00	100.00
NNO	Primo	25.00	60.00
	Epico/10		
NNO	S.Rollins/R.Reigns/10	60.00	120.00

2017 Topps Heritage WWE Kiss

*GOLD/10: UNPRICED DUE TO SCARCITY
*RED/1: UNPRICED DUE TO SCARCITY
STATED ODDS 1:685

NNO	Alexa Bliss	60.00	120.00
NNO	Asuka	25.00	60.00
NNO	Carmella	30.00	80.00
NNO	Charlotte Flair	25.00	60.00
NNO	Dana Brooke	20.00	50.00
NNO	Ember Moon	20.00	50.00
NNO	Liv Morgan	50.00	100.00

2017 Topps Heritage WWE Kiss Autographs

*GOLD/10: UNPRICED DUE TO SCARCITY
*RED/1: UNPRICED DUE TO SCARCITY
STATED ODDS 1:2,717

NNO	Alexa Bliss	200.00	350.00
NNO	Asuka	75.00	150.00
NNO	Carmella	60.00	120.00
NNO	Charlotte Flair	60.00	120.00
NNO	Dana Brooke	75.00	150.00
NNO	Ember Moon	50.00	100.00
NNO	Liv Morgan	50.00	100.00

2017 Topps Heritage WWE NXT TakeOver Toronto 2016 Mat Relics

*BRONZE/99: .5X TO 1.2X BASIC MEM
*BLUE/50: .6X TO 1.5X BASIC MEM
*SILVER/25: .75X TO 2X BASIC MEM
*GOLD/10: UNPRICED DUE TO SCARCITY
*RED/1: UNPRICED DUE TO SCARCITY
*P.P.BLACK/1: UNPRICED DUE TO SCARCITY
*P.P.CYAN/1: UNPRICED DUE TO SCARCITY
*P.P.MAGENTA/1: UNPRICED DUE TO SCARCITY
*P.P.YELLOW/1: UNPRICED DUE TO SCARCITY
RANDOMLY INSERTED INTO PACKS

NNO	Akam	1.50	4.00
NNO	Asuka	5.00	12.00
NNO	Bobby Roode	4.00	10.00
NNO	Johnny Gargano	1.50	4.00
NNO	Mickie James	2.50	6.00
NNO	Rezar	1.50	4.00
NNO	Samoa Joe	5.00	12.00
NNO	Shinsuke Nakamura	4.00	10.00
NNO	Tommaso Ciampa	1.50	4.00
NNO	Tye Dillinger	3.00	8.00

2017 Topps Heritage WWE Roster Updates

COMPLETE SET (10) 12.00 30.00
*P.P.BLACK/1: UNPRICED DUE TO SCARCITY
*P.P.CYAN/1: UNPRICED DUE TO SCARCITY
*P.P.MAGENTA/1: UNPRICED DUE TO SCARCITY
*P.P.YELLOW/1: UNPRICED DUE TO SCARCITY
RANDOMLY INSERTED INTO PACKS

R1	Alexander Wolfe	2.00	5.00
R2	Kassius Ohno	1.50	4.00
R3	Nikki Cross	3.00	8.00
R4	Roderick Strong	2.00	5.00
R5	Tye Dillinger	3.00	8.00
R6	Cedric Alexander	2.50	6.00
R7	Gentleman Jack Gallagher	3.00	8.00
R8	Neville	2.50	6.00
R9	Rich Swann	1.50	4.00
R10	TJ Perkins	1.50	4.00

2017 Topps Heritage WWE Shirt Relics

*BLUE/50: .5X TO 1.2X BASIC MEM
*SILVER/25: .6X TO 1.5X BASIC MEM
*GOLD/10: UNPRICED DUE TO SCARCITY
*RED/1: UNPRICED DUE TO SCARCITY

RC	Carmella	5.00	12.00
RN	Naomi	4.00	10.00
RS	Sheamus	4.00	10.00
RAA	Andrade Cien Almas	2.00	5.00
RAC	Apollo Crews	2.50	6.00
RAE	Aiden English	2.00	5.00
RAF	Alicia Fox	3.00	8.00
RBK	Becky Lynch	6.00	15.00
RBL	Brock Lesnar	10.00	25.00
RBR	Bobby Roode	5.00	12.00
RCA	Curtis Axel	2.00	5.00
RCF	Charlotte Flair	8.00	20.00
RDY	Darren Young	2.00	5.00
RHI	Hideo Itami	3.00	8.00
RJC	John Cena	10.00	25.00
RJG	Johnny Gargano	2.00	5.00
RJJ	JoJo	3.00	8.00
RKA	Karl Anderson	2.00	5.00
RLH	Luke Harper	2.00	5.00
RNJ	No Way Jose	2.00	5.00
RNN	Natalya	4.00	10.00
RRO	Randy Orton	5.00	12.00
RSB	Sasha Banks	6.00	15.00
RSN	Shinsuke Nakamura	5.00	12.00
RSR	Seth Rollins	6.00	15.00
RSU	Summer Rae	5.00	12.00
RTC	Tommaso Ciampa	2.00	5.00
RZR	Zack Ryder	2.00	5.00

2017 Topps Heritage WWE SummerSlam All-Stars

COMPLETE SET (30) 6.00 15.00
*P.P.BLACK/1: UNPRICED DUE TO SCARCITY
*P.P.CYAN/1: UNPRICED DUE TO SCARCITY
*P.P.MAGENTA/1: UNPRICED DUE TO SCARCITY
*P.P.YELLOW/1: UNPRICED DUE TO SCARCITY
STATED ODDS 1:1

1	Undertaker	1.50	4.00
2	Edge	1.00	2.50
3	Triple H	1.00	2.50
4	Bret Hit Man Hart	.75	2.00
5	Shawn Michaels	1.00	2.50
6	Randy Orton	1.00	2.50
7	Kane	.50	1.25
8	Ultimate Warrior	.75	2.00
9	Rob Van Dam	.75	2.00
10	Brock Lesnar	2.00	5.00
11	Big Show	.50	1.25
12	Chris Jericho	1.00	2.50
13	Kurt Angle	.75	2.00
14	John Cena	2.00	5.00
15	Tatanka	.40	1.00
16	Jerry The King Lawler	.50	1.25
17	Earthquake	.40	1.00
18	Irwin R. Schyster	.40	1.00
19	British Bulldog	.30	.75
20	Stone Cold Steve Austin	1.50	4.00
21	Daniel Bryan	1.50	4.00
22	Mick Foley	1.00	2.50
23	The Rock	1.50	4.00
24	Sheamus	.75	2.00
25	Kofi Kingston	.50	1.25
26	X-Pac	.40	1.00
27	Dolph Ziggler	.60	1.50
28	Ric Flair	1.00	2.50
29	Texas Tornado	.40	1.00
30	Typhoon	.40	1.00

2017 Topps Heritage WWE Survivor Series 2016 Mat Relics

*BRONZE/99: .5X TO 1.2X BASIC MEM
*BLUE/50: .6X TO 1.5X BASIC MEM
*SILVER/25: .75X TO 2X BASIC MEM
*GOLD/10: UNPRICED DUE TO SCARCITY
*RED/1: UNPRICED DUE TO SCARCITY
*P.P.BLACK/1: UNPRICED DUE TO SCARCITY
*P.P.CYAN/1: UNPRICED DUE TO SCARCITY
*P.P.MAGENTA/1: UNPRICED DUE TO SCARCITY
*P.P.YELLOW/1: UNPRICED DUE TO SCARCITY
STATED ODDS 1:175

NNO	AJ Styles	6.00	15.00
NNO	Alexa Bliss	15.00	40.00
NNO	Alicia Fox	5.00	12.00
NNO	Bayley	6.00	15.00
NNO	Becky Lynch	6.00	15.00
NNO	Braun Strowman	5.00	12.00
NNO	Bray Wyatt	6.00	15.00
NNO	Brock Lesnar	8.00	20.00
NNO	Carmella	5.00	12.00
NNO	Charlotte Flair	6.00	15.00
NNO	Chris Jericho	6.00	15.00
NNO	Dean Ambrose	4.00	10.00
NNO	Goldberg	6.00	15.00
NNO	Kevin Owens	5.00	12.00
NNO	Natalya	4.00	10.00
NNO	Randy Orton	5.00	12.00
NNO	Roman Reigns	5.00	12.00
NNO	Sasha Banks	8.00	20.00
NNO	Seth Rollins	5.00	12.00
NNO	Shane McMahon	6.00	15.00

2018 Topps Heritage WWE

COMPLETE SET W/SP (119) 25.00 60.00
COMPLETE SET W/O SP (110) 10.00 25.00
UNOPENED BOX (24 PACKS)
UNOPENED PACK (6 CARDS)
*BRONZE: .6X TO 1.5X BASIC CARDS
*BLUE/99: .75X TO 2X BASIC CARDS
*SILVER/25: 2X TO 5X BASIC CARDS
*GOLD/10: UNPRICED DUE TO SCARCITY
*RED/1: UNPRICED DUE TO SCARCITY
*P.P.BLACK/1: UNPRICED DUE TO SCARCITY
*P.P.CYAN/1: UNPRICED DUE TO SCARCITY
*P.P.MAGENTA/1: UNPRICED DUE TO SCARCITY
*P.P.YELLOW/1: UNPRICED DUE TO SCARCITY

1	AJ Styles	1.00	2.50
2	Akira Tozawa	.40	1.00
3	Alexa Bliss	1.25	3.00
4	Alicia Fox	.40	1.00
5	Apollo Crews	.25	.60
6	Ariya Daivari	.25	.60
7	Asuka	.75	2.00
8	Baron Corbin	.40	1.00
9	Bayley	.40	1.00
10	Becky Lynch	.60	1.50
11	Big Cass	.30	.75
12	Big E	.30	.75
13	Big Show	.25	.60
14	Bobby Roode	.40	1.00
15	Braun Strowman	.60	1.50
16	Bray Wyatt	.60	1.50
17	Brie Bella	.50	1.25
18	Carmella	.50	1.25
19	Cedric Alexander	.25	.60
20	Cesaro	.50	1.25

21	Chad Gable	.25	.60
22	Charlotte Flair	.75	2.00
23	Chris Jericho	.60	1.50
24	Dean Ambrose	.50	1.25
25	Drew Gulak	.25	.60
26	Elias	.60	1.50
27	Fandango	.25	.60
28	Finn Balor	.60	1.50
29	Gentleman Jack Gallagher	.30	.75
30	Goldust	.50	1.25
31	Jason Jordan	.25	.60
32	Jeff Hardy	.50	1.25
33	Jey Uso	.25	.60
34	Jimmy Uso	.25	.60
35	Jinder Mahal	.30	.75
36	John Cena	1.00	2.50
37	Kalisto	.25	.60
38	Kane	.40	1.00
39	Karl Anderson	.25	.60
40	Kevin Owens	.60	1.50
41	Kofi Kingston	.30	.75
42	Kurt Angle	.60	1.50
43	Lana	.60	1.50
44	Liv Morgan	.50	1.25
45	Luke Gallows	.30	.75
46	Mandy Rose	.60	1.50
47	Maria Kanellis	.50	1.25
48	Maryse	.50	1.25
49	Woken Matt Hardy	.60	1.50
50	Mickie James	.50	1.25
51	Mojo Rawley	.25	.60
52	Mustafa Ali	.25	.60
53	Naomi	.30	.75
54	Natalya	.30	.75
55	Nia Jax	.40	1.00
56	Nikki Bella	.50	1.25
57	Noam Dar	.25	.60
58	Paige	.60	1.50
59	Pete Dunne	.25	.60
60	R-Truth	.30	.75
61	Randy Orton	.60	1.50
62	Rhyno	.25	.60
63	Roman Reigns	.60	1.50
64	Ruby Riott	.40	1.00
65	Rusev	.40	1.00
66	Sami Zayn	.25	.60
67	Samoa Joe	.50	1.25
68	Sarah Logan	.25	.60
69	Sasha Banks	.75	2.00
70	Seth Rollins	.60	1.50
71	Shane McMahon	.50	1.25
72	Sheamus	.50	1.25
73	Shelton Benjamin	.30	.75
74	Shinsuke Nakamura	.60	1.50
75	Sin Cara	.30	.75
76	Sonya Deville	.50	1.25
77	Stephanie McMahon	.50	1.25
78	Tamina	.25	.60
79	The Brian Kendrick	.40	1.00
80	The Miz	.50	1.25
81	The Rock	1.25	3.00
82	Titus O'Neil	.25	.60
83	Tony Nese	.25	.60
84	Triple H	.60	1.50
85	Tye Dillinger	.25	.60
86	Tyler Bate	.25	.60
87	Tyler Breeze	.25	.60
88	Undertaker	1.00	2.50

89	Xavier Woods	.30	.75
90	Zack Ryder	.25	.60
91	Adam Cole	.30	.75
92	Aleister Black	.30	.75
93	Alexander Wolfe	.25	.60
94	Andrade Cien Almas	.40	1.00
95	Billie Kay	.50	1.25
96	Bobby Fish	.25	.60
97	Drew McIntyre	.40	1.00
98	Ember Moon	.50	1.25
99	Eric Young	.30	.75
100	Johnny Gargano	.25	.60
101	Kairi Sane	.60	1.50
102	Kassius Ohno	.25	.60
103	Killian Dain	.30	.75
104	Kyle O'Reilly	.30	.75
105	Nikki Cross	.40	1.00
106	Oney Lorcan	.30	.75
107	Peyton Royce	.60	1.50
108	Roderick Strong	.25	.60
109	Tommaso Ciampa	.25	.60
110	Velveteen Dream	.25	.60
111	Aiden English SP	1.25	3.00
112	Ariya Daivari SP	1.25	3.00
113	Dash Wilder SP	1.50	4.00
114	Harper SP	2.00	5.00
115	Konnor SP	1.25	3.00
116	R-Truth SP	1.50	4.00
117	Rowan SP	2.00	5.00
118	Scott Dawson SP	1.50	4.00
119	Viktor SP	1.25	3.00

2018 Topps Heritage WWE Autographed NXT TakeOver War Games 2017 Mat Relics

STATED PRINT RUN 10 SER.#'d SETS
UNPRICED DUE TO SCARCITY

NXTAAC Adam Cole
NXTABF Bobby Fish
NXTADM Drew McIntyre
NXTAEM Ember Moon
NXTAKD Killian Dain
NXTAKO Kyle O'Reilly
NXTARS Roderick Strong

2018 Topps Heritage WWE Autographed Survivor Series 2017 Mat Relics

STATED PRINT RUN 10 SER.#'d SETS
UNPRICED DUE TO SCARCITY

SSAAJ AJ Styles
SSAAS Asuka
SSABR Booby Roode
SSABS Braun Strowman
SSAKA Kurt Angle
SSANJ Nia Jax
SSARO Randy Orton
SSASB Sasha Banks
SSASJ Samoa Joe
SSASN Shinsuke Nakamura
SSATH Triple H

2018 Topps Heritage WWE Autographed TLC 2017 Mat Relics

STATED PRINT RUN 10 SER.#'d SETS
UNPRICED DUE TO SCARCITY

TLCAAJ AJ Styles

TLCABS Braun Strowman
TLCAKA Kurt Angle
TLCASH Sheamus
TLCATM The Miz

2018 Topps Heritage WWE Autographed TLC Commemorative Medallion Relics

STATED PRINT RUN 10 SER.#'d SETS
UNPRICED DUE TO SCARCITY

CTMAAJ AJ Styles
CTMABC Baron Corbin
CTMABS Braun Strowman
CTMADZ Dolph Ziggler
CTMAKA Kane
CTMAKA Kurt Angle
CTMAMZ The Miz
CTMASA Sheamus
CTMASH Sheamus
CTMATM The Miz

2018 Topps Heritage WWE Autographs

*BLUE/50: .5X TO 1.2X BASIC AUTOS
*SILVER/25: .6X TO 1.5X BASIC AUTOS
*GOLD/10: UNPRICED DUE TO SCARCITY
*RED/1: UNPRICED DUE TO SCARCITY
STATED PRINT RUN 99 SER.#'d SETS

AAB	Alexa Bliss	50.00	100.00
AAC	Adam Cole	15.00	40.00
AAS	AJ Styles	15.00	40.00
AAS	Asuka	12.00	30.00
ABA	Bayley	12.00	30.00
ABE	Big E	5.00	12.00
ABL	Becky Lynch	15.00	40.00
ABS	Braun Strowman	12.00	30.00
ACF	Charlotte Flair	15.00	40.00
AFB	Finn Balor	12.00	30.00
AJH	Jeff Hardy	12.00	30.00
AKA	Kurt Angle	10.00	25.00
AKK	Kofi Kingston	6.00	15.00
AKO	Kevin Owens	6.00	15.00
ALM	Liv Morgan	10.00	25.00
AMH	Matt Hardy	10.00	25.00
AMR	Mandy Rose	15.00	40.00
ASB	Sasha Banks	12.00	30.00
ASN	Shinsuke Nakamura	10.00	25.00
AXW	Xavier Woods	5.00	12.00
AALB	Aleister Black	6.00	15.00

2018 Topps Heritage WWE Autographs Silver

ACA	Carmella	12.00	30.00
ASM	Stephanie McMahon	75.00	150.00
ATH	Triple H	150.00	300.00
AUN	Undertaker	125.00	250.00

2018 Topps Heritage WWE Big Legends

COMPLETE SET (50)	12.00	30.00

*BRONZE/99: .75X TO 2X BASIC CARDS
*BLUE/50: 1.2X TO 3X BASIC CARDS
*SILVER/25: 1.5X TO 4X BASIC CARDS
*GOLD/10: UNPRICED DUE TO SCARCITY
*RED/1: UNPRICED DUE TO SCARCITY
*P.P.BLACK/1: UNPRICED DUE TO SCARCITY
*P.P.CYAN/1: UNPRICED DUE TO SCARCITY

*P.P.MAGENTA/1: UNPRICED DUE TO SCARCITY
*P.P.YELLOW/1: UNPRICED DUE TO SCARCITY
STATED ODDS 2:1; 4:1 FAT PACK

BL1	Alundra Blayze	.30	.75
BL2	Andre the Giant	.60	1.50
BL3	Bam Bam Bigelow	.50	1.25
BL4	Bob Backlund	.30	.75
BL5	Booker T	.50	1.25
BL6	Bret Hit Man Hart	.75	2.00
BL7	British Bulldog	.60	1.50
BL8	Bruno Sammartino	.50	1.25
BL9	Brutus The Barber Beefcake	.30	.75
BL10	Cowboy Bob Orton	.30	.75
BL11	Dean Malenko	.30	.75
BL12	Diamond Dallas Page	.50	1.25
BL13	Dusty Rhodes	.60	1.50
BL14	Eddie Guerrero	.75	2.00
BL15	Edge	.75	2.00
BL16	George The Animal Steele	.40	1.00
BL17	Greg The Hammer Valentine	.30	.75
BL18	Hacksaw Jim Duggan	.30	.75
BL19	Harley Race	.30	.75
BL20	The Honky Tonk Man	.30	.75
BL21	Iron Sheik	.30	.75
BL22	Irwin R. Schyster	.30	.75
BL23	Jake The Snake Roberts	.40	1.00
BL24	Jerry The King Lawler	.60	1.50
BL25	Jim The Anvil Neidhart	.50	1.25
BL26	Kerry Von Erich	.30	.75
BL27	Kevin Nash	.60	1.50
BL28	Kevin Von Erich	.50	1.25
BL29	Larry Zbyszko	.30	.75
BL30	Lex Luger	.40	1.00
BL31	Lita	.75	2.00
BL32	Macho Man Randy Savage	1.00	2.50
BL33	Michael P.S. Hayes	.30	.75
BL34	Mick Foley	.60	1.50
BL35	Million Dollar Man Ted DiBiase	.40	1.00
BL36	Mr. Perfect	.40	1.00
BL37	Mr. Wonderful Paul Orndorff	.30	.75
BL38	Nikolai Volkoff	.30	.75
BL39	Ravishing Rick Rude	.40	1.00
BL40	Ric Flair	1.00	2.50
BL41	Ricky The Dragon Steamboat	.50	1.25
BL42	Ron Simmons	.40	1.00
BL43	Rowdy Roddy Piper	.75	2.00
BL44	Scott Hall	.60	1.50
BL45	Sgt. Slaughter	.40	1.00
BL46	Sid Vicious	.30	.75
BL47	Sting	.75	2.00
BL48	Stone Cold Steve Austin	1.50	4.00
BL49	Trish Stratus	1.25	3.00
BL50	Ultimate Warrior	1.25	3.00

2018 Topps Heritage WWE Big Legends Autographs

*SILVER/25: UNPRICED DUE TO SCARCITY
*GOLD/10: UNPRICED DUE TO SCARCITY
*RED/1: UNPRICED DUE TO SCARCITY

BLAAB	Alundra Blayze	6.00	15.00
BLABB	Brutus The Barber Beefcake	6.00	15.00
BLABH	Bret Hit Man Hart	25.00	60.00
BLAIS	Irwin R. Schyster	10.00	25.00
BLAJD	Hacksaw Jim Duggan	8.00	20.00
BLAJR	Jake The Snake Roberts	15.00	40.00
BLAST	Sting	25.00	60.00
BLATD	Million Dollar Man Ted DiBiase	12.00	30.00

BLATS Trish Stratus	30.00	75.00
BLADDP Diamond Dallas Page	10.00	25.00

2018 Topps Heritage WWE Dual Autographs

STATED PRINT RUN 10 SER.#'d SETS
UNPRICED DUE TO SCARCITY
DACC Epico/Primo/9
DAKR B.Kay/P.Royce/10
DALC M.Cole/J.Lawler/10
DATM S.McMahon/Triple H/10
DAUT Triple H/Undertaker/10

2018 Topps Heritage WWE Kiss

*GOLD/10: UNPRICED DUE TO SCARCITY
*RED/1: UNPRICED DUE TO SCARCITY
STATED ODDS

KCAB Alexa Bliss	60.00	120.00
KCAF Alicia Fox	15.00	40.00
KCAS Asuka	30.00	75.00
KCCC Charly Caruso	50.00	100.00
KCDB Dana Brooke	20.00	50.00
KCDF Dasha Fuentes	15.00	40.00
KCMR Mandy Rose	50.00	100.00
KCNA Natalya	15.00	40.00
KCNA Naomi	15.00	40.00
KCRY Renee Young	20.00	50.00

2018 Topps Heritage WWE Kiss Autographs

*GOLD/10: UNPRICED DUE TO SCARCITY
*RED/1: UNPRICED DUE TO SCARCITY
STATED PRINT RUN 25 SER.#'d SETS

KAAB Alexa Bliss	150.00	300.00
KAAF Alicia Fox	50.00	100.00
KAAS Asuka	60.00	120.00
KACC Charly Caruso	30.00	75.00
KADB Dana Brooke	50.00	100.00
KADF Dasha Fuentes	30.00	75.00
KAMR Mandy Rose	75.00	150.00
KANA Natalya	25.00	60.00
KARY Renee Young	30.00	75.00

2018 Topps Heritage WWE Manufactured Coins

1 John Cena	8.00	20.00
2 Brock Lesnar	6.00	15.00
3 AJ Styles	5.00	12.00
4 Roman Reigns	5.00	12.00
5 Seth Rollins	5.00	12.00
6 Dean Ambrose	4.00	10.00
7 Braun Strowman	4.00	10.00
8 Samoa Joe	4.00	10.00
9 Shinsuke Nakamura	5.00	12.00
10 Kevin Owens	4.00	10.00

2018 Topps Heritage WWE NXT TakeOver War Games 2017 Mat Relics

*BRONZE/99: .5X TO 1.2X BASIC MEM
*BLUE/50: .6X TO 1.5X BASIC MEM
*SILVER/25: .75X TO 2X BASIC MEM
*GOLD/10: UNPRICED DUE TO SCARCITY
*RED/1: UNPRICED DUE TO SCARCITY
STATED PRINT RUN 299 SER.#'d SETS

NXTAA Andrade Cien Almas	2.50	6.00
NXTAC Adam Cole	8.00	20.00
NXTAW Alexander Wolfe	2.50	6.00
NXTBF Bobby Fish	4.00	10.00
NXTDM Drew McIntyre	2.50	6.00
NXTEM Ember Moon	3.00	8.00
NXTEY Eric Young	3.00	8.00
NXTKD Killian Dain	3.00	8.00
NXTKO Kyle O'Reilly	3.00	8.00
NXTRS Roderick Strong	2.50	6.00

2018 Topps Heritage WWE Shirt Relics

*BLUE/50: .5X TO 1.2X BASIC MEM
*SILVER/25: .6X TO 1.5X BASIC MEM
*GOLD/10: UNPRICED DUE TO SCARCITY
*RED/1: UNPRICED DUE TO SCARCITY
STATED PRINT RUN 99 SER.#'d SETS

SRAB Alexa Bliss	12.00	30.00
SRAE Aiden English	4.00	10.00
SRAF Alicia Fox	3.00	8.00
SRAK Akam	3.00	8.00
SRAW Alexander Wolfe	3.00	8.00
SRBE Becky Lynch	5.00	12.00
SRBL Brock Lesnar	6.00	15.00
SRCA Carmella	5.00	12.00
SRDW Dash Wilder	3.00	8.00
SREM Ember Moon	5.00	12.00
SREY Eric Young	3.00	8.00
SRGD Goldust	3.00	8.00
SRJC John Cena	6.00	15.00
SRJJ JoJo	5.00	12.00
SRNC Nikki Cross	5.00	12.00
SRRE Rezar	3.00	8.00
SRRR Roman Reigns	8.00	20.00
SRRY Renee Young	5.00	12.00
SRSD Scott Dawson	3.00	8.00
SRSR Seth Rollins	5.00	12.00

2018 Topps Heritage WWE Survivor Series 2017 Mat Relics

*BRONZE/99: .5X TO 1.2X BASIC MEM
*BLUE/50: .6X TO 1.5X BASIC MEM
*SILVER/25: .75X TO 2X BASIC MEM
*GOLD/10: UNPRICED DUE TO SCARCITY
*RED/1: UNPRICED DUE TO SCARCITY
STATED PRINT RUN 299 SER.#'d SETS

SSAB Alexa Bliss	10.00	25.00
SSAJ AJ Styles	3.00	8.00
SSAS Asuka	5.00	12.00
SSBA Bayley	3.00	8.00
SSBL Brock Lesnar	4.00	10.00
SSBR Bobby Roode	3.00	8.00
SSBS Braun Strowman	4.00	10.00
SSCF Charlotte Flair	5.00	12.00
SSDA Dean Ambrose	2.50	6.00
SSFB Finn Balor	3.00	8.00
SSJC John Cena	4.00	10.00
SSKA Kurt Angle	2.50	6.00
SSNJ Nia Jax	2.50	6.00
SSRO Randy Orton	2.50	6.00
SSRR Roman Reigns	3.00	8.00
SSSB Sasha Banks	6.00	15.00
SSSJ Samoa Joe	4.00	10.00
SSSN Shinsuke Nakamura	3.00	8.00
SSSR Seth Rollins	3.00	8.00
SSTH Triple H	4.00	10.00

2018 Topps Heritage WWE Tag Teams and Stables

COMPLETE SET (20)	6.00	15.00

*BRONZE/99: .5X TO 1.2X BASIC CARDS
*BLUE/50: .6X TO 1.5X BASIC CARDS
*SILVER/25: 1.2X TO 3X BASIC CARDS
*GOLD/10: UNPRICED DUE TO SCARCITY
*RED/1: UNPRICED DUE TO SCARCITY
STATED ODDS 1:2; 2:1 FAT PACK

TT1 Cesaro & Sheamus	.75	2.00
TT2 The Shield	1.00	2.50
TT3 The Hardy Boyz	1.00	2.50
TT4 Heath Slater & Rhyno	.40	1.00
TT5 Luke Gallows & Karl Anderson	.50	1.25
TT6 The Miz & The Miztourage	.75	2.00
TT7 The Revival	.50	1.25
TT8 Bludgeon Brothers	.60	1.50
TT9 Breezango	.40	1.00
TT10 Shelton Benjamin & Chad Gable	.50	1.25
TT11 Kevin Owens & Sami Zayn	1.00	2.50
TT12 The Hype Bros	.40	1.00
TT13 Jinder Mahal & The Singh Brothers	.50	1.25
TT14 The New Day	.60	1.50
TT15 The Authors of Pain	.40	1.00
TT16 Heavy Machinery	.40	1.00
TT17 The Iiconics	1.00	2.50
TT18 SAnitY	.60	1.50
TT19 The Street Profits	.40	1.00
TT20 Undisputed ERA	.50	1.25

2018 Topps Heritage WWE TLC 2017 Mat Relics

*BRONZE/99: .5X TO 1.2X BASIC MEM
*BLUE/50: .6X TO 1.5X BASIC MEM
*SILVER/25: .75X TO 2X BASIC MEM
*GOLD/10: UNPRICED DUE TO SCARCITY
*RED/1: UNPRICED DUE TO SCARCITY
STATED PRINT RUN 299 SER.#'d SETS

TLCAJ AJ Styles	4.00	10.00
TLCBS Braun Strowman	2.00	5.00
TLCCE Cesaro	2.00	5.00
TLCDA Dean Ambrose	3.00	8.00
TLCFB Finn Balor	4.00	10.00
TLCKA Kurt Angle	4.00	10.00
TLCKN Kane	3.00	8.00
TLCSH Sheamus	2.00	5.00
TLCSR Seth Rollins	5.00	12.00
TLCTM The Miz	2.00	5.00

2018 Topps Heritage WWE TLC Commemorative Medallion Relics

*BRONZE/99: .5X TO 1.2X BASIC MEM
*BLUE/50: .6X TO 1.5X BASIC MEM
*SILVER/25: .75X TO 2X BASIC MEM
*GOLD/10: UNPRICED DUE TO SCARCITY
*RED/1: UNPRICED DUE TO SCARCITY
STATED PRINT RUN 199 SER.#'d SETS

CTMAB Alexa Bliss	10.00	25.00
CTMAJ AJ Styles	5.00	12.00
CTMBC Baron Corbin	4.00	10.00
CTMBL Becky Lynch	6.00	15.00
CTMBS Braun Strowman	5.00	12.00
CTMCE Cesaro	3.00	8.00
CTMDA Dean Ambrose	3.00	8.00
CTMDE Dean Ambrose	3.00	8.00
CTMDZ Dolph Ziggler	3.00	8.00
CTMJC John Cena	5.00	12.00
CTMKA Kurt Angle	3.00	8.00
CTMKA Kane	3.00	8.00
CTMKL Kalisto	3.00	8.00
CTMMZ The Miz	3.00	8.00
CTMRL Seth Rollins	4.00	10.00
CTMRR Roman Reigns	5.00	12.00
CTMSA Sheamus	3.00	8.00
CTMSH Sheamus	3.00	8.00
CTMSR Seth Rollins	3.00	8.00
CTMTM The Miz	3.00	8.00

2018 Topps Heritage WWE Top 10 Rookies

COMPLETE SET (10)	4.00	10.00

*BRONZE/99: .5X TO 1.2X BASIC CARDS
*BLUE/50: .6X TO 1.5X BASIC CARDS
*SILVER/25: .75X TO 2X BASIC CARDS
*GOLD/10: UNPRICED DUE TO SCARCITY
*RED/1: UNPRICED DUE TO SCARCITY
*P.P.BLACK/1: UNPRICED DUE TO SCARCITY
*P.P.CYAN/1: UNPRICED DUE TO SCARCITY
*P.P.MAGENTA/1: UNPRICED DUE TO SCARCITY
*P.P.YELLOW/1: UNPRICED DUE TO SCARCITY
STATED ODDS 1:3; 1:1 FAT PACK

TR1 Asuka	1.25	3.00
TR2 Shinsuke Nakamura	1.00	2.50
TR3 Bobby Roode	.60	1.50
TR4 Samoa Joe	.75	2.00
TR5 Tyler Bate	.40	1.00
TR6 Pete Dunne	.40	1.00
TR7 Dash Wilder	.50	1.25
TR8 Scott Dawson	.50	1.25
TR9 Elias	1.00	2.50
TR10 Tye Dillinger	.40	1.00

2018 Topps Heritage WWE Top 10 Rookies Autographs

*SILVER/25: .5X TO 1.2X BASIC AUTOS
*GOLD/10: UNPRICED DUE TO SCARCITY
*RED/1: UNPRICED DUE TO SCARCITY
STATED PRINT RUN 50 SER.#'d SETS

TTRAAS Asuka	15.00	40.00
TTRABR Bobby Roode	10.00	25.00
TTRADW Dash Wilder	5.00	12.00
TTRAEL Elias	25.00	60.00
TTRASD Scott Dawson	5.00	12.00
TTRASJ Samoa Joe	10.00	25.00
TTRASN Shinsuke Nakamura	12.00	30.00
TTRATD Tye Dillinger	6.00	15.00

2018 Topps Heritage WWE Triple Mat Relics

*SILVER/25: .5X TO 1.2X BASIC MEM
*GOLD/10: UNPRICED DUE TO SCARCITY
*RED/1: UNPRICED DUE TO SCARCITY
STATED PRINT RUN 50 SER.#'d SETS

TMBL Brock Lesnar	8.00	20.00
TMCF Charlotte Flair	12.00	30.00
TMDA Dean Ambrose	10.00	25.00
TMJC John Cena	10.00	25.00
TMKO Kevin Owens	8.00	20.00
TMTH Triple H	8.00	20.00
TMTM The Miz	8.00	20.00
TMUD Undertaker	15.00	40.00

2020 Topps Immortal Championship Wrestling Series 1

NNO Axel Lennox
NNO Bin Hamin
NNO Brut VanSlyke
NNO Christina Marie
NNO Greek God Papadon
NNO Justin Credible
NNO Mattick
NNO Mike Skyros
NNO Pat Sawyer
NNO Referee Sideburns
NNO Richard Holliday
NNO Rick Recon
NNO Sean Carr
NNO Sean Carr
NNO Slyck Wagner Brown

2017 Topps Legends of WWE

COMPLETE SET (100) 8.00 20.00
UNOPENED BOX (12 PACKS)
UNOPENED PACK (5 CARDS)
*BRONZE: .6X TO 1.5X BASIC CARDS
*SILVER/99: .75X TO 2X BASIC CARDS
*BLUE/50: 1.2X TO 3X BASIC CARDS
*GOLD/10: UNPRICED DUE TO SCARCITY
*RED/1: UNPRICED DUE TO SCARCITY

1	Brock Lesnar	1.25	3.00
2	Goldberg	1.00	2.50
3	The Rock	1.25	3.00
4	Hunter Hearst Helmsley	.60	1.50
5	Undertaker	1.00	2.50
6	Afa	.25	.60
7	Alundra Blayze	.30	.75
8	Andre the Giant	.50	1.25
9	Bam Bam Bigelow	.40	1.00
10	The Berzerker	.25	.60
11	Big Boss Man	.30	.75
12	Big John Studd	.30	.75
13	Bob Backlund	.25	.60
14	Bobby The Brain Heenan	.40	1.00
15	The Boogeyman	.25	.60
16	Booker T	.30	.75
17	Bret Hit Man Hart	.50	1.25
18	Brian Knobbs	.25	.60
19	British Bulldog	.25	.60
20	Bruno Sammartino	.40	1.00
21	Brutus The Barber Beefcake	.25	.60
22	Cowboy Bob Orton	.40	1.00
23	D'Lo Brown	.25	.60
24	Daniel Bryan	1.00	2.50
25	Dean Malenko	.30	.75
26	Diamond Dallas Page	.30	.75
27	Don Muraco	.25	.60
28	Dory Funk Jr.	.25	.60
29	Dusty Rhodes	.30	.75
30	Earthquake	.25	.60
31	Eddie Guerrero	.50	1.25
32	Edge	.60	1.50
33	Eve Torres	.40	1.00
34	Fit Finlay	.25	.60
35	General Adnan	.25	.60
36	George The Animal Steele	.40	1.00
37	Gerald Brisco	.25	.60
38	The Goon	.25	.60
39	Greg The Hammer Valentine	.30	.75
40	Hacksaw Jim Duggan	.40	1.00
41	Haku	.25	.60
42	Harley Race	.30	.75
43	The Honky Tonk Man	.30	.75
44	Iron Sheik	.30	.75
45	Irwin R. Schyster	.25	.60
46	Jake The Snake Roberts	.30	.75
47	The Godfather	.25	.60
48	Jerry The King Lawler	.30	.75
49	Jerry Sags	.25	.60
50	Jim The Anvil Neidhart	.25	.60
51	Junkyard Dog	.30	.75
52	Mike Rotunda	.25	.60
53	Ken Shamrock	.25	.60
54	Kerry Von Erich	.25	.60
55	Kevin Nash	.40	1.00
56	Kevin Von Erich	.40	1.00
57	Larry Zbyszko	.30	.75
58	Lex Luger	.30	.75
59	Macho Man Randy Savage	.50	1.25
60	Magnum T.A.	.25	.60
61	Michael P.S. Hayes	.30	.75
62	Mick Foley	.60	1.50
63	Million Dollar Man Ted DiBiase	.30	.75
64	Miss Elizabeth	.40	1.00
65	Mr. Perfect	.50	1.25
66	Mr. Wonderful Paul Orndorff	.30	.75
67	Nikolai Volkoff	.30	.75
68	Norman Smiley	.30	.75
69	Papa Shango	.25	.60
70	Pat Patterson	.25	.60
71	Ravishing Rick Rude	.40	1.00
72	Ric Flair	.60	1.50
73	Ricky The Dragon Steamboat	.50	1.25
74	Road Dogg	.40	1.00
75	Rob Van Dam	.50	1.25
76	Rocky Johnson	.25	.60
77	Ron Simmons	.30	.75
78	Rowdy Roddy Piper	.50	1.25
79	Scott Hall	.30	.75
80	Sgt. Slaughter	.30	.75
81	Sensational Sherri	.30	.75
82	Sid Vicious	.30	.75
83	Sika	.25	.60
84	Stevie Ray	.25	.60
85	Sting	.75	2.00
86	Stone Cold Steve Austin	1.00	2.50
87	Tatanka	.25	.60
88	Tatsumi Fujinami	.25	.60
89	Terri Runnels	.25	.60
90	Terry Taylor	.25	.60
91	Trish Stratus	1.00	2.50
92	Tully Blanchard	.30	.75
93	Typhoon	.25	.60
94	Ultimate Warrior	.50	1.25
95	Umaga	.25	.60
96	Virgil	.25	.60
97	The Warlord	.25	.60
98	Wendi Richter	.30	.75
99	X-Pac	.25	.60
100	Yokozuna	.40	1.00

2017 Topps Legends of WWE Autographed Retired Championship Belt Relics

*GOLD/10: UNPRICED DUE TO SCARCITY
*BLACK/5: UNPRICED DUE TO SCARCITY
*RED/1: UNPRICED DUE TO SCARCITY
RANDOMLY INSERTED INTO PACKS

ARCAB	Alundra Blayze	8.00	20.00
ARCBH	Bret Hit Man Hart	15.00	40.00
ARCBP	Beth Phoenix	8.00	20.00
ARCBR	Bret Hit Man Hart	15.00	40.00
ARCBS	Big Show	10.00	25.00
ARCBT	Booker T	12.00	30.00
ARCCF	Charlotte Flair	15.00	40.00
ARCCH	Chris Jericho	12.00	30.00
ARCCJ	Chris Jericho	12.00	30.00
ARCDM	Dean Malenko	6.00	15.00
ARCET	Eve Torres	12.00	30.00
ARCGO	Goldberg	20.00	50.00
ARCIV	Ivory	10.00	25.00
ARCJA	Jim The Anvil Neidhart	6.00	15.00
ARCJB	JBL	8.00	20.00
ARCMA	Maryse	12.00	30.00
ARCMD	Alundra Blayze	6.00	15.00
ARCRD	Road Dogg	6.00	15.00
ARCRF	Ric Flair	60.00	120.00
ARCST	Sting	25.00	60.00
ARCTD	Ted DiBiase	10.00	25.00
ARCTS	Trish Stratus	25.00	60.00
ARCWR	Wendi Richter	10.00	25.00

2017 Topps Legends of WWE Autographed Shirt Relics

*SILVER/50: X TO X BASIC AUTOS
*BLUE/25: X TO X BASIC AUTOS
*GOLD/10: UNPRICED DUE TO SCARCITY
*BLACK/5: UNPRICED DUE TO SCARCITY
*RED/1: UNPRICED DUE TO SCARCITY
STATED ODDS

ARBH Bret Hit Man Hart
ARBS Big Show
ARDP Diamond Dallas Page
ARED Edge
ARIR The Iron Sheik
ARKN Kevin Nash
ARLL Lex Luger
ARMA Mankind
ARMF Mick Foley
ARRD Road Dogg
ARRS Ricky The Dragon Steamboat
ARSM Shawn Michaels
ARST Sting
ARTB Tully Blanchard
ARTD Million Dollar Man Ted DiBiase

2017 Topps Legends of WWE Autographs

*BRONZE/99: .5X TO 1.2X BASIC AUTOS
*SILVER/50: .6X TO 1.5X BASIC AUTOS
*BLUE/25: .75X TO 2X BASIC AUTOS
*GOLD/10: UNPRICED DUE TO SCARCITY
*BLACK/5: UNPRICED DUE TO SCARCITY
*RED/1: UNPRICED DUE TO SCARCITY
STATED PRINT RUN 199 SER.#'d SETS

LAAB	Alundra Blayze	8.00	20.00
LAAL	Albert	4.00	10.00
LABF	Brutus The Barber Beefcake	8.00	20.00
LABM	Bret Hit Man Hart	15.00	40.00
LABT	Booker T	6.00	15.00
LADP	Diamond Dallas Page	8.00	20.00
LAED	Edge	6.00	15.00
LAET	Eve Torres	10.00	25.00
LAFF	Fit Finlay	4.00	10.00
LAGD	Goldust	8.00	20.00
LAGV	Greg The Hammer Valentine	6.00	15.00
LAHA	Hacksaw Jim Duggan	4.00	10.00
LAIR	Irwin R. Schyster	5.00	12.00
LAJA	Jim The Anvil Neidhart	8.00	20.00
LAKE	Kane	10.00	25.00
LAKN	Kevin Nash	8.00	20.00
LAKS	Ken Shamrock	6.00	15.00
LALL	Lex Luger	8.00	20.00
LAMF	Mick Foley	10.00	25.00
LAMP	Michael P.S. Hayes	6.00	15.00
LANS	Norman Smiley	5.00	12.00
LAPE	Paul Ellering	4.00	10.00
LARS	Ricky The Dragon Steamboat	15.00	40.00
LASM	Shawn Michaels	15.00	40.00
LASS	Sgt. Slaughter	12.00	30.00
LAST	Sting	20.00	50.00
LASV	Sid Vicious	6.00	15.00
LATA	Tatanka	4.00	10.00
LATD	Million Dollar Man Ted DiBiase	8.00	20.00
LATH	The Boogeyman	6.00	15.00
LAWE	Wendi Richter	6.00	15.00
LAWR	William Regal	4.00	10.00

2017 Topps Legends of WWE Autographs Bronze

*BRONZE: .5X TO 1.2X BASIC AUTOS

LAGO Goldberg 20.00 50.00

2017 Topps Legends of WWE Autographs Silver

STATED PRINT RUN 50 SER.#'d SETS

LAUN Undertaker 125.00 250.00

2017 Topps Legends of WWE Dual Autographs

STATED PRINT RUN 10 SER.#'d SETS
RANDOMLY INSERTED INTO PACKS

DADS	T.DiBiase/IRS	50.00	100.00
DAFB	R.Flair/T.Blanchard	50.00	100.00
DAHN	J.Neidhart/B.Hart	75.00	150.00
DARB	A.Blayze/W.Richter	30.00	60.00
DASV	I.Sheik/N.Volkoff	30.00	75.00
DASZ	L.Zbyszko/B.Sammartino	30.00	75.00
DATM	HHH/S.McMahon	500.00	1000.00
DAUK	Kane/Undertaker	300.00	500.00
DAUS	Sting/Undertaker	300.00	600.00
DASTL	L.Luger Sting	100.00	200.00

2017 Topps Legends of WWE Legendary Bouts

COMPLETE SET (20) 6.00 15.00
RANDOMLY INSERTED INTO PACKS

1	Undertaker/Shawn Michaels	1.25	3.00
2	Bret Hart/Steve Austin	1.25	3.00
3	Randy Savage/Ricky Steamboat	.60	1.50
4	Ultimate Warrior/Randy Savage	.60	1.50
5	Bret Hart/The British Bulldog	.30	.75
6	Bret Hart/Shawn Michaels	.75	2.00
7	The Rock/Steve Austin	1.50	4.00
8	Undertaker/Shawn Michaels	1.25	3.00
9	John Cena/Brock Lesnar	1.50	4.00
10	Mr. Perfect/Bret Hart	.60	1.50
11	Razor Ramon/Shawn Michaels	.75	2.00
12	Ric Flair/Mr. Perfect	.60	1.50
13	Randy Orton/Cactus Jack	.75	2.00
14	Ric Flair Wins 1992 Royal Rumble	.75	2.00

#			
15	Undertaker/Triple H	1.25	3.00
16	Ric Flair/Randy Savage	.75	2.00
17	Chris Jericho/Shawn Michaels	.75	2.00
18	Triple H/Cactus Jack	.75	2.00
19	Sting's Squad./Dangerous Alliance	1.00	2.50
20	Edge/John Cena	1.50	4.00

2017 Topps Legends of WWE Retired Titles

COMPLETE SET (22) 5.00 12.00
RANDOMLY INSERTED INTO PACKS

#			
1	Bret Hit Man Hart	.75	2.00
2	Ric Flair	1.00	2.50
3	Terry Funk	.40	1.00
4	Triple H	1.00	2.50
5	Money Inc.	.50	1.25
6	The Outsiders	.60	1.50
7	Terry Taylor & Greg Valentine	.50	1.25
8	The Glamour Girls	.40	1.00
9	Trish Stratus	1.50	4.00
10	Nikki Bella	1.00	2.50
11	Ted DiBiase	.50	1.25
12	Tatsumi Fujinami	.40	1.00
13	British Bulldog	.40	1.00
14	Ricky Steamboat	.75	2.00
15	Rob Van Dam	.75	2.00
16	Chris Jericho	1.00	2.50
17	Dean Malenko	.50	1.25
18	Tatsumi Fujinami	.40	1.00
19	Brian Pillman	.40	1.00
20	Bradshaw	.50	1.25
21	Norman Smiley	.50	1.25
22	Virgil	.40	1.00

2017 Topps Legends of WWE Shirt Relics

STATED PRINT RUN 299 SER.#'d SETS

ARBH	Bret Hit Man Hart	5.00	12.00
ARBL	Brock Lesnar	4.00	10.00
ARBS	Big Show	3.00	8.00
ARDP	Diamond Dallas Page	3.00	8.00
ARED	Edge	3.00	8.00
ARIR	The Iron Sheik	2.50	6.00
ARKN	Kevin Nash	2.50	6.00
ARLL	Lex Luger	2.50	6.00
ARMA	Mankind	2.50	6.00
ARMF	Mick Foley	3.00	8.00
ARRD	Road Dogg	2.50	6.00
ARRS	Ricky The Dragon Steamboat	3.00	8.00
ARSM	Shawn Michaels	6.00	15.00
ARST	Sting	6.00	15.00
ARTB	Tully Blanchard	2.50	6.00
ARTD	Million Dollar Man Ted DiBiase	3.00	8.00

2017 Topps Legends of WWE Triple Autographs

TAFSG	Flair/Sting/Goldberg	150.00	300.00
TAHNH	Neidhart/J.Hart/B.Hart	125.00	250.00
TALJM	D.Love/Cactus Jack/Mankind	100.00	250.00
TANSL	Luger/Nash/Sting	100.00	200.00

2018 Topps Legends of WWE

COMPLETE SET (100)
UNOPENED BOX (12 PACKS)
UNOPENED PACK (5 CARDS)
*BRONZE: .6X TO 1.5X BASIC CARDS
*SILVER/50: 1X TO 2.5X BASIC CARDS
*BLUE/25: 1.5X TO 4X BASIC CARDS
*GOLD/10: UNPRICED DUE TO SCARCITY
*BLACK/5: UNPRICED DUE TO SCARCITY
*RED/1: UNPRICED DUE TO SCARCITY
*P.P.BLACK/1: UNPRICED DUE TO SCARCITY
*P.P.CYAN/1: UNPRICED DUE TO SCARCITY
*P.P.MAGENTA/1: UNPRICED DUE TO SCARCITY
*P.P.YELLOW/1: UNPRICED DUE TO SCARCITY

#			
1	Andre the Giant	.60	1.50
2	Bam Bam Bigelow	.50	1.25
3	Batista	.50	1.25
4	Big John Studd	.30	.75
5	Bob Backlund	.50	1.25
6	Bobby The Brain Heenan	.50	1.25
7	Booker T	.50	1.25
8	Bret Hit Man Hart	.75	2.00
9	Chief Jay Strongbow	.50	1.25
10	Classy Freddie Blassie	.50	.75
11	Cowboy Bob Orton	.30	.75
12	D'Lo Brown	.30	.75
13	Diamond Dallas Page	.50	1.25
14	Don Muraco	.30	.75
15	Dusty Rhodes	.60	1.50
16	Eddie Guerrero	.75	2.00
17	Edge	.75	2.00
18	Fit Finlay	.30	.75
19	George The Animal Steele	.40	1.00
20	Gorilla Monsoon	.60	1.50
21	Hacksaw Jim Duggan	.30	.75
22	Harley Race	.30	.75
23	Honky Tonk Man	.30	.75
24	Jake The Snake Roberts	.40	1.00
25	Jim Ross	.50	1.25
26	Jerry The King Lawler	.60	1.50
27	Jim The Anvil Neidhart	.50	1.25
28	Junkyard Dog	.30	.75
29	Ken Shamrock	.40	1.00
30	Kevin Nash	.60	1.50
31	Kevin Von Erich	.50	1.25
32	Kurt Angle	.75	2.00
33	Lex Luger	.40	1.00
34	Mark Henry	.40	1.00
35	Million Dollar Man Ted DiBiase	.40	1.00
36	Mr. Perfect	.40	1.00
37	Mr. Wonderful Paul Orndorff	.30	.75
38	Papa Shango	.30	.75
39	Pat Patterson	.30	.75
40	Ravishing Rick Rude	.40	1.00
41	Ric Flair	1.00	2.50
42	Ricky The Dragon Steamboat	.50	1.25
43	Rowdy Roddy Piper	.75	2.00
44	Sgt. Slaughter	.40	1.00
45	Shawn Michaels	1.00	2.50
46	Sid Vicious	.30	.75
47	Stevie Ray	.30	.75
48	Sting	.75	2.00
49	Stone Cold Steve Austin	1.50	4.00
50	Tatanka	.30	.75
51	Tatsumi Fujinami	.30	.75
52	Ultimate Warrior	1.25	3.00
53	Vader	.40	1.00
54	William Regal	.50	1.25
55	Yokozuna	.40	1.00
56	Big Show	.30	.75
57	Bobby Lashley	.60	1.50
58	The Brian Kendrick	.50	1.25
59	Daniel Bryan	.75	2.00
60	Dolph Ziggler	.40	1.00
61	Jeff Hardy	.60	1.50
62	Goldust	.60	1.50
63	John Cena	1.25	3.00
64	Kane	.50	1.25
65	Woken Matt Hardy	.75	2.00
66	Randy Orton	.75	2.00
67	The Rock	1.50	4.00
68	Shelton Benjamin	.40	1.00
69	Undertaker	1.25	3.00
70	Triple H	.75	2.00
IC1	X-Pac/1-2-3 Kid	.40	1.00
IC2	Albert/Tensai	.30	.75
IC3	Big Bubba Rogers/Big Boss Man	.30	.75
IC4	Brutus Beefcake/The Zodiac	.30	.75
IC5	The Booty Man/The Disciple	.30	.75
IC6	Earthquake/The Shark	.30	.75
IC7	Kama Mustafa/Kama	.30	.75
IC8	The Godfather/Goodfather	.30	.75
IC9	Trillionaire/Million Dollar Man	.40	1.00
WD1	Alundra Blayze	.30	.75
WD2	Beth Phoenix	.60	1.50
WD3	Eve Torres	.60	1.50
WD4	Lita	.75	2.00
WD5	Miss Elizabeth	.75	2.00
WD6	Sherri Martel	.60	1.50
WD7	Stephanie McMahon	.60	1.50
WD8	Terri Runnels	.40	1.00
WD9	Trish Stratus	1.25	3.00
IC10	Colonel Mustafa/Iron Sheik	.30	.75
IC11	Michael Wallstreet/IRS	.30	.75
IC12	Umaga/Jamal	.30	.75
IC13	Road Dogg/Jesse James	.30	.75
IC14	Macho Man/Macho King R.Savage	1.00	2.50
IC15	Dok Hendrix/Michael P.S. Hayes	.30	.75
IC16	Scott Hall/Razor Ramon	.60	1.50
IC17	Faarooq/Ron Simmons	.40	1.00
IC18	Terry Taylor/Red Rooster	.30	.75
IC19	Tugboat/Typhoon	.30	.75
IC20	Virgil/Vincent	.30	.75
WD10	Wendi Richter	.30	.75

2018 Topps Legends of WWE Autographed Commemorative Hall of Fame Rings

*SILVER/50: .5X TO 1.2X BASIC AUTOS
*BLUE/25: .6X TO 1.5X BASIC AUTOS
*GOLD/10: UNPRICED DUE TO SCARCITY
*BLACK/5: UNPRICED DUE TO SCARCITY
*RED/1: UNPRICED DUE TO SCARCITY
STATED PRINT RUN 99 SER.#'d SETS

HOFAB	Alundra Blayze	10.00	25.00
HOFBH	Bret Hit Man Hart	15.00	40.00
HOFBP	Beth Phoenix	12.00	30.00
HOFBT	Booker T	15.00	40.00
HOFDP	Diamond Dallas Page	10.00	25.00
HOFEG	Edge	10.00	25.00
HOFHR	Harley Race	15.00	40.00
HOFJD	Hacksaw Jim Duggan	10.00	25.00
HOFJL	Jerry The King Lawler	20.00	50.00
HOFJR	Jake The Snake Roberts	12.00	30.00
HOFKA	Kurt Angle	12.00	30.00
HOFKN	Kevin Nash	12.00	30.00
HOFLT	Lita	20.00	50.00
HOFMH	Mark Henry	10.00	25.00
HOFPO	Mr. Wonderful Paul Orndorff	12.00	30.00
HOFRD	Ricky The Dragon Steamboat	10.00	25.00
HOFRF	Ric Flair/84	30.00	75.00
HOFRR	Razor Ramon	15.00	40.00
HOFSS	Sgt. Slaughter	12.00	30.00
HOFST	Sting	25.00	60.00
HOFWR	Wendi Richter	10.00	25.00

2018 Topps Legends of WWE Autographed Dual Relics

*GOLD/10: UNPRICED DUE TO SCARCITY
*BLACK/5: UNPRICED DUE TO SCARCITY
*RED/1: UNPRICED DUE TO SCARCITY
STATED PRINT RUN 25 SER.#'d SETS

ADRGD	Goldust	12.00	30.00
ADRJH	Jeff Hardy	15.00	40.00
ADRMH	Woken Matt Hardy	20.00	50.00

2018 Topps Legends of WWE Autographed Shirt Relics

*SILVER/50: .5X TO 1.2X BASIC AUTOS
*BLUE/25: .6X TO 1.5X BASIC AUTOS
*GOLD/10: UNPRICED DUE TO SCARCITY
*BLACK/5: UNPRICED DUE TO SCARCITY
*RED/1: UNPRICED DUE TO SCARCITY
STATED PRINT RUN 99 SER.#'d SETS

ASRDP	Diamond Dallas Page	10.00	25.00
ASREG	Edge	12.00	30.00
ASRIS	The Iron Sheik	10.00	25.00
ASRKN	Kevin Nash	15.00	40.00
ASRLL	Lex Luger	10.00	25.00
ASRMH	Woken Matt Hardy	8.00	20.00
ASRRD	Road Dogg		
ASRRS	Ricky The Dragon Steamboat	8.00	20.00
ASRST	Sting	15.00	40.00

2018 Topps Legends of WWE Autographs

*BRONZE/99: SAME VALUE AS BASIC AUTOS
*SILVER/50: .5X TO 1.2X BASIC AUTOS
*BLUE/25: .6X TO 1.5X BASIC AUTOS
*GOLD/10: UNPRICED DUE TO SCARCITY
*BLACK/5: UNPRICED DUE TO SCARCITY
*RED/1: UNPRICED DUE TO SCARCITY
*P.P.BLACK/1: UNPRICED DUE TO SCARCITY
*P.P.CYAN/1: UNPRICED DUE TO SCARCITY
*P.P.MAGENTA/1: UNPRICED DUE TO SCARCITY
*P.P.YELLOW/1: UNPRICED DUE TO SCARCITY
STATED ODDS

AAB	Alundra Blayze	6.00	15.00
AAF	Afa	5.00	12.00
ABE	Brutus The Barber Beefcake	8.00	20.00
ABH	Bret Hit Man Hart	12.00	30.00
ABN	Brian Knobbs	6.00	15.00
ABS	Big Show	8.00	20.00
ABT	Booker T	8.00	20.00
ACB	Cowboy Bob Orton	5.00	12.00
ACJ	Chris Jericho	12.00	30.00
ADB	Daniel Bryan	10.00	25.00
ADP	Diamond Dallas Page	6.00	15.00
AED	Edge	12.00	30.00
AFA	Faarooq	5.00	12.00
AFF	Fit Finlay	6.00	15.00
AGD	Goldust	6.00	15.00
AGO	The Goon	10.00	25.00
AHA	Haku	8.00	20.00
AHR	Harley Race	8.00	20.00
AHT	Honky Tonk Man	6.00	15.00
AIR	Irwin R. Schyster	5.00	12.00
AJD	Hacksaw Jim Duggan	10.00	25.00
AJH	Jimmy Hart	6.00	15.00

AJJ	JJ Dillon	6.00	15.00
AJL	Jerry The King Lawler	8.00	20.00
AJS	Jake The Snake Roberts	10.00	25.00
AKA	Kurt Angle	12.00	30.00
AKE	Kane	6.00	15.00
AKN	Kevin Nash	6.00	15.00
ALL	Lex Luger	8.00	20.00
ALT	Lita	12.00	30.00
AMA	Mankind	6.00	15.00
AMC	Michael Cole	5.00	12.00
AMD	Million Dollar Man Ted DiBiase	8.00	20.00
ANB	Jerry Sags	5.00	12.00
ANS	Norman Smiley	6.00	15.00
APE	Paul Ellering	8.00	20.00
APS	Michael P.S. Hayes	6.00	15.00
ARH	Rhyno	5.00	12.00
ARO	Randy Orton	10.00	25.00
ARS	Ricky The Dragon Steamboat	10.00	25.00
ASI	Sika	6.00	15.00
ASR	Stevie Ray	6.00	15.00
ASS	Sgt. Slaughter	6.00	15.00
AST	Sting	15.00	40.00
ASV	Sid Vicious	6.00	15.00
ATA	Magnum T.A.	6.00	15.00
ATG	The Godfather	6.00	15.00
ATK	Tatanka	5.00	12.00
ATS	Trish Stratus	20.00	50.00
ATT	Terry Taylor	5.00	12.00
ATW	The Warlord	5.00	12.00
AWD	Wendi Richter	6.00	15.00
AWR	William Regal	8.00	20.00

2018 Topps Legends of WWE Autographs Silver

STATED PRINT RUN 50 SER.#'d SETS

ASM	Stephanie McMahon	75.00	150.00
ATH	Triple H	125.00	250.00
AUD	Undertaker	100.00	200.00

2018 Topps Legends of WWE Dual Autographs

DABW	Bushwhackers
DADX	HHH/HBK
DAGG	J.Martin/L.Kai
DAHF	P.Orndorff/H.Race
DAHH	Booker T/S.Ray

2018 Topps Legends of WWE Relics

RANDOMLY INSERTED INTO PACKS

SRBH	Bret Hit Man Hart	5.00	12.00
SRDP	Diamond Dallas Page	3.00	8.00
SREG	Edge	3.00	8.00
SRGD	Goldust	2.50	6.00
SRIS	The Iron Sheik	2.50	6.00
SRJC	John Cena	5.00	12.00
SRKN	Kevin Nash	3.00	8.00
SRLL	Lex Luger	2.50	6.00
SRMH	Woken Matt Hardy	2.00	5.00
SRRD	Road Dogg	2.00	5.00
SRRS	Ricky The Dragon Steamboat	2.00	5.00
SRST	Sting	3.00	8.00
SRTD	Million Dollar Man Ted DiBiase	2.00	5.00

2018 Topps Legends of WWE Triple Autographs

STATED PRINT RUN 10 SER.#'d SETS
UNPRICED DUE TO SCARCITY

TAMHF	K.Angle/HHH/S.McMahon
TAMOD	Faarooq/Edge/Undertaker
TATCM	HHH/Undertaker/Faarooq

2021 Topps Living WWE

1	Stone Cold Steve Austin/
2	Trish Stratus/
3	The Miz/
4	Maryse/
5	Erik/
6	Ivar/

2016-18 Topps Now WWE

1	Brock Lesnar/132*	6.00	15.00
2	Finn Balor/221*	5.00	12.00
3	Dean Ambrose/114*	6.00	15.00
4	Charlotte/124*	6.00	15.00
5	AJ Styles/127*	8.00	20.00
6	AJ Styles/191*	6.00	15.00
7	Becky Lynch/212*	8.00	20.00
8	Heath Slater and Rhyno/104*	4.00	10.00
9	Kane/81*	12.00	30.00
10	The Miz/85*	6.00	15.00
11	Kevin Owens/68*	5.00	12.00
12	The New Day/61*	15.00	40.00
13	Charlotte/88*	5.00	12.00
14	Roman Reigns/61*	8.00	20.00
15	Chris Jericho/62*	10.00	25.00
16	AJ Styles/73*	5.00	12.00
17	Naomi/70*	8.00	20.00
18	Heath Slater & Rhyno/65*	8.00	20.00
19	Dolph Ziggler/73*	5.00	12.00
20	Bray Wyatt/86*	5.00	12.00
21	Nikki Bella/87*	5.00	12.00
22	Goldberg/249*	6.00	15.00
23	Kevin Owens/98*	8.00	20.00
24	Charlotte Flair/151*	6.00	15.00
25	Roman Reigns/69*	5.00	12.00
26	New Day/70*	5.00	12.00
27	Brian Kendrick/72*	5.00	12.00
28	The Miz/59*	5.00	12.00
29	Edge/58*	5.00	12.00
30	Undertaker/126*	8.00	20.00
31	Goldberg/125*	6.00	15.00
32	Team Smackdown Live Men/62*	5.00	12.00
33	Team Raw Women/88*	4.00	10.00
34	Team Raw Tag Team/60*	5.00	12.00
35	The Brian Kendrick/59*	5.00	12.00
36	The Miz/60*	5.00	12.00
37	AJ Styles/122*	4.00	10.00
38	Alexa Bliss/180*	15.00	40.00
39	The Miz/82*	4.00	10.00
40	Nikki Bella/93*	6.00	15.00
41	Baron Corbin/91*	4.00	10.00
42	Randy Orton & Bray Wyatt/115*	5.00	12.00
43A	Kevin Owens/65*	4.00	10.00
44	Cesaro & Sheamus/65*	4.00	10.00
45	Sami Zayn/68*	4.00	10.00
46	Seth Rollins/63*	4.00	10.00
47	Rich Swann/65*	4.00	10.00
48A	Charlotte Flair/108*	6.00	15.00
49	Naomi/Nikki Bella/Becky Lynch/88*	4.00	10.00
50	Luke Gallows & Karl Anderson/64*	4.00	10.00
51	Charlotte Flair/100*	4.00	10.00
52	Kevin Owens/62*	6.00	15.00
53	Neville/61*	5.00	12.00
54A	John Cena/82*	6.00	15.00
55	Goldberg/Undertaker/73*	6.00	15.00

56A	Randy Orton/85*	5.00	12.00
57	Nia Jax/83*	6.00	15.00
58	Bray Wyatt/102*	5.00	12.00
59	Naomi/82*	6.00	15.00
60	Randy Orton/54*	6.00	15.00
61	Nikki Bella & Natalya/74*	6.00	15.00
62	American Alpha/39*	4.00	10.00
63	Becky Lynch/73*	6.00	15.00
64	Bayley/288*	6.00	15.00
65	Goldberg/223*	8.00	20.00
66	Bayley/153*	5.00	12.00
67	Roman Reigns/64*	5.00	12.00
68	Neville/73*	5.00	12.00
69	Sasha Banks/141*	5.00	12.00
70	Luke Gallows & Karl Anderson/74*	5.00	12.00
71	Samoa Joe/81*	5.00	12.00
72	Undertaker/172*	6.00	15.00
73	Naomi/72*	5.00	12.00
74	Goldberg/64*	8.00	20.00
75	Randy Orton/69*	5.00	12.00
76	John Cena/Nikki Bella/91*	5.00	12.00
77	Hardy Boyz/114*	8.00	20.00
78	Bayley/97*	5.00	12.00
79	Kevin Owens/71*	5.00	12.00
80	Shinsuke Nakamura/78*	8.00	20.00
82	Tye Dillinger/37*	10.00	25.00
81	Finn Balor/46*	10.00	25.00
83	The Revival/46*	5.00	12.00
84	Dean Ambrose/Miz/Maryse/40*	5.00	12.00
85	Alexa Bliss/123*	10.00	25.00
86	Kevin Owens/49*	5.00	12.00
87	Charlotte Flair/57*	8.00	20.00
88	Braun Strowman/55*	5.00	12.00
89	Bray Wyatt/49*	5.00	12.00
90	Seth Rollins/50*	5.00	12.00
91	Alexa Bliss/223*	10.00	25.00
92	The Hardy Boyz/65*	5.00	12.00
93	Chris Jericho/56*	5.00	12.00
94	Shinsuka Nakamura/96*	5.00	12.00
95	The Usos/		
96	Sami Zayn/41*	5.00	12.00
97	Natalya Carmella Tamina/49*	5.00	12.00
98	Kevin Owens/44*	5.00	12.00
99	Jinder Mahal/69*	5.00	12.00
100	The Miz/60*	5.00	12.00
101	Sasha Banks/Rich Swann/78*	6.00	15.00
102	Alexa Bliss/264*	8.00	20.00
103	Cesaro & Sheamus/53*	4.00	10.00
104	Neville/53*	4.00	10.00
105	Samoa Joe/56*	4.00	10.00
106	Carmella/112*	6.00	15.00
107	The Usos/41*	5.00	12.00
108	Naomi/49*	5.00	12.00
109	Jinder Mahal/41*	4.00	10.00
110	Baron Corbin/60*	4.00	10.00
111	Brock Lesnar/61*	6.00	15.00
112	Braun Strowman/39*	4.00	10.00
113	The Miz/33*	4.00	10.00
114	Sasha Banks/103*	5.00	12.00
115	Cesaro & Sheamus/33*	4.00	10.00
116	Big Cass/32*	4.00	10.00
117	Bray Wyatt/37*	4.00	10.00
118	Neville/32*	4.00	10.00
119	Jinder Mahal/50*	4.00	10.00
120	The New Day/49*	4.00	10.00
121	John Cena/59*	4.00	10.00
122	Kevin Owens/44*	4.00	10.00
123	Natalya/44*	4.00	10.00

124	Baron Corbin/38*	4.00	10.00
125	HHH & Stephanie/Connor's Cure/216*	4.00	10.00
126	Natalya/62*	4.00	10.00
127	Sasha Banks/114*	6.00	15.00
128	Dean Ambrose & Seth Rollins/80*	5.00	12.00
129	AJ Styles/63*	5.00	12.00
130	Jinder Mahal/38*	5.00	12.00
131	Brock Lesnar/50*	5.00	12.00
132	Brock Lesnar/51*	5.00	12.00
133	Enzo Amore/48*	5.00	12.00
134	Roman Reigns/46*	5.00	12.00
135	Alexa Bliss/138*	10.00	25.00
136	Ambrose/Rollins/38*	5.00	12.00
137	Finn Balor/40*	5.00	12.00
138	Kevin Owens/39*	5.00	12.00
139	Bobby Roode/32*	5.00	12.00
140	Jinder Mahal/29*	5.00	12.00
141	Natalya/53*	5.00	12.00
142	Baron Corbin/30*	5.00	12.00
143	The Usos/32*	5.00	12.00
144	Angle/Rollins/Ambrose/75*	5.00	12.00
145	Alexa Bliss/191*	8.00	20.00
146	The Demon Finn Balor/94*	5.00	12.00
147	Asuka/146*	6.00	15.00
148	Enzo Amore/55*	4.00	10.00
149	Sasha Banks/100*	5.00	12.00
150	The Shield/50*	4.00	10.00
151	Team Raw Women/35*	4.00	10.00
152	Charlotte Flair/102*	6.00	15.00
153	Team Raw Men/	4.00	10.00
154	AJ Styles/65*	4.00	10.00
155	Kevin Owens & Sami Zayn/34*	4.00	10.00
156	Charlotte Flair/63*	6.00	15.00
157	The Usos/33*	4.00	10.00
158	Dolph Ziggler/33*	4.00	10.00
159	Scott Hall/89*	4.00	10.00
160	Undertaker/147*	6.00	15.00
161	The Miz/88*	4.00	10.00
162	John Cena/91*	6.00	15.00
163	Stone Cold Steve Austin/153*	8.00	20.00

2016-18 Topps Now WWE Relics

STATED PRINT RUN 25 SER.#'d SETS

43B	Kevin Owens	20.00	50.00
48B	Charlotte Flair	60.00	120.00
54B	John Cena	50.00	100.00
56B	Randy Orton	25.00	60.00
72A	Undertaker	80.00	150.00
74A	Goldberg	15.00	40.00
75A	Randy Orton	20.00	50.00
76A	John Cena/Nikki Bella	30.00	75.00
127A	Sasha Banks	60.00	120.00
128A	Dean Ambrose & Seth Rollins	30.00	75.00
131A	Brock Lesnar	30.00	75.00
144A	Kurt Angle	30.00	75.00
147A	Asuka	50.00	100.00
163A	Stone Cold Steve Austin	60.00	120.00

2018 Topps Now WWE

COMPLETE SET (72)		300.00	600.00
1	AJ Styles/99*	6.00	15.00
2	Shinsuke Nakamura/127*	5.00	12.00
3	Cesaro & Sheamus/82*	5.00	12.00
4	Lita/102*	6.00	15.00
5	Trish Stratus/186*	8.00	20.00
6	Asuka/145*	6.00	15.00
7	Alexa Bliss/171*	10.00	25.00

#	Card	Low	High
8	Asuka/140*	6.00	15.00
9	Woken Matt Hardy/56*	6.00	15.00
10	Roman Reigns/59*	6.00	15.00
11	AJ Styles/53*	5.00	12.00
12	Asuka/103*	6.00	15.00
13	Charlotte Flair/101*	6.00	15.00
14	Randy Orton/67*	5.00	12.00
15	Shinsuke Nakamura/50*	5.00	12.00
16	Daniel Bryan/125*	6.00	15.00
17	Woken Matt Hardy/76*	8.00	20.00
18	Cedric Alexander/74*	8.00	20.00
19	Naomi/87*	8.00	20.00
20	Seth Rollins/77*	8.00	20.00
21	Charlotte Flair/261*	8.00	20.00
22	Jinder Mahal/64*	5.00	12.00
23	The Bludgeon Brothers/67*	5.00	12.00
24	The Undertaker/145*	8.00	20.00
25	Daniel Bryan/93*	8.00	20.00
26	Nia Jax/115*	5.00	12.00
27	AJ Styles/85*	5.00	12.00
28	Braun Strowman/67*	5.00	12.00
29	Brock Lesnar/44*	5.00	12.00
30	Ronda Rousey/1342*	12.00	30.00
31	Braun Strowman/66*	5.00	12.00
32	Daniel Bryan/52*	6.00	15.00
33	Undertaker/62*	8.00	20.00
34	AJ Styles/52*	6.00	15.00
35	John Cena/66*	5.00	12.00
36	Seth Rollins/37*	6.00	15.00
37	Daniel Bryan/30*	12.00	30.00
38	Roman Reigns/33*	8.00	20.00
39	Alexa Bliss/301*	8.00	20.00
40	AJ Styles/101*	6.00	15.00
41	Alexa Bliss/304*	10.00	25.00
42	Braun Strowman/101*	5.00	12.00
43	Bobby Lashley/47*	8.00	20.00
44	Alexa Bliss/175*	10.00	25.00
45	AJ Styles/58*	8.00	20.00
46	Dolph Ziggler/48*	6.00	15.00
47	Seth Rollins/80*	6.00	15.00
48	Charlotte Flair/191*	8.00	20.00
49	Ronda Rousey/970*	8.00	20.00
50	Roman Reigns/79*	12.00	30.00
51	Becky Lynch/172*	5.00	12.00
52	Dolph Ziggler/Drew McIntyre/73*	5.00	12.00
53	AJ Styles/74*	5.00	12.00
54	Ronda Rousey/299*	6.00	15.00
55	John Cena/64*	5.00	12.00
56	Ilconics/146*	5.00	12.00
57	AJ Styles/64*	4.00	10.00
58	Ronda Rousey/Bellas/166*	6.00	15.00
59	Triple H/72*	4.00	10.00
60	Buddy Murphy/64*	10.00	25.00
61	Trish Stratus & Lita/212*	6.00	15.00
62	Nia Jax/139*	12.00	30.00
63	Toni Storm/239*	8.00	20.00
64	Shayna Baszler/149*	6.00	15.00
65	Becky Lynch/325*	5.00	12.00
66	Ronda Rousey/324*	5.00	12.00
67	Seth Rollins/63*	10.00	25.00
68	Charlotte Flair/143*	8.00	20.00
69	Brock Lesnar/63*	10.00	25.00
70	Asuka/270*	4.00	10.00
71	Daniel Bryan/70*	6.00	15.00
72	Ronda Rousey/295*	5.00	12.00

2018 Topps Now WWE Relics

*GOLD/1: UNPRICED/SCARCITY

#	Card	Low	High
2A	Shinsuke Nakamura	25.00	60.00
6A	Asuka	75.00	150.00
24A	The Undertaker	25.00	60.00
25A	Daniel Bryan	30.00	75.00
29A	Brock Lesnar	60.00	120.00
30A	Ronda Rousey	150.00	300.00
48A	Charlotte Flair	30.00	75.00
49A	Ronda Rousey	100.00	200.00
50A	Roman Reigns		
68A	Charlotte Flair	50.00	100.00
69A	Brock Lesnar		

2019 Topps Now WWE

#	Card	Low	High
1	Women's Royal Rumble/166*	8.00	20.00
2	Men's Royal Rumble/75*	5.00	12.00
3	Asuka/186*	6.00	15.00
4	Ronda Rousey/268*	6.00	15.00
5	Daniel Bryan/90*	5.00	12.00
6	Brock Lesnar/91*	6.00	15.00
7	Becky Lynch/279*	6.00	15.00
8	Seth Rollins/113*	5.00	12.00
9	WM35 Men's Preview/100*	4.00	10.00
10	WM35 Women's Preview/215*	5.00	12.00
11	Seth Rollins/157*	4.00	10.00
12	Roman Reigns/119*	4.00	10.00
13	Kurt Angle/127*	6.00	15.00
14	Kofi Kingston/217*	4.00	10.00
15	The Ilconics/211*	3.00	8.00
16	Triple H/95*	3.00	8.00
17	John Cena/136*	4.00	10.00
18	Becky Lynch/710*	6.00	15.00
19	Seth Rollins/58*	6.00	15.00
20	Kofi Kingston/49*	5.00	12.00
21	Rey Mysterio/48*	8.00	20.00
22	Bayley/164*	5.00	12.00
23	Charlotte Flair/140*	6.00	15.00
24	Becky Lynch/163*	5.00	12.00
25	Bayley/138*	5.00	12.00
26	Brock Lesnar/49*	5.00	12.00
27	Mansoor/29*	12.00	30.00
28	Randy Orton/26*	6.00	15.00
29	Undertaker/31*	6.00	15.00
30	Drew Gulak/45*	5.00	12.00
31	Becky Lynch/109*	6.00	15.00
32	Ricochet/48*	5.00	12.00
33	Bayley/81*	8.00	20.00
34	Seth Rollins w/Becky Lynch/111*	6.00	15.00
35	Undertaker & Roman Reigns/58*	6.00	15.00
36	AJ Styles/57*	5.00	12.00
37	Bayley/81*	5.00	12.00
38	Seth Rollins & Becky Lynch/91*	5.00	12.00
39	Brock Lesnar/55*	5.00	12.00
40	Becky Lynch vs. Natalya/58*	6.00	15.00
41	Kofi Kingston vs. Randy Orton/29*	4.00	10.00
42	Brock Lesnar vs. Seth Rollins/29*	8.00	20.00
43	Becky Lynch/159*	8.00	20.00
44	AJ Styles/67*	4.00	10.00
45	Charlotte Flair/171*	6.00	15.00
46	The Fiend Bray Wyatt/	8.00	20.00
47	Seth Rollins/96*	4.00	10.00
48	Bayley//96*	5.00	12.00
49	Samoa Joe/26*	6.00	15.00
50	Cedric Alexander/26*	3.00	8.00
51	Elias/29*	3.00	8.00
52	Andrade/28*	5.00	12.00
53	Ricochet/31*	4.00	10.00
54	Baron Corbin/31*	4.00	10.00
55	Ali/20*		
56	Chad Gable/56*	6.00	15.00
57	Baron Corbin/21*		
58	Samoa Joe and Ricochet/21*		
59	Elias/21*		
60	Chad Gable/20*		
61	Baron Corbin/30*		
62	Chad Gable/31*	6.00	15.00
63	Bayley/101*		
64	Sasha Banks/172*	5.00	12.00
65	Kofi Kingston/55*		
66	Erick Rowan/55*		
67	Seth Rollins/66*		
68	Baron Corbin/		
69	Rock & Becky Lynch/118*	6.00	15.00
70	Becky & Charlotte/81*	6.00	15.00
71	Kevin Owens/41*	5.00	12.00
72	Roman Reigns/38*		
73	Roman Reigns & Daniel Bryan/44*		
74	Kabuki Warriors/74*	5.00	12.00
75	Charlotte Flair/75*	6.00	15.00
76	Becky Lynch/110*	4.00	10.00
77	The Fiend Bray Wyatt/182*	8.00	20.00
78	Team Hogan/36*	5.00	12.00
79	Natalya/Lacey Evans/104*		
80	AJ Styles/34*		
81	Mansoor/34*		
82	The OC/34*	5.00	12.00
83	Brock Lesnar/34*	6.00	15.00
84	Team NXT Women/79*	6.00	15.00
85	Roderick Strong/43*	6.00	15.00
86	Adam Cole/43*	6.00	15.00
87	The Fiend Bray Wyatt/80*	8.00	20.00
88	Team SmackDown Men/38*	8.00	20.00
89	Brock Lesnar/43*	5.00	12.00
90	Shayna Baszler/61*	8.00	20.00
91	The New Day/29*		
92	Aleister Black/29*		
93	King Corbin/24*		
94	Bray Wyatt/50*	6.00	15.00
95	The Kabuki Warriors/70*	5.00	12.00

2020 Topps Now WWE

#	Card	Low	High
1	Roman Reigns/51*	6.00	15.00
2	Charlotte Flair/170*	5.00	12.00
3	Bayley/77*	4.00	10.00
4	The Fiend/85*	6.00	15.00
5	Becky Lynch/152*	8.00	20.00
6	Drew McIntyre/*76	5.00	12.00
7	Undertaker/77*	5.00	12.00
8	The Miz & John Morrison/40*		
9	Roman Reigns/41*	6.00	15.00
10	Bayley/83*	5.00	12.00
11	Goldberg/67*	4.00	10.00
12	Alexa Bliss & Nikki Cross/160*	6.00	15.00
13	Becky Lynch/162*	6.00	15.00
14	Sami Zayn/66*		
15	John Morrison/56*		
16	Kevin Owens/61*		
17	Braun Strowman/75*		
18	Undertaker/141*		
19	Rob Gronkowski/393*	5.00	12.00
20	Charlotte Flair/153*		
21	Aleister Black/55*		
22	Edge/96*		
23	Street Profits/71*		
24	Bayley/105*		
25	The Fiend Bray Wyatt/107*		
26	Drew McIntyre/105*		
27	The New Day/45*		
28	Bayley/75*		
29	Braun Strowman/55*		
30	Drew McIntyre/59*		
31	Asuka/155*		
32	Otis/78*		
33	Bayley & Sasha Banks/148*		
34	Sheamus/38*		
35	Braun Strowman/40*		
36	Drew McIntyre/41*		
37	Randy Orton/84*		
38	Cesaro & Nakamura/38*		
39	Seth Rollins/31*		
40	Drew McIntyre/36*		
41	Bayley/73*		
42	The Fiend Bray Wyatt/116*		
43	Drew McIntyre/79*		
44	Asuka/209*		
45	Seth Rollins/57*		
46	Mandy Rose/93*		
47	Bayley/128*		
48	Roman Reigns/86*		
49	Roman Reigns/73*		
50	Rey & Dominik Mysterio/97*		
51	Shayna Baszler & Nia Jax/72*		
52	Bobby Lashley/45*		
53	Roman Reigns/62*		
54	Drew McIntyre/52*		
55	Asuka/102*		
56	Sami Zayn/52*		
57	Roman Reigns/61*		
58	The Miz/39*		
59	Sasha Banks/163*		
60	Randy Orton/73*		
61	Team RAW (men)/68*		
62	Street Profits/55*		
63	Bobby Lashley/65*		
64	Sasha Banks/261*		
65	Team RAW (women)/129*		
66	Roman Reigns/65*		
67	Undertaker/736*		
68	Drew McIntyre		
69	Sasha Banks		
70	The Hurt Business		
71	Asuka & Charlotte Flair		
72	Roman Reigns		
73	Randy Orton		

2020 Topps Now WWE Autographs

*RED/10: UNPRICED DUE TO SCARCITY
*GOLD/1: UNPRICED DUE TO SCARCITY
STATED PRINT RUN 25 SER.#'d SETS

#	Card	Low	High
31A	Asuka	75.00	150.00
32A	Otis	30.00	75.00
DMA	Dominik Mysterio	60.00	120.00

2020 Topps Now WWE Relics

#	Card	Low	High
1A	Drew McIntyre	30.00	75.00
2A	Charlotte Flair	50.00	100.00

2021 Topps Now WWE

1 Drew McIntyre/
2 Sasha Banks/
3 Bianca Belair/
4 Roman Reigns/
5 Edge/

2017 Topps Now WWE Countdown to NXT TakeOver Orlando

#			
1	Asuka vs. Ember Moon	5.00	12.00
2	Bobby Roode vs. Nakamura	5.00	12.00
3	AOP vs. Revival vs. #DIY	5.00	12.00
4	Aleister Black vs. Andrade	5.00	12.00
5	Dillinger/Strong/Jose/Ruby vs. Sanity	5.00	12.00

2017 Topps Now WWE Countdown to WrestleMania

#			
1	Goldberg vs. Brock Lesnar	5.00	12.00
2	Bray Wyatt vs. Randy Orton	5.00	12.00
3	Chris Jericho vs. Kevin Owens	6.00	15.00
4	Undertaker vs. Roman Reigns	8.00	20.00
5	Bayley/Charlotte/Sasha/Nia	8.00	20.00
6	SD Women's Title Match	12.00	30.00
7	Cena & Nikki vs. Miz & Maryse	5.00	12.00
8	Seth Rollins vs. HHH	5.00	12.00
9	AJ Styles vs. Shane McMahon	5.00	12.00
10	Dean Ambrose vs. Baron Corbin	5.00	12.00
11	Neville vs. Austin Aries	5.00	12.00

2017 Topps Now WWE SummerSlam

#	
1	Lesnar/Reigns/Samoa Joe/Strowman
2	Jinder Mahal vs. Nakamura
3	Alexa Bliss vs. Sasha Banks
4	Naomi vs. Natalya
5	AJ Styles vs. Kevin Owens
6	Akira Tozawa vs. Neville
7	Cesaro/Sheamus vs. Ambrose/Rollins
8	New Day vs. Usos
9	John Cena vs. Baron Corbin
10	Randy Orton vs. Rusev
11	The Demon Finn Balor vs. Bray Wyatt
12	Big Show vs. Big Cass

2016-18 Topps Now WWE NXT

#			
1	Samoa Joe/43*		
2	Asuka/77*	20.00	50.00
3	DIY/58*		
4	Authors of Pain/44*		
5	Bobby Roode/40*		
7	Eric Young/50*	6.00	15.00
8	Roderick Strong/71*	6.00	15.00
9	The Authors of Pain/49*	5.00	12.00
10	Asuka/87*	5.00	12.00
11	Bobby Roode/56*	6.00	15.00
12	Seth Rollins/62*	6.00	15.00
13	Bobby Roode/74*	5.00	12.00
14	Asuka/117*	5.00	12.00
15	Roderick Strong/27*	4.00	10.00
16	Asuka/74*	4.00	10.00
17	Bobby Roode/25*	4.00	10.00
18	The Authors of Pain/27*	4.00	10.00
19	Tommaso Ciampa/43*	4.00	10.00
20	Sanity/47*	5.00	12.00
21	Asuka/86*	5.00	12.00
22	Drew McIntyre/46*	5.00	12.00
23	Adam Cole/104*	5.00	12.00
24	Undisputed Era/57*	5.00	12.00
25	Andrade Cien Almas/46*	5.00	12.00
26	Ember Moon/63*	5.00	12.00

2016-18 Topps Now WWE NXT Relics

#			
4B	Asuka	30.00	75.00
5B	Bobby Roode	8.00	20.00

2018 Topps Now WWE NXT

#			
1	The Undisputed Era/38*	5.00	12.00
2	Ember Moon/56*	5.00	12.00
3	Aleister Black/54*	5.00	12.00
4	Andrade Cien Almas/31*	5.00	12.00
5	Adam Cole/80*	8.00	20.00
6	Shayna Baszler/80*	8.00	20.00
7	The Undisputed Era/50*	8.00	20.00
8	Aleister Black/56*	8.00	20.00
9	Johnny Gargano/51*	8.00	20.00
10	Kairi Sane/196*		
11	Tommaso Ciampa/66*		

2019 Topps Now WWE NXT

#			
1	War Raiders/67*	6.00	15.00
2	Johnny Gargano/77*	3.00	8.00
3	Shayna Baszler/71*	6.00	15.00
4	Tommaso Ciampa/65*	4.00	10.00
5	War Raiders/91*	4.00	10.00
6	Johnny Gargano/131*	4.00	10.00
7	Shayna Baszler/104*	5.00	12.00
8	Velveteen Dream/93*	6.00	15.00
9	Matt Riddle/36*	4.00	10.00
10	Street Profits/34*	5.00	12.00
11	Velveteen Dream/36*	5.00	12.00
12	Shayna Baszler/36*	5.00	12.00
13	Adam Cole/56*	5.00	12.00
14	The Street Profits/64*	4.00	10.00
15	Io Shirai/93*	5.00	12.00
16	The Velveteen Dream/65*	4.00	10.00
17	Shayna Baszler/80*	5.00	12.00
18	Adam Cole/86*	4.00	10.00
19	Candice LeRae/110*	8.00	20.00
20	Roderick Strong/31*	6.00	15.00
21	Team Ripley/79*		
22	Pete Dunne/46*		
23	Finn Balor/38*		
25	The Undisputed Era/22*		
26	Tyler Bate/24*		
27	Kay Lee Ray/45*		
28	Gallus/36*		

2020 Topps Now WWE NXT

#			
1	Jordan Devlin/48*	6.00	15.00
2	#DIY/		
3	Rhea Ripley/131*	5.00	12.00
4	Imperium/37*	8.00	20.00
5	Adam Cole/35*	5.00	12.00
6	The Broserweights/38*	6.00	15.00
7	Rhea Ripley/81*	5.00	12.00
8	Finn Balor/29*	8.00	20.00
9	Dakota Kai/88*	4.00	10.00
10	Keith Lee/34*	5.00	12.00
11	Finn Balor/42*		
12	Keith Lee/48*		
13	Adam Cole/64*		
14	Karrion Kross/88*		
15	Io Shirai/314*		
16	Io Shirai/94*		
17	Dexter Lumis/67*		
18	Tegan Nox/227*		
19	Candice LeRae/85*		
20	Keith Lee/125*		
21A	Karrion Kross/		
21B	Damian Priest/35*		
22A	Io Shirai/		
22B	Kushida/57*		
23A	Damian Priest/		
23B	Santos Escobar/47*		
24	Io Shirai/110*		
25	Finn Balor/*40		
26	Johnny Gargano/28*		
27	Dexter Lumis/36*		
28	Rhea Ripley/83*		
29	Io Shirai/96*		
30	Team Candice/95*		
31	Johnny Gargano/42*		
32	The Undisputed Era/61*		
LR	Leon Ruff/148*		

2017 Topps Now WWE NXT TakeOver Brooklyn III

#			
1	Bobby Roode vs. Drew McIntyre	6.00	15.00
2	Asuka vs. Ember Moon	8.00	20.00
3	AOP vs. SAnitY	6.00	15.00
4	Aleister Black vs. Hideo Itami	6.00	15.00
5	Andrade vs. Johnny Gargano	6.00	15.00

2019 Topps On-Demand WWE Mother's Day

COMPLETE SET (9)		12.00	30.00
STATED PRINT RUN 107 ANNCD SETS			

#			
1	Beth Phoenix	2.00	5.00
2	Eve Torres	1.50	4.00
3	Lacey Evans	2.50	6.00
4	Maryse	1.50	4.00
5	Mickie James	3.00	8.00
6	Naomi	2.00	5.00
7	Tamina	1.25	3.00
8	Trish Stratus	6.00	15.00
9	Stephanie McMahon	3.00	8.00

2020 Topps On-Demand WWE 30 Years of the Deadman

COMPLETE SET (40)		12.00	30.00
STATED PRINT RUN 278 SER.#'d SETS			

2020 Topps On-Demand WWE 30 Years of the Deadman Rest in Peace Relic

*NAVY BLUE/50: .75X TO 2X BASIC MEM
*PURPLE/30: 1X TO 2.5X BASIC MEM
*GRAY/15: UNPRICED DUE TO SCARCITY
*BLACK/5: UNPRICED DUE TO SCARCITY
*GOLD/1: UNPRICED DUE TO SCARCITY

C1	Undertaker	12.00	30.00

2019 Topps On-Demand WWE WrestleMania 35 Roster

COMPLETE SET (10)		25.00	60.00
STATED PRINT RUN 75 SER.#'d SETS			

#			
1	Kurt Angle	3.00	8.00
2	Kofi Kingston	2.50	6.00
3	The New Daniel Bryan	6.00	15.00
4	Becky Lynch	6.00	15.00
5	Charlotte Flair	6.00	15.00
6	Ronda Rousey	8.00	20.00
7	Seth Rollins	4.00	10.00
8	Brock Lesnar	6.00	15.00
9	Triple H	4.00	10.00
10	Dave Batista	4.00	10.00

2010 Topps Platinum WWE

COMPLETE SET (125)		12.00	30.00

UNOPENED BOX (24 PACKS)
UNOPENED PACK (7 CARDS)
*RAINBOW: .8X TO 2X BASIC CARDS
*X-FRACTOR: 1X TO 2.5X BASIC CARDS
*GREEN/499: 1.25X TO 3X BASIC CARDS
*BLUE/199: 2X TO 5X BASIC CARDS
*GOLD/50: 3X TO 8X BASIC CARDS
*RED/1: UNPRICED DUE TO SCARCITY
*P.P.BLACK/1: UNPRICED DUE TO SCARCITY
*P.P.CYAN/1: UNPRICED DUE TO SCARCITY
*P.P.MAGENTA/1: UNPRICED DUE TO SCARCITY
*P.P.YELLOW/1: UNPRICED DUE TO SCARCITY

#			
1	John Cena	1.00	2.50
2	Finlay	.30	.75
3	Shad	.20	.50
4	Dean Malenko	.30	.75
5	Christian	.30	.75
6	Kane	.50	1.25
7	Luke Gallows	.20	.50
8	The Miz	.30	.75
9	Gail Kim	.50	1.25
10	Iron Sheik	.50	1.25
11	Eli Cottonwood	.20	.50
12	High Chief Peter Maivia	.20	.50
13	Earthquake	.30	.75
14	Melina	.75	2.00
15	Paul Bearer	.30	.75
16	Rosa Mendes	.30	.75
17	Ricky The Dragon Steamboat	.30	.75
18	Darren Young	.30	.75
19	Animal UER/Hawk on Front	.20	.50
20	JTG	.20	.50
21	Evan Bourne	.20	.50
22	Jake The Snake Roberts	.50	1.25
23	Edge	.75	2.00
24	Beth Phoenix	.75	2.00
25	Jey Uso	.20	.50
26	The Great Khali	.20	.50
27	Jimmy Superfly Snuka	.50	1.25
28	Layla	.50	1.25
29	Mark Henry	.30	.75
30	Arn Anderson	.30	.75
31	Jimmy Uso	.20	.50
32	Bushwhacker Luke	.20	.50
33	Jerry The King Lawler	.30	.75
34	Chris Masters	.20	.50
35	Bushwhacker Butch	.20	.50
36	Hawk UER/Animal on Front	.20	.50
37	Big Show	.50	1.25
38	Tamina	.20	.50
39	Hacksaw Jim Duggan	.30	.75
40	Cowboy Bob Orton	.30	.75
41	Percy Watson	.20	.50
42	Ted DiBiase	.30	.75
43	Curt Hawkins	.20	.50
44	Husky Harris	.40	1.00
45	Tyler Reks	.20	.50
46	Mr. Perfect Curt Hennig	.30	.75
47	Jillian	.75	2.00
48	CM Punk	.75	2.00
49	Vance Archer	.20	.50
50	Tiffany	.30	.75
51	Hillbilly Jim	.30	.75
52	David Otunga	.30	.75
53	Jack Swagger	.20	.50
54	Maryse	.75	2.00
55	Triple H	1.00	2.50
56	Michelle McCool	.75	2.00

57	Alex Riley	.20	.50
58	One Man Gang	.30	.75
59	Kofi Kingston	.30	.75
60	Zack Ryder	.20	.50
61	Doink	.30	.75
62	Sergeant Slaughter	.50	1.25
63	Dusty Rhodes	.50	1.25
64	Kelly Kelly	.75	2.00
65	Theodore Long	.20	.50
66	Chris Jericho	.50	1.25
67	Heath Slater	.30	.75
68	Natalya	.75	2.00
69	Rocky Johnson	.20	.50
70	Kaval	.20	.50
71	Eve	.75	2.00
72	Bobby The Brain Heenan	.30	.75
73	Undertaker	.75	2.00
74	Bam Bam Bigelow	.30	.75
75	Classy Freddie Blassie	.50	1.25
76	MVP	.30	.75
77	Goldust	.30	.75
78	Chavo Guerrero	.30	.75
79	Brian Pillman	.50	1.25
80	Lucky Cannon	.20	.50
81	Drew McIntyre	.30	.75
82	Ranjin Singh	.20	.50
83	Papa Shango	.20	.50
84	William Regal	.50	1.25
85	Titus O'Neil	.20	.50
86	Trent Barreta	.20	.50
87	Nikki Bella	.75	2.00
88	R-Truth	.20	.50
89	Vader	.30	.75
90	Skip Sheffield	.30	.75
91	Tyson Kidd	.20	.50
92	Michael Tarver	.30	.75
93	John Morrison	.30	.75
94	Michael McGillicutty	.20	.50
95	Koko B. Ware	.30	.75
96	Don Muraco	.30	.75
97	Randy Orton	.75	2.00
98	Harley Race	.30	.75
99	British Bulldog	.30	.75
100	Sheamus	.30	.75
101	Justin Gabriel	.30	.75
102	Yoshi Tatsu	.20	.50
103	Ezekiel Jackson	.20	.50
104	Terry Funk	.50	1.25
105	Mr. Wonderful Paul Orndorff	.50	1.25
106	David Hart Smith	.20	.50
107	Ravishing Rick Rude	.30	.75
108	Nikolai Volkoff	.30	.75
109	Cody Rhodes	.20	.50
110	Hornswoggle	.30	.75
111	Primo	.20	.50
112	Santino Marella	.20	.50
113	Rey Mysterio	.50	1.25
114	Wade Barrett	.30	.75
115	Dolph Ziggler	.30	.75
116	Million Dollar Man Ted DiBiase	.30	.75
117	Chief Jay Strongbow	.20	.50
118	Vladimir Kozlov	.30	.75
119	Junkyard Dog	.50	1.25
120	Vickie Guerrero	.20	.50
121	Rowdy Roddy Piper	.75	2.00
122	Kamala	.30	.75
123	Brie Bella	.75	2.00
124	Caylen Croft	.20	.50

125	Alicia Fox	.30	.75
CL	Checklist	.20	.50

2010 Topps Platinum WWE Autographed Relics

*BLUE/99: .75X TO 1.5X BASIC AUTOS
*GOLD/25: 1X TO 2X BASIC AUTOS
STATED PRINT RUN 275 SER. #'d SETS

1	John Cena	20.00	50.00
5	Christian	10.00	25.00
8	The Miz	10.00	25.00
21	Evan Bourne	12.00	30.00
23	Edge	15.00	40.00
37	Big Show	15.00	40.00
48	CM Punk	35.00	70.00
59	Kofi Kingston	12.00	30.00
76	MVP	10.00	25.00
97	Randy Orton	15.00	40.00

2010 Topps Platinum WWE Autographs

*BLUE/99: .75X TO 1.5X BASIC AUTOS
*GOLD/25: 1X TO 2X BASIC AUTOS
*RED/1: UNPRICED DUE TO SCARCITY
*P.P.BLACK/1: UNPRICED DUE TO SCARCITY
*P.P.CYAN/1: UNPRICED DUE TO SCARCITY
*P.P.MAGENTA/1: UNPRICED DUE TO SCARCITY
*P.P.YELLOW/1: UNPRICED DUE TO SCARCITY
STATED PRINT RUN 271 SER.#'d SETS

6	Kane	15.00	40.00
42	Ted DiBiase	12.00	30.00
43	Curt Hawkins	6.00	15.00
45	Tyler Reks	6.00	15.00
52	David Otunga	8.00	20.00
54	Maryse	20.00	50.00
56	Michelle McCool	20.00	50.00
60	Zack Ryder	8.00	20.00
64	Kelly Kelly	20.00	50.00
65	Theodore Long	8.00	20.00
66	Chris Jericho	25.00	60.00
81	Drew McIntyre	12.00	30.00
86	Trent Barreta	8.00	20.00
114	Wade Barrett	12.00	30.00
115	Dolph Ziggler	12.00	30.00
124	Caylen Croft UER/Misspelled Caylan	8.00	20.00
125	Alicia Fox	12.00	30.00

2010 Topps Platinum WWE Legendary Superstars

COMPLETE SET (25) 5.00 12.00
*GREEN/499: .5X TO 1.25X BASIC CARDS
*BLUE/199: .6X TO 1.5X BASIC CARDS
*GOLD/50: 1.2X TO 3X BASIC CARDS
*RED/1: UNPRICED DUE TO SCARCITY
STATED ODDS 1:4

LS1	Evan Bourne/Jimmy Snuka	.60	1.50
LS2	Dolph Ziggler/Paul Orndorff	.60	1.50
LS3	Randy Orton/Jake Roberts	1.00	2.50
LS4	Goldust/Papa Shango	.40	1.00
LS5	R-Truth/Koko B. Ware	.40	1.00
LS6	The Miz/Michael Hayes	.40	1.00
LS7	Mark Henry/One Man Gang	.40	1.00
LS8	Big Show/Vader	.60	1.50
LS9	William Regal/Arn Anderson	.60	1.50
LS10	John Cena/Dusty Rhodes	1.25	3.00
LS11	Drew McIntyre/Rick Rude	.40	1.00
LS12	Edge/Brian Pillman	1.00	2.50

LS13	Chris Jericho/Roddy Piper	1.00	2.50
LS14	The Usos/Wild Samoans	.40	1.00
LS15	Kane/Bam Bam Bigelow	.60	1.50
LS16	Daniel Bryan/Dean Malenko	.40	1.00
LS17	Sheamus/Iron Sheik	.60	1.50
LS18	Triple H/Harley Race	1.25	3.00
LS19	Curt Hawkins/Curt Hennig	.40	1.00
LS20	Ted DiBiase/Tully Blanchard	.40	1.00
LS21	MVP/Ted DiBiase	.40	1.00
LS22	Rey Mysterio/Ricky Steamboat	.60	1.50
LS23	CM Punk/Terry Funk	1.00	2.50
LS24	Brothers of Destruction	1.00	2.50
	Legion of Doom		
LS25	Wade Barrett/British Bulldog	.40	1.00

2010 Topps Platinum WWE Platinum Performance

COMPLETE SET (25) 6.00 15.00
*GREEN/499: .5X TO 1.25X BASIC CARDS
*BLUE/199: .6X TO 1.5X BASIC CARDS
*GOLD/50: 1.2X TO 3X BASIC CARDS
*RED/1: UNPRICED DUE TO SCARCITY
STATED ODDS 1:4

PP1	Pat Patterson	.40	1.00
PP2	Bobby The Brain Heenan	.40	1.00
PP3	Chris Jericho	.60	1.50
PP4	Randy Orton	1.00	2.50
PP5	Hacksaw Jim Duggan	.40	1.00
PP6	Triple H	1.25	3.00
PP7	CM Punk	1.00	2.50
PP8	The British Bulldog	.40	1.00
PP9	Beth Phoenix	1.00	2.50
PP10	John Cena	1.25	3.00
PP11	Jimmy Superfly Snuka	.60	1.50
PP12	Sheamus	.40	1.00
PP13	Chris Jericho	.60	1.50
PP14	Big Show	.60	1.50
PP15	Rey Mysterio	.60	1.50
PP16	The Hart Dynasty	.40	1.00
PP17	Undertaker	1.00	2.50
PP18	Million Dollar Man Ted DiBiase	.40	1.00
PP19	Vladimir Kozlov	.40	1.00
PP20	Edge	1.00	2.50
PP21	John Morrison	.40	1.00
PP22	Harley Race	.40	1.00
PP23	MVP	.40	1.00
PP24	Eve	1.00	2.50
PP25	Ricky The Dragon Steamboat	.40	1.00

2010 Topps Platinum WWE Relics

*GREEN/399: .5X TO 1.25X BASIC MEM
*BLUE/99: .6X TO 1.5X BASIC MEM
*GOLD/50: 1.2X TO 3X BASIC MEM
*RED/10: UNPRICED DUE TO SCARCITY
STATED ODDS ONE PER HOBBY BOX

1	John Cena	8.00	20.00
5	Christian	5.00	12.00
8	The Miz	5.00	12.00
23	Edge	6.00	15.00
37	Big Show	6.00	15.00
48	CM Punk	8.00	20.00
55	Triple H	8.00	20.00
59	Kofi Kingston	5.00	12.00
76	MVP	5.00	12.00
88	R-Truth	5.00	12.00
91	Tyson Kidd	6.00	15.00
93	John Morrison	8.00	20.00

97	Randy Orton	10.00	25.00
100	Sheamus	6.00	15.00
106	David Hart Smith	5.00	12.00

2010 Topps Platinum WWE Triple Relics

STATED PRINT RUN 99 SER.#'d SETS

PTR1	TripleH/Cena/Edge	25.00	50.00
PTR2	Morrison/Kingston/Miz	20.00	40.00
PTR3	Bourne/Truth/Christian	20.00	40.00
PTR4	Rhodes/Bourne/MVP	20.00	40.00
PTR5	Christian/Edge/Kidd	20.00	40.00
PTR6	Sheamus/Mysterio/Orton/75	25.00	50.00
PTR7	Cena/Sheamus/Morrison	25.00	50.00
PTR8	Orton/Smith/Marella	25.00	50.00
PTR9	Show/Edge/Punk	20.00	40.00
PTR10	Punk/Miz/Mysterio/75	20.00	40.00

2006 Topps UK WWE Insider English

COMPLETE SET (82)
UNOPENED BOX (24 PACKS)
UNOPENED PACK (5 CARDS)
*GERMAN: X TO X BASIC CARDS
*ITALIAN: X TO X BASIC CARDS

1	Antonio
2	Big Show FOIL
3	Carlito
4	Chris Masters
5	Christy Hemme FOIL
6	Danny Basham
7	Edge
8	Eric Bischoff
9	Eugene
10	Gene Snitsky
11	Hulk Hogan FOIL
12	Jerry The King Lawler
13	Jim Ross
14	John Cena FOIL
15	Jonathan Coachman
16	Kane FOIL
17	Chavo Guerrero
18	Kurt Angle FOIL
19	Lance Cade FOIL
20	Lilian Garcia
21	Lita
22	Maria
23	Matt Hardy
24	Rene Dupree
25	Ric Flair FOIL
26	Rob Conway
27	Rob Van Dam
28	Romeo
29	Rosey
30	Shawn Michaels
31	Shelton Benjamin
32	Stacy Keibler
33	Stone Cold Steve Austin
34	Tajiri
35	The Hurricane
36	Trevor Murdoch FOIL
37	Triple H
38	Trish Stratus
39	Tyson Tomko
40	Val Venis
41	Victoria
42	Viscera
43	Batista FOIL

44	Booker T
45	Candice
46	Chris Benoit FOIL
47	Christian
48	Doug Basham
49	The Boogeyman FOIL
50	Funaki
51	Hardcore Holly
52	Heidenreich FOIL
53	JBL
54	Joey Mercury
55	Johnny Nitro
56	Josh Mathews
57	Juventud
58	Ken Kennedy
59	Melina
60	Michael Cole
61	Michelle McCool
62	Nunzio FOIL
63	Orlando Jordan
64	Paul London
65	Psicosis
66	Randy Orton
67	Rey Mysterio FOIL
68	Road Warrior Animal FOIL
69	Scotty 2 Hotty
70	Sharmell
71	Simon Dean
72	Steven Richards
73	Super Crazy
74	Sylvan
75	Tazz
76	Theodore Long
77	Torrie Wilson
78	Undertaker FOIL
79	Vito
80	William Regal
81	WWE Logo FOIL
82	WrestleMania 22 Logo

2006 Topps UK WWE Insider English Checklists

COMPLETE SET (2)
*GERMAN: X TO X BASIC CARDS
*ITALIAN: X TO X BASIC CARDS

| CK1 | Checklist 1 |
| CK2 | Checklist 2 |

1999 Topps WCW Embossed

Subsets within the set include: P = Personalities (47-49); DHD = Danger: Hardcore Division (50-54); WOW = Women of WCW (62-72)

COMPLETE SET (72)		10.00	25.00
UNOPENED BOX (36 PACKS)			
UNOPENED PACK (8 CARDS)			

1	Title Card	.12	.30
2	Buff Bagwell	.12	.30
3	Lash LeRoux	.12	.30
4	Chris Benoit	.20	.50
5	Rick Steiner	.20	.50
6	Diamond Dallas Page	.25	.60
7	Disco Inferno	.12	.30
8	Bobby Duncum, Jr.	.12	.30
9	Vampiro	.12	.30
10	Rowdy Roddy Piper	.40	1.00
11	Arn Anderson	.25	.60
12	Sid Vicious	.12	.30

13	Macho Man Randy Savage	.40	1.00
14	Ric Flair	1.00	2.50
15	Saturn	.12	.30
16	Goldberg	.30	1.00
17	Steven Regal	.12	.30
18	Juventud Guerrera	.20	.50
19	Chavo Guerrero, Jr.	.12	.30
20	Eddy Guerrero	.20	.50
21	Shane Douglas	.12	.30
22	Sting	.60	1.50
23	Rey Mysterio, Jr.	.30	.75
24	Booker T.	.20	.50
25	Stevie Ray	.12	.30
26	Bret Hart	.20	.50
27	Barry Windham	.12	.30
28	Scott Norton	.12	.30
29	Curt Hennig	.25	.60
30	Kaos	.12	.30
31	Scotty Riggs	.12	.30
32	Hugh Morrus	.12	.30
33	Ernest The Cat Miller	.12	.30
34	Kanyon	.12	.30
35	Kaz Hayashi	.12	.30
36	Billy Kidman	.12	.30
37	Konnan	.12	.30
38	Psychosis	.12	.30
39	Lenny Lane	.12	.30
40	Lodi	.12	.30
41	Meng	.12	.30
42	Dean Malenko	.12	.30
43	Prince Iaukea	.12	.30
44	Berlyn	.12	.30
45	David Flair	.12	.30
46	Evan Karagias	.12	.30
47	Jimmy Hart P	.20	.50
48	JJ Dillon P	.12	.30
49	Charles Robinson P	.12	.30
50	Hardcore Hak DHD	.12	.30
51	Brian Knobs DHD	.12	.30
52	Bam Bam Bigelow DHD	.20	.50
53	Jerry Flynn DHD	.12	.30
54	Fit Finlay DHD	.12	.30
55	Hulk Hogan	2.00	5.00
56	Kevin Nash	.30	.75
57	Scott Steiner	.30	.75
58	Lex Luger	.25	.60
59	Scott Hall	.12	.30
60	Horace Hogan	.12	.30
61	Vincent	.12	.30
62	Kimberly WOW	.20	.50
63	Chae WOW	.20	.50
64	Spice WOW	.20	.50
65	Tygress WOW	.20	.50
66	Fyre WOW	.20	.50
67	A.C. Jazz WOW	.20	.50
68	Storm WOW	.20	.50
69	Asya WOW	.20	.50
70	Madusa WOW	.20	.50
71	Gorgeous George WOW	.20	.50
72	Miss Elizabeth WOW	.30	.75
NNO	Hulk Hogan RR	25.00	50.00

1999 Topps WCW Embossed Authentic Signatures

STATED ODDS 1:49

NNO	Asya	20.00	50.00
NNO	Barbarian	50.00	100.00
NNO	Blitzkrieg	15.00	40.00

NNO	Brad Armstrong	25.00	60.00
NNO	Buff Bagwell	75.00	150.00
NNO	Chastity	30.00	75.00
NNO	Chris Adams	50.00	100.00
NNO	Dave Taylor	20.00	50.00
NNO	Doug Dillinger	15.00	40.00
NNO	Eric Watts	30.00	75.00
NNO	Gorgeous George	100.00	200.00
NNO	Hacksaw Jim Duggan	30.00	75.00
NNO	Horace Hogan	25.00	60.00
NNO	Jerry Flynn	25.00	60.00
NNO	Kendall Windham	30.00	75.00
NNO	Lash Laroux	20.00	50.00
NNO	Lex Luger	60.00	120.00
NNO	Lizmark, Jr.	20.00	50.00
NNO	Madusa	50.00	100.00
NNO	Outrageous Evan Karagios	20.00	50.00
NNO	Sarge Buddy Lee Parker	20.00	50.00
NNO	Scott Hudson	30.00	75.00
NNO	Scotty Putsky	25.00	60.00
NNO	Steve Regal	50.00	100.00
NNO	Tank Abbott	50.00	100.00
NNO	Tough Tom	20.00	50.00
NNO	Van Hammer	30.00	75.00

1999 Topps WCW Embossed Chrome

| COMPLETE SET (5) | | | 12.00 |
| STATED ODDS 1:6 | | | |

1	Buff Bagwell/Lex Luger	1.50	4.00
2	Goldberg/Kevin Nash	2.50	6.00
3	Randy Savage/Gorgeous George	2.50	6.00
4	Ric Flair/David Flair	2.00	5.00
5	Scott Steiner/Rick Steiner	1.25	3.00

1999 Topps WCW Embossed Promos

| P1 | Buff Bagwell | 1.00 | 2.50 |
| P2 | Gorgeous George | 1.50 | 4.00 |

1992 Topps UK WCW

COMPLETE SET (66)

1	Lex Luger
2	Sting
3	Brian Pillman
4	Arn Anderson
5	Tom Zenk
6	Scott Steiner
7	Rick Steiner
8	Barry Windham
9	Butch Reed
10	Ron Simmons
11	Doom
12	El Gigante
13	Michael PS Hayes
14	Jimmy Garvin
15	The Fabulous Freebirds
16	The Steiner Brothers
17	Brian Pillman
18	Diamond Studd
19	P.N. News
20	Johnny B. Badd
21	Paul E. Dangerously
22	Bobby Eaton
23	Richard Morton
24	One Man Gang
25	Diamond Dallas Page
26	Checklist
27	Tommy Rich

28	P.N. News
29	Van Hammer
30	Lex Luger
31	Missy Hyatt
32	Van Hammer
33	Arn Anderson
34	Bobby Eaton
35	Jimmy Garvin UER/Scott Hall Image
36	Big Josh
37	Dustin Rhodes
38	Tom Zenk
39	Johnny B. Badd
40	Lex Luger
41	Sting
42	Terrence Taylor
43	Big Van Vader
44	Arn Anderson
45	Barry Windham
46	One Man Gang
47	Sting
48	Checklist
49	Jimmy Garvin UER/Scott Hall Image
50	Lex Luger
51	Dustin Rhodes
52	Diamond Studd
53	Tommy Rich
54	Lex Luger
55	Bobby Eaton
56	Johnny B. Badd
57	Sting
58	Big Josh
59	Tracy Smothers
60	Brian Pillman
61	Big Van Vader
62	Terrence Taylor
63	Ron Simmons
64	Tom Zenk
65	P.N. News
66	El Gigante

1999 Topps WCW VHS Promos

COMPLETE SET (5)

1	Hollywood Hogan
2	Ric Flair
3	Sting
4	Lex Luger
5	Randy Savage

1998 Topps WCW/nWo

This all-new 72 premium-card set on 20 point heavy-duty stock, UV coated on both sides, features all of the WCW and nWo's hard-hitting, body-slamming superstars like Goldberg, Sting, Hollywood Hogan and Kevin Nash. Subsets within this set include: NG = Nitro Girls (58-64); ICON = Icons (65-67); and CH = Champions (68-71)

COMPLETE SET (72)		30.00	75.00
UNOPENED BOX (36 PACKS)			
UNOPENED PACK (4 CARDS)			

1	Hollywood Hogan	2.00	5.00
2	Sting	.75	2.00
3	Kevin Nash	.40	1.00
4	Macho Man Randy Savage	.40	1.00
5	Bret Hart	.30	.75
6	Lex Luger	.30	.75
7	Giant	.20	.50
8	Diamond Dallas Page	.20	.50

9 Goldberg	10.00	25.00
10 Scott Hall	.12	.30
11 Rick Steiner	.20	.50
12 Scott Steiner	.30	.75
13 Buff Bagwell	.60	1.50
14 Scott Norton	.12	.30
15 Booker T	.20	.50
16 Rowdy Roddy Piper	.40	1.00
17 Chris Benoit	.20	.50
18 Raven	.12	.30
19 Chris Jericho	6.00	15.00
20 Ravishing Rick Rude	.30	.75
21 Konnan	.12	.30
22 Saturn	.12	.30
23 Sick Boy	.12	.30
24 British Bulldog	.20	.50
25 Juventud Guerrera	.12	.30
26 Dean Malenko	.12	.30
27 Eddy Guerrero	8.00	20.00
28 Chavo Guerrero Jr.	.12	.30
29 Ultimo Dragon	.12	.30
30 Disco Inferno	.12	.30
31 Wrath	.12	.30
32 Rey Mysterio Jr.	10.00	25.00
33 Psychosis	.12	.30
34 Stevie Ray	.12	.30
35 Jimmy Hart	.20	.50
36 Steve McMichael	.20	.50
37 Curt Hennig	.30	.75
38 Meng	.12	.30
39 Vincent	.12	.30
40 Fit Finley	.12	.30
41 Jay Leno	1.25	3.00
42 Alex Wright	.12	.30
43 Tenay/Schiavone/Heenan	.12	.30
44 Hugh Morrus	.12	.30
45 Kaz Hayashi	.12	.30
46 Kanyon	.12	.30
47 The Disciple	.20	.50
48 Jim Neidhart	.12	.30
49 Arn Anderson	.20	.50
50 Eric Bischoff	1.25	3.00
51 Ernest Miller	.12	.30
52 Miss Elizabeth	.30	.75
53 Gene Okerlund	.20	.50
54 Ric Flair	.75	2.00
55 Brian Adams	.20	.50
56 Lodi	.12	.30
57 Riggs	.12	.30
58 Fyre NG	.20	.50
59 Chae NG	.20	.50
60 Kimberly NG	.20	.50
61 Spice NG	.20	.50
62 A.C. Jazz NG	.20	.50
63 Tygress NG	.20	.50
64 Whisper NG	.20	.50
65 Hollywood Hogan ICON	2.00	5.00
66 Macho Man Randy Savage ICON	.40	1.00
67 Rowdy Roddy Piper ICON	.40	1.00
68 Goldberg CH	2.50	6.00
69 Chris Jericho CH	3.00	8.00
70 Bret Hart CH	.30	.75
71 Kidman CH	.12	.30
72 Checklist	.12	2.00

1998 Topps WCW/nWo Authentic Signatures

This 37-card insert set features authentic autograph

---

cards of the most popular wrestlers, WCW/nWo personalities and NITRO girl dancers including Goldberg. Cards are unnumbered.

COMPLETE SET (37)
STATED ODDS 1:40 HOBBY

NNO Alex Wright	25.00	60.00
NNO Arn Anderson	75.00	150.00
NNO Bobby Heenan	125.00	250.00
NNO Chris Benoit	225.00	450.00
NNO Chris Jericho	100.00	200.00
NNO Dean Malenko	60.00	120.00
NNO Diamond Dallas Page	125.00	250.00
NNO The Disciple	25.00	60.00
NNO Disco Inferno	25.00	60.00
NNO Eddy Guerrero	300.00	500.00
NNO Ernest Miller	100.00	200.00
NNO Fit Finley	30.00	75.00
NNO Fyre	30.00	75.00
NNO Gene Okerlund	100.00	200.00
NNO Giant	50.00	100.00
NNO Hollywood Hogan	300.00	500.00
NNO Jimmy Hart	30.00	75.00
NNO Juventud Guerrera	30.00	75.00
NNO Kanyon	25.00	60.00
NNO Kaz Hayashi	30.00	75.00
NNO Kevin Nash	50.00	100.00
NNO Kidman	50.00	100.00
NNO Konnan	30.00	75.00
NNO Lodi	20.00	50.00
NNO Meng	20.00	50.00
NNO Mike Tenay	15.00	40.00
NNO Psychosis	30.00	75.00
NNO Raven	50.00	100.00
NNO Riggs	50.00	100.00
NNO Saturn	30.00	75.00
NNO Sick Boy	20.00	50.00
NNO Spice	30.00	75.00
NNO Tony Schiavone	50.00	100.00
NNO Tygress	25.00	60.00
NNO Vincent	15.00	40.00
NNO Whisper	25.00	60.00
NNO Wrath	30.00	75.00

1998 Topps WCW/nWo Chrome

This 10 card insert set features twelve randomly inserted Topps Chrome cards featuring images, logos and sparkling photography based on all twelve 1998 Pay Per View WCW/nWo Events.

COMPLETE SET (10) 20.00 40.00
STATED ODDS 1:12 HOBBY EXCLUSIVE

C1 Goldberg	3.00	8.00
C2 Diamond Dallas Page	2.50	6.00
C3 Macho Man Randy Savage	3.00	8.00
C4 Sting	3.00	8.00
C5 Hollywood Hogan	4.00	10.00
C6 Kevin Nash	2.50	6.00
C7 Konnan	1.25	3.00
C8 Bret Hart	2.00	5.00
C9 Giant	2.00	5.00
C10 Lex Luger	2.50	6.00

1998 Topps WCW/nWo Retail Stickers

This is a 10 sticker set of your favorite WCW/nWo wrestlers.

COMPLETE SET (10) 5.00 12.00
STATED ODDS 1:1 RETAIL EXCLUSIVE

S1 Goldberg	2.00	5.00
S2 Diamond Dallas Page	.60	1.50
S3 Macho Man Randy Savage	1.25	3.00
S4 Sting	1.00	2.50
S5 Hollywood Hogan	2.00	5.00
S6 Kevin Nash	.50	1.25
S7 Konnan	.40	1.00
S8 Bret Hart	1.25	3.00
S9 Giant	.60	1.50
S10 Lex Luger	.40	1.00

1998 Topps WCW/nWo Promos

P1 Hollywood Hogan	1.00	2.50
P2 Sting	.60	1.50
P3 Macho Man	.75	2.00
P4 Diamond Dallas Page	.60	1.50
P5 Goldberg	1.00	2.50

1999 Topps WCW/nWo Nitro

This all-new 72 premium-card set on 20 point heavy-duty stock, UV coated on both sides, features all of the WCW and nWo's hard-hitting, body-slamming superstars like Goldberg, Sting, Hollywood Hogan and Kevin Nash. This set also has seven never before seen subsets. Suggested retail price of this set with 8 cards per pack is $1.99 per pack.

COMPLETE SET (72) 6.00 15.00
UNOPENED BOX (36 PACKS)
UNOPENED PACK (8 CARDS)

1 Checklist	.12	.30
2 Bret Hart	.25	.60
3 Diamond Dallas Page	.25	.60
4 Goldberg	.30	.75
5 Rick Steiner	.20	.50
6 Booker T	.20	.50
7 Chris Jericho	.20	.50
8 Saturn	.12	.30
9 Bam Bam Bigelow	.20	.50
10 Chavo Guerrero, Jr.	.12	.30
11 Disco Inferno	.12	.30
12 Wrath	.12	.30
13 Rey Misterio, Jr.	.25	.60
14 Meng	.12	.30
15 Super Calo	.12	.30
16 Glacier	.12	.30
17 Silver King	.12	.30
18 Kaos	.12	.30
19 Lenny Lane	.12	.30
20 Norman Smiley	.12	.30
21 Kidman	.12	.30
22 Alex Wright	.12	.30
23 Kanyon	.12	.30
24 Raven	.12	.30
25 Lodi	.12	.30
26 Ernest Miller	.20	.50
27 The Disciple	.20	.50
28 Bobby Duncum, Jr.	.12	.30
29 Barry Windham	.12	.30
30 Konnan	.12	.30
31 Buff Bagwell	.12	.30
32 Eric Bischoff	.12	.30
33 Hollywood Hogan	1.50	4.00
34 Scott Hall	.12	.30
35 Horace Hogan	.12	.30
36 Scott Steiner	.25	.60
37 Stevie Ray	.12	.30
38 Brian Adams	.12	.30
39 Vincent	.12	.30

---

40 Curt Hennig	.25	.60
41 Macho Man Randy Savage	.40	1.00
42 Sting	.60	1.50
43 Kevin Nash	.30	.75
44 Lex Luger	.25	.60
45 Ric Flair	1.00	2.50
46 Arn Anderson	.20	.50
47 Dean Malenko	.12	.30
48 Chris Benoit	.25	.60
49 Steve McMichael	.20	.50
50 Juventud Guerrera	.12	.30
51 Eddie Guerrero	.20	.50
52 Psychosis	.12	.30
53 La Parka	.12	.30
54 Damian	.12	.30
55 Hector Garza	.12	.30
56 Miss Elizabeth	.30	.75
57 Kimberly	.20	.50
58 Spice	.20	.50
59 A.C. Jazz	.20	.50
60 Tygress	.20	.50
61 Whisper	.20	.50
62 Chae	.20	.50
63 Fyre	.20	.50
64 Storm	.20	.50
65 Goldberg Triumphant	.30	.75
66 The Venomous Bite of Sting	.40	1.00
67 Hogan for President	.60	1.50
68 Kevin Nash Is God	.30	.75
69 DDP Is Back Again	.25	.60
70 Larry Zbyszko/Bobby Heenan	.20	.50
71 Doug Dellinger	.12	.30
72 Sonny Onoo	.12	.30

1999 Topps WCW/nWo Nitro Authentic Signatures

This 37 card insert set features authentic autograph cards of the most popular wrestlers, WCW/nWo personalities and NITRO girl dancers including superstar GOLDBERG.

COMPLETE SET (37)
STATED ODDS 1:40 HOBBY

NNO A.C. Jazz	25.00	60.00
NNO Bam Bam Bigelow	150.00	300.00
NNO Billy Silverman	20.00	50.00
NNO Bret Hart	100.00	200.00
NNO Brian Adams	100.00	200.00
NNO Chae	20.00	50.00
NNO Charles Robinson	15.00	40.00
NNO Chavo Guerrero, Jr.	15.00	40.00
NNO Curt Hennig	250.00	400.00
NNO Cyclope	12.00	30.00
NNO Damian	12.00	30.00
NNO David Penzer	15.00	40.00
NNO El Dandy	10.00	25.00
NNO Glacier	15.00	40.00
NNO Goldberg	150.00	300.00
NNO Hector Garza	12.00	30.00
NNO Hugh Morrus	25.00	60.00
NNO Jim Neidhart	50.00	100.00
NNO Kenny Kaos	15.00	40.00
NNO Kimberly	125.00	250.00
NNO La Parka	50.00	100.00
NNO Larry Zbyszko	25.00	60.00
NNO Lenny Lane	12.00	30.00
NNO Macho Man Randy Savage	500.00	1000.00
NNO Ms. Elizabeth	400.00	800.00
NNO Nick Patrick	10.00	25.00

NNO Norman Smiley	12.00	30.00
NNO Prince Iaukea	10.00	25.00
NNO Rick Steiner	50.00	100.00
NNO Scott Hall	125.00	250.00
NNO Scott Norton	12.00	30.00
NNO Silver King	10.00	25.00
NNO Sonny Onoo	10.00	25.00
NNO Sting	100.00	200.00
NNO Storm	10.00	25.00
NNO Super Calo	10.00	25.00
NNO Ultimo Dragon	30.00	75.00

1999 Topps WCW/nWo Nitro Chrome

This 12-card insert set features randomly inserted Topps Chrome cards featuring images, logos and sparkling photography based on all twelve 1998 Pay Per View WCW/nWo Events.

COMPLETE SET (12)	30.00	60.00
STATED ODDS 1:12 HOBBY		
C1 Sting/Luger v. Hogan/Nash	3.00	8.00
C2 Hogan v. Sting	4.00	10.00
C3 Hogan v. Savage	3.00	8.00
C4 Savage v. Sting	2.50	6.00
C5 Nash v. Giant	3.00	8.00
C6 Hogan/Hart v. Savage/Piper	4.00	10.00
C7 DDP v. Hogan	3.00	8.00
C8 DDP v. Hogan	3.00	8.00
C9 WCW v. The Pac v. Hollywood	3.00	8.00
C10 Goldberg v. DDP	2.50	6.00
C11 60 Man 3 Ring Battle Royal	1.50	4.00
C12 Nash v. Goldberg	3.00	8.00

1999 Topps WCW/nWo Nitro Stickers

COMPLETE SET (12)	3.00	6.00
STATED ODDS 1:1 RETAIL		
S1 Sting/Luger v. Hogan/Nash	.40	1.00
S2 Hogan v. Sting	.40	1.00
S3 Hogan v. Savage	.30	.75
S4 Savage v. Sting	.20	.50
S5 Nash v. Giant	.20	.50
S6 Hogan/Hart v. Savage/Piper	.40	1.00
S7 DDP v. Hogan	.40	1.00
S8 DDP v. Hogan	.40	1.00
S9 WCW v. The Pac v. Hollywood	.40	1.00
S10 Goldberg v. DDP	.30	.75
S11 60 Man 3 Ring Battle Royal	.20	.50
S12 Nash v. Goldberg	.30	.75

1999 Topps WCW/nWo Nitro Promos

D1 IS DEALER EXCLUSIVE		
B1 Nash and Nitro Girls DE	3.00	8.00
H1 Goldberg	2.00	5.00
H2 Kevin Nash	.75	2.00
H3 Goldberg	1.25	3.00
R1 Goldberg		

2009 Topps WWE

COMPLETE SET (90)	15.00	30.00
UNOPENED BOX (24 PACKS)		
UNOPENED PACK (7 CARDS)		
*GOLD/500: 1.2X TO 3X BASIC CARDS		
*BLACK/40: 5X TO 12X BASIC CARDS		
*PLATINUM/1: UNPRICED DUE TO SCARCITY		
1 Hurricane Helms	.15	.40
2 Carlito	.40	1.00
3 CM Punk	.25	.60
4 Maria	.60	1.50

5 Kofi Kingston	.15	.40
6 Primo	.15	.40
7 Rey Mysterio	.40	1.00
8 Natalya	.60	1.50
9 Tommy Dreamer	.15	.40
10 Michelle McCool	.60	1.50
11 Undertaker	.75	2.00
12 Big Show	.40	1.00
13 Charlie Haas	.15	.40
14 Chris Jericho	.40	1.00
15 Evan Bourne	.15	.40
16 Layla	.40	1.00
17 Christian	.40	1.00
18 Cody Rhodes	.15	.40
19 Dolph Ziggler	.25	.60
20 Randy Orton	.40	1.00
21 Edge	.60	1.50
22 Mickie James	.75	2.00
23 Festus	.15	.40
24 Finlay	.25	.60
25 Ted DiBiase	.25	.60
26 Goldust	.25	.60
27 Melina	.60	1.50
28 Hornswoggle	.25	.60
29 Jack Swagger	.15	.40
30 Jim Ross	.15	.40
31 Mark Henry	.25	.60
32 Katie Lea Burchill	.40	1.00
33 Mike Knox	.15	.40
34 Kelly Kelly	.60	1.50
35 Matt Hardy	.60	1.50
36 Montel Vontavious Porter	.25	.60
37 R-Truth	.15	.40
38 John Cena	1.00	2.50
39 William Regal	.40	1.00
40 Santino Marella	.15	.40
41 Tyson Kidd	.15	.40
42 Maryse	.40	1.00
43 Shelton Benjamin	.15	.40
44 The Brian Kendrick	.25	.60
45 The Great Khali	.15	.40
46 Eve	.60	1.50
47 The Miz	.25	.60
48 Triple H	1.00	2.50
49 Vladimir Kozlov	.25	.60
50 Alicia Fox	.25	.60
51 Beth Phoenix	.75	2.00
52 Gail Kim	.40	1.00
53 Jerry The King Lawler	.25	.60
54 Theodore Long	.15	.40
55 Batista	.60	1.50
56 Tiffany	.25	.60
57 Ranjin Singh	.15	.40
58 Tony Atlas	.15	.40
59 Kane	.60	1.50
60 Shawn Michaels	1.00	2.50
61 Chavo Guerrero	.25	.60
62 John Morrison	.25	.60
63 Jamie Noble	.15	.40
64 Jimmy Wang Yang	.15	.40
65 Kung Fu Naki	.15	.40
66 Paul Burchill	.15	.40
67 Jillian Hall	.60	1.50
68 David Hart Smith	.15	.40
69 Curt Hawkins	.15	.40
70 DJ Gabriel	.15	.40
71 Ezekiel Jackson	.15	.40
72 Jesse	.15	.40

73 Zack Ryder	.15	.40
74 JTG	.15	.40
75 Shad Gaspard	.15	.40
76 Ricky Ortiz	.15	.40
77 Brie Bella	.60	1.50
78 Nikki Bella	.60	1.50
79 CM Punk	.25	.60
80 Santina Marella	.15	.40
81 Chris Jericho	.40	1.00
82 Matt Hardy	.60	1.50
83 Rey Mysterio	.40	1.00
84 Undertaker/Shawn Michaels	1.00	2.50
85 Edge	.60	1.50
86 John Cena	1.00	2.50
87 Randy Orton	.40	1.00
88 Triple H	1.00	2.50
89 Stone Cold Steve Austin	1.00	2.50
90 John Cena CL	1.00	2.50

2009 Topps WWE Autographs

Hobby Exclusives include: Arn Anderson, Beth Phoenix, Evan Bourne, Gail Kim, Jim Ross, John Cena, Michelle McCool, Ricky Steamboat, and Tiffany; Retail Exclusives include: John Morrison, Maryse, Mickie James, and Santino Marella.

STATED ODDS 1:54 HOBBY; 1:172 RETAIL		
NNO Arn Anderson	25.00	60.00
NNO Beth Phoenix	12.00	30.00
NNO Evan Bourne	6.00	15.00
NNO Gail Kim	12.00	30.00
NNO Jim Ross	10.00	25.00
NNO John Cena	20.00	50.00
NNO John Morrison	15.00	40.00
NNO Maryse	25.00	60.00
NNO Michelle McCool	12.00	30.00
NNO Mickie James	15.00	40.00
NNO Ricky Steamboat	15.00	40.00
NNO Santino Marella	6.00	15.00
NNO Tiffany	12.00	30.00

2009 Topps WWE Dual Autographs

STATED ODDS 1:55 HOBBY EXCLUSIVE		
NNO Bob & Randy Orton	20.00	50.00
NNO Carlito/Primo	8.00	20.00
NNO Dusty & Cody Rhodes	30.00	75.00
NNO Ted DiBiase Sr. & Jr.	15.00	40.00

2009 Topps WWE Event-Worn Ringside Relics

Hobby Exclusives include: The Miz (looking left), Santino Marella (hands apart), Shawn Michaels (w/o hat), and Triple H; Retail Exclusives include: Christian, Cody Rhodes, The Miz (looking right), Santino Marella (hands clasped), Shawn Michaels (w/hat), and Ted Dibiase.

STATED ODDS 1:24 HOBBY; 1:84 RETAIL		
NNO Christian	6.00	15.00
NNO Cody Rhodes	6.00	15.00
NNO Miz (looking left)	5.00	12.00
NNO Miz (looking right)	5.00	12.00
NNO Santino Marella (hands apart)	6.00	15.00
NNO Santino Marella (hands clasped)	6.00	15.00
NNO Shawn Michaels (no hat)	8.00	20.00
NNO Shawn Michaels (w/hat)	8.00	20.00
NNO Ted DiBiase	6.00	15.00
NNO Triple H	8.00	20.00

2009 Topps WWE Historical Commemorative Patches

COMPLETE SET (4)	12.00	30.00
STATED ODDS 1:RETAIL BLASTER BOX		
P1 John Cena	6.00	15.00
WrestleMania		
P2 John Cena	6.00	15.00
The Bash		
P3 John Cena	6.00	15.00
SummerSlam		
P4 John Cena	6.00	15.00
Royal Rumble		

2009 Topps WWE Judgment Day Mat Relic Autographs

STATED ODDS 1:215 HOBBY EXCLUSIVE		
NNO Christian	25.00	60.00
NNO Edge	30.00	75.00
NNO Randy Orton	30.00	75.00
NNO Rey Mysterio	20.00	50.00

2009 Topps WWE Legends of the Ring

COMPLETE SET (20)	8.00	20.00
*GOLD/2250: .75X TO 2X BASIC CARDS		
*PLATINUM/1: UNPRICE DUE TO SCARCITY		
STATED ODDS 1:1 HOBBY AND RETAIL		
1 Bam Bam Bigelow	1.00	2.50
2 British Bulldog	1.00	2.50
3 Chief Jay Strongbow	.60	1.50
4 Dean Malenko	1.00	2.50
5 Don Muraco	.40	1.00
6 Dusty Rhodes	1.00	2.50
7 Iron Sheik	1.00	2.50
8 Jake The Snake Roberts	1.00	2.50
9 Jimmy Superfly Snuka	1.00	2.50
10 Junkyard Dog	1.00	2.50
11 Mr. Perfect	1.00	2.50
12 Nikolai Volkoff	.60	1.50
13 Ravishing Rick Rude	1.00	2.50
14 Sgt. Slaughter	1.00	2.50
15 Superstar Billy Graham	1.00	2.50
16 Terry Funk	.60	1.50
17 Vader	.60	1.50
18 The Wild Samoans	.60	1.50
19 Gorilla Monsoon	1.00	2.50
20 Mr. Wonderful Paul Orndorff	.60	1.50

2009 Topps WWE Reign of Honor

COMPLETE SET (10)	6.00	15.00
STATED ODDS 1:6 HOBBY AND RETAIL		
1 John Cena	1.50	4.00
2 Triple H	1.50	4.00
3 Jack Swagger	.25	.60
4 Rey Mysterio	.60	1.50
5 MVP	.40	1.00
6 Melina	1.00	2.50
7 Maryse	.60	1.50
8 Primo & Carlito	.60	1.50
9 Shawn Michaels	1.50	4.00
10 Undertaker	1.25	3.00

2009 Topps WWE Sketches

STATED ODDS 1:2,857 HOBBY EXCLUSIVE
UNPRICED DUE TO SCARCITY

NNO Eve

Beauty Is in the Eye of the Owner
NNO Eve/Musical Notes		
NNO Eve/Passion		
NNO Eve/Speak What You Feel		
NNO J.Lawler/Batista		
NNO J.Lawler/Big Show		
NNO J.Lawler/Edge		
NNO J.Lawler/Jack Swagger		
NNO J.Lawler/Rey Mysterio		
NNO J.Lawler/Triple H		
NNO J.Lawler/Undertaker		
NNO Natalya/Balance		
NNO Natalya/Calm		
NNO Natalya/Energy		
NNO Natalya		
Glory		
NNO Natalya/Happy		
NNO Natalya/Honour		
NNO Natalya/Peace		
NNO Natalya/Pride		
NNO Natalya/Sparkle		
NNO Natalya/Spirit		
NNO Santino/Island		
NNO Santino/Landscape		
NNO Santino/Map of Italy		
NNO Santino/Muscle		
NNO Santino/Santina		
NNO Santino/Santino		
NNO Santino/Self Portrait 1		
NNO Santino/Self Portrait 2		
NNO Santino/Self Portrait 3		
NNO Santino/Self Portrait w/belt		

2009 Topps WWE Tin Inserts

COMPLETE SET (4)
STATED ODDS 1:

1 Jack Swagger
2 Triple H
3 Chris Jericho
4 Rey Mysterio

2009 Topps WWE Topps Town

COMPLETE SET (30) 6.00 15.00
STATED ODDS 1:1 HOBBY AND RETAIL

1 Batista	.50	1.25
2 Beth Phoenix	.60	1.50
3 Chris Jericho	.30	.75
4 Christian	.30	.75
5 CM Punk	.20	.50
6 Cody Rhodes	.12	.30
7 Dolph Ziggler	.20	.50
8 Edge	.50	1.25
9 Evan Bourne	.12	.30
10 Gail Kim	.30	.75
11 Jack Swagger	.12	.30
12 John Cena	.75	2.00
13 John Morrison	.20	.50
14 Kofi Kingston	.12	.30
15 Maria	.50	1.25
16 Maryse	.30	.75
17 Matt Hardy	.50	1.25
18 Melina	.50	1.25
19 Michelle McCool	.50	1.25
20 Mickie James	.60	1.50
21 Montel Vontavious Porter	.20	.50
22 Randy Orton	.30	.75
23 Rey Mysterio	.30	.75
24 R-Truth	.12	.30
25 Santino Marella	.12	.30
26 Shawn Michaels	.75	2.00
27 Ted DiBiase	.20	.50
28 The Miz	.20	.50
29 Triple H	.75	2.00
30 Undertaker	.60	1.50

2010 Topps WWE

COMPLETE SET (110) 10.00 25.00
UNOPENED BOX (24 PACKS)
UNOPENED PACK (7 CARDS)
*BLUE/2010: 1X TO 2.5X BASIC CARDS
*SILVER/999: 1.2X TO 3X BASIC CARDS
*GOLD/50: 4X TO 10X BASIC CARDS
*RED/1: UNPRICED DUE TO SCARCITY
*P.P.BLACK/1: UNPRICED DUE TO SCARCITY
*P.P.CYAN/1: UNPRICED DUE TO SCARCITY
*P.P.MAGENTA/1: UNPRICED DUE TO SCARCITY
*P.P.YELLOW/1: UNPRICED DUE TO SCARCITY

1 John Cena	.75	2.00
2 Layla	.40	1.00
3 William Regal	.40	1.00
4 John Morrison	.25	.60
5 Matt Hardy	.40	1.00
6 Alicia Fox	.25	.60
7 Yoshi Tatsu	.15	.40
8 Nikki Bella	.60	1.50
9 Randy Orton	.60	1.50
10 Luke Gallows	.15	.40
11 MVP	.25	.60
12 Michelle McCool	.60	1.50
13 JTG	.15	.40
14 Rosa Mendes	.25	.60
15 Beth Phoenix	.60	1.50
16 Chris Jericho	.40	1.00
17 Kane	.40	1.00
18 Mark Henry	.25	.60
19 Tyson Kidd	.15	.40
20 Santino Marella	.15	.40
21 Theodore Long	.15	.40
22 Big Show	.40	1.00
23 Kofi Kingston	.25	.60
24 Vladimir Kozlov	.25	.60
25 Vance Archer	.15	.40
26 Brie Bella	.60	1.50
27 Ezekiel Jackson	.15	.40
28 David Hart Smith	.15	.40
29 Trent Bareta	.15	.40
30 Kelly Kelly	.60	1.50
31 Goldust	.25	.60
32 Maryse	.60	1.50
33 Tyler Reks	.15	.40
34 Serena	.25	.60
35 Melina	.60	1.50
36 CM Punk	.60	1.50
37 Drew McIntyre	.25	.60
38 Jillian	.60	1.50
39 Cody Rhodes	.15	.40
40 Ted DiBiase	.25	.60
41 Finlay	.25	.60
42 Dolph Ziggler	.25	.60
43 Triple H	.75	2.00
44 Hornswoggle	.25	.60
45 R-Truth	.15	.40
46 The Miz	.25	.60
47 Primo	.15	.40
48 Jack Swagger	.15	.40
49 Caylen Croft	.15	.40
50 Rey Mysterio	.40	1.00
51 Chris Masters	.15	.40
52 Chavo Guerrero	.25	.60
53 Shad	.15	.40
54 Ranjin Singh	.15	.40
55 Sheamus	.25	.60
56 Vickie Guerrero	.15	.40
57 Evan Bourne	.15	.40
58 Edge	.60	1.50
59 The Undertaker	.60	1.50
60 Zack Ryder	.15	.40
61 Natalya	.60	1.50
62 The Great Khali	.15	.40
63 Eve	.60	1.50
64 Christian	.25	.60
65 Michael Tarver	.25	.60
66 Skip Sheffield	.25	.60
67 Wade Barrett	.25	.60
68 Daniel Bryan	.25	.60
69 Darren Young	.25	.60
70 David Otunga	.25	.60
71 Heath Slater	.25	.60
72 Justin Gabriel	.25	.60
73 Undertaker 18-0	.60	1.50
74 ShowMiz	.40	1.00
75 The Dude Busters	.15	.40
76 The Straight Edge Society	.60	1.50
77 Hart Dynasty	.60	1.50
78 Mr. Perfect Curt Hennig	.25	.60
79 Dean Malenko	.25	.60
80 Don Muraco	.25	.60
81 Akeem	.25	.60
82 Doink the Clown	.15	.40
83 Earthquake	.25	.60
84 Hillbilly Jim	.25	.60
85 Mr. Wonderful Paul Orndorff	.40	1.00
86 Nikolai Volkoff	.25	.60
87 Papa Shango	.15	.40
88 Vader	.25	.60
89 Sgt. Slaughter	.40	1.00
90 Junkyard Dog	.40	1.00
91 Bobby The Brain Heenan	.25	.60
92 Harley Race	.25	.60
93 The American Dream Dusty Rhodes	.40	1.00
94 Jake The Snake Roberts	.40	1.00
95 The Iron Sheik	.40	1.00
96 Koko B. Ware	.25	.60
97 Brian Pillman	.40	1.00
98 Jimmy Superfly Snuka	.40	1.00
99 Mean Gene Okerland UER	.25	.60
100 Million Dollar Man Ted DiBiase	.25	.60
101 The Bushwackers	.15	.40
102 Paul Bearer	.25	.60
103 Rowdy Roddy Piper	.60	1.50
104 Terry Funk	.40	1.00
105 Kamala	.25	.60
106 Cowboy Bob Orton	.25	.60
107 The Road Warriors	.40	1.00
108 Ravishing Rick Rude	.25	.60
109 Bam Bam Bigelow	.25	.60
110 Classy Freddie Blassie	.40	1.00
CH1 Checklist 1/2	.15	.40
CH3 Checklist 3/4	.15	.40

2010 Topps WWE Autographs

Triple H never signed for the set so when customers redeemed his exchange card they instead received a John Cena autograph.
*GOLD/25: .6X TO 1.5X BASIC AUTOS
*RED/1: UNPRICED DUE TO SCARCITY
*P.P.BLACK/1: UNPRICED DUE TO SCARCITY
*P.P.CYAN/1: UNPRICED DUE TO SCARCITY
*P.P.MAGENTA/1: UNPRICED DUE TO SCARCITY
*P.P.YELLOW/1: UNPRICED DUE TO SCARCITY
OVERALL AUTO ODDS 1:BOX

ABP Beth Phoenix		
ABS Big Show	12.00	30.00
ACC Caylen Croft	6.00	15.00
ACH Christian		
ACM CM Punk	20.00	50.00
ACR Cody Rhodes	8.00	20.00
ADM Drew McIntyre	10.00	25.00
ADS David Hart Smith	8.00	20.00
AEB Evan Bourne	6.00	15.00
AED Edge	12.00	30.00
AEJ Ezekiel Jackson	6.00	15.00
AGK Gail Kim	12.00	30.00
AJC John Cena	30.00	75.00
AJM John Morrison	10.00	25.00
AJT JTG	6.00	15.00
AKK Kofi Kingston	8.00	20.00
ALG Luke Gallows	6.00	15.00
AMM Michelle McCool	12.00	30.00
ARM Rosa Mendes	10.00	25.00
ARO Randy Orton	20.00	50.00
ART R-Truth	8.00	20.00
ASE Serena	10.00	25.00
ASH Shad	6.00	15.00
ATB Trent Baretta	6.00	15.00
ATD Ted DiBiase	10.00	25.00
ATH Triple H		
ATK Tyson Kidd	8.00	20.00
ATM Miz	12.00	30.00
AVA Vance Archer	6.00	15.00
AZR Zack Ryder	8.00	20.00
ASAN Santino Marella	10.00	25.00
ASHE Sheamus	12.00	30.00
JCA1 John Cena	50.00	100.00

2010 Topps WWE Championship Material

COMPLETE SET (50) 20.00 50.00
*PUZZLE BACK: .5X TO 1.2X BASIC CARDS
*IC PUZZLE: .5X TO 1.2X BASIC CARDS
STATED ODDS 1:6 HOBBY AND RETAIL

C1 Christian	.50	1.25
C2 John Morrison	.50	1.25
C3 John Morrison	.50	1.25
C4 The Miz & John Morrison	.50	1.25
C5 CM Punk	1.25	3.00
C6 CM Punk	1.25	3.00
C7 Kofi Kingston & CM Punk	1.25	3.00
C8 The Miz	.50	1.25
C9 The Hart Dynasty	1.25	3.00
C10 Goldust	.50	1.25
C11 Triple H	1.50	4.00
C12 Edge & Chris Jericho	1.25	3.00
C13 Christian	.50	1.25
C14 Chris Jericho & Big Show	.75	2.00
C15 Chris Jericho	.75	2.00
C16 Randy Orton	1.25	3.00
C17 Big Show & The Miz	.75	2.00
C18 Edge & Christian	1.25	3.00
C19 Edge	1.25	3.00

C20	Mark Henry	.50	1.25
C21	Chavo Guerrero	.50	1.25
C22	Matt Hardy	.75	2.00
C23	Undertaker & Kane	1.25	3.00
C24	Kane	.75	2.00
C25	Kane	.75	2.00
C26	R-Truth	.30	.75
C27	John Cena	1.50	4.00
C28	Big Show	.75	2.00
C29	Ted DiBiase & Cody Rhodes	.50	1.25
C30	Drew McIntyre	.50	1.25
C31	Rey Mysterio	.75	2.00
C32	Jack Swagger	.30	.75
C33	William Regal	.75	2.00
C34	Kofi Kingston	.50	1.25
C35	Santino Marella	.30	.75
C36	Ted DiBiase	.75	2.00
C37	Michelle McCool	1.25	3.00
C38	Maryse	1.25	3.00
C39	Edge & Randy Orton	1.25	3.00
C40	Jillian	1.25	3.00
C41	Melina	1.25	3.00
C42	MVP	.50	1.25
C43	Kofi Kingston	.50	1.25
C44	Matt Hardy	.75	2.00
C45	Finlay	.50	1.25
C46	Mr. Perfect	.50	1.25
C47	Don Muraco	.50	1.25
C48	Ravishing Rick Rude	.50	1.25
C49	Rowdy Roddy Piper	1.25	3.00
C50	British Bulldog	.50	1.25

2010 Topps WWE Dual Autographs

*GOLD/25: .5X TO 1.2X BASIC AUTOS
*RED/1: UNPRICED DUE TO SCARCITY
*P.P.BLACK/1: UNPRICED DUE TO SCARCITY
*P.P.CYAN/1: UNPRICED DUE TO SCARCITY
*P.P.MAGENTA/1: UNPRICED DUE TO SCARCITY
*P.P.YELLOW/1: UNPRICED DUE TO SCARCITY
STATED PRINT RUN 99 SER.#'d SETS

DABM	E.Bourne/D.McIntyre	10.00	25.00
DACB	C.Croft/T.Baretta	8.00	20.00
DACO	J.Cena/R.Orton	50.00	100.00
DADR	T.DiBiase/C.Rhodes	12.00	30.00
DAES	Edge	15.00	40.00
	Big Show		
DAJC	E.Jackson/Christian		
DAJS	JTG	8.00	20.00
	Shad		
DAJT	E.Jackson/R-Truth	8.00	20.00
DAKM	K.Kingston/Miz	12.00	30.00
DAMP	J.Morrison/CM Punk	20.00	50.00
DAPG	CM Punk/L.Gallows	20.00	50.00
DAPS	CM Punk	15.00	40.00
	Serena		
DARM	Z.Ryder/R.Mendes	12.00	30.00
DASK	D.Smith/T.Kidd	8.00	20.00
DASP	S.Marella/B.Phoenix		
DASS	S.Marella/Sheamus	12.00	30.00
DAKMC	G.Kim/M.McCool	15.00	40.00

2010 Topps WWE Elimination Chamber Canvas

COMPLETE SET (19) 60.00 120.00
*GOLD/50: .75X TO 2X BASIC CARDS
*RED/1: UNPRICED DUE TO SCARCITY
OVERALL RELIC ODDS 1:2 RETAIL EXCLUSIVE

EC1	John Cena	8.00	20.00
EC2	Sheamus	2.50	6.00
EC3	Triple H	8.00	20.00
EC4	Randy Orton	6.00	15.00
EC5	Ted DiBiase Jr.	2.50	6.00
EC6	Kofi Kingston	2.50	6.00
EC7	Drew McIntyre	2.50	6.00
EC8	Kane	4.00	10.00
EC9	Michelle McCool	6.00	15.00
EC10	Layla	4.00	10.00
EC11	Maryse	6.00	15.00
EC12	The Miz	2.50	6.00
EC13	MVP	2.50	6.00
EC14	Chris Jericho	4.00	10.00
EC15	The Undertaker	6.00	15.00
EC16	John Morrison	2.50	6.00
EC17	CM Punk	6.00	15.00
EC18	Rey Mysterio	4.00	10.00
EC19	R-Truth	2.50	6.00

2010 Topps WWE Favorite Finishers

COMPLETE SET (25) 8.00 20.00
STATED ODDS 1:4 HOBBY AND RETAIL

FF1	Dolph Ziggler	.40	1.00
FF2	Jack Swagger	.25	.60
FF3	Edge	1.00	2.50
FF4	CM Punk	1.00	2.50
FF5	Sheamus	.40	1.00
FF6	Evan Bourne	.25	.60
FF7	Undertaker	1.00	2.50
FF8	John Cena	1.25	3.00
FF9	The Hart Dynasty	1.00	2.50
FF10	Yoshi Tatsu	.25	.60
FF11	Drew McIntyre	.40	1.00
FF12	MVP	.40	1.00
FF13	John Morrison	.40	1.00
FF14	Randy Orton	1.00	2.50
FF15	Big Show	.60	1.50
FF16	Kofi Kingston	.40	1.00
FF17	Matt Hardy	.60	1.50
FF18	Kane	.60	1.50
FF19	Christian	.40	1.00
FF20	Mark Henry	.40	1.00
FF21	Triple H	1.25	3.00
FF22	Beth Phoenix	1.00	2.50
FF23	Rey Mysterio	.60	1.50
FF24	Chris Jericho	.60	1.50
FF25	The Miz	.40	1.00

2010 Topps WWE History Of

COMPLETE SET (25) 10.00 25.00
STATED ODDS 1:8 HOBBY AND RETAIL

HO1	Chris Jericho	.75	2.00
HO2	Triple H	1.50	4.00
HO3	Edge	1.25	3.00
HO4	Jack Swagger	.30	.75
HO5	John Morrison	.50	1.25
HO6	The Undertaker	1.25	3.00
HO7	Kane	.75	2.00
HO8	The Miz	.50	1.25
HO9	Finlay	.50	1.25
HO10	Michelle McCool	1.25	3.00
HO11	Rey Mysterio	.75	2.00
HO12	Natalya	1.25	3.00
HO13	John Cena	1.50	4.00
HO14	Kelly Kelly	1.25	3.00
HO15	Ted DiBiase	.50	1.25
HO16	Randy Orton	1.25	3.00
HO17	Kofi Kingston	.50	1.25
HO18	Big Show	.75	2.00
HO19	Santino Marella	.30	.75
HO20	Goldust	.50	1.25
HO21	Christian	.50	1.25
HO22	William Regal	.75	2.00
HO23	British Bulldog	.50	1.25
HO24	Junkyard Dog	.75	2.00
HO25	Mr. Perfect	.50	1.25

2010 Topps WWE National Heroes

COMPLETE SET (25) 10.00 25.00
STATED ODDS 1:8 HOBBY AND RETAIL

NH1	John Cena	1.50	4.00
NH2	Maryse	1.25	3.00
NH3	Jack Swagger	.30	.75
NH4	Edge	1.25	3.00
NH5	Chris Jericho	.75	2.00
NH6	William Regal	.75	2.00
NH7	Finlay	.50	1.25
NH8	Yoshi Tatsu	.30	.75
NH9	Sheamus	.50	1.25
NH10	Sgt. Slaughter	.75	2.00
NH11	Vladimir Kozlov	.50	1.25
NH12	The Great Khali	.30	.75
NH13	Kamala	.50	1.25
NH14	Nikolai Volkoff	.50	1.25
NH15	Iron Shiek	.75	2.00
NH16	Wild Samoans	.30	.75
NH17	Kofi Kingston	.50	1.25
NH18	Drew McIntyre	.50	1.25
NH19	Santino Marella	.30	.75
NH20	Rey Mysterio	.75	2.00
NH21	Mark Henry	.50	1.25
NH22	Christian	.50	1.25
NH23	Tyson Kidd	.30	.75
NH24	Chavo Guerrero	.50	1.25
NH25	The British Bulldog	.50	1.25

2010 Topps WWE Signature Swatches

STATED PRINT RUN 25 SER. #'d SETS

SSSBS	Big Show	60.00	120.00
SSSCG	Chavo Guerrero	25.00	60.00
SSSCH	Christian	30.00	80.00
SSSCJ	Chris Jericho	50.00	100.00
SSSCM	CM Punk	60.00	120.00
SSSCR	Cody Rhodes	25.00	60.00
SSSDS	David Hart Smith	25.00	60.00
SSSEB	Evan Bourne	25.00	60.00
SSSED	Edge	50.00	100.00
SSSJC	John Cena	100.00	200.00
SSSJM	John Morrison	50.00	100.00
SSSKK	Kofi Kingston	30.00	80.00
SSSMH	Matt Hardy	30.00	80.00
SSSRM	Rey Mysterio	50.00	100.00
SSSRO	Randy Orton	100.00	200.00
SSSSA	Santino Marella EXCH	50.00	100.00
SSSSH	Shad	25.00	60.00
SSSTD	Ted DiBiase Jr.	25.00	60.00
SSSTK	Tyson Kidd	30.00	80.00
SSSTM	The Miz	30.00	80.00
SSSJTG	JTG	25.00	60.00
SSSMVP	MVP	30.00	80.00

2010 Topps WWE Superstar Jumbo Swatches

STATED PRINT RUN 30 SER.#'d SETS

SSSBS	Big Show	50.00	100.00
SSSCG	Chavo Guerrero		
SSSCH	Christian	40.00	80.00
SSSCJ	Chris Jericho		
SSSCM	CM Punk	50.00	100.00
SSSCR	Cody Rhodes	20.00	50.00
SSSDS	David Hart Smith	25.00	60.00
SSSEB	Evan Bourne	25.00	60.00
SSSED	Edge	50.00	100.00
SSSJC	John Cena	60.00	120.00
SSSJM	John Morrison	40.00	80.00
SSSKK	Kofi Kingston	40.00	80.00
SSSMH	Matt Hardy EXCH	50.00	100.00
SSSRM	Rey Mysterio	40.00	80.00
SSSRO	Randy Orton	40.00	80.00
SSSSA	Santino Marella EXCH	25.00	60.00
SSSSH	Shad		
SSSTD	Ted DiBiase Jr.		
SSSTH	Triple H		
SSSTK	Tyson Kidd	25.00	60.00
SSSTM	The Miz	40.00	80.00
SSSTU	The Undertaker		
SSSJTG	JTG		
SSSMVP	MVP	25.00	60.00

2010 Topps WWE Superstar Swatches

*GOLD/99: .5X TO 1.2X BASIC CARDS
*RED/1: UNPRICED DUE TO SCARCITY
OVERALL RELIC ODDS 1:BOX

JCR1	John Cena	15.00	30.00
SBS	Big Show	5.00	12.00
SCG	Chavo Guerrero		
SCH	Christian	5.00	12.00
SCJ	Chris Jericho		
SCM	CM Punk	5.00	12.00
SCR	Cody Rhodes	4.00	10.00
SDS	David Hart Smith	4.00	10.00
SEB	Evan Bourne	5.00	12.00
SED	Edge	6.00	15.00
SJC	John Cena	10.00	25.00
SJM	John Morrison	6.00	15.00
SKK	Kofi Kingston	5.00	12.00
SMH	Matt Hardy EXCH	8.00	20.00
SRM	Rey Mysterio	8.00	20.00
SRO	Randy Orton	10.00	25.00
SSA	Santino Marella EXCH	5.00	12.00
SSH	Shad		
STD	Ted DiBiase EXCH	6.00	15.00
STH	Triple H EXCH	20.00	50.00
STK	Tyson Kidd	4.00	10.00
STM	The Miz	4.00	10.00
STU	The Undertaker		
SJTG	JTG		
SMVP	MVP	4.00	10.00

2010 Topps WWE Topps Town

COMPLETE SET (25) 10.00 25.00
STATED ODDS 1:6 HOBBY AND RETAIL

TT1	John Cena	1.25	3.00
TT2	Jack Swagger	.25	.60
TT3	Rey Mysterio	.60	1.50
TT4	The Miz	.40	1.00
TT5	Kane	.60	1.50

TT6	Triple H	1.25	3.00
TT7	MVP	.40	1.00
TT8	The Undertaker	1.00	2.50
TT9	John Morisson	.40	1.00
TT10	Randy Orton	1.00	2.50
TT11	Kofi Kingston	.40	1.00
TT12	Michelle McCool	1.00	2.50
TT13	Cody Rhodes	.25	.60
TT14	Edge	1.00	2.50
TT15	Kelly Kelly	1.00	2.50
TT16	Ted DiBiase	.40	1.00
TT17	Chris Jericho	.60	1.50
TT18	CM Punk	1.00	2.50
TT19	Big Show	.60	1.50
TT20	Beth Phoenix	1.00	2.50
TT21	Sheamus	.40	1.00
TT22	Christian	.40	1.00
TT23	R-Truth	.25	.60
TT24	Ezekiel Jackson	.25	.60
TT25	Maryse	1.00	2.50

2010 Topps WWE When They Were Young

RANDOMLY INSERTED INTO PACKS

WTWY1 John Cena
WTWY2 William Regal
WTWY3 Jack Swagger
WTWY4 Chris Jericho
WTWY5 Big Show
WTWY6 Natalya
WTWY7 The Miz
WTWY8 Sheamus
WTWY9 Chavo Guerrero
WTWY10 Shad
WTWY11 Hornswoggle
WTWY12 Jerry Lawler
WTWY13 Santino Marella
WTWY14 Melina
WTWY15 Ted DiBiase Jr.
WTWY16 Cody Rhodes
WTWY17 Christian
WTWY18 Kelly Kelly
WTWY19 Rosa Mendes
WTWY20 CM Punk
WTWY21 Shelton Benjamin
WTWY22 Evan Bourne
WTWY23 R-Truth
WTWY24 Zack Ryder
WTWY25 Triple H

2010 Topps WWE World Championship Material

COMPLETE SET (25)		12.00	30.00
*PUZZLE: .5X TO 1.2X BASIC CARDS			
STATED ODDS 1:6 HOBBY AND RETAIL			
W1	John Cena	1.50	4.00
W2	John Cena	1.50	4.00
W3	Triple H	1.50	4.00
W4	Triple H	1.50	4.00
W5	Chris Jericho	.75	2.00
W6	Superstar Billy Graham	.75	2.00
W7	Chris Jericho	.75	2.00
W8	Sheamus	.50	1.25
W9	Randy Orton	1.25	3.00
W10	Randy Orton	1.25	3.00
W11	Kane	.75	2.00
W12	Undertaker	1.25	3.00

W13	Undertaker	1.25	3.00
W14	Rey Mysterio	.75	2.00
W15	Jack Swagger	.30	.75
W16	Melina	1.25	3.00
W17	Edge	1.25	3.00
W18	Beth Phoenix	1.25	3.00
W19	Edge	1.25	3.00
W20	Michelle McCool	1.25	3.00
W21	Big Show	.75	2.00
W22	CM Punk	1.25	3.00
W23	Sgt. Slaughter	.75	2.00
W24	The Iron Sheik	.75	2.00
W25	John Cena	1.50	4.00

2011 Topps WWE

COMPLETE SET (113)		10.00	25.00
UNOPENED BOX (24 PACKS)			
UNOPENED PACK (7 CARDS)			
*BLUE/2011: .8X TO 2X BASIC CARDS			
*BLACK/999: 1.5X TO 4X BASIC CARDS			
*GOLD/50: 4X TO 10X BASIC CARDS			
*RED/1: UNPRICED DUE TO SCARCITY			
*P.P.BLACK/1: UNPRICED DUE TO SCARCITY			
*P.P.CYAN/1: UNPRICED DUE TO SCARCITY			
*P.P.MAGENTA/1: UNPRICED DUE TO SCARCITY			
*P.P.YELLOW/1: UNPRICED DUE TO SCARCITY			
1	John Cena	.75	2.00
2	Randy Orton	.60	1.50
3	Rey Mysterio	.40	1.00
4	Wade Barrett	.15	.40
5	John Morrison	.25	.60
6	Natalya	.60	1.50
7	Primo	.15	.40
8	Justin Gabriel	.15	.40
9	Johnny Curtis	.15	.40
10	Josh Mathews	.15	.40
11	Michael McGillicutty	.15	.40
12	Jey Uso	.15	.40
13	Dolph Ziggler	.25	.60
14	Alex Riley	.15	.40
15	Kharma	.25	.60
16	Ranjin Singh	.15	.40
17	Chris Masters	.15	.40
18	Ted DiBiase	.25	.60
19	Percy Watson	.15	.40
20	Hornswoggle	.25	.60
21	David Otunga	.15	.40
22	Booker T	.25	.60
23	Mason Ryan	.15	.40
24	Tamina	.15	.40
25	CM Punk	.40	1.00
26	Jack Korpela	.15	.40
27	Kelly Kelly	.60	1.50
28	William Regal	.25	.60
29	Beth Phoenix	.40	1.00
30	The Great Khali	.15	.40
31	Michael Cole	.15	.40
32	Brodus Clay	.15	.40
33	Goldust	.15	.40
34	Jimmy Uso	.15	.40
35	Kofi Kingston	.15	.40
36	Matt Striker	.15	.40
37	Nikki Bella	.60	1.50
38	Yoshi Tatsu	.15	.40
39	Ricardo Rodriguez	.15	.40
40	Cody Rhodes	.15	.40
41	Brie Bella	.60	1.50
42	Ezekiel Jackson	.25	.60

43	Vladimir Kozlov	.25	.60
44	Sheamus	.25	.60
45	Vickie Guerrero	.25	.60
46	Alicia Fox	.25	.60
47	Drew McIntyre	.15	.40
48	Todd Grisham	.15	.40
49	Jack Swagger	.25	.60
50	Tyson Kidd	.15	.40
51	Alberto Del Rio	.40	1.00
52	Heath Slater	.15	.40
53	Evan Bourne	.15	.40
54	JTG	.15	.40
55	Kaitlyn	.40	1.00
56	Big Show	.40	1.00
57	Tyler Reks	.15	.40
58	Layla	.40	1.00
59	Justin Roberts	.15	.40
60	R-Truth	.15	.40
61	Daniel Bryan	.15	.40
62	Gail Kim	.40	1.00
63	The Miz	.25	.60
64	Chavo Guerrero	.15	.40
65	Curt Hawkins	.15	.40
66	Maryse	.60	1.50
67	Kane	.40	1.00
68	Santino Marella	.25	.60
69	Mark Henry	.25	.60
70	David Hart Smith	.15	.40
71	Rosa Mendes	.25	.60
72	Jerry The King Lawler	.40	1.00
73	Undertaker	.60	1.50
74	Melina	.60	1.50
75	Sin Cara	.40	1.00
76	Eve	.60	1.50
77	Theodore Long	.15	.40
78	Zack Ryder	.15	.40
79	Christian	.15	.40
80	Triple H	.75	2.00
81	Edge	.60	1.50
82	The Rock	.75	2.00
83	Darren Young	.15	.40
84	Lucky Cannon	.15	.40
85	Titus O'Neil	.15	.40
86	Byron Saxton	.15	.40
87	Conor O'Brian	.15	.40
88	Jacob Novak	.15	.40
89	The American Dream Dusty Rhodes	.25	.60
90	The British Bulldog	.25	.60
91	Million Dollar Man Ted DiBiase	.25	.60
92	Rowdy Roddy Piper	.60	1.50
93	Mr. Perfect	.40	1.00
94	The Iron Sheik	.40	1.00
95	Cowboy Bob Orton	.25	.60
96	Jake The Snake Roberts	.40	1.00
97	Ravishing Rick Rude	.25	.60
98	Doink the Clown	.25	.60
99	Big Boss Man	.25	.60
100	Bushwhacker Luke	.25	.60
101	Bushwhacker Butch	.25	.60
102	Yokozuna	.25	.60
103	Sgt. Slaughter	.40	1.00
104	Papa Shango	.15	.40
105	Hawk	.40	1.00
106	Animal	.40	1.00
107	Kamala	.25	.60
108	Terry Funk	.25	.60
109	Junkyard Dog	.40	1.00
110	Hacksaw Jim Duggan	.40	1.00

CL1	Checklist 1	.15	.40
CL2	Checklist 2	.15	.40
CL3	Checklist 3	.15	.40

2011 Topps WWE Autographs

NNO	Alberto Del Rio	15.00	40.00
NNO	Alex Riley	10.00	25.00
NNO	Big Show	12.00	30.00
NNO	Brie Bella	20.00	50.00
NNO	Christian	10.00	25.00
NNO	David Otunga	6.00	15.00
NNO	Drew McIntyre	8.00	20.00
NNO	Evan Bourne	6.00	15.00
NNO	Eve	12.00	30.00
NNO	Ezekiel Jackson	10.00	25.00
NNO	John Cena	25.00	60.00
NNO	Kane	12.00	30.00
NNO	Kofi Kingston	10.00	25.00
NNO	Mark Henry	10.00	25.00
NNO	Michael McGillicutty	6.00	15.00
NNO	Nikki Bella	20.00	50.00
NNO	Randy Orton	20.00	50.00
NNO	R-Truth	8.00	20.00
NNO	Sin Cara	10.00	25.00
NNO	The Miz	10.00	25.00

2011 Topps WWE Catchy Phrases

COMPLETE SET (10)		5.00	10.00
*P.P.BLACK/1: UNPRICED DUE TO SCARCITY			
*P.P.CYAN/1: UNPRICED DUE TO SCARCITY			
*P.P.MAGENTA/1: UNPRICED DUE TO SCARCITY			
*P.P.YELLOW/1: UNPRICED DUE TO SCARCITY			
STATED ODDS 1:8 HOBBY AND RETAIL			
CP1	John Cena	1.50	4.00
CP2	The Miz	.50	1.25
CP3	The Rock	1.50	4.00
CP4	Undertaker	1.25	3.00
CP5	Triple H	1.50	4.00
CP6	Rey Mysterio	.75	2.00
CP7	Christian	.30	.75
CP8	Zack Ryder	.30	.75
CP9	Goldust	.30	.75
CP10	Vickie Guerrero	.50	1.25

2011 Topps WWE Dual Autographs

STATED PRINT RUN 70 SER.#'d SETS			
NNO	A.Del Rio/Christian	25.00	60.00
NNO	Big Show/M.Henry	20.00	50.00
NNO	Brie Bella & Nikki Bella	60.00	120.00
NNO	D.Otunga/M.McGillicutty	12.00	30.00
NNO	Eve/K.Kingston	25.00	60.00
NNO	J.Cena/R-Truth	30.00	75.00
NNO	Kane/E.Jackson	15.00	40.00
NNO	R.Orton/E.Bourne	25.00	60.00
NNO	S.Cara/D.McIntyre	15.00	40.00
NNO	Miz/A.Riley	20.00	50.00

2011 Topps WWE Electrifying Entrances

COMPLETE SET (25)		10.00	25.00
*P.P.BLACK/1: UNPRICED DUE TO SCARCITY			
*P.P.CYAN/1: UNPRICED DUE TO SCARCITY			
*P.P.MAGENTA/1: UNPRICED DUE TO SCARCITY			
*P.P.YELLOW/1: UNPRICED DUE TO SCARCITY			
STATED ODDS 1:8 HOBBY AND RETAIL			
EE1	Undertaker	1.25	3.00
EE2	John Cena	1.50	4.00

EE3	Triple H	1.50	4.00
EE4	Rey Mysterio	.75	2.00
EE5	R-Truth	.30	.75
EE6	Randy Orton	1.25	3.00
EE7	The Miz	.50	1.25
EE8	Big Show	.75	2.00
EE9	Kofi Kingston	.30	.75
EE10	Sheamus	.50	1.25
EE11	Alberto Del Rio	.75	2.00
EE12	Kane	.75	2.00
EE13	Christian	.30	.75
EE14	Jack Swagger	.50	1.25
EE15	Sin Cara	.75	2.00
EE16	Wade Barrett	.30	.75
EE17	John Morrison	.50	1.25
EE18	Drew McIntyre	.30	.75
EE19	Daniel Bryan	.30	.75
EE20	Cody Rhodes	.30	.75
EE21	Ted DiBiase	.50	1.25
EE22	Dolph Ziggler	.50	1.25
EE23	Santino Marella	.50	1.25
EE24	The Great Khali	.30	.75
EE25	Kharma	.50	1.25

2011 Topps WWE Heritage

COMPLETE SET (50)		12.00	30.00
P.P.BLACK/1: UNPRICED DUE TO SCARCITY			
P.P.CYAN/1: UNPRICED DUE TO SCARCITY			
P.P.MAGENTA/1: UNPRICED DUE TO SCARCITY			
P.P.YELLOW/1: UNPRICED DUE TO SCARCITY			
STATED ODDS 1:4 HOBBY AND RETAIL			
H1	Stone Cold Steve Austin	1.00	2.50
H2	Shawn Michaels	1.00	2.50
H3	Trish Stratus	1.25	3.00
H4	Booker T	.40	1.00
H5	Jerry The King Lawler	.60	1.50
H6	Michael PS Hayes	.25	.60
H7	The American Dream Dusty Rhodes	.40	1.00
H8	The British Bulldog	.40	1.00
H9	Million Dollar Man Ted DiBiase	.40	1.00
H10	Rowdy Roddy Piper	1.00	2.50
H11	Mr. Perfect	.60	1.50
H12	Mean Gene Okerlund	.40	1.00
H13	Jimmy Superfly Snuka	.60	1.50
H14	Paul Bearer	.40	1.00
H15	Irwin R. Schyster	.25	.60
H16	Vader	.40	1.00
H17	Akeem	.25	.60
H18	Bobby The Brain Heenan	.40	1.00
H19	Kama Mustafa	.25	.60
H20	Howard Finkel	.25	.60
H21	Don Muraco	.40	1.00
H22	Harley Race	.40	1.00
H23	Brian Pillman	.40	1.00
H24	The Iron Sheik	.60	1.50
H25	Koko B. Ware	.40	1.00
H26	Gorilla Monsoon	.40	1.00
H27	Jake The Snake Roberts	.60	1.50
H28	Ravishing Rick Rude	.40	1.00
H29	Doink the Clown	.25	.60
H30	Big Boss Man	.40	1.00
H31	Jim Ross	.25	.60
H32	Rocky Johnson	.40	1.00
H33	Terry Funk	.40	1.00
H34	Big John Studd	.25	.60
H35	The Godfather	.25	.60
H36	Hillbilly Jim	.40	1.00
H37	Barry Windham	.25	.60

H38	Tito Santana	.25	.60
H39	Nikolai Volkoff	.40	1.00
H40	Arn Anderson	.40	1.00
H41	Tully Blanchard	.40	1.00
H42	One Man Gang	.25	.60
H43	Dean Malenko	.25	.60
H44	Classy Freddie Blassie	.40	1.00
H45	Tom Prichard	.25	.60
H46	Yokozuna	.40	1.00
H47	Mr. Wonderful Paul Orndorff	.40	1.00
H48	Sgt. Slaughter	.60	1.50
H49	Diesel	.40	1.00
H50	Batista	.40	1.00

2011 Topps WWE Masters of the Mat Relics

*GOLD/50: 1X TO 2.5X BASIC MEM			
*RED/1: UNPRICED DUE TO SCARCITY			
STATED ODDS 1:69			
NNO	Alberto Del Rio	2.50	6.00
NNO	Big Show	2.50	6.00
NNO	Christian	2.50	6.00
NNO	Cody Rhodes	2.50	6.00
NNO	Daniel Bryan	2.50	6.00
NNO	Dolph Ziggler	2.50	6.00
NNO	Drew McIntyre	2.50	6.00
NNO	Jack Swagger	2.50	6.00
NNO	John Cena	5.00	12.00
NNO	John Morrison	2.50	6.00
NNO	Kane	2.50	6.00
NNO	Kofi Kingston	2.50	6.00
NNO	Mark Henry	2.50	6.00
NNO	Randy Orton	4.00	10.00
NNO	Rey Mysterio	3.00	8.00
NNO	R-Truth	2.50	6.00
NNO	Santino Marella	2.50	6.00
NNO	Sheamus	2.50	6.00
NNO	Sin Cara	2.50	6.00
NNO	Ted DiBiase	2.50	6.00
NNO	The Great Khali	2.50	6.00
NNO	The Miz	2.50	6.00
NNO	Triple H	4.00	10.00
NNO	Undertaker	4.00	10.00
NNO	Wade Barrett	2.50	6.00

2011 Topps WWE Prestigious Pairings

COMPLETE SET (15)		6.00	15.00
*P.P.BLACK/1: UNPRICED DUE TO SCARCITY			
*P.P.CYAN/1: UNPRICED DUE TO SCARCITY			
*P.P.MAGENTA/1: UNPRICED DUE TO SCARCITY			
*P.P.YELLOW/1: UNPRICED DUE TO SCARCITY			
STATED ODDS 1:8 HOBBY AND RETAIL			
PP1	Big Show/Kane	.75	2.00
PP2	Marella/Kozlov	.50	1.25
PP3	Phoenix/Kelly	1.25	3.00
PP4	Lawler/Ross	.75	2.00
PP5	Swagger/Cole	.50	1.25
PP6	Orton/Mysterio	1.25	3.00
PP7	Cena/Cara	1.50	4.00
PP8	Jimmy Uso/Jay Uso	.30	.75
PP9	Ziggler/Guerrero	.50	1.25
PP10	Edge/Christian	1.25	3.00
PP11	Del Rio/Clay	.75	2.00
PP12	Ziggler/Sheamus	.50	1.25
PP13	Morrison/Bryan	.50	1.25

PP14	Torres/Kim	1.25	3.00
PP15	R-Truth/Morrison	.50	1.25

2011 Topps WWE Ringside Relics Ring Skirts

*GOLD/50: .6X TO 1.5X BASIC MEM			
*RED/1: UNPRICED DUE TO SCARCITY			
STATED ODDS 1:180			
NNO	Alberto Del Rio	3.00	8.00
NNO	Big Show	3.00	8.00
NNO	Christian	3.00	8.00
NNO	Daniel Bryan	3.00	8.00
NNO	Dolph Ziggler	3.00	8.00
NNO	Jack Swagger	3.00	8.00
NNO	John Cena	6.00	15.00
NNO	John Morrison	3.00	8.00
NNO	Kane	3.00	8.00
NNO	Kofi Kingston	3.00	8.00
NNO	Randy Orton	5.00	12.00
NNO	Rey Mysterio	4.00	10.00
NNO	R-Truth	3.00	8.00
NNO	Santino Marella	3.00	8.00
NNO	Sheamus	3.00	8.00
NNO	Sin Cara	3.00	8.00
NNO	The Miz	3.00	8.00
NNO	Triple H	5.00	12.00
NNO	Undertaker	6.00	15.00
NNO	Wade Barrett	3.00	8.00

2011 Topps WWE Superstar Swatches

*GOLD/50: .6X TO 1.5X BASIC CARDS			
*RED/1: UNPRICED DUE TO SCARCITY			
STATED ODDS 1:126			
NNO	Christian	4.00	10.00
NNO	Cody Rhodes	4.00	10.00
NNO	Daniel Bryan	5.00	12.00
NNO	Drew McIntyre	4.00	10.00
NNO	Heath Slater	4.00	10.00
NNO	Jack Swagger	4.00	10.00
NNO	Kofi Kingston	4.00	10.00
NNO	Randy Orton	5.00	12.00
NNO	R-Truth	4.00	10.00
NNO	Santino Marella	4.00	10.00
NNO	Sheamus	4.00	10.00
NNO	Stone Cold Steve Austin	6.00	15.00
NNO	Ted DiBiase	4.00	10.00
NNO	The Miz	4.00	10.00
NNO	Wade Barrett	4.00	10.00

2012 Topps WWE

COMPLETE SET (93)		15.00	40.00
COMPLETE SET W/O SP (90)		10.00	25.00
UNOPENED BOX (24 PACKS)			
UNOPENED PACK (7 CARDS)			
*BLUE: 1X TO 2.5X BASIC CARDS			
*GOLD: 2.5X TO 6X BASIC CARDS			
*PURPLE: 2.5X TO 6X BASIC CARDS			
*RED: 2.5X TO 6X BASIC CARDS			
*SILVER: 2.5X TO 6X BASIC CARDS			
*BLACK: 8X TO 20X BASIC CARDS			
*PLATINUM/1: UNPRICED DUE TO SCARCITY			
*P.P.BLACK/1: UNPRICED DUE TO SCARCITY			
*P.P.CYAN/1: UNPRICED DUE TO SCARCITY			
*P.P.MAGENTA/1: UNPRICED DUE TO SCARCITY			
*P.P.YELLOW/1: UNPRICED DUE TO SCARCITY			
1	John Cena	.75	2.00

2	Randy Orton	.60	1.50
3	Beth Phoenix	.40	1.00
4	Sheamus	.40	1.00
5	Brock Lesnar	.60	1.50
6	Daniel Bryan	.15	.40
7A	Mick Foley	.60	1.50
7B	Cactus Jack SP	4.00	10.00
7C	Dude Love SP	4.00	10.00
7D	Mankind SP	4.00	10.00
8	Cody Rhodes	.15	.40
9	Cameron	.25	.60
10	Christian	.15	.40
11	Kelly Kelly	.60	1.50
12	Hornswoggle	.25	.60
13	Brodus Clay	.15	.40
14	Aksana	.40	1.00
15	Epico	.15	.40
16	Mark Henry	.25	.60
17	Maxine	.40	1.00
18	Jey Uso	.15	.40
19	Zack Ryder	.15	.40
20	Ricardo Rodriguez	.15	.40
21	JTG	.15	.40
22	Hunico	.15	.40
23	Kofi Kingston	.15	.40
24	Matt Striker	.15	.40
25	Kane	.40	1.00
26	Jimmy Uso	.15	.40
27	Naomi	.25	.60
28	The Great Khali	.15	.40
29	Tyler Reks	.15	.40
30	Josh Matthews	.15	.40
31	Derrick Bateman	.15	.40
32	Camacho	.15	.40
33	Kharma	.25	.60
34	Heath Slater	.15	.40
35	Evan Bourne	.15	.40
36	Yoshi Tatsu	.15	.40
37	Big Show	.40	1.00
38	Ryback	.15	.40
39	Percy Watson	.15	.40
40	Kaitlyn	.40	1.00
41	The Miz	.25	.60
42	William Regal	.25	.60
43	Michael Cole	.15	.40
44	Wade Barrett	.15	.40
45	Rey Mysterio	.40	1.00
46	Alicia Fox	.25	.60
47	Triple H	.60	1.50
48	Layla	.40	1.00
49	Chris Jericho	.60	1.50
50	Jinder Mahal	.15	.40
51	Eve	.60	1.50
52	Johnny Curtis	.15	.40
53	Tensai	.15	.40
54	Titus O'Neil	.15	.40
55	Vickie Guerrero	.25	.60
56	Justin Gabriel	.15	.40
57	Primo	.15	.40
58	Booker T	.25	.60
59	Goldust	.15	.40
60	Natalya	.60	1.50
61	Jack Swagger	.25	.60
62	Ezekiel Jackson	.25	.60
63	John Laurinaitis	.15	.40
64	Ted DiBiase	.25	.60
65	R-Truth	.15	.40
66	Trent Barreta	.15	.40

67	Jerry The King Lawler	.40	1.00
68	Tyson Kidd	.15	.40
69	David Otunga	.15	.40
70	Rosa Mendes	.25	.60
71	Michael McGillicutty	.15	.40
72	Drew McIntyre	.15	.40
73	Alex Riley	.15	.40
74	Theodore Long	.15	.40
75	Dolph Ziggler	.25	.60
76	Sin Cara	.40	1.00
77	Justin Roberts	.15	.40
78	Alberto Del Rio	.40	1.00
79	Curt Hawkins	.15	.40
80	Tamina Snuka	.25	.60
81	Mason Ryan	.15	.40
82	Darren Young	.15	.40
83	Scott Stanford	.15	.40
84	Lilian Garcia	.40	1.00
85	Santino Marella	.25	.60
86	Antonio Cesaro	.15	.40
87	The Rock	.75	2.00
88	AJ	.75	2.00
89	CM Punk	.60	1.50
90	Undertaker	.60	1.50

2012 Topps WWE Autographs

STATED ODDS 1:470 HOBBY AND RETAIL

NNO	Booker T	15.00	40.00
NNO	Cactus Jack	50.00	100.00
NNO	Chris Jericho	30.00	75.00
NNO	Dude Love	50.00	100.00
NNO	Epico	8.00	20.00
NNO	Hunico	8.00	20.00
NNO	John Laurinaitis	12.00	30.00
NNO	Mankind	50.00	100.00
NNO	Mick Foley	30.00	75.00
NNO	Primo	8.00	20.00
NNO	Triple H		

2012 Topps WWE Classic Hall of Famers

COMPLETE SET (35)   10.00   25.00
*P.P.BLACK/1: UNPRICED DUE TO SCARCITY
*P.P.CYAN/1: UNPRICED DUE TO SCARCITY
*P.P.MAGENTA/1: UNPRICED DUE TO SCARCITY
*P.P.YELLOW/1: UNPRICED DUE TO SCARCITY
STATED ODDS 1:4 HOBBY AND RETAIL

1	Chief Jay Strongbow	.40	1.00
2	Classy Freddie Blassie	.40	1.00
3	Gorilla Monsoon	.40	1.00
4	Jimmy Superfly Snuka	.40	1.00
5	Big John Studd	.40	1.00
6	Bobby The Brain Heenan	.40	1.00
7	Don Muraco	.40	1.00
8	Greg The Hammer Valentine	.40	1.00
9	Harley Race	.40	1.00
10	Junkyard Dog	.40	1.00
11	Sgt. Slaughter	.40	1.00
12	Tito Santana	.40	1.00
13	Cowboy Bob Orton	.40	1.00
14	The Iron Sheik	.40	1.00
15	Mr. Wonderful Paul Orndorff	.40	1.00
16	Nikolai Volkoff	.40	1.00
17	Rowdy Roddy Piper	.60	1.50
18	Mean Gene Okerlund	.40	1.00
19	The American Dream Dusty Rhodes	.40	1.00
20	Mr. Perfect Curt Hennig	.40	1.00

21	Rocky Johnson	.40	1.00
22	Terry Funk	.40	1.00
23	Howard Finkel	.40	1.00
24	Koko B. Ware	.40	1.00
25	Ricky The Dragon Steamboat	.40	1.00
26	Stone Cold Steve Austin	1.25	3.00
27	Million Dollar Man Ted DiBiase	.40	1.00
28	Hacksaw Jim Duggan	.40	1.00
29	Road Warrior Hawk	.40	1.00
30	Road Warrior Animal	.40	1.00
31	Shawn Michaels	1.00	2.50
32	Edge	.60	1.50
33	Arn Anderson	.40	1.00
34	Barry Windham	.40	1.00
35	Tully Blanchard	.40	1.00

2012 Topps WWE Classic Hall of Famers Autographs

STATED ODDS 1:269 HOBBY AND RETAIL

NNO	Animal	30.00	60.00
NNO	Barry Windham	12.00	30.00
NNO	Don Muraco	20.00	50.00
NNO	Greg The Hammer Valentine	20.00	50.00
NNO	Harley Race	12.00	30.00
NNO	Jimmy Superfly Snuka	20.00	50.00
NNO	Koko B. Ware	15.00	40.00
NNO	Mr. Wonderful Paul Orndorff	15.00	40.00
NNO	Nikolai Volkoff	15.00	30.00
NNO	Terry Funk	20.00	50.00
NNO	Tito Santana	20.00	50.00
NNO	Tully Blanchard	15.00	40.00

2012 Topps WWE Diva Kiss

STATED ODDS 1:1,125

NNO	AJ	100.00	175.00
NNO	Aksana	30.00	80.00
NNO	Alicia Fox	30.00	80.00
NNO	Beth Phoenix	30.00	80.00
NNO	Kaitlyn	20.00	50.00
NNO	Kelly Kelly	25.00	60.00
NNO	Layla	50.00	100.00
NNO	Maxine	20.00	50.00
NNO	Natalya	30.00	80.00
NNO	Rosa Mendes	30.00	80.00
NNO	Cameron	20.00	50.00
NNO	Naomi	30.00	80.00
NNO	Tamina Snuka	30.00	80.00

2012 Topps WWE Divas Class of 2012

COMPLETE SET (15)   8.00   20.00
*P.P.BLACK/1: UNPRICED DUE TO SCARCITY
*P.P.CYAN/1: UNPRICED DUE TO SCARCITY
*P.P.MAGENTA/1: UNPRICED DUE TO SCARCITY
*P.P.YELLOW/1: UNPRICED DUE TO SCARCITY
STATED ODDS 1:4 HOBBY AND RETAIL

1	AJ	2.50	6.00
2	Aksana	1.25	3.00
3	Alicia Fox	.75	2.00
4	Beth Phoenix	1.25	3.00
5	Cameron	.75	2.00
6	Eve	2.00	5.00
7	Kaitlyn	1.25	3.00
8	Kelly Kelly	2.00	5.00
9	Layla	1.25	3.00
10	Lilian Garcia	1.25	3.00
11	Maxine	1.25	3.00

12	Naomi	.75	2.00
13	Natalya	2.00	5.00
14	Rosa Mendes	.75	2.00
15	Tamina Snuka	.75	2.00

2012 Topps WWE Divas Class of 2012 Autographs

STATED ODDS 1:364

NNO	Aksana	15.00	40.00
NNO	Alicia Fox	15.00	40.00
NNO	Beth Phoenix	15.00	40.00
NNO	Kaitlyn	35.00	70.00
NNO	Kelly Kelly	35.00	70.00
NNO	Lilian Garcia	25.00	50.00
NNO	Maxine	15.00	40.00
NNO	Rosa Mendes	15.00	40.00
NNO	Tamina Snuka	25.00	50.00

2012 Topps WWE Dual Autographs

STATED ODDS 1:2,245 HOBBY EXCLUSIVE

NNO	Jimmy & Tamina Snuka	75.00	150.00
NNO	Maxine/Kaitlyn	30.00	75.00
NNO	Primo/Epico	20.00	50.00
NNO	T.Blanchard/B.Windham	25.00	60.00

2012 Topps WWE First Class Champions

COMPLETE SET (20)   10.00   25.00
*P.P.BLACK/1: UNPRICED DUE TO SCARCITY
*P.P.CYAN/1: UNPRICED DUE TO SCARCITY
*P.P.MAGENTA/1: UNPRICED DUE TO SCARCITY
*P.P.YELLOW/1: UNPRICED DUE TO SCARCITY
STATED ODDS 1:6 HOBBY AND RETAIL

1	The Iron Shiek	.50	1.25
2	Sgt. Slaughter	.50	1.25
3	Undertaker	1.25	3.00
4	Yokozuna	.50	1.25
5	Diesel	.50	1.25
6	Shawn Michaels	1.25	3.00
7	Stone Cold Steve Austin	1.50	4.00
8	The Rock	1.50	4.00
9	Mankind	1.25	3.00
10	Triple H	1.25	3.00
11	Big Show	.75	2.00
12	Chris Jericho	1.25	3.00
13	Brock Lesnar	1.25	3.00
14	John Cena	1.50	4.00
15	Edge	.75	2.00
16	Randy Orton	1.25	3.00
17	Batista	.50	1.25
18	Sheamus	.75	2.00
19	The Miz	.50	1.25
20	CM Punk	1.25	3.00

2012 Topps WWE Shirt Relics

*BLACK/50: .8X TO 2X BASIC MEM
*PLATINUM/1: UNPRICED DUE TO SCARCITY
STATED ODDS 1:112

NNO	Alberto Del Rio	5.00	12.00
NNO	Big Show	6.00	15.00
NNO	Brodus Clay	5.00	12.00
NNO	Camacho	5.00	12.00
NNO	CM Punk	6.00	15.00
NNO	Cody Rhodes	5.00	12.00
NNO	Daniel Bryan	5.00	12.00
NNO	Dolph Ziggler	6.00	15.00
NNO	Hornswoggle	5.00	12.00

NNO	Hunico	4.00	10.00
NNO	Jerry Lawler	6.00	15.00
NNO	John Cena	10.00	25.00
NNO	Kofi Kingston	5.00	12.00
NNO	Mark Henry	4.00	10.00
NNO	Randy Orton	6.00	15.00
NNO	R-Truth	4.00	10.00
NNO	Santino Marella	4.00	10.00
NNO	Sheamus	5.00	12.00
NNO	The Miz	5.00	12.00
NNO	Zack Ryder	5.00	12.00
NNO	Natalya	5.00	12.00
NNO	Christian	5.00	12.00
NNO	Chris Jericho	6.00	15.00
NNO	Evan Bourne	3.00	8.00
NNO	Heath Slater	4.00	10.00
NNO	Jack Swagger	4.00	10.00
NNO	Justin Gabriel	3.00	8.00
NNO	Michael McGillicutty	3.00	8.00
NNO	Ted DiBiase	3.00	8.00
NNO	Wade Barrett	4.00	10.00

2012 Topps WWE Top Class Matches Punk's Picks

COMPLETE SET (10)   5.00   12.00
*P.P.BLACK/1: UNPRICED DUE TO SCARCITY
*P.P.CYAN/1: UNPRICED DUE TO SCARCITY
*P.P.MAGENTA/1: UNPRICED DUE TO SCARCITY
*P.P.YELLOW/1: UNPRICED DUE TO SCARCITY
STATED ODDS 1:6

1	Wins ECW Championship	1.00	2.50
2	Wins Money in the Bank	1.00	2.50
3	Wins Intercontinental Title	1.00	2.50
4	Wins World Heavyweight Championship	1.00	2.50
5	Loses His Hair	1.00	2.50
6	Wins the WWE Championship	1.00	2.50
7	Unifies the WWE Championship	1.00	2.50
8	Reclaims the WWE Championship	1.00	2.50
9	Victorious at WrestleMania XXVIII	1.00	2.50
10	Turns Back Jericho Again	1.00	2.50

2012 Topps WWE World Class Events

COMPLETE SET (10)   5.00   12.00
*P.P.BLACK/1: UNPRICED DUE TO SCARCITY
*P.P.CYAN/1: UNPRICED DUE TO SCARCITY
*P.P.MAGENTA/1: UNPRICED DUE TO SCARCITY
*P.P.YELLOW/1: UNPRICED DUE TO SCARCITY
STATED ODDS 1:6

1	WrestleMania XXVII	1.00	2.50
2	Money in the Bank 2011	1.00	2.50
3	SummerSlam 2011	1.00	2.50
4	Hell in a Cell 2011	1.00	2.50
5	Vengeance 2011	1.00	2.50
6	Survivor Series 2011	1.00	2.50
7	Tables, Ladders and Chairs 2011	1.00	2.50
8	Royal Rumble 2012	1.00	2.50
9	Elimination Chamber 2012	1.00	2.50
10	WrestleMania XXVIII	1.00	2.50

2012 Topps WWE WrestleMania XXVIII Mat Relics

*BLACK/50: .8X TO 2X BASIC MEM
*PLATINUM/1: UNPRICED DUE TO SCARCITY
STATED ODDS 1:109

NNO	Beth Phoenix	6.00	15.00
NNO	Big Show	6.00	15.00
NNO	Booker T	5.00	12.00

NNO	Chris Jericho	6.00	15.00
NNO	CM Punk	6.00	15.00
NNO	Cody Rhodes	5.00	12.00
NNO	Daniel Bryan	5.00	12.00
NNO	David Otunga	5.00	12.00
NNO	Dolph Ziggler	5.00	12.00
NNO	Eve	6.00	15.00
NNO	Jack Swagger	6.00	15.00
NNO	John Cena	10.00	25.00
NNO	Kane	6.00	15.00
NNO	Kelly Kelly	8.00	20.00
NNO	Kofi Kingston	5.00	12.00
NNO	Mark Henry	5.00	12.00
NNO	Randy Orton	6.00	15.00
NNO	R-Truth	5.00	12.00
NNO	Santino Marella	5.00	12.00
NNO	Sheamus	6.00	15.00
NNO	The Miz	5.00	12.00
NNO	The Rock	10.00	25.00
NNO	Triple H	8.00	20.00
NNO	Undertaker	10.00	25.00
NNO	Zack Ryder	6.00	15.00

2013 Topps WWE

COMPLETE SET (110)		8.00	20.00
UNOPENED BOX (24 PACKS)			
UNOPENED PACK (7 CARDS)			

*BLACK: 2.5X TO 6X BASIC CARDS
*SILVER: 4X TO 10X BASIC CARDS
*GOLD/10: 15X TO 40X BASIC CARDS
*P.P.BLACK/1: UNPRICED DUE TO SCARCITY
*P.P.CYAN/1: UNPRICED DUE TO SCARCITY
*P.P.MAGENTA/1: UNPRICED DUE TO SCARCITY
*P.P.YELLOW/1: UNPRICED DUE TO SCARCITY

1	AJ Lee	.75	2.00
2	Alex Riley	.15	.40
3	Big E Langston	.15	.40
4	Big Show	.30	.75
5	Brock Lesnar	.60	1.50
6	Brodus Clay	.15	.40
7	Cameron	.25	.60
8	CM Punk	.60	1.50
9	Daniel Bryan	.40	1.00
10	David Otunga	.15	.40
11	Dean Ambrose	.25	.60
12	Dolph Ziggler	.25	.60
13	Epico	.15	.40
14	Evan Bourne	.15	.40
15	Eve	.60	1.50
16	Jack Swagger	.25	.60
17	Jerry The King Lawler	.30	.75
18	John Cena	.75	2.00
19	JTG	.15	.40
20	Justin Roberts	.15	.40
21	Kane	.30	.75
22	Kofi Kingston	.15	.40
23	Mason Ryan	.15	.40
24	Michael Cole	.15	.40
25	Michael McGillicutty	.15	.40
26	The Miz	.25	.60
27	Naomi	.40	1.00
28	Paul Heyman	.15	.40
29	Primo	.15	.40
30	R-Truth	.15	.40
31	Rey Mysterio	.40	1.00
32	The Rock	.75	2.00
33	Roman Reigns	.25	.60
34	Rosa Mendes	.25	.60

35	Ryback	.15	.40
36	Santino Marella	.15	.40
37	Scott Stanford	.15	.40
38	Seth Rollins	.15	.40
39	Tamina Snuka	.20	.50
40	Tensai	.15	.40
41	Triple H	.60	1.50
42	Vickie Guerrero	.25	.60
43	Zack Ryder	.15	.40
44	Aksana	.25	.60
45	Alberto Del Rio	.30	.75
46	Alicia Fox	.25	.60
47	Antonio Cesaro	.15	.40
48	Booker T	.25	.60
49	Camacho	.15	.40
50	Christian	.15	.40
51	Cody Rhodes	.15	.40
52	Damien Sandow	.15	.40
53	Darren Young	.15	.40
54	Drew McIntyre	.15	.40
55	Ezekiel Jackson	.15	.40
56	The Great Khali	.15	.40
57	Heath Slater	.15	.40
58	Hornswoggle	.15	.40
59	Hunico	.15	.40
60	Jey Uso	.15	.40
61	Jimmy Uso	.15	.40
62	Jinder Mahal	.15	.40
63	Fandango	.15	.40
64	Josh Mathews	.15	.40
65	Justin Gabriel	.15	.40
66	Kaitlyn	.30	.75
67	Layla	.30	.75
68	Lilian Garcia	.40	1.00
69	Mark Henry	.20	.50
70	Matt Striker	.15	.40
71	Natalya	.30	.75
72	Percy Watson	.15	.40
73	Randy Orton	.50	1.25
74	Ricardo Rodriguez	.15	.40
75	Sheamus	.30	.75
76	Sin Cara	.25	.60
77	Ted DiBiase	.20	.50
78	Theodore Long	.15	.40
79	Titus O'Neil	.15	.40
80	Tyson Kidd	.15	.40
81	Undertaker	.60	1.50
82	Wade Barrett	.15	.40
83	William Regal	.20	.50
84	Yoshi Tatsu	.15	.40
85	The American Dream Dusty Rhodes	.25	.60
86	Big John Studd	.25	.60
87	The British Bulldog	.25	.60
88	The Bushwhackers	.15	.40
89	Cowboy Bob Orton	.25	.60
90	Dean Malenko	.15	.40
91	Hacksaw Jim Duggan	.25	.60
92	Greg The Hammer Valentine	.15	.40
93	Harley Race	.25	.60
94	The Iron Sheik	.25	.60
95	Jake The Snake Roberts	.25	.60
96	Jimmy Superfly Snuka	.25	.60
97	Junkyard Dog	.25	.60
98	Million Dollar Man Ted DiBiase	.25	.60
99	Mr. Perfect	.25	.60
100	Mr. Wonderful Paul Orndorff	.25	.60
101	Nikolai Volkoff	.25	.60
102	Ravishing Rick Rude	.25	.60

103	Ricky The Dragon Steamboat	.25	.60
104	Rowdy Roddy Piper	.40	1.00
105	Sgt. Slaughter	.25	.60
106	Terry Funk	.25	.60
107	Tito Santana	.25	.60
108	Tom Prichard	.15	.40
109	Vader	.15	.40
110	Yokozuna	.15	.40

2013 Topps WWE Autographed Relics

STATED ODDS 1:9,550
UNPRICED DUE TO SCARCITY

NNO	Alicia Fox	
NNO	Daniel Bryan	
NNO	Dolph Ziggler	
NNO	Kofi Kingston	
NNO	Ryback	
NNO	Sin Cara	

2013 Topps WWE Autographs

STATED ODDS 1:79 HOBBY AND RETAIL

NNO	AJ Lee	30.00	75.00
NNO	Alicia Fox	8.00	20.00
NNO	Antonio Cesaro	10.00	25.00
NNO	Bushwhacker Butch	12.00	30.00
NNO	Bushwhacker Luke	8.00	20.00
NNO	Cowboy Bob Orton	10.00	25.00
NNO	Daniel Bryan	15.00	40.00
NNO	Dean Malenko	12.00	30.00
NNO	Dolph Ziggler	12.00	30.00
NNO	Eve	12.00	30.00
NNO	Jack Swagger	10.00	25.00
NNO	Kaitlyn	15.00	40.00
NNO	Kofi Kingston	8.00	20.00
NNO	Michael Cole	8.00	20.00
NNO	Million Dollar Man Ted DiBiase	12.00	30.00
NNO	Randy Orton	20.00	50.00
NNO	Rosa Mendes	10.00	25.00
NNO	Ryback	15.00	40.00
NNO	Sin Cara	10.00	25.00
NNO	Tom Prichard	8.00	20.00

2013 Topps WWE Diva Kiss

STATED ODDS 1:568 HOBBY AND RETAIL

NNO	AJ Lee	100.00	175.00
NNO	Aksana	25.00	50.00
NNO	Alicia Fox	15.00	40.00
NNO	Cameron	25.00	50.00
NNO	Eve	40.00	80.00
NNO	Kaitlyn	40.00	80.00
NNO	Layla	30.00	60.00
NNO	Naomi	15.00	40.00
NNO	Natalya	30.00	60.00
NNO	Rosa Mendes	25.00	50.00

2013 Topps WWE Diva Snapshots

COMPLETE SET (10)		20.00	40.00

STATED ODDS 1:24 HOBBY AND RETAIL

NNO	AJ Lee	6.00	15.00
NNO	Aksana	2.00	5.00
NNO	Alicia Fox	2.00	5.00
NNO	Cameron	2.00	5.00
NNO	Eve	5.00	12.00
NNO	Kaitlyn	2.50	6.00
NNO	Layla	2.50	6.00
NNO	Naomi	3.00	8.00

NNO	Natalya	2.50	6.00
NNO	Rosa Mendes	2.00	5.00

2013 Topps WWE Shirt Relics

STATED ODDS 1:24 HOBBY; 1:96 RETAIL

NNO	Alicia Fox	6.00	15.00
Skirt			
NNO	Big Show/Hat	6.00	15.00
NNO	Brodus Clay/Pants	4.00	10.00
NNO	CM Punk/Shirt	6.00	15.00
NNO	Damien Sandow/Shirt	5.00	12.00
NNO	Daniel Bryan/Shirt	5.00	12.00
NNO	Dolph Ziggler/Shirt	5.00	12.00
NNO	Kofi Kingston/Shirt	5.00	12.00
NNO	Paul Heyman/Suit	6.00	15.00
NNO	R-Truth/Shirt	5.00	12.00
NNO	Rey Mysterio/Shirt	6.00	15.00
NNO	Ryback/Shirt	8.00	20.00
NNO	Santino Marella/Puppet	6.00	15.00
NNO	Sheamus/Shirt	6.00	15.00
NNO	Sin Cara/Shirt	5.00	12.00
Shirt			
NNO	The Miz/Shirt	4.00	10.00
NNO	Titus O'Neil/Shirt	4.00	10.00
NNO	Wade Barrett/Shirt	5.00	12.00
NNO	CM Punk/Sock SP	30.00	60.00

2013 Topps WWE SummerSlam Mat Relics

STATED ODDS 1:102

NNO	AJ Lee	8.00	20.00
NNO	Aksana	4.00	10.00
NNO	Alberto Del Rio	5.00	12.00
NNO	Antonio Cesaro	4.00	10.00
NNO	Big Show	4.00	10.00
NNO	Brock Lesnar	6.00	15.00
NNO	CM Punk	6.00	15.00
NNO	Daniel Bryan	4.00	10.00
NNO	Darren Young	4.00	10.00
NNO	Dolph Ziggler	5.00	12.00
NNO	Jerry The King Lawler	5.00	12.00
NNO	John Cena	8.00	20.00
NNO	Kane	5.00	12.00
NNO	Kofi Kingston	5.00	12.00
NNO	Paul Heyman	5.00	12.00
NNO	R-Truth	4.00	10.00
NNO	Santino Marella	4.00	10.00
NNO	Sheamus	4.00	10.00
NNO	The Miz	4.00	10.00
NNO	Titus O'Neil	4.00	10.00
NNO	Triple H	6.00	15.00
NNO	Vickie Guerrero	4.00	10.00

2013 Topps WWE Triple Autographs

STATED ODDS 1:12,637 HOBBY AND RETAIL
UNPRICED DUE TO SCARCITY

NNO	Luke/Butch/DiBiase
NNO	Bryan/Cesaro/Kaitlyn
NNO	Eve/Fox/Mendes
NNO	Swagger/SinCara/Ryback
NNO	R.Orton/B.Orton/Cole

2013 Topps WWE Triple Threat Tier Three

COMPLETE SET (30)		5.00	12.00

*TIER TWO: .5X TO 1.2X TIER THREE
*TIER ONE: .8X TO 2X TIER THREE

TT1 Dolph Ziggler	.30	.75
TT2 John Cena	1.00	2.50
TT3 Jack Swagger	.30	.75
TT4 The Miz	.30	.75
TT5 Prime Time Players	.20	.50
TT6 Wade Barrett	.20	.50
TT7 Santino Marella	.20	.50
TT8 Brock Lesnar	.75	2.00
TT9 Sin Cara	.30	.75
TT10 Rey Mysterio	.50	1.25
TT11 Damien Sandow	.20	.50
TT12 Randy Orton	.60	1.50
TT13 Cody Rhodes	.20	.50
TT14 Eve	.75	2.00
TT15 Kane	.40	1.00
TT16 Big Show	.40	1.00
TT17 AJ Lee	1.00	2.50
TT18 Mark Henry	.25	.60
TT19 Triple H	.75	2.00
TT20 Ryback	.20	.50
TT21 Zack Ryder	.20	.50
TT22 Daniel Bryan	.50	1.25
TT23 Alberto Del Rio	.40	1.00
TT24 Christian	.20	.50
TT25 Tyson Kidd	.20	.50
TT26 CM Punk	.75	2.00
TT27 The Rock	1.00	2.50
TT28 Undertaker	.75	2.00
TT29 Kofi Kingston	.20	.50
TT30 Sheamus	.40	1.00

2013 Topps WWE 2K14 Phenom Edition Promo

NNO Undertaker

2014 Topps WWE

Subsets include: L = Legends (96-110)

COMPLETE SET (110)	10.00	25.00
UNOPENED BOX (24 PACKS)		
UNOPENED PACK (7 CARDS)		

1 AJ Lee	.75	2.00
2 Alex Riley	.15	.40
3 Big E Langston	.15	.40
4 Bo Dallas	.15	.40
5 Brad Maddox	.15	.40
6 Bray Wyatt	.40	1.00
7 Brie Bella	.50	1.25
8 Brock Lesnar	.60	1.50
9 Brodus Clay	.15	.40
10 Cameron	.25	.60
11 Chris Jericho	.40	1.00
12 CM Punk	.60	1.50
13 Curtis Axel	.15	.40
14 Daniel Bryan	.25	.60
15 David Otunga	.15	.40
16 Dean Ambrose	.40	1.00
17 Diego	.15	.40
18 Dolph Ziggler	.25	.60
19 Erick Rowan	.25	.60
20 Eva Marie	.60	1.50
21 Fandango	.25	.60
22 Fernando	.15	.40
23 Jack Swagger	.25	.60
24 Jerry The King Lawler	.40	1.00
25 John Cena	.75	2.00
26 Jojo	.25	.60
27 Justin Roberts	.15	.40
28 Kane	.40	1.00
29 Kofi Kingston	.15	.40
30 Luke Harper	.25	.60
31 El Torito	.15	.40
32 Michael Cole	.15	.40
33 The Miz	.25	.60
34 Naomi	.25	.60
35 Nikki Bella	.50	1.25
36 Paul Heyman	.15	.40
37 R-Truth	.15	.40
38 Randy Orton	.60	1.50
39 Rey Mysterio	.40	1.00
40 The Rock	.75	2.00
41 Rob Van Dam	.40	1.00
42 Roman Reigns	.40	1.00
43 Ryback	.15	.40
44 Santino Marella	.25	.60
45 Scott Stanford	.15	.40
46 Seth Rollins	.15	.40
47 Stephanie McMahon	.25	.60
48 Summer Rae	.60	1.50
49 Tamina Snuka	.25	.60
50 Tensai	.15	.40
51 Triple H	.60	1.50
52 Zack Ryder	.15	.40
53 Zeb Colter	.25	.60
54 Aksana	.40	1.00
55 Alberto Del Rio	.40	1.00
56 Alicia Fox	.25	.60
57 Antonio Cesaro	.15	.40
58 Big Show	.40	1.00
59 Booker T	.25	.60
60 Camacho	.15	.40
61 Christian	.15	.40
62 Cody Rhodes	.15	.40
63 Curt Hawkins	.15	.40
64 Damien Sandow	.15	.40
65 Darren Young	.15	.40
66 Drew McIntyre	.15	.40
67 Ezekiel Jackson	.25	.60
68 The Great Khali	.15	.40
69 Heath Slater	.15	.40
70 Hornswoggle	.25	.60
71 Hunico	.15	.40
72 JBL	.25	.60
73 Jey Uso	.15	.40
74 Jimmy Uso	.15	.40
75 Jinder Mahal	.15	.40
76 Josh Mathews	.15	.40
77 Justin Gabriel	.15	.40
78 Kaitlyn	.40	1.00
79 Layla	.40	1.00
80 Lilian Garcia	.40	1.00
81 Mark Henry	.25	.60
82 Natalya	.50	1.25
83 Renee Young	.60	1.50
84 Ricardo Rodriguez	.15	.40
85 Rosa Mendes	.25	.60
86 Sheamus	.40	1.00
87 Sin Cara	.40	1.00
88 Theodore Long	.15	.40
89 Titus O'Neil	.15	.40
90 Tony Chimel	.15	.40
91 Tyson Kidd	.15	.40
92 Undertaker	.60	1.50
93 Vickie Guerrero	.25	.60
94 Wade Barrett	.15	.40
95 William Regal	.25	.60
96 Andre The Giant L	.60	1.50
97 Billy Gunn L	.25	.60
98 Bob Backlund L	.25	.60
99 Diamond Dallas Page L	.25	.60
100 Eddie Guerrero L	.25	.60
101 Honky Tonk Man L	.25	.60
102 Jim Ross L	.25	.60
103 Junkyard Dog L	.25	.60
104 Kevin Nash L	.40	1.00
105 Larry Zbyszko L	.25	.60
106 Mick Foley L	.40	1.00
107 Paul Bearer L	.25	.60
108 Road Dogg L	.25	.60
109 Shawn Michaels L	.60	1.50
110 X-Pac L	.15	.40

2014 Topps WWE Autographs

NNO AJ Lee	30.00	75.00
NNO Billy Gunn	8.00	20.00
NNO Bray Wyatt	20.00	50.00
NNO Daniel Bryan	15.00	40.00
NNO Erick Rowan	6.00	15.00
NNO Eva Marie	20.00	50.00
NNO Jack Swagger	8.00	20.00
NNO John Cena	25.00	60.00
NNO Jojo	6.00	15.00
NNO Luke Harper	8.00	20.00
NNO Randy Orton	15.00	40.00
NNO Renee Young	15.00	40.00
NNO Road Dogg	12.00	30.00
NNO Shawn Michaels	30.00	75.00
NNO Summer Rae	12.00	30.00
NNO X-Pac	8.00	20.00

2014 Topps WWE Champions

COMPLETE SET (30)	10.00	25.00

1 Bruno Sammartino	.40	1.00
2 Bob Backlund	.40	1.00
3 The Iron Sheik	.40	1.00
4 Andre The Giant	1.00	2.50
5 Sgt. Slaughter	.60	1.50
6 Undertaker	1.00	2.50
7 Yokozuna	.40	1.00
8 Diesel	.60	1.50
9 Shawn Michaels	1.00	2.50
10 Stone Cold Steve Austin	1.25	3.00
11 Kane	.60	1.50
12 The Rock	1.25	3.00
13 Mankind	.60	1.50
14 Triple H	1.00	2.50
15 Big Show	.60	1.50
16 Chris Jericho	.60	1.50
17 Brock Lesnar	1.00	2.50
18 Eddie Guerrero	.40	1.00
19 JBL	.40	1.00
20 John Cena	1.25	3.00
21 Edge	.60	1.50
22 Rob Van Dam	.60	1.50
23 Randy Orton	1.00	2.50
24 Batista	.75	2.00
25 Sheamus	.60	1.50
26 The Miz	.40	1.00
27 CM Punk	1.00	2.50
28 Rey Mysterio	.60	1.50
29 Alberto Del Rio	.60	1.50
30 Daniel Bryan	.40	1.00

2014 Topps WWE Championship Belts

STATED PRINT RUN 400 SETS

NNO AJ Lee	10.00	25.00
NNO Andre The Giant	8.00	20.00
NNO Brie Bella	6.00	15.00
NNO British Bulldog	4.00	10.00
NNO Chris Jericho	5.00	12.00
NNO Christian	2.00	5.00
NNO CM Punk	8.00	20.00
NNO Daniel Bryan	3.00	8.00
NNO D-Generation X	4.00	10.00
NNO Edge	5.00	12.00
NNO Jeri-Show	5.00	12.00
NNO Jimmy Superfly Snuka	3.00	8.00
NNO John Cena	10.00	25.00
NNO Kaitlyn	5.00	12.00
NNO Kofi Kingston	2.00	5.00
NNO Kofi Kingston/R-Truth	2.00	5.00
NNO Layla	5.00	12.00
NNO The Miz	3.00	8.00
NNO Mr. Perfect Curt Hennig	2.50	6.00
NNO Nikki Bella	6.00	15.00
NNO Randy Orton	8.00	20.00
NNO Ravishing Rick Rude	2.00	5.00
NNO Rey Mysterio/Eddie Guerrero	5.00	12.00
NNO Ricky The Dragon Steamboat	2.00	5.00
NNO The Rock	10.00	25.00
NNO Rowdy Roddy Piper	5.00	12.00
NNO Stone Cold Steve Austin	10.00	25.00
NNO Team Hell No	5.00	12.00
NNO Triple H	8.00	20.00
NNO Undertaker	8.00	20.00

2014 Topps WWE Diva Kiss

STATED PRINT RUN 100 SETS

NNO	AJ Lee	150.00	225.00
NNO	Brie Bella	50.00	100.00
NNO	Eva Marie	30.00	75.00
NNO	Jojo	25.00	60.00
NNO	Kaitlyn	25.00	60.00
NNO	Lilian Garcia	25.00	60.00
NNO	Natalya	25.00	60.00
NNO	Nikki Bella	50.00	100.00
NNO	Renee Young	35.00	75.00
NNO	Summer Rae	60.00	120.00

2014 Topps WWE Diva Kiss Autographs

COMMON AUTO		60.00	120.00

STATED PRINT RUN 20 SETS

NNO	AJ Lee	200.00	400.00
NNO	Eva Marie	125.00	250.00
NNO	Jojo	60.00	120.00
NNO	Renee Young	75.00	150.00
NNO	Summer Rae	125.00	250.00

2014 Topps WWE Greatest Championship Contenders

COMPLETE SET (10)		5.00	12.00

*P.P.BLACK/1: UNPRICED DUE TO SCARCITY
*P.P.CYAN/1: UNPRICED DUE TO SCARCITY
*P.P.MAGENTA/1: UNPRICED DUE TO SCARCITY
*P.P.YELLOW/1: UNPRICED DUE TO SCARCITY
STATED ODDS 1:12

1	Ricky The Dragon Steamboat	.50	1.25
2	Mr. Perfect	.60	1.50
3	Ravishing Rick Rude	.50	1.25
4	Million Dollar Man Ted DiBiase	.60	1.50
5	Rowdy Roddy Piper	1.25	3.00
6	Mr. Wonderful Paul Orndorff	.50	1.25
7	Jake The Snake Roberts	.75	2.00
8	Jimmy Superfly Snuka	.75	2.00
9	The British Bulldog	1.00	2.50
10	The American Dream Dusty Rhodes	1.00	2.50

2014 Topps WWE Greatest Championship Matches

COMPLETE SET (20)		8.00	20.00

*P.P.BLACK/1: UNPRICED DUE TO SCARCITY
*P.P.CYAN/1: UNPRICED DUE TO SCARCITY
*P.P.MAGENTA/1: UNPRICED DUE TO SCARCITY
*P.P.YELLOW/1: UNPRICED DUE TO SCARCITY
STATED ODDS 1:8 HOBBY AND RETAIL

1	The Rock	.75	2.00
	Stone Cold Steve Austin		
2	John Cena/CM Punk	.75	2.00
3	John Cena/HBK	.75	2.00
4	The Rock/Mankind	.75	2.00
5	Triple H/Cactus Jack	.60	1.50
6	HBK/Mankind	.60	1.50
7	John Cena/RVD	.75	2.00
8	Brock Lesnar/Undertaker	.60	1.50
9	Rey Mysterio/John Cena	.75	2.00
10	HHH/Chris Jericho	.60	1.50
11	Steve Austin/The Rock	.75	2.00
12	Randy Orton/John Cena	.75	2.00
13	CM Punk/John Cena	.75	2.00
14	The Rock/HHH	.75	2.00
15	Brock Lesnar/Eddie Guerrero	.60	1.50

16	John Cena/JBL	.75	2.00
17	The Rock/Brock Lesnar	.75	2.00
18	Steve Austin/Chris Jericho	.75	2.00
19	CM Punk/Chris Jericho	.60	1.50
20	Mankind/The Rock	.75	2.00

2014 Topps WWE NXT Prospects

COMPLETE SET (20)		15.00	40.00

*P.P.BLACK/1: UNPRICED DUE TO SCARCITY
*P.P.CYAN/1: UNPRICED DUE TO SCARCITY
*P.P.MAGENTA/1: UNPRICED DUE TO SCARCITY
*P.P.YELLOW/1: UNPRICED DUE TO SCARCITY
STATED ODDS 1:2 HOBBY AND RETAIL

1	Adrian Neville	.60	1.50
2	Alexander Rusev	.75	2.00
3	Baron Corbin	.30	.75
4	Bayley	3.00	8.00
5	Charlotte	6.00	15.00
6	CJ Parker	.30	.75
7	Konnor O'Brian	.30	.75
8	Corey Graves	.30	.75
9	Emma	1.50	4.00
10	Enzo Amore	.60	1.50
11	Jason Jordan	.30	.75
12	Leo Kruger	.30	.75
13	Mojo Rawley	.30	.75
14	Paige	5.00	12.00
15	Rick Viktor	.30	.75
16	Sami Zayn	.60	1.50
17	Sasha Banks	8.00	20.00
18	Sylvester Lefort	.30	.75
19	Tyler Breeze	.30	.75
20	Xavier Woods	.30	.75

2014 Topps WWE Quad Autograph

NNO Shawn Michaels/X-Pac
Road Dogg/Billy Gunn

2014 Topps WWE Stone Cold Steve Austin Tribute

COMPLETE SET (10)		5.00	12.00

*P.P.BLACK/1: UNPRICED DUE TO SCARCITY
*P.P.CYAN/1: UNPRICED DUE TO SCARCITY
*P.P.MAGENTA/1: UNPRICED DUE TO SCARCITY
*P.P.YELLOW/1: UNPRICED DUE TO SCARCITY
STATED ODDS 1:12 HOBBY AND RETAIL

1	Stone Cold Steve Austin	1.00	2.50
2	Stone Cold Steve Austin	1.00	2.50
3	Stone Cold Steve Austin	1.00	2.50
4	Stone Cold Steve Austin	1.00	2.50
5	Stone Cold Steve Austin	1.00	2.50
6	Stone Cold Steve Austin	1.00	2.50
7	Stone Cold Steve Austin	1.00	2.50
8	Stone Cold Steve Austin	1.00	2.50
9	Stone Cold Steve Austin	1.00	2.50
10	Stone Cold Steve Austin	1.00	2.50

2014 Topps WWE SummerSlam Mat Relics

NNO	AJ Lee	12.00	30.00
NNO	Alberto Del Rio	6.00	15.00
NNO	Big E Langston	2.50	6.00
NNO	Bray Wyatt	6.00	15.00
NNO	Brie Bella	8.00	20.00
NNO	Brock Lesnar	10.00	25.00
NNO	Christian	2.50	6.00
NNO	CM Punk	10.00	25.00

NNO	Cody Rhodes	2.50	6.00
NNO	Damien Sandow	2.50	6.00
NNO	Daniel Bryan	4.00	10.00
NNO	Dean Ambrose	6.00	15.00
NNO	Dolph Ziggler	4.00	10.00
NNO	John Cena	12.00	30.00
NNO	Kaitlyn	6.00	15.00
NNO	Kane	6.00	15.00
NNO	Natalya	8.00	20.00
NNO	Randy Orton	10.00	25.00
NNO	Rob Van Dam	6.00	15.00
NNO	Triple H	10.00	25.00

2014 Topps WWE Swatch Relics

NNO	Brodus Clay/Shirt	3.00	8.00
NNO	Christian/Shirt	3.00	8.00
NNO	CM Punk/Shirt	6.00	15.00
NNO	Damien Sandow/Shirt	3.00	8.00
NNO	Daniel Bryan/Shirt	4.00	10.00
NNO	Darren Young/Shirt	3.00	8.00
NNO	Dean Ambrose/Shirt	8.00	20.00
NNO	Dolph Ziggler/Shirt	5.00	12.00
NNO	Hornswoggle/Shirt	3.00	8.00
NNO	John Cena/Shirt	8.00	20.00
NNO	Mark Henry/Shirt	4.00	10.00
NNO	The Miz/Shirt	3.00	8.00
NNO	Randy Orton/Shirt	6.00	15.00
NNO	Roman Reigns/Shirt	12.00	30.00
NNO	Ryback/Shirt	3.00	8.00
NNO	Seth Rollins/Shirt	6.00	15.00
	Shirt		
NNO	Undertaker/Pants	12.00	30.00
NNO	Wade Barrett/Shirt	3.00	8.00

2014 Topps WWE Triple Autographs

OVERALL TRIPLE AUTO PRINT RUN 25
UNPRICED DUE TO SCARCITY

NNO AJ Lee
Summer Rae/Renee Young
NNO Bray Wyatt
Luke Harper/Erick Rowan
NNO Eva Marie
Jojo/Jack Swagger
NNO John Cena
Daniel Bryan/Randy Orton

2014 Topps WWE Promo

P1 Shawn Michaels
(WWE 50 Book Exclusive)

2015 Topps WWE

COMPLETE SET (100)		8.00	20.00
UNOPENED BOX (24 PACKS)			
UNOPENED PACK (7 CARDS)			

*BLACK: 2X TO 5X BASIC CARDS
*SILVER: 3X TO 8X BASIC CARDS
*GOLD/10: 6X TO 15X BASIC CARDS
*RED/1: UNPRICED DUE TO SCARCITY
*P.P.BLACK/1: UNPRICED DUE TO SCARCITY
*P.P.CYAN/1: UNPRICED DUE TO SCARCITY
*P.P.MAGENTA/1: UNPRICED DUE TO SCARCITY
*P.P.YELLOW/1: UNPRICED DUE TO SCARCITY

1	Adam Rose	.20	.50
2	AJ Lee	.75	2.00
3	Alex Riley	.15	.40
4	Alicia Fox	.30	.75
5	Bad News Barrett	.15	.40
6	Batista	.40	1.00
7	Big E	.25	.60
8	Big Show	.40	1.00
9	Bo Dallas	.15	.40
10	Booker T	.25	.60
11	Bray Wyatt	.60	1.50
12	Brie Bella	.50	1.25
13	Brock Lesnar	.60	1.50
14	Byron Saxton	.15	.40
15	Cameron	.25	.60
16	Cesaro	.15	.40
17	Chris Jericho	.40	1.00
18	Christian	.15	.40
19	Curtis Axel	.15	.40
20	Damien Mizdow	.15	.40
21	Daniel Bryan	.60	1.50
22	Darren Young	.15	.40
23	David Otunga	.15	.40
24	Dean Ambrose	.40	1.00
25	Diego	.15	.40
26	Dolph Ziggler	.25	.60
27	Eden	.25	.60
28	Emma	.25	.60
29	Erick Rowan	.25	.60
30	Eva Marie	.60	1.50
31	Fandango	.15	.40
32	Fernando	.15	.40
33	Goldust	.15	.40
34	Heath Slater	.15	.40
35	Hornswoggle	.25	.60
36	Jack Swagger	.25	.60
37	Jason Albert	.15	.40
38	JBL	.15	.40
39	Jerry The King Lawler	.25	.60
40	Jey Uso	.15	.40
41	Jimmy Uso	.15	.40
42	John Cena	.75	2.00
43	Justin Gabriel	.15	.40
44	Kane	.40	1.00
45	Kofi Kingston	.15	.40
46	Lana	.60	1.50
47	Layla	.40	1.00
48	Lilian Garcia	.40	1.00
49	Luke Harper	.25	.60
50	Mark Henry	.25	.60
51	Michael Cole	.15	.40
52	The Miz	.25	.60
53	Naomi	.25	.60
54	Natalya	.50	1.25
55	Nikki Bella	.50	1.25
56	Paige	.75	2.00
57	Paul Heyman	.15	.40
58	R-Truth	.15	.40
59	Randy Orton	.60	1.50
60	Renee Young	.60	1.50
61	Rey Mysterio	.40	1.00
62	The Rock	.75	2.00
63	Rob Van Dam	.40	1.00
64	Roman Reigns	.40	1.00
65	Rosa Mendes	.25	.60
66	Rusev	.40	1.00
67	Ryback	.15	.40
68	Santino Marella	.15	.40
69	Scott Stanford	.15	.40
70	Seth Rollins	.25	.60
71	Sheamus	.40	1.00
72	Sin Cara	.25	.60
73	Stardust	.15	.40

74	Stephanie McMahon	.25	.60
75	Summer Rae	.60	1.50
76	Tamina Snuka	.25	.60
77	Titus O'Neil	.15	.40
78	Tom Phillips	.15	.40
79	Tony Chimel	.15	.40
80	El Torito	.15	.40
81	Triple H	.60	1.50
82	Tyson Kidd	.15	.40
83	Undertaker	.60	1.50
84	William Regal	.25	.60
85	Xavier Woods	.25	.60
86	Zack Ryder	.15	.40
87	Zeb Colter	.25	.60
88	Bret The Hit Man Hart	.50	1.25
89	Bruno Sammartino	.40	1.00
90	George The Animal Steele	.20	.50
91	Gerald Brisco	.25	.60
92	Hulk Hogan	.75	2.00
93	Larry Zbyszko	.25	.60
94	Mouth of the South Jimmy Hart	.20	.50
95	Pat Patterson	.15	.40
96	Ric Flair	.75	2.00
97	Rowdy Roddy Piper	.50	1.25
98	Sting	.40	1.00
99	Ultimate Warrior	.50	1.25
100	Virgil	.15	.40

2015 Topps WWE Athletic Tape Relics

*RED/1: UNPRICED DUE TO SCARCITY
STATED PRINT RUN 20 SER.#'d SETS

NNO	Cesaro	30.00	80.00
NNO	Curtis Axel	25.00	60.00
NNO	Daniel Bryan	120.00	200.00
NNO	Darren Young	15.00	40.00
NNO	Jack Swagger	15.00	40.00
NNO	Rey Mysterio	30.00	80.00
NNO	Ryback	25.00	60.00
NNO	Zack Ryder	50.00	100.00

2015 Topps WWE Autographs

*BLACK/50: .6X TO 1.5X BASIC AUTOS
*SILVER/25: .75X to 2X BASIC AUTOS
*GOLD/10: 1X TO 2.5X BASIC AUTOS
*RED/1: UNPRICED DUE TO SCARCITY
*P.P.BLACK/1: UNPRICED DUE TO SCARCITY
*P.P.CYAN/1: UNPRICED DUE TO SCARCITY
*P.P.MAGENTA/1: UNPRICED DUE TO SCARCITY
*P.P.YELLOW/1: UNPRICED DUE TO SCARCITY
RANDOMLY INSERTED INTO PACKS

NNO	AJ Lee	50.00	100.00
NNO	Bray Wyatt	15.00	40.00
NNO	Bret Hit Man Hart	25.00	60.00
NNO	Eden	6.00	15.00
NNO	Emma	20.00	50.00
NNO	George The Animal Steele	15.00	40.00
NNO	Hulk Hogan	125.00	250.00
NNO	Jack Swagger	6.00	15.00
NNO	John Cena	25.00	60.00
NNO	Larry Zbyszko	6.00	15.00
NNO	Mouth of the South Jimmy Hart	6.00	15.00
NNO	Paige	100.00	200.00
NNO	Ric Flair	15.00	40.00
NNO	Rowdy Roddy Piper	25.00	60.00
NNO	Rusev	20.00	50.00
NNO	Seth Rollins	15.00	40.00

2015 Topps WWE Championship Plates

*GOLD/10: UNPRICED DUE TO SCARCITY
*RED/1: UNPRICED DUE TO SCARCITY
RANDOMLY INSERTED INTO PACKS

NNO	AJ Lee	15.00	40.00
NNO	Batista and Rey Mysterio	6.00	15.00
NNO	Big Show	6.00	15.00
NNO	Booker T	6.00	15.00
NNO	Brie Bella	8.00	20.00
NNO	Brock Lesnar	8.00	20.00
NNO	Bruno Sammartino	6.00	15.00
NNO	Cesaro	6.00	15.00
NNO	Dean Ambrose	8.00	20.00
NNO	Dolph Ziggler	8.00	20.00
NNO	Edge and Chris Jericho	6.00	15.00
NNO	Eve	10.00	25.00
NNO	Hulk Hogan	12.00	30.00
NNO	John Cena	10.00	25.00
NNO	Kane	6.00	15.00
NNO	Kane and Big Show	6.00	15.00
NNO	Lex Luger	6.00	15.00
NNO	New Age Outlaws	8.00	20.00
NNO	Nikki Bella	12.00	30.00
NNO	Paige	15.00	40.00
NNO	Randy Orton	6.00	15.00
NNO	Razor Ramon	8.00	20.00
NNO	Rey Mysterio	6.00	15.00
NNO	Ric Flair/US Title	10.00	25.00
NNO	Ric Flair/WWE Title	12.00	30.00
NNO	Rock	8.00	20.00
NNO	Triple H	6.00	15.00
NNO	Ultimate Warrior/IC Title	6.00	15.00
NNO	Ultimate Warrior/WWE Title	10.00	25.00
NNO	Usos	8.00	20.00

2015 Topps WWE Crowd Chants Oh No

COMPLETE SET (10)		4.00	10.00

*P.P.BLACK/1: UNPRICED DUE TO SCARCITY
*P.P.CYAN/1: UNPRICED DUE TO SCARCITY
*P.P.MAGENTA/1: UNPRICED DUE TO SCARCITY
*P.P.YELLOW/1: UNPRICED DUE TO SCARCITY
RANDOMLY INSERTED INTO PACKS

1	The Montreal Incident	.40	1.00
2	Mr. McMahon/The Rock	.40	1.00
3	Eve/Zack Ryder	1.00	2.50
4	Brad Maddox/Ryback	.40	1.00
5	Damien Sandow/Cody Rhodes	.40	1.00
6	Big Show/John Cena	.40	1.00
7	Randy Orton/Daniel Bryan	1.25	3.00
8	Triple H/Daniel Bryan	.75	2.00
9	Wyatt Family/John Cena	.50	1.25
10	Streak Ends	1.00	2.50

2015 Topps WWE Crowd Chants One More Match

COMPLETE SET (10)		4.00	10.00

*P.P.BLACK/1: UNPRICED DUE TO SCARCITY
*P.P.CYAN/1: UNPRICED DUE TO SCARCITY
*P.P.MAGENTA/1: UNPRICED DUE TO SCARCITY
*P.P.YELLOW/1: UNPRICED DUE TO SCARCITY
RANDOMLY INSERTED INTO PACKS

1	Cowboy Bob Orton	.40	1.00
2	Edge	.50	1.25
3	Shawn Michaels	.50	1.25
4	Million Dollar Man Ted DiBiase	.40	1.00

5	Bruno Sammartino	.40	1.00
6	Ric Flair	.75	2.00
7	Rowdy Roddy Piper	.50	1.25
8	Hulk Hogan	1.25	3.00
9	Jake The Snake Roberts	.40	1.00
10	Stone Cold Steve Austin	1.25	3.00

2015 Topps WWE Crowd Chants This Is Awesome

COMPLETE SET (10)		4.00	10.00

*P.P.BLACK/1: UNPRICED DUE TO SCARCITY
*P.P.CYAN/1: UNPRICED DUE TO SCARCITY
*P.P.MAGENTA/1: UNPRICED DUE TO SCARCITY
*P.P.YELLOW/1: UNPRICED DUE TO SCARCITY
RANDOMLY INSERTED INTO PACKS

1	Rock beats Cena	.75	2.00
2	DX Reunites	.75	2.00
3	Bob Backlund HOF	.40	1.00
4	Dolph Ziggler/Alberto Del Rio	.40	1.00
5	Big Show/Triple H	.40	1.00
6	Kofi Kingston	.40	1.00
7	Wyatt Family/The Shield	.40	1.00
8	Hogan/Austin/Rock	1.25	3.00
9	Daniel Bryan	.40	1.00
10	Paige/AJ Lee	2.50	6.00

2015 Topps WWE Crowd Chants USA

COMPLETE SET (10)		5.00	12.00

*P.P.BLACK/1: UNPRICED DUE TO SCARCITY
*P.P.CYAN/1: UNPRICED DUE TO SCARCITY
*P.P.MAGENTA/1: UNPRICED DUE TO SCARCITY
*P.P.YELLOW/1: UNPRICED DUE TO SCARCITY
RANDOMLY INSERTED INTO PACKS

1	Hulk Hogan	1.50	4.00
2	Sgt. Slaughter	.75	2.00
3	Hacksaw Jim Duggan	.40	1.00
4	Lex Luger	.40	1.00
5	The US Express	.40	1.00
6	Jack Swagger	.40	1.00
7	The American Dream Dusty Rhodes	.40	1.00
8	John Cena	1.25	3.00
9	The Rock	1.50	4.00
10	Undertaker	1.25	3.00

2015 Topps WWE Crowd Chants WOOOOOO

COMPLETE SET (10)		4.00	10.00

*P.P.BLACK/1: UNPRICED DUE TO SCARCITY
*P.P.CYAN/1: UNPRICED DUE TO SCARCITY
*P.P.MAGENTA/1: UNPRICED DUE TO SCARCITY
*P.P.YELLOW/1: UNPRICED DUE TO SCARCITY
RANDOMLY INSERTED INTO PACKS

1	Ric Flair/Royal Rumble	.75	2.00
2	Ric Flair/Randy Savage	.60	1.50
3	Ric Flair/Eric Bischoff	.60	1.50
4	Ric Flair/Jeff Jarrett	.60	1.50
5	Evolution	.60	1.50
6	Ric Flair/Carlito	.60	1.50
7	Ric Flair/Roddy Piper	.60	1.50
8	Ric Flair HOF	1.25	3.00
9	Shawn Michaels/Ric Flair	.60	1.50
10	Four Horsemen HOF	1.25	3.00

2015 Topps WWE Crowd Chants YES! YES! YES!

COMPLETE SET (10)		5.00	12.00

*P.P.BLACK/1: UNPRICED DUE TO SCARCITY

*P.P.CYAN/1: UNPRICED DUE TO SCARCITY
*P.P.MAGENTA/1: UNPRICED DUE TO SCARCITY
*P.P.YELLOW/1: UNPRICED DUE TO SCARCITY
RANDOMLY INSERTED INTO PACKS

1	Daniel Bryan/Kane	.75	2.00
2	Team Hell No/Tag Champs	1.25	3.00
3	Team Hell No/Ziggler & Big-E	.75	2.00
4	Daniel Bryan/WWE Title	.75	2.00
5	Locker Room/Daniel Bryan	.75	2.00
6	Daniel Bryan/Second Title	.75	2.00
7	Daniel Bryan/Wyatt Family	.75	2.00
8	Yes Movement	.75	2.00
9	Daniel Bryan/Triple H	.75	2.00
10	Daniel Bryan WWE World Title	1.25	3.00

2015 Topps WWE Crowd Chants You Still Got It

COMPLETE SET (10)		2.50	6.00

*P.P.BLACK/1: UNPRICED DUE TO SCARCITY
*P.P.CYAN/1: UNPRICED DUE TO SCARCITY
*P.P.MAGENTA/1: UNPRICED DUE TO SCARCITY
*P.P.YELLOW/1: UNPRICED DUE TO SCARCITY
RANDOMLY INSERTED INTO PACKS

1	Ricky The Dragon Steamboat	.40	1.00
2	Booker T	.40	1.00
3	Chris Jericho	.40	1.00
4	Vader	.40	1.00
5	Road Warrior Animal	.40	1.00
6	Jerry The King Lawler	.40	1.00
7	Rob Van Dam	.40	1.00
8	Goldust	.40	1.00
9	Billy Gunn	.40	1.00
10	Road Dogg	.40	1.00

2015 Topps WWE Diva Kiss

*GOLD/10: .5X TO 1.2X BASIC KISS
*RED/1: UNPRICED DUE TO SCARCITY
RANDOMLY INSERTED INTO PACKS

NNO	Alicia Fox	20.00	50.00
NNO	Eva Marie	25.00	60.00
NNO	Eve Torres	25.00	60.00
NNO	Lana	30.00	80.00
NNO	Layla	15.00	40.00
NNO	Lilian Garcia	15.00	40.00
NNO	Paige	150.00	300.00
NNO	Rosa Mendes	15.00	40.00
NNO	Trish Stratus	30.00	80.00
NNO	Lita	25.00	60.00

2015 Topps WWE Diva Kiss Autographs

*GOLD/10: UNPRICED DUE TO SCARCITY
*RED/1: UNPRICED DUE TO SCARCITY
STATED PRINT RUN 15 SER.#'d SETS

NNO	Alicia Fox	40.00	100.00
NNO	Eva Marie	80.00	200.00
NNO	Eve Torres	40.00	100.00
NNO	Lana	80.00	200.00
NNO	Layla	50.00	125.00
NNO	Lilian Garcia	50.00	125.00
NNO	Paige	100.00	250.00
NNO	Rosa Mendes	30.00	80.00
NNO	Trish Stratus	100.00	250.00
NNO	Lita	80.00	200.00

2015 Topps WWE King of the Ring Relics

*RED/1: UNPRICED DUE TO SCARCITY
RANDOMLY INSERTED INTO PACKS

NNO	Billy Gunn	12.00	30.00
NNO	Bret Hit Man Hart	25.00	60.00
NNO	Brock Lesnar	15.00	40.00
NNO	Don Muraco	12.00	30.00
NNO	Edge	20.00	50.00
NNO	Harley Race	20.00	50.00
NNO	King Booker	15.00	40.00
NNO	Million Dollar Man Ted DiBiase	20.00	50.00
NNO	Sheamus	15.00	40.00
NNO	Stone Cold Steve Austin	25.00	60.00
NNO	Tito Santana	15.00	40.00
NNO	Triple H	25.00	60.00
NNO	William Regal	12.00	30.00

2015 Topps WWE NXT Prospects

COMPLETE SET (10)		6.00	15.00
STATED ODDS 1:3			
1	Aiden English	1.00	2.50
2	Alexa Bliss	4.00	10.00
3	Angelo Dawkins	1.00	2.50
4	Bull Dempsey	1.50	4.00
5	Colin Cassady	1.25	3.00
6	Hideo Itami	2.00	5.00
7	Kalisto	1.25	3.00
8	Marcus Louis	1.00	2.50
9	Sawyer Fulton	1.00	2.50
10	Tye Dillinger	1.00	2.50

2015 Topps WWE SummerSlam Mat Relics

*GOLD/10: UNPRICED DUE TO SCARCITY
*RED/1: UNPRICED DUE TO SCARCITY
RANDOMLY INSERTED INTO PACKS

NNO	AJ Lee	12.00	30.00
NNO	Bray Wyatt	6.00	15.00
NNO	Brie Bella	6.00	15.00
NNO	Brock Lesnar	8.00	20.00
NNO	Cesaro	5.00	12.00
NNO	Chris Jericho	8.00	20.00
NNO	Dean Ambrose	6.00	15.00
NNO	Dolph Ziggler	8.00	20.00
NNO	Jack Swagger	5.00	12.00
NNO	John Cena	6.00	15.00
NNO	Miz	5.00	12.00
NNO	Nikki Bella	6.00	15.00
NNO	Paige	15.00	40.00
NNO	Randy Orton	5.00	12.00
NNO	Rob Van Dam	5.00	12.00
NNO	Roman Reigns	8.00	20.00
NNO	Rusev	6.00	15.00
NNO	Seth Rollins	5.00	12.00
NNO	Stephanie McMahon	8.00	20.00
NNO	Triple H	8.00	20.00

2015 Topps WWE Swatch Relics

*GOLD/10: UNPRICED DUE TO SCARCITY
*RED/1: UNPRICED DUE TO SCARCITY
RANDOMLY INSERTED INTO PACKS

NNO	AJ Lee	15.00	40.00
NNO	Big E	5.00	12.00
NNO	Big Show	5.00	12.00
NNO	Bo Dallas	6.00	15.00
NNO	Bray Wyatt	10.00	25.00

NNO	Brie Bella	6.00	15.00
NNO	Dolph Ziggler	6.00	15.00
NNO	Fandango	5.00	12.00
NNO	Goldust	5.00	12.00
NNO	Jey Uso	5.00	12.00
NNO	John Cena	6.00	15.00
NNO	The Miz	5.00	12.00
NNO	Natalya	6.00	15.00
NNO	Nikki Bella	6.00	15.00
NNO	Paige	15.00	40.00
NNO	Randy Orton	6.00	15.00
NNO	Seth Rollins	6.00	15.00
NNO	Stardust	5.00	12.00

2015 Topps WWE Triple Autographs

STATED PRINT RUN 5 SER.#'d SETS
UNPRICED DUE TO SCARCITY

NNO	AJ/Paige/Emma
NNO	Wyatt/Rusev/Hart
NNO	Hogan/Flair/Piper
NNO	Cena/Ambrose/Rollins
NNO	Paige/Emma/Eden

2016 Topps WWE

COMPLETE SET (100)		10.00	25.00
UNOPENED BOX (24 PACKS)			
UNOPENED PACK (8 CARDS)			
*BRONZE: 1.2X TO 3X BASIC CARDS			
*SILVER: 2X TO 5X BASIC CARDS			
*GOLD/10: UNPRICED DUE TO SCARCITY			
*RED/1: UNPRICED DUE TO SCARCITY			
*P.P.BLACK/1: UNPRICED DUE TO SCARCITY			
*P.P.CYAN/1: UNPRICED DUE TO SCARCITY			
*P.P.MAGENTA/1: UNPRICED DUE TO SCARCITY			
*P.P.YELLOW/1: UNPRICED DUE TO SCARCITY			
1	Adam Rose	.20	.50
2	Alberto Del Rio	.30	.75
3	Alicia Fox	.30	.75
4	The Ascension	.20	.50
5	Becky Lynch	.60	1.50
6	Big Show	.40	1.00
7	Bo Dallas	.20	.50
8	Booker T	.40	1.00
9	Brie Bella	.40	1.00
10	Bubba Ray Dudley	.40	1.00
11	The Bunny	.20	.50
12	Byron Saxton	.20	.50
13	Cesaro	.40	1.00
14	Charlotte	.60	1.50
15	Corey Graves	.12	.30
16	Curtis Axel	.20	.50
17	D-Von Dudley	.30	.75
18	Damien Sandow	.20	.50
19	Dolph Ziggler	.25	.60
20	Fandango	.20	.50
21	Goldust	.30	.75
22	Jason Albert	.20	.50
23	JBL	.25	.60
24	Jerry The King Lawler	.40	1.00
25	Kalisto	.50	1.25
26	Kevin Owens	.50	1.25
27	Lana	.75	2.00
28	Mandy Rose	.50	1.25
29	Mark Henry	.25	.60
30	The Miz	.30	.75
31	Naomi	.30	.75
32	Natalya	.30	.75

33	Neville	.50	1.25
34	Nikki Bella	.60	1.50
35	Paige	.60	1.50
36	Titus O'Neil	.20	.50
37	R-Truth	.20	.50
38	Rusev	.50	1.25
39	Ryback	.25	.60
40	Sasha Banks	.60	1.50
41	Sin Cara	.25	.60
42	Stardust	.20	.50
43	Summer Rae	.50	1.25
44	Tamina	.25	.60
45	Tyler Breeze	.20	.50
46	Tyson Kidd	.20	.50
47	The Usos	.20	.50
48	William Regal	.20	.50
49	Zeb Colter	.20	.50
50	Alundra Blayze L	.25	.60
51	American Dream Dusty Rhodes L	.20	.50
52	Andre the Giant L	.60	1.50
53	Bam Bam Bigelow L	.25	.60
54	Barry Windham L	.20	.50
55	Batista L	.40	1.00
56	The Brain Busters L	.20	.50
57	The British Bulldog L	.25	.60
58	The Bushwhackers L	.20	.50
59	Christian L	.30	.75
60	Dangerous Danny Davis L	.20	.50
61	Doink the Clown L	.20	.50
62	Edge L	.50	1.25
63	Eve Torres L	.40	1.00
64	George The Animal Steele L	.25	.60
65	The Godfather L	.25	.60
66	Irwin R. Schyster L	.20	.50
67	Jake The Snake Roberts L	.40	1.00
68	Jim Ross L	.30	.75
69	J.J. Dillon L	.20	.50
70	Kamala L	.20	.50
71	Kerry Von Erich L	.30	.75
72	Kevin Nash L	.50	1.25
73	Kevin Von Erich L	.30	.75
74	Lita L	.60	1.50
75	Macho King Randy Savage L	.50	1.25
76	Mike Rotunda L	.20	.50
77	Million Dollar Man Ted DiBiase L	.25	.60
78	Miss Elizabeth L	.20	.50
79	Mr. X L	.20	.50
80	The Nasty Boys L	.20	.50
81	The Natural Disasters L	.20	.50
82	Bret Hit Man Hart L	.50	1.25
83	Papa Shango L	.25	.60
84	Ric Flair L	.75	2.00
85	Rikishi L	.25	.60
86	Road Dogg L	.30	.75
87	Rob Van Dam L	.40	1.00
88	Faarooq L	.50	1.25
89	Rowdy Roddy Piper L	.60	1.50
90	Santino Marella L	.25	.60
91	Scott Hall L	.50	1.25
92	Sensational Sherri L	.30	.75
93	Shawn Michaels L	.75	2.00
94	Stevie Ray L	.20	.50
95	Superstar Billy Graham L	.20	.50
96	Tatsumi Fujinami L	.20	.50
97	Trish Stratus L	1.00	2.50
98	Ultimate Warrior L	.50	1.25
99	Virgil L	.20	.50
100	X-Pac L	.30	.75

2016 Topps WWE 2K17 NXT TakeOver London Mat Relics

*PURPLE/299: SAME VALUE AS BASIC
*GREEN/199: .5X TO 1.2X BASIC MEM
*BRONZE/99: X TO 1.5X BASIC MEM
*SILVER/50: .75X TO 2X BASIC MEM
*BLUE/25: UNPRICED DUE TO SCARCITY
*GOLD/10: UNPRICED DUE TO SCARCITY
RANDOMLY INSERTED INTO PACKS

NNO	Asuka	5.00	12.00
NNO	Emma	6.00	15.00
NNO	Dana Brooke	3.00	8.00
NNO	Dash Wilder	2.50	6.00
NNO	Scott Dawson	2.50	6.00
NNO	Enzo Amore	3.00	8.00
NNO	Colin Cassady	3.00	8.00
NNO	Carmella	6.00	15.00
NNO	Baron Corbin	4.00	10.00
NNO	Apollo Crews	3.00	8.00
NNO	Bayley	5.00	12.00
NNO	Nia Jax	3.00	8.00
NNO	Finn Balor	5.00	12.00
NNO	Samoa Joe	3.00	8.00

2016 Topps WWE Authority Perspectives

COMPLETE SET (18)		12.00	30.00
*P.P.BLACK/1: UNPRICED DUE TO SCARCITY			
*P.P.CYAN/1: UNPRICED DUE TO SCARCITY			
*P.P.MAGENTA/1: UNPRICED DUE TO SCARCITY			
*P.P.YELLOW/1: UNPRICED DUE TO SCARCITY			
RANDOMLY INSERTED INTO PACKS			
*ANTI-AUTHORITY: SAME VALUE			
1A	Triple H	2.50	6.00
2A	Stephanie McMahon	1.00	2.50
3A	Seth Rollins	1.00	2.50
4A	Kane	1.00	2.50
5A	J&J Security	.60	1.50
6A	The New Day	1.50	4.00
7A	The Wyatt Family	1.25	3.00
8A	King Barrett	.60	1.50
9A	Sheamus	1.50	4.00
10A	John Cena	3.00	8.00
11A	Sting	1.50	4.00
12A	The Rock	3.00	8.00
13A	Reigns/Ambrose	2.00	5.00
14A	Randy Orton	1.50	4.00
15A	Brock Lesnar	3.00	8.00
16A	Undertaker	2.50	6.00
17A	Chris Jericho	1.50	4.00
18A	Daniel Bryan	2.50	6.00

2016 Topps WWE Autographs

*BRONZE/50: .5X TO 1.2X BASIC AUTOS
*SILVER/25: .75X TO 2X BASIC AUTOS
*GOLD/10: UNPRICED DUE TO SCARCITY
*RED/1: UNPRICED DUE TO SCARCITY
*P.P.BLACK/1: UNPRICED DUE TO SCARCITY
*P.P.CYAN/1: UNPRICED DUE TO SCARCITY
*P.P.MAGENTA/1: UNPRICED DUE TO SCARCITY
*P.P.YELLOW/1: UNPRICED DUE TO SCARCITY
RANDOMLY INSERTED INTO PACKS

NNO	Apollo Crews	10.00	25.00
NNO	Alberto Del Rio	10.00	25.00
NNO	Asuka	30.00	80.00
NNO	Bayley	25.00	60.00
NNO	Becky Lynch	15.00	40.00

NNO	Braun Strowman	10.00	25.00
NNO	Bray Wyatt	10.00	25.00
NNO	Bubba Ray Dudley	8.00	20.00
NNO	Charlotte	12.00	30.00
NNO	D-Von Dudley	6.00	15.00
NNO	Dean Ambrose	10.00	25.00
NNO	Finn Balor	15.00	40.00
NNO	JJ Dillion	6.00	15.00
NNO	John Cena	15.00	40.00
NNO	Luke Harper	10.00	25.00
NNO	Natalya	8.00	20.00
NNO	Nia Jax	12.00	30.00
NNO	Ric Flair	15.00	40.00
NNO	Rikishi	6.00	15.00
NNO	Roman Reigns	10.00	25.00
NNO	Samoa Joe	8.00	20.00
NNO	Seth Rollins	8.00	20.00
NNO	Sting	25.00	60.00
NNO	Superstar Billy Graham	15.00	40.00

2016 Topps WWE Diva Kiss

*GOLD/10: UNPRICED DUE TO SCARCITY
*RED/1: UNPRICED DUE TO SCARCITY
STATED PRINT RUN 99 SER.#'d SETS

NNO	Alicia Fox	25.00	60.00
NNO	Alundra Blayze	25.00	60.00
NNO	Bayley	50.00	100.00
NNO	Becky Lynch	50.00	100.00
NNO	Brie Bella	30.00	80.00
NNO	Charlotte	30.00	80.00
NNO	Lana	50.00	100.00
NNO	Lita	25.00	60.00
NNO	Nikki Bella	60.00	120.00
NNO	Sasha Banks	80.00	150.00
NNO	Trish Stratus	50.00	100.00

2016 Topps WWE Diva Kiss Autographs

*GOLD/10: UNPRICED DUE TO SCARCITY
*RED/1: UNPRICED DUE TO SCARCITY
*P.P.BLACK/1: UNPRICED DUE TO SCARCITY
*P.P.CYAN/1: UNPRICED DUE TO SCARCITY
*P.P.MAGENTA/1: UNPRICED DUE TO SCARCITY
*P.P.YELLOW/1: UNPRICED DUE TO SCARCITY
STATED PRINT RUN 25 SER.#'d SETS

NNO	Alicia Fox	30.00	80.00
NNO	Alundra Blayze	30.00	80.00
NNO	Bayley	100.00	200.00
NNO	Becky Lynch	100.00	200.00
NNO	Brie Bella	50.00	100.00
NNO	Charlotte	100.00	200.00
NNO	Lana	60.00	120.00
NNO	Lita	50.00	100.00
NNO	Nikki Bella	50.00	100.00
NNO	Sasha Banks	200.00	400.00
NNO	Trish Stratus	120.00	250.00

2016 Topps WWE Medallions

*BRONZE/50: .5X TO 1.2X BASIC MEM
*SILVER/25: .6X TO 1.5X BASIC MEM
*GOLD/10: UNPRICED DUE TO SCARCITY
*RED/1: UNPRICED DUE TO SCARCITY
STATED PRINT RUN 299 SER.#'d SETS

NNO	Big E	2.00	5.00
NNO	Braun Strowman	2.50	6.00
NNO	Bray Wyatt	8.00	20.00
NNO	Brock Lesnar	10.00	25.00

NNO	Chris Jericho	5.00	12.00
NNO	Daniel Bryan	8.00	20.00
NNO	Dean Ambrose	6.00	15.00
NNO	Jamie Noble	2.00	5.00
NNO	Joey Mercury	2.00	5.00
NNO	John Cena	10.00	25.00
NNO	Kane	3.00	8.00
NNO	King Barrett	2.00	5.00
NNO	Kofi Kingston	2.00	5.00
NNO	Luke Harper	2.00	5.00
NNO	Randy Orton	5.00	12.00
NNO	The Rock	10.00	25.00
NNO	Roman Reigns	6.00	15.00
NNO	Seth Rollins	3.00	8.00
NNO	Sheamus	5.00	12.00
NNO	Stephanie McMahon	3.00	8.00
NNO	Sting	5.00	12.00
NNO	Triple H	8.00	20.00
NNO	Undertaker	8.00	20.00
NNO	Xavier Woods	2.00	5.00

2016 Topps WWE NXT Inserts

COMPLETE SET (28)		8.00	20.00

*P.P.BLACK/1: UNPRICED DUE TO SCARCITY
*P.P.CYAN/1: UNPRICED DUE TO SCARCITY
*P.P.MAGENTA/1: UNPRICED DUE TO SCARCITY
*P.P.YELLOW/1: UNPRICED DUE TO SCARCITY
STATED ODDS 1:1

1	Aiden English	.30	.75
2	Alexa Bliss	4.00	10.00
3	Angelo Dawkins	.30	.75
4	Apollo Crews	.30	.75
5	Asuka	4.00	10.00
6	Baron Corbin	.40	1.00
7	Bayley	.75	2.00
8	Billie Kay	.75	2.00
9	Blake	.30	.75
10	Carmella	.75	2.00
11	Chad Gable	.40	1.00
12	Colin Cassady	.60	1.50
13	Dana Brooke	.75	2.00
14	Dash Wilder	.40	1.00
15	Scott Dawson	.30	.75
16	Enzo Amore	.60	1.50
17	Finn Balor	2.00	5.00
18	Hideo Itami	.40	1.00
19	Jason Jordan	.40	1.00
20	Mojo Rawley	.30	.75
21	Murphy	.30	.75
22	Nia Jax	.50	1.25
23	Peyton Royce	.75	2.00
24	Sami Zayn	.50	1.25
25	Samoa Joe	.75	2.00
26	Sawyer Fulton	.40	1.00
27	Simon Gotch	.50	1.25
28	Tye Dillinger	.40	1.00

2016 Topps WWE NXT TakeOver Brooklyn Mat Relics

*BRONZE/50: .5X TO 1.2X BASIC MEM
*SILVER/25: .6X TO 1.5X BASIC MEM
*GOLD/10: UNPRICED DUE TO SCARCITY
*RED/1: UNPRICED DUE TO SCARCITY
*P.P.BLACK/1: UNPRICED DUE TO SCARCITY
*P.P.CYAN/1: UNPRICED DUE TO SCARCITY
*P.P.MAGENTA/1: UNPRICED DUE TO SCARCITY
*P.P.YELLOW/1: UNPRICED DUE TO SCARCITY

STATED PRINT RUN 199 SER.#'d SETS

NNO	Aiden English	2.50	6.00
NNO	Alexa Bliss	12.00	30.00
NNO	Apollo Crews	2.50	6.00
NNO	Baron Corbin	3.00	8.00
NNO	Bayley	6.00	15.00
NNO	Blake	2.50	6.00
NNO	Finn Balor	8.00	20.00
NNO	Kevin Owens	6.00	15.00
NNO	Murphy	2.50	6.00
NNO	Samoa Joe	6.00	15.00
NNO	Sasha Banks	8.00	20.00
NNO	Simon Gotch	4.00	10.00
NNO	Tye Dillinger	3.00	8.00
NNO	Tyler Breeze	2.50	6.00

2016 Topps WWE Shirt Relics

*BRONZE/50: .5X TO 1.2X BASIC MEM
*SILVER/25: .6X TO 1.5X BASIC MEM
*GOLD/10: UNPRICED DUE TO SCARCITY
*RED/1: UNPRICED DUE TO SCARCITY
*P.P.BLACK/1: UNPRICED DUE TO SCARCITY
*P.P.CYAN/1: UNPRICED DUE TO SCARCITY
*P.P.MAGENTA/1: UNPRICED DUE TO SCARCITY
*P.P.YELLOW/1: UNPRICED DUE TO SCARCITY
RANDOMLY INSERTED INTO PACKS

NNO	Aiden English	3.00	8.00
NNO	Alberto Del Rio	5.00	12.00
NNO	Alicia Fox	5.00	12.00
NNO	Apollo Crews	3.00	8.00
NNO	Bayley	8.00	20.00
NNO	Becky Lynch	10.00	25.00
NNO	Braun Strowman	4.00	10.00
NNO	Bray Wyatt	12.00	30.00
NNO	Brie Bella	6.00	15.00
NNO	Cesaro	6.00	15.00
NNO	Charlotte	10.00	25.00
NNO	Dean Ambrose	10.00	25.00
NNO	D-Von Dudley	5.00	12.00
NNO	Finn Balor	10.00	25.00
NNO	John Cena	15.00	40.00
NNO	Kevin Owens	8.00	20.00
NNO	Luke Harper	3.00	8.00
NNO	Naomi	5.00	12.00
NNO	Natalya	5.00	12.00
NNO	Neville	8.00	20.00
NNO	Paige	10.00	25.00
NNO	Roman Reigns	10.00	25.00
NNO	Samoa Joe	8.00	20.00
NNO	Sasha Banks	10.00	25.00
NNO	Seth Rollins	5.00	12.00
NNO	Simon Gotch	5.00	12.00
NNO	Tamina	4.00	10.00
NNO	Tyler Breeze	3.00	8.00
NNO	Zack Ryder	3.00	8.00

2016 Topps WWE SummerSlam Mat Relics

*BRONZE/50: .5X TO 1.2X BASIC MEM
*SILVER/25: .6X TO 1.5X BASIC MEM
*GOLD/10: UNPRICED DUE TO SCARCITY
*RED/1: UNPRICED DUE TO SCARCITY
*P.P.BLACK/1: UNPRICED DUE TO SCARCITY
*P.P.CYAN/1: UNPRICED DUE TO SCARCITY
*P.P.MAGENTA/1: UNPRICED DUE TO SCARCITY
*P.P.YELLOW/1: UNPRICED DUE TO SCARCITY

STATED PRINT RUN 199 SER.#'d SETS

NNO	Big Show	4.00	10.00
NNO	Bray Wyatt	8.00	20.00
NNO	Brock Lesnar	10.00	25.00
NNO	Cesaro	4.00	10.00
NNO	Dean Ambrose	6.00	15.00
NNO	Dolph Ziggler	2.50	6.00
NNO	John Cena	10.00	25.00
NNO	Kevin Owens	5.00	12.00
NNO	King Barrett	2.00	5.00
NNO	Luke Harper	2.00	5.00
NNO	The Miz	3.00	8.00
NNO	Neville	5.00	12.00
NNO	Randy Orton	5.00	12.00
NNO	Roman Reigns	6.00	15.00
NNO	Rusev	5.00	12.00
NNO	Ryback	2.50	6.00
NNO	Seth Rollins	3.00	8.00
NNO	Sheamus	5.00	12.00
NNO	Stardust	2.00	5.00
NNO	Undertaker	8.00	20.00

2016 Topps WWE Superstars of Canada Autographs

STATED PRINT RUN 25 SER.#'d SETS

NNO	Chris Jericho	15.00	40.00
NNO	Christian	12.00	30.00
NNO	Edge	25.00	60.00
NNO	Kevin Owens	12.00	30.00
NNO	Natalya	12.00	30.00
NNO	Renee Young	15.00	40.00
NNO	Sami Zayn	10.00	25.00
NNO	Trish Stratus	50.00	100.00
NNO	Tyson Kidd	6.00	15.00
NNO	Viktor	6.00	15.00

2016 Topps WWE Triple Autographs

STATED PRINT RUN 11 SER.#'d SETS

NNO	Alberto Del Rio Superstar Billy Graham/Rikishi	50.00	100.00
NNO	Bayley/Asuka/Nia Jax	75.00	150.00
NNO	Wyatt/Harper/Strowman	100.00	200.00
NNO	Charlotte Becky Lynch/Natalya	100.00	200.00
NNO	Balor/Samoa Joe/Crews	100.00	200.00
NNO	Cena/Dudley Boyz	75.00	150.00
NNO	Rollins/Ambrose/Reigns	125.00	250.00
NNO	Sting/Flair/Dillon	150.00	300.00

2017 Topps WWE

COMPLETE SET W/O SP (100)	8.00	20.00
COMPLETE SET W/SP (120)		
UNOPENED BOX (24 PACKS)		
UNOPENED PACK (7 CARDS)		

*BRONZE: .5X TO 1.2X BASIC CARDS
*BLUE/99: 1X TO 2.5X BASIC CARDS
*SILVER/25: 2X TO 5X BASIC CARDS
*GOLD/10: 4X TO 10X BASIC CARDS
*RED/1: UNPRICED DUE TO SCARCITY
*P.P.BLACK/1: UNPRICED DUE TO SCARCITY
*P.P.CYAN/1: UNPRICED DUE TO SCARCITY
*P.P.MAGENTA/1: UNPRICED DUE TO SCARCITY
*P.P.YELLOW/1: UNPRICED DUE TO SCARCITY

1A	The Rock	1.25	3.00
1B	The Rock SP Just Bring It	10.00	25.00
2	Tyson Kidd	.25	.60
3	Booker T	.30	.75

4	Byron Saxton	.25	.60
5A	Bayley	.75	2.00
5B	Bayley SP Leaping	5.00	12.00
6	Big Cass	.30	.75
7A	Big E	.30	.75
7B	Big E SP Big Splash	3.00	8.00
8	Bob Backlund	.25	.60
9A	Brian Kendrick	.25	.60
9B	Brian Kendrick SP Jacket	3.00	8.00
10A	Brock Lesnar	1.25	3.00
10B	Brock Lesnar SP Outside Ring	8.00	20.00
11	Chad Patton	.25	.60
12	Charly Caruso	.25	.60
13A	Chris Jericho	.60	1.50
13B	Chris Jericho SP Walls of Jericho	6.00	15.00
14	Corey Graves	.25	.60
15	Darrick Moore	.25	.60
16	Enzo Amore	.75	2.00
17A	Finn Balor	1.00	2.50
17B	Finn Balor SP Entrance/No Logo	10.00	25.00
18A	Goldberg	1.00	2.50
18B	Goldberg SP Jacket	12.00	30.00
19	JoJo	.40	1.00
20	John Cone	.25	.60
21	Karl Anderson	.25	.60
22A	Kofi Kingston	.30	.75
22B	Kofi Kingston SP Leaping	6.00	15.00
23	Luke Gallows	.40	1.00
24	Michael Cole	.25	.60
25	Mick Foley	.60	1.50
26A	Nia Jax	.40	1.00
26B	Nia Jax SP Pink Gear	5.00	12.00
27	Paige	.60	1.50
28	Paul Heyman	.25	.60
29	Rod Zapata	.25	.60
30	Shawn Bennett	.25	.60
31	TJ Perkins	.25	.60
32	Titus O'Neil	.25	.60
33A	Triple H	.60	1.50
33B	Triple H SP No Mic	10.00	25.00
34A	Xavier Woods	.30	.75
34B	Xavier Woods	2.50	6.00
35A	AJ Styles	1.25	3.00
35B	AJ Styles	12.00	30.00
36A	Alexa Bliss	1.25	3.00
36B	Alexa Bliss SP Flip	15.00	40.00
37	Andrea D'Marco	.25	.60
38A	Carmella	.60	1.50
38B	Carmella SP Microphone	6.00	15.00
39	Chad Gable	.30	.75
40	Charles Robinson	.25	.60
41	Dan Engler	.25	.60
42	David Otunga	.25	.60
43	Greg Hamilton	.25	.60
44	Jason Ayers	.25	.60
45	Jason Jordan	.30	.75
46	JBL	.30	.75
47A	John Cena	1.25	3.00
47B	John Cena SP		
48A	Kane	.30	.75
48B	Kane SP Facing Forward	8.00	20.00
49	Luke Harper	.25	.60
50	Maryse	.50	1.25
51	Mauro Ranallo	.25	.60
52	Mike Chioda	.25	.60
53A	The Miz	.50	1.25
53B	Miz SP In the Ring	8.00	20.00
54	Mojo Rawley	.30	.75
55A	Randy Orton	.60	1.50
55B	Randy Orton SP RKO	6.00	15.00
56	Renee Young	.40	1.00
57	Ryan Tran	.25	.60
58A	Undertaker	1.00	2.50
58B	Undertaker SP Silhouette	20.00	50.00
59	Zack Ryder	.25	.60
60	Alexander Wolfe	.30	.75
61	Aliyah	.30	.75
62A	Asuka	.75	2.00
62B	Asuka SP/(mask)	8.00	20.00
63A	Austin Aries	.50	1.25
63B	Austin Aries SP Cape	6.00	15.00
64	Billie Kay	.30	.75
65A	Bobby Roode	.60	1.50
65B	Bobby Roode SP	8.00	20.00
66	Cathy Kelley	.25	.60
67	Dash Wilder	.25	.60
68	Dasha Fuentes	.30	.75
69	Danilo Anfibio	.25	.60
70	Drake Wuertz	.25	.60
71	Eddie Orengo	.25	.60
72	Ember Moon	.60	1.50
73	Eric Young	.50	1.25
74	Hideo Itami	.40	1.00
75	Johnny Gargano	.25	.60
76	Liv Morgan	.40	1.00
77	Nick Miller	.25	.60
78	Nikki Cross	.50	1.25
79	Oney Lorcan	.25	.60
80	Paul Ellering	.25	.60
81	Peyton Royce	.40	1.00
82	Roderick Strong	.30	.75
83A	Samoa Joe	.75	2.00
83B	Samoa Joe SP		
84	Scott Dawson	.25	.60
85	Shane Thorne	.25	.60
86A	Shinsuke Nakamura	.60	1.50
86B	Shinsuke Nakamura SP Jacket	6.00	15.00
87	Tommaso Ciampa	.25	.60
88	Tye Dillinger	.50	1.25
89	William Regal	.30	.75
90	Norman Smiley	.30	.75
91	Ric Flair	.60	1.50
92	Terri Runnels	.25	.60
93	Beth Phoenix	.25	.60
94	Eric Bischoff	.25	.60
95	Ivory	.25	.60
96	Judy Martin	.25	.60
97	Kelly Kelly	.50	1.25
98	Leilani Kai	.25	.60
99	Princess Victoria	.25	.60
100	Torrie Wilson	.60	1.50

2017 Topps WWE Autographed Shirt Relics

STATED ODDS 1:3,524

NNO	Bayley	30.00	75.00
NNO	Big E	15.00	40.00
NNO	Bray Wyatt	30.00	75.00
NNO	Carmella	25.00	60.00
NNO	Cesaro	15.00	40.00
NNO	Dolph Ziggler	15.00	40.00
NNO	John Cena	50.00	100.00
NNO	Karl Anderson	15.00	40.00
NNO	Kevin Owens	15.00	40.00
NNO	Kofi Kingston	15.00	40.00
NNO	The Miz	30.00	75.00
NNO	Randy Orton	30.00	80.00
NNO	Roman Reigns		
NNO	Seth Rollins	25.00	60.00
NNO	Shinsuke Nakamura		
NNO	Xavier Woods		

2017 Topps WWE Autographs

*BLUE/50: .6X TO 1.5X BASIC AUTOS
*SILVER/25: .75X TO 2X BASIC AUTOS
*GOLD/10: UNPRICED DUE TO SCARCITY
*RED/1: UNPRICED DUE TO SCARCITY
STATED ODDS 1:50

5	Bayley	15.00	40.00
6	Big Cass	8.00	20.00
7	Big E	6.00	15.00
10	Brock Lesnar	50.00	100.00
13	Chris Jericho	12.00	30.00
16	Enzo Amore	10.00	25.00
18	Goldberg	50.00	100.00
21	Karl Anderson	6.00	15.00
22	Kofi Kingston	6.00	15.00
23	Luke Gallows	5.00	12.00
34	Xavier Woods	6.00	15.00
38	Carmella	10.00	25.00
53	The Miz	5.00	12.00
62	Asuka	15.00	40.00
64	Billie Kay	8.00	20.00
81	Peyton Royce	10.00	25.00
83	Samoa Joe	6.00	15.00
91	Ric Flair	15.00	40.00
92	Terri Runnels	10.00	25.00
93	Beth Phoenix	6.00	15.00
94	Eric Bischoff	8.00	20.00
96	Judy Martin	6.00	15.00
97	Kelly Kelly	15.00	40.00
98	Leilani Kai	6.00	15.00
100	Torrie Wilson	10.00	25.00

2017 Topps WWE Autographs Blue

STATED ODDS 1:99
STATED PRINT RUN 50 SER.#'d SETS

58	Undertaker	150.00	300.00

2017 Topps WWE Autographs Silver

STATED ODDS 1:116
STATED PRINT RUN 25 SER.#'d SETS

25	Mick Foley	15.00	40.00

2017 Topps WWE Breaking Ground

COMPLETE SET (10)		5.00	12.00

STATED ODDS 1:2

1	Baron Corbin	1.00	2.50
2	Dana Brooke	1.25	3.00
3	Tyler Breeze	.60	1.50
4	Jason Jordan	.75	2.00
5	Tyler Breeze	.60	1.50
6	The Superstars	1.00	2.50
7	Bayley	2.00	5.00
8	Scott Hall	.75	2.00
9	Sami Zayn	.75	2.00
10	Tyler Breeze	.60	1.50

2017 Topps WWE Championship Relics

*BLUE/50: .5X TO 1.2X BASIC MEM
*SILVER/25: .6X TO 1.5X BASIC MEM
*GOLD/10: 1X TO 2.5X BASIC MEM
*RED/1: UNPRICED DUE TO SCARCITY
STATED ODDS 1:277

NNO	AJ Styles	10.00	25.00
NNO	Becky Lynch	6.00	15.00
NNO	Charlotte Flair	8.00	20.00
NNO	Dean Ambrose	6.00	15.00
NNO	Dean Ambrose	6.00	15.00
NNO	Dolph Ziggler	3.00	8.00
NNO	Finn Balor	8.00	20.00
NNO	Kalisto	3.00	8.00
NNO	Kevin Owens/NXT Title	5.00	12.00
NNO	Kevin Owens/Universal Title	5.00	12.00
NNO	The Miz	4.00	10.00
NNO	The New Day	4.00	10.00
NNO	Rhyno & Heath Slater	2.00	5.00
NNO	Roman Reigns/US Title	6.00	15.00
NNO	Roman Reigns/WWE Title	6.00	15.00
NNO	Rusev	4.00	10.00
NNO	Sasha Banks	6.00	15.00
NNO	Seth Rollins	6.00	15.00
NNO	Triple H	5.00	12.00
NNO	Zack Ryder	2.00	5.00

2017 Topps WWE Kiss

*GOLD/10: .6X TO 1.5X BASIC KISS
*RED/1: UNPRICED DUE TO SCARCITY
STATED ODDS 1:125

NNO	Asuka	25.00	60.00
NNO	Becky Lynch	15.00	40.00
NNO	Charlotte Flair	25.00	60.00
NNO	Maryse	20.00	50.00
NNO	Naomi	15.00	40.00
NNO	Summer Rae	12.00	30.00

2017 Topps WWE NXT Autographed TakeOver Brooklyn II Mat Relics

STATED PRINT RUN 10 SER.#'d SETS

NNO Asuka
NNO Austin Aries
NNO Bayley
NNO Samoa Joe
NNO Shinsuke Nakamura

2017 Topps WWE NXT TakeOver Brooklyn II Mat Relics

*BRONZE/199: SAME VALUE AS BASIC MEM
*BLUE/50: .5X TO 1.2X BASIC MEM
*SILVER/25: .6X TO 1.5X BASIC MEM
*GOLD/10: 1X TO 2.5X BASIC MEM
*RED/1: UNPRICED DUE TO SCARCITY
STATED ODDS 1:369

NNO	Andrade Cien Almas	2.00	5.00
NNO	Asuka	6.00	15.00
NNO	Austin Aries	4.00	10.00
NNO	Bayley	6.00	15.00
NNO	Bobby Roode	5.00	12.00
NNO	Johnny Gargano	2.00	5.00
NNO	No Way Jose	2.00	5.00
NNO	Samoa Joe	6.00	15.00
NNO	Shinsuke Nakamura	5.00	12.00
NNO	Tommaso Ciampa	2.00	5.00

2017 Topps WWE Roster Updates

COMPLETE SET (20)		8.00	20.00

RANDOMLY INSERTED INTO PACKS

R1	Tamina	1.25	3.00
R2	Cedric Alexander	1.50	4.00

R3	Gran Metalik	2.00	5.00
R4	Jack Gallagher	2.00	5.00
R5	Lince Dorado	1.25	3.00
R6	Noam Dar	1.00	2.50
R7	Rich Swann	1.00	2.50
R8	Stephanie McMahon	1.25	3.00
R9	Shane McMahon	1.50	4.00
R10	Tom Phillips	1.00	2.50
R11	Andrade Cien Almas	1.00	2.50
R12	Mandy Rose	1.25	3.00
R13	Mike Rome	1.00	2.50
R14	No Way Jose	1.00	2.50
R15	Otis Dozovic	1.25	3.00
R16	Riddick Moss	1.25	3.00
R17	Tian Bing	1.00	2.50
R18	Tino Sabbatelli	1.25	3.00
R19	Tye Dillinger	2.00	5.00
R20	Tucker Knight	2.50	6.00

2017 Topps WWE Shirt Relics

*BLUE/50: .5X TO 1.2X BASIC MEM
*SILVER/25: .6X TO 1.5X BASIC MEM
*GOLD/10: 1X TO 2.5X BASIC MEM
*RED/1: UNPRICED DUE TO SCARCITY
STATED ODDS 1:185
STATED PRINT RUN 199 SER.#'d SETS

NNO	Andrade Cien Almas	2.00	5.00
NNO	Baron Corbin	3.00	8.00
NNO	Bayley	6.00	15.00
NNO	Big E	2.50	6.00
NNO	Bobby Roode	5.00	12.00
NNO	Bray Wyatt	5.00	12.00
NNO	Carmella	5.00	12.00
NNO	Cesaro	4.00	10.00
NNO	Chad Gable	2.50	6.00
NNO	Dolph Ziggler	3.00	8.00
NNO	Heath Slater	2.00	5.00
NNO	Jason Jordan	2.50	6.00
NNO	John Cena	10.00	25.00
NNO	Johnny Gargano	2.00	5.00
NNO	Karl Anderson	2.00	5.00
NNO	Kevin Owens	5.00	12.00
NNO	Kofi Kingston	2.50	6.00
NNO	The Miz	4.00	10.00
NNO	No Way Jose	2.00	5.00
NNO	Randy Orton	5.00	12.00
NNO	Roman Reigns	6.00	15.00
NNO	Seth Rollins	6.00	15.00
NNO	Shinsuke Nakamura	5.00	12.00
NNO	Tommaso Ciampa	2.00	5.00
NNO	Xavier Woods	2.50	6.00

2017 Topps WWE Stone Cold Podcast

COMPLETE SET (8)		8.00	20.00
STATED ODDS 1:4			
1	Triple H	2.00	5.00
2	Paul Heyman	.75	2.00
3	Edge & Christian	2.00	5.00
4	Brock Lesnar	4.00	10.00
5	Big Show	1.00	2.50
6	Mick Foley	2.00	5.00
7	AJ Styles	4.00	10.00
8	Dean Ambrose	2.50	6.00

2017 Topps WWE Autographed SummerSlam 2016 Mat Relics

STATED PRINT RUN 10 SER.#'d SETS

UNPRICED DUE TO SCARCITY

NNO	AJ Styles
NNO	Big Cass
NNO	Brock Lesnar
NNO	Charlotte Flair
NNO	Chris Jericho
NNO	Dean Ambrose
NNO	Dolph Ziggler
NNO	Enzo Amore
NNO	Finn Balor
NNO	John Cena
NNO	Karl Anderson
NNO	Kevin Owens
NNO	Kofi Kingston
NNO	Luke Gallows
NNO	Randy Orton
NNO	Roman Reigns
NNO	Rusev
NNO	Sasha Banks
NNO	Seth Rollins
NNO	Xavier Woods

2017 Topps WWE SummerSlam 2016 Mat Relics

*BRONZE/199: SAME VALUE AS BASIC MEM
*BLUE/50: .5X TO 1.2X BASIC MEM
*SILVER/25: .6X TO 1.5X BASIC MEM
*GOLD/10: 1X TO 2.5X BASIC MEM
*RED/1: UNPRICED DUE TO SCARCITY
STATED ODDS 1:184
STATED PRINT RUN 299 SER.#'d SETS

NNO	AJ Styles	10.00	25.00
NNO	Big Cass	2.50	6.00
NNO	Brock Lesnar	10.00	25.00
NNO	Charlotte Flair	8.00	20.00
NNO	Chris Jericho	5.00	12.00
NNO	Dean Ambrose	6.00	15.00
NNO	Dolph Ziggler	3.00	8.00
NNO	Enzo Amore	6.00	15.00
NNO	Finn Balor	8.00	20.00
NNO	John Cena	10.00	25.00
NNO	Karl Anderson	2.00	5.00
NNO	Kevin Owens	5.00	12.00
NNO	Kofi Kingston	2.50	6.00
NNO	Luke Gallows	3.00	8.00
NNO	Randy Orton	5.00	12.00
NNO	Roman Reigns	6.00	15.00
NNO	Rusev	4.00	10.00
NNO	Sasha Banks	6.00	15.00
NNO	Seth Rollins	6.00	15.00
NNO	Xavier Woods	2.50	6.00

2017 Topps WWE Total Divas

COMPLETE SET (20)		12.00	30.00
STATED ODDS 1:2			
1	Nikki Bella	1.25	3.00
2	Brie Bella	1.25	3.00
3	Natalya	1.00	2.50
4	The Bellas	1.25	3.00
5	Mandy Rose	.60	1.50
6	Natalya	1.00	2.50
7	Nikki Bella	1.25	3.00
8	Nikki Bella	1.25	3.00
9	Alicia Fox	.75	2.00
10	Natalya	1.00	2.50
11	Brie Bella	1.25	3.00
12	Brie Bella	1.25	3.00
13	John Cena	2.50	6.00
14	Daniel Bryan	2.00	5.00
15	Natalya	1.00	2.50
16	The Bella Twins	1.25	3.00
17	Nikki Bella	1.25	3.00
18	Mandy Rose	.60	1.50
19	Alicia Fox	.75	2.00
20	Nikki Bella	1.25	3.00

2017 Topps WWE Triple Autographs

STATED ODDS 1:1,762

NNO	Bayley/Jax/Morgan		
NNO	Big E/Kingston/Woods	60.00	120.00
NNO	Kay/Royce/Aliyah		
NNO	Lesnar/Goldberg/Bischoff	250.00	400.00
NNO	C.Kelly/Fuentes/Young	75.00	150.00
NNO	Martin/Kai/Victoria		
NNO	K.Kelly/Wilson/Phoenix	75.00	150.00

2017 Topps WWE Undertaker Tribute

This was a continuation series across four different products in 2017. 10-Card sets were inserted in the following products: Topps WWE Road to WrestleMania (1-10), Topps WWE (11-20), Topps Heritage WWE (21-30), and Topps WWE Then Now Forever (31-40).

COMPLETE SET (40)		15.00	40.00
1	Undertaker	2.00	5.00
2	Undertaker	2.00	5.00
3	Undertaker	2.00	3.00
4	Undertaker	2.00	5.00
5	Undertaker	2.00	5.00
6	Undertaker	2.00	5.00
7	Undertaker	2.00	5.00
8	Undertaker	2.00	5.00
9	Undertaker	2.00	5.00
10	Undertaker	2.00	5.00
11	Undertaker	2.00	5.00
12	Undertaker	2.00	5.00
13	Undertaker	2.00	5.00
14	Undertaker	2.00	5.00
15	Undertaker	2.00	5.00
16	Undertaker	2.00	5.00
17	Undertaker	2.00	5.00
18	Undertaker	2.00	5.00
19	Undertaker	2.00	5.00
20	Undertaker	2.00	5.00
21	Undertaker	2.00	5.00
22	Undertaker	2.00	5.00
23	Undertaker	2.00	5.00
24	Undertaker	2.00	5.00
25	Undertaker	2.00	5.00
26	Undertaker	2.00	5.00
27	Undertaker	2.00	5.00
28	Undertaker	2.00	5.00
29	Undertaker	2.00	5.00
30	Undertaker	2.00	5.00
31	Undertaker	2.00	5.00
32	Undertaker	2.00	5.00
33	Undertaker	2.00	5.00
34	Undertaker	2.00	5.00
35	Undertaker	2.00	5.00
36	Undertaker	2.00	5.00
37	Undertaker	2.00	5.00
38	Undertaker	2.00	5.00
39	Undertaker	2.00	5.00
40	Undertaker	2.00	5.00

2018 Topps WWE

COMPLETE SET W/O SP (100)	8.00	20.00
UNOPENED BOX (24 PACKS)		
UNOPENED PACK (7 CARDS)		

*BRONZE: .5X TO 1.2X BASIC CARDS
*BLUE/99: .75X TO 2X BASIC CARDS
*SILVER/25: 2X TO 5X BASIC CARDS
*GOLD/10: UNPRICED DUE TO SCARCITY
*RED/1: UNPRICED DUE TO SCARCITY
*P.P.BLACK/1: UNPRICED DUE TO SCARCITY
*P.P.CYAN/1: UNPRICED DUE TO SCARCITY
*P.P.MAGENTA/1: UNPRICED DUE TO SCARCITY
*P.P.YELLOW/1: UNPRICED DUE TO SCARCITY

1A	Adam Cole	.30	.75
1B	Adam Cole SP Shirtless	12.00	30.00
2A	AJ Styles	1.00	2.50
2B	AJ Styles SP Shirtless	20.00	50.00
3	Akam	.25	.60
4	Akira Tozawa	.40	1.00
5A	Aleister Black	.30	.75
5B	Aleister Black SP Mid-Air	6.00	15.00
6	Alicia Fox	.40	1.00
7	Andrade Cien Almas	.40	1.00
8	Apollo Crews	.25	.60
9	Ariya Daivari	.25	.60
10	Asuka	.75	2.00
11A	Big E	.30	.75
11B	Big E SP Microphone	2.50	6.00
12	Billie Kay	.50	1.25
13	Bo Dallas	.25	.60
14A	Bobby Roode	.40	1.00
14B	Bobby Roode SP In Action	10.00	25.00
15	Bobby Fish	.25	.60
16	Booker T	.40	1.00
17	The Brian Kendrick	.40	1.00
18	Brie Bella	.50	1.25
19	Byron Saxton	.25	.60
20A	Carmella	.50	1.25
20B	Carmella SP In Ring	12.00	30.00
21	Cathy Kelley	.50	1.25
22	Cedric Alexander	.25	.60
23	Chad Gable	.25	.60
24A	Charlotte Flair	.75	2.00
24B	Charlotte Flair SP Close-Up	12.00	30.00
25	Christy St. Cloud	.30	.75
26	Curt Hawkins	.25	.60
27	Curtis Axel	.25	.60
28	Daniel Bryan	.60	1.50
29	Drew Gulak	.25	.60
30A	Drew McIntyre	.40	1.00
30B	Drew McIntyre SP Close-Up	2.50	6.00
31	Elias	.60	1.50
32A	Ember Moon	.50	1.25
32B	Ember Moon SP In Between Ropes	6.00	15.00
33	Gentleman Jack Gallagher	.30	.75
34	Gran Metalik	.25	.60
35	Greg Hamilton	.40	1.00
36	Heath Slater	.25	.60
37	Hideo Itami	.25	.60
38	Jerry The King Lawler	.50	1.25
39	Jey Uso	.25	.60
40	Jim Ross	.40	1.00
41	Jimmy Uso	.25	.60
42A	Jinder Mahal	.30	.75
42B	Jinder Mahal SP Shirtless		

43 John Cena	1.00	2.50
44 Johnny Gargano	.25	.60
45A Kairi Sane	.60	1.50
45B Kairi Sane SP Mid-Air		
46 Kayla Braxton	.25	.60
47A Kevin Owens	.60	1.50
47B Kevin Owens SP Red Background	8.00	20.00
48A Kofi Kingston	.30	.75
48B Kofi Kingston SP Cross Body	2.50	6.00
49 Kurt Angle	.60	1.50
50A Kyle O'Reilly	.30	.75
50B Kyle O'Reilly SP Straightfaced	2.50	6.00
51 Lana	.60	1.50
52 Lita	.60	1.50
53 Maria Kanellis	.60	1.50
54 Maryse	.50	1.25
55 Mauro Ranallo	.25	.60
56 Mean Gene Okerlund	.30	.75
57 Michael Cole	.25	.60
58 Mickie James	.50	1.25
59 Mike Kanellis	.60	1.50
60 Mike Rome	.25	.60
61 The Miz	.50	1.25
62 Montez Ford	.25	.60
63 Mr. McMahon	.50	1.25
64 Mustafa Ali	.25	.60
65 Naomi	.30	.75
66A Natalya	.30	.75
66B Natalya SP Pointing Up	12.00	30.00
67 Neville	.40	1.00
68 Nia Jax	.40	1.00
69 Nigel McGuinness	.25	.60
70 Noam Dar	.25	.60
71 Paige	.60	1.50
72 Paul Ellering	.30	.75
73 Percy Watson	.25	.60
74 Pete Dunne	.25	.60
75 Peyton Royce	.60	1.50
76 Rezar	.25	.60
77 Rhyno	.25	.60
78 Big Cass	.30	.75
79 The Rock	1.25	3.00
80 Roderick Strong	.25	.60
81 Samir Singh	.25	.60
82 Shane McMahon	.50	1.25
83 Shelton Benjamin	.30	.75
84 Sin Cara	.30	.75
85 Sonya Deville	.50	1.25
86 Stephanie McMahon	.50	1.25
87 Sunil Singh	.25	.60
88 Tamina	.25	.60
89 Titus O'Neil	.25	.60
90 TJP	.30	.75
91 Tommaso Ciampa	.25	.60
92 Tony Nese	.25	.60
93 Tony Chimel	.25	.60
94 Triple H	.60	1.50
95 Tyler Bate	.25	.60
96A Undertaker	1.00	2.50
96B Undertaker SP Kneeling	10.00	25.00
97 William Regal	.40	1.00
98A Xavier Woods	.30	.75
98B Xavier Woods SP Cross Body	5.00	12.00
99 Zack Ryder	.25	.60
100 Zelina Vega	.25	.60

2018 Topps WWE Autographed Commemorative Championship Medallions

STATED PRINT RUN 10 SER.#'d SETS
UNPRICED DUE TO SCARCITY

CCAJ AJ Styles	
CCAT Akira Tozawa	
CCBW Bray Wyatt	
CCCJ Chris Jericho	
CCJM Jinder Mahal	
CCKO Kevin Owens	
CCNA Natalya	
CCNO Naomi	
CCRO Randy Orton	
CCTM The Miz	

2018 Topps WWE Autographed Dual Mat Relics

STATED PRINT RUN 10 SER.#'d SETS
UNPRICED DUE TO SCARCITY

DMRDB Daniel Bryan	
DMRSM Stephanie McMahon	
DMRTH Triple H	
DMRUT Undertaker	
DNRDA Dean Ambrose	

2018 Topps WWE Autographed NXT TakeOver Brooklyn III Mat Relics

STATED PRINT RUN 10 SER.#'d SETS
UNPRICED DUE TO SCARCITY

TBRAB Aleister Black	
TBRAC Adam Cole	
TBRAS Asuka	
TBRBR Bobby Roode	
TBRDM Drew McIntyre	
TBREM Ember Moon	
TBREY Eric Young	
TBRHI Hideo Itami	
TBRJG Johnny Gargano	

2018 Topps WWE Autographed Shirt Relics

STATED PRINT RUN 10 SER.#'d SETS
UNPRICED DUE TO SCARCITY

SRAE Aiden English	
SRAF Alicia Fox	
SREY Eric Young	
SRGD Goldust	
SRJJ Jojo	
SRNA Natalya	
SRRY Renee Young	
SRSJ Samoa Joe	

2018 Topps WWE Autographed SummerSlam 2017 Mat Relics

STATED PRINT RUN 10 SER.#'d SETS
UNPRICED DUE TO SCARCITY

SMRAJ AJ Styles	
SMRBC Baron Corbin	
SMRBS Braun Strowman	
SMRBW Bray Wyatt	
SMRCO Cesaro	
SMRDA Dean Ambrose	
SMRJM Jinder Mahal	
SMRKO Kevin Owens	
SMRNA Natalya	
SMRNO Naomi	
SMRSB Sasha Banks	
SMRSH Sheamus	
SMRSJ Samoa Joe	
SMRSN Shinsuke Nakamura	

2018 Topps WWE Autographs

*BLUE/50: .5X TO 1.2X BASIC AUTOS
*SILVER/25: .6X TO 1.5X BASIC AUTOS
*GOLD/10: UNPRICED DUE TO SCARCITY
*RED/1: UNPRICED DUE TO SCARCITY

1 Adam Cole	20.00	50.00
2 AJ Styles	15.00	40.00
4 Akira Tozawa	5.00	12.00
5 Aleister Black	10.00	25.00
8 Apollo Crews	4.00	10.00
10 Asuka	15.00	40.00
11 Big E	8.00	20.00
14 Bobby Roode	6.00	15.00
15 Bobby Fish	12.00	30.00
18 Brie Bella	10.00	25.00
20 Carmella	12.00	30.00
24 Charlotte Flair	15.00	40.00
30 Drew McIntyre	8.00	20.00
32 Ember Moon	10.00	25.00
42 Jinder Mahal	5.00	12.00
45 Kairi Sane	30.00	75.00
47 Kevin Owens	6.00	15.00
48 Kofi Kingston	6.00	15.00
49 Kurt Angle	12.00	30.00
50 Kyle O'Reilly	12.00	30.00
61 The Miz	5.00	12.00
65 Naomi	4.00	10.00
66 Natalya	6.00	15.00
68 Nia Jax	10.00	25.00
80 Roderick Strong	5.00	12.00
83 Shelton Benjamin	5.00	12.00
88 Tamina	4.00	10.00
89 Titus O'Neil	5.00	12.00
98 Xavier Woods	6.00	15.00

2018 Topps WWE Commemorative Championship Medallions

*BRONZE/99: .5X TO 1.2X BASIC MEM
*BLUE/50: .6X TO 1.5X BASIC MEM
*SILVER/25: .75X TO 2X BASIC MEM
*GOLD/10: UNPRICED DUE TO SCARCITY
*RED/1: UNPRICED DUE TO SCARCITY

CCAA American Alpha	3.00	8.00
CCAB Alexa Bliss	10.00	25.00
CCAJ AJ Styles	6.00	15.00
CCAS Dean Ambrose & Seth Rollins	8.00	20.00
CCAT Akira Tozawa	3.00	8.00
CCAX Alexa Bliss	8.00	20.00
CCBA Bayley	8.00	20.00
CCBL Brock Lesnar	10.00	25.00
CCBW Bray Wyatt	3.00	8.00
CCCJ Chris Jericho	4.00	10.00
CCCS Cesaro & Sheamus	2.50	6.00
CCGA Luke Gallows & Karl Anderson	2.50	6.00
CCHB The Hardy Boyz	6.00	15.00
CCJC John Cena	5.00	12.00
CCJM Jinder Mahal	2.50	6.00
CCKA Kalisto	2.50	6.00
CCKO Kevin Owens	4.00	10.00
CCNA Natalya	2.50	6.00
CCND The New Day	2.50	6.00
CCNO Naomi	2.50	6.00
CCRO Randy Orton	4.00	10.00
CCTM The Miz	2.50	6.00
CCTU The Usos	3.00	8.00
CCWF The Wyatt Family	5.00	12.00

2018 Topps WWE Dual Mat Relics

*SILVER/25: .6X TO 1.5X BASIC MEM
*GOLD/10: UNPRICED DUE TO SCARCITY
*RED/1: UNPRICED DUE TO SCARCITY

DMRBL Brock Lesnar	10.00	25.00
DMRBY Bayley	10.00	25.00
DMRDA Dean Ambrose	6.00	15.00
DMRDB Daniel Bryan	8.00	20.00
DMRRR Roman Reigns	6.00	15.00
DMRSM Stephanie McMahon	15.00	40.00
DMRSR Seth Rollins	5.00	12.00
DMRTH Triple H	6.00	15.00
DMRTR The Rock	8.00	20.00
DMRUT Undertaker	12.00	30.00

2018 Topps WWE Evolution

COMPLETE SET (50)	15.00	40.00
E1 The Giant	.40	1.00
E2 Big Show	.40	1.00
E3 Big Show	.40	1.00
E4 Booker T	.60	1.50
E5 G.I. Bro	.60	1.50
E6 King Booker	.60	1.50
E7 Booker T	.60	1.50
E8 Brock Lesnar	1.50	4.00
E9 Brock Lesnar	1.50	4.00
E10 Chris Jericho	1.00	2.50
E11 Chris Jericho	1.00	2.50
E12 Daniel Bryan	1.00	2.50
E13 Daniel Bryan	1.00	2.50
E14 Daniel Bryan	1.00	2.50
E15 The Rock	2.00	5.00
E16 The Rock	2.00	5.00
E17 Goldust	.75	2.00
E18 Seven	.75	2.00
E19 American Nightmare Dustin Rhodes	.75	2.00
E20 Goldust	.75	2.00
E21 Jerry The King Lawler	.75	2.00
E22 Jerry The King Lawler	.75	2.00
E23 John Cena	1.50	4.00
E24 Doctor of Thuganomics John Cena	1.50	4.00
E25 John Cena	1.50	4.00
E26 Kane	.60	1.50
E27 Kane	.60	1.50
E28 Corporate Kane	.60	1.50
E29 Kane	.60	1.50
E30 Kurt Angle	1.00	2.50
E31 Kurt Angle	1.00	2.50
E32 Mark Henry	.50	1.25
E33 Mark Henry	.50	1.25
E34 Mark Henry	.50	1.25
E35 Cactus Jack	.75	2.00
E36 Mankind	.75	2.00
E37 Dude Love	.75	2.00
E38 Mick Foley	.75	2.00
E39 Randy Orton	1.00	2.50
E40 Randy Orton	1.00	2.50
E41 Hunter Hearst Helmsley	1.00	2.50
E42 Triple H	1.00	2.50
E43 The Game Triple H	1.00	2.50
E44 COO Triple H	1.00	2.50

E45	Undertaker	1.50	4.00
E46	Undertaker	1.50	4.00
E47	Undertaker	1.50	4.00
E48	The American Bad-Ass Undertaker	1.50	4.00
E49	Big Evil Undertaker	1.50	4.00
E50	Undertaker	1.50	4.00

2018 Topps WWE Kiss

*GOLD/10: UNPRICED DUE TO SCARCITY
*RED/1: UNPRICED DUE TO SCARCITY

KBX	Billie Kay	20.00	50.00
KDB	Dana Brooke	15.00	40.00
KEM	Ember Moon	20.00	50.00
KKS	Kairi Saine	30.00	75.00
KLM	Liv Morgan	25.00	60.00
KMA	Maryse	15.00	40.00
KNA	Natalya	15.00	40.00
KPR	Peyton Royce	25.00	60.00
KSD	Sonya Deville	50.00	100.00

2018 Topps WWE Kiss Autographs

*GOLD/10: UNPRICED DUE TO SCARCITY
*RED/1: UNPRICED DUE TO SCARCITY
STATED PRINT RUN 25 SER.#'d SETS

NNO	Billie Kay	30.00	75.00
NNO	Dana Brooke	30.00	75.00
NNO	Ember Moon	60.00	120.00
NNO	Kairi Saine	50.00	100.00
NNO	Liv Morgan	50.00	100.00
NNO	Maryse	50.00	100.00
NNO	Mickie James	75.00	150.00
NNO	Natalya	30.00	75.00
NNO	Peyton Royce	30.00	75.00
NNO	Sonya Deville	60.00	120.00

2018 Topps WWE NXT TakeOver Brooklyn III Mat Relics

*BRONZE/199: .5X TO 1.2X BASIC MEM
*BLUE/50: .6X TO 1.5X BASIC MEM
*SILVER/25: .75X TO 2X BASIC MEM
*GOLD/10: UNPRICED DUE TO SCARCITY
*RED/1: UNPRICED DUE TO SCARCITY

TBRAA	Andrade Cien Almas	3.00	8.00
TBRAB	Aleister Black	3.00	8.00
TBRAC	Adam Cole	6.00	15.00
TBRAS	Asuka	6.00	15.00
TBRBR	Bobby Roode	3.00	8.00
TBRDM	Drew McIntyre	3.00	8.00
TBREM	Ember Moon	4.00	10.00
TBREY	Eric Young	3.00	8.00
TBRHI	Hideo Itami	3.00	8.00
TBRJG	Johnny Gargano	3.00	8.00

2018 Topps WWE Roster Updates

COMPLETE SET (20)		15.00	40.00
R1	Aiden English	1.00	2.50
R2	Aliyah	1.50	4.00
R3	Angelo Dawkins	1.00	2.50
R4	Buddy Murphy	1.25	3.00
R5	Charly Caruso	1.50	4.00
R6	Corey Graves	1.25	3.00
R7	Dana Brooke	2.00	5.00
R8	Dasha Fuentes	1.50	4.00
R9	Epico Colon		2.50
R10	JoJo	1.00	2.50
R11	Konnor	1.00	2.50
R12	Lars Sullivan	1.00	2.50

R13	Lio Rush	1.00	2.50
R14	Primo Colon	1.00	2.50
R15	R-Truth	1.25	3.00
R16	Renee Young	1.50	4.00
R17	Sarah Logan	1.00	2.50
R18	Tom Phillips	1.00	2.50
R19	Viktor	1.00	2.50
R20	Wesley Blake	1.25	3.00

2018 Topps WWE Shirt Relics

*BLUE/50: .6X TO 1.5X BASIC MEM
*SILVER/25: .75X TO 2X BASIC MEM
*GOLD/10: UNPRICED DUE TO SCARCITY
*RED/1: UNPRICED DUE TO SCARCITY

SRAE	Aiden English	3.00	8.00
SRAF	Alicia Fox	3.00	8.00
SRAW	Alexander Wolfe	2.50	6.00
SRBL	Brock Lesnar	6.00	15.00
SRDW	Dash Wilder	2.50	6.00
SREY	Eric Young	3.00	8.00
SRGD	Goldust	3.00	8.00
SRJC	John Cena	8.00	20.00
SRJJ	JoJo	5.00	12.00
SRNA	Natalya	3.00	8.00
SRNC	Nikki Cross	6.00	15.00
SRRR	Roman Reigns	4.00	10.00
SRRY	Renee Young	6.00	15.00
SRSD	Scott Dawson	3.00	8.00
SRSJ	Samoa Joe	4.00	10.00

2018 Topps WWE SummerSlam 2017 Mat Relics

*BRONZE/199: .5X TO 1.2X BASIC MEM
*BLUE/50: .6X TO 1.5X BASIC MEM
*SILVER/25: .75X TO 2X BASIC MEM
*GOLD/10: UNPRICED DUE TO SCARCITY
*RED/1: UNPRICED DUE TO SCARCITY

SMRAB	Alexa Bliss	8.00	20.00
SMRAJ	AJ Styles	5.00	12.00
SMRBC	Baron Corbin	2.50	6.00
SMRBL	Brock Lesnar	4.00	10.00
SMRBS	Braun Strowman	5.00	12.00
SMRBW	Bray Wyatt	2.50	6.00
SMRCO	Cesaro	2.50	6.00
SMRDA	Dean Ambrose	2.50	6.00
SMRFB	Finn Balor	4.00	10.00
SMRJC	John Cena	5.00	12.00
SMRJM	Jinder Mahal	2.50	6.00
SMRKO	Kevin Owens	2.50	6.00
SMRNA	Natalya	3.00	8.00
SMRNO	Naomi	2.50	6.00
SMRRR	Roman Reigns	3.00	8.00
SMRSB	Sasha Banks	8.00	20.00
SMRSH	Sheamus	2.50	6.00
SMRSJ	Samoa Joe	2.50	6.00
SMRSN	Shinsuke Nakamura	4.00	10.00
SMRSR	Seth Rollins	2.50	6.00

2018 Topps WWE Triple Autographs

STATED PRINT RUN 10 SER.#'d SETS
UNPRICED DUE TO SCARCITY

TADAY Big E
Kofi Kingston/Xavier Woods
TAERA Cole/Fish/O'Reilly
TAHOJ Ambrose/Rollins/Reigns
TAMIZ Miz/Axel/Dallas
TARAW HHH/S.McMahon/Angle

| TATWF | Bray Wyatt |
Luke Harper/Erick Rowan

2007 Topps WWE Action

COMPLETE SET (90)		8.00	20.00
UNOPENED BOX (24 PACKS)			
UNOPENED PACK (7 CARDS)			
1	John Cena	.60	1.50
2	Carlito	.40	1.00
3	Charlie Haas	.10	.25
4	Chris Masters	.40	1.00
5	Edge	.40	1.00
6	Eugene	.10	.25
7	Jim Duggan	.40	1.00
8	John Morrison	.10	.25
9	JTG	.10	.25
10	Kenny Dykstra	.15	.40
11	Lance Cade	.15	.40
12	Randy Orton	.40	1.00
13	Robbie McAllister	.10	.25
14	Rory McAllister	.10	.25
15	Shad	.10	.25
16	Shawn Michaels	.60	1.50
17	Shelton Benjamin	.10	.25
18	Super Crazy	.15	.40
19	Trevor Murdoch	.10	.25
20	Triple H	.60	1.50
21	Umaga	.15	.40
22	Val Venis	.25	.60
23	Viscera	.25	.60
24	Ric Flair	.40	1.00
25	The Great Khali	.15	.40
26	Jeff Hardy	.25	.60
27	Matt Hardy	.25	.60
28	Batista	.40	1.00
29	Boogeyman	.15	.40
30	Brian Kendrick	.15	.40
31	Chavo Guerrero	.15	.40
32	Santino Marella	.25	.60
33	Dave Taylor	.10	.25
34	Deuce	.10	.25
35	Domino	.10	.25
36	Finlay	.25	.60
37	Funaki	.15	.40
38	Gregory Helms	.10	.25
39	Hornswoggle	.15	.40
40	Jamie Noble	.10	.25
41	Jimmy Wang Yang	.10	.25
42	Kane	.40	1.00
43	King Booker	.40	1.00
44	Mark Henry	.15	.40
45	Montel Vontavious Porter	.15	.40
46	Mr. Kennedy	.25	.60
47	Paul London	.25	.60
48	Rey Mysterio	.25	.60
49	Scotty 2 Hotty	.15	.40
50	The Miz	.40	1.00
51	Balls Mahoney	.10	.25
52	Bobby Lashley	.40	1.00
53	CM Punk	.15	.40
54	Elijah Burke	.10	.25
55	Hardcore Holly	.25	.60
56	Kevin Thorn	.10	.25
57	Nunzio	.15	.40
58	Marcus CorVan	.10	.25
59	Matt Striker	.10	.25
60	Tazz	.15	.40
61	Joey Styles	.10	.25

62	Sabu	.10	.25
63	Sandman	.15	.40
64	Snitsky	.15	.40
65	Steve Richards	.15	.40
66	Tommy Dreamer	.15	.40
67	Undertaker/Batista	.50	1.25
68	Undertaker/Batista	.50	1.25
69	Undertaker/Batista	.50	1.25
70	J. Cena/S. Michaels	.60	1.50
71	J. Cena/S. Michaels	.60	1.50
72	J. Cena/S. Michaels	.60	1.50
73	Bobby Lashley/Umaga	.40	1.00
74	Bobby Lashley/Umaga	.40	1.00
75	Bobby Lashley/Umaga	.40	1.00
76	Mr. Kennedy	.25	.60
77	Mr. Kennedy	.25	.60
78	Mr. Kennedy	.25	.60
79	ECW Originals/New Breed	.10	.25
80	ECW Originals/New Breed	.10	.25
81	ECW Originals/New Breed	.10	.25
82	The Great Khali/Kane	.40	1.00
83	The Great Khali/Kane	.40	1.00
84	The Great Khali/Kane	.40	1.00
85	The Great Khali/Kane	.40	1.00
86	Mr. McMahon	.40	1.00
87	Mr. McMahon	.40	1.00
88	Mr. McMahon	.40	1.00
89	Mr. McMahon	.40	1.00
90	Checklist Card	.10	.25

2007 Topps WWE Action Autographs

STATED ODDS 1:48 HOBBY EXCLUSIVE
WILLIAM PERRY ODDS 1:1,392

NNO	Bobby Lashley	10.00	25.00
NNO	Carlito	5.00	12.00
NNO	CM Punk	30.00	60.00
NNO	Edge	10.00	25.00
NNO	Jeff Hardy	20.00	40.00
NNO	John Cena	25.00	50.00
NNO	Matt Hardy	10.00	25.00
NNO	Mr. Kennedy	10.00	25.00
NNO	William Refrigerator Perry	40.00	80.00

2007 Topps WWE Action Lenticular Motion

COMPLETE SET (10)		5.00	12.00
STATED ODDS 1:8 RETAIL EXCLUSIVE			
1	John Cena	1.25	3.00
2	Carlito	.60	1.50
3	Shawn Michaels	1.00	2.50
4	Batista	1.00	2.50
5	Mr. Kennedy	.40	1.00
6	Bobby Lashley	.40	1.00
7	Ric Flair	1.50	4.00
8	Edge	.75	2.00
9	Rey Mysterio	.75	2.00
10	Rob Van Dam	.40	1.00

2007 Topps WWE Action Ringside Relics

COMPLETE SET (4)		10.00	25.00
STATED ODDS 1:48 HOBBY EXCLUSIVE			
NNO	Carlito	3.00	8.00
NNO	Edge	4.00	10.00
NNO	Mr. Kennedy	3.00	8.00
NNO	Shawn Michaels	5.00	12.00

2007 Topps WWE Action Tattoos

COMPLETE SET (10)	4.00	10.00
STATED ODDS 1:4 RETAIL EXCLUSIVE		
1 Batista	.50	1.25
2 Booker T	.50	1.25
3 John Cena	.75	2.00
4 Edge	.50	1.25
5 Triple H	.75	2.00
6 Undertaker	.60	1.50
7 Carlito	.50	1.25
8 Ric Flair	.50	1.25
9 Rob Van Dam	.50	1.25
10 Rey Mysterio	.30	.75

2015-16 Topps WWE Bret Hart Tribute

Cards #1-10 are exclusive to 2015 Topps WWE Road to WrestleMania while cards #11-20 are exclusive to 2016 Topps WWE.

COMPLETE SET (20)	15.00	40.00
CANADIAN EXCLUSIVES		
1 Bret Hit Man Hart	2.50	6.00
2 Bret Hit Man Hart	2.50	6.00
3 Bret Hit Man Hart	2.50	6.00
4 Bret Hit Man Hart	2.50	6.00
5 Bret Hit Man Hart	2.50	6.00
6 Bret Hit Man Hart	2.50	6.00
7 Bret Hit Man Hart	2.50	6.00
8 Bret Hit Man Hart	2.50	6.00
9 Bret Hit Man Hart	2.50	6.00
10 Bret Hit Man Hart	2.50	6.00
11 Bret Hit Man Hart	2.50	6.00
12 Bret Hit Man Hart	2.50	6.00
13 Bret Hit Man Hart	2.50	6.00
14 Bret Hit Man Hart	2.50	6.00
15 Bret Hit Man Hart	2.50	6.00
16 Bret Hit Man Hart	2.50	6.00
17 Bret Hit Man Hart	2.50	6.00
18 Bret Hit Man Hart	2.50	6.00
19 Bret Hit Man Hart	2.50	6.00
20 Bret Hit Man Hart	2.50	6.00

2015-16 Topps WWE Bret Hart Tribute Autographs and Relics

NNO Bret Hart AU/100	50.00	100.00
NNO Bret Hart MEM/100	30.00	80.00
NNO Bret Hart AU MEM/10	150.00	300.00

2016 Topps WWE Brock Lesnar Tribute

This was a continuation series across four different products in 2016. 10-Card sets were inserted in the following products: Topps WWE Road to WrestleMania (1-10), Topps WWE (11-20), Topps Heritage WWE (21-30), and Topps WWE Then Now Forever (31-40). The entire series were exclusive to Walmart Jumbo Packs and Relic Boxes.

COMPLETE SET (10)	15.00	40.00
WALMART EXCLUSIVE		
1 Brock Lesnar	1.00	2.50
2 Brock Lesnar	1.00	2.50
3 Brock Lesnar	1.00	2.50
4 Brock Lesnar	1.00	2.50
5 Brock Lesnar	1.00	2.50
6 Brock Lesnar	1.00	2.50
7 Brock Lesnar	1.00	2.50
8 Brock Lesnar	1.00	2.50
9 Brock Lesnar	1.00	2.50
10 Brock Lesnar	1.00	2.50
11 Brock Lesnar	1.00	2.50
12 Brock Lesnar	1.00	2.50
13 Brock Lesnar	1.00	2.50
14 Brock Lesnar	1.00	2.50
15 Brock Lesnar	1.00	2.50
16 Brock Lesnar	1.00	2.50
17 Brock Lesnar	1.00	2.50
18 Brock Lesnar	1.00	2.50
19 Brock Lesnar	1.00	2.50
20 Brock Lesnar	1.00	2.50
21 Brock Lesnar	1.00	2.50
22 Brock Lesnar	1.00	2.50
23 Brock Lesnar	1.00	2.50
24 Brock Lesnar	1.00	2.50
25 Brock Lesnar	1.00	2.50
26 Brock Lesnar	1.00	2.50
27 Brock Lesnar	1.00	2.50
28 Brock Lesnar	1.00	2.50
29 Brock Lesnar	1.00	2.50
30 Brock Lesnar	1.00	2.50
31 Brock Lesnar	1.00	2.50
32 Brock Lesnar	1.00	2.50
33 Brock Lesnar	1.00	2.50
34 Brock Lesnar	1.00	2.50
35 Brock Lesnar	1.00	2.50
36 Brock Lesnar	1.00	2.50
37 Brock Lesnar	1.00	2.50
38 Brock Lesnar	1.00	2.50
39 Brock Lesnar	1.00	2.50
40 Brock Lesnar	1.00	2.50

2016 Topps WWE Brock Lesnar Tribute Autographs and Relics

NNO Brock Lesnar AUTO		
NNO Brock Lesnar RELIC		
NNO Brock Lesnar RELIC AUTO		

2011 Topps WWE Champions

COMPLETE SET (90)	10.00	25.00
UNOPENED BOX (24 PACKS)		
UNOPENED PACK (7 CARDS)		
1 Undertaker/Shawn Michaels	.60	1.50
2 ShowMiz/Morrison & R-Truth	.40	1.00
3 Randy Orton/Rhodes & DiBiase	.60	1.50
4 Jack Swagger MITB	.25	.60
5 Triple H/Sheamus	.75	2.00
6 Rey Mysterio/CM Punk	.40	1.00
7 10-Diva Tag Match	.60	1.50
8 John Cena/Batista	.75	2.00
9 Sheamus	.25	.60
10 Randy Orton	.60	1.50
11 The Miz	.60	1.50
12 Rey Mysterio	.40	1.00
13 Kane	.40	1.00
14 Edge	.60	1.50
15 Dolph Ziggler	.25	.60
16 Edge	.60	1.50
17 Kofi Kingston	.15	.40
18 Dolph Ziggler	.25	.60
19 Kofi Kingston	.15	.40
20 Wade Barrett	.15	.40
21 R-Truth	.15	.40
22 The Miz	.25	.60
23 Daniel Bryan	.15	.40
24 Sheamus	.25	.60
25 David Hart Smith/Tyson Kidd	.15	.40
26 Cody Rhodes/Drew McIntyre	.15	.40
27 David Otunga/John Cena	.75	2.00
28 Heath Slater/Justin Gabriel	.15	.40
29 Santino Marella/Vladimir Kozlov	.25	.60
30 Heath Slater/Justin Gabriel	.15	.40
31 John Cena/The Miz	.75	2.00
32 Heath Slater/Justin Gabriel	.15	.40
33 Eve	.60	1.50
34 Alicia Fox	.25	.60
35 Melina	.60	1.50
36 Michelle McCool	.60	1.50
37 Natalya	.60	1.50
38 Eve	.60	1.50
39 Beth Phoenix	.40	1.00
40 Layla	.40	1.00
41 Nexus	.15	.40
42 Alberto Del Rio	.40	1.00
43 Alex Riley	.15	.40
44 Mason Ryan	.15	.40
45 Sin Cara	.40	1.00
46 Ted DiBiase	.25	.60
47 Big Show/Miz	.40	1.00
48 Randy Orton/Evan Bourne	.60	1.50
49 Big Show/CM Punk	.40	1.00
50 Kane MITB	.40	1.00
51 The Miz MITB	.25	.60
52 Kane/Undertaker	.60	1.50
53 Team SmackDown	.60	1.50
54 Sheamus KOTR	.25	.60
55 Team Mysterio	.40	1.00
56 CM Punk	.40	1.00
57 Wade Barrett	.15	.40
58 John Morrison	.25	.60
59 Booker T	.25	.60
60 Diesel	.25	.60
61 Alberto Del Rio	.40	1.00
62 Edge	.60	1.50
63 John Cena	.75	2.00
64 The Rock Returns	.75	2.00
65 Stone Cold Steve Austin	.60	1.50
66 Trish Stratus/Vickie Guerrero	.75	2.00
67 Mean Gene Okerlund	.25	.60
68 Cowboy Bob Orton	.25	.60
69 Nikolai Volkoff	.25	.60
70 Jimmy Superfly Snuka	.40	1.00
71 Tito Santana	.15	.40
72 Sgt. Slaughter	.40	1.00
73 Jim Ross	.15	.40
74 Rowdy Roddy Piper	.60	1.50
75 Daniel Bryan	.15	.40
76 The Miz	.25	.60
77 CM Punk/John Cena	.75	2.00
78 Wade Barrett	.15	.40
79 John Morrison	.25	.60
80 Drew McIntyre	.15	.40
81 Daniel Bryan	.15	.40
82 Cody Rhodes	.15	.40
83 Edge/Alberto Del Rio	.60	1.50
84 Big Show/Kane/Santino/Kofi	.40	1.00
85 Randy Orton/CM Punk	.60	1.50
86 Michael Cole/Jerry Lawler	.40	1.00
87 Undertaker/Triple H	.75	2.00
88 Trish & Morrison/LayCool & Ziggler	.75	2.00
89 The Miz/John Cena	.75	2.00
90 Checklist	.15	.40

2011 Topps WWE Champions Autographs

STATED ODDS 1:150		
NNO Dolph Ziggler	8.00	20.00
NNO Edge	15.00	40.00
NNO John Cena	25.00	60.00
NNO Kofi Kingston	12.00	30.00
NNO Layla	10.00	25.00
NNO Michelle McCool	12.00	30.00
NNO The Miz	12.00	30.00
NNO Natalya	12.00	30.00
NNO Randy Orton	20.00	50.00
NNO Santino Marella	8.00	20.00
NNO Sheamus	12.00	30.00
NNO Vladimir Kozlov	8.00	20.00

2011 Topps WWE Champions Foil

COMPLETE SET (10)	4.00	10.00
STATED ODDS 1:3		
F1 Stone Cold Steve Austin	1.00	2.50
F2 Triple H	1.25	3.00
F3 Ravishing Rick Rude	.40	1.00
F4 John Morrison	.40	1.00
F5 Edge & Christian	1.00	2.50
F6 Michelle McCool	1.00	2.50
F7 Melina	1.00	2.50
F8 The British Bulldog	.40	1.00
F9 Terry Funk	.40	1.00
F10 Booker T	.40	1.00

2009 Topps WWE Chipz

COMPLETE SET (63)	15.00	30.00
UNOPENED BOX (24 PACKS)		
UNOPENED PACK (3 CHIPS)		
1 John Cena	1.00	2.50
2 Randy Orton	.40	1.00
3 Charlie Haas	.15	.40
4 JTG	.15	.40
5 Snitsky	.25	.60
6 Shad	.15	.40
7 Shawn Michaels	1.00	2.50
8 Santino Marella	.15	.40
9 D-Lo Brown	.25	.60
10 William Regal	.40	1.00
11 Jerry Lawler	.25	.60
12 Chris Jericho	.40	1.00
13 Ted DiBiase	.40	1.00
14 Cody Rhodes	.15	.40
15 Hardcore Holly	.25	.60
16 JBL	.25	.60
17 Michael Cole	.15	.40
18 Rey Mysterio	.40	1.00
19 Batista	.60	1.50
20 Chuck Palumbo	.25	.60
21 Jamie Noble	.15	.40
22 CM Punk	.25	.60
23 Kofi Kingston	.15	.40
24 Kane	.60	1.50
25 Triple H	1.00	2.50
26 Brian Kendrick	.25	.60
27 Undertaker	.75	2.00
28 Jeff Hardy	.60	1.50
29 Umaga	.25	.60
30 Jim Ross	.15	.40
31 Edge	.60	1.50
32 Big Show	.40	1.00
33 Kenny Dykstra	.25	.60

34	Jimmy Wang Yang	.15	.40
35	Zack Ryder	.15	.40
36	Curt Hawkins	.15	.40
37	Deuce	.15	.40
38	Kung Fu Naki	.15	.40
39	R-Truth	.15	.40
40	MVP	.25	.60
41	Vladimir Kozlov	.25	.60
42	Primo	.15	.40
43	Jesse	.15	.40
44	Festus	.15	.40
45	Tazz	.15	.40
46	Shelton Benjamin	.15	.40
47	Elijah Burke	.15	.40
48	Hornswoggle	.25	.60
49	Tommy Dreamer	.15	.40
50	Mike Knox	.15	.40
51	Evan Bourne	.15	.40
52	Matt Striker	.15	.40
53	Matt Hardy	.60	1.50
54	John Morrison	.25	.60
55	Chavo Guerrero	.25	.60
56	Candice	.75	2.00
57	Jillian	.60	1.50
58	Maria	.60	1.50
59	Melina	.60	1.50
60	Michelle McCool	.60	1.50
61	Eve	.60	1.50
62	Kelly Kelly	.60	1.50
63	Victoria	.60	1.50

2009 Topps WWE Chipz Foil

COMPLETE SET (17)		10.00	20.00
STATED ODDS 1:2			
1	Randy Orton	.50	1.25
2	Shawn Michaels	1.25	3.00
3	Mr. Kennedy	.50	1.25
4	Carlito	.50	1.25
5	Shad	.20	.50
6	Chris Jericho	.50	1.25
7	The Great Khali	.20	.50
8	Matt Hardy	.75	2.00
9	MVP	.30	.75
10	Hurricane Helms	.20	.50
11	Mark Henry	.30	.75
12	Finlay	.30	.75
13	John Morrison	.30	.75
14	Boogeyman	.30	.75
15	The Miz	.30	.75
16	Beth Phoenix	1.00	2.50
17	Mickie James	1.00	2.50

2009 Topps WWE Chipz Silver

SILVER STATED ODDS 1:24			
GOLD STATED ODDS 1:72			
1	Shawn Michaels	12.00	30.00
2	Rey Mysterio	10.00	25.00
3	CM Punk	8.00	20.00
4	Kane	10.00	25.00
5	Triple H	10.00	25.00
6	Batista	10.00	25.00
7	Jeff Hardy	10.00	25.00
8	Edge	8.00	20.00
9	Randy Orton	10.00	25.00
10	John Cena GOLD	10.00	25.00

2011 Topps WWE Classic

COMPLETE SET (90)		8.00	20.00
UNOPENED BOX (24 PACKS)			
UNOPENED PACK (8 CARDS)			
*GOLD: 4X TO 10X BASIC CARDS			
1	A.J.	.75	2.00
2	Alberto Del Rio	.40	1.00
3	Alex Riley	.15	.40
4	Alicia Fox	.25	.60
5	Batista	.25	.60
6	Beth Phoenix	.40	1.00
7	Big Show	.40	1.00
8	Booker T	.25	.60
9	Brie Bella	.60	1.50
10	Brodus Clay	.15	.40
11	Christian	.15	.40
12	CM Punk	.40	1.00
13	Cody Rhodes	.15	.40
14	Curt Hawkins	.15	.40
15	Daniel Bryan	.15	.40
16	David Otunga	.15	.40
17	Dolph Ziggler	.25	.60
18	Drew McIntyre	.15	.40
19	Eden Stiles	.60	1.50
20	Edge	.60	1.50
21	Evan Bourne	.15	.40
22	Eve	.60	1.50
23	Ezekiel Jackson	.25	.60
24	Goldust	.15	.40
25	Heath Slater	.15	.40
26	Hornswoggle	.25	.60
27	Jack Swagger	.25	.60
28	Jerry The King Lawler	.40	1.00
29	Jey Uso	.15	.40
30	Jim Ross	.15	.40
31	Jimmy Uso	.15	.40
32	Jinder Mahal	.25	.60
33	John Cena	.75	2.00
34	John Morrison	.25	.60
35	Johnny Curtis	.15	.40
36	JTG	.15	.40
37	Justin Gabriel	.15	.40
38	Kaitlyn	.40	1.00
39	Kane	.40	1.00
40	Kelly Kelly	.60	1.50
41	Kofi Kingston	.15	.40
42	Layla	.40	1.00
43	Mark Henry	.25	.60
44	Mason Ryan	.15	.40
45	Matt Striker	.15	.40
46	Michael Cole	.15	.40
47	Michael McGillicutty	.15	.40
48	The Miz	.25	.60
49	Natalya	.60	1.50
50	Nikki Bella	.60	1.50
51	Percy Watson	.15	.40
52	Primo	.15	.40
53	R-Truth	.15	.40
54	Randy Orton	.60	1.50
55	Rey Mysterio	.40	1.00
56	Ricardo Rodriguez	.15	.40
57	The Rock	.75	2.00
58	Rosa Mendes	.25	.60
59	Santino Marella	.25	.60
60	Shawn Michaels	.60	1.50
61	Sheamus	.25	.60
62	Sin Cara	.40	1.00

63	Stone Cold Steve Austin	.60	1.50
64	Tamina	.15	.40
65	Ted DiBiase	.25	.60
66	Theodore Long	.15	.40
67	Trent Barreta	.15	.40
68	Triple H	.75	2.00
69	Trish Stratus	.75	2.00
70	Tyler Reks	.15	.40
71	Tyson Kidd	.15	.40
72	Undertaker	.60	1.50
73	Vickie Guerrero	.25	.60
74	Wade Barrett	.15	.40
75	William Regal	.25	.60
76	Yoshi Tatsu	.15	.40
77	Zack Ryder	.15	.40
78	The American Dream Dusty Rhodes	.25	.60
79	Arn Anderson	.25	.60
80	Big Boss Man	.25	.60
81	Bobby The Brain Heenan	.25	.60
82	Diesel	.25	.60
83	Jimmy Superfly Snuka	.40	1.00
84	Junkyard Dog	.40	1.00
85	Michael PS Hayes	.15	.40
86	Ricky The Dragon Steamboat	.40	1.00
87	The Road Warriors	.40	1.00
88	Rowdy Roddy Piper	.60	1.50
89	Sgt. Slaughter	.40	1.00
90	Yokozuna	.25	.60

2011 Topps WWE Classic Autographs

STATED ODDS 1:24 HOBBY; 1:153 RETAIL			
NNO	A.J.	75.00	150.00
NNO	CM Punk	15.00	40.00
NNO	Daniel Bryan	15.00	40.00
NNO	Dolph Ziggler	8.00	20.00
NNO	Hornswoggle	8.00	20.00
NNO	Jack Swagger	8.00	20.00
NNO	Jinder Mahal	15.00	40.00
NNO	Johnny Curtis	8.00	20.00
NNO	Justin Gabriel	8.00	20.00
NNO	Mason Ryan	8.00	20.00
NNO	Rey Mysterio	20.00	50.00
NNO	R-Truth	10.00	25.00
NNO	Santino Marella	8.00	20.00
NNO	Sheamus	12.00	30.00
NNO	Wade Barrett	8.00	20.00
NNO	Zack Ryder	8.00	20.00

2011 Topps WWE Classic Relics

STATED ODDS 1:24 HOBBY; 1:48 RETAIL			
NNO	Alberto Del Rio	5.00	12.00
NNO	Christian	5.00	12.00
NNO	CM Punk	8.00	20.00
NNO	Daniel Bryan	5.00	12.00
NNO	Dolph Ziggler	6.00	15.00
NNO	Drew McIntyre	5.00	12.00
NNO	Hornswoggle	5.00	12.00
NNO	Jack Swagger	5.00	12.00
NNO	Kofi Kingston	5.00	12.00
NNO	The Miz	5.00	12.00
NNO	Santino Marella	8.00	20.00
NNO	Sheamus	5.00	12.00
NNO	Zack Ryder	6.00	15.00

2011 Topps WWE Classic Promo

P1	The Rock vs. John Cena		
	(WWE '12 People's Edition Exclusive)		

2020 Topps WWE Countdown to WrestleMania

COMPLETE SET (20)			
1	Hulk Hogan/Andre the Giant/207*	6.00	15.00
2	Hulk Hogan/Randy Savage/207*	5.00	12.00
3	Ultimate Warrior/Hulk Hogan/208*	6.00	15.00
4	Razor Ramon/170*	4.00	10.00
5	Shawn Michaels/Bret Hart/147*	5.00	12.00
6	Bret Hart/Steve Austin/149*	5.00	12.00
7	Stone Cold Steve Austin/164*	5.00	12.00
8	The Rock/172*	4.00	10.00
9	Brock Lesnar/132*		
10	Eddie Guerrero/134*		
11	Undertaker/123*	5.00	12.00
12	Undertaker/129*	4.00	10.00
13	John Cena/113*	4.00	10.00
14	Daniel Bryan/116*	4.00	10.00
15	Brock Lesnar/106*	8.00	20.00
16	Seth Rollins/116*	4.00	10.00
17	Charlotte Flair/183*	5.00	12.00
18	Kurt Angle & Ronda Rousey/194*	10.00	25.00
19	Becky Lynch/206*	8.00	20.00
20	Kofi Kingston/113*	4.00	10.00

2017 Topps WWE Daniel Bryan Tribute

COMPLETE SET (20)		8.00	20.00
1	Daniel Bryan	1.25	3.00
2	Daniel Bryan	1.25	3.00
3	Daniel Bryan	1.25	3.00
4	Daniel Bryan	1.25	3.00
5	Daniel Bryan	1.25	3.00
6	Daniel Bryan	1.25	3.00
7	Daniel Bryan	1.25	3.00
8	Daniel Bryan	1.25	3.00
9	Daniel Bryan	1.25	3.00
10	Daniel Bryan	1.25	3.00
11	Daniel Bryan	1.25	3.00
12	Daniel Bryan	1.25	3.00
13	Daniel Bryan	1.25	3.00
14	Daniel Bryan	1.25	3.00
15	Daniel Bryan	1.25	3.00
16	Daniel Bryan	1.25	3.00
17	Daniel Bryan	1.25	3.00
18	Daniel Bryan	1.25	3.00
19	Daniel Bryan	1.25	3.00
20	Daniel Bryan	1.25	3.00
21	Daniel Bryan	1.25	3.00
22	Daniel Bryan	1.25	3.00
23	Daniel Bryan	1.25	3.00
24	Daniel Bryan	1.25	3.00
25	Daniel Bryan	1.25	3.00
26	Daniel Bryan	1.25	3.00
27	Daniel Bryan	1.25	3.00
28	Daniel Bryan	1.25	3.00
29	Daniel Bryan	1.25	3.00
30	Daniel Bryan	1.25	3.00
31	Daniel Bryan	1.25	3.00
32	Daniel Bryan	1.25	3.00
33	Daniel Bryan	1.25	3.00
34	Daniel Bryan	1.25	3.00
35	Daniel Bryan	1.25	3.00
36	Daniel Bryan	1.25	3.00
37	Daniel Bryan	1.25	3.00
38	Daniel Bryan	1.25	3.00

39	Daniel Bryan	1.25	3.00
40	Daniel Bryan	1.25	3.00

2017 Topps WWE Daniel Bryan Tribute Autographs and Relics

NNO	Daniel Bryan AU	
NNO	Daniel Bryan MEM	
NNO	Daniel Bryan AU MEM	

2017 Topps WWE Daniel Bryan Tribute Topps Heritage WWE Autographs and Relics

RANDOMLY INSERTED INTO PACKS

1	Daniel Bryan AUTO	
2	Daniel Bryan RELIC	
3	Daniel Bryan AUTO RELIC	

2017 Topps WWE Daniel Bryan Tribute Topps WWE Road to WrestleMania Autographs and Relics

NNO	Daniel Bryan AU	
NNO	Daniel Bryan MEM	
NNO	Daniel Bryan AU MEM	

2017 Topps WWE Daniel Bryan Tribute Topps WWE Then Now Forever Autographs and Relics

STATED ODDS

NNO	Daniel Bryan AUTO	12.00	30.00
NNO	Daniel Bryan RELIC	8.00	20.00
NNO	Daniel Bryan AUTO RELIC		

2008 Topps WWE Decade of Decadence Ultimate Fan Edition DVD Memorabilia Promo

NNO	Edge	
Shirt		

2016 Topps WWE Divas Revolution

COMPLETE SET (43)		10.00	25.00

*SILVER/50: 1X TO 2.5X BASIC CARDS
*PINK/25: 2.5X TO 6X BASIC CARDS
*GOLD/10: 4X TO 10X BASIC CARDS
*RED/1: UNPRICED DUE TO SCARCITY

1	Wendi Richter	.25	.60
2	Miss Elizabeth	.25	.60
3	Sensational Sherri	.40	1.00
4	Alundra Blayze	.30	.75
5	Ivory	.25	.60
6	Lita	.75	2.00
7	Trish Stratus	1.25	3.00
8	Torrie Wilson	.60	1.50
9	Leilani Kai	.25	.60
10	Kelly Kelly	.40	1.00
11	Beth Phoenix	.40	1.00
12	Eve Torres	.50	1.25
13	Alexa Bliss	1.25	3.00
14	Alicia Fox	.40	1.00
15	Cathy Kelley	.25	.60
16	Becky Lynch	.75	2.00
17	Brie Bella	.50	1.25
18	Carmella	.60	1.50
19	Charlotte	.75	2.00
20	Dana Brooke	.60	1.50
21	Dasha Fuentes	.25	.60
22	Emma	.50	1.25

23	Eva Marie	.50	1.25
24	JoJo	.25	.60
25	Lana	1.00	2.50
26	Maryse	.50	1.25
27	Naomi	.40	1.00
28	Natalya	.40	1.00
29	Nia Jax	.40	1.00
30	Nikki Bella	.75	2.00
31	Renee Young	.60	1.50
32	Rosa Mendes	.25	.60
33	Sasha Banks	.75	2.00
34	Stephanie McMahon	.40	1.00
35	Summer Rae	.60	1.50
36	Tamina	.30	.75
37	Aliyah	.30	.75
38	Asuka	1.00	2.50
39	Bayley	.60	1.50
40	Billie Kay	.60	1.50
41	Liv Morgan	.30	.75
42	Peyton Royce	.60	1.50
43	Mandy Rose	.60	1.50

2016 Topps WWE Divas Revolution Autographs

*SILVER/50: .6X TO 1.5X BASIC AUTOS
*PINK/25: .75X TO 2X BASIC AUTOS
*GOLD/10: 1.2X TO 3X BASIC AUTOS
*RED/1: UNPRICED DUE TO SCARCITY
STATED ODDS 1:9

1	Wendi Richter	12.00	30.00
4	Alundra Blayze	10.00	25.00
6	Lita	15.00	40.00
7	Trish Stratus	20.00	50.00
8	Torrie Wilson	20.00	50.00
9	Leilani Kai	6.00	15.00
10	Kelly Kelly	15.00	40.00
11	Beth Phoenix	10.00	25.00
12	Eve Torres	20.00	50.00
13	Alexa Bliss	60.00	120.00
14	Alicia Fox	12.00	30.00
16	Becky Lynch	15.00	40.00
17	Brie Bella	12.00	30.00
18	Carmella	15.00	40.00
19	Charlotte	20.00	50.00
22	Emma	15.00	40.00
26	Maryse	12.00	30.00
27	Naomi	10.00	25.00
28	Natalya	12.00	30.00
30	Nikki Bella	15.00	40.00
32	Rosa Mendes	6.00	15.00
33	Sasha Banks	20.00	50.00
35	Summer Rae	10.00	25.00
36	Tamina	10.00	25.00
38	Asuka	15.00	40.00
43	Mandy Rose	15.00	40.00

2016 Topps WWE Divas Revolution Best Matches

COMPLETE SET (9)		6.00	15.00

*SILVER/50: .5X TO 1.5X BASIC CARDS
*PINK/25: X TO 2X BASIC CARDS
*GOLD/10: 1.2X TO 3X BASIC CARDS
*RED/1: UNPRICED DUE TO SCARCITY

1	Alundra Blayze/Bull Nakano	.60	1.50
2	Trish Stratus/Lita	2.50	6.00
3	Charlotte/Natalya	1.50	4.00
4	Stephanie McMahon/Brie Bella	.75	2.00

5	Charlotte/Sasha Banks	1.50	4.00
6	Sasha Banks/Becky Lynch	1.50	4.00
7	Bayley	1.25	3.00
8	Bayley/Sasha Banks	1.25	3.00
9	Asuka/Bayley	2.00	5.00

2016 Topps WWE Divas Revolution Diva Kiss

*GOLD/10: .75X TO 2X BASIC KISS
*RED/1: UNPRICED DUE TO SCARCITY
STATED ODDS 1:15

NNO	Alexa Bliss	60.00	120.00
NNO	Alicia Fox	12.00	30.00
NNO	Asuka	25.00	60.00
NNO	Becky Lynch	20.00	50.00
NNO	Billie Kay	25.00	60.00
NNO	Carmella	25.00	60.00
NNO	Charlotte	20.00	50.00
NNO	Dana Brooke	25.00	60.00
NNO	Emma	25.00	60.00
NNO	Mandy Rose	20.00	40.00
NNO	Maryse	20.00	50.00
NNO	Natalya	20.00	50.00
NNO	Nia Jax	12.00	30.00
NNO	Peyton Royce	12.00	30.00
NNO	Renee Young	20.00	50.00

2016 Topps WWE Divas Revolution Diva Kiss Autographs

*GOLD/10: .75X TO 2X BASIC AUTOS
*RED/1: UNPRICED DUE TO SCARCITY
STATED ODDS 1:56

NNO	Alexa Bliss	120.00	200.00
NNO	Alicia Fox	15.00	40.00
NNO	Asuka	40.00	100.00
NNO	Becky Lynch	60.00	120.00
NNO	Billie Kay	25.00	60.00
NNO	Carmella	60.00	120.00
NNO	Charlotte	60.00	120.00
NNO	Dana Brooke	25.00	60.00
NNO	Emma	25.00	60.00
NNO	Mandy Rose	25.00	60.00
NNO	Maryse	25.00	60.00
NNO	Natalya	15.00	40.00
NNO	Nia Jax	15.00	40.00
NNO	Peyton Royce	15.00	40.00
NNO	Renee Young	20.00	50.00

2016 Topps WWE Divas Revolution Historic Women's Champions

COMPLETE SET (10)		6.00	15.00

*SILVER/50: .75X TO 2X BASIC CARDS
*PINK/25: 2X TO 5X BASIC CARDS
*GOLD/10: 3X TO 8X BASIC CARDS
*RED/1: UNPRICED DUE TO SCARCITY

1	Alundra Blayze	.50	1.25
2	Lita	1.25	3.00
3	Trish Stratus	2.00	5.00
4	Maryse	.75	2.00
5	Eve Torres	.75	2.00
6	Nikki Bella	1.25	3.00
7	Charlotte	1.25	3.00
8	Charlotte	1.25	3.00
9	Bayley	1.00	2.50
10	Charlotte	1.25	3.00

2016 Topps WWE Divas Revolution Mat Relics

*SILVER/50: .5X TO 1.2X BASIC MEM
*PINK/25: .6X TO 1.5X BASIC MEM
*GOLD/10: .75X TO 2X BASIC MEM
*RED/1: UNPRICED DUE TO SCARCITY
STATED ODDS 1:8

NNO	Alexa Bliss Belfast	10.00	25.00
NNO	Alexa Bliss DMF	10.00	25.00
NNO	Alicia Fox Summerslam	3.00	8.00
NNO	Alicia Fox WrestleMania	3.00	8.00
NNO	Asuka Belfast	8.00	20.00
NNO	Asuka DMF	8.00	20.00
NNO	Bayley Takeover	5.00	12.00
NNO	Bayley DMF	5.00	12.00
NNO	Bayley Belfast	5.00	12.00
NNO	Becky Lynch SummerSlam	6.00	15.00
NNO	Becky Lynch NXT	6.00	15.00
NNO	Brie Bella SummerSlam	4.00	10.00
NNO	Brie Bella WrestleMania	4.00	10.00
NNO	Carmella Belfast	5.00	12.00
NNO	Carmella DMF	5.00	12.00
NNO	Charlotte SummerSlam	6.00	15.00
NNO	Charlotte NXT	6.00	15.00
NNO	Dana Brooke NXT	5.00	12.00
NNO	Emma WrestleMania	4.00	10.00
NNO	Emma NXT	4.00	10.00
NNO	Eve Torres WrestleMania	4.00	10.00
NNO	Naomi SummerSlam	3.00	8.00
NNO	Naomi WrestleMania	3.00	8.00
NNO	Naomi WrestleMania	3.00	8.00
NNO	Nia Jax Belfast	3.00	8.00
NNO	Nia Jax DMF	3.00	8.00
NNO	Nikki Bella MITB	6.00	15.00
NNO	Nikki Bella SummerSlam	6.00	15.00
NNO	Nikki Bella WrestleMania	6.00	15.00
NNO	Peyton Royce Belfast	5.00	12.00
NNO	Peyton Royce DMF	5.00	12.00
NNO	Rosa Mendes WrestleMania	2.00	5.00
NNO	Sasha Banks Takeover	6.00	15.00
NNO	Sasha Banks SummerSlam	6.00	15.00
NNO	Tamina SummerSlam	2.50	6.00

2016 Topps WWE Divas Revolution Power Couples

COMPLETE SET (10)		6.00	15.00

*RED/50: .75X TO 2X BASIC CARDS
*PINK/25: 1.2X TO 3X BASIC CARDS
*GOLD/10: 2X TO 5X BASIC CARDS
RANDOMLY INSERTED INTO PACKS

1	Miss Elizabeth/Randy Savage	1.00	2.50
2	Stephanie McMahon/HHH	1.50	4.00
3	Lita/Edge	1.25	3.00
4	Sensational Sherri/HBK	1.50	4.00
5	Trish Stratus/Christian	2.00	5.00
6	Brie Bella/Daniel Bryan	1.50	4.00
7	Queen Sherri/Randy Savage	1.00	2.50
8	Naomi/Jimmy Uso	.60	1.50
9	Rusev/Lana	1.50	4.00
10	Lita/Kane	1.25	3.00

2016 Topps WWE Divas Revolution The Revolution

COMPLETE SET (4)		4.00	10.00

*SILVER/50: .75X TO 2X BASIC CARDS
*PINK/25: 1.2X TO 3X BASIC CARDS
*GOLD/10: 1.5X TO 4X BASIC CARDS

*RED/1: UNPRICED DUE TO SCARCITY

1 Charlotte	1.50	4.00
2 Team PCB	1.25	3.00
3 Charlotte	1.50	4.00
4 Charlotte	1.50	4.00

2016 Topps WWE Divas Revolution Rivalries

COMPLETE SET (8)	5.00	12.00

*SILVER/50: 1X TO 2.5X BASIC CARDS
*PINK/25: 1.2X TO 3X BASIC CARDS
*GOLD/10: 1.5X TO 4X BASIC CARDS
*RED//1: UNPRICED DUE TO SCARCITY
RANDOMLY INSERTED INTO PACKS

1 Trish Stratus/Lita	2.00	5.00
2 Trish Stratus/Stephanie McMahon	2.00	5.00
3 Bayley/Sasha Banks	1.25	3.00
4 Charlotte/Sasha Banks	1.25	3.00
5 Charlotte/Nikki Bella	1.25	3.00
6 Becky Lynch/Charlotte	1.25	3.00
7 Brie Bella/Nikki Bella	1.25	3.00
8 Miss Elizabeth	.60	1.50
Sensational Sherri		

2016 Topps WWE Divas Revolution Shirt Relics

*SILVER/50: .5X TO 1.2X BASIC MEM
*PINK/25: .6X TO 1.5X BASIC MEM
*GOLD/10: UNPRICED DUE TO SCARCITY
*RED/1: UNPRICED DUE TO SCARCITY

NNO Alexa Bliss	12.00	30.00
NNO Alicia Fox	4.00	10.00
NNO Asuka	10.00	25.00
NNO Becky Lynch	8.00	20.00
NNO Brie Bella	5.00	12.00
NNO Carmella	6.00	15.00
NNO Charlotte	8.00	20.00
NNO JoJo	2.50	6.00
NNO Lana	10.00	25.00
NNO Naomi	4.00	10.00
NNO Natalya	4.00	10.00
NNO Renee Young	6.00	15.00
NNO Sasha Banks	8.00	20.00
NNO Summer Rae	6.00	15.00
NNO Tamina	3.00	8.00

2007 Topps WWE Dog Tags

COMPLETE SET (24)	40.00	80.00
UNOPENED BOX (24 PACKS)		
UNOPENED PACK (1 TAG+1 CARD)		

*GOLD: 1X TO 2.5X BASIC TAGS

1 John Cena	4.00	10.00
2 Batista	2.50	6.00
3 Johnny Nitro	1.00	2.50
4 Carlito	2.50	6.00
5 Ric Flair	2.50	6.00
6 Undertaker	3.00	8.00
7 Chris Benoit	1.50	4.00
8 CM Punk	1.00	2.50
9 Booker T	2.50	6.00
10 Rob Van Dam	2.50	6.00
11 Ken Kennedy	1.50	4.00
12 Shawn Michaels	4.00	10.00
13 The Rock	5.00	12.00
14 Jeff Hardy	1.50	4.00
15 Stone Cold Steve Austin	4.00	10.00
16 Edge	2.50	6.00
17 Rey Mysterio	1.50	4.00
18 Kane	2.50	6.00
19 Randy Orton	2.50	6.00
20 Triple H	4.00	10.00
21 Sabu	.60	1.50
22 Umaga	1.00	2.50
23 Sandman	1.00	2.50
24 Bobby Lashley	2.50	6.00

2007 Topps WWE Dog Tags Trading Cards

COMPLETE SET (25)	15.00	40.00
1 John Cena	2.00	5.00
2 Batista	1.25	3.00
3 Johnny Nitro	.50	1.25
4 Carlito	1.25	3.00
5 Ric Flair	1.25	3.00
6 Undertaker	1.50	4.00
7 Chris Benoit	.75	2.00
8 CM Punk	.50	1.25
9 Booker T	1.25	3.00
10 Rob Van Dam	1.25	3.00
11 Ken Kennedy	.75	2.00
12 Shawn Michaels	2.00	5.00
13 The Rock	2.50	6.00
14 Jeff Hardy	.75	2.00
15 Stone Cold Steve Austin	2.00	5.00
16 Edge	1.25	3.00
17 Rey Mysterio	.75	2.00
18 Kane	1.25	3.00
19 Randy Orton	1.25	3.00
20 Triple H	2.00	5.00
21 Sabu	.30	.75
22 Umaga	.50	1.25
23 Sandman	.50	1.25
24 Bobby Lashley	1.25	3.00
NNO Checklist	.30	.75

2015 Topps WWE Dog Tags

COMPLETE SET (30)	15.00	40.00

*GOLD: X TO X BASIC TAGS

1 AJ Lee	1.50	4.00
2 Bad News Barrett	.30	.75
3 Batista	.75	2.00
4 Big Show	.75	2.00
5 Bray Wyatt	1.25	3.00
6 Brock Lesnar	1.25	3.00
7 Cesaro	.30	.75
8 Chris Jericho	.75	2.00
9 Daniel Bryan	1.25	3.00
10 Dean Ambrose	.75	2.00
11 Dolph Ziggler	.50	1.25
12 Edge	.75	2.00
13 Hulk Hogan	1.50	4.00
14 Jake The Snake Roberts	.50	1.25
15 John Cena	1.50	4.00
16 Kane	.75	2.00
17 Kofi Kingston	.30	.75
18 Randy Orton	1.25	3.00
19 Rey Mysterio	.75	2.00
20 Ric Flair	1.50	4.00
21 Rob Van Dam	.75	2.00
22 The Rock	1.50	4.00
23 Roman Reigns	.75	2.00
24 Seth Rollins	.50	1.25
25 Shawn Michaels	1.25	3.00
26 Sheamus	.75	2.00
27 Stone Cold Steve Austin	1.50	4.00
28 Triple H	1.25	3.00
29 Ultimate Warrior	1.00	2.50
30 Undertaker	1.25	3.00

2015 Topps WWE Dog Tags Trading Cards

COMPLETE SET (30)	8.00	20.00
STATED ODDS 1:1		
1 AJ Lee	.75	2.00
2 Bad News Barrett	.15	.40
3 Batista	.40	1.00
4 Big Show	.40	1.00
5 Bray Wyatt	.60	1.50
6 Brock Lesnar	.60	1.50
7 Cesaro	.15	.40
8 Chris Jericho	.40	1.00
9 Daniel Bryan	.60	1.50
10 Dean Ambrose	.40	1.00
11 Dolph Ziggler	.25	.60
12 Edge	.40	1.00
13 Hulk Hogan	.75	2.00
14 Jake The Snake Roberts	.25	.60
15 John Cena	.75	2.00
16 Kane	.40	1.00
17 Kofi Kingston	.15	.40
18 Randy Orton	.60	1.50
19 Rey Mysterio	.40	1.00
20 Ric Flair	.75	2.00
21 Rob Van Dam	.40	1.00
22 The Rock	.75	2.00
23 Roman Reigns	.40	1.00
24 Seth Rollins	.25	.60
25 Shawn Michaels	.60	1.50
26 Sheamus	.40	1.00
27 Stone Cold Steve Austin	.75	2.00
28 Triple H	.60	1.50
29 Ultimate Warrior	.50	1.25
30 Undertaker	.60	1.50

2015 Topps WWE Dog Tags Relic Tags

*GOLD: X TO X BASIC MEM
STATED ODDS

1 Bad News Barrett	
2 Big Show	
3 Bray Wyatt	
4 Cesaro	
5 Chris Jericho	
6 Daniel Bryan	
7 Dolph Ziggler	
8 Edge	
9 Hulk Hogan	
10 Kofi Kingston	
11 John Cena	
12 Randy Orton	
13 Rey Mysterio	
14 Rob Van Dam	
15 Roman Reigns	
16 Seth Rollins	

2010 Topps WWE Dog Tags Pyrotechno Edition

COMPLETE SET (24)	12.00	30.00
UNOPENED BOX (24 PACKS)		
UNOPENED PACK (1 TAG+1 CARD)		

*GOLD: .75X TO 2X BASIC TAGS

1 John Cena	2.50	6.00
2 Kofi Kingston	.75	2.00
3 Big Show	1.25	3.00
4 Cody Rhodes	.50	1.25
5 Ted DiBiase	.75	2.00
6 Santino Marella	.50	1.25
7 The Miz	.75	2.00
8 Triple H	2.50	6.00
9 Shawn Michaels	3.00	8.00
10 CM Punk	2.00	5.00
11 John Morrison	.75	2.00
12 Chris Jericho	1.25	3.00
13 Matt Hardy	1.25	3.00
14 Christian	.75	2.00
15 Tommy Dreamer	.50	1.25
16 Undertaker	2.00	5.00
17 Yoshi Tatsu	.50	1.25
18 Sheamus	.75	2.00
19 Finlay	.75	2.00
20 Hornswoggle	.75	2.00
21 Edge	2.00	5.00
22 Batista	2.00	5.00
23 Evan Bourne	.50	1.25
24 Randy Orton	2.00	5.00

2010 Topps WWE Dog Tags Pyrotechno Edition Trading Cards

COMPLETE SET (24)	10.00	25.00
1 John Cena	2.00	5.00
2 Kofi Kingston	.60	1.50
3 Big Show	1.00	2.50
4 Cody Rhodes	.40	1.00
5 Ted DiBiase	.60	1.50
6 Santino Marella	.40	1.00
7 The Miz	.60	1.50
8 Triple H	2.00	5.00
9 Shawn Michaels	2.50	6.00
10 CM Punk	1.50	4.00
11 John Morrison	.60	1.50
12 Chris Jericho	1.00	2.50
13 Matt Hardy	1.00	2.50
14 Christian	.60	1.50
15 Tommy Dreamer	.40	1.00
16 Undertaker	1.50	4.00
17 Yoshi Tatsu	.40	1.00
18 Sheamus	.60	1.50
19 Finlay	.60	1.50
20 Hornswoggle	.60	1.50
21 Edge	1.50	4.00
22 Batista	1.50	4.00
23 Evan Bourne	.40	1.00
24 Randy Orton	1.50	4.00

2011 Topps WWE Dog Tags Ringside Relic Edition

COMPLETE SET (24)	10.00	20.00
UNOPENED BOX (24 PACKS)		
UNOPENED PACK (1 TAG+1 CARD)		
1 CM Punk	1.00	2.50
2 Daniel Bryan	.40	1.00
3 David Otunga	.40	1.00
4 John Cena	2.00	5.00
5 John Morrison	.60	1.50
6 Justin Gabriel	.40	1.00
7 Ezekiel Jackson	.60	1.50
8 Randy Orton	1.50	4.00
9 Sheamus	.60	1.50

10 The Miz	.60	1.50
11 Wade Barrett	.40	1.00
12 Heath Slater	.40	1.00
13 Dolph Ziggler	.60	1.50
14 Edge	1.50	4.00
15 Kane	1.00	2.50
16 Undertaker	1.50	4.00
17 Alberto Del Rio	1.00	2.50
18 Jack Swagger	.60	1.50
19 Tyler Reks	.40	1.00
20 Drew McIntyre	.40	1.00
21 Rey Mysterio	1.00	2.50
22 Kaval	1.00	2.50
23 Kofi Kingston	.40	1.00
24 Big Show	1.00	2.50

2011 Topps WWE Dog Tags Ringside Relic Edition Memorabilia Tags

STATED ODDS 1:24

1 Hornswoggle	2.50	6.00
2 Sheamus	2.50	6.00
3 Kofi Kingston	2.50	6.00
4 Edge	6.00	15.00
5 Jack Swagger	2.50	6.00
6 Justin Gabriel	2.50	6.00
7 David Hart Smith	2.50	6.00
8 The Miz	2.50	6.00
9 John Cena	8.00	20.00
10 Randy Orton	6.00	15.00
11 Alex Riley	2.50	6.00
12 Heath Slater	2.50	6.00
13 Wade Barrett	2.50	6.00
14 John Morrison	2.50	6.00
15 David Otunga	2.50	6.00
16 Tyson Kidd	2.50	6.00
17 Rey Mysterio	4.00	10.00
18 Big Show	4.00	10.00

2011 Topps WWE Dog Tags Ringside Relic Edition Trading Cards

COMPLETE SET (24)	4.00	10.00
1 CM Punk	.40	1.00
2 Daniel Bryan	.15	.40
3 David Otunga	.15	.40
4 John Cena	.75	2.00
5 John Morrison	.25	.60
6 Justin Gabriel	.15	.40
7 Ezekiel Jackson	.25	.60
8 Randy Orton	.60	1.50
9 Sheamus	.25	.60
10 The Miz	.25	.60
11 Wade Barrett	.15	.40
12 Heath Slater	.15	.40
13 Dolph Ziggler	.25	.60
14 Edge	.60	1.50
15 Kane	.40	1.00
16 Undertaker	.60	1.50
17 Alberto Del Rio	.40	1.00
18 Jack Swagger	.25	.60
19 Tyler Reks	.15	.40
20 Drew McIntyre	.15	.40
21 Rey Mysterio	.40	1.00
22 Kaval	.40	1.00
23 Kofi Kingston	.15	.40
24 Big Show	.40	1.00

2011 Topps WWE Dog Tags Ringside Relic Edition Silver Insert Cards

COMPLETE SET (18)	4.00	10.00

STATED ODDS 1:24

1 Hornswoggle	.40	1.00
2 Sheamus	.40	1.00
3 Kofi Kingston	.25	.60
4 Edge	1.00	2.50
5 Jack Swagger	.40	1.00
6 Justin Gabriel	.25	.60
7 David Hart Smith	.25	.60
8 The Miz	.40	1.00
9 John Cena	1.25	3.00
10 Randy Orton	1.00	2.50
11 Alex Riley	.25	.60
12 Heath Slater	.25	.60
13 Wade Barrett	.25	.60
14 John Morrison	.40	1.00
15 David Otunga	.25	.60
16 Tyson Kidd	.25	.60
17 Rey Mysterio	.60	1.50
18 Big Show	.60	1.50

2012 Topps WWE Dog Tags Ringside Relic Edition

COMPLETE SET (24)	15.00	40.00
UNOPENED BOX (24 PACKS)		
UNOPENED PACK (1 TAG+1 CARD)		

STATED ODDS 1:1

1 CM Punk	2.50	6.00
2 Ted Dibiase	1.00	2.50
3 Sheamus	1.50	4.00
4 David Otunga	.60	1.50
5 The Miz	1.00	2.50
6 Jack Swagger	1.00	2.50
7 R-Truth	.60	1.50
8 Heath Slater	.60	1.50
9 Christian	.60	1.50
10 John Cena	3.00	8.00
11 Zack Ryder	.60	1.50
12 Daniel Bryan	.60	1.50
13 Hornswoggle	1.00	2.50
14 Rey Mysterio	1.50	4.00
15 Dolph Ziggler	1.00	2.50
16 Kofi Kingston	.60	1.50
17 Evan Bourne	.60	1.50
18 Santino Marella	1.00	2.50
19 Triple H	2.50	6.00
20 Sin Cara	1.50	4.00
21 The Miz	1.00	2.50
22 Stone Cold Steve Austin	3.00	8.00
23 Undertaker	2.50	6.00
24 Randy Orton	2.50	6.00

2012 Topps WWE Dog Tags Ringside Relic Edition Memorabilia Tags

STATED ODDS 1:24

1 CM Punk	6.00	15.00
2 Ted Dibiase	2.50	6.00
3 Sheamus	4.00	10.00
4 David Otunga	1.50	4.00
5 The Miz	2.50	6.00
6 Jack Swagger	2.50	6.00
7 R-Truth	1.50	4.00
8 Heath Slater	1.50	4.00
9 Christian	1.50	4.00
10 John Cena	8.00	20.00

11 Zack Ryder	1.50	4.00
12 Daniel Bryan	1.50	4.00
13 Hornswoggle	2.50	6.00
14 Rey Mysterio	4.00	10.00
15 Dolph Ziggler	2.50	6.00
16 Kofi Kingston	1.50	4.00
17 Evan Bourne	1.50	4.00

2012 Topps WWE Dog Tags Ringside Relic Edition Trading Cards

COMPLETE SET (24)	5.00	12.00
1 CM Punk	1.00	2.50
2 Ted Dibiase	.40	1.00
3 Sheamus	.60	1.50
4 David Otunga	.25	.60
5 The Miz	.40	1.00
6 Jack Swagger	.40	1.00
7 R-Truth	.25	.60
8 Heath Slater	.25	.60
9 Christian	.25	.60
10 John Cena	1.25	3.00
11 Zack Ryder	.25	.60
12 Daniel Bryan	.25	.60
13 Hornswoggle	.40	1.00
14 Rey Mysterio	.60	1.50
15 Dolph Ziggler	.40	1.00
16 Kofi Kingston	.25	.60
17 Evan Bourne	.25	.60
18 Santino Marella	.40	1.00
19 Triple H	1.00	2.50
20 Sin Cara	.60	1.50
21 The Miz	.40	1.00
22 Stone Cold Steve Austin	1.25	3.00
23 Undertaker	1.00	2.50
24 Randy Orton	1.00	2.50

2013 Topps WWE Dog Tags Signature Series

COMPLETE SET (30)		
UNOPENED BOX (24 PACKS)		
UNOPENED PACK (1 TAG+1 CARD)		

STATED ODDS 1:1

1 John Cena	3.00	8.00
2 CM Punk	2.50	6.00
3 Ryback	.60	1.50
4 Sheamus	1.25	3.00
5 Big Show	1.25	3.00
6 Randy Orton	2.00	5.00
7 Alberto Del Rio	1.25	3.00
8 Christian	.60	1.50
9 Cody Rhodes	.60	1.50
10 Rey Mysterio	1.50	4.00
11 Sin Cara	1.00	2.50
12 Dolph Ziggler	1.00	2.50
13 Zack Ryder	.60	1.50
14 Santino	.60	1.50
15 Triple H	2.50	6.00
16 Undertaker	2.50	6.00
17 Kane	1.25	3.00
18 Daniel Bryan	1.50	4.00
19 The Miz	1.00	2.50
20 Kofi Kingston	.60	1.50
21 R-Truth	.60	1.50
22 Brodus Clay	.60	1.50
23 Wade Barrett	.60	1.50
24 The Rock	3.00	8.00
25 Cactus Jack	2.50	6.00

26 Jerry King Lawler	1.25	3.00
27 Shawn Michaels	2.50	6.00
28 Kevin Nash	.75	2.00
29 Booker T	1.00	2.50
30 Stone Cold Steve Austin	2.50	6.00

2013 Topps WWE Dog Tags Signature Series Autographed Tags

STATED ODDS 1:107

NNO AJ Lee	75.00	150.00
NNO Aksana	6.00	15.00
NNO Booker T	12.00	30.00
NNO Brodus Clay	6.00	15.00
NNO Daniel Bryan	15.00	40.00
NNO Kane	12.00	30.00
NNO Layla	6.00	15.00
NNO Natalya	10.00	25.00
NNO Tamina	6.00	15.00
NNO Zack Ryder	6.00	15.00

2013 Topps WWE Dog Tags Signature Series Divas Trading Cards

COMPLETE SET (5)		
STATED ODDS 1:107		
1 AJ Lee	15.00	40.00
2 Aksana	5.00	12.00
3 Layla	6.00	15.00
4 Natalya	6.00	15.00
5 Tamina	4.00	10.00

2013 Topps WWE Dog Tags Signature Series Memorabilia Tags

STATED ODDS 1:24

NNO Alberto Del Rio	3.00	8.00
NNO Brodus Clay	1.50	4.00
NNO CM Punk	6.00	15.00
NNO Cody Rhodes	1.50	4.00
NNO Daniel Bryan	4.00	10.00
NNO Dolph Ziggler	2.50	6.00
NNO John Cena	8.00	20.00
NNO Kofi Kingston	1.50	4.00
NNO The Miz	2.50	6.00
NNO Rey Mysterio	4.00	10.00
NNO R-Truth	1.50	4.00
NNO Ryback	1.50	4.00
NNO Santino	1.50	4.00
NNO Shawn Michaels	6.00	15.00
NNO Sheamus	3.00	8.00
NNO Sin Cara	2.50	6.00
NNO Wade Barrett	1.50	4.00
NNO Zack Ryder	1.50	4.00

2013 Topps WWE Dog Tags Signature Series Trading Cards

COMPLETE SET (30)	6.00	15.00
1 John Cena	1.25	3.00
2 CM Punk	1.00	2.50
3 Ryback	.25	.60
4 Sheamus	.50	1.25
5 Big Show	.50	1.25
6 Randy Orton	.75	2.00
7 Alberto Del Rio	.50	1.25
8 Christian	.25	.60
9 Cody Rhodes	.25	.60
10 Rey Mysterio	.60	1.50
11 Sin Cara	.40	1.00
12 Dolph Ziggler	.40	1.00

13	Zack Ryder	.25	.60
14	Santino	.25	.60
15	Triple H	1.00	2.50
16	Undertaker	1.00	2.50
17	Kane	.50	1.25
18	Daniel Bryan	.60	1.50
19	The Miz	.40	1.00
20	Kofi Kingston	.25	.60
21	R-Truth	.25	.60
22	Brodus Clay	.25	.60
23	Wade Barrett	.25	.60
24	The Rock	1.25	3.00
25	Cactus Jack	1.00	2.50
26	Jerry King Lawler	.50	1.25
27	Shawn Michaels	1.00	2.50
28	Kevin Nash	.30	.75
29	Booker T	.40	1.00
30	Stone Cold Steve Austin	1.00	2.50

2007 Topps WWE Dog Tags UK

COMPLETE SET (21)		25.00	60.00
UNOPENED BOX (24 PACKS)			
UNOPENED PACK (1 TAG+1 CARD)			
*GOLD: 1X TO 2.5X BASIC TAGS			
1	John Cena	4.00	10.00
2	Batista	2.50	6.00
3	Johnny Nitro	1.00	2.50
4	Carlito	2.50	6.00
5	Ric Flair	2.50	6.00
6	Undertaker	3.00	8.00
7	CM Punk	1.00	2.50
8	Booker T	2.50	6.00
9	Ken Kennedy	1.50	4.00
10	Shawn Michaels	4.00	10.00
11	The Rock	5.00	12.00
12	Jeff Hardy	1.50	4.00
13	Stone Cold Steve Austin	4.00	10.00
14	Edge	2.50	6.00
15	Rey Mysterio	1.50	4.00
16	Kane	2.50	6.00
17	Randy Orton	2.50	6.00
18	Triple H	4.00	10.00
19	Umaga	1.00	2.50
20	Sandman	1.00	2.50
21	Bobby Lashley	2.50	6.00

2007 Topps WWE Dog Tags UK Trading Cards

COMPLETE SET (21)		12.00	30.00
1	John Cena	2.00	5.00
2	Batista	1.25	3.00
3	Johnny Nitro	.50	1.25
4	Carlito	1.25	3.00
5	Ric Flair	1.25	3.00
6	Undertaker	1.50	4.00
7	CM Punk	.50	1.25
8	Booker T	1.25	3.00
9	Ken Kennedy	.75	2.00
10	Shawn Michaels	2.00	5.00
11	The Rock	2.50	6.00
12	Jeff Hardy	.75	2.00
13	Stone Cold Steve Austin	2.00	5.00
14	Edge	1.25	3.00
15	Rey Mysterio	.75	2.00
16	Kane	1.25	3.00
17	Randy Orton	1.25	3.00
18	Triple H	2.00	5.00
19	Umaga	.50	1.25
20	Sandman	.50	1.25
21	Bobby Lashley	1.25	3.00
CL	Checklist	.30	.75

2007-08 Topps WWE DVD Collection

Produced by Topps and released as a Best Buy DVD exclusive, this set was released in four blocks: Wrestlemania 23 (D1-D4), SummerSlam (D5-D8), Survivor Series (D9-D12), and Royal Rumble (D13-D16). The set is rounded out with an unnumbered checklist.

COMPLETE SET (17)

D1 Iron Sheik & Nikolai Volkoff
D2 Ravishing Rick Rude
D3 Mr. Perfect/Roddy Piper
D4 The Rock
D5 The Million Dollar Man Ted DiBiase
D6 The British Bulldog Davey Boy Smith
D7 Mankind
D8 Shawn Michaels
D9 Jake The Snake Roberts
D10 Sgt. Slaughter
D11 Undertaker
D12 Edge
D13 Hacksaw Jim Duggan
D14 Ric Flair
D15 Stone Cold Steve Austin
D16 Triple H
CL Checklist

2007 Topps WWE Face-Off

COMPLETE SET (132)		20.00	50.00
1	Bobby Lashley	1.25	3.00
2	Armando Estrada	.30	.75
3	Brian Kendrick	.50	1.25
4	Carlito	1.25	3.00
5	Charlie Haas	.30	.75
6	Daivari	.30	.75
7	Jim Duggan	.50	1.25
8	Jeff Hardy	.75	2.00
9	Jerry Lawler	.75	2.00
10	Jim Ross	.40	1.00
11	John Cena	2.00	5.00
12	Jonathan Coachman	.30	.75
13	JTG	.30	.75
14	King Booker	1.25	3.00
15	Lance Cade	.30	.75
16	Mr. Kennedy	.75	2.00
17	Paul London	.75	2.00
18	Randy Orton	1.25	3.00
19	Robbie McAllister	.30	.75
20	Rory McAllister	.30	.75
21	Roddy Piper	1.25	3.00
22	Sandman	.50	1.25
23	Santino Marella	.40	1.00
24	Shad	.30	.75
25	Shane McMahon	.75	2.00
26	Shawn Michaels	2.00	5.00
27	Shelton Benjamin	.30	.75
28	Snitsky	.50	1.25
29	Stone Cold	2.00	5.00
30	Super Crazy	.50	1.25
31	Todd Grisham	.30	.75
32	Trevor Murdoch	.30	.75
33	Triple H	2.00	5.00
34	Umaga	.50	1.25
35	Val Venis	.75	2.00
36	William Regal	.75	2.00
37	Batista	1.25	3.00
38	Brett Major	.50	1.25
39	Brian Major	.30	.75
40	Chavo Guerrero	.50	1.25
41	Chris Masters	1.25	3.00
42	Dave Taylor	.30	.75
43	Deuce	.30	.75
44	Domino	.30	.75
45	Edge	1.25	3.00
46	Eugene	.30	.75
47	Finlay	.75	2.00
48	Funaki	.50	1.25
49	Gregory Helms	.30	.75
50	Hardcore Holly	.75	2.00
51	Hornswoggle	.40	1.00
52	Jamie Noble	.30	.75
53	JBL	.75	2.00
54	Jimmy Wang Yang	.30	.75
55	Kane	1.25	3.00
56	Kenny Dykstra	.50	1.25
57	Mark Henry	.50	1.25
58	Matt Hardy	.75	2.00
59	Michael Cole	.30	.75
60	MVP	.50	1.25
61	Rey Mysterio	.75	2.00
62	Ric Flair	1.25	3.00
63	Shannon Moore	.30	.75
64	The Great Khali	.50	1.25
65	Theodore Long	.40	1.00
66	Undertaker	1.50	4.00
67	Ashley	1.25	3.00
68	Candice	1.50	4.00
69	Cherry	.30	.75
70	Jillian	1.50	4.00
71	Kelly Kelly	.75	2.00
72	Maria	1.25	3.00
73	Melina	1.25	3.00
74	Michelle McCool	1.50	4.00
75	Mickie James	1.50	4.00
76	Queen Sharmell	.75	2.00
77	Torrie Wilson	2.50	6.00
78	Victoria	1.50	4.00
79	Balls Mahoney	.30	.75
80	Boogeyman	.50	1.25
81	CM Punk	.50	1.25
82	Elijah Burke	.30	.75
83	Joey Styles	.30	.75
84	John Morrison	.50	1.25
85	Kevin Thorn	.30	.75
86	Nunzio	.50	1.25
87	Marcus Cor Von	.30	.75
88	Matt Striker	.30	.75
89	Mike Knox	.30	.75
90	Stevie Richards	.50	1.25
91	Tazz	.50	1.25
92	The Miz	.60	1.50
93	Tommy Dreamer	.40	1.00
94	Big Daddy V	.30	.75
95	Kendrick / London	.75	2.00
96	Hass / Benjamin	.30	.75
97	Carlito / Masters	1.25	3.00
98	Cryme Tyme	.30	.75
99	Taylor / Regal	.75	2.00
100	Deuce / Domino	.30	.75
101	D-Generation X	1.00	2.50
102	Burke / Cor Von	.30	.75
103	Undertaker / Kane	1.50	4.00
104	Finlay / Hornswoggle	.75	2.00
105	Michaels / Cena	2.00	5.00
106	Cade / Murdoch	.30	.75
107	Kane / Boogeyman	1.25	3.00
108	Flair / Piper	1.25	3.00
109	Hardy Boys	.75	2.00
110	Highlanders	.50	1.25
111	Major Brothers	.50	1.25
112	Dusty / Cody Rhodes	.75	2.00
113	Candice / Victoria	1.50	4.00
114	Vince / Shane McMahon	1.25	3.00
115	Junkyard Dog	.60	1.50
116	British Bulldog	1.25	3.00
117	Bushwhacker Butch	.50	1.25
118	Bushwhacker Luke	.50	1.25
119	Curt Hennig	.50	1.25
120	Doink the Clown	.30	.75
121	Dusty Rhodes	.75	2.00
122	Jake Roberts	.75	2.00
123	Jimmy Snuka	.50	1.25
124	Ted Dibiase	.60	1.50
125	Nikolai Volkoff	.60	1.50
126	Paul Bearer	.50	1.25
127	Sgt. Slaughter	.75	2.00
128	Billy Graham	.50	1.25
129	Terry Funk	.30	.75
130	Bobby Heenan	.60	1.50
131	Checklist 1 CL		
132	Checklist 2 CL		.75

2007 Topps WWE Face-Off Royal Rumble Champions

COMPLETE SET (10)		12.00	30.00
RANDOMLY INSERTED INTO PACKS			
R1	Batista	2.00	5.00
R2	Triple H	3.00	8.00
R3	The Rock	4.00	10.00
R4	Jim Duggan	.75	2.00
R5	Rey Mysterio	1.25	3.00
R6	Ric Flair	2.00	5.00
R7	Shawn Michaels	3.00	8.00
R8	Stone Cold Steve Austin	3.00	8.00
R9	Undertaker	2.50	6.00
R10	Mr. McMahon	2.00	5.00

2007 Topps WWE Face-Off Superstar Foil

COMPLETE SET (22)		12.00	30.00
RANDOMLY INSERTED INTO PACKS			
S1	Bobby Lashley	1.50	4.00
S2	Boogeyman	.60	1.50
S3	Carlito	1.50	4.00
S4	Chavo Guerrero	.60	1.50
S5	Chris Masters	1.50	4.00
S6	CM Punk	.60	1.50
S7	Edge	1.50	4.00
S8	Fit Finlay	1.00	2.50
S9	Jeff Hardy	1.00	2.50
S10	John Cena	2.50	6.00
S11	John Morrison	.60	1.50
S12	Kane	1.50	4.00
S13	King Booker	1.50	4.00
S14	Mark Henry	.60	1.50
S15	Matt Hardy	1.00	2.50
S16	Mr. Kennedy	1.00	2.50
S17	MVP	.60	1.50
S18	Randy Orton	1.50	4.00

S19	Shelton Benjamin	.40	1.00
S20	The Great Khali	.60	1.50
S21	Tommy Dreamer	.50	1.25
S22	Umaga	.60	1.50

2021 Topps WWE Fully Loaded Autographed Gear Relics

*GREEN/50: .5X TO 1.2X BASIC AUTOS
*PURPLE/25: UNPRICED DUE TO SCARCITY
*BLUE/10: UNPRICED DUE TO SCARCITY
*RED/5: UNPRICED DUE TO SCARCITY
*GOLD/1: UNPRICED DUE TO SCARCITY
STATED ODDS 1:23
STATED PRINT RUN 199 SER.#'d SETS

SGAJ	AJ Styles	20.00	50.00
SGBL	Becky Lynch	75.00	150.00
SGFB	Finn Balor	20.00	50.00
SGSN	Shinsuke Nakamura	20.00	50.00

2021 Topps WWE Fully Loaded Autographed Chair Relics

*GREEN/50: .5X TO 1.2X BASIC AUTOS
*PURPLE/25: UNPRICED DUE TO SCARCITY
*BLUE/10: UNPRICED DUE TO SCARCITY
*RED/5: UNPRICED DUE TO SCARCITY
*GOLD/1: UNPRICED DUE TO SCARCITY
STATED ODDS 1:20
STATED PRINT RUN 99 SER.#'d SETS

CAS	Asuka	50.00	100.00
CCL	Candice LeRae	30.00	75.00
CDK	Dakota Kai	30.00	75.00
CKC	King Corbin	12.00	30.00
CRR	Rhea Ripley	60.00	120.00
CSB	Shayna Baszler	15.00	40.00
CTN	Tegan Nox	30.00	75.00

2021 Topps WWE Fully Loaded Autographed Kiss

*GREEN/50: .5X TO 1.2X BASIC AUTOS
*PURPLE/25: UNPRICED DUE TO SCARCITY
*BLUE/10: UNPRICED DUE TO SCARCITY
*RED/5: UNPRICED DUE TO SCARCITY
*GOLD/1: UNPRICED DUE TO SCARCITY
STATED ODDS 1:118
STATED PRINT RUN 50 SER.#'d SETS

KBK	Billie Kay		
KBL	Becky Lynch		
KCC	Charly Caruso		
KCF	Charlotte Flair		
KCM	Carmella		
KEM	Ember Moon		
KLM	Liv Morgan		
KMJ	Mickie James	75.00	150.00
KMM	Maryse		
KMR	Mandy Rose		
KNC	Nikki Cross	125.00	250.00
KNJ	Nia Jax		
KNT	Natalya	50.00	100.00
KPR	Peyton Royce		
KRR	Ruby Riott		
KRY	Renee Young		
KSD	Sonya Deville		
KVB	Vanessa Borne		

2021 Topps WWE Fully Loaded Autographed Ladder Relics

*GREEN/50: .5X TO 1.2X BASIC AUTOS

*PURPLE/25: UNPRICED DUE TO SCARCITY
*BLUE/10: UNPRICED DUE TO SCARCITY
*RED/5: UNPRICED DUE TO SCARCITY
*GOLD/1: UNPRICED DUE TO SCARCITY
STATED ODDS 1:15
STATED PRINT RUN 99 SER.#'d SETS

LAJ	AJ Styles	25.00	60.00
LAS	Asuka	30.00	75.00
LBE	Big E	15.00	40.00
LCS	Cesaro	15.00	40.00
LKC	King Corbin	12.00	30.00
LKK	Kofi Kingston	15.00	40.00
LKO	Kevin Owens	25.00	60.00
LLE	Lacey Evans	30.00	75.00
LNJ	Nia Jax	20.00	50.00
LOT	Otis	12.00	30.00
LSZ	Sami Zayn	12.00	30.00

2021 Topps WWE Fully Loaded Autographed Microphone Box Relics

*GOLD/1: UNPRICED DUE TO SCARCITY
STATED PRINT RUN 5 SER.#'d SETS
UNPRICED DUE TO SCARCITY

MCBE Big E
MCRT R-Truth
MCTM The Miz

2021 Topps WWE Fully Loaded Autographed Oversized Mat Relics

*GREEN/50: .5X TO 1.2X BASIC AUTOS
*PURPLE/25: UNPRICED DUE TO SCARCITY
*BLUE/10: UNPRICED DUE TO SCARCITY
*RED/5: UNPRICED DUE TO SCARCITY
*GOLD/1: UNPRICED DUE TO SCARCITY
STATED ODDS 1:6
STATED PRINT RUN 199 SER.#'d SETS

MAB	Alexa Bliss	75.00	150.00
MAJ	AJ Styles	20.00	50.00
MBA	Bayley	30.00	75.00
MBL	The Fiend Bray Wyatt	60.00	120.00
MBS	Braun Strowman	15.00	40.00
MCF	Becky Lynch	60.00	120.00
MCM	Carmella	30.00	75.00
MJG	Johnny Gargano	12.00	30.00
MKK	Kofi Kingston	12.00	30.00
MSB	Sasha Banks	75.00	150.00
MSH	Sheamus	15.00	40.00
MSN	Shinsuke Nakamura	15.00	40.00
MSR	Seth Rollins	20.00	50.00
MTM	The Miz	15.00	40.00

2021 Topps WWE Fully Loaded Autographed Table Relics

*GREEN/50: .5X TO 1.2X BASIC AUTOS
*PURPLE/25: UNPRICED DUE TO SCARCITY
*BLUE/10: UNPRICED DUE TO SCARCITY
*RED/5: UNPRICED DUE TO SCARCITY
*GOLD/1: UNPRICED DUE TO SCARCITY
STATED ODDS 1:11
STATED PRINT RUN 99 SER.#'d SETS

TAB	Aleister Black	20.00	50.00
TAC	Adam Cole	20.00	50.00
TAJ	AJ Styles	20.00	50.00
TAS	Asuka	50.00	100.00
TBF	Bobby Fish	15.00	40.00
TBS	Braun Strowman	15.00	40.00
TCM	Carmella	30.00	75.00

TCS	Cesaro	15.00	40.00
TDD	Dominik Dijakovic	12.00	30.00
TKL	Keith Lee	15.00	40.00
TKO	Kevin Owens	15.00	40.00
TKR	Kyle O'Reilly	12.00	30.00
TLA	Bobby Lashley	12.00	30.00
TRS	Roderick Strong	15.00	40.00
TSN	Shinsuke Nakamura	15.00	40.00
TTC	Tommaso Ciampa	15.00	40.00

2021 Topps WWE Fully Loaded Autographed Turnbuckle Relics

*GREEN/50: .5X TO 1.2X BASIC AUTOS
*PURPLE/25: UNPRICED DUE TO SCARCITY
*BLUE/10: UNPRICED DUE TO SCARCITY
*RED/5: UNPRICED DUE TO SCARCITY
*GOLD/1: UNPRICED DUE TO SCARCITY
STATED ODDS 1:11
STATED PRINT RUN 99 SER.#'d SETS

AAC	Apollo Crews	12.00	30.00
AAG	Angel Garza	12.00	30.00
AAN	Andrade	15.00	40.00
AAT	Austin Theory	20.00	50.00
ADM	Drew McIntyre	20.00	50.00
ADZ	Dolph Ziggler	12.00	30.00
AJH	Jeff Hardy	25.00	60.00
ALE	Lacey Evans	25.00	60.00
AMA	Mustafa Ali	12.00	30.00
AMR	Mandy Rose	75.00	150.00
AOT	Otis	15.00	40.00
ARC	Ricochet	12.00	30.00
ART	R-Truth	15.00	40.00
ASB	Shayna Baszler		
ASJ	Samoa Joe	15.00	40.00
ATM	The Miz	12.00	30.00

2021 Topps WWE Fully Loaded Autographs

STATED ODDS 1:430

AVM	Mr. McMahon	300.00	600.00

2019 Topps WWE Garbage Pail Kids

Launch Date: 3/12/2019; Total Print Run :

COMPLETE SET (13)		25.00	60.00

STATED PRINT RUN 1028 SETS PRODUCED

1	Gigantic Andre	2.50	6.00
2	Breakin' Becky	8.00	20.00
3	C-Thru Cena	4.00	10.00
4	Savage Randy	2.50	6.00
5	Mixed-Up Mick	3.00	8.00
6	Mouthy Miz & Maryse	2.50	6.00
7	Slick Ric	4.00	10.00
8	Rowdy Ronda	6.00	15.00
9	Brawlin' Rollins	3.00	8.00
10	Seething Steve	3.00	8.00
11	Chipped Rock	4.00	10.00
12	Unravelled Warrior	3.00	8.00
13	Undead Taker	5.00	10.00

2018 Topps WWE Hall of Fame Tribute

This is a continuation series across several products in 2018. 10-card sets were inserted into the following products: Topps WWE Road to WrestleMania - Andre the Giant (1-10), Topps WWE - Ultimate Warrior (11-20), Topps Heritage WWE - Ric Flair (21-30), and Topps WWE Then Now Forever - "Rowdy" Roddy Piper

(31-40).			
1	Andre the Giant	.60	1.50
2	Andre the Giant	.60	1.50
3	Andre the Giant	.60	1.50
4	Andre the Giant	.60	1.50
5	Andre the Giant	.60	1.50
6	Andre the Giant	.60	1.50
7	Andre the Giant	.60	1.50
8	Andre the Giant	.60	1.50
9	Andre the Giant	.60	1.50
10	Andre the Giant	.60	1.50
11	Ultimate Warrior	.60	1.50
12	Ultimate Warrior	.60	1.50
13	Ultimate Warrior	.60	1.50
14	Ultimate Warrior	.60	1.50
15	Ultimate Warrior	.60	1.50
16	Ultimate Warrior	.60	1.50
17	Ultimate Warrior	.60	1.50
18	Ultimate Warrior	.60	1.50
19	Ultimate Warrior	.60	1.50
20	Ultimate Warrior	.60	1.50
21	Ric Flair	.60	1.50
22	Ric Flair	.60	1.50
23	Ric Flair	.60	1.50
24	Ric Flair	.60	1.50
25	Ric Flair	.60	1.50
26	Ric Flair	.60	1.50
27	Ric Flair	.60	1.50
28	Ric Flair	.60	1.50
29	Ric Flair	.60	1.50
30	Ric Flair	.60	1.50
31	Rowdy Roddy Piper	.60	1.50
32	Rowdy Roddy Piper	.60	1.50
33	Rowdy Roddy Piper	.60	1.50
34	Rowdy Roddy Piper	.60	1.50
35	Rowdy Roddy Piper	.60	1.50
36	Rowdy Roddy Piper	.60	1.50
37	Rowdy Roddy Piper	.60	1.50
38	Rowdy Roddy Piper	.60	1.50
39	Rowdy Roddy Piper	.60	1.50
40	Rowdy Roddy Piper	.60	1.50

2015 Topps WWE Hulk Hogan Tribute

This was a continuation series across four different products in 2015. 10-Card sets were inserted in the following products: Topps WWE (1-10), Topps Chrome WWE (11-20), and Topps WWE Road to WrestleMania (21-30). The fourth set (31-40) was never produced due to Hogan being suspended by WWE.

COMPLETE SET (30)		12.00	30.00

*GOLD/10: 4X TO 10X BASIC CARDS
*RED/1: UNPRICED DUE TO SCARCITY

1	Hulk Hogan	.75	2.00
2	Hulk Hogan	.75	2.00
3	Hulk Hogan	.75	2.00
4	Hulk Hogan	.75	2.00
5	Hulk Hogan	.75	2.00
6	Hulk Hogan	.75	2.00
7	Hulk Hogan	.75	2.00
8	Hulk Hogan	.75	2.00
9	Hulk Hogan	.75	2.00
10	Hulk Hogan	.75	2.00
11	Hulk Hogan	.75	2.00
12	Hulk Hogan	.75	2.00
13	Hulk Hogan	.75	2.00
14	Hulk Hogan	.75	2.00
15	Hulk Hogan	.75	2.00

16	Hulk Hogan	.75	2.00
17	Hulk Hogan	.75	2.00
18	Hulk Hogan	.75	2.00
19	Hulk Hogan	.75	2.00
20	Hulk Hogan	.75	2.00
21	Hulk Hogan	.75	2.00
22	Hulk Hogan	.75	2.00
23	Hulk Hogan	.75	2.00
24	Hulk Hogan	.75	2.00
25	Hulk Hogan	.75	2.00
26	Hulk Hogan	.75	2.00
27	Hulk Hogan	.75	2.00
28	Hulk Hogan	.75	2.00
29	Hulk Hogan	.75	2.00
30	Hulk Hogan	.75	2.00

2007 Topps WWE Payback

COMPLETE SET (96)

1. Shawn Michaels
2 Triple H
3 Edge
4 John Cena
5 Randy Orton
6 Val Venis
7 Kane
8 Eugene
9 Jerry Lawler
10 Lita
11 Viscera
12 Rob Conway
13 Chris Masters
14 Shelton Benjamin
15 Mickie James
16 Ric flair
17 Victoria
18 Umaga
19 Carlito
20 Johnny Nitro
21 Candice
22 torrie Wilson
23 Mick Foley
24 Hulk Hogan
25 Kenny
26 Jeff Hardy
27 Stone Cold Steve Austin
28 Charlie Haas
29 Mikey
30 Melina
31 Rory McAllister
32 Robbie McAllister
33 Rey Mysterio
34 Undertaker
35 JBL
36 Jillian Hall
37 Brian Kendrick
38 Chris Benoit
39 King Booker
40 Batista
41 Paul London
42 Chavo Guerrero Jr.
43 Gregory Helms
44 Matt Hardy
45 Tatanka
46 Paul Burchill
47 Bobby Lashley
48 Snitsky
49 Finlay
50 The Miz

51 Ashley
52 Joey Mercury
53 Psicosis
54 Super Crazy
55 The Great Khali
56 Kid Kash
57 Ken Kennedy
58 Funaki
59 Scotty 2 Hotty
60 William Regal
61 Vito
62 Michelle McCool
63 Mark Henry
64 Jamie Noble
65 Al Snow
66 Test
67 Little Guido Maritato
68 Jazz
69 Justin Credible
70 Roadkill
71 Sandman
72 Big Show
73 Tommy Dreamer
74 Tony Mamaluke
75 CM Punk
76 Hardcore Holly
77 Francine
78 Tazz
79 Rob Van Dam
80 Sabu
81 Balls Mahoney
82 C.W. Anderson
83 Danny Doring
84 Matt Striker
85 Mike Knox
86 Stevie Richards
87 Kevin Thorn
88 Terry Funk
89 British Bulldog
90 Sgt. Slaughter
91 Rowdy Roddy Piper
92 Million Dollar Man Ted DiBiase
93 Dusty Rhodes
94 Junkyard Dog
95 Doink The Clown
96 Jake "The Snake" Roberts

2010 Topps WWE Icons Stickers

1 WWE Logo
2 HHH
3 John Cena
4 Raw Logo
5 Mark Henry
6 Vladimir Kozlov
7 Sheamus
8 R-Truth
9 The Miz
10 David Hart Smith
11 John Cena
12 Ezekiel Jackson
13 William Regal
14 Smackdown Logo
15 Kane
16 Cody Rhodes
17 Kofi Kingston
18 Drew McIntyre
19 Matt Hardy
20 Chris Masters

21 Jack Swagger
22 Rey Mysterio
23 Vance Archer
24 NXT Logo
25 Matt Striker
26 NXT Team
27 Wade Barrett
28 Skip Sheffield
29 Heath Slater
30 David Otunga
31 Justin Gabriel
32 Darren Young
33 Michael Tarver
34 Royal Rumble Logo
35 The Miz
36 The Miz vs MVP
37 The Miz vs MVP
38 The Miz vs MVP
39 Sheamus vs Randy Orton
40 Sheamus vs Randy Orton
41 Sheamus vs Randy Orton
42 Sheamus vs Randy Orton
43 Sheamus
44 Undertaker vs Rey Mysterio
45 Undertaker vs Rey Mysterio
46 Undertaker vs Rey Mysterio
47 Undertaker vs Rey Mysterio
48 Royal Rumble Moments
49 Royal Rumble Moments
50 Royal Rumble Moments
51 Edge
52 Edge
53 Edge
54 Elimination Chamber Logo
55 Undertaker
56 CM Punk vs R-Truth
57 Chris Jericho vs John Morrison
58 Chris Jericho vs John Morrison
59 Sheamus
60 HHH vs Sheamus
61 HHH vs Sheamus
62 John Cena vs HHH
63 John Cena vs Randy Orton
64 Wrestlemania Logo
65 John Morrison
66 Randy Orton vs Cody Rhodes
67 Randy Orton vs Cody Rhodes
68 Randy Orton vs Cody Rhodes
69 Randy Orton
70 Edge
71 Chris Jericho vs Edge
72 John Cena vs. Batista
73 John Cena vs. Batista
74 Undertaker Logo
75 Shawn Michaels Logo
76 Undertaker vs Shawn Michaels
77 Undertaker vs Shawn Michaels
78 Undertaker vs Shawn Michaels
79 Undertaker vs Shawn Michaels
80 Undertaker vs Shawn Michaels
81 Undertaker vs Shawn Michaels
82 Undertaker vs Shawn Michaels
83 Undertaker vs Shawn Michaels
84 Extreme Rules Logo
85 Jack Swagger vs Randy Orton
86 Jack Swagger vs Randy Orton
87 HHH vs Sheamus
88 HHH vs Sheamus

89 Chris Jericho vs Edge
90 Chris Jericho vs Edge
91 John Cena vs Batista
92 John Cena vs Batista
93 John Cena vs Batista
94 Sheamus
95 Sheamus
96 Sheamus vs Santino Marella
97 R-Truth
98 R-Truth
99 Ted DiBiase
100 Ted DiBiase
101 Ted DiBiase
102 Mark Henry
103 Mark Henry
104 Jack Swagger
105 Jack Swagger
106 Jack Swagger
107 Kofi Kingston
108 Kofi Kingston
109 CM Punk Team
110 CM Punk
111 CM Punk Team
112 Dolph Ziggler
113 Dolph Ziggler
114 Heath Slater
115 Skip Sheffield
116 Michael Tarver
117 John Cena vs Michael Tarver
118 Michael Tarver
119 Wade Barrett
120 Wade Barrett
121 Justin Gabriel
122 Darren Young
123 Darren Young
124 WWE Champion Belt
125 John Cena
126 John Cena
127 Sheamus
128 Sheamus
129 Randy Orton
130 Randy Orton
131 Randy Orton
132 HHH
133 HHH
134 WWE World Heavywight Belt
135 Jack Swagger
136 Jack Swagger
137 Jack Swagger
138 Undertaker
139 Undertaker
140 CM Punk
141 CM Punk
142 Chris Jericho
143 Chris Jericho
144 WWE Intercontinental Belt
145 Kofi Kingston
146 Kofi Kingston
147 Chris Jericho
148 Chris Jericho
149 Drew McIntyre
150 Drew McIntyre
151 Drew McIntyre
152 Rey Mysterio
153 Rey Mysterio
154 WWE Divas Belt
155 Eve
156 Eve

2006 Topps WWE Insider

COMPLETE SET (72)	8.00	20.00
UNOPENED BOX (24 PACKS)		
UNOPENED PACK (7 CARDS)		
1 Lashley	.30	.75
2 Big Show	.50	1.25
3 Carlito	.50	1.25
4 Chris Masters	.20	.50
5 Edge	.50	1.25
6 Gene Snitsky	.20	.50
7 Hulk Hogan	.75	2.00
8 Jerry The King Lawler	.40	1.00
9 John Cena	.75	2.00
10 Jonathan Coachman	.12	.30
11 Kane	.50	1.25
12 Chavo Guerrero	.20	.50
13 Kurt Angle	.50	1.25
14 Lance Cade	.12	.30
15 Lilian Garcia	.60	1.50
16 Lita	.75	2.00
17 Maria	.50	1.25
18 Matt Hardy	.30	.75
19 Rene Dupree	.20	.50
20 Ric Flair	.60	1.50
21 Rob Conway	.20	.50
22 Rob Van Dam	.30	.75
23 Paul Burchill	.12	.30
24 Kid Kash	.12	.30
25 Shawn Michaels	.75	2.00
26 Shelton Benjamin	.12	.30
27 Mickie James	.75	2.00
28 Stone Cold	.75	2.00
29 Gregory Helms	.12	.30
30 Trevor Murdoch	.12	.30
31 Triple H	.75	2.00
32 Trish Stratus	1.25	3.00
33 Mark Henry	.20	.50
34 Val Venis	.20	.50
35 Victoria	.75	2.00
36 Viscera	.20	.50
37 Batista	.50	1.25
38 Booker T	.30	.75
39 Candice Michelle	.75	2.00
40 Chris Benoit	.50	1.25
41 Boogeyman	.20	.50
42 Funaki	.20	.50
43 Hardcore Holly	.20	.50
44 Joey Styles	.12	.30
45 JBL	.30	.75
46 Joey Mercury	.12	.30
47 Johnny Nitro	.20	.50
48 Ashley	.50	1.25
49 Finlay	.30	.75
50 Ken Kennedy	.30	.75
51 Melina	.50	1.25
52 Michael Cole	.12	.30
53 Nunzio	.12	.30
54 Orlando Jordan	.12	.30
55 Paul London	.12	.30
56 Psicosis	.12	.30
57 Randy Orton	.30	.75
58 Rey Mysterio	.50	1.25
59 Road Warrior Animal	.25	.60
60 Kristal	.30	.75
61 Sharmell	.50	1.25
62 Simon Dean	.12	.30
63 Steven Richards	.20	.50
64 Super Crazy	.20	.50
65 Goldust	.20	.50
66 Tazz	.20	.50
67 Theodore Long	.12	.30
68 Torrie Wilson	1.25	3.00
69 Undertaker	.60	1.50
70 Vito	.12	.30
71 William Regal	.30	.75
72 Checklist	.10	.25

2006 Topps WWE Insider Autographs

STATED ODDS 1:24 HOBBY EXCLUSIVE		
NNO Ashley	6.00	15.00
NNO Candice Michelle	25.00	60.00
NNO Carlito	30.00	80.00
NNO Chris Masters	6.00	15.00
NNO Edge	15.00	40.00
NNO Eugene	12.00	30.00
NNO Goldust	8.00	20.00
NNO Gregory Helms	8.00	20.00
NNO John Cena	12.00	30.00
NNO Kristal	8.00	20.00
NNO Lita	6.00	15.00
NNO Maria	20.00	50.00
NNO Matt Hardy	25.00	60.00
NNO Melina	8.00	20.00
NNO Mickie James	20.00	50.00
NNO Randy Orton	8.00	20.00
NNO Road Warrior	15.00	40.00
NNO Shelton Benjamin	12.00	30.00
NNO Torrie Wilson	6.00	15.00
NNO Trish Stratus	6.00	15.00
NNO Victoria	12.00	30.00
NNO Viscera	20.00	50.00

2006 Topps WWE Insider Champions

COMPLETE SET (12)	5.00	12.00
STATED ODDS 1:6 RETAIL EXCLUSIVE		
C1 John Cena	.75	2.00
C2 Ric Flair	.60	1.50
C3 Trish Stratus	1.25	3.00
C4 Rey Mysterio	.50	1.25
C5 Eddie Guerrero	.50	1.25
C6 Booker T	.30	.75
C7 Chris Benoit	.50	1.25
C8 Kurt Angle	.50	1.25
C9 Undertaker	.60	1.50
C10 Triple H	.75	2.00
C11 Stone Cold	.75	2.00
C12 Hulk Hogan	.75	2.00

2006 Topps WWE Insider Coins

COMPLETE SET (24)	4.00	10.00
STATED ODDS 1:1 RETAIL EXCLUSIVE		
1 John Cena	.40	1.00
2 Edge	.25	.60
3 Carlito	.25	.60
4 Kurt Angle	.25	.60
5 Randy Orton	.15	.40
6 Shawn Michaels	.40	1.00
7 Undertaker	.30	.75
8 Batista	.25	.60
9 Ric Flair	.30	.75
10 Chris Masters	.10	.25
11 Triple H	.40	1.00
12 Kane	.25	.60
13 Boogeyman	.10	.25
14 Steve Austin	.40	1.00
15 Trish Stratus	.60	1.50
16 Rob Van Dam	.15	.40
17 Chris Benoit	.25	.60
18 Hulk Hogan	.40	1.00
19 JBL	.15	.40
20 Rey Mysterio	.25	.60
21 Big Show	.25	.60
22 Booker T	.15	.40
23 Torrie Wilson	.60	1.50
24 Candice Michelle	.40	1.00

2006 Topps WWE Insider Divas

COMPLETE SET (12)	4.00	10.00
STATED ODDS 1:3 RETAIL EXCLUSIVE		
D1 Candice Michelle	.60	1.50
D2 Ashley	.40	1.00
D3 Mickie James	.60	1.50
D4 Sharmell	.40	1.00
D5 Torrie Wilson	1.00	2.50
D6 Trish Stratus	1.00	2.50
D7 Jillian Hall	.40	1.00
D8 Lilian Garcia	.50	1.25
D9 Lita	.60	1.50
D10 Maria	.40	1.00
D11 Kristal	.25	.60
D12 Victoria	.60	1.50

2006 Topps WWE Insider Memorabilia

STATED ODDS 1:24 HOBBY EXCLUSIVE		
NNO John Cena	6.00	15.00
NNO Kurt Angle	3.00	8.00
NNO Matt Hardy	2.00	5.00
NNO Rey Mysterio	2.00	5.00
NNO Shawn Michaels	8.00	20.00

2006 Topps WWE Insider Promos

COMPLETE SET (2)	
P1 Undertaker	
P2 Batista	

2019 Topps WWE Intercontinental Championship 40th Anniversary

This is a continuation series across four different products in 2019. This particular set highlights some of the prominent WWE Intercontinental Champions during the storied history of the title. 10-Card sets were inserted in the following products: Topps WWE Road to WrestleMania (IC1-IC10), Topps WWE RAW (IC11-IC20), Topps WWE SummerSlam (IC21-IC30), and SmackDown Live (IC31-IC40).

COMPLETE SET (40)
RANDOMLY INSERTED INTO PACKS

IC1 Don Muraco		.50	1.25
IC2 Macho Man Randy Savage		1.25	3.00
IC3 Ricky The Dragon Steamboat		.60	1.50
IC4 The Honky Tonk Man		.50	1.25
IC5 Ultimate Warrior		1.25	3.00
IC6 Ravishing Rick Rude		.60	1.50
IC7 Mr. Perfect		.75	2.00
IC8 Texas Tornado		.75	2.00
IC9 Bret Hit Man Hart		1.25	3.00
IC10 Rowdy Roddy Piper		1.25	3.00
IC11 Shawn Michaels		1.25	3.00
IC12 Razor Ramon		.75	2.00
IC13 Diesel		.75	2.00
IC14 Triple H		1.25	3.00
IC15 The Rock		2.50	6.00
IC16 Stone Cold Steve Austin		2.50	6.00
IC17 Ken Shamrock		.75	2.00
IC18 Road Dogg		.50	1.25
IC19 The Godfather		.50	1.25
IC20 Edge		1.25	3.00
IC21 D'Lo Brown		.50	1.25
IC22 Kurt Angle		1.00	2.50
IC23 Eddie Guerrero		1.25	3.00
IC24 Billy Gunn		.60	1.50
IC25 Jeff Hardy		1.25	3.00
IC26 Kane		.75	2.00
IC27 Albert		.50	1.25
IC28 William Regal		.75	2.00
IC29 Booker T		1.25	3.00
IC30 Randy Orton		1.25	3.00
IC31 Shelton Benjamin		.60	1.50
IC32 Ric Flair		1.50	4.00
IC33 Umaga		.50	1.25
IC34 Kofi Kingston		.75	2.00
IC35 Rey Mysterio		1.25	3.00
IC36 Drew McIntyre		.60	1.50
IC37 Dolph Ziggler		1.00	2.50
IC38 Big Show		.75	2.00
IC39 The Miz		1.00	2.50
IC40 Curtis Axel		.60	1.50

2017 Topps WWE John Cena Tribute

This was a continuation series across four different products in 2017. 10-Card sets were inserted in the following products: Topps WWE Road to WrestleMania (1-10), Topps WWE (11-20), Topps Heritage WWE (21-30), and Topps WWE Then Now Forever (31-40).

COMPLETE SET (40)   6.00   15.00
STATED ODDS 1:6

1 John Cena		1.00	2.50
2 John Cena		1.00	2.50
3 John Cena		1.00	2.50
4 John Cena		1.00	2.50
5 John Cena		1.00	2.50
6 John Cena		1.00	2.50
7 John Cena		1.00	2.50
8 John Cena		1.00	2.50
9 John Cena		1.00	2.50
10 John Cena		1.00	2.50
11 John Cena		1.00	2.50
12 John Cena		1.00	2.50
13 John Cena		1.00	2.50
14 John Cena		1.00	2.50
15 John Cena		1.00	2.50
16 John Cena		1.00	2.50
17 John Cena		1.00	2.50
18 John Cena		1.00	2.50
19 John Cena		1.00	2.50
20 John Cena		1.00	2.50
21 John Cena		1.00	2.50
22 John Cena		1.00	2.50
23 John Cena		1.00	2.50
24 John Cena		1.00	2.50
25 John Cena		1.00	2.50
26 John Cena		1.00	2.50
27 John Cena		1.00	2.50
28 John Cena		1.00	2.50
29 John Cena		1.00	2.50
30 John Cena		1.00	2.50
31 John Cena		1.00	2.50
32 John Cena		1.00	2.50
33 John Cena		1.00	2.50
34 John Cena		1.00	2.50
35 John Cena		1.00	2.50
36 John Cena		1.00	2.50
37 John Cena		1.00	2.50
38 John Cena		1.00	2.50
39 John Cena		1.00	2.50
40 John Cena		1.00	2.50

2018 Topps WWE Macho Man Randy Savage Tribute

This was a continuation series across four different products in 2018. 10-Card sets are inserted in the following products: Topps WWE Road to WrestleMania (1-10), Topps WWE (11-20), Topps Heritage WWE (21-30), and Topps WWE Then Now Forever (31-40).

1 Macho Man Randy Savage		1.25	3.00
2 Macho Man Randy Savage		1.25	3.00
3 Macho Man Randy Savage		1.25	3.00
4 Macho Man Randy Savage		1.25	3.00
5 Macho Man Randy Savage		1.25	3.00
6 Macho Man Randy Savage		1.25	3.00
7 Macho Man Randy Savage		1.25	3.00
8 Macho Man Randy Savage		1.25	3.00
9 Macho Man Randy Savage		1.25	3.00
10 Macho Man Randy Savage		1.25	3.00
11 Macho Man Randy Savage		1.25	3.00
12 Macho Man Randy Savage		1.25	3.00
13 Macho Man Randy Savage		1.25	3.00
14 Macho Man Randy Savage		1.25	3.00
15 Macho Man Randy Savage		1.25	3.00
16 Macho Man Randy Savage		1.25	3.00
17 Macho Man Randy Savage		1.25	3.00
18 Macho Man Randy Savage		1.25	3.00
19 Macho Man Randy Savage		1.25	3.00
20 Macho Man Randy Savage		1.25	3.00
21 Macho Man Randy Savage		1.25	3.00
22 Macho Man Randy Savage		1.25	3.00
23 Macho Man Randy Savage		1.25	3.00
24 Macho Man Randy Savage		1.25	3.00
25 Macho Man Randy Savage		1.25	3.00
26 Macho Man Randy Savage		1.25	3.00
27 Macho Man Randy Savage		1.25	3.00
28 Macho Man Randy Savage		1.25	3.00
29 Macho Man Randy Savage		1.25	3.00
30 Macho Man Randy Savage		1.25	3.00
31 Macho Man Randy Savage		1.25	3.00
32 Macho Man Randy Savage		1.25	3.00
33 Macho Man Randy Savage		1.25	3.00
34 Macho Man Randy Savage		1.25	3.00
35 Macho Man Randy Savage		1.25	3.00
36 Macho Man Randy Savage		1.25	3.00
37 Macho Man Randy Savage		1.25	3.00
38 Macho Man Randy Savage		1.25	3.00
39 Macho Man Randy Savage		1.25	3.00
40 Macho Man Randy Savage		1.25	3.00

2019 Topps WWE Money in the Bank

COMPLETE SET (90)   10.00   25.00
*BRONZE: .5X TO 1.2X BASIC CARDS
*GREEN/99: .75X TO 2X BASIC CARDS
*BLUE/50: 1.2X TO 3X BASIC CARDS
*PURPLE/25: 2X TO 5X BASIC CARDS
*GOLD/10: UNPRICED DUE TO SCARCITY
*BLACK/5: UNPRICED DUE TO SCARCITY
*RED/1: UNPRICED DUE TO SCARCITY

1 Aiden English		.25	.60
2 AJ Styles		1.25	3.00
3 Alexa Bliss		1.25	3.00
4 Alicia Fox		.50	1.25
5 Andrade		.30	.75
6 Ariya Daivari		.25	.60
7 Apollo Crews		.30	.75
8 Asuka		.75	2.00
9 Baron Corbin		.40	1.00
10 Bayley		.50	1.25
11 Becky Lynch		1.00	2.50
12 Beth Phoenix		.40	1.00
13 Big Show		.40	1.00
14 Big E		.25	.60
15 Bobby Lashley		.50	1.25
16 Robert Roode		.50	1.25
17 Booker T		.60	1.50
18 Braun Strowman		.60	1.50
19 Bray Wyatt		.60	1.50
20 Brock Lesnar		1.00	2.50
21 Carmella		.60	1.50
22 Cesaro		.30	.75
23 Charlotte Flair		1.00	2.50
24 Christian		.40	1.00
25 Curt Hawkins		.25	.60
26 Curtis Axel		.30	.75
27 Dana Brooke		.50	1.25
28 Daniel Bryan		1.00	2.50
29 Drew McIntyre		.30	.75
30 Elias		.50	1.25
31 Ember Moon		.60	1.50
32 Eve Torres		.30	.75
33 Fandango		.25	.60
34 Finlay		.25	.60
35 Finn Balor		.60	1.50
36 Gran Metalik		.25	.60
37 Heath Slater		.25	.60
38 Jeff Hardy		.60	1.50
39 Jey Uso		.30	.75
40 Jimmy Uso		.30	.75
41 Jinder Mahal		.50	1.25
42 John Cena		1.00	2.50
43 Kalisto		.25	.60
44 Kane		.40	1.00
45 Karl Anderson		.40	1.00
46 Kevin Owens		.60	1.50
47 Kofi Kingston		.40	1.00
48 Lacey Evans		.50	1.25
49 Lince Dorado		.25	.60
50 Luke Gallows		.40	1.00
51 Mark Henry		.30	.75
52 Maria Kanellis		.60	1.50
53 Mandy Rose		.60	1.50
54 Matt Hardy		.50	1.25
55 Mike Kanellis		.25	.60
56 Mojo Rawley		.30	.75
57 Ali		.25	.60
58 Naomi		.40	1.00
59 Natalya		.50	1.25
60 Nikki Cross		.40	1.00
61 Nia Jax		.50	1.25
62 Paige		1.00	2.50
63 Paul Heyman		.30	.75
64 Randy Orton		.60	1.50
65 Rey Mysterio		.60	1.50
66 Ric Flair		.75	2.00
67 Ricochet		.60	1.50
68 Roman Reigns		.60	1.50
69 Ronda Rousey		1.25	3.00
70 Rowan		.25	.60
71 R-Truth		.30	.75
72 Sami Zayn		.50	1.25
73 Samir Singh		.25	.60
74 Samoa Joe		.50	1.25
75 Sonya Deville		.50	1.25
76 Seth Rollins		.60	1.50
77 Sheamus		.40	1.00
78 Shelton Benjamin		.30	.75
79 Shinsuke Nakamura		.60	1.50
80 Sunil Singh		.25	.60
81 Tamina		.25	.60
82 Lord Tensai		.25	.60
83 The Miz		.50	1.25
84 Titus O'Neil		.30	.75
85 Tony Nese		.25	.60
86 Tyler Breeze		.30	.75
87 Xavier Woods		.30	.75
88 William Regal		.40	1.00
89 Zack Ryder		.30	.75
90 Zelina Vega		.40	1.00

2019 Topps WWE Money in the Bank Autographed Mat Relics

COMMON AUTO   5.00   12.00
*BLUE/50: .5X TO 1.2X BASIC AUTOS
*PURPLE/25: UNPRICED DUE TO SCARCITY
*GOLD/10: UNPRICED DUE TO SCARCITY
*BLACK/5: UNPRICED DUE TO SCARCITY
*RED/1: UNPRICED DUE TO SCARCITY
STATED ODDS 1:227
STATED PRINT RUN 99 SER.#'d SETS

MRACM Carmella		12.00	30.00
MRAFB Finn Balor		10.00	25.00
MRAKA Karl Anderson		8.00	20.00
MRAKK Kofi Kingston		6.00	15.00
MRAKO Kevin Owens		8.00	20.00
MRALG Luke Gallows		6.00	15.00
MRANT Natalya		6.00	15.00
MRART R-Truth		6.00	15.00
MRASA Samir Singh		5.00	12.00
MRASJ Samoa Joe		6.00	15.00

MRASM	Sheamus	8.00	20.00
MRASN	Shinsuke Nakamura	6.00	15.00
MRASR	Seth Rollins	8.00	20.00
MRASU	Sunil Singh	5.00	12.00
MRATO	Titus O'Neil	5.00	12.00
MRATS	Tamina	5.00	12.00
MRAXW	Xavier Woods	5.00	12.00
MRAZR	Zack Ryder	6.00	15.00

2019 Topps WWE Money in the Bank
Autographed Shirt Relics

*BLUE/50: .5X TO 1.2X BASIC AUTOS
*PURPLE/25: .6X TO 1.5X BASIC AUTOS
*GOLD/10: UNPRICED DUE TO SCARCITY
*BLACK/5: UNPRICED DUE TO SCARCITY
*RED/1: UNPRICED DUE TO SCARCITY
STATED ODDS 1:453
STATED PRINT RUN 99 SER.#'d SETS

SRAAC	Apollo Crews	5.00	12.00
SRAAJ	AJ Styles	10.00	25.00
SRABS	Braun Strowman	12.00	30.00
SRACS	Cesaro	5.00	12.00
SRAHS	Heath Slater	5.00	12.00
SRAKK	Kofi Kingston	6.00	15.00
SRARI	Ricochet	10.00	25.00
SRARR	Roman Reigns		
SRASR	Seth Rollins	12.00	30.00
SRASZ	Sami Zayn		

2019 Topps WWE Money in the Bank
Autographs

*GREEN/99: .5X TO 1.2X BASIC AUTOS
*BLUE/50: .6X TO 1.5X BASIC AUTOS
*PURPLE/25: UNPRICED DUE TO SCARCITY
*GOLD/10: UNPRICED DUE TO SCARCITY
*BLACK/5: UNPRICED DUE TO SCARCITY
*RED/1: UNPRICED DUE TO SCARCITY
STATED ODDS 1:41
STATED PRINT RUN 99 SER.#'d SETS

AAB	Alexa Bliss	20.00	50.00
AAD	Andrade	4.00	10.00
AAE	Aiden English	4.00	10.00
AAJ	AJ Styles	8.00	20.00
AAK	Asuka	10.00	25.00
AAL	Ali	4.00	10.00
ABC	Baron Corbin	4.00	10.00
ABE	Big E	4.00	10.00
ABJ	Shelton Benjamin	4.00	10.00
ABK	Dana Brooke	10.00	25.00
ABL	Becky Lynch	12.00	30.00
ABM	Matt Hardy	5.00	12.00
ABR	Robert Roode	4.00	10.00
ABS	Braun Strowman	5.00	12.00
ABW	Bray Wyatt	6.00	15.00
ACF	Charlotte Flair EXCH	12.00	30.00
ACM	Carmella	6.00	15.00
ACS	Cesaro	4.00	10.00
ADB	Daniel Bryan	6.00	15.00
ADM	Drew McIntyre	4.00	10.00
ADZ	Dolph Ziggler	4.00	10.00
AEL	Elias	5.00	12.00
AEM	Ember Moon	6.00	15.00
AFB	Finn Balor	5.00	12.00
AKK	Kofi Kingston	4.00	10.00
AKL	Kalisto	4.00	10.00
AKO	Kevin Owens	5.00	12.00
AMA	Maria Kanellis	8.00	20.00

AMG	Karl Anderson	4.00	10.00
AMI	Mike Kanellis	4.00	10.00
ANT	Natalya	5.00	12.00
ARM	Rey Mysterio	10.00	25.00
ARS	Rusev	4.00	10.00
ARW	Rowan	4.00	10.00
ASA	Samir Singh	4.00	10.00
ASB	Sasha Banks	10.00	25.00
ASJ	Samoa Joe	4.00	10.00
ASM	Sheamus	4.00	10.00
ASN	Shinsuke Nakamura	5.00	12.00
ASR	Seth Rollins	.60	15.00
ASU	Sunil Singh	4.00	10.00
ASZ	Sami Zayn	4.00	10.00
ATM	The Miz	5.00	12.00
ATO	Titus O'Neil	4.00	10.00
AXW	Xavier Woods	4.00	10.00
AZR	Zack Ryder	5.00	12.00
AZV	Zelina Vega	8.00	20.00

2019 Topps WWE Money in the Bank
Cash-In Moments

COMPLETE SET (13)		8.00	20.00
STATED ODDS 1:6			
CM1	Kane	.60	1.50
CM2	The Miz	.75	2.00
CM3	Daniel Bryan	1.50	4.00
CM4	John Cena	1.50	4.00
CM5	Randy Orton	1.00	2.50
CM6	Seth Rollins	1.00	2.50
CM7	Sheamus	.60	1.50
CM8	Baron Corbin	.60	1.50
CM9	Braun Strowman	1.00	2.50
CM10	Carmella	1.00	2.50
CM11	Alexa Bliss	2.00	5.00
CM12	Bayley	.75	2.00
CM13	Brock Lesnar	1.50	4.00

2019 Topps WWE Money in the Bank
Dual Autographs

*GOLD/10: UNPRICED DUE TO SCARCITY
*BLACK/5: UNPRICED DUE TO SCARCITY
*RED/1: UNPRICED DUE TO SCARCITY
STATED ODDS 1:3,663
STATED PRINT RUN 25 SER.#'d SETS

DANEW	X.Woods/Big E	25.00	60.00
DABROS	The Singhs	25.00	60.00
DAGOOD	K.Anderson/L.Gallows	20.00	50.00
DAHRDY	The Hardys	30.00	75.00

2019 Topps WWE Money in the Bank
Greatest Matches and Moments

COMPLETE SET (22)		6.00	15.00
STATED ODDS 1:3			
GMM1	Shelton Benjamin	.40	1.00
GMM2	Matt Hardy	.60	1.50
GMM3	Kofi Kingston	.50	1.25
GMM4	Kofi Kingston	.50	1.25
GMM5	Kofi Kingston	.50	1.25
GMM6	The Miz	.60	1.50
GMM7	Daniel Bryan	1.25	3.00
GMM8	Christian	.50	1.25
GMM9	Big Show	.50	1.25
GMM10	The Shield	.75	2.00
GMM11	John Cena	1.25	3.00
GMM12	Seth Rollins	.75	2.00
GMM13	John Cena	1.25	3.00

GMM14	Bray Wyatt	.75	2.00
GMM15	AJ Styles	1.50	4.00
GMM16	Seth Rollins	.75	2.00
GMM17	Mike & Maria Kanellis	.75	2.00
GMM18	Carmella	.75	2.00
GMM19	AJ Styles and Nakamura	1.50	4.00
GMM20	Carmella	.75	2.00
GMM21	Ember Moon	.75	2.00
GMM22	Brock Lesnar	1.25	3.00

2019 Topps WWE Money in the Bank
Mat Relics

*GREEN/99: .5X TO 1.2X BASIC MEM
*BLUE/50: .6X TO 1.5X BASIC MEM
*PURPLE/25: UNPRICED DUE TO SCARCITY
*GOLD/10: UNPRICED DUE TO SCARCITY
*BLACK/5: UNPRICED DUE TO SCARCITY
*RED/1: UNPRICED DUE TO SCARCITY
STATED ODDS 1:20

MRBC	Baron Corbin	2.50	6.00
MRBE	Big E	2.50	6.00
MRBL	Bobby Lashley	2.50	6.00
MRBR	Robert Roode	2.50	6.00
MRCM	Carmella	4.00	10.00
MRFB	Finn Balor	5.00	12.00
MRJE	Jey Uso	2.50	6.00
MRJI	Jimmy Uso	2.50	6.00
MRKK	Kofi Kingston	3.00	8.00
MRKO	Kevin Owens	4.00	10.00
MRLK	Becky Lynch	5.00	12.00
MRNM	Naomi	2.50	6.00
MRNT	Natalya	2.50	6.00
MRRO	Randy Orton	3.00	8.00
MRRT	R-Truth	3.00	8.00
MRSJ	Samoa Joe	2.50	6.00
MRSM	Sheamus	2.50	6.00
MRSR	Seth Rollins	4.00	10.00
MRTO	Titus O'Neil	2.50	6.00
MRTS	Tamina	2.50	6.00
MRXW	Xavier Woods	2.50	6.00
MRZR	Zack Ryder	2.50	6.00

2019 Topps WWE Money in the Bank
Money Cards

COMPLETE SET (13)		8.00	20.00
STATED ODDS 1:6			
MC1	Kane	.60	1.50
MC2	The Miz	.75	2.00
MC3	Daniel Bryan	1.50	4.00
MC4	John Cena	1.50	4.00
MC5	Randy Orton	1.00	2.50
MC6	Seth Rollins	1.00	2.50
MC7	Sheamus	.60	1.50
MC8	Baron Corbin	.60	1.50
MC9	Braun Strowman	1.00	2.50
MC10	Carmella	1.00	2.50
MC11	Alexa Bliss	2.00	5.00
MC12	Bayley	.75	2.00
MC13	Brock Lesnar	1.50	4.00

2019 Topps WWE Money in the Bank
Quad Autograph

STATED ODDS 1:47,616
STATED PRINT RUN 5 SER.#'d SETS
UNPRICED DUE TO SCARCITY

QABC Owens/Styles/Nakamura/Corbin

2019 Topps WWE Money in the Bank
Shirt Relics

*GREEN/99: .5X TO 1.2X BASIC MEM
*BLUE/50: .6X TO 1.5X BASIC MEM
*PURPLE/25: UNPRICED DUE TO SCARCITY
*GOLD/10: UNPRICED DUE TO SCARCITY
*BLACK/5: UNPRICED DUE TO SCARCITY
*RED/1: UNPRICED DUE TO SCARCITY
STATED ODDS 1:23
STATED PRINT RUN 199 SER.#'d SETS

SRAC	Apollo Crews	1.50	4.00
SRAJ	AJ Styles		
SRBL	Brock Lesnar	5.00	12.00
SRBS	Braun Strowman	2.50	6.00
SRCS	Cesaro	4.00	10.00
SRFB	Finn Balor		
SRHS	Heath Slater		
SRJE	Jey Uso		
SRJI	Jimmy Uso		
SRKB	Booker T	3.00	8.00
SRKK	Kofi Kingston	3.00	8.00
SRKO	Kevin Owens	3.00	8.00
SRLA	Bobby Lashley	2.50	6.00
SRMZ	The Miz	3.00	8.00
SRRI	Ricochet	5.00	12.00
SRRM	Rey Mysterio	5.00	12.00
SRRR	Roman Reigns		
SRSR	Seth Rollins	5.00	12.00
SRSZ	Sami Zayn	2.50	6.00

2019 Topps WWE Money in the Bank
Triple Autographs

*GOLD/10: UNPRICED DUE TO SCARCITY
*BLACK/5: UNPRICED DUE TO SCARCITY
*RED/1: UNPRICED DUE TO SCARCITY
STATED ODDS 1:6,802
STATED PRINT RUN SER.#'d SETS

TABC	Anderson/Gallows/Styles	60.00	120.00
TANEW	Woods/Big E/Kingston	50.00	100.00

2019 Topps WWE Money in the Bank
Promo

NYCC19	John Cena NYCC	5.00	12.00

2016 Topps WWE NXT

*BRONZE/50: .6X TO 1.5X BASIC CARDS
*SILVER/25: .75X TO 2X BASIC CARDS
*GOLD/10: 1.5X TO 4X BASIC CARDS
*RED/1: UNPRICED DUE TO SCARCITY

1	Aliyah	.75	2.00
2	Akam	.60	1.50
3	Andrade "Cien" Almas	.60	1.50
4	Angelo Dawkins	.60	1.50
5	Asuka	2.50	6.00
6	Austin Aries	.75	2.00
7	Billie Kay	1.50	4.00
8	Blake	.60	1.50
9	Dash Wilder	.75	2.00
10	Elias Samson	.60	1.50
11	Hideo Itami	.75	2.00
12	Johnny Gargano	.60	1.50
13	Liv Morgan	.75	2.00
14	Buddy Murphy	.60	1.50
15	No Way Jose	.60	1.50
16	Peyton Royce	1.50	4.00
17	Rezar	.60	1.50
18	Samoa Joe	1.50	4.00

#	Player	Lo	Hi
19	Sawyer Fulton	.75	2.00
20	Scott Dawson	.60	1.50
21	Shinsuke Nakamura	2.50	6.00
22	Tommaso Ciampa	.75	2.00
23	Tye Dillinger	.75	2.00
24	Roman Reigns	2.00	5.00
25	Seth Rollins	1.00	2.50
26	Big E	.60	1.50
27	Bray Wyatt	2.50	6.00
28	Xavier Woods	.60	1.50
29	Rusev	1.50	4.00
30	Kalisto	1.50	4.00
31	Neville	1.50	4.00
32	Kevin Owens	1.50	4.00
33	Charlotte	2.00	5.00
34	Sasha Banks	2.00	5.00
35	Becky Lynch	2.00	5.00
36	Sami Zayn	1.00	2.50
37	Baron Corbin	.75	2.00
38	Big Cass	1.25	3.00
39	Enzo Amore	1.25	3.00
40	Aiden English	.60	1.50
41	Simon Gotch	1.00	2.50
42	Dana Brooke	1.50	4.00
43	Alexa Bliss	3.00	8.00
44	Carmella	1.50	4.00
45	Chad Gable	.75	2.00
46	Finn Balor	2.00	5.00
47	Jason Jordan	.75	2.00
48	Mojo Rawley	.60	1.50
49	Nia Jax	1.00	2.50
50	Bayley	1.50	4.00

2016 Topps WWE NXT Autographs

*BRONZE/50: .5X TO 1.2X BASIC AUTOS
*SILVER/25: .6X TO 1.5X BASIC AUTOS
*GOLD/10: UNPRICED DUE TO SCARCITY
*RED/1: UNPRICED DUE TO SCARCITY
STATED OVERALL ODDS 1:MINIBOX

	Player	Lo	Hi
NNO	Alexa Bliss	50.00	100.00
NNO	Aliyah	8.00	15.00
NNO	Andrade Cien Almas	6.00	15.00
NNO	Angelo Dawkins	6.00	15.00
NNO	Asuka	20.00	50.00
NNO	Austin Aries	10.00	25.00
NNO	Bayley	15.00	40.00
NNO	Billie Kay	20.00	50.00
NNO	Blake	6.00	15.00
NNO	Buddy Murphy	6.00	15.00
NNO	Dash Wilder	12.00	30.00
NNO	Elias Samson	15.00	40.00
NNO	Finn Balor	15.00	40.00
NNO	Hideo Itami	6.00	15.00
NNO	Johnny Gargano	6.00	15.00
NNO	Liv Morgan	12.00	30.00
NNO	Nia Jax	8.00	20.00
NNO	No Way Jose	10.00	25.00
NNO	Peyton Royce	15.00	40.00
NNO	Samoa Joe	10.00	25.00
NNO	Sawyer Fulton	10.00	25.00
NNO	Scott Dawson	6.00	15.00
NNO	Shinsuke Nakamura	10.00	25.00
NNO	Tommaso Ciampa	6.00	15.00
NNO	Tye Dillinger	10.00	25.00

2017 Topps WWE NXT

COMPLETE SET (50)
UNOPENED BOX (10 PACKS)
UNOPENED PACK (7 CARDS)
*BRONZE: .6X TO 1.5X BASIC CARDS
*BLUE/50: X TO 2X BASIC CARDS
*SILVER/25: X TO 3X BASIC CARDS
*GOLD/10: UNPRICED DUE TO SCARCITY
*RED/1: UNPRICED DUE TO SCARCITY
*P.P.BLACK/1: UNPRICED DUE TO SCARCITY
*P.P.CYAN/1: UNPRICED DUE TO SCARCITY
*P.P.MAGENTA/1: UNPRICED DUE TO SCARCITY
*P.P.YELLOW/1: UNPRICED DUE TO SCARCITY

#	Player	Lo	Hi
1	Asuka	1.25	3.00
2	Akam	.40	1.00
3	Alexander Wolfe	.50	1.25
4	Aliyah	.50	1.25
5	Andrade Cien Almas	.40	1.00
6	Angelo Dawkins	.40	1.00
7	Killian Dain	.40	1.00
8	Billie Kay	.50	1.25
9	Bobby Roode	1.00	2.50
10	Buddy Murphy	.40	1.00
11	Elias Samson	.60	1.50
12	Ember Moon	1.00	2.50
13	Eric Young	.75	2.00
14	Hideo Itami	.60	1.50
15	Johnny Gargano	.40	1.00
16	Liv Morgan	.60	1.50
17	Mandy Rose	.50	1.25
18	Nick Miller	.40	1.00
19	Nikki Cross	.75	2.00
20	No Way Jose	.40	1.00
21	Oney Lorcan	.40	1.00
22	Otis Dozovic	.50	1.25
23	Peyton Royce	.60	1.50
24	Rezar	.40	1.00
25	Riddick Moss	.50	1.25
26	Roderick Strong	.50	1.25
27	Ruby Riot	.50	1.25
28	Sawyer Fulton	.40	1.00
29	Shane Thorne	.40	1.00
30	Tian Bing	.40	1.00
31	Tino Sabbatelli	.50	1.25
32	Tommaso Ciampa	.40	1.00
33	Tucker Knight	1.00	2.50
34	Wesley Blake	.40	1.00
35	Cathy Kelley	.40	1.00
36	Charly Caruso	.40	1.00
37	Mike Rome	.40	1.00
38	Paul Ellering	.40	1.00
39	Tom Phillips	.40	1.00
40	William Regal	.50	1.25
41	Corey Graves	.40	1.00
42	Dasha Fuentes	.50	1.25
43	Baron Corbin	.60	1.50
44	Bayley	1.25	3.00
45	Dash Wilder	.40	1.00
46	Finn Balor	1.50	4.00
47	Samoa Joe	1.25	3.00
48	Scott Dawson	.40	1.00
49	Shinsuke Nakamura	1.00	2.50
50	Tye Dillinger	.75	2.00

2017 Topps WWE NXT Autographs

*BRONZE/99: .5X TO 1.2X BASIC AUTOS
*BLUE/50: .6X TO 1.5X BASIC AUTOS
*SILVER/25: .75X TO 2X BASIC AUTOS
*GOLD/10: UNPRICED DUE TO SCARCITY
*RED/1: UNPRICED DUE TO SCARCITY
*P.P.BLACK/1: UNPRICED DUE TO SCARCITY
*P.P.CYAN/1: UNPRICED DUE TO SCARCITY
*P.P.MAGENTA/1: UNPRICED DUE TO SCARCITY
*P.P.YELLOW/1: UNPRICED DUE TO SCARCITY
RANDOMLY INSERTED INTO PACKS

	Player	Lo	Hi
RAAC	Andrade Cien Almas	5.00	12.00
RAAD	Angelo Dawkins	5.00	12.00
RAAK	Akam	8.00	20.00
RAAL	Aliyah	6.00	15.00
RAAS	Asuka	15.00	40.00
RAAW	Alexander Wolfe	8.00	20.00
RABD	Killian Dain	5.00	12.00
RABK	Billie Kay	10.00	25.00
RABM	Buddy Murphy	5.00	12.00
RABR	Bobby Roode	10.00	25.00
RACC	Charly Caruso	8.00	20.00
RACK	Cathy Kelley	8.00	20.00
RADF	Dasha Fuentes	8.00	20.00
RADW	Dash Wilder	5.00	12.00
RAEM	Ember Moon	10.00	25.00
RAEY	Eric Young	6.00	15.00
RAHI	Hideo Itami	5.00	12.00
RAJG	Johnny Gargano	5.00	12.00
RALM	Liv Morgan	10.00	25.00
RAMR	Mandy Rose	8.00	20.00
RANC	Nikki Cross	10.00	25.00
RANM	Nick Miller	5.00	12.00
RANW	No Way Jose	5.00	12.00
RAOD	Otis Dozovic	5.00	12.00
RAOL	Oney Lorcan	6.00	15.00
RAPR	Peyton Royce	8.00	20.00
RARE	Rezar	5.00	12.00
RARM	Riddick Moss	5.00	12.00
RARS	Roderick Strong	5.00	12.00
RASD	Scott Dawson	5.00	12.00
RASF	Sawyer Fulton	5.00	12.00
RASN	Shinsuke Nakamura	12.00	30.00
RAST	Shane Thorne	5.00	12.00
RATB	Tian Bing	5.00	12.00
RATC	Tommaso Ciampa	5.00	12.00
RATK	Tucker Knight	5.00	12.00
RATP	Tom Phillips	5.00	12.00
RATS	Tino Sabbatelli	5.00	12.00
RAWB	Wesley Blake	5.00	12.00

2017 Topps WWE NXT Dual Relics

RANDOMLY INSERTED INTO PACKS
STATED PRINT RUN 25 SER.#'d SETS
UNPRICED DUE TO SCARCITY

DRAA Andrade Cien Almas
DRAS Asuka
DRBR Bobby Roode
DRBY Bayley
DREM Ember Moon
DRFB Finn Balor
DRJG Johnny Gargano
DRNJ No Way Jose
DRSD Scott Dawson
DRSJ Samoa Joe
DRSN Shinsuke Nakamura
DRTC Tommaso Ciampa

2017 Topps WWE NXT Mat Relics

*BRONZE/99: .5X TO 1.2X BASIC MEM
*BLUE/50: .6X TO 1.5X BASIC MEM
*SILVER/25: .75X TO 2X BASIC MEM
*GOLD/10: UNPRICED DUE TO SCARCITY
*RED/1: UNPRICED DUE TO SCARCITY
RANDOMLY INSERTED INTO PACKS

	Player	Lo	Hi
MRAA	Andrade Cien Almas	2.00	5.00
MRAC	Apollo Crews	2.50	6.00
MRAE	Aiden English	2.00	5.00
MRAK	Asuka	6.00	15.00
MRAS	Asuka	6.00	15.00
MRAU	Austin Aries	4.00	10.00
MRBC	Big Cass	2.50	6.00
MRBR	Bobby Roode	5.00	12.00
MRBY	Bayley	6.00	15.00
MRCG	Chad Gable	2.50	6.00
MRDW	Dash Wilder	2.00	5.00
MREA	Enzo Amore	6.00	15.00
MREM	Ember Moon	5.00	12.00
MRFB	Finn Balor	8.00	20.00
MRJG	Johnny Gargano	2.00	5.00
MRJJ	Jason Jordan	2.50	6.00
MRKO	Kevin Owens	5.00	12.00
MRMR	Mojo Rawley	2.50	6.00
MRSB	Sasha Banks	6.00	15.00
MRSD	Scott Dawson	2.00	5.00
MRSH	Shinsuke Nakamura	5.00	12.00
MRSJ	Samoa Joe	6.00	15.00
MRSK	Asuka	6.00	15.00
MRSN	Shinsuke Nakamura	5.00	12.00
MRSZ	Sami Zayn	2.50	6.00
MRTB	Tyler Breeze	2.00	5.00
MRTC	Tommaso Ciampa	2.00	5.00
MRTD	Tye Dillinger	4.00	10.00
MRZR	Zack Ryder	2.00	5.00
MRBCB	Baron Corbin	3.00	8.00
MRBEY	Bayley	6.00	15.00
MRBLY	Bayley	6.00	15.00
MRBRD	Bobby Roode	5.00	12.00
MRBRH	Bobby Roode	5.00	12.00
MRBYY	Bayley	6.00	15.00
MRFBL	Finn Balor	8.00	20.00
MRFBR	Finn Balor	8.00	20.00
MRNWJ	No Way Jose	2.00	5.00
MRNYJ	No Way Jose	2.00	5.00
MRSJE	Samoa Joe	6.00	15.00
MRSJO	Samoa Joe	6.00	15.00
MRSNK	Shinsuke Nakamura	5.00	12.00
MRSZN	Sami Zayn	2.50	6.00
MRTDL	Tye Dillinger	4.00	10.00

2017 Topps WWE NXT Matches and Moments

*BRONZE: .5X TO 1.5X BASIC CARDS
*BLUE/50: .75X TO 2X BASIC CARDS
*SILVER/25: 1.2X TO 3X BASIC CARDS
*GOLD/10: UNPRICED DUE TO SCARCITY
*RED/1: UNPRICED DUE TO SCARCITY
*P.P.BLACK/1: UNPRICED DUE TO SCARCITY
*P.P.CYAN/1: UNPRICED DUE TO SCARCITY
*P.P.MAGENTA/1: UNPRICED DUE TO SCARCITY
*P.P.YELLOW/1: UNPRICED DUE TO SCARCITY

#	Player	Lo	Hi
1	Jason Jordan & Chad Gable	.50	1.25
2	Finn Balor/Samoa Joe	1.50	4.00
3	Apollo Crews	.50	1.25
4	Finn Balor/Samoa Joe	1.50	4.00
5	Finn Balor/Samoa Joe	1.50	4.00
6	Bayley	1.25	3.00
7	Apollo Crews	.50	1.25
8	Baron Corbin	.60	1.50
9	Samoa Joe	1.25	3.00
10	Samoa Joe	1.25	3.00

11	Dash/Dawson	.40	1.00
12	Dash/Dawson	.40	1.00
13	Jason Jordan/Chad Gable	.50	1.25
14	Samoa Joe/Baron Corbin	1.25	3.00
15	Dash/Dawson	.40	1.00
16	Finn Balor	1.50	4.00
17	Elias Samson	.60	1.50
18	Sami Zayn	.75	2.00
19	Finn Balor	1.50	4.00
20	Sami Zayn vs. Samoa Joe	1.25	3.00
21	Baron Corbin	.60	1.50
22	Finn Balor	1.50	4.00
23	Samoa Joe	1.25	3.00
24	The Revival	.40	1.00
25	American Alpha	.50	1.25
26	Finn Balor	1.50	4.00
27	American Alpha	.50	1.25
28	Shinsuke Nakamura	1.00	2.50
29	Asuka	1.25	3.00
30	Finn Balor	1.50	4.00
31	Apollo Crews	.50	1.25
32	Shinsuke Nakamura	1.00	2.50
33	No Way Jose	.40	1.00
34	Samoa Joe	1.25	3.00
35	Samoa Joe	1.50	4.00
36	Shinsuke Nakamura	1.00	2.50
37	Finn Balor	1.50	4.00
38	Blake/Murphy	.40	1.00
39	Johnny Gargano/Tommaso Ciampa	.40	1.00
40	Andrade Cien Almas	.40	1.00
41	The Revival	.50	1.25
42	The Authors of Pain	.40	1.00
43	Samoa Joe	1.50	4.00
44	TM-61	.40	1.00
45	Oney Lorcan	.40	1.00
46	Johnny Gargano/Tommaso Ciampa	.40	1.00
47	The Revival	.50	1.25
48	Shinsuke Nakamura	1.50	4.00
49	Shinsuke Nakamura	1.00	2.50
50	Bobby Roode	1.00	2.50

2017 Topps WWE NXT Shirt Relics

*BRONZE/99: .5X TO 1.2X BASIC MEM
*BLUE/50: .6X TO 1.5X BASIC MEM
*SILVER/25: .75X TO 2X BASIC MEM
*GOLD/10: UNPRICED DUE TO SCARCITY
*RED/1: UNPRICED DUE TO SCARCITY
RANDOMLY INSERTED INTO PACKS

SRAK	Akam	2.00	5.00
SRAW	Alexander Wolfe	2.50	6.00
SRBR	Bobby Roode	5.00	12.00
SREM	Ember Moon	5.00	12.00
SREY	Eric Young	4.00	10.00
SRHI	Hideo Itami	3.00	8.00
SRNC	Nikki Cross	4.00	10.00
SRRZ	Rezar	2.00	5.00
SRSD	Scott Dawson	2.00	5.00
SRSN	Shinsuke Nakamura	5.00	12.00
SRACA	Andrade Cien Almas	2.00	5.00
SRAKA	Asuka	6.00	15.00
SRBLY	Bayley	6.00	15.00
SRNWJ	No Way Jose	2.00	5.00

2018 Topps WWE NXT

COMPLETE SET (50)
UNOPENED BOX (10 PACKS)
UNOPENED PACK (7 CARDS)
*BRONZE: .6X TO 1.5X BASIC CARDS
*BLUE/50: .75X TO 2X BASIC CARDS
*SILVER/25: 1.2X TO 3X BASIC CARDS
*GOLD/10: UNPRICED DUE TO SCARCITY
*RED/1: UNPRICED DUE TO SCARCITY
*P.P.BLACK/1: UNPRICED DUE TO SCARCITY
*P.P.CYAN/1: UNPRICED DUE TO SCARCITY
*P.P.MAGENTA/1: UNPRICED DUE TO SCARCITY
*P.P.YELLOW/1: UNPRICED DUE TO SCARCITY

R1	Adam Cole	.50	1.25
R2	Akam	.40	1.00
R3	Aleister Black	.50	1.25
R4	Alexander Wolfe	.40	1.00
R5	Andrade Cien Almas	.60	1.50
R6	Angelo Dawkins	.40	1.00
R7	Bobby Fish	.40	1.00
R8	Buddy Murphy	.50	1.25
R9	Cezar Bononi	.40	1.00
R10	Drew McIntyre	.60	1.50
R11	Eric Young	.50	1.25
R12	Fabian Aichner	.40	1.00
R13	Gabriel Ealy	.40	1.00
R14	Kassius Ohno	.40	1.00
R15	Killian Dain	.50	1.25
R16	Kyle O'Reilly	.50	1.25
R17	Lars Sullivan	.40	1.00
R18	Lio Rush	.40	1.00
R19	Montez Ford	.40	1.00
R20	Nick Miller	.40	1.00
R21	No Way Jose	.50	1.25
R22	Oney Lorcan	.50	1.25
R23	Otis Dozovic	.40	1.00
R24	Paul Ellering	.50	1.25
R25	Pete Dunne	.40	1.00
R26	Rezar	.40	1.00
R27	Riddick Moss	.40	1.00
R28	Roderick Strong	.40	1.00
R29	Shane Thorne	.40	1.00
R30	Tino Sabbatelli	.50	1.25
R31	Tommaso Ciampa	.40	1.00
R32	Tucker Knight	.40	1.00
R33	Tyler Bate	.40	1.00
R34	Trent Seven	.40	1.00
R35	Velveteen Dream	.40	1.00
R36	Wesley Blake	.50	1.25
R37	Aliyah	.60	1.50
R38	Bianca Belair	.50	1.25
R39	Billie Kay	.75	2.00
R40	Ember Moon	.75	2.00
R41	Kairi Sane	1.00	2.50
R42	Lacey Evans	.50	1.25
R43	Nikki Cross	.60	1.50
R44	Peyton Royce	1.00	2.50
R45	Shayna Baszler	1.00	2.50
R46	Taynara Conti	.40	1.00
R47	Vanessa Borne	.40	1.00
R48	Zelina Vega	.40	1.00
R49	William Regal	.50	1.25
R50	Triple H	1.00	2.50

2018 Topps WWE NXT Autographed Shirt Relics

*BLUE/50: .5X TO 1.2X BASIC AUTOS
*SILVER/25: .6X TO 1.5X BASIC AUTOS
*GOLD/10: UNPRICED DUE TO SCARCITY
*RED/1: UNPRICED DUE TO SCARCITY
STATED PRINT RUN 99 SER.#'d SETS

ARAA	Andrade Cien Almas	8.00	20.00
ARAK	Akam	6.00	15.00
ARAW	Alexander Wolfe	5.00	12.00
AREM	Ember Moon	12.00	30.00
AREY	Eric Young	8.00	20.00
ARNC	Nikki Cross	10.00	25.00
ARNW	No Way Jose	8.00	20.00
ARRZ	Rezar	6.00	15.00

2018 Topps WWE NXT Autographs

*BRONZE/99: SAME VALUE AS BASIC
*BLUE/50: .5X TO 1.2X BASIC AUTOS
*SILVER/25: .6X TO 1.5X BASIC AUTOS
*GOLD/10: UNPRICED DUE TO SCARCITY
*RED/1: UNPRICED DUE TO SCARCITY
*P.P.BLACK/1: UNPRICED DUE TO SCARCITY
*P.P.CYAN/1: UNPRICED DUE TO SCARCITY
*P.P.MAGENTA/1: UNPRICED DUE TO SCARCITY
*P.P.YELLOW/1: UNPRICED DUE TO SCARCITY
RANDOMLY INSERTED INTO PACKS

AAA	Andrade Cien Almas	4.00	10.00
AAB	Aleister Black	6.00	15.00
AAC	Adam Cole	8.00	20.00
AAD	Angelo Dawkins	4.00	10.00
AAK	Akam	4.00	10.00
AAW	Alexander Wolfe	4.00	10.00
AAY	Aliyah	6.00	15.00
ABB	Bianca Belair	10.00	25.00
ABF	Bobby Fish	10.00	25.00
ABK	Billie Kay	10.00	25.00
ABM	Buddy Murphy	5.00	12.00
ABY	Bayley	8.00	20.00
ACB	Cezar Bononi	5.00	12.00
ADA	Dean Ambrose	20.00	50.00
ADM	Drew McIntyre	8.00	20.00
AEM	Ember Moon	8.00	20.00
AEY	Eric Young	5.00	12.00
AFA	Fabian Aichner	6.00	15.00
AJG	Johnny Gargano	6.00	15.00
AKD	Killian Dain	5.00	12.00
AKS	Kairi Sane	20.00	50.00
ALE	Lacey Evans	10.00	25.00
ALR	Lio Rush	10.00	25.00
ALS	Lars Sullivan	10.00	25.00
AMF	Montez Ford	10.00	25.00
ANC	Nikki Cross	6.00	15.00
ANM	Nick Miller	5.00	12.00
ANW	No Way Jose	4.00	10.00
AOD	Otis Dozovic	5.00	12.00
AOL	Oney Lorcan	5.00	12.00
AON	Kassius Ohno	4.00	10.00
APD	Pete Dunne	15.00	40.00
APR	Peyton Royce	6.00	15.00
ARE	Rezar	4.00	10.00
ARM	Riddick Moss	4.00	10.00
ARS	Roderick Strong	4.00	10.00
ASH	Shayna Baszler	12.00	30.00
AST	Shane Thorne	5.00	12.00
ATB	Tyler Bate	10.00	25.00
ATC	Tommaso Ciampa	5.00	12.00
ATK	Tucker Knight	4.00	10.00
ATS	Tino Sabbatelli	4.00	10.00
ATY	Taynara Conti	20.00	50.00
AUA	Kyle O'Reilly	6.00	15.00
AVB	Vanessa Borne	12.00	30.00
AVD	Velveteen Dream	6.00	15.00
AWB	Wesley Blake	4.00	10.00
AZV	Zelina Vega	20.00	50.00

2018 Topps WWE NXT Dual Autographs

*GOLD/10: UNPRICED DUE TO SCARCITY
*RED/1: UNPRICED DUE TO SCARCITY
STATED PRINT RUN 25 SER.#'d SETS

DADY	Triple H/William Regal	75.00	150.00
DAID	Peyton Royce/Billie Kay	75.00	150.00

2018 Topps WWE NXT Matches and Moments

*BRONZE: .6X TO 1.5X BASIC CARDS
*BLUE/50: .75X TO 2X BASIC CARDS
*SILVER/25: 1.2X TO 3X BASIC CARDS
*GOLD/10: UNPRICED DUE TO SCARCITY
*RED/1: UNPRICED DUE TO SCARCITY
*P.P.BLACK/1: UNPRICED DUE TO SCARCITY
*P.P.CYAN/1: UNPRICED DUE TO SCARCITY
*P.P.MAGENTA/1: UNPRICED DUE TO SCARCITY
*P.P.YELLOW/1: UNPRICED DUE TO SCARCITY

1	Samoa Joe	.75	2.00
2	Bobby Roode	.60	1.50
3	The Revival	.50	1.25
4	Shinsuke Nakamura	1.00	2.50
5	The Authors of Pain	.50	1.25
6	Tye Dillinger	.40	1.00
7	Bobby Roode	.60	1.50
8	Andrade "Cien" Almas	.60	1.50
9	SAnitY Debut	.60	1.50
10	#DIY Advance	.40	1.00
11	Shane Thorne	.40	1.00
12	The Authors of Pain	.50	1.25
13	Andrade "Cien" Almas	.60	1.50
14	Bobby Roode	.60	1.50
15	The Authors of Pain	.50	1.25
16	#DIY	.40	1.00
17	Samoa Joe	.75	2.00
18	SAnitY	.60	1.50
19	Samoa Joe	.75	2.00
20	Shinsuke Nakamura	1.00	2.50
21	Shinsuke Nakamura	1.00	2.50
22	Bobby Roode	.60	1.50
23	#DIY	.40	1.00
24	#DIY	.50	1.25
25	TM61	.50	1.25
26	Eric Young	.50	1.25
27	The Authors of Pain	.50	1.25
28	Seth Rollins	1.00	2.50
29	Bobby Roode	1.00	2.50
30	SAnitY	.50	1.25
31	Kassius Ohno	.40	1.00
32	The Authors of Pain	.50	1.25
33	Shinsuke Nakamura	1.00	2.50
34	Bobby Roode	.60	1.50
35	Kassius Ohno	1.00	2.50
36	SAnitY	.50	1.25
37	Aleister Black	.50	1.25
38	The Authors of Pain	.50	1.25
39	Bobby Roode	1.00	2.50
40	Oney Lorcan	.50	1.25
41	Drew McIntyre	.60	1.50
42	Tye Dillinger	.40	1.00
43	Tyler Bate	.50	1.25
44	Hideo Itami	.40	1.00
45	Hideo Itami	.40	1.00
46	Roderick Strong	.50	1.25
47	Pete Dunne	.40	1.00
48	Bobby Roode	.60	1.50

49 The Authors of Pain	.40	1.00
50 Tommaso Ciampa	.40	1.00

2018 Topps WWE NXT Triple Autographs

*GOLD/10: UNPRICED DUE TO SCARCITY
*RED/1: UNPRICED DUE TO SCARCITY
STATED ODDS

TAERA Cole/Fish/O'Reilly	50.00	100.00
TAMAG McIntyre/Almas/Gargano	30.00	75.00
TAMCA Moon/Cross/Aliyah	50.00	100.00
TASAY Young/Wolfe/Dain	25.00	60.00

2019 Topps WWE NXT

COMPLETE SET (100) 12.00 30.00
*BRONZE: .6X TO 1.5X BASIC CARDS
*BLUE/50: .75X TO 2X BASIC CARDS
*SILVER/25: 2X TO 5X BASIC CARDS
*GOLD/10: UNPRICED DUE TO SCARCITY
*RED/1: UNPRICED DUE TO SCARCITY

1 Velveteen Dream	.50	1.25
2 The Undisputed Era	.40	1.00
3 Aleister Black	.30	.75
4 Andrade	.30	.75
5 Roderick Strong	.50	1.25
6 Pete Dunne	.50	1.25
7 Johnny Gargano	.25	.60
8 Pete Dunne & Roderick Strong	.50	1.25
9 Adam Cole	.30	.75
10 Johnny Gargano	.25	.60
11 Pete Dunne & Roderick Strong	.50	1.25
12 EC3	.25	.60
13 Ricochet	.60	1.50
14 Adam Cole	.30	.75
15 Roderick Strong	.50	1.25
16 Aleister Black	.30	.75
17 Johnny Gargano	.50	1.25
18 The Viking Raiders	.30	.75
19 Ricochet	.60	1.50
20 Lars Sullivan	.25	.60
21 Kona Reeves	.30	.75
22 Pete Dunne	.50	1.25
23 The Viking Raiders	.30	.75
24 Tommaso Ciampa	.40	1.00
25 Kona Reeves	.30	.75
26 Dunne/Danny Burch/Oney Lorcan	.50	1.25
27 Lars Sullivan	.25	.60
28 EC3	.40	1.00
29 Pete Dunne	.50	1.25
30 The Undisputed Era	.50	1.25
31 Ricochet	.60	1.50
32 Aleister Black	.30	.75
33 Tommaso Ciampa	.25	.60
34 British Strong Style	.50	1.25
35 Aleister Black & Ricochet	.60	1.50
36 Moustache Mountain	.40	1.00
37 The Undisputed Era	.50	1.25
38 Johnny Gargano	.25	.60
39 The Undisputed Era	.50	1.25
40 Tommaso Ciampa	.30	.75
41 EC3	.25	.60
42 Aleister Black	.30	.75
43 Keith Lee	.25	.60
44 The Undisputed Era	.50	1.25
45 Velveteen Dream	.50	1.25
46 Ricochet	.60	1.50
47 Tommaso Ciampa	.25	.60
48 Lars Sullivan	.25	.60
49 The Undisputed Era	.50	1.25
50 The Forgotten Sons	.40	1.00
51 Jaxson Ryker	.25	.60
52 Pete Dunne	.60	1.50
53 Lars Sullivan	.25	.60
54 Keith Lee	.25	.60
55 Ricochet	.60	1.50
56 Bobby Fish	.40	1.00
57 Pete Dunne	.50	1.25
58 EC3	.25	.60
59 Johnny Gargano	.30	.75
60 Matt Riddle	.40	1.00
61 Heavy Machinery	.25	.60
62 Pete Dunne	.50	1.25
63 Aleister Black	.30	.75
64 Tommaso Ciampa	.25	.60
65 Dunne/Ricochet/Viking Raiders	.60	1.50
66 The Forgotten Sons	.40	1.00
67 EC3	.25	.60
68 Ricochet	.60	1.50
69 Dominik Dijakovic	.25	.60
70 Walter	.50	1.25
71 Tommaso Ciampa	.25	.60
72 The Viking Raiders	.30	.75
73 Johnny Gargano	.25	.60
74 Matt Riddle	.40	1.00
75 Black/Ricochet/Velveteen Dream	.25	.60
76 Rik Bugez	.40	1.00
77 Ricochet	.60	1.50
78 Velveteen Dream	.50	1.25
79 Keith Lee	.25	.60
80 DIY	.25	.60
81 Aleister Black/Ricochet	.60	1.50
82 Aleister Black/Ricochet	.60	1.50
83 Johnny Gargano	.25	.60
84 Adam Cole	.30	.75
85 Aleister Black & Ricochet	.60	1.50
86 The Viking Raiders	.30	.75
87 Velveteen Dream	.50	1.25
88 Walter	.50	1.25
89 Johnny Gargano	.50	1.25
90 Velveteen Dream	.50	1.25
91 Kushida	.25	.60
92 Matt Riddle	.40	1.00
93 The Viking Raiders	.30	.75
94 Tyler Breeze	.30	.75
95 Walter	.50	1.25
96 Imperium	.50	1.25
97 Matt Riddle	.50	1.25
98 The Street Profits	.30	.75
99 Velveteen Dream	.50	1.25
100 Adam Cole	.30	.75

2019 Topps WWE NXT Autographed Shirt Relics

*BLUE/50: .5X TO 1.2X BASIC AUTOS
*SILVER/25: UNPRICED DUE TO SCARCITY
*GOLD/10: UNPRICED DUE TO SCARCITY
*RED/1: UNPRICED DUE TO SCARCITY
STATED ODDS 1:364
STATED PRINT RUN 99 SER.#'d SETS

ASAC Adam Cole	8.00	20.00
ASRS Roderick Strong	6.00	15.00
ASSB Shayna Baszler	10.00	25.00
ASVD Velveteen Dream	6.00	15.00

2019 Topps WWE NXT Autographs

*BRONZE/99: SAME VALUE AS BASIC
*BLUE/50: .5X TO 1.2X BASIC AUTOS
*SILVER/25: UNPRICE DUE TO SCARCITY
*GOLD/10: UNPRICED DUE TO SCARCITY
*RED/1: UNPRICED DUE TO SCARCITY
*P.P.BLACK/1: UNPRICED DUE TO SCARCITY
*P.P.CYAN/1: UNPRICED DUE TO SCARCITY
*P.P.MAGENTA/1: UNPRICED DUE TO SCARCITY
*P.P.YELLOW/1: UNPRICED DUE TO SCARCITY
STATED ODDS 1:20

AE Erik	5.00	12.00
AI Ivar	5.00	12.00
AAC Adam Cole	8.00	20.00
ABB Bianca Belair	10.00	25.00
ABF Bobby Fish	5.00	12.00
ABM Buddy Murphy	5.00	12.00
ACG Chelsea Green	15.00	40.00
ACL Candice LeRae	6.00	15.00
ADD Dominik Dijakovic	6.00	15.00
ADP Deonna Purrazzo	6.00	15.00
AIS Io Shirai	25.00	60.00
AJD Jessamyn Duke	8.00	20.00
AJG Johnny Gargano	5.00	12.00
AKL Keith Lee	12.00	30.00
AKY Kyle O'Reilly	5.00	12.00
ALE Lacey Evans	15.00	40.00
AMS Marina Shafir	5.00	12.00
AMY Mia Yim	10.00	25.00
ANC Nikki Cross	8.00	20.00
AOD Otis	6.00	15.00
AOH Kassius Ohno	5.00	12.00
APD Pete Dunne	8.00	20.00
APM Damian Priest	5.00	12.00
ARC Ricochet	12.00	30.00
ARS Roderick Strong	5.00	12.00
ASB Shayna Baszler	6.00	15.00
ATK Tucker	5.00	12.00
ATM Tommaso Ciampa	8.00	20.00
ATS Toni Storm	75.00	150.00
AVD Velveteen Dream	5.00	12.00
AWT Walter	15.00	40.00
ABRO Matt Riddle	15.00	40.00

2019 Topps WWE NXT Dual Autographs

*GOLD/10: UNPRICED DUE TO SCARCITY
*RED/1: UNPRICED DUE TO SCARCITY
STATED ODDS 1:1,149
STATED PRINT RUN 25 SER.#'d SETS

DAAB M.Barthel/F.Aichner	25.00	60.00
DAGL C.LeRae/J.Gargano	60.00	120.00
DAMG V.Borne/Aliyah	50.00	100.00
DASO K.O'Reilly/R.Strong	20.00	50.00

2019 Topps WWE NXT Kiss Autographs

*GOLD/10: UNPRICED DUE TO SCARCITY
*RED/1: UNPRICED DUE TO SCARCITY
STATED ODDS 1:1,910
STATED PRINT RUN 25 SER.#'d SETS

AKAL Aliyah	50.00	100.00
AKBB Bianca Belair	100.00	200.00
AKCG Chelsea Green	100.00	200.00
AKIS Io Shirai	200.00	350.00

2019 Topps WWE NXT Roster

COMPLETE SET (50) 15.00 40.00
STATED ODDS 2:1

1 Adam Cole	.60	1.50
2 Jordan Myles	.30	.75
3 Aliyah	.50	1.25
4 Angelo Dawkins	.50	1.25
5 Bianca Belair	.30	.75
6 Bobby Fish	.75	2.00
7 Candice LeRae	1.00	2.50
8 Cathy Kelly	1.25	3.00
9 Chelsea Green	.50	1.25
10 Dakota Kai	1.00	2.50
11 Damian Priest	.50	1.25
12 Danny Burch	.50	1.25
13 Deonna Purrazzo	.50	1.25
14 Dominik Dijakovic	.50	1.25
15 Fabian Aichner	1.00	2.50
16 Humberto Carrillo	1.00	2.50
17 Io Shirai	.50	1.25
18 Jaxson Ryker	.50	1.25
19 Jessamyn Duke	.60	1.50
20 Jessi Kamea	.50	1.25
21 Johnny Gargano	.50	1.25
22 Kacy Catanzaro	1.25	3.00
23 Kassius Ohno	.75	2.00
24 Keith Lee	.50	1.25
25 Kona Reeves	.60	1.50
26 Kushida	.50	1.25
27 Kyle O'Reilly	.75	2.00
28 Marcel Barthel	1.00	2.50
29 Marina Shafir	.50	1.25
30 Matt Riddle	.75	2.00
31 Mauro Ranallo	.50	1.25
32 Mia Yim	.50	1.25
33 Montez Ford	.50	1.25
34 Oney Lorcan	.60	1.50
35 Pete Dunne	1.00	2.50
36 Raul Mendoza	.50	1.25
37 Rik Bugez	.50	1.25
38 Riddick Moss	.50	1.25
39 Roderick Strong	1.00	2.50
40 Shayna Baszler	1.00	2.50
41 Steve Cutler	.75	2.00
42 Toni Storm	2.00	5.00
43 Trent Seven	.75	2.00
44 Tyler Bate	.60	1.50
45 Vanessa Borne	.60	1.50
46 Velveteen Dream	1.00	2.50
47 Walter	1.00	2.50
48 Wesley Blake	.75	2.00
49 William Regal	.75	2.00
50 Xia Li	.50	1.25

2019 Topps WWE NXT Triple Autographs

*GOLD/10: UNPRICED DUE TO SCARCITY
*RED/1: UNPRICED DUE TO SCARCITY
STATED ODDS 1:1,442
STATED PRINT RUN 25 SER.#'d SETS

TA4H Shafir/Baszler/Duke	60.00	120.00
TAFS Ryker/Blake/Cutler	30.00	75.00
TAMYC Purrazzo/Shirai/Yim	100.00	200.00

2020 Topps WWE NXT

COMPLETE SET (100) 8.00 20.00
*BRONZE: .5X TO 1.2X BASIC CARDS

1	Imperium	.60	1.50
2	Alexander Wolfe	.60	1.50
3	Angel Garza	.40	1.00
4	Adam Cole	.75	2.00
5	Imperium	.50	1.25
6	Isaiah Swerve Scott	.40	1.00
7	Trent Seven	.30	.75
8	Killian Dain	.40	1.00
9	Johnny Gargano	.75	2.00
10	WALTER	.60	1.50
11	Pete Dunne	.30	.75
12	Tyler Bate	.50	1.25
13	Pete Dunne	.60	1.50
14	Dave Mastiff	.40	1.00
15	Street Profits	.30	.75
16	Velveteen Dream	.40	1.00
17	Adam Cole	.75	2.00
18	Flash Morgan Webster	.40	1.00
19	Mark Andrews	.30	.75
20	Moustache Mountain	.60	1.50
21	Killian Dain	.40	1.00
22	Dominik Dijakovic	.30	.75
23	Undisputed ERA	.75	2.00
24	Joe Coffey	.40	1.00
25	Mark Andrews	.40	1.00
26	WALTER	.60	1.50
27	Roderick Strong	.60	1.50
28	Mark Andrews & Flash Webster	.40	1.00
29	Roderick Strong	.60	1.50
30	Matt Riddle	.60	1.50
31	Keith Lee	.30	.75
32	Matt Riddle	.60	1.50
33	Adam Cole	.75	2.00
34	Undisputed ERA	.60	1.50
35	Finn Balor	.75	2.00
36	Tommaso Ciampa	.75	2.00
37	Gallus	.40	1.00
38	Roderick Strong	.60	1.50
39	Tommaso Ciampa	.60	1.50
40	Pete Dunne	.30	.75
41	Damian Priest	.30	.75
42	Gallus	.40	1.00
43	Angel Garza	.40	1.00
44	Roderick Strong	.60	1.50
45	Finn Balor	.75	2.00
46	Undisputed ERA	.75	2.00
47	NXT Invades SmackDown	1.00	2.50
48	Adam Cole	.75	2.00
49	Pete Dunne	.30	.75
50	Angel Garza	.40	1.00
51	Ilja Dragunov	.60	1.50
52	Imperium	.30	.75
53	WALTER	.60	1.50
54	Finn Balor	.75	2.00
55	Keith Lee	.60	1.50
56	Damian Priest	.30	.75
57	Adam Cole	.75	2.00
58	Alexander Wolfe	.30	.75
59	NXT Invades SD DX-Style	.75	2.00
60	Pete Dunne	.30	.75
61	Finn Balor	.75	2.00
62	Team Ciampa	.60	1.50
63	Roderick Strong	.60	1.50
64	Adam Cole	.75	2.00
65	Keith Lee	.75	2.00
66	Undisputed ERA	.75	2.00
67	Finn Balor	.75	2.00
68	Gallus & Ilja Dragunov	.60	1.50
69	Tommaso Ciampa	.30	.75
70	Imperium	.60	1.50
71	Angel Garza	.40	1.00
72	Finn Balor	.75	2.00
73	Brawl Leads to Ladder Match	.30	.75
74	Johnny Gargano	.60	1.50
75	Isaiah Swerve Scott	.40	1.00
76	Austin Theory	.50	1.25
77	Ilja Dragunov	.50	1.25
78	Austin Theory	.50	1.25
79	Imperium	.30	.75
80	Undisputed ERA	.75	2.00
81	Keith Lee	.30	.75
82	Tyler Bate	.50	1.25
83	Gallus	.40	1.00
84	WALTER	.60	1.50
85	Undisputed ERA	.75	2.00
86	BroserWeights	.60	1.50
87	Johnny Gargano	.60	1.50
88	Grizzled Young Veterans	.40	1.00
89	Isaiah Swerve Scott	.40	1.00
90	Imperium	.75	2.00
91	Grizzled Young Veterans	.40	1.00
92	BroserWeights	.60	1.50
93	Keith Lee	.60	1.50
94	Jordan Devlin	.30	.75
95	Travis Banks	.30	.75
96	Finn Balor	.75	2.00
97	Jordan Devlin	.40	1.00
98	Imperium	.60	1.50
99	#DIY	.60	1.50
100	BroserWeights	.60	1.50

2020 Topps WWE NXT Autographed Mat Relics

MRAAC	Adam Cole	20.00	50.00
MRABB	Bianca Belair	15.00	40.00
MRABF	Bobby Fish	12.00	30.00
MRACL	Candice LeRae	25.00	60.00
MRADK	Dakota Kai	30.00	75.00
MRAIS	Io Shirai	30.00	75.00
MRAJG	Johnny Gargano	10.00	25.00
MRAKL	Keith Lee	12.00	30.00
MRAKO	Kyle O'Reilly	10.00	25.00
MRAMR	Matt Riddle	15.00	40.00
MRARR	Rhea Ripley	50.00	100.00
MRATC	Tommaso Ciampa	12.00	30.00
MRATN	Tegan Nox	25.00	60.00
MRAVT	Velveteen Dream	12.00	30.00

2020 Topps WWE NXT Autographed Shirt Relics

SRAAC	Adam Cole	20.00	50.00
SRABF	Bobby Fish	12.00	30.00
SRAFB	Finn Balor	15.00	40.00
SRAJG	Johnny Gargano	12.00	30.00
SRAKO	Kyle O'Reilly	10.00	25.00
SRAKU	Kushida	10.00	25.00
SRAMY	Mia Yim	12.00	30.00
SRAT7	Trent Seven	20.00	50.00
SRATC	Tommaso Ciampa	10.00	25.00
SRAVD	Velveteen Dream		

2020 Topps WWE NXT Called Up

COMPLETE SET (9)		6.00	15.00
RANDOMLY INSERTED INTO PACKS			
CU1	Aleister Black	1.50	4.00
CU2	Angelo Dawkins	.75	2.00
CU3	Lacey Evans	2.00	5.00
CU4	Lars Sullivan	.75	2.00
CU5	Montez Ford	.75	2.00
CU6	Nikki Cross	1.50	4.00
CU7	Otis	.75	2.00
CU8	Ricochet	1.25	3.00
CU9	Tucker	.75	2.00

2020 Topps WWE NXT Called Up Autographs

CUAAB	Aleister Black		
CUAAD	Angelo Dawkins		
CUALE	Lacey Evans		
CUAMF	Montez Ford	15.00	40.00
CUANC	Nikki Cross		
CUAOT	Otis		
CUARC	Ricochet		

2020 Topps WWE NXT Dual Autographs

DABB	V.Borne/Aliyah	100.00	200.00
DATK	T.Nox/D.Kai	125.00	250.00
DAUE	B.Fish/K.O'Reilly	25.00	60.00

2020 Topps WWE NXT Johnny Gargano Tribute

COMPLETE SET (20)		12.00	30.00
RANDOMLY INSERTED INTO PACKS			
JG1	Johnny Gargano	1.50	4.00
JG2	Johnny Gargano	1.50	4.00
JG3	Johnny Gargano	1.50	4.00
JG4	Johnny Gargano	1.50	4.00
JG5	Johnny Gargano	1.50	4.00
JG6	Johnny Gargano	1.50	4.00
JG7	Johnny Gargano	1.50	4.00
JG8	Johnny Gargano	1.50	4.00
JG9	Johnny Gargano	1.50	4.00
JG10	Johnny Gargano	1.50	4.00
JG11	Johnny Gargano	1.50	4.00
JG12	Johnny Gargano	1.50	4.00
JG13	Johnny Gargano	1.50	4.00
JG14	Johnny Gargano	1.50	4.00
JG15	Johnny Gargano	1.50	4.00
JG16	Johnny Gargano	1.50	4.00
JG17	Johnny Gargano	1.50	4.00
JG18	Johnny Gargano	1.50	4.00
JG19	Johnny Gargano	1.50	4.00
JG20	Johnny Gargano	1.50	4.00

2020 Topps WWE NXT Johnny Gargano Tribute Autographs

JG15	Johnny Gargano	10.00	25.00
JG16	Johnny Gargano	10.00	25.00
JG17	Johnny Gargano	10.00	25.00
JG18	Johnny Gargano	10.00	25.00
JG19	Johnny Gargano	10.00	25.00

2020 Topps WWE NXT Roster

COMPLETE SET (66)		15.00	40.00
RANDOMLY INSERTED INTO PACKS			
NXT1	Adam Cole	.75	2.00
NXT2	Aliyah	.60	1.50
NXT3	Angel Garza	.40	1.00
NXT4	Austin Theory	.50	1.25
NXT5	Bianca Belair	.75	2.00
NXT6	Boa	.30	.75
NXT7	Bobby Fish	.30	.75
NXT8	Bronson Reed	.30	.75
NXT9	Cameron Grimes	.30	.75
NXT10	Candice LeRae	1.00	2.50
NXT11	Chelsea Green	1.50	4.00
NXT12	Dakota Kai	.60	1.50
NXT13	Damian Priest	.30	.75
NXT14	Danny Burch	.40	1.00
NXT15	Dexter Lumis	.30	.75
NXT16	Dominik Dijakovic	.30	.75
NXT17	Fandango	.30	.75
NXT18	Finn Balor	.75	2.00
NXT19	Io Shirai	.50	1.25
NXT20	Isaiah "Swerve" Scott	.40	1.00
NXT21	Jaxson Ryker	.40	1.00
NXT22	Jessamyn Duke	.50	1.25
NXT23	Joaquin Wilde	.30	.75
NXT24	Johnny Gargano	.60	1.50
NXT25	Keith Lee	.30	.75
NXT26	Killian Dain	.40	1.00
NXT27	Kona Reeves	.30	.75
NXT28	Kyle O'Reilly	.40	1.00
NXT29	Kushida	.40	1.00
NXT30	Mansoor	.30	.75
NXT31	Marina Shafir	.50	1.25
NXT32	Matt Riddle	.60	1.50
NXT33	Mia Yim	.60	1.50
NXT34	Oney Lorcan	.40	1.00
NXT35	Pete Dunne	.30	.75
NXT36	Raul Mendoza	.30	.75
NXT37	Rhea Ripley	.75	2.00
NXT38	Roderick Strong	.60	1.50
NXT39	Santana Garrett	.30	.75
NXT40	Shane Thorne	.30	.75
NXT41	Shayna Baszler	1.00	2.50
NXT42	Shotzi Blackheart	1.00	2.50
NXT43	Steve Cutler	.30	.75
NXT44	Tegan Nox	.75	2.00
NXT45	Tommaso Ciampa	.60	1.50
NXT46	Tyler Breeze	.40	1.00
NXT47	Vanessa Borne	.60	1.50
NXT48	Velveteen Dream	.40	1.00
NXT49	Wesley Blake	.40	1.00
NXT50	Xia Li	.60	1.50

NXT51	Alexander Wolfe	.30	.75
NXT52	Fabian Aichner	.30	.75
NXT53	Flash Morgan Webster	.40	1.00
NXT54	Joe Coffey	.30	.75
NXT55	Jordan Devlin	.30	.75
NXT56	Kay Lee Ray	.50	1.25
NXT57	Marcel Barthel	.30	.75
NXT58	Mark Andrews	.30	.75
NXT59	Mark Coffey	.40	1.00
NXT60	Toni Storm	.75	2.00
NXT61	Trent Seven	.30	.75
NXT62	Tyler Bate	.50	1.25
NXT63	WALTER	.60	1.50
NXT64	Wolfgang	.30	.75
NXT65	James Drake	.40	1.00
NXT66	Zack Gibson	.30	.75

2020 Topps WWE NXT Roster Autographs

*BRONZE/99: .5X TO 1.2X BASIC AUTOS
*BLUE/50: .6X TO 1.5X BASIC AUTOS
*SILVER/25: UNPRICED DUE TO SCARCITY
*GOLD/10: UNPRICED DUE TO SCARCITY
*RED/1: UNPRICED DUE TO SCARCITY
STATED ODDS

AAC	Adam Cole	10.00	25.00
AAG	Angel Garza	6.00	15.00
AAL	Aliyah	10.00	25.00
AAR	Arturo Ruas	6.00	15.00
AAT	Austin Theory	12.00	30.00
ABB	Bianca Belair	20.00	50.00
ABF	Bobby Fish	5.00	12.00
ABL	Shotzi Blackheart	60.00	120.00
ABR	Bronson Reed	10.00	25.00
ACG	Cameron Grimes	6.00	15.00
ACL	Candice LeRae	20.00	50.00
ADD	Dominik Dijakovic	5.00	12.00
ADK	Dakota Kai	15.00	40.00
ADL	Dexter Lumis	20.00	50.00
ADP	Damian Priest	6.00	15.00
AFA	Fabian Aichner	5.00	12.00
AFB	Finn Balor	10.00	25.00
AIO	Io Shirai	20.00	50.00
AIS	Isaiah Swerve Scott	5.00	12.00
AJG	Johnny Gargano	8.00	20.00
AJW	Joaquin Wilde	8.00	20.00
AKC	Kayden Carter	10.00	25.00
AKL	Keith Lee	6.00	15.00
AKU	Kushida	10.00	25.00
AMB	Marcel Barthel	5.00	12.00
AMR	Matt Riddle	15.00	40.00
AMY	Mia Yim	8.00	20.00
AOL	Oney Lorcan	5.00	12.00
ARM	Raul Mendoza	6.00	15.00
ARR	Rhea Ripley	30.00	75.00
ARS	Roderick Strong	5.00	12.00
ATN	Tegan Nox	30.00	75.00
ATO	Tommaso Ciampa	6.00	15.00
AVD	Velveteen Dream	5.00	12.00

2011 Topps WWE Power Chipz

COMPLETE SET (74)
UNOPENED BOX (24 PACKS)
UNOPENED PACK (4 CHIPZ)

1 Undertaker
2 Edge
3 John Cena
4 Triple H
5 Rey Mysterio
6 CM Punk
7 Randy Orton
8 The Miz
9 Big Show
10 Kofi Kingston
11 Sheamus
12 Alberto Del Rio
13 Stone Cold Steve Austin
14 Shawn Michaels
15 Christian
16 Kane
17 Jack Swagger
18 Daniel Bryan
19 Eve
20 John Morrison
21 The Great Khali
22 Dolph Ziggler
23 Mark Henry
24 Chavo Guerrero
25 Wade Barrett
26 Natalya
27 Batista
28 Santino Marella
29 Cody Rhodes
30 Ted DiBiase, Jr.
31 Hornswoggle
32 Drew McIntyre
33 Alex Riley
34 William Regal
35 Vladimir Kozlov
36 Primo
37 Ezekiel Jackson
38 R-Truth
39 Beth Phoenix
40 Trish Stratus
41 Goldust
42 David Hart Smith
43 Jerry Lawler
44 Curt Hawkins
45 Tyson Kidd
46 Zack Ryder
47 Melina
48 JTG
49 Evan Bourne
50 Michael McGillicutty
51 Yoshi Tatsu
52 Chris Masters
53 Tyler Reks
54 Skip Sheffield
55 Darren Young
56 Husky Harris
57 Jey Uso
58 Jimmy Uso
59 David Otunga
60 Heath Slater
61 Justin Gabriel
62 Trent Barreta
63 Kaitlyn
64 Gail Kim
65 Alicia Fox
66 Kelly Kelly
67 Layla
68 Brie Bella
69 Nikki Bella
70 Maryse
71 Tamina
72 Rosa Mendes
73 Vickie Guerrero
74 Teddy Long

2011 Topps WWE Power Chipz Finishing Moves

COMPLETE SET (12)
RANDOMLY INSERTED INTO PACKS

F1 John Cena/Attitude Adjustment
F2 Randy Orton/RKO
F3 Undertaker/Last Ride
F4 Edge/Spear
F5 Triple H/Pedigree
F6 Rey Mysterio/619
F7 CM Punk/Go To Sleep
F8 The Miz/Skull-Crushing Finale
F9 Big Show/Choke Slam
F10 Kofi Kingston/Trouble In Paradise
F11 Sheamus/High Cross
F12 Kane/Tombstone Piledriver

2011 Topps WWE Power Chipz Gold

COMPLETE SET (12)
RANDOMLY INSERTED INTO PACKS

G1 Undertaker
G2 Edge
G3 John Cena
G4 Triple H
G5 Rey Mysterio
G6 CM Punk
G7 Randy Orton
G8 The Miz
G9 Big Show
G10 Kofi Kingston
G11 Sheamus
G12 Alberto Del Rio

2011 Topps WWE Power Chipz Legends

COMPLETE SET (24)
RANDOMLY INSERTED INTO PACKS

L1 Booker T
L2 Rowdy Roddy Piper
L3 Jake The Snake Roberts
L4 Mr. Perfect
L5 The British Bulldog
L6 Ted DiBiase The Million Dollar Man
L7 Dusty Rhodes The American Dream
L8 Cowboy Bob Orton
L9 Junkyard Dog
L10 One Man Gang
L11 Papa Shango
L12 Sgt. Slaughter
L13 Hacksaw Jim Duggan
L14 Yokozuna
L15 Vader
L16 Doink The Clown
L17 Ravishing Rick Rude
L18 Jimmy Superfly Snuka
L19 Big Boss Man
L20 Terry Funk
L21 Kamala
L22 Hillbilly Jim
L23 Classy Freddie Blassie
L24 Mean Gene Okerlund

2011 Topps WWE Power Chipz Ruby

COMPLETE SET (12)
RANDOMLY INSERTED INTO PACKS

R1 Santino Marella
R2 Cody Rhodes
R3 Ted DiBiase, Jr.
R4 Hornswoggle
R5 Drew McIntyre
R6 Alex Riley
R7 William Regal
R8 Vladimir Kozlov
R9 Primo
R10 Ezekiel Jackson
R11 R-Truth
R12 Beth Phoenix

2011 Topps WWE Power Chipz Silver

COMPLETE SET (12)
RANDOMLY INSERTED INTO PACKS

S1 Christian
S2 Kane
S3 Jack Swagger
S4 Daniel Bryan
S5 Eve
S6 John Morrison
S7 The Great Khali
S8 Dolph Ziggler
S9 Mark Henry
S10 Chavo Guerrero
S11 Wade Barrett
S12 Natalya

2012 Topps WWE Power Plates

NNO Alberto Del Rio
Destiny
NNO The American Dream Dusty Rhodes
Dream SP
NNO Big Show
Giant
NNO The British Bulldog
Bulldog SP
NNO Christian
Charisma
NNO CM Punk
GTS
NNO Cody Rhodes
Xrhodes
NNO Daniel Bryan
Skills
NNO Evan Bourne
Air
NNO John Cena
Champ
NNO Kane
Big Red
NNO Kevin Nash
Diesel
NNO Kofi Kingston
SOS
NNO Mark Henry
Strongman
NNO Million Dollar Man Ted DiBiase
$$$ SP
NNO The Miz
Awesome
NNO Randy Orton
RKO

NNO Rey Mysterio
619
NNO Rowdy Roddy Piper
Hotrod SP
NNO R-Truth
Truth
NNO Santino Marella
Cobra
NNO Sgt. Slaughter
USA SP
NNO Sheamus
Celtic
NNO Zack Ryder
WWWYKI

2005 Topps WWE Push Pop Italian

1 The Basham Brothers
2 Trish Stratus
3 Big Show
4 Randy Orton
5 John Cena
6 Dawn Marie
7 Edge
8 Akio
9 Dudley Boyz
10 Eugene
11 Funaki
12 Eddie Guerrero
13 The Hurricane
14 Charlie Haas
15 Chris Benoit
16 Hardcore Holly
17 Triple H
18 Jerry "The King" Lawler
19 John Cena
20 Batista
21 Kane
22 Kurt Angle
23 Mark Jindrak
24 Matt Hardy
25 Booker T
26 Maven
27 Gene Snitsky
28 Muhammad Hassan
29 Miss Jackie
30 Shelton Benjamin
31 Victoria
32 Nunzio
33 Orlando Jordan
34 Randy Orton
35 Rey Mysterio
36 Chris Benoit
37 La Resistance
38 Rhyno
39 Chavo
40 Ric Flair
41 The Rock
42 RVD
43 Christian
44 Scotty 2 Hotty
45 Eric Bischoff
46 Spike Dudley
47 Carlito
48 Simon Dean
49 Steven Richards
50 Tajiri
51 Tazz
52 Chris Jericho

53 Tyson Tomko
54 Stone Cold Steve Austin
55 Undertaker
56 Val Venis
57 Luther Reigns
58 William Regal
59 Evolution
60 Kenzo Suzuki
61 Rey Mysterio
62 Eddie Guerrero
63 Undertaker
64 Triple H
65 Batista
66 Heidenreich
67 Ric Flair
68 JBL
69 WWE Logo
70 Lita
71 RAW Logo
72 SmackDown Logo

2019 Topps WWE RAW

COMPLETE SET (90)	10.00	25.00

*BRONZE: .6X TO 1.5X BASIC CARDS
*BLUE/99: .75X TO 2X BASIC CARDS
*SILVER/25: 2X TO 5X BASIC CARDS
*GOLD/10: UNPRICED DUE TO SCARCITY
*BLACK/1: UNPRICED DUE TO SCARCITY
*P.P.BLACK/1: UNPRICED DUE TO SCARCITY
*P.P.CYAN/1: UNPRICED DUE TO SCARCITY
*P.P.MAGENTA/1: UNPRICED DUE TO SCARCITY
*P.P.YELLOW/1: UNPRICED DUE TO SCARCITY

1 Akam	.25	.60
2 Alexa Bliss	1.25	3.00
3 Alicia Fox	.50	1.25
4 Apollo Crews	.30	.75
5 Baron Corbin	.40	1.00
6 Batista	.60	1.50
7 Bayley	.50	1.25
8 Bo Dallas	.30	.75
9 Bobby Lashley	.50	1.25
10 Bobby Roode	.50	1.25
11 Booker T	.60	1.50
12 Braun Strowman	.60	1.50
13 Bray Wyatt	.60	1.50
14 Brie Bella	.60	1.50
15 Brock Lesnar	1.00	2.50
16 Chad Gable	.25	.60
17 Charly Caruso	.40	1.00
18 Corey Graves	.30	.75
19 Curt Hawkins	.25	.60
20 Curtis Axel	.30	.75
21 Dana Brooke	.50	1.25
22 Dash Wilder	.25	.60
23 David Otunga	.25	.60
24 Dean Ambrose	.60	1.50
25 Dolph Ziggler	.50	1.25
26 Drake Maverick	.25	.60
27 Drew McIntyre	.30	.75
28 Elias	.50	1.25
29 Ember Moon	.60	1.50
30 Fandango	.25	.60
31 Finn Balor	.60	1.50
32 Gran Metalik	.25	.60
33 Heath Slater	.25	.60
34 Jason Jordan	.30	.75
35 Jinder Mahal	.50	1.25
36 Jonathan Coachman	.25	.60

37 John Cena	1.00	2.50
38 JoJo	.40	1.00
39 Kalisto	.25	.60
40 Kane	.40	1.00
41 Kayla Braxton	.40	1.00
42 Kevin Owens	.60	1.50
43 Konnor	.25	.60
44 Kurt Angle	.50	1.25
45 Lince Dorado	.25	.60
46 Lio Rush	.30	.75
47 Liv Morgan	.75	2.00
48 Michael Cole	.25	.60
49 Mickie James	.60	1.50
50 Mike Rome	.30	.75
51 Mojo Rawley	.30	.75
52 Natalya	.50	1.25
53 Nia Jax	.50	1.25
54 Nikki Bella	.60	1.50
55 No Way Jose	.30	.75
56 Paul Heyman	.30	.75
57 Renee Young	.40	1.00
58 Rezar	.25	.60
59 Rhyno	.25	.60
60 Roman Reigns	.60	1.50
61 Ronda Rousey	1.25	3.00
62 Ruby Riott	.50	1.25
63 Sami Zayn	.50	1.25
64 Samir Singh	.25	.60
65 Sarah Logan	.30	.75
66 Sasha Banks	1.00	2.50
67 Scott Dawson	.25	.60
68 Seth Rollins	.60	1.50
69 Stephanie McMahon	.60	1.50
70 Sunil Singh	.25	.60
71 Titus O'Neil	.30	.75
72 Tyler Breeze	.30	.75
73 Viktor	.25	.60
74 Zack Ryder	.30	.75
75 Akira Tozawa	.25	.60
76 Ariya Daivari	.25	.60
77 Buddy Murphy	.30	.75
78 Cedric Alexander	.25	.60
79 Drew Gulak	.25	.60
80 Gentleman Jack Gallagher	.30	.75
81 Hideo Itami	.25	.60
82 Maria Kanellis	.60	1.50
83 Mark Andrews	.25	.60
84 Mike Kanellis	.25	.60
85 Nigel McGuinness	.25	.60
86 Noam Dar	.25	.60
87 The Brian Kendrick	.40	1.00
88 TJP	.40	1.00
89 Tony Nese	.25	.60
90 Vic Joseph	.25	.60

2019 Topps WWE RAW Autographed Commemorative Intercontinental Championship Relics

STATED PRINT RUN 10 SER.#'d SETS

ICRAHH Triple H
ICRASM Shawn Michaels

2019 Topps WWE RAW Autographed Commemorative RAW Championship Relics

STATED PRINT RUN 10 SER.#'d SETS
UNPRICED DUE TO SCARCITY

RACAB Alexa Bliss
RACBL Bayley
RACBS Braun Strowman
RACCF Charlotte Flair
RACDA Dean Ambrose
RACFB Finn Balor
RACKO Kevin Owens
RACRRR Ronda Rousey
RACSB Sasha Banks
RACSR Seth Rollins
RACTM The Miz

2019 Topps WWE RAW Autographed Mat Relics

STATED PRINT RUN 10 SER.#'d SETS
UNPRICED DUE TO SCARCITY

DMARAB Aleister Black
DMARAJ AJ Styles
DMARAK Asuka
DMARAS Shayna Baszler
DMARBL Bobby Lashley
DMARBR Bobby Roode
DMARBS Braun Strowman
DMARCF Charlotte Flair
DMAREM Ember Moon
DMARFB Finn Balor
DMARJG Johnny Gargano
DMARJN Natalya
DMARKK Kofi Kingston
DMARKO Kevin Owens
DMARKR Kyle O'Reilly
DMARLK Becky Lynch
DMARMB Alexa Bliss
DMARNC Nikki Cross
DMARNM Naomi
DMARRC Ricochet
DMARRD Rusev
DMARRS Roderick Strong
DMARSB Sasha Banks
DMARSJ Samoa Joe
DMARSN Shinsuke Nakamura
DMARSR Seth Rollins
DMARSZ Sami Zayn
DMARTC Tomasso Ciampa
DMARTM The Miz
DMARVD Velveteen Dream
DMARRRR Ronda Rousey

2019 Topps WWE RAW Autographed Shirt Relics

STATED PRINT RUN 10 SER.#'d SETS
UNPRICED DUE TO SCARCITY

SARAB Alexa Bliss
SARDA Dean Ambrose
SARFB Finn Balor
SARKO Kevin Owens
SARRY Renee Young
SARSR Seth Rollins
SARWJ No Way Jose

2019 Topps WWE RAW Autographed Women's Revolution Relics

STATED PRINT RUN 10 SER.#'d SETS
UNPRICED DUE TO SCARCITY

DRACAB Alexa Bliss
DRACSB Sasha Banks
DRACRRR Ronda Rousey

2019 Topps WWE RAW Autographs

*BLUE/50: .5X TO 1.2X BASIC AUTOS
*SILVER/25: .6X TO 1.5X BASIC AUTOS
*GOLD/10: UNPRICED DUE TO SCARCITY
*BLACK/1: UNPRICED DUE TO SCARCITY
STATED PRINT RUN 99 SER.#'d SETS

AAB	Alexa Bliss	25.00	60.00
AAC	Apollo Crews		
ABC	Baron Corbin	5.00	12.00
ABL	Bobby Lashley	5.00	12.00
ABR	Bobby Roode	4.00	10.00
ABS	Braun Strowman/94	5.00	12.00
ABT	Booker T	5.00	12.00
ACA	Cedric Alexander	4.00	10.00
ACC	Charly Caruso	6.00	15.00
ACG	Chad Gable	3.00	8.00
ADA	Dean Ambrose	6.00	15.00
ADB	Dana.Brooke	6.00	15.00
ADM	Drew McIntyre	5.00	12.00
AEM	Ember Moon/63	8.00	20.00
AFB	Finn Balor/88	12.00	30.00
AGR	Corey Graves	6.00	15.00
AHO	Hideo Itami	3.00	8.00
AJG	Gentleman Jack Gallagher	12.00	30.00
AJJ	Jason Jordan/77	5.00	12.00
AJN	Natalya		
AKA	Kurt Angle	8.00	20.00
AKT	Kalisto	4.00	10.00
ALD	Lince Dorado/98	10.00	25.00
ALR	Lio Rush	6.00	15.00
ARY	Renee Young	6.00	12.00
ASL	Sarah Logan	6.00	15.00
ASR	Seth Rollins	8.00	20.00
ATB	Tyler Breeze	4.00	10.00
ATN	Titus O'Neil	4.00	10.00

2019 Topps WWE RAW Commemorative Intercontinental Championship Relics

RANDOMLY INSERTED INTO PACKS

ICRED	Edge		
ICRHH	Triple H		
ICRRM	The Rock		
ICRRR	Razor Ramon		
ICRSM	Shawn Michaels		

2019 Topps WWE RAW Commemorative RAW Championship Relics

*BRONZE/99: SAME VALUE AS BASIC
*BLUE/50: .5X TO 1.2X BASIC MEM
*SILVER/25: .6X TO 1.5X BASIC MEM
*GOLD/10: UNPRICED DUE TO SCARCITY
*BLACK/1: UNPRICED DUE TO SCARCITY
RANDOMLY INSERTED INTO PACKS

RCAB	Alexa Bliss	10.00	25.00
RCBC	Karl Anderson/Luke Gallows	2.00	5.00
RCBD	Roman Reigns	5.00	12.00
RCBL	Bayley	5.00	12.00
RCBS	Braun Strowman	2.50	6.00
RCBT	Curtis Axel/Bo Dallas	2.50	6.00
RCCF	Charlotte Flair	4.00	10.00
RCDA	Dean Ambrose	5.00	12.00
RCDZ	Dolph Ziggler	2.50	6.00
RCFB	Finn Balor	3.00	8.00
RCGB	Goldberg	6.00	15.00
RCKO	Kevin Owens	2.00	5.00

RCNJ	Nia Jax	2.00	5.00
RCRR	Roman Reigns	5.00	12.00
RCSB	Sasha Banks	6.00	15.00
RCSD	Seth Rollins/Dean Ambrose	3.00	8.00
RCSR	Seth Rollins	4.00	10.00
RCTB	Cesaro/Sheamus	2.00	5.00
RCTM	The Miz	2.00	5.00
RCZM	Drew McIntyre/Dolph Ziggler	2.50	6.00
RCRRR	Ronda Rousey	12.00	30.00

2019 Topps WWE RAW Hometown Heroes

COMPLETE SET (48)		12.00	30.00

RANDOMLY INSERTED INTO PACKS

HH1	Alexa Bliss	2.00	5.00
HH2	Apollo Crews	.50	1.25
HH3	Baron Corbin	.60	1.50
HH4	Bayley	.75	2.00
HH5	Big Show	.60	1.50
HH6	Bo Dallas	.50	1.25
HH7	Bobby Lashley	.75	2.00
HH8	Bobby Roode	.75	2.00
HH9	Booker T	1.00	2.50
HH10	Curtis Axel	.50	1.25
HH11	Dana Brooke	.75	2.00
HH12	Dean Ambrose	1.00	2.50
HH13	Dolph Ziggler	.75	2.00
HH14	Drew McIntyre	.50	1.25
HH15	Elias	.75	2.00
HH16	Ember Moon	1.00	2.50
HH17	Finn Balor	1.00	2.50
HH18	Heath Slater	.40	1.00
HH19	Jason Jordan	.50	1.25
HH20	Jinder Mahal	.75	2.00
HH21	John Cena	1.50	4.00
HH22	Kevin Owens	1.00	2.50
HH23	Liv Morgan	1.25	3.00
HH24	Mickie James	1.00	2.50
HH25	Mojo Rawley	.50	1.25
HH26	Natalya	.75	2.00
HH27	Nia Jax	.75	2.00
HH28	No Way Jose	.50	1.25
HH29	Lince Dorado	.40	1.00
HH30	Lio Rush	.50	1.25
HH31	Rhyno	.40	1.00
HH32	Roman Reigns	1.00	2.50
HH33	Ronda Rousey	2.00	5.00
HH34	Ruby Riott	.75	2.00
HH35	Sarah Logan	.50	1.25
HH36	Sasha Banks	1.50	4.00
HH37	Seth Rollins	1.00	2.50
HH38	Titus O'Neil	.50	1.25
HH39	Zack Ryder	.50	1.25
HH40	Buddy Murphy	.50	1.25
HH41	Cedric Alexander	.40	1.00
HH42	Drew Gulak	.40	1.00
HH43	Gentleman Jack Gallagher	.50	1.25
HH44	Gran Metalik	.40	1.00
HH45	Hideo Itami	.40	1.00
HH46	Kalisto	.40	1.00
HH47	Mark Andrews	.40	1.00
HH48	TJP	.60	1.50

2019 Topps WWE RAW Image Variations

RANDOMLY INSERTED INTO PACKS

IVAB	Alexa Bliss	30.00	75.00

IVAC	Apollo Crews	2.50	6.00
IVBL	Bobby Lashley	12.00	30.00
IVBR	Bobby Roode		
IVBY	Bayley	8.00	20.00
IVDG	Drew Gulak		
IVDM	Drew McIntyre	3.00	8.00
IVDZ	Dolph Ziggler		
IVEM	Ember Moon	4.00	10.00
IVFB	The Demon Finn Balor	15.00	40.00
IVJN	Natalya	5.00	12.00
IVKO	Kevin Owens	4.00	10.00
IVLL	Kalisto	2.50	6.00
IVLR	Lio Rush	3.00	8.00
IVMK	Mike Kanellis	4.00	10.00
IVMR	Mojo Rawley	4.00	10.00
IVNJ	Nia Jax	4.00	10.00
IVRR	Roman Reigns	6.00	15.00
IVRS	Drake Maverick	6.00	15.00
IVSB	Sasha Banks	12.00	30.00
IVSR	Seth Rollins	5.00	12.00
IVSZ	Sami Zayn	3.00	8.00
IVTJ	TJP	5.00	12.00
IVZR	Zack Ryder	8.00	20.00

2019 Topps WWE RAW Intercontinental Champions Autographs

*GOLD/10: UNPRICED DUE TO SCARCITY
STATED PRINT RUN 25 SER.#'d SETS

ICAHH	Triple H	100.00	200.00
ICASM	Shawn Michaels	50.00	100.00

2019 Topps WWE RAW Kiss

*SILVER/25: .6X TO 1.5X BASIC KISS
*GOLD/10: UNPRICED DUE TO SCARCITY
*BLACK/1: UNPRICED DUE TO SCARCITY
STATED PRINT RUN 50 SER.#'d SETS

KCAF	Alicia Fox	15.00	40.00
KCEM	Ember Moon	15.00	40.00
KCNJ	Nia Jax	12.00	30.00

2019 Topps WWE RAW Kiss Autographs

*GOLD/10: UNPRICED DUE TO SCARCITY
*BLACK/1: UNPRICED DUE TO SCARCITY
STATED PRINT RUN 25 SER.#'d SETS

KARAF	Alicia Fox	30.00	75.00
KARMJ	Mickie James	60.00	120.00
KARNJ	Nia Jax	20.00	50.00

2019 Topps WWE RAW Legends of RAW

COMPLETE SET (20)		6.00	15.00

RANDOMLY INSERTED INTO PACKS

LR1	Batista	.60	1.50
LR2	Bret Hitman Hart	.60	1.50
LR3	Edge	.60	1.50
LR4	Faarooq	.40	1.00
LR5	Goldberg	.75	2.00
LR6	Jerry The King Lawler	.50	1.25
LR7	Ken Shamrock	.40	1.00
LR8	Lita	.60	1.50
LR9	Mr. Perfect	.40	1.00
LR10	Mark Henry	.30	.75
LR11	Mankind	.50	1.25
LR12	Sycho Sid	.25	.60
LR13	Rikishi	.25	.60

LR14	Ric Flair	.75	2.00
LR15	Road Dogg	.25	.60
LR16	Shawn Michaels	.60	1.50
LR17	Stone Cold Steve Austin	1.25	3.00
LR18	Trish Stratus	1.25	3.00
LR19	Vader	.30	.75
LR20	X-Pac	.25	.60

2019 Topps WWE RAW Mat Relics

SEMISTARS		2.00	5.00
UNLISTED STARS		2.50	6.00

*BRONZE/99: .5X TO 1.2X BASIC MEM
*BLUE/50: .6X TO 1.5X BASIC MEM
*SILVER/25: .75X TO 2X BASIC MEM
*GOLD/10: UNPRICED DUE TO SCARCITY
*BLACK/1: UNPRICED DUE TO SCARCITY
RANDOMLY INSERTED INTO PACKS

DMRAB	Aleister Black	1.50	4.00
DMRAJ	AJ Styles	3.00	8.00
DMRAK	Asuka	6.00	15.00
DMRAS	Shayna Baszler	4.00	10.00
DMRBL	Bobby Lashley	1.50	4.00
DMRBR	Bobby Roode	2.50	6.00
DMRBS	Braun Strowman	2.00	5.00
DMRCF	Charlotte Flair	4.00	10.00
DMRCM	Carmella	5.00	12.00
DMRDB	Daniel Bryan	2.50	6.00
DMRDN	Danny Burch	2.50	6.00
DMREM	Ember Moon	3.00	8.00
DMRFB	Finn Balor	4.00	10.00
DMRJG	Johnny Gargano	2.00	5.00
DMRJN	Natalya	3.00	8.00
DMRKK	Kofi Kingston	3.00	8.00
DMRKO	Kevin Owens	2.50	6.00
DMRKR	Kyle O'Reilly	3.00	8.00
DMRLD	Lana	2.50	6.00
DMRLK	Becky Lynch	6.00	15.00
DMRLS	Lars Sullivan	1.50	4.00
DMRMB	Alexa Bliss	12.00	30.00
DMRNC	Nikki Cross	1.50	4.00
DMRNJ	Nia Jax	2.00	5.00
DMRNM	Naomi	2.50	6.00
DMROL	Oney Lorcan	2.00	5.00
DMRRC	Ricochet	3.00	8.00
DMRRD	Rusev	2.50	6.00
DMRRR	Roman Reigns	4.00	10.00
DMRRS	Roderick Strong	2.00	5.00
DMRSB	Sasha Banks	8.00	20.00
DMRSJ	Samoa Joe	2.00	5.00
DMRSN	Shinsuke Nakamura	3.00	8.00
DMRSR	Seth Rollins	4.00	10.00
DMRSZ	Sami Zayn	2.00	5.00
DMRTC	Tommaso Ciampa	2.00	5.00
DMRTM	The Miz	2.50	6.00
DMRVD	Velveteen Dream	2.00	5.00
DMRWE	Elias	2.00	5.00
DMRRRR	Ronda Rousey	10.00	25.00

2019 Topps WWE RAW Shirt Relics

*BRONZE/99: .5X TO 1.2X BASIC MEM
*BLUE/50: .6X TO 1.5X BASIC MEM
*SILVER/25: .75X TO 2X BASIC MEM
*GOLD/10: UNPRICED DUE TO SCARCITY
*BLACK/1: UNPRICED DUE TO SCARCITY
STATED PRINT RUN 199 SER.#'d SETS

SRAB	Alexa Bliss	15.00	40.00
SRDA	Dean Ambrose	6.00	15.00

SREL	Elias	4.00	10.00
SRFB	Finn Balor	8.00	20.00
SRKO	Kevin Owens	3.00	8.00
SRRR	Roman Reigns	5.00	15.00
SRSR	Seth Rollins	6.00	15.00
SRWJ	No Way Jose	3.00	6.00

2019 Topps WWE RAW Triple Autographs

*BLACK/1: UNPRICED DUE TO SCARCITY
STATED PRINT RUN 10 SER.#'d SETS
UNPRICED DUE TO SCARCITY

TAAB	Bliss/Fox/James	
TARS	Morgan/Riott/Logan	

2019 Topps WWE RAW Women's Revolution Autographs

*GOLD/10: UNPRICED DUE TO SCARCITY
*BLACK/1: UNPRICED DUE TO SCARCITY
STATED ODDS

WABL	Bayley	20.00	50.00
WARR	Ronda Rousey		
WASB	Sasha Banks	30.00	75.00

2019 Topps WWE RAW Women's Revolution Relics

STATED ODDS

DRCAB	Alexa Bliss
DRCNJ	Nia Jax
DRCSB	Sasha Banks

2009 Topps WWE Rivals Stickers

1	Emblem WWE	.12	.30
2	WWE 1	.12	.30
3	WWE 2		.30
4	John Cena	.75	2.00
5	John Cena	.75	2.00
6	John Cena	.75	2.00
7	John Cena	.75	2.00
8	John Cena	.75	2.00
9	John Cena	.75	2.00
10	John Cena	.75	2.00
11	John Cena	.75	2.00
12	John Cena	.75	2.00
13	John Cena	.75	2.00
14	Edge	.50	1.25
15	Edge	.50	1.25
16	Edge	.50	1.25
17	Edge	.50	1.25
18	Edge	.50	1.25
19	Edge	.50	1.25
20	Edge	.50	1.25
21	Edge	.50	1.25
22	Edge	.50	1.25
23	Edge	.50	1.25
24	Kane	.50	1.25
25	Kane	.50	1.25
26	Kane	.50	1.25
27	Kane	.50	1.25
28	Kane	.50	1.25
29	The Miz	.20	.50
30	The Miz	.20	.50
31	The Miz	.20	.50
32	The Miz	.20	.50
33	The Miz	.20	.50
34	Mr. Kennedy	.30	.75
35	Mr. Kennedy	.30	.75
36	Mr. Kennedy	.30	.75
37	Mr. Kennedy	.30	.75
38	Mr. Kennedy	.30	.75
39	William Regal	.30	.75
40	William Regal	.30	.75
41	William Regal	.30	.75
42	William Regal	.30	.75
43	William Regal	.30	.75
44	Chavo Guerrero	.20	.50
45	Chavo Guerrero	.20	.50
46	Chavo Guerrero	.20	.50
47	Chavo Guerrero	.20	.50
48	Chavo Guerrero	.20	.50
49	Chavo Guerrero	.20	.50
50	Chavo Guerrero	.20	.50
51	Chavo Guerrero	.20	.50
52	Chavo Guerrero	.20	.50
53	Chavo Guerrero	.20	.50
54	CM Punk	.20	.50
55	CM Punk	.20	.50
56	CM Punk	.20	.50
57	CM Punk	.20	.50
58	CM Punk	.20	.50
59	CM Punk	.20	.50
60	CM Punk	.20	.50
61	CM Punk	.20	.50
62	CM Punk	.20	.50
63	CM Punk	.20	.50
64	The Great Khali	.12	.30
65	The Great Khali	.12	.30
66	The Great Khali	.12	.30
67	The Great Khali	.12	.30
68	The Great Khali	.12	.30
69	Finlay & Hornswoggle	.20	.50
70	Finlay & Hornswoggle	.20	.50
71	Finlay & Hornswoggle	.20	.50
72	Finlay & Hornswoggle	.20	.50
73	Finlay & Hornswoggle	.20	.50
74	Kofi Kingston	.12	.30
75	Kofi Kingston	.12	.30
76	Kofi Kingston	.12	.30
77	Kofi Kingston	.12	.30
78	Kofi Kingston	.12	.30
79	Carlito	.30	.75
80	Carlito	.30	.75
81	Carlito	.30	.75
82	Carlito	.30	.75
83	Carlito	.30	.75
84	Jeff Hardy	.50	1.25
85	Jeff Hardy	.50	1.25
86	Jeff Hardy	.50	1.25
87	Jeff Hardy	.50	1.25
88	Jeff Hardy	.50	1.25
89	Jeff Hardy	.50	1.25
90	Jeff Hardy	.50	1.25
91	Jeff Hardy	.50	1.25
92	Jeff Hardy	.50	1.25
93	Jeff Hardy	.50	1.25
94	John Morrison	.20	.50
95	John Morrison	.20	.50
96	John Morrison	.20	.50
97	John Morrison	.20	.50
98	John Morrison	.20	.50
99	John Morrison	.20	.50
100	John Morrison	.20	.50
101	John Morrison	.20	.50
102	John Morrison	.20	.50
103	John Morrison	.20	.50
104	Shawn Michaels	.75	2.00
105	Shawn Michaels	.75	2.00
106	Shawn Michaels	.75	2.00
107	Shawn Michaels	.75	2.00
108	Shawn Michaels	.75	2.00
109	Vladimir Kozlov	.20	.50
110	Vladimir Kozlov	.20	.50
111	Vladimir Kozlov	.20	.50
112	Vladimir Kozlov	.20	.50
113	Vladimir Kozlov	.20	.50
114	Big Show	.30	.75
115	Big Show	.30	.75
116	Big Show	.30	.75
117	Big Show	.30	.75
118	Big Show	.30	.75
119	JBL	.20	.50
120	JBL	.20	.50
121	JBL	.20	.50
122	JBL	.20	.50
123	JBL	.20	.50
124	Beth Phoenix	.60	1.50
125	Beth Phoenix	.60	1.50
126	Maria	.50	1.25
127	Maria	.50	1.25
128	Candice	.50	1.25
129	Melina	.60	1.50
130	Mickie James	.60	1.50
131	Candice	.60	1.50
132	Melina	.50	1.25
133	Mickie James	.60	1.50
134	Matt Hardy	.50	1.25
135	Matt Hardy	.50	1.25
136	Matt Hardy	.50	1.25
137	Matt Hardy	.50	1.25
138	Matt Hardy	.50	1.25
139	Matt Hardy	.50	1.25
140	Matt Hardy	.50	1.25
141	Matt Hardy	.50	1.25
142	Matt Hardy	.50	1.25
143	Matt Hardy	.50	1.25
144	MVP	.20	.50
145	MVP	.20	.50
146	MVP	.20	.50
147	MVP	.20	.50
148	MVP	.20	.50
149	Chris Jericho	.30	.75
150	Chris Jericho	.30	.75
151	Chris Jericho	.30	.75
152	Chris Jericho	.30	.75
153	Chris Jericho	.30	.75
154	Cody Rhodes & Ted Dibiase	.20	.50
155	Cody Rhodes & Ted Dibiase	.20	.50
156	Cody Rhodes & Ted Dibiase	.20	.50
157	Cody Rhodes & Ted Dibiase	.20	.50
158	Cody Rhodes & Ted Dibiase	.20	.50
159	Cryme Tyme	.12	.30
160	Cryme Tyme	.12	.30
161	Cryme Tyme	.12	.30
162	Cryme Tyme	.12	.30
163	Cryme Tyme	.12	.30
164	Triple H	.75	2.00
165	Triple H	.75	2.00
166	Triple H	.75	2.00
167	Triple H	.75	2.00
168	Triple H	.75	2.00
169	Triple H	.75	2.00
170	Triple H	.75	2.00
171	Triple H	.75	2.00
172	Triple H	.75	2.00
173	Triple H	.75	2.00
174	Rey Mysterio	.30	.75
175	Rey Mysterio	.30	.75
176	Rey Mysterio	.30	.75
177	Rey Mysterio	.30	.75
178	Rey Mysterio	.30	.75
179	Rey Mysterio	.30	.75
180	Rey Mysterio	.30	.75
181	Rey Mysterio	.30	.75
182	Rey Mysterio	.30	.75
183	Rey Mysterio	.30	.75
184	Shelton Benjamin	.12	.30
185	Shelton Benjamin	.12	.30
186	Shelton Benjamin	.12	.30
187	Shelton Benjamin	.12	.30
188	Shelton Benjamin	.12	.30
189	Tommy Dreamer	.12	.30
190	Tommy Dreamer	.12	.30
191	Tommy Dreamer	.12	.30
192	Tommy Dreamer	.12	.30
193	Tommy Dreamer	.12	.30
194	Santino Marella	.12	.30
195	Santino Marella	.12	.30
196	Santino Marella	.12	.30
197	Santino Marella	.12	.30
198	Santino Marella	.12	.30
199	Umaga	.20	.50
200	Umaga	.20	.50
201	Umaga	.20	.50
202	Umaga	.20	.50
203	Umaga	.20	.50
204	Randy Orton	.30	.75
205	Randy Orton	.30	.75
206	Randy Orton	.30	.75
207	Randy Orton	.30	.75
208	Randy Orton	.30	.75
209	Randy Orton	.30	.75
210	Randy Orton	.30	.75
211	Randy Orton	.30	.75
212	Randy Orton	.30	.75
213	Randy Orton	.30	.75
214	Undertaker	.60	1.50
215	Undertaker	.60	1.50
216	Undertaker	.60	1.50
217	Undertaker	.60	1.50
218	Undertaker	.60	1.50
219	Undertaker	.60	1.50
220	Undertaker	.60	1.50
221	Undertaker	.60	1.50
222	Undertaker	.60	1.50
223	Undertaker	.60	1.50
224	Mark Henry	.20	.50
225	Mark Henry	.20	.50
226	Mark Henry	.20	.50
227	Mark Henry	.20	.50
228	Mark Henry	.20	.50
229	Batista	.50	1.25
230	Batista	.50	1.25
231	Batista	.50	1.25
232	Batista	.50	1.25
233	Batista	.50	1.25
234	Jack Swagger	.12	.30
235	Jack Swagger	.12	.30
236	Jack Swagger	.12	.30
P1	RAW	.12	.30
P2	John Cena	.75	2.00
P3	Randy Orton	.30	.75

2014 Topps WWE Road to WrestleMania (promos continued)

P4	JBL	.20	.50
P5	Rey Mysterio	.30	.75
P6	ECW	.12	.30
P7	John Morrison	.20	.50
P8	Mark Henry	.20	.50
P9	Chavo Guerrero	.20	.50
P10	SMACK DOWN	.12	.30
P11	Edge	.50	1.25
P12	Triple H	.75	2.00
P13	Jeff Hardy	.50	1.25
P14	Vladimir Kozlov	.20	.50

2014 Topps WWE Road to WrestleMania

COMPLETE SET (110)		12.00	30.00
UNOPENED BOX (24 PACKS)			
UNOPENED PACK (7 CARDS)			
*BRONZE: .6X TO 1.5X BASIC CARDS			
*BLUE: .75X TO 2X BASIC CARDS			
*PURPLE: .75X TO 2X BASIC CARDS			
*BLACK: 2.5X TO 6X BASIC CARDS			
*GOLD/10: UNPRICED DUE TO SCARCITY			
*P.P.BLACK/1: UNPRICED DUE TO SCARCITY			
*P.P.CYAN/1: UNPRICED DUE TO SCARCITY			
*P.P.MAGENTA/1: UNPRICED DUE TO SCARCITY			
*P.P.YELLOW/1: UNPRICED DUE TO SCARCITY			

1	Wade Barrett	.15	.40
2	Dolph Ziggler	.25	.60
3	Ryback	.15	.40
4	Kofi Kingston	.15	.40
5	Undertaker	.60	1.50
6	AJ Lee	.75	2.00
7	Brock Lesnar	.60	1.50
8	Mark Henry	.15	.40
9	Dean Ambrose	.60	1.50
10	The Shield	.75	2.00
11	Brock Lesnar	.60	1.50
12	Curtis Axel	.15	.40
13	Team Hell No	.50	1.25
14	Curtis Axel	.15	.40
15	AJ Lee	.75	2.00
16	Alberto Del Rio	.40	1.00
17	John Cena	.75	2.00
18	Mark Henry	.15	.40
19	Brad Maddox	.15	.40
20	Wyatt Family	.60	1.50
21	Damien Sandow	.25	.60
22	John Cena	.75	2.00
23	Randy Orton	.60	1.50
24	AJ Lee	.75	2.00
25	Rob Van Dam	.40	1.00
26	Vickie Guerrero	.15	.40
27	Eva Marie and Jojo	.15	.40
28	Cody Rhodes	.15	.40
29	Daniel Bryan	.75	2.00
30	Alberto Del Rio	.40	1.00
31	Bray Wyatt	.75	2.00
32	Cody Rhodes	.15	.40
33	Daniel Bryan	.75	2.00
34	Randy Orton	.60	1.50
35	Daniel Bryan	.75	2.00
36	Randy Orton	.60	1.50
37	Randy Orton	.60	1.50
38	Edge	.60	1.50
39	Randy Orton	.60	1.50
40	The Miz	.25	.60
41	Natalya & Tyson Kidd	.75	2.00
42	Daniel Bryan	.75	2.00
43	Triple H	.60	1.50
44	Daniel Bryan	.75	2.00
45	The Rhodes Brothers	.25	.60
46	Los Matadores	.15	.40
47	The Rhodes Brothers	.25	.60
48	Big Show	.40	1.00
49	The Rhodes Brothers	.25	.60
50	The Rhodes Brothers	.25	.60
51	John Cena	.75	2.00
52	Randy Orton	.60	1.50
53	John Cena	.75	2.00
54	The Authority	.25	.60
55	Big E	.15	.40
56	Xavier Woods	.15	.40
57	Rey Mysterio	.40	1.00
58	The Shield	.75	2.00
59	Team Total Divas	1.25	3.00
60	Titus O'Neil	.15	.40
61	Sin Cara	.15	.40
62	Triple H	.60	1.50
63	Daniel Bryan	.75	2.00
64	Randy Orton	.60	1.50
65	Brodus Clay	.15	.40
66	The Total Divas	1.25	3.00
67	Brock Lesnar	.60	1.50
68	Jake The Snake Roberts	.40	1.00
69	Daniel Bryan	.75	2.00
70	Batista	.60	1.50
71	New Age Outlaws	.25	.60
72	Rusev	.40	1.00
73	Kevin Nash	.40	1.00
74	Sheamus	.40	1.00
75	Batista	.40	1.00
76	Titus O'Neil	.15	.40
77	Christian	.25	.60
78	Emma	.40	1.00
79	The Wyatt Family	.60	1.50
80	Randy Orton	.60	1.50
81	Hulk Hogan	.75	2.00
82	Undertaker	.60	1.50
83	Lana	.60	1.50
84	The Usos	.25	.60
85	Big Show	.40	1.00
86	Hulk Hogan	.75	2.00
87	Daniel Bryan	.75	2.00
88	The Shield	.75	2.00
89	Kane	.40	1.00
90	The Wyatt Family	.60	1.50
91	Undertaker	.60	1.50
92	Brock Lesnar	.60	1.50
93	The Wyatt Family	.60	1.50
94	Rowdy Roddy Piper	.40	1.00
95	Jake The Snake Roberts	.40	1.00
96	Kane	.40	1.00
97	Razor Ramon	.40	1.00
98	Ultimate Warrior	.40	1.00
99	The Usos	.25	.60
100	The Real Americans	.25	.60
101	Triple H	.60	1.50
102	Daniel Bryan	.75	2.00
103	The Shield	.75	2.00
104	Kofi Kingston	.15	.40
105	Cesaro	.25	.60
106	John Cena	.75	2.00
107	Brock Lesnar	.60	1.50
108	AJ Lee	.75	2.00
109	Daniel Bryan	.75	2.00
110	Daniel Bryan	.75	2.00

2014 Topps WWE Road to WrestleMania 30 Years of WrestleMania

COMPLETE SET (60)		12.00	30.00
*P.P.BLACK/1: UNPRICED DUE TO SCARCITY			
*P.P.CYAN/1: UNPRICED DUE TO SCARCITY			
*P.P.MAGENTA/1: UNPRICED DUE TO SCARCITY			
*P.P.YELLOW/1: UNPRICED DUE TO SCARCITY			
STATED ODDS 2:1			

1	The Foreign Legion	.20	.50
2	Hulk Hogan & Mr. T	1.25	3.00
3	The British Bulldogs	.20	.50
4	Hulk Hogan/King Kong Bundy	1.25	3.00
5	Ricky "The Dragon" Steamboat	.20	.50
6	Hulk Hogan vs. Andre	1.25	3.00
7	Hulk Hogan vs. Andre	1.25	3.00
8	Macho Man Randy Savage	.20	.50
9	Rick Rude	.20	.50
10	Hulk Hogan	1.25	3.00
11	Million Dollar Man Ted DiBiase	.20	.50
12	Ultimate Warrior	1.50	4.00
13	Ultimate Warrior	.60	1.50
14	Hulk Hogan	1.25	3.00
15	Macho Man Randy Savage	.75	2.00
16	Hulk Hogan	1.25	3.00
17	Yokozuna	.20	.50
18	Hulk Hogan	1.25	3.00
19	Yokozuna	.20	.50
20	Bret "Hit Man" Hart	.20	.50
21	Yokozuna & Owen Hart	.20	.50
22	Diesel	.20	.50
23	Ultimate Warrior	.60	1.50
24	Shawn Michaels	.60	1.50
25	British Bulldog & Owen Hart	.40	1.00
26	Bret "Hit Man" Hart	1.00	2.50
27	Triple H	.75	2.00
28	Stone Cold Steve Austin	1.25	3.00
29	Road Dogg	.20	.50
30	Stone Cold Steve Austin	2.00	5.00
31	Edge & Christian	.60	1.50
32	Triple H	.75	2.00
33	Edge & Christian	.60	1.50
34	Stone Cold Steve Austin	1.00	2.50
35	The Rock	2.00	5.00
36	Triple H	.75	2.00
37	Triple H	.75	2.00
38	Brock Lesnar	.75	2.00
39	Eddie Guerrero	.20	.50
40	Triple Threat Match	1.25	3.00
41	John Cena	1.00	2.50
42	Batista	.20	.50
43	Rey Mysterio	.20	.50
44	John Cena	1.25	3.00
45	Vince McMahon	.20	.50
46	John Cena	1.25	3.00
47	Shawn Michaels Retires Ric Flair	.60	1.50
48	Randy Orton	1.25	3.00
49	John Cena	1.25	3.00
50	Triple H	.75	2.00
51	Chris Jericho	.60	1.50
52	John Cena	1.25	3.00
53	Edge	.60	1.50
54	The Miz	1.25	3.00
55	CM Punk	.50	1.25
56	The Rock	1.50	4.00
57	Triple H	1.00	2.50
58	John Cena	1.50	4.00
59	Daniel Bryan	1.25	3.00
60	Daniel Bryan	1.25	3.00

2014 Topps WWE Road to WrestleMania Autographed WrestleMania 30 Mat Relics

RANDOMLY INSERTED INTO PACKS

NNO	Bray Wyatt	40.00	100.00
NNO	Cameron	12.00	30.00
NNO	Cesaro	15.00	40.00
NNO	Eve	20.00	50.00
NNO	Hulk Hogan	150.00	300.00
NNO	Jimmy Hart	20.00	30.00
NNO	Kane	25.00	60.00
NNO	Kevin Nash	30.00	80.00
NNO	Layla	12.00	30.00
NNO	Lex Luger	30.00	80.00
NNO	Naomi	20.00	50.00
NNO	Nikki Bella	30.00	80.00
NNO	Roman Reigns	40.00	100.00
NNO	Ron Simmons	30.00	80.00
NNO	Summer Rae	40.00	100.00
NNO	Trish Stratus	60.00	120.00

2014 Topps WWE Road to WrestleMania Dual Autographs

RANDOMLY INSERTED INTO PACKS

NNO	Bray Wyatt	120.00	250.00
	Roman Reigns		
NNO	H.Hogan/J.Hart	125.00	250.00
NNO	Kane/Layla	20.00	50.00
NNO	K.Nash/R.Simmons	30.00	80.00
NNO	Lex Luger/Cesaro	50.00	100.00
NNO	Naomi/N.Bella	25.00	60.00
NNO	Trish Stratus	50.00	100.00
	Eve		

2014 Topps WWE Road to WrestleMania Queen of WrestleMania

COMPLETE SET (8)		10.00	25.00
*P.P.BLACK/1: UNPRICED DUE TO SCARCITY			
*P.P.CYAN/1: UNPRICED DUE TO SCARCITY			
*P.P.MAGENTA/1: UNPRICED DUE TO SCARCITY			
*P.P.YELLOW/1: UNPRICED DUE TO SCARCITY			
STATED ODDS 1:12			

1	Leads T&A to Victory	2.00	5.00
2	Triple Threat Match/Women's Title	2.00	5.00
3	Defeats Victoria and Jazz	2.00	5.00
4	Turns on Chris Jericho	2.00	5.00
5	Defeats Christy Hemme	2.00	5.00
6	Battles Mickie James	2.00	5.00
7	With John Morrison and Snooki	2.00	5.00
8	Hall of Fame Induction	2.00	5.00

2014 Topps WWE Road to WrestleMania The Streak

COMPLETE SET (22)		8.00	20.00
*P.P.BLACK/1: UNPRICED DUE TO SCARCITY			
*P.P.CYAN/1: UNPRICED DUE TO SCARCITY			
*P.P.MAGENTA/1: UNPRICED DUE TO SCARCITY			
*P.P.YELLOW/1: UNPRICED DUE TO SCARCITY			
STATED ODDS 1:1			

1	Jimmy Superfly Snuka	.60	1.50
2	Jake The Snake Roberts	.60	1.50
3	Giant Gonzales	.60	1.50
4	King Kong Bundy	.60	1.50

5 Diesel		.60	1.50
6 Sycho Sid		.60	1.50
7 Kane		.60	1.50
8 Big Boss Man		.60	1.50
9 Triple H		.60	1.50
10 Ric Flair		.60	1.50
11 Big Show/A-Train		.60	1.50
12 Kane		.60	1.50
13 Randy Orton		.60	1.50
14 Mark Henry		.60	1.50
15 Batista		.60	1.50
16 Edge		.60	1.50
17 Shawn Michaels		.60	1.50
18 Shawn Michaels		.60	1.50
19 Triple H		.60	1.50
20 Triple H		.60	1.50
21 CM Punk		.60	1.50
22 Brock Lesnar		2.00	5.00

2014 Topps WWE Road to WrestleMania Swatch Relics

*P.P.BLACK/1: UNPRICED DUE TO SCARCITY
*P.P.CYAN/1: UNPRICED DUE TO SCARCITY
*P.P.MAGENTA/1: UNPRICED DUE TO SCARCITY
*P.P.YELLOW/1: UNPRICED DUE TO SCARCITY
RANDOMLY INSERTED INTO PACKS

NNO Alberto Del Rio/Shirt	3.00	8.00
NNO Big Show/Shirt	3.00	8.00
NNO Billy Gunn/Shirt	3.00	8.00
NNO Bray Wyatt/Shirt	4.00	10.00
NNO Curtis Axel/Shirt	3.00	8.00
NNO Damien Sandow/Shirt	3.00	8.00
NNO Daniel Bryan/Shirt	10.00	25.00
NNO Darren Young/Shirt	4.00	10.00
NNO Dolph Ziggler/Shirt	5.00	12.00
NNO Goldust/Shirt	3.00	8.00
NNO Jack Swagger/Shirt	3.00	8.00
NNO Jey Uso/Shirt	8.00	20.00
NNO John Cena/Shirt	120.00	200.00
NNO John Cena/Shoe	8.00	20.00
NNO Mark Henry/Shirt	4.00	10.00
NNO The Miz/Shirt	3.00	8.00
NNO Natalya/Shirt	4.00	10.00
NNO Ryback/Shirt	3.00	8.00
NNO Tamina Snuka/Shirt	3.00	8.00
NNO T.Stratus/Green Pants	30.00	60.00
NNO T.Stratus/Purple Pants	30.00	60.00
NNO Undertaker/Pants & Hat	150.00	300.00

2014 Topps WWE Road to WrestleMania Ultimate Warrior Tribute

COMPLETE SET (10)   5.00   12.00
*P.P.BLACK/1: UNPRICED DUE TO SCARCITY
*P.P.CYAN/1: UNPRICED DUE TO SCARCITY
*P.P.MAGENTA/1: UNPRICED DUE TO SCARCITY
*P.P.YELLOW/1: UNPRICED DUE TO SCARCITY
STATED ODDS 1:4

1 Defeats Honky Tonk Man	.75	2.00
2 Defeats Ravishing Rick Rude	.75	2.00
3 Defeats The Heenan Family	.75	2.00
4 Defeats Hulk Hogan for WWE Title	.75	2.00
5 Defeats Ravishing Rick Rude	.75	2.00
6 Wins Match at Survivor Series	.75	2.00
7 Defeats Macho King Randy Savage	.75	2.00
8 Returns to WWE, Defeats Triple H	.75	2.00

9 Joins WCW	.75	2.00
10 Addresses WWE Universe	.75	2.00

2014 Topps WWE Road to WrestleMania WrestleMania 30 Mat Relics

RANDOMLY INSERTED INTO PACKS

NNO AJ Lee	12.00	30.00
NNO Batista	4.00	10.00
NNO Big Show	5.00	12.00
NNO Bray Wyatt	6.00	15.00
NNO Brock Lesnar	4.00	10.00
NNO Cesaro	3.00	8.00
NNO Daniel Bryan	8.00	20.00
NNO Dean Ambrose	5.00	12.00
NNO Hulk Hogan	10.00	25.00
NNO Jey Uso	3.00	8.00
NNO Jimmy Uso	3.00	8.00
NNO John Cena	8.00	20.00
NNO Randy Orton	6.00	15.00
NNO The Rock	6.00	15.00
NNO Roman Reigns	8.00	20.00
NNO Seth Rollins	6.00	15.00
NNO Sheamus	3.00	8.00
NNO Stone Cold Steve Austin	6.00	15.00
NNO Triple H	5.00	12.00
NNO Undertaker	6.00	15.00

2014 Topps WWE Road to WrestleMania WrestleMania Autographs

*BRONZE/25: .5X TO 1.2X BASIC AUTOS
RANDOMLY INSERTED INTO PACKS

NNO Bray Wyatt	15.00	40.00
NNO Cameron	8.00	20.00
NNO Cesaro	12.00	30.00
NNO Eve	12.00	20.00
NNO Hulk Hogan	80.00	150.00
NNO Jimmy Hart	12.00	25.00
NNO Kane	15.00	40.00
NNO Kevin Nash	20.00	50.00
NNO Layla	12.00	25.00
NNO Lex Luger	12.00	30.00
NNO Naomi	12.00	30.00
NNO Nikki Bella	15.00	40.00
NNO Roman Reigns	20.00	50.00
NNO Ron Simmons	12.00	30.00
NNO Summer Rae	15.00	40.00
NNO Trish Stratus	20.00	50.00

2014 Topps WWE Road to WrestleMania WWE 2K15

STATED ODDS 1:613

1 AJ Lee	50.00	100.00
2 Bray Wyatt	15.00	40.00
3 Brock Lesnar	10.00	25.00
4 Cesaro	8.00	20.00
5 Daniel Bryan	15.00	40.00
6 Dolph Ziggler	8.00	20.00
7 Hulk Hogan	30.00	80.00
8 John Cena	30.00	80.00
9 Roman Reigns	20.00	50.00
10 Seth Rollins	20.00	50.00

2015 Topps WWE Road to WrestleMania

COMPLETE SET (110)   .10   25.00

UNOPENED BOX (24 PACKS)
UNOPENED PACK (7 CARDS)
*BRONZE: .6X TO 1.5X BASIC CARDS
*BLUE: .75X TO 2X BASIC CARDS
*PURPLE: .75X TO 2X BASIC CARDS
*SILVER: 2.5X TO 6X BASIC CARDS
*GOLD/10: UNPRICED DUE TO SCARCITY
*RED/1: UNPRICED DUE TO SCARCITY
*P.P. BLACK/1: UNPRICED DUE TO SCARCITY
*P.P. CYAN/1: UNPRICED DUE TO SCARCITY
*P.P. MAGENTA/1: UNPRICED DUE TO SCARCITY
*P.P. YELLOW/1: UNPRICED DUE TO SCARCITY

1 Paige	.60	1.50
2 The Shield/Daniel Bryan	.30	.75
3 Daniel Bryan/Hulk Hogan	.50	1.25
4 Fandango/Summer Rae/Layla	.12	.30
5 Ultimate Warrior Tribute	.12	.30
6 Cesaro/Mark Henry	.12	.30
7 Evolution/The Shield	.50	1.25
8 Jimmy Uso/Naomi	.12	.30
9 Kane/Daniel Bryan	.30	.75
10 Bray Wyatt/John Cena	.50	1.25
11 Kane/Brie Bella	.30	.75
12 Bad News Barrett/Big E	.12	.30
13 The Shield/Evolution	.30	.75
14 Bray Wyatt/John Cena	.50	1.25
15 Daniel Bryan/Kane	.50	1.25
16 Sheamus/Dean Ambrose	.30	.75
17 Adam Rose	.15	.40
18 Bo Dallas	.12	.30
19 The Authority/Brad Maddox	.50	1.25
20 Daniel Bryan/Brie Bella	.50	1.25
21 Brie Bella	.40	1.00
22 John Cena/Bray Wyatt	.60	1.50
23 The Shield/Evolution	.30	.75
24 Batista	.30	.75
25 Seth Rollins/The Shield	.20	.50
26 The Authority/Daniel Bryan	.50	1.25
27 John Cena/Shield/Wyatts	.60	1.50
28 Stardust	.12	.30
29 John Cena/Kane	.60	1.50
30 Seth Rollins MITB	.20	.50
31 John Cena	.60	1.50
32 Bret Hit Man Hart/Damien Sandow	.40	1.00
33 Funkadactyls	.20	.50
34 Summer Rae/Layla/Fandango	.50	1.25
35 The Miz	.20	.50
36 John Cena	.60	1.50
37 Brock Lesnar/John Cena	.50	1.25
38 Stephanie McMahon/Brie Bella	.20	.50
39 Brock Lesnar/Hulk Hogan	.50	1.25
40 Dolph Ziggler/The Miz	.20	.50
41 Paige/AJ Lee	.60	1.50
42 Seth Rollins/Dean Ambrose	.20	.50
43 Roman Reigns/Randy Orton	.30	.75
44 Brock Lesnar/John Cena	.50	1.25
45 Gold & Stardust/Usos	.12	.30
46 The Miz/Dolph Ziggler	.20	.50
47 Dean Ambrose/Seth Rollins	.30	.75
48 John Cena/Brock Lesnar	.60	1.50
49 Dolph Ziggler/The Miz	.20	.50
50 The Bunny	.12	.30
51 Seth Rollins/Dean Ambrose	.20	.50
52 The Rock/Rusev	.60	1.50
53 Dean Ambrose/The Authority	.30	.75
54 Dean Ambrose/John Cena	.30	.75
55 Nikki Bella/Brie Bella	.40	1.00
56 John Cena/Randy Orton	.60	1.50

57 Bray Wyatt/Dean Ambrose	.50	1.25
58 The Authority/Randy Orton	.50	1.25
59 Rusev/Sheamus	.30	.75
60 Luke Harper/Dolph Ziggler	.20	.50
61 Miz & Mizdow/Goldust & Stardust	.20	.50
62 Divas Survivor Series Match	.12	.30
63 Nikki Bella/AJ Lee	.40	1.00
64 Sting WWE Debut	.30	.75
65 Team Cena/Team Authority	.60	1.50
66 Dolph Ziggler/Luke Harper	.20	.50
67 John Cena/Seth Rollins	.60	1.50
68 Roman Reigns	.30	.75
69 Bray Wyatt/Dean Ambrose	.50	1.25
70 Brock Lesnar/Chris Jericho	.50	1.25
71 Seth Rollins/John Cena	.20	.50
72 Dean Ambrose/Bray Wyatt	.30	.75
73 Edge & Christian	.30	.75
74 Usos/The Miz & Mizdow	.12	.30
75 The Ascension/Miz & Mizdow	.12	.30
76 Seth Rollins/John Cena	.20	.50
77 Bad New Barrett/Dolph Ziggler	.12	.30
78 Authority/Ziggler/Ryback/Rowan	.50	1.25
79 Rollins/Cena/Lesnar	.20	.50
80 Daniel Bryan	.50	1.25
81 The Ascension/nWo	.12	.30
82 Sting/Team Cena	.30	.75
83 Lesnar/Rollins/Cena	.50	1.25
84 Kane	.30	.75
85 Roman Reigns	.30	.75
86 Daniel Bryan/Kane	.50	1.25
87 Daniel Bryan/Seth Rollins	.50	1.25
88 Stardust/Goldust	.12	.30
89 Ric Flair/Triple H	.60	1.50
90 Prime Time Players	.12	.30
91 Randy Orton/The Authority	.50	1.25
92 Tyson Kidd & Cesaro/Usos	.12	.30
93 Sting/Triple H	.30	.75
94 Rusev/John Cena	.30	.75
95 Roman Reigns/Daniel Bryan	.30	.75
96 Sting/Randy Orton	.30	.75
97 Larry Zbyszko HOF	.20	.50
98 Bushwackers HOF	.12	.30
99 Hulk Hogan/Macho Man HOF	.60	1.50
100 Kevin Nash HOF	.30	.75
101 Tyson Kidd & Cesaro	.12	.30
102 Big Show	.30	.75
103 Daniel Bryan	.50	1.25
104 Randy Orton/Seth Rollins	.50	1.25
105 Triple H/Sting	.50	1.25
106 AJ Lee & Paige/Bella Twins	.60	1.50
107 John Cena/Rusev	.60	1.50
108 The Rock/The Authority	.60	1.50
109 Undertaker/Bray Wyatt	.50	1.25
110 Rollins/Lesnar/Reigns	.20	.50

2015 Topps WWE Road to WrestleMania Autographs

*BRONZE/50: .5X TO 1.2X BASIC AUTOS
*SILVER/25: .6X TO 1.5X BASIC AUTOS
*GOLD/10: .75X TO 2X BASIC AUTOS
*P.P.BLACK/1: UNPRICED DUE TO SCARCITY
*P.P.CYAN/1: UNPRICED DUE TO SCARCITY
*P.P.MAGENTA/1: UNPRICED DUE TO SCARCITY
*P.P.YELLOW/1: UNPRICED DUE TO SCARCITY
RANDOMLY INSERTED INTO PACKS

NNO Afa	8.00	20.00
NNO Alicia Fox	6.00	15.00
NNO Bray Wyatt	12.00	30.00

NNO	Brie Bella	12.00	30.00
NNO	Brock Lesnar	60.00	120.00
NNO	Damien Mizdow	6.00	15.00
NNO	Daniel Bryan	12.00	30.00
NNO	Dean Ambrose	12.00	30.00
NNO	Dolph Ziggler	8.00	20.00
NNO	Emma	10.00	25.00
NNO	Hulk Hogan	30.00	80.00
NNO	Jack Swagger	6.00	15.00
NNO	Jimmy Hart	10.00	25.00
NNO	Nikki Bella	15.00	40.00
NNO	Razor Ramon	20.00	50.00
NNO	Roman Reigns	15.00	40.00
NNO	R-Truth	8.00	20.00
NNO	Ryback	8.00	20.00
NNO	Sika	8.00	20.00

2015 Topps WWE Road to WrestleMania Bizarre WrestleMania Matches

COMPLETE SET (10)		5.00	12.00
*P.P.BLACK/1: UNPRICED DUE TO SCARCITY			
*P.P.CYAN/1: UNPRICED DUE TO SCARCITY			
*P.P.MAGENTA/1: UNPRICED DUE TO SCARCITY			
*P.P.YELLOW/1: UNPRICED DUE TO SCARCITY			
STATED ODDS 1:4			
1	Andre the Giant/Big John Studd	1.00	2.50
2	Mr.T/Rowdy Roddy Piper	1.00	2.50
3	Corporal Kirchner/Nikolai Volkoff	1.00	2.50
4	Battle Royal	1.00	2.50
5	Rowdy Roddy Piper/Adrian Adonis	1.00	2.50
6	Jake Roberts/Rick Martel	1.00	2.50
7	Rowdy Roddy Piper/Goldust	1.00	2.50
8	C.Jack & C.Charlie/New Age Outlaws	1.00	2.50
9	Gimmick Battle Royal	1.00	2.50
10	Akebono/Big Show	1.00	2.50

2015 Topps WWE Road to WrestleMania Classic WrestleMania Matches

COMPLETE SET (30)		6.00	15.00
*P.P.BLACK/1: UNPRICED DUE TO SCARCITY			
*P.P.CYAN/1: UNPRICED DUE TO SCARCITY			
*P.P.MAGENTA/1: UNPRICED DUE TO SCARCITY			
*P.P.YELLOW/1: UNPRICED DUE TO SCARCITY			
RANDOMLY INSERTED INTO PACKS			
1	Harley Race/JYD	.50	1.25
2	Honky Tonk Man	.50	1.25
	Jake The Snake Roberts		
3	Twin Towers/Rockers	.50	1.25
4	Nasty Boys/Hart Foundation	.50	1.25
5	Bret Hit Man Hart	.50	1.25
	Rowdy Roddy Piper		
6	Money Inc/Mega-Maniacs	.50	1.25
7	Lex Luger/Mr. Perfect	.50	1.25
8	Bret Hit Man Hart	.50	1.25
9	Razor Ramon/Shawn Michaels	.50	1.25
10	Stone Cold Steve Austin	.50	1.25
	Savio Vega		
11	Chris Jericho/Kurt Angle	.50	1.25
12	Chris Jericho/William Regal	.50	1.25
13	Eddie Guerrero/Test	.50	1.25
14	Stone Cold Steve Austin	.50	1.25
	Chris Jericho		
15	Shawn Michaels/Chris Jericho	.50	1.25
16	John Cena/Big Show	.50	1.25
17	Christian/Chris Jericho	.50	1.25

18	Goldberg/Brock Lesnar	.50	1.25
19	Rey Mysterio/Eddie Guerrero	.50	1.25
20	Edge MITB	.50	1.25
21	Kurt Angle/Shawn Michaels	.50	1.25
22	Rob Van Dam MITB	.50	1.25
23	Edge/Mick Foley	.50	1.25
24	Shawn Michaels/Mr. McMahon	.50	1.25
25	Jack Swagger MITB	.50	1.25
26	Bret Hit Man Hart	.50	1.25
	Mr. McMahon		
27	Randy Orton/CM Punk	.50	1.25
28	Sheamus/Daniel Bryan	.50	1.25
29	Shield/Orton Sheamus Big Show	.50	1.25
30	Team Hell No/Ziggler & Big E	.50	1.25

2015 Topps WWE Road to WrestleMania Dual Autographs

STATED PRINT RUN 10 SER.#'d SETS
UNPRICED DUE TO SCARCITY

NNO	Afa/Sika
NNO	Brie & Nikki Bella
NNO	D.Mizdow/J.Hart
NNO	D.Bryan/B.Wyatt
NNO	D.Ambrose/R.Reigns
NNO	D.Ziggler/Ryback
NNO	Emma/A.Fox
NNO	H.Hogan/R.Ramon

2015 Topps WWE Road to WrestleMania Hall of Fame

COMPLETE SET (30)		4.00	10.00
*P.P.BLACK/1: UNPRICED DUE TO SCARCITY			
*P.P.CYAN/1: UNPRICED DUE TO SCARCITY			
*P.P.MAGENTA/1: UNPRICED DUE TO SCARCITY			
*P.P.YELLOW/1: UNPRICED DUE TO SCARCITY			
STATED ODDS 1:1			
1	Chief Jay Strongbow	.40	1.00
2	Classy Freddie Blassie	.25	.60
3	Gorilla Monsoon	.30	.75
4	George The Animal Steele	.30	.75
5	Jimmy Superfly Snuka	.40	1.00
6	Pat Patterson	.25	.60
7	The Magnificent Don Muraco	.40	1.00
8	Greg The Hammer Valentine	.30	.75
9	The King Harley Race	.40	1.00
10	Sgt. Slaughter	.40	1.00
11	Tito Santana	.40	1.00
12	Hulk Hogan	1.25	3.00
13	Rowdy Roddy Piper	.75	2.00
14	Cowboy Bob Orton	.25	.60
15	Mr. Wonderful Paul Orndorff	.40	1.00
16	Nikolai Volkoff	.25	.60
17	The Iron Sheik	.40	1.00
18	Bret Hit Man Hart	.75	2.00
19	The American Dream Dusty Rhodes	.40	1.00
20	Jerry The King Lawler	.40	1.00
21	Nature Boy Ric Flair	1.25	3.00
22	Rocky Johnson	.40	1.00
23	Stone Cold Steve Austin	1.25	3.00
24	Ricky The Dragon Steamboat	.40	1.00
25	Koko B. Ware	.30	.75
26	Million Dollar Man Ted DiBiase	.40	1.00
27	Heartbreak Kid Shawn Michaels	1.00	2.50
28	Hacksaw Jim Duggan	.40	1.00
29	Edge	.60	1.50
30	Ron Simmons	.40	1.00

2015 Topps WWE Road to WrestleMania HHH at WrestleMania

COMPLETE SET (10)		4.00	10.00
*P.P.BLACK/1: UNPRICED DUE TO SCARCITY			
*P.P.CYAN/1: UNPRICED DUE TO SCARCITY			
*P.P.MAGENTA/1: UNPRICED DUE TO SCARCITY			
*P.P.YELLOW/1: UNPRICED DUE TO SCARCITY			
STATED ODDS 1:2			
1	Defeats Goldust	.75	2.00
2	Battles Kane	.75	2.00
3	Wins 4-Way Elimination Match	.75	2.00
4	Defeats Y2J for WWE Title	.75	2.00
5	Defeats Booker T	.75	2.00
6	Defeats Randy Orton	.75	2.00
7	Defeats Sheamus	.75	2.00
8	Faces Undertaker No Holds Barred	.75	2.00
9	Faces Undertaker Hell in a Cell	.75	2.00
10	Defeats Brock Lesnar	.75	2.00

2015 Topps WWE Road to WrestleMania Mat Relics

*SILVER/25: .6X TO 1.5X BASIC MEM			
*GOLD/10: UNPRICED DUE TO SCARCITY			
*P.P.BLACK/1: UNPRICED DUE TO SCARCITY			
*P.P.CYAN/1: UNPRICED DUE TO SCARCITY			
*P.P.MAGENTA/1: UNPRICED DUE TO SCARCITY			
*P.P.YELLOW/1: UNPRICED DUE TO SCARCITY			
RANDOMLY INSERTED INTO PACKS			
NNO	Bad News Barrett	2.00	5.00
NNO	Big Show	2.50	6.00
NNO	Bray Wyatt	3.00	8.00
NNO	Brie Bella	4.00	10.00
NNO	Brock Lesnar	3.00	8.00
NNO	Damien Mizdow	2.50	6.00
NNO	Daniel Bryan	5.00	12.00
NNO	Dean Ambrose	3.00	8.00
NNO	Dolph Ziggler	2.00	5.00
NNO	John Cena	4.00	10.00
NNO	Nikki Bella	4.00	10.00
NNO	Paige	6.00	15.00
NNO	Randy Orton	3.00	8.00
NNO	Roman Reigns	4.00	10.00
NNO	Rusev	2.50	6.00
NNO	Ryback	2.00	5.00
NNO	Seth Rollins	3.00	8.00
NNO	Sting	6.00	15.00
NNO	Triple H	3.00	8.00
NNO	Undertaker	5.00	12.00

2015 Topps WWE Road to WrestleMania Rocking WrestleMania

COMPLETE SET (8)		5.00	12.00
*P.P.BLACK/1: UNPRICED DUE TO SCARCITY			
*P.P.CYAN/1: UNPRICED DUE TO SCARCITY			
*P.P.MAGENTA/1: UNPRICED DUE TO SCARCITY			
*P.P.YELLOW/1: UNPRICED DUE TO SCARCITY			
RANDOMLY INSERTED INTO PACKS			
1	Faces Stone Cold Steve Austin	1.25	3.00
2	Takes on Stone Cold Steve Austin	1.25	3.00
3	Defeats Hollywood Hulk Hogan	1.25	3.00
4	Defeats Stone Cold Steve Austin	1.25	3.00
5	Rock 'n' Sock Reunite	1.25	3.00
6	Rock Bottoms John Cena	1.25	3.00
7	Defeats John Cena	1.25	3.00
8	Battles John Cena	1.25	3.00

2015 Topps WWE Road to WrestleMania Superstars of Canada

COMPLETE SET (10)		25.00	60.00
RANDOMLY INSERTED INTO PACKS			
1	Chris Jericho	5.00	12.00
2	Christian	2.00	5.00
3	Edge	5.00	12.00
4	Kevin Owens	6.00	15.00
5	Natalya	6.00	15.00
6	Renee Young	8.00	20.00
7	Sami Zayn	3.00	8.00
8	Trish Stratus	10.00	25.00
9	Tyson Kidd	2.00	5.00
10	Viktor	2.00	5.00

2015 Topps WWE Road to WrestleMania Superstars of Canada Autographs

RANDOMLY INSERTED INTO PACKS
STATED PRINT RUN 25 SER.#'d SETS
CANADIAN EXCLUSIVES

NNO	Chris Jericho	50.00	100.00
NNO	Christian	25.00	60.00
NNO	Edge	50.00	100.00
NNO	Kevin Owens	15.00	40.00
NNO	Natalya	20.00	50.00
NNO	Renee Young	20.00	50.00
NNO	Sami Zayn	10.00	25.00
NNO	Trish Stratus	100.00	200.00
NNO	Tyson Kidd	6.00	15.00
NNO	Viktor	6.00	15.00

2015 Topps WWE Road to WrestleMania Swatch Relics

*P.P.BLACK/1: UNPRICED DUE TO SCARCITY			
*P.P.CYAN/1: UNPRICED DUE TO SCARCITY			
*P.P.MAGENTA/1: UNPRICED DUE TO SCARCITY			
*P.P.YELLOW/1: UNPRICED DUE TO SCARCITY			
RANDOMLY INSERTED INTO PACKS			
NNO	Adam Rose	4.00	10.00
NNO	Brie Bella	6.00	15.00
NNO	Cesaro	4.00	10.00
NNO	Charlotte	10.00	25.00
NNO	Dean Ambrose	8.00	20.00
NNO	Damien Mizdow	4.00	10.00
NNO	Dolph Ziggler	4.00	10.00
NNO	Goldust	6.00	15.00
NNO	Hulk Hogan	10.00	25.00
NNO	John Cena	6.00	15.00
NNO	Jack Swagger	5.00	12.00
NNO	Nikki Bella	10.00	25.00
NNO	Paige	12.00	30.00
NNO	Roman Reigns	8.00	20.00
NNO	Rusev	5.00	12.00
NNO	Ryback	5.00	12.00
NNO	Stardust	5.00	12.00
NNO	Sami Zayn	6.00	15.00

2015 Topps WWE Road to WrestleMania Turnbuckle Pad Relics

RANDOMLY INSERTED INTO PACKS
STATED PRINT RUN 25 SER.#'d SETS

NNO	Bad News Barrett	6.00	15.00
NNO	Big Show	15.00	40.00
NNO	Bray Wyatt	25.00	60.00
NNO	Brie Bella	20.00	50.00

NNO Brock Lesnar 25.00 60.00
NNO Damien Mizdow 6.00 15.00
NNO Daniel Bryan 25.00 60.00
NNO Dean Ambrose 15.00 40.00
NNO Dolph Ziggler 10.00 25.00
NNO John Cena 30.00 80.00
NNO Nikki Bella 20.00 50.00
NNO Paige 30.00 80.00
NNO Randy Orton 25.00 60.00
NNO Roman Reigns 15.00 40.00
NNO Rusev 15.00 40.00
NNO Ryback 6.00 15.00
NNO Seth Rollins 10.00 25.00
NNO Sting 15.00 40.00
NNO Triple H 25.00 60.00
NNO Undertaker 25.00 60.00

2016 Topps WWE Road to WrestleMania

COMPLETE SET (110) 12.00 30.00
UNOPENED BOX (24 PACKS)
UNOPENED PACK (7 CARDS)
*BRONZE: .5X TO 1.2X BASIC CARDS
*SILVER: 2X TO 5X BASIC CARDS
*GOLD/10: UNPRICED DUE TO SCARCITY
*RED/1: UNPRICED DUE TO SCARCITY
*PP BLACK/1: UNPRICED DUE TO SCARCITY
*PP CYAN/1: UNPRICED DUE TO SCARCITY
*PP MAGENTA/1: UNPRICED DUE TO SCARCITY
*PP YELLOW/1: UNPRICED DUE TO SCARCITY
NUMBERS 111-113 ARE WWE DVD EXCLUSIVES

1 Daniel Bryan .75 2.00
2 The Usos .20 .50
3 Alundra Blayze .25 .60
4 Ric Flair .75 2.00
5 Triple H .75 2.00
6 Hideo Itami .25 .60
7 Damien Mizdow .30 .75
8 Sting .50 1.25
9 Triple H .75 2.00
10 D-Generation X .60 1.50
11 Rusev .50 1.25
12 Bray Wyatt .75 2.00
13 Roman Reigns 1.00 2.50
14 Sheamus .50 1.25
15 Kalisto .50 1.25
16 Brock Lesnar 1.00 2.50
17 Neville .50 1.25
18 Big Show .60 1.50
19 Fandango .20 .50
20 Daniel Bryan/John Cena 1.00 2.50
21 The Miz .30 .75
22 The New Day .50 1.25
23 Roman Reigns .60 1.50
24 Seth Rollins .30 .75
25 Bad New Barrett .20 .50
26 Sami Zayn 1.00 2.50
27 Erick Rowan .20 .50
28 Neville 1.00 2.50
29 Daniel Bryan .75 2.00
30 John Cena 1.00 2.50
31 Seth Rollins .30 .75
32 Rusev .75 2.00
33 Kevin Owens 1.00 2.50
34 Lana .75 2.00
35 The New Day .50 1.25
36 Kalisto .50 1.25
37 The New Day .50 1.25

38 Nikki Bella .60 1.50
39 Kevin Owens .50 1.25
40 Ryback .25 .60
41 Dean Ambrose .60 1.50
42 Dusty Rhodes Tribute .20 .50
43 Bray Wyatt .75 2.00
44 Sheamus .50 1.25
45 Nikki Bella .60 1.50
46 John Cena 1.00 2.50
47 The Prime Time Players .20 .50
48 Seth Rollins .60 1.50
49 Brock Lesnar 1.00 2.50
50 Brock Lesnar 1.00 2.50
51 Cesaro 1.00 2.50
52 Chris Jericho .50 1.25
53 Nikki Bella .60 1.50
54 Brock Lesnar 1.00 2.50
55 Rusev/Summer Rae .75 2.00
56 Brock Lesnar 1.00 2.50
57 John Cena 1.00 2.50
58 Rusev .50 1.25
59 Stardust .20 .50
60 Brock Lesnar 1.00 2.50
61 Cesaro .50 1.25
62 Bray Wyatt .75 2.00
63 Charlotte .60 1.50
64 John Cena 1.00 2.50
65 Undertaker 1.00 2.50
66 Brock Lesnar 1.00 2.50
67 John Cena/Cesaro/Randy Orton 1.00 2.50
68 Seth Rollins .30 .75
69 John Cena 1.00 2.50
70 Dean Ambrose/Cesaro .60 1.50
71 Rowdy Roddy Piper Tribute .60 1.50
72 Ambrose/Reigns/Orton .50 1.25
73 The New Day .50 1.25
74 Undertaker 1.00 2.50
75 Ryback .30 .75
76 Roman Reigns/Dean Ambrose .75 2.00
77 Seth Rollins .30 .75
78 Team PCB .60 1.50
79 Undertaker 1.00 2.50
80 Brock Lesnar 1.00 2.50
81 The Dudley Boyz .40 1.00
82 Braun Strowman .25 .60
83 Sting .50 1.25
84 Charlotte .60 1.50
85 Sting/John Cena 1.00 2.50
86 Hideo Itami .25 .60
87 Sami Zayn .30 .75
88 Becky Lynch .60 1.50
89 Kevin Owens .50 1.25
90 Tyler Breeze/Adam Rose .20 .50
91 Finn Balor .60 1.50
92 Charlotte/Bayley .60 1.50
93 Sasha Banks .60 1.50
94 Kevin Owens .50 1.25
95 Samoa Joe .50 1.25
96 Kevin Owens .50 1.25
97 Samoa Joe .50 1.25
98 Samoa Joe .50 1.25
99 Finn Balor/Samoa Joe .60 1.50
100 Finn Balor .60 1.50
101 The Vaudevillains .20 .50
102 Sasha Banks .60 1.50
103 Blake/Murphy .20 .50
104 Bayley .60 1.50
105 Bayley .50 1.25

106 The Vaudevillains .20 .50
107 Apollo Crews .20 .50
108 Samoa Joe .50 1.25
109 Bayley .50 1.25
110 Finn Balor .60 1.50
111 The Dudley Boyz SP
112 Stone Cold Steve Austin SP
113 Daniel Bryan SP

2016 Topps WWE Road to WrestleMania Autographs

*BRONZE/50: .5X TO 1.2X BASIC AUTOS
*SILVER/25: .60X TO 1.5X BASIC AUTOS
*GOLD/10: UNPRICED DUE TO SCARCITY
*RED/1: UNPRICED DUE TO SCARCITY
*PP BLACK/1: UNPRICED DUE TO SCARCITY
*PP CYAN/1: UNPRICED DUE TO SCARCITY
*PP MAGENTA/1: UNPRICED DUE TO SCARCITY
*PP YELLOW/1: UNPRICED DUE TO SCARCITY
STATED PRINT RUN 99 SER.#'d SETS

NNO Baron Corbin 10.00 25.00
NNO Bayley 60.00 120.00
NNO Becky Lynch 25.00 60.00
NNO Brie Bella 10.00 25.00
NNO Brock Lesnar 100.00 200.00
NNO Charlotte 15.00 40.00
NNO Daniel Bryan 10.00 25.00
NNO Dean Ambrose 10.00 25.00
NNO Dory Funk Jr. 12.00 30.00
NNO Dusty Rhodes 50.00 100.00
NNO Eva Marie 15.00 40.00
NNO Gerald Brisco 6.00 15.00
NNO John Cena 20.00 50.00
NNO Kalisto 12.00 30.00
NNO Kevin Von Erich 10.00 25.00
NNO Lana 20.00 50.00
NNO Michael P.S. Hayes 10.00 25.00
NNO Neville 6.00 15.00
NNO Nikki Bella 15.00 40.00
NNO Pat Patterson 6.00 15.00
NNO Ric Flair 15.00 40.00
NNO Roman Reigns 12.00 30.00
NNO Samoa Joe 8.00 20.00
NNO Sasha Banks 25.00 60.00
NNO Seth Rollins 10.00 25.00
NNO Sting 30.00 80.00
NNO Terry Funk 15.00 40.00

2016 Topps WWE Road to WrestleMania Battleground Mat Relics

*BRONZE/50: .5X TO 1.2X BASIC MEM
*SILVER/25: .6X TO 1.5X BASIC MEM
*GOLD/10: UNPRICED DUE TO SCARCITY
*RED/1: UNPRICED DUE TO SCARCITY
*PP BLACK/1: UNPRICED DUE TO SCARCITY
*PP CYAN/1: UNPRICED DUE TO SCARCITY
*PP MAGENTA/1: UNPRICED DUE TO SCARCITY
*PP YELLOW/1: UNPRICED DUE TO SCARCITY
STATED PRINT RUN 199 SER.#'d SETS

NNO Big E 2.00 5.00
NNO Bray Wyatt 8.00 20.00
NNO Brie Bella 4.00 10.00
NNO Brock Lesnar 10.00 25.00
NNO Charlotte 6.00 15.00
NNO Darren Young 2.00 5.00
NNO John Cena 10.00 25.00

NNO Kevin Owens 5.00 12.00
NNO Kofi Kingston 2.00 5.00
NNO Luke Harper 2.00 5.00
NNO Randy Orton 5.00 12.00
NNO Roman Reigns 6.00 15.00
NNO R-Truth 2.00 5.00
NNO Sasha Banks 6.00 15.00
NNO Seth Rollins 3.00 8.00
NNO Sheamus 5.00 12.00
NNO Titus O'Neil 2.00 5.00
NNO Undertaker 8.00 20.00
NNO Wade Barrett 2.00 5.00
NNO Xavier Woods 2.00 5.00

2016 Topps WWE Road to WrestleMania Battleground Turnbuckle Pad Relics

STATED PRINT RUN 25 SER.#'d SETS

NNO Big E 5.00 12.00
NNO Bray Wyatt 20.00 50.00
NNO Brie Bella 10.00 25.00
NNO Brock Lesnar 25.00 60.00
NNO Charlotte 15.00 40.00
NNO Darren Young 5.00 12.00
NNO John Cena 25.00 60.00
NNO Kevin Owens 12.00 30.00
NNO Kofi Kingston 5.00 12.00
NNO Luke Harper 5.00 12.00
NNO Randy Orton 12.00 30.00
NNO Roman Reigns 15.00 40.00
NNO R-Truth 5.00 12.00
NNO Sasha Banks 15.00 40.00
NNO Seth Rollins 8.00 20.00
NNO Sheamus 12.00 30.00
NNO Titus O'Neil 5.00 12.00
NNO Undertaker 20.00 50.00
NNO Wade Barrett 5.00 12.00
NNO Xavier Woods 5.00 12.00

2016 Topps WWE Road to WrestleMania Dual Autographs

STATED PRINT RUN 11 SER.#'d SETS

NNO Charlotte 100.00 200.00
Bayley
NNO Lana 100.00 200.00
Eva Marie
NNO Neville 30.00 75.00
Kalisto
NNO Pat Patterson 25.00 60.00
Gerald Brisco
NNO Samoa Joe 50.00 100.00
Baron Corbin
NNO Sasha Banks 200.00 300.00
Becky Lynch
NNO Sting 225.00 350.00
Ric Flair
NNO Terry Funk 50.00 100.00
Dory Funk Jr.

2016 Topps WWE Road to WrestleMania Dusty Rhodes Tribute

COMPLETE SET (10) 3.00 8.00
STATED ODDS 1:6

1 Dusty Rhodes .60 1.50
2 Dusty Rhodes .60 1.50
3 Dusty Rhodes .60 1.50
4 Dusty Rhodes 1.00 2.50

5	Dusty Rhodes	.60	1.50
6	Dusty Rhodes	1.00	2.50
7	Dusty Rhodes	.60	1.50
8	Dusty Rhodes	.60	1.50
9	Dusty Rhodes	.60	1.50
10	Dusty Rhodes	1.50	4.00

2016 Topps WWE Road to WrestleMania Immortals

COMPLETE SET (10) 6.00 15.00
STATED ODDS 1:6

1	Roman Reigns	1.00	2.50
2	Daniel Bryan	1.25	3.00
3	Randy Orton	.75	2.00
4	The Bellas	1.00	2.50
5	Paige	1.00	2.50
6	Triple H	1.25	3.00
7	Undertaker	1.25	3.00
8	The Rock	1.50	4.00
9	Brock Lesnar	1.50	4.00
10	John Cena	1.50	4.00

2016 Topps WWE Road to WrestleMania NXT Diva Kiss

STATED PRINT RUN 99 SER.#'d SETS

NNO	Alexa Bliss	50.00	100.00
NNO	Bayley	80.00	150.00
NNO	Becky Lynch	50.00	100.00
NNO	Carmella	25.00	60.00
NNO	Charlotte	50.00	100.00
NNO	Dana Brooke	20.00	50.00
NNO	Eva Marie	30.00	80.00
NNO	Jojo	20.00	50.00
NNO	Sasha Banks	100.00	200.00

2016 Topps WWE Road to WrestleMania NXT Diva Kiss Autographs

*GOLD/10: UNPRICED DUE TO SCARCITY
*RED/1: UNPRICED DUE TO SCARCITY
*PP BLACK/1: UNPRICED DUE TO SCARCITY
*PP CYAN/1: UNPRICED DUE TO SCARCITY
*PP MAGENTA/1: UNPRICED DUE TO SCARCITY
*PP YELLOW/1: UNPRICED DUE TO SCARCITY
STATED PRINT RUN 25 SER.#'d SETS

NNO	Alexa Bliss	250.00	500.00
NNO	Bayley	75.00	150.00
NNO	Becky Lynch	120.00	200.00
NNO	Carmella	60.00	120.00
NNO	Charlotte	150.00	250.00
NNO	Dana Brooke	50.00	100.00
NNO	Eva Marie	50.00	100.00
NNO	Jojo	50.00	100.00
NNO	Sasha Banks	150.00	250.00

2016 Topps WWE Road to WrestleMania Roster

COMPLETE SET (30) 10.00 25.00
*P.P.BLACK/1: UNPRICED DUE TO SCARCITY
*P.P.CYAN/1: UNPRICED DUE TO SCARCITY
*P.P.MAGENTA/1: UNPRICED DUE TO SCARCITY
*P.P.YELLOW/1: UNPRICED DUE TO SCARCITY
STATED ODDS 1:1

1	The Rock	1.50	4.00
2	Triple H	1.25	3.00
3	Undertaker	1.25	3.00
4	Sting	.75	2.00
5	Brock Lesnar	1.50	4.00
6	Seth Rollins	.50	1.25
7	Roman Reigns	1.00	2.50
8	Randy Orton	.75	2.00
9	Dean Ambrose	1.00	2.50
10	John Cena	1.50	4.00
11	Rusev	.75	2.00
12	Daniel Bryan	1.25	3.00
13	Dolph Ziggler	.40	1.00
14	King Barrett	.30	.75
15	Luke Harper	.30	.75
16	Bray Wyatt	1.25	3.00
17	The Miz	.50	1.25
18	Ryback	.40	1.00
19	Big Show	.60	1.50
20	Cesaro	.60	1.50
21	Tyson Kidd	.30	.75
22	Kofi Kingston	.30	.75
23	Big E	.30	.75
24	Xavier Woods	.30	.75
25	Brie Bella	.60	1.50
26	Nikki Bella	1.00	2.50
27	Paige	1.00	2.50
28	Naomi	.50	1.25
29	Natalya	.50	1.25
30	Lana	1.25	3.00

2016 Topps WWE Road to WrestleMania Rowdy Roddy Piper Tribute

COMPLETE SET (10) 4.00 10.00
STATED ODDS 1:6

1	Rowdy Roddy Piper	.75	2.00
2	Rowdy Roddy Piper	1.25	3.00
3	Rowdy Roddy Piper	.75	2.00
4	Rowdy Roddy Piper	.75	2.00
5	Rowdy Roddy Piper	.75	2.00
6	Rowdy Roddy Piper	.75	2.00
7	Rowdy Roddy Piper	.75	2.00
8	Rowdy Roddy Piper	.75	2.00
9	Rowdy Roddy Piper	.75	2.00
10	Rowdy Roddy Piper	.75	2.00

2016 Topps WWE Road to WrestleMania Shirt Relics

*BRONZE/50: .5X TO 1.2X BASIC MEM
*SILVER/25: .6X TO 1.5X BASIC MEM
*GOLD/10: UNPRICED DUE TO SCARCITY
*RED/1: UNPRICED DUE TO SCARCITY
*PP BLACK/1: UNPRICED DUE TO SCARCITY
*PP CYAN/1: UNPRICED DUE TO SCARCITY
*PP MAGENTA/1: UNPRICED DUE TO SCARCITY
*PP YELLOW/1: UNPRICED DUE TO SCARCITY
STATED PRINT RUN 350 SER.#'d SETS

NNO	Alicia Fox	3.00	8.00
NNO	Baron Corbin	2.50	6.00
NNO	Bayley	10.00	25.00
NNO	Becky Lynch	10.00	25.00
NNO	Big Show	4.00	10.00
NNO	Bray Wyatt	8.00	20.00
NNO	Colin Cassady	4.00	10.00
NNO	Darren Young	2.00	5.00
NNO	Dean Ambrose	6.00	15.00
NNO	John Cena	10.00	25.00
NNO	Kalisto	5.00	12.00
NNO	Kevin Owens	5.00	12.00
NNO	Kofi Kingston	2.00	5.00
NNO	Miz	3.00	8.00
NNO	Mojo Rawley	2.00	5.00
NNO	Neville	5.00	12.00
NNO	Paige	8.00	20.00
NNO	Randy Orton	5.00	12.00
NNO	Rob Van Dam	4.00	10.00
NNO	Roman Reigns	6.00	15.00
NNO	Ryback	2.50	6.00
NNO	Sami Zayn	3.00	8.00
NNO	Samoa Joe	5.00	12.00
NNO	Sasha Banks	8.00	20.00
NNO	Seth Rollins	3.00	8.00
NNO	Sheamus	5.00	12.00
NNO	Sin Cara	2.50	6.00
NNO	Summer Rae	5.00	12.00
NNO	Tyler Breeze	2.00	5.00
NNO	Xavier Woods	2.00	5.00

2016 Topps WWE Road to WrestleMania SP Inserts

STATED ODDS 1:24 HOBBY EXCLUSIVE

1	Kevin Owens	4.00	10.00
2	Charlotte	5.00	12.00
3	John Cena	8.00	20.00
4	Seth Rollins	4.00	10.00
5	Brock Lesnar	8.00	20.00
6	Tyler Breeze	1.50	4.00
7	Alberto Del Rio	8.00	20.00
8	Roman Reigns	6.00	15.00
9	Seth Rollins	2.50	6.00
10	Brock Lesnar	8.00	20.00
11	Paige	5.00	12.00
12	Goldust	2.50	6.00
13	Ryback	2.00	5.00
14	Undertaker/Kane	6.00	15.00
15	Roman Reigns	5.00	12.00
16	Sheamus	5.00	12.00
17	The New Day	1.50	4.00
18	Alberto Del Rio	2.50	6.00
19	Dean Ambrose	5.00	12.00
20	Sheamus	5.00	12.00

2016 Topps WWE Road to WrestleMania Triple Threat Autographed Dual Relics

STATED PRINT RUN 11 SER.#'d SETS

NNO	Bray Wyatt	50.00	100.00
NNO	Daniel Bryan	100.00	150.00
NNO	Dean Ambrose	25.00	60.00
NNO	John Cena	50.00	100.00
NNO	Nikki Bella	60.00	120.00
NNO	Roman Reigns	60.00	120.00
NNO	Seth Rollins	30.00	80.00

2016 Topps WWE Road to WrestleMania WWE Hall of Fame Commemorative Ring Relics

*BRONZE/50: .5X TO 1.2X BASIC MEM
*SILVER/25: .6X TO 1.5X BASIC MEM
*GOLD/10: UNPRICED DUE TO SCARCITY
RED/1: UNPRICED DUE TO SCARCITY
*P.P. BLACK/1: UNPRICED DUE TO SCARCITY
*P.P. CYAN/1: UNPRICED DUE TO SCARCITY
*P.P. MAGENTA/1: UNPRICED DUE TO SCARCITY
*P.P. YELLOW/1: UNPRICED DUE TO SCARCITY
STATED PRINT RUN 299 SER.#'d SETS

NNO	Alundra Blayze	2.00	5.00
NNO	American Dream Dusty Rhodes	1.50	4.00
NNO	Bob Backlund	1.50	4.00
NNO	Booker T	3.00	8.00
NNO	Bret Hit Man Hart	4.00	10.00
NNO	Bruno Sammartino	2.00	5.00
NNO	Don Muraco	1.50	4.00
NNO	Edge	4.00	10.00
NNO	George The Animal Steele	2.00	5.00
NNO	Hacksaw Jim Duggan	1.50	4.00
NNO	Harley Race	1.50	4.00
NNO	Iron Sheik	1.50	4.00
NNO	Jake The Snake Roberts	3.00	8.00
NNO	Jerry The King Lawler	3.00	8.00
NNO	Kevin Nash	4.00	10.00
NNO	Koko B. Ware	1.50	4.00
NNO	Larry Zbyszko	1.50	4.00
NNO	Lita	5.00	12.00
NNO	Million Dollar Man Ted DiBiase	2.00	5.00
NNO	Mr. Wonderful Paul Orndorff	1.50	4.00
NNO	Razor Ramon	4.00	10.00
NNO	Ric Flair	6.00	15.00
NNO	Ricky The Dragon Steamboat	2.00	5.00
NNO	Ron Simmons	4.00	10.00
NNO	Rowdy Roddy Piper	5.00	12.00
NNO	Sgt. Slaughter	2.00	5.00
NNO	Shawn Michaels	6.00	15.00
NNO	Stone Cold Steve Austin	8.00	20.00
NNO	Trish Stratus	8.00	20.00
NNO	Ultimate Warrior	4.00	10.00

2017 Topps WWE Road to WrestleMania

COMPLETE SET (100) 10.00 25.00
UNOPENED BOX (24 PACKS)
UNOPENED PACK (7 CARDS)
*BRONZE: .5X TO 1.2X BASIC CARDS
*BLUE/99: 1X TO 2.5X BASIC CARDS
*SILVER/25: 1.5X TO 4X BASIC CARDS
*GOLD/10: 3X TO 8X BASIC CARDS
*RED/1: UNPRICED DUE TO SCARCITY
*P.P.BLACK/1: UNPRICED DUE TO SCARCITY
*P.P.CYAN/1: UNPRICED DUE TO SCARCITY
*P.P.MAGENTA/1: UNPRICED DUE TO SCARCITY
*P.P.YELLOW/1: UNPRICED DUE TO SCARCITY

1	Roman Reigns	.60	1.50
2	Dean Ambrose	.60	1.50
3	Dean Ambrose	.60	1.50
4	John Cena	1.00	2.50
5	Charlotte	.75	2.00
6	Kalisto	.30	.75
7	Brock Lesnar	1.00	2.50
8	The Wyatt Family	.50	1.25
9	Dean Ambrose	.60	1.50
10	Kalisto	.30	.75
11	Sasha Banks	.60	1.50
12	AJ Styles	1.00	2.50
13	The Wyatt Family	.50	1.25
14	Triple H	.50	1.25
15	Triple H	.50	1.25
16	AJ Styles	1.00	2.50
17	The Rock	1.00	2.50
18	Roman Reigns/Dean Ambrose	.60	1.50
19	Brock Lesnar	1.00	2.50
20	Brock Lesnar	1.00	2.50
21	Daniel Bryan Retires	.75	2.00
22	Chris Jericho	.50	1.25
23	Kevin Owens	.50	1.25
24	Brock Lesnar	1.00	2.50

25	Kalisto	.30	.75
26	Charlotte	.75	2.00
27	AJ Styles	1.00	2.50
28	Roman Reigns/Dean Ambrose	.60	1.50
29	Brock Lesnar	1.00	2.50
30	Roman Reigns	.60	1.50
31	Shane McMahon	.30	.75
32	Dean Ambrose	.60	1.50
33	Triple H	.50	1.25
34	Undertaker	.75	2.00
35	Triple H	.50	1.25
36	Shane McMahon	.30	.75
37	Sami Zayn	.25	.60
38	The New Day	.40	1.00
39	Dean Ambrose	.60	1.50
40	Brock Lesnar	1.00	2.50
41	Triple H	.50	1.25
42	Triple H	.50	1.25
43	Roman Reigns	.60	1.50
44	Undertaker	.75	2.00
45	Brock Lesnar	1.00	2.50
46	Shane McMahon	.30	.75
47	The Godfather	.20	.50
48	Vader	.20	.50
49	The Fabulous Freebirds	.20	.50
50	John Cena	1.00	2.50
51	Sting Retires	.60	1.50
52	Kalisto	.30	.75
53	Team Total Divas	.20	.50
54	Lita	.40	1.00
55	The Usos	.25	.60
56	Zack Ryder	.20	.50
57	Chris Jericho	.50	1.25
58	Brock Lesnar	1.00	2.50
59	Charlotte	.75	2.00
60	Shane McMahon	.30	.75
61	Undertaker	.75	2.00
62	Diamond Dallas Page	.25	.60
63	Tatanka	.20	.50
64	Baron Corbin	.30	.75
65	The Rock	1.00	2.50
66	HHH/Stephanie	.50	1.25
67	Roman Reigns	.60	1.50
68	Apollo Crews	.25	.60
69	The Miz	.40	1.00
70	Maryse	.40	1.00
71	Enzo Amore/Big Cass	.60	1.50
72	Cesaro	.40	1.00
73	AJ Styles	1.00	2.50
74	Vaudevillains	.20	.50
75	Cesaro	.40	1.00
76	Gallows & Anderson	.30	.75
77	Roman Reigns	.60	1.50
	Bray Wyatt		
78	Sami Zayn	.25	.60
79	League of Nations	.20	.50
80	Dean Ambrose	.60	1.50
81	Charlotte	.75	2.00
82	Shane & Stephanie McMahon	.30	.75
83	Roman Reigns	.60	1.50
84	Dana Brooke	.40	1.00
85	Rusev	.40	1.00
86	Dean Ambrose	.60	1.50
87	Charlotte	.75	2.00
88	Roman Reigns	.60	1.50
89	Seth Rollins	.60	1.50
90	The Club	.20	.50
91	AJ Styles	1.00	2.50

92	Dean Ambrose	.60	1.50
93	Seth Rollins	.60	1.50
94	Dean Ambrose	.60	1.50
95	Team USA	.20	.50
96	Daniel Bryan	.75	2.00
	Mick Foley		
97	WWE Draft	.20	.50
98	Sasha Banks/Bayley	.60	1.50
99	John Cena/Enzo & Cass	1.00	2.50
100	Dean Ambrose	.60	1.50

2017 Topps WWE Road to WrestleMania Autographed Andre the Giant Battle Royal Trophy Relics

STATED ODDS 1:33,024

UNPRICED DUE TO SCARCITY

NNO Big Show
NNO Cesaro
NNO Curtis Axel
NNO Darren Young
NNO Goldust
NNO Heath Slater
NNO Hideo Itami
NNO Jack Swagger
NNO Kane
NNO Konnor
NNO Mark Henry
NNO The Miz
NNO Viktor

2017 Topps WWE Road to WrestleMania Andre the Giant Battle Royal Trophy Relics

*BLUE/50: .5X TO 1.2X BASIC MEM
*SILVER/25: .6X TO 1.5X BASIC MEM
*GOLD/10: .75X TO 2X BASIC MEM
*RED/1: UNPRICED DUE TO SCARCITY
*P.P.BLACK/1: UNPRICED DUE TO SCARCITY
*P.P.CYAN/1: UNPRICED DUE TO SCARCITY
*P.P.MAGENTA/1: UNPRICED DUE TO SCARCITY
*P.P.YELLOW/1: UNPRICED DUE TO SCARCITY
STATED ODDS 1:1,296

NNO	Baron Corbin	3.00	8.00
NNO	Big Show	2.50	6.00
NNO	Bo Dallas	2.00	5.00
NNO	Cesaro	4.00	10.00
NNO	Curtis Axel	2.00	5.00
NNO	Darren Young	2.00	5.00
NNO	Diamond Dallas Page	2.50	6.00
NNO	Fandango	2.00	5.00
NNO	Goldust	2.50	6.00
NNO	Heath Slater	2.00	5.00
NNO	Hideo Itami	3.00	8.00
NNO	Jack Swagger	2.00	5.00
NNO	Kane	2.50	6.00
NNO	Konnor	2.00	5.00
NNO	Mark Henry	2.00	5.00
NNO	R-Truth	2.00	5.00
NNO	Tatanka	2.00	5.00
NNO	The Miz	4.00	10.00
NNO	Tyler Breeze	2.00	5.00
NNO	Viktor	2.00	5.00

2017 Topps WWE Road to WrestleMania Autographed Shirt Relics

STATED ODDS 1:22,016

UNPRICED DUE TO SCARCITY

NNO Asuka
NNO Austin Aries
NNO Bayley
NNO Becky Lynch
NNO Big Cass
NNO Big E
NNO Bray Wyatt
NNO Cesaro
NNO Darren Young
NNO Dolph Ziggler
NNO Enzo Amore
NNO Hideo Itami
NNO John Cena
NNO Kevin Owens
NNO Kofi Kingston
NNO Natalya
NNO Randy Orton
NNO Roman Reigns
NNO Sami Zayn
NNO Sasah Banks
NNO Seth Rollins
NNO Shinsuke Nakamura
NNO Simon Gotch
NNO Xavier Woods
NNO Zack Ryder

2017 Topps WWE Road to WrestleMania Autographs

*BLUE/50: .6X TO 1.5X BASIC AUTOS
*SILVER/25: .75X TO 2X BASIC AUTOS
*GOLD/10: 1X TO 2.5X BASIC AUTOS
*RED/1: UNPRICED DUE TO SCARCITY
*P.P.BLACK/1: UNPRICED DUE TO SCARCITY
*P.P.CYAN/1: UNPRICED DUE TO SCARCITY
*P.P.MAGENTA/1: UNPRICED DUE TO SCARCITY
*P.P.YELLOW/1: UNPRICED DUE TO SCARCITY
STATED ODDS 1:36

NNO	Asuka	15.00	40.00
NNO	Austin Aries	8.00	20.00
NNO	Bayley	20.00	50.00
NNO	Becky Lynch	15.00	40.00
NNO	Big E	8.00	20.00
NNO	Bray Wyatt	12.00	30.00
NNO	Cesaro	10.00	25.00
NNO	Charlotte	12.00	30.00
NNO	Dean Ambrose	12.00	30.00
NNO	Finn Balor	12.00	30.00
NNO	Hideo Itami	6.00	15.00
NNO	John Cena		
NNO	Kevin Owens	15.00	40.00
NNO	Kofi Kingston	6.00	15.00
NNO	Lana	8.00	20.00
NNO	Lex Luger	10.00	25.00
NNO	Maryse	12.00	30.00
NNO	The Miz	6.00	15.00
NNO	Nikki Bella	15.00	40.00
NNO	Roman Reigns	10.00	25.00
NNO	Rusev	6.00	15.00
NNO	Sasha Banks	20.00	50.00
NNO	Seth Rollins	10.00	25.00
NNO	Shinsuke Nakamura	20.00	50.00
NNO	Sting	25.00	60.00

2017 Topps WWE Road to WrestleMania Kiss

*GOLD/10: .6X TO 1.5X BASIC KISS

UNPRICED DUE TO SCARCITY
NNO Asuka
NNO Austin Aries
NNO Bayley
NNO Becky Lynch
NNO Big Cass
NNO Big E
NNO Bray Wyatt
NNO Cesaro
NNO Darren Young
NNO Dolph Ziggler
NNO Enzo Amore
NNO Hideo Itami
NNO John Cena
NNO Kevin Owens
NNO Kofi Kingston
NNO Natalya
NNO Randy Orton
NNO Roman Reigns
NNO Sami Zayn
NNO Sasah Banks
NNO Seth Rollins
NNO Shinsuke Nakamura
NNO Simon Gotch
NNO Xavier Woods
NNO Zack Ryder

*RED/1: UNPRICED DUE TO SCARCITY
STATED ODDS 1:91

NNO	Alexa Bliss	60.00	120.00
NNO	Becky Lynch	20.00	50.00
NNO	Carmella	20.00	50.00
NNO	Charlotte	15.00	40.00
NNO	Liv Morgan	20.00	50.00
NNO	Natalya	12.00	30.00
NNO	Nia Jax	12.00	30.00
NNO	Renee Young	12.00	30.00

2017 Topps WWE Road to WrestleMania Kiss Autographs

*GOLD/10: UNPRICED DUE TO SCARCITY
*RED/1: UNPRICED DUE TO SCARCITY
STATED ODDS 1:354

NNO	Alexa Bliss	100.00	200.00
NNO	Becky Lynch	50.00	100.00
NNO	Carmella	30.00	80.00
NNO	Charlotte	50.00	100.00
NNO	Liv Morgan	60.00	120.00
NNO	Natalya	25.00	60.00
NNO	Nia Jax	20.00	50.00
NNO	Nikki Bella	60.00	120.00
NNO	Renee Young	25.00	60.00

2017 Topps WWE Road to WrestleMania Dual Autographs

STATED ODDS 1:726
STATED PRINT RUN 10 SER.#'d SETS

NNO	Asuka/Bayley	100.00	200.00
NNO	Charlotte/R.Flair	100.00	200.00
NNO	F.Balor/H.Itami	60.00	120.00
NNO	J.Cena/N.Bella	125.00	250.00
NNO	K.Kingston/Big E	30.00	75.00
NNO	Miz/Maryse	60.00	120.00
NNO	R.Reigns/D.Ambrose		
NNO	Rusev/Lana	75.00	150.00
NNO	S.Banks/B.Lynch	100.00	200.00
NNO	S.Rollins/Cesaro	60.00	120.00
NNO	S.Nakamura/A.Aries		
NNO	Sting/L.Luger	75.00	150.00

2017 Topps WWE Road to WrestleMania Autographed NXT TakeOver Dallas Mat Relics

STATED PRINT RUN 10 SER.#'d SETS
UNPRICED DUE TO SCARCITY

NNO Asuka
NNO Austin Aries
NNO Bayley
NNO Sami Zayn
NNO Samoa Joe
NNO Shinsuke Nakamura

2017 Topps WWE Road to WrestleMania NXT TakeOver Dallas Mat Relics

*BLUE/50: .5X TO 1.2X BASIC MEM
*SILVER/25: .6X TO 1.5X BASIC MEM
*GOLD/10: .75X TO 2X BASIC MEM
*RED/1: UNPRICED DUE TO SCARCITY
*P.P.BLACK/1: UNPRICED DUE TO SCARCITY
*P.P.CYAN/1: UNPRICED DUE TO SCARCITY
*P.P.MAGENTA/1: UNPRICED DUE TO SCARCITY
*P.P.YELLOW/1: UNPRICED DUE TO SCARCITY

STATED ODDS 1:2,642

NNO	Asuka	5.00	12.00
NNO	Austin Aries	3.00	8.00
NNO	Baron Corbin	2.50	6.00
NNO	Bayley	5.00	12.00
NNO	Chad Gable	2.00	5.00
NNO	Finn Balor	6.00	15.00
NNO	Jason Jordan	2.00	5.00
NNO	Sami Zayn	2.00	5.00
NNO	Samoa Joe	5.00	12.00
NNO	Shinsuke Nakamura	4.00	10.00

2017 Topps WWE Road to WrestleMania Shirt Relics

*BLUE/50: .5X TO 1.2X BASIC MEM
*SILVER/25: .6X TO 1.5X BASIC MEM
*GOLD/10: UNPRICED DUE TO SCARCITY
*RED/1: UNPRICED DUE TO SCARCITY
*P.P.BLACK/1: UNPRICED DUE TO SCARCITY
*P.P.CYAN/1: UNPRICED DUE TO SCARCITY
*P.P.MAGENTA/1: UNPRICED DUE TO SCARCITY
*P.P.YELLOW/1: UNPRICED DUE TO SCARCITY
STATED ODDS 1:870

NNO	Asuka	4.00	10.00
NNO	Austin Aries	2.50	6.00
NNO	Becky Lynch	4.00	10.00
NNO	Big Cass	1.50	4.00
NNO	Bray Wyatt	3.00	8.00
NNO	Cesaro	2.50	6.00
NNO	Charlotte	5.00	12.00
NNO	Darren Young	1.25	3.00
NNO	Dolph Ziggler	2.00	5.00
NNO	Finn Balor	5.00	12.00
NNO	Hideo Itami	2.00	5.00
NNO	John Cena	6.00	15.00
NNO	Kofi Kingston	1.50	4.00
NNO	Natalya	2.50	6.00
NNO	No Way Jose	1.25	3.00
NNO	Randy Orton	3.00	8.00
NNO	Roman Reigns	4.00	10.00
NNO	Sasha Banks	4.00	10.00
NNO	Seth Rollins	4.00	10.00
NNO	Shinsuke Nakamura	3.00	8.00
NNO	Simon Gotch	1.25	3.00
NNO	Zack Ryder	1.25	3.00

2017 Topps WWE Road to WrestleMania Autographed Triple Threat Dual Relics

STATED ODDS 1:66,048
STATED PRINT RUN 10 SER.#'d SETS

NNO	Brock Lesnar	125.00	250.00
NNO	John Cena	125.00	200.00
NNO	Roman Reigns	60.00	120.00
NNO	Sasha Banks	120.00	200.00

2017 Topps WWE Road to WrestleMania Autographed WrestleMania 32 Mat Relics

STATED ODDS 1:33,024
UNPRICED DUE TO SCARCITY

NNO AJ Styles
NNO Becky Lynch
NNO Bray Wyatt
NNO Brie Bella
NNO Brock Lesnar
NNO Chris Jericho

NNO Dean Ambrose
NNO John Cena
NNO Kevin Owens
NNO Natalya
NNO Roman Reigns
NNO Sasha Banks
NNO Zack Ryder

2017 Topps WWE Road to WrestleMania WrestleMania 32 Mat Relics

*BLUE/50: .5X TO 1.2X BASIC MEM
*SILVER/25: .6X TO 1.5X BASIC MEM
*GOLD/10: .75X TO 2X BASIC MEM
*RED/1: UNPRICED DUE TO SCARCITY
*P.P.BLACK/1: UNPRICED DUE TO SCARCITY
*P.P.CYAN/1: UNPRICED DUE TO SCARCITY
*P.P.MAGENTA/1: UNPRICED DUE TO SCARCITY
*P.P.YELLOW/1: UNPRICED DUE TO SCARCITY
STATED ODDS 1:1,296

NNO	AJ Styles	10.00	25.00
NNO	Baron Corbin	3.00	8.00
NNO	Becky Lynch	6.00	15.00
NNO	Bray Wyatt	5.00	12.00
NNO	Brie Bella	5.00	12.00
NNO	Brock Lesnar	10.00	25.00
NNO	Charlotte	8.00	20.00
NNO	Chris Jericho	5.00	12.00
NNO	Dean Ambrose	6.00	15.00
NNO	John Cena	10.00	25.00
NNO	Kevin Owens	5.00	12.00
NNO	Lana	6.00	15.00
NNO	Natalya	4.00	10.00
NNO	The Rock	10.00	25.00
NNO	Roman Reigns	6.00	15.00
NNO	Sasha Banks	6.00	15.00
NNO	Shane McMahon	3.00	8.00
NNO	Triple H	5.00	12.00
NNO	Undertaker	8.00	20.00
NNO	Zack Ryder	2.00	5.00

2017 Topps WWE Road to WrestleMania WrestleMania 33 Roster

COMPLETE SET (50) 10.00 25.00
STATED ODDS 2:1

WMR1	Triple H	.75	2.00
WMR2	Stephanie McMahon	.40	1.00
WMR3	Roman Reigns	1.00	2.50
WMR4	The Rock	1.50	4.00
WMR5	John Cena	1.50	4.00
WMR6	Bray Wyatt	.75	2.00
WMR7	Erick Rowan	.30	.75
WMR8	Braun Strowman	.40	1.00
WMR9	Luke Harper	.30	.75
WMR10	Undertaker	1.25	3.00
WMR11	Shane McMahon	.50	1.25
WMR12	Brock Lesnar	1.50	4.00
WMR13	Dean Ambrose	1.00	2.50
WMR14	Charlotte	1.25	3.00
WMR15	Ric Flair	.75	2.00
WMR16	Sasha Banks	1.00	2.50
WMR17	Becky Lynch	1.00	2.50
WMR18	Chris Jericho	.75	2.00
WMR19	AJ Styles	1.50	4.00
WMR20	Baron Corbin	.50	1.25
WMR21	Kane	.40	1.00

WMR22	Big Show	.40	1.00
WMR23	Mark Henry	.30	.75
WMR24	Zack Ryder	.30	.75
WMR25	Kevin Owens	.75	2.00
WMR26	Sami Zayn	.40	1.00
WMR27	The Miz	.60	1.50
WMR28	Dolph Ziggler	.50	1.25
WMR29	Sin Cara	.40	1.00
WMR30	Kalisto	.50	1.25
WMR31	Kofi Kingston	.40	1.00
WMR32	Big E	.40	1.00
WMR33	Xavier Woods	.40	1.00
WMR34	Sheamus	.60	1.50
WMR35	Rusev	.60	1.50
WMR36	Jey Uso	.40	1.00
WMR37	Jimmy Uso	.40	1.00
WMR38	Darren Young	.30	.75
WMR39	R-Truth	.30	.75
WMR40	Goldust	.40	1.00
WMR41	Heath Slater	.30	.75
WMR42	Brie Bella	.75	2.00
WMR43	Natalya	.60	1.50
WMR44	Alicia Fox	.50	1.25
WMR45	Eva Marie	.75	2.00
WMR46	Lana	1.00	2.50
WMR47	Naomi	.60	1.50
WMR48	Tamina	.40	1.00
WMR49	Emma	.75	2.00
WMR50	Summer Rae	.75	2.00

2018 Topps WWE Road to WrestleMania

COMPLETE SET (100) 8.00 20.00
UNOPENED BOX (24 PACKS)
UNOPENED PACK (7 CARDS)
*BRONZE: .5X TO 1.2X BASIC CARDS
*BLUE/99: .75X TO 2X BASIC CARDS
*SILVER/25: 2X TO 5X BASIC CARDS
*GOLD/10: UNPRICED DUE TO SCARCITY
*RED/1: UNPRICED DUE TO SCARCITY
*P.P.BLACK/1: UNPRICED DUE TO SCARCITY
*P.P.CYAN/1: UNPRICED DUE TO SCARCITY
*P.P.MAGENTA/1: UNPRICED DUE TO SCARCITY
*P.P.YELLOW/1: UNPRICED DUE TO SCARCITY

1	Roman Reigns	.60	1.50
2	Cesaro & Sheamus	.50	1.25
3	Roman Reigns	.60	1.50
4	Universal Champion Kevin Owens	.60	1.50
5	Roman Reigns	.60	1.50
6	Kevin Owens	.60	1.50
7	Team Raw defeats Team SmackDown	.50	1.25
8	Cesaro & Sheamus	.50	1.25
9	Undertaker Returns	1.00	2.50
10	Chris Jericho	.60	1.50
11	Luke Gallows & Karl Anderson	.30	.75
12	Kevin Owens	.60	1.50
13	Samoa Joe Debuts	.50	1.25
14	Kevin Owens	.60	1.50
15	Roman Reigns	.60	1.50
16	Kevin Owens	1.00	2.50
17	Roman Reigns	1.00	2.50
18	Mick Foley	.60	1.50
19	Undertaker	1.00	2.50
20	Undertaker	1.00	2.50
21	Ricky The Dragon Steamboat	.40	1.00
22	Diamond Dallas Page	.40	1.00
23	Kurt Angle Returns	.60	1.50
24	Kevin Owens	.60	1.50

25	The Hardy Boyz Return	.60	1.50
26	Seth Rollins	.60	1.50
27	Brock Lesnar	1.00	2.50
28	Roman Reigns	.60	1.50
29	Kurt Angle	.60	1.50
30	The Revival	.30	.75
31	Finn Balor	.60	1.50
32	Alexa Bliss	1.25	3.00
33	Elias	.60	1.50
34	Chris Jericho	.60	1.50
35	Bray Wyatt	.60	1.50
36	Braun Strowman	.60	1.50
37	Goldust	.50	1.25
38	The Miz	.50	1.25
39	Cesaro & Sheamus	.50	1.25
40	Samoa Joe	.50	1.25
41	Big Cass Turns	.30	.75
42	Cesaro & Sheamus	.50	1.25
43	Universal Champion Brock Lesnar	1.00	2.50
44	Kurt Angle	.60	1.50
45	Braun Strowman	.60	1.50
46	Dean Ambrose	.60	1.50
47	TJP	.30	.75
48	The Brian Kendrick	.40	1.00
49	The Brian Kendrick	.40	1.00
50	Rich Swann	.30	.75
51	Neville Returns	.40	1.00
52	Neville	.40	1.00
53	Neville	.40	1.00
54	Noam Dar	.40	1.00
55	Akira Tozawa	.40	1.00
56	WWE Champion AJ Styles	1.00	2.50
57	Dolph Ziggler	.50	1.25
58	Bray Wyatt	.60	1.50
59	Randy Orton	.60	1.50
60	The Miz	.50	1.25
61	Edge and Undertaker Return	1.00	2.50
62	Team SmackDown defeats Team Raw	1.00	2.50
63	James Ellsworth	.25	.60
64	The New Wyatt Family	.60	1.50
65	The Miz	.50	1.25
66	Baron Corbin	.40	1.00
67	AJ Styles	1.00	2.50
68	American Alpha	.25	.60
69	Dean Ambrose	.50	1.25
70	John Cena	1.00	2.50
71	Randy Orton	.60	1.50
72	Randy Orton	.60	1.50
73	Bray Wyatt	.60	1.50
74	Randy Orton	.60	1.50
75	The Usos	.40	1.00
76	Shane McMahon	1.00	2.50
77	Mojo Rawley	.25	.60
78	Dean Ambrose	.50	1.25
79	AJ Styles	1.00	2.50
80	John Cena Proposes to Nikki Bella	1.00	2.50
81	Randy Orton	.60	1.50
82	Tye Dillinger	.25	.60
83	Shinsuke Nakamura	.60	1.50
84	The Superstar Shake-Up	.75	2.00
85	Jinder Mahal	.30	.75
86	Kevin Owens	.60	1.50
87	Shinsuke Nakamura	.60	1.50
88	The Usos	.40	1.00
89	Jinder Mahal	.30	.75
90	Maria Kanellis	.60	1.50
91	WWE Champion Jinder Mahal	.30	.75
92	Baron Corbin	.40	1.00

93 AJ Styles	1.00	2.50
94 The New Day	.40	1.00
95 Kevin Owens	.60	1.50
96 John Cena	1.00	2.50
97 WWE Champion Jinder Mahal	.30	.75
98 AJ Styles	1.00	2.50
99 Shinsuke Nakamura	1.00	2.50
100 Jinder Mahal	.30	.75

2018 Topps WWE Road to WrestleMania Commemorative Andre the Giant Battle Royal Trophy Relics

*BRONZE/99: .5X TO 1.2X BASIC MEM
*BLUE/50: .6X TO 1.5X BASIC MEM
*SILVER/25: .75X TO 2X BASIC MEM
*GOLD/10: UNPRICED DUE TO SCARCITY
*RED/1: UNPRICED DUE TO SCARCITY
STATED ODDS 1:936

ACBR Braun Strowman	6.00	15.00
ACBS Big Show	2.50	6.00
ACCG Chad Gable	2.50	6.00
ACDZ Dolph Ziggler	2.50	6.00
ACFA Fandango	5.00	12.00
ACGO Goldust	2.50	6.00
ACHS Heath Slater	2.50	6.00
ACJI Jimmy Uso	5.00	12.00
ACJJ Jason Jordan	2.50	6.00
ACJM Jinder Mahal	2.50	6.00
ACJU Jey Uso	2.50	6.00
ACKD Killian Dain	3.00	8.00
ACLH Luke Harper	3.00	8.00
ACMH Mark Henry	2.50	6.00
ACMR Mojo Rawley	3.00	8.00
ACRH Rhyno	3.00	8.00
ACRT R-Truth	2.50	6.00
ACSZ Sami Zayn	4.00	10.00
ACTB Tian Bing	2.50	6.00
ACTBR Tyler Breeze	2.50	6.00

2018 Topps WWE Road to WrestleMania Autographed Commemorative Andre the Giant Battle Royal Trophy Re

STATED ODDS 1:24,096
STATED PRINT RUN 10 SER.#'d SETS
UNPRICED DUE TO SCARCITY

NNO Big Show
NNO Braun Strowman
NNO Dolph Ziggler
NNO Fandango
NNO Goldust
NNO Heath Slater
NNO Jey Uso
NNO Jimmy Uso
NNO Jinder Mahal
NNO Killian Dain
NNO Luke Harper
NNO Mark Henry
NNO Mojo Rawley
NNO Sami Zayn
NNO Tyler Breeze

2018 Topps WWE Road to WrestleMania Autographed Dual Relics

STATED ODDS 1:96,384
STATED PRINT RUN 10 SER.#'d SETS

UNPRICED DUE TO SCARCITY
NNO Alexa Bliss
NNO John Cena
NNO Kevin Owens
NNO Naomi
NNO Roman Reigns
NNO Shinsuke Nakamura

2018 Topps WWE Road to WrestleMania Autographed NXT TakeOver Orlando Mat Relics

STATED ODDS 1:32,128
STATED PRINT RUN 10 SER.#'d SETS
UNPRICED DUE TO SCARCITY

NNO Aleister Black
NNO Asuka
NNO Bobby Roode
NNO Eric Young
NNO Johnny Gargano
NNO Kassius Ohno
NNO Nikki Cross
NNO Roderick Strong
NNO Ruby Riot
NNO Shinsuke Nakamura
NNO Tommaso Ciampa

2018 Topps WWE Road to WrestleMania Autographed Shirt Relics

STATED ODDS 1:32,128
STATED PRINT RUN 10 SER.#'d SETS
UNPRICED DUE TO SCARCITY

NNO Becky Lynch
NNO Carmella
NNO Cesaro
NNO Goldust
NNO Karl Anderson
NNO Kevin Owens
NNO Luke Gallows
NNO Luke Harper
NNO Naomi
NNO Roman Reigns
NNO Sting
NNO Xavier Woods

2018 Topps WWE Road to WrestleMania Autographed Wrestlemania 33 Mat Relics

STATED ODDS 1:24,096
STATED PRINT RUN 10 SER.#'d SETS
UNPRICED DUE TO SCARCITY

NNO AJ Styles
NNO Charlotte Flair
NNO Chris Jericho
NNO Jeff Hardy
NNO Kevin Owens
NNO Maryse
NNO Naomi
NNO Randy Orton
NNO Roman Reigns
NNO Sasha Banks
NNO Stephanie McMahon
NNO The Miz
NNO Triple H
NNO Undertaker

2018 Topps WWE Road to WrestleMania Autographs

*BLUE/50: .5X TO 1.2X BASIC AUTOS
*SILVER/25: .6X TO 1.5X BASIC AUTOS
*GOLD/10: UNPRICED DUE TO SCARCITY
*RED/1: UNPRICED DUE TO SCARCITY
*P.P.BLACK/1: UNPRICED DUE TO SCARCITY
*P.P.CYAN/1: UNPRICED DUE TO SCARCITY
*P.P.MAGENTA/1: UNPRICED DUE TO SCARCITY
*P.P.YELLOW/1: UNPRICED DUE TO SCARCITY
STATED ODDS 1:32

AAB Aleister Black	12.00	30.00
AAL Alexa Bliss	30.00	75.00
AAS AJ Styles	15.00	40.00
ABA Bayley	12.00	30.00
ABL Becky Lynch	15.00	40.00
ABW Bray Wyatt	8.00	20.00
ACA Carmella	10.00	25.00
ACF Charlotte Flair	15.00	40.00
ADA Dean Ambrose	12.00	30.00
ADW Dash Wilder	6.00	15.00
AEM Ember Moon	12.00	30.00
AEY Eric Young	5.00	12.00
AFB Finn Balor	15.00	40.00
AJG Johnny Gargano	10.00	25.00
AJH Jeff Hardy	15.00	40.00
AJM Jinder Mahal	10.00	25.00
AKA Kassius Ohno	6.00	15.00
AKO Kevin Owens	8.00	20.00
AMH Matt Hardy	15.00	40.00
ANA Naomi	6.00	15.00
ANC Nikki Cross	10.00	25.00
ARS Roderick Strong	5.00	12.00
ASB Sasha Banks	20.00	50.00
ASD Scott Dawson	5.00	12.00
ASJ Samoa Joe	8.00	20.00
ASN Shinsuke Nakamura	12.00	30.00
ASR Seth Rollins	12.00	30.00
ATC Tommaso Ciampa	5.00	12.00
ATD Tye Dillinger	6.00	15.00
ATM The Miz	8.00	20.00
AASU Asuka	15.00	40.00
ABOR Bobby Roode	10.00	25.00
AKUA Kurt Angle	15.00	40.00
ARRI Ruby Riot	12.00	30.00

2018 Topps WWE Road to WrestleMania Autographs Silver

STATED ODDS 1:105
STATED PRINT RUN 25 SER.#'d SETS

ASM Stephanie McMahon	125.00	250.00
ATH Triple H	150.00	300.00
AUN Undertaker	150.00	300.00
ANAT Natalya	10.00	25.00

2018 Topps WWE Road to WrestleMania Dual Autographs

STATED ODDS 1:1,928
STATED PRINT RUN 10 SER.#'d SETS

DABR A.Black/B.Roode/10	60.00	120.00
DAFS F.Balor/Samoa Joe/4		
DAJT T.Ciampa/J.Gargano/10	30.00	75.00
DAMJ Matt & Jeff Hardy/10	30.00	75.00
DARK K.Ohno/R.Strong/10		
DARN N.Cross/R.Riot/10	20.00	50.00
DAUK K.Angle/Undertaker/10	250.00	400.00

2018 Topps WWE Road to WrestleMania Dual Relics

*SILVER/25: .5X TO 1.2X BASIC MEM
*GOLD/10: UNPRICED DUE TO SCARCITY
*RED/1: UNPRICED DUE TO SCARCITY
STATED PRINT RUN 50 SER.#'d SETS

DRAB Alexa Bliss	30.00	75.00
DRBL Brock Lesnar	10.00	25.00
DRJC John Cena	15.00	40.00
DRKO Kevin Owens	10.00	25.00
DRNA Naomi	12.00	30.00
DRRR Roman Reigns	10.00	25.00
DRSN Shinsuke Nakamura		
DRSR Seth Rollins	12.00	30.00

2018 Topps WWE Road to WrestleMania Kiss

*GOLD/10: UNPRICED DUE TO SCARCITY
*RED/1: UNPRICED DUE TO SCARCITY
STATED ODDS 1:112

KAB Alexa Bliss	60.00	120.00
KAS Asuka	30.00	75.00
KCA Carmella	25.00	60.00
KCF Charlotte Flair	25.00	60.00
KMA Maryse	20.00	50.00
KNA Naomi	12.00	30.00
KRR Ruby Riot	20.00	50.00

2018 Topps WWE Road to WrestleMania Kiss Autographs

*GOLD/10: UNPRICED DUE TO SCARCITY
*RED/1: UNPRICED DUE TO SCARCITY
STATED ODDS 1:445

NNO Alexa Bliss	120.00	250.00
NNO Asuka	50.00	100.00
NNO Becky Lynch	60.00	120.00
NNO Carmella	50.00	100.00
NNO Charlotte Flair	75.00	150.00
NNO Goldust	75.00	150.00
NNO Maryse	50.00	100.00
NNO Nikki Cross	50.00	100.00
NNO Ruby Riot	50.00	100.00

2018 Topps WWE Road to WrestleMania NXT TakeOver Orlando Mat Relics

*BRONZE/99: SAME VALUE AS BASIC MEM
*BLUE/50: .5X TO 1.2X BASIC MEM
*SILVER/25: .6X TO 1.5X BASIC MEM
*GOLD/10: UNPRICED DUE TO SCARCITY
*RED/1: UNPRICED DUE TO SCARCITY
STATED ODDS 1:1,236

MRAB Aleister Black	6.00	15.00
MRAS Asuka	6.00	15.00
MRBR Bobby Roode	6.00	15.00
MRDW Dash Wilder	2.50	6.00
MREM Ember Moon	3.00	8.00
MREY Eric Young	2.50	6.00
MRJG Johnny Gargano	3.00	8.00
MRKO Kassius Ohno	6.00	15.00
MRNC Nikki Cross	4.00	10.00
MRRR Ruby Riot	5.00	12.00
MRRS Roderick Strong	2.50	6.00
MRSD Scott Dawson	3.00	8.00
MRSN Shinsuke Nakamura	4.00	10.00

MRTC Tommaso Ciampa	3.00	8.00	
MRTD Tye Dillinger	3.00	8.00	

2018 Topps WWE Road to WrestleMania Road to WrestleMania 34

RTW1 The Miz & Miztourage	1.25	3.00
RTW2 Big Cass	.75	2.00
RTW3 Finn Balor	1.50	4.00
RTW4 Dean Ambrose & Seth Rollins	1.50	4.00
RTW5 Brock Lesnar	2.50	6.00
RTW6 Braun Strowman	1.50	4.00
RTW7 John Cena	2.50	6.00
RTW8 Jeff Hardy	1.25	3.00
RTW9 John Cena and Roman Reigns	2.50	6.00
RTW10 Neville	1.00	2.50
RTW11 Enzo Amore	.60	1.50
RTW12 The Brian Kendrick	1.00	2.50
RTW13 The Usos	.60	1.50
RTW14 John Cena	2.50	6.00
RTW15 Randy Orton	1.50	4.00
RTW16 AJ Styles	2.50	6.00
RTW17 Jinder Mahal	.75	2.00
RTW18 Bobby Roode	1.00	2.50
RTW19 Shelton Benjamin	.75	2.00
RTW20 Shinsuke Nakamura	1.50	4.00

2018 Topps WWE Road to WrestleMania Shirt Relics

*BLUE/50: .5X TO 1.2X BASIC MEM
*SILVER/25: .6X TO 1.5X BASIC MEM
*GOLD/10: UNPRICED DUE TO SCARCITY
*RED/1: UNPRICED DUE TO SCARCITY
STATED ODDS 1:1,890
STATED PRINT RUN 99 SER.#'d SETS

SRAB Alexa Bliss	12.00	30.00
SRBL Becky Lynch	10.00	25.00
SRBR Brock Lesnar	5.00	12.00
SRCA Carmella	6.00	15.00
SRCE Cesaro	3.00	8.00
SRCG Chad Gable	2.50	6.00
SRGO Goldust	3.00	8.00
SRJC John Cena	6.00	15.00
SRJI Jimmy Uso	2.50	6.00
SRJJ Jason Jordan	3.00	8.00
SRKA Karl Anderson	2.50	6.00
SRKO Kevin Owens	2.50	6.00
SRLG Luke Gallows	2.50	6.00
SRLH Luke Harper	3.00	8.00
SRNA Naomi	4.00	10.00
SRNW No Way Jose	2.50	6.00
SRRR Roman Reigns	4.00	10.00
SRSR Seth Rollins	4.00	10.00
SRST Sting	10.00	25.00
SRXW Xavier Woods	2.50	6.00

2018 Topps WWE Road to WrestleMania WrestleMania 33 Mat Relics

*BRONZE/99: SAME VALUE AS BASIC MEM
*BLUE/50: .5X TO 1.2X BASIC MEM
*SILVER/25: .6X TO 1.5X BASIC MEM
*GOLD/10: UNPRICED DUE TO SCARCITY
*RED/1: UNPRICED DUE TO SCARCITY
STATED ODDS 1:748
STATED PRINT RUN 199 SER.#'d SETS

WMAB Alexa Bliss	10.00	25.00
WMAS AJ Styles	8.00	20.00
WMBA Bayley	6.00	15.00
WMBR Brock Lesnar	6.00	15.00
WMBY Bray Wyatt	10.00	25.00
WMCA Carmella	5.00	12.00
WMCF Charlotte Flair	6.00	15.00
WMCJ Chris Jericho	4.00	10.00
WMDA Dean Ambrose	5.00	12.00
WMJC John Cena	6.00	15.00
WMJH Jeff Hardy	6.00	15.00
WMKO Kevin Owens	4.00	10.00
WMMA Maryse	6.00	15.00
WMMH Matt Hardy	4.00	10.00
WMNA Naomi	4.00	10.00
WMNB Nikki Bella	5.00	12.00
WMRO Randy Orton	3.00	8.00
WMRR Roman Reigns	10.00	25.00
WMSB Sasha Banks	6.00	15.00
WMSM Stephanie McMahon	6.00	15.00
WMSR Seth Rollins	5.00	12.00
WMTH Triple H	8.00	20.00
WMTM The Miz	3.00	8.00
WMUN Undertaker	15.00	40.00
WMNAT Natalya	3.00	8.00

2018 Topps WWE Road to WrestleMania WrestleMania 34 Roster

COMPLETE SET (50)	12.00	30.00
R1 Roman Reigns	.75	2.00
R2 Brock Lesnar	1.25	3.00
R3 Randy Orton	.75	2.00
R4 Bray Wyatt	.75	2.00
R5 Seth Rollins	.75	2.00
R6 Triple H	.75	2.00
R7 John Cena	1.25	3.00
R8 The Miz	.60	1.50
R9 Kevin Owens	.75	2.00
R10 Chris Jericho	.75	2.00
R11 AJ Styles	1.25	3.00
R12 Dean Ambrose	.60	1.50
R13 Baron Corbin	.50	1.25
R14 Mojo Rawley	.30	.75
R15 Jinder Mahal	.40	1.00
R16 Asuka	1.00	2.50
R17 Matt Hardy	.75	2.00
R18 Jeff Hardy	.60	1.50
R19 Luke Gallows	.40	1.00
R20 Karl Anderson	.30	.75
R21 Cesaro	.60	1.50
R22 Sheamus	.60	1.50
R23 Enzo Amore	.30	.75
R24 Big Cass	.40	1.00
R25 Bayley	.50	1.25
R26 Charlotte Flair	1.00	2.50
R27 Sasha Banks	1.00	2.50
R28 Nia Jax	.50	1.25
R29 Naomi	.40	1.00
R30 Alexa Bliss	1.50	4.00
R31 Becky Lynch	.75	2.00
R32 Mickie James	.60	1.50
R33 Natalya	.40	1.00
R34 Carmella	.60	1.50
R35 Braun Strowman	.75	2.00
R36 Big Show	.30	.75
R37 Sami Zayn	.30	.75
R38 Luke Harper	.50	1.25
R39 Dolph Ziggler	.40	1.00
R40 Fandango	.30	.75
R41 Tyler Breeze	.30	.75
R42 Jason Jordan	.30	.75
R43 Chad Gable	.30	.75
R44 Jey Uso	.30	.75
R45 Jimmy Uso	.30	.75
R46 Heath Slater	.30	.75
R47 Rhyno	.30	.75
R48 Goldust	.60	1.50
R49 R-Truth	.40	1.00
R50 Titus O'Neil	.30	.75

2019 Topps WWE Road to WrestleMania

COMPLETE SET (100)	10.00	25.00
UNOPENED BOX (24 PACKS)		
UNOPENED PACK (7 CARDS)		

*BRONZE: .5X TO 1.2X BASIC CARDS
*BLUE/99: .75X TO 2X BASIC CARDS
*SILVER/25: 2X TO 5X BASIC CARDS
*GOLD/10: UNPRICED DUE TO SCARCITY
*RED/1: UNPRICED DUE TO SCARCITY
*P.P.BLACK/1: UNPRICED DUE TO SCARCITY
*P.P.CYAN/1: UNPRICED DUE TO SCARCITY
*P.P.MAGENTA/1: UNPRICED DUE TO SCARCITY
*P.P.YELLOW/1: UNPRICED DUE TO SCARCITY

1 Braun Strowman	.60	1.50
2 Braun Strowman	1.00	2.50
3 Roman Reigns	1.00	2.50
4 The Shield	.60	1.50
5 Kane	.40	1.00
6 Demon Finn Balor	.60	1.50
7 Kurt Angle	.50	1.25
8 SmackDown Live Siege	.50	1.25
9 Cesaro & Sheamus	.40	1.00
10 The Shield	.60	1.50
11 Triple H	.60	1.50
12 Braun Strowman	.60	1.50
13 The Shield	.60	1.50
14 Team Raw Defeat Team SmackDown	.60	1.50
15 Roman Reigns	.60	1.50
16 Matt Hardy Snaps	.50	1.25
17 Braun Strowman	.60	1.50
18 Seth Rollins & Jason Jordan	.60	1.50
19 Roman Reigns	.60	1.50
20 The Balor Club	.60	1.50
21 Stone Cold Steve Austin Returns	1.25	3.00
22 The Miz	.50	1.25
23 Cesaro & Sheamus	.40	1.00
24 John Cena	1.00	2.50
25 Elias	.50	1.25
26 Finn Balor and Seth Rollins	.60	1.50
27 Braun Strowman	.60	1.50
28 Roman Reigns	.60	1.50
29 Kurt Angle	.50	1.25
30 Braun Strowman	.60	1.50
31 John Cena	1.00	2.50
32 Braun Strowman	.60	1.50
33 John Cena	1.00	2.50
34 Woken Matt Hardy	.60	1.50
35 Seth Rollins	.60	1.50
36 Kurt Angle & Ronda Rousey	1.25	3.00
37 Undertaker	1.25	3.00
38 Braun Strowman	.60	1.50
39 Breezango	.30	.75
40 Gentleman Jack Gallagher	.40	1.00
41 Kalisto	.25	.60
42 Kalisto	.25	.60
43 Drew Gulak	.25	.60
44 Akira Tozawa	.25	.60
45 Hideo Itami	.25	.60
46 Cedric Alexander & Goldust	.25	.60
47 Drake Maverick	.25	.60
48 Mark Andrews	.25	.60
49 Buddy Murphy	.30	.75
50 Cedric Alexander	.25	.60
51 Mustafa Ali	.25	.60
52 Cedric Alexander	.25	.60
53 Buddy Murphy	.30	.75
54 Cedric Alexander	.25	.60
55 Shinsuke Nakamura	.60	1.50
56 The New Day	.40	1.00
57 Rusev	.50	1.25
58 Kevin Owens	.60	1.50
59 The Usos	.30	.75
60 Baron Corbin	.40	1.00
61 Jinder Mahal	.60	1.50
62 Kevin Owens	.60	1.50
63 Kevin Owens and Sami Zayn	.60	1.50
64 Baron Corbin	.40	1.00
65 Kevin Owens & Sami Zayn	.60	1.50
66 Shinsuka Nakamura	.60	1.50
67 AJ Styles	1.25	3.00
68 Raw Launches Counter-Siege	.60	1.50
69 Baron Corbin	.40	1.00
70 The Usos	.30	.75
71 Kevin Owens & Sami Zayn	.60	1.50
72 Mojo Rawley	.30	.75
73 Kevin Owens	.60	1.50
74 Rusev & Aiden English	.50	1.25
75 Kevin Owens & Sami Zayn	1.00	2.50
76 Kevin Owens	.60	1.50
77 Dolph Ziggler	.50	1.25
78 Kevin Owens & Sami Zayn	1.00	2.50
79 AJ Styles	1.25	3.00
80 Dolph Ziggler	.50	1.25
81 Kevin Owens	.60	1.50
82 Sami Zayn	1.25	3.00
83 Bobby Roode	.50	1.25
84 AJ Styles	1.25	3.00
85 Shinsuke Nakamura	.60	1.50
86 AJ Styles & Nakamura	1.25	3.00
87 John Cena	1.00	2.50
88 Sami Zayn	.50	1.25
89 Randy Orton	.60	1.50
90 AJ Styles	1.25	3.00
91 Daniel Bryan	1.00	2.50
92 Daniel Bryan	1.00	2.50
93 Jinder Mahal	.60	1.50
94 Bludgeon Brothers	.30	.75
95 Daniel Bryan & Shane McMahon	1.00	2.50
96 AJ Styles	1.25	3.00
97 Braun Strowman	.60	1.50
98 Shinsuka Nakamura	.60	1.50
99 The Usos	.30	.75
100 Woken Matt Hardy	.50	1.25

2019 Topps WWE Road to WrestleMania Autographed Commemorative Andre the Giant Battle Royal Trophy Re

STATED PRINT RUN 10 SER.#'d SETS
UNPRICED DUE TO SCARCITY

BRABC Baron Corbin
BRACG Chad Gable

BRADZ Dolph Ziggler
BRAFN Fandango
BRAGD Goldust
BRAKA Karl Anderson
BRALG Luke Gallows
BRAMH Woken Matt Hardy
BRAMR Mojo Rawley
BRASB Shelton Benjamin
BRASC Sin Cara
BRATB Tyler Breeze
BRATO Titus O'Neil

2019 Topps WWE Road to WrestleMania Autographed Commemorative Intercontinental Championship Relics

STATED PRINT RUN 10 SER.#'d SETS
UNPRICED DUE TO SCARCITY

ICRBH Bret Hit Man Hart
ICRRS Ricky The Dragon Steamboat

2019 Topps WWE Road to WrestleMania Autographed Divas Revolution Relic

UNPRICED DUE TO SCARCITY

DRRABB Brie Bella

2019 Topps WWE Road to WrestleMania Autographed Mat Relics

STATED PRINT RUN 10 SER.#'d SETS
UNPRICED DUE TO SCARCITY

MRAAB Alexa Bliss
MRAAC Adam Cole
MRAAS Asuka
MRACF Charlotte Flair
MRAEM Ember Moon
MRAJG Johnny Gargano
MRAKA Kurt Angle
MRAKD Killian Dain
MRAKO Kevin Owens
MRAMH Woken Matt Hardy
MRANA Naomi
MRARC Ricochet
MRASB Shayna Baszler
MRASN Shinsuke Nakamura
MRASR Seth Rollins
MRASZ Sami Zayn
MRATC Tommaso Ciampa
MRAUN Undertaker
MRAALB Aleister Black
MRAERA Kyle O'Reilly
MRAHHH Triple H
MRARRR Ronda Rousey
MRASMC Stephanie McMahon

2019 Topps WWE Road to WrestleMania Autographed Shirt Relics

STATED PRINT RUN 10 SER.#'d SETS
UNPRICED DUE TO SCARCITY

SRAAB Alexa Bliss
SRAAF Alicia Fox
SRACM Carmella
SRAFB Finn Balor
SRAMH Woken Matt Hardy

SRARD Rusev
SRARY Renee Young
SRASR Seth Rollins

2019 Topps WWE Road to WrestleMania Autographs

*BLUE/50: .5X TO 1.2X BASIC AUTOS
*SILVER/25: .6X TO 1.5X BASIC AUTOS
*GOLD/10: UNPRICED DUE TO SCARCITY
*RED/1: UNPRICED DUE TO SCARCITY
*P.P.BLACK/1: UNPRICED DUE TO SCARCITY
*P.P.CYAN/1: UNPRICED DUE TO SCARCITY
*P.P.MAGENTA/1: UNPRICED DUE TO SCARCITY
*P.P.YELLOW/1: UNPRICED DUE TO SCARCITY
RANDOMLY INSERTED INTO PACKS

AAB	Alexa Bliss	30.00	75.00
AAE	Aiden English	5.00	12.00
AAJ	AJ Styles	15.00	40.00
AAS	Asuka	15.00	40.00
ABE	Big E	6.00	15.00
ABR	Bobby Roode	6.00	15.00
ABS	Braun Strowman	15.00	40.00
ACE	Cesaro	5.00	12.00
ACF	Charlotte Flair	20.00	50.00
ACM	Carmella	12.00	30.00
ADB	Daniel Bryan	10.00	25.00
AEM	Ember Moon	10.00	25.00
AFB	Finn Balor	15.00	40.00
AJH	Jeff Hardy	15.00	40.00
AKA	Kurt Angle	10.00	25.00
AKK	Kofi Kingston	6.00	15.00
AKO	Kevin Owens	10.00	25.00
ALM	Liv Morgan EXCH	15.00	40.00
AMH	Woken Matt Hardy	8.00	20.00
ANA	Naomi	8.00	20.00
ANJ	Nia Jax	6.00	15.00
ARD	Rusev	8.00	20.00
ARW	Rowan	5.00	12.00
ASB	Sasha Banks	20.00	50.00
ASH	Sheamus	6.00	15.00
ASJ	Samoa Joe	8.00	20.00
ASN	Shinsuke Nakamura	10.00	25.00
ASR	Seth Rollins	10.00	25.00
ASZ	Sami Zayn	5.00	12.00
ATM	The Miz	6.00	15.00
AXW	Xavier Woods	6.00	15.00
ARRR	Ronda Rousey	125.00	250.00
ARTT	Ruby Riott	12.00	30.00
AWWE	Elias	12.00	30.00

2019 Topps WWE Road to WrestleMania Autographs Blue

AJM	Jinder Mahal	8.00	20.00
AJEY	Jey Uso	6.00	15.00
AJIM	Jimmy Uso	6.00	15.00

2019 Topps WWE Road to WrestleMania Autographs Silver

AUN	Undertaker	125.00	250.00
AHHH	Triple H	100.00	200.00
ASMC	Stephanie McMahon	75.00	150.00

2019 Topps WWE Road to WrestleMania Commemorative Andre the Giant Battle Royal Trophy Relics

*BRONZE/99: .5X TO 1.2X BASIC MEM
*BLUE/50: .6X TO 1.5X BASIC MEM

*SILVER/25: .75X TO 2X BASIC MEM
*GOLD/10: UNPRICED DUE TO SCARCITY
*RED/1: UNPRICED DUE TO SCARCITY
RANDOMLY INSERTED INTO PACKS

BRAE	Aiden English	2.00	5.00
BRBC	Baron Corbin	2.50	6.00
BRCG	Chad Gable	3.00	8.00
BRDZ	Dolph Ziggler	2.50	6.00
BRFN	Fandango	2.00	5.00
BRGD	Goldust	2.50	6.00
BRHS	Heath Slater	2.00	5.00
BRKA	Karl Anderson	2.50	6.00
BRKN	Kane	3.00	8.00
BRLG	Luke Gallows	2.50	6.00
BRMH	Woken Matt Hardy	3.00	8.00
BRMR	Mojo Rawley	2.00	5.00
BRRT	R-Truth	2.00	5.00
BRRY	Rhyno	2.50	6.00
BRSB	Shelton Benjamin	3.00	8.00
BRSC	Sin Cara	4.00	10.00
BRTB	Tyler Breeze	2.50	6.00
BRTD	Tye Dillinger	2.50	6.00
BRTO	Titus O'Neil	2.50	6.00
BRZR	Zack Ryder	3.00	8.00

2019 Topps WWE Road to WrestleMania Divas Revolution Autographs

RANDOMLY INSERTED INTO PACKS

DRABB Brie Bella
DRABL Becky Lynch
DRACF Charlotte Flair

2019 Topps WWE Road to WrestleMania Divas Revolution Relics

RANDOMLY INSERTED INTO PACKS

DRRBB Brie Bella
DRRNB Nikki Bella

2019 Topps WWE Road to WrestleMania Dual Autographs

STATED PRINT RUN 10 SER.#'d SETS
UNPRICED DUE TO SCARCITY

DAAP Akam/Rezar
DABB Rowan/Harper
DABR T.Breeze/Fandango
DABT B.Dallas/C.Axel
DADW B.Wyatt/M.Hardy
DAUSO The Usos
DAYEP S.Zayn/K.Owens

2019 Topps WWE Road to WrestleMania Intercontinental Champions Autographs

*GOLD/10: UNPRICED DUE TO SCARCITY
*RED/1: UNPRICED DUE TO SCARCITY
*P.P.BLACK/1: UNPRICED DUE TO SCARCITY
*P.P.CYAN/1: UNPRICED DUE TO SCARCITY
*P.P.MAGENTA/1: UNPRICED DUE TO SCARCITY
*P.P.YELLOW/1: UNPRICED DUE TO SCARCITY
RANDOMLY INSERTED INTO PACKS

ICABH Bret Hit Man Hart
ICARS Ricky The Dragon Steamboat

2019 Topps WWE Road to WrestleMania Kiss

*SILVER/25: .6X TO 1.2X BASIC KISS
*GOLD/10: UNPRICED DUE TO SCARCITY
*RED/1: UNPRICED DUE TO SCARCITY
STATED PRINT RUN 50 SER.#'d SETS

KCEM	Ember Moon	20.00	50.00
KCKS	Kairi Sane	25.00	60.00
KCLE	Lacey Evans	30.00	75.00
KCNA	Naomi	15.00	40.00
KCTC	Taynara Conti	30.00	75.00
KCVB	Vanessa Borne	15.00	40.00

2019 Topps WWE Road to WrestleMania Mat Relics

*BRONZE/99: .5X TO 1.2X BASIC MEM
*BLUE/50: .6X TO 1.5X BASIC MEM
*SILVER/25: .75X TO 2X BASIC MEM
*GOLD/10: UNPRICED DUE TO SCARCITY
*RED/1: UNPRICED DUE TO SCARCITY
RANDOMLY INSERTED INTO PACKS

MRAA	Andrade Cien Almas	2.50	6.00
MRAB	Alexa Bliss	10.00	25.00
MRAC	Adam Cole	3.00	8.00
MRAJ	AJ Styles	3.00	8.00
MRAS	Asuka	5.00	12.00
MRBA	Batista		
MRBS	Braun Strowman	2.50	6.00
MRCA	Cedric Alexander	2.00	5.00
MRCF	Charlotte Flair	5.00	12.00
MRDB	Daniel Bryan	3.00	8.00
MREM	Ember Moon	3.00	8.00
MRFB	Finn Balor	3.00	8.00
MRJC	John Cena	4.00	10.00
MRJG	Johnny Gargano	2.50	6.00
MRKA	Kurt Angle	3.00	8.00
MRKD	Killian Dain	2.00	5.00
MRKO	Kevin Owens	2.00	5.00
MRLS	Lars Sullivan	1.50	4.00
MRMH	Woken Matt Hardy	2.50	6.00
MRNA	Naomi	4.00	10.00
MRNJ	Nia Jax	2.00	5.00
MRPD	Pete Dunne	3.00	8.00
MRRC	Ricochet	3.00	8.00
MRRR	Roman Reigns	4.00	10.00
MRRS	Roderick Strong		
MRSB	Shayna Baszler	3.00	8.00
MRSN	Shinsuke Nakamura	2.50	6.00
MRSR	Seth Rollins	3.00	8.00
MRSZ	Sami Zayn	1.50	4.00
MRTC	Tommaso Ciampa	2.50	6.00
MRTM	The Miz	2.00	5.00
MRUN	Undertaker	5.00	12.00
MRVD	Velveteen Dream	3.00	8.00
MRALB	Aleister Black	3.00	8.00
MREC3	EC3	1.50	4.00
MRERA	Kyle O'Reilly	2.50	6.00
MRHHH	Triple H	3.00	8.00
MRRRR	Ronda Rousey	6.00	15.00
MRSMC	Stephanie McMahon	3.00	8.00
MRWWE	Elias	2.00	5.00

2019 Topps WWE Road to WrestleMania Shirt Relics

*BRONZE/99: .5X TO 1.2X BASIC MEM
*BLUE/50: .6X TO 1.5X BASIC MEM
*SILVER/25: .75X TO 2X BASIC MEM

*GOLD/10: UNPRICED DUE TO SCARCITY
*RED/1: UNPRICED DUE TO SCARCITY
RANDOMLY INSERTED INTO PACKS

SRAB	Alexa Bliss	15.00	30.00
SRAE	Aiden English	2.50	6.00
SRAF	Alicia Fox	5.00	12.00
SRBS	Braun Strowman	2.50	6.00
SRCM	Carmella	4.00	10.00
SRDB	Daniel Bryan	3.00	8.00
SRFB	Finn Balor	3.00	8.00
SRJC	John Cena	4.00	10.00
SRJH	Jeff Hardy	2.50	6.00
SRMH	Woken Matt Hardy	4.00	10.00
SRRD	Rusev		
SRRR	Roman Reigns	5.00	12.00
SRRY	Renee Young	2.50	6.00
SRSR	Seth Rollins	4.00	10.00
SRTM	The Miz	2.50	6.00
SRWWE	Elias	5.00	12.00

2019 Topps WWE Road to WrestleMania Update

COMPLETE SET (20) 8.00 20.00
RANDOMLY INSERTED INTO PACKS

U1	No Way Jose	.50	1.25
U2	Jeff Hardy	1.00	2.50
U3	Bobby Lashley	.75	2.00
U4	Samoa Joe	.75	2.00
U5	Jeff Hardy	1.00	2.50
U6	AOP	.60	1.50
U7	Kevin Owens and Sami Zayn	1.00	2.50
U8	Dolph Ziggler and Drew McIntyre	.75	2.00
U9	Kalisto	.40	1.00
U10	Drew Gulak	.40	1.00
U11	Buddy Murphy	.50	1.25
U12	Lince Dorado	.40	1.00
U13	Paige	1.50	4.00
U14	Usos	.50	1.25
U15	Randy Orton	1.00	2.50
U16	Shinsuke Nakamura	1.00	2.50
U17	Jeff Hardy	1.00	2.50
U18	Harper	.50	1.25
U19	Samoa Joe	.75	2.00
U20	AJ Styles & Daniel Bryan	2.00	5.00

2019 Topps WWE Road to WrestleMania WrestleMania 35 Roster

COMPLETE SET (50) 6.00 15.00
RANDOMLY INSERTED INTO PACKS

WM1	Paul Heyman	.40	1.00
WM2	AJ Styles	1.50	4.00
WM3	Shinsuke Nakamura	.75	2.00
WM4	Undertaker	1.50	4.00
WM5	John Cena	1.25	3.00
WM6	Elias	.60	1.50
WM7	Kurt Angle	.60	1.50
WM8	Ronda Rousey	1.50	4.00
WM9	Triple H	.75	2.00
WM10	Stephanie McMahon	.75	2.00
WM11	Charlotte Flair	1.25	3.00
WM12	Asuka	1.00	2.50
WM13	Nia Jax	.60	1.50
WM14	Alexa Bliss	1.50	4.00
WM15	Daniel Bryan	1.25	3.00
WM16	Shane McMahon	.75	2.00
WM17	Kevin Owens	.75	2.00

WM18	Sami Zayn	.60	1.50
WM19	Seth Rollins	.75	2.00
WM20	The Miz	.60	1.50
WM21	Finn Balor	.75	2.00
WM22	Jinder Mahal	.60	1.50
WM23	Randy Orton	.75	2.00
WM24	Bobby Roode	.60	1.50
WM25	Rusev	.60	1.50
WM26	Aiden English	.30	.75
WM27	Braun Strowman	.75	2.00
WM28	Cesaro	.40	1.00
WM29	Sheamus	.50	1.25
WM30	Harper	.40	1.00
WM31	Rowan	.30	.75
WM32	Jey Uso	.40	1.00
WM33	Jimmy Uso	.40	1.00
WM34	Big E	.30	.75
WM35	Kofi Kingston	.50	1.25
WM36	Xavier Woods	.40	1.00
WM37	Cedric Alexander	.30	.75
WM38	Mustafa Ali	.30	.75
WM39	Woken Matt Hardy	.60	1.50
WM40	Bray Wyatt	.75	2.00
WM41	Naomi	.50	1.25
WM42	Bayley	.60	1.50
WM43	Sasha Banks	1.25	3.00
WM44	Samoa Joe	.60	1.50
WM45	Jeff Hardy	.75	2.00
WM46	Bobby Lashley	.60	1.50
WM47	Ember Moon	.75	2.00
WM48	Carmella	.75	2.00
WM49	Ruby Riott	.60	1.50
WM50	Liv Morgan	1.00	2.50

2020 Topps WWE Road to WrestleMania

COMPLETE SET (100) 12.00 30.00
*FOILBOARD: .5X TO 1.2X BASIC CARDS
*BLUE/99: 1.2X TO 3X BASIC CARDS
*SILVER/25: UNPRICED DUE TO SCARCITY
*GOLD/10: UNPRICED DUE TO SCARCITY
*RED/1: UNPRICED DUE TO SCARCITY
*P.P.BLACK/1: UNPRICED DUE TO SCARCITY
*P.P.CYAN/1: UNPRICED DUE TO SCARCITY
*P.P.MAGENTA/1: UNPRICED DUE TO SCARCITY
*P.P.YELLOW/1: UNPRICED DUE TO SCARCITY

1	Lince Dorado & Gran Metalik	.25	.60
2	Buddy Murphy	.30	.75
3	Buddy Murphy	.30	.75
4	Buddy Murphy	.30	.75
5	Buddy Murphy	.30	.75
6	Noam Dar	.25	.60
7	Buddy Murphy	.40	1.00
8	Buddy Murphy	.30	.75
9	Tony Nese	.25	.60
10	Buddy Murphy	.30	.75
11	Tony Nese	.25	.60
12	Tony Nese	.25	.60
13	Tony Nese	.25	.60
14	Tony Nese	.25	.60
15	Roman Reigns	.60	1.50
16	Seth Rollins	.50	1.25
17	Dolph Ziggler & Drew McIntyre	.50	1.25
18	Brock Lesnar	1.00	2.50
19	Dolph Ziggler & Drew McIntyre	.50	1.25
20	Seattle Hates The Elias & KO Show	.30	.75
21	Triple H	1.00	2.50
22	Roman Reigns	.60	1.50

23	Dolph Ziggler	.25	.60
24	Brock Lesnar	1.00	2.50
25	D-Generation X	1.00	2.50
26	Drew McIntyre	.50	1.25
27	AOP	.30	.75
28	Seth Rollins	.50	1.25
29	Brock Lesnar	1.00	2.50
30	Team RAW Def. Team SmackDown	.60	1.50
31	AOP	.30	.75
32	Robert Roode & Chad Gable	.25	.60
33	Finn Balor	.60	1.50
34	Cena/Balor/Rollins	.60	1.50
35	Bobby Lashley	.50	1.25
36	Seth Rollins	.50	1.25
37	Brock Lesnar	1.00	2.50
38	The Revival	.25	.60
39	Baron Corbin	.30	.75
40	Seth Rollins	1.00	2.50
41	The Revival	.25	.60
42	Finn Balor	.60	1.50
43	Baron Corbin	.30	.75
44	Batista Returns	.40	1.00
45	Roman Reigns Returns	.60	1.50
46	Seth Rollins	.50	1.25
47	Bobby Lashley	.50	1.25
48	Kurt Angle	.60	1.50
49	Kurt Angle	.60	1.50
50	Drew McIntyre	.50	1.25
51	Baron Corbin	.30	.75
52	Curt Hawkins & Zack Ryder	.25	.60
53	Braun Strowman	.60	1.50
54	Seth Rollins	.50	1.25
55	Roman Reigns	.60	1.50
56	Triple H	.60	1.50
57	Baron Corbin	.30	.75
58	The Demon Finn Balor	.60	1.50
59	The New Day	.40	1.00
60	Daniel Bryan	.75	2.00
61	Randy Orton	.60	1.50
62	AJ Styles	.75	2.00
63	Shinsuke Nakamura	.50	1.25
64	The New Day	.40	1.00
65	AJ Styles	.75	2.00
66	Randy Orton	.60	1.50
67	Big Show Helps The Bar	.30	.75
68	The Miz	.40	1.00
69	The Miz	.50	1.25
70	Rey Mysterio	.50	1.25
71	Daniel Bryan	.75	2.00
72	The New Daniel Bryan	.75	2.00
73	The New Daniel Bryan	.75	2.00
74	The Bar	.30	.75
75	AJ Styles & Mustafa Ali	.75	2.00
76	Mustafa Ali	.40	1.00
77	Rusev	.30	.75
78	AJ Styles	.75	2.00
79	Samoa Joe & Andrade	.40	1.00
80	Andrade	.50	1.25
81	Rey Mysterio and Andrade	.50	1.25
82	Shinsuke Nakamura	.50	1.25
83	The Miz & Shane McMahon	.40	1.00
84	Erick Rowan	.25	.60
85	R-Truth	.25	.60
86	R-Truth	.25	.60
87	The Usos	.25	.60
88	The New Daniel Bryan	.75	2.00
89	Samoa Joe	.40	1.00
90	The Usos	.25	.60

91	The Bar	.30	.75
92	Samoa Joe	.40	1.00
93	The New Daniel Bryan	.75	2.00
94	Kofi Kingston	.40	1.00
95	The New Day	.25	.60
96	AJ Styles	.75	2.00
97	The Usos	.25	.60
98	Shane McMahon	.40	1.00
99	Samoa Joe	.40	1.00
100	Kofi Kingston	.75	2.00

2020 Topps WWE Road to WrestleMania Andre the Giant Battle Royal Commemorative Trophy Relics

*BRONZE/99: .5X TO 1.2X BASIC MEM
*BLUE/50: .6X TO 1.5X BASIC MEM
*SILVER/25: UNPRICED DUE TO SCARCITY
*GOLD/10: UNPRICED DUE TO SCARCITY
*RED/1: UNPRICED DUE TO SCARCITY
STATED PRINT RUN 199 SER.#'d SETS

AGAC	Apollo Crews	2.00	5.00
AGAD	Andrade	2.50	6.00
AGAL	Ali	2.50	6.00
AGBS	Braun Strowman	4.00	10.00
AGCA	Curtis Axel	2.00	5.00
AGGM	Gran Metalik	4.00	10.00
AGJH	Jeff Hardy	5.00	12.00
AGJM	Jinder Mahal	2.00	5.00
AGKA	Karl Anderson	2.50	6.00
AGKL	Kalisto	2.50	6.00
AGLD	Lince Dorado	2.00	5.00
AGMH	Matt Hardy	4.00	10.00
AGOT	Otis	6.00	15.00
AGRR	Robert Roode	3.00	8.00
AGSB	Shelton Benjamin	2.50	6.00
AGTB	Tyler Breeze	2.50	6.00
AGTK	Tucker	2.00	5.00

2020 Topps WWE Road to WrestleMania Autographed Andre the Giant Battle Royal Commemorative Trophy Re

*RED/1: UNPRICED DUE TO SCARCITY
STATED PRINT RUN 10 SER.#'d SETS
UNPRICED DUE TO SCARCITY

AGAAC Apollo Crews
AGAAD Andrade
AGAAL Ali
AGABS Braun Strowman
AGAGM Gran Metalik
AGAJH Jeff Hardy
AGAJM Jinder Mahal
AGAMH Matt Hardy
AGAOT Otis
AGATK Tucker

2020 Topps WWE Road to WrestleMania Autographed Hall of Fame Headliner Tribute Relic

HOFHTM Honky Tonk Man

2020 Topps WWE Road to WrestleMania Autographed Mat Relics

*RED/1: UNPRICED DUE TO SCARCITY
STATED PRINT RUN 10 SER.#'d SETS
UNPRICED DUE TO SCARCITY

MRAAC	Adam Cole		
MRAAJ	AJ Styles		
MRABC	Becky Lynch		
MRABK	Billie Kay		
MRABP	Beth Phoenix		
MRACM	Carmella		
MRAKA	Kurt Angle		
MRAKK	Kofi Kingston		
MRAPR	Peyton Royce		
MRARR	Roman Reigns		
MRASB	Shayna Baszler		
MRASJ	Samoa Joe		
MRAVD	Velveteen Dream		
MRAZR	Zack Ryder		

2020 Topps WWE Road to WrestleMania Autographed Shirt Relics

*RED/1: UNPRICED DUE TO SCARCITY
STATED PRINT RUN 10 SER.#'d SETS
UNPRICED DUE TO SCARCITY

SRAAB	Aleister Black
SRAAD	Andrade
SRAAJ	AJ Styles
SRABB	Bobby Lashley
SRABD	Bo Dallas
SRABS	Braun Strowman
SRACA	Curtis Axel
SRAEL	Elias
SRAFB	Finn Balor
SRANJ	No Way Jose
SRARC	Ricochet
SRARR	Ronda Rousey
SRAZR	Zack Ryder

2020 Topps WWE Road to WrestleMania Autographed Women's WrestleMania Battle Royal Commemorative Trop

*RED/1: UNPRICED DUE TO SCARCITY
STATED PRINT RUN 10 SER.#'d SETS
UNPRICED DUE TO SCARCITY

WRAAS	Asuka
WRACM	Carmella
WRADB	Dana Brooke
WRAEM	Ember Moon
WRAKS	Kairi Sane
WRAMJ	Mickie James
WRAMK	Maria Kanellis
WRAMR	Mandy Rose
WRANC	Nikki Cross
WRANM	Naomi
WRASD	Sonya Deville
WRASL	Sarah Logan
WRAZV	Zelina Vega

2020 Topps WWE Road to WrestleMania Autographs

*BLUE/50: .5X TO 1.2X BASIC AUTOS
*SILVER/25: UNPRICED DUE TO SCARCITY
*GOLD/10: UNPRICED DUE TO SCARCITY
*RED/1: UNPRICED DUE TO SCARCITY
*P.P.BLACK/1: UNPRICED DUE TO SCARCITY
*P.P.CYAN/1: UNPRICED DUE TO SCARCITY
*P.P.MAGENTA/1: UNPRICED DUE TO SCARCITY
*P.P.YELLOW/1: UNPRICED DUE TO SCARCITY
STATED PRINT RUN 99 SER.#'d SETS

AAB	Alexa Bliss	60.00	120.00
AAJ	AJ Styles	10.00	25.00
AAL	Aleister Black	12.00	30.00
AAS	Asuka	25.00	60.00
ABK	Becky Lynch	30.00	75.00
ABS	Braun Strowman	15.00	40.00
ABW	Bray Wyatt	12.00	30.00
ACM	Carmella	15.00	40.00
ADB	Daniel Bryan	10.00	25.00
AKK	Kofi Kingston	6.00	15.00
AKO	Kevin Owens	8.00	20.00
AKS	Kairi Sane	15.00	40.00
ALE	Lacey Evans	12.00	30.00
AMA	Ali	6.00	15.00
ARC	Ricochet	10.00	25.00
ARR	Roman Reigns	10.00	25.00
ASB	Sasha Banks	25.00	60.00
ASJ	Samoa Joe	6.00	15.00
ASN	Shinsuke Nakamura	8.00	20.00
ASR	Seth Rollins	12.00	30.00
ATM	The Miz	6.00	15.00

2020 Topps WWE Road to WrestleMania Dual Autographs

*GOLD/10: UNPRICED DUE TO SCARCITY
*RED/1: UNPRICED DUE TO SCARCITY
STATED PRINT RUN 25 SER.#'d SETS

DAGB	K.Anderson/L.Gallows	25.00	60.00
DAHB	The Hardy Boyz	100.00	200.00
DAHM	Tucker/Otis	60.00	120.00
DAIG	Andrade/Z.Vega	30.00	75.00
DAII	B.Kay/P.Royce	100.00	200.00
DARV	S.Dawson/D.Wilder		

2020 Topps WWE Road to WrestleMania Hall of Fame Headliner Tribute

COMPLETE SET (16)　10.00　25.00
RANDOMLY INSERTED INTO PACKS

HF1	Honky Tonk Man	1.00	2.50
HF2	Honky Tonk Man	1.00	2.50
HF3	Honky Tonk Man	1.00	2.50
HF4	Honky Tonk Man	1.50	4.00
HF5	Honky Tonk Man	1.00	2.50
HF6	Honky Tonk Man	1.00	2.50
HF7	Honky Tonk Man	1.00	2.50
HF8	Honky Tonk Man	1.00	2.50
HF9	Honky Tonk Man	1.00	2.50
HF10	Honky Tonk Man	1.00	2.50
HF11	Honky Tonk Man	1.00	2.50
HF12	Honky Tonk Man	1.00	2.50
HF13	Honky Tonk Man	1.00	2.50
HF14	Honky Tonk Man	1.00	2.50
HF15	Honky Tonk Man	1.00	2.50
HF16	Honky Tonk Man	1.00	2.50

2020 Topps WWE Road to WrestleMania Hall of Fame Headliner Tribute Autographs

STATED PRINT RUN 10 SER.#'d SETS
UNPRICED DUE TO SCARCITY

HFA1	Honky Tonk Man
HFA2	Honky Tonk Man
HFA3	Honky Tonk Man
HFA4	Honky Tonk Man
HFA5	Honky Tonk Man
HFA6	Honky Tonk Man
HFA7	Honky Tonk Man
HFA8	Honky Tonk Man
HFA9	Honky Tonk Man
HFA10	Honky Tonk Man
HFA11	Honky Tonk Man
HFA12	Honky Tonk Man
HFA13	Honky Tonk Man
HFA14	Honky Tonk Man
HFA15	Honky Tonk Man
HFA16	Honky Tonk Man

2020 Topps WWE Road to WrestleMania Mat Relics

*BRONZE/99: .5X TO 1.2X BASIC MEM
*BLUE/50: .6X TO 1.5X BASIC MEM
*SILVER/25: UNPRICED DUE TO SCARCITY
*GOLD/10: UNPRICED DUE TO SCARCITY
*RED/1: UNPRICED DUE TO SCARCITY
STATED PRINT RUN 199 SER.#'d SETS

MRAB	Aleister Black	2.00	5.00
MRAC	Adam Cole	5.00	12.00
MRAJ	AJ Styles	5.00	12.00
MRBB	Bianca Belair	4.00	10.00
MRBC	Becky Lynch	10.00	25.00
MRBK	Billie Kay	8.00	20.00
MRBM	Buddy Murphy	2.00	5.00
MRBP	Beth Phoenix	2.50	6.00
MRBS	Braun Strowman	4.00	10.00
MRBT	Batista	6.00	15.00
MRCF	Charlotte Flair	6.00	15.00
MRCH	Curt Hawkins	2.00	5.00
MRCM	Carmella	5.00	12.00
MRDB	Daniel Bryan	3.00	8.00
MRDM	Drew McIntyre	4.00	10.00
MRER	Erik	2.00	5.00
MRIS	Io Shirai	2.00	5.00
MRIV	Ivar	2.00	5.00
MRJG	Johnny Gargano	2.50	6.00
MRKA	Kurt Angle	3.00	8.00
MRKK	Kofi Kingston	4.00	10.00
MRKS	Kairi Sane	2.50	6.00
MRMR	Matt Riddle	2.00	5.00
MRNT	Natalya	3.00	8.00
MRPD	Pete Dunne	2.00	5.00
MRPR	Peyton Royce	6.00	15.00
MRRC	Ricochet	2.50	6.00
MRRM	Rey Mysterio	2.50	6.00
MRRR	Roman Reigns	4.00	10.00
MRRS	Ronda Rousey	8.00	20.00
MRSB	Shayna Baszler	5.00	12.00
MRSJ	Samoa Joe	3.00	8.00
MRTH	Triple H	3.00	8.00
MRTM	The Miz	2.50	6.00
MRTN	Tony Nese	2.00	5.00
MRVD	Velveteen Dream	2.00	5.00
MRWT	Walter	2.50	6.00
MRZR	Zack Ryder	10.00	25.00
MRJEY	Jey Uso	2.50	6.00
MRJIM	Jimmy Uso	2.50	6.00

2020 Topps WWE Road to WrestleMania Shirt Relics

*BRONZE/99: .5X TO 1.2X BASIC MEM
*BLUE/50: .6X TO 1.5X BASIC MEM
*SILVER/25: UNPRICED DUE TO SCARCITY
*GOLD/10: UNPRICED DUE TO SCARCITY
*RED/1: UNPRICED DUE TO SCARCITY
STATED PRINT RUN 199 SER.#'d SETS

SRAB	Aleister Black	4.00	10.00
SRAD	Andrade	2.50	6.00
SRAJ	AJ Styles	5.00	12.00
SRBB	Bobby Lashley	3.00	8.00
SRBD	Bo Dallas	2.00	5.00
SRBH	Bret Hit Man Hart	8.00	20.00
SRBL	Brock Lesnar	4.00	10.00
SRBS	Braun Strowman	3.00	8.00
SRBT	Booker T	3.00	8.00
SRCA	Curtis Axel	2.50	6.00
SREL	Elias	2.50	6.00
SRFB	Finn Balor	5.00	12.00
SRNJ	No Way Jose	2.00	5.00
SRRR	Ronda Rousey	20.00	50.00
SRSM	Shawn Michaels	5.00	12.00
SRSR	Stevie Ray	2.00	5.00
SRZR	Zack Ryder	2.50	6.00

2020 Topps WWE Road to WrestleMania Six-Person Autograph Booklet

STATED PRINT RUN 10 SER.#'d SETS
UNPRICED DUE TO SCARCITY

ABCMITB	Rousey/Flair/Rollins/Reigns/Kingston/Lynch

2020 Topps WWE Road to WrestleMania Triple Autographs

*GOLD/10: UNPRICED DUE TO SCARCITY
*RED/1: UNPRICED DUE TO SCARCITY
STATED PRINT RUN 25 SER.#'d SETS

TALP	Dorado/Metalik/Kalisto	60.00	120.00
TAND	Woods/Big E/Kingston	75.00	150.00

2020 Topps WWE Road to WrestleMania Winningest Superstars in WrestleMania History

COMPLETE SET (10)　6.00　15.00
RANDOMLY INSERTED INTO PACKS

WS1	Randy Orton	1.00	2.50
WS2	Shawn Michaels	1.00	2.50
WS3	Seth Rollins	.75	2.00
WS4	Macho Man Randy Savage	1.25	3.00
WS5	Rey Mysterio	.75	2.00
WS6	Kane	.50	1.25
WS7	Bret Hit Man Hart	1.00	2.50
WS8	Triple H	1.00	2.50
WS9	John Cena	1.50	4.00
WS10	Undertaker	1.50	4.00

2020 Topps WWE Road to WrestleMania Winningest Superstars in WrestleMania History Autographs

*RED/1: UNPRICED DUE TO SCARCITY
STATED PRINT RUN 10 SER.#'d SETS
UNPRICED DUE TO SCARCITY

WSA1	Randy Orton
WSA2	Shawn Michaels
WSA3	Seth Rollins
WSA4	Rey Mysterio
WSA5	Bret Hit Man Hart

2020 Topps WWE Road to WrestleMania Women's WrestleMania Battle Royal Commemorative Trophy Relics

*BRONZE/99: .5X TO 1.2 X BASIC MEM

*BLUE/50: .6X TO 1.5 X BASIC MEM
*SILVER/25: UNPRICED DUE TO SCARCITY
*GOLD/10: UNPRICED DUE SCARCITY
*RED/1: UNPRICED DUE TO SCARCITY
STATED PRINT RUN 199 SER.#'d SETS

WRAS	Asuka	6.00	15.00
WRCM	Carmella	5.00	12.00
WRDB	Dana Brooke	2.50	6.00
WREM	Ember Moon	3.00	8.00
WRKS	Kairi Sane	2.50	6.00
WRMJ	Mickie James	4.00	10.00
WRMK	Maria Kanellis	5.00	12.00
WRMR	Mandy Rose	8.00	20.00
WRNC	Nikki Cross	4.00	10.00
WRNM	Naomi	2.50	6.00
WRSD	Sonya Deville	3.00	8.00
WRSL	Sarah Logan	2.50	6.00
WRZV	Zelina Vega	3.00	8.00

2020 Topps WWE Road to WrestleMania WrestleMania Roster

COMPLETE SET (50) 12.00 30.00
RANDOMLY INSERTED INTO PACKS

WM1	AJ Styles	1.00	2.50
WM2	Aleister Black	.60	1.50
WM3	Alexa Bliss	1.50	4.00
WM4	Mustafa Ali	.50	1.25
WM5	Andrade	.50	1.25
WM6	Asuka	.60	1.50
WM7	King Corbin	.40	1.00
WM8	Bayley	.60	1.50
WM9	Becky Lynch	1.25	3.00
WM10	Big E	.30	.75
WM11	Billie Kay	.60	1.50
WM12	Bobby Lashley	.60	1.50
WM13	Braun Strowman	.75	2.00
WM14	The Fiend Bray Wyatt	1.00	2.50
WM15	Brock Lesnar	1.25	3.00
WM16	Buddy Murphy	.40	1.00
WM17	Carmella	.75	2.00
WM18	Cesaro	.30	.75
WM19	Charlotte Flair	1.25	3.00
WM20	Daniel Bryan	1.00	2.50
WM21	Drew McIntyre	.60	1.50
WM22	Elias	.30	.75
WM23	Ember Moon	.60	1.50
WM24	Erik	.30	.75
WM25	Finn Balor	.75	2.00
WM26	Ivar	.30	.75
WM27	Jeff Hardy	.75	2.00
WM28	John Cena	1.25	3.00
WM29	Kairi Sane	.60	1.50
WM30	Kevin Owens	.40	1.00
WM31	Kofi Kingston	.50	1.25
WM32	Lacey Evans	.75	2.00
WM33	Lars Sullivan	.30	.75
WM34	Mandy Rose	1.50	4.00
WM35	Matt Hardy	.60	1.50
WM36	Nikki Cross	.60	1.50
WM37	Peyton Royce	.60	1.50
WM38	Randy Orton	.75	2.00
WM39	Rey Mysterio	.60	1.50
WM40	Ricochet	.50	1.25
WM41	Roman Reigns	.75	2.00
WM42	R-Truth	.30	.75
WM43	Sami Zayn	.40	1.00
WM44	Samoa Joe	.50	1.25
WM45	Seth Rollins	.60	1.50
WM46	Shinsuke Nakamura	.60	1.50
WM47	Sonya Deville	.75	2.00
WM48	The Miz	.50	1.25
WM49	Xavier Woods	.30	.75
WM50	Zelina Vega	.60	1.50

2020 Topps WWE Road to WrestleMania Yearly Records

COMPLETE SET (10) 8.00 20.00
BLASTER EXCLUSIVE

YR1	Asuka	1.25	3.00
YR2	Braun Strowman	1.50	4.00
YR3	Brock Lesnar	2.50	6.00
YR4	Carmella	1.50	4.00
YR5	Charlotte Flair	2.50	6.00
YR6	Daniel Bryan	2.00	5.00
YR7	Kofi Kingston	1.00	2.50
YR8	Mickie James	1.00	2.50
YR9	Pete Dunne	.60	1.50
YR10	Seth Rollins	1.25	3.00

2020 Topps WWE Road to WrestleMania Yearly Records Autographs

*RED/1: UNPRICED DUE TO SCARCITY
STATED PRINT RUN 10 SER.#'d SETS
UNPRICED DUE TO SCARCITY

YRA1 Asuka
YRA2 Braun Strowman
YRA3 Carmella
YRA4 Kofi Kingston
YRA5 Seth Rollins

2021 Topps WWE Road to WrestleMania Stickers

COMPLETE SET (304)

1 Intro
2 Intro
3 Intro
4 Intro
5 Drew McIntyre
6 Drew McIntyre
7 Drew McIntyre
8 Drew McIntyre
9 Drew McIntyre
10 Drew McIntyre
11 Drew McIntyre
12 Drew McIntyre
13 Drew McIntyre
14 Drew McIntyre
15 Becky Lynch
16 Becky Lynch
17 Becky Lynch
18 Becky Lynch
19 Becky Lynch
20 Becky Lynch
21 Becky Lynch
22 Becky Lynch
23 Becky Lynch
24 Becky Lynch
25 The Fiend Bray Wyatt
26 The Fiend Bray Wyatt
27 The Fiend Bray Wyatt
28 The Fiend Bray Wyatt
29 The Fiend Bray Wyatt
30 The Fiend Bray Wyatt
31 The Fiend Bray Wyatt
32 The Fiend Bray Wyatt
33 The Fiend Bray Wyatt
34 The Fiend Bray Wyatt
35 Charlotte Flair
36 Charlotte Flair
37 Charlotte Flair
38 Charlotte Flair
39 Angel Garza
40 Drew Gulak
41 Big Show
42 Shayna Baszler
43 Lacey Evans
44 AJ Styles
45 AJ Styles
46 AJ Styles
47 AJ Styles
48 Mandy Rose
49 Dana Brooke
50 Elias
51 Nia Jax
52 Braun Strowman
53 Braun Strowman
54 Bobby Lashley
55 Bobby Lashley
56 Cedric Alexander
57 MVP
58 Shelton Benjamin
59 Akira Tozawa
60 Randy Orton
61 Viking Raiders
62 R-Truth
63 Naomi
64 Andrade
65 Nikki Cross
66 The New Day
67 The New Day
68 The Miz
69 Ricochet
70 Keith Lee
71 Keith Lee
72 Keith Lee
73 Keith Lee
74 Ali
75 Retribution
76 Retribution
77 Lana
78 Sheamus
79 Alexa Bliss
80 Alexa Bliss
81 Alexa Bliss
82 Gran Metalik
83 John Morrison
84 Humberto Carrillo
85 Humberto Carrillo
86 Humberto Carrillo
87 Jeff Hardy
88 Tucker
89 Asuka
90 Asuka
91 Asuka
92 Edge
93 Edge
94 Charlotte Flair
95 Number One
96 Surprise
97 Most Eliminations
98 Most Wins
99 Champion
100 History Maker
101 1988
102 The People's Rumble
103 Undertaker The Streak
104 Undertaker The Streak #1
105 Undertaker The Streak #6
106 Undertaker The Streak #7
107 Undertaker The Streak #9
108 Undertaker The Streak #12
109 Undertaker The Streak #14
110 Undertaker The Streak #17
111 Undertaker The Streak #21
112 WrestleMania
113 WrestleMania X
114 WrestleMania 13
115 WrestleMania XV
116 WrestleMania X-Seven
117 WrestleMania XX
118 WrestleMania 25
119 WrestleMania XXX
120 WrestleMania 36
121 Adam Cole
122 Adam Cole
123 Adam Cole
124 The Undisputed Era
125 Shotzi Blackheart
126 Dexter Lumis
127 Johnny Gargano
128 Candice LeRae
129 Rhea Ripley
130 Damian Priest
131 Finn Balor
132 Karrion Kross
133 Dakota Kai
134 Pete Dunne
135 Kushida
136 Kushida
137 Kushida
138 Ember Moon
139 Tommaso Ciampa
140 NXT UK
141 Moustache Mountain
142 Moustache Mountain
143 Trent Seven
144 Tyler Bate
145 Ilja Dragunov
146 Jordan Devlin
147 Piper Niven
148 Gallus
149 Kay Lee Ray
150 Andre the Giant
151 Macho Man Randy Savage
152 Ultimate Warrior
153 Rowdy Roddy Piper
154 Bret "Hit Man" Hart
155 Shawn Michaels
156 Undertaker
157 Stone Cold Steve Austin
158 The Rock
159 Triple H
160 Trish Stratus
161 Eddie Guerrero
162 Edge
163 John Cena
164 Randy Orton
165 Batista
166 Charlotte Flair

167	Becky Lynch	
168	Roman Reigns	
169	Roman Reigns	
170	Roman Reigns	
171	Roman Reigns	
172	Roman Reigns	
173	Roman Reigns	
174	Roman Reigns	
175	Roman Reigns	
176	Roman Reigns	
177	Roman Reigns	
178	Roman Reigns	
179	Sasha Banks	
180	Sasha Banks	
181	Sasha Banks	
182	Sasha Banks	
183	Sasha Banks	
184	Sasha Banks	
185	Sasha Banks	
186	Sasha Banks	
187	Sasha Banks	
188	Sasha Banks	
189	Seth Rollins	
190	Seth Rollins	
191	Seth Rollins	
192	Seth Rollins	
193	Seth Rollins	
194	Seth Rollins	
195	Seth Rollins	
196	Seth Rollins	
197	Seth Rollins	
198	Seth Rollins	
199	Bayley	
200	Bayley	
201	Bayley	
202	Bayley	
203	Rey Mysterio	
204	Rey Mysterio	
205	Rey Mysterio	
206	Baron Corbin	
207	Baron Corbin	
208	SmackDown Fact	
209	Usos	
210	Usos	
211	Kevin Owens	
212	Bo Dallas	
213	Big E	
214	Big E	
215	Big E	
216	Mojo Rawley	
217	Tamina	
218	Cesaro	
219	Cesaro	
220	Cesaro	
221	Billie Kay	
222	Dolph Ziggler	
223	Dolph Ziggler	
224	Dolph Ziggler	
225	Street Profits	
226	Street Profits	
227	Street Profits	
228	Chad Gable	
229	Apollo Crews	
230	Murphy	
231	The Riott Squad	
232	The Riott Squad	
233	Aleister Black	
234	Bianca Belair	

235	Bianca Belair	
236	Bianca Belair	
237	Sami Zayn	
238	Kalisto	
239	SmackDown Fact	
240	Daniel Bryan	
241	Daniel Bryan	
242	Daniel Bryan	
243	Natalya	
244	Lars Sullivan	
245	Otis	
246	Otis	
247	Kane	
248	Shinsuke Nakamura	
249	Shinsuke Nakamura	
250	Wesley Blake	
251	Jaxson Ryker	
252	Steve Cutler	
253	Carmella	
254	Carmella	
255	Carmella	
256	Robert Roode	
257	Mickie James	
258	Main Event Shocker	
259	Fantastic Flair	
260	Super Cena	
261	Hardcore Hell	
262	Air Shane	
263	Macho Marathon	
264	Asuka's Run Ended	
265	Magic Mysterio	
266	Money, Money, Money	
267	Mega Match	
268	Bret Wins Big	
269	His Time Is Now	
270	KO to Big Show	
271	The Last Ride	
272	I'm Sorry, I Love You	
273	You Never Saw It Coming	
274	Warrior to the Rescue	
275	Greatest Rivals	
276	Wyatt's World	
277	Legends of the Ladder	
278	Super Spear	
279	The Boyz Are Back	
280	Dream Match	
281	Austin Era Begins	
282	Match Made in Heaven	
283	Kofi-Mania	
284	The Ultimate Challenge	
285	Best of British	
286	The Boyhood Dream	
287	Becky Two Belts	
288	Stone Cold Classic	
289	Icon vs. Icon	
290	Drama in the Cell	
291	Yes	
292	End of the Streak	
293	Heist of the Century	
294	The Greatest of Them All	
295	Sami Zayn	
296	Bianca Belair	
297	Seth Rollins	
298	Alexa Bliss	
299	Kofi Kingston	
300	Big Show	
301	Becky Lynch	
302	Charlotte Flair	

303	Cesaro		
304	Mandy Rose		

2021 Topps WWE Road to WrestleMania Stickers Autographs

STATED PRINT RUN 100 ANNCD SETS

AA1	Big E	20.00	50.00
AA2	Becky Lynch	60.00	120.00
AA3	Walter	30.00	75.00
AA4	Trent Seven	30.00	75.00
AA5	Naomi	50.00	100.00

2021 Topps WWE Road to WrestleMania Stickers Firefly Funhouse Pop-Up Card

NNO Bray Wyatt

2021 Topps WWE Road to WrestleMania Stickers Gold XL

COMPLETE SET (3)

T1	Icons
T2	Superstars
T3	Future Legends

2021 Topps WWE Road to WrestleMania Stickers Limiited Edition

COMPLETE SET (4)

LE1	The Rock	2.00	5.00
LE2	The Fiend Bray Wyatt	2.50	6.00
LE3	Roman Reigns	1.50	4.00
LE4	Sasha Banks	1.50	4.00

2021 Topps WWE Road to WrestleMania Stickers Tins

NNO	McIntyre/Bliss/Orton/Lashley/Strowman
NNO	Rose/Banks/Bayley/Rollins/Styles
NNO	Ripley/Fiend/Shirai/Reigns/Big E

2016 Topps WWE The Rock Tribute

This was a continuation series across four different products in 2016. 10-Card sets were inserted in the following products: Topps WWE Road to WrestleMania (1-10), Topps WWE (11-20), Topps Heritage WWE (21-30), and Topps Then Now Forever.

COMPLETE SET (40)		6.00	15.00
STATED ODDS 1:6			
1	The Rock	1.00	2.50
2	The Rock	1.00	2.50
3	The Rock	1.00	2.50
4	The Rock	1.00	2.50
5	The Rock	1.00	2.50
6	The Rock	1.00	2.50
7	The Rock	1.00	2.50
8	The Rock	1.00	2.50
9	The Rock	1.00	2.50
10	The Rock	1.00	2.50
11	The Rock	1.00	2.50
12	The Rock	1.00	2.50
13	The Rock	1.00	2.50
14	The Rock	1.00	2.50
15	The Rock	1.00	2.50
16	The Rock	1.00	2.50

17	The Rock	1.00	2.50
18	The Rock	1.00	2.50
19	The Rock	1.00	2.50
20	The Rock	1.00	2.50
21	The Rock	1.00	2.50
22	The Rock	1.00	2.50
23	The Rock	1.00	2.50
24	The Rock	1.00	2.50
25	The Rock	1.00	2.50
26	The Rock	1.00	2.50
27	The Rock	1.00	2.50
28	The Rock	1.00	2.50
29	The Rock	1.00	2.50
30	The Rock	1.00	2.50
31	The Rock	1.00	2.50
32	The Rock	1.00	2.50
33	The Rock	1.00	2.50
34	The Rock	1.00	2.50
35	The Rock	1.00	2.50
36	The Rock	1.00	2.50
37	The Rock	1.00	2.50
38	The Rock	1.00	2.50
39	The Rock	1.00	2.50
40	The Rock	1.00	2.50

2019 Topps WWE Roman Reigns Leukemia and Lymphoma Society Set

COMPLETE SET (11)		8.00	20.00
STATED PRINT RUN 101 ANNCD SETS			
1	Survivor Series 2013	1.25	3.00
2	Royal Rumble 2014	1.25	3.00
3	Fastlane 2015	1.25	3.00
4	Extreme Rules 2015	1.25	3.00
5	WrestleMania 32	1.25	3.00
6	Extreme Rules 2016	1.25	3.00
7	WrestleMania 33	1.25	3.00
8	No Mercy 2017	1.25	3.00
9	SummerSlam 2018	1.25	3.00
10	RAW Return 2019	1.25	3.00
11	LLS	1.25	3.00

2019 Topps WWE Ronda Rousey Spotlight Complete Series

This is a continuation series across four different products in 2019. 10-Card sets were inserted in the following products: Topps WWE Road to WrestleMania (1-10), Topps WWE RAW (11-20), Topps WWE SummerSlam (21-30), and SmackDown Live (31-40).

COMPLETE SET (40)		25.00	60.00
1	Helps The Rock Fend Off Triple H and Stephanie McMahon	1.25	3.00
2	Crashes Women's Royal Rumble	1.25	3.00
3	WWE Contract	1.25	3.00
4	Confronts HHH & Stephanie	1.25	3.00
5	Takes Down Stephanie	1.25	3.00
6	Rebuffs Absolution	1.25	3.00
7	Teams w/Kurt Angle	1.25	3.00
8	Armbars Stephanie Twice	1.25	3.00
9	Helps Natalya	1.25	3.00
10	Armbars Mickie James	1.25	3.00
11	Chases off Alexa Bliss	1.25	3.00
12	Confronts Nia Jax	1.25	3.00
13	Signs Contract for Title Match	1.25	3.00
14	Armbars Nia Jax	1.25	3.00
15	Defeats Nia Jax by DQ	1.25	3.00
16	Is Suspended	1.25	3.00

17	Violates Her Suspension	1.25	3.00
18	Wins Her RAW Debut	1.25	3.00
19	Defeats Alexa Bliss for Women's Title	1.25	3.00
20	Attacks Stephanie McMahon	1.25	3.00
21	Works with Trish Stratus	1.25	3.00
22	Stops Alexa Bliss & Alicia Fox	1.25	3.00
23	Teams with Natalya	1.25	3.00
24	Successfully Defends Title Against Bliss	1.25	3.00
25	Defeats Rudy Riott	1.25	3.00
26	Crashes Negotiations	1.25	3.00
27	Goes Toe-to-Toe with Charlotte Flair	1.25	3.00
28	Defeats Mickie James	1.25	3.00
29	Teams with Ember Moon	1.25	3.00
30	Watches Ember Moon's Back	1.25	3.00
31	Defends Women's Title Against Nia	1.25	3.00
32	Tries to Issue Open Challenge	1.25	3.00
33	Defeats Natalya to Retain Title	1.25	3.00
34	Teams with Natalya	1.25	3.00
35	Appears A Moment of Bliss	1.25	3.00
36	Tags with Sasha Banks	1.25	3.00
37	Defeats Bayley in Open Challenge	1.25	3.00
38	Defeats Liv Morgan & Sarah Logan	1.25	3.00
39	Attacks Becky Lynch	1.25	3.00
40	Defeats Dana Brooke	1.25	3.00

2010 Topps WWE Rumble Pack

COMPLETE SET (50)		5.00	12.00
UNOPENED BOX (24 PACKS)			
UNOPENED PACK (6 CARDS)			
1	Big Show	.30	.75
2	Big Show	.30	.75
3	Carlito	.30	.75
4	Chris Jericho	.30	.75
5	Christian	.20	.50
6	Christian	.20	.50
7	CM Punk	.50	1.25
8	Cody Rhodes	.12	.30
9	Cody Rhodes	.12	.30
10	Evan Bourne	.12	.30
11	Evan Bourne	.12	.30
12	Hornswoggle	.20	.50
13	Hornswoggle	.20	.50
14	Yoshi Tatsu	.12	.30
15	Yoshi Tatsu	.12	.30
16	Jack Swagger	.12	.30
17	Jack Swagger	.12	.30
18	John Cena	.60	1.50
19	John Cena	.60	1.50
20	John Morrison	.15	.40
21	John Morrison	.15	.40
22	Kane	.30	.75
23	Kane	.30	.75
24	Kofi Kingston	.20	.50
25	Kofi Kingston	.20	.50
26	Kung Fu Naki	.12	.30
27	Matt Hardy	.30	.75
28	MVP	.20	.50
29	MVP	.20	.50
30	Primo	.12	.30
31	R-Truth	.12	.30
32	R-Truth	.12	.30
33	Randy Orton	.50	1.25
34	Randy Orton	.50	1.25
35	Rey Mysterio	.30	.75
36	Rey Mysterio	.30	.75
37	Santino Marella	.12	.30
38	Shawn Michaels	.75	2.00
39	Shawn Michaels	.75	2.00

40	Sheamus	.20	.50
41	Ted DiBiase	.20	.50
42	The Miz	.20	.50
43	Undertaker	.50	1.25
44	Triple H	.60	1.50
45	Triple H	.60	1.50
46	Edge	.50	1.25
47	Edge	.50	1.25
48	Batista	.50	1.25
49	Batista	.50	1.25
50	Checklist	.12	.30

2010 Topps WWE Rumble Pack
Finger Puppets

COMPLETE SET (10)		3.00	8.00
STATED ODDS 1:4			
1	Shawn Michaels	1.25	3.00
2	Rey Mysterio	.50	1.25
3	CM Punk	.75	2.00
4	Hornswoggle	.30	.75
5	Mark Henry	.30	.75
6	Hurricane Helms	.20	.50
7	Triple H	1.00	2.50
8	R-Truth	.20	.50
9	Dolph Ziggler	.30	.75
10	MVP	.30	.75

2010 Topps WWE Rumble Pack
Glow-in-the-Dark

COMPLETE SET (10)		4.00	10.00
STATED ODDS 1:6			
1	John Cena	1.25	3.00
2	Undertaker	1.00	2.50
3	Rey Mysterio	.60	1.50
4	Yoshi Tatsu	.25	.60
5	The Miz	.40	1.00
6	Big Show	.60	1.50
7	Shawn Michaels	1.50	4.00
8	Triple H	1.25	3.00
9	Carlito	.60	1.50
10	Jack Swagger	.25	.60

2010 Topps WWE Rumble Pack
Hidden Images

COMPLETE SET (10)		4.00	10.00
STATED ODDS 1:6			
1	John Cena	1.25	3.00
2	MVP	.40	1.00
3	Undertaker	1.00	2.50
4	Evan Bourne	.25	.60
5	CM Punk	1.00	2.50
6	Triple H	1.25	3.00
7	Christian	.40	1.00
8	Kane	.60	1.50
9	Chris Jericho	.60	1.50
10	Rey Mysterio	.60	1.50

2010 Topps WWE Rumble Pack Pop-
Ups

COMPLETE SET (9)		3.00	8.00
STATED ODDS 1:4			
1	John Cena	1.00	2.50
2	Sheamus	.30	.75
3	Undertaker	.75	2.00
4	Triple H	1.00	2.50
5	Evan Bourne	.20	.50
6	Randy Orton	.75	2.00

7	John Morrison	.25	.60
8	The Miz	.30	.75
9	Edge	.75	2.00

2010 Topps WWE Rumble Pack
Stickers

COMPLETE SET (30)		6.00	15.00
STATED ODDS 2:1			
1	John Cena	.75	2.00
2	John Cena	.75	2.00
3	John Cena	.75	2.00
4	Triple H	.75	2.00
5	Triple H	.75	2.00
6	Triple H	.75	2.00
7	Undertaker	.60	1.50
8	Undertaker	.60	1.50
9	Undertaker	.60	1.50
10	Rey Mysterio	.40	1.00
11	Rey Mysterio	.40	1.00
12	Rey Mysterio	.40	1.00
13	Edge	.60	1.50
14	Edge	.60	1.50
15	Edge	.60	1.50
16	Batista	.60	1.50
17	Batista	.60	1.50
18	Batista	.60	1.50
19	Shawn Michaels	1.00	2.50
20	Shawn Michaels	1.00	2.50
21	Shawn Michaels	1.00	2.50
22	CM Punk	.60	1.50
23	CM Punk	.60	1.50
24	CM Punk	.60	1.50
25	Randy Orton	.60	1.50
26	Randy Orton	.60	1.50
27	Randy Orton	.60	1.50
28	Kane	.40	1.00
29	Kofi Kingston	.25	.60
30	DX CL	1.00	2.50

2010 Topps WWE Rumble Pack
Tattoos

COMPLETE SET (10)		5.00	12.00
STATED ODDS 1:6			
1	Kofi Kingston/Randy Orton	1.00	2.50
2	Christian/William Regal	.60	1.50
3	Triple H/Edge	1.25	3.00
4	Kane/Big Show	.60	1.50
5	Batista/The Undertaker	1.00	2.50
6	MVP/Jack Swagger	.40	1.00
7	Shawn Michaels/Chris Jericho	1.50	4.00
8	Rey Mysterio/CM Punk	1.00	2.50
9	John Morrison/The Miz	.40	1.00
10	John Cena/Sheamus	1.25	3.00

2018 Topps WWE Shawn Michaels
Tribute

This is a continuation series across four different products in 2018. 10-Card sets were inserted in the following products: Topps WWE Road to WrestleMania (1-10), Topps WWE (11-20), Topps Heritage WWE (21-30), and Topps WWE Then Now Forever (31-40).

1	Shawn Michaels	1.25	3.00
2	Shawn Michaels	1.25	3.00
3	Shawn Michaels	1.25	3.00

4	Shawn Michaels	1.25	3.00
5	Shawn Michaels	1.25	3.00
6	Shawn Michaels	1.25	3.00
7	Shawn Michaels	1.25	3.00
8	Shawn Michaels	1.25	3.00
9	Shawn Michaels	1.25	3.00
10	Shawn Michaels	1.25	3.00
11	Shawn Michaels	1.25	3.00
12	Shawn Michaels	1.25	3.00
13	Shawn Michaels	1.25	3.00
14	Shawn Michaels	1.25	3.00
15	Shawn Michaels	1.25	3.00
16	Shawn Michaels	1.25	3.00
17	Shawn Michaels	1.25	3.00
18	Shawn Michaels	1.25	3.00
19	Shawn Michaels	1.25	3.00
20	Shawn Michaels	1.25	3.00
21	Shawn Michaels	1.25	3.00
22	Shawn Michaels	1.25	3.00
23	Shawn Michaels	1.25	3.00
24	Shawn Michaels	1.25	3.00
25	Shawn Michaels	1.25	3.00
26	Shawn Michaels	1.25	3.00
27	Shawn Michaels	1.25	3.00
28	Shawn Michaels	1.25	3.00
29	Shawn Michaels	1.25	3.00
30	Shawn Michaels	1.25	3.00
31	Shawn Michaels	1.25	3.00
32	Shawn Michaels	1.25	3.00
33	Shawn Michaels	1.25	3.00
34	Shawn Michaels	1.25	3.00
35	Shawn Michaels	1.25	3.00
36	Shawn Michaels	1.25	3.00
37	Shawn Michaels	1.25	3.00
38	Shawn Michaels	1.25	3.00
39	Shawn Michaels	1.25	3.00
40	Shawn Michaels	1.25	3.00

2018 Topps WWE Shawn Michaels
Tribute Topps Heritage WWE
Autographs and Relics

SMA1	Shawn Michaels AU	30.00	75.00
SMR1	Shawn Michaels RELIC	8.00	20.00
SMAR1	Shawn Michaels AU RELIC	60.00	120.00

2018 Topps WWE Shawn Michaels
Tribute Topps WWE Road to
WrestleMania Autographs and Relics

SM	Shawn Michaels AU	30.00	75.00
SMR	Shawn Michaels RELIC	10.00	25.00
SMAR	Shawn Michaels AU RELIC	50.00	100.00

2020 Topps WWE Signature
Performance Autographs

*BLUE/25: UNPRICED DUE TO SCARCITY
*RED/10: UNPRICED DUE TO SCARCITY
*ORANGE/5: UNPRICED DUE TO SCARCITY
*GOLD/1: UNPRICED DUE TO SCARCITY
STATED PRINT RUN 50 SER.#'d SETS

NNO	Drew McIntyre	50.00	100.00

2008 Topps WWE Slam Attax

COMPLETE SET (172)		15.00	40.00
1	John Cena CH	1.25	3.00
2	Edge CH	.75	2.00
3	Chavo Guerrero CH	.30	.75

4	Matt Hardy CH	.75	2.00
5	Chris Jericho CH	.50	1.25
6	Triple H CH	1.25	3.00
7	Jeff Hardy CH	.75	2.00
8	Rey Mysterio CH	.50	1.25
9	Randy Orton CH	.50	1.25
10	CM Punk CH	.20	.50
11	William Regal CH	.50	1.25
12	Batista CH	.75	2.00
13	Shawn Michaels CH	1.25	3.00
14	Beth Phoenix CH	1.00	2.50
15	Kofi Kingston CH	.50	1.25
16	Undertaker CH	1.00	2.50
17	Montel Vontavious Porter FM	.30	.75
18	Kane FM	.75	2.00
19	Mr. Kennedy FM	.50	1.25
20	Big Show FM	.50	1.25
21	Carlito FM	.50	1.25
22	D-Generation X FM	.60	1.50
23	The Hardys FM	.75	2.00
24	Cryme Tyme FM	.25	.60
25	Umaga FM	.30	.75
26	JBL FM	.20	.50
27	Mark Henry FM	.30	.75
28	John Morrison FM	.20	.50
29	The Great Khali FM	.20	.50
30	Snitsky FM	.30	.75
31	Shelton Benjamin FM	.20	.50
32	Stone Cold Steve Austin FM	1.25	3.00
33	Mickie James FM	1.25	3.00
34	Finlay FM	.30	.75
35	Vladimir Kozlov FM	.20	.50
36	WWE Championship TC	.20	.50
37	Intercontinental Championship TC	.20	.50
38	Women's Championship TC	.20	.50
39	World Tag Team Championship TC	.20	.50
40	World Heavyweight Championship TC	.20	.50
41	United States Championship TC	.20	.50
42	WWE Tag Team Championship TC	.20	.50
43	WWE Diva Championship TC	.20	.50
44	ECW Championship TC	.20	.50
45	WWE Money in the Bank Briefcase TC	.20	.50
46	Deuce	.20	.50
47	Kofi Kingston	.50	1.25
48	JBL	.20	.50
49	Charlie Haas	.20	.50
50	Ron Simmons	.20	.50
51	CM Punk	.20	.50
52	Chuck Palumbo	.30	.75
53	William Regal	.50	1.25
54	Paul Burchill	.20	.50
55	Rey Mysterio	.50	1.25
56	Snitsky	.30	.75
57	Paul London	.20	.50
58	Chris Jericho	.50	1.25
59	Val Venis	.25	.60
60	Jerry Lawler	.40	1.00
61	Ted DiBiase Jr.	.50	1.25
62	Stone Cold Steve Austin	1.25	3.00
63	Hacksaw Jim Duggan	.50	1.25
64	Todd Grisham	.20	.50
65	Jamie Noble	.20	.50
66	Batista	.75	2.00
67	D'Lo Brown	.30	.75
68	Santino Marella	.20	.50
69	Shawn Michaels	1.25	3.00
70	Michael Cole	.20	.50
71	John Cena	1.25	3.00
72	JTG	.20	.50
73	Shad	.20	.50
74	Randy Orton	.50	1.25
75	Lance Cade	.20	.50
76	Hardcore Holly	.30	.75
77	Cody Rhodes	.20	.50
78	Kane	.75	2.00
79	Mike Adamle	.20	.50
80	Ezekiel Jackson	.20	.50
81	Montel Vontavious Porter	.30	.75
82	Funaki	.20	.50
83	Undertaker	1.00	2.50
84	DH Smith	.20	.50
85	Gregory Helms	.25	.60
86	Jeff Hardy	.75	2.00
87	Vladimir Kozlov	.20	.50
88	The Great Khali	.20	.50
89	Jesse	.20	.50
90	Festus	.20	.50
91	Edge	.75	2.00
92	Carlito	.50	1.25
93	Vickie Guerrero	.25	.60
94	Kenny Dykstra	.30	.75
95	Mr. Kennedy	.50	1.25
96	Shelton Benjamin	.20	.50
97	Triple H	1.25	3.00
98	Justin Roberts	.20	.50
99	Jimmy Wang Yang	.20	.50
100	Curt Hawkins	.20	.50
101	Zack Ryder	.20	.50
102	Brian Kendrick	.30	.75
103	Big Show	.50	1.25
104	Jim Ross	.40	1.00
105	Umaga	.30	.75
106	Tazz	.30	.75
107	John Morrison	.20	.50
108	Tommy Dreamer	.20	.50
109	Mike Knox	.20	.50
110	Super Crazy	.30	.75
111	Boogeyman	.30	.75
112	Mark Henry	.30	.75
113	Chavo Guerrero	.30	.75
114	Tony Chimel	.20	.50
115	Finlay	.30	.75
116	Bam Neely	.20	.50
117	Matt Hardy	.75	2.00
118	Armando Estrada	.20	.50
119	Elijah Burke	.20	.50
120	Hornswoggle	.30	.75
121	The Miz	.30	.75
122	Ricky Ortiz	.20	.50
123	Evan Bourne	.20	.50
124	Theodore Long	.25	.60
125	Matt Striker	.20	.50
126	Natalya DV	.40	1.00
127	Eve DV	.40	1.00
128	Maria DV	.75	2.00
129	Tiffany DV	.30	.75
130	Katie Lea Burchill DV	.25	.60
131	Kelly Kelly DV	.75	2.00
132	Layla DV	.50	1.25
133	Beth Phoenix DV	1.00	2.50
134	Candice DV	1.00	2.50
135	Lilian Garcia DV	.50	1.25
136	Lena Yada DV	.25	.60
137	Victoria DV	1.00	2.50
138	Melina DV	.75	2.00
139	Maryse DV	.75	2.00
140	Michelle McCool DV	1.00	2.50
141	Jillian DV	.75	2.00
142	Mickie James DV	1.25	3.00
143	Kane & Undertaker	1.00	2.50
144	The Bushwhackers	.25	.60
145	Curt Hawkins & Zack Ryder	.20	.50
146	Finlay & Hornswoggle	.30	.75
147	Chris Jericho & Lance Cade	.50	1.25
148	Cody Rhodes & Ted Dibiase	.50	1.25
149	John Morrison & The Miz	.30	.75
150	The Hardys TT	.75	2.00
151	Jesse & Festus TT	.20	.50
152	Cryme Tyme TT	.25	.60
153	D-Generation X TT	.60	1.50
154	Chavo Guerrero / Bam Neely TT	.30	.75
155	Sgt. Slaughter HOF	.50	1.25
156	The Mouth of the South Jimmy Hart HOF	.30	.75
157	Cowboy Bob Orton HOF	.50	1.25
158	The Iron Sheik HOF	.75	2.00
159	Rowdy Roddy Piper HOF	.75	2.00
160	Pat Patterson HOF	.20	.50
161	Gerald Brisco HOF	.20	.50
162	Junkyard Dog HOF	.30	.75
163	Dusty Rhodes HOF	.50	1.25
164	Jimmy Superfly Snuka	.50	1.25
165	Tony Atlas HOF	.20	.50
166	Bobby The Brain Heenan	.50	1.25
167	Superstar Billy Graham	.25	.60
168	Gorilla Monsoon L	.50	1.25
169	Nikolai Volkoff L	.30	.75
170	Curt Hennig L	.50	1.25
171	Vader L	.30	.75
172	Stone Cold Steve Austin L	1.25	3.00

2010 Topps WWE Slam Attax

	COMPLETE SET (130)	12.00	30.00
	UNOPENED BOX (24 PACKS)		
	UNOPENED PACK (8 CARDS)		
1	Kofi Kingston	.20	.50
2	Carlito	.30	.75
3	Primo	.12	.30
4	Jerry Lawler	.20	.50
5	Ted DiBiase	.20	.50
6	Jim Duggan	.20	.50
7	Festus	.12	.30
8	Chris Masters	.12	.30
9	Hornswoggle	.20	.50
10	Jamie Noble	.12	.30
11	Mark Henry	.20	.50
12	Justin Roberts	.12	.30
13	Santino Marella	.12	.30
14	Shawn Michaels	.75	2.00
15	Jack Swagger	.12	.30
16	Michael Cole	.12	.30
17	The Miz	.20	.50
18	Triple H	.60	1.50
19	Chavo Guerrero	.20	.50
20	Evan Bourne	.12	.30
21	Big Show	.30	.75
22	Montel Vontavious Porter	.20	.50
23	John Cena	.60	1.50
24	Randy Orton	.50	1.25
25	Cody Rhodes	.12	.30
26	Eve	.50	1.25
27	Melina	.50	1.25
28	Alicia Fox	.20	.50
29	Kelly Kelly	.50	1.25
30	Gail Kim	.30	.75
31	Jillian	.50	1.25
32	Maryse	.50	1.25
33	Sheamus	.20	.50
34	Brie Bella	.50	1.25
35	Nikki Bella	.50	1.25
36	Kung Fu Naki	.12	.30
37	Undertaker	.50	1.25
38	Charlie Haas	.12	.30
39	Kane	.30	.75
40	CM Punk	.50	1.25
41	Dolph Ziggler	.20	.50
42	Rey Mysterio	.30	.75
43	Chris Jericho	.30	.75
44	The Great Khali	.12	.30
45	Slam Master J	.12	.30
46	Matt Hardy	.30	.75
47	Edge	.50	1.25
48	JTG	.12	.30
49	Shad	.12	.30
50	David Hart Smith	.12	.30
51	Tyson Kidd	.12	.30
52	Mike Knox	.12	.30
53	R-Truth	.12	.30
54	John Morrison	.20	.50
55	Finlay	.20	.50
56	Beth Phoenix	.50	1.25
57	Batista	.50	1.25
58	Theodore Long	.12	.30
59	Todd Grisham	.12	.30
60	Ranjin Singh	.12	.30
61	Jimmy Wang Yang	.12	.30
62	Curt Hawkins	.12	.30
63	Jim Ross	.12	.30
64	Natalya	.50	1.25
65	Michelle McCool	.50	1.25
66	Mickie James	.60	1.50
67	Layla	.30	.75
68	Maria	.50	1.25
69	Tommy Dreamer	.12	.30
70	The Hurricane	.12	.30
71	Vladimir Kozlov	.20	.50
72	Tony Chimel	.12	.30
73	Ezekiel Jackson	.12	.30
74	Shelton Benjamin	.12	.30
75	Josh Mathews	.12	.30
76	William Regal	.30	.75
77	Paul Burchill	.12	.30
78	Gabriel	.12	.30
79	Goldust	.20	.50
80	Zack Ryder	.12	.30
81	Yoshi Tatsu	.12	.30
82	Abraham Washington	.12	.30
83	Tyler Reks	.12	.30
84	Savannah	.20	.50
85	Matt Striker	.12	.30
86	Christian	.20	.50
87	Rosa Mendes	.20	.50
88	Katie Lea Burchill	.30	.75
89	Tiffany	.20	.50
90	C.Rhodes/T.DiBiase	.20	.50
91	Cryme Tyme	.12	.30
92	D.Smith/T.Kidd	.12	.30
93	S.Benjamin/C.Haas	.12	.30
94	C.Jericho/Big Show	.30	.75
95	M.Henry/Hornswoggle	.20	.50
96	Iron Sheik	.30	.75
97	Ted DiBiase	.20	.50

98	Jake Roberts	.30	.75
99	Koko B. Ware	.20	.50
100	British Bulldog	.20	.50
101	Sgt. Slaughter	.30	.75
102	Rick Rude	.20	.50
103	Bam Bam Bigelow	.20	.50
104	Junkyard Dog	.30	.75
105	Roddy Piper	.50	1.25
106	Paul Orndorff	.30	.75
107	Jimmy Snuka	.30	.75
108	Nikolai Volkoff	.20	.50
109	Dusty Rhodes	.30	.75
110	Bobby Heenan	.20	.50
111	Hillbilly Jim	.20	.50
112	Curt Hennig	.20	.50
113	Bob Orton	.20	.50
114	Jerry Lawler	.20	.50
115	Earthquake	.20	.50
116	TLC Match	.12	.30
117	Steel Cage Match	.12	.30
118	Hell in a Cell Match	.12	.30
119	Stretcher Match	.12	.30
120	Casket Match	.12	.30
121	Royal Rumble	.12	.30
122	No Way Out	.12	.30
123	WrestleMania	.12	.30
124	Backlash	.12	.30
125	Judgement Day	.12	.30
126	Extreme Rules	.12	.30
127	The Bash	.12	.30
128	Night Of Champions	.12	.30
129	Summerslam	.12	.30
130	Survivor Series	.12	.30

2010 Topps WWE Slam Attax Champions

COMPLETE SET (16)		8.00	20.00
STATED ODDS 1:5			
1	John Cena	2.00	5.00
2	Edge	1.50	4.00
3	Matt Hardy	1.00	2.50
4	Chris Jericho	1.00	2.50
5	Triple H	2.00	5.00
6	Rey Mysterio	1.00	2.50
7	Randy Orton	1.50	4.00
8	CM Punk	1.50	4.00
9	Batista	1.50	4.00
10	C.Jericho/Big Show	1.00	2.50
11	Michelle McCool	1.50	4.00
12	Kofi Kingston	.60	1.50
13	Christian	.60	1.50
14	Montel Vontavious Porter	.60	1.50
15	Maryse	1.50	4.00
16	Undertaker	1.50	4.00

2010 Topps WWE Slam Attax Finishing Moves

COMPLETE SET (19)		6.00	15.00
STATED ODDS 1:6			
1	Kane	.75	2.00
2	Cody Rhodes	.30	.75
3	Ted DiBiase	.50	1.25
4	Shawn Michaels	2.00	5.00
5	John Morrison	.50	1.25
6	Carlito	.75	2.00
7	Beth Phoenix	1.25	3.00
8	Jack Swagger	.30	.75

9	Mark Henry	.50	1.25
10	Tommy Dreamer	.30	.75
11	Evan Bourne	.30	.75
12	The Great Khali	.30	.75
13	Chavo Guerrero	.50	1.25
14	Melina	1.25	3.00
15	Finlay	.50	1.25
16	Big Show	.75	2.00
17	Shelton Benjamin	.30	.75
18	R-Truth	.30	.75
19	Maria	1.25	3.00

2010 Topps WWE Slam Attax Props

COMPLETE SET (10)		5.00	12.00
STATED ODDS 1:5			
1	Steel Chair	.75	2.00
2	Sledgehammer	.75	2.00
3	Table	.75	2.00
4	Trash Can	.75	2.00
5	Ladder	.75	2.00
6	Steel Steps	.75	2.00
7	Ring Bell	.75	2.00
8	Brass Knuckles	.75	2.00
9	Shillelagh	.75	2.00
10	Kendo Stick	.75	2.00

2010 Topps WWE Slam Attax Starter Box Exclusives

COMPLETE SET (5)		6.00	15.00
STATED ODDS ONE PER STARTER BOX			
1	Chris Jericho	1.25	3.00
2	Undertaker	2.00	5.00
3	Randy Orton	2.00	5.00
4	Triple H	2.50	6.00
5	John Cena	2.50	6.00

2010 Topps WWE Slam Attax Titles

COMPLETE SET (11)		5.00	12.00
STATED ODDS 1:6			
1	WWE Championship	.75	2.00
2	Intercontinental Championship	.75	2.00
3	Women's Championship	.75	2.00
4	Word Tag Team Championship	.75	2.00
5	World Heavyweight Championship	.75	2.00
6	United States Championship	.75	2.00
7	WWE Tag Team Championship	.75	2.00
8	WWE Divas Championship	.75	2.00
9	ECW Championship	.75	2.00
10	WWE Money in the Bank Briefcase	.75	2.00
11	WWE Slammy Award	.75	2.00

2010 Topps WWE Slam Attax WrestleMania XXVI

COMPLETE SET (5)		6.00	15.00
ONE SET PER WRESTLEMANIA XXVI TIN			
1	Chris Jericho	1.00	2.50
2	John Cena	2.00	5.00
3	Randy Orton	1.50	4.00
4	Triple H	2.00	5.00
5	Undertaker	1.50	4.00

2018 Topps WWE Slam Attax Live!

COMPLETE SET (392)		25.00	60.00
1	Alexa Bliss FOIL	1.00	2.50
2	Baron Corbin FOIL	.30	.75
3	Bobby Roode FOIL	.30	.75
4	Braun Strowman FOIL	.50	1.25

5	Elias FOIL	.50	1.25
6	Finn Balor FOIL	.50	1.25
7	John Cena FOIL	.75	2.00
8	Kevin Owens FOIL	.50	1.25
9	Nia Jax FOIL	.30	.75
10	Roman Reigns FOIL	.50	1.25
11	Sami Zayn FOIL	.20	.50
12	Seth Rollins FOIL	.50	1.25
13	AJ Styles FOIL	.75	2.00
14	Rusev FOIL	.30	.75
15	Asuka FOIL	.60	1.50
16	Bludgeon Brothers FOIL	.30	.75
17	Carmella FOIL	.40	1.00
18	Charlotte Flair FOIL	.60	1.50
19	Jeff Hardy FOIL	.40	1.00
20	The Miz FOIL	.40	1.00
21	Rusev FOIL	.30	.75
22	Samoa Joe FOIL	.40	1.00
23	Shinsuke Nakamura FOIL	.50	1.25
24	The Usos FOIL	.30	.75
25	Adam Cole FOIL	.25	.60
26	Aleister Black FOIL	.25	.60
27	Kairi Sane FOIL	.50	1.25
28	Pete Dunne FOIL	.20	.50
29	Roderick Strong FOIL	.20	.50
30	Shayna Baszler FOIL	.50	1.25
31	Undisputed Era FOIL	.25	.60
32	Cedric Alexander FOIL	.20	.50
33	Alexa Bliss/Nia Jax FOIL	1.00	2.50
34	Bray Wyatt/Woken Matt Hardy FOIL	.50	1.25
35	Roman Reigns/Jinder Mahal FOIL	.50	1.25
36	Seth Rollins/Finn Balor FOIL	.50	1.25
37	AJ Styles/Nakamura FOIL	.75	2.00
38	Asuka/Charlotte Flair FOIL	.60	1.50
39	Bobby Roode/Randy Orton FOIL	.50	1.25
40	Daniel Bryan/The Miz FOIL	.50	1.25
41	Adam Cole/Velveteen Dream FOIL	.25	.60
42	Andrade/Aleister Black FOIL	.30	.75
43	Ember Moon/Shayna Baszler FOIL	.50	1.25
44	Bret Hart/Shawn Michaels FOIL	.60	1.50
45	Ric Flair/Chris Jericho FOIL	.60	1.50
46	Trish Stratus/Lita FOIL	.75	2.00
47	Undertaker/Kane FOIL	.75	2.00
48	X-Pac/Shane McMahon FOIL	.40	1.00
49	1-2-3 Kid	.25	.60
50	Braun Strowman	.50	1.25
51	Bret Hit Man Hart	.50	1.25
52	Chris Jericho	.50	1.25
53	Chris Jericho	.50	1.25
54	D-Generation X	.60	1.50
55	Daniel Bryan	.50	1.25
56	Daniel Bryan	.50	1.25
57	Finn Balor	.50	1.25
58	Jeff Hardy	.40	1.00
59	John Cena	.75	2.00
60	John Cena & Shawn Michaels	.75	2.00
61	Kane	.30	.75
62	Mark Henry	.25	.60
63	The Miz	.40	1.00
64	Paige	.50	1.25
65	Randy Orton	.50	1.25
66	Ric Flair	.60	1.50
67	Roman Reigns	.50	1.25
68	Sasha Banks	.60	1.50
69	Seth Rollins	.50	1.25
70	Shane McMahon	.40	1.00
71	Stephanie McMahon	.40	1.00
72	Sting	.50	1.25

73	Stone Cold Steve Austin	1.00	2.50
74	Stone Cold Steve Austin	1.00	2.50
75	Stone Cold Steve Austin	1.00	2.50
76	The Rock	1.00	2.50
77	Trish Stratus & Lita	.75	2.00
78	Ultimate Warrior	.75	2.00
79	Undertaker & Triple H	.75	2.00
80	Yokozuna	.25	.60
81	Akam	.20	.50
82	Alexa Bliss	1.00	2.50
83	Alicia Fox	.30	.75
84	Apollo Crews	.20	.50
85	Baron Corbin	.30	.75
86	Bayley	.30	.75
87	Big Show	.20	.50
88	Bo Dallas	.20	.50
89	Bobby Roode	.30	.75
90	Braun Strowman	.50	1.25
91	Bray Wyatt	.50	1.25
92	Chad Gable	.20	.50
93	Charly Caruso	.30	.75
94	Corey Graves	.25	.60
95	Curt Hawkins	.20	.50
96	Curtis Axel	.20	.50
97	Dana Brooke	.40	1.00
98	Dash Wilder	.25	.60
99	David Otunga	.25	.60
100	Dean Ambrose	.40	1.00
101	Drew McIntyre	.30	.75
102	Elias	.50	1.25
103	Ember Moon	.40	1.00
104	Fandango	.20	.50
105	Finn Balor	.50	1.25
106	Goldust	.40	1.00
107	Heath Slater	.20	.50
108	Jason Jordan	.20	.50
109	Jinder Mahal	.25	.60
110	John Cena	.75	2.00
111	Jojo	.20	.50
112	Jonathan Coachman	.20	.50
113	Kane	.30	.75
114	Kevin Owens	.50	1.25
115	Konnor	.20	.50
116	Kurt Angle	.50	1.25
117	Bobby Lashley	.40	1.00
118	Liv Morgan	.40	1.00
119	Maryse	.40	1.00
120	Woken Matt Hardy	.50	1.25
121	Michael Cole	.20	.50
122	Mickie James	.40	1.00
123	Mike Kanellis	.20	.50
124	Mike Rome	.20	.50
125	Mojo Rawley	.25	.60
126	Natalya	.25	.60
127	Nia Jax	.30	.75
128	No Way Jose	.25	.60
129	Renee Young	.30	.75
130	Rezar	.20	.50
131	Rhyno	.20	.50
132	Roman Reigns	.50	1.25
133	Ronda Rousey	1.00	2.50
134	Ruby Riott	.30	.75
135	Sami Zayn	.20	.50
136	Sarah Logan	.20	.50
137	Sasha Banks	.60	1.50
138	Scott Dawson	.25	.60
139	Seth Rollins	.50	1.25
140	Stephanie McMahon	.40	1.00

#	Name			#	Name		
141	Titus O'Neil	.20	.50	209	Johnny Gargano	.20	.50
142	Triple H	.50	1.25	210	Kairi Sane	.50	1.25
143	Tyler Breeze	.20	.50	211	Kassius Ohno	.20	.50
144	Viktor	.20	.50	212	Kyle O'Reilly	.25	.60
145	Zack Ryder	.20	.50	213	Lacey Evans	.25	.60
146	Aiden English	.20	.50	214	Lars Sullivan	.20	.50
147	AJ Styles	.75	2.00	215	Lio Rush	.20	.50
148	Alexander Wolfe	.20	.50	216	Mauro Ranallo	.20	.50
149	Andrade Cien Almas	.30	.75	217	Montez Ford	.20	.50
150	Asuka	.60	1.50	218	Nick Miller	.20	.50
151	Becky Lynch	.50	1.25	219	Nigel McGuinness	.20	.50
152	Big Cass	.25	.60	220	Nikki Cross	.30	.75
153	Big E	.25	.60	221	Oney Lorcan	.25	.60
154	Billie Kay	.40	1.00	222	Otis Dozovic	.20	.50
155	Byron Saxton	.20	.50	223	Percy Watson	.20	.50
156	Carmella	.40	1.00	224	Pete Dunne	.20	.50
157	Cesaro	.40	1.00	225	Ricochet	.40	1.00
158	Charlotte Flair	.60	1.50	226	Riddick Moss	.20	.50
159	Chris Jericho	.50	1.25	227	Roderick Strong	.20	.50
160	Daniel Bryan	.50	1.25	228	Shane Thorne	.20	.50
161	Dasha Fuentes	.30	.75	229	Shayna Baszler	.50	1.25
162	Eric Young	.25	.60	230	Taynara Conti	.20	.50
163	Greg Hamilton	.30	.75	231	Tino Sabatelli	.25	.60
164	Harper	.30	.75	232	Tommaso Ciampa	.20	.50
165	Jeff Hardy	.40	1.00	233	Trent Seven	.20	.50
166	Jey Uso	.20	.50	234	Tucker Knight	.20	.50
167	Jimmy Uso	.20	.50	235	Tyler Bate	.20	.50
168	Karl Anderson	.20	.50	236	Vanessa Borne	.20	.50
169	Killian Dain	.25	.60	237	Velveteen Dream	.20	.50
170	Kofi Kingston	.25	.60	238	Wesley Blake	.25	.60
171	Lana	.50	1.25	239	William Regal	.30	.75
172	Luke Gallows	.25	.60	240	Akira Tozawa	.30	.75
173	Mandy Rose	.50	1.25	241	Ariya Daivari	.20	.50
174	Maria Kanellis	.50	1.25	242	The Brian Kendrick	.30	.75
175	The Miz	.40	1.00	243	Cedric Alexander	.20	.50
176	Naomi	.25	.60	244	Drake Maverick	.25	.60
177	Nikki Bella	.40	1.00	245	Drew Gulak	.20	.50
178	Paige	.50	1.25	246	Gentleman Jack Gallagher	.25	.60
179	Peyton Royce	.50	1.25	247	Gran Metalik	.20	.50
180	R-Truth	.25	.60	248	Hideo Itami	.20	.50
181	Randy Orton	.50	1.25	249	Kalisto	.20	.50
182	Rowan	.30	.75	250	Lince Dorado	.20	.50
183	Rusev	.30	.75	251	Mustafa Ali	.20	.50
184	Samir Singh	.20	.50	252	Neville	.30	.75
185	Samoa Joe	.40	1.00	253	Noam Dar	.20	.50
186	Shane McMahon	.40	1.00	254	TJP	.25	.60
187	Sheamus	.40	1.00	255	Tony Nese	.20	.50
188	Shelton Benjamin	.25	.60	256	Alundra Blayze	.20	.50
189	Shinsuke Nakamura	.50	1.25	257	Andre the Giant	.40	1.00
190	Sin Cara	.25	.60	258	Bam Bam Bigelow	.30	.75
191	Sonya Deville	.40	1.00	259	Batista	.30	.75
192	Sunil Singh	.20	.50	260	Beth Phoenix	.40	1.00
193	Tamina	.20	.50	261	Big Boss Man	.20	.50
194	Tom Phillips	.20	.50	262	Billy Gunn	.25	.60
195	Tye Dillinger	.20	.50	263	Bob Backlund	.20	.50
196	Xavier Woods	.25	.60	264	Bobby The Brain Heenan	.30	.75
197	Zelina Vega	.20	.50	265	Booker T	.30	.75
198	Adam Cole	.25	.60	266	Bret Hit Man Hart	.50	1.25
199	Aleister Black	.25	.60	267	British Bulldog	.30	.75
200	Aliyah	.30	.75	268	Bruno Sammartino	.30	.75
201	Angelo Dawkins	.20	.50	269	Chief Jay Strongbow	.30	.75
202	Bianca Belair	.25	.60	270	Classy Freddie Blassie	.20	.50
203	Bobby Fish	.20	.50	271	Cowboy Bob Orton	.20	.50
204	Buddy Murphy	.25	.60	272	D'Lo Brown	.20	.50
205	Cezar Bononi	.20	.50	273	Dean Malenko	.20	.50
206	Danny Burch	.20	.50	274	Diamond Dallas Page	.30	.75
207	EC3	.20	.50	275	Dusty Rhodes	.40	1.00
208	Fabian Aichner	.20	.50	276	Eddie Guerrero	.50	1.25

#	Name			#	Name		
277	Edge	.50	1.25	345	The Singh Brothers	.25	.60
278	Eve	.40	1.00	346	The Usos	.30	.75
279	The Godfather	.20	.50	347	Danny Burch & Oney Lorcan	.25	.60
280	Hacksaw Jim Duggan	.20	.50	348	Heavy Machinery	.20	.50
281	Harley Race	.20	.50	349	Moustache Mountain	.20	.50
282	Honky Tonk Man	.20	.50	350	Riddick Moss & Tino Sabbatelli	.25	.60
283	Howard Finkel	.20	.50	351	The Street Profits	.20	.50
284	Iron Sheik	.20	.50	352	TM-61	.20	.50
285	Irwin R. Schyster	.20	.50	353	Undisputed Era	.25	.60
286	Jake The Snake Roberts	.25	.60	354	Bushwhackers		.50
287	Jerry The King Lawler	.40	1.00	355	D-Generation X	.60	1.50
288	Jim The Anvil Neidhart	.30	.75	356	Nasty Boys	.20	.50
289	Jimmy Hart	.30	.75	357	nWo	.40	1.00
290	Junkyard Dog	.20	.50	358	WWE Title	.20	.50
291	Ken Shamrock	.25	.60	359	Intercontinental Title	.20	.50
292	Kevin Nash	.40	1.00	360	RAW Women's Title	.20	.50
293	Lex Luger	.25	.60	361	WWE UK Title	.20	.50
294	Lita	.50	1.25	362	SmackDown Women's Title	.20	.50
295	Macho Man Randy Savage	.60	1.50	363	NXT Title	.20	.50
296	Magnificent Don Muraco	.20	.50	364	WWE Universal Title	.20	.50
297	Mark Henry	.25	.60	365	NXT Women's Title	.20	.50
298	Mean Gene Okerlund	.25	.60	366	RAW Tag Team Title	.20	.50
299	Million Dollar Man Ted DiBiase	.25	.60	367	SmackDown Tag Team Title	.20	.50
300	Mr. Perfect Curt Hennig	.25	.60	368	United States Title	.20	.50
301	Mr. Wonderful Paul Orndorff	.20	.50	369	WWE Cruiserweight Title	.20	.50
302	Norman Smiley	.20	.50	370	NXT Tag Team Title	.20	.50
303	Papa Shango	.20	.50	371	Puzzle	.50	1.25
304	Paul Bearer	.30	.75	372	Puzzle	.75	2.00
305	Prince Albert	.20	.50	373	Puzzle	.30	.75
306	Psycho Sid	.20	.50	374	Puzzle	.50	1.25
307	Ravishing Rick Rude	.25	.60	375	Puzzle	1.00	2.50
308	Razor Ramon	.40	1.00	376	Puzzle	.50	1.25
309	Ric Flair	.60	1.50	377	Puzzle	.40	1.00
310	Ricky The Dragon Steamboat	.30	.75	378	Puzzle	.75	2.00
311	Rikishi	.20	.50	379	Puzzle	.50	1.25
312	Road Dogg	.20	.50	380	Puzzle	.50	1.25
313	The Rock	1.00	2.50	381	Puzzle	.75	2.00
314	Rowdy Roddy Piper	.50	1.25	382	Puzzle	.60	1.50
315	Sgt. Slaughter	.25	.60	383	Puzzle	1.00	2.50
316	Shawn Michaels	.60	1.50	384	Puzzle	1.00	2.50
317	Sting	.50	1.25	385	Puzzle	.75	2.00
318	Stone Cold Steve Austin	1.00	2.50	386	Puzzle	.20	.50
319	Tatanka	.20	.50	387	Puzzle	.20	.50
320	Trish Stratus	.75	2.00	388	Puzzle	.20	.50
321	Ultimate Warrior	.75	2.00	389	Steel Chair	.20	.50
322	Umaga	.20	.50	390	Table	.20	.50
323	Undertaker	.75	2.00	391	Ladder	.20	.50
324	Viscera	.20	.50	392	Trash Can	.20	.50
325	X-Pac	.25	.60				
326	Yokozuna	.25	.60				
327	The Ascension	.20	.50				
328	Authors of Pain	.20	.50				
329	Bray Wyatt & Woken Matt Hardy	.50	1.25				
330	Breezango	.20	.50				
331	Heath Slater & Rhyno	.20	.50				
332	The Miztourage	.40	1.00				
333	The Revival	.25	.60				
334	The Riott Squad	.40	1.00				
335	The Shield	.50	1.25				
336	Titus Worldwide	.40	1.00				
337	Absolution	.50	1.25				
338	The Bar	.40	1.00				
339	Bludgeon Brothers	.30	.75				
340	Gallows & Anderson	.25	.60				
341	The New Day	.30	.75				
342	Rusev Day	.30	.75				
343	The Iconics	.50	1.25				
344	SanitY	.30	.75				

**2018 Topps WWE Slam Attax Live!
Authentic Ring Mat Memorabilia**

RMAA	John Cena & Nikki Bella
RMAB	Triple H & Stephanie McMahon
RMAC	Seth Rollins
RMBA	The Usos
RMBB	Carmella
RMBC	Baron Corbin
RMCA	Sasha Banks
RMCB	Braun Strowman
RMCC	AJ Styles
RMDA	Kurt Angle
RMDB	The Miz
RMDC	Dean Ambrose/Seth Rollins
RMEA	Charlotte Flair
RMEB	Alexa Bliss
RMEC	Finn Balor
RMFA	Shinsuke Nakamura
RMFB	Kevin Owens

RMFC Asuka
RMGA Drew McIntyre
RMGB Braun Strowman
RMGC Andrade Cien Almas
RMHA Undisputed Era
RMHB Velveteen Dream
RMHC Kairi Sane
RMIA Aleister Black
RMIB Adam Cole
RMIC Ember Moon
RMJA Finn Balor
RMJB Elias
RMJC Jason Jordan

2018 Topps WWE Slam Attax Live! Authentic T-Shirt Memorabilia

TS1 AJ Styles
TS3 Bayley
TS5 John Cena
TS7 Karl Anderson
TS9 Roman Reigns
TS10 Sami Zayn
TS11 Tye Dillinger

2018 Topps WWE Slam Attax Live! Collector Cards

CC1 Bret Hit Man Hart
CC2 Eddie Guerrero
CC3 Shawn Michaels
CC4 Sting
CC5 Stone Cold Steve Austin
CC6 Ultimate Warrior

2018 Topps WWE Slam Attax Live! Gold Limited Edition

LEPA Roman Reigns
LEPB Daniel Bryan
LEPC Andrade Cien Almas
LEPD Sasha Banks
LEPE Asuka
LEPF Seth Rollins
LEPG John Cena
LEPH Kevin Owens

2018 Topps WWE Slam Attax Live! Silver Limited Edition

LEMB Braun Strowman
LEMC Adam Cole
LEMD Charlotte Flair
LEMF Randy Orton
LESA Ronda Rousey

2010 Topps WWE Slam Attax Mayhem

COMPLETE SET (161)	12.00	30.00
UNOPENED BOX (24 PACKS)		
UNOPENED PACK (8 CARDS)		
1 Chris Jericho	.30	.75
2 David Hart Smith	.12	.30
3 Edge	.50	1.25
4 Evan Bourne	.12	.30
5 Ezekiel Jackson	.12	.30
6 Goldust	.20	.50
7 Jerry Lawler	.20	.50
8 Jay Uso	.12	.30
9 Jimmy Uso	.12	.30
10 John Cena	.60	1.50
11 John Morrison	.20	.50
12 Justin Roberts	.12	.30
13 Mark Henry	.20	.50
14 Michael Cole	.12	.30
15 Primo	.12	.30
16 R-Truth	.12	.30
17 Randy Orton	.50	1.25
18 Ranjin Singh	.12	.30
19 Santino Marella	.12	.30
20 Sheamus	.20	.50
21 Ted DiBiase	.20	.50
22 The Great Khali	.12	.30
23 The Miz	.20	.50
24 Triple H	.60	1.50
25 Tyson Kidd	.12	.30
26 Vladimir Kozlov	.20	.50
27 William Regal	.30	.75
28 Yoshi Tatsu	.12	.30
29 Zack Ryder	.12	.30
30 Alicia Fox	.20	.50
31 Brie Bella	.50	1.25
32 Eve	.50	1.25
33 Gail Kim	.30	.75
34 Jillian	.50	1.25
35 Maryse	.50	1.25
36 Melina	.50	1.25
37 Natalya	.50	1.25
38 Nikki Bella	.50	1.25
39 Tamina	.12	.30
40 Big Show	.30	.75
41 Caylen Croft	.12	.30
42 Chavo Guerrero	.20	.50
43 Chris Masters	.12	.30
44 Christian	.20	.50
45 CM Punk	.50	1.25
46 Cody Rhodes	.12	.30
47 Curt Hawkins	.12	.30
48 Dolph Ziggler	.20	.50
49 Drew McIntyre	.20	.50
50 Finlay	.20	.50
51 Hornswoggle	.20	.50
52 Jack Swagger	.12	.30
53 JTG	.12	.30
54 Kane	.30	.75
55 Kofi Kingston	.20	.50
56 Luke Gallows	.12	.30
57 Matt Hardy	.30	.75
58 Matt Striker	.12	.30
59 Montel Vontavious Porter	.20	.50
60 Rey Mysterio	.30	.75
61 Shad	.12	.30
62 Theodore Long	.12	.30
63 Todd Grisham	.12	.30
64 Tony Chimel	.12	.30
65 Trent Barreta	.12	.30
66 Tyler Reks	.12	.30
67 Undertaker	.50	1.25
68 Vance Archer	.12	.30
69 Beth Phoenix	.50	1.25
70 Kelly Kelly	.50	1.25
71 Layla	.30	.75
72 Michelle McCool	.50	1.25
73 Rosa Mendes	.20	.50
74 Serena	.20	.50
75 Darren Young	.20	.50
76 David Otunga	.20	.50
77 Heath Slater	.20	.50
78 Justin Gabriel	.20	.50
79 Michael Tarver	.20	.50
80 Skip Sheffield	.20	.50
81 Wade Barrett	.20	.50
82 Alex Riley	.12	.30
83 Husky Harris	.25	.60
84 Kaval	.12	.30
85 Lucky Cannon	.12	.30
86 Eli Cottonwood	.12	.30
87 Michael McGillicutty	.12	.30
88 Percy Watson	.12	.30
89 Titus O'Neil	.12	.30
90 Jamie Keyes	.12	.30
91 David Hart Smith/Tyson Kidd	.12	.30
92 Trent Barreta/Caylen Croft	.12	.30
93 Chris Jericho/The Miz	.30	.75
94 Montel Vontavious Porter/JTG	.20	.50
95 Curt Hawkins/Vance Archer	.12	.30
96 William Regal/Vladimir Kozlov	.30	.75
97 THE USO Brothers	.12	.30
98 Iron Sheik	.30	.75
99 Jake The Snake Roberts	.30	.75
100 Koko B. Ware	.20	.50
101 British Bulldog	.20	.50
102 Sgt. Slaughter	.30	.75
103 Ravishing Rick Rude	.20	.50
104 Bam Bam Bigelow	.20	.50
105 Junkyard Dog	.30	.75
106 Ted DiBiase	.20	.50
107 Rowdy Roddy Piper	.50	1.25
108 Mr. Wonderful Paul Orndorff	.30	.75
109 Jimmy Superfly Snuka	.30	.75
110 Nikolai Volkoff	.20	.50
111 Dusty Rhodes	.30	.75
112 Bobby The Brain Heenan	.20	.50
113 Hillbilly Jim	.20	.50
114 Mr. Perfect Curt Hennig	.20	.50
115 Barry Windham	.20	.50
116 Cowboy Bob Orton	.20	.50
117 Jerry The King Lawler	.20	.50
118 Earthquake	.20	.50
119 Ricky Dragon Steamboat	.20	.50
120 Vader	.20	.50
121 Gorilla Monsoon	.12	.30
122 Terry Funk	.30	.75
123 IRS	.12	.30
124 Yokozuna	.12	.30
125 Steel Chair	.12	.30
126 Sledgehammer	.12	.30
127 Table	.12	.30
128 Trash Can	.12	.30
129 Ladder	.12	.30
130 Steel Steps	.12	.30
131 Ring Bell	.12	.30
132 Brass Knuckles	.12	.30
133 Baseball Bat	.12	.30
134 Handcuffs	.12	.30
135 Fire Extinguisher	.12	.30
136 Announcers Table	.12	.30
137 Steel Pipe	.12	.30
138 Microphone	.12	.30
139 Steel Cage Match	.12	.30
140 Hell in a Cell Match	.12	.30
141 Stretcher Match	.12	.30
142 Casket Match	.12	.30
143 Elimination Chamber Match	.12	.30
144 Ambulance Match	.12	.30
145 Backstage Brawl	.12	.30
146 Royal Rumble	.12	.30
147 Elimination Chamber	.12	.30
148 WrestleMania XXVI	.12	.30
149 Extreme Rules	.12	.30
150 WWE Over The Limit	.12	.30
151 Fatal 4 Way	.12	.30
152 Money In The Bank	.12	.30
153 SummerSlam	.12	.30
154 Night Of Champions	.12	.30
155 Hell In A Cell	.12	.30
156 WWE Bragging Rights	.12	.30
157 TLC:Tables, Ladders and Chairs	.12	.30
158 John Cena	.60	1.50
159 The Miz	.20	.50
160 Undertaker	.50	1.25
161 Rey Mysterio	.30	.75

2010 Topps WWE Slam Attax Mayhem Champions

COMPLETE SET (16)	8.00	20.00
STATED ODDS 1:6		
1 Jack Swagger	.40	1.00
2 Drew McIntyre	.60	1.50
3 John Cena	2.00	5.00
4 The Miz	.60	1.50
5 David Hart Smith/Tyson Kidd	.40	1.00
6 Eve	1.50	4.00
7 Layla	1.00	2.50
8 Triple H	2.00	5.00
9 Randy Orton	1.50	4.00
10 Chris Jericho	1.00	2.50
11 Undertaker	1.50	4.00
12 Big Show	1.00	2.50
13 Edge	1.50	4.00
14 Sheamus	.60	1.50
15 Melina	1.50	4.00
16 Kofi Kingston	.60	1.50

2010 Topps WWE Slam Attax Mayhem Finishing Moves

COMPLETE SET (26)	10.00	25.00
STATED ODDS		
1 Chavo Guerrero	.50	1.25
2 Chris Masters	.30	.75
3 Christian	.50	1.25
4 Dolph Ziggler	.50	1.25
5 Kane	.75	2.00
6 Luke Gallows	.30	.75
7 Matt Hardy	.75	2.00
8 Montel Vontavious Porter	.50	1.25
9 Undertaker	1.25	3.00
10 Evan Bourne	.30	.75
11 Mark Henry	.50	1.25
12 Rey Mysterio	.75	2.00
13 R-Truth	.30	.75
14 Ted DiBiase	.50	1.25
15 The Great Khali	.30	.75
16 The Miz	.50	1.25
17 Zack Ryder	.30	.75
18 Edge	1.25	3.00
19 Randy Orton	1.25	3.00
20 John Cena	1.50	4.00
21 John Morrison	.50	1.25
22 Jack Swagger	.30	.75
23 Beth Phoenix	1.25	3.00
24 Michelle McCool	1.25	3.00
25 Maryse	1.25	3.00
26 Gail Kim	.75	2.00

2010 Topps WWE Slam Attax Mayhem General Managers

COMPLETE SET (6)	2.50	6.00
STATED ODDS 1:6		
1 T.Long/You're Kicked Out	.75	2.00
2 T.Long/You're Kicked Out	.75	2.00
3 T.Long/You're Kicked Out	.75	2.00
4 T.Long/Return to the Ring	.75	2.00
5 T.Long/Return to the Ring	.75	2.00
6 T.Long/Return to the Ring	.75	2.00

2010 Topps WWE Slam Attax Mayhem Starter Box Exclusives

COMPLETE SET (3)	2.50	6.00
STATED ODDS ONE PER STARTER BOX		
1 Montel Vontavious Porter	.75	2.00
2 Triple H	2.50	6.00
3 Drew McIntyre	.75	2.00

2010 Topps WWE Slam Attax Mayhem Titles

COMPLETE SET (10)	5.00	12.00
STATED ODDS		
1 WWE Championship	.75	2.00
2 Intercontinental Championship	.75	2.00
3 Women's Championship	.75	2.00
4 World Tag Team Championship	.75	2.00
5 World Heavyweight Championship	.75	2.00
6 United States Championship	.75	2.00
7 WWE Tag Team Championship	.75	2.00
8 WWE Divas Championship	.75	2.00
9 WWE Money in the Bank Briefcase	.75	2.00
10 WWE Slammy Award	.75	2.00

2020 Topps WWE Slam Attax Reloaded

COMPLETE SET (352)	20.00	50.00
1 Akam	.40	1.00
2 Akira Tozawa	.30	.75
3 Aleister Black	.60	1.50
4 Andrade	.50	1.25
5 Angel Garza	.40	1.00
6 Angelo Dawkins	.30	.75
7 Apollo Crews	.40	1.00
8 Asuka	.60	1.50
9 Becky Lynch	1.25	3.00
10 Bianca Belair	.75	2.00
11 Big Show	.40	1.00
12 Billie Kay	.60	1.50
13 Bobby Lashley	.60	1.50
14 Cedric Alexander	.30	.75
15 Charlotte Flair	1.25	3.00
16 Drew McIntyre	.60	1.50
17 Edge	.60	1.50
18 Erik	.30	.75
19 Humberto Carrillo	.50	1.25
20 Ivar	.30	.75
21 Jason Jordan	.30	.75
22 Jinder Mahal	.30	.75
23 Kairi Sane	.60	1.50
24 Kevin Owens	.40	1.00
25 Liv Morgan	.75	2.00
26 Montez Ford	.30	.75
27 Murphy	.40	1.00
28 Natalya	.50	1.25
29 Nia Jax	.50	1.25

30 Peyton Royce	.60	1.50
31 R-Truth	.30	.75
32 Randy Orton	.75	2.00
33 Rey Mysterio	.60	1.50
34 Rezar	.30	.75
35 Ricochet	.50	1.25
36 Shayna Baszler	1.00	2.50
37 Ruby Riott	.50	1.25
38 Samoa Joe	.50	1.25
39 Seth Rollins	.60	1.50
40 Shelton Benjamin	.40	1.00
41 Titus O'Neil	.30	.75
42 Undertaker	1.25	3.00
43 Zelina Vega	.60	1.50
44 AJ Styles	1.00	2.50
45 Alexa Bliss	1.50	4.00
46 Bayley	.60	1.50
47 Big E	.30	.75
48 Bo Dallas	.30	.75
49 Braun Strowman	.75	2.00
50 Carmella	.75	2.00
51 Cesaro	.30	.75
52 Dana Brooke	.50	1.25
53 Daniel Bryan	1.00	2.50
54 Dolph Ziggler	.30	.75
55 Elias	.30	.75
56 Ember Moon	.60	1.50
57 Goldberg	1.25	3.00
58 Gran Metalik	.30	.75
59 Jaxson Ryker	.40	1.00
60 Jeff Hardy	.75	2.00
61 Jey Uso	.30	.75
62 Jimmy Uso	.30	.75
63 John Morrison	.30	.75
64 Kalisto	.30	.75
65 Kane	.40	1.00
66 King Corbin	.40	1.00
67 Kofi Kingston	.50	1.25
68 Lacey Evans	.75	2.00
69 Lars Sullivan	.30	.75
70 Lince Dorado	.30	.75
71 Mandy Rose	1.50	4.00
72 Maryse	.60	1.50
73 Mickie James	.50	1.25
74 Mojo Rawley	.30	.75
75 Mustafa Ali	.50	1.25
76 Naomi	.60	1.50
77 Nikki Cross	.60	1.50
78 Otis	.30	.75
79 Robert Roode	.30	.75
80 Roman Reigns	.75	2.00
81 Sami Zayn	.40	1.00
82 Sasha Banks	1.25	3.00
83 Sheamus	.40	1.00
84 Shinsuke Nakamura	.60	1.50
85 Shorty G	.30	.75
86 Sonya Deville	.75	2.00
87 Steve Cutler	.30	.75
88 Tamina	.40	1.00
89 The Fiend Bray Wyatt	1.00	2.50
90 The Miz	.50	1.25
91 Tucker	.30	.75
92 Wesley Blake	.40	1.00
93 Xavier Woods	.30	.75
94 Adam Cole	.75	2.00
95 Aliyah	.60	1.50
96 Arturo Ruas	.30	.75
97 Mercedes Martinez	.50	1.25

98 Boa	.30	.75
99 Bobby Fish	.30	.75
100 Bronson Reed	.30	.75
101 Cameron Grimes	.30	.75
102 Candice LeRae	1.00	2.50
103 Chelsea Green	1.50	4.00
104 Dakota Kai	.60	1.50
105 Damian Priest	.30	.75
106 Danny Burch	.40	1.00
107 Dexter Lumis	.30	.75
108 Dominik Dijakovic	.30	.75
109 Fandango	.30	.75
110 Finn Balor	.75	2.00
111 Io Shirai	.50	1.25
112 Isaiah Swerve Scott	.40	1.00
113 Jessamyn Duke	.50	1.25
114 Joaquin Wilde	.30	.75
115 Johnny Gargano	.60	1.50
116 Kacy Catanzaro	.60	1.50
117 Karrion Kross	.60	1.50
118 Keith Lee	.30	.75
119 Killian Dain	.40	1.00
120 Kona Reeves	.30	.75
121 Kushida	.40	1.00
122 Kyle O'Reilly	.40	1.00
123 Mansoor	.30	.75
124 Marina Shafir	.50	1.25
125 Matt Riddle	.60	1.50
126 Mia Yim	.60	1.50
127 Pete Dunne	.30	.75
128 Racquel Gonzalez	.50	1.25
129 Rhea Ripley	.75	2.00
130 Roderick Strong	.60	1.50
131 Scarlett	1.25	3.00
132 Shane Thorne	.30	.75
133 Santana Garett	.30	.75
134 Shotzi Blackheart	1.00	2.50
135 Tegan Nox	.75	2.00
136 Tommaso Ciampa	.60	1.50
137 Tyler Breeze	.40	1.00
138 Vanessa Borne	.60	1.50
139 Velveteen Dream	.40	1.00
140 Xia Li	.60	1.50
141 Alexander Wolfe	.30	.75
142 Dave Mastiff	.40	1.00
143 Fabian Aichner	.12	.30
144 Flash Morgan Webster	.40	1.00
145 Ilja Dragunov	.50	1.25
146 James Drake	.40	1.00
147 Joe Coffey	.30	.75
148 Jordan Devlin	.30	.75
149 Kay Lee Ray	.50	1.25
150 Ligero	.30	.75
151 Marcel Barthel	.30	.75
152 Mark Andrews	.30	.75
153 Mark Coffey	.40	1.00
154 Noam Dar	.30	.75
155 Piper Niven	.40	1.00
156 Toni Storm	.75	2.00
157 Travis Banks	.30	.75
158 Trent Seven	.30	.75
159 Tyler Bate	.50	1.25
160 Walter	.60	1.50
161 Wolfgang	.30	.75
162 Zack Gibson	.30	.75
163 Ariya Daivari	.30	.75
164 Gentleman Jack Gallagher	.40	1.00
165 Oney Lorcan	.40	1.00

166 Raul Mendoza	.30	.75
167 Samir Singh	.30	.75
168 Sunil Singh	.30	.75
169 The Brian Kendrick	.30	.75
170 Tony Nese	.30	.75
171 AOP TT	.40	1.00
172 Murphy/Austin Theory TT	.50	1.25
173 Miz/John Morrison TT	.50	1.25
174 Seth Rollins/Murphy TT	.60	1.50
175 Usos TT	.30	.75
176 Heavy Machinery TT	.30	.75
177 Robert Roode/Dolph Ziggler TT	.30	.75
178 Street Profits TT	.30	.75
179 Viking Raiders TT	.30	.75
180 Broserweights TT	.60	1.50
181 Ever Rise TT	.30	.75
182 Danny Burch/Oney Lorcan TT	.40	1.00
183 Ricochet/Cedric Alexander TT	.50	1.25
184 Grizzled Young Veterans TT	.40	1.00
185 Alexa Bliss/Nikki Cross TT	1.50	4.00
186 Kabuki Warriors TT	.60	1.50
187 Nakamura/Cesaro TT	.60	1.50
188 Lucha House Party TT	.30	.75
189 New Day TT	.50	1.25
190 Forgotten Sons TT	.40	1.00
191 British Strong Style TT	.50	1.25
192 Gallus TT	.40	1.00
193 The Undisputed Era TT	.75	2.00
194 Imperium TT	.60	1.50
195 Adam Cole FL	.75	2.00
196 Aleister Black FL	.60	1.50
197 Bianca Belair FL	.75	2.00
198 Dominik Dijakovic FL	.30	.75
199 Io Shirai FL	.50	1.25
200 Keith Lee FL	.30	.75
201 King Corbin FL	.40	1.00
202 Liv Morgan FL	.75	2.00
203 Matt Riddle FL	.60	1.50
204 Pete Dunne FL	.30	.75
205 Rhea Ripley FL	.75	2.00
206 Ricochet FL	.50	1.25
207 Shayna Baszler FL	1.00	2.50
208 Tommaso Ciampa FL	.60	1.50
209 Velveteen Dream FL	.40	1.00
210 Walter FL	.60	1.50
211 Angel Garza FL	.40	1.00
212 Austin Theory FL	.50	1.25
213 Cameron Grimes FL	.30	.75
214 Candice LeRae FL	1.00	2.50
215 Dakota Kai FL	.60	1.50
216 Johnny Gargano FL	.60	1.50
217 Montez Ford FL	.30	.75
218 Toni Storm FL	.75	2.00
219 Lacey Evans FL	.75	2.00
220 Otis FL	.30	.75
221 AJ Styles R	1.00	2.50
222 Asuka R	.60	1.50
223 Rey Mysterio R	.60	1.50
224 Ruby Riott R	.50	1.25
225 Table	.20	.50
226 Ladder	.20	.50
227 Steel Chair	.20	.50
228 Trash Can	.20	.50
229 The Fiend Bray Wyatt FFH	1.00	2.50
230 Bray Wyatt FFH	1.00	2.50
231 Mercy the Buzzard FFH		1.00
232 Huskus the Pig Boy FFH	.40	
233 Ramblin' Rabbit FFH		1.00

234	Abby the Witch FFH	1.00	2.50
235	Beth Phoenix HOF	.50	1.25
236	Brutus Beefcake HOF	.30	.75
237	Dusty Rhodes HOF	.60	1.50
238	Jerry Lawler HOF	.75	2.00
239	Mark Henry HOF	.50	1.25
240	Road Dogg HOF	.40	1.00
241	Faarooq HOF	.50	1.25
242	X-Pac HOF	.30	.75
243	Big Boss Man HOF	.50	1.25
244	British Bulldog HOF	.50	1.25
245	Diamond Dallas Page HOF	.60	1.50
246	Hacksaw Jim Duggan HOF	.60	1.50
247	Kevin Nash HOF	.50	1.25
248	Mr. Perfect HOF	.50	1.25
249	Rick Rude HOF	.40	1.00
250	Razor Ramon HOF	.50	1.25
251	Ricky Steamboat HOF	.50	1.25
252	Rikishi HOF	.30	.75
253	Rowdy Roddy Piper HOF	.75	2.00
254	Sgt. Slaughter HOF	.60	1.50
255	The Honky Tonk Man HOF	.50	1.25
256	The Million Dollar Man HOF	.60	1.50
257	Andre the Giant HOF	.75	2.00
258	Batista HOF	.50	1.25
259	Booker T HOF	.60	1.50
260	Bret Hit Man Hart HOF	.75	2.00
261	Chyna HOF	.75	2.00
262	Eddie Guerrero HOF	.75	2.00
263	Lita HOF	.75	2.00
264	Randy Savage HOF	1.00	2.50
265	Mick Foley HOF	.60	1.50
266	Ric Flair HOF	1.25	3.00
267	Shawn Michaels HOF	.75	2.00
268	Diesel HOF	.50	1.25
269	Sting HOF	1.00	2.50
270	Trish Stratus HOF	1.50	4.00
271	Ultimate Warrior HOF	.75	2.00
272	Yokozuna HOF	.50	1.25
273	Andrade B	.50	1.25
274	Charlotte Flair B	1.25	3.00
275	Drew McIntyre B	.60	1.50
276	Edge B	.60	1.50
277	Sheamus B	.40	1.00
278	AJ Styles B	1.00	2.50
279	Alexa Bliss B	1.50	4.00
280	Murphy B	.40	1.00
281	The Fiend Bray Wyatt B	1.00	2.50
282	Nikki Cross B	.60	1.50
283	Adam Cole B	.75	2.00
284	Dolph Ziggler B	.30	.75
285	Rhea Ripley B	.75	2.00
286	Io Shirai B	.50	1.25
287	Shayna Baszler B	1.00	2.50
288	Seth Rollins B	.60	1.50
289	Angel Garza B	.40	1.00
290	Goldberg B	1.25	3.00
291	Roman Reigns B	.75	2.00
292	The Miz B	.50	1.25
293	Bayley B	.60	1.50
294	Natalya B	.50	1.25
295	Randy Orton B	.75	2.00
296	Daniel Bryan B	1.00	2.50
297	Kairi Sane B	.60	1.50
298	Shorty G B	.30	.75
299	Aleister Black B	.60	1.50
300	Kevin Owens B	.40	1.00
301	Kofi Kingston B	.50	1.25

302	Shinsuke Nakamura B	.60	1.50
303	Asuka MITB	.60	1.50
304	Otis MITB	.30	.75
305	Universal Title	.20	.50
306	WWE Title	.20	.50
307	RAW Women's Title	.20	.50
308	SmackDown Women's Title	.20	.50
309	Intercontinental Title	.20	.50
310	United States Title	.20	.50
311	24/7 Title	.20	.50
312	RAW Tag Team Title	.20	.50
313	SmackDown Tag Team Title	.20	.50
314	WWE Women's Tag Team Title	.20	.50
315	NXT Title	.20	.50
316	NXT Women's Title	.20	.50
317	NXT North American Title	.20	.50
318	NXT Cruiserweight Title	.20	.50
319	NXT Tag Team Title	.20	.50
320	NXT UK Title	.20	.50
321	NXT UK Women's Title	.20	.50
322	NXT UK Tag Team Title	.20	.50
323	Orton/RKO	.75	2.00
324	Balor/Coup de Grace	.75	2.00
325	Goldberg/Jackhammer	1.25	3.00
326	Black/Black Mass	.60	1.50
327	Edge/Spear	.60	1.50
328	Styles/Phenomenal Forearm	1.00	2.50
329	Hardy/Swanton Bomb	.75	2.00
330	McIntyre/Claymore Kick	.60	1.50
331	Hart/Sharpshooter	.75	2.00
332	Austin/Stone Cold Stunner	1.50	4.00
333	Undertaker/Tombstone	1.25	3.00
334	Triple H/Pedigree	.75	2.00
335	Kane/Chokeslam	.40	1.00
336	Cena/Attitude Adjustment	1.25	3.00
337	Braun Strowman B	.75	2.00
338	Otis B	.30	.75
339	Sasha Banks ICONS	1.25	3.00
340	Charlotte Flair ICONS	1.25	3.00
341	Daniel Bryan ICONS	1.00	2.50
342	Seth Rollins ICONS	.60	1.50
343	Triple H ICONS	.75	2.00
344	The Rock ICONS	1.50	4.00
345	Bret Hart ICONS	.75	2.00
346	Steve Austin ICONS	1.50	4.00
347	Roman Reigns 100 CLUB	.75	2.00
348	Asuka 100 CLUB	.60	1.50
349	Drew McIntyre 100 CLUB	.60	1.50
350	Bray Wyatt 100 CLUB	1.00	2.50
351	Undertaker SR	1.25	3.00
352	John Cena SR	1.25	3.00

2020 Topps WWE Slam Attax Reloaded Autographs

AAB	Alexa Bliss
AAC	Adam Cole
AAD	Angelo Dawkins
AAJ	AJ Styles
AAN	Andrade
AAS	Asuka
ABA	Bayley
ABB	Bianca Belair
ABE	Big E
ABL	Becky Lynch
ABM	Murphy
ACS	Cesaro
ADB	Daniel Bryan
ADM	Drew McIntyre
AED	Edge
AEL	Elias
AEM	Ember Moon
AFB	Finn Balor
AJG	Johnny Gargano
AKO	Kevin Owens
AKS	Kairi Sane
ALA	Bobby Lashley
ALE	Lacey Evans
AMA	Mustafa Ali
AMR	Mandy Rose
ANJ	Nia Jax
ANM	Naomi
ANT	Natalya
AOO	Otis
APD	Pete Dunne
ARB	Ruby Riott
ARC	Ricochet
ARR	Robert Roode
ARS	Roderick Strong
ART	R-Truth
ASB	Shayna Baszler
ASD	Sonya Deville
ASG	Shorty G
ASH	Shinsuke Nakamura
ATB	Tyler Bate
ATC	Tommaso Ciampa
ATE	Aleister Black
ATM	The Miz
ATS	Trent Seven
AVD	Velveteen Dream/50
	(Topps.com Exclusive)
AXW	Xavier Woods

2020 Topps WWE Slam Attax Reloaded Collector Tins

NNO	Edge
NNO	John Cena
NNO	Sasha Banks

2020 Topps WWE Slam Attax Reloaded Exclusives

T1	Bret Hit Man Hart
T2	British Bulldog
T3	Eddie Guerrero
T4	Yokozuna
T5	Batista
T6	Diesel
T7	Lita
T8	Bayley
T9	The Fiend Bray Wyatt
T10	Kofi Kingston
T11	Velveteen Dream
T12	Kevin Owens
T13	Rhea Ripley
T14	Sasha Banks
T15	Macho Man Randy Savage
T16	Ric Flair
T17	Shawn Michaels
T18	Stone Cold Steve Austin
T19	Papa Shango
T20	Vader
T21	Booker T
T22	Daniel Bryan
T23	Drew McIntyre
T24	Randy Orton
T25	Roman Reigns
T26	King Corbin
T27	Alexa Bliss
T28	Becky Lynch
T29	Andre the Giant
T30	Bam Bam Bigelow
T31	Ultimate Warrior
T32	Rowdy Roddy Piper
T33	Razor Ramon
T34	Chyna
T35	Trish Stratus
T36	AJ Styles
T37	Braun Strowman
T38	The Miz
T39	Seth Rollins
T40	Adam Cole
T41	Charlotte Flair
T42	Asuka

2020 Topps WWE Slam Attax Reloaded Limited Edition Bronze

LEBB	Becky Lynch
LECB	Drew McIntyre
LERB	Roman Reigns

2020 Topps WWE Slam Attax Reloaded Limited Edition Gold

LEDA	The Rock
	(Mega Tins Exclusive)
LEDB	Undertaker
	(Mega Tins Exclusive)
LEDC	Stone Cold Steve Austin
	(Mega Tins Exclusive)
LESA	The Fiend Bray Wyatt
LETA	John Cena
	(Collector Tins Exclusive)
LETB	Sasha Banks
	(Collector Tins Exclusive)
LETC	Edge
	(Collector Tins Exclusive)
LEXA	Daniel Bryan
	(Web Wednesday Exclusive)
LEXB	Charlotte Flair
	(WWE Kids Magazine Exclusive)
LEXC	Seth Rollins
	(Web Wednesday Exclusive)
LEXD	Nikki Cross
	(Web Wednesday Exclusive)

2020 Topps WWE Slam Attax Reloaded Relics

M1	Drew McIntyre/T-Shirt
M2	Humberto Carrllo/T-Shirt
M3	Samoa Joe/T-Shirt
M4	Shayna Baszler/T-Shirt
M5	Sonya Deville/T-Shirt
M6	Roman Reigns vs. King Corbin/Table
M7	Triple H vs. Batista/Mat

2020 Topps WWE Slam Attax Reloaded XL

XL1	John Cena
XL2	Charlotte Flair
XL3	Braun Strowman
XL4	Bayley
XL5	Becky Lynch
XL6	Roman Reigns
XL7	Undertaker
XL8	The Fiend Bray Wyatt

XL9 Drew McIntyre
XL10 Rhea Ripley
XL11 Kofi Kingston

2016 Topps WWE Slam Attax TakeOver

	COMPLETE SET (299)	25.00	60.00
1	AJ Styles	.50	1.25
2	Asuka	.50	1.25
3	Alberto Del Rio	.20	.50
4	Brock Lesnar	.60	1.50
5	Charlotte	.40	1.00
6	Dean Ambrose	.40	1.00
7	Finn Balor	.40	1.00
8	John Cena	.60	1.50
9	Kalisto	.30	.75
10	Kevin Owens	.30	.75
11	Roman Reigns	.40	1.00
12	Samoa Joe	.30	.75
13	Sasha Banks	.40	1.00
14	Seth Rollins	.20	.50
15	The New Day	.30	.75
16	Triple H	.50	1.25
17	AJ Styles	.50	1.25
18	Asuka	.50	1.25
19	Alberto Del Rio	.20	.50
20	Brock Lesnar	.60	1.50
21	Charlotte	.40	1.00
22	Dean Ambrose	.40	1.00
23	Finn Balor	.40	1.00
24	John Cena	.60	1.50
25	Kalisto	.30	.75
26	Kevin Owens	.30	.75
27	Roman Reigns	.40	1.00
28	Samoa Joe	.30	.75
29	Sasha Banks	.40	1.00
30	Seth Rollins	.20	.50
31	The New Day	.30	.75
32	Triple H	.50	1.25
33	Becky Lynch	.40	1.00
34	Big E	.12	.30
35	Bo Dallas	.12	.30
36	Bray Wyatt	.50	1.25
37	Charlotte	.40	1.00
38	Kalisto	.30	.75
39	Kevin Owens	.30	.75
40	Luke Harper	.12	.30
41	Neville	.25	.60
42	Paige	.40	1.00
43	Roman Reigns	.40	1.00
44	Rusev	.30	.75
45	Sasha Banks	.40	1.00
46	Seth Rollins	.20	.50
47	Tyler Breeze	.12	.30
48	Xavier Woods	.12	.30
49	MITB Briefcase	.12	.30
50	NXT Women's Title	.12	.30
51	NXT Title	.12	.30
52	NXT Tag Team Title	.12	.30
53	WWE Tag Team Title	.12	.30
54	WWE Women's Title	.12	.30
55	WWE United States Title	.12	.30
56	WWE Title	.12	.30
57	AJ Styles	.50	1.25
58	Alberto Del Rio	.20	.50
59	Apollo Crews	.12	.30
60	Asuka	.50	1.25
61	Baron Corbin	.15	.40
62	Bayley	.30	.75
63	Becky Lynch	.40	1.00
64	Big Cass	.25	.60
65	Braun Strowman	.15	.40
66	Bray Wyatt	.50	1.25
67	Brock Lesnar	.60	1.50
68	Charlotte	.40	1.00
69	Chris Jericho	.30	.75
70	Dean Ambrose	.40	1.00
71	Dolph Ziggler	.15	.40
72	Elias Samson	.12	.30
73	Erick Rowan	.12	.30
74	Heath Slater	.12	.30
75	Hideo Itami	.15	.40
76	Jason Jordan	.15	.40
77	John Cena	.60	1.50
78	Kalisto	.30	.75
79	Kevin Owens	.30	.75
80	Mojo Rawley	.12	.30
81	Neville	.25	.60
82	Paige	.40	1.00
83	Roman Reigns	.40	1.00
84	Rusev	.30	.75
85	Samoa Joe	.30	.75
86	Sasha Banks	.40	1.00
87	Sheamus	.30	.75
88	Triple H	.50	1.25
89	Aiden English	.12	.30
90	AJ Styles	.50	1.25
91	Alberto Del Rio	.20	.50
92	Alicia Fox	.20	.50
93	Apollo Crews	.12	.30
94	Baron Corbin	.15	.40
95	Becky Lynch	.40	1.00
96	Big Cass	.25	.60
97	Big E	.12	.30
98	Big Show	.25	.60
99	Bo Dallas	.12	.30
100	Booker T	.25	.60
101	Braun Strowman	.15	.40
102	Bray Wyatt	.50	1.25
103	Brie Bella	.25	.60
104	Brock Lesnar	.60	1.50
105	Bubba Ray Dudley	.25	.60
106	Byron Saxton	.12	.30
107	Cesaro	.25	.60
108	Charlotte	.40	1.00
109	Chris Jericho	.30	.75
110	Curtis Axel	.12	.30
111	Dana Brooke	.30	.75
112	Daniel Bryan	.50	1.25
113	Darren Young	.12	.30
114	David Otunga	.12	.30
115	Dean Ambrose	.40	1.00
116	Dolph Ziggler	.15	.40
117	D-Von Dudley	.20	.50
118	Emma	.25	.60
119	Enzo Amore	.25	.60
120	Epico	.12	.30
121	Erick Rowan	.12	.30
122	Eva Marie	.25	.60
123	Fandango	.12	.30
124	Goldust	.20	.50
125	Heath Slater	.12	.30
126	Jack Swagger	.12	.30
127	JBL	.15	.40
128	Jerry Lawler	.25	.60
129	Jey Uso	.12	.30
130	Jimmy Uso	.12	.30
131	John Cena	.60	1.50
132	Jojo	.12	.30
133	Kalisto	.30	.75
134	Kane	.20	.50
135	Karl Anderson	.12	.30
136	Kevin Owens	.30	.75
137	Kofi Kingston	.12	.30
138	Konnor	.12	.30
139	Lana	.50	1.25
140	Luke Gallows	.15	.40
141	Luke Harper	.12	.30
142	Mark Henry	.15	.40
143	Maryse	.25	.60
144	Mauro Ranallo	.12	.30
145	Michael Cole	.12	.30
146	Naomi	.20	.50
147	Natalya	.20	.50
148	Neville	.25	.60
149	Nikki Bella	.40	1.00
150	Paige	.40	1.00
151	Primo	.12	.30
152	Randy Orton	.30	.75
153	Renee Young	.30	.75
154	Roman Reigns	.40	1.00
155	Rosa Mendes	.12	.30
156	R-Truth	.12	.30
157	Rusev	.30	.75
158	Ryback	.15	.40
159	Sami Zayn	.20	.50
160	Sasha Banks	.40	1.00
161	Seth Rollins	.20	.50
162	Sheamus	.30	.75
163	Simon Gotch	.20	.50
164	Sin Cara	.15	.40
165	Summer Rae	.30	.75
166	Tamina	.15	.40
167	The Miz	.20	.50
168	The Rock	.60	1.50
169	Titus O'Neil	.12	.30
170	Tony Chimel	.12	.30
171	Triple H	.50	1.25
172	Tyler Breeze	.12	.30
173	Tyson Kidd	.12	.30
174	Undertaker	.50	1.25
175	Viktor	.12	.30
176	Xavier Woods	.12	.30
177	Zack Ryder	.12	.30
178	Alexa Bliss	.60	1.50
179	Angelo Dawkins	.12	.30
180	Asuka	.50	1.25
181	Austin Aries	.15	.40
182	Bayley	.30	.75
183	Billie Kay	.30	.75
184	Blake	.12	.30
185	Carmella	.30	.75
186	Cathy Kelley	.12	.30
187	Chad Gable	.15	.40
188	Corey Graves	.12	.30
189	Dash Wilder	.15	.40
190	Dasha Fuentes	.12	.30
191	Elias Samson	.12	.30
192	Finn Balor	.40	1.00
193	Greg Hamilton	.12	.30
194	Hideo Itami	.15	.40
195	Jason Jordan	.15	.40
196	Mandy Rose	.30	.75
197	Mojo Rawley	.12	.30
198	Murphy	.12	.30
199	Nia Jax	.20	.50
200	No Way Jose	.12	.30
201	Peyton Royce	.30	.75
202	Samoa Joe	.30	.75
203	Sawyer Fulton	.15	.40
204	Scott Dawson	.12	.30
205	Shinsuke Nakamura	.50	1.25
206	Tom Phillips	.12	.30
207	Tye Dillinger	.15	.40
208	William Regal	.12	.30
209	Adrienne Reese	.30	.75
210	Bronson Matthews	.12	.30
211	Oney Lorcan	.12	.30
212	Hugo Knox	.12	.30
213	King Constantine	.12	.30
214	Manny Andrade	.20	.50
215	Noah Kekoa	.12	.30
216	Tino Sabbatelli	.12	.30
217	Bam Bam Bigelow	.15	.40
218	Big Boss Man	.20	.50
219	Bob Backlund	.12	.30
220	Bobby Heenan	.20	.50
221	Booker T	.25	.60
222	Bret Hart	.30	.75
223	Brian Pillman	.15	.40
224	British Bulldog	.15	.40
225	Bruno Sammartino	.15	.40
226	Chief Jay Strongbow	.20	.50
227	Freddie Blassie	.15	.40
228	Bob Orton	.20	.50
229	Dean Malenko	.12	.30
230	Diamond Dallas Page	.20	.50
231	Diesel	.30	.75
232	Doink The Clown	.12	.30
233	Dusty Rhodes	.12	.30
234	Eddie Guerrero	.30	.75
235	Edge	.30	.75
236	Greg Valentine	.15	.40
237	Jim Duggan	.12	.30
238	Harley Race	.12	.30
239	Honky Tonk Man	.12	.30
240	Iron Shiek	.12	.30
241	Irwin R. Schyster	.12	.30
242	Jake Roberts	.25	.60
243	Jim Neidhart	.12	.30
244	Jimmy Hart	.15	.40
245	Junkyard Dog	.20	.50
246	Kevin Nash	.30	.75
247	Lex Luger	.20	.50
248	Lita	.40	1.00
249	Randy Savage	.30	.75
250	Don Muraco	.12	.30
251	Gene Okerlund	.15	.40
252	Ted Dibiase	.15	.40
253	Curt Hennig	.30	.75
254	Paul Orndorf	.12	.30
255	Paul Bearer	.20	.50
256	Rick Rude	.20	.50
257	Razor Ramon	.30	.75
258	Ric Flair	.50	1.25
259	Ricky Steamboat	.15	.40
260	Rikishi	.15	.40
261	Rhyno	.12	.30
262	Road Dogg	.20	.50
263	Ron Simmons	.30	.75
264	Rowdy Roddy Piper	.40	1.00
265	Sgt. Slaughter	.15	.40

266	Shawn Michaels	.50	1.25
267	Sting	.30	.75
268	Stone Cold Steve Austin	.60	1.50
269	Terry Funk	.12	.30
270	The Godfather	.15	.40
271	Trish Stratus	.60	1.50
272	Ultimate Warrior	.30	.75
273	Vader	.25	.60
274	X-Pac	.20	.50
275	Yokozuna	.25	.60
276	American Alpha	.15	.40
277	Blake/Murphy	.12	.30
278	Enzo/Cass	.25	.60
279	Gargano/Ciampa	.15	.40
280	Gallows/Anderson	.15	.40
281	The Shining Stars	.12	.30
282	Team B.A.D.	.40	1.00
283	The Ascension	.12	.30
284	The Bella Twins	.40	1.00
285	The Bushwhackers	.12	.30
286	The Dudley Boyz	.25	.60
287	The Hype Bros	.12	.30
288	The Lucha Dragons	.30	.75
289	The New Day	.30	.75
290	The Prime Time Players	.12	.30
291	The Revival	.15	.40
292	The Social Outcasts	.12	.30
293	The Usos	.12	.30
294	The Vaudevillains	.20	.50
295	The Wyatt Family	.50	1.25
296	Ladder	.12	.30
297	Steel Chair	.12	.30
298	Table	.12	.30
299	Trash Can	.12	.30

2019 Topps WWE SmackDown Live

COMPLETE SET (90) 10.00 25.00
*GREEN: .5X TO 1.5X BASIC CARDS
*PURPLE/99: .75X TO 3X BASIC CARDS
*20TH ANN./20: UNPRICED DUE TO SCARCITY
*GOLD/10: UNPRICED DUE TO SCARCITY
*RED/1: UNPRICED DUE TO SCARCITY
*P.P.BLACK/1: UNPRICED DUE TO SCARCITY
*P.P.CYAN/1: UNPRICED DUE TO SCARCITY
*P.P.MAGENTA/1: UNPRICED DUE TO SCARCITY
*P.P.YELLOW/1: UNPRICED DUE TO SCARCITY

1	Aiden English	.25	.60
2	Aleister Black	.30	.75
3	Ali	.25	.60
4	Andrade	.30	.75
5	Apollo Crews	.30	.75
6	Asuka	.75	2.00
7	Bayley	.50	1.25
8	Becky Lynch	1.00	2.50
9	Big E	.25	.60
10	Billie Kay	.50	1.25
11	Bo Dallas	.30	.75
12	Buddy Murphy	.30	.75
13	Byron Saxton	.25	.60
14	Carmella	.60	1.50
15	Cesaro	.30	.75
16	Chad Gable	.25	.60
17	Charlotte Flair	1.00	2.50
18	Corey Graves	.30	.75
19	Curtis Axel	.30	.75
20	Daniel Bryan	1.00	2.50
21	Elias	.50	1.25
22	Ember Moon	.60	1.50
23	Finn Balor	.60	1.50
24	Greg Hamilton	.25	.60
25	Jeff Hardy	.60	1.50
26	Jinder Mahal	.50	1.25
27	Kairi Sane	.50	1.25
28	Kevin Owens	.60	1.50
29	Kofi Kingston	.40	1.00
30	Lana	.50	1.25
31	Lars Sullivan	.25	.60
32	Liv Morgan	.75	2.00
33	Mandy Rose	.60	1.50
34	Maryse	.30	.75
35	Matt Hardy	.50	1.25
36	Mickie James	.60	1.50
37	Otis	.25	.60
38	Paige	1.00	2.50
39	Peyton Royce	.60	1.50
40	R-Truth	.30	.75
41	Randy Orton	.60	1.50
42	Roman Reigns	.60	1.50
43	Rowan	.25	.60
44	Rusev	.50	1.25
45	Samir Singh	.25	.60
46	Sarah Schreiber	.25	.60
47	Sheamus	.40	1.00
48	Shelton Benjamin	.30	.75
49	Shinsuke Nakamura	.60	1.50
50	Sin Cara	.25	.60
51	Sonya Deville	.50	1.25
52	Sunil Singh	.25	.60
53	Tom Phillips	.25	.60
54	Tucker	.25	.60
55	Xavier Woods	.30	.75
56	Zelina Vega	.40	1.00
57	Big Show	.40	1.00
58	The Rock	1.25	3.00
59	Triple H	.60	1.50
60	Undertaker	1.25	3.00
61	Albert	.25	.60
62	Beth Phoenix	.40	1.00
63	Big Boss Man	.30	.75
64	The British Bulldog	.60	1.50
65	Boogeyman	.25	.60
66	King Booker	.60	1.50
67	Cactus Jack	.50	1.25
68	Christian	.40	1.00
69	Chyna	.50	1.25
70	Cowboy Bob Orton	.25	.60
71	D-Lo Brown	.25	.60
72	Diamond Dallas Page	.50	1.25
73	Eddie Guerrero	.60	1.50
74	Faarooq	.40	1.00
75	Finlay	.25	.60
76	The Godfather	.25	.60
77	Goldberg	.75	2.00
78	Jerry The King Lawler	.50	1.25
79	Kevin Nash	.40	1.00
80	Lita	.60	1.50
81	Mankind	.50	1.25
82	Paul Bearer	.30	.75
83	Rikishi	.25	.60
84	Road Dogg Jesse James	.25	.60
85	Rowdy Roddy Piper	.60	1.50
86	Scott Hall	.40	1.00
87	Stone Cold Steve Austin	1.25	3.00
88	Tatanka	.25	.60
89	Trish Stratus	1.25	3.00
90	X-Pac	.25	.60

2019 Topps WWE SmackDown Live 20 Years of SmackDown

COMPLETE SET (46) 12.00 30.00
RANDOMLY INSERTED INTO PACKS

SD1	Undertaker & Big Show	1.50	4.00
SD2	The Rock & Mankind	1.50	4.00
SD3	Stone Cold Steve Austin	1.50	4.00
SD4	Jeff Hardy	.75	2.00
SD5	Kurt Angle	.60	1.50
SD6	Batista	.75	2.00
SD7	Rey Mysterio	.75	2.00
SD8	John Cena	1.25	3.00
SD9	Kurt Angle	.60	1.50
SD10	Kurt Angle	.60	1.50
SD11	Rey Mysterio	.75	2.00
SD12	Brock Lesnar	1.25	3.00
SD13	Brock Lesnar	1.25	3.00
SD14	Eddie Guerrero	.75	2.00
SD15	Stone Cold Steve Austin	1.50	4.00
SD16	Eddie Guerrero	.75	2.00
SD17	Undertaker	1.50	4.00
SD18	Kurt Angle	.60	1.50
SD19	Eddie Guerrero	.75	2.00
SD20	Undertaker	1.50	4.00
SD21	Kurt Angle	.60	1.50
SD22	Booker T	.75	2.00
SD23	Shawn Michaels	.75	2.00
SD24	Jeff Hardy	.75	2.00
SD25	Jeff Hardy	.75	2.00
SD26	Shawn Michaels	.75	2.00
SD27	Randy Orton	.75	2.00
SD28	Daniel Bryan	1.25	3.00
SD29	Beth Phoenix	.50	1.25
SD30	Daniel Bryan	1.25	3.00
SD31	John Cena	1.25	3.00
SD32	Cesaro	.40	1.00
SD33	Batista	.75	2.00
SD34	Wyatt Family	.40	1.00
SD35	Kevin Owens	.75	2.00
SD36	The Miz	.60	1.50
SD37	Alexa Bliss	1.50	4.00
SD38	Bray Wyatt	.75	2.00
SD39	The Usos	.40	1.00
SD40	Carmella	.75	2.00
SD41	Shinsuke Nakamura	.75	2.00
SD42	The New Day	.60	1.50
SD43	AJ Styles	1.50	4.00
SD44	John Cena	1.25	3.00
SD45	Rusev	.60	1.50
SD46	The New Day	.60	1.50

2019 Topps WWE SmackDown Live Autographed Intercontinental Championship 40th Anniversary Relics

RANDOMLY INSERTED INTO PACKS
ICRKK Kofi Kingston
ICRSB Shelton Benjamin
ICRTM The Miz

2019 Topps WWE SmackDown Live Autographed Mat Relics

STATED PRINT RUN 10 SER.#'d SETS
UNPRICED DUE TO SCARCITY
MRAAJ AJ Styles
MRABD Daniel Bryan
MRABE Big E
MRABM Buddy Murphy
MRACM Carmella
MRAJE Jey Uso
MRAJH Jeff Hardy
MRAJI Jimmy Uso
MRAKA Karl Anderson
MRAKK Kofi Kingston
MRAKS Shinsuke Nakamura
MRALG Luke Gallows
MRAMA Ali
MRAMR Mandy Rose
MRARJ Rey Mysterio
MRARM Rey Mysterio
MRART R-Truth
MRASD Sonya Deville
MRASN Shinsuke Nakamura
MRAXW Xavier Woods

2019 Topps WWE SmackDown Live Autographed Shirt Relics

STATED PRINT RUN 10 SER.#'d SETS
UNPRICED DUE TO SCARCITY
SRAC Apollo Crews
SREM Ember Moon
SRMH Matt Hardy
SRXW Xavier Woods
SRAAA Andrade
SRAAB Aleister Black
SRAEL Elias
SRAKK Kofi Kingston

2019 Topps WWE SmackDown Live Autographed SmackDown Championship Commemorative Relics

STATED PRINT RUN 10 SER.#'d SETS
UNPRICED DUE TO SCARCITY
ASCAB Alexa Bliss
ASCAJ AJ Styles
ASCBC Baron Corbin
ASCBL Becky Lynch
ASCBR Robert Roode
ASCCM Carmella
ASCKK Kofi Kingston
ASCKO Kevin Owens
ASCNM Naomi
ASCNT Natalya
ASCRO Randy Orton
ASCRT R-Truth
ASCSJ Samoa Joe
ASCSN Shinsuke Nakamura

2019 Topps WWE SmackDown Live Autographed Women's Evolution Relics

DRACCM Carmella

2019 Topps WWE SmackDown Live Autographs

*ORANGE/50: .5X TO 1.2X BASIC AUTOS
*20TH ANN./20: UNPRICED DUE TO SCARCITY
*GOLD/10: UNPRICED DUE TO SCARCITY
*RED/1: UNPRICED DUE TO SCARCITY
STATED PRINT RUN 99 SER.#'d SETS

AAA	Andrade	4.00	10.00
AAL	Aleister Black	12.00	30.00
ABA	Bayley	10.00	25.00

ABE Becky Lynch		
ABK Billie Kay	8.00	20.00
ABL Big E	4.00	10.00
ABU Buddy Murphy	8.00	20.00
ACH Chad Gable	4.00	10.00
ACM Carmella	10.00	25.00
AEL Elias	4.00	10.00
AEM Ember Moon	8.00	20.00
AFI Finn Balor	12.00	30.00
AGH Greg Hamilton	4.00	10.00
AKE Kevin Owens	6.00	15.00
AKK Kofi Kingston	6.00	15.00
ALI Liv Morgan	15.00	40.00
AMA Ali	4.00	10.00
AMH Matt Hardy	6.00	15.00
AMR Mandy Rose	15.00	40.00
AOT Otis	10.00	25.00
APR Peyton Royce	10.00	25.00
ARR Roman Reigns	10.00	25.00
ART R-Truth	5.00	12.00
ARW Rowan	4.00	10.00
ASD Sonya Deville	6.00	15.00
ASN Shinsuke Nakamura	5.00	12.00
ATU Tucker	4.00	10.00
AXW Xavier Woods	5.00	12.00
AZV Zelina Vega	12.00	30.00

2019 Topps WWE SmackDown Live Corey Says

COMPLETE SET (19)	6.00	15.00
RANDOMLY INSERTED INTO PACKS		
CG1 AJ Styles	1.50	4.00
CG2 Asuka	1.00	2.50
CG3 Becky Lynch	1.25	3.00
CG4 Carmella	.75	2.00
CG5 Cesaro	.40	1.00
CG6 Charlotte Flair	1.25	3.00
CG7 Daniel Bryan	1.25	3.00
CG8 Jeff Hardy	.75	2.00
CG9 Randy Orton	.75	2.00
CG10 Rey Mysterio	.75	2.00
CG11 Rusev	.60	1.50
CG12 Samoa Joe	.60	1.50
CG13 Shane McMahon	.75	2.00
CG14 Sheamus	.50	1.25
CG15 Shinsuke Nakamura	.75	2.00
CG16 The Miz	.60	1.50
CG17 The New Day	.60	1.50
CG18 The Usos	.40	1.00
CG19 Undertaker	1.50	4.00

2019 Topps WWE SmackDown Live Dual Autographs

*GOLD/10: UNPRICED DUE TO SCARCITY
*RED/1: UNPRICED DUE TO SCARCITY
STATED PRINT RUN 25 SER.#'d SETS

DADB R-Truth/Carmella	20.00	50.00
DAGB K.Anderson/L.Gallows	30.00	75.00
DAII B.Kay/P.Royce	75.00	150.00
DATQ Z.Vega/Andrade	20.00	50.00
DAABS S.Deville/M.Rose	75.00	150.00

2019 Topps WWE SmackDown Live Image Variations

IV1 Aleister Black		
IV2 Andrade	6.00	15.00
IV3 Big E		
IV4 Billie Kay	6.00	15.00
IV5 Charlotte Flair	15.00	40.00
IV6 Daniel Bryan	12.00	30.00
IV7 Jeff Hardy	4.00	10.00
IV8 Killian Dain		
IV9 Kofi Kingston	6.00	15.00
IV10 Mandy Rose	12.00	30.00
IV11 Peyton Royce		
IV12 R-Truth		
IV13 Shinsuke Nakamura		
IV14 Sheamus		
IV15 Shelton Benjamin	8.00	20.00
IV16 Sonya Deville	10.00	25.00
IV17 Xavier Woods	4.00	10.00
IV18 Zelina Vega		
IV19 Ali		
IV20 Matt Hardy	8.00	20.00

2019 Topps WWE SmackDown Live Intercontinental Championship 40th Anniversary Autographs

ICAKK Kofi Kingston	8.00	20.00
ICASB Shelton Benjamin	12.00	30.00
ICATM The Miz	10.00	25.00

2019 Topps WWE SmackDown Live Intercontinental Championship 40th Anniversary Relics

RANDOMLY INSERTED INTO PACKS
ICRDM Drew McIntyre
ICRKK Kofi Kingston
ICRRM Rey Mysterio
ICRSB Shelton Benjamin
ICRTM The Miz

2019 Topps WWE SmackDown Live Mat Relics

*PURPLE/99: .6X TO 1.5X BASIC MEM
*ORANGE/50: .75X TO 2X BASIC MEM
*20TH ANN./20: UNPRICED DUE TO SCARCITY
*GOLD/10: UNPRICED DUE TO SCARCITY
*RED/1: UNPRICED DUE TO SCARCITY
STATED PRINT RUN 199 SER.#'d SETS

MR4H Charlotte Flair	8.00	20.00
MRAJ AJ Styles	4.00	10.00
MRAS Asuka	6.00	15.00
MRAW Alexander Wolfe	3.00	8.00
MRBD Daniel Bryan	4.00	10.00
MRBE Big E	2.50	6.00
MRBL Becky Lynch	6.00	15.00
MRBM Buddy Murphy	2.50	6.00
MRBS Big Show	2.50	6.00
MRBT Batista	3.00	8.00
MRCF Charlotte Flair	6.00	15.00
MRCM Carmella	4.00	10.00
MRCS Cesaro	2.50	6.00
MRDB Daniel Bryan	4.00	10.00
MREY Eric Young	2.50	6.00
MRJE Jey Uso	2.50	6.00
MRJH Jeff Hardy	4.00	10.00
MRJI Jimmy Uso	2.50	6.00
MRKA Karl Anderson	2.50	6.00
MRKD Killian Dain	2.50	6.00
MRKK Kofi Kingston	3.00	8.00
MRKS Shinsuke Nakamura	3.00	8.00
MRLG Luke Gallows	2.50	6.00
MRLN Lana	3.00	8.00
MRMA Ali	2.50	6.00
MRMH Stephanie McMahon	4.00	10.00
MRMR Mandy Rose	6.00	15.00
MRRF Ric Flair	5.00	12.00
MRRJ Rey Mysterio	4.00	10.00
MRRM Rey Mysterio	4.00	10.00
MRRO Randy Orton	4.00	10.00
MRRS Rusev	2.50	6.00
MRRT R-Truth	2.50	6.00
MRSD Sonya Deville	3.00	8.00
MRSH Sheamus	2.50	6.00
MRSJ Samoa Joe	2.50	6.00
MRSN Shinsuke Nakamura	3.00	8.00
MRTH Triple H	3.00	8.00
MRTM The Miz	2.50	6.00
MRUT Undertaker	6.00	15.00
MRXW Xavier Woods	2.50	6.00

2019 Topps WWE SmackDown Live Shirt Relics

*PURPLE/99: .6X TO 1.5X BASIC MEM
*ORANGE/50: .75X TO 2X BASIC MEM
20TH ANN./20: UNPRICED DUE TO SCARCITY
*GOLD/10: UNPRICED DUE TO SCARCITY
*RED/1: UNPRICED DUE TO SCARCITY
STATED PRINT RUN 199 SER.#'d SETS

SRAA Andrade/199	5.00	12.00
SRAB Aleister Black/199	5.00	12.00
SRAC Apollo Crews/199	4.00	10.00
SREL Elias/199	5.00	12.00
SREM Ember Moon/199	6.00	15.00
SRJH Jeff Hardy/199	5.00	12.00
SRKA Karl Anderson/199	4.00	10.00
SRKK Kofi Kingston/199	4.00	10.00
SRKS Kairi Sane/199	5.00	12.00
SRLG Luke Gallows/199	4.00	10.00
SRLM Liv Morgan/160	12.00	30.00
SRMH Matt Hardy/199	4.00	10.00
SRSM Sheamus/199	4.00	10.00
SRXW Xavier Woods/199	6.00	15.00

2019 Topps WWE SmackDown Live SmackDown Championship Commemorative Relics

*PURPLE/99: .6X TO 1.5X BASIC MEM
*ORANGE/50: .75X TO 2X BASIC MEM
20TH ANN./20: UNPRICED DUE TO SCARCITY
*GOLD/10: UNPRICED DUE TO SCARCITY
*RED/1: UNPRICED DUE TO SCARCITY
STATED PRINT RUN 199 SER.#'d SETS

SCAB Alexa Bliss	8.00	20.00
SCAJ AJ Styles	5.00	12.00
SCAS Asuka	6.00	15.00
SCBC Baron Corbin	2.50	6.00
SCBL Becky Lynch	10.00	25.00
SCBR Robert Roode	2.50	6.00
SCBW Bray Wyatt	6.00	15.00
SCCF Charlotte Flair	4.00	10.00
SCCM Carmella	8.00	20.00
SCDB Daniel Bryan	5.00	12.00
SCJC John Cena	6.00	15.00
SCJH Jeff Hardy	5.00	12.00
SCKK Kofi Kingston	5.00	12.00
SCKO Kevin Owens	2.50	6.00
SCMH Jinder Mahal	2.50	6.00
SCNM Naomi	2.50	6.00
SCNT Natalya	2.50	6.00
SCRO Randy Orton	5.00	12.00
SCRT R-Truth	3.00	8.00
SCRV Rusev	2.50	6.00
SCSJ Samoa Joe	2.50	6.00
SCSN Shinsuke Nakamura	4.00	10.00
SCVP Randy Orton	5.00	12.00

2019 Topps WWE SmackDown Live SmackDown Tag Team Championship Commemorative Relics

*PURPLE/99: .6X TO 1.5X BASIC MEM
*ORANGE/50: .75X TO 2X BASIC MEM
20TH ANN./20: UNPRICED DUE TO SCARCITY
*GOLD/10: UNPRICED DUE TO SCARCITY
*RED/1: UNPRICED DUE TO SCARCITY
STATED PRINT RUN 199 SER.#'d SETS

SCAA Jason Jordan/Chad Gable	4.00	10.00
SCBB Matt Hardy/Jeff Hardy	6.00	15.00
SCND Xavier Woods/Kofi Kingston	5.00	12.00
SCPE Rowan/Daniel Bryan	4.00	10.00
SCTB Cesaro/Sheamus	4.00	10.00
SCUS Jey Uso/Jimmy Uso	6.00	15.00
SCWF Randy Orton/Bray Wyatt	5.00	12.00

2019 Topps WWE SmackDown Live Triple Autographs

*GOLD/10: UNPRICED DUE TO SCARCITY
*RED/1: UNPRICED DUE TO SCARCITY
STATED PRINT RUN 25 SER.#'d SETS

TAND Woods/Big E/Kingston	100.00	200.00

2019 Topps WWE SmackDown Live Women's Evolution Autographs

RANDOMLY INSERTED INTO PACKS
WACM Carmella
WAMR Mandy Rose
WASD Sonya Deville

2019 Topps WWE SmackDown Live Women's Evolution Relics

RANDOMLY INSERTED INTO PACKS
DRCAK Asuka
DRCCM Carmella
DRCKS Kairi Sane

2015 Topps WWE Sting Tribute

This was a continuation series across four different products in 2015. 10-Card sets were inserted in the following products: Topps WWE (1-10), Topps Chrome WWE (11-20), Topps Road to WrestleMania (21-30), and Topps Heritage WWE (31-40).

COMPLETE SET (40)	15.00	40.00
*GOLD/10: 2X TO 5X BASIC CARDS		
*RED/1: UNPRICED DUE TO SCARCITY		
1 4 Horsemen	1.25	3.00
2 Round Robin	1.25	3.00
3 Sting/Flair	1.25	3.00
4 Sting/Sid Vicious	1.25	3.00
5 Sting/Luger/Steiners	1.25	3.00
6 Sting/Rick Rude	1.25	3.00
7 Battlebowl	1.25	3.00
8 Sting/Luger/WCW Title	1.25	3.00
9 Sting's Squadron	1.25	3.00
10 Sting/Vader	1.25	3.00
11 vs. Jake the Snake Roberts	1.25	3.00
12 vs. Big Van Vader	1.25	3.00

13 w/Hawk vs. Nasty Boys	1.25	3.00
14 w/B.Pillman and Dustin Rhodes	1.25	3.00
15 Wins European Cup	1.25	3.00
16 vs. Ravishing Rick Rude	1.25	3.00
17 vs. Ric Flair	1.25	3.00
18 w/Hogan vs. 3 Faces of Fear	1.25	3.00
19 vs. Avalanche	1.25	3.00
20 w/Savage vs. Avalanche and Rogers	1.25	3.00
21 Sting/Arn Anderson	1.25	3.00
22 Sting/Meng US Title Match	1.25	3.00
23 Sting/Meng Retains US Title	1.25	3.00
24 First Nitro	1.25	3.00
25 Sting/Flair/Pillman/Anderson	1.25	3.00
26 Sting/Hogan	1.25	3.00
27 Sting/Flair/Luger	1.25	3.00
28 Sting/Regal	1.25	3.00
29 Abandons Team WCW	1.25	3.00
30 Joins n.W.o. Wolfpac	1.25	3.00
31 vs. The Giant	1.25	3.00
32 Four Corners WCW Title Match	1.25	3.00
33 vs. DDP	1.25	3.00
34 w/Kevin Nash tag team	1.25	3.00
35 Battles to a No-Contest	1.25	3.00
36 w/Luger and DDP vs. Flair and Hart	1.25	3.00
37 Retains WCW Title	1.25	3.00
38 vs. Booker T US Title	1.25	3.00
39 vs. Booker T World Title	1.25	3.00
40 vs. Vampiro/Great Muta	1.25	3.00

2015 Topps WWE Sting Tribute Autographs and Relics

*GOLD/10: UNPRICED DUE TO SCARCITY
*RED/1: UNPRICED DUE TO SCARCITY

NNO Sting AU/Red White Blue	25.00	60.00
NNO Sting MEM/Shirt	10.00	25.00
NNO Sting AU MEM/Shirt	50.00	100.00

2015 Topps WWE Sting Tribute Topps Chrome WWE Autographs and Relics

*GOLD/10: UNPRICED DUE TO SCARCITY

NNO Sting AU/WCW Belt	50.00	100.00
NNO Sting MEM/Tights	15.00	40.00
NNO Sting AU MEM/Tights	75.00	150.00

2015 Topps WWE Sting Tribute Topps Heritage WWE Autographs and Relics

*GOLD/10: UNPRICED DUE TO SCARCITY
*RED/1: UNPRICED DUE TO SCARCITY

NNO Sting AU	50.00	100.00
NNO Sting AU MEM/Glove		

2015 Topps WWE Sting Tribute Topps WWE Road to WrestleMania Autographs and Relics

*GOLD/10: UNPRICED DUE TO SCARCITY
*RED/1: UNPRICED DUE TO SCARCITY

NNO Sting AU	50.00	100.00
NNO Sting MEM/Boots	30.00	75.00
NNO Sting AU MEM/Boots	75.00	150.00

2019 Topps WWE SummerSlam

COMPLETE SET (100)	10.00	25.00
*BRONZE: .6X TO 1.5X BASIC CARDS		
*BLUE/99: .75X TO 2X BASIC CARDS		
*SILVER/25: 2X TO 5X BASIC CARDS		

*GOLD/10: UNPRICED DUE TO SCARCITY
*RED/1: UNPRICED DUE TO SCARCITY
*P.P.BLACK/1: UNPRICED DUE TO SCARCITY
*P.P.CYAN/1: UNPRICED DUE TO SCARCITY
*P.P.MAGENTA/1: UNPRICED DUE TO SCARCITY
*P.P.YELLOW/1: UNPRICED DUE TO SCARCITY

1 Akam	.25	.60
2 Baron Corbin	.40	1.00
3 Bobby Lashley	.50	1.25
4 Braun Strowman	.60	1.50
5 Bray Wyatt	.60	1.50
6 Brock Lesnar	1.00	2.50
7 Dolph Ziggler	.50	1.25
8 Drew McIntyre	.30	.75
9 Elias	.50	1.25
10 Finn Balor	.60	1.50
11 Kevin Owens	.60	1.50
12 Kurt Angle	.50	1.25
13 Rezar	.25	.60
14 Roman Reigns	.60	1.50
15 Sami Zayn	.50	1.25
16 Seth Rollins	.60	1.50
17 Titus O'Neil	.30	.75
18 Alexa Bliss	1.25	3.00
19 Bayley	.50	1.25
20 Ember Moon	.60	1.50
21 Liv Morgan	.75	2.00
22 Natalya	.50	1.25
23 Nia Jax	.50	1.25
24 Ronda Rousey	1.25	3.00
25 Ruby Riott	.50	1.25
26 Sarah Logan	.30	.75
27 Sasha Banks	1.00	2.50
28 Ali	.25	.60
29 AJ Styles	1.25	3.00
30 Andrade	.30	.75
31 Big E	.25	.60
32 Cesaro	.30	.75
33 Daniel Bryan	1.00	2.50
34 Jeff Hardy	.60	1.50
35 Kofi Kingston	.40	1.00
36 The Miz	.50	1.25
37 Randy Orton	.60	1.50
38 Rey Mysterio	.60	1.50
39 Samoa Joe	.50	1.25
40 Sheamus	.40	1.00
41 Shinsuke Nakamura	.60	1.50
42 Xavier Woods	.30	.75
43 Asuka	.75	2.00
44 Becky Lynch	1.00	2.50
45 Carmella	.60	1.50
46 Charlotte Flair	1.00	2.50
47 Mandy Rose	.60	1.50
48 Naomi	.40	1.00
49 Peyton Royce	.60	1.50
50 Zelina Vega	.40	1.00
51 Matt Hardy & Bray Wyatt	.60	1.50
52 Shelton Benjamin	.60	1.50
53 Nakamura, Rusev & English	1.25	3.00
54 The Deleters of Worlds	.60	1.50
55 Cedric Alexander	.25	.60
56 Jeff Hardy	.60	1.50
57 The Bludgeon Brothers	.30	.75
58 Seth Rollins	.60	1.50
59 AJ Styles	1.25	3.00
60 Brock Lesnar	1.00	2.50
61 Seth Rollins	.60	1.50
62 Jeff Hardy	.60	1.50

63 AJ Styles and Nakamura	.60	1.50
64 Braun Strowman	.60	1.50
65 The Deleters of Worlds	.60	1.50
66 Finn Balor	.60	1.50
67 Rusev	1.00	2.50
68 Andrade	.40	1.00
69 Cedric Alexander	.30	.75
70 The B-Team	.30	.75
71 Braun Strowman	.60	1.50
72 Shinsuke Nakamura	.60	1.50
73 Seth Rollins	.60	1.50
74 AJ Styles	1.25	3.00
75 Braun Strowman	.60	1.50
76 Dolph Ziggler	.50	1.25
77 Rusev	1.25	3.00
78 Drew McIntyre	.30	.75
79 AJ Styles & Jeff Hardy	1.25	3.00
80 The B-Team	.30	.75
81 Bobby Lashley	.50	1.25
82 AJ Styles	1.25	3.00
83 Dolph Ziggler	.60	1.50
84 Roman Reigns	.60	1.50
85 Bobby Lashley	.50	1.25
86 Randy Orton	.60	1.50
87 Drew Gulak	.25	.60
88 Baron Corbin	.60	1.50
89 Nakamura & Randy Orton	.60	1.50
90 The New Day	.40	1.00
91 Brock Lesnar	1.00	2.50
92 Cedric Alexander	.25	.60
93 Seth Rollins	.60	1.50
94 The New Day	.25	.60
95 Braun Strowman	.60	1.50
96 Samoa Joe	.50	1.25
97 The Miz	1.00	2.50
98 Finn Balor	.60	1.50
99 Shinsuke Nakamura	.60	1.50
100 Roman Reigns	.60	1.50

2019 Topps WWE SummerSlam Autographed Intercontinental Championship Manufactured Relics

UNPRICED DUE TO SCARCITY

ICRAJH Jeff Hardy
ICRAKA Kurt Angle
ICRAWR William Regal

2019 Topps WWE SummerSlam Autographed Manufactured Logo Relics

STATED PRINT RUN 10 SER.#'d SETS
UNPRICED DUE TO SCARCITY

LRABS Braun Strowman
LRAKA Kurt Angle
LRALL Lex Luger
LRAMK Mankind
LRARO Randy Orton
LRATD Ted DiBiase

2019 Topps WWE SummerSlam Autographed Mat Relics

STATED PRINT RUN 10 SER.#'d SETS
UNPRICED DUE TO SCARCITY

MRAAB Alexa Bliss
MRAAC Adam Cole
MRAAJ AJ Styles
MRABC Baron Corbin

MRABE Big E
MRABL Becky Lynch
MRABM Drew McIntyre
MRABS Braun Strowman
MRACM Carmella
MRADB Daniel Bryan
MRAEC Velveteen Dream
MRAFB Finn Balor
MRAJG Johnny Gargano
MRAJH Jeff Hardy
MRAKK Kofi Kingston
MRAKO Kevin Owens
MRAKR Kyle O'Reilly
MRAKS Kairi Sane
MRANT Natalya
MRARC Ricochet
MRARS Roderick Strong
MRARW Rowan
MRASB Shayna Baszler
MRASJ Samoa Joe
MRASN Shinsuke Nakamura
MRASR Seth Rollins
MRATB Tyler Bate
MRATM The Miz
MRATS Trent Seven
MRAVD EC3
MRAXW Xavier Woods

2019 Topps WWE SummerSlam Autographed Superstar Relics

STATED PRINT RUN 10 SER.#'d SETS
UNPRICED DUE TO SCARCITY

SRAAE Aiden English
SRAAW Alexander Wolfe
SRABS Braun Strowman
SRACS Cesaro
SRADW Dash Wilder
SRAEY Eric Young
SRAKD Killian Dain
SRASD Scott Dawson
SRASM Shawn Michaels
SRASZ Sami Zayn

2019 Topps WWE SummerSlam Autographed Women's Evolution Relics

UNPRICED DUE TO SCARCITY

ERARR Ruby Riott
ERATS Tamina

2019 Topps WWE SummerSlam Autographs

*BLUE/50: .5X TO 1.2X BASIC AUTOS
*SILVER/25: .6X TO 1.5X BASIC AUTOS
*GOLD/10: UNPRICED DUE TO SCARCITY
*RED/1: UNPRICED DUE TO SCARCITY
*P.P.BLACK/1: UNPRICED DUE TO SCARCITY
*P.P.CYAN/1: UNPRICED DUE TO SCARCITY
*P.P.MAGENTA/1: UNPRICED DUE TO SCARCITY
*P.P.YELLOW/1: UNPRICED DUE TO SCARCITY
STATED ODDS 1:24

OCAA Andrade	4.00	10.00
OCAB Alexa Bliss	30.00	75.00
OCAJ AJ Styles	12.00	30.00
OCBE Big E	4.00	10.00
OCBL Bayley	10.00	25.00
OCBR Bobby Roode	5.00	12.00

OCBS	Braun Strowman	6.00	15.00
OCCF	Charlotte Flair	15.00	40.00
OCCM	Carmella	8.00	20.00
OCDM	Drew McIntyre	6.00	15.00
OCEL	Elias	8.00	20.00
OCFB	Finn Balor	12.00	30.00
OCJH	Jeff Hardy	12.00	30.00
OCKK	Kofi Kingston	8.00	20.00
OCKO	Kevin Owens	5.00	12.00
OCMM	Bobby Lashley	5.00	12.00
OCMR	Mandy Rose	20.00	50.00
OCRM	Rey Mysterio	12.00	30.00
OCRR	Ruby Riott	15.00	40.00
OCRT	R-Truth	4.00	10.00
OCSD	Sonya Deville	10.00	25.00
OCSJ	Samoa Joe	6.00	15.00
OCSN	Shinsuke Nakamura	8.00	20.00
OCTM	The Miz	6.00	15.00
OCXW	Xavier Woods	4.00	10.00
OCZV	Zelina Vega	12.00	30.00

2019 Topps WWE SummerSlam Dual Autographs

STATED PRINT RUN 10 SER.#'d SETS
UNPRICED DUE TO SCARCITY

DAAB	S.Deville/M.Rose
DABT	B.Dallas/C.Axel
DAII	B.Kay/P.Royce
DAMK	Maria & Mike Kanellis
DAND	X.Woods/K.Kingston

2019 Topps WWE SummerSlam Greatest Matches and Moments

COMPLETE SET (40)		6.00	15.00
RANDOMLY INSERTED INTO PACKS			
GM1	Ult.Warrior/Honky Tonk Man	.50	1.25
GM2	Warrior/Rick Rude	.60	1.50
GM3	Dusty Rhodes/Honky Tonk Man	.50	1.25
GM4	The Texas Tornado Def. Mr. Perfect	.30	.75
GM5	Macho Man Marries Elizabeth	.60	1.50
GM6	Virgil/Ted DiBiase	.25	.60
GM7	British Bulldog/Bret Hart	.50	1.25
GM8	Warrior/Randy Savage	.60	1.50
GM9	Lex Luger/Yokozuna	.30	.75
GM10	Alundra Blayze/Bull Nakano	.25	.60
GM11	Shawn Michaels/Razor Ramon	.50	1.25
GM12	Mankind/Undertaker	.40	1.00
GM13	Shawn Michaels/Vader	.60	1.50
GM14	Mankind/Triple H	.50	1.25
GM15	Steve Austin wins IC Title	1.00	2.50
GM16	Ken Shamrock/Owen Hart	.40	1.00
GM17	Steve Austin/Undertaker	1.25	3.00
GM18	Mankind/Steve Austin/HHH	.50	1.25
GM19	Rock/HHH/Kurt Angle	1.00	2.50
GM20	Kurt Angle/Steve Austin	1.25	3.00
GM21	Shawn Michaels/HHH	.60	1.50
GM22	Kurt Angle/Rey Mysterio	.40	1.00
GM23	Kurt Angle/Brock Lesnar	.50	1.25
GM24	Kurt Angle/Eddie Guerrero	.40	1.00
GM25	Rey Mysterio/Eddie Guerrero	.60	1.50
GM26	Ric Flair/Mick Foley	.75	2.00
GM27	John Cena/Randy Orton	1.00	2.50
GM28	Batista/John Cena	.50	1.25
GM29	Rey Mysterio/Dolph Ziggler	.60	1.50
GM30	Randy Orton/Sheamus	.50	1.25
GM31	Randy Orton/Christian	.60	1.50
GM32	Kane/Rey Mysterio/Undertaker	.30	.75

GM33	Miz/Rey Mysterio	.50	1.25
GM34	Daniel Bryan/John Cena	.75	2.00
GM35	Roman Reigns/Randy Orton	.60	1.50
GM36	Seth Rollins/John Cena	.50	1.25
GM37	Charlotte.Flair/Sasha Banks	1.00	2.50
GM38	Finn Balor/Seth Rollins	.60	1.50
GM39	AJ Styles/John Cena	1.25	3.00
GM40	Usos/New Day	.30	.75

2019 Topps WWE SummerSlam Intercontinental Champion Autographs

STATED PRINT RUN 25 SER.#'d SETS

ICRJH	Jeff Hardy	15.00	40.00
ICRWR	William Regal	10.00	25.00

2019 Topps WWE SummerSlam Intercontinental Championship Manufactured Relics

RANDOMLY INSERTED INTO PACKS

ICRBT	Booker T
ICRDL	D'Lo Brown
ICRJH	Jeff Hardy
ICRKA	Kurt Angle
ICRWR	William Regal

2019 Topps WWE SummerSlam Manufactured Logo Relics

*BRONZE/99: .5X TO 1.2X BASIC MEM
*BLUE/50: .6X TO 1.5X BASIC MEM
*SILVER/25: .75X TO 2X BASIC MEM
*GOLD/10: UNPRICED DUE TO SCARCITY
*RED/1: UNPRICED DUE TO SCARCITY
STATED ODDS 1:152

LRBH	Bret Hit Man Hart	3.00	8.00
LRBL	Brock Lesnar	6.00	15.00
LRBS	Braun Strowman	3.00	8.00
LRBT	Booker T	3.00	8.00
LRED	Edge	3.00	8.00
LRJC	John Cena	4.00	10.00
LRKA	Kurt Angle	3.00	8.00
LRLL	Lex Luger	2.50	6.00
LRMK	Mankind	2.50	6.00
LRRO	Randy Orton	4.00	10.00
LRSA	Stone Cold Steve Austin	6.00	15.00
LRSM	Shawn Michaels	4.00	10.00
LRTD	Ted DiBiase	2.50	6.00
LRUT	Undertaker	4.00	10.00
LRBDC	Diesel	3.00	8.00

2019 Topps WWE SummerSlam Mat Relics

*BRONZE/99: .5X TO 1.2X BASIC MEM
*BLUE/50: .6X TO 1,5X BASIC MEM
*SILVER/25: .75X TO 2X BASIC MEM
*GOLD/10: UNPRICED DUE TO SCARCITY
*RED/1: UNPRICED DUE TO SCARCITY
RANDOMLY INSERTED INTO PACKS

MRAB	Alexa Bliss	12.00	30.00
MRAC	Adam Cole	3.00	8.00
MRAJ	AJ Styles	3.00	8.00
MRBC	Baron Corbin	1.50	4.00
MRBD	Roman Reigns	3.00	8.00
MRBE	Big E	1.50	4.00
MRBI	Brock Lesnar	3.00	8.00
MRBL	Becky Lynch	6.00	15.00
MRBM	Drew McIntyre	2.50	6.00

MRBS	Braun Strowman	2.50	6.00
MRCF	Charlotte Flair	5.00	12.00
MRCM	Carmella	4.00	10.00
MRDB	Daniel Bryan		
MRDZ	Dolph Ziggler	2.50	6.00
MREC	Velveteen Dream	2.50	6.00
MRFB	Finn Balor	4.00	10.00
MRHP	Harper	2.50	6.00
MRJG	Johnny Gargano	2.50	6.00
MRJH	Jeff Hardy	4.00	10.00
MRKK	Kofi Kingston	3.00	8.00
MRKO	Kevin Owens	2.00	5.00
MRKR	Kyle O'Reilly	2.00	5.00
MRKS	Kairi Sane	3.00	8.00
MRNT	Natalya	3.00	8.00
MRPH	Paul Heyman	2.50	6.00
MRRC	Ricochet	3.00	8.00
MRRR	Ronda Rousey	10.00	25.00
MRRS	Roderick Strong	2.50	6.00
MRRW	Rowan	1.50	4.00
MRSB	Shayna Baszler		
MRSJ	Samoa Joe	2.00	5.00
MRSN	Shinsuke Nakamura	2.00	5.00
MRSR	Seth Rollins	3.00	8.00
MRTB	Tyler Bate	2.50	6.00
MRTC	Tommaso Ciampa	2.50	6.00
MRTM	The Miz	2.00	5.00
MRTS	Trent Seven	1.50	4.00
MRVD	EC3	1.50	4.00
MRXW	Xavier Woods	1.50	4.00

2019 Topps WWE SummerSlam Mr. SummerSlam

RANDOMLY INSERTED INTO PACKS

MSS1	Lesnar/Rock	1.25	3.00
MSS2	Lesnar/HHH	1.00	2.50
MSS3	Lesnar/Cena	1.00	2.50
MSS4	Lesnar/Orton	1.00	2.50
MSS5	Lesnar/Joe/Strowman/Reigns	1.00	2.50
MSS6	Undertaker Returns	1.25	3.00
MSS7	Undertaker/Kama	1.25	3.00
MSS8	Unholy Alliance/Kane/X-Pac	.40	1.00
MSS9	Undertaker/Edge	1.25	3.00
MSS10	Undertaker/Brock Lesnar	1.25	3.00
MSS11	Edge & Christian	.60	1.50
MSS12	Edge/Eddie Guerrero	.60	1.50
MSS13	Edge IC Title	.60	1.50
MSS14	Edge/Matt Hardy	.60	1.50
MSS15	Edge/John Cena	.60	1.50
MSS16	HHH PPV Debut	.60	1.50
MSS17	Triple H/Rock	1.25	3.00
MSS18	DX/Mr. McMahon & Shane	.60	1.50
MSS19	HHH/King Booker	.60	1.50
MSS20	HHH/A Giant	.60	1.50
MSS21	Hart Foundation	.60	1.50
MSS22	Bret Hart/Mr. Perfect	.60	1.50
MSS23	Bret Hart/Lawler	.60	1.50
MSS24	Bret Hart/Undertaker	.60	1.50
MSS25	Bret Hart Returns	.60	1.50

2019 Topps WWE SummerSlam Posters Spotlight

COMPLETE SET (4)		3.00	8.00
STATED ODDS 1:6			
SS14	'14 Cena/Lesnar	1.25	3.00
SS15	'15 Lesnar/Undertaker	1.00	2.50

SS16	'17 Collage	1.00	2.50
SS17	'18 Lesnar/Bliss/Rousey/Reigns	1.50	4.00

2019 Topps WWE SummerSlam Superstar Relics

*BRONZE/99: SAME VALUE AS BASIC
*BLUE/50: .5X TO 1.2X BASIC MEM
*SILVER/25: .6X TO 1.5X BASIC MEM
*GOLD/10: UNPRICED DUE TO SCARCITY
*RED/1: UNPRICED DUE TO SCARCITY
RANDOMLY INSERTED INTO PACKS

SRAC	Apollo Crews	2.50	6.00
SRAW	Alexander Wolfe	2.50	6.00
SRBS	Braun Strowman	5.00	12.00
SRCS	Cesaro	3.00	8.00
SRDW	Dash Wilder	2.50	6.00
SRED	Edge	4.00	10.00
SREY	Eric Young	2.50	6.00
SRHS	Heath Slater	2.50	6.00
SRJC	John Cena	5.00	12.00
SRKD	Killian Dain	2.50	6.00
SRRR	Roman Reigns	4.00	10.00
SRSD	Scott Dawson	2.50	6.00
SRSM	Shawn Michaels	4.00	10.00
SRSR	Seth Rollins	3.00	8.00
SRSZ	Sami Zayn	2.50	6.00

2019 Topps WWE SummerSlam Women's Evolution Autographs

*GOLD/10: UNPRICED DUE TO SCARCITY
*P.P.BLACK/1: UNPRICED DUE TO SCARCITY
*P.P.CYAN/1: UNPRICED DUE TO SCARCITY
*P.P.MAGENTA/1: UNPRICED DUE TO SCARCITY
*P.P.YELLOW/1: UNPRICED DUE TO SCARCITY
STATED PRINT RUN 25 SER.#'d SETS
UNPRICED DUE TO SCARCITY

WAAF	Alicia Fox
WAEM	Ember Moon
WAMJ	Mickie James
WANL	Natalya
WARR	Ruby Riott
WATS	Tamina

2019 Topps WWE SummerSlam Women's Evolution Relics

STATED PRINT RUN 25 SER.#'d SETS
UNPRICED DUE TO SCARCITY

ERAF	Alicia Fox
EREM	Ember Moon
ERRR	Ruby Riott
ERTS	Tamina

2005 Topps WWE Tattoos Italian

1 The Basham Brothers
2 Trish Stratus
3 Big Show
4 Randy Orton
5 John Cena
6 Dawn Marie
7 Edge
8 Akio
9 Dudley Boyz
10 Eugene
11 Funaki
12 Eddie Guerrero
13 The Hurricane
14 Charlie Haas

15	Chris Benoit		
16	Hardcore Holly		
17	Triple H		
18	Jerry "The King" Lawler		
19	John Cena		
20	Batista		
21	Kane		
22	Kurt Angle		
23	Mark Jindrak		
24	Matt Hardy		
25	Booker T		
26	Maven		
27	Gene Snitsky		
28	Muhammad Hassan		
29	Miss Jackie		
30	Shelton Benjamin		
31	Victoria		
32	Nunzio		
33	Orlando Jordan		
34	Randy Orton		
35	Rey Mysterio		
36	Chris Benoit		
37	La Resistance		
38	Rhyno		
39	Chavo		
40	Ric Flair		
41	The Rock		
42	RVD		
43	Christian		
44	Scotty 2 Hotty		
45	Eric Bischoff		
46	Spike Dudley		
47	Carlito		
48	Simon Dean		
49	Steven Richards		
50	Tajiri		
51	Tazz		
52	Chris Jericho		
53	Tyson Tomko		
54	Stone Cold Steve Austin		
55	Undertaker		
56	Val Venis		
57	Luther Reigns		
58	William Regal		
59	Evolution		
60	Kenzo Suzuki		
61	Rey Mysterio		
62	Eddie Guerrero		
63	Undertaker		
64	Triple H		
65	Batista		
66	Heidenreich		
67	Ric Flair		
68	JBL		
69	WWE Logo		
70	Lita		
71	RAW Logo		
72	SmackDown Logo		

2016 Topps WWE Then Now Forever

COMPLETE SET (100)		10.00	25.00
UNOPENED BOX (24 PACKS)			
UNOPENED PACK (7 CARDS)			
*BRONZE: 1.2X TO 3X BASIC CARDS			
*SILVER: 2X TO 5X BASIC CARDS			
*GOLD/10: 4X TO 10X BASIC CARDS			
*RED/1: UNPRICED DUE TO SCARCITY			
*P.P.BLACK/1: UNPRICED DUE TO SCARCITY			
*P.P.CYAN/1: UNPRICED DUE TO SCARCITY			
*P.P.MAGENTA/1: UNPRICED DUE TO SCARCITY			
*P.P.YELLOW/1: UNPRICED DUE TO SCARCITY			

101	Aiden English	.20	.50
102	AJ Styles	.75	2.00
103	Apollo Crews	.20	.50
104	Baron Corbin	.25	.60
105	Big Cass	.40	1.00
106	Big E	.20	.50
107	Braun Strowman	.25	.60
108	Bray Wyatt	.75	2.00
109	Brock Lesnar	1.00	2.50
110	Cathy Kelley	.20	.50
111	Chris Jericho	.50	1.25
112	Dana Brooke	.50	1.25
113	Darren Young	.20	.50
114	Dasha Fuentes	.20	.50
115	David Otunga	.20	.50
116	Dean Ambrose	.60	1.50
117	Emma	.40	1.00
118	Enzo Amore	.40	1.00
119	Epico	.20	.50
120	Erick Rowan	.20	.50
121	Eva Marie	.40	1.00
122	Greg Hamilton	.20	.50
123	Heath Slater	.20	.50
124	Jack Swagger	.20	.50
125	John Cena	1.00	2.50
126	JoJo	.20	.50
127	Kane	.30	.75
128	Karl Anderson	.20	.50
129	Kofi Kingston	.20	.50
130	Luke Gallows	.25	.60
131	Luke Harper	.20	.50
132	Maryse	.40	1.00
133	Mauro Ranallo	.20	.50
134	Primo	.20	.50
135	Randy Orton	.50	1.25
136	Renee Young	.50	1.25
137	The Rock	1.00	2.50
138	Roman Reigns	.60	1.50
139	Rosa Mendes	.20	.50
140	Sami Zayn	.30	.75
141	Scott Stanford	.20	.50
142	Seth Rollins	.30	.75
143	Shane McMahon	.30	.75
144	Sheamus	.50	1.25
145	Simon Gotch	.30	.75
146	Stephanie McMahon	.30	.75
147	Tom Phillips	.20	.50
148	Tony Chimel	.20	.50
149	Triple H	.75	2.00
150	Undertaker	.75	2.00
151	Xavier Woods	.20	.50
152	Zack Ryder	.20	.50
153	Big Boss Man L	.30	.75
154	Big John Studd L	.30	.75
155	Bob Backlund L	.20	.50
156	Bobby The Brain Heenan L	.30	.75
157	Brian Pillman L	.25	.60
158	Bruno Sammartino L	.25	.60
159	Chief Jay Strongbow L	.30	.75
160	Cowboy Bob Orton L	.30	.75
161	Daniel Bryan L	.75	2.00
162	Dean Malenko L	.20	.50
163	Diamond Dallas Page L	.30	.75
164	Eddie Guerrero L	.50	1.25
165	The Funks L	.20	.50
166	Gerald Brisco L	.20	.50
167	Gorilla Monsoon L	.30	.75
168	General Adnan L	.20	.50
169	Greg The Hammer Valentine L	.25	.60
170	Hacksaw Jim Duggan L	.20	.50
171	High Chief Peter Maivia L	.20	.50
172	The Honky Tonk Man L	.20	.50
173	Howard Finkel L	.20	.50
174	Jamie Noble L	.20	.50
175	Jim The Anvil Neidhart L	.20	.50
176	Joey Mercury L	.20	.50
177	Junkyard Dog L	.30	.75
178	The King Harley Race L	.20	.50
179	Larry Zbyszko L	.20	.50
180	Lex Luger L	.30	.75
181	Mean Gene Okerlund L	.25	.60
182	Michael P.S. Hayes L	.20	.50
183	Mouth of the South Jimmy Hart L	.25	.60
184	Mr. Perfect Curt Henning L	.50	1.25
185	Mr. Wonderful Paul Orndorff L	.20	.50
186	Nikolai Volkoff L	.25	.60
187	Norman Smiley L	.20	.50
188	Pat Patterson L	.20	.50
189	Paul Bearer L	.30	.75
190	Ravishing Rick Rude L	.30	.75
191	Ricky The Dragon Steamboat L	.25	.60
192	Rocky Johnson L	.25	.60
193	Sgt. Slaughter L	.25	.60
194	Sting L	.50	1.25
195	Stone Cold Steve Austin L	1.00	2.50
196	Tatanka L	.20	.50
197	Tom Prichard L	.20	.50
198	Vader L	.40	1.00
199	Viscera L	.20	.50
200	Yokozuna L	.40	1.00

2016 Topps WWE Then Now Forever Autographs

*BRONZE/50: .5X TO 1.2X BASIC AUTOS			
*SILVER/25: .75X TO 2X BASIC AUTOS			
*GOLD/10: 1.2X TO 3X BASIC AUTOS			
*RED/1: UNPRICED DUE TO SCARCITY			
*P.P.BLACK/1: UNPRICED DUE TO SCARCITY			
*P.P.CYAN/1: UNPRICED DUE TO SCARCITY			
*P.P.MAGENTA/1: UNPRICED DUE TO SCARCITY			
*P.P.YELLOW/1: UNPRICED DUE TO SCARCITY			
STATED ODDS 1:51			

NNO	Aiden English	6.00	15.00
NNO	AJ Styles	20.00	50.00
NNO	Becky Lynch	15.00	40.00
NNO	Charlotte	12.00	30.00
NNO	Chris Jericho	15.00	40.00
NNO	Dean Ambrose	10.00	25.00
NNO	Enzo Amore	12.00	30.00
NNO	Hideo Itami	6.00	15.00
NNO	Karl Anderson	8.00	20.00
NNO	Luke Gallows	8.00	20.00
NNO	Maryse	12.00	30.00
NNO	Naomi	6.00	15.00
NNO	Natalya	8.00	20.00
NNO	Norman Smiley	6.00	15.00
NNO	Ric Flair	15.00	40.00
NNO	Roman Reigns	10.00	25.00
NNO	R-Truth	6.00	15.00
NNO	Sami Zayn	10.00	25.00
NNO	Samoa Joe	6.00	15.00
NNO	Sasha Banks	20.00	50.00
NNO	Seth Rollins	8.00	20.00
NNO	Shinsuke Nakamura	30.00	80.00
NNO	Simon Gotch	6.00	15.00
NNO	Sting	20.00	50.00

2016 Topps WWE Then Now Forever Diva Kiss

*GOLD/10: UNPRICED DUE TO SCARCITY			
*RED/1: UNPRICED DUE TO SCARCITY			
STATED ODDS 1:125			
STATED PRINT RUN 99 SER.#'d SETS			

NNO	Alicia Fox	15.00	40.00
NNO	Asuka	30.00	80.00
NNO	Bayley	30.00	80.00
NNO	Becky Lynch	25.00	60.00
NNO	Brie Bella	20.00	50.00
NNO	Carmella	25.00	60.00
NNO	Charlotte	20.00	50.00
NNO	Lana	20.00	50.00
NNO	Nikki Bella	20.00	50.00
NNO	Sasha Banks	30.00	80.00

2016 Topps WWE Then Now Forever Diva Kiss Autographs

*GOLD/10: UNPRICED DUE TO SCARCITY			
*RED/1: UNPRICED DUE TO SCARCITY			
STATED ODDS 1:482			
STATED PRINT RUN 25 SER.#'d SETS			

NNO	Alicia Fox	25.00	60.00
NNO	Asuka	80.00	150.00
NNO	Bayley	150.00	300.00
NNO	Becky Lynch	60.00	120.00
NNO	Brie Bella	80.00	150.00
NNO	Carmella	50.00	100.00
NNO	Charlotte	60.00	120.00
NNO	Lana	50.00	100.00
NNO	Nikki Bella	60.00	120.00
NNO	Sasha Banks	150.00	300.00

2016 Topps WWE Then Now Forever Mask and Face Paint Medallions

*BRONZE: .5X TO 1.2X BASIC MEM			
*SILVER: .6X TO 1.5X BASIC MEM			
*GOLD/10: UNPRICED DUE TO SCARCITY			
*RED/1: UNPRICED DUE TO SCARCITY			
*P.P.BLACK/1: UNPRICED DUE TO SCARCITY			
*P.P.CYAN/1: UNPRICED DUE TO SCARCITY			
*P.P.MAGENTA/1: UNPRICED DUE TO SCARCITY			
*P.P.YELLOW/1: UNPRICED DUE TO SCARCITY			
STATED ODDS 1:338			

NNO	Asuka	8.00	20.00
NNO	Braun Strowman	5.00	12.00
NNO	Goldust	10.00	25.00
NNO	Kalisto	6.00	15.00
NNO	Kane	5.00	12.00
NNO	Papa Shango	5.00	12.00
NNO	Sin Cara	5.00	12.00
NNO	Sting	8.00	20.00
NNO	Undertaker	10.00	25.00

2016 Topps WWE Then Now Forever NXT Prospects

COMPLETE SET (15)		12.00	30.00
STATED ODDS 1:1			

1	Angelo Dawkins	1.00	2.50
2	Austin Aries	1.25	3.00
3	Asuka	4.00	10.00
4	Billie Kay	2.50	6.00

5 Blake	1.00	2.50
6 Dash Wilder	1.25	3.00
7 Elias Samson	1.00	2.50
8 Hideo Itami	1.25	3.00
9 No Way Jose	1.00	2.50
10 Peyton Royce	2.50	6.00
11 Samoa Joe	2.50	6.00
12 Sawyer Fulton	1.25	3.00
13 Scott Dawson	1.00	2.50
14 Shinsuke Nakamura	2.50	6.00
15 Tye Dillinger	1.25	3.00

2016 Topps WWE Then Now Forever NXT Rivalries

COMPLETE SET (20)	10.00	25.00
STATED ODDS 1:2		
1 Shinsuke Nakamura vs. Samoa Joe	2.00	5.00
2 Finn Balor vs. Samoa Joe	1.25	3.00
3 Kevin Owens vs. Finn Balor	1.25	3.00
4 Asuka vs. Bayley	.75	2.00
5 Nia Jax vs. Asuka	1.25	3.00
6 Nia Jax vs. Bayley	1.50	4.00
7 Emma vs. Asuka	.75	2.50
8 No Way Jose vs. Austin Aries	.75	2.00
9 Baron Corbin vs. Austin Aries	.75	2.00
10 Elias Samson vs. Apollo Crews	.75	2.00
11 Baron Corbin vs. Samoa Joe	1.25	3.00
12 Emma vs. Bayley	1.25	3.00
13 Sami Zayn vs. Cesaro	.75	2.00
14 Tyler Breeze vs. Hideo Itami	.75	2.00
15 Tyler Breeze vs. Neville	.75	2.00
16 Summer Rae vs. Paige	2.00	5.00
17 Bo Dallas vs. Neville	.75	2.00
18 Bray Wyatt vs. Neville	.75	2.00
19 Big E vs. Bo Dallas	.75	2.00
20 Big E vs. Seth Rollins	.75	2.00

2016 Topps WWE Then Now Forever Royal Rumble 2016 Mat Relics

*BRONZE/50: .5X TO 1.2X BASIC MEM
*SILVER/25: .6X TO 1.5X BASIC MEM
*GOLD/10: UNPRICED DUE TO SCARCITY
*RED/1: UNPRICED DUE TO SCARCITY
*P.P.BLACK/1: UNPRICED DUE TO SCARCITY
*P.P.CYAN/1: UNPRICED DUE TO SCARCITY
*P.P.MAGENTA/1: UNPRICED DUE TO SCARCITY
*P.P.YELLOW/1: UNPRICED DUE TO SCARCITY
STATED ODDS 1:92

NNO AJ Styles	8.00	20.00
NNO Alberto Del Rio	3.00	8.00
NNO Becky Lynch	6.00	15.00
NNO Big E	2.00	5.00
NNO Big Show	4.00	10.00
NNO Braun Strowman	2.50	6.00
NNO Bray Wyatt	8.00	20.00
NNO Brock Lesnar	10.00	25.00
NNO Charlotte	6.00	15.00
NNO Chris Jericho	5.00	12.00
NNO Dean Ambrose	6.00	15.00
NNO Dolph Ziggler	2.50	6.00
NNO Erick Rowan	2.00	5.00
NNO Kalisto	5.00	12.00
NNO Kane	3.00	8.00
NNO Kevin Owens	5.00	12.00
NNO Kofi Kingston	2.00	5.00
NNO Luke Harper	2.00	5.00
NNO The Miz	3.00	8.00
NNO Ric Flair	8.00	20.00
NNO Roman Reigns	6.00	15.00
NNO Sami Zayn	3.00	8.00
NNO Sheamus	5.00	12.00
NNO Triple H	8.00	20.00
NNO Xavier Woods	2.00	5.00

2016 Topps WWE Then Now Forever Shirt Relics

*BRONZE/50: .5X TO 1.2X BASIC MEM
*SILVER/25: .6X TO 1.5X BASIC MEM
*GOLD/10: UNPRICED DUE TO SCARCITY
*RED/1: UNPRICED DUE TO SCARCITY
*P.P.BLACK/1: UNPRICED DUE TO SCARCITY
*P.P.CYAN/1: UNPRICED DUE TO SCARCITY
*P.P.MAGENTA/1: UNPRICED DUE TO SCARCITY
*P.P.YELLOW/1: UNPRICED DUE TO SCARCITY
STATED ODDS 1:102

1 Aiden English	2.00	5.00
2 Alberto Del Rio	3.00	8.00
3 Apollo Crews	2.00	5.00
4 Asuka	8.00	20.00
5 Austin Aries	2.50	6.00
6 Baron Corbin	2.50	6.00
7 Bayley	5.00	12.00
8 Big Cass	4.00	10.00
9 Big Show	4.00	10.00
10 Bo Dallas	2.00	5.00
11 Braun Strowman	2.50	6.00
12 Bray Wyatt	8.00	20.00
13 Bubba Ray Dudley	4.00	10.00
14 Cesaro	4.00	10.00
15 Curtis Axel	2.00	5.00
16 Darren Young	2.00	5.00
17 Finn Balor	6.00	15.00
18 Heath Slater	2.00	5.00
19 Jey Uso	2.00	5.00
20 Jimmy Uso	2.00	5.00
21 John Cena	10.00	25.00
22 Kalisto	5.00	12.00
23 Kevin Owens	5.00	12.00
24 Luke Harper	2.00	5.00
25 Randy Orton	5.00	12.00
26 Roman Reigns	6.00	15.00
27 Sheamus	5.00	12.00
28 Simon Gotch	3.00	8.00
29 Xavier Woods	2.00	5.00
30 Zack Ryder	2.00	5.00

2016 Topps WWE Then Now Forever Triple Autographs

STATED ODDS 1:1,362
STATED PRINT RUN 11 SER.#'d SETS

NNO Aiden English Simon Gotch/Enzo Amore	50.00	100.00
NNO Styles Anderson/Gallows	125.00	250.00
NNO Cena Jericho/R-Truth	75.00	150.00
NNO Naomi Banks/Bayley	125.00	250.00
NNO Natalya Charlotte/Lynch	125.00	250.00
NNO Samoa Joe Balor/Itami	100.00	200.00
NNO Rollins Ambrose/Reigns	120.00	250.00
NNO Nakamura Zayn/Asuka	100.00	200.00

2016 Topps WWE Then Now Forever WWE Rivalries

COMPLETE SET (20)	10.00	25.00
STATED ODDS 1:2		
1 AJ Styles vs. John Cena	1.00	2.50
2 Seth Rollins vs. Roman Reigns	1.00	2.50
3 Seth Rollins vs. Dean Ambrose	1.25	3.00
4 Dean Ambrose vs. Chris Jericho	1.25	3.00
5 Roman Reigns vs. AJ Styles	1.50	4.00
6 Chris Jericho vs. AJ Styles	.75	2.00
7 Sami Zayn vs. Kevin Owens	1.25	3.00
8 Kevin Owens vs. Cesaro	1.50	4.00
9 Kevin Owens vs. Dolph Ziggler	1.25	3.00
10 Undertaker vs. Brock Lesnar	2.00	5.00
11 Roman Reigns vs. Triple H	1.25	3.00
12 Dean Ambrose vs. Triple H	1.25	3.00
13 Natalya vs. Charlotte	1.00	2.50
14 Natalya vs. Becky Lynch	1.25	3.00
15 Dolph Ziggler vs. Baron Corbin	.75	2.00
16 Enzo Amore vs. Chris Jericho	1.00	2.50
17 Kalisto vs. Rusev	.75	2.00
18 Rusev vs. Jack Swagger	.75	2.00
19 Lana vs. Brie Bella	1.50	4.00
20 Dolph Ziggler vs. The Miz	.75	2.00

2017 Topps WWE Then Now Forever

COMPLETE SET (100)	10.00	25.00
UNOPENED BOX (24 PACKS)		
UNOPENED PACK (7 CARDS)		
*BRONZE: .5X TO 1.2X BASIC CARDS		
*BLUE/99: 1X TO 2.5X BASIC CARDS		
*SILVER/25: 2X TO 5X BASIC CARDS		
*GOLD/10: 4X TO 10X BASIC CARDS		
*RED/1: UNPRICED DUE TO SCARCITY		
*P.P.BLACK/1: UNPRICED DUE TO SCARCITY		
*P.P.CYAN/1: UNPRICED DUE TO SCARCITY		
*P.P.MAGENTA/1: UNPRICED DUE TO SCARCITY		
*P.P.YELLOW/1: UNPRICED DUE TO SCARCITY		
101 Tyler Bate		
102 Brie Bella	.60	1.50
103 Jerry The King Lawler	.30	.75
104A Akira Tozawa	.25	.60
104B Akira Tozawa SP Arms Up	8.00	20.00
105 Alicia Fox	.40	1.00
106 Apollo Crews	.30	.75
107 Ariya Daivari	.25	.60
108 Harley Race	.30	.75
109A Big Show	.30	.75
109B Big Show SP Red/White/Blue	4.00	10.00
110 Bo Dallas	.25	.60
111A Braun Strowman	.30	.75
111B Braun Strowman SP Stomping	5.00	12.00
112A Bray Wyatt	.60	1.50
112B Bray Wyatt SP White Ropes	5.00	12.00
113A Cesaro	.50	1.25
113B Cesaro SP Mid-Air	5.00	12.00
114 Charly Caruso	.25	.60
115 Curt Hawkins	.25	.60
116 Curtis Axel	.25	.60
117 Dana Brooke	.50	1.25
118 Darren Young	.25	.60
119 Dean Ambrose	.75	2.00
120 Emma	.60	1.50
121 Jeff Hardy	.50	1.25
122 Goldust	.30	.75
123 Heath Slater	.25	.60
124 JoJo	.40	1.00
125 Kalisto	.40	1.00
126 Kurt Angle	.50	1.25
127 Mark Henry	.25	.60
128 Matt Hardy	.60	1.50
129 Mickie James	.40	1.00
130 Neville	.40	1.00
131 R-Truth	.25	.60
132 Rhyno	.25	.60
133 Roman Reigns	.75	2.00
134 Sasha Banks	.75	2.00
135 Seth Rollins	.75	2.00
136A Sheamus	.50	1.25
136B Sheamus SP Mid-Air	4.00	10.00
137 Summer Rae	.60	1.50
138 Aiden English	.25	.60
139 Baron Corbin	.40	1.00
140 Becky Lynch	.75	2.00
141 Charlotte Flair	1.00	2.50
142A Daniel Bryan	1.00	2.50
142B Daniel Bryan SP YES!	5.00	12.00
143A Dolph Ziggler	.40	1.00
143B Dolph Ziggler SP Drops Elbow	5.00	12.00
144 Epico	.25	.60
145 Erick Rowan	.25	.60
146 Fandango	.25	.60
147 James Ellsworth	.25	.60
148 Jey Uso	.30	.75
149 Jimmy Uso	.30	.75
150 Jinder Mahal	.40	1.00
151A Kevin Owens	.60	1.50
151B Kevin Owens SP Red/White/Blue	5.00	12.00
152 Konnor	.25	.60
153 Lana	.75	2.00
154 Naomi	.50	1.25
155A Natalya	.50	1.25
155B Natalya SP Arms Raised	6.00	15.00
156 Nikki Bella	.60	1.50
157 Primo	.25	.60
158A Rusev	.50	1.25
158B Rusev SP Man Bun	5.00	12.00
159 Sami Zayn	.30	.75
160 Shinsuke Nakamura	.60	1.50
161 Sin Cara	.30	.75
162 Tyler Breeze	.25	.60
163 Viktor	.25	.60
164 Akam	.25	.60
165 Aleister Black	.25	.60
166 Andrade Cien Almas	.25	.60
167 Angelo Dawkins	.25	.60
168 Buddy Murphy	.25	.60
169 Drew McIntyre	.25	.60
170 Elias	.40	1.00
171 Kassius Ohno	.25	.60
172 Killian Dain	.25	.60
173 Abbey Laith	.25	.60
174 Lacey Evans	.40	1.00
175 Mandy Rose	.30	.75
176 No Way Jose	.25	.60
177 Rezar	.25	.60
178 Ruby Riot	.30	.75
179 Sawyer Fulton	.25	.60
180 Wesley Blake	.25	.60
181 Alundra Blayze	.30	.75
182 Andre the Giant	.50	1.25
183 Bret Hit Man Hart	.50	1.25

184	British Bulldog	.25	.60
185	Bruno Sammartino	.40	1.00
186	Dusty Rhodes	.30	.75
187	Edge	.60	1.50
188	Jake The Snake Roberts	.30	.75
189	Lex Luger	.30	.75
190	Macho Man Randy Savage	.50	1.25
191	Million Dollar Man Ted DiBiase	.30	.75
192	Mr. Perfect	.50	1.25
193	Ravishing Rick Rude	.40	1.00
194	Rowdy Roddy Piper	.50	1.25
195	Shawn Michaels	.60	1.50
196	Sting	.75	2.00
197	Stone Cold Steve Austin	1.00	2.50
198	Trish Stratus	1.00	2.50
199	Ultimate Warrior	.50	1.25
200	Wendi Richter	.30	.75

2017 Topps WWE Then Now Forever Autographed Dual Relics

STATED PRINT RUN 10 SER. #'d SETS
UNPRICED DUE TO SCARCITY

NNO Asuka
NNO Bayley
NNO Bobby Roode
NNO Bray Wyatt
NNO Charlotte Flair
NNO John Cena
NNO Nikki Bella
NNO Randy Orton
NNO Shinsuke Nakamura

2017 Topps WWE Then Now Forever Autographed NXT TakeOver San Antonio 2017 Mat Relics

STATED PRINT RUN 10 SER.#'d SETS
UNPRICED DUE TO SCARCITY

NNO Asuka
NNO Billie Kay
NNO Bobby Roode
NNO Eric Young
NNO Peyton Royce
NNO Roderick Strong
NNO Shinsuke Nakamura

2017 Topps WWE Then Now Forever Autographed Royal Rumble 2017 Mat Relics

STATED PRINT RUN 10 SER. #'d SETS
UNPRICED DUE TO SCARCITY

NNO AJ Styles
NNO Braun Strowman
NNO Bray Wyatt
NNO Charlotte Flair
NNO Chris Jericho
NNO Goldberg
NNO Karl Anderson
NNO Kevin Owens
NNO Luke Gallows
NNO Naomi
NNO Neville
NNO Nia Jax
NNO Nikki Bella
NNO Randy Orton
NNO Roman Reigns
NNO Undertaker

2017 Topps WWE Then Now Forever Autographed Shirt Relics

STATED PRINT RUN 10 SER.#'d SETS
UNPRICED DUE TO SCARCITY

NNO Aiden English
NNO Becky Lynch
NNO Big Show
NNO Charlotte Flair
NNO Curtis Axel
NNO JoJo
NNO Kevin Owens
NNO Naomi
NNO Natalya
NNO Sasha Banks
NNO Seth Rollins
NNO Sheamus
NNO Sting
NNO Summer Rae

2017 Topps WWE Then Now Forever Autographs

*BLUE/50: .6X TO 1.5X BASIC AUTOS
*SILVER/25: .75X TO 2X BASIC AUTOS
*GOLD/10: UNPRICED DUE TO SCARCITY
*RED/1: UNPRICED DUE TO SCARCITY
STATED ODDS

102	Brie Bella	10.00	25.00
104	Akira Tozawa	8.00	20.00
105	Alicia Fox	8.00	20.00
106	Apollo Crews	6.00	15.00
111	Braun Strowman	12.00	30.00
112	Bray Wyatt	8.00	20.00
113	Cesaro	6.00	15.00
119	Dean Ambrose	10.00	25.00
121	Jeff Hardy	15.00	40.00
123	Heath Slater	5.00	12.00
126	Kurt Angle	15.00	40.00
128	Matt Hardy	15.00	40.00
134	Sasha Banks	20.00	50.00
136	Sheamus	5.00	12.00
139	Baron Corbin	5.00	12.00
140	Becky Lynch	15.00	40.00
154	Naomi	10.00	25.00
159	Sami Zayn	5.00	12.00
160	Shinsuke Nakamura	15.00	40.00
165	Aleister Black	20.00	50.00
169	Drew McIntyre	8.00	20.00
171	Kassius Ohno	6.00	15.00
172	Killian Dain	6.00	15.00
174	Lacey Evans	12.00	30.00
178	Ruby Riot	15.00	40.00
189	Lex Luger	8.00	20.00

2017 Topps WWE Then Now Forever Championship Medallion Relics

*BRONZE/99: .5X TO 1.2X BASIC MEM
*BLUE/50: .6X TO 1.5X BASIC MEM
*SILVER/25: .75X TO 2X BASIC MEM
*GOLD/10: UNPRICED DUE TO SCARCITY
*RED/1: UNPRICED DUE TO SCARCITY
RANDOMLY INSERTED INTO PACKS

NNO	Aiden English	1.50	4.00
NNO	American Alpha	2.00	5.00
NNO	Asuka	5.00	12.00
NNO	The Authors of Pain	1.50	4.00
NNO	Bayley	5.00	12.00
NNO	Blake & Murphy	1.50	4.00

NNO	Bobby Roode	4.00	10.00
NNO	The Brian Kendrick	1.50	4.00
NNO	DIY	1.50	4.00
NNO	Finn Balor	6.00	15.00
NNO	Kevin Owens	4.00	10.00
NNO	Neville	2.50	6.00
NNO	The Revival	1.50	4.00
NNO	Rich Swann	1.50	4.00
NNO	Sami Zayn	2.00	5.00
NNO	Samoa Joe	5.00	12.00
NNO	Sasha Banks	5.00	12.00
NNO	Shinsuke Nakamura	4.00	10.00
NNO	TJ Perkins	1.50	4.00

2017 Topps WWE Then Now Forever Dual Relics

*SILVER/25: .6X TO 1.5X BASIC MEM
*GOLD/10: UNPRICED DUE TO SCARCITY
*RED/1: UNPRICED DUE TO SCARCITY
STATED PRINT RUN 50 SER.#'d SETS

NNO	Asuka		
NNO	Bayley		
NNO	Bobby Roode	10.00	25.00
NNO	Bray Wyatt		
NNO	Brock Lesnar		
NNO	Charlotte Flair		
NNO	John Cena	12.00	30.00
NNO	Nikki Bella	10.00	25.00
NNO	Randy Orton		
NNO	Shinsuke Nakamura	20.00	50.00

2017 Topps WWE Then Now Forever Finishers and Signature Moves

COMPLETE SET (50) 10.00 25.00
STATED ODDS 2:1

F1	John Cena	1.50	4.00
F2	John Cena	1.50	4.00
F3	Brock Lesnar	1.50	4.00
F4	Brock Lesnar	1.50	4.00
F5	Goldberg	1.25	3.00
F6	Goldberg	1.25	3.00
F7	The Rock	1.50	4.00
F8	The Rock	1.50	4.00
F9	Triple H	.75	2.00
F10	Randy Orton	.75	2.00
F11	Undertaker	1.25	3.00
F12	Undertaker	1.25	3.00
F13	Undertaker	1.25	3.00
F14	Kane	.40	1.00
F15	Big Show	.40	1.00
F16	Big Show	.40	1.00
F17	Chris Jericho	.75	2.00
F18	Chris Jericho	.75	2.00
F19	Chris Jericho	.75	2.00
F20	Daniel Bryan	1.25	3.00
F21	Mick Foley	.75	2.00
F22	Mick Foley	.75	2.00
F23	Booker T	.40	1.00
F24	AJ Styles	1.50	4.00
F25	AJ Styles	1.50	4.00
F26	AJ Styles	1.50	4.00
F27	Finn Balor	1.25	3.00
F28	Finn Balor	1.25	3.00
F29	The Miz	.60	1.50
F30	The Miz	.60	1.50
F31	Bobby Roode	.75	2.00
F32	Shinsuke Nakamura	.75	2.00
F33	Drew McIntyre	.30	.75
F34	Aliyah	.40	1.00
F35	Andrade Cien Almas	.30	.75
F36	Dean Ambrose	1.00	2.50
F37	No Way Jose	.30	.75
F38	Ember Moon	.75	2.00
F39	Eric Young	.60	1.50
F40	Hideo Itami	.50	1.25
F41	Nikki Cross	.60	1.50
F42	Billie Kay	.40	1.00
F43	Tye Dillinger	.60	1.50
F44	Buddy Murphy	.30	.75
F45	Peyton Royce	.50	1.25
F46	The Authors of Pain	.30	.75
F47	The Revival	.30	.75
F48	TM-61	.30	.75
F49	The Hype Bros.	.40	1.00
F50	#DIY	.30	.75

2017 Topps WWE Then Now Forever Kiss

*GOLD/10: UNPRICED DUE TO SCARCITY
*RED/1: UNPRICED DUE TO SCARCITY
STATED PRINT RUN 99 SER.#'d SETS

NNO	Alexa Bliss	50.00	100.00
NNO	Asuka	50.00	100.00
NNO	Becky Lynch	30.00	80.00
NNO	Billie Kay	15.00	40.00
NNO	Charlotte Flair	20.00	50.00
NNO	Ember Moon	15.00	40.00
NNO	Liv Morgan	30.00	80.00
NNO	Peyton Royce	15.00	40.00

2017 Topps WWE Then Now Forever Kiss Autographs

*GOLD/10: UNPRICED DUE TO SCARCITY
*RED/1: UNPRICED DUE TO SCARCITY
STATED PRINT RUN 25 SER.#'d SETS

NNO	Alexa Bliss		
NNO	Asuka	50.00	100.00
NNO	Becky Lynch	50.00	100.00
NNO	Billie Kay	30.00	75.00
NNO	Charlotte Flair	60.00	120.00
NNO	Ember Moon	25.00	60.00
NNO	Liv Morgan	50.00	100.00
NNO	Mickie James	60.00	120.00
NNO	Nikki Bella	50.00	100.00
NNO	Peyton Royce	30.00	75.00

2017 Topps WWE Then Now Forever NXT TakeOver San Antonio 2017 Mat Relics

*BRONZE/99: .5X TO 1.2X BASIC MEM
*BLUE/50: .6X TO 1.5X BASIC MEM
*SILVER/25: .75X TO 2X BASIC MEM
*GOLD/10: UNPRICED DUE TO SCARCITY
*RED/1: UNPRICED DUE TO SCARCITY
STATED PRINT RUN 350 SER.#'d SETS

NNO	Akam	1.50	4.00
NNO	Asuka	5.00	12.00
NNO	Billie Kay	2.00	5.00
NNO	Bobby Roode	4.00	10.00
NNO	Eric Young	3.00	8.00
NNO	Peyton Royce	2.50	6.00
NNO	Rezar	1.50	4.00
NNO	Roderick Strong	2.00	5.00

2017 Topps WWE Then Now Forever

Card		Low	High
NNO	Shinsuke Nakamura	4.00	10.00
NNO	Tye Dillinger	3.00	8.00

2017 Topps WWE Then Now Forever Roster Updates

Card		Low	High
	COMPLETE SET (20)	12.00	30.00
R21	Alexa Bliss	5.00	12.00
R22	Dash Wilder	1.00	2.50
R23	Jason Jordan	1.25	3.00
R24	Maryse	2.00	5.00
R25	The Miz	2.00	5.00
R26	Mustafa Ali	1.00	2.50
R27	Scott Dawson	1.00	2.50
R28	Tony Nese	1.00	2.50
R29	The New Day	2.00	5.00
R30	Samir Singh	1.00	2.50
R31	Sunil Singh	1.00	2.50
R32	Tamina	1.25	3.00
R33	Tye Dillinger	2.00	5.00
R34	Dan Matha	1.00	2.50
R35	Vanessa Borne	1.25	3.00
R36	Gabriel Ealy	1.00	2.50
R37	Kona Reeves	1.00	2.50
R38	The Velveteen Dream	1.25	3.00
R39	Steve Cutler	1.00	2.50
R40	Uriel Ealy	1.00	2.50

2017 Topps WWE Then Now Forever Royal Rumble 2017 Mat Relics

*BRONZE/99: .5X TO 1.2X BASIC MEM
*BLUE/50: .6X TO 1.5X BASIC MEM
*SILVER/25: .75X TO 2X BASIC MEM
*GOLD/10: UNPRICED DUE TO SCARCITY
*RED/1: UNPRICED DUE TO SCARCITY
RANDOMLY INSERTED INTO PACKS

Card		Low	High
NNO	AJ Styles	6.00	15.00
NNO	Bayley	4.00	10.00
NNO	Braun Strowman	1.50	4.00
NNO	Bray Wyatt	3.00	8.00
NNO	Brock Lesnar	6.00	15.00
NNO	Charlotte Flair	5.00	12.00
NNO	Chris Jericho	3.00	8.00
NNO	Goldberg	5.00	12.00
NNO	John Cena	6.00	15.00
NNO	Karl Anderson	1.25	3.00
NNO	Kevin Owens	3.00	8.00
NNO	Luke Gallows	2.00	5.00
NNO	Naomi	2.50	6.00
NNO	Neville	2.00	5.00
NNO	Nia Jax	2.00	5.00
NNO	Nikki Bella	3.00	8.00
NNO	Randy Orton	3.00	8.00
NNO	Rich Swann	1.25	3.00
NNO	Roman Reigns	4.00	10.00
NNO	Undertaker	5.00	12.00

2017 Topps WWE Then Now Forever Shirt Relics

*BLUE/50: .5X TO 1.2X BASIC MEM
*SILVER/25: .6X TO 1.5X BASIC MEM
*GOLD/10: UNPRICED DUE TO SCARCITY
*RED/1: UNPRICED DUE TO SCARCITY
RANDOMLY INSERTED INTO PACKS

Card		Low	High
NNO	Aiden English	1.25	3.00
NNO	Andrade Cien Almas	1.25	3.00
NNO	Becky Lynch	4.00	10.00
NNO	Big Show	1.50	4.00

Card		Low	High
NNO	Brock Lesnar	6.00	15.00
NNO	Charlotte Flair	5.00	12.00
NNO	Curtis Axel	1.25	3.00
NNO	Darren Young	1.25	3.00
NNO	John Cena	6.00	15.00
NNO	JoJo	2.00	5.00
NNO	Kevin Owens	3.00	8.00
NNO	Naomi	2.50	6.00
NNO	Natalya	2.50	6.00
NNO	No Way Jose	1.25	3.00
NNO	Sasha Banks	4.00	10.00
NNO	Seth Rollins	4.00	10.00
NNO	Sheamus	2.50	6.00
NNO	Sting	4.00	10.00
NNO	Summer Rae	3.00	8.00

2017 Topps WWE Then Now Forever Triple Autographs

STATED PRINT RUN 10 SER.#'d SETS
RANDOMLY INSERTED INTO PACKS

Card		Low	High
NNO	Bayley	125.00	250.00
	Sasha Banks/Charlotte Flair		
NNO	Wyatt	75.00	150.00
	Orton/Harper		
NNO	Rollins	150.00	300.00
	Reigns/Ambrose		
NNO	Undertaker	400.00	600.00
	Lesnar/Goldberg		
NNO	Undertaker	250.00	400.00
	Kane/Bryan		

2018 Topps WWE Then Now Forever

	Low	High
COMPLETE SET W/SP (124)		
COMPLETE SET W/O SP (100)	8.00	20.00
UNOPENED BOX (24 PACKS)		
UNOPENED PACK (7 CARDS)		

*BRONZE: .5X TO 1.2X BASIC CARDS
*BLUE/99: .75X TO 2X BASIC CARDS
*SILVER/25: 2X TO 5X BASIC CARDS
*GOLD/10: UNPRICED DUE TO SCARCITY
*RED/1: UNPRICED DUE TO SCARCITY
*P.P.BLACK/1: UNPRICED DUE TO SCARCITY
*P.P.CYAN/1: UNPRICED DUE TO SCARCITY
*P.P.MAGENTA/1: UNPRICED DUE TO SCARCITY
*P.P.YELLOW/1: UNPRICED DUE TO SCARCITY

Card		Low	High
101	Ronda Rousey	2.50	6.00
102	Alexa Bliss	1.25	3.00
102A	Alexa Bliss SP		
103	Akam	.25	.60
104	Alexander Wolfe	.25	.60
105	Andrade	.40	1.00
105A	Andrade SP		
106	Constable Baron Corbin	.40	1.00
107	Bayley	.40	1.00
107A	Bayley SP		
108	Becky Lynch	.60	1.50
108A	Becky Lynch SP		
109	Bianca Belair	.30	.75
110	Big Show	.25	.60
111	Billie Kay	.50	1.25
112	Bobby Lashley	.50	1.25
112A	Bobby Lashley SP		
113	Braun Strowman	.60	1.50
113A	Braun Strowman SP		
114	Bray Wyatt	.60	1.50
114A	Bray Wyatt SP		
115	Candice LeRae	.30	.75

Card		Low	High
116	Cesaro	.50	1.25
116A	Cesaro SP		
117	Cezar Bononi	.25	.60
118	Dakota Kai	.30	.75
119	Danny Burch	.25	.60
120	Dash Wilder	.30	.75
121	David Otunga	.30	.75
122	Dean Ambrose	.50	1.25
122A	Dean Ambrose SP		
123	Dolph Ziggler	.30	.75
124	Drake Maverick	.30	.75
125	Drew McIntyre	.40	1.00
125A	Drew McIntyre SP		
126	EC3	.30	.75
127	Ember Moon	.50	1.25
127A	Ember Moon SP		
128	Eric Young	.30	.75
128A	Eric Young SP		
129	Fabian Aichner	.25	.60
130	Fandango	.25	.60
131	Finn Balor	.60	1.50
131A	Finn Balor SP		
132	Goldust	.50	1.25
133	Hanson	.30	.75
134	Harper	.40	1.00
135	Hideo Itami	.25	.60
136	Jason Jordan	.25	.60
137	Jeff Hardy	.50	1.25
137A	Jeff Hardy SP		
138	Jonathan Coachman	.25	.60
139	Kalisto	.25	.60
140	Kane	.40	1.00
141	Karl Anderson	.25	.60
142	Kassius Ohno	.25	.60
143	Killian Dain	.30	.75
144	Kona Reeves	.25	.60
145	Lacey Evans	.30	.75
146	Lince Dorado	.25	.60
147	Liv Morgan	.50	1.25
148	Luke Gallows	.30	.75
149	Mandy Rose	.60	1.50
150	Mark Andrews	.25	.60
151	Woken Matt Hardy	.60	1.50
152	Mojo Rawley	.25	.60
153	Nick Miller	.25	.60
154	Nikki Bella	.50	1.25
155	Nikki Cross	.40	1.00
156	No Way Jose	.30	.75
157	Otis Dozovic	.25	.60
158	Peyton Royce	.60	1.50
159	Randy Orton	.60	1.50
159A	Randy Orton SP		
160	Raul Mendoza	.25	.60
161	Rezar	.25	.60
162	Ricochet	.50	1.25
163	Riddick Moss	.25	.60
164	Roman Reigns	.60	1.50
164A	Roman Reigns SP		
165	Rowan	.40	1.00
166	Rowe	.25	.60
167	Ruby Riott	.40	1.00
167A	Ruby Riott SP		
168	Rusev	.40	1.00
168A	Rusev SP		
169	Sami Zayn	.25	.60
169A	Sami Zayn SP		
170	Samoa Joe	.50	1.25
170A	Samoa Joe SP		

Card		Low	High
171	Sasha Banks	.75	2.00
171A	Sasha Banks SP		
172	Scott Dawson	.30	.75
173	Scott Stanford	.25	.60
174	Seth Rollins	.60	1.50
174A	Seth Rollins SP		
175	Shane Thorne	.25	.60
176	Shayna Baszler	.60	1.50
177	Sheamus	.50	1.25
177A	Sheamus SP		
178	Shinsuke Nakamura	.60	1.50
178A	Shinsuke Nakamura SP		
179	Taynara Conti	.25	.60
180	Tino Sabbatelli	.30	.75
181	Trent Seven	.25	.60
182	Tucker Knight	.25	.60
183	Tye Dillinger	.25	.60
184	Tyler Breeze	.25	.60
185	Vanessa Borne	.25	.60
186	Velveteen Dream	.25	.60
187	Zelina Vega	.25	.60
188	Andre the Giant	.50	1.25
189	Beth Phoenix	.50	1.25
190	Bret Hit Man Hart	.60	1.50
191	Eddie Guerrero	.60	1.50
192	Edge	.60	1.50
193	Jake The Snake Roberts	.30	.75
194	Lita	.60	1.50
195	Macho Man Randy Savage	.75	2.00
196	Million Dollar Man Ted DiBiase	.30	.75
197	Mr. Perfect	.30	.75
198	Shawn Michaels	.75	2.00
199	Sting	.60	1.50
200	Stone Cold Steve Austin	1.25	3.00

2018 Topps WWE Then Now Forever 25 Years of RAW

	Low	High
COMPLETE SET (50)	12.00	30.00
RANDOMLY INSERTED INTO PACKS		

Card		Low	High
RAW1	Monday Night RAW Premieres	.40	1.00
RAW2	Mr. Perfect Def. Ric Flair	.40	1.00
RAW3	123 Kid vs. Bret Hart	.40	1.00
RAW4	Ringmaster Debuts	1.50	4.00
RAW5	Bret Hart Snaps	.75	2.00
RAW6	Austin injures Bret Hart	1.50	4.00
RAW7	NA Outlaws/Chainsaw Charlie	.40	1.00
RAW8	HHH Leads DX	.75	2.00
RAW9	DX Invades WCW	.75	2.00
RAW10	Stone Cold/Zamboni	1.50	4.00
RAW11	Undertaker Captures Austin	1.25	3.00
RAW12	Stone Cold/Beer Truck	1.50	4.00
RAW13	The Higher Power	.40	1.00
RAW14	Rock/This Is Your Life	.40	1.00
RAW15	HHH and Stephanie Elope	.75	2.00
RAW16	Angle/Milk Truck	.75	2.00
RAW17	HHH Returns	.75	2.00
RAW18	WWE Draft	.40	1.00
RAW19	Hardy/Undertaker	.60	1.50
RAW20	HHH Turns on HBK	.75	2.00
RAW21	HHH/Evolution	.75	2.00
RAW22	Goldberg Debuts	1.25	3.00
RAW23	HHH Def. Ric Flair	.75	2.00
RAW24	Lita Def. Trish	.75	2.00
RAW25	Batista Thumbs Down	.50	1.25
RAW26	Cena Joins RAW	1.25	3.00
RAW27	HBK/Montreal	1.00	2.50
RAW28	Mr. McMahon's Limo	.60	1.50
RAW29	Hardy Swantons Orton	.60	1.50

RAW30	Ric Flair Retires	1.00	2.50
RAW31	Bret Hart Returns	.75	2.00
RAW32	HBK Farewell	1.00	2.50
RAW33	Nexus Invades	.40	1.00
RAW34	Miz Cashes In	.60	1.50
RAW35	HHH/Taker WrestleMania	.75	2.00
RAW36	Edge Retires	.75	2.00
RAW37	Daniel Bryan Kane Hug	.75	2.00
RAW38	Dolph Ziggler Cashes In	.40	1.00
RAW39	Mark Henry Fake Retires	.40	1.00
RAW40	Yes! Movement	.75	2.00
RAW41	Seth Rollins Turns	.75	2.00
RAW42	Kevin Owens Debuts	.75	2.00
RAW43	Shane McMahon Returns	.60	1.50
RAW44	Styles Confronts Cena	1.25	3.00
RAW45	Goldberg Returns	1.25	3.00
RAW46	Angle New GM	.75	2.00
RAW47	Roman Reigns/My Yard	.75	2.00
RAW48	The Shield Reunite	.40	1.00
RAW49	Miz Wins 8th IC Title	.60	1.50
RAW50	Scott Hall Returns	.60	1.50

2018 Topps WWE Then Now Forever Autographed Royal Rumble 2018 Mat Relics

STATED PRINT RUN 10 SER.#'d SETS
UNPRICED DUE TO SCARCITY

MRARRAC	Adam Cole
MRARRAJ	AJ Styles
MRARRAS	Asuka
MRARRBS	Braun Strowman
MRARRFB	Finn Balor
MRARRKK	Kofi Kingston
MRARRKO	Kevin Owens
MRARRMH	Woken Matt Hardy
MRARRRS	Rusev
MRARRSN	Shinsuke Nakamura
MRARRSR	Seth Rollins
MRARRSZ	Sami Zayn

2018 Topps WWE Then Now Forever Autographed Shirt Relics

STATED PRINT RUN 10 SER.#'d SETS
UNPRICED DUE TO SCARCITY

SRAB	Alexa Bliss
SRAK	Akam
SRCG	Chad Gable
SRCR	Carmella
SRDZ	Dolph Ziggler
SRJC	John Cena
SRJJ	Jason Jordan
SRKA	Karl Anderson
SRLG	Luke Gallows
SRNA	Naomi
SRRZ	Rezar
SRSR	Seth Rollins

2018 Topps WWE Then Now Forever Autographs

*BLUE/99: .5X TO 1.2X BASIC AUTOS
*SILVER/25: .6X TO 1.5X BASIC AUTOS
*GOLD/10: UNPRICED DUE TO SCARCITY
*RED/1: UNPRICED DUE TO SCARCITY
RANDOMLY INSERTED INTO PACKS

102	Alexa Bliss	30.00	75.00
106	Baron Corbin	4.00	10.00
108	Becky Lynch	15.00	40.00

111	Billie Kay	10.00	25.00
113	Braun Strowman	10.00	25.00
114	Bray Wyatt	8.00	20.00
115	Candice LeRae	12.00	30.00
125	Drew McIntyre	6.00	15.00
126	EC3	10.00	25.00
127	Ember Moon	8.00	20.00
128	Eric Young	5.00	12.00
131	Finn Balor	8.00	20.00
133	Hanson	12.00	30.00
137	Jeff Hardy	8.00	20.00
142	Kassius Ohno	4.00	10.00
147	Liv Morgan	15.00	40.00
151	Woken Matt Hardy	8.00	20.00
152	Mojo Rawley	5.00	12.00
158	Peyton Royce	12.00	30.00
162	Ricochet	25.00	60.00
166	Rowe	8.00	20.00
167	Ruby Riott	12.00	30.00
168	Rusev	6.00	15.00
169	Sami Zayn	6.00	15.00
170	Samoa Joe	5.00	12.00
178	Shinsuke Nakamura	10.00	25.00
189	Beth Phoenix	10.00	25.00

2018 Topps WWE Then Now Forever Four Corner Mat Relics

*SILVER/25: .5X TO 1.2X BASIC MEM
*GOLD/10: UNPRICED DUE TO SCARCITY
STATED PRINT RUN 50 SER.#'d SETS

FCAJ	AJ Styles	12.00	30.00
FCAS	Asuka	10.00	25.00
FCDA	Dean Ambrose	4.00	10.00
FCJC	John Cena	12.00	30.00
FCRO	Randy Orton	6.00	15.00
FCRR	Roman Reigns	6.00	15.00
FCSN	Shinsuke Nakamura	10.00	25.00
FCSR	Seth Rollins	12.00	30.00
FCTH	Triple H	10.00	25.00
FCUN	Undertaker	15.00	40.00

2018 Topps WWE Then Now Forever Kiss

*GOLD/10: UNPRICED DUE TO SCARCITY
*RED/1: UNPRICED DUE TO SCARCITY

KCAB	Alexa Bliss		
KCAS	Asuka		
KCMR	Mandy Rose	30.00	75.00

2018 Topps WWE Then Now Forever Kiss Autographs

*GOLD/10: UNPRICED DUE TO SCARCITY
*RED/1: UNPRICED DUE TO SCARCITY
STATED PRINT RUN 25 SER.#'d SETS

KCMJ	Mickie James	60.00	120.00
KCMR	Mandy Rose	50.00	100.00
KCRR	Ruby Riott		

2018 Topps WWE Then Now Forever Money in the Bank 2017 Mat Relics

*BRONZE/99: .5X TO 1.2X BASIC MEM
*BLUE/50: .6X TO 1.5X BASIC MEM
*SILVER/25: .75X TO 2X BASIC MEM
*GOLD/10: UNPRICED DUE TO SCARCITY
*RED/1: UNPRICED DUE TO SCARCITY

MRMBAJ	AJ Styles	8.00	20.00
MRMBBC	Baron Corbin	2.50	6.00

MRMBBL	Becky Lynch	6.00	15.00
MRMBCF	Charlotte Flair	10.00	25.00
MRMBCR	Carmella	5.00	12.00
MRMBDZ	Dolph Ziggler	3.00	8.00
MRMBKO	Kevin Owens	2.50	6.00
MRMBNT	Natalya	3.00	8.00
MRMBSN	Shinsuke Nakamura	4.00	10.00
MRMBSZ	Sami Zayn	2.50	6.00
MRMBTA	Tamina	2.50	6.00

2018 Topps WWE Then Now Forever NXT TakeOver Philadelphia 2018 Mat Relics

*BRONZE/99: .5X TO 1.2X BASIC MEM
*BLUE/50: .6X TO 1.5X BASIC MEM
*SILVER/25: .75X TO 2X BASIC MEM
*GOLD/10: UNPRICED DUE TO SCARCITY
*RED/1: UNPRICED DUE TO SCARCITY

MRPHAA	Andrade Cien Almas	4.00	10.00
MRPHAB	Aleister Black	2.50	6.00
MRPHAC	Adam Cole	3.00	8.00
MRPHBF	Bobby Fish	2.00	5.00
MRPHEM	Ember Moon	3.00	8.00
MRPHJG	Johnny Gargano	2.00	5.00
MRPHKO	Kassius Ohno	3.00	8.00
MRPHOR	Kyle O'Reilly	4.00	10.00
MRPHSB	Shayna Baszler	3.00	8.00
MRPHVD	Velveteen Dream	5.00	12.00

2018 Topps WWE Then Now Forever RAW 25 Mat Relics

*BRONZE/99: .5X TO 1.2X BASIC MEM
*BLUE/50: .6X TO 1.5X BASIC MEM
*SILVER/25: .75X TO 2X BASIC MEM
*GOLD/10: UNPRICED DUE TO SCARCITY
*RED/1: UNPRICED DUE TO SCARCITY

MR25AS	Asuka	5.00	12.00
MR25EL	Elias	2.50	6.00
MR25JC	John Cena	6.00	15.00
MR25RR	Roman Reigns	4.00	10.00
MR25SA	Stone Cold Steve Austin	12.00	30.00
MR25TM	The Miz	3.00	8.00

2018 Topps WWE Then Now Forever Roster Updates

COMPLETE SET (20)		15.00	40.00
RANDOMLY INSERTED INTO PACKS			
R21	Asuka	2.50	6.00
R22	Bobby Roode	1.25	3.00
R23	Chad Gable	.75	2.00
R24	Jinder Mahal	1.00	2.50
R25	Kevin Owens	2.00	5.00
R26	Konnor	.75	2.00
R27	Maria Kanellis	2.00	5.00
R28	Mike Kanellis	2.00	5.00
R29	Natalya	1.00	2.50
R30	Paige	2.00	5.00
R31	R-Truth	1.00	2.50
R32	Samir Singh	.75	2.00
R33	Sarah Logan	.75	2.00
R34	Sonya Deville	1.50	4.00
R35	Sunil Singh	.75	2.00
R36	The Miz	1.50	4.00
R37	Vic Joseph	.75	2.00
R38	Viktor	.75	2.00
R39	Zack Ryder	.75	2.00
R40	Maryse	1.50	4.00

2018 Topps WWE Then Now Forever Royal Rumble 2018 Mat Relics

*BRONZE/199: .5X TO 1.2X BASIC MEM
*BLUE/99: .6X TO 1.5X BASIC MEM
*SILVER/25: .75X TO 2X BASIC MEM
*GOLD/10: UNPRICED DUE TO SCARCITY
*RED/1: UNPRICED DUE TO SCARCITY

MRRRAA	Andrade Cien Almas	2.00	5.00
MRRRAC	Adam Cole	4.00	10.00
MRRRAJ	AJ Styles	6.00	15.00
MRRRAS	Asuka	4.00	10.00
MRRRBE	Big E	2.00	5.00
MRRRBS	Braun Strowman	3.00	8.00
MRRRCE	Cesaro	2.50	6.00
MRRRDZ	Dolph Ziggler	2.50	6.00
MRRREL	Elias	3.00	8.00
MRRRFB	Finn Balor	5.00	12.00
MRRRJC	John Cena	6.00	15.00
MRRRJJ	Jason Jordan	2.50	6.00
MRRRJM	Jinder Mahal	2.00	5.00
MRRRKK	Kofi Kingston	2.50	6.00
MRRRKN	Kane	2.50	6.00
MRRRKO	Kevin Owens	2.00	5.00
MRRRMH	Woken Matt Hardy	2.50	6.00
MRRRNB	Nikki Bella	5.00	12.00
MRRRRO	Randy Orton	4.00	10.00
MRRRRR	Roman Reigns	4.00	10.00
MRRRRS	Rusev	2.50	6.00
MRRRSH	Sheamus	3.00	8.00
MRRRSN	Shinsuke Nakamura	3.00	8.00
MRRRSR	Seth Rollins	4.00	10.00
MRRRSZ	Sami Zayn	2.50	6.00
MRRRTM	The Miz	2.50	6.00
MRRRXW	Xavier Woods	2.50	6.00

2018 Topps WWE Then Now Forever Shirt Relics

*BLUE/99: .5X TO 1.2X BASIC MEM
*SILVER/25: .75X TO 2X BASIC MEM
*GOLD/10: UNPRICED DUE TO SCARCITY
*RED/1: UNPRICED DUE TO SCARCITY

SRAB	Alexa Bliss	8.00	20.00
SRAK	Akam		
SRCG	Chad Gable	1.50	4.00
SRCR	Carmella	3.00	8.00
SRDZ	Dolph Ziggler	1.50	4.00
SRJC	John Cena	4.00	10.00
SRJJ	Jason Jordan	2.00	5.00
SRKA	Karl Anderson		
SRLG	Luke Gallows		
SRNA	Naomi		
SRRZ	Rezar		
SRSR	Seth Rollins		

2018 Topps WWE Then Now Forever Triple Autographs

STATED PRINT RUN 10 SER.#'d SETS
UNPRICED DUE TO SCARCITY

TAABS	Paige/Rose/Deville
TACLB	Styles/Gallows/Anderson
TATRS	Riott/Morgan/Logan
TATWW	O'Neil/Crews/Brooke

2018 Topps WWE Then Now Forever Promo

NYCC2	Alexa Bliss NYCC	4.00	10.00

2016 Topps WWE Then Now Forever Stickers

1	WWE Logo FOIL	.20	.50
2	Raw Logo	.20	.50
3	Smackdown Logo	.20	.50
4	NXT Logo	.20	.50
5	WWE Legends Logo	.20	.50
6	Brock Lesnar FOIL	.60	1.50
7	Brock Lesnar	.60	1.50
8	Brock Lesnar	.60	1.50
9	Brock Lesnar	.60	1.50
10	Brock Lesnar	.60	1.50
11	Neville	.30	.75
12	Neville	.30	.75
13	Neville	.30	.75
14	Neville	.30	.75
15	Neville	.30	.75
16	The New Day FOIL	.30	.75
17	The New Day	.30	.75
18	The New Day	.30	.75
19	The New Day	.30	.75
20	The New Day	.30	.75
21	Dudley Boyz	.12	.30
22	Dudley Boyz	.12	.30
23	D-Von Dudley	.20	.50
24	Bubba Ray Dudley	.25	.60
25	Dudley Boyz	.12	.30
26	Finn Balor FOIL	.40	1.00
27	Finn Balor	.40	1.00
28	Finn Balor	.40	1.00
29	Finn Balor	.40	1.00
30	Finn Balor	.40	1.00
31	Samoa Joe	.30	.75
32	Samoa Joe	.30	.75
33	Samoa Joe	.30	.75
34	Samoa Joe	.30	.75
35	Samoa Joe	.30	.75
36	Apollo Crews	.12	.30
37	Apollo Crews	.12	.30
38	Apollo Crews	.12	.30
39	Apollo Crews	.12	.30
40	Apollo Crews	.12	.30
41	Baron Corbin	.15	.40
42	Baron Corbin	.15	.40
43	Baron Corbin	.15	.40
44	Baron Corbin	.15	.40
45	Baron Corbin	.15	.40
46	John Cena FOIL	.60	1.50
47	John Cena	.60	1.50
48	John Cena	.60	1.50
49	John Cena	.60	1.50
50	John Cena	.60	1.50
51	Seth Rollins	.20	.50
52	Seth Rollins	.20	.50
53	Seth Rollins	.20	.50
54	Seth Rollins	.20	.50
55	Seth Rollins	.20	.50
56	Roman Reigns FOIL	.40	1.00
57	Roman Reigns	.40	1.00
58	Roman Reigns	.40	1.00
59	Roman Reigns	.40	1.00
60	Roman Reigns	.40	1.00
61	Dean Ambrose FOIL	.40	1.00
62	Dean Ambrose	.40	1.00
63	Dean Ambrose	.40	1.00
64	Dean Ambrose	.40	1.00
65	Dean Ambrose	.40	1.00
66	The Wyatt Family FOIL	.50	1.25
67	Bray Wyatt	.50	1.25
68	Braun Strowman	.15	.40
69	Luke Harper	.12	.30
70	Erick Rowan	.12	.30
71	Kalisto FOIL	.30	.75
72	Kalisto	.30	.75
73	Kalisto	.30	.75
74	Kalisto	.30	.75
75	Kalisto	.30	.75
76	Bret Hart FOIL	.30	.75
77	Bret Hart	.30	.75
78	Bret Hart	.30	.75
79	Bret Hart	.30	.75
80	Bret Hart	.30	.75
81	Edge FOIL	.30	.75
82	Edge	.30	.75
83	Edge	.30	.75
84	Edge	.30	.75
85	Edge	.30	.75
86	Sting	.30	.75
87	Sting	.30	.75
88	Sting	.30	.75
89	Sting	.30	.75
90	Sting	.30	.75
91	Shawn Michaels FOIL	.50	1.25
92	Shawn Michaels	.50	1.25
93	Shawn Michaels	.50	1.25
94	Shawn Michaels	.50	1.25
95	Shawn Michaels	.50	1.25
96	Charlotte FOIL	.40	1.00
97	Alicia Fox	.20	.50
98	Becky Lynch	.40	1.00
99	Brie Bella	.25	.60
100	Lana	.50	1.25
101	Nikki Bella FOIL	.40	1.00
102	Natalya	.20	.50
103	Paige	.40	1.00
104	Sasha Banks	.40	1.00
105	Summer Rae	.30	.75
106	Naomi	.20	.50
107	Bayley FOIL	.30	.75
108	Alexa Bliss	.60	1.50
109	Asuka	.50	1.25
110	Billie Kay	.30	.75
111	Carmella	.30	.75
112	Eva Marie FOIL	.25	.60
113	Dana Brooke	.30	.75
114	Emma	.25	.60
115	Nia Jax	.20	.50
116	Peyton Royce	.30	.75
117	Dasha Fuentes	.12	.30
118	Randy Orton FOIL	.30	.75
119	Randy Orton	.30	.75
120	Randy Orton	.30	.75
121	Randy Orton	.30	.75
122	Randy Orton	.30	.75
123	Daniel Bryan FOIL	.50	1.25
124	Daniel Bryan	.50	1.25
125	Daniel Bryan	.50	1.25
126	Daniel Bryan	.50	1.25
127	Daniel Bryan	.50	1.25
128	Ryback FOIL	.15	.40
129	Ryback	.15	.40
130	Ryback	.15	.40
131	Ryback	.15	.40
132	Ryback	.15	.40
133	Dolph Ziggler FOIL	.15	.40
134	Dolph Ziggler	.15	.40
135	Dolph Ziggler	.15	.40
136	Dolph Ziggler	.15	.40
137	Dolph Ziggler	.15	.40
138	Chris Jericho	.30	.75
139	Shawn Michaels	.50	1.25
140	Steve Austin/Beer Truck	.60	1.50
141	Samoa Joe	.30	.75
142	no info		
143	Randy Orton	.30	.75
144	Bayley/Sasha Banks	.40	1.00
145	Bray Wyatt	.50	1.25
146	no info		
147	The Rock	.60	1.50
148	Ric Flair	.50	1.25
149	Daniel Bryan	.50	1.25
150	Brock Lesnar	.60	1.50
151	Kevin Owens	.30	.75
152	Finn Balor	.40	1.00
153	Bret Hart	.30	.75
154	The Rock/John Cena	.60	1.50
155	The Bellas	.40	1.00
156	Seth Rollins		
157	no info		
158	Ultimate Warrior	.30	.75
159	Roman Reigns	.40	1.00
160	League of Nations FOIL	.30	.75
161	Alberto Del Rio	.20	.50
162	Sheamus	.30	.75
163	Wade Barrett	.20	
164	Rusev	.30	.75
165	Kane FOIL	.20	.50
166	Kane	.20	.50
167	Kane	.20	.50
168	Kane	.20	.50
169	Kane	.20	.50
170	Kevin Owens FOIL	.30	.75
171	Kevin Owens	.30	.75
172	Kevin Owens	.30	.75
173	Kevin Owens	.30	.75
174	Kevin Owens	.30	.75
175	Chris Jericho FOIL	.30	.75
176	Chris Jericho	.30	.75
177	Chris Jericho	.30	.75
178	Chris Jericho	.30	.75
179	Chris Jericho	.30	.75
180	Dash/Dawson	.15	.40
181	Dash/Dawson	.15	.40
182	Dash/Dawson	.15	.40
183	Dash/Dawson	.15	.40
184	Dash/Dawson	.15	.40
185	Blake/Murphy FOIL	.12	.30
186	Murphy	.12	.30
187	Blake	.12	.30
188	Alexa Bliss/Murphy/Blake	.60	1.50
189	Blake	.12	.30
190	Enzo Amore	.25	.60
191	Enzo Amore	.25	.60
192	Enzo Amore	.25	.60
193	Enzo Amore	.25	.60
194	Enzo Amore	.25	.60
195	Colin Cassady FOIL	.25	.60
196	Colin Cassady	.25	.60
197	Colin Cassady	.25	.60
198	Colin Cassady	.25	.60
199	Colin Cassady	.25	.60
200	Eddie Guerrero FOIL	.30	.75
201	Eddie Guerrero	.30	.75
202	Eddie Guerrero	.30	.75
203	Eddie Guerrero	.30	.75
204	Eddie Guerrero	.30	.75
205	Stone Cold Steve Austin FOIL	.60	1.50
206	Stone Cold Steve Austin	.60	1.50
207	Stone Cold Steve Austin	.60	1.50
208	Stone Cold Steve Austin	.60	1.50
209	Stone Cold Steve Austin	.60	1.50
210	Razor Ramon	.30	.75
211	Razor Ramon	.30	.75
212	Razor Ramon	.30	.75
213	Razor Ramon	.30	.75
214	Razor Ramon	.30	.75
215	Ultimate Warrior FOIL	.30	.75
216	Ultimate Warrior	.30	.75
217	Ultimate Warrior	.30	.75
218	Ultimate Warrior	.30	.75
219	Ultimate Warrior	.30	.75
220	The Usos FOIL	.12	.30
221	The Usos	.12	.30
222	The Usos	.12	.30
223	The Usos	.12	.30
224	The Usos	.12	.30
225	Cesaro	.25	.60
226	Cesaro	.25	.60
227	Cesaro	.25	.60
228	Cesaro	.25	.60
229	Cesaro	.25	.60
230	The Rock FOIL	.60	1.50
231	The Rock	.60	1.50
232	The Rock	.60	1.50
233	The Rock/John Cena	.60	1.50
234	The Rock	.60	1.50
235	Undertaker FOIL	.50	1.25
236	Undertaker	.50	1.25
237	Undertaker	.50	1.25
238	Undertaker	.50	1.25
239	Undertaker	.50	1.25
240	Brock Lesnar	.60	1.50
241	Kalisto	.30	.75
242	Brock Lesnar/Undertaker	.60	1.50
243	Sting	.30	.75
244	Seth Rollins	.20	.50

2020-21 Topps WWE This Month in History

COMPLETE SET
DEC.'20 PRINT RUN SETS
JAN.'21 PRINT RUN SETS

1	Jeff Hardy/95*
2	Evolution/85*
3	Boogeyman/85*
4	Trish Stratus/188*
5	Wade Barrett/78*
6	Sgt. Slaughter/89*
7	Eddie Guerrero/
8	Daniel Bryan/
9	Andre the Giant/

2020 Topps WWE 3:16 Day

	COMPLETE SET (6)	15.00	40.00
	STATED PRINT RUN 137 SETS		
1	Stone Cold Steve Austin	4.00	10.00
2	Stone Cold Steve Austin	4.00	10.00
3	Stone Cold Steve Austin	4.00	10.00
4	Stone Cold Steve Austin	4.00	10.00
5	Stone Cold Steve Austin	4.00	10.00
6	Stone Cold Steve Austin	6.00	15.00

2019 Topps WWE Transcendent

*BLUE/15: UNPRICED DUE TO SCARCITY
*PURPLE/10: UNPRICED DUE TO SCARCITY
*BLACK/5: UNPRICED DUE TO SCARCITY
*GOLD/1: UNPRICED DUE TO SCARCITY
*RED/1: UNPRICED DUE TO SCARCITY
STATED PRINT RUN 25 SER.#'d SETS

AAB	Alexa Bliss	150.00	300.00
AAC	Adam Cole	50.00	100.00
AAJ	AJ Styles	75.00	150.00
AAL	Aleister Black	50.00	100.00
AAS	Asuka	100.00	200.00
ABB	Brie Bella	30.00	75.00
ABE	Becky Lynch	75.00	150.00
ABH	Bret Hit Man Hart	60.00	120.00
ABK	Billie Kay	30.00	75.00
ABL	Brock Lesnar	50.00	100.00
ABO	Bobby Lashley	25.00	60.00
ABR	Bobby Roode	20.00	50.00
ABS	Braun Strowman	30.00	75.00
ABY	Bayley	50.00	100.00
ACA	Carmella	30.00	75.00
ACF	Charlotte Flair	100.00	200.00
ACJ	Chris Jericho	60.00	120.00
ADA	Dean Ambrose	30.00	75.00
ADB	Daniel Bryan	50.00	100.00
AEL	Elias	15.00	40.00
AFB	Finn Balor	20.00	50.00
AJC	John Cena	100.00	200.00
AJG	Johnny Gargano	30.00	75.00
AKO	Kevin Owens	15.00	40.00
ALL	Lex Luger	25.00	60.00
ALV	Liv Morgan	75.00	150.00
AMA	Maryse	20.00	50.00
AMJ	Mickie James	30.00	75.00
AMM	Mr. McMahon	500.00	1000.00
AMR	Mandy Rose	60.00	120.00
ANA	Naomi	15.00	40.00
ANB	Nikki Bella	50.00	100.00
ANT	Natalya	25.00	60.00
APG	Paige	100.00	200.00
APR	Peyton Royce	75.00	150.00
ARD	Ricky The Dragon Steamboat	20.00	50.00
ARO	Randy Orton	30.00	75.00
ASA	Stone Cold Steve Austin	225.00	450.00
ASB	Sasha Banks	75.00	150.00
ASH	Shane McMahon	200.00	400.00
ASJ	Samoa Joe	15.00	40.00
ASM	Stephanie McMahon	100.00	200.00
ASN	Shinsuke Nakamura	25.00	60.00
ASR	Seth Rollins	20.00	50.00
AST	Sting	60.00	120.00
ASW	Shawn Michaels	100.00	200.00
ATH	Triple H	150.00	300.00
ATS	Trish Stratus	75.00	150.00
AUN	Undertaker	175.00	350.00
ARRR	Ronda Rousey	200.00	400.00

2019 Topps WWE Transcendent Autographed Championship Titles

NNO Dean Ambrose
NNO Jeff Hardy
NNO Randy Orton
NNO Rey Mysterio
NNO Seth Rollins

2019 Topps WWE Transcendent Autographed Kiss

*BLACK/5: UNPRICED DUE TO SCARCITY
*GOLD/1: UNPRICED DUE TO SCARCITY
*RED/1: UNPRICED DUE TO SCARCITY
STATED PRINT RUN 10 SER.#'d SETS
UNPRICED DUE TO SCARCITY

KAS Asuka
KBB Brie Bella
KNB Nikki Bella
KPR Peyton Royce

2019 Topps WWE Transcendent Autographed Sketches

STATED PRINT RUN 1 SER.#'d SET
UNPRICED DUE TO SCARCITY

1 Adam Cole
2 AJ Styles
3 Aleister Black
4 Alexa Bliss
5 Asuka
6 Bayley
7 Becky Lynch
8 Billie Kay
9 Bobby Lashley
10 Bobby Roode
11 Braun Strowman
12 Bray Wyatt
13 Bret Hart
14 Brie Bella
15 Charlotte Flair
16 Daniel Bryan
17 Dean Ambrose
18 Dolph Ziggler
19 Drew McIntyre
20 Elias
21 Ember Moon
22 Finn Balor
23 Jeff Hardy
24 John Cena
25 Johnny Gargano
26 Kairi Sane
27 Kane
28 Kevin Owens
29 Kofi Kingston
30 Matt Hardy
31 Naomi
32 Nikki Bella
33 Randy Orton
34 Ric Flair
35 Ricochet
36 Roman Reigns
37 Ronda Rousey
38 Samoa Joe
39 Sasha Banks
40 Seth Rollins
41 Shawn Michaels
42 Shinsuke Nakamura
43 Sting
44 Stone Cold Steve Austin
45 The Miz
46 The Rock
47 Tommaso Ciampa
48 Triple H
49 Trish Stratus
50 Undertaker

2019 Topps WWE Transcendent Oversized Tribute Cut Signatures

STATED PRINT RUN 1 SER.#'d SET
UNPRICED DUE TO SCARCITY

CAG Andre The Giant
CBH Bobby Heenan
CBS Bruno Sammartino
CCH Mr. Perfect
CDR Dusty Rhodes
CEG Eddie Guerrero
CFB Freddie Blassie
CGM Gorilla Monsoon
CGS George Steele
CJN Jim The Anvil Neidhart
CJS Chief Jay Strongbow
CKV Kerry Von Erich
CME Miss Elizabeth
CMY Mae Young
CPB Paul Bearer
CRR Ravishing Rick Rude
CRS Macho Man Randy Savage
CSM Sherri Martel
CUG Umaga
CUM Ultimate Warrior
CYK Yokozuna
CBBB Bam Bam Bigelow
CBJS Big John Studd
CBVV Vader
CJYD Junkyard Dog
CRRR Rowdy Roddy Piper

2019 Topps WWE Transcendent Oversized Tribute Dual Cut Signatures

STATED PRINT RUN 1 SER.#'d SET
UNPRICED DUE TO SCARCITY

DCAB Andre the Giant/B.Heenan
DCBC P. Bearer/Vader
DCDS G.Steele/Junkyard Dog
DCEM Elizabeth/S.Martel
DCES G.Steele/Elizabeth
DCHH Mr. Perfect/B.Heenan
DCPE K.Von Erich/R.Piper
DCPG E.Guerrero/R.Piper
DCPW Warrior/R.Piper
DCRE D.Rhodes/Elizabeth
DCRS R.Savage/S.Martel
DCSB G.Steele/F.Blassie
DCSE R.Savage/Elizabeth
DCSH B.Heenan/J.Studd
DCSN J.Neidhart/R.Savage
DCSR B.Sammartino/R.Piper
DCSS B.Sammartino/J.Strongbow
DCSW Warrior/R.Savage
DCVB B.Bigelow/Vader
DCVM Vader/R.Savage
DCYU Umaga/Yokozuna
DCYV Vader/Yokozuna
DCNWO1 C.Hennig/D.Rhodes
DCNWO2 R.Savage/C.Hennig

2019 Topps WWE Transcendent VIP Party Autographs

B1	Big Show	15.00	40.00
B2	Big Show	15.00	40.00
F1	Ric Flair	75.00	150.00
F2	Ric Flair	75.00	150.00
S1	Sting	50.00	100.00
S2	Sting	50.00	100.00

2019 Topps WWE Transcendent VIP Party Dual Autograph

NNO	Stephanie McMahon/Triple H	225.00	450.00

2020 Topps WWE Transcendent

COMPLETE SET (50)   500.00   750.00
STATED PRINT RUN 50 SER.#'d SETS

1	Adam Cole	15.00	40.00
2	Andre the Giant	30.00	75.00
3	Angelo Dawkins	6.00	15.00
4	Bianca Belair	15.00	40.00
5	Big Show	8.00	20.00
6	Bruno Sammartino	15.00	40.00
7	Cain Velasquez	6.00	15.00
8	Cameron Grimes	6.00	15.00
9	Candice LeRae	20.00	50.00
10	Chyna	15.00	40.00
11	Damian Priest	6.00	15.00
12	Dusty Rhodes	12.00	30.00
13	Eddie Guerrero	15.00	40.00
14	Harley Race	10.00	25.00
15	Hulk Hogan	20.00	50.00
16	Io Shirai	10.00	25.00
17	Jim The Anvil Neidhart	8.00	20.00
18	John Cena	25.00	60.00
19	John Morrison	6.00	15.00
20	Johnny Gargano	12.00	30.00
21	Keith Lee	6.00	15.00
22	Kevin Nash	10.00	25.00
23	Lana	15.00	40.00
24	Lio Rush	6.00	15.00
25	Macho Man Randy Savage	20.00	50.00
26	Mandy Rose	30.00	80.00
27	Mr. Perfect Curt Hennig	10.00	25.00
28	Montez Ford	6.00	15.00
29	Mustafa Ali	10.00	25.00
30	Naomi	12.00	30.00
31	Natalya	10.00	25.00
32	Nikki Cross	12.00	30.00
33	Paul Heyman	6.00	15.00
34	Ravishing Rick Rude	8.00	20.00
35	Renee Young	8.00	20.00
36	Rhea Ripley	15.00	40.00
37	Robert Roode	6.00	15.00
38	Roderick Strong	12.00	30.00
39	Rowdy Roddy Piper	15.00	40.00
40	Rusev	8.00	20.00
41	Scott Hall	10.00	25.00
42	Shorty G	6.00	15.00
43	Sting	20.00	50.00
44	Sonya Deville	15.00	40.00
45	The British Bulldog	10.00	25.00
46	The Rock	30.00	80.00
47	Ultimate Warrior	30.00	75.00
48	Undertaker	25.00	60.00
49	Vader	10.00	25.00
50	Yokozuna	10.00	25.00

2020 Topps WWE Transcendent Autographed Replica Championship Side Plates

UNPRICED DUE TO SCARCITY

NNO AJ Styles
NNO Becky Lynch

NNO Charlotte Flair
NNO Daniel Bryan
NNO Kofi Kingston
NNO Randy Orton
NNO Roman Reigns
NNO Seth Rollins
NNO Triple H

2020 Topps WWE Transcendent Autographs

*GREEN/15: UNPRICED DUE TO SCARCITY
*PURPLE/10: UNPRICED DUE TO SCARCITY
*BLUE/5: UNPRICED DUE TO SCARCITY
*RED/1: UNPRICED DUE TO SCARCITY

AAA	Andrade	25.00	60.00
AAB	Aleister Black	30.00	75.00
AAJ	AJ Styles	60.00	120.00
AAK	Asuka	100.00	200.00
AAX	Alexa Bliss	150.00	300.00
ABC	King Corbin	25.00	60.00
ABD	Diesel	30.00	75.00
ABH	Bret Hit Man Hart	75.00	150.00
ABI	Brock Lesnar	125.00	250.00
ABL	Becky Lynch	75.00	150.00
ABR	Braun Strowman	50.00	100.00
ABT	Booker T	30.00	75.00
ABW	The Fiend Bray Wyatt	100.00	200.00
ABY	Bayley	50.00	100.00
ACF	Charlotte Flair	100.00	200.00
ACW	Sheamus	25.00	60.00
ADB	Daniel Bryan	50.00	100.00
ADR	Drew McIntyre	60.00	120.00
AFB	Finn Balor	50.00	100.00
AGB	Goldberg	75.00	150.00
AHH	Hulk Hogan	250.00	500.00
AJH	Jeff Hardy	60.00	120.00
AKA	Kurt Angle	50.00	100.00
AKK	Kofi Kingston	60.00	120.00
AKN	Kane	50.00	100.00
AKO	Kevin Owens	50.00	100.00
AKS	Kairi Sane	75.00	150.00
ALE	Lacey Evans	60.00	120.00
ALT	Lita	75.00	150.00
AMF	Mick Foley	30.00	75.00
AMR	Matt Riddle	60.00	120.00
AQS	Shayna Baszler	50.00	100.00
ARC	Ricochet	25.00	60.00
ARO	Randy Orton	60.00	120.00
ARR	Roman Reigns	75.00	150.00
ASB	Sasha Banks	125.00	250.00
ASC	Stone Cold Steve Austin	350.00	700.00
ASM	Shane McMahon	125.00	250.00
ASN	Shinsuke Nakamura	30.00	75.00
ASR	Seth Rollins	50.00	100.00
AST	Stephanie McMahon	250.00	400.00
ATC	Tommaso Ciampa	50.00	100.00
ATM	The Miz	30.00	75.00
AUT	Undertaker	300.00	500.00
AZV	Zelina Vega	60.00	120.00
AHBK	Shawn Michaels	125.00	250.00
AHHH	Triple H	250.00	400.00
AVKM	Mr. McMahon	600.00	1000.00

2020 Topps WWE Transcendent Bat Relic Autographs

RCST	Sting	250.00	400.00

2020 Topps WWE Transcendent Dual Autographs

*GREEN/15: UNPRICED DUE TO SCARCITY
*PURPLE/10: UNPRICED DUE TO SCARCITY
*BLUE/5: UNPRICED DUE TO SCARCITY
*RED/1: UNPRICED DUE TO SCARCITY
STATED PRINT RUN 25 SER.#'d SETS

DAVR	Erik/Ivar	75.00	150.00
DAUSO	Jimmy Uso/Jey Uso	75.00	150.00

2020 Topps WWE Transcendent Image Variation Autographs

STATED PRINT RUN 1 SER.#'d SET
UNPRICED DUE TO SCARCITY

AIVAA Andrade
AIVAB Aleister Black
AIVAJ AJ Styles
AIVAK Asuka
AIVAX Alexa Bliss
AIVBC King Corbin
AIVBD Diesel
AIVBH Bret Hit Man Hart
AIVBI Brock Lesnar
AIVBL Becky Lynch
AIVBR Braun Strowman
AIVBT Booker T
AIVBW Bray Wyatt
AIVBY Bayley
AIVCF Charlotte Flair
AIVCW Sheamus
AIVDB Daniel Bryan
AIVDR Drew McIntyre
AIVFB Finn Balor
AIVGB Goldberg
AIVHH Hulk Hogan
AIVJH Jeff Hardy
AIVKA Kurt Angle
AIVKK Kofi Kingston
AIVKN Kane
AIVKO Kevin Owens
AIVKS Kairi Sane
AIVLE Lacey Evans
AIVLT Lita
AIVMF Mick Foley
AIVMR Matt Riddle
AIVQS Shayna Baszler
AIVRC Ricochet
AIVRO Randy Orton
AIVRR Roman Reigns
AIVSB Sasha Banks
AIVSC Stone Cold Steve Austin
AIVSJ Samoa Joe
AIVSM Shane McMahon
AIVSN Shinsuke Nakamura
AIVSR Seth Rollins
AIVST Stephanie McMahon
AIVTC Tommaso Ciampa
AIVTM The Miz
AIVUT Undertaker
AIVZV Zelina Vega
AIVHBK Shawn Michaels
AIVHHH Triple H
AIVVKM Mr. McMahon

2020 Topps WWE Transcendent Image Variation Dual Autographs

STATED PRINT RUN 1 SER.#'d SET

UNPRICED DUE TO SCARCITY
DAIVVR Erik/Ivar
DAIVUSO Jimmy Uso/Jey Uso

2020 Topps WWE Transcendent John Cena Superstar Tribute

COMPLETE SET (50)		250.00	500.00
JCRP1	John Cena	10.00	25.00
JCRP2	John Cena	10.00	25.00
JCRP3	John Cena	10.00	25.00
JCRP4	John Cena	10.00	25.00
JCRP5	John Cena	10.00	25.00
JCRP6	John Cena	10.00	25.00
JCRP7	John Cena	10.00	25.00
JCRP8	John Cena	10.00	25.00
JCRP9	John Cena	10.00	25.00
JCRP10	John Cena	10.00	25.00
JCRP11	John Cena	10.00	25.00
JCRP12	John Cena	10.00	25.00
JCRP13	John Cena	10.00	25.00
JCRP14	John Cena	10.00	25.00
JCRP15	John Cena	10.00	25.00
JCRP16	John Cena	10.00	25.00
JCRP17	John Cena	10.00	25.00
JCRP18	John Cena	10.00	25.00
JCRP19	John Cena	10.00	25.00
JCRP20	John Cena	10.00	25.00
JCRP21	John Cena	10.00	25.00
JCRP22	John Cena	10.00	25.00
JCRP23	John Cena	10.00	25.00
JCRP24	John Cena	10.00	25.00
JCRP25	John Cena	10.00	25.00
JCRP26	John Cena	10.00	25.00
JCRP27	John Cena	10.00	25.00
JCRP28	John Cena	10.00	25.00
JCRP29	John Cena	10.00	25.00
JCRP30	John Cena	10.00	25.00
JCRP31	John Cena	10.00	25.00
JCRP32	John Cena	10.00	25.00
JCRP33	John Cena	10.00	25.00
JCRP34	John Cena	10.00	25.00
JCRP35	John Cena	10.00	25.00
JCRP36	John Cena	10.00	25.00
JCRP37	John Cena	10.00	25.00
JCRP38	John Cena	10.00	25.00
JCRP39	John Cena	10.00	25.00
JCRP40	John Cena	10.00	25.00
JCRP41	John Cena	10.00	25.00
JCRP42	John Cena	10.00	25.00
JCRP43	John Cena	10.00	25.00
JCRP44	John Cena	10.00	
25.00xxxxxxxxxx			
JCRP45	John Cena	10.00	25.00
JCRP46	John Cena	10.00	25.00
JCRP47	John Cena	10.00	25.00
JCRP48	1John Cena	10.00	25.00
JCRP49	John Cena	10.00	25.00
JCRP50	John Cena	10.00	25.00

2020 Topps WWE Transcendent John Cena Superstar Tribute Autographs

STATED PRINT RUN 1 SER.#'d SET
UNPRICED DUE TO SCARCITY

2020 Topps WWE Transcendent Sketches

STATED PRINT RUN 1 SER.#'d SET
UNPRICED DUE TO SCARCITY
ART BY DAN BERGREN

NNO AJ Styles
NNO Alexa Bliss
NNO Andrade
NNO Angel Garza
NNO Asuka
NNO Batista
NNO Bayley
NNO Becky Lynch
NNO Braun Strowman
NNO The Fiend Bray Wyatt
NNO Bret Hit Man Hart
NNO Brock Lesnar
NNO Charlotte Flair
NNO Eddie Guerrero
NNO Ember Moon
NNO Finn Balor
NNO Goldberg
NNO Hulk Hogan
NNO Jeff Hardy
NNO John Cena
NNO Kairi Sane
NNO Kane
NNO Keith Lee
NNO Kevin Owens
NNO Kofi Kingston
NNO Lacey Evans
NNO Lita
NNO Matt Riddle
NNO Mustafa Ali
NNO Pete Dunne
NNO Randy Orton
NNO Macho Man Randy Savage
NNO Ricochet
NNO Rowdy Roddy Piper
NNO Roman Reigns
NNO Ronda Rousey
NNO Sami Zayn
NNO Samoa Joe
NNO Sasha Banks
NNO Seth Rollins
NNO Shawn Michaels
NNO Shayna Baszler
NNO Shinsuke Nakamura
NNO Sting
NNO Stone Cold Steve Austin
NNO The Miz
NNO The Rock
NNO Triple H
NNO Ultimate Warrior
NNO Undertaker

2016 Topps WWE Triple H Tribute

This was a continuation series across four different products in 2016. 10-Card sets were inserted in the following products: Topps WWE Road to WrestleMania (1-10), Topps WWE (11-20), Topps Heritage WWE (21-30), and Topps WWE Then Now Forever (31-40).

COMPLETE SET (10)		12.00	30.00
TARGET EXCLUSIVES			
1	Triple H	.50	1.25

2 Triple H	.50	1.25
3 Triple H	.50	1.25
4 Triple H	.50	1.25
5 Triple H	.50	1.25
6 Triple H	1.25	3.00
7 Triple H	1.50	4.00
8 Triple H	1.25	3.00
9 Triple H	1.25	3.00
10 Triple H	1.25	3.00
11 Triple H	.50	1.25
12 Triple H	.50	1.25
13 Triple H	.50	1.25
14 Triple H	.50	1.25
15 Triple H	.50	1.25
16 Triple H	1.25	3.00
17 Triple H	1.25	3.00
18 Triple H	1.25	3.00
19 Triple H	1.25	3.00
20 Triple H	1.25	3.00
21 Triple H	.50	1.25
22 Triple H	.50	1.25
23 Triple H	.50	1.25
24 Triple H	.50	1.25
25 Triple H	.50	1.25
26 Triple H	1.25	3.00
27 Triple H	1.25	3.00
28 Triple H	1.25	3.00
29 Triple H	1.25	3.00
30 Triple H	1.25	3.00
31 Triple H	.50	1.25
32 Triple H	.50	1.25
33 Triple H	.50	1.25
34 Triple H	.50	1.25
35 Triple H	.50	1.25
36 Triple H	1.25	3.00
37 Triple H	1.25	3.00
38 Triple H	1.25	3.00
39 Triple H	1.25	3.00
40 Triple H	1.25	3.00

2020 Topps WWE Triple H 25th Anniversary

COMPLETE SET (25)

1 Triple H
2 Triple H
3 Triple H
4 Triple H
5 Triple H
6 Triple H
7 Triple H
8 Triple H
9 Triple H
10 Triple H
11 Triple H
12 Triple H
13 Triple H
14 Triple H
15 Triple H
16 Triple H
17 Triple H
18 Triple H
19 Triple H

20 Triple H
21 Triple H
22 Triple H
23 Triple H
24 Triple H
25 Triple H

2020 Topps WWE Triple H 25th Anniversary Autographs

COMMON AUTO (1A-5A)
*GREEN/9: UNPRICED DUE TO SCARCITY
*GOLD/1: UNPRICED DUE TO SCARCITY
STATED OVERALL ODDS 1:2 W/RELICS
STATED PRINT RUN 99 SER.#'d SETS

1A Triple H
2A Triple H
3A Triple H
4A Triple H
5A Triple H

2020 Topps WWE Triple H 25th Anniversary Cerebral Moments

COMPLETE SET (11)
STATED PRINT RUN 460 SETS

C1 Triple H
C2 Triple H
C3 Triple H
C4 Triple H
C5 Triple H
C6 Triple H
C7 Triple H
C8 Triple H
C9 Triple H
C10 Triple H
C11 Triple H
C12 Triple H

2020 Topps WWE Triple H 25th Anniversary Relics

STATED OVERALL ODDS 1:2 W/AUTOGRAPHS
STATED PRINT RUN 15 SER.#'d SETS
UNPRICED DUE TO SCARCITY

1R Triple H
2R Triple H
3R Triple H
4R Triple H
5R Triple H

2020 Topps WWE Triple H 25th Anniversary World Title Victories

COMPLETE SET (14)
STATED PRINT RUN 460 SETS

T1 Triple H
T2 Triple H
T3 Triple H
T4 Triple H
T5 Triple H
T6 Triple H
T7 Triple H
T8 Triple H

T9 Triple H
T10 Triple H
T11 Triple H
T12 Triple H
T13 Triple H

2017 Topps WWE Ultimate Collection Stickers

1 General managers
2 General managers
3 General managers
4 General managers
5 General managers
6 Enzo Amore & Big Cass
7 Enzo Amore & Big Cass
8 Enzo Amore & Big Cass
9 Enzo Amore & Big Cass
10 Enzo Amore & Big Cass
11 American Alpha
12 American Alpha
13 American Alpha
14 American Alpha
15 American Alpha
16 AJ Styles
17 AJ Styles
18 AJ Styles
19 AJ Styles
20 AJ Styles
21 Finn Balor
22 Finn Balor
23 Finn Balor
24 Finn Balor
25 Finn Balor
26 Austin Aries
27 Austin Aries
28 Austin Aries
29 Austin Aries
30 Austin Aries
31 Bobby Roode
32 Bobby Roode
33 Bobby Roode
34 Bobby Roode
35 Bobby Roode
36 Braun Strowman
37 Braun Strowman
38 Braun Strowman
39 Braun Strowman
40 Braun Strowman
41 Baron Corbin
42 Baron Corbin
43 Baron Corbin
44 Baron Corbin
45 Baron Corbin
46 Chris Jericho
47 Chris Jericho
48 Chris Jericho
49 Chris Jericho
50 Chris Jericho
51 Randy Orton
52 Randy Orton
53 Randy Orton
54 Randy Orton
55 Randy Orton

56 Tye Dillinger
57 Tye Dillinger
58 Tye Dillinger
59 Tye Dillinger
60 Tye Dillinger
61 No Way Jose
62 No Way Jose
63 No Way Jose
64 No Way Jose
65 No Way Jose
66 Brock Lesnar
67 Brock Lesnar
68 Brock Lesnar
69 Brock Lesnar
70 Brock Lesnar
71 Dean Ambrose
72 Dean Ambrose
73 Dean Ambrose
74 Dean Ambrose
75 Dean Ambrose
76 Kevin Owens
77 Kevin Owens
78 Kevin Owens
79 Kevin Owens
80 Kevin Owens
81 Bray Wyatt
82 Bray Wyatt
83 Bray Wyatt
84 Bray Wyatt
85 Bray Wyatt
86 Samoa Joe
87 Samoa Joe
88 Samoa Joe
89 Samoa Joe
90 Samoa Joe
91 Shinsuke Nakamura
92 Shinsuke Nakamura
93 Shinsuke Nakamura
94 Shinsuke Nakamura
95 Shinsuke Nakamura
96 Women's Division
97 Women's Division
98 Women's Division
99 Women's Division
100 Women's Division
101 Women's Division
102 Women's Division
103 Women's Division
104 Women's Division
105 Women's Division
106 Women's Division
107 Women's Division
108 Women's Division
109 Women's Division

2008 Topps WWE Ultimate Rivals

COMPLETE SET (90)	8.00	20.00
UNOPENED BOX (24 PACKS)		
UNOPENED PACK (7 CARDS)		
1 Kane vs. Chavo Guerrero	.40	1.00
2 Batista vs. Mark Henry	.40	1.00
3 Batisita vs. The Great Khali	.40	1.00
4 Batista vs. Undertaker	.50	1.25
5 Big Daddy V vs. Boogeyman	.15	.40
6 Kendrick/London vs. Regal/Taylor	.25	.60
7 Chris Jericho vs. JBL	.25	.60
8 CM Punk vs. John Morrison	.10	.25
9 CM Punk vs. Mike Knox	.10	.25
10 CM Punk vs. Shannon Moore	.10	.25
11 C.Rhodes vs. Hardcore Holly	.15	.40
12 D-Generation X vs. Rated RKO	.25	.60
13 Elijah Burke vs. CM Punk	.10	.25
14 Finlay vs. Rey Mysterio	.25	.60
15 Finlay vs. JBL	.15	.40
16 Jamie Noble vs. The Hurricane	.12	.30
17 Jamie Noble vs. Hornswoggle	.15	.40
18 Jeff Hardy vs. John Morrison	.40	1.00
19 Jeff Hardy vs. Umaga	.40	1.00
20 John Cena vs. Carlito	.60	1.50
21 John Cena vs. Edge	.60	1.50
22 John Cena vs. Randy Orton	.60	1.50
23 Kane vs. MVP	.40	1.00
24 Kane vs. Snitsky	.40	1.00
25 Umaga vs. Kane	.40	1.00
26 Kane vs. Undertaker	.50	1.25
27 K.Dykstra vs. Chuck Palumbo	.15	.40
28 K.Dykstra vs. Shawn Michaels	.60	1.50
29 Cade/Murdoch vs. Rhodes/Holly	.15	.40
30 Deuce/Domino vs. London/Kendrick	.15	.40
31 Matt Hardy vs. Edge	.40	1.00
32 Matt Hardy vs. MVP	.40	1.00
33 T.Dreamer vs. Matt Striker	.10	.25
34 Mr. Kennedy vs. Undertaker	.50	1.25
35 Big Show vs. John Cena	.60	1.50
36 R.Mysterio vs. Chavo Guerrero	.25	.60
37 Rey Mysterio vs. MVP	.25	.60
38 Ric Flair vs. Carlito	.40	1.00
39 S.Marella vs. Steve Austin	.60	1.50
40 Shawn Michaels vs. Undertaker	.60	1.50
41 Funaki vs. Val Venis	.10	.25
42 Steve Austin vs. Mr. McMahon	.60	1.50
43 Kevin Thorn vs. Stevie Richards	.15	.40
44 Tommy Dreamer vs. Mick Foley	.50	1.25
45 Triple H vs. Batista	.60	1.50
46 Triple H vs. Mick Foley	.60	1.50
47 Randy Orton vs. Triple H	.60	1.50
48 Triple H vs. Umaga	.60	1.50
49 Shane McMahon vs. Mr. McMahon	.25	.60
50 Randy Orton vs. Jeff Hardy	.40	1.00
51 Steve Austin vs. Brian Pillman	.60	1.50
52 S.Michaels vs. British Bulldog	.60	1.50
53 Chris Jericho vs. Dean Malenko	.25	.60
54 Big Show vs. Undertaker	.50	1.25
55 Randy Orton vs. Dusty Rhodes	.25	.60
56 Shane McMahon vs. Chris Jericho	.25	.60
57 Jerry Lawler vs. Tazz	.25	.60
58 Ric Flair vs. Terry Funk	.40	1.00
59 Paul Bearer vs. Undertaker	.50	1.25
60 Rey Mysterio vs. JBL	.25	.60
61 Arn Anderson vs. Ric Flair	.40	1.00
62 Ric Flair vs. Mr.Perfect	.40	1.00
63 Ric Flair vs. Dusty Rhodes	.40	1.00
64 Kama Mustafa vs. Undertaker	.50	1.25
65 Santino Marella vs. Maria	.40	1.00
66 Mickie James vs. Melina	.60	1.50
67 Candice Michelle vs. Beth Phoenix	.50	1.25
68 Melina vs. Candice Michelle	.50	1.25
69 Kelly Kelly vs. Layla	.40	1.00
70 Victoria vs. Michelle McCool	.50	1.25
71 Mickie James vs. Beth Phoenix	.60	1.50
72 Maria vs. Melina	.40	1.00
73 Doink vs. Bam Bam Bigelow	.25	.60
74 Iron Shiek vs. Sgt. Slaughter	.40	1.00
75 Paul Orndorff vs. Bobby Heenan	.25	.60
76 J.Strongbow vs. Peter Maivia	.25	.60
77 Mick Foley vs. Terry Funk	.25	.60
78 Dusty Rhodes vs. Billy Graham	.25	.60
79 Ron Simmons vs. Vader	.15	.40
80 Jake Roberts vs. Kamala	.25	.60
81 Jake Roberts vs. Rick Rude	.25	.60
82 Jake Roberts vs. Ted DiBiase	.25	.60
83 Jake Roberts vs. Jerry Lawler	.25	.60
84 Bam Bam vs. One Man Gang	.25	.60
85 Ric Flair vs. Roddy Piper	.40	1.00
86 Rocky Johnson vs. Wild Samoans	.15	.40
87 Ted DiBiase vs. Dusty Rhodes	.25	.60
88 Sgt. Slaughter vs. Pat Patterson	.25	.60
89 Gorilla Monsoon vs. Vader	.25	.60
90 Checklist	.10	.25

2008 Topps WWE Ultimate Rivals Autographs

STATED ODDS 1:48 HOBBY EXCLUSIVE

NNO CM Punk	15.00	40.00
NNO Edge	12.00	30.00
NNO Elijah Burke	6.00	15.00
NNO John Morrison	8.00	20.00
NNO Matt Hardy	8.00	20.00
NNO Michelle McCool	12.00	30.00
NNO The Miz	8.00	20.00
NNO Stevie Richards	6.00	15.00
NNO Super Crazy	6.00	15.00
NNO Victoria	8.00	20.00

2008 Topps WWE Ultimate Rivals Motion Cards

COMPLETE SET (10)	4.00	10.00
STATED ODDS 1:8 HOBBY AND RETAIL		
1 Batista vs. Edge	.60	1.50
2 Lance Cade vs. Hardcore Holly	.20	.50
3 Carlito vs. Brian Kendrick	.30	.75
4 Chavo Guerrero vs. CM Punk	.30	.75
5 Hornswoggle/Finley vs. Edge	.60	1.50
6 Lance Cade	.20	.50
7 Jeff Hardy vs. Randy Orton	.60	1.50
8 Rey Mysterio vs. Edge	.60	1.50
9 Triple H vs. Umaga	1.00	2.50
10 Undertaker vs. MVP	1.00	2.50

2008 Topps WWE Ultimate Rivals Ringside Relics

STATED ODDS 1:48 HOBBY EXCLUSIVE

NNO Carlito	3.00	8.00
NNO Charlie Haas	3.00	8.00
NNO CM Punk	3.00	8.00
NNO Edge	4.00	10.00
NNO John Cena	6.00	15.00
NNO Matt Hardy	5.00	12.00
NNO Mr. Kennedy	3.00	8.00

2008 Topps WWE Ultimate Rivals Tattoos

COMPLETE SET (10)   4.00   10.00
STATED ODDS 1:4 RETAIL EXCLUSIVE

1	John Cena	1.00	3.00
2	Batista	.60	1.50
3	Shawn Michaels	1.00	2.50
4	Edge	.60	1.50
5	Mr. Kennedy	.30	.75
6	The Undertaker	.60	1.50
7	Ric Flair	.60	1.50
8	Triple H	1.00	2.50
9	Rey Mysterio	.30	.75
10	John Morrison	.30	.75

2008 Topps WWE Ultimate Rivals Promos

P1	John Cena vs. Edge	1.00	2.50

2015 Topps WWE Undisputed

COMPLETE SET (100)   30.00   80.00
UNOPENED BOX (10 PACKS)
UNOPENED PACKS (5 CARDS)
*RED: .5X TO 1.2X BASIC CARDS
*BLACK/99: .6X TO 1.5X BASIC CARDS
*PURPLE/50: .75X TO 2X BASIC CARDS
*SILVER/25: 1.2X TO 3X BASIC CARDS
*GOLD/1: UNPRICED DUE TO SCARCITY
*PP BLACK/1: UNPRICED DUE TO SCARCITY
*PP CYAN/1: UNPRICED DUE TO SCARCITY
*PP MAGENTA/1: UNPRICED DUE TO SCARCITY
*PP YELLOW/1: UNPRICED DUE TO SCARCITY

1	Undertaker	2.50	6.00
2	Rosa Mendes	1.00	2.50
3	Lita	2.50	6.00
4	Kofi Kingston	.60	1.50
5	George The Animal Steele	.75	2.00
6	Titus O'Neil	.60	1.50
7	Stardust	.60	1.50
8	The American Dream Dusty Rhodes	1.00	2.50
9	Alicia Fox	1.25	3.00
10	Brock Lesnar	2.50	6.00
11	Zack Ryder	.60	1.50
12	Summer Rae	2.50	6.00
13	The Miz	1.00	2.50
14	Roman Reigns	1.50	4.00
15	Natalya	2.00	5.00
16	Rob Van Dam	1.50	4.00
17	Lana	2.50	6.00
18	Shawn Michaels	2.50	6.00
19	R-Truth	.60	1.50
20	Nature Boy Ric Flair	3.00	8.00
21	Jey Uso	.60	1.50
22	Hacksaw Jim Duggan	1.00	2.50
23	Booker T	1.00	2.50
24	Randy Orton	2.50	6.00
25	John Cena	3.00	8.00
26	Big Show	1.50	4.00
27	Cesaro	.60	1.50
28	Kevin Nash	1.50	4.00
29	Honky Tonk Man	1.00	2.50
30	Bret Hit Man Hart	2.00	5.00
31	Paige	3.00	8.00
32	Dolph Ziggler	1.00	2.50
33	Christian	.60	1.50
34	Ricky The Dragon Steamboat	1.00	2.50
35	Chris Jericho	1.50	4.00
36	Jerry The King Lawler	1.00	2.50
37	Kane	1.50	4.00
38	Bo Dallas	.60	1.50
39	Darren Young	.60	1.50
40	Daniel Bryan	2.50	6.00
41	Paul Heyman	.60	1.50
42	Big E	1.00	2.50
43	Sin Cara	1.00	2.50
44	Doink The Clown	.60	1.50
45	Naomi	1.00	2.50
46	Paul Bearer	1.00	2.50
47	Rusev	1.50	4.00
48	Mark Henry	1.00	2.50
49	Erick Rowan	1.00	2.50
50	Triple H	2.50	6.00
51	Diamond Dallas Page	1.25	3.00
52	Tyson Kidd	.60	1.50
53	The British Bulldog	1.00	2.50
54	Razor Ramon	1.50	4.00
55	Million Dollar Man Ted DiBiase	1.00	2.50
56	King Barrett	.60	1.50
57	Seth Rollins	1.00	2.50
58	Rowdy Roddy Piper	2.00	5.00
59	Ultimate Warrior	2.00	5.00
60	Trish Stratus	3.00	8.00
61	Eve Torres	1.25	3.00
62	Adam Rose	.75	2.00
63	Bruno Sammartino	1.50	4.00
64	JBL	.60	1.50
65	The Iron Sheik	1.00	2.50
66	Emma	1.00	2.50
67	Jack Swagger	1.00	2.50
68	Luke Harper	1.00	2.50
69	Konnor	.75	2.00
70	Sting	1.50	4.00
71	Bray Wyatt	2.50	6.00
72	Bob Backlund	.60	1.50
73	Eva Marie	2.50	6.00
74	Jake The Snake Roberts	1.00	2.50
75	Yokozuna	1.00	2.50
76	Nikki Bella	2.00	5.00
77	Sheamus	1.50	4.00
78	Jimmy Uso	.60	1.50
79	Fandango	.60	1.50
80	Neville	1.25	3.00
81	Viktor	.60	1.50
82	Cowboy Bob Orton	.60	1.50
83	Arn Anderson	.75	2.00
84	Damien Sandow	.60	1.50
85	Edge	1.50	4.00
86	Classy Freddie Blassie	.60	1.50
87	Dean Ambrose	1.50	4.00
88	Stephanie McMahon	1.00	2.50
89	Sgt. Slaughter	1.00	2.50
90	Mr. Perfect Curt Hennig	1.00	2.50
91	Ryback	.60	1.50
92	Big Boss Man	.60	1.50
93	Bam Bam Bigelow	.75	2.00
94	Pat Patterson	.60	1.50
95	Brie Bella	2.00	5.00
96	Cameron	1.00	2.50
97	Kalisto	1.00	2.50
98	The Rock	3.00	8.00
99	Goldust	.60	1.50
100	Ravishing Rick Rude	1.00	2.50

2015 Topps WWE Undisputed Autographed Relics

*BLACK/50: .6X TO 1.5X BASIC AUTOS
*PURPLE/25: 1X TO 2.5X BASIC AUTOS
*GOLD/1: UNPRICED DUE TO SCARCITY

UARAF	Alicia Fox	6.00	15.00
UARAR	Adam Rose	5.00	12.00
UARBB	Brie Bella	12.00	30.00
UARBD	Bo Dallas	5.00	12.00
UARBS	Big Show	8.00	20.00
UARBW	Bray Wyatt	12.00	30.00
UARCA	Curtis Axel	5.00	12.00
UARCE	Cesaro	10.00	25.00
UARDA	Dean Ambrose	12.00	30.00
UARDB	Daniel Bryan	15.00	40.00
UARDM	Damien Sandow	5.00	12.00
UARDY	Darren Young	5.00	12.00
UARDZ	Dolph Ziggler	6.00	15.00
UARFA	Fandango	5.00	12.00
UARGO	Goldust	8.00	20.00
UARHS	Heath Slater	5.00	12.00
UARJC	John Cena	25.00	60.00
UARJS	Jack Swagger	5.00	12.00
UARJU	Jimmy Uso	8.00	20.00
UARKO	Konnor	5.00	12.00
UARMH	Mark Henry	6.00	15.00
UARNA	Natalya	8.00	20.00
UARNB	Nikki Bella	12.00	30.00
UARRO	Randy Orton	12.00	30.00
UARRR	Roman Reigns	10.00	25.00
UARSH	Sheamus	10.00	25.00
UARSR	Seth Rollins	12.00	30.00
UARTK	Tyson Kidd	5.00	12.00
UARTM	The Miz	8.00	20.00
UARTO	Titus O'Neil	5.00	12.00
UARVI	Viktor	5.00	12.00
UARZR	Zack Ryder	5.00	12.00
UARBNB	King Barrett	6.00	15.00
UARJKL	Jerry The King Lawler	8.00	20.00
UARSRA	Summer Rae	10.00	25.00

2015 Topps WWE Undisputed Autographs

*BLACK/50: .6X TO 1.5X BASIC AUTOS
*PURPLE/25: 1X TO 2.5X BASIC AUTOS
*GOLD/1: UNPRICED DUE TO SCARCITY

UAAB	Alundra Blayze	6.00	15.00
UABB	Brie Bella	8.00	20.00
UABL	Brock Lesnar	120.00	200.00
UABS	Bruno Sammartino	10.00	25.00
UABW	Bray Wyatt	8.00	20.00
UACJ	Chris Jericho	8.00	20.00
UADA	Dean Ambrose	8.00	20.00
UADB	Daniel Bryan	10.00	25.00
UADZ	Dolph Ziggler	6.00	15.00
UAED	Edge	10.00	25.00
UAEV	Eve Torres	6.00	15.00
UAIS	The Iron Sheik	6.00	15.00
UAJC	John Cena	20.00	50.00
UAJL	Jerry The King Lawler	8.00	20.00
UALI	Lita	10.00	25.00
UALT	Lawrence Taylor	25.00	60.00
UAMM	Million Dollar Man Ted DiBiase	8.00	20.00
UANA	Natalya	6.00	15.00
UANB	Nikki Bella	12.00	30.00
UANE	Neville	6.00	15.00
UAPH	Paul Heyman	8.00	20.00

2015 Topps WWE Undisputed Cut Signatures

STATED PRINT RUN 1 SER.#'d SET
UNPRICED DUE TO SCARCITY

CUTBB   British Bulldog
CUTJD   Junkyard Dog
CUTMP   Mr. Perfect Curt Hennig
CUTBBM   Big Boss Man
CUTCJS   Chief Jay Strongbow

2015 Topps WWE Undisputed Famous Finishers

COMPLETE SET (30)   12.00   30.00
*RED: .5X TO 1.2X BASIC CARDS
*BLACK/99: .6X TO 1.5X BASIC CARDS
*PURPLE/50: .75X TO 2X BASIC CARDS
*SILVER/25: 1.2X TO 3X BASIC CARDS

UAPR	Pete Rose	20.00	50.00
UARF	Nature Boy Ric Flair	15.00	40.00
UARO	Randy Orton	12.00	30.00
UARR	Razor Ramon	12.00	30.00
UARU	Rusev	6.00	15.00
UARY	Ryback	6.00	15.00
UASM	Shawn Michaels	30.00	80.00
UASR	Seth Rollins	10.00	25.00
UATM	The Miz	6.00	15.00
UATS	Trish Stratus	15.00	40.00
UABHH	Bret Hit Man Hart	25.00	60.00
UABSH	Big Show	6.00	15.00
UARRE	Roman Reigns	10.00	25.00
UASRA	Summer Rae	8.00	20.00

2015 Topps WWE Undisputed Cage Evolution Moments

COMPLETE SET (20)   10.00   25.00
*RED: .5X TO 1.2X BASIC CARDS
*BLACK/99: .6X TO 1.5X BASIC CARDS
*PURPLE/50: .75X TO 2X BASIC CARDS
*SILVER/25: 1.2X TO 3X BASIC CARDS
*GOLD/1: UNPRICED DUE TO SCARCITY
*PP BLACK/1: UNPRICED DUE TO SCARCITY
*PP CYAN/1: UNPRICED DUE TO SCARCITY
*PP MAGENTA/1: UNPRICED DUE TO SCARCITY
*PP YELLOW/1: UNPRICED DUE TO SCARCITY

CEM1	Ultimate Warrior/Rick Rude	1.25	3.00
CEM2	Undertaker/Shawn Michaels	1.50	4.00
CEM3	Edge/Christian	1.00	2.50
CEM4	John Cena/Big Show	2.00	5.00
CEM5	Sheamus/Ryback/R-Truth	1.00	2.50
	Barrett/Ziggler/Henry		
CEM6	Triple H/Randy Orton	1.50	4.00
CEM7	JBL/Big Show	1.00	2.50
CEM8	John Cena/Edge	2.00	5.00
CEM9	Undertaker/Edge	1.50	4.00
CEM10	Mark Henry/Big Show	1.00	2.50
CEM11	Big Show/Bryan/Henry	1.50	4.00
CEM12	Undertaker/Triple H	1.50	4.00
CEM13	Triple H/Brock Lesnar	1.50	4.00
CEM14	Cesaro/Orton/Bryan	2.00	5.00
CEM15	John Cena/Bray Wyatt	2.00	5.00
CEM16	RVD/Jericho/HHH	1.50	4.00
	Booker T/Kane/HBK		
CEM17	Shawn Michaels/Triple H	1.50	4.00
CEM18	Dean Ambrose/Seth Rollins	1.00	2.50
CEM19	Randy Orton/Seth Rollins	1.50	4.00
CEM20	John Cena/Seth Rollins	2.00	5.00

*GOLD/1: UNPRICED DUE TO SCARCITY
*PP BLACK/1: UNPRICED DUE TO SCARCITY
*PP CYAN/1: UNPRICED DUE TO SCARCITY
*PP MAGENTA/1: UNPRICED DUE TO SCARCITY
*PP YELLOW/1: UNPRICED DUE TO SCARCITY

FF1	Sweet Chin Music	2.00	5.00
FF2	Pedigree	2.00	5.00
FF3	Stratusfaction	2.50	6.00
FF4	Zig Zag	.75	2.00
FF5	Tombstone	2.00	5.00
FF6	Figure-4 Leglock	2.50	6.00
FF7	RKO	2.00	5.00
FF8	Rude Awakening	.75	2.00
FF9	Codebreaker	1.25	3.00
FF10	Brogue Kick	1.25	3.00
FF11	Sharpshooter	1.50	4.00
FF12	Attitude Adjustment	2.50	6.00
FF13	Million Dollar Dream	.75	2.00
FF14	KO Punch	1.25	3.00
FF15	Sister Abigail	2.00	5.00
FF16	F-5	2.00	5.00
FF17	Running Knee Smash	2.00	5.00
FF18	Camel Clutch	.75	2.00
FF19	Texas Cloverleaf	.75	2.00
FF20	World's Strongest Slam	.75	2.00
FF21	Razor's Edge	1.25	3.00
FF22	Banzai Drop	.75	2.00
FF23	Patriot Lock	.75	2.00
FF24	Spear	1.25	3.00
FF25	Perfectplex	.75	2.00
FF26	DDT	.75	2.00
FF27	Coup de Grace	1.50	4.00
FF28	Figure Eight	1.50	4.00
FF29	Skull-Crushing Finale	.75	2.00
FF30	Red Arrow	1.00	2.50

2015 Topps WWE Undisputed Famous Rivalries Dual Autographed Jumbo Relics

STATED PRINT RUN 5 SER.#'d SETS
UNPRICED DUE TO SCARCITY

FRARAR D.Ambrose/S.Rollins
FRARBB Nikki & Brie Bella
FRARCO J.Cena/R.Orton
FRARSH Big Show/M.Henry
FRARZM D.Ziggler/Miz

2015 Topps WWE Undisputed Famous Rivalries Dual Autographs

STATED PRINT RUN 25 SER.#'d SETS

FRACO	J.Cena/R.Orton	150.00	300.00
FRAHL	B.Hart/J.Lawler	75.00	150.00
FRAMR	S.Michaels/R.Ramon	100.00	200.00

2015 Topps WWE Undisputed Fistographs

STATED PRINT RUN 10 SER.#'d SETS

NNO	Big Show	100.00	200.00
NNO	Bray Wyatt	100.00	200.00
NNO	Bret Hit Man Hart	125.00	250.00
NNO	Bruno Sammartino	125.00	250.00
NNO	Daniel Bryan		
NNO	Dean Ambrose	150.00	300.00
NNO	Edge	125.00	250.00
NNO	Jack Swagger		
NNO	John Cena		
NNO	Kane	100.00	200.00
NNO	King Barrett		
NNO	Lita	150.00	300.00
NNO	Mark Henry	75.00	150.00
NNO	Randy Orton	125.00	250.00
NNO	Ric Flair		
NNO	Roman Reigns	100.00	200.00
NNO	Rowdy Roddy Piper		
NNO	Rusev	75.00	150.00
NNO	Shawn Michaels	300.00	450.00
NNO	Sheamus		
NNO	Trish Stratus	250.00	400.00

2015 Topps WWE Undisputed Four Corners Quadragraphs

STATED PRINT RUN 10 SER.#'d SETS

FCQBBSL	Lita/Trish/Bellas	300.00	600.00
FCQBBYS	Bryan/Young/Barrett/Slater	125.00	250.00
FCQDNZO	Dallas/Neville/Zayn/Owens	125.00	250.00
FCQHHLD	J.Hart/B.Hart/Lawler/DiBiase	150.00	300.00

2015 Topps WWE Undisputed NXT In Line Autographs

*BLACK/50: .6X TO 1.5X BASIC AUTOS
*PURPLE/25: 1X TO 2.5X BASIC AUTOS
*GOLD/1: UNPRICED DUE TO SCARCITY

NABD	Bull Dempsey	5.00	12.00
NABL	Becky Lynch	20.00	50.00
NABM	Murphy	5.00	12.00
NACC	Colin Cassady	6.00	15.00
NACH	Charlotte	20.00	50.00
NAEA	Enzo Amore	10.00	25.00
NAFB	Finn Balor	25.00	60.00
NAHI	Hideo Itami	8.00	20.00
NAKO	Kevin Owens	15.00	40.00
NASB	Sasha Banks	20.00	50.00
NASJ	Samoa Joe	10.00	25.00
NASZ	Sami Zayn	10.00	25.00
NATB	Tyler Breeze	8.00	20.00
NAWB	Blake	5.00	12.00
NABCO	Baron Corbin	6.00	15.00

2015 Topps WWE Undisputed NXT Prospects

COMPLETE SET (25)		15.00	40.00

*RED: .5X TO 1.2X BASIC CARDS
*BLACK/99: .6X TO 1.5X BASIC CARDS
*PURPLE/50: .75X TO 2X BASIC CARDS
*SILVER/25: 1.2X TO 3X BASIC CARDS
*GOLD/1: UNPRICED DUE TO SCARCITY
*PP BLACK/1: UNPRICED DUE TO SCARCITY
*PP CYAN/1: UNPRICED DUE TO SCARCITY
*PP MAGENTA/1: UNPRICED DUE TO SCARCITY
*PP YELLOW/1: UNPRICED DUE TO SCARCITY

NXT1	Angelo Dawkins	1.50	4.00
NXT2	Sasha Banks	5.00	12.00
NXT3	Finn Balor	4.00	10.00
NXT4	Sami Zayn	2.00	5.00
NXT5	Charlotte	4.00	10.00
NXT6	Blake	1.25	3.00
NXT7	Murphy	1.25	3.00
NXT8	Carmella	2.00	5.00
NXT9	Enzo Amore	1.25	3.00
NXT10	Baron Corbin	2.00	5.00
NXT11	Hideo Itami	1.25	3.00
NXT12	Tyler Breeze	1.25	3.00
NXT13	Solomon Crowe	1.25	3.00
NXT14	Becky Lynch	4.00	10.00
NXT15	Bayley	2.50	6.00
NXT16	Bull Dempsey	2.00	5.00
NXT17	Alexa Bliss	6.00	15.00
NXT18	Tye Dillinger	2.00	5.00
NXT19	Jason Jordan	1.25	3.00
NXT20	Colin Cassady	2.00	5.00
NXT21	Aiden English	1.50	4.00
NXT22	Simon Gotch	1.25	3.00
NXT23	Mojo Rawley	1.25	3.00
NXT24	Marcus Louis	2.00	5.00
NXT25	Samoa Joe	3.00	8.00

2016 Topps WWE Undisputed

COMPLETE SET (100)		25.00	60.00
UNOPENED BOX (10 PACKS)			
UNOPENED PACK (5 CARDS)			

*BRONZE/99: .5X TO 1.2X BASIC CARDS
*SILVER/50: .75X TO 2X BASIC CARDS
*BLUE/25: 1.2X TO 3X BASIC CARDS
*GOLD/10: 2X TO 5X BASIC CARDS
*RED/1: UNPRICED DUE TO SCARCITY
*P.P.BLACK/1: UNPRICED DUE TO SCARCITY
*P.P.CYAN/1: UNPRICED DUE TO SCARCITY
*P.P.MAGENTA/1: UNPRICED DUE TO SCARCITY
*P.P.YELLOW/1: UNPRICED DUE TO SCARCITY

1	Alberto Del Rio	1.00	2.50
2	Big E	.60	1.50
3	Big Show	1.25	3.00
4	Braun Strowman	.75	2.00
5	Bray Wyatt	2.50	6.00
6	Brock Lesnar	3.00	8.00
7	Bubba Ray Dudley	1.25	3.00
8	Cesaro	1.25	3.00
9	Chris Jericho	1.50	4.00
10	D-Von Dudley	1.00	2.50
11	Dean Ambrose	2.00	5.00
12	Dolph Ziggler	.75	2.00
13	Erick Rowan	.60	1.50
14	Goldust	1.00	2.50
15	Jerry The King Lawler	1.25	3.00
16	John Cena	3.00	8.00
17	Kane	1.00	2.50
18	Kevin Owens	1.50	4.00
19	King Barrett	.60	1.50
20	Kofi Kingston	.60	1.50
21	Luke Harper	.60	1.50
22	Mark Henry	.75	2.00
23	The Miz	1.00	2.50
24	Neville	1.50	4.00
25	Paul Heyman	.75	2.00
26	R-Truth	.60	1.50
27	Randy Orton	1.50	4.00
28	The Rock	3.00	8.00
29	Roman Reigns	2.00	5.00
30	Rusev	1.50	4.00
31	Ryback	.75	2.00
32	Seth Rollins	1.00	2.50
33	Sheamus	1.50	4.00
34	Sting	1.50	4.00
35	Triple H	2.50	6.00
36	Tyler Breeze	.60	1.50
37	Tyson Kidd	.60	1.50
38	Undertaker	2.50	6.00
39	Xavier Woods	.60	1.50
40	Zack Ryder	.60	1.50
41	The American Dream Dusty Rhodes	.60	1.50
42	Andre the Giant	2.00	5.00
43	Bam Bam Bigelow	.75	2.00
44	Batista	1.25	3.00
45	Big Boss Man	1.00	2.50
46	Big John Studd	1.00	2.50
47	Bob Backlund	.60	1.50
48	Bobby The Brain Heenan	1.00	2.50
49	Bret Hit Man Hart	1.50	4.00
50	Brian Pillman	.75	2.00
51	The British Bulldog	.75	2.00
52	Cowboy Bob Orton	1.00	2.50
53	Diamond Dallas Page	1.00	2.50
54	Doink the Clown	.60	1.50
55	Eddie Guerrero	1.50	4.00
56	Edge	1.50	4.00
57	General Adnan	.60	1.50
58	George The Animal Steele	.75	2.00
59	Hacksaw Jim Duggan	.60	1.50
60	High Chief Peter Maivia	.60	1.50
61	Honky Tonk Man	.60	1.50
62	Jake The Snake Roberts	1.25	3.00
63	Jim The Anvil Neidhart	.60	1.50
64	Jim Ross	1.00	2.50
65	J.J. Dillon	.60	1.50
66	Junkyard Dog	1.00	2.50
67	Kamala	.60	1.50
68	The King Harley Race	.60	1.50
69	Kevin Nash	1.50	4.00
70	Lex Luger	1.00	2.50
71	Macho Man Randy Savage	1.50	4.00
72	Mean Gene Okerlund	.75	2.00
73	Michael P.S. Hayes	.60	1.50
74	Million Dollar Man Ted DiBiase	.75	2.00
75	The Mouth of the South Jimmy Hart	.75	2.00
76	Mr. Perfect Curt Hennig	1.50	4.00
77	Mr. Wonderful Paul Orndorff	.60	1.50
78	Papa Shango	.75	2.00
79	Paul Bearer	1.00	2.50
80	Ravishing Rick Rude	1.00	2.50
81	Ric Flair	2.50	6.00
82	Ricky The Dragon Steamboat	.75	2.00
83	Rikishi	.75	2.00
84	Road Dogg	1.00	2.50
85	Rob Van Dam	1.25	3.00
86	Rocky Johnson	.75	2.00
87	Rowdy Roddy Piper	2.00	5.00
88	Scott Hall	1.50	4.00
89	Sgt. Slaughter	.75	2.00
90	Shawn Michaels	2.50	6.00
91	Superstar Billy Graham	.60	1.50
92	Stone Cold Steve Austin	3.00	8.00
93	Tatanka	.60	1.50
94	Tatsumi Fujinami	.60	1.50
95	Tito Santana	.75	2.00
96	Ultimate Warrior	1.50	4.00
97	Vader	1.25	3.00
98	Virgil	.60	1.50
99	X-Pac	1.00	2.50
100	Yokozuna	1.25	3.00

2016 Topps WWE Undisputed Autographed Diva Kiss and Relic Booklets

STATED PRINT RUN 5 SER. #'d SETS
UNPRICED DUE TO SCARCITY

ADRAF Alicia Fox
ADRBA Bayley
ADRBB Brie Bella
ADRLA Lana
ADRNB Nikki Bella

2016 Topps WWE Undisputed Autographed Relics

*SILVER/50: .6X TO 1.5X BASIC AUTOS
*BLUE/25: 1X TO 2.5X BASIC MEM
*GOLD/10: 1.2X TO 3X BASIC AUTOS
*RED/1: UNPRICED DUE TO SCARCITY
*P.P.BLACK/1: UNPRICED DUE TO SCARCITY
*P.P.CYAN/1: UNPRICED DUE TO SCARCITY
*P.P.MAGENTA/1: UNPRICED DUE TO SCARCITY
*P.P.YELLOW/1: UNPRICED DUE TO SCARCITY
STATED PRINT RUN 99 SER.#'d SETS

UARAC	Alicia Fox	6.00	15.00
UARAE	Aiden English	6.00	15.00
UARBB	Brie Bella	12.00	30.00
UARBC	Baron Corbin	6.00	15.00
UARBE	Big E	6.00	15.00
UARBL	Becky Lynch	20.00	50.00
UARBW	Bray Wyatt	10.00	25.00
UARCC	Colin Cassady	8.00	20.00
UARCH	Charlotte	15.00	40.00
UARDA	Dean Ambrose	12.00	30.00
UARDD	D-Von Dudley	6.00	15.00
UARDZ	Dolph Ziggler	6.00	15.00
UAREA	Enzo Amore	12.00	30.00
UARFB	Finn Balor	15.00	40.00
UARJU	Jey Uso	6.00	15.00
UARKA	Kalisto	6.00	15.00
UARKK	Kofi Kingston	6.00	15.00
UARKO	Kevin Owens	12.00	30.00
UARMR	Mojo Rawley	6.00	15.00
UARNE	Neville	8.00	20.00
UARRR	Roman Reigns	10.00	25.00
UARRY	Ryback	6.00	15.00
UARSB	Sasha Banks	25.00	60.00
UARSC	Sin Cara	8.00	20.00
UARSG	Simon Gotch	6.00	15.00
UARSH	Sheamus	6.00	15.00
UARSJ	Samoa Joe	6.00	15.00
UARSR	Seth Rollins	10.00	25.00
UARTB	Tyler Breeze	6.00	15.00
UARTM	The Miz	6.00	15.00
UARXW	Xavier Woods	6.00	15.00
UARZR	Zack Ryder	6.00	15.00
UARADR	Alberto Del Rio	6.00	15.00
UARAPC	Apollo Crews	6.00	15.00
UARBAY	Bayley	20.00	50.00
UARBRD	Bubba Ray Dudley	6.00	15.00
UARJIU	Jimmy Uso	8.00	20.00

2016 Topps WWE Undisputed Autographs

*BRONZE/99: .5X TO 1.2X BASIC AUTOS
*SILVER/50: .75X TO 2X BASIC AUTOS
*BLUE/25: 1.2X TO 3X BASIC AUTOS
*GOLD/10: 1.5X TO 4X BASIC AUTOS
*RED/1: UNPRICED DUE TO SCARCITY
*P.P.BLACK/1: UNPRICED DUE TO SCARCITY
*P.P.CYAN/1: UNPRICED DUE TO SCARCITY
*P.P.MAGENTA/1: UNPRICED DUE TO SCARCITY
*P.P.YELLOW/1: UNPRICED DUE TO SCARCITY
RANDOMLY INSERTED INTO PACKS

UAAF	Alicia Fox	5.00	12.00
UAAS	Asuka	10.00	25.00
UABA	Bayley	15.00	40.00
UABB	Brie Bella	8.00	20.00
UABE	Big E	6.00	15.00
UABH	Bret Hit Man Hart	12.00	30.00

UABL	Becky Lynch	15.00	40.00
UABS	Braun Strowman	6.00	15.00
UABT	Booker T	6.00	15.00
UACA	Carmella	15.00	40.00
UACC	Colin Cassady	8.00	20.00
UACE	Cesaro	6.00	15.00
UACH	Charlotte	12.00	30.00
UADA	Dean Ambrose	10.00	25.00
UADB	Daniel Bryan	8.00	20.00
UADD	D-Von Dudley	6.00	15.00
UAEA	Enzo Amore	12.00	30.00
UAER	Erick Rowan	5.00	12.00
UAFB	Finn Balor	10.00	25.00
UAGO	Goldust	5.00	12.00
UAHI	Hideo Itami	5.00	12.00
UAJC	John Cena	20.00	50.00
UAJN	Jim The Anvil Neidhart	6.00	15.00
UAKA	Kalisto	5.00	12.00
UAKK	Kofi Kingston	5.00	12.00
UALA	Lana	10.00	25.00
UALH	Luke Harper	6.00	15.00
UALI	Lita	8.00	20.00
UANA	Natalya	5.00	12.00
UANB	Nikki Bella	10.00	25.00
UANJ	Nia Jax	5.00	12.00
UARR	Roman Reigns	8.00	20.00
UASB	Sasha Banks	15.00	40.00
UASC	Sin Cara	6.00	15.00
UASJ	Samoa Joe	5.00	12.00
UASR	Seth Rollins	8.00	20.00
UAST	Sting	20.00	50.00
UATS	Trish Stratus	10.00	25.00
UAXW	Xavier Woods	5.00	12.00
UAAJS	AJ Styles	20.00	50.00
UABAC	Baron Corbin	6.00	15.00
UABRD	Bubba Ray Dudley	5.00	12.00
UABRW	Bray Wyatt	6.00	15.00
UANAO	Naomi	5.00	12.00
UASTR	Stevie Ray	5.00	12.00

2016 Topps WWE Undisputed Cut Signatures

STATED PRINT RUN 1 SER.#'d SET
UNPRICED DUE TO SCARCITY

UCSRS	Macho Man Randy Savage	
UCSCFB	Classy Freddie Blassie	
UCSMIE	Miss Elizabeth	

2016 Topps WWE Undisputed Divas Revolution

COMPLETE SET (30)		60.00	120.00

*BRONZE/99: .5X TO 1.2X BASIC CARDS
*SILVER/50: .75X TO 2X BASIC CARDS
*BLUE/25: 1.2X TO 3X BASIC CARDS
*GOLD/10: UNPRICED DUE TO SCARCITY
*RED/1: UNPRICED DUE TO SCARCITY
*P.P.BLACK/1 UNPRICED DUE TO SCARCITY
*P.P.CYAN/1 UNPRICED DUE TO SCARCITY
*P.P.MAGENTA/1 UNPRICED DUE TO SCARCITY
*P.P.YELLOW/1 UNPRICED DUE TO SCARCITY
RANDOMLY INSERTED INTO PACKS

DR1	Alundra Blayze	1.50	4.00
DR2	Eve	2.50	6.00
DR3	Lita	4.00	10.00
DR4	Miss Elizabeth	1.25	3.00
DR5	Sensational Sherri	2.00	5.00
DR6	Trish Stratus	6.00	15.00

DR7	Alicia Fox	2.00	5.00
DR8	Asuka	5.00	12.00
DR9	Bayley	3.00	8.00
DR10	Becky Lynch	4.00	10.00
DR11	Brie Bella	2.50	6.00
DR12	Cameron	1.25	3.00
DR13	Charlotte	4.00	10.00
DR14	Dasha Fuentes	1.25	3.00
DR15	Eden	1.50	4.00
DR16	Emma	2.50	6.00
DR17	Eva Marie	2.50	6.00
DR18	JoJo	1.25	3.00
DR19	Lana	5.00	12.00
DR20	Mandy Rose	3.00	8.00
DR21	Naomi	2.00	5.00
DR22	Natalya	2.00	5.00
DR23	Nikki Bella	4.00	10.00
DR24	Paige	4.00	10.00
DR25	Renee Young	3.00	8.00
DR26	Rosa Mendes	1.25	3.00
DR27	Sasha Banks	4.00	10.00
DR28	Maryse	2.50	6.00
DR29	Summer Rae	3.00	8.00
DR30	Tamina	1.50	4.00

2016 Topps WWE Undisputed Faction Triple Autograph Booklets

STATED PRINT RUN 10 SER.#'d SETS

FTAARR	Ambrose/Rollins/Reigns	125.00	250.00
FTABBF	The Bellas/Fox	100.00	200.00
FTAKBW	Kingston/Big E/Woods	75.00	150.00
FTANBT	Naomi/Banks/Tamina	125.00	250.00
FTASKV	Stardust/Konnor/Viktor	60.00	120.00

2016 Topps WWE Undisputed Family Ties Dual Autographs

STATED PRINT RUN 25 SER.#'d SETS

FTABB	Nikki & Brie Bella	120.00	200.00
FTAFC	Ric & Charlotte Flair	120.00	200.00
FTAGS	Goldust/Stardust	60.00	120.00
FTANN	J.Neidhart/Natalya	60.00	120.00
FTATR	Booker T/S. Ray	30.00	75.00

2016 Topps WWE Undisputed NXT Prospects

COMPLETE SET (30)		30.00	80.00

*BRONZE/99: .5X TO 1.2X BASIC CARDS
*SILVER/50: .75X TO 2X BASIC CARDS
*BLUE/25: 1.2X TO 3X BASIC CARDS
*GOLD/10: UNPRICED DUE TO SCARCITY
*RED/1: UNPRICED DUE TO SCARCITY
*P.P.BLACK/1: UNPRICED DUE TO SCARCITY
*P.P.CYAN/1: UNPRICED DUE TO SCARCITY
*P.P.MAGENTA/1: UNPRICED DUE TO SCARCITY
*P.P.YELLOW/1: UNPRICED DUE TO SCARCITY
RANDOMLY INSERTED INTO PACKS

NXT1	Aiden English	1.25	3.00
NXT2	Alexa Bliss	6.00	15.00
NXT3	Angelo Dawkins	1.25	3.00
NXT4	Apollo Crews	1.25	3.00
NXT5	Asuka	5.00	12.00
NXT6	Austin Aries	1.50	4.00
NXT7	Baron Corbin	1.50	4.00
NXT8	Bayley	3.00	8.00
NXT9	Billie Kay	3.00	8.00
NXT10	Blake	1.25	3.00
NXT11	Carmella	3.00	8.00

NXT12	Chad Gable	1.50	4.00
NXT13	Colin Cassady	2.50	6.00
NXT14	Dana Brooke	3.00	8.00
NXT15	Dash Wilder	1.50	4.00
NXT16	Elias Samson	1.25	3.00
NXT17	Enzo Amore	2.50	6.00
NXT18	Finn Balor	4.00	10.00
NXT19	Hideo Itami	1.50	4.00
NXT20	Jason Jordan	1.50	4.00
NXT21	Mojo Rawley	1.25	3.00
NXT22	Murphy	1.25	3.00
NXT23	Nia Jax	2.00	5.00
NXT24	Peyton Royce	3.00	8.00
NXT25	Sami Zayn	2.00	5.00
NXT26	Samoa Joe	3.00	8.00
NXT27	Sawyer Fulton	1.50	4.00
NXT28	Scott Dawson	1.25	3.00
NXT29	Simon Gotch	2.00	5.00
NXT30	Tye Dillinger	1.50	4.00

2016 Topps WWE Undisputed Relics

STATED PRINT RUN 175 SER.#'d SETS

UARAC	Alicia Fox	3.00	8.00
UARAE	Aiden English	2.00	5.00
UARBB	Brie Bella	4.00	10.00
UARBC	Baron Corbin	2.50	6.00
UARBE	Big E	2.00	5.00
UARBL	Becky Lynch	6.00	15.00
UARBW	Bray Wyatt	8.00	20.00
UARCC	Colin Cassady	4.00	10.00
UARCH	Charlotte	6.00	15.00
UARDA	Dean Ambrose	6.00	15.00
UARDD	D-Von Dudley	3.00	8.00
UARDZ	Dolph Ziggler	2.50	6.00
UAREA	Enzo Amore	4.00	10.00
UARFB	Finn Balor	6.00	15.00
UARJU	Jey Uso	2.00	5.00
UARKA	Kalisto	5.00	12.00
UARKB	King Barrett	2.00	5.00
UARKK	Kofi Kingston	2.00	5.00
UARKO	Kevin Owens	5.00	12.00
UARMR	Mojo Rawley	2.00	5.00
UARNE	Neville	5.00	12.00
UARRR	Roman Reigns	6.00	15.00
UARRY	Ryback	2.50	6.00
UARSB	Sasha Banks	6.00	15.00
UARSC	Sin Cara	2.50	6.00
UARSG	Simon Gotch	3.00	8.00
UARSH	Sheamus	5.00	12.00
UARSJ	Samoa Joe	5.00	12.00
UARSR	Seth Rollins	3.00	8.00
UARTB	Tyler Breeze	2.00	5.00
UARTM	The Miz	3.00	8.00
UARXW	Xavier Woods	2.00	5.00
UARZR	Zack Ryder	2.00	5.00
UARADR	Alberto Del Rio	3.00	8.00
UARAPC	Apollo Crews	2.00	5.00
UARBAY	Bayley	5.00	12.00
UARBRD	Bubba Ray Dudley	4.00	10.00
UARJIU	Jimmy Uso	2.00	5.00

2016 Topps WWE Undisputed Tag Teams

COMPLETE SET (40)		50.00	100.00

*BRONZE/99: .5X TO 1.2X BASIC CARDS
*SILVER/50: .75X TO 2X BASIC CARDS
*BLUE/25: 1.2X TO 3X BASIC CARDS
*GOLD/10: UNPRICED DUE TO SCARCITY

UTT1	The Allied Powers	1.50	4.00
UTT2	The APA	2.50	6.00
UTT3	The Ascension	1.00	2.50
UTT4	Blake and Murphy	1.00	2.50
UTT5	The Brain Busters	1.00	2.50
UTT6	Brothers of Destruction	4.00	10.00
UTT7	The Bushwhackers	1.00	2.50
UTT8	D-Generation X	3.00	8.00
UTT9	The Dudley Boyz	2.00	5.00
UTT10	Edge and Christian	2.50	6.00
UTT11	The Enforcers	1.00	2.50
UTT12	The Foreign Legion	1.25	3.00
UTT13	The Funks	1.00	2.50
UTT14	Gold and Stardust	1.50	4.00
UTT15	Harlem Heat	2.00	5.00
UTT16	The Hart Foundation	2.50	6.00
UTT17	The Hollywood Blonds	5.00	12.00
UTT18	The Hype Bros.	1.00	2.50
UTT19	J and J Security	1.00	2.50
UTT20	Jeri-Show	2.50	6.00
UTT21	The Insiders	2.50	6.00
UTT22	The Lucha Dragons	2.50	6.00
UTT23	The Mega Bucks	3.00	8.00
UTT24	Money Inc.	1.25	3.00
UTT25	The Nasty Boys	1.25	3.00
UTT26	The Natural Disasters	1.00	2.50
UTT27	The Outsiders	2.50	6.00
UTT28	The Prime Time Players	1.00	2.50
UTT29	Rated-RKO	2.50	6.00
UTT30	Rhythm and Blues	1.25	3.00
UTT31	ShoMiz	2.00	5.00
UTT32	Team Hell No	4.00	10.00
UTT33	Team Rhodes Scholars	1.00	2.50
UTT34	Dudes with Attitude	4.00	10.00
UTT35	Two Man Power Trip	5.00	12.00
UTT36	Unholy Alliance	4.00	10.00
UTT37	Miz/Mizdow	1.50	4.00
UTT38	The Usos	1.00	2.50
UTT39	The Vaudevillains	1.50	4.00
UTT40	The Revival	1.25	3.00

2017 Topps WWE Undisputed

COMPLETE SET (70)		20.00	50.00
UNOPENED BOX (10 PACKS)			
UNOPENED PACK (5 CARDS)			

1	John Cena	3.00	8.00
2	AJ Styles	3.00	8.00
3	Big Cass	.75	2.00
4	Big E	.75	2.00
5	The Brian Kendrick	.60	1.50
6	Bray Wyatt	1.50	4.00
7	Brock Lesnar	3.00	8.00
8	Cesaro	1.25	3.00
9	Chad Gable	.75	2.00
10	Chris Jericho	1.50	4.00
11	Daniel Bryan	2.50	6.00
12	Dean Ambrose	2.00	5.00
13	Dolph Ziggler	1.00	2.50
14	Finn Balor	2.50	6.00
15	Goldberg	2.50	6.00
16	James Ellsworth	.60	1.50
17	Jason Jordan	.75	2.00
18	Kane	.75	2.00
19	Karl Anderson	.60	1.50
20	Kevin Owens	1.50	4.00
21	Kofi Kingston	.75	2.00
22	Luke Gallows	1.00	2.50
23	Luke Harper	.60	1.50
24	Mick Foley	1.50	4.00
25	The Miz	1.25	3.00
26	Neville	1.00	2.50
27	Randy Orton	1.50	4.00
28	Rich Swann	.60	1.50
29	The Rock	3.00	8.00
30	Roman Reigns	2.00	5.00
31	Rusev	1.25	3.00
32	Sami Zayn	.75	2.00
33	Seth Rollins	2.00	5.00
34	Shane McMahon	1.00	2.50
35	Sheamus	1.25	3.00
36	TJ Perkins	.60	1.50
37	Triple H	1.50	4.00
38	Undertaker	2.50	6.00
39	Xavier Woods	.75	2.00
40	Zack Ryder	.60	1.50
41	Alexander Wolfe	.75	2.00
42	Andrade Cien Almas	.60	1.50
43	Austin Aries	1.25	3.00
44	Bobby Roode	1.50	4.00
45	Dash Wilder	.60	1.50
46	Eric Young	1.25	3.00
47	Hideo Itami	1.00	2.50
48	Johnny Gargano	.60	1.50
49	Nick Miller	.60	1.50
50	No Way Jose	.60	1.50
51	Oney Lorcan	.60	1.50
52	Roderick Strong	.75	2.00
53	Samoa Joe	2.00	5.00
54	Sawyer Fulton	.60	1.50
55	Scott Dawson	.60	1.50
56	Shane Thorne	.60	1.50
57	Shinsuke Nakamura	1.50	4.00
58	Tommaso Ciampa	.60	1.50
59	Tye Dillinger	1.25	3.00
60	William Regal	.75	2.00
61	Andre the Giant	1.25	3.00
62	Bret Hit Man Hart	1.25	3.00
63	Macho Man Randy Savage	1.25	3.00
64	Million Dollar Man Ted DiBiase	.75	2.00
65	Ric Flair	1.50	4.00
66	Rowdy Roddy Piper	1.25	3.00
67	Shawn Michaels	1.50	4.00
68	Sting	2.00	5.00
69	Stone Cold Steve Austin	2.50	6.00
70	Ultimate Warrior	1.25	3.00

2017 Topps WWE Undisputed Autographed Relics

UARAE	Aiden English	5.00	12.00
UARAB	Alexa Bliss	60.00	120.00
UARAF	Alicia Fox	6.00	15.00
UARAS	Asuka	25.00	60.00
UARAA	Austin Aries	5.00	12.00
UARBC	Baron Corbin	6.00	15.00
UARBE	Becky Lynch	25.00	60.00
UARBCA	Big Cass	5.00	12.00
UARBIG	Big E	6.00	15.00
UARBS	Big Show	6.00	15.00
UARBD	Bo Dallas	6.00	15.00
UARBR	Bobby Roode	6.00	15.00
UARBRS	Braun Strowman	15.00	40.00
UARBW	Bray Wyatt	10.00	25.00
UARBB	Brie Bella	12.00	30.00
UARCA	Carmella	12.00	30.00
UARCU	Curtis Axel	5.00	12.00
UARDY	Darren Young	6.00	15.00
UARDZ	Dolph Ziggler	6.00	15.00
UARFA	Fandango	5.00	12.00
UARFB	Finn Balor	12.00	30.00
UARGO	Goldust	6.00	15.00
UARHS	Heath Slater	5.00	12.00
UARJG	Johnny Gargano	5.00	12.00
UARJO	Jojo	6.00	15.00
UARKA	Kalisto	8.00	20.00
UARLH	Luke Harper	6.00	15.00
UARMR	Mojo Rawley	5.00	12.00
UARNA	Natalya	6.00	15.00
UARNE	Neville	8.00	20.00
UARRO	Randy Orton	15.00	40.00
UARRY	Renee Young	8.00	20.00
UARRR	Roman Reigns	15.00	40.00
UARSJ	Samoa Joe	6.00	15.00
UARSB	Sasha Banks	15.00	40.00
UARSR	Seth Rollins	12.00	30.00
UARSH	Sheamus	6.00	15.00
UARSG	Simon Gotch	5.00	12.00
UARSU	Summer Rae	8.00	20.00
UARTA	Tamina	6.00	15.00
UARTC	Tommaso Ciampa	8.00	20.00
UARVI	Viktor	5.00	12.00
UARZR	Zack Ryder	6.00	15.00

2017 Topps WWE Undisputed Autographs

UAA	Asuka	15.00	40.00
UAC	Cesaro	6.00	15.00
UAE	Edge	10.00	25.00
UAM	Maryse	12.00	30.00
UAN	Natalya	8.00	20.00
UAR	Rhyno	6.00	15.00
UAS	Sting	20.00	50.00
UAAA	Austin Aries	6.00	15.00
UAAB	Alexa Bliss	60.00	120.00
UAAF	Alicia Fox	8.00	20.00
UAAS	AJ Styles	20.00	50.00
UABA	Bayley	15.00	40.00
UABC	Big Cass	6.00	15.00
UABE	Big E	.5.00	12.00
UABH	Bret Hit Man Hart	15.00	40.00
UABL	Becky Lynch	15.00	40.00
UABR	Bobby Roode	10.00	25.00
UABW	Bray Wyatt	8.00	20.00
UACA	Carmella	12.00	30.00
UACF	Charlotte Flair	15.00	40.00
UACJ	Chris Jericho	10.00	25.00
UADA	Dean Ambrose	10.00	25.00
UADB	Dana Brooke	10.00	25.00
UADD	Diamond Dallas Page	12.00	30.00
UAEA	Enzo Amore	8.00	20.00
UAEM	Ember Moon	20.00	50.00
UAEY	Eric Young	6.00	15.00
UAFB	Finn Balor	15.00	40.00
UAHS	Heath Slater	5.00	12.00
UAJG	Johnny Gargano	6.00	15.00
UAKA	Karl Anderson	6.00	15.00
UAKO	Kevin Owens	8.00	20.00
UALG	Luke Gallows	5.00	12.00
UALM	Liv Morgan	12.00	30.00
UANA	Naomi	8.00	20.00
UANB	Nikki Bella	10.00	25.00
UARR	Roman Reigns	8.00	20.00
UARS	Roderick Strong	6.00	15.00
UARY	Renee Young	8.00	20.00
UASB	Sasha Banks	15.00	40.00
UASH	Sheamus	5.00	12.00
UASN	Shinsuke Nakamura	20.00	50.00
UASR	Seth Rollins	10.00	25.00
UASZ	Sami Zayn	6.00	15.00
UATC	Tommaso Ciampa	6.00	15.00
UATM	The Miz	5.00	12.00
UATP	TJ Perkins	5.00	12.00
UATS	Trish Stratus	15.00	40.00
UAXW	Xavier Woods	5.00	12.00
UABAC	Baron Corbin	8.00	20.00
UAEMM	Emma	10.00	25.00
UAKOK	Kofi Kingston	5.00	12.00

2017 Topps WWE Undisputed Autographs Bronze

UAG	Goldberg	50.00	100.00
UAU	Undertaker	150.00	300.00
UARO	Randy Orton	15.00	40.00
UABRL	Brock Lesnar	50.00	100.00

2017 Topps WWE Undisputed Dream Matches

COMPLETE SET (10)		10.00	25.00

D1	Sting/Undertaker	2.00	5.00

D2	Goldberg/Steve Austin	1.50	4.00
D3	Steve Austin/Brock Lesnar	1.50	4.00
D4	Shawn Michaels/The Rock	2.00	5.00
D5	Shawn Michaels/Eddie Guerrero	1.25	3.00
D6	John Cena/Steve Austin	1.50	4.00
D7	Edge/Bret Hit Man Hart	1.00	2.50
D8	Undertaker/Goldberg	1.50	4.00
D9	Batista/Brock Lesnar	1.25	3.00
D10	Nakamura/Daniel Bryan	1.00	2.50

2017 Topps WWE Undisputed Dual Autographs

STATED PRINT RUN 25 SER.#'d SETS

UDAAE	Asuka/E.Moon	60.00	120.00
UDABA	B.Roode/A.Aries	30.00	75.00
UDABG	B.Lesnar/Goldberg	120.00	250.00
UDACR	Charlotte & Ric Flair	75.00	150.00
UDAJT	J.Gargano/T.Ciampa	50.00	100.00
UDAKC	K.Owens/C.Jericho	60.00	120.00
UDASB	S.Banks/Bayley	75.00	150.00
UDASR	S.Rollins/R.Reigns	100.00	200.00

2017 Topps WWE Undisputed Quad Autographed Booklets

STATED PRINT RUN 5 SER.#'d SETS
UNPRICED DUE TO SCARCITY

UQACSBB Charlotte/Banks/Lynch/Bayley
UQAFAKL Balor/Styles/Anderson/Gallows
UQAGBJR Goldberg/Lesnar/Cena/Orton
UQASBER Nakamura/Roode/Young/Strong

2017 Topps WWE Undisputed Relics

*SILVER/50: .5X TO 1.2X BASIC MEM
*GREEN/25: .6X TO 1.5X BASIC MEM
*GOLD/10: UNPRICED DUE TO SCARCITY
*RED/1: UNPRICED DUE TO SCARCITY
RANDOMLY INSERTED INTO PACKS

URAA	Austin Aries	3.00	8.00
URAB	Alexa Bliss	8.00	20.00
URAE	Aiden English	1.50	4.00
URAF	Alicia Fox	2.50	6.00
URAS	Asuka	5.00	12.00
URBB	Brie Bella	4.00	10.00
URBD	Bo Dallas	1.50	4.00
URBE	Becky Lynch	5.00	12.00
URBL	Brock Lesnar	8.00	20.00
URBR	Bobby Roode	4.00	10.00
URBS	Big Show	2.00	5.00
URBW	Bray Wyatt	4.00	10.00
URCA	Carmella	4.00	10.00
URCU	Curtis Axel	1.50	4.00
URDY	Darren Young	1.50	4.00
URFB	Finn Balor	6.00	15.00
URGO	Goldust	2.00	5.00
URJC	John Cena	8.00	20.00
URJO	Jojo	2.50	6.00
URLH	Luke Harper	1.50	4.00
URMR	Mojo Rawley	2.00	5.00
URNA	Natalya	3.00	8.00
URNE	Neville	2.50	6.00
URRO	Randy Orton	4.00	10.00
URRY	Renee Young	2.50	6.00
URSB	Sasha Banks	5.00	12.00
URSG	Simon Gotch	1.50	4.00
URSH	Sheamus	3.00	8.00
URSJ	Samoa Joe	5.00	12.00
URSR	Seth Rollins	5.00	12.00

URSR	Summer Rae	4.00	10.00
URTA	Tamina	2.00	5.00
URVI	Viktor	1.50	4.00
URXW	Xavier Woods	2.00	5.00
URZR	Zack Ryder	1.50	4.00
URBCA	Big Cass	2.00	5.00
URBIG	Big E	2.00	5.00

2017 Topps WWE Undisputed Cut Signature

STATED PRINT RUN 1 SER.#'d SET
UNPRICED DUE TO SCARCITY

UTCYO Yokozuna

2017 Topps WWE Undisputed Triple Autographs

STATED PRINT RUN 10 SER.#'d SETS

UTAAKL	Styles/Anderson/Gallows	100.00	200.00
UTABAE	Bayley/Asuka/Moon	150.00	300.00
UTACSB	Flair/Banks/Lynch	250.00	400.00
UTADSR	Ambrose/Rollins/Reigns	125.00	250.00
UTANCA	N.Bella/Carmella/Bliss	200.00	350.00

2017 Topps WWE Undisputed Women's Division

*BRONZE/99: .75X TO 2X BASIC CARDS
*SILVER/50: 1X TO 2.5X BASIC CARDS
*GREEN/25: 1.5X TO 4X BASIC CARDS
*GOLD/10: UNPRICED DUE TO SCARCITY
*RED/1: UNPRICED DUE TO SCARCITY
*P.P.BLACK/1: UNPRICED DUE TO SCARCITY
*P.P.CYAN/1: UNPRICED DUE TO SCARCITY
*P.P.MAGENTA/1: UNPRICED DUE TO SCARCITY
*P.P.YELLOW/1: UNPRICED DUE TO SCARCITY
RANDOMLY INSERTED INTO PACKS

W1	Alexa Bliss	4.00	10.00
W2	Alicia Fox	1.25	3.00
W3	Bayley	2.50	6.00
W4	Becky Lynch	2.50	6.00
W5	Carmella	2.00	5.00
W6	Charlotte Flair	3.00	8.00
W7	Dana Brooke	1.50	4.00
W8	Eva Marie	2.00	5.00
W9	Lana	2.50	6.00
W10	Maryse	1.50	4.00
W11	Mickie James	1.25	3.00
W12	Naomi	1.50	4.00
W13	Natalya	1.50	4.00
W14	Nia Jax	1.25	3.00
W15	Nikki Bella	2.00	5.00
W16	Sasha Banks	2.50	6.00
W17	Asuka	2.50	6.00
W18	Ember Moon	2.00	5.00
W19	Liv Morgan	1.25	3.00

2018 Topps WWE Undisputed

COMPLETE SET (50)		20.00	50.00
UNOPENED BOX (10 PACKS)		200.00	250.00
UNOPENED PACK (5 CARDS)		20.00	25.00

*ORANGE/99: .6X TO 1.5X BASIC CARDS
*GREEN/50: .75X TO 2X BASIC CARDS
*BLUE/25: 1X TO 2.5X BASIC CARDS
*GOLD/10: 2X TO 5X BASIC CARDS
*PURPLE/5: UNPRICED DUE TO SCARCITY
*RED/1: UNPRICED DUE TO SCARCITY
*P.P.BLACK/1: UNPRICED DUE TO SCARCITY
*P.P.CYAN/1: UNPRICED DUE TO SCARCITY

*P.P.MAGENTA/1: UNPRICED DUE TO SCARCITY
*P.P.YELLOW/1: UNPRICED DUE TO SCARCITY

1	AJ Styles	2.50	6.00
2	Alexa Bliss	3.00	8.00
3	Asuka	2.00	5.00
4	Bayley	1.00	2.50
5	Becky Lynch	1.50	4.00
6	Big E	.75	2.00
7	Bobby Roode	1.00	2.50
8	Brie Bella	1.25	3.00
9	Braun Strowman	1.50	4.00
10	Bray Wyatt	1.50	4.00
11	Brock Lesnar	2.50	6.00
12	Carmella	1.25	3.00
13	Cesaro	1.25	3.00
14	Charlotte Flair	2.00	5.00
15	Chris Jericho	1.50	4.00
16	Daniel Bryan	1.50	4.00
17	Dean Ambrose	1.25	3.00
18	Finn Balor	1.50	4.00
19	Jason Jordan	.60	1.50
20	Jeff Hardy	1.25	3.00
21	John Cena	2.50	6.00
22	Kane	1.00	2.50
23	Kevin Owens	1.50	4.00
24	Kofi Kingston	.75	2.00
25	Kurt Angle	1.50	4.00
26	Woken Matt Hardy	1.50	4.00
27	Mickie James	1.25	3.00
28	Naomi	.75	2.00
29	Natalya	.75	2.00
30	Nia Jax	1.00	2.50
31	Nikki Bella	1.25	3.00
32	Paige	1.50	4.00
33	Randy Orton	1.50	4.00
34	Roman Reigns	1.50	4.00
35	Ruby Riott	1.00	2.50
36	Sami Zayn	.60	1.50
37	Samoa Joe	1.25	3.00
38	Sasha Banks	2.00	5.00
39	Seth Rollins	1.50	4.00
40	Sheamus	1.25	3.00
41	Shinsuke Nakamura	1.50	4.00
42	The Miz	1.25	3.00
43	Triple H	1.50	4.00
44	Undertaker	2.50	6.00
45	Xavier Woods	.75	2.00
46	Adam Cole	.75	2.00
47	Aleister Black	.75	2.00
48	Drew McIntyre	1.00	2.50
49	Ember Moon	1.25	3.00
50	Kairi Sane	1.50	4.00

2018 Topps WWE Undisputed 30 Years of Royal Rumble

COMPLETE SET (25)		12.00	30.00

*ORANGE/99: .5X TO 1.2X BASIC CARDS
*GREEN/50: .6X TO 1.5X BASIC CARDS
*BLUE/25: .75X TO 2X BASIC CARDS
*GOLD/10: 1.2X TO 3X BASIC CARDS
*PURPLE/5: UNPRICED DUE TO SCARCITY
*RED/1: UNPRICED DUE TO SCARCITY
*P.P.BLACK/1: UNPRICED DUE TO SCARCITY
*P.P.CYAN/1: UNPRICED DUE TO SCARCITY
*P.P.MAGENTA/1: UNPRICED DUE TO SCARCITY
*P.P.YELLOW/1: UNPRICED DUE TO SCARCITY
RANDOMLY INSERTED INTO PACKS

RR1	Hacksaw Jim Duggan	.60	1.50
RR2	Big John Studd	.60	1.50
RR3	Ric Flair	2.00	5.00
RR4	Yokozuna	.75	2.00
RR5	Bret Hit Man Hart	1.50	4.00
RR6	Lex Luger	.75	2.00
RR7	Shawn Michaels	2.00	5.00
RR8	Shawn Michaels	2.00	5.00
RR9	Stone Cold Steve Austin	3.00	8.00
RR10	Stone Cold Steve Austin	3.00	8.00
RR11	The Rock	3.00	8.00
RR12	Stone Cold Steve Austin	3.00	8.00
RR13	Triple H	1.50	4.00
RR14	Brock Lesnar	2.50	6.00
RR15	Batista	1.00	2.50
RR16	Undertaker	2.50	6.00
RR17	John Cena	2.50	6.00
RR18	Randy Orton	1.50	4.00
RR19	Edge	1.50	4.00
RR20	Sheamus	1.25	3.00
RR21	John Cena	2.50	6.00
RR22	Batista	1.00	2.50
RR23	Roman Reigns	1.50	4.00
RR24	Triple H	1.50	4.00
RR25	Randy Orton	1.50	4.00

2018 Topps WWE Undisputed 30 Years of Survivor Series

COMPLETE SET (25)		12.00	30.00

*ORANGE/99: .5X TO 1.2X BASIC CARDS
*GREEN/50: .6X TO 1.5X BASIC CARDS
*BLUE/25: .75X TO 2X BASIC CARDS
*GOLD/10: 1.2X TO 3X BASIC CARDS
*PURPLE/5: UNPRICED DUE TO SCARCITY
*RED/1: UNPRICED DUE TO SCARCITY
*P.P.BLACK/1: UNPRICED DUE TO SCARCITY
*P.P.CYAN/1: UNPRICED DUE TO SCARCITY
*P.P.MAGENTA/1: UNPRICED DUE TO SCARCITY
*P.P.YELLOW/1: UNPRICED DUE TO SCARCITY
RANDOMLY INSERTED INTO PACKS

SS1	Andre The Giant	1.25	3.00
SS2	Macho Man Randy Savage	2.00	5.00
SS3	Ultimate Warrior	2.50	6.00
SS4	Ultimate Warrior	2.50	6.00
SS5	Big Boss Man	.60	1.50
SS6	The Nasty Boys	.60	1.50
SS7	Lex Luger	.75	2.00
SS8	Million Dollar Man Ted DiBiase	.75	2.00
SS9	Shawn Michaels	2.00	5.00
SS10	Ken Shamrock	.75	2.00
SS11	The Rock	3.00	8.00
SS12	Chris Jericho	1.50	4.00
SS13	Randy Orton	1.50	4.00
SS14	Batista	1.00	2.50
SS15	John Cena	2.50	6.00
SS16	Randy Orton	1.50	4.00
SS17	Mickie James	1.25	3.00
SS18	Kofi Kingston	.75	2.00
SS19	Dolph Ziggler	.75	2.00
SS20	Dolph Ziggler	.75	2.00
SS21	Natalya	.75	2.00
SS22	John Cena	2.50	6.00
SS23	The Usos	1.00	2.50
SS24	AJ Styles	2.50	6.00
SS25	Kurt Angle	1.50	4.00

2018 Topps WWE Undisputed Autographed Kiss and Shirt Relic Booklets

STATED ODDS 1:1,500
STATED PRINT RUN 5 SER.#'d SETS
UNPRICED DUE TO SCARCITY

KSAF Alicia Fox
KSEM Ember Moon
KSNA Natalya
KSNB Nikki Bella
KSRY Renee Young

2018 Topps WWE Undisputed Autographed Relics

*SILVER/50: .5X TO 1.2X BASIC AUTOS
*BLUE/25: UNPRICED DUE TO SCARCITY
*GOLD/10: UNPRICED DUE TO SCARCITY
*PURPLE/5: UNPRICED DUE TO SCARCITY
*RED/1: UNPRICED DUE TO SCARCITY
*P.P.BLACK/1: UNPRICED DUE TO SCARCITY
*P.P.CYAN/1: UNPRICED DUE TO SCARCITY
*P.P.MAGENTA/1: UNPRICED DUE TO SCARCITY
*P.P.YELLOW/1: UNPRICED DUE TO SCARCITY
STATED ODDS 1:10
STATED PRINT RUN 99 SER.#'d SETS

URAA Andrade Cien Almas	8.00	20.00
URAB Alexa Bliss	60.00	120.00
URAE Aiden English	5.00	12.00
URAF Alicia Fox	15.00	40.00
URAK Akam	6.00	15.00
URAP Apollo Crews	5.00	12.00
URAW Alexander Wolfe	6.00	15.00
URAX Curtis Axel	5.00	12.00
URBK Becky Lynch	30.00	75.00
URCA Carmella	20.00	50.00
URCF Charlotte Flair	20.00	50.00
URCG Chad Gable	6.00	15.00
URDW Dash Wilder	6.00	15.00
UREY Eric Young	8.00	20.00
URFN Fandango	5.00	12.00
URGD Goldust	10.00	25.00
URHA Harper	6.00	15.00
URJJ JoJo	15.00	40.00
URJO Jason Jordan	5.00	12.00
URJU Jimmy Uso	6.00	15.00
URKA Karl Anderson	5.00	12.00
URLG Luke Gallows	6.00	15.00
URNA Naomi	10.00	25.00
URNC Nikki Cross	10.00	25.00
URNT Natalya	12.00	30.00
URNW No Way Jose	8.00	20.00
URRE Rezar	6.00	15.00
URRY Renee Young	15.00	40.00
URSB Sasha Banks	25.00	60.00
URSD Scott Dawson	6.00	15.00
URSR Seth Rollins	15.00	40.00
URTC Tommaso Ciampa	8.00	20.00
URZR Zack Ryder	6.00	15.00

2018 Topps WWE Undisputed Autographs

*ORANGE/99: .5X TO 1.2X BASIC AUTOS
*GREEN/50: .6X TO 1.5X BASIC AUTOS
*BLUE/25: UNPRICED DUE TO SCARCITY
*GOLD/10: UNPRICED DUE TO SCARCITY
*PURPLE/5: UNPRICED DUE TO SCARCITY
*RED/1: UNPRICED DUE TO SCARCITY

*P.P.BLACK/1: UNPRICED DUE TO SCARCITY
*P.P.CYAN/1: UNPRICED DUE TO SCARCITY
*P.P.MAGENTA/1: UNPRICED DUE TO SCARCITY
*P.P.YELLOW/1: UNPRICED DUE TO SCARCITY
RANDOMLY INSERTED INTO PACKS

UAAB Alexa Bliss	30.00	75.00
UAAC Adam Cole	12.00	30.00
UAAJ AJ Styles	20.00	50.00
UAAS Asuka	15.00	40.00
UABA Bayley	15.00	40.00
UABC Baron Corbin	6.00	15.00
UABE Big E	6.00	15.00
UABF Bobby Fish	8.00	20.00
UABL Becky Lynch	25.00	60.00
UABR Bobby Roode	10.00	25.00
UABW Bray Wyatt	10.00	25.00
UACA Carmella	12.00	30.00
UACE Cesaro	6.00	15.00
UACF Charlotte Flair	15.00	40.00
UACG Chad Gable	4.00	10.00
UADA Dean Ambrose	8.00	20.00
UADB Daniel Bryan	15.00	40.00
UADM Drew McIntyre	10.00	25.00
UADW Dash Wilder	5.00	12.00
UAEL Elias	15.00	40.00
UAEY Eric Young	5.00	12.00
UAFA Fandango	8.00	20.00
UAFB Finn Balor	15.00	40.00
UAHI Hideo Itami	6.00	15.00
UAJH Jeff Hardy	12.00	30.00
UAJJ Jason Jordan	6.00	15.00
UAJM Jinder Mahal	6.00	15.00
UAKA Karl Anderson	4.00	10.00
UAKK Kofi Kingston	4.00	10.00
UAKO Kevin Owens	12.00	30.00
UAKS Kairi Sane	25.00	60.00
UALA Lana	8.00	20.00
UAMH Matt Hardy	10.00	25.00
UAMK Maria Kanellis	8.00	20.00
UAMR Mojo Rawley	4.00	10.00
UANA Naomi	5.00	12.00
UANJ Nia Jax	10.00	25.00
UARS Roderick Strong	6.00	15.00
UARU Rusev	5.00	12.00
UASB Sasha Banks	20.00	50.00
UASD Scott Dawson	4.00	10.00
UASH Sheamus	6.00	15.00
UASJ Samoa Joe	10.00	25.00
UASN Shinsuke Nakamura	10.00	25.00
UASR Seth Rollins	12.00	30.00
UAST Sting	15.00	40.00
UASZ Sami Zayn	5.00	12.00
UATB Tyler Breeze	6.00	15.00
UATD Tye Dillinger	5.00	12.00
UATM The Miz	8.00	20.00
UAVD Velveteen Dream	15.00	40.00
UAXW Xavier Woods	5.00	12.00
UAZR Zack Ryder	4.00	10.00
UAABL Aleister Black	10.00	20.00
UABCA Big Cass	5.00	12.00
UABRS Braun Strowman	12.00	30.00
UAEMB Ember Moon	12.00	30.00
UAKOH Kassius Ohno	6.00	15.00
UAKUA Kurt Angle	12.00	30.00
UAKYO Kyle O'Reilly	6.00	15.00
UAMAR Maryse	10.00	25.00
UANAT Natalya	8.00	20.00

UARRI Ruby Riott	8.00	20.00
UASBE Shelton Benjamin	6.00	15.00

2018 Topps WWE Undisputed Classic Matches Dual Autographed Relics

*PURPLE/5: UNPRICED DUE TO SCARCITY
*RED/1: UNPRICED DUE TO SCARCITY
STATED ODDS 1:766
STATED PRINT RUN 10 SER.#'d SETS
UNPRICED DUE TO SCARCITY

ARBH HHH/D.Bryan
ARDS Sheamus/D.Bryan
ARRH HHH/S.Rollins
ARRU Undertaker/R.Reigns

2018 Topps WWE Undisputed Cut Signatures

STATED ODDS 1:19,120
STATED PRINT RUN 1 SER.#'d SET
UNPRICED DUE TO SCARCITY

CSCH Mr. Perfect Curt Hennig
CSEG Eddie Guerrero

2018 Topps WWE Undisputed Dual Autographs

*GOLD/10: UNPRICED DUE TO SCARCITY
*PURPLE/5: UNPRICED DUE TO SCARCITY
*RED/1: UNPRICED DUE TO SCARCITY
STATED ODDS 1:154
STATED PRINT RUN 25 SER.#'d SETS

DAAJ K.Angle/J.Jordan	25.00	60.00
DAAR D.Ambrose/S.Rollins	30.00	75.00
DABG S.Benjamin/C.Gable	15.00	40.00
DACS Sheamus/Cesaro	15.00	40.00
DAFB T.Breeze/Fandango	30.00	75.00
DAGA K.Anderson/L.Gallows	25.00	60.00
DAHH J.Hardy/M.Hardy	60.00	120.00
DARR M.Rawley/Z.Ryder	30.00	75.00
DATM HHH/S.McMahon	150.00	300.00
DAWD S.Dawson/D.Wilder	15.00	40.00

2018 Topps WWE Undisputed Quad Autographed Booklets

QAAUTH HHH/McMahon/Rollins/Orton
QATEAMA Benjamin/Jordan/Gable/Angle
QAWYATT Wyatt/Strowman/Harper/Rowan
QASANITY Cross/Wolfe/Dain/Young
QATHEMIZ Axel/Maryse/Miz/Dallas

2018 Topps WWE Undisputed Relics

*GREEN/50: .6X TO 1.2X BASIC MEM
*BLUE/25: .75X TO 2X BASIC MEM
*GOLD/10: 1.5X TO 4X BASIC MEM
*PURPLE/5: UNPRICED DUE TO SCARCITY
*RED/1: UNPRICED DUE TO SCARCITY
*P.P.BLACK/1: UNPRICED DUE TO SCARCITY
*P.P.CYAN/1: UNPRICED DUE TO SCARCITY
*P.P.MAGENTA/1: UNPRICED DUE TO SCARCITY
*P.P.YELLOW/1: UNPRICED DUE TO SCARCITY
STATED ODDS 1:10
STATED PRINT RUN 99 SER.#'d SETS

URAA Andrade Cien Almas	5.00	12.00
URAB Alexa Bliss	12.00	30.00
URAE Aiden English	2.00	5.00
URAF Alicia Fox	5.00	12.00
URAK Akam	2.00	5.00
URAW Alexander Wolfe	2.50	6.00

URAX Curtis Axel	3.00	8.00
URBC Baron Corbin	2.50	6.00
URBE Big E	2.50	6.00
URBK Becky Lynch	10.00	25.00
URBL Brock Lesnar	6.00	15.00
URBR Bobby Roode	2.50	6.00
URCA Carmella	8.00	20.00
URCF Charlotte Flair	6.00	15.00
URCG Chad Gable	2.50	6.00
URDB Daniel Bryan	5.00	12.00
URDW Dash Wilder	3.00	8.00
UREM Ember Moon	5.00	12.00
UREY Eric Young	2.50	6.00
URGD Goldust	3.00	8.00
URHA Harper	2.00	5.00
URHI Hideo Itami	2.00	5.00
URJC John Cena	10.00	25.00
URJJ JoJo	6.00	15.00
URJO Jason Jordan	2.00	5.00
URJU Jimmy Uso	3.00	8.00
URKA Karl Anderson	3.00	8.00
URKK Kofi Kingston	2.50	6.00
URKO Kevin Owens	2.50	6.00
URLG Luke Gallows	2.00	5.00
URNA Naomi	2.50	6.00
URNC Nikki Cross	6.00	15.00
URNT Natalya	3.00	8.00
URNW No Way Jose	2.00	5.00
URRE Rezar	2.00	5.00
URRR Roman Reigns	6.00	15.00
URRY Renee Young	5.00	12.00
URSB Sasha Banks	12.00	30.00
URSD Scott Dawson	2.00	5.00
URSR Seth Rollins	2.50	6.00
URTC Tommaso Ciampa	6.00	15.00
URXW Xavier Woods	2.50	6.00

2018 Topps WWE Undisputed Rivals Dual Autograph and Championship Booklets

STATED ODDS 1:1,500
STATED PRINT RUN 5 SER.#'d SETS
UNPRICED DUE TO SCARCITY

ACAC B.Corbin/D.Ambrose
ACBF Bayley/C.Flair
ACNB A.Bliss/Naomi
ACOJ C.Jericho/K.Owens
ACOW B.Wyatt/R.Orton

2018 Topps WWE Undisputed Triple Autographs

*PURPLE/5: UNPRICED DUE TO SCARCITY
*RED/1: UNPRICED DUE TO SCARCITY
STATED ODDS 1:475
STATED PRINT RUN 10 SER.#'d SETS

TACFO O'Reilly/Cole/Fish
TAKBW Kingston/Woods/Big E
TAMAD Miz/Axel/Dallas
TAOTC O'Neil/Crews/Tozawa
TASGA Anderson/Gallows/Styles
TAUUN J.Uso/J.Uso/Naomi
TAYWD Dain/Young/Wolfe

2018 Topps WWE Undisputed Triple Shirt Relics

*GOLD/10: UNPRICED DUE TO SCARCITY
*PURPLE/5: UNPRICED DUE TO SCARCITY

*RED/1: UNPRICED DUE TO SCARCITY
STATED ODDS 1:310
STATED PRINT RUN 25 SER.#'d SETS

TSBGA Gallows/Balor/Anderson	20.00	50.00
TSDAY Woods/Kingston/Big E	12.00	30.00
TSNUU The Usos/Naomi	15.00	40.00
TSOZB Zayn/Bryan/Owens	12.00	30.00
TSRRJ Rollins/Reigns/Jordan	15.00	40.00

2019 Topps WWE Undisputed

COMPLETE SET (100) 25.00 60.00
UNOPENED BOX (10 PACKS)
UNOPENED PACK (5 CARDS)
*ORANGE/99: .6X TO 1.5X BASIC CARDS
*GREEN/50: .75X TO 2X BASIC CARDS
*BLUE/25: 1X TO 2.5X BASIC CARDS
*GOLD/10: UNPRICED DUE TO SCARCITY
*PURPLE/5: UNPRICED DUE TO SCARCITY
*RED/1: UNPRICED DUE TO SCARCITY
*P.P.BLACK/1: UNPRICED DUE TO SCARCITY
*P.P.CYAN/1: UNPRICED DUE TO SCARCITY
*P.P.MAGENTA/1: UNPRICED DUE TO SCARCITY
*P.P.YELLOW/1: UNPRICED DUE TO SCARCITY

1 Aiden English	.50	1.25
2 AJ Styles	2.50	6.00
3 Alexa Bliss	2.50	6.00
4 Alexander Wolfe	.50	1.25
5 Andrade	.60	1.50
6 Asuka	1.50	4.00
7 Baron Corbin	.75	2.00
8 Bayley	1.00	2.50
9 Becky Lynch	2.00	5.00
10 Big E	.50	1.25
11 Billie Kay	1.00	2.50
12 Bo Dallas	.60	1.50
13 Bobby Lashley	1.00	2.50
14 Bobby Roode	1.00	2.50
15 Braun Strowman	1.25	3.00
16 Bray Wyatt	1.25	3.00
17 Carmella	1.25	3.00
18 Cedric Alexander	.50	1.25
19 Cesaro	.60	1.50
20 Charlotte Flair	2.00	5.00
21 Curtis Axel	.60	1.50
22 Daniel Bryan	2.00	5.00
23 Dash Wilder	.50	1.25
24 Dolph Ziggler	1.00	2.50
25 Drake Maverick	.50	1.25
26 Drew Gulak	.50	1.25
27 Drew McIntyre	.60	1.50
28 Elias	1.00	2.50
29 Ember Moon	1.25	3.00
30 Eric Young	.60	1.50
31 Finn Balor	1.25	3.00
32 Harper	.60	1.50
33 Jeff Hardy	1.25	3.00
34 Jey Uso	.60	1.50
35 Jimmy Uso	.60	1.50
36 Jinder Mahal	1.00	2.50
37 John Cena	2.00	5.00
38 Karl Anderson	.75	2.00
39 Kevin Owens	1.25	3.00
40 Killian Dain	.50	1.25
41 Kofi Kingston	.75	2.00
42 Kurt Angle	1.00	2.50
43 Lacey Evans	1.00	2.50
44 Lio Rush	.60	1.50
45 Liv Morgan	1.50	4.00
46 Luke Gallows	.75	2.00
47 Mustafa Ali	.50	1.25
48 Naomi	.75	2.00
49 Natalya	1.00	2.50
50 Nia Jax	1.00	2.50
51 Paige	2.00	5.00
52 Peyton Royce	1.25	3.00
53 Randy Orton	1.25	3.00
54 Rey Mysterio	1.25	3.00
55 Roman Reigns	1.25	3.00
56 Ronda Rousey	2.50	6.00
57 Rowan	.50	1.25
58 Ruby Riott	1.00	2.50
59 Rusev	1.00	2.50
60 Sami Zayn	1.00	2.50
61 Samoa Joe	1.00	2.50
62 Sarah Logan	.60	1.50
63 Sasha Banks	2.00	5.00
64 Scott Dawson	.50	1.25
65 Seth Rollins	1.25	3.00
66 Sheamus	.75	2.00
67 Shelton Benjamin	.60	1.50
68 Shinsuke Nakamura	1.25	3.00
69 The Miz	1.00	2.50
70 The Rock	2.50	6.00
71 Titus O'Neil	.60	1.50
72 Triple H	1.25	3.00
73 Undertaker	2.50	6.00
74 Xavier Woods	.60	1.50
75 Zelina Vega	.75	2.00
76 Adam Cole	.60	1.50
77 Aleister Black	.60	1.50
78 Deonna Purrazzo	.50	1.25
79 EC3	.50	1.25
80 Johnny Gargano	.50	1.25
81 Kairi Sane	1.00	2.50
82 Keith Lee	.50	1.25
83 Nikki Cross	.75	2.00
84 Ricochet	1.25	3.00
85 Shayna Baszler	1.00	2.50
86 Tommaso Ciampa	.50	1.25
87 Goldberg	1.50	4.00
88 Shawn Michaels	1.25	3.00
89 Sting	1.25	3.00
90 Trish Stratus	2.50	6.00
RS1 Finn Balor	1.25	3.00
RS2 Jeff Hardy	1.25	3.00
RS3 Sasha Banks	2.00	5.00
RS4 Bayley	1.00	2.50
RS5 Seth Rollins	1.25	3.00
RS6 Shinsuke Nakamura	1.25	3.00
RS7 Aleister Black	.60	1.50
RS8 Ricochet	1.25	3.00
RS9 Sting	1.25	3.00
RS10 Ric Flair	1.50	4.00

2019 Topps WWE Undisputed Autographed Kiss and Shirt Relic Booklet

STATED PRINT RUN 5 SER.#'d SETS
UNPRICED DUE TO SCARCITY

AKSAF Alicia Fox

2019 Topps WWE Undisputed Autographed Relics

*GREEN/50: .5X TO 1.2X BASIC AUTOS
*BLUE/25: .6X TO 1.5X BASIC AUTOS
*GOLD/10: UNPRICED DUE TO SCARCITY
*PURPLE/5: UNPRICED DUE TO SCARCITY
*RED/1: UNPRICED DUE TO SCARCITY
STATED PRINT RUN 120 SER.#'d SETS

UAR4H Shayna Baszler	10.00	25.00
UARAA Andrade	12.00	30.00
UARAB Alexa Bliss	60.00	120.00
UARAC Adam Cole	10.00	25.00
UARAE Aiden English	6.00	15.00
UARAK Asuka	20.00	50.00
UARBD Bo Dallas	6.00	15.00
UARBS Braun Strowman	12.00	30.00
UARCA Curtis Axel	6.00	15.00
UARCM Carmella	15.00	40.00
UARCS Cesaro	6.00	15.00
UARDW Dash Wilder	6.00	15.00
UAREL Elias	10.00	25.00
UARFB Finn Balor	12.00	30.00
UARJH Jeff Hardy	12.00	30.00
UARKD Killian Dain	6.00	15.00
UARKK Kofi Kingston	12.00	30.00
UARLG Luke Gallows	6.00	15.00
UARLM Liv Morgan	25.00	60.00
UARMG Karl Anderson	6.00	15.00
UARNJ Nia Jax	8.00	20.00
UARNM Naomi	8.00	20.00
UARNN Natalya	10.00	25.00
UARNW No Way Jose	6.00	15.00
UARRB Ruby Riott	12.00	30.00
UARRC Ricochet	20.00	50.00
UARSB Sasha Banks	20.00	50.00
UARSD Scott Dawson	6.00	15.00
UARSM Sheamus	6.00	15.00
UARSR Seth Rollins	8.00	20.00
UARSZ Sami Zayn	6.00	15.00
UARTC Tommaso Ciampa	10.00	25.00
UARTM The Miz	10.00	25.00
UARVD Velveteen Dream	10.00	25.00
UARXW Xavier Woods	6.00	15.00
UARZR Zack Ryder	6.00	15.00

2019 Topps WWE Undisputed Autographed Relics Blue

UARCH Curt Hawkins 10.00 25.00

2019 Topps WWE Undisputed Autographed Relics Green

UARAF Alicia Fox 8.00 20.00

2019 Topps WWE Undisputed Autographed Tag Team Championship Medallion Booklets

STATED PRINT RUN 5 SER.#'d SETS
UNPRICED DUE TO SCARCITY

DACBT C.Axel/B.Dallas
DACND X.Woods/K.Kingston
DACTB Cesaro/Sheamus
DACUSO Jey and Jimmy Uso

2019 Topps WWE Undisputed Autographs

Ronda Rousey, Triple H, and Undertaker do not have regular base autographs. Undertaker's base autograph is in the Orange parallel set while the base autographs of Ronda Rousey and Triple H are in the Gold parallel set.

*GOLD/10: UNPRICED DUE TO SCARCITY
*PURPLE/5: UNPRICED DUE TO SCARCITY
*RED/1: UNPRICED DUE TO SCARCITY
*P.P.BLACK/1: UNPRICED DUE TO SCARCITY
*P.P.CYAN/1: UNPRICED DUE TO SCARCITY
*P.P.MAGENTA/1: UNPRICED DUE TO SCARCITY
*P.P.YELLOW/1: UNPRICED DUE TO SCARCITY
STATED PRINT RUN 199 SER.#'d SETS

AAA Andrade Almas	5.00	12.00
AAB Alexa Bliss	50.00	100.00
AAC Adam Cole	10.00	25.00
AAL Aleister Black	8.00	20.00
AAS AJ Styles	15.00	40.00
AAW Alexander Wolfe	5.00	12.00
ABC Baron Corbin	5.00	12.00
ABD Bo Dallas	5.00	12.00
ABE Big E	6.00	15.00
ABL Becky Lynch	25.00	60.00
ABR Bobby Roode	8.00	20.00
ABS Braun Strowman	10.00	25.00
ACA Cedric Alexander	5.00	12.00
ACE Cesaro	5.00	12.00
ACF Charlotte Flair	20.00	50.00
ACJ Cactus Jack	15.00	40.00
ACU Curtis Axel	5.00	12.00
ADK Dakota Kai	12.00	30.00
ADM Drew McIntyre	6.00	15.00
ADP Deonna Purrazzo	20.00	50.00
AEC EC3	5.00	12.00
AEY Eric Young	5.00	12.00
AFB Finn Balor	12.00	30.00
AJF Jeff Hardy	12.00	30.00
AJG Johnny Gargano	6.00	15.00
AJM Jinder Mahal	5.00	12.00
AKA Kurt Angle	10.00	25.00
AKD Killian Dain	5.00	12.00
AKK Kofi Kingston	10.00	25.00
AKL Keith Lee	6.00	15.00
AKR Kyle O'Reilly	5.00	12.00
AKS Kairi Sane	15.00	40.00
ALR Lio Rush	5.00	12.00
AMA Maryse	10.00	25.00
AME Carmella	10.00	25.00
AMR Mandy Rose	15.00	40.00
ANA Naomi	6.00	15.00
ANJ Nia Jax	8.00	20.00
ANN Natalya	5.00	12.00
APD Pete Dunne	6.00	15.00
ARI Ricochet	20.00	50.00
ARM Rey Mysterio	12.00	30.00
ARS Roderick Strong	5.00	12.00
ARU Rusev	5.00	12.00
ARY Renee Young	6.00	15.00
ASD Sonya Deville	12.00	30.00
ASH Sheamus	5.00	12.00
ASN Shinsuke Nakamura	10.00	25.00
AST Sting	15.00	40.00
ASU Asuka	15.00	40.00
ASZ Sami Zayn	5.00	12.00
ATC Tommaso Ciampa	8.00	20.00
ATM The Miz	10.00	25.00
ATN Titus O'Neil	5.00	12.00
AVD Velveteen Dream	10.00	25.00
AXW Xavier Woods	5.00	12.00
AZV Zelina Vega	12.00	30.00
ABAS Shayna Baszler	10.00	25.00
AE Elias	8.00	20.00

2019 Topps WWE Undisputed Cut Signatures

STATED PRINT RUN 1 SER.#'d SET
UNPRICED DUE TO SCARCITY

CSDR Dusty Rhodes
CSEG Eddie Guerrero
CSJN Jim "The Anvil" Neidhart

2019 Topps WWE Undisputed Dual Autographs

*GOLD/10: UNPRICED DUE TO SCARCITY
*PURPLE/5: UNPRICED DUE TO SCARCITY
*RED/1: UNPRICED DUE TO SCARCITY
STATED PRINT RUN 25 SER.#'d SETS

DTI B.Kay/P.Royce	125.00	250.00
DTR D.Wilder/S.Dawson	50.00	100.00
DUE R.Strong/K.O'Reilly	25.00	60.00
DWR Hanson/Rowe	100.00	200.00

2019 Topps WWE Undisputed Quad Autographs Booklets

STATED PRINT RUN 5 SER.#'d SETS
UNPRICED DUE TO SCARCITY

QHW Flair/Lynch/Banks/Bayley
QUE Strong/O'Reilly/Fish/Cole

2019 Topps WWE Undisputed Relics

*GREEN/50: .5X TO 1.2X BASIC MEM
*BLUE/25: .6X TO 1.5X BASIC MEM
*GOLD/10: UNPRICED DUE TO SCARCITY
*PURPLE/5: UNPRICED DUE TO SCARCITY
*RED/1: UNPRICED DUE TO SCARCITY
STATED PRINT RUN 99 SER.#'d SETS

UR4H Shayna Baszler	4.00	10.00
URAA Andrade	4.00	10.00
URAB Alexa Bliss	12.00	30.00
URAC Adam Cole	6.00	15.00
URAF Alicia Fox	4.00	10.00
URAK Asuka	5.00	12.00
URBD Bo Dallas	4.00	10.00
URBS Braun Strowman	5.00	12.00
URCA Curtis Axel	5.00	12.00
URCF Charlotte Flair	10.00	25.00
URCM Carmella	6.00	15.00
URCS Cesaro	3.00	8.00
URDW Dash Wilder	3.00	8.00
URDZ Dolph Ziggler	4.00	10.00
UREL Elias	3.00	8.00
UREM Ember Moon	5.00	12.00
URFB Finn Balor	5.00	12.00
URJC John Cena	6.00	15.00
URJH Jeff Hardy	5.00	12.00
URKD Killian Dain	5.00	12.00
URKK Kofi Kingston	4.00	10.00
URKO Kevin Owens	5.00	12.00
URLG Luke Gallows	4.00	10.00
URLM Liv Morgan	10.00	25.00
URMG Karl Anderson	4.00	10.00
URNJ Nia Jax	5.00	12.00
URNM Naomi	3.00	8.00
URNN Natalya	4.00	10.00
URNW No Way Jose	4.00	10.00
URRB Ruby Riott	4.00	10.00
URRC Ricochet	5.00	12.00
URRR Roman Reigns	6.00	15.00
URSB Sasha Banks	8.00	20.00
URSD Scott Dawson	3.00	8.00
URSM Sheamus	3.00	8.00
URSR Seth Rollins	5.00	12.00
URSZ Sami Zayn	3.00	8.00
URTC Tommaso Ciampa	5.00	12.00
URTM The Miz	3.00	8.00
URVD Velveteen Dream	4.00	10.00
URXW Xavier Woods	4.00	10.00
URZR Zack Ryder	5.00	12.00
URUCE Jey Uso	3.00	8.00
URUSO Jimmy Uso	3.00	8.00

2019 Topps WWE Undisputed Triple Autographs

*PURPLE/5: UNPRICED DUE TO SCARCITY
*RED/1: UNPRICED DUE TO SCARCITY
STATED PRINT RUN 10 SER.#'d SETS
UNPRICED DUE TO SCARCITY

TLP Kalisto/Metalik/Dorado
TND Big E/Woods/Kingston
TRD Rusev/Lana/English
TRS Logan/Riott/Morgan

2020 Topps WWE Undisputed

COMPLETE SET (90)	25.00	60.00

*ORANGE/99: .75X TO 2X BASIC CARDS
*GREEN/50: 1.2X TO 3X BASIC CARDS
*BLUE/25: UNPRICED DUE TO SCARCITY
*GOLD/10: UNPRICED DUE TO SCARCITY
*PURPLE/5: UNPRICED DUE TO SCARCITY
*RED/1: UNPRICED DUE TO SCARCITY
*P.P.BLACK/1: UNPRICED DUE TO SCARCITY
*P.P.CYAN/1: UNPRICED DUE TO SCARCITY
*P.P.MAGENTA/1: UNPRICED DUE TO SCARCITY
*P.P.YELLOW/1: UNPRICED DUE TO SCARCITY

1 Aleister Black	1.00	2.50
2 Andrade	.75	2.00
3 Asuka	1.00	2.50
4 Becky Lynch	2.00	5.00
5 Bianca Belair	1.25	3.00
6 Bobby Lashley	1.00	2.50
7 Buddy Murphy	.60	1.50
8 Charlotte Flair	2.00	5.00
9 Drew McIntyre	1.00	2.50
10 Edge	1.00	2.50
11 Erik	.50	1.25
12 Humberto Carrillo	.75	2.00
13 Ivar	.50	1.25
14 Kairi Sane	1.00	2.50
15 Kevin Owens	.60	1.50
16 Lana	1.25	3.00
17 Nia Jax	.75	2.00
18 Randy Orton	1.25	3.00
19 Ricochet	.75	2.00
20 Ruby Riott	.75	2.00
21 R-Truth	.50	1.25
22 Samoa Joe	.75	2.00
23 Seth Rollins	1.00	2.50
24 Zelina Vega	1.00	2.50
25 AJ Styles	1.50	4.00
26 Alexa Bliss	2.50	6.00
27 Bayley	1.00	2.50
28 Big E	.50	1.25
29 Braun Strowman	1.25	3.00
30 The Fiend Bray Wyatt	1.50	4.00
31 Carmella	1.25	3.00
32 Cesaro	.50	1.25
33 Dana Brooke	.75	2.00
34 Daniel Bryan	1.50	4.00
35 Dolph Ziggler	.50	1.25
36 Elias	.50	1.25
37 King Corbin	.60	1.50
38 Kofi Kingston	.75	2.00
39 Lacey Evans	1.25	3.00
40 Matt Riddle	1.00	2.50
41 Mustafa Ali	.75	2.00
42 Naomi	1.00	2.50
43 Nikki Cross	1.00	2.50
44 Robert Roode	.50	1.25
45 Roman Reigns	1.25	3.00
46 Sami Zayn	.60	1.50
47 Sasha Banks	2.00	5.00
48 Sheamus	.60	1.50
49 Shinsuke Nakamura	1.00	2.50
50 The Miz	.75	2.00
51 Xavier Woods	.50	1.25
52 Adam Cole	1.25	3.00
53 Bobby Fish	.50	1.25
54 Candice LeRae	1.50	4.00
55 Dakota Kai	1.00	2.50
56 Damian Priest	.50	1.25
57 Dominik Dijakovic	.50	1.25
58 Finn Balor	1.25	3.00
59 Io Shirai	.75	2.00
60 Johnny Gargano	1.00	2.50
61 Kay Lee Ray	.75	2.00
62 Karrion Kross	1.00	2.50
63 Keith Lee	.50	1.25
64 Kushida	.60	1.50
65 Kyle O'Reilly	.60	1.50
66 Mia Yim	1.00	2.50
67 Pete Dunne	.50	1.25
68 Rhea Ripley	1.25	3.00
69 Roderick Strong	1.00	2.50
70 Scarlett	2.00	5.00
71 Shayna Baszler	1.50	4.00
72 Tommaso Ciampa	1.00	2.50
73 Toni Storm	1.25	3.00
74 Velveteen Dream	.60	1.50
75 Walter	1.00	2.50
76 John Cena	2.00	5.00
77 Ronda Rousey	2.50	6.00
78 Undertaker	2.00	5.00
79 Batista	.75	2.00
80 Booker T	1.00	2.50
81 Bret Hit Man Hart	1.25	3.00
82 Diesel	.75	2.00
83 Howard Finkel	.50	1.25
84 Hulk Hogan	1.50	4.00
85 Lita	1.25	3.00
86 Mr. T	1.00	2.50
87 Razor Ramon	.75	2.00
88 Rowdy Roddy Piper	1.25	3.00
89 Trish Stratus	2.50	6.00
90 Stone Cold Steve Austin	2.50	6.00

2020 Topps WWE Undisputed Autographed Dual Relics

*GREEN/50: .75X TO 2X BASIC AUTOS
*BLUE/25: UNPRICED DUE TO SCARCITY
*GOLD/10: UNPRICED DUE TO SCARCITY
*PURPLE/5: UNPRICED DUE TO SCARCITY
*RED/1: UNPRICED DUE TO SCARCITY
*P.P.BLACK/1: UNPRICED DUE TO SCARCITY
*P.P.CYAN/1: UNPRICED DUE TO SCARCITY
*P.P.MAGENTA/1: UNPRICED DUE TO SCARCITY
*P.P.YELLOW/1: UNPRICED DUE TO SCARCITY
STATED PRINT RUN 99 SER.#'d SETS

DRAAB Aleister Black	12.00	30.00
DRAAC Adam Cole	8.00	20.00
DRAAD Angelo Dawkins	8.00	20.00
DRAAJ AJ Styles	15.00	40.00
DRAAN Andrade/62	8.00	20.00
DRABB Bianca Belair	15.00	40.00
DRABF Bobby Fish	8.00	20.00
DRABO Bobby Lashley	8.00	20.00
DRABS Braun Strowman	10.00	25.00
DRACC Cesaro	6.00	15.00
DRACF Charlotte Flair	25.00	60.00
DRACS Cesaro	6.00	15.00
DRADZ Dolph Ziggler	6.00	15.00
DRAEK Erik	6.00	15.00
DRAFB Finn Balor	10.00	25.00
DRAJD Mia Yim	12.00	30.00
DRAJG Johnny Gargano	10.00	25.00
DRAKD Killian Dain	6.00	15.00
DRAKE Kevin Owens	8.00	20.00
DRAKK Kofi Kingston	8.00	20.00
DRAKO Kevin Owens	8.00	20.00
DRAKR Kyle O'Reilly	6.00	15.00
DRALE Lacey Evans	15.00	40.00
DRALS Bobby Lashley	8.00	20.00
DRAMR Matt Riddle	12.00	30.00
DRAMZ The Miz	8.00	20.00
DRANJ Nia Jax	6.00	15.00
DRANT Natalya	10.00	25.00
DRAOT Otis	12.00	30.00
DRAPD The Demon Finn Balor	15.00	40.00
DRAPP Ricochet	10.00	25.00
DRARB Ruby Riott	15.00	40.00
DRARC Ricochet	10.00	25.00
DRARH Rhea Ripley	50.00	100.00
DRARS Roderick Strong	6.00	15.00
DRASH Shayna Baszler	15.00	40.00
DRASR Seth Rollins	8.00	20.00
DRATC Tommaso Ciampa	6.00	15.00
DRAVD Velveteen Dream/46		
DRAXW Xavier Woods	6.00	15.00

2020 Topps WWE Undisputed Autographed Match Books

STATED PRINT RUN 5 SER.#'d SETS
UNPRICED DUE TO SCARCITY

MBCAS AJ Styles/Samoa Joe
MBCDT D.Bryan/Miz
MBCJT J.Gargano/T.Ciampa

2020 Topps WWE Undisputed Autographed Oversized Boxloaders

STATED PRINT RUN 5 SER.#'d SETS
UNPRICED DUE TO SCARCITY

BLAC Adam Cole
BLAJ AJ Styles
BLBA Bayley
BLBW The Fiend Bray Wyatt
BLKK Kofi Kingston
BLMR Matt Riddle
BLSB Sasha Banks
BLSN Shinsuke Nakamura
BLTM The Miz
BL4HW Shayna Baszler

2020 Topps WWE Undisputed Autographs

*ORANGE/99: .5X TO 1.2X BASIC AUTOS
*GREEN/50: .6X TO 1.5X BASIC AUTOS
*BLUE/25: UNPRICED DUE TO SCARCITY
*GOLD/10: UNPRICED DUE TO SCARCITY
*PURPLE/5: UNPRICED DUE TO SCARCITY
*RED/1: UNPRICED DUE TO SCARCITY
*P.P.BLACK/1: UNPRICED DUE TO SCARCITY
*P.P.CYAN/1: UNPRICED DUE TO SCARCITY
*P.P.MAGENTA/1: UNPRICED DUE TO SCARCITY
*P.P.YELLOW/1: UNPRICED DUE TO SCARCITY
STATED PRINT RUN 199 SER.#'d SETS

AAB	Alexa Bliss	50.00	100.00
AAC	Adam Cole	10.00	25.00
AAJ	AJ Styles	12.00	30.00
AAN	Andrade	6.00	15.00
AAS	Asuka	30.00	75.00
AAT	Aleister Black	8.00	20.00
AAZ	Zelina Vega	15.00	40.00
ABA	Bayley EXCH	15.00	40.00
ABB	Bianca Belair	12.00	30.00
ABD	Daniel Bryan	10.00	25.00
ABE	Big E	6.00	15.00
ABF	Bobby Fish	8.00	20.00
ABM	Buddy Murphy	6.00	15.00
ABS	Braun Strowman EXCH	10.00	25.00
ABT	Booker T	10.00	25.00
ABW	The Fiend Bray Wyatt	50.00	100.00
ACF	Charlotte Flair	20.00	50.00
ACL	Candice LeRae	15.00	40.00
ACM	Carmella EXCH	15.00	40.00
ACS	Cesaro	5.00	15.00
ADB	Dana Brooke	10.00	25.00
ADD	Dominik Dijakovic	8.00	20.00
ADK	Dakota Kai	20.00	50.00
ADM	Drew McIntyre	12.00	30.00
ADP	Damian Priest	8.00	20.00
ADZ	Dolph Ziggler	8.00	20.00
AHC	Humberto Carrillo	6.00	15.00
AIO	Io Shirai	30.00	75.00
AIV	Ivar	6.00	15.00
AJG	Johnny Gargano	6.00	15.00
AKC	King Corbin	8.00	20.00
AKK	Kofi Kingston	6.00	15.00
AKO	Kevin Owens	6.00	15.00
AKS	Kairi Sane	20.00	50.00
AKU	Kushida	8.00	20.00
ALE	Lacey Evans	15.00	40.00
ALN	Lana EXCH	10.00	25.00
ALT	Lita	20.00	50.00
AMA	Mustafa Ali	8.00	20.00
AMR	Matt Riddle	12.00	30.00
AMY	Mia Yim	10.00	25.00
ANC	Nikki Cross	10.00	25.00
ARB	Ruby Riott	12.00	30.00
ARC	Ricochet	8.00	20.00
ARD	Kyle O'Reilly	6.00	15.00
ARR	Roman Reigns EXCH	15.00	40.00
ART	R-Truth	12.00	30.00
ASB	Sasha Banks	30.00	75.00
ASG	Shorty G EXCH	8.00	20.00
ASJ	Samoa Joe	6.00	15.00
ASM	Sheamus	8.00	20.00
ASN	Shinsuke Nakamura	6.00	15.00
ASR	Seth Rollins	10.00	25.00
ASZ	Sami Zayn	6.00	15.00

ATC	Tommaso Ciampa	8.00	20.00
ATM	The Miz	8.00	20.00
AVD	Velveteen Dream EXCH	6.00	15.00
AVR	Erik	8.00	20.00
A4HW	Shayna Baszler	12.00	30.00
ABOB	Bobby Lashley	8.00	20.00
ALEE	Keith Lee	10.00	25.00
ARIP	Rhea Ripley	60.00	120.00
AROD	Roderick Strong EXCH	8.00	20.00

2020 Topps WWE Undisputed Cut Signatures

CSBB	Bam Bam Bigelow		
CSBH	Bobby The Brain Heenan		
CSBM	Big Boss Man		
CSBS	Bruno Sammartino		
CSDR	Dusty Rhodes		
CSEG	Eddie Guerrero		
CSGO	Mean Gene Okerlund		
CSJN	Jim The Anvil Neidhart		
CSJS	Big John Studd		
CSJT	Earthquake		
CSMP	Mr. Perfect		
CSNV	Nikolai Volkoff		
CSPB	Paul Bearer		
CSRP	Rowdy Roddy Piper		
CSRR	Ravishing Rick Rude		
CSRS	Macho Man Randy Savage		
CSUM	Umaga		
CSUW	Ultimate Warrior		
CSVD	Big Van Vader		
CSYO	Yokozuna		
CSDBS	Davey Boy Smith		

2020 Topps WWE Undisputed Dual Relics

*GREEN/50: .75X TO 2X BASIC MEM
*BLUE/25: UNPRICED DUE TO SCARCITY
*GOLD/10: UNPRICED DUE TO SCARCITY
*PURPLE/5: UNPRICED DUE TO SCARCITY
*RED/1: UNPRICED DUE TO SCARCITY
*P.P.BLACK/1: UNPRICED DUE TO SCARCITY
*P.P.CYAN/1: UNPRICED DUE TO SCARCITY
*P.P.MAGENTA/1: UNPRICED DUE TO SCARCITY
*P.P.YELLOW/1: UNPRICED DUE TO SCARCITY
STATED PRINT RUN 99 SER.#'d SETS

DRAB	Aleister Black	3.00	8.00
DRAC	Adam Cole	2.50	6.00
DRAD	Angelo Dawkins	2.50	6.00
DRAJ	AJ Styles	4.00	10.00
DRAN	Andrade	2.00	5.00
DRBB	Bianca Belair	3.00	8.00
DRBF	Bobby Fish	2.00	5.00
DRBO	Bobby Lashley	2.50	6.00
DRBS	Braun Strowman	3.00	8.00
DRCF	Charlotte Flair	5.00	12.00
DRCM	Carmella	8.00	20.00
DRCS	Cesaro	2.50	6.00
DRDZ	Dolph Ziggler	2.50	6.00
DREK	Erik	2.00	5.00
DREL	Elias	2.50	6.00
DRFB	Finn Balor	6.00	15.00
DRJD	Mia Yim	5.00	12.00
DRJG	Johnny Gargano	4.00	10.00
DRKD	Killian Dain	2.00	5.00
DRKE	Kevin Owens	3.00	8.00
DRKK	Kofi Kingston	3.00	8.00

DRKO	Kevin Owens	3.00	8.00
DRKR	Kyle O'Reilly	2.50	6.00
DRKS	Kairi Sane	12.00	30.00
DRLE	Lacey Evans	6.00	15.00
DRMR	Matt Riddle	4.00	10.00
DRMZ	The Miz	2.50	6.00
DRNJ	Nia Jax	2.50	6.00
DRNT	Natalya	3.00	8.00
DROT	Otis	2.00	5.00
DRPD	The Demon Finn Balor	6.00	15.00
DRRB	Ruby Riott	5.00	12.00
DRRC	Ricochet	3.00	8.00
DRRO	Randy Orton	3.00	8.00
DRRR	Roman Reigns	4.00	10.00
DRRS	Roderick Strong	2.00	5.00
DRSM	Shawn Michaels	4.00	10.00
DRSR	Seth Rollins	3.00	8.00
DRTC	Tommaso Ciampa	2.50	6.00
DRVD	Velveteen Dream	2.00	5.00
DRXW	Xavier Woods	2.50	6.00
DRHHH	Triple H	4.00	10.00

2020 Topps WWE Undisputed Framed Autograph

STATED PRINT RUN 150 SER.#'d SETS

AFF	Bray Wyatt	50.00	100.00

2020 Topps WWE Undisputed Quad Autographs

STATED PRINT RUN 5 SER.#'d SETS
UNPRICED DUE TO SCARCITY

QHW	Banks/Flair/Lynch/Bayley
QIP	Walter/Barthel/Aichner/Wolfe
QUE	Cole/Fish/O'Reilly/Strong

2020 Topps WWE Undisputed Schamberger Art

COMPLETE SET (10)		20.00	50.00
RANDOMLY INSERTED INTO PACKS			
RS1	Mustafa Ali	3.00	8.00
RS2	Asuka	5.00	12.00
RS3	Becky Lynch	5.00	12.00
RS4	Bianca Belair	3.00	8.00
RS5	Eddie Guerrero	4.00	10.00
RS6	Macho Man Randy Savage	6.00	15.00
RS7	The Miz	2.50	6.00
RS8	Toni Storm	6.00	15.00
RS9	Undertaker	4.00	10.00
RS10	Walter	2.00	5.00

2020 Topps WWE Undisputed Schamberger Art Autographs

STATED PRINT RUN 10 SER.#'d SETS
UNPRICED DUE TO SCARCITY

RSRSAS	Schamberger/Ali
RSRSBB	Schamberger/Asuka
RSRSBL	Schamberger/Lynch
RSRSMA	Schamberger/Belair
RSRSRG	Schamberger/Guerrero
RSRSRS	Schamberger/Savage
RSRSTM	Schamberger/Miz
RSRSTS	Schamberger/Storm
RSRSUT	Schamberger/Undertaker
RSRSWT	Schamberger/WALTER

2020 Topps WWE Undisputed Schamberger Art Superstar Autographs

STATED PRINT RUN 10 SER.#'d SETS
UNPRICED DUE TO SCARCITY

ARSAS	Asuka
ARSBB	Bianca Belair
ARSMA	Mustafa Ali
ARSTM	The Miz

2020 Topps WWE Undisputed Tag Team Autographs

*GOLD/10: UNPRICED DUE TO SCARCITY
*PURPLE/5: UNPRICED DUE TO SCARCITY
*RED/1: UNPRICED DUE TO SCARCITY
STATED PRINT RUN 25 SER.#'d SETS

DAKW	K.Sane/Asuka	125.00	250.00
DASP	A.Dawkins/M.Ford	30.00	75.00
DAVR	Erik/Ivar	20.00	50.00

2020 Topps WWE Undisputed Triple Autographs

*PURPLE/5: UNPRICED DUE TO SCARCITY
*RED/1: UNPRICED DUE TO SCARCITY
STATED PRINT RUN 10 SER.#'d SETS
UNPRICED DUE TO SCARCITY

TALP	Dorado/Metalik/Kalisto
TAND	Woods/Big E/Kingston

2017 Topps WWE Women's Division

Also known as the Roster set.
UNOPENED BLASTER BOX (81 CARDS)
UNOPENED HANGER BOX (40 CARDS)
UNOPENED FAT PACK (18 CARDS)
*SILVER/50: 1.2X TO 3X BASIC CARDS
*BLUE/25: 2X TO 5X BASIC CARDS
*GOLD/10: UNPRICED DUE TO SCARCITY
*RED/1: UNPRICED DUE TO SCARCITY

R1	Aliyah	.40	1.00
R2	Asuka	1.00	2.50
R3	Billie Kay	.40	1.00
R4	Cathy Kelley	.30	.75
R5	Ember Moon	.75	2.00
R6	Kimberly Frankele	.30	.75
R7	Liv Morgan	.50	1.25
R8	Mandy Rose	.40	1.00
R9	Nikki Cross	.60	1.50
R10	Peyton Royce	.50	1.25
R11	Ruby Riot	.40	1.00
R12	Brie Bella	.75	2.00
R13	Alexa Bliss	1.50	4.00
R14	Alicia Fox	.50	1.25
R15	Bayley	1.00	2.50
R16	Charly Caruso	.30	.75
R17	Dana Brooke	.60	1.50
R18	Emma	.75	2.00
R19	JoJo	.50	1.25
R20	Maryse	.60	1.50
R21	Mickie James	.50	1.25
R22	Nia Jax	.50	1.25
R23	Sasha Banks	1.00	2.50
R24	Stephanie McMahon	.40	1.00
R25	Summer Rae	.75	2.00
R26	Lita	.60	1.50
R27	Becky Lynch	1.00	2.50
R28	Carmella	.75	2.00

R29	Charlotte Flair	1.25	3.00
R30	Dasha Fuentes	.40	1.00
R31	Lana	1.00	2.50
R32	Naomi	.60	1.50
R33	Natalya	.60	1.50
R34	Nikki Bella	.75	2.00
R35	Renee Young	.50	1.25
R36	Tamina	.40	1.00
R37	Alundra Blayze	.40	1.00
R38	Eve Torres	.50	1.25
R39	Miss Elizabeth	.50	1.25
R40	Sherri Martel	.40	1.00
R41	Terri Runnels	.30	.75
R42	Trish Stratus	1.25	3.00
R43	Wendi Richter	.40	1.00
R44	Beth Phoenix	.30	.75
R45	Ivory	.30	.75
R46	Judy Martin	.30	.75
R47	Kelly Kelly	.60	1.50
R48	Leilani Kai	.30	.75
R49	Princess Victoria	.30	.75
R50	Torrie Wilson	.75	2.00

2017 Topps WWE Women's Division Autographed Kiss and Mat Relics

STATED ODDS 1:1,054 BLASTER BOX EXCLUSIVE
STATED PRINT RUN 5 SER.#'d SETS
UNPRICED DUE TO SCARCITY

WARCA Carmella
WARNA Natalya

2017 Topps WWE Women's Division Autographed Mat Relics

STATED ODDS 1:68 BLASTER BOX
STATED ODDS 1:6,012 HANGER BOX
STATED ODDS 1:11,988 HANGER PACK
STATED PRINT RUN 10 SER.#'d SETS
UNPRICED DUE TO SCARCITY

MRAB Alexa Bliss
MRAF Alicia Fox
MRAS Asuka
MRBA Bayley
MRBL Becky Lynch
MRCA Carmella
MRCF Charlotte Flair
MRNJ Nia Jax
MRSR Summer Rae
MRSU Summer Rae
MRTA Tamina
MRASA Asuka
MRASU Asuka
MRBAY Bayley
MRBEC Becky Lynch
MRBLY Bayley
MRCAR Carmella
MRCHA Charlotte Flair
MRCHF Charlotte Flair
MRCRM Carmella
MREMM Emma
MRNAO Naomi
MRNAT Natalya
MRNIA Nia Jax
MRSUM Summer Rae
MRTAM Tamina
MRCHAR Charlotte Flair
MREMMA Emma

2017 Topps WWE Women's Division Autographs

*SILVER/50: .5X TO 1.2X BASIC AUTOS
*BLUE/25: .6X TO 1.5X BASIC AUTOS
*GOLD/10: UNPRICED DUE TO SCARCITY
*RED/1: UNPRICED DUE TO SCARCITY
STATED ODDS 1:13 BLASTER BOX
STATED ODDS 1:802 HANGER BOX
STATED ODDS 1:1,599 HANGER PACK
STATED PRINT RUN 99 OR FEWER SER.#'d SETS

R1	Aliyah/99	6.00	15.00
R2	Asuka/99	20.00	50.00
R3	Billie Kay/99	10.00	25.00
R4	Cathy Kelley/99	8.00	20.00
R5	Ember Moon/94	8.00	20.00
R7	Liv Morgan/99	12.00	30.00
R8	Mandy Rose/99	15.00	40.00
R10	Peyton Royce/99	10.00	25.00
R11	Ruby Riot/99	20.00	50.00
R12	Brie Bella/56	10.00	25.00
R13	Alexa Bliss/99	50.00	100.00
R14	Alicia Fox/61	10.00	25.00
R18	Emma/99	12.00	30.00
R19	JoJo/99	6.00	15.00
R22	Nia Jax/99	10.00	25.00
R23	Sasha Banks/68	25.00	60.00
R27	Becky Lynch/99	15.00	40.00
R28	Carmella/99	20.00	50.00
R29	Charlotte Flair/57	20.00	50.00
R30	Dasha Fuentes/99	6.00	15.00
R32	Naomi/99	8.00	20.00
R33	Natalya/78	8.00	20.00
R34	Nikki Bella/99	10.00	25.00
R36	Tamina/99	6.00	15.00
R37	Alundra Blayze/99	8.00	20.00
R41	Terri Runnels/99	10.00	25.00
R43	Wendi Richter/99	6.00	15.00
R44	Beth Phoenix/99	8.00	20.00
R45	Ivory/99	6.00	15.00
R46	Judy Martin/99	6.00	15.00
R47	Kelly Kelly/99	10.00	25.00
R48	Leilani Kai/99	6.00	15.00
R49	Princess Victoria/99	10.00	25.00
R50	Torrie Wilson/99	12.00	30.00

2017 Topps WWE Women's Division Autographs Blue

STATED ODDS 1:39 BLASTER BOX
STATED ODDS 1:3,280 HANGER BOX
STATED ODDS 1:6,539 HANGER PACK
STATED PRINT RUN 25 SER.#'d SETS

R25	Summer Rae	15.00	40.00

2017 Topps WWE Women's Division Autographs Silver

STATED ODDS 1:20 BLASTER BOX
STATED ODDS 1:1,569 HANGER BOX
STATED ODDS 1:3,128 HANGER PACK
STATED PRINT RUN 50 SER.#'d SETS

R15	Bayley	15.00	40.00
R20	Maryse	8.00	20.00
R38	Eve Torres	20.00	50.00
R42	Trish Stratus	25.00	60.00

2017 Topps WWE Women's Division Diva's Championship Medallions

*SILVER/50: .5X TO 1.2X BASIC MEM

*BLUE/25: .6X TO 1.5X BASIC MEM
*GOLD/10: UNPRICED DUE TO SCARCITY
*RED/1: UNPRICED DUE TO SCARCITY
STATED ODDS 1:15 BLASTER BOX
STATED ODDS 1:1,203 HANGER BOX
STATED ODDS 1:2,398 HANGER PACK
STATED PRINT RUN 99 SER.#'d SETS

DCM	Maryse	5.00	12.00
DCN	Natalya	5.00	12.00
DCAF	Alicia Fox	4.00	10.00
DCBB	Brie Bella	6.00	15.00
DCBP	Beth Phoenix	2.50	6.00
DCCF	Charlotte Flair	10.00	25.00
DCET	Eve Torres	4.00	10.00
DCKK	Kelly Kelly	5.00	12.00
DCMJ	Mickie James	4.00	10.00
DCNB	Nikki Bella	6.00	15.00

2017 Topps WWE Women's Division Finishers and Signature Moves

*SILVER/50: 1X TO 2.5X BASIC CARDS
*BLUE/25: 1.2X TO 3X BASIC CARDS
*GOLD/10: 2X TO 5X BASIC CARDS
*RED/1: UNPRICED DUE TO SCARCITY
STATED ODDS 5:1 HANGER BOX EXCLUSIVE

F1	Alexa Bliss	3.00	8.00
F2	Nikki Bella	1.50	4.00
F3	Bayley	2.00	5.00
F4	Natalya	1.25	3.00
F5	Brie Bella	1.50	4.00
F6	Sasha Banks	2.00	5.00
F7	Becky Lynch	2.00	5.00
F8	Beth Phoenix	.60	1.50
F9	Sasha Banks	2.00	5.00
F10	Charlotte Flair	2.50	6.00
F11	Eve Torres	1.00	2.50
F12	Mickie James	1.00	2.50
F13	Trish Stratus	2.50	6.00
F14	Naomi	1.25	3.00
F15	Alicia Fox	1.00	2.50
F16	Tamina	.75	2.00
F17	Dana Brooke	1.25	3.00
F18	Emma	1.50	4.00
F19	Carmella	1.50	4.00
F20	Summer Rae	1.50	4.00
F21	Nia Jax	1.00	2.50
F22	Stephanie McMahon	.75	2.00
F23	Kelly Kelly	1.25	3.00
F24	Charlotte Flair	2.50	6.00

2017 Topps WWE Women's Division Kiss

*GOLD/10: UNPRICED DUE TO SCARCITY
*RED/1: UNPRICED DUE TO SCARCITY
STATED ODDS 1:67 BLASTER BOX
STATED ODDS 1:1,503 HANGER BOX
STATED ODDS 1:2,997 HANGER PACK
STATED PRINT RUN 99 SER.#'d SETS

KAF	Alicia Fox/99	15.00	40.00
KBK	Billie Kay/99	25.00	60.00
KCA	Carmella/99	25.00	60.00
KDB	Dana Brooke/69	15.00	40.00
KNA	Naomi/54	15.00	40.00
KPR	Peyton Royce/99	20.00	50.00
KRY	Renee Young/68	25.00	60.00

2017 Topps WWE Women's Division Kiss Autographs

*GOLD/10: UNPRICED DUE TO SCARCITY
*RED/1: UNPRICED DUE TO SCARCITY
STATED ODDS 1:211 BLASTER BOX
STATED ODDS 1:6,012 HANGER BOX
STATED ODDS 1:11,988 HANGER PACK
STATED PRINT RUN 25 SER.#'d SETS

KAF	Alicia Fox		
KAS	Asuka		
KBK	Billie Kay	50.00	100.00
KCA	Carmella	50.00	100.00
KDB	Dana Brooke	30.00	75.00
KMR	Mandy Rose	60.00	120.00
KPR	Peyton Royce	125.00	250.00
KRY	Renee Young	30.00	75.00

2017 Topps WWE Women's Division Mat Relics

*SILVER/50: .5X TO 1.2X BASIC MEM
*BLUE/25: .6X TO 1.5X BASIC MEM
*GOLD/10: UNPRICED DUE TO SCARCITY
*RED/1: UNPRICED DUE TO SCARCITY
STATED ODDS 1:10 BLASTER BOX
STATED ODDS 1:262 HANGER BOX
STATED ODDS 1:522 HANGER PACK
STATED PRINT RUN 199 SER.#'d SETS

MRAB	Alexa Bliss	8.00	20.00
MRAF	Alicia Fox	2.50	6.00
MRAL	Alexa Bliss	8.00	20.00
MRAS	Asuka	5.00	12.00
MRBA	Bayley	5.00	12.00
MRBB	Brie Bella	4.00	10.00
MRBL	Becky Lynch	5.00	12.00
MRBR	Brie Bella	4.00	10.00
MRCA	Carmella	4.00	10.00
MRCF	Charlotte Flair	6.00	15.00
MRDB	Dana Brooke	3.00	8.00
MRLA	Lana	5.00	12.00
MRNB	Nikki Bella	4.00	10.00
MRNC	Nikki Cross	3.00	8.00
MRNI	Nikki Bella	4.00	10.00
MRNJ	Nia Jax	2.50	6.00
MRSB	Sasha Banks	5.00	12.00
MRSM	Stephanie McMahon	2.00	5.00
MRSR	Summer Rae	4.00	10.00
MRSU	Summer Rae	4.00	10.00
MRTA	Tamina	2.00	5.00
MRASA	Asuka	5.00	12.00
MRASU	Asuka	5.00	12.00
MRBAY	Bayley	5.00	12.00
MRBEC	Becky Lynch	5.00	12.00
MRBLY	Bayley	5.00	12.00
MRBRI	Brie Bella	4.00	10.00
MRCAR	Carmella	4.00	10.00
MRCHA	Charlotte Flair	6.00	15.00
MRCHF	Charlotte Flair	6.00	15.00
MRCRM	Carmella	4.00	10.00
MREMM	Emma	4.00	10.00
MRLAA	Lana	5.00	12.00
MRLAN	Lana	5.00	12.00
MRNAO	Naomi	3.00	8.00
MRNAT	Natalya	3.00	8.00
MRNIA	Nia Jax	2.50	6.00
MRNIK	Nikki Cross	3.00	8.00
MRSAS	Sasha Banks	5.00	12.00
MRSTE	Stephanie McMahon	2.00	5.00

MRSUM	Summer Rae	4.00	10.00
MRTAM	Tamina	2.00	5.00
MRCHAR	Charlotte Flair	6.00	15.00
MREMMA	Emma	4.00	10.00

2017 Topps WWE Women's Division NXT Matches and Moments

*SILVER/50: 1.2X TO 3X BASIC CARDS
*BLUE/25: 2X TO 5X BASIC CARDS
*GOLD/10: UNPRICED DUE TO SCARCITY
*RED/1: UNPRICED DUE TO SCARCITY

NXT1	Emma	.75	2.00
NXT2	Billie Kay	.40	1.00
NXT3	Peyton Royce	.50	1.25
NXT4	Asuka	1.00	2.50
NXT5	Asuka	1.00	2.50
NXT6	Bayley	1.00	2.50
NXT7	Nia Jax	.50	1.25
NXT8	Bayley	1.50	4.00
NXT9	Bayley	1.00	2.50
NXT10	Carmella	1.00	2.50
NXT11	Bayley	1.00	2.50
NXT12	Bayley	1.00	2.50
NXT13	Asuka	1.00	2.50
NXT14	Asuka	1.00	2.50
NXT15	Nia Jax	.50	1.25
NXT16	Nia Jax	.50	1.25
NXT17	Asuka	1.00	2.50
NXT18	Bayley	1.00	2.50
NXT19	Mandy Rose	.40	1.00
NXT20	Ember Moon	.75	2.00
NXT21	Asuka	1.00	2.50
NXT22	Asuka	1.00	2.50
NXT23	Nikki Cross	.60	1.50
NXT24	Asuka	1.00	2.50
NXT25	Asuka	1.00	2.50
NXT26	Ember Moon	.75	2.00

2017 Topps WWE Women's Division Rivalries

*SILVER/50: 1.2X TO 3X BASIC CARDS
*BLUE/25: 2X TO 5X BASIC CARDS
*GOLD/10: UNPRICED DUE TO SCARCITY
*RED/1: UNPRICED DUE TO SCARCITY
STATED ODDS 3:1 HANGER PACK EXCLUSIVE

RV1	Charlotte Flair/Bayley	1.25	3.00
RV2	Charlotte Flair/Dana Brooke	1.25	3.00
RV3	Sasha Banks/Dana Brooke	1.00	2.50
RV4	Sasha Banks/Nia Jax	1.00	2.50
RV5	Bayley/Dana Brooke	1.00	2.50
RV6	Nikki Bella/Maryse	.75	2.00
RV7	Nikki Bella/Natalya	.75	2.00
RV8	Nikki Bella/Carmella	.75	2.00
RV9	Becky Lynch/Alexa Bliss	1.50	4.00
RV10	Becky Lynch/Mickie James	1.00	2.50
RV11	Alexa Bliss/Mickie James	1.50	4.00
RV12	Alexa Bliss/Naomi	1.50	4.00
RV13	Alexa Bliss/Bayley	1.50	4.00
RV14	Naomi/Charlotte Flair	1.25	3.00
RV15	Asuka/Ember Moon	1.00	2.50
RV16	Asuka/Peyton Royce	1.00	2.50
RV17	Asuka/Billie Kay	1.00	2.50
RV18	Asuka/Nikki Cross	1.00	2.50
RV19	Ruby Riot/Nikki Cross	.60	1.50
RV20	Wendi Richter/Leilani Kai	.40	1.00
RV21	Trish Stratus/Mickie James	1.25	3.00
RV22	Mickie James/Beth Phoenix	.50	1.25

RV23	Mickie James/Maryse	.60	1.50
RV24	Eve Torres/Maryse	.60	1.50
RV25	Eve Torres/Natalya	.60	1.50

2017 Topps WWE Women's Division Shirt Relics

*SILVER/50: .5X TO 1.2X BASIC MEM
*BLUE/25: .6X TO 1.5X BASIC MEM
*GOLD/10: UNPRICED DUE TO SCARCITY
*RED/1: UNPRICED DUE TO SCARCITY
STATED ODDS 1:12 BLASTER BOX
STATED ODDS 1:950 HANGER BOX
STATED ODDS 1:1,893 HANGER PACK
STATED PRINT RUN 199 SER.#'d SETS

SRAB	Alexa Bliss	15.00	40.00
SRAF	Alicia Fox	5.00	12.00
SRBA	Bayley	10.00	25.00
SRBL	Becky Lynch	10.00	25.00
SRCA	Carmella	8.00	20.00
SRCF	Charlotte Flair	12.00	30.00
SRJO	JoJo	5.00	12.00
SRNA	Naomi	6.00	15.00
SRNT	Natalya	6.00	15.00
SRRY	Renee Young	5.00	12.00
SRSB	Sasha Banks	10.00	25.00
SRSR	Summer Rae	8.00	20.00

2017 Topps WWE Women's Division Women's Championship Medallions

*SILVER/50: .5X TO 1.2X BASIC MEM
*BLUE/25: .6X TO 1.5X BASIC MEM
*GOLD/10: UNPRICED DUE TO SCARCITY
*RED/1: UNPRICED DUE TO SCARCITY
STATED ODDS 1:15 BLASTER BOX
STATED ODDS 1:1,203 HANGER BOX
STATED ODDS 1:2,398 HANGER PACK
STATED PRINT RUN 99 SER.#'d SETS

WCI	Ivory	2.50	6.00
WCAB	Alundra Blayze	3.00	8.00
WCBP	Beth Phoenix	2.50	6.00
WCLK	Leilani Kai	2.50	6.00
WCMJ	Mickie James	4.00	10.00
WCSM	Stephanie McMahon	3.00	8.00
WCSS	Sensational Sherri	3.00	8.00
WCTS	Trish Stratus	10.00	25.00
WCWR	Wendi Richter	3.00	8.00

2017 Topps WWE Women's Division WWE Matches and Moments

*SILVER/50: 1.2X TO 3X BASIC CARDS
*BLUE/25: 2X TO 5X BASIC CARDS
*GOLD/10: UNPRICED DUE TO SCARCITY
*RED/1: UNPRICED DUE TO SCARCITY

WWE1	Sasha Banks	1.00	2.50
WWE2	Charlotte	1.25	3.00
WWE3	Nikki Bella	.75	2.00
WWE4	Bayley	1.00	2.50
WWE5	Becky Lynch	1.00	2.50
WWE6	Alexa Bliss	1.50	4.00
WWE7	Charlott Flair	1.25	3.00
WWE8	Alexa Bliss	1.50	4.00
WWE9	Charlotte Flair	1.25	3.00
WWE10	Sasha Banks	1.00	2.50
WWE11	Nikki Bella	.75	2.00
WWE12	Charlotte Flair	1.25	3.00
WWE13	Team Raw	1.25	3.00
WWE14	Sasha Banks	1.00	2.50

WWE15	Nikki Bella	.75	2.00
WWE16	Alexa Bliss	1.50	4.00
WWE17	Charlotte Flair	1.25	3.00
WWE18	Charlotte Flair	1.25	3.00
WWE19	Bayley	1.00	2.50
WWE20	Natalya	.75	2.00
WWE21	La Luchadora	.50	1.25
WWE22	Bayley	1.00	2.50
WWE23	Alexa Bliss	1.50	4.00
WWE24	Mickie James	1.50	4.00

2018 Topps WWE Women's Division

UNOPENED BOX (24 PACKS)
UNOPENED PACK (7 CARDS)
*SILVER/50: .6X TO 1.5X BASIC CARDS
*BLUE/25: 1.2X TO 3X BASIC CARDS
*GOLD/10: UNPRICED DUE TO SCARCITY
*RED/1: UNPRICED DUE TO SCARCITY

1	Alexa Bliss	2.00	5.00
2	Alicia Fox	.60	1.50
3	Asuka	1.25	3.00
4	Bayley	.60	1.50
5	Becky Lynch	1.00	2.50
6	Brie Bella	.75	2.00
7	Carmella	.75	2.00
8	Cathy Kelley	.75	2.00
9	Charlotte Flair	1.25	3.00
10	Charly Caruso	.60	1.50
11	Dana Brooke	.75	2.00
12	Dasha Fuentes	.60	1.50
13	JoJo	.40	1.00
14	Lana	1.00	2.50
15	Liv Morgan	.75	2.00
16	Mandy Rose	1.00	2.50
17	Maria Kanellis	1.00	2.50
18	Maryse	.75	2.00
19	Mickie James	.75	2.00
20	Naomi	.50	1.25
21	Natalya	.50	1.25
22	Nia Jax	.60	1.50
23	Nikki Bella	.75	2.00
24	Renee Young	.60	1.50
25	Ronda Rousey	2.00	5.00
26	Ruby Riott	.60	1.50
27	Sarah Logan	.40	1.00
28	Sasha Banks	1.25	3.00
29	Sonya Deville	.75	2.00
30	Stephanie McMahon	.75	2.00
31	Tamina	.40	1.00
32	Aliyah	.60	1.50
33	Bianca Belair	.50	1.25
34	Billie Kay	.75	2.00
35	Candice LeRae	.50	1.25
36	Dakota Kai	.50	1.25
37	Ember Moon	.75	2.00
38	Kairi Sane	1.00	2.50
39	Kayla Braxton	.40	1.00
40	Lacey Evans	.50	1.25
41	Nikki Cross	.60	1.50
42	Peyton Royce	1.00	2.50
43	Shayna Baszler	1.00	2.50
44	Taynara Conti	.40	1.00
45	Vanessa Borne	.40	1.00
46	Zelina Vega	.40	1.00
47	Alundra Blayze	.40	1.00
48	Lita	1.00	2.50
49	Trish Stratus	1.50	4.00
50	Wendi Richter	.40	1.00

2018 Topps WWE Women's Division Autographed Kiss and Shirt Relic Booklets

STATED PRINT RUN 5 SER.#'d SETS
UNPRICED DUE TO SCARCITY

ASKAB Alexa Bliss
ASKCF Charlotte Flair
ASKCR Carmella
ASKEM Ember Moon

2018 Topps WWE Women's Division Autographed Mat Relics

STATED ODDS 1:1,866
STATED PRINT RUN 10 SER.#'d SETS
UNPRICED DUE TO SCARCITY

AMRAK Asuka
AMRAS Asuka
AMRBB Brie Bella
AMRBL Becky Lynch
AMRBP Beth Phoenix
AMRBY Bayley
AMRCR Carmella
AMRDB Dana Brooke
AMREB Ember Moon
AMREM Ember Moon
AMRKR Kairi Sane
AMRKS Kairi Sane
AMRLA Lana
AMRLM Liv Morgan
AMRLT Lita
AMRMJ Mickie James
AMRMR Mandy Rose
AMRNA Naomi
AMRNB Nikki Bella
AMRNC Nikki Cross
AMRNJ Nia Jax
AMRNT Natalya
AMRNY Natalya
AMRPR Peyton Royce
AMRRR Ruby Riott
AMRSB Sasha Banks
AMRSD Sonya Deville
AMRSL Sarah Logan
AMRTM Tamina
AMRTS Trish Stratus

2018 Topps WWE Women's Division Autographed Shirt Relics

STATED ODDS 1:4,547
STATED PRINT RUN 10 SER.#'d SETS
UNPRICED DUE TO SCARCITY

ASRAB Alexa Bliss
ASRAF Alicia Fox
ASRBL Becky Lynch
ASRCF Charlotte Flair
ASRCM Carmella
ASREM Ember Moon
ASRJO JoJo
ASRNA Naomi
ASRNC Nikki Cross
ASRNT Natalya
ASRRY Renee Young
ASRSB Sasha Banks

2018 Topps WWE Women's Division Autographs

*GREEN/150: SAME VALUE AS BASIC AUTOS

*PURPLE/99: .5X TO 1.2X BASIC AUTOS		
*BRONZE/75: .6X TO 1.5X BASIC AUTOS		
*SILVER/50: .75X TO 2X BASIC AUTOS		
*BLUE/25: 1X TO 2.5X BASIC AUTOS		
*GOLD/10: UNPRICED DUE TO SCARCITY		
*BLACK/5: UNPRICED DUE TO SCARCITY		
*RED/1: UNPRICED DUE TO SCARCITY		
*P.P.BLACK/1: UNPRICED DUE TO SCARCITY		
*P.P.CYAN/1: UNPRICED DUE TO SCARCITY		
*P.P.MAGENTA/1: UNPRICED DUE TO SCARCITY		
*P.P.YELLOW/1: UNPRICED DUE TO SCARCITY		
STATED ODDS 1:86		
STATED PRINT RUN 199 SER.#'d SETS		

1	Alexa Bliss	30.00	75.00
2	Alicia Fox	5.00	12.00
3	Asuka	12.00	30.00
4	Bayley	10.00	25.00
5	Becky Lynch	12.00	30.00
6	Brie Bella	10.00	25.00
7	Carmella	8.00	20.00
9	Charlotte Flair	15.00	40.00
11	Dana Brooke	6.00	15.00
12	Dasha Fuentes	5.00	12.00
14	Lana	6.00	15.00
15	Liv Morgan	15.00	40.00
16	Mandy Rose	12.00	30.00
19	Mickie James	10.00	25.00
20	Naomi	6.00	15.00
21	Natalya	8.00	20.00
22	Nia Jax	12.00	30.00
23	Nikki Bella	10.00	25.00
26	Ruby Riott	15.00	40.00
27	Sarah Logan	10.00	25.00
28	Sasha Banks	15.00	40.00
29	Sonya Deville	8.00	20.00
31	Tamina	5.00	12.00
32	Aliyah	6.00	15.00
33	Bianca Belair	8.00	20.00
34	Billie Kay	10.00	25.00
35	Candice LeRae	15.00	40.00
36	Dakota Kai	25.00	60.00
37	Ember Moon	10.00	25.00
38	Kairi Sane	15.00	40.00
40	Lacey Evans	12.00	30.00
42	Peyton Royce	15.00	40.00
43	Shayna Baszler	8.00	20.00
44	Taynara Conti	12.00	30.00
45	Vanessa Borne	8.00	20.00

2018 Topps WWE Women's Division
Autographs Green

24	Renee Young	6.00	15.00

2018 Topps WWE Women's Division
Commemorative Championship Relics

*PURPLE/99: SAME VALUE AS BASIC
*SILVER/50: .5X TO 1.2X BASIC MEM
*BLUE/25: .6X TO 1.5X BASIC MEM
*GOLD/10: UNPRICED DUE TO SCARCITY
*BLACK/5: UNPRICED DUE TO SCARCITY
*RED/1: UNPRICED DUE TO SCARCITY
STATED ODDS 1:183
STATED PRINT RUN 199 SER.#'d SETS

CCAB	Alundra Blayze	2.00	5.00
CCAL	Alexa Bliss	10.00	25.00
CCAS	Asuka	5.00	12.00

CCBL	Becky Lynch	8.00	20.00
CCBP	Beth Phoenix	2.50	6.00
CCBY	Bayley	2.50	6.00
CCCF	Charlotte Flair	6.00	15.00
CCCH	Charlotte Flair	6.00	15.00
CCET	Eve Torres	2.00	5.00
CCLT	Lita	4.00	10.00
CCMJ	Mickie James	5.00	12.00
CCMR	Maryse	2.00	5.00
CCNA	Naomi	2.50	6.00
CCNB	Nikki Bella	3.00	8.00
CCNT	Natalya	3.00	8.00
CCPG	Paige	10.00	25.00
CCSB	Sasha Banks	6.00	15.00
CCSS	Sensational Sherri	2.00	5.00
CCTS	Trish Stratus	4.00	10.00
CCWR	Wendi Richter	2.00	5.00

2018 Topps WWE Women's Division
Kiss

*GOLD/10: UNPRICED DUE TO SCARCITY
*RED/1: UNPRICED DUE TO SCARCITY
STATED ODDS 1:1,797
STATED PRINT RUN 99 SER.#'d SETS

KCCF	Charlotte Flair	30.00	75.00
KCCR	Carmella	25.00	60.00
KCEM	Ember Moon	25.00	60.00
KCLM	Liv Morgan	20.00	50.00

2018 Topps WWE Women's Division
Kiss Autographs

*GOLD/10: UNPRICED DUE TO SCARCITY
*RED/1: UNPRICED DUE TO SCARCITY
STATED ODDS 1:7,658
STATED PRINT RUN 25 SER.#'d SETS

AKCAB	Alexa Bliss	150.00	300.00
AKCCF	Charlotte Flair	200.00	400.00
AKCLM	Liv Morgan	60.00	120.00

2018 Topps WWE Women's Division
Mat Relics

*GREEN/150: SAME AS BASIC MEM
*PURPLE/99: .5X TO 1.2X BASIC MEM
*BRONZE/75: .6X TO 1.5X BASIC MEM
*SILVER/50: .75X TO 2X BASIC MEM
*BLUE/25: 1X TO 2.5X BASIC MEM
*GOLD/10: UNPRICED DUE TO SCARCITY
*BLACK/5: UNPRICED DUE TO SCARCITY
*RED/1: UNPRICED DUE TO SCARCITY
STATED ODDS 1:123

AMRAK	Asuka	4.00	10.00
AMRAS	Asuka	4.00	10.00
AMRBB	Brie Bella	3.00	8.00
AMRBL	Becky Lynch	5.00	12.00
AMRBP	Beth Phoenix	3.00	8.00
AMRBY	Bayley	2.50	6.00
AMRCR	Carmella	4.00	10.00
AMRDB	Dana Brooke	2.50	6.00
AMREB	Ember Moon	5.00	12.00
AMREM	Ember Moon	5.00	12.00
AMRKR	Kairi Sane	5.00	12.00
AMRKS	Kairi Sane	5.00	12.00
AMRLA	Lana	5.00	12.00
AMRLM	Liv Morgan	4.00	10.00
AMRLT	Lita	3.00	8.00
AMRMJ	Mickie James	4.00	10.00
AMRMR	Mandy Rose	3.00	8.00

AMRNA	Naomi	2.00	5.00
AMRNB	Nikki Bella	5.00	12.00
AMRNC	Nikki Cross	2.00	5.00
AMRNJ	Nia Jax	2.00	5.00
AMRNT	Natalya	5.00	12.00
AMRNY	Natalya	5.00	12.00
AMRPR	Peyton Royce	3.00	8.00
AMRRR	Ruby Riott	4.00	10.00
AMRSB	Sasha Banks	6.00	15.00
AMRSD	Sonya Deville	3.00	8.00
AMRSL	Sarah Logan	3.00	8.00
AMRTM	Tamina	2.00	5.00
AMRTS	Trish Stratus	8.00	20.00

2018 Topps WWE Women's Division
Matches and Moments

*SILVER/50: .6X TO 1.5X BASIC CARDS
*BLUE/25: 1.2X TO 3X BASIC CARDS
*GOLD/10: UNPRICED DUE TO SCARCITY
*RED/1: UNPRICED DUE TO SCARCITY

NXT1	Ember Moon	.75	2.00
NXT2	Asuka	1.25	3.00
NXT3	Asuka	1.25	3.00
NXT4	Ruby Riott	.60	1.50
NXT5	Asuka	1.25	3.00
NXT6	Asuka	1.25	3.00
NXT7	Asuka	1.25	3.00
NXT8	Sarah Logan	.40	1.00
NXT9	NXT Women's Triple Threat	1.25	3.00
NXT10	Asuka	1.25	3.00
NXT11	Bianca Belair	.50	1.25
NXT12	Vanessa Borne	.40	1.00
NXT13	Ember Moon	.75	2.00
NXT14	Asuka	1.25	3.00
NXT15	Shayna Baszler	1.00	2.50
NXT16	Dakota Kai	.50	1.25
NXT17	Bianca Belair	.50	1.25
NXT18	Candice LeRae	.50	1.25
NXT19	Lacey Evans	.50	1.25
NXT20	Kairi Sane	1.00	2.50
NXT21	Kairi Sane	1.00	2.50
NXT22	Shayna Baszler	1.00	2.50
NXT23	Dakota Kai	.50	1.25
NXT24	Candice LeRae	.50	1.25
NXT25	Shayna Baszler	1.00	2.50
NXT26	Kairi Sane	1.00	2.50
NXT27	Shayna Baszler	1.00	2.50
NXT28	Kairi Sane	1.00	2.50
NXT29	Asuka	1.25	3.00
NXT30	Kairi Sane	1.00	2.50
RAW1	Charlotte Flair	1.25	3.00
RAW2	Bayley	.60	1.50
RAW3	Sasha Banks	1.25	3.00
RAW4	Sasha Banks	1.25	3.00
RAW5	Bayley	.60	1.50
RAW6	Sasha Banks	1.25	3.00
RAW7	Nia Jax	.60	1.50
RAW8	Bayley & Sasha Banks	1.25	3.00
RAW9	Bayley	.60	1.50
RAW10	Alexa Bliss/Mickie James	2.00	5.00
SDL1	Becky Lynch	1.00	2.50
SDL2	Naomi	.50	1.25
SDL3	Naomi	.50	1.25
SDL4	Alexa Bliss	2.00	5.00
SDL5	Natalya	.50	1.25
SDL6	Mickie James	.75	2.00
SDL7	John Cena & Nikki Bella	1.50	4.00
SDL8	Naomi	.50	1.25

SDL9	Charlotte Flair	1.25	3.00
SDL10	Charlotte Flair	1.25	3.00

2018 Topps WWE Women's Division
Mixed Match Challenge

COMPLETE SET (24)	8.00	20.00

*SILVER/50: .6X TO 1.5X BASIC CARDS
*BLUE/25: .75X TO 2X BASIC CARDS
*GOLD/10: UNPRICED DUE TO SCARCITY
*RED/1: UNPRICED DUE TO SCARCITY
RANDOMLY INSERTED INTO PACKS

MM1	Bliss/Strowman	1.50	4.00
MM2	Banks/Balor	1.00	2.50
MM3	Jax/Crews	.50	1.25
MM4	Miz/Asuka	1.00	2.50
MM5	Rose/Goldust	.75	2.00
MM6	Bayley/Elias	.75	2.00
MM7	Roode/Flair	1.00	2.50
MM8	Lana/Rusev	.75	2.00
MM9	Natalya/Nakamura	.75	2.00
MM10	Jimmy Uso/Naomi	.40	1.00
MM11	Zayn/Lynch	.75	2.00
MM12	Big E/Carmella	.60	1.50
MM13	The Boss Club	1.00	2.50
MM14	Team Awe-ska	1.00	2.50
MM15	Team Little Big	1.50	4.00
MM16	Glowish	.30	.75
MM17	Ravishing Rusev Day!	.50	1.25
MM18	The Robe Warriors	.50	1.25
MM19	Team Awe-ska	1.00	2.50
MM20	Team Little Big	.75	2.00
MM21	The Robe Warriors	1.00	2.50
MM22	Team Awe-ska	1.00	2.50
MM23	Roode & Lynch	.75	2.00
MM24	Team Awe-ska	1.00	2.50

2018 Topps WWE Women's Division
Power Couples

*SILVER/50: .5X TO 1.2X BASIC CARDS
*BLUE/25: .6X TO 1.5X BASIC CARDS
*GOLD/10: UNPRICED DUE TO SCARCITY
*RED/1: UNPRICED DUE TO SCARCITY
RANDOMLY INSERTED INTO PACKS

PC1	Brie Bella/Daniel Bryan	1.50	4.00
PC2	Stephanie McMahon/Triple H	1.50	4.00
PC3	Maryse/The Miz	1.25	3.00
PC4	Renee Young/Dean Ambrose	1.25	3.00
PC5	Naomi/Jimmy Uso	.75	2.00
PC6	Lana/Rusev	1.50	4.00
PC7	Maria Kanellis/Mike Kanellis	1.50	4.00
PC8	Candice LeRae/Johnny Gargano	.75	2.00
PC9	Beth Phoenix/Edge	1.50	4.00
PC10	Alicia Fox/Noam Dar	1.00	2.50
PC11	Alicia Fox/Cedric Alexander	1.00	2.50
PC12	Lana/Dolph Ziggler	1.50	4.00
PC13	Eve Torres/Zack Ryder	1.25	3.00
PC14	Maria Kanellis/Dolph Ziggler	1.50	4.00
PC15	Stephanie McMahon/Kurt Angle	1.50	4.00
PC16	Trish Stratus/Chris Jericho	2.50	6.00
PC17	Trish Stratus/Jeff Hardy	2.50	6.00
PC18	Marlena/Goldust	1.25	3.00
PC19	Miss Elizabeth/Randy Savage	2.00	5.00
PC20	Queen Sherri/Randy Savage	2.00	5.00
PC21	Sherri/Shawn Michaels	2.00	5.00
PC22	Lita/Kane	1.50	4.00

2018 Topps WWE Women's Division Shirt Relics

*PURPLE/99: .5X TO 1.2X BASIC MEM
*SILVER/50: .6X TO 1.5X BASIC MEM
*BLUE/25: .75X TO 2X BASIC MEM
*GOLD/10: UNPRICED DUE TO SCARCITY
*BLACK/5: UNPRICED DUE TO SCARCITY
*RED/1: UNPRICED DUE TO SCARCITY
STATED ODDS 1:516

ASRAB	Alexa Bliss	15.00	40.00
ASRAF	Alicia Fox	5.00	12.00
ASRBL	Becky Lynch	8.00	20.00
ASRCF	Charlotte Flair	10.00	25.00
ASRCM	Carmella	6.00	15.00
ASREM	Ember Moon	6.00	15.00
ASRJO	JoJo	5.00	10.00
ASRNA	Naomi	5.00	12.00
ASRNC	Nikki Cross	4.00	10.00
ASRNT	Natalya	6.00	15.00
ASRRY	Renee Young	5.00	12.00
ASRSB	Sasha Banks	8.00	20.00

2018 Topps WWE Women's Division Women's Champion

COMPLETE SET (25)   10.00   25.00
RANDOMLY INSERTED INTO PACKS

WC1	Maryse	.75	2.00
WC2	Mickie James	.75	2.00
WC3	Eve Torres	.75	2.00
WC4	Alicia Fox	.60	1.50
WC5	Natalya	.50	1.25
WC6	Brie Bella	.75	2.00
WC7	Beth Phoenix	.75	2.00
WC8	Nikki Bella	.75	2.00
WC9	Paige	1.00	2.50
WC10	Charlotte Flair	1.25	3.00
WC11	Paige	1.00	2.50
WC12	Charlotte Flair	1.25	3.00
WC13	Sasha Banks	1.25	3.00
WC14	Bayley	.60	1.50
WC15	Asuka	1.25	3.00
WC16	Ember Moon	.75	2.00
WC17	Charlotte Flair	1.25	3.00
WC18	Sasha Banks	1.25	3.00
WC19	Bayley	.60	1.50
WC20	Alexa Bliss	2.00	5.00
WC21	Becky Lynch	1.00	2.50
WC22	Alexa Bliss	2.00	5.00
WC23	Naomi	.50	1.25
WC24	Natalya	.50	1.25
WC25	Charlotte Flair	1.25	3.00

2018 Topps WWE Women's Division Women's Royal Rumble

COMPLETE SET (24)   12.00   30.00
*SILVER/50: .5X TO 1.5X BASIC CARDS
*BLUE/25: 1.2X TO 3X BASIC CARDS
*GOLD/10: UNPRICED DUE TO SCARCITY
*RED/1: UNPRICED DUE TO SCARCITY
STATED ODDS 1:2

RR1	Sasha Banks	2.00	5.00
RR2	Becky Lynch	1.50	4.00
RR3	Sarah Logan	.60	1.50
RR4	Mandy Rose	1.50	4.00
RR5	Lita	1.50	4.00
RR6	Kairi Sane	1.50	4.00
RR7	Tamina	.60	1.50
RR8	Dana Brooke	1.25	3.00
RR9	Sonya Deville	1.25	3.00
RR10	Liv Morgan	1.25	3.00
RR11	Lana	1.50	4.00
RR12	Ruby Riott	1.00	2.50
RR13	Carmella	1.25	3.00
RR14	Natalya	.75	2.00
RR15	Naomi	.75	2.00
RR16	Nia Jax	1.00	2.50
RR17	Ember Moon	1.25	3.00
RR18	Beth Phoenix	1.25	3.00
RR19	Asuka	2.00	5.00
RR20	Mickie James	1.25	3.00
RR21	Nikki Bella	1.25	3.00
RR22	Brie Bella	1.25	3.00
RR23	Bayley	1.00	2.50
RR24	Trish Stratus	2.50	6.00

2019 Topps WWE Women's Division

COMPLETE SET (100)   8.00   20.00
*PURPLE/99: .6X TO 1.5X BASIC CARDS
*BRONZE/75: .75X TO 2X BASIC CARDS
*ORANGE/50: 1X TO 2.5X BASIC CARDS
*BLUE/25: 1.5X TO 4X BASIC CARDS
*GOLD/10: UNPRICED DUE TO SCARCITY
*RED/1: UNPRICED DUE TO SCARCITY
*P.P.BLACK/1: UNPRICED DUE TO SCARCITY
*P.P.CYAN/1: UNPRICED DUE TO SCARCITY
*P.P.MAGENTA/1: UNPRICED DUE TO SCARCITY
*P.P.YELLOW/1: UNPRICED DUE TO SCARCITY

1	Alexa Bliss	1.25	3.00
2	Alicia Fox	.50	1.25
3	Bayley	.50	1.25
4	Dana Brooke	.50	1.25
5	Ember Moon	.60	1.50
6	Lacey Evans	.50	1.25
7	Liv Morgan	.75	2.00
8	Mickie James	.60	1.50
9	Natalya	.50	1.25
10	Nia Jax	.50	1.25
11	Ronda Rousey	1.25	3.00
12	Ruby Riott	.50	1.25
13	Sarah Logan	.30	.75
14	Sasha Banks	1.00	2.50
15	Tamina	.25	.60
16	Renee Young	.40	1.00
17	Stephanie McMahon	.60	1.50
18	Maria Kanellis	.60	1.50
19	Asuka	.75	2.00
20	Becky Lynch	1.00	2.50
21	Billie Kay	.50	1.25
22	Carmella	.60	1.50
23	Mandy Rose	.60	1.50
24	Maryse	.30	.75
25	Naomi	.40	1.00
26	Nikki Cross	.40	1.00
27	Peyton Royce	.60	1.50
28	Sonya Deville	.50	1.25
29	Zelina Vega	.40	1.00
30	Paige	1.00	2.50
31	Aliyah	.25	.60
32	Bianca Belair	.25	.60
33	Candice LeRae	.50	1.25
34	Chelsea Green	.25	.60
35	Dakota Kai	.50	1.25
36	Deonna Purrazzo	.25	.60
37	Io Shirai	.25	.60
38	Jessamyn Duke	.30	.75
39	Jessi Kamea	.25	.60
40	Kacy Catanzaro	.60	1.50
41	Kairi Sane	.50	1.25
42	Lacey Lane	.25	.60
43	Marina Shafir	.25	.60
44	Mia Yim	.25	.60
45	MJ Jenkins	.25	.60
46	Shayna Baszler	.50	1.25
47	Taynara Conti	.30	.75
48	Vanessa Borne	.30	.75
49	Xia Li	.25	.60
50	Toni Storm	1.00	2.50
51	Nina Samuels	.30	.75
52	Alundra Blayze	.30	.75
53	Beth Phoenix	.40	1.00
54	Eve Torres	.30	.75
55	Marlena	.25	.60
56	Lita	.60	1.50
57	Sherri Martel	.40	1.00
58	Miss Elizabeth	.50	1.25
59	Trish Stratus	1.25	3.00
60	Wendi Richter	.25	.60
61	Asuka	.75	2.00
62	Ember Moon	.60	1.50
63	Asuka	.75	2.00
64	Asuka	.75	2.00
65	Alexa Bliss	1.25	3.00
66	Shayna Baszler	.50	1.25
67	Naomi	.40	1.00
68	Nia Jax	1.25	3.00
69	Ronda Rousey	1.25	3.00
70	Candice LeRae	.50	1.25
71	Carmella	.60	1.50
72	Asuka	.75	2.00
73	Shayna Baszler	.50	1.25
74	Kairi Sane	.50	1.25
75	Shayna Baszler	.50	1.25
76	Bayley	.50	1.25
77	Alexa Bliss	1.25	3.00
78	Carmella	.75	2.00
79	Alexa Bliss	1.25	3.00
80	Sasha Banks & Bayley	1.00	2.50
81	Kairi Sane	.50	1.25
82	Ronda Rousey	1.25	3.00
83	Asuka	.75	2.00
84	Ronda Rousey	1.25	3.00
85	Iiconics	.60	1.50
86	Io Shirai	.25	.60
87	Becky Lynch	1.00	2.50
88	Bianca Belair	.25	.60
89	Shayna Baszler	.50	1.25
90	Team RAW/Team SmackDown	.75	2.00
91	Nikki Cross	.40	1.00
92	Mia Yim	.25	.60
93	Io Shirai	.50	1.25
94	Natalya	.50	1.25
95	Ronda Rousey	1.25	3.00
96	Asuka	.75	2.00
97	Natalya	.50	1.25
98	Asuka	.75	2.00
99	Bayley/Sasha Banks/Ember Moon	.60	1.50
100	Bianca Belair	.25	.60

2019 Topps WWE Women's Division Autographed Mat Relics

*RED/1: UNPRICED DUE TO SCARCITY
STATED PRINT RUN 10 SER.#'d SETS
UNPRICED DUE TO SCARCITY

MRAAS	Asuka		

MRABL	Becky Lynch
MRABY	Bayley
MRACA	Carmella
MRAIS	Io Shirai
MRAKS	Kairi Sane
MRANA	Natalya
MRANM	Naomi
MRAQA	Shayna Baszler
MRASD	Sonya Deville
MRATA	Tamina

2019 Topps WWE Women's Division Autographed Shirt Relics

*RED/1: UNPRICED DUE TO SCARCITY
STATED PRINT RUN 10 SER.#'d SETS
UNPRICED DUE TO SCARCITY

SRAAB	Alexa Bliss
SRACM	Carmella
SRALE	Lacey Evans
SRANM	Naomi
SRANT	Natalya
SRAQA	Shayna Baszler
SRARY	Renee Young
SRATM	Tamina

2019 Topps WWE Women's Division Autographs

*GREEN/150: SAME VALUE AS BASIC
*PURPLE/99: .5X TO 1.2X BASIC AUTOS
*BRONZE/75: .5X TO 1.2X BASIC AUTOS
*ORANGE/50: .6X TO 1.5X BASIC AUTOS
*BLUE/25: UNPRICED DUE TO SCARCITY
*GOLD/10: UNPRICED DUE TO SCARCITY
*BLACK/5: UNPRICED DUE TO SCARCITY
*RED/1: UNPRICED DUE TO SCARCITY
*P.P.BLACK/1: UNPRICED DUE TO SCARCITY
*P.P.CYAN/1: UNPRICED DUE TO SCARCITY
*P.P.MAGENTA/1: UNPRICED DUE TO SCARCITY
*P.P.YELLOW/1: UNPRICED DUE TO SCARCITY
RANDOMLY INSERTED INTO PACKS

AAB	Alexa Bliss	30.00	75.00
ABE	Bayley	12.00	30.00
ABK	Billie Kay	10.00	25.00
ABZ	Shayna Baszler	8.00	20.00
ACG	Chelsea Green	20.00	50.00
ACL	Candice LeRae	10.00	25.00
ACM	Carmella	12.00	30.00
ADB	Dana Brooke	6.00	15.00
ADK	Dakota Kai	10.00	25.00
ADP	Deonna Purrazzo	6.00	15.00
AEM	Ember Moon	8.00	20.00
AIS	Io Shirai	30.00	75.00
AJD	Jessamyn Duke	10.00	25.00
AJE	Jessi Kamea	8.00	20.00
AKC	Kacy Catanzaro	15.00	40.00
ALE	Lacey Evans	10.00	25.00
AMR	Mandy Rose	15.00	40.00
AMS	Marina Shafir	8.00	20.00
AMY	Mia Yim	12.00	30.00
ANC	Nikki Cross	8.00	20.00
ANT	Natalya	6.00	15.00
APR	Peyton Royce	10.00	25.00
ARY	Renee Young	6.00	15.00
ASD	Sonya Deville	10.00	25.00
ATC	Taynara Conti	6.00	15.00
ATM	Tamina	6.00	15.00
AVB	Vanessa Borne	6.00	15.00
AEST	Bianca Belair	6.00	15.00

2019 Topps WWE Women's Division Championship Side Plate Commemorative Patches

*PURPLE/99: .5X TO 1.2X BASIC MEM
*ORANGE/50: .6X TO 1.5X BASIC MEM
*BLUE/25: .75X TO 2X BASIC MEM
*GOLD/10: UNPRICED DUE TO SCARCITY
*RED/1: UNPRICED DUE TO SCARCITY
STATED PRINT RUN 199 SER.#'d SETS

PCAB	Alexa Bliss	15.00	40.00
PCAK	Asuka	8.00	20.00
PCBL	Becky Lynch	10.00	25.00
PCBY	Bayley	8.00	20.00
PCCM	Carmella	6.00	15.00
PCEM	Ember Moon	5.00	12.00
PCKS	Kairi Sane	12.00	30.00
PCNJ	Nia Jax	5.00	12.00
PCNM	Naomi	4.00	10.00
PCNT	Natalya	4.00	10.00
PCQA	Shayna Baszler	5.00	12.00
PCRR	Ronda Rousey	12.00	30.00
PCSB	Sasha Banks	8.00	20.00

2019 Topps WWE Women's Division Dual Autographs

*GOLD/10: UNPRICED DUE TO SCARCITY
*BLACK/5: UNPRICED DUE TO SCARCITY
*RED/1: UNPRICED DUE TO SCARCITY
RANDOMLY INSERTED INTO PACKS
STATED PRINT RUN 25 SER.#'d SETS

DABC	A.Bliss/N.Cross	200.00	300.00
DADD	B.Phoenix/Natalya	60.00	120.00
DAII	B.Kay/P/Royce	125.00	250.00

2019 Topps WWE Women's Division Mat Relics

*GREEN/150: SAME VALUE AS BASIC
*PURPLE/99: .5X TO 1.2X BASIC MEM
*BRONZE/75: .6X TO 1.5X BASIC MEM
*ORANGE/50: .75X TO 2X BASIC MEM
*BLUE/25: 1.2X TO 3X BASIC MEM
*GOLD/10: UNPRICED DUE TO SCARCITY
*BLACK/5: UNPRICED DUE TO SCARCITY
*RED/1: UNPRICED DUE TO SCARCITY
RANDOMLY INSERTED INTO PACKS
STATED PRINT RUN 199 SER.#'d SETS

MRAB	Alexa Bliss	10.00	25.00
MRAF	Alicia Fox	3.00	8.00
MRAK	Asuka	5.00	12.00
MRAS	Asuka	4.00	10.00
MRBE	Becky Lynch	10.00	25.00
MRBK	Billie Kay	4.00	10.00
MRBL	Becky Lynch	10.00	25.00
MRBP	Beth Phoenix	3.00	8.00
MRBY	Bayley	2.50	6.00
MRCA	Carmella	3.00	8.00
MRCH	Charlotte Flair	4.00	10.00
MRCM	Carmella	3.00	8.00
MREM	Ember Moon	4.00	10.00
MRIS	Io Shirai	6.00	15.00
MRJJ	JoJo	2.50	6.00
MRKS	Kairi Sane	5.00	12.00
MRLI	Liv Morgan	6.00	15.00
MRLM	Liv Morgan	5.00	12.00
MRLT	Lita	3.00	8.00
MRMD	Alundra Blayze	2.50	6.00
MRMJ	Mickie James	2.50	6.00

MRNA	Natalya	2.50	6.00
MRNI	Nia Jax	3.00	8.00
MRNJ	Nia Jax	3.00	8.00
MRNM	Naomi	2.50	6.00
MRNT	Natalya	2.50	6.00
MRQA	Shayna Baszler	2.50	6.00
MRRB	Ruby Riott	3.00	8.00
MRRO	Ronda Rousey	10.00	25.00
MRRR	Ronda Rousey	10.00	25.00
MRRU	Ruby Riott	3.00	8.00
MRRY	Renee Young	3.00	8.00
MRSA	Sarah Logan	2.50	6.00
MRSB	Sasha Banks	6.00	15.00
MRSD	Sonya Deville	5.00	12.00
MRSF	Trish Stratus	4.00	10.00
MRSL	Sarah Logan	2.50	6.00
MRTA	Tamina	2.50	6.00
MRTM	Tamina	2.50	6.00
MRTS	Toni Storm	8.00	20.00

2019 Topps WWE Women's Division Mixed Match Challenge Season 2

COMPLETE SET (25)
*ORANGE/50: 1.2X TO 3X BASIC CARDS
*BLUE/25: 2X TO 5X BASIC CARDS
*GOLD/10: UNPRICED DUE TO SCARCITY
*RED/1: UNPRICED DUE TO SCARCITY
RANDOMLY INSERTED INTO PACKS

MMC1	Monster Eclipse	.60	1.50
MMC2	Country Dominance	.60	1.50
MMC3	B'N'B	.60	1.50
MMC4	Mahalicia	.50	1.25
MMC5	Team Pawz	.50	1.25
MMC6	Awe-ska	.75	2.00
MMC7	Day One Glow	.40	1.00
MMC8	Ravishing Rusev Day	.50	1.25
MMC9	Fabulous Truth	.60	1.50
MMC10	Monster Eclipse	.60	1.50
MMC11	Country Dominance	.60	1.50
MMC12	Awe-ska	.75	2.00
MMC13	B'N'B	.60	1.50
MMC14	Robert Roode/Team Pawz	.50	1.25
MMC15	Awe-ska	.75	2.00
MMC16	Monster Eclipse	.60	1.50
MMC17	Fabulous Truth	.60	1.50
MMC18	Curt Hawkins/Monster Eclipse	.60	1.50
MMC19	Mahalicia	.50	1.25
MMC20	B'N'B	.60	1.50
MMC21	Awe-ska	.75	2.00
MMC22	Apollo Crews/B'N'B	.50	1.25
MMC23	Mahalicia	.50	1.25
MMC24	Fabulous Truth	.60	1.50
MMC25	Fabulous Truth Win	.60	1.50

2019 Topps WWE Women's Division Shirt Relics

*PURPLE/99: .5X TO 1.2X BASIC CARDS
*ORANGE/50: .6X TO 1.5X BASIC CARDS
*BLUE/25: .75X TO 2X BASIC CARDS
*GOLD/10: UNPRICED DUE TO SCARCITY
*RED/1: UNPRICED DUE TO SCARCITY
STATED PRINT RUN 199 SER.#'d SETS

SRAB	Alexa Bliss	12.00	30.00
SRAF	Alicia Fox	5.00	12.00
SRAS	Asuka	6.00	15.00
SRCM	Carmella	5.00	12.00
SRJJ	JoJo	4.00	10.00

SRLE	Lacey Evans	5.00	12.00
SRNM	Naomi	4.00	10.00
SRNT	Natalya	4.00	10.00
SRQA	Shayna Baszler	4.00	10.00
SRSB	Sasha Banks		

2019 Topps WWE Women's Division Team Bestie

COMPLETE SET (20)   8.00   20.00
*ORANGE/50: 1.5X TO 4X BASIC CARDS
*BLUE/25: 2.5X TO 6X BASIC CARDS
*GOLD/10: UNPRICED DUE TO SCARCITY
*RED/1: UNPRICED DUE TO SCARCITY
RANDOMLY INSERTED INTO PACKS

TB1	Trish Stratus	.75	2.00
TB2	Trish Stratus	.75	2.00
TB3	Trish Stratus	.75	2.00
TB4	Trish Stratus	.75	2.00
TB5	Team Bestie	1.00	2.50
TB6	Trish Stratus	.75	2.00
TB7	Trish Stratus	.75	2.00
TB8	Trish Stratus	.75	2.00
TB9	Trish Stratus	1.25	3.00
TB10	Trish Stratus	.75	2.00
TB11	Lita	.60	1.50
TB12	Lita/The Rock	1.00	2.50
TB13	Lita	.60	1.50
TB14	Team Bestie	.75	2.00
TB15	Lita	.60	1.50
TB16	Lita	.60	1.50
TB17	Lita	.60	1.50
TB18	Lita	.60	1.50
TB19	Lita	.60	1.50
TB20	Lita	.60	1.50

2019 Topps WWE Women's Division Triple Autographs

STATED PRINT RUN 10 SER.#'d SETS
UNPRICED DUE TO SCARCITY

TA4H   Shafir/Duke/Baszler

2019 Topps WWE Women's Division Women's Evolution

COMPLETE SET (10)   8.00   20.00
*ORANGE/50: 1.2X TO 1.5X BASIC CARDS
*BLUE/25: 2X TO 3X BASIC CARDS
*GOLD/10: UNPRICED DUE TO SCARCITY
*RED/1: UNPRICED DUE TO SCARCITY

WE1	Lita	1.50	4.00
WE2	Alundra Blayze	.75	2.00
WE3	Nia Jax/Tamina	.60	1.50
WE4	Carmella	1.50	4.00
WE5	Mandy Rose	1.50	4.00
WE6	Toni Storm	2.50	6.00
WE7	Sasha/Bayley/Natalya	2.50	6.00
WE8	Jessamyn Duke/Marina Shafir	.75	2.00
WE9	Becky Lynch	2.50	6.00
WE10	Women's Division	3.00	8.00

2019 Topps WWE Women's Division Women's Royal Rumble

COMPLETE SET (25)   12.00   30.00
*ORANGE/50: 2X TO 5X BASIC CARDS
*BLUE/25: 3X TO 8X BASIC CARDS
*GOLD/10: UNPRICED DUE TO SCARCITY
*RED/1: UNPRICED DUE TO SCARCITY
RANDOMLY INSERTED INTO PACKS

RR1	Lacey Evans	1.00	2.50
RR2	Natalya	1.00	2.50
RR3	Mandy Rose	1.25	3.00
RR4	Mickie James	1.25	3.00
RR5	Ember Moon	1.25	3.00
RR6	Billie Kay	1.00	2.50
RR7	Nikki Cross	.75	2.00
RR8	Peyton Royce	1.25	3.00
RR9	Tamina	.50	1.25
RR10	Kairi Sane	1.00	2.50
RR11	Naomi	.75	2.00
RR12	Candice LeRae	1.00	2.50
RR13	Alicia Fox	1.00	2.50
RR14	Kacy Catanzaro	1.25	3.00
RR15	Zelina Vega	.75	2.00
RR16	Ruby Riott	1.00	2.50
RR17	Io Shirai	.50	1.25
RR18	Sonya Deville	1.00	2.50
RR19	Alexa Bliss	2.50	6.00
RR20	Bayley	1.00	2.50
RR21	Becky Lynch	2.00	5.00
RR22	Nia Jax	1.00	2.50
RR23	Carmella	1.25	3.00
RR24	Maria Kanellis	1.25	3.00
RR25	Xia Li	.50	1.25

2019 Topps WWE Women's Revolution

This is a continuation series across four different products in 2019. It was initially known as Divas Revolution but changed to Women's Revolution in the second product release. However, the prefix on the numbers still remains DR for Divas Revolution. 10-Card sets were inserted in the following products: Topps WWE Road to WrestleMania (DR1-DR10), Topps WWE RAW (DR11-DR20), Topps WWE SummerSlam (DR21-DR30), and Topps WWE SmackDown Live (DR31-DR40).

COMPLETE SET (40)		25.00	60.00
SEMISTARS		1.00	2.50
UNLISTED STARS		1.25	3.00

RANDOMLY INSERTED INTO PACKS

DR1	Paige	2.00	5.00
DR2	Charlotte/Becky/Sasha	2.00	5.00
DR3	Charlotte Flair	2.00	5.00
DR4	Team PCB	2.00	5.00
DR5	Charlotte Flair	2.00	5.00
DR6	Nikki Bella	2.00	5.00
DR7	Charlotte Flair	2.00	5.00
DR8	Paige	2.00	5.00
DR9	Natalya	2.00	5.00
DR10	Charlotte Flair	2.00	5.00
DR11	Paige	2.00	5.00
DR12	Charlotte Flair	2.00	5.00
DR13	Paige	2.00	5.00
DR14	Charlotte Flair	2.00	5.00
DR15	Charlotte Flair	2.00	5.00
DR16	Nikki Bella	1.25	3.00
DR17	Charlotte Flair	2.00	5.00
DR18	Sasha Banks	2.00	5.00
DR19	Brie Bella	1.25	3.00
DR20	Team B.A.D./Sasha Banks	2.00	5.00
DR21	Lita	1.25	3.00
DR22	Charlotte Flair	2.00	5.00
DR23	Charlotte Flair	2.00	5.00
DR24	SD Women's Championship	2.50	6.00
DR25	Becky Lynch	2.00	5.00
DR26	Charlotte Flair	2.00	5.00

1985 Topps WWF (continued — Divas Revolution)

DR27	Sasha Banks & Charlotte Flair	2.00	5.00
DR28	Mickie James & Asuka	1.25	3.00
DR29	Alexa Bliss	2.50	6.00
DR30	Mickie James & Alexa Bliss	2.50	6.00
DR31	Bayley	1.00	2.50
DR32	Naomi	.75	2.00
DR33	Naomi & Charlotte	.75	2.00
DR34	Alexa Bliss	2.50	6.00
DR35	Carmella	1.25	3.00
DR36	Asuka	1.50	4.00
DR37	Charlotte Flair	2.00	5.00
DR38	Absolution	2.00	5.00
DR39	Riott Squad	1.50	4.00
DR40	Asuka	1.50	4.00

1985 Topps WWF

COMPLETE SET W/HOGAN (66)	200.00	400.00
COMPLETE SET W/O HOGAN (60)	30.00	75.00
UNOPENED BOX (36 PACKS)	1000.00	1500.00
UNOPENED PACK (9 CARDS+1 STICKER)	30.00	40.00
RACK PACK (26 CARDS+3 STICKERS)	150.00	200.00
RINGSIDE ACTION (22-56)		
SUPERSTARS SPEAK (57-66)		
*OPC: SAME VALUE AS TOPPS		

1	Hulk Hogan	75.00	150.00
2	The Iron Sheik	1.00	2.50
3	Captain Lou Albano	.75	2.00
4	Junk Yard Dog	1.00	2.50
5	Paul Mr. Wonderful Orndorff	.60	1.50
6	Jimmy Superfly Snuka	.60	1.50
7	Rowdy Roddy Piper	6.00	15.00
8	Wendi Richter	.75	2.00
9	Greg The Hammer Valentine	1.00	2.50
10	Brutus Beefcake	1.00	2.50
11	Jesse The Body Ventura	3.00	8.00
12	Big John Studd	.60	1.50
13	Fabulous Moolah	1.25	3.00
14	Tito Santana	1.25	3.00
15	Hillbilly Jim	1.00	2.50
16	Hulk Hogan	100.00	200.00
17	Mr. Fuji	.75	2.00
18	Rotundo & Windham	.75	2.00
19	Moondog Spot	.50	1.25
20	Chief Jay Strongbow	.50	1.25
21	George The Animal Steele	1.25	3.00
22	Let Go of My Toe! RA	.50	1.25
23	Lock 'Em Up! RA	.50	1.25
24	Scalp 'Em! RA	.50	1.25
25	Going for the Midsection! RA	.75	2.00
26	Up in the Air! RA	.60	1.50
27	All Tied Up! RA	1.50	4.00
28	Here She Comes! RA	.50	1.25
29	Stretched to the Limit! RA	3.00	8.00
30	Over He Goes! RA	1.00	2.50
31	An Appetite for Mayhem! RA	.60	1.50
32	Putting on Pressure! RA	.50	1.25
33	Smashed on a Knee! RA	.75	2.00
34	A Fist Comes Flying! RA	.50	1.25
35	Lemme' Out of This! RA	.50	1.25
36	No Fair Chokin'! RA	.50	1.25
37	Attacked by an Animal! RA	.50	1.25
38	One Angry Man! RA	1.25	3.00
39	Someone's Going Down! RA	1.25	3.00
40	Strangle Hold! RA	2.00	5.00
41	Bending an Arm! RA	.50	1.25
42	Ready for a Pile Driver! RA	.75	2.00
43	Face to the Canvas! RA	.50	1.25
44	Paul Wants It All! RA	.75	2.00
45	Kick to the Face! RA	3.00	8.00
46	Ready for Action! RA	.50	1.25
47	Putting on the Squeeze! RA	.60	1.50
48	Giants in Action! RA	1.50	4.00
49	Camel Clutch! RA	.60	1.50
50	Pile Up! RA	2.00	5.00
51	Can't Get Away! RA	.60	1.50
52	Going for the Pin! RA	.50	1.25
53	Ready to Fly! RA	2.00	5.00
54	Crusher in a Crusher! RA	.50	1.25
55	Fury of the Animal! RA	.75	2.00
56	Wrong Kind of Music! RA	6.00	15.00
57	Who's your next challenger? SS	2.50	6.00
58	This dog has got a mean bite! SS	.75	2.00
59	I don't think I'll ask that... SS	1.25	3.00
60	You Hulkster fans lift... SS	8.00	20.00
61	This ain't my idea... SS	1.00	2.50
62	You mean Freddie Blassie is... SS	1.25	3.00
63	Mppgh Ecch Oong. SS	1.00	2.50
64	It's the rock n' wrestling... SS	.75	2.00
65	Arrrggghhhh! SS	.60	1.50
66	They took my reindeer! SS	.60	1.50

1985 Topps WWF Stickers

COMPLETE SET W/HOGAN (22)	50.00	100.00
COMPLETE SET W/O HOGAN (17)	12.00	30.00

1	Hulk Hogan	15.00	40.00
2	Captain Lou Albano	.75	2.00
3	Brutus Beefcake	1.25	3.00
4	Jesse Ventura	2.00	5.00
5	The Iron Sheik	1.50	4.00
6	Wendi Richter	1.25	3.00
7	Jimmy Snuka	.75	2.00
8	Ivan Putski	1.00	2.50
9	Hulk Hogan	4.00	10.00
10	Junk Yard Dog	1.25	3.00
11	Hulk Hogan	6.00	15.00
12	Captain Lou Albano	.75	2.00
13	Captain Lou Albano	.75	2.00
14	Freddie Blassie & The Iron Sheik	.75	2.00
15	Jimmy Snuka	.75	2.00
16	Hulk Hogan	10.00	25.00
17	Iron Sheik	1.50	4.00
18	Rene Goulet & S.D. Jones	1.25	3.00
19	Junk Yard Dog	.75	2.00
20	Wendi Richter	1.25	3.00
21	Andre the Giant	3.00	8.00
22	Hulk Hogan	8.00	20.00

1987 Topps WWF

COMPLETE SET (75)	60.00	120.00
UNOPENED BOX (36 PACKS)		
UNOPENED PACK (9 CARDS+1 STICKER)		

1	Bret "Hit Man" Hart	25.00	60.00
2	Andre the Giant	6.00	15.00
3	Hulk Hogan	5.00	12.00
4	Frankie	.75	2.00
5	Koko B. Ware	.75	2.00
6	Tito Santana	.60	1.50
7	Randy Savage & Elizabeth	10.00	25.00
8	Billy Jack Haynes	.40	1.00
9	Hercules & Bobby Heenan	.40	1.00
10	King Harley Race	.60	1.50
11	Kimchee & Kamala	.40	1.00
12	Bravo/Johnny V/Valentine	.50	1.25
13	Honky Tonk Man	1.00	2.50
14	Outback Jack	.40	1.00
15	King Kong Bundy	1.25	3.00
16	The Magnificent Muraco	.40	1.00
17	Mr. Fuji and Killer Khan	.75	2.00
18	The Natural Butch Reed	.60	1.50
19	Davey Boy Smith	.75	2.00
20	The Dynamite Kid	.40	1.00
21	Ricky The Dragon Steamboat	1.50	4.00
22	Two-Man Clothesline RA	.40	1.00
23	Ref Turned Wrestler RA	.75	2.00
24	Ready to Strike RA	.60	1.50
25	In the Outback RA	.40	1.00
26	The Hulkster Explodes RA	2.00	5.00
27	Double Whammy RA	.40	1.00
28	Spoiling for a Fight RA	.40	1.00
29	Flip Flop RA	.40	1.00
30	Islanders Attack RA	.40	1.00
31	King Harley Parades RA	.40	1.00
32	Backbreaker RA	.40	1.00
33	Double Dropkick RA	.40	1.00
34	The Loser Must Bow RA	.40	1.00
35	American-Made RA	2.50	6.00
36	A Challenge Answered RA	2.00	5.00
37	Champ in the Ring RA	4.00	10.00
38	Listening to Hulkamania RA	2.00	5.00
39	Heading for the Ring RA	.40	1.00
40	Out to Destroy RA	.40	1.00
41	Tama Takes a Beating RA	.40	1.00
42	Bundy in Mid-Air RA	.40	1.00
43	Karate Stance RA	.40	1.00
44	Her Eyes on Randy RA	2.50	6.00
45	The Olympian Returns RA	.40	1.00
46	Reed Is Riled RA	.40	1.00
47	Flying Bodypress RA	.40	1.00
48	Hooking the Leg RA	.40	1.00
49	A Belly Buster WMIII	.40	1.00
50	Revenge on Randy WMIII	.75	2.00
51	Fighting the Full Nelson WMIII	.40	1.00
52	Honky Tonk Goes Down WMIII	.40	1.00
53	Over the Top WMIII	.40	1.00
54	The Giant Is Slammed WMIII	1.25	3.00
55	Out of the Ring WMIII	.75	2.00
56	And Still Champion WMIII	1.50	4.00
57	Harts Hit Concrete WMIII	.40	1.00
58	The Challenge RA	1.25	3.00
59	Bearhug RA	.40	1.00
60	Fantastic Bodypress RA	.40	1.00
61	Aerial Maneuvers RA	.40	1.00
62	Ready to Sting! RA	.40	1.00
63	Showing Off RA	.40	1.00
64	Scare Tactics RA	.40	1.00
65	Taking a Bow RA	.60	1.50
66	Out to Eat a Turnbuckle RA	.40	1.00
67	Nice guys finish last! SS	.40	1.00
68	Here's how we keep... SS	.40	1.00
69	Urrggh. Nice! SS	.40	1.00
70	No Kamala...him not dinner! SS	.40	1.00
71	We are the original destroyers. SS	.40	1.00
72	I think the fans are mad at me. SS	.40	1.00
73	You ain't nothin'... SS	.40	1.00
74	I'm gonna take a big bit... SS	.40	1.00
75	Good! SS	.40	1.00

1987 Topps WWF Stickers

COMPLETE SET (22)	7.50	15.00

1	Bret Hit Man Hart	1.00	2.50
2	Hulk Hogan	1.50	4.00
3	Koko B. Ware	.40	1.00
4	Randy Savage & Elizabeth	1.25	3.00
5	Billy Jack Haynes	.40	1.00
6	Hercules & Bobby Heenan	.60	1.50
7	King Harley Race	.60	1.50
8	Kimchee & Kamala	.40	1.00
9	Bravo/Johnny V/Valentine	.60	1.50
10	Honky Tonk Man	.60	1.50
11	Outback Jack	.40	1.00
12	King Kong Bundy	.60	1.50
13	Magnificent Muraco	.40	1.00
14	Mr. Fuji & Killer Khan	.40	1.00
15	Ricky The Dragon Steamboat	.60	1.50
16	Danny Davis	.40	1.00
17	Andre the Giant	1.25	3.00
18	Ken Patera	.40	1.00
19	Smash Demolition	.40	1.00
20	Jim The Anvil Neidhart	.40	1.00
21	George The Animal Steele	.60	1.50
22	WWF Logo	.40	1.00

1985 Topps WWF 3-D Pro Wrestling Stars

COMPLETE SET (12)	500.00	1000.00
UNOPENED BOX		
UNOPENED PACK (1 CARD)		

1	Hulk Hogan	250.00	500.00
2	Wendi Richter	50.00	100.00
3	Jimmy Superfly Snuka	50.00	100.00
4	The Iron Sheik	60.00	120.00
5	Hillbilly Jim	30.00	75.00
6	Captain Lou Albano	50.00	100.00
7	Paul Orndorff	75.00	150.00
8	Jesse The Body Ventura	60.00	120.00
9	Brutus Beefcake	30.00	75.00
10	Andre the Giant	200.00	350.00
11	Rocky Johnson	30.00	75.00
12	Junk Yard Dog	60.00	120.00

1993 Topps Ireland Wacky Wrestling

COMPLETE SET (66)	15.00	40.00

1	Randy Savage
2	Undertaker
3	Papa Shango & Ultimate Warrior
4	Hulk Hogan
5	Hacksaw Jim Duggan
6	Sid Vicious
7	Ric Flair & Rowdy Roddy Piper
8	El Matador
9	Bushwhackers
10	Scott Steiner
11	Ultimate Warrior & Undertaker
12	Papa Shango
13	Hulk Hogan
14	Shawn Michaels
15	Shawn Michaels & Virgil
16	Razor Ramon
17	Bret Hart
18	Bret Hart
19	El Matador
20	Papa Shango
21	Big Bossman & The Mountie
22	Hulk Hogan
23	Hulk Hogan & Ultimate Warrior
24	Ultimate Warrior
25	Ric Flair & Michael Hayes
26	Ric Flair
27	Ric Flair
28	Ric Flair & El Gigante
29	Undertaker
30	Kamala & Bushwhacker Luke
31	Kamala

32 Honky Tonk Man
33 Honky Tonk Man
34 Honky Tonk Man & Greg Valentine
35 Sid Vicious
36 Sid Vicious & Scott Steiner
37 Lanny Poffo
38 Ted DiBiase
39 Brian Knobbs & Scott Steiner
40 Sgt. Slaughter
41 Steiner Brothers
42 Iron Sheik & Sgt. Slaughter
43 Randy Savage
44 Koko B. Ware
45 Road Warrior Animal
46 Road Warrior Animal
47 Road Warrior Animal
48 Hercules
49 Bam Bam Bigelow
50 Bushwhackers
51 Bushwhackers
52 Brooklyn Brawler
53 Ravishing Rick Rude
54 Tony Atlas & Greg Valentine
55 Jim Neidhart & Ivan Koloff
56 Terry Taylor
57 Big Bossman & Nailz
58 Davey Boy Smith
59 Ravishing Rick Rude & Paul Orndorff
60 Ric Flair & Sting
61 DDP & Diamond Studd
62 Road Warrior Hawk & Ric Flair
63 Papa Shango
64 Ric Flair & Lex Luger
65 Tony Atlas & Nikolai Volkoff
66 Randy Savage

2006 Topps UK WWE Insider English WWE Champions

COMPLETE SET (14)
*GERMAN: X TO X BASIC CARDS
*ITALIAN: X TO X BASIC CARDS

C1 John Cena (Super Foil Card)
C2 Ric Flair
C3 Trish Stratus
C4 Undertaker
C5 JBL
C6 Batista
C7 Chris Benoit
C8 Triple H
C9 Road Warrior Animal
C10 Edge
C11 Stone Cold Steve Austin
C12 Hulk Hogan
C13 Rey Mysterio
C14 Booker T

2006 Topps UK WWE Insider English WWE Divas

COMPLETE SET (12)
*GERMAN: X TO X BASIC CARDS
*ITALIAN: X TO X BASIC CARDS

D1 Candice
D2 Melina
D3 Michelle McCool
D4 Sharmell
D5 Torrie Wilson
D6 Trish Stratus
D7 Christy Hemme

D8 Lilian Garcia
D9 Lita
D10 Maria
D11 Stacy Keibler
D12 Victoria

2006 Topps UK WWE Insider English WWE Legends

COMPLETE SET (22)
*GERMAN: X TO X BASIC CARDS
*ITALIAN: X TO X BASIC CARDS

L1 Ted DiBiase
L2 Dusty Rhodes
L3 Paul Bearer
L4 Earthquake
L5 Hillbilly Jim
L6 Nicolai Volkoff
L7 Paul Orndorff
L8 Doink the Clown
L9 Bam Bam Bigelow
L10 The Junkyard Dog
L11 Freebird Michael Hayes
L12 Freebird Terry Gordy
L13 The British Bulldog
L14 Rowdy Roddy Piper
L15 Sgt. Slaughter
L16 The Iron Sheik
L17 Bobby The Brain Heenan
L18 The Mouth of the South Jimmy Hart
L19 Superstar Billy Graham
L20 Jake The Snake Roberts
L21 Vader
L22 Gorilla Monsoon

2009 TRISTAR Hulk Hogan Joins TNA Commemoratives

COMPLETE SET (2)

H1 Hulk Hogan
H2 Hulk Hogan

2008 TRISTAR TNA Cross The Line

COMPLETE SET (100)	8.00	20.00
UNOPENED BOX (20 PACKS)		
UNOPENED PACK (6 CARDS)		
*GOLD/50: 2X TO 5X BASIC CARDS		
*RED/10: UNPRICED DUE TO SCARCITY		
*PURPLE/1: UNPRICED DUE TO SCARCITY		
1 A.J. Styles	.40	1.00
2 Motor City Machineguns	.15	.40
3 Brother Ray	.20	.50
4 LAX	.15	.40
5 Consequences Creed	.15	.40
6 Taylor Wilde	.60	1.50
7 Sheik Abdul Bashir	.20	.50
8 Main Event Mafia	.20	.50
9 Hector Guerrero & Willie Urbina	.12	.30
10 Lauren	.40	1.00
11 Kyra Angle	.40	1.00
12 Suicide	.12	.30
13 Rhaka Khan	.20	.50
14 Mick Foley	.60	1.50
15 Shane Sewell	.12	.30
16 Dutch Mantel	.12	.30
17 Beer Money Inc.	.15	.40
18 Prince Justice Brotherhood	.12	.30
19 Jeff Jarrett	.75	2.00
20 A.J. Styles	.40	1.00
21 Cowboy James Storm	.15	.40
22 Mike Tenay	.15	.40
23 Don West	.12	.30
24 Rudy Charles	.12	.30
25 Andrew Thomas	.12	.30
26 Jeremy Borash	.12	.30
27 Hermie Sadler	.12	.30
28 Kevin Nash	.60	1.50
29 Brother Devon	.20	.50
30 Beautiful People	.60	1.50
31 Roxxi	.40	1.00
32 Abyss	.40	1.00
33 Dixie Carter	.30	.75
34 Christian Cage	.30	.75
35 Booker T	.75	2.00
36 Shark Boy	.12	.30
37 Johnny Devine	.15	.40
38 Petey Williams	.12	.30
39 Homicide	.15	.40
40 Angelina Love	.60	1.50
41 Scott Steiner	.60	1.50
42 Alex Shelley	.15	.40
43 Jacqueline	.40	1.00
44 Curry Man	.12	.30
45 Kip James	.15	.40
46 Earl Hebner	.15	.40
47 Velvet Sky	.50	1.25
48 Kurt Angle	.75	2.00
49 Jim Cornette	.15	.40
50 Sting	.60	1.50
51 Traci Brooks	.50	1.25
52 Jay Lethal	.12	.30
53 Robert Roode	.12	.30
54 Petey Williams	.12	.30
55 Sonjay Dutt	.12	.30
56 Sharmell	.40	1.00
57 Chris Sabin	.12	.30
58 Matt Morgan	.15	.40
59 ODB	.40	1.00
60 Tomko	.12	.30
61 Kurt Angle	.75	2.00
62 Christian Cage	.30	.75
63 ODB	.40	1.00
64 Team 3D	.20	.50
65 A.J. Styles	.40	1.00
66 James Storm	.15	.40
67 Raisha Saeed	.30	.75
68 Sonjay Dutt	.12	.30
69 Kevin Nash	.60	1.50
70 Matt Morgan	.15	.40
71 BG James	.12	.30
72 Hernandez	.15	.40
73 A.J. Styles	.40	1.00
74 Kurt Angle	.75	2.00
75 Christian Cage	.30	.75
76 Jeff Jarrett	.75	2.00
77 Sting	.60	1.50
78 Christian Cage	.30	.75
79 Jeff Jarrett	.75	2.00
80 Kurt Angle Meets Samoa Joe	.75	2.00
81 Sharmell	.40	1.00
82 Sting	.60	1.50
83 Most Important Moment in TNA History	.12	.30
84 Christian†Cage vs. Abyss	.40	1.00
85 Samoa Joe vs. Daniels vs. Styles	.40	1.00
86 Kurt Angle	.75	2.00
87 Styles vs. Angle	.75	2.00
88 Eric Young	.12	.30
89 Rhino	.30	.75
90 Samoa Joe	.20	.50
91 SoCal Val	.60	1.50
92 Curry Man	.12	.30
93 Lance Rock	.15	.40
94 Jimmy Rave	.15	.40
95 Sting vs. Samoa Joe	.60	1.50
96 Kurt Angle vs. Jeff Jarrett	.75	2.00
97 Awesome Kong/TNA Knockouts	.30	.75
98 Beer Money vs. LAX	.15	.40
99 Steve McMichael	.30	.75
100 Checklist	.12	.30

2008 TRISTAR TNA Cross the Line Autographed Memorabilia Silver

*GOLD/50: .6X TO 1.2X BASIC AU MEM
*RED/25: .75X TO 1.5 BASIC AU MEM
*GREEN/5: UNPRICED DUE TO SCARCITY
*PURPLE/1: UNPRICED DUE TO SCARCITY
STATED PRINT RUN 99 SER.#'d SETS

MAA Abyss	15.00	30.00
MOA ODB	15.00	30.00
MSA Sting	25.00	50.00
MABA Sheik Abdul-Bashir	10.00	20.00
MALA Angelina Love	20.00	40.00
MASA A.J. Styles	20.00	40.00
MCCA Christian Cage	15.00	30.00
MCHA Christy Hemme	20.00	40.00
MCMA Curry Man	10.00	20.00
MDCA Dixie Carter	15.00	30.00
MJBA Jeremy Borash	10.00	20.00
MKAA Kurt Angle	15.00	30.00
MKNA Kevin Nash	20.00	40.00
MRCA Rudy Charles	10.00	20.00
MRSA Raisha Saeed	10.00	20.00
MSEA Super Eric	10.00	20.00
MSJA Samoa Joe	20.00	40.00
MSVA SoCal Val	15.00	30.00
MTWA Taylor Wilde	15.00	30.00
MVSA Velvet Sky	20.00	40.00

2008 TRISTAR TNA Cross the Line Autographs Silver

*GOLD/50: .5X TO 1.2X BASIC AUTOS
*RED/25: .6X TO 1.5X BASIC AUTOS
*PURPLE/1: UNPRICED DUE TO SCARCITY
*P.P.BLACK/1: UNPRICED DUE TO SCARCITY
*P.P.CYAN/1: UNPRICED DUE TO SCARCITY
*P.P.MAGENTA/1: UNPRICED DUE TO SCARCITY
*P.P.YELLOW/1: UNPRICED DUE TO SCARCITY

CA Abyss	8.00	20.00
CJ Jacqueline	6.00	15.00
CL Lauren	6.00	15.00
CO ODB	6.00	15.00
CS Sting	20.00	50.00
CAB Sheik Abdul Bashir	6.00	15.00
CAJ A.J. Styles	10.00	25.00
CAK Awesome Kong	6.00	15.00
CAL Angelina Love	10.00	25.00
CAS Alex Shelley	6.00	15.00
CAT Andrew Thomas	6.00	15.00
CBD Brother Devon	8.00	20.00
CBR Brother Ray	8.00	20.00
CBT Booker T	8.00	20.00
CCC Christian Cage	8.00	20.00
CCH Christy Hemme	10.00	25.00
CCM Curry Man	8.00	20.00
CCS Chris Sabin	6.00	15.00

2008 TRISTAR TNA Cross the Line Dual Autographs Silver

*GOLD/50: .5X TO 1.2X BASIC AUTOS
*RED/25: .6X TO 1.5X BASIC AUTOS
*BLUE/5: UNPRICED DUE TO SCARCITY
*PURPLE/1: UNPRICED DUE TO SCARCITY
*P.P.BLACK/1: UNPRICED DUE TO SCARCITY
*P.P.CYAN/1: UNPRICED DUE TO SCARCITY
*P.P.MAGENTA/1: UNPRICED DUE TO SCARCITY
*P.P.YELLOW/1: UNPRICED DUE TO SCARCITY
RANDOMLY INSERTED INTO PACKS

C2BS	Booker T/Sharmell	15.00	30.00
C2CB	J.Cornette/T.Brooks	12.50	25.00
C2CR	C.Cage/Rhino	12.50	25.00
C2HH	Hernandez/Homicide	7.50	15.00
C2JK	S.Joe/K.Nash	15.00	30.00
C2KS	A.Kong/R.Saeed	12.50	25.00
C2KW	A.Kong/T.Wilde	20.00	40.00
C2LS	A.Love/V.Sky	20.00	40.00
C2RD	BroRay/BroDevon	15.00	30.00
C2SA	A.J.Styles/K.Angle	15.00	30.00
C2SA	Sting/K.Angle	20.00	40.00
C2SR	J.Storm/R.Roode	15.00	30.00
C2SS	A.Shelley/C.Sabin	15.00	30.00
C2SW	S.Steiner/P.Williams	12.50	25.00
C2WC	P.Williams/C.Creed	7.50	15.00

2008 TRISTAR TNA Cross the Line Dual Memorabilia Silver

*GOLD/50: .5X TO 1.2X BASIC MEM
*RED/25: .6X TO 1.5X BASIC MEM
*GREEN/5: UNPRICED DUE TO SCARCITY
*PURPLE/1: UNPRICED DUE TO SCARCITY
STATED PRINT RUN 99 SER.#'d SETS

MS2	Sting	20.00	50.00
MAS2	Kurt Angle/A.J. Styles	8.00	20.00
MDL2	Sonjay Dutt/Jay Lethal	6.00	15.00
MLV2	Jay Lethal	5.00	12.00
	SoCal Val		

2008 TRISTAR TNA Cross the Line High Impact Championship Inserts

STATED ODDS 1:CASE
NO PRICING DUE TO SCARCITY
NNO A.J. Styles Auto Baseball EXCH
NNO TNA Wrestler Auto Photo EXCH
NNO Velvet Sky Auto Baseball EXCH
NNO Booker T Auto Baseball EXCH

2008 TRISTAR TNA Cross the Line Memorabilia Silver

*GOLD/50: .5X TO 1.2X BASIC MEM
*RED/25: .6X TO 1.5X BASIC MEM
*GREEN/5: UNPRICED DUE TO SCARCITY
*PURPLE/1: UNPRICED DUE TO SCARCITY
STATED PRINT RUN 99 SER.#'d SETS

MA	Abyss	8.00	20.00
MS	Sting	10.00	25.00
MAB	Sheik Abdul Bashir	6.00	15.00
MAS	A.J. Styles	8.00	20.00
MBP	The Beautiful People	10.00	25.00
MCC	Christian Cage	8.00	20.00
MCM	Curry Man	6.00	15.00
MDC	Dixie Carter	8.00	20.00
MKA	Kurt Angle	10.00	25.00
MKN	Kevin Nash	8.00	20.00
MSE	Super Eric	6.00	15.00
MTW	Taylor Wilde	8.00	20.00

2008 TRISTAR TNA Cross the Line Quad Autographs Silver

*GOLD/50: .6X TO 1.2X BASIC AUTOS
*RED/25: .75X TO 1.5X BASIC AUTOS
*BLUE/5: UNPRICED DUE TO SCARCITY
*PURPLE/1: UNPRICED DUE TO SCARCITY
*P.P.BLACK/1: UNPRICED DUE TO SCARCITY
*P.P.CYAN/1: UNPRICED DUE TO SCARCITY
*P.P.MAGENTA/1: UNPRICED DUE TO SCARCITY
*P.P.YELLOW/1: UNPRICED DUE TO SCARCITY
RANDOMLY INSERTED INTO PACKS

1	Love/Sky/Brooks/Hemme	60.00	120.00
2	Sting/Nash/Jarrett/Steiner	125.00	200.00
3	Hebner/Johnson/Thomas/Charles	25.00	50.00
4	Tenay/West/Guerrero/Urbina	25.00	50.00
5	Storm/Roode/Homic/Hrndz	25.00	50.00
6	Love/Sky/Kong/Jacqueline	30.00	60.00
7	Bashir/Dutt/Curry/Guer	25.00	50.00

2008 TRISTAR TNA Cross the Line Triple Autographs Silver

*GOLD/50: .6X TO 1.2X BASIC AUTOS
*RED/25: .75X TO 1.5X BASIC AUTOS
*BLUE/5: UNPRICED DUE TO SCARCITY
*PURPLE/1: UNPRICED DUE TO SCARCITY
*P.P.BLACK/1: UNPRICED DUE TO SCARCITY
*P.P.CYAN/1: UNPRICED DUE TO SCARCITY
*P.P.MAGENTA/1: UNPRICED DUE TO SCARCITY
*P.P.YELLOW/1: UNPRICED DUE TO SCARCITY
RANDOMLY INSERTED INTO PACKS

C3B	Tenay/West/Borash	20.00	40.00
C3BP	Love/Sky/James	40.00	80.00
C3RR	Hemme/Rock/Rave	25.00	50.00
C3BSS	Booker/Sting/Samoa	40.00	80.00
C3LVD	Lethal/SoCal/Dutt	25.00	50.00
C3PJB	Shark/Curry/SuperEric	20.00	40.00

2010 TRISTAR TNA Icons

COMPLETE SET (100) 10.00 25.00
UNOPENED BOX (20 PACKS)
UNOPENED PACK (6 CARDS)
*GOLD/25: 2.5X TO 6X BASIC CARDS
*RED/5: UNPRICED DUE TO SCARCITY
*PURPLE/1: UNPRICED DUE TO SCARCITY

1	Hulk Hogan	1.00	2.50
2	Ric Flair	.75	2.00
3	Sting	.60	1.50
4	Jeff Hardy	.60	1.50
5	Mick Foley	.75	2.00
6	Kevin Nash	.60	1.50
7	Rob Van Dam	.40	1.00
8	Jeff Jarrett	.40	1.00
9	Kurt Angle	.60	1.50
10	Eric Bischoff	.15	.40
11	Earl Hebner	.15	.40
12	Mr. Anderson	.25	.60
13	Team 3D	.25	.60
14	AJ Styles	.40	1.00
15	Tara	.60	1.50
16	Tommy Dreamer	.15	.40
17	Ric Flair	.75	2.00
18	Sting	.60	1.50
19	Jeff Hardy	.60	1.50
20	Jeff Jarrett	.40	1.00
21	Kevin Nash	.60	1.50
22	Kurt Angle	.60	1.50
23	Mick Foley	.75	2.00
24	Rob Van Dam	.40	1.00
25	Ric Flair	.75	2.00
26	Sting	.60	1.50
27	Jeff Hardy	.60	1.50
28	Mick Foley	.75	2.00
29	Kevin Nash	.60	1.50
30	Rob Van Dam	.40	1.00
31	Team 3D	.25	.60
32	Kurt Angle	.60	1.50
33	Eric Bischoff	.15	.40
34	Dixie Carter	.40	1.00
35	Desmond Wolfe	.15	.40
36	Jay Lethal	.15	.40
37	Matt Morgan	.15	.40
38	Abyss	.25	.60
39	AJ Styles	.40	1.00
40	Hulk Hogan	1.00	2.50
41	Velvet Sky	.75	2.00
42	Angelina Love	.60	1.50
43	Taylor Wilde	.40	1.00
44	Sarita	.40	1.00
45	Daffney	.60	1.50
46	Madison Rayne	.60	1.50
47	Lacey Von Erich	.75	2.00
48	Christy Hemme	.60	1.50
49	SoCal Val	.60	1.50
50	Chelsea	.60	1.50
51	Miss Tessmacher	.75	2.00
52	Rosie Lottalove	.40	1.00
53	Motor City Machineguns	.20	.50
54	Rob Terry	.15	.40
55	Kazarian	.15	.40
56	D'Angelo Dinero	.15	.40
57	Douglas Williams	.15	.40
58	Desmond Wolfe	.15	.40
59	Eric Young	.15	.40
60	Generation Me	.15	.40
61	Beer Money Inc.	.25	.60
62	Abyss	.25	.60
63	Matt Morgan	.15	.40
64	Samoa Joe	.25	.60
65	Hernandez	.15	.40
66	Ink Inc.	.15	.40
67	Jay Lethal	.15	.40
68	Magnus	.15	.40
69	Lacey Von Erich	.75	2.00
70	Hulk Hogan	.75	2.00
71	Ric Flair	.60	1.50
72	Sting	.50	1.25
73	Jeff Hardy	.50	1.25
74	Mick Foley	.60	1.50
75	Kevin Nash	.50	1.25
76	Rob Van Dam	.30	.75
77	Jeff Jarrett	.30	.75
78	Kurt Angle	.50	1.25
79	Mr. Anderson	.20	.50
80	Tommy Dreamer	.15	.40
81	Hulk Hogan	.75	2.00
82	Ric Flair	.60	1.50
83	Sting	.50	1.25
84	Jeff Hardy	.50	1.25
85	Mick Foley	.60	1.50
86	Kevin Nash	.50	1.25
87	Rob Van Dam	.30	.75
88	Jeff Jarrett	.30	.75
89	Kurt Angle	.50	1.25
90	Mick Foley	.60	1.50
91	Mick Foley	.60	1.50
92	Mick Foley	.60	1.50
93	Mick Foley	.60	1.50
94	Mick Foley	.60	1.50
95	Sting	.50	1.25
96	Kevin Nash	.50	1.25
97	Rob Van Dam	.30	.75
98	Mr. Anderson	.20	.50
99	Jeff Jarrett	.30	.75
100	Kurt Angle	.50	1.25

2010 TRISTAR TNA Icons Dual Memorabilia Silver

STATED PRINT RUN 199 SER.#'d SETS

M8	Rob Van Dam
	Jeff Hardy
M9	Ric Flair
	AJ Styles

2010 TRISTAR TNA Icons Hogangraphs Green

OVERALL AUTO ODDS TWO PER BOX

H1	Hulk Hogan	75.00	150.00
H2	Hulk Hogan	75.00	150.00
H3	Hulk Hogan	75.00	150.00
H4	Hulk Hogan	75.00	150.00
H5	Hulk Hogan	75.00	150.00

2010 TRISTAR TNA Icons Hulk Hogan Die-Cut Letter Memorabilia Silver

*GOLD/50: .5X TO 1.2X BASIC MEM
*RED/25: .6X TO 1.5 BASIC MEM
*PURPLE/1: UNPRICED DUE TO SCARCITY
STATED ODDS OVERALL MEM 1:BOX
STATED PRINT RUN 199 SER.#'d SETS

HH1	Hulk Hogan Bandana H	12.00	30.00
HH2	Hulk Hogan Bandana O	12.00	30.00
HH3	Hulk Hogan Bandana G	12.00	30.00
HH4	Hulk Hogan Bandana A	12.00	30.00
HH5	Hulk Hogan Bandana N	12.00	30.00

2010 TRISTAR TNA Icons Hulk Hogan Dual Autographs Gold

*GREEN/50: UNPRICED DUE TO SCARCITY
*RED/5: UNPRICED DUE TO SCARCITY
*PURPLE/1: UNPRICED DUE TO SCARCITY
STATED PRINT RUN 99 SER.#'d SETS

H21	Hulk Hogan/Abyss
H22	Hulk Hogan/AJ Styles
H23	Hulk Hogan/Jeff Hardy
H24	Hulk Hogan/Jeff Jarrett
H25	Hulk Hogan/Kevin Nash
H26	Hulk Hogan/Kurt Angle
H27	Hulk Hogan/Lacey Von Erich
H28	Hulk Hogan/Mick Foley
H29	Hulk Hogan/Ric Flair
H210	Hulk Hogan/Rob Van Dam
H211	Hulk Hogan/Sting
H212	Hulk Hogan/Tara
H213	Hulk Hogan/Velvet Sky

2010 TRISTAR TNA Icons Hulk Hogan Quad Autographs Gold

*GREEN/50: UNPRICED DUE TO SCARCITY
*RED/5: UNPRICED DUE TO SCARCITY
*PURPLE/1: UNPRICED DUE TO SCARCITY
STATED PRINT RUN 99 SER. #'d SETS

H41	Hogan/Sky/Rayne/Von Erich
H42	Hogan/Magnus/Williams/Terry
H43	Hogan/Flair/Abyss/Styles
H44	Hogan/Flair/Sting/Foley

2010 TRISTAR TNA Icons Iconigraphs Gold

*GREEN/25: .5X TO 1.2X BASIC AUTOS
*RED/5: UNPRICED DUE TO SCARCITY
*PURPLE/1: UNPRICED DUE TO SCARCITY
STATED ODDS OVERALL 2:BOX
STATED PRINT RUN 50 SER.#'d SETS

I1	Ric Flair		
I2	Sting		
I3	Jeff Hardy	25.00	50.00
I4	Mick Foley	12.00	30.00
I5	Kevin Nash	10.00	20.00
I6	Rob Van Dam	20.00	40.00
I7	Jeff Jarrett	10.00	20.00
I8	Kurt Angle	12.00	25.00
I9	Earl Hebner	12.00	25.00
I10	Mr. Anderson	12.00	25.00
I11	AJ Styles	10.00	20.00
I12	Syxx-Pac	12.00	25.00
I13	Tara	12.00	25.00
I14	Tommy Dreamer	10.00	20.00
I15	Sting/Icon		
I16	Jeff Hardy/Twist of Fate		
I17	Mick Foley/Bang Bang		
I18	Kevin Nash (inscribed)		
I19	Rob Van Dam/Mr. Monday Night		
I20	Rob Van Dam/Whole F'n Show		
I21	Rob Van Dam/420		
I22	Jeff Jarrett/TNA Founder		
I23	Jeff Jarrett/Guitar Show		
I24	Jeff Jarrett/Slapnutz		
I25	Jeff Jarrett/The Chosen One		
I26	Jeff Jarrett/Music City USA		
I27	Kurt Angle/Olympic Champ		
I28	Kurt Angle/It's Real		
I29	Earl Hebner/Montreal Screw Job		
I30	Mr. Anderson/Mic Check		
I31	Mr. Anderson/Go Pack Go		
I32	AJ Styles/Grand Slam Winner		
I33	AJ Styles/Phenomenal		
I34	AJ Styles/TNA Original		
I35	Tommy Dreamer/Extreme Original		

2010 TRISTAR TNA Icons Memorabilia Silver

*GOLD: .5X TO 1.2X BASIC MEM
*RED: .6X TO 1.5X BASIC MEM
*PURPLE/1: UNPRICED DUE TO SCARCITY
STATED ODDS OVERALL 1:BOX
STATED PRINT RUN 199 SER.#'d SETS

M1	Ric Flair		
M2	Rob Van Dam	4.00	10.00
M3	Jeff Hardy	6.00	15.00
M4	Sting		
M5	Mick Foley	8.00	20.00
M6	Kevin Nash	6.00	15.00
M7	Tommy Dreamer	4.00	10.00

2010 TRISTAR TNA Icons Memorabilia Gold

*GOLD: .5X TO 1.2X BASIC MEM
STATED PRINT RUN 50 SER.#'d SETS

M1	Ric Flair		
M2	Rob Van Dam	5.00	12.00
M3	Jeff Hardy	8.00	20.00
M4	Sting	10.00	25.00
M5	Mick Foley	10.00	25.00
M6	Kevin Nash	8.00	20.00
M7	Tommy Dreamer	5.00	12.00

2010 TRISTAR TNA Icons The Next Generation Autographs Gold

*GREEN/25: .5X TO 1.2X BASIC AUTOS
*RED/5: UNPRICED DUE TO SCARCITY
*PURPLE/1: UNPRICED DUE TO SCARCITY
STATED ODDS OVERALL 2:BOX
STATED PRINT RUN 50 SER.#'d SETS

NEXT1	Alex Shelley	6.00	15.00
NEXT2	Chris Sabin	4.00	10.00
NEXT3	Rob Terry	4.00	10.00
NEXT4	Kazarian	4.00	10.00
NEXT5	D'Angelo Dinero	4.00	10.00
NEXT6	Douglas Williams	4.00	10.00
NEXT7	Desmond Wolfe	4.00	10.00
NEXT8	Eric Young	4.00	10.00
NEXT9	Abyss	6.00	15.00
NEXT10	Matt Morgan	4.00	10.00
NEXT11	Samoa Joe	6.00	15.00
NEXT12	Hernandez	4.00	10.00
NEXT13	Jay Lethal	4.00	10.00
NEXT14	Magnus	4.00	10.00

2010 TRISTAR TNA Icons Quad Memorabilia Silver

COMPLETE SET (1)

HH8	Hogan/Flair/Sting/Foley

2010 TRISTAR TNA Icons Six Autographs Gold

*GREEN/50: UNPRICED DUE TO SCARCITY
*RED/5: UNPRICED DUE TO SCARCITY
*PURPLE/1: UNPRICED DUE TO SCARCITY
STATED PRINT RUN 99 SER.#'d SETS

A61	Hogan/Foley/Sting/Nash/Flair/Jarr
A62	RVD/Moore/Hardy/Foley/Anderson/Angle
A63	Devon/Young/Ray/Storm/Nash/Roode
A64	Sky/Love/Rayne/Wilde/Von Erich/Sarita

2010 TRISTAR TNA Icons Sugar and Spice Autographs Gold

*GREEN/25: .5X TO 1.2X BASIC AUTOS
*RED/5: UNPRICED DUE TO SCARCITY
*PURPLE/1: UNPRICED DUE TO SCARCITY
STATED ODDS OVERALL 2:BOX
STATED PRINT RUN 50 SER.#'d SETS

SS1	Velvet Sky	10.00	25.00
SS2	Angelina Love	8.00	20.00
SS3	Taylor Wilde	8.00	20.00
SS4	Sarita	8.00	20.00
SS5	Daffney	10.00	25.00
SS6	Madison Rayne	8.00	20.00
SS7	Lacey Von Erich	12.00	30.00
SS8	Christy Hemme	8.00	20.00
SS9	SoCal Val	8.00	20.00
SS10	Chelsea	10.00	25.00
SS11	Miss Tessmacher	12.00	30.00
SS12	Rosie Lottalove	10.00	25.00

2010 TRISTAR TNA Icons Triple Memorabilia Silver

STATED PRINT RUN 199 SER.#'d SETS

HH6	Hulk Hogan/Bandana
HH7	Hulk Hogan/Bandana/Shirt/Mat
M10	Sky/Rayne/Von Erich

2008 TRISTAR TNA Impact

COMPLETE SET (69)	8.00	20.00
UNOPENED BOX (18 PACKS)	30.00	50.00
UNOPENED PACK (8 CARDS)		

*GOLD/50: 2X TO 5X BASIC CARDS
*RUBY/10: UNPRICED DUE TO SCARCITY
*P.P.BLACK/1: UNPRICED DUE TO SCARCITY
*P.P.CYAN/1: UNPRICED DUE TO SCARCITY
*P.P.MAGENTA/1: UNPRICED DUE TO SCARCITY
*P.P.YELLOW/1: UNPRICED DUE TO SCARCITY

1	Kurt Angle	.75	2.00
2	Christian Cage	.30	.75
3	Samoa Joe	.20	.50
4	A.J. Styles	.40	1.00
5	Tomko	.12	.30
6	Booker T	.75	2.00
7	Jay Lethal	.12	.30
8	Jeff Jarrett	.75	2.00
9	Rhino	.30	.75
10	Curry Man	.12	.30
11	Sting	.60	1.50
12	Scott Steiner	.60	1.50
13	Robert Roode	.12	.30
14	Eric Young	.12	.30
15	Homicide	.15	.40
16	Hernandez	.15	.40
17	Petey Williams	.12	.30
18	Shark Boy	.12	.30
19	Consequences Creed	.15	.40
20	Alex Shelley	.15	.40
21	Jimmy Rave	.15	.40
22	Rellik	.15	.40
23	Brother Devon	.20	.50
24	Brother Ray	.20	.50
25	Kip James	.15	.40
26	Abyss	.40	1.00
27	Lance Hoyt	.15	.40
28	BG James	.12	.30
29	Chris Sabin	.12	.30
30	Kaz	.12	.30
31	Johnny Devine	.15	.40
32	Super Eric	.12	.30
33	Black Reign	.15	.40
34	James Storm	.15	.40
35	Sonjay Dutt	.12	.30
36	A.Styles/Tomko	.40	1.00
37	Team 3D	.20	.50
38	LAX	.40	1.00
39	Rock n' Rave Infection	.75	2.00
40	Motor Sity Machineguns	.15	.40
41	Karen Angle	.50	1.25
42	ODB	.40	1.00
43	Awesome Kong	.30	.75
44	Traci Brooks	.50	1.25
45	Christy Hemme	.75	2.00
46	Sharmell	.40	1.00
47	Gail Kim	.40	1.00
48	Angelina Love	.60	1.50
49	Raisha Saeed	.30	.75
50	SoCal Val	.60	1.50
51	Velvet Sky	.50	1.25
52	Hermie Sadler	.40	1.00
53	Jacqueline	.40	1.00
54	Roxxi Laveaux	.40	1.00
55	Salinas	.40	1.00
56	Vince Russo	.12	.30
57	James Mitchell	.15	.40
58	Matt Morgan	.15	.40
59	Jim Cornette	.15	.40
60	Earl Hebner	.15	.40
61	Andrew Thomas	.12	.30
62	Rudy Charles	.12	.30
63	Mark Johnson	.12	.30
64	Mike Tenay	.15	.40
65	Don West	.12	.30
66	Jeremy Borash	.12	.30
67	Terry Taylor	.12	.30
68	Dixie Carter	.30	.75
69	Kevin Nash	.60	1.50

2008 TRISTAR TNA Impact Autographs Silver

*GOLD/50: .5X TO 1.2X BASIC AUTOS
*RED/25: .6X TO 1.5X BASIC AUTOS
*BLUE/5: UNPRICED DUE TO SCARCITY
*PURPLE/1: UNPRICED DUE TO SCARCITY

AA	Abyss	6.00	15.00
AJ	Jacqueline	4.00	10.00

AK	Kaz	4.00	10.00
AO	ODB	4.00	10.00
AR	Rellik	4.00	10.00
AS	Sting SP	40.00	80.00
AT	Tomko	6.00	15.00
AAJ	A.J. Styles	15.00	40.00
AAK	Awesome Kong	5.00	12.00
AAL	Angelina Love	6.00	15.00
AAS	Alex Shelley	5.00	12.00
ABD	Brother Devon	6.00	15.00
ABG	BG James	5.00	12.00
ABR	Black Reign	4.00	10.00
ABR	Brother Ray	6.00	15.00
ABT	Booker T SP	15.00	40.00
ACC	Christian Cage SP	6.00	15.00
ACH	Christy Hemme	10.00	25.00
ACM	Curry Man	4.00	10.00
ACS	Chris Sabin	5.00	12.00
ADC	Dixie Carter SP	15.00	40.00
ADW	Don West	4.00	10.00
AEY	Eric Young	4.00	10.00
AGK	Gail Kim	20.00	40.00
AH1	Hernandez	4.00	10.00
AH2	Homicide	4.00	10.00
AJB	Jeremy Borash	4.00	10.00
AJC	Jim Cornette	5.00	12.00
AJD	Johnny Devine	4.00	10.00
AJJ	Jeff Jarrett	6.00	15.00
AJL	Jay Lethal	4.00	10.00
AJM	James Mitchell	4.00	10.00
AJR	Jimmy Rave	5.00	12.00
AJS	James Storm	4.00	10.00
AKA	Kurt Angle SP	30.00	60.00
AKJ	Kip James	5.00	12.00
AKN	Kevin Nash	12.00	30.00
ALH	Lance Hoyt	4.00	10.00
AMM	Matt Morgan	5.00	12.00
AMT	Mike Tenay	4.00	10.00
APB	Payton Banks	5.00	12.00
APW	Petey Williams	4.00	10.00
AR2	Rhino	5.00	12.00
ARL	Roxxi Laveaux	5.00	12.00
ARR	Robert Roode	5.00	12.00
ARS	Raisha Saeed	4.00	10.00
AS2	Sharmell	4.00	10.00
AS3	Salinas	5.00	12.00
ASB	Shark Boy	4.00	10.00
ASD	Sonjay Dutt	4.00	10.00
ASE	Super Eric	4.00	10.00
ASJ	Samoa Joe SP	15.00	40.00
ASS	Scott Steiner	12.00	30.00
ASV	SoCal Val	5.00	12.00
ATB	Traci Brooks	5.00	12.00
AVS	Velvet Sky	10.00	25.00
ACC2	Consequences Creed	4.00	10.00
AKA2	Karen Angle SP	20.00	40.00

2008 TRISTAR TNA Impact Dual Autographs Gold

COMPLETE SET (10)
*RED/25: .5X TO 1.2X BASIC AUTOS
*BLUE/5: UNPRICED DUE TO SCARCITY
*PURPLE/1: UNPRICED DUE TO SCARCITY
STATED PRINT RUN 50 SER.#'d SETS

A2AA	Ku.Angle/Ka.Angle	50.00	100.00
A2BS	Booker T/Sharmell	25.00	50.00
A2DR	Brothers Devon & Ray	25.00	50.00
A2HH	Homicide/Hernandez	20.00	40.00
A2LS	A.Love/V.Sky	40.00	80.00
A2LV	J.Lethal/S.Val	20.00	40.00
A2RB	R.Roode/P.Banks	25.00	50.00
A2SJ	J.Storm/Jacqueline	20.00	40.00
A2SS	A.Shelley/C.Sabin	30.00	60.00
A2TW	M.Tenay/D.West	15.00	30.00

2008 TRISTAR TNA Impact Memorabilia Black

*RAINBOW FOIL/10-50
*GOLD/25: .5X TO 1.2X BASIC MEM
*RED/1: UNPRICED DUE TO SCARCITY
STATED PRINT RUN 250 SER.#'d SETS

AAO	ODB	6.00	15.00
AAS	Sting	10.00	25.00
AAT	Tomko	5.00	12.00
AAAL	Angelina Love	10.00	25.00
AAAS	A.J. Styles	6.00	15.00
AACC	Christian Cage	5.00	12.00
AACH	Christy Hemme	8.00	20.00
AAGK	Gail Kim	8.00	20.00
AAJL	Jay Lethal	6.00	15.00
AAKA	Kurt Angle	8.00	20.00
AAKN	Kevin Nash	8.00	20.00
AASD	Sonjay Dutt	5.00	12.00
AASJ	Samoa Joe	5.00	12.00
AASS	Scott Steiner	8.00	20.00
AASV	SoCal Val	8.00	20.00
AATB	Traci Brooks	8.00	20.00
AAVS	Velvet Sky	10.00	25.00
AAKA2	Karen Angle	10.00	25.00

2008 TRISTAR TNA Impact Mike's Magical Moments

COMPELETE SET (5) 1.00 2.50
*GOLD/50: 2X TO 5X BASIC CARDS
*RED/10: UNPRICED DUE TO SCARCITY
*PURPLE/1: UNPRICED DUE TO SCARCITY
*P.P.BLACK/1: UNPRICED DUE TO SCARCITY
*P.P.CYAN/1: UNPRICED DUE TO SCARCITY
*P.P.MAGENTA/1: UNPRICED DUE TO SCARCITY
*P.P.YELLOW/1: UNPRICED DUE TO SCARCITY

M1	First Night	.12	.30
M2	Kurt Angle/Samoa Joe	.75	2.00
M3	Big Name Newcomers/Arrivals	.12	.30
M4	X Division	.12	.30
M5	Sporting Superstars	.12	.30

2008 TRISTAR TNA Impact Muscles Ink

COMPLETE SET (10) 3.00 8.00
*GOLD/50: 2X TO 5X BASIC CARDS
*RED/10: UNPRICED DUE TO SCARCITY
*PURPLE/1: UNPRICED DUE TO SCARCITY
*P.P.BLACK/1: UNPRICED DUE TO SCARCITY
*P.P.CYAN/1: UNPRICED DUE TO SCARCITY
*P.P.MAGENTA/1: UNPRICED DUE TO SCARCITY
*P.P.YELLOW/1: UNPRICED DUE TO SCARCITY

MI1	Scott Steiner	.60	1.50
MI2	Robert Roode	.12	.30
MI3	Petey Williams	.12	.30
MI4	Traci Brooks	.50	1.25
MI5	Brother Devon	.20	.50
MI6	Booker T	.75	2.00
MI7	Christy Hemme	.75	2.00
MI8	Kevin Nash	.60	1.50
MI9	Tomko	.12	.30
MI10	Kurt Angle	.75	2.00

2008 TRISTAR TNA Impact Then and Now

COMPLETE SET (4) 1.50 4.00
*GOLD/50: 2X TO 5X BASIC CARDS
*RED/10: UNPRICED DUE TO SCARCITY
*PURPLE/1: UNPRICED DUE TO SCARCITY
*P.P.BLACK/1: UNPRICED DUE TO SCARCITY
*P.P.CYAN/1: UNPRICED DUE TO SCARCITY
*P.P.MAGENTA/1: UNPRICED DUE TO SCARCITY
*P.P.YELLOW/1: UNPRICED DUE TO SCARCITY

TN1	Jeff Jarrett	.75	2.00
TN2	Robert Roode	.12	.30
TN3	Kevin Nash	.60	1.50
TN4	Scott Steiner	.60	1.50

2008 TRISTAR TNA Impact Thoughts by Big Sexy Kevin Nash

COMPLETE SET (5) 2.00 5.00
*GOLD/50: 2X TO 5X BASIC CARDS
*RED/10: UNPRICED DUE TO SCARCITY
*PURPLE/1: UNPRICED DUE TO SCARCITY
*P.P.BLACK/1: UNPRICED DUE TO SCARCITY
*P.P.CYAN/1: UNPRICED DUE TO SCARCITY
*P.P.MAGENTA/1: UNPRICED DUE TO SCARCITY
*P.P.YELLOW/1: UNPRICED DUE TO SCARCITY

BS1	TNA's X-Division	.60	1.50
BS2	Samoa Joe	.60	1.50
BS3	Sting	.60	1.50
BS4	Scott Steiner	.60	1.50
BS5	Trading Cards	.60	1.50

2008 TRISTAR TNA Impact Triple Autographs Red

STATED PRINT RUN 25 SER.#'d SETS

A3AAS	Angle/Angle/Styles	75.00	150.00
A3RHH	Rave/Hoyt/Hemme	25.00	50.00

2008 TRISTAR TNA Impact We Are TNA

COMPLETE SET (7) 2.50 6.00
*GOLD/50: 2X TO 5X BASIC CARDS
*RED/10: UNPRICED DUE TO SCARCITY
*PURPLE/1: UNPRICED DUE TO SCARCITY
*P.P.BLACK/1: UNPRICED DUE TO SCARCITY
*P.P.CYAN/1: UNPRICED DUE TO SCARCITY
*P.P.MAGENTA/1: UNPRICED DUE TO SCARCITY
*P.P.YELLOW/1: UNPRICED DUE TO SCARCITY

T1	6-Sided Ring	.40	1.00
T2	X-Division	.20	.50
T3	History	.75	2.00
T4	TNA World Championship	.75	2.00
T5	TNA X-Division Championship	.40	1.00
T6	TNA World Tag Team Champ.	.40	1.00
T7	TNA Womens Championship	.40	1.00

2009 TRISTAR TNA Impact

COMPLETE SET (100) 12.50 25.00
UNOPENED BOX (20 PACKS)
UNOPENED PACK (6 CARDS)
*WHITE: SAME VALUE
*SILVER/20: 4X TO 10X BASIC CARDS
*GOLD/5: UNPRICED DUE TO SCARCITY
*PURPLE/1: UNPRICED DUE TO SCARCITY

1	Sting	.60	1.50
2	Mick Foley	.60	1.50
3	Daniels	.12	.30
4	Angelina Love	.60	1.50
5	Bobby Lashley	.30	.75
6	James Storm	.15	.40
7	Jeff Jarrett	.60	1.50
8	Taz	.12	.30
9	Brother Ray	.20	.50
10	Tara	.50	1.25
11	Samoa Joe	.20	.50
12	Kevin Nash	.75	2.00
13	Suicide	.12	.30
14	Velvet Sky	.60	1.50
15	Scott Steiner	.60	1.50
16	Daffney	.30	.75
17	Amazing Red	.12	.30
18	Matt Morgan	.15	.40
19	Hernandez	.15	.40
20	ODB	.20	.50
21	AJ Styles	.30	.75
22	Jay Lethal	.12	.30
23	Awesome Kong	.20	.50
24	Robert Roode	.15	.40
25	Kurt Angle	.75	2.00
26	Brutus Magnus	.12	.30
27	SoCal Val	.50	1.25
28	Mike Tenay	.12	.30
29	Jenna Morasca	.50	1.25
30	Booker T	.12	.30
31	Alex Shelley	.15	.40
32	Kiyoshi	.12	.30
33	Sojournor Bolt	.20	.50
34	Abyss	.30	.75
35	Christy Hemme	.75	2.00
36	Doug Williams	.12	.30
37	Consequences Creed	.12	.30
38	Taylor Wilde	.50	1.25
39	Jesse Neal	.12	.30
40	Brother Devon	.20	.50
41	Lauren Brooke	.30	.75
42	Shark Boy	.12	.30
43	Homicide	.15	.40
44	Sharmell	.20	.50
45	Jim Cornette	.12	.30
46	Cody Deaner	.12	.30
47	Eric Young	.12	.30
48	Raisha Saeed	.20	.50
49	Rhino	.20	.50
50	Sarita	.30	.75
51	Don West	.12	.30
52	Traci Brooks	.50	1.25
53	Sheik Abdul Bashir	.12	.30
54	Dr. Stevie	.15	.40
55	Madison Rayne	.50	1.25
56	Chris Sabin	.12	.30
57	Kip James	.15	.40
58	Dixie Carter	.30	.75
59	Jeremy Borash	.12	.30
60	Rob Terry	.12	.30
61	Hermie Sadler	.12	.30
62	Rocco & Sally Boy	.12	.30
63	Ayako Hamada	.30	.75
64	The Beautiful People	.60	1.50
65	Beer Money, Inc.	.15	.40
66	Danny Bonaduce	.30	.75
67	Curtis Granderson	.20	.50
68	THE ICON: STING	.60	1.50
69	THE ICON: STING	.60	1.50
70	THE ICON: STING	.60	1.50
71	THE ICON: STING	.60	1.50

72	THE ICON: STING	.60	1.50
73	Mick Foley	.60	1.50
74	Kurt Angle	.75	2.00
75	Booker T	.12	.30
76	AJ Styles	.30	.75
77	Suicide	.12	.30
78	Daniels	.12	.30
79	Team 3D	.20	.50
80	Sting/Kurt Angle	.75	2.00
81	Angelina Love	.60	1.50
82	Awesome Kong	.20	.50
83	Kurt Angle	.75	2.00
84	Jenna Morasca	.50	1.25
85	Daniels	.12	.30
86	Madison Rayne	.50	1.25
87	Mike Tenay	.12	.30
88	Alex Shelley	.15	.40
89	Sheik Abdul Bashir	.12	.30
90	Jeff Jarrett	.60	1.50
91	Consequences Creed	.12	.30
92	Lauren Brooke	.30	.75
93	Mick Foley	.60	1.50
94	James Storm	.15	.40
95	Jenna Morasca	.50	1.25
96	Kip James	.15	.40
97	Mike Tenay	.12	.30
98	Daniels	.12	.30
99	Tweet n' Tweak Connection	.20	.50
NNO	Checklist	.12	.30

2009 TRISTAR TNA Impact Autographs Silver

SEMISTARS (IA1-IA84)
UNLISTED STARS (IA1-IA84)
*GOLD/60: .5X TO 1.2X BASIC AUTOS
*BLUE/25: .6X TO 1.5X BASIC AUTOS
*GREEN/10: UNPRICED DUE TO SCARCITY
*PURPLE/1: UNPRICED DUE TO SCARCITY

IA1	Abyss	5.00	12.00
IA2	AJ Styles	6.00	15.00
IA3	Alex Shelley	4.00	10.00
IA4	Amazing Red	4.00	10.00
IA5	Angelina Love	8.00	20.00
IA6	Awesome Kong	5.00	12.00
IA7	Bobby Lashley		
IA8	Booker T		
IA9	Brother Devon	4.00	10.00
IA10	Brother Ray	4.00	10.00
IA11	Brutus Magnus	4.00	10.00
IA12	Chris Sabin	5.00	12.00
IA13	Christy Hemme		
IA14	Cody Deaner	4.00	10.00
IA15	Consequences Creed	4.00	10.00
IA16	Curtis Granderson		
IA17	Daffney	8.00	20.00
IA18	Daniels	5.00	12.00
IA19	Danny Bonaduce	6.00	15.00
IA20	Dixie Carter	5.00	12.00
IA21	Doug Williams	4.00	10.00
IA22	Dr. Stevie	5.00	12.00
IA23	Eric Young	4.00	10.00
IA24	Hernandez		
IA25	Homicide	4.00	10.00
IA26	Hermie Sadler	4.00	10.00
IA27	James Storm	5.00	12.00
IA28	Jay Lethal	4.00	10.00
IA29	Jeff Jarrett	6.00	15.00
IA30	Jenna Morasca	6.00	15.00

IA31	Jesse Neal	4.00	10.00
IA32	Jeremy Borash	4.00	10.00
IA33	Jim Cornette		
IA34	Kevin Nash		
IA35	Kip James	4.00	10.00
IA36	Kiyoshi	4.00	10.00
IA37	Kurt Angle		
IA38	Lauren Brooke	5.00	12.00
IA39	Madison Rayne	6.00	15.00
IA40	Matt Morgan		
IA41	Mick Foley		
IA42	ODB	4.00	10.00
IA43	Raisha Saeed	5.00	12.00
IA44	Rhino		
IA45	Rob Terry	5.00	12.00
IA46	Robert Roode	5.00	12.00
IA47	Samoa Joe	5.00	12.00
IA48	Sarita	6.00	15.00
IA49	Scott Steiner		
IA50	Shark Boy	5.00	12.00
IA51	Sharmell		
IA52	Sheik Abdul Bashir		10.00
IA53	SoCal Val	6.00	15.00
IA54	Sojournor Bolt		
IA55	Sting		
IA56	Suicide	4.00	10.00
IA57	Tara	8.00	20.00
IA58	Taylor Wilde	8.00	20.00
IA59	Traci Brooks	6.00	15.00
IA60	Velvet Sky	8.00	20.00
IA61	Jeff Jarrett		
	Mick Foley		
IA62	Angelina Love	12.00	30.00
	Velvet Sky		
IA63	Chris Sabin		
	Alex Shelley		
IA64	Daffney	12.00	30.00
	The Governor		
IA65	Bobby Lashley		
	Kurt Angle		
IA66	Kevin Nash		
	Jenna Morasca		
IA67	Abyss		
	Lauren		
IA68	Mick Foley		
	Sting		
IA69	Consequences Creed		
	Jay Lethal		
IA70	Jesse Neal		
	Rhino		
IA71	Mike Tenay		
	Don West		
IA72	ODB		
	Cody Deaner		
IA73	Brother Devon		
	Brother Ray		
IA74	Sting		
	Kurt Angle		
IA75	Kevin Nash		
	Samoa Joe		
IA76	Scott Steiner		
	Booker T		
IA77	Angelina Love		
	Velvet Sky/Madison Rayne		
IA78	Sting		
	Kurt Angle/Mick Foley		
IA79	Tara		
	Christy Hemme/Traci Brooks		

IA80	Brutus Magnus		
	Rob Terry/Doug Williams		
IA81	Brother Devon		
	Brother Ray/James Storm/Robert Roode		
IA82	Kurt Angle		
	Kevin Nash/Booker T/Scott Steiner		
IA83	Angelina Love		
	Velvet Sky/Tara/Christy Hemme		
IA84	Chris Sabin		
	Alex Shelley/Jay Lethal/Consequences Creed		

2009 TRISTAR TNA Impact High Impact Championship Inserts

NNO Phone Call EXCH
NNO 2 Tickets and Backstage Pass EXCH
NNO 2 Tickets EXCH
NNO Autographed Baseball EXCH
NNO Autographed Photo EXCH

2009 TRISTAR TNA Impact Knockout Autographed Dual Kiss Gold

*BLUE/10: UNPRICED DUE TO SCARCITY
*PURPLE/1: UNPRICED DUE TO SCARCITY
STATED PRINT RUN 25 SER.#'d SETS

2K1	A.Love/V.Sky		
2K2	C.Hemme/T.Brooks		
2K3	J.Morasca/Sharmell	15.00	30.00
2K4	SoCal Val/L.Brooke	25.00	50.00

2009 TRISTAR TNA Impact Knockout Kiss Gold

*BLUE/25: .6X TO 1.5X BASIC KISS
*GREEN/10: UNPRICED DUE TO SCARCITY
*PURPLE/1: UNPRICED DUE TO SCARCITY
STATED PRINT RUN 99 SER.#'d SETS

K1	Angelina Love	15.00	40.00
K2	Awesome Kong	8.00	20.00
K3	Christy Hemme	15.00	40.00
K4	Jenna Morasca	10.00	25.00
K5	ODB	8.00	20.00
K6	Sharmell	8.00	20.00
K7	Tara	15.00	40.00
K8	Taylor Wilde	12.00	30.00
K9	Traci Brooks	12.00	30.00
K10	Velvet Sky	15.00	40.00

2009 TRISTAR TNA Impact Sting Autographed Face Paint Silver

STATED PRINT RUN 10 SER. #'d SETS
NOT PRICED DUE TO SCARCITY

S1 Sting Black
S2 Sting White

2009 TRISTAR TNA Impact Sting Event-Worn Face Paint Silver

*PURPLE/1: UNPRICED DUE TO SCARCITY
STATED PRINT RUN 5 SER. #'d SETS
UNPRICED DUE TO SCARCITY

S1 Sting Black
S2 Sting White

2009 TRISTAR TNA Impact Sting Face Paint Gold

*GREEN/10: UNPRICED DUE TO SCARCITY
*PURPLE/1: UNPRICED DUE TO SCARCITY
STATED PRINT RUN 60 SER.#'d SETS

S1	Sting Black	25.00	60.00
S2	Sting White	25.00	60.00

2013 TRISTAR TNA Impact Glory

There were only 1,800 serial-numbered boxes produced for this set.

COMPLETE SET (109)		20.00	50.00
COMPLETE SET W/O SP (100)		8.00	20.00
UNOPENED BOX (20 PACKS)			
UNOPENED PACK (6 CARDS)			

*RED/40: 2X TO 5X BASIC CARDS
*RED SP/40: .5X TO 1.2X BASIC CARDS
*BLUE/10: UNPRICED DUE TO SCARCITY
*BLUE SP/10: UNPRICED DUE TO SCARCITY
*RAINBOW/1: UNPRICED DUE TO SCARCITY
*RAINBOW SP/1: UNPRICED DUE TO SCARCITY
STATED ODDS SP 1:1 HOBBY BOX

1	Jeff Hardy	.60	1.50
2	Hulk Hogan	.75	2.00
3	Kurt Angle	.25	.60
4	Sting	.60	1.50
5	Rampage Jackson	.25	.60
6	Tito Ortiz	.25	.60
7	Mickie James	.75	2.00
8	Chris Sabin	.15	.40
9	Bully Ray	.15	.40
10	Bobby Roode	.15	.40
11	AJ Styles	.25	.60
12	Gail Kim	.40	1.00
13	Velvet Sky	.60	1.50
14	Chavo Guerrero Jr.	.15	.40
15	James Storm	.15	.40
16	ODB	.15	.40
17	Christopher Daniels	.15	.40
18	Sting	.60	1.50
19	Joseph Park	.25	.60
20	Jessie Godderz	.15	.40
21	Mr. Anderson	.25	.60
22	Garett Bischoff	.25	.60
23	Samoa Joe	.15	.40
24	Austin Aries	.25	.60
25	Hernandez	.15	.40
26	Jeremy Borash	.15	.40
27	Manik	.15	.40
28	Velvet Sky	.60	1.50
29	Jeff Hardy	.60	1.50
30	Christy Hemme	.50	1.25
31	Robbie E	.15	.40
32	Dixie Carter	.25	.60
33	Christopher Daniels	.15	.40
34	Taryn Terrell	.40	1.00
35	Eric Young	.15	.40
36	Miss Tessmacher	.40	1.00
37	Magnus	.15	.40
38	AJ Styles	.25	.60
39	Hulk Hogan	.75	2.00
40	Sting	.60	1.50
41	Gail Kim	.40	1.00
42	Wes Brisco	.15	.40
43	Rob Terry	.15	.40
44	Chavo Guerrero Jr.	.15	.40
45	Gunner	.15	.40
46	Velvet Sky	.60	1.50
47	Knux	.15	.40
48	Jeff Hardy	.60	1.50
49	Chris Sabin	.15	.40
50	Kazarian	.15	.40
51	King Mo	.15	.40
52	Austin Aries	.25	.60

53	Jay Bradley	.15	.40
54	Kenny King	.15	.40
55	Taz	.15	.40
56	Hernandez	.15	.40
57	Eric Young	.15	.40
58	Hulk Hogan	.75	2.00
59	Velvet Sky	.60	1.50
60	Sting	.60	1.50
61	AJ Styles	.25	.60
62	Rockstar Spud	.15	.40
63	Bully Ray	.15	.40
64	Dixie Carter	.25	.60
65	Velvet Sky	.60	1.50
66	Rampage Jackson	.25	.60
67	Jeff Hardy	.60	1.50
68	Christopher Daniels	.15	.40
69	Abyss	.25	.60
70	Chris Sabin	.15	.40
71	Mike Tenay	.15	.40
72	Mickie James	.75	2.00
73	AJ Styles	.25	.60
74	ODB	.15	.40
75	Magnus	.15	.40
76	Hector Guerrero	.15	.40
77	Hulk Hogan	.75	2.00
78	Brooke Hogan	.40	1.00
79	Austin Aries	.25	.60
80	Jessie Godderz	.15	.40
81	Jessie Godderz	.15	.40
82	Jessie Godderz	.15	.40
83	Garett Bischoff	.25	.60
84	Chavo Guerrero Jr.	.15	.40
85	Sam Shaw	.15	.40
86	Bobby Roode	.15	.40
87	Dixie Carter	.25	.60
88	Jeff Hardy	.60	1.50
89	Hulk Hogan	.75	2.00
90	Jeff Hardy Original Art	.50	1.25
91	Jeff Hardy Original Art	.50	1.25
92	Jeff Hardy Original Art	.50	1.25
93	Jeff Hardy Original Art	.50	1.25
94	Jeff Hardy Original Art	.50	1.25
95	Jeff Hardy Original Art	.50	1.25
96	Jeff Hardy Original Art	.50	1.25
97	Jeff Hardy Original Art	.50	1.25
98	Jeff Hardy Original Art	.50	1.25
99	Jeff Hardy Original Art	.50	1.25
100	Aces and Eights SP	3.00	8.00
101	Jeff Hardy SP	3.00	8.00
102	Rampage Jackson SP	1.25	3.00
103	Velvet Sky SP	3.00	8.00
104	AJ Styles SP	1.25	3.00
105	Gail Kim SP	2.00	5.00
106	Sting SP	3.00	8.00
107	Jeff Hardy SP	3.00	8.00
108	Dixie Carter SP	1.25	3.00
109	Hulk Hogan SP	4.00	10.00

2013 TRISTAR TNA Impact Glory Autographed Mat Relics Gold

*BLUE/10: UNPRICED DUE TO SCARCITY
*RED/5: UNPRICED DUE TO SCARCITY
*RAINBOW/1: UNPRICED DUE TO SCARCITY
STATED PRINT RUN 50 SER.#'d SETS

MAS	AJ Styles	12.00	30.00
MBH	Brooke Hogan	20.00	50.00
MBR	Bully Ray	8.00	20.00
MBR	Bobby Roode	8.00	20.00

MCG	Chavo Guerrero Jr.	8.00	20.00
MCH	Christy Hemme	12.00	30.00
MCS	Chris Sabin	8.00	20.00
MD	Devon	8.00	20.00
MHH	Hulk Hogan	50.00	100.00
MJG	Jessie Godderz	8.00	20.00
MJH	Jeff Hardy	20.00	50.00
MKA	Kurt Angle	15.00	40.00
MMA	Mr. Anderson	8.00	20.00
MMJ	Mickie James	20.00	50.00
MRJ	Rampage Jackson	12.00	30.00
MS	Sting	30.00	60.00
MT	Tara	8.00	20.00
MTT	Taryn Terrell	12.00	30.00

2013 TRISTAR TNA Impact Glory Autographed Memorabilia Red

M1	Hulk Hogan		
M2	Jeff Hardy		
M3	Sting	40.00	80.00
M4	Austin Aries		
M5	Rampage Jackson	15.00	40.00
M6	Tito Ortiz		

2013 TRISTAR TNA Impact Glory Dual Autographs Gold

*RED/50: .5X TO 1.2X BASIC AUTOS
*BLUE/10: UNPRICED DUE TO SCARCITY
*GREEN/5: UNPRICED DUE TO SCARCITY
*RAINBOW/1: UNPRICED DUE TO SCARCITY
*P.P.BLACK/1: UNPRICED DUE TO SCARCITY
*P.P.CYAN/1: UNPRICED DUE TO SCARCITY
*P.P.MAGENTA/1: UNPRICED DUE TO SCARCITY
*P.P.YELLOW/1: UNPRICED DUE TO SCARCITY
STATED PRINT RUN 99 SER.#'d SETS

4	J.Park/Abyss	8.00	20.00
7	M.James/G.Kim	10.00	25.00
8	C.Daniels/Kazarian	4.00	10.00
10	E.Young/ODB	4.00	10.00
12	G.Kim/V.Sky	8.00	20.00
14	B.Roode/J.Storm	5.00	12.00
16	J.Storm/Gunner	5.00	12.00
20	A.Styles/S.Joe	8.00	20.00
21	C.Hemme/S.Val	8.00	20.00

2013 TRISTAR TNA Impact Glory Dual Memorabilia Gold

*RED/50: .5X TO 1.2X BASIC MEM
*BLUE/10: UNPRICED DUE TO SCARCITY
*GREEN/5: UNPRICED DUE TO SCARCITY
*RAINBOW/1: UNPRICED DUE TO SCARCITY
STATED PRINT RUN 99 SER.#'d SETS

M8	B.Ray/M.Tessmacher	5.00	12.00
M9	T.Ortiz/R.Jackson	5.00	12.00

2013 TRISTAR TNA Impact Glory Dual Memorabilia Red

*RED/50: .5X TO 1.2X BASIC MEM

M8	B.Ray/M.Tessmacher	6.00	15.00
M9	T.Ortiz/R.Jackson	6.00	15.00

2013 TRISTAR TNA Impact Glory Jeff Hardy Autographed Face Paint Green

H1	Jeff Hardy		
H2	Jeff Hardy		

2013 TRISTAR TNA Impact Glory Memorabilia Red

STATED PRINT RUN 50 SER.#'d SETS

M10	Tito Ortiz	5.00	12.00
M11	Rampage Jackson	5.00	12.00
M12	Bully Ray	5.00	12.00
M13	Mickie James	15.00	40.00
M14	Sting	12.00	30.00

2013 TRISTAR TNA Impact Glory On-Card Autographs Gold

*RED/50: .5X TO 1.2X BASIC AUTOS
*BLUE/10: UNPRICED DUE TO SCARCITY
*GREEN/5: UNPRICED DUE TO SCARCITY
*RAINBOW/1: UNPRICED DUE TO SCARCITY
STATED PRINT RUN 199 SER.#'d SETS

GAS	AJ Styles	8.00	20.00
GBR	Bobby Roode	6.00	15.00
GCH	Christy Hemme	6.00	15.00
GGK	Gail Kim	8.00	20.00
GJG	Jessie Godderz	5.00	12.00
GJS	James Storm	5.00	12.00
GKA	Kurt Angle	12.00	30.00
GMJ	Mickie James	8.00	20.00
GT	Tara	6.00	15.00
GVS	Velvet Sky	10.00	25.00

2013 TRISTAR TNA Impact Glory Quad Memorabilia Gold

*RED/50: X TO X BASIC MEM
*BLUE/10: UNPRICED DUE TO SCARCITY
*GREEN/5: UNPRICED DUE TO SCARCITY
*RAINBOW/1: UNPRICED DUE TO SCARCITY
STATED PRINT RUN 99 SER.#'d SETS

M7	Kim/James/Tessmacher/Sky		

2013 TRISTAR TNA Impact Glory Sticker Autographs Gold

*RED/50: .5X TO 1.2X BASIC AUTOS
*BLUE/10: UNPRICED DUE TO SCARCITY
*GREEN/5: UNPRICED DUE TO SCARCITY
*RAINBOW/1: UNPRICED DUE TO SCARCITY
*P.P.BLACK/1: UNPRICED DUE TO SCARCITY
*P.P.CYAN/1: UNPRICED DUE TO SCARCITY
*P.P.MAGENTA/1: UNPRICED DUE TO SCARCITY
*P.P.YELLOW/1: UNPRICED DUE TO SCARCITY
STATED PRINT RUN 99 SER.#'d SETS

G5	Chris Sabin	4.00	10.00
G11	Manik	4.00	10.00
G15	Knux	4.00	10.00
G26	Wes Brisco	4.00	10.00
G27	Jay Bradley	4.00	10.00
G31	Brooke Hogan	15.00	40.00
G32	Garett Bischoff	4.00	10.00
G33	Magnus	4.00	10.00
G37	Devon	4.00	10.00

2013 TRISTAR TNA Impact Glory Triple Autographs Red

*BLUE/10: UNPRICED DUE TO SCARCITY
*GREEN/5: UNPRICED DUE TO SCARCITY
*RAINBOW/1: UNPRICED DUE TO SCARCITY
STATED PRINT RUN 50 SER.#'d SETS

1	Bobby Roode	8.00	20.00
	Christopher Daniels/ Kazarian		

3	Brisco/G.Bischoff/Knux	8.00	20.00
5	James/ODB/Tessmacher	12.00	30.00

2013 TRISTAR TNA Impact Live

COMPLETE SET (109)		25.00	50.00
COMPLETE SET W/O SP (99)		8.00	20.00
UNOPENED BOX (20 PACKS)			
UNOPENED PACK (6 CARDS)			

*GOLD/50: 2X TO 5X BASIC CARDS
*GOLD SP/50: .6X TO 1.5X BASIC CARDS
*RED/10: UNPRICED DUE TO SCARCITY
*RED SP/10: UNPRICED DUE TO SCARCITY
*RAINBOW/1: UNPRICED DUE TO SCARCITY
*RAINBOW/1: UNPRICED DUE TO SCARCITY
STATED SP ODDS 1:BOX

1	Hulk Hogan	.75	2.00
2	Brooke Hogan	.40	1.00
3	Hulk Hogan/Brooke Hogan	.75	2.00
4	Sting	.60	1.50
5	Jeff Hardy	.60	1.50
6	Austin Aries	.25	.60
7	Gail Kim	.40	1.00
8	AJ Styles	.25	.60
9	Bobby Roode	.15	.40
10	Bully Ray	.15	.40
11	Kurt Angle	.25	.60
12	Garett Bischoff	.25	.60
13	Hernandez	.15	.40
14	King Mo	.15	.40
15	Jessie Godderz	.15	.40
16	Tara	.50	1.25
17	James Storm	.15	.40
18	Kazarian	.15	.40
19	Christopher Daniels	.15	.40
20	Matt Morgan	.15	.40
21	Rob Van Dam	.25	.60
22	Douglas Williams	.15	.40
23	SoCal Val	.40	1.00
24	Sting	.60	1.50
25	Christy Hemme	.50	1.25
26	Jesse Sorensen	.15	.40
27	Taz	.15	.40
28	Earl Hebner	.15	.40
29	Magnus	.15	.40
30	AJ Styles	.25	.60
31	Kenny King	.15	.40
32	Taryn Terrell	.40	1.00
33	Devon	.15	.40
34	Velvet Sky	.60	1.50
35	Jeff Hardy	.60	1.50
36	Joseph Park	.25	.60
37	Eric Young	.15	.40
38	Tara	.50	1.25
39	Chris Sabin	.15	.40
40	Sting	.60	1.50
41	Bully Ray	.15	.40
42	Robbie E	.15	.40
43	Rob Terry	.15	.40
44	James Storm	.15	.40
45	Crimson	.15	.40
46	DOC	.15	.40
47	Jessie Godderz	.15	.40
48	Samoa Joe	.15	.40
49	Rob Van Dam	.25	.60
50	Hulk Hogan	.75	2.00
51	Jeff Hardy	.60	1.50
52	Christy Hemme	.50	1.25
53	Jessie Godderz	.15	.40

54	Madison Rayne	.40	1.00
55	TNA Referees	.15	.40
56	Zema Ion	.15	.40
57	Christopher Daniels	.15	.40
58	Mr. Anderson	.25	.60
59	Garett Bischoff	.25	.60
60	AJ Styles	.25	.60
61	Mike Tenay	.15	.40
62	Aces and Eights	.15	.40
63	Matt Morgan	.15	.40
64	James Storm	.15	.40
65	Hernandez	.15	.40
66	Kurt Angle	.25	.60
67	Douglas Williams	.15	.40
68	Jeff Hardy	.60	1.50
69	ODB	.15	.40
70	Abyss	.25	.60
71	Bully Ray	.15	.40
72	Jeremy Borash	.15	.40
73	Gunner	.15	.40
74	Christopher Daniels	.15	.40
75	AJ Styles	.25	.60
76	Gut Check	.15	.40
77	Alex Silva	.15	.40
78	Christian York	.15	.40
79	Sam Shaw	.15	.40
80	Joey Ryan	.15	.40
81	Taeler Hendrix	.25	.60
82	Wes Brisco	.15	.40
83	Al Snow	.25	.60
84	D'Lo Brown	.15	.40
85	Chavo Guerrero Jr.	.15	.40
86	Hector Guerrero	.15	.40
87	World Tag Team Champions: Hernandez and Chavo Guerrero Jr.	.15	.40
88	The Guerrero Legacy	.15	.40
89	Gail Kim	.40	1.00
90	Mr. Anderson	.25	.60
91	Miss Tessmacher	.40	1.00
92	Robbie E	.15	.40
93	Tara	.50	1.25
94	Mickie James	.75	2.00
95	Chavo Guerrero Jr.	.15	.40
96	Destination X	.15	.40
97	Slammiversary	.15	.40
98	Bound For Glory	.15	.40
99	Sting's Hall of Fame Induction	.60	1.50
100	Hulk Hogan SP	4.00	10.00
101	Sting SP	3.00	8.00
102	Bully Ray SP	.75	2.00
103	Samoa Joe SP	.75	2.00
104	Kurt Angle SP	1.25	3.00
105	Hulk Hogan SP	4.00	10.00
106	Sting SP	3.00	8.00
107	Kurt Angle SP	1.25	3.00
108	Miss Tessmacher SP	2.00	5.00
109	Jeff Hardy SP	3.00	8.00
CL	Checklist	.15	.40

2013 TRISTAR TNA Impact Live Autographed Memorabilia Gold

M17 Gail Kim

2013 TRISTAR TNA Impact Live Autographed Memorabilia Rainbow

STATED PRINT RUN 1 SER.#'d SET
UNPRICED DUE TO SCARCITY

M15	Hulk Hogan		
M16	Jeff Hardy		
M17	Gail Kim		
M18	Sting		

2013 TRISTAR TNA Impact Live Autographs Gold

*GREEN/50: .5X TO 1.2X BASIC AUTOS
*BLUE/25: .6X TO 1.5X BASIC AUTOS
*RED/5: UNPRICED DUE TO SCARCITY
*RAINBOW/1: UNPRICED DUE TO SCARCITY
STATED PRINT RUN 99 SER. #'d SETS

L16	Gail Kim	8.00	20.00
L17	James Storm	5.00	12.00
L20	Mr. Anderson	6.00	15.00
L23	Taryn Terrell	12.00	30.00
L24	Doug Williams	3.00	8.00
L25	Matt Morgan	5.00	12.00
L26	Christy Hemme	10.00	25.00
L27	Abyss	3.00	8.00
L29	Samoa Joe	3.00	8.00
L32	Bully Ray	5.00	12.00
L33	Robbie E	3.00	8.00
L34	Winter	4.00	10.00
L35	Jesse Sorensen	3.00	8.00
L36	Kazarian	4.00	10.00
L37	Garett Bischoff	3.00	8.00
L38	Kenny King	6.00	15.00
L39	Christian York	8.00	20.00
L40	Hector Guerrero	3.00	8.00
L41	ODB	5.00	12.00
L42	Bobby Roode	3.00	8.00
L43	Chris Sabin	4.00	10.00
L44	SoCal Val	5.00	12.00
L45	Rosita	5.00	12.00
L46	Hernandez	3.00	8.00
L47	Kid Kash	3.00	8.00
L48	Austin Aries	8.00	20.00

2013 TRISTAR TNA Impact Live Dual Autographs Gold

*GREEN/50: .5X TO 1.2X BASIC AUTOS
*BLUE/25: .6X TO 1.5X BASIC AUTOS
*RED/5: UNPRICED DUE TO SCARCITY
*RAINBOW/1: UNPRICED DUE TO SCARCITY
STATED PRINT RUN 99 SER.#'d SETS

2	Chavo & Hector Guerrero		
3	K.Angle/W.Brisco		
4	E.Young/ODB		
5	C.Daniels/Kazarian	4.00	10.00
6	Tara/J.Godderz	6.00	15.00
7	C.Hemme/J.Borash	6.00	15.00
8	M.Morgan/J.Ryan	6.00	15.00
9	Sarita/Rosita	5.00	12.00
10	C.Guerrero/Hernandez		
11	G.Kim/M.James	12.00	30.00
12	J.Storm/B.Roode		
13	B.Roode/J.Hardy		
14	B.Hogan/B.Ray		
15	A.Aries/M.Morgan		
16	M.Tessmacher/Tara	8.00	20.00
17	W.Brisco/G.Bischoff	5.00	12.00
18	S.Shaw/C.York		
19	M.James/Tara		
20	C.Daniels/C.Sabin	4.00	10.00
21	C.Sabin/J.Sorensen	4.00	10.00
22	K.Angle/M.Anderson		

23	B.Roode/A.Aries		
24	M.Anderson/Devon		
25	Sting/J.Hardy		

2013 TRISTAR TNA Impact Live Dual Memorabilia Silver

*GOLD/50: .5X TO 1.2X BASIC MEM
*BLUE/25: .6X TO 1.5X BASIC MEM
*RED/5: UNPRICED DUE TO SCARCITY
*RAINBOW/1: UNPRICED DUE TO SCARCITY
STATED ODDS OVERALL 1:BOX

M11	Tara Jessie Godderz	4.00	10.00
M12	C.Guerrero Jr./Hernandez	4.00	10.00

2013 TRISTAR TNA Impact Live Eight Autographs Gold

*GREEN/50: X TO X BASIC AUTOS
*BLUE/25: UNPRICED DUE TO SCARCITY
*RED/5: UNPRICED DUE TO SCARCITY
*RAINBOW/1: UNPRICED DUE TO SCARCTIY
STATED PRINT RUN 99 SER.#'d SETS

3 Brooke Hogan
Tara/ Velvet Sky/ Madison Rayne/ Gail Kim/ Mickie James/ Christy Hemme/ Ms. Tessmacher

2013 TRISTAR TNA Impact Live Jeff Hardy Die-Cut Letter Memorabilia Gold

*BLUE/25: .5X TO 1.2X BASIC MEM
*RED/5: .75X TO 2X BASIC MEM
*RAINBOW/1: UNPRICED DUE TO SCARCITY
STATED PRINT RUN 50 SER.#'d SETS

M1	Jeff Hardy H	15.00	40.00
M2	Jeff Hardy A	15.00	40.00
M3	Jeff Hardy R	15.00	40.00
M4	Jeff Hardy D	15.00	40.00
M5	Jeff Hardy Y	15.00	40.00

2013 TRISTAR TNA Impact Live Memorabilia Silver

*GOLD/50: .5X TO 1.2X BASIC MEM
*BLUE/25: .6X TO 1.5X BASIC MEM
*RED/5: UNPRICED DUE TO SCARCITY
*RAINBOW/1: UNPRICED DUE TO SCARCITY
STATED ODDS OVERALL 1:BOX

M6	Hulk Hogan	10.00	25.00
M7	Sting	8.00	20.00
M8	Kurt Angle	6.00	15.00
M9	Austin Aries	4.00	10.00
M10	Chavo Guerrero Jr.	4.00	10.00

2013 TRISTAR TNA Impact Live Quad Autographs Gold

*GREEN/50: X TO X BASIC AUTOS
*BLUE/25: UNPRICED DUE TO SCARCITY
*RED/5: UNPRICED DUE TO SCARCITY
*RAINBOW/1: UNPRICED DUE TO SCARCITY
STATED PRINT RUN 99 SER.#'d SETS

1 Gail Kim
Mickie James/ Tara/ Velvet Sky
2 Angle/Brisco/G.Bischoff/Samoa Joe

2013 TRISTAR TNA Impact Live Quad Memorabilia Silver

*GOLD/50: .5X TO 1.2X BASIC MEM

---

*BLUE/25: .6X TO 1.5X BASIC MEM
*RED/5: UNPRICED DUE TO SCARCITY
*RAINBOW/1: UNPRICED DUE TO SCARCITY
STATED ODDS OVERALL 1:BOX

M13 Hulk Hogan
Sting/ Jeff Hardy/ Kurt Angle

M14	Kim/James/Tessmacher/Sky	12.00	30.00

2013 TRISTAR TNA Impact Live Six Autographs Gold

2 Kim/Tara/James
Sky/Tessmacher/Rayne

2013 TRISTAR TNA Impact Live Ten Autographs Gold

2 Styles/Morgan/Sabin/Daniels/Roode
Young/Hernandez/Kazarian/Storm/Robbie

2013 TRISTAR TNA Impact Live Triple Autographs Gold

2 Jeff Hardy
Austin Aries/ Bobby Roode
4 Angle/Anderson/Hardy

2013 TRISTAR TNA Impact Live Twelve Autographs Gold

2 Brooke/Tara/Hemme/Sarita
Kim/Sky/Tessmacher/Terrell/James/Rayne/ODB/Val

2012 TRISTAR TNA Impact Reflexxions

COMPLETE SET (100) 10.00 25.00
UNOPENED BOX (20 PACKS)
UNOPENED PACK (6 CARDS)
*SILVER/40: 2.5X TO 6X BASIC CARDS
*GOLD/10: UNPRICED DUE TO SCARCITY
*PURPLE/1: UNPRICED DUE TO SCARCITY
SUBSET CARDS SAME PRICE AS BASE CARDS
EXCHANGE DEADLINE 6/1/2013

1	Hulk Hogan	1.00	2.50
2	Ric Flair	.75	2.00
3	Sting	.60	1.50
4	Bobby Roode	.15	.40
5	James Storm	.15	.40
6	Jeff Hardy	.60	1.50
7	AJ Styles	.25	.60
8	Dixie Carter	.40	1.00
9	Jeff Jarrett	.25	.60
10	Rob Van Dam	.25	.60
11	Velvet Sky	.75	2.00
12	Bully Ray	.15	.40
13	Angelina Love	.60	1.50
14	Kurt Angle	.25	.60
15	Crimson	.15	.40
16	Christy Hemme	.60	1.50
17	Gail Kim	.40	1.00
18	Austin Aries	.25	.60
19	Mickie James	1.00	2.50
20	Samoa Joe	.15	.40
21	Eric Bischoff	.15	.40
22	Garrett Bischoff	.25	.60
23	Mr. Anderson	.25	.60
24	Alex Shelley	.15	.40
25	Mark Haskins	.15	.40
26	Rob Terry	.15	.40
27	Karen Jarrett	.25	.60
28	Douglas Williams	.15	.40

29	Rosita	.25	.60
30	Kazarian	.15	.40
31	Scott Steiner	.25	.60
32	Zema Ion	.15	.40
33	Anarquia	.15	.40
34	Gunner	.15	.40
35	Kid Kash	.25	.60
36	D'Angelo Dinero	.15	.40
37	Magnus	.15	.40
38	Tara	.60	1.50
39	Abyss	.25	.60
40	Matt Morgan	.15	.40
41	ODB	.15	.40
42	Chris Sabin	.15	.40
43	Jesse Sorensen	.15	.40
44	Mike Tenay	.15	.40
45	Madison Rayne	.40	1.00
46	Devon	.15	.40
47	Sarita	.25	.60
48	Eric Young	.15	.40
49	Traci Brooks	.40	1.00
50	Anthony Nese	.15	.40
51	Taz	.15	.40
52	Hernandez	.15	.40
53	Brooke Tessmacher	.40	1.00
54	Christopher Daniels	.15	.40
55	Jesse Neal	.15	.40
56	Robbie E	.15	.40
57	SoCal Val	.40	1.00
58	Brian Kendrick	.15	.40
59	Jeremy Borash	.15	.40
60	Shannon Moore	.15	.40
61	Winter	.60	1.50
62	Ric Flair US	.75	2.00
63	Sting US	.60	1.50
64	Christy Hemme US	.60	1.50
65	Jeff Jarrett US	.25	.60
66	Velvet Sky US	.75	2.00
67	Mr. Anderson US	.25	.60
68	Gail Kim US	.40	1.00
69	Scott Steiner US	.25	.60
70	Traci Brooks US	.40	1.00
71	Jeff Hardy US	.60	1.50
72	Dixie Carter US	.40	1.00
73	Sting FT	.60	1.50
74	Ric Flair FT	.75	2.00
75	Velvet Sky FT	.75	2.00
76	Jeff Jarrett FT	.25	.60
77	Scott Steiner FT	.25	.60
78	Jeff Hardy FT	.60	1.50
79	Mr. Anderson FT	.25	.60
80	Velvet Sky BMV	.75	2.00
81	Christy Hemme BMV	.60	1.50
82	Gail Kim BMV	.40	1.00
83	Karen Jarrett BMV	.25	.60
84	Traci Brooks BMV	.40	1.00
85	Madison Rayne BMV	.40	1.00
86	Brooke Tessmacher BMV	.40	1.00
87	Hulk Hogan SW	1.00	2.50
88	Sting SW	.60	1.50
89	Kurt Angle SW	.25	.60
90	Crimson SW	.15	.40
91	Jeff Hardy LH	.60	1.50
92	Sting LH	.60	1.50
93	Christy Hemme LH	.60	1.50
94	Ric Flair LH	.75	2.00
95	Mr. Anderson LH	.25	.60
96	Velvet Sky LH	.75	2.00
97	Scott Steiner LH	.25	.60
98	Gail Kim LH	.40	1.00
99	Jeff Jarrett LH	.25	.60
CL	Checklist	.15	.40
NNO	Jeff Hardy Art Redemption EXCH		

2012 TRISTAR TNA Impact Reflexxions Autographed Mat Relics Gold

*BLUE/25: X TO X BASIC AU RELICS
*RED/5: UNPRICED DUE TO SCARCITY
*PURPLE/1: UNPRICED DUE TO SCARCITY
STATED PRINT RUN 50 SER.#'d SETS

M3	Kurt Angle		
M4	Velvet Sky	25.00	50.00
M5	AJ Styles		
M6	Bobby Roode		
M7	Tara		
M8	Mr. Anderson		
M9	James Storm	15.00	30.00
M10	Angelina Love	20.00	40.00
M11	Jeff Jarrett		
M12	Gail Kim	20.00	40.00
M13	Rob Van Dam		

2012 TRISTAR TNA Impact Reflexxions Autographed Memorabilia Blue

*RED/5: UNPRICED DUE TO SCARCITY
*PURPLE/1: UNPRICED DUE TO SCARCITY
STATED PRINT RUN 25 SER.#'d SETS

M14	Hulk Hogan		
M15	Ric Flair	75.00	125.00
M16	Sting	50.00	100.00
M17	Rob Van Dam	20.00	40.00
M18	Kurt Angle	25.00	50.00
M19	Mickie James	75.00	125.00
M20	Jeff Hardy	40.00	80.00
M21	Mr. Anderson	15.00	30.00
M22	Garett Bischoff	15.00	30.00
M23	Velvet Sky	40.00	80.00

2012 TRISTAR TNA Impact Reflexxions Autographs Silver

*GOLD/50: .5X TO 1.2X BASIC AUTOS
*RED/25: X TO X BASIC AUTOS
*GREEN/5: UNPRICED DUE TO SCARCITY
*PURPLE/1: UNPRICED DUE TO SCARCITY
STATED PRINT RUN 99 SER.#'d SETS

16	Christy Hemme	10.00	25.00
20	Samoa Joe	4.00	10.00
22	Garrett Bischoff	4.00	10.00
26	Rob Terry	4.00	10.00
29	Rosita	6.00	15.00
30	Kazarian	4.00	10.00
33	Anarquia	4.00	10.00
34	Gunner	4.00	10.00
35	Kid Kash	6.00	15.00
36	D'Angelo Dinero	4.00	10.00
37	Magnus	4.00	10.00
39	Abyss	5.00	12.00
41	ODB	4.00	10.00
43	Jesse Sorensen	5.00	12.00
45	Madison Rayne	6.00	15.00
47	Sarita	5.00	12.00
48	Eric Young	4.00	10.00
49	Traci Brooks	5.00	12.00
52	Hernandez	4.00	10.00
53	Brooke Tessmacher	8.00	20.00
55	Jesse Neal	4.00	10.00
56	Robbie E	4.00	10.00
57	SoCal Val	5.00	12.00
61	Winter	8.00	20.00

2012 TRISTAR TNA Impact Reflexxions Blue Foil Inserts

COMPLETE SET (50)		60.00	120.00

*RED/10: UNPRICED DUE TO SCARCITY
*PURPLE/1: UNPRICED DUE TO SCARCITY
STATED PRINT RUN 40 SER.#'d SETS

R1	Hulk Hogan	4.00	10.00
R2	Hulk Hogan	4.00	10.00
R3	Hulk Hogan	4.00	10.00
R4	Hulk Hogan	4.00	10.00
R5	Hulk Hogan	4.00	10.00
R6	Ric Flair	3.00	8.00
R7	Ric Flair	3.00	8.00
R8	Sting	2.50	6.00
R9	Sting	2.50	6.00
R10	Kurt Angle	1.00	2.50
R11	Kurt Angle	1.00	2.50
R12	Jeff Jarrett	1.00	2.50
R13	Rob Van Dam	1.00	2.50
R14	Velvet Sky	3.00	8.00
R15	AJ Styles	1.00	2.50
R16	Eric Bischoff	.60	1.50
R17	Scott Steiner	1.00	2.50
R18	Angelina Love	2.50	6.00
R19	Mr. Anderson	1.00	2.50
R20	Bobby Roode	.60	1.50
R21	James Storm	.60	1.50
R22	Abyss	1.00	2.50
R23	Gail Kim	1.50	4.00
R24	Samoa Joe	.60	1.50
R25	Crimson	.60	1.50
R26	Dixie Carter	1.50	4.00
R27	Tara	2.50	6.00
R28	Hernandez	.60	1.50
R29	Christopher Daniels	.60	1.50
R30	Devon	.60	1.50
R31	Mickie James	4.00	10.00
R32	Matt Morgan	.60	1.50
R33	Bully Ray	.60	1.50
R34	Garett Bischoff	1.00	2.50
R35	Brooke Tessmacher	1.50	4.00
R36	Karen Jarrett	1.00	2.50
R37	The Immortal Battles	4.00	10.00
R38	The Immortal Battles	4.00	10.00
R39	The Immortal Battles	4.00	10.00
R40	Jeff Hardy	2.50	6.00
R41	Jeff Hardy Original Art	5.00	12.00
R42	Jeff Hardy Original Art	5.00	12.00
R43	Jeff Hardy Original Art	5.00	12.00
R44	Jeff Hardy Original Art	5.00	12.00
R45	Jeff Hardy Original Art	5.00	12.00
R46	Jeff Hardy Original Art	5.00	12.00
R47	Jeff Hardy Original Art	5.00	12.00
R48	Jeff Hardy Original Art	5.00	12.00
R49	Jeff Hardy Original Art	5.00	12.00
R50	Jeff Hardy Original Art	5.00	12.00

2012 TRISTAR TNA Impact Reflexxions Dual Autographs Silver

*GOLD/50: .5X TO 1.25X BASIC AUTOS
*RED/25: .6X TO 1.5X BASIC AUTOS
*GREEN/5: UNPRICED DUE TO SCARCITY
*PURPLE/1: UNPRICED DUE TO SCARCITY
STATED PRINT RUN 99 SER.#'d SETS

7	Tara/Tessmacher	8.00	20.00
8	Crimson/Morgan	6.00	15.00
9	Kim/Sky	15.00	30.00
10	K.Jarrett/Brooks	10.00	25.00
12	Hernandez/Anarquia	5.00	12.00
14	Robbie E/Robbie T	5.00	12.00
15	Sarita/Rosita	8.00	20.00
17	Aries/Kash	8.00	20.00
19	Hemme/SoCal Val	8.00	20.00
20	Tenay/Borash	5.00	12.00
29	Aries/Kendrick	6.00	15.00
30	Sky/Love	8.00	20.00

2012 TRISTAR TNA Impact Reflexxions Dual Memorabilia Silver

*GOLD/50: .5X TO 1.2X BASIC MEM
*BLUE/25: .6X TO 1.5X BASIC MEM
*RED/5: UNPRICED DUE TO SCARCITY
*PURPLE/1: UNPRICED DUE TO SCARCITY
STATED PRINT RUN 199 SER.#'d SETS

M26	J.Jarrett/K.Jarrett	4.00	10.00
M27	Roode/Storm	4.00	10.00
M29	Jarrett/Brooks	5.00	12.00

2012 TRISTAR TNA Impact Reflexxions Quad Memorabilia Silver

*GOLD/50: X TO X BASIC MEM
*BLUE/25: X TO X BASIC MEM
*RED/5: UNPRICED DUE TO SCARCITY
*PURPLE/1: UNPRICED DUE TO SCARCITY
STATED PRINT RUN 199 SER.#'d SETS

M36	Styles/Abyss/Mrgn/Dnls	8.00	20.00

2012 TRISTAR TNA Impact Reflexxions Quad Memorabilia Gold

*GOLD: .5X TO 1.2X BASIC MEM
STATED PRINT RUN 50 SER.#'d SETS

M34	James/Tara/Sky/Love	15.00	40.00
M36	Styles/Abyss/Mrgn/Dnls	10.00	25.00

2012 TRISTAR TNA Impact Reflexxions Quad Memorabilia Red

STATED PRINT RUN 5 SER.#'d SETS
UNPRICED DUE TO SCARCITY

M34 James/Tara/Sky/Love
M35 Hulk/Flair/Sting/Angle
M36 Styles/Abyss/Mrgn/Dnls

2012 TRISTAR TNA Impact Reflexxions Six Autographs Red

*GREEN/5: UNPRICED DUE TO SCARCITY
*PURPLE/1: UNPRICED DUE TO SCARCITY
STATED PRINT RUN 25 SER.#'d SETS

1 Sky/Tara/Tess/Love/Wint/Rayn
3 Rood/Strm/Styl/VDam/Hard/Angle

2012 TRISTAR TNA Impact Reflexxions Triple Autographs Red

*GREEN/5: UNPRICED DUE TO SCARCITY
*PURPLE/1: UNPRICED DUE TO SCARCITY
STATED PRINT RUN 25 SER.#'d SETS

2	Angle/Jarrett/Jarrett	20.00	40.00

2012 TRISTAR TNA Impact Reflexxions Triple Memorabilia Silver

3	Roode/Styles/Hardy	40.00	80.00
4	Kim/James/Sky	40.00	80.00
5	Hemme/Kim/Brooks	30.00	60.00

*GOLD/50: .5X TO 1.2X BASIC MEM
*BLUE/25: X TO X BASIC MEM
*RED/5: UNPRICED DUE TO SCARCITY
*PURPLE/1: UNPRICED DUE TO SCARCITY
STATED PRINT RUN 199 SER.#'d SETS

M32	Sting/Steiner/Jarrett	8.00	20.00
M33	RVD/Anderson/Styles	6.00	15.00

2012 TRISTAR TNA Impact Reflexxions Triple Memorabilia Blue

*BLUE: .6X TO 1.5X BASIC MEM
STATED PRINT RUN 25 SER.#'d SETS

M31	Hogan/Flair/Sting		
M32	Sting/Steiner/Jarrett	12.00	30.00
M33	RVD/Anderson/Styles	10.00	25.00

2012 TRISTAR TNA Impact Reflexxions Triple Memorabilia Purple

STATED PRINT RUN 1 SER.#'d SET
UNPRICED DUE TO SCARCITY

M31 Hogan/Flair/Sting
M32 Sting/Steiner/Jarrett
M33 RVD/Anderson/Styles

2012 TRISTAR TNA Impact TENacious

COMPLETE SET (120)

COMPLETE SET W/O SP (100)	8.00	20.00

UNOPENED BOX (20 PACKS)
UNOPENED PACK (6 CARDS)
*SILVER/30: 2.5X TO 6X BASIC CARDS
*GOLD/RED/10: UNPRICED DUE TO SCARCITY
*PURPLE/1: UNPRICED DUE TO SCARCITY

1	Jeff Jarrett	.25	.60
2	AJ Styles	.25	.60
3	James Storm	.15	.40
4	Jeremy Borash	.15	.40
5	Mike Tenay	.15	.40
6	Hulk Hogan	1.00	2.50
7	Brooke Hogan	.60	1.50
8	Sting	.60	1.50
9	Gail Kim	.40	1.00
10	Jeff Jarrett	.25	.60
11	Jeff Hardy	.60	1.50
12	Kurt Angle	.25	.60
13	Chris Sabin	.15	.40
14	Austin Aries	.25	.60
15	Bully Ray	.15	.40
16	Hector Guerrero	.15	.40
17	Kazarian	.15	.40
18	Eric Bischoff	.15	.40
19	Hernandez	.15	.40
20	Jeff Jarrett	.25	.60
21	Mickie James	1.00	2.50
22	Christopher Daniels	.15	.40
23	Mr. Anderson	.25	.60
24	ODB	.15	.40
25	Devon	.15	.40
26	Matt Morgan	.15	.40
27	Ric Flair	.75	2.00
28	AJ Styles	.25	.60
29	Rob Terry	.15	.40
30	Jeff Jarrett	.25	.60
31	Rob Van Dam	.25	.60
32	Jeff Hardy	.60	1.50
33	Kid Kash	.25	.60
34	Robbie E	.15	.40
35	Madison Rayne	.40	1.00
36	Bobby Roode	.15	.40
37	Bobby Roode	.15	.40
38	Bobby Roode	.15	.40
39	Bobby Roode	.15	.40
40	Jeff Jarrett	.25	.60
41	Jeremy Borash	.15	.40
42	Jeremy Borash	.15	.40
43	Jeremy Borash	.15	.40
44	Joseph Park	.25	.60
45	Alex Silva	.15	.40
46	Gunner	.15	.40
47	Mr. Anderson	.25	.60
48	Rosita	.25	.60
49	Samoa Joe	.15	.40
50	Jeff Jarrett	.25	.60
51	Sarita	.25	.60
52	Eric Young	.15	.40
53	Kurt Angle	.25	.60
54	Miss Tessmacher	.40	1.00
55	Sting	.60	1.50
56	Tara	.60	1.50
57	Garett Bischoff	.25	.60
58	Taz	.15	.40
59	SoCal Val	.40	1.00
60	Jeff Jarrett	.25	.60
61	Velvet Sky	.75	2.00
62	Angelina Love	.60	1.50
63	Jeff Hardy	.60	1.50
64	Zema Ion	.15	.40
65	Winter	.60	1.50
66	James Storm	.15	.40
67	Jessie Godderz	.15	.40
68	Matt Morgan	.15	.40
69	ODB	.15	.40
70	Jeff Jarrett	.25	.60
71	Christopher Daniels	.15	.40
72	Gail Kim	.40	1.00
73	Velvet Sky	.75	2.00
74	Doug Williams	.15	.40
75	Abyss	.25	.60
76	Crimson	.15	.40
77	Karen Jarrett	.25	.60
78	Eric Young	.15	.40
79	Magnus	.15	.40
80	Jeff Jarrett	.25	.60
81	D'Angelo Dinero	.15	.40
82	Jesse Sorensen	.15	.40
83	Jeff Hardy	.60	1.50
84	Christy Hemme	.60	1.50
85	Christopher Daniels	.15	.40
86	Hulk Hogan	1.00	2.50
87	Tara	.60	1.50
88	ODB	.15	.40
89	Magnus	.15	.40
90	AJ Styles	.25	.60
91	Miss Tessmacher	.40	1.00
92	Joe vs. Daniels vs. Styles	.15	.40
93	MSG Hulk Hogan Press Conference	1.00	2.50
94	IMPACT Wrestling Live on 1/4/2010	1.00	2.50
95	Beer Money vs. MCMG Best of 5	.15	.40
96	RVD Defeats Hardy and Styles	.25	.60
97	Sting Defeats Jarrett	.60	1.50
98	Samoa Joe vs. Kurt Angle	.25	.60
99	Gail Kim Wins 1st Knockouts Title	.40	1.00
100	Jeff Hardy/100	8.00	20.00
101	Team 3D/100	2.50	6.00
102	Kurt Angle/100	3.00	8.00
103	Hulk Hogan/100	4.00	10.00
104	Ric Flair/100	4.00	10.00
105	Jeff Hardy ART/100	8.00	20.00
106	Jeff Hardy ART/100	8.00	20.00
107	Jeff Hardy ART/100	8.00	20.00
108	Jeff Hardy ART/100	8.00	20.00
109	Jeff Hardy ART/100	8.00	20.00
110	Hulk Hogan/100	4.00	10.00
111	Hulk Hogan/100	4.00	10.00
112	Hulk Hogan/100	4.00	10.00
113	Hulk Hogan/100	4.00	10.00
114	Hulk Hogan/100	4.00	10.00
115	Sting/100	3.00	8.00
116	Sting/100	3.00	8.00
117	Sting/100	3.00	8.00
118	Sting/100	3.00	8.00
119	Sting/100	3.00	8.00
CL	Checklist	.15	.40

2012 TRISTAR TNA Impact TENacious Autographed Memorabilia Silver

COMPLETE SET (5)
*GOLD/80: .5X TO 1.2X BASIC AU MEM
*BLUE/50: .6X TO 1.5X BASIC AU MEM
*RED/10: UNPRICED DUE TO SCARCITY
*PURPLE/1: UNPRICED DUE TO SCARCITY
STATED PRINT RUN 100 SER.#'d SETS

T2	Jeff Hardy	12.00	30.00
T3	Bobby Roode	5.00	12.00
T4	Sting	25.00	60.00
T5	Mickie James	15.00	40.00
T6	Rob Van Dam	10.00	25.00

2012 TRISTAR TNA Impact TENacious Autographed Memorabilia Blue

T2	Jeff Hardy	20.00	50.00
T3	Bobby Roode	8.00	20.00
T4	Sting	50.00	100.00
T5	Mickie James	30.00	60.00
T6	Rob Van Dam	15.00	40.00

2012 TRISTAR TNA Impact TENacious Autographs Gold

*RED/10: UNPRICED DUE TO SCARCITY
*PURPLE/1: UNPRICED DUE TO SCARCITY
STATED PRINT RUN 100 SER.#'d SETS

TEN1	Jeff Jarrett	6.00	15.00
TEN2	AJ Styles	5.00	12.00
TEN3	James Storm	4.00	10.00
TEN4	Gail Kim		
TEN8	Sting		
TEN9	Bobby Roode	4.00	10.00
TEN10	Jeff Hardy	25.00	50.00
TEN11	Kurt Angle	10.00	25.00
TEN12	Eric Bischoff		
TEN13	Mickie James	12.00	30.00
TEN14	Mr. Anderson	5.00	12.00
TEN15	Ric Flair		
TEN16	Rob Van Dam	10.00	25.00
TEN17	Austin Aries	10.00	25.00
TEN18	Brooke Tessmacher	10.00	25.00
TEN19	Samoa Joe	4.00	10.00
TEN20	Tara	8.00	20.00
TEN21	Bully Ray	5.00	12.00
TEN22	Devon	4.00	10.00
TEN23	Velvet Sky	8.00	20.00
TEN24	Garett Bischoff	4.00	10.00
TEN25	Abyss	4.00	10.00
TEN26	Christy Hemme	10.00	25.00
TEN27	Jeremy Borash	4.00	10.00
TEN28	ODB	4.00	10.00
TEN29	Magnus	4.00	10.00
TEN30	Crimson	4.00	10.00
TEN31	Doug Williams	4.00	10.00
TEN32	Robbie E	4.00	10.00
TEN33	Alex Shelley	4.00	10.00
TEN34	Rosita	5.00	12.00
TEN35	Gunner	5.00	12.00
TEN36	Kazarian	4.00	10.00
TEN37	Angelina Love	8.00	20.00
TEN38	Matt Morgan	4.00	10.00
TEN39	Chris Sabin	4.00	10.00
TEN40	Gail Kim	10.00	25.00
TEN41	Hernandez	5.00	12.00
TEN42	Madison Rayne	8.00	20.00
TEN43	Anarquia		
TEN44	Winter	6.00	15.00
TEN45	Eric Young	5.00	12.00
TEN46	Sarita	5.00	12.00
TEN47	Shannon Moore	4.00	10.00
TEN48	Christopher Daniels	4.00	10.00
TEN49	Mike Tenay	4.00	10.00
TEN50	SoCal Val	5.00	12.00

2012 TRISTAR TNA Impact TENacious Celebrity Cut Signatures Gold

STATED PRINT RUN 5 SER.#'d SETS
UNPRICED DUE TO SCARCITY

1 Ace Young
2 Adam Pac-Man Jones
3 AJ Pierzynski
4 Brandon Jacobs
5 Brian Urlacher
6 Brooke Hogan
7 Chris Rock
8 Curtis Granderson
9 David Eckstein
10 Dennis Rodman
11 Johnny Damon
12 Juan Pablo Montoya
13 Ken Shamrock
14 Rowdy Roddy Piper
15 Steve McMichael
16 Tito Ortiz
17 Toby Keith
18 Tom Arnold

2012 TRISTAR TNA Impact TENacious Dual Autographs Gold

*RED/10: UNPRICED DUE TO SCARCITY
*PURPLE/1: UNPRICED DUE TO SCARCITY
STATED PRINT RUN 100 SER. #'d SETS

TEN21	B.Roode/J.Storm	8.00	20.00
TEN22	Eric & Garett Bischoff		
TEN23	J.Hardy/K.Angle		
TEN24	V.Sky/G.Kim	12.00	30.00
TEN25	K.Angle/AJ Styles		
TEN26	Sting/J.Hardy		

TEN28 ODB/E.Young	5.00	12.00
TEN210 B.Roode/E.Young	5.00	12.00
TEN211 A.Shelley/C.Sabin	5.00	12.00
TEN212 K.Angle/Samoa Joe	10.00	25.00
TEN213 Sting/B.Roode		
TEN214 Sting/J.Jarrett		
TEN215 B.Ray/Devon		
TEN216 Jeff & Karen Jarrett		
TEN217 Kazarian/T.Brooks	8.00	20.00
TEN218 K.Angle/Sting		
TEN219 Hernandez/Anarquia	5.00	12.00
TEN220 Kazarian/C.Daniels	5.00	12.00

2012 TRISTAR TNA Impact TENacious
Dual Memorabilia Silver

*GOLD/80: .5X TO 1.2X BASIC MEM
*BLUE/50: .6X TO 1.5X BASIC MEM
*RED/10: UNPRICED DUE TO SCARCITY
*PURPLE/1: UNPRICED DUE TO SCARCITY
STATED PRINT RUN 100 SER.#'d SETS

T10 Eric & Garett Bischoff	3.00	8.00
T11 Devon/B.Ray	3.00	8.00
T12 B.Roode/J.Storm	3.00	8.00
T13 J.Hardy/Mr.Anderson	6.00	15.00
T14 K.Angle/AJ Styles	3.00	8.00

2012 TRISTAR TNA Impact TENacious
Quad Autographs Gold

*RED/10: UNPRICED DUE TO SCARCITY
*PURPLE/1: UNPRICED DUE TO SCARCITY

TEN41 Jarrett/Styles/Storm/Borash		
TEN43 Storm/Roode/Sabin/Shelley	10.00	25.00

2012 TRISTAR TNA Impact TENacious
Six Autographs Gold

*RED/10: UNPRICED DUE TO SCARCITY
*PURPLE/1: UNPRICED DUE TO SCARCITY
STATED ODDS

TEN61 Styles/Samoa Joe/Daniels
Aries/Sabin/Kash
TEN62 Young/Styles/Terry
Abyss/Williams/Devon
TEN63 Angle/Sting/Styles
Roode/RVD/Hardy
TEN64 Kim/Love/Tara
Rayne/James/Sky

2012 TRISTAR TNA Impact TENacious
Triple Autographs Gold

*RED/10: UNPRICED DUE TO SCARCITY
*PURPLE/1: UNPRICED DUE TO SCARCITY
STATED ODDS

TEN31 Styles/Samoa Joe/Daniels
TEN32 Kurt & Karen Angle/Jarrett

2012 TRISTAR TNA Impact TENacious
Triple Memorabilia Blue

T15 Jarrett/Storm/Styles	6.00	15.00
T17 Kim/Sky/James	10.00	25.00

2009 TRISTAR TNA Knockouts

COMPLETE SET W/SP (108)	20.00	50.00
COMPLETE SET W/O SP (90)	12.00	30.00
UNOPENED BOX (18 PACKS)		
UNOPENED PACK (4 CARDS)		

*SILVER: 4X TO 10X BASIC CARDS
*GOLD/10: UNPRICED DUE TO SCARCITY

*PURPLE/1: UNPRICED DUE TO SCARCITY
*P.P.BLACK/1: UNPRICED DUE TO SCARCITY
*P.P.CYAN/1: UNPRICED DUE TO SCARCITY
*P.P.MAGENTA/1: UNPRICED DUE TO SCARCITY
*P.P.YELLOW/1: UNPRICED DUE TO SCARCITY
INSTANT WIN CARD RANDOMLY INSERTED
90-107 ARE REVEALED PACKS EXCLUSIVE

1 Angelina Love	.50	1.25
2 Awesome Kong	.15	.40
3 Christy Hemme	.60	1.50
4 The Governor	.25	.60
5 Jacqueline	.20	.50
6 Jenna Morasca	.40	1.00
7 Lauren	.25	.60
8 Madison Rayne	.40	1.00
9 ODB	.15	.40
10 Raisha Saeed	.15	.40
11 Rhaka Khan	.20	.50
12 Roxxi	.20	.50
13 Sharmell	.15	.40
14 SoCal Val	.40	1.00
15 Sojournor Bolt	.15	.40
16 Taylor Wilde	.40	1.00
17 Traci Brooks	.40	1.00
18 Velvet Sky	.50	1.25
19 Cute Kip	.12	.30
20 The Beautiful People	.50	1.25
21 Angelina Love	.50	1.25
22 Christy Hemme	.60	1.50
23 Lauren	.25	.60
24 ODB	.15	.40
25 Roxxi	.20	.50
26 Sharmell	.15	.40
27 SoCal Val	.40	1.00
28 Taylor Wilde	.40	1.00
29 Traci Brooks	.40	1.00
30 Velvet Sky	.50	1.25
31 Angelina Love	.50	1.25
32 Awesome Kong	.15	.40
33 Dixie Carter	.25	.60
34 Jacqueline	.20	.50
35 Lauren	.25	.60
36 ODB	.15	.40
37 Raisha Saeed	.15	.40
38 Traci Brooks	.40	1.00
39 Christy Hemme	.60	1.50
40 Rhaka Khan	.20	.50
41 Roxxi	.20	.50
42 Sharmell	.15	.40
43 SoCal Val	.40	1.00
44 Sojournor Bolt	.15	.40
45 Taylor Wilde	.40	1.00
46 Velvet Sky	.50	1.25
47 Jacqueline	.20	.50
48 Sojournor Bolt	.15	.40
49 ODB	.15	.40
50 Traci Brooks	.40	1.00
51 Angelina Love	.50	1.25
52 Awesome Kong	.15	.40
53 Christy Hemme	.60	1.50
54 Jacqueline	.20	.50
55 Lauren	.25	.60
56 ODB	.15	.40
57 Sharmell	.15	.40
58 SoCal Val	.40	1.00
59 Sojournor Bolt	.15	.40
60 Taylor Wilde	.40	1.00
61 Traci Brooks	.40	1.00

62 Velvet Sky	.50	1.25
63 Angelina Love	.50	1.25
64 Awesome Kong	.15	.40
65 Christy Hemme	.60	1.50
66 Dixie Carter	.25	.60
67 Roxxi	.20	.50
68 Sharmell	.15	.40
69 ODB	.15	.40
70 Taylor Wilde	.40	1.00
71 Traci Brooks	.40	1.00
72 Velvet Sky	.50	1.25
73 Angelina Love / AJ Styles	.50	1.25
74 Awesome Kong / Samoa Joe	.15	.40
75 Christy Hemme / Robert Roode	.60	1.50
76 Dixie Carter / Mick Foley	.50	1.25
77 Jacqueline / James Storm	.20	.50
78 Jenna Morasca / Brother Ray	.40	1.00
79 Lauren / Chris Sabin	.25	.60
80 ODB / Rhino	.15	.40
81 Raisha Saeed / Alex Shelley	.15	.40
82 Rhaka Khan / Kurt Angle	.60	1.50
83 Roxxi / Jim Cornette	.20	.50
84 Sharmell / Mike Tenay	.15	.40
85 SoCal Val / Consequences Creed	.40	1.00
86 Sojournor Bolt / Don West	.15	.40
87 Taylor Wilde / Jay Lethal	.40	1.00
88 Traci Brooks / Sting	.50	1.25
89 Velvet Sky / Brother Devon	.50	1.25
90 Traci Brooks	1.25	3.00
91 Angelina Love	1.50	4.00
92 SoCal Val	1.25	3.00
93 Christy Hemme	2.00	5.00
94 Velvet Sky	1.50	4.00
95 Lauren	.75	2.00
96 ODB	.50	1.25
97 Traci Brooks	1.25	3.00
98 SoCal Val	1.25	3.00
99 Christy Hemme	2.00	5.00
100 Angelina Love	1.50	4.00
101 Roxxi	.60	1.50
102 Jenna Morasca	1.25	3.00
103 Velvet Sky	1.50	4.00
104 SoCal Val	1.25	3.00
105 Christy Hemme	2.00	5.00
106 Angelina Love/Velvet Sky	1.50	4.00
107 Traci Brooks/SoCal Val	1.25	3.00
CL Checklist	.20	.50
NNO Instant Winner		

2009 TRISTAR TNA Knockouts
Autographed Dual Kiss Gold

*TURQUOISE/10: UNPRICED DUE TO SCARCITY
*PURPLE/1: UNPRICED DUE TO SCARCITY
STATED PRINT RUN 25 SER.#'d SETS

2K1 A.Love/V.Sky
2K2 C.Hemme/T.Brooks
2K3 Jenna/Sharmell
2K4 S.Val/Lauren

2009 TRISTAR TNA Knockouts
Autographed Kiss

STATED PRINT RUN 10 SER.#'d SETS

K1 Angelina Love
K2 Awesome Kong
K3 Jacqueline
K4 Jenna
K5 Lauren

K6 Madison Rayne		
K7 ODB		
K8 Roxxi		
K9 Sharmell		
K10 Sojournor Bolt		
K11 Taylor Wilde		
K12 Velvet Sky		
K13 Christy Hemme		
K14 SoCal Val		
K15 Traci Brooks		

2009 TRISTAR TNA Knockouts
Knockout Kiss

*TURQUOISE/25: .5X TO 1.25X BASIC KISS
*GREEN/5: UNPRICED DUE TO SCARCITY
*PURPLE/1: UNPRICED DUE TO SCARCITY
*P.P.BLACK/1: UNPRICED DUE TO SCARCITY
*P.P.CYAN/1: UNPRICED DUE TO SCARCITY
*P.P.MAGENTA/1: UNPRICED DUE TO SCARCITY
*P.P.YELLOW/1: UNPRICED DUE TO SCARCITY
STATED PRINT RUN 75 SER.#'d SETS
K12-K15 ARE REVEALED PACKS EXCLUSIVE

K1 Angelina Love	30.00	60.00
K2 Awesome Kong	12.00	30.00
K3 Jacqueline	8.00	20.00
K4 Jenna	25.00	50.00
K5 Lauren	15.00	40.00
K6 Madison Rayne	25.00	50.00
K7 ODB	12.00	30.00
K8 Roxxi	10.00	25.00
K9 Sharmell	10.00	25.00
K10 Sojournor Bolt	8.00	20.00
K11 Taylor Wilde	25.00	50.00
K12 Velvet Sky	30.00	60.00
K13 Christy Hemme	25.00	50.00
K14 SoCal Val	15.00	40.00
K15 Traci Brooks	12.00	30.00

2009 TRISTAR TNA Knockouts
Signature Curves

*GOLD/75: .5X TO 1.2X BASIC AUTOS
*TURQUOISE/25: UNPRICED DUE TO SCARCITY
*PINK/10: UNPRICED DUE TO SCARCITY
*GREEN/5: UNPRICED DUE TO SCARCITY
*PURPLE/1: UNPRICED DUE TO SCARCITY
*P.P.BLACK/1: UNPRICED DUE TO SCARCITY
*P.P.CYAN/1: UNPRICED DUE TO SCARCITY
*P.P.MAGENTA/1: UNPRICED DUE TO SCARCITY
*P.P.YELLOW/1: UNPRICED DUE TO SCARCITY
STATED ODDS 1:9

KA1 Angelina Love	10.00	25.00
KA2 Awesome Kong	6.00	15.00
KA3 Christy Hemme	10.00	25.00
KA4 Dixie Carter	6.00	15.00
KA5 Jacqueline	6.00	15.00
KA6 Jenna	8.00	20.00
KA7 Madison Rayne	10.00	25.00
KA8 Raisha Saeed	6.00	15.00
KA9 Roxxi	6.00	15.00
KA10 Sharmell	6.00	15.00
KA11 SoCal Val	8.00	20.00
KA12 Sojournor Bolt	8.00	20.00
KA13 Taylor Wilde	8.00	20.00
KA14 Traci Brooks	8.00	20.00
KA15 Velvet Sky	10.00	25.00
KA24 Lauren	10.00	25.00
KA25 ODB	8.00	20.00

2009 TRISTAR TNA Knockouts Six-Person Signature Curves Gold

*TURQUOISE/25: X TO X BASIC AUTOS
*GREEN/5: UNPRICED DUE TO SCARCITY
*PURPLE/1: UNPRICED DUE TO SCARCITY
*P.P.BLACK/1: UNPRICED DUE TO SCARCITY
*P.P.CYAN/1: UNPRICED DUE TO SCARCITY
*P.P.MAGENTA/1: UNPRICED DUE TO SCARCITY
*P.P.YELLOW/1: UNPRICED DUE TO SCARCITY
STATED ODDS

KA27 Sharmell/Booker T/Nash
Angle/Sting/Steiner

2009 TRISTAR TNA Knockouts Top Drawer Memorabilia Gold

*TURQUOISE/75: .5X TO 1.2X BASIC MEM
*PINK/10: UNPRICED DUE TO SCARCITY
*PURPLE/1: UNPRICED DUE TO SCARCITY
STATED PRINT RUN 175 SER.#'d SETS

TD1	Angelina Love	10.00	25.00
TD2	Christy Hemme	10.00	25.00
TD3	Jenna Morasca	6.00	15.00
TD4	Lauren	10.00	25.00
TD5	Madison Rayne	10.00	25.00
TD6	Roxxi	6.00	15.00
TD7	SoCal Val	8.00	20.00
TD8	Sojournor Bolt	6.00	15.00
TD9	Taylor Wilde	10.00	25.00
TD10	Traci Brooks	6.00	15.00
TD11	Velvet Sky	10.00	25.00

2010 TRISTAR TNA New Era

COMPLETE SET (101)		30.00	75.00
UNOPENED BOX (20 PACKS)			
UNOPENED PACK (6 CARDS)			
COMPLETE SET W/O SP (90)		10.00	25.00

*SILVER: 2.5X TO 6X BASIC CARDS
*GOLD/10: UNPRICED DUE TO SCARCITY
*PURPLE/1: UNPRICED DUE TO SCARCITY
OBAK STATED ODDS 2:HOBBY BOX
OBAK ANNOUNCED PRINT RUN 600

1	Hulk Hogan	1.00	2.50
2	Hulk Hogan	1.00	2.50
3	Hulk Hogan	1.00	2.50
4	Hulk Hogan	1.00	2.50
5	Hulk Hogan	1.00	2.50
6	Hulk Hogan	1.00	2.50
7	Hulk Hogan	1.00	2.50
8	Ric Flair	.75	2.00
9	Jeff Hardy	.60	1.50
10	Scott Hall	.15	.40
11	Syxx-Pac	.25	.60
12	Eric Bischoff	.15	.40
13	Shannon Moore	.15	.40
14	Orlando Jordan	.15	.40
15	Bubba The Love Sponge	.25	.60
16	Mr. Anderson	.25	.60
17	The Nasty Boys	.15	.40
18	Generation Me	.15	.40
19	The Pope D'Angelo Dinero	.15	.40
20	Desmond Wolfe	.15	.40
21	Brian Kendrick	.25	.60
22	Jimmy Hart	.25	.60
23	Sting	.60	1.50
24	Kurt Angle	.60	1.50
25	Mick Foley	.75	2.00
26	Kevin Nash	.60	1.50
27	Jeff Jarrett	.40	1.00
28	James Storm	.25	.60
29	Alex Shelley	.25	.60
30	AJ Styles	.40	1.00
31	Team 3D	.25	.60
32	British Invasion	.15	.40
33	Taz & Mike Tenay	.15	.40
34	Motor City Machineguns	.25	.60
35	Matt Morgan	.15	.40
36	Amazing Red	.15	.40
37	Robert Roode	.15	.40
38	Suicide	.15	.40
39	Abyss	.25	.60
40	Lethal Consequences	.15	.40
41	Eric Young	.15	.40
42	Beer Money, Inc.	.25	.60
43	Samoa Joe	.25	.60
44	Daniels	.15	.40
45	Taylor Wilde	.40	1.00
46	Homicide	.20	.50
47	Daffney	.60	1.50
48	Hernandez	.15	.40
49	The Beautiful People	.75	2.00
50	Rob Terry	.15	.40
51	Lacey Von Erich	.75	2.00
52	Tara	.60	1.50
53	Hamada	.40	1.00
54	Sarita	.40	1.00
55	ODB	.25	.60
56	Jesse Neal	.15	.40
57	Velvet Sky	.75	2.00
58	Magnus	.15	.40
59	Angelina Love	.60	1.50
60	Doug Williams	.15	.40
61	Madison Rayne	.60	1.50
62	Rhino	.25	.60
63	Kazarian	.15	.40
64	Chris Sabin	.15	.40
65	Dr. Stevie	.15	.40
66	Christy Hemme	.60	1.50
67	Jeremy Borash	.15	.40
68	Dixie Carter	.40	1.00
69	Bob Carter	.15	.40
70	Rob Van Dam	.40	1.00
71	Destination X	.15	.40
72	Lockdown	.15	.40
73	Hulk Hogan/Eric Bischoff	.75	2.00
74	Ric Flair/AJ Styles	.60	1.50
75	Scott Hall/Syxx-Pac	.20	.50
76	Hulk Hogan/Abyss	.75	2.00
77	Matt Morgan/Hernandez	.15	.40
78	Ric Flair	.60	1.50
79	Ric Flair	.60	1.50
80	Ric Flair	.60	1.50
81	TNA iMPACT! Moves	.75	2.00
82	Hogan's Wrestling Return	.75	2.00
83	H.Hogan/R.Flair	.75	2.00
84	The Main Event	.75	2.00
85	Why, Sting, Why?	.50	1.25
86	Van Dam Arrives in TNA	.30	.75
87	The Band: Off Key	.20	.50
88	Kurt Angle	.50	1.25
89	Jeff Hardy Returns	.50	1.25
90	What A Night!	.75	2.00
91	Hulk Hogan OBAK SP	4.00	10.00
92	Ric Flair OBAK SP	3.00	8.00
93	Sting OBAK SP	2.50	6.00
94	Kevin Nash OBAK SP	2.50	6.00
95	Jeff Jarrett OBAK SP	1.50	4.00
96	Kurt Angle OBAK SP	2.50	6.00
97	Mick Foley OBAK SP	3.00	8.00
98	AJ Styles OBAK SP	1.50	4.00
99	Beautiful People OBAK SP	3.00	8.00
100	Hogan/Flair OBAK SP	4.00	10.00
CL	Checklist	.15	.40

2010 TRISTAR TNA New Era Autographed Hulk Hogan Bonus Red

*PURPLE/1: UNPRICED DUE TO SCARCITY
STATED PRINT RUN 9 SER.#'d SETS
UNPRICED DUE TO SCARCITY

H1 Hulk Hogan holding rope
H2 Hulk Hogan black shirt in ring
H3 Hulk Hogan ripping shirt
H4 Hulk Hogan no shirt white bkgrnd
H5 Hulk Hogan w/boa
H6 Hulk Hogan black shirt white bkgrnd

2010 TRISTAR TNA New Era Autographed Memorabilia Silver

STATED PRINT RUN 199 SER.#'d SETS

M13	Hulk Hogan		
M14	Ric Flair		
M15	Mick Foley		
M16	Sting		
M17	AJ Styles		
M18	Velvet Sky	15.00	40.00

2010 TRISTAR TNA New Era Autographs Silver

*GOLD/50: .5X TO 1.2X BASIC AUTOS
*GREEN/15-25: X TO X BASIC AUTOS
*RED/5: UNPRICED DUE TO SCARCITY
*PURPLE/1: UNPRICED DUE TO SCARCITY

A1	Hulk Hogan		
A2	Sting		
A3	Mick Foley	10.00	25.00
A4	Kurt Angle	8.00	20.00
A5	Sean Morley	6.00	15.00
A6	Mr. Anderson	8.00	20.00
A7	Orlando Jordan	8.00	20.00
A8	D'Angelo Dinero	8.00	20.00
A9	Tara	6.00	15.00
A10	Desmond Wolfe	4.00	10.00
A11	Taz	4.00	10.00
A12	Kevin Nash	8.00	20.00
A13	Brian Kendrick	6.00	15.00
A14	AJ Styles	8.00	20.00
A15	Jeff Jarrett	5.00	12.00
A16	Sarita	6.00	15.00
A17	Amazing Red	4.00	10.00
A18	Lacey Von Erich	12.00	30.00
A19	Abyss	4.00	10.00
A20	Rob Van Dam	12.00	30.00
A21	Hernandez	4.00	10.00
A22	Taylor Wilde	6.00	15.00
A23	Samoa Joe	8.00	20.00
A24	Awesome Kong	5.00	12.00
A25	Dr. Stevie	5.00	12.00
A26	Brutus Magnus	4.00	10.00
A27	Velvet Sky	10.00	25.00
A28	Jeremy Borash	4.00	10.00
A29	Madison Rayne	8.00	20.00
A30	Doug Williams	4.00	10.00
A31	Christy Hemme	10.00	25.00
A32	Suicide	4.00	10.00
A33	Hamada	8.00	20.00
A34	Robert Roode	4.00	10.00
A35	Brian Knobs	4.00	10.00
A36	Dixie Carter	5.00	12.00
A37	Daniels	4.00	10.00
A38	Bubba The Love Sponge	10.00	25.00
A39	ODB	5.00	12.00
A40	Homicide	4.00	10.00
A41	Matt Morgan	4.00	10.00
A42	Daffney	10.00	25.00
A43	Jesse Neal	4.00	10.00
A44	James Storm	4.00	10.00
A45	SoCal Val	6.00	15.00
A46	Jeff Hardy	20.00	40.00
A47	Traci Brooks	6.00	15.00
A48	Jerry Sags	4.00	10.00
A49	Angelina Love	8.00	20.00
A50	Alex Shelley	4.00	10.00
A51	Syxx-Pac	6.00	15.00
A52	Shannon Moore	6.00	15.00
A53	Jay Lethal	4.00	10.00
A54	Rob Terry	4.00	10.00
A55	Ric Flair		

2010 TRISTAR TNA New Era Dual Autographs Silver

*GOLD/50: X TO X BASIC AUTOS
*GREEN/25: X TO X BASIC AUTOS
*RED/5: UNPRICED DUE TO SCARCITY
*PURPLE/1: UNPRICED DUE TO SCARCITY
RANDOMLY INSERTED INTO RETAIL PACKS

1 H.Hogan/Sting
2 M.Foley/Abyss
3 H.Hogan/D.Carter
4 K.Angle/J.Jarrett
5 K.Nash/E.Young
6 H.Hogan/M.Foley
7 K.Angle/Mr.Anderson
8 Taz/M.Tenay
9 H.Hogan/K.Nash
10 A.Love/Lacey Von Erich
11 D.Dinero/O.Jordan
12 B.Knobs/J.Sags
13 A.Kong/Hamada
14 K.Angle/D.Wolfe
15 M.Morgan/Hernandez
16 V.Sky/M.Rayne
17 H.Hogan/K.Angle
18 A.Shelley/C.Sabin
19 J.Storm/R.Roode
20 R.Flair/AJ Styles
21 Sting/R.Flair
22 H.Hogan/R.Flair

2010 TRISTAR TNA New Era Dual Autographs Gold

STATED PRINT RUN 50 SER.#'d SETS

1 H.Hogan/Sting
2 M.Foley/Abyss
3 H.Hogan/D.Carter
4 K.Angle/J.Jarrett
5 K.Nash/E.Young
6 H.Hogan/M.Foley
7 K.Angle/Mr.Anderson
8 Taz/M.Tenay
9 H.Hogan/K.Nash

10 Angelina Love/L.Von Erich
11 D.Dinero/O.Jordan
12 B.Knobs/J.Sags
13 A.Kong/Hamada
14 K.Angle/D.Wolfe
15 M.Morgan/Hernandez
16 V.Sky/M.Rayne
17 H.Hogan/K.Angle
18 A.Shelley/C.Sabin
19 J.Storm/R.Roode
20 R.Flair/AJ Styles
21 Sting/R.Flair
22 H.Hogan/R.Flair

2010 TRISTAR TNA New Era Dual Autographs Green

*GREEN: X TO X BASIC AUTOS
STATED PRINT RUN 25 SER.#'d SETS

1 H.Hogan/Sting		
2 M.Foley/Abyss	20.00	40.00
3 H.Hogan/D.Carter		
4 K.Angle/J.Jarrett	25.00	50.00
5 K.Nash/E.Young	15.00	30.00
6 H.Hogan/M.Foley		
7 K.Angle/Mr.Anderson	20.00	40.00
8 Taz/M.Tenay	10.00	20.00
9 H.Hogan/K.Nash		
10 Angelina Love/L.Von Erich	20.00	40.00
11 D.Dinero/O.Jordan	20.00	40.00
12 B.Knobs/J.Sags	15.00	30.00
13 A.Kong/Hamada	15.00	30.00
14 K.Angle/D.Wolfe	20.00	40.00
15 M.Morgan/Hernandez	15.00	30.00
16 V.Sky/M.Rayne	20.00	40.00
17 H.Hogan/K.Angle		
18 A.Shelley/C.Sabin	10.00	20.00
19 J.Storm/R.Roode	15.00	30.00
20 R.Flair/AJ Styles		
21 Sting/R.Flair		
22 H.Hogan/R.Flair		

2010 TRISTAR TNA New Era Dual Memorabilia Silver

STATED ODDS

M10 J.Storm/R.Roode	4.00	10.00

2010 TRISTAR TNA New Era Memorabilia Silver

*GOLD/50: .5X TO 1.2X BASIC MEM
*RED/25: .6X TO 1.5X BASIC MEM
*PURPLE/1: UNPRICED DUE TO SCARCITY
OVERALL MEM ODDS ONE PER HOBBY BOX
STATED PRINT RUN 99-199

M1 Hulk Hogan		
M2 Ric Flair		
M3 Mick Foley	5.00	12.00
M4 Sting	6.00	15.00
M5 Kurt Angle	5.00	12.00
M6 Rob Van Dam	4.00	10.00
M7 Mr. Anderson	4.00	10.00
M8 Syxx-Pac	4.00	10.00

2010 TRISTAR TNA New Era Quad Autographs Silver

*GOLD/50: X TO X BASIC AUTOS
*GREEN/25: X TO X BASIC AUTOS
*RED/5: UNPRICED DUE TO SCARCITY

*PURPLE/1: UNPRICED DUE TO SCARCITY
RANDOMLY INSERTED INTO RETAIL PACKS

1 Hogan/Jarrett/Angle/Foley
2 Sky/Rayne/Von Erich/Love
3 Hogan/Flair/Sting/Nash
4 Wilde/Sarita/Hamada/A.Kong
5 Hogan/Abyss/Flair/Styles

2010 TRISTAR TNA New Era Triple Autographs Silver

*GOLD/50: X TO X BASIC AUTOS
*GREEN/25: X TO X BASIC AUTOS
*RED/5: UNPRICED DUE TO SCARCITY
*PURPLE/1: UNPRICED DUE TO SCARCITY
RANDOMLY INSERTED INTO RETAIL PACKS

1 Hogan/Nash/6-Pac
2 Sky/Rayne/Von Erich
3 Terry/Magnus/Williams
4 Tara/Hemme/Brooks

2010 TRISTAR TNA New Era Triple Autographs Green

*GREEN: X TO X BASIC AUTOS
STATED PRINT RUN 25 SER.#'d SETS

1 Hogan/Nash/6-Pac		
2 Sky/Rayne/Von Erich	30.00	60.00
3 Terry/Magnus/Williams	15.00	30.00
4 Tara/Hemme/Brooks	20.00	40.00

2010 TRISTAR TNA New Era Triple Autographs Red

STATED PRINT RUN 5 SER.#'d SETS
UNPRICED DUE TO SCARCITY

1 Hogan/Nash/6-Pac
2 Sky/Rayne/Von Erich
3 Terry/Magnus/Williams
4 Tara/Hemme/Brooks

2010 TRISTAR TNA Obak National Convention

COMPLETE SET (3)	4.00	10.00
TNA1 Rob Van Dam	2.00	5.00
TNA2 Mick Foley	2.50	6.00
TNA3 Kurt Angle	2.00	5.00

2011 TRISTAR TNA Signature Impact

COMPLETE SET (100)	20.00	40.00
COMPLETE SET W/O SP (90)	10.00	25.00
UNOPENED BOX (20 PACKS)		
UNOPENED PACK (6 CARDS)		

*SILVER/50: 2.5X TO 6X BASIC CARDS
*SILVER SP/50: .75X TO 2X BASIC CARDS
*GOLD/5: UNPRICED DUE TO SCARCITY
*PURPLE/1: UNPRICED DUE TO SCARCITY

1 Hulk Hogan	1.00	2.50
2 Ric Flair	.75	2.00
3 Sting	.60	1.50
4 Jeff Jarrett	.25	.60
5 Scott Steiner	.25	.60
6 Jeff Hardy	.60	1.50
7 Matt Hardy	.40	1.00
8 Velvet Sky	.75	2.00
9 Abyss	.25	.60
10 Kurt Angle	.25	.60
11 Sting	.60	1.50
12 Ric Flair	.75	2.00
13 Matt Hardy/Jeff Hardy	.60	1.50
14 AJ Styles	.25	.60
15 Velvet Sky	.75	2.00
16 Scott Steiner	.25	.60
17 Mr. Anderson	.25	.60
18 Anarquia	.15	.40
19 Devon	.15	.40
20 Dixie Carter	.40	1.00
21 Crimson	.15	.40
22 Angelina Love	.60	1.50
23 Eric Bischoff	.15	.40
24 AJ Styles	.25	.60
25 Daniels	.15	.40
26 Gunner	.15	.40
27 Murphy	.15	.40
28 Tara	.60	1.50
29 Ric Flair	.75	2.00
30 Hulk Hogan	1.00	2.50
31 Mickie James	1.00	2.50
32 Sting	.60	1.50
33 Abyss	.25	.60
34 Mr. Anderson	.25	.60
35 James Storm	.15	.40
36 Karen Jarrett	.25	.60
37 Bully Ray	.15	.40
38 Douglas Williams	.15	.40
39 Mickie James	1.00	2.50
40 Mr. Anderson	.25	.60
41 Alex Shelley	.15	.40
42 Chris Sabin	.15	.40
43 Matt Morgan	.15	.40
44 Rob Van Dam	.25	.60
45 Hulk Hogan	1.00	2.50
46 Samoa Joe	.15	.40
47 Taz	.15	.40
48 RVD	.25	.60
49 Madison Rayne	.40	1.00
50 Orlando Jordan	.15	.40
51 Mike Tenay	.15	.40
52 Taz	.15	.40
53 Jeremy Borash	.15	.40
54 Christy Hemme	.60	1.50
55 Eric Young	.15	.40
56 Ms. Tessmacher	.40	1.00
57 Rob Terry	.15	.40
58 Amazing Red	.15	.40
59 Hernandez	.15	.40
60 Magnus	.15	.40
61 K.Angle/J.Jarrett	.25	.60
62 Lockdown 2011	.15	.40
63 Karen Jarrett's TNA Return	.25	.60
64 Karen on Angle & Jarrett	.25	.60
65 The Jarrett/Angle Bunch	.15	.40
66 Robbie E	.15	.40
67 Robert Roode	.15	.40
68 Shannon Moore	.15	.40
69 Jesse Neal	.15	.40
70 Cookie	.15	.40
71 D'Angelo Dinero	.15	.40
72 Rosita	.25	.60
73 Generation Me	.15	.40
74 Samoa Joe	.15	.40
75 Mexican America	.15	.40
76 Sarita	.25	.60
77 Suicide	.15	.40
78 Brian Kendrick	.15	.40
79 Winter	.60	1.50
80 Kazarian	.15	.40
81 Immortal	.15	.40
82 Fortune	.15	.40
83 Bully Ray	.15	.40
84 Christy Hemme	.60	1.50
85 Kurt Angle	.25	.60
86 Beer Money	.15	.40
87 Eric Bischoff	.15	.40
88 Scott Steiner	.25	.60
89 Samoa Joe	.15	.40
90 Hogan/Flair/Sting	3.00	8.00
91 Hulk Hogan SP	3.00	8.00
92 Hulk Hogan SP	3.00	8.00
93 Hulk Hogan SP	3.00	8.00
94 Ric Flair SP	3.00	8.00
95 Ric Flair SP	3.00	8.00
96 Ric Flair SP	3.00	8.00
97 Sting SP	3.00	8.00
98 Sting SP	3.00	8.00
99 Sting SP	3.00	8.00
CL Checklist	.15	.40

2011 TRISTAR TNA Signature Impact Autographs Silver

*GOLD/25: .6X TO 1.25X BASIC AUTOS
*RED/5: UNPRICED DUE TO SCARCITY
*PURPLE/1: UNPRICED DUE TO SCARCITY
STATED PRINT RUN 99 SER.#'d SETS

S8 Jeff Hardy	25.00	50.00
S9 Matt Hardy	15.00	30.00
S10 Rob Van Dam	15.00	30.00
S11 Mickie James	30.00	60.00
S12 Scott Steiner		
S13 Anarquia	15.00	30.00
S14 Jeff Jarrett	12.00	25.00
S15 Kazarian	6.00	15.00
S16 Winter	12.00	25.00
S17 Kurt Angle	20.00	40.00
S18 Karen Jarrett	6.00	15.00
S19 Abyss	6.00	15.00
S20 Matt Morgan	6.00	15.00
S21 Kendrick	6.00	15.00
S22 Mr. Anderson	10.00	20.00
S23 Velvet Sky	20.00	40.00
S24 Robert Roode	10.00	20.00
S25 Ms. Tessmacher	12.00	25.00
S26 Sarita	6.00	15.00
S27 Jesse Neal	6.00	15.00
S28 Amazing Red	6.00	15.00
S29 D'Angelo Dinero	6.00	15.00
S30 Magnus	6.00	15.00
S31 Angelina Love	10.00	20.00
S32 Orlando Jordan	6.00	15.00
S33 Mick Foley	10.00	20.00
S34 Crimson	6.00	15.00
S35 Daniels	6.00	15.00
S36 Madison Rayne	10.00	20.00
S37 Murphy		
S38 Tara	10.00	20.00
S39 James Storm	6.00	15.00
S40 Jeremy Buck	6.00	15.00
S41 Rosita	12.00	25.00
S42 Rob Terry	6.00	15.00
S43 SoCal Val	10.00	20.00
S44 Jay Lethal	6.00	15.00
S45 Mike Tenay	6.00	15.00
S46 Jeremy Borash	6.00	15.00
S47 Samoa Joe	6.00	15.00
S48 Eric Young	6.00	15.00

S49 AJ Styles	10.00	20.00
S50 Christy Hemme	10.00	20.00
S51 Shannon Moore	6.00	15.00
S52 Max Buck	6.00	15.00
S53 Chyna	10.00	25.00
S54 Eric Bischoff		

2011 TRISTAR TNA Signature Impact Dual Autographs Silver

*GOLD/25: .6X TO 1.25X BASIC AUTOS
*RED/5: UNPRICED DUE TO SCARCITY
*PURPLE/1: UNPRICED DUE TO SCARCITY
STATED PRINT RUN 99 SER.#'d SETS

1 H.Hogan/R.Flair		
2 Jeff & Matt Hardy		
3 Jeff & Karen Jarrett		
4 Sting/RVD		
5 H.Hogan/Sting		
6 M.Hardy/RVD		
7 H.Hogan/M.Hardy		
8 Sarita/Rosita	10.00	20.00
9 Hernandez/Anarquia		
10 AJ Styles/Daniels	10.00	20.00
11 RVD/H.Hogan		
12 M.James/Tara	20.00	40.00
13 Tara/M.Rayne	10.00	20.00
14 Gunner/Murphy	6.00	15.00
15 Magnus/D.Williams	6.00	15.00
16 Max & Jeremy Buck	6.00	15.00
17 S.Steiner/H.Hogan		
18 Crimson/Abyss	6.00	15.00
19 K.Angle/J.Jarrett		
20 S.Moore/J.Neal		
21 M.Foley/RVD		
22 C.Hemme/S.Val	10.00	20.00
23 Hernandez/M.Morgan	6.00	15.00
24 Robbie E/Cookie	6.00	15.00
25 Winter/A.Love	10.00	20.00
26 A.Love/V.Sky	15.00	30.00
27 Chyna/K.Angle		

2011 TRISTAR TNA Signature Impact Dual Memorabilia Silver

STATED PRINT RUN 199 SER.#'d SETS
M11 Jeff & Matt Hardy

2011 TRISTAR TNA Signature Impact Eight Autographs Silver

*GOLD/25: UNPRICED DUE TO SCARCITY
*RED/5: UNPRICED DUE TO SCARCITY
*PURPLE/1: UNPRICED DUE TO SCARCITY
STATED PRINT RUN 99 SER.#'d SETS

1 Hogan/Flair/Sting/Steiner
Angle/J.Hardy/RVD/M.Hardy
2 Hogan/Tara/Flair/James
Sting/Sky/J.Hardy/Love
3 James/Tara/Love/Sky
Rayne/Winter/Rosita/Sarita

2011 TRISTAR TNA Signature Impact Five Autographs Silver

*GOLD/25: X TO X BASIC AUTOS
*RED/5: UNPRICED DUE TO SCARCITY
*PURPLE/1: UNPRICED DUE TO SCARCITY
STATED PRINT RUN 99 SER.#'d SETS

1 Hogan/Steiner/Sting/Jarrett/Flair		
2 Love/Sky/Tara/James/Rayne	30.00	60.00
3 Jeff & Matt Hardy/RVD/Foley/Angle		

2011 TRISTAR TNA Signature Impact Memorabilia Silver

*GOLD/50: .6X TO 1.25X BASIC MEM
*BLUE/25: .75X TO 1.5X BASIC MEM
*RED/5: UNPRICED DUE TO SCARCITY
*PURPLE/1: UNPRICED DUE TO SCARCITY
STATED PRINT RUN 199 SER.#'d SETS

M6 Hulk Hogan		
M7 Sting	12.00	25.00
M8 Chyna	12.00	25.00
M9 Jeff Hardy		
M10 Rob Van Dam	10.00	20.00

2011 TRISTAR TNA Signature Impact Quad Autographs Silver

*GOLD/25: .6X TO 1.25X BASIC AUTOS
*RED/5: UNPRICED DUE TO SCARCITY
*PURPLE/1: UNPRICED DUE TO SCARCITY
STATED PRINT RUN 99 SER.#'d SETS

1 Flair/Hardy/Abyss/Styles		
2 Hogan/Flair/The Hardys		
3 Hernandez/Anarquia/Sarita/Rosita	15.00	30.00
4 Angle/Chyna/Karen & Jeff Jarrett		

2011 TRISTAR TNA Signature Impact Quad Memorabilia Silver

M14 Sky/Love/Winter/James	15.00	40.00
M15 Hernandez/Anarquia	8.00	20.00
Sarita/Rosita		

2011 TRISTAR TNA Signature Impact Ric Flair Die-Cut Letter Memorabilia Silver

COMPLETE SET (5)
M1 Ric Flair F
M2 Ric Flair L
M3 Ric Flair A
M4 Ric Flair I
M5 Ric Flair R

2011 TRISTAR TNA Signature Impact Seven Autographs Silver

*GOLD/25: UNPRICED DUE TO SCARCITY
*RED/5: UNPRICED DUE TO SCARCITY
*PURPLE/1: UNPRICED DUE TO SCARCITY
STATED PRINT RUN 99 SER.#'d SETS
UNPRICED DUE TO SCARCITY

1 Sting/RVD/Anderson/Hogan
Flair/Jeff & Matt Hardy
2 Hogan/James/Flair
Love/RVD/Sky/J.Hardy

2011 TRISTAR TNA Signature Impact Six Autographs Silver

*GOLD/25: UNPRICED DUE TO SCARCITY
*RED/5: UNPRICED DUE TO SCARCITY
*PURPLE/1: UNPRICED DUE TO SCARCITY
STATED PRINT RUN 99 SER.#'d SETS
UNPRICED DUE TO SCARCITY

1 Hogan/Flair/Sting
Angle/Jarrett/Steiner
2 Tara/James/Sky
Love/Rayne/Hemme

2011 TRISTAR TNA Signature Impact Triple Autographs Silver

*GOLD/25: UNPRICED DUE TO SCARCITY
*RED/5: UNPRICED DUE TO SCARCITY
*PURPLE/1: UNPRICED DUE TO SCARCITY
STATED PRINT RUN 99 SER.#'d SETS
UNPRICED DUE TO SCARCITY

1 Jeff & Karen Jarrett/Angle
2 Sky/Winter/Love
3 Sting/RVD/Anderson
4 Hogan/Flair/Sting
5 Jeff & Matt Hardy/RVD

2011 TRISTAR TNA Signature Impact Triple Memorabilia Silver

M12 Hogan/Flair/Sting		
M13 Jeff & Karen Jarrett/Angle	8.00	20.00

2010 TRISTAR TNA Xtreme

COMPLETE SET W/SP (111)	60.00	120.00
COMPLETE SET W/O SP (101)	10.00	25.00
UNOPENED BOX (20 PACKS)		
UNOPENED PACK (6 CARDS)		

*SILVER/40: 3X TO 8X BASIC CARDS
*GOLD/10: UNPRICED DUE TO SCARCITY
*PURPLE/1: UNPRICED DUE TO SCARCITY
SP STATED ODDS 1:BOX

1 Hulk Hogan	1.00	2.50
2 Eric Bischoff	.15	.40
3 Jeff Jarrett	.40	1.00
4 Samoa Joe	.25	.60
5 Robbie E	.15	.40
6 Sting	.60	1.50
7 Ric Flair	.75	2.00
8 AJ Styles	.40	1.00
9 Matt Morgan	.15	.40
10 Cowboy James Storm	.25	.60
11 Robert Roode	.15	.40
12 Kazarian	.15	.40
13 Tommy Dreamer	.15	.40
14 Mick Foley	.75	2.00
15 Brother Devon	.25	.60
16 Stevie Richards	.15	.40
17 Rhino	.25	.60
18 Brian Kendrick	.25	.60
19 Raven	.25	.60
20 Taz	.15	.40
21 Sabu	.15	.40
22 Al Snow	.40	1.00
23 Hardcore Justice	.15	.40
24 RVD/Sabu	.40	1.00
25 Raven/Tommy Dreamer	.25	.60
26 So.Philly Street Fight	.15	.40
27 Rhino/Al Snow/Brother Runt	.40	1.00
28 Stevie Richards/PJ Polaco	.15	.40
29 Too Cold Scorpio/CW Anderson	.15	.40
30 The FBI/Kash/Diamond/Swinger	.15	.40
31 Jason Hervey	.15	.40
32 Rob Van Dam	.40	1.00
33 Jeff Hardy	.60	1.50
34 Kurt Angle	.60	1.50
35 D'Angelo Dinero	.15	.40
36 Brother Ray	.25	.60
37 Mr. Anderson	.25	.60
38 TNA Tag Team Champ	.15	.40
39 Falls Count Anywhere	.25	.60
40 Jarrett/Joe/Sting/Nash	.60	1.50
41 Tommy Dreamer/AJ Styles	.40	1.00
42 Jeff Hardy/Kurt Angle	.60	1.50
43 London Brawling	.15	.40
44 Generation Me	.15	.40
45 Rob Terry	.15	.40
46 Douglas Williams	.15	.40
47 Motorcity Machine Guns	.25	.60
48 Amazing Red	.15	.40
49 Magnus	.15	.40
50 Hernandez	.15	.40
51 Jeremy Borash	.15	.40
52 Orlando Jordan	.15	.40
53 TNA Tag Team Champ	.15	.40
54 Classic Knockouts	.25	.60
55 RVD Overcomes the Odds	.40	1.00
56 Lethal Lockdown	.15	.40
57 Cookie	.25	.60
58 Mickie James	.75	2.00
59 Angelina Love	.60	1.50
60 Velvet Sky	.75	2.00
61 Lacey Von Erich	.75	2.00
62 Madison Rayne	.60	1.50
63 Taylor Wilde	.40	1.00
64 Hamada	.40	1.00
65 Daffney	.60	1.50
66 Sarita	.40	1.00
67 SoCal Val	.60	1.50
68 Tara	.60	1.50
69 Miss Tessmacher	.75	2.00
70 Ink Inc.	.15	.40
71 Abyss SS	.25	.60
72 AJ Styles SS	.40	1.00
73 Hulk Hogan SS	1.00	2.50
74 Kurt Angle SS	.60	1.50
75 Jeff Jarrett SS	.40	1.00
76 Jeff Hardy SS	.60	1.50
77 Dixie Carter SS	.40	1.00
78 Rob Van Dam SS	.40	1.00
79 Lacey Von Erich SS	.75	2.00
80 Jay Lethal SS	.15	.40
81 Tommy Dreamer SS	.15	.40
82 Mick Foley SS	.75	2.00
83 Sting PC	.60	1.50
84 Madison Rayne PC	.60	1.50
85 D'Angelo Dinero PC	.15	.40
86 Christy Hemme PC	.60	1.50
87 Jeff Hardy PC	.60	1.50
88 Angelina Love PC	.60	1.50
89 Mickie James PC	.75	2.00
90 Dixie Carter PC	.40	1.00
91 Kurt Angle PC	.60	1.50
92 Mike Tenay PC	.15	.40
93 Mickie James	.75	2.00
94 Rob Van Dam UX	.40	1.00
95 Sting UX	.60	1.50
96 Jeff Hardy UX	.60	1.50
97 Abyss UX	.25	.60
98 Tommy Dreamer UX	.15	.40
99 AJ Styles UX	.40	1.00
100 Hulk Hogan UX	1.00	2.50
101 Jeff Hardy Original Art SP	6.00	15.00
102 Jeff Hardy Original Art SP	6.00	15.00
103 Jeff Hardy Original Art SP	6.00	15.00
104 Jeff Hardy Original Art SP	6.00	15.00
105 Jeff Hardy Original Art SP	6.00	15.00
106 Jeff Hardy Original Art SP	6.00	15.00
107 Jeff Hardy Original Art SP	6.00	15.00
108 Jeff Hardy Original Art SP	6.00	15.00
109 Jeff Hardy Original Art SP	6.00	15.00
110 Jeff Hardy Original Art SP	6.00	15.00
CL Checklist	.15	.40

2010 TRISTAR TNA Xtreme Autographed Memorabilia Gold

*GREEN/25: UNPRICED DUE TO SCARCITY
*RED/5: UNPRICED DUE TO SCARCITY
*PURPLE/1: UNPRICED DUE TO SCARCITY
STATED PRINT RUN 99 SER.#'d SETS
UNPRICED DUE TO SCARCITY

XA1 Hulk Hogan
XA2 Mickie James
XA3 Rob Van Dam
XA4 Jeff Hardy
XA5 Sting
XA6 AJ Styles

2010 TRISTAR TNA Xtreme Autographs Gold

COMMON AUTO	5.00	12.00

*GREEN/25: .6X TO 1.5X BASIC AUTOS
*RED/5: UNPRICED DUE TO SCARCITY
*PURPLE/1: UNPRICED DUE TO SCARCITY
STATED PRINT RUN 99 SER.#'d SETS

X1 Rob Van Dam		
X2 Rhino	6.00	15.00
X3 Mick Foley		
X4 Tommy Dreamer	6.00	15.00
X5 Sabu	6.00	15.00
X6 Raven		
X7 Stevie Richards	6.00	15.00
X8 Al Snow	8.00	20.00
X9 Kid Kash	5.00	12.00
X10 New Jack	5.00	12.00
X11 P.J. Polaco	5.00	12.00
X12 Tracy Smothers	5.00	12.00
X13 Axl Rotten	5.00	12.00
X14 Too Cold Scorpio	5.00	12.00
X15 Bill Alfonso	5.00	12.00
X16 Tony Luke	5.00	12.00
X17 Blue Tillie	5.00	12.00
X18 Swinger	5.00	12.00
X19 Brother Runt	5.00	12.00
X20 Stephen DeAngelis	5.00	12.00
X21 Simon Diamond	5.00	12.00
X22 Nova	5.00	12.00
X23 Guido Maritato	5.00	12.00
X24 Big Sal	5.00	12.00
X25 Mustafa	5.00	12.00
X26 C.W. Anderson	5.00	12.00
X27 Joel Gertner		
X28 John Rechner		
X29 Taz	5.00	12.00
X30 Brian Kendrick	6.00	15.00
X31 Tara	8.00	20.00
X32 Jason Hervey	6.00	15.00
X33 Mickie James	15.00	30.00
X34 Jeremy Borash	5.00	12.00
X35 Samoa Joe	8.00	20.00
X36 Alex Shelley	5.00	12.00
X37 Shannon Moore	8.00	20.00
X38 Jay Lethal	5.00	12.00
X39 Jeff Hardy		
X40 Chris Sabin	5.00	12.00
X41 Kazarian	5.00	12.00
X42 Mr. Anderson	6.00	15.00
X43 Sting		
X44 Abyss	6.00	15.00
X45 AJ Styles	8.00	20.00
X46 Angelina Love	10.00	25.00
X47 Madison Rayne	10.00	25.00
X48 Velvet Sky	10.00	25.00
X49 Lacey Von Erich	10.00	25.00
X50 Christy Hemme	10.00	25.00
X51 Kevin Nash	10.00	25.00
X52 Kurt Angle	10.00	25.00
X53 Ric Flair		
X54 Hulk Hogan		
X55 Hulk Hogan		
X56 Hulk Hogan		

2010 TRISTAR TNA Xtreme Autographs Green

*GREEN: .6X TO 1.5X BASIC AUTOS
STATED PRINT RUN 25 SER.#'d SETS

X1 Rob Van Dam		
X2 Rhino	10.00	25.00
X3 Mick Foley		
X4 Tommy Dreamer	10.00	25.00
X5 Sabu	10.00	25.00
X6 Raven		
X7 Stevie Richards	10.00	25.00
X8 Al Snow	12.00	30.00
X9 Kid Kash	8.00	20.00
X10 New Jack	8.00	20.00
X11 P.J. Polaco	8.00	20.00
X12 Tracy Smothers	8.00	20.00
X13 Axl Rotten	8.00	20.00
X14 Too Cold Scorpio	8.00	20.00
X15 Bill Alfonso	8.00	20.00
X16 Tony Luke	8.00	20.00
X17 Blue Tillie	8.00	20.00
X18 Swinger	8.00	20.00
X19 Brother Runt	8.00	20.00
X20 Stephen DeAngelis	8.00	20.00
X21 Simon Diamond	8.00	20.00
X22 Nova	8.00	20.00
X23 Guido Maritato	8.00	20.00
X24 Big Sal	8.00	20.00
X25 Mustafa	8.00	20.00
X26 C.W. Anderson	8.00	20.00
X27 Joel Gertner		
X28 John Rechner		
X29 Taz	8.00	20.00
X30 Brian Kendrick	10.00	25.00
X31 Tara	15.00	30.00
X32 Jason Hervey	10.00	25.00
X33 Mickie James	25.00	50.00
X34 Jeremy Borash	8.00	20.00
X35 Samoa Joe	12.00	30.00
X36 Alex Shelley	8.00	20.00
X37 Shannon Moore	12.00	30.00
X38 Jay Lethal	8.00	20.00
X39 Jeff Hardy		
X40 Chris Sabin	8.00	20.00
X41 Kazarian	8.00	20.00
X42 Mr. Anderson	10.00	25.00
X43 Sting		
X44 Abyss	10.00	25.00
X45 AJ Styles	12.00	30.00
X46 Angelina Love	20.00	40.00
X47 Madison Rayne	20.00	40.00
X48 Velvet Sky	20.00	40.00
X49 Lacey Von Erich	20.00	40.00
X50 Christy Hemme	20.00	40.00
X51 Kevin Nash	20.00	40.00
X52 Kurt Angle	20.00	40.00
X53 Ric Flair		
X54 Hulk Hogan		
X55 Hulk Hogan		
X56 Hulk Hogan		

2010 TRISTAR TNA Xtreme Dual Autographed Memorabilia Gold

STATED PRINT RUN 50 SER.#'d SETS

XA7 RVD/Sabu		
XA8 A.Love/V.Sky	35.00	70.00
XA9 J.Hardy/RVD		

2010 TRISTAR TNA Xtreme Dual Autographs Gold

1 R.Flair/M.Foley		
2 Sting/K.Nash		
3 RVD/Sabu		
4 A.Love/V.Sky	12.00	30.00
5 A.Shelley/C.Sabin	8.00	20.00
6 Max & Jeremy Buck	8.00	20.00
7 J.Neal/S.Moore	12.00	25.00
8 Robbie E/Cookie	12.00	30.00
9 Tommy & Trisa Dreamer	12.00	30.00
10 N.Jack/Mustafa		
11 J.Finegan/M.Kehner		
12 Scorpio/C.Anderson		
13 M.Tenay/Taz		
14 Raven/T.Dreamer		
15 H.Hogan/R.Flair		

2010 TRISTAR TNA Xtreme Dual Memorabilia

*GOLD/50: .5X TO 1.2X BASIC MEM
*GREEN/25: .6X TO 1.5X BASIC MEM
*RED/5: UNPRICED DUE TO SCARCITY
*PURPLE/1: UNPRICED DUE TO SCARCITY
STATED PRINT RUN 199 SER.#'d SETS

X12 Robbie E/Cookie	8.00	20.00
X13 Jeremy & Max Buck	6.00	15.00

2010 TRISTAR TNA Xtreme Dual Memorabilia Gold

*GOLD: .5X TO 1.2X BASIC MEM
STATED PRINT RUN 50 SER.#'d SETS

X12 Robbie E/Cookie	10.00	25.00
X13 Jeremy & Max Buck	8.00	20.00

2010 TRISTAR TNA Xtreme Lovely Locks Hair Autographs Turquoise

*PINK/1: UNPRICED DUE TO SCARCITY
STATED PRINT RUN 3 SER.#'d SETS
UNPRICED DUE TO SCARCITY

LL1 Velvet Sky
LL2 Angelina Love
LL3 SoCal Val
LL4 Christy Hemme

2010 TRISTAR TNA Xtreme Memorabilia

*GOLD/50: .5X TO 1.2X BASIC MEM
*GREEN/10: UNPRICED DUE TO SCARCITY
*RED/5: UNPRICED DUE TO SCARCITY
*PURPLE/1: UNPRICED DUE TO SCARCITY
OVERALL MEMORABILIA ODDS ONE PER HOBBY BOX
STATED PRINT RUN 199 SER.#'d SETS

X1 Hulk Hogan
X2 Rob Van Dam

2010 TRISTAR TNA Xtreme Obak

X3 Jeff Hardy		
X4 Mr. Anderson	6.00	15.00
X5 Kurt Angle	6.00	15.00
X6 Mickie James		
X7 AJ Styles		
X8 D'Angelo Dinero		
X9 Sabu	6.00	15.00
X10 Al Snow	6.00	15.00
X11 Brother Runt	6.00	15.00

COMPLETE SET (8)	15.00	40.00
STATED PRINT RUN 310 SER.#'d SETS		
X1 Hulk Hogan	8.00	20.00
X2 Jeff Hardy	5.00	12.00
X3 Rob Van Dam	3.00	8.00
X4 Mickie James	6.00	15.00
X5 AJ Styles	3.00	8.00
X6 Tommy Dreamer	1.25	3.00
X7 Jeff Jarrett	3.00	8.00
X8 Sting	5.00	12.00

2010 TRISTAR TNA Xtreme Quad Autographs

*GOLD/99: UNPRICED DUE TO SCARCITY
*GREEN/25: UNPRICED DUE TO SCARCITY
*RED/5: UNPRICED DUE TO SCARCITY
*PURPLE/1: UNPRICED DUE TO SCARCITY
UNPRICED DUE TO SCARCITY

1 Hogan/Flair/Jarrett/Hardy
2 Angle/Sting/Nash/Foley
3 Sky/Love/Rayne/Tara
4 Tommy & Trisa Dreamer/Kimberly/Brianna

2010 TRISTAR TNA Xtreme Quad Memorabilia Gold

*GREEN/10: UNPRICED DUE TO SCARCITY
*RED/5: UNPRICED DUE TO SCARCITY
*PURPLE/1: UNPRICED DUE TO SCARCITY
STATED PRINT RUN 50 SER.#'d SETS

X14 Hogan/Sting/RVD/Hardy		
X15 Sky/Love/Von Erich/Rayne		
X16 Hogan/Flair/Foley/Sting		
X17 Tara/James/Sky/Love		
X18 Snow/B.Runt/Scorpio/Tillie	15.00	30.00
X19 Dreamer/RVD/Sabu/Snow	15.00	30.00

2010 TRISTAR TNA Xtreme Six Autographs

*GOLD/99: UNPRICED DUE TO SCARCITY
*GREEN/25: UNPRICED DUE TO SCARCITY
*RED/5: UNPRICED DUE TO SCARCITY
*PURPLE/1: UNPRICED DUE TO SCARCITY
UNPRICED DUE TO SCARCITY

1 Flair/Styles/Storm
Roode/Kazarian/Morgan
2 Hogan/Flair/Hardy
Jarrett/Angle/Sting
3 Dreamer/Foley/Richards
Rhino/Raven/Sabu
4 Smothers/Luke/Maritato
Kash/Diamond/Swinger

2010 TRISTAR TNA Xtreme Six Autographs Gold

STATED PRINT RUN 99 SER. #'d SETS

1 Flair/Styles/Storm
  Roode/Kazarian/Morgan
2 Hogan/Flair/Hardy
  Jarrett/Angle/Sting
3 Dreamer/Foley/Richards
  Rhino/Raven/Sabu
4 Smothers/Luke/Maritato
  Kash/Diamond/Swinger

2010 TRISTAR TNA Xtreme Sting Die-Cut Letter Memorabilia Green

STATED PRINT RUN 10 SER.#'d SETS

S1 Sting S		20.00	40.00
S2 Sting T		20.00	40.00
S3 Sting I		20.00	40.00
S4 Sting N		20.00	40.00
S5 Sting G		20.00	40.00

2010 TRISTAR TNA Xtreme Sting Face Paint Red

STATED PRINT RUN 5 SER.#'d SETS
UNPRICED DUE TO SCARCITY

S3 Sting
S4 Sting

2010 TRISTAR TNA Xtreme Triple Autographs Gold

STATED PRINT RUN 99 SER.#'d SETS

1 Hogan/Jarrett/Flair
2 Foley/Angle/Anderson
3 Raven/Dreamer/Foley
4 Richards/Nova/Polaco
5 Rhino/Runt/Snow
6 Ray/Devon/Gertner
7 Sabu/VanDam/Alfonso

2010 TRISTAR TNA Xtreme Velvet Sky Die-Cut Letter Memorabilia Gold

STATED PRINT RUN 50 SER.#'d SETS

VS1 Velvet Sky S		25.00	50.00
VS2 Velvet Sky K		25.00	50.00
VS3 Velvet Sky Y		25.00	50.00

1993 Unbeatables Mid-South Wrestling

COMPLETE SET (25)
STATED PRINT RUN 1,000 SETS

1 Big Mike Norman
2 Ricky Morton
3 The Sheik
4 Ben Jordan
5 Chris Champion
6 Reno Riggins
7 The Mongolian Mauler
8 Billy Montana
9 Gary Valiant
10 The Scorpion
11 The Medic
12 Jeff Daniels with Dominique
13 PG-13
14 Mephisto and Dante
15 Wild Boys
16 The Hickersons
17 Rhodes and Lawler
18 Woodrow Foundation
19 Madd Maxx

20 Little Farmer John
21 Cowabunga
22 Willie the Wrestling Clown
23 Chris Keirn
24 Freddie Morton
25 The Fireball

2006 Unilever WWE

NNO Batista		5.00	12.00
NNO Booker T		3.00	8.00
NNO Carlito		5.00	12.00
NNO Hulk Hogan		8.00	20.00
NNO The Hurricane		1.25	3.00
NNO John Cena		8.00	20.00
NNO Kurt Angle		8.00	20.00
NNO Rey Mysterio		5.00	12.00
NNO Stone Cold Steve Austin		8.00	20.00
NNO The Undertaker		6.00	15.00

2008 Unilever WWE

COMPLETE SET (10)

NNO Batista
NNO Bobby Lashley
NNO Carlito
NNO CM Punk
NNO Edge
NNO Jeff Hardy
NNO John Cena
NNO Rob Van Dam
NNO Shawn Michaels
NNO Triple H

1998 Up Front Sports WCW/nWo American Pop 3-D

COMPLETE SET (3)

NNO Goldberg
NNO Randy Savage
NNO Sting

1998 Up Front Sports WCW/nWo Pop-Up Real Action

COMPLETE SET (10)

1 Bret Hart
2 Sting
3 DDP
4 Goldberg
5 Hollywood Hogan
6 Kevin Nash
7 Lex Luger
8 Macho Man Randy Savage
9 Scott Steiner
10 Scott Hall

2000 Waldenbooks WWF Limited Edition

COMPLETE SET (2)		8.00	20.00
1 Have a Nice Day!		3.00	8.00
2 The Rock Says		6.00	15.00

1997 WCW Chromium Stickers

COMPLETE SET (5)

NNO DDP
NNO The Giant
NNO Lex Luger
NNO Ric Flair
NNO Sting

1992 WCW Magazine Collector's Special 2

COMPLETE SET (9)

1 Sting
2 Sting
3 Sting
4 Sting
5 Sting
6 Sting
7 Sting
8 Sting
9 Sting

1992 WCW Magazine Collector's Special 2 Postcards

COMPLETE SET (4)

1 Sting
2 Sting
3 Sting
4 Sting

1993 WCW Magazine Collector's Special 3

COMPLETE SET (18)

10 Steve Austin
11 Johnny B. Badd
12 Cactus Jack
13 Shane Douglas
14 Van Hammer
15 Missy Hyatt
16 Jushin Liger
17 Madusa
18 Brian Pillman
19 Dustin Rhodes
20 Rick Rude
21 Ron Simmons
22 Ricky Steamboat
23 Sting
24 Big Van Vader
25 Erik Watts
26 Barry Windham
27 Tom Zenk

2000 WCW Magazine Limited Edition

COMPLETE SET (48)

1 Tank Abbott
2 The Artist
3 Mike Awesome
4 Buff Bagwell
5 Shawn Stasiak
6 Eric Bischoff
7 Booker T.
8 Johnny the Bull
9 Chris Candido
10 The Cat
11 Crowbar
12 Daffney
13 The Demon
14 Disqo
15 Shane Douglas
16 3 Count
17 Kronik
18 David Flair
19 Ric Flair
20 Goldberg
21 Lance Storm

22 Juventud Guerrera
23 Miss Hancock
24 Major Gunns
25 Rick Steiner
26 Bret Hart
27 Chuck Palumbo
28 Curt Hennig
29 Hulk Hogan
30 Jeff Jarrett
31 Midajah
32 Billy Kidman
33 Kimberly
38 Rey Mysterio Jr.
39 Kevin Nash
40 Diamond Dallas Page
41 Jindrak & O'Haire
44 Norman Smiley
45 Paisley
46 Scott Steiner
47 Stevie Ray
48 Sting
49 Terry Funk
50 Vampiro
51 Sid Vicious
52 Big Vito
53 The Wall
54 Torrie Wilson

2000 Wizards of the Coast WCW Nitro

COMPLETE SET (171)

1 450 Splash C
2 Angry Fans U
3 Arm Bar C
4 Arm Drag and Twist U
5 Arm Toss C
6 Aysa UR
7 Aysa at Work U
8 Backbreaker U
9 Backdrop U
10 Baseball Bat U
11 Bear Hug U
12 Belly-to-Belly Suplex C
13 Berlyn UR
14 Berlyn's Chain R
15 Berlyn's Old Friend R
16 Big Block U
17 Big Splash C
18 Billy Kidman UR
19 Block C
20 Body Slam C
21 Boot to the Head C
22 Bounce off the Ropes C
23 Bret Hart UR
24 Bret's Sharpshooter R
25 Bret's the Best there Is R
26 Buff Bagwell UR
27 Buff is the Stuff R
28 Buff's Blockbuster R
29 Buff's Fans R
30 Call for Help R
31 Camel Clutch U
32 Chae UR
33 Chaos in the Ring U
34 Choke Hold C
35 Choke Slam U
36 Chop C
37 Closed Fist C

38 Clothesline C
39 Come From Behind R
40 Continue the Hold U
41 Corner Chaos U
42 Crowd Chants "Goldberg" R
43 DDP Gets Help From Kimberly R
44 DDP's Diamond Cutter R
45 DDP's Rapid-Fire Punches R
46 DDT U
47 Desperate Block U
48 Desperate Dodge U
49 Diamond Dallas Page UR
50 Disco Inferno UR
51 Disco's Boogie Punch R
52 Disco, The Gamblin' Man R
53 Dive From the Top Rope U
54 Dodge C
55 Doug Dillinger R
56 Down But Not Out R
57 DQ R
58 Dropkick C
59 European Uppercut U
60 Extra Effort U
61 Eye Rake C
62 Face Punch U
63 Fans Boo the Other Wrestler U
64 Fans Want Action R
65 Fast Punch C
66 Figure-Four Leg-Lock U
67 Flying Body-Press C
68 Flying Dropkick from the Top Rope U
69 Flying Elbow from the Top Rope C
70 Flying Forearm C
71 Flying Headbutt U
72 Flying Knee-Drop U
73 Folding Chair C
74 Full Stop U
75 Garbage Can U
76 Goldberg UR
77 Goldberg's Jackhammer R
78 Goldberg's Spear R
79 Good Night, Everybody U
80 Gouging C
81 Gut Check U
82 Hair Pull C
83 Head Stomp C
84 Headlock C
85 Heckling Fans U
86 Help U
87 Hidden Weapon U
88 Instant Replay C
89 Irish Whip to the Corner C
90 Irish Whip to the Ropes U
91 Jeff Jarrett UR
92 Jeff's Guitar R
93 Jeff's Punch R
94 Jimmy Hart U
95 Jump from the Top Rope C
96 Keeping it Clean R
97 Kevin Nash UR
98 Kick C
99 Kidman Gets Help R
100 Kidman's Shooting-Star Press R
101 KidmanCam R
102 Larry Zybysko R
103 Late Nitro U
104 Loud Fans C
105 Low Blow C

106 Low Kick C
107 Making It Look Easy U
108 Mentor U
109 Missile Dropkick C
110 Mix in Some Nitro C
111 Moonsault C
112 Ms. Hancock Shows Off U
113 Nash's Elbow Smash R
114 Nash's Jackknife Power Bomb R
115 Nash's nWo Support R
116 Nitro F
117 Nitro Girls UR
118 Nitro Girls, Center Stage UR
119 No Holds Barred R
120 One On One R
121 Outside Interference R
122 Outta Here U
123 Payback C
124 Piledriver C
125 Pin U
126 Practiced Block C
127 Practiced Dodge C
128 Punch C
129 Quick Hit U
130 Resistance is Useless U
131 Reversal R
132 Reverse Somersault from the Top Rope U
133 Rey Mysterio Jr. UR
134 Rey's Too Fast to Catch R
135 Ringside Reinforcements R
136 Rope Burn U
137 Rowdy Roddy Piper Takes Charge C
138 Running Start C
139 Scott Hall UR
140 Scott's Abdominal Stretch R
141 Scott's Outsider's Edge R
142 Scott's Survey Time R
143 Second Wind U
144 Seeing Red? U
145 Sid Vicious UR
146 Sid's Choke Slam R
147 Sid's Rules R
148 Sleeper Hold C
149 Snap Suplex C
150 Spice UR
151 Spinning Kick C
152 Sting UR
153 Sting's Mask R
154 Sting's Scorpion Death-lock R
155 Stinger Splash R
156 Stopped Cold C
157 Strong Block U
158 Swinging Neckbreaker C
159 Table R
160 Taking One For a Friend R
161 The Artist C
162 The Total Package (TTP) UR
163 Thrust to the Throat C
164 Tongan Death-Grip C
165 Top-Rope Punch U
166 Torrie at Work R
167 TTP's Flex Posedown R
168 TTP's Torture Rack R
169 Tygress UR
170 Vertical Suplex U
171 You Can't Stop Me! U

2000 Wizards of the Coast WCW Nitro Hardcore Edition

1 Baby UR
2 Big Poppa Pump Scott Steiner UR
3 Brian Knobs UR
4 Cat, the commissioner UR
5 Chameleon UR
6 Chiquita UR
7 Date with a nitro girl UR
8 Hollywood Hogan UR
9 Norman Smiley UR
10 Paisley UR
11 Ric Flair UR
12 Starr UR
13 Syren UR
14 Tank Abbott UR
15 Terry Funk UR
16 Vampiro UR
17 4 percent body fat R
18 Berlyn's Neckbreaker R
19 Bret shows his true Allegiance R
20 Brian is the nasty boy R
21 Brian's boot camp training R
22 Disco, Manager of Champions R
23 Hogan's F.U.N.B. R
24 Hogan's leg drop R
25 Jealousy among the nitro girls R
26 Jeff, Charter Member of the New Blood R
27 Kevin Nash Joins the Millionaire's Club R
28 More new blood R
29 No-Nonsense Man R
30 Norman's Big Wiggle R
31 One for the Kidmancam R
32 Pretty Evil R
33 Rey's bronco-buster R
34 Ric is the dirtiest player in the game R
35 Ric's chop to the chest R
36 Ric's Figure Four Leg Lock R
37 Screamin' Norman R
38 Sid wins the world title R
39 Steiner Recliner R
40 Steiner, genetic freak R
41 Sting gains momentum R
42 Tank's Knockout Punch R
43 Terry is middle-aged and crazy R
44 Terry is the hardcore icon R
45 TTP's Elizabeth R
46 Vampiro turns on sting R
47 Vampiro's knee drop R
48 Vampiro's red liquid R
49 Years of Experience R
50 Always Bring an Extra weapon U
51 Always have a backup plan U
52 Announcer's Table U
53 Axe Handle outside of the Ring U
54 Backwards Low Blow U
55 Change of Momentum U
56 Clothesline over the Top Rope U
57 Crossface U
58 David flair joins vince russo U
59 Elizabeth steps in U
60 Flying Shoulder U
61 Front face-lock U
62 Get out of my Ring U
63 Giving the fans what they want U
64 Got Anything Left? U
65 Heave Onto the Concrete U
66 High-Impact Kick U

67 High Risk Body Press U
68 Hold and shove through the ropes U
69 Humiliating block U
70 It gets dangerous for the fans U
71 Lets take this outside U
72 Metal steps to the ring U
73 Punch in the Nose U
74 Shove out of the Ring U
75 Surprise guest referee U
76 Tackle over the ropes U
77 Throw ?em out U
78 Toss from the Turnbuckle U
79 Toss over the rope U
80 Two-Count U
81 We're Going Outside Again U
82 Wicked hair pull U
83 Bischoff on your Side C
84 Block and Hope for the Best C
85 Brass Knuckles C
86 Choke with the Camera Cord C
87 Down-on-the-mat-Punch C
88 Drag to the Post C
89 Eat the Railing C
90 Enjoy the Pain C
91 Fans Love Hardcore C
92 Fans Love Lucha-Libre Style C
93 Fans Love Old-Style Wrestling C
94 Flyin' High C
95 Flying Shoulder from the apron C
96 Head Slap C
97 Headfirst to the Concrete C
98 Human Shield C
99 Meet the Announcers Up Close C
100 Military Press-Drop C
101 One Ring Can't Contain these two C
102 Over-the-Rope Choke C
103 Savate Kick C
104 Shoulder Mounted Suplex C
105 Slam into the Railing C
106 Slammed by a Girl C
107 Snapmare C
108 Stick Check outside the ring C
109 Stunned C
110 Swinging DDT C
111 Take the Microphone C
112 Toss over the Railing C
113 Wearing 'em Down for the fans C
114 What a Display of Power for the fans C

1999 WCW 24K Gold Signature Series

COMPLETE SET (4)
NNO Goldberg
NNO Hollywood Hogan
NNO Kevin Nash
NNO Sting

1985 Wieser and Wieser All-Star Wrestling Postcards

NNO Andre the Giant
NNO Barry Windham
NNO Carlos Colon
NNO Chris Adams
NNO Dusty Rhodes
NNO The Fabulous Freebirds
NNO The Fabulous Ones
NNO Gorgeous Jimmy Garvin

NNO Greg Valentine
NNO Hulk Hogan
NNO Iron Sheik
NNO Jerry The King Lawler
NNO Jesse The Body Ventura
NNO Jimmy Valiant
NNO Junkyard Dog
NNO Kamala
NNO Kerry Von Erich
NNO Kevin Sullivan
NNO Kevin Von Erich
NNO Lou Albano
NNO Paul Orndorff
NNO Ric Flair
NNO Rick Martel
NNO Ricky Steamboat
NNO The Road Warriors
NNO The Rock & Roll Express
NNO Rowdy Roddy Piper
NNO Sergeant Slaughter
NNO Superfly Jimmy Snuka
NNO Terry Allen
NNO Tommy Rich
NNO Tony Atlas

2009 WK Promotions ETH Brimstone

COMPLETE SET (20)

1 Brimstone
2 Brimstone
3 Brimstone
4 Brimstone
5 Brimstone
6 Brimstone
7 Brimstone
8 Brimstone
9 Brimstone
10 Brimstone
11 Brimstone
12 Brimstone
13 Brimstone
14 Brimstone
15 Brimstone
16 Brimstone
17 Brimstone
18 Brimstone
19 Brimstone
20 Brimstone

1985 WMMC AWA Vending Prism Stickers

COMPLETE SET (15)

NNO Baron Von Raschke
NNO Gorgeous Jimmy Garvin & Precious
NNO High Flyers
NNO It's Not My Fault
("Gorgeous" Jimmy Garvin)
NNO Larry Zbyszko
NNO Legion of Doom
NNO Magnum TA
NNO Mr. Electricity
NNO Rick Martel
NNO The Road Warriors
NNO Sgt. Slaughter (American Flag)
NNO Sgt. Slaughter (tank)
NNO Steve Regal
NNO The Tonga Kid
NNO The Wild Samoans

1987 Wonderama NWA Wrestling Supercards

COMPLETE SET (51)

1 Ric Flair
2 Tommy Angel
3 Dusty Rhodes vs. Tully Blanchard
4 Baby Doll
5 Eddie Hotstuff Gilbert
6 Rocky King
7 Lex Luger vs. Arn Anderson
8 Mike Rotunda vs. Ivan Koloff
9 Barry Windham & Sting
10 Ron Simmons
11 Mighty Wilbur
12 Skandor Akbar
13 Precious
14 Shaska Whatley vs. Jimmy Valiant
15 Curtis Thompson
16 Kendall Windham
17 Sting
18 Paul Ellering
19 Johnny Ace
20 Kat Leroux & Linda Dallas
21 Michael P.S. Hayes
22 Terry Taylor
23 Barry Windham
24 Johnny Weaver vs. J.J. Dillion
25 Tully Blanchard
26 Dick Murdoch
27 Sweet Stan Lane
28 Barbarian & Paul Jones
29 Linda Dallas & Misty Blue
30 Road Warriors
31 Stan Lane vs Sean Royal
32 Ricky Santana
33 Jimmy Valiant
34 Larry Zbyszko vs Kendall Windham
35 Lex Luger
36 Shaska Whatley
37 Warlord
38 Beautiful Bobby Eaton
39 Dusty Rhodes
40 Paul Jones
41 Eddie Gilbert vs. Sting
42 Rowdy Roddy Piper
43 Barry Windham vs. Arn Anderson
44 Michael Hayes
45 Larry Stephens
46 Black Bart
47 Gladiator #2
48 Ric Flair vs. Sting
49 Ivan Koloff
CL Checklist
NNO Ric Flair Header

1988 Wonderama NWA

COMPLETE SET (343)	300.00	600.00
1 Ric Flair	75.00	150.00
2 Tommy Angel	.40	1.00
3 Dusty Rhodes/Tully Blanchard	2.50	6.00
4 Baby Doll	1.25	3.00
5 Eddie Gilbert	2.00	5.00
6 Rocky King	.75	2.00
7 Lex Luger/Arn Anderson	1.50	4.00
8 Mike Rotunda vs. Ivan Koloff	.60	1.50
9 Barry Windham/Sting	5.00	12.00
10 Ron Simmons	.20	3.00
11 Mighty Wilbur	.40	1.00
12 Skandor Akbar	.60	1.50
13 Precious	1.50	4.00
14 Shaska Whatley vs. Jimmy Valiant	.40	1.00
15 Curtis Thompson	.75	2.00
16 Kendall Windham	2.00	5.00
17 Sting	20.00	50.00
18 Paul Ellering	1.25	3.00
19 Johnny Ace	.75	2.00
20 Kat Leroux w/Linda Dallas	.75	2.00
21 Michael Hayes	1.00	2.50
22 Terry Taylor	.40	1.00
23 Barry Windham	2.50	6.00
24 Johnny Weaver vs. J.J. Dillon	.40	1.00
25 Tully Blanchard	1.00	2.50
26 Dick Murdoch	.75	2.00
27 Stan Lane	.75	2.00
28 Barbarian w/Paul Jones	.40	1.00
29 Linda Dallas w/Misty Blue	.75	2.00
30 Road Warriors	15.00	40.00
31 Stan Lane vs. Sean Royal	.50	1.25
32 Ricky Santana	.40	1.00
33 Jimmy Valiant	1.25	3.00
34 Larry Zbyszko vs. Kendall Windham	.75	2.00
35 Lex Luger	2.00	5.00
36 Shaska Whatley	.40	1.00
37 Warlord	.40	1.00
38 Bobby Eaton	2.00	5.00
39 Dusty Rhodes	2.50	6.00
40 Paul Jones	.40	1.00
41 Eddie Gilbert/Sting	2.00	5.00
42 Butch Miller	.40	1.00
43 Barry Windham/Arn Anderson	3.00	8.00
44 Michael Hayes	1.00	2.50
45 Larry Stephens	.40	1.00
46 Black Bart	.40	1.00
47 Gladiator #2	.40	.30
48 Ric Flair/Sting	3.00	8.00
49 Ivan Koloff	1.25	3.00
50 Jamie West	.40	1.00
51 Larry Zbyszko	.75	2.00
52 Sean Royal vs. Bobby Eaton	.40	1.00
53 Arn Anderson vs. Lex Luger	2.00	5.00
54 Baby Doll	.60	1.50
55 Tim Horner vs. Shaska Whatley	.40	1.00
56 Jimmy Garvin vs. Tully Blanchard	1.00	2.50
57 Kendall Windham vs. Gladiator	.40	1.00
58 Terry Taylor vs. Eddie Gilbert	.75	2.00
59 Dick Murdoch	.50	1.25
60 Stan Lane vs. Sean Royal	.40	.30
61 Magnum T.A.	.75	.75
62 Ricky Santana	.40	.30
63 Luke Williams	.40	.30
64 Robert Gibson	1.50	4.00
65 Ron Garvin	.40	1.00
66 Ivan Koloff	.50	.50
67 Larry Zbyszko vs. Kendall Windham	.50	.50
68a Butch Miller	1.25	3.00
68b Ric Flair logo	6.00	15.00
69 Ricky Morton	1.50	4.00
70 Tommy Angel	.40	1.00
71 Stan Lane vs. Sean Royal	.40	.30
72 Kendall Windham	.40	.30
73 Baby Doll	.50	.50
74a Black Bart		
74b Barry Windham logo	1.00	2.50
75 Road Warrior Hawk	1.50	4.00
76 Mike Rotunda	.60	1.50
77 Ron Simmons/Arn Anderson	1.00	2.50
78 J.J. Dillon	.40	1.00
79 Shaska Whatley vs. Jimmy Valiant	.60	1.50
80 Kat Leroux	.50	1.25
81 Kendall Windham vs. Larry Zbyszko	.50	1.25
82 Road Warrior Animal	2.00	5.00
83 D.Murdoch/Steve Williams	.50	1.25
84 Tully Blanchard	2.50	6.00
85 Barbarian	.75	2.00
86 Robert Gibson	1.25	3.00
87 Ricky Santana	.40	1.00
88 Jimmy Valiant	.60	1.50
89 Nikita Koloff/Ric Flair	4.00	10.00
90 Kat Leroux vs. Misty Blue	.50	1.25
91 Kevin Sullivan	6.00	15.00
92 Luke Williams	.40	1.00
93 Lex Luger/Arn Anderson	1.00	2.50
94 Big Bubba Rogers	1.25	3.00
95 Bobby Eaton	.60	1.50
96 Paul Jones	.40	1.00
97 Butch Miller	.40	.30
98 Jimmy Garvin w/Precious	1.25	3.00
99a Warlord vs. Sting	2.00	5.00
99b Dusty Rhodes logo	3.00	8.00
100 Ivan Koloff	.50	1.25
101 Larry Zbyszko	.50	.50
102 Sting	20.00	50.00
103 Larry Zbyszko/Baby Doll	.60	1.50
104 Eddie Gilbert/Sting	1.00	2.50
105 Dusty Rhodes	2.00	5.00
106 Mighty Wilbur	.40	1.00
107 Michael Hayes/Ric Flair	.60	1.50
108 Brad Armstrong w/Tom Horner	.40	.30
109 Terry Taylor	.40	.30
110 Dick Murdoch	.50	.50
111 Tully Blanchard	.75	2.00
112 Ricky Santana vs. Warlord	.40	1.00
113 Jimmy Valiant	1.25	3.00
114 Kevin Sullivan	.60	1.50
115 Paul Jones	.40	1.00
116 Lex Luger/Sting	8.00	20.00
117 Ivan Koloff	.50	1.25
118 Larry Zbyszko/Barry Windham	.50	.50
119 Italian Stallion	.40	.30
120 Dusty Rhodes	2.00	5.00
121 Tim Horner vs. Chris Champion	.40	1.00
122 Eddie Gilbert/Sting	1.50	4.00
123 Mighty Wilbur vs. Ivan Koloff	.50	1.25
124 Barry Windham	.50	.50
125 Dick Murdoch	.50	1.25
126 Lex Luger	3.00	8.00
127 Dusty Rhodes/Nikita Koloff	1.00	2.50
128 Barbarian/Warlord/Ivan Koloff	.50	1.25
129 Paul Jones	.40	.30
130 Arn Anderson/Barry Windham	.75	2.00
131 Ivan Koloff	.75	2.00
132 Baby Doll/Dusty Rhodes	1.50	4.00
133 Eddie Gilbert w/Terry Taylor	.60	1.50
134 Rocky King w/Kendall Windham	.40	1.00
135 Jimmy Garvin vs. Tully Blanchard	.75	2.00
136a Ricky Morton vs. Ric Flair	1.50	4.00
136b Lex Luger logo	1.50	4.00
137 Tim Horner vs. Gladiator	.40	1.00
138 Kendall Windham	.40	.30
139 Magnum T.A.	.75	.75
140 Terry Taylor	.40	.30
141 Dick Murdoch/Steve Williams	.60	.60
142 Barbarian	.40	.30

1995 WWF Magazine Trading Cards

COMPLETE SET (90)

64 H.O.G. (Henry Orpheus Godwinn)
65 WrestleMania (Andre vs Studd)
66 Harvey Wippleman
67 King Kong Bundy
68 The Grand Wizard
69 Bam Bam Bigelow
70 Jim Ross (Commentator)
71 Federation Blimp
72 Tatanka
73 King Mabel and Sir Mo
74 Survivor Series '94 (Casket Match-Yokozuna vs Undertaker)
75 Mr. Bob Backlund
76 Fatu
77 George The Animal Steele
78 Shawn Michaels
79 Gorilla Monsoon (Interim President)
80 Diesel vs Bob Backlund (Nov. 26th, 1996)
81 Isaac Yankem D.D.S.
82 Backlund Snaps! (Sep. 19th, 1994)
83 The Kid Comes into His Own! (May 17th, 1993)
84 Shawn Introduces The Psycho! (Feb. 20th 1995)
85 Sid Snaps as Blayze is Torched! (Apr.3rd 1995)
86 Monday Night Raw
87 Backlund to Run For President? (May 15th, 1995)
88 Razor Captures the Gold! (Oct. 11th, 1993)
89 Friends Reunite! (May 22nd, 1995)
90 Checklist 46-90

1996-98 WWF Magazine Trading Cards

COMPLETE SET (201)

1 Ahmed Johnson
2 SummerSlam '88 (Warrior vs Honky-Intercontinental Match)
3 Goldust
4 Dean Douglas
5 The Fabulous Moolah
6 Two Dudes With Attitudes (Michaels & Diesel)
7 Marty Jannetty
8 Bret Hitman Hart
9 Barry Horowitz
10 Hakushi
11 Royal Rumble '95 (HBK Wins Rumble)
12 Sunny of the Body Donnas
13 Smoking Gunns (Billy & Bart Gunn)
14 Ivan Putski
15 King King Bundy
16 Avatar
17 Rowdy Roddy Piper vs Bret Hart
18 Razor Ramon
19 Hunter Hearst-Helmsley
20 WrestleMania III (Roberts vs Honky Tonk Man)
21 Million Dollar Man
22 Undertaker
23 Ernie Ladd
24 1-2-3 Kid vs Sid
25 Henry Godwinn
26 Tornado Rips Through Perfect!
27 Brother Love
28 Battle Royal (WrestleMania II)
29 Junk Yard Dog vs King Harley Race (WrestleMania III)
30 Strike Force vs Demolition (WrestleMania IV)
31 Hart Foundation vs Honky & Valentine (WrestleMania V)
32 WrestleMania
33 The Rockers vs Orient Express (WrestleMania VI)

34 Roberts vs Martel (WrestleMania VII)
35 The Undertaker vs Roberts (WrestleMania VIII)
36 Bret Hart vs Yokozuna (WrestleMania X)
37 Undertaker Left for Dead!
38 Rebirth at Survivor Series
39 In Your Casket!
NNO The King of the Mountain!
NNO Another One Bites The Dust!
NNO The "Ultimate" Gorilla Press!
NNO A Rude Awakening!
NNO Look, Up in the Sky....
NNO A Caged Warrior!
NNO No Time For Sergeants!
NNO One Word: Icon!!!
NNO Raw Power Unleashed!
49 And the Winner Is... (Slammy Awards)
50 The Kid's Dream Comes True! (WrestleMania XII)
51 Good Friends...Better Enemies!
52 Ahmed Survives Series!!!
53 New Sensation!!!
54 One For the Record Books!!!
55 The Sycho BodyGuard!
56 Sid Snaps On Raw
57 Wild Card!
58 It's Vader Time!
59 Vader Vetos the President!
60 A Bomb Falls on the Heartbreak Kid
61 The First Reign of Excellence!
62 Bret Reclaims the Gold!
63 The Hit Man Takes Aim at Big Daddy!
64 Edged by Goldust!
65 Shattered Dreams at the Oscars!
66 The Curtain Falls on the Wildman!
67 The Stone Cold King!
68 Friends Like This...
69 Knocked "Stone Cold" By the Hit Man
70 Uncle Paul?!
71 That's What Friends Are For!
72 Mankind Gets "Stone Cold" Raw!
73 Hair Today...Gone Tomorrow!
74 Getting Down and Dirty!
75 Purebreed Champion!
76 Sable Finds Her "Wild" Man!
77 Debut of a Wild and Crazy Guy!
78 The King of Pain?
79 A Wild Ride to the Top!
80 Karate Fighting The King
81 Even Marc and Sable Have Their Bad Days
82 The Gentle Cat Becomes a Tigress?
83 Sable-The Queen of the Wild!
84 That "Wild Thing" He Does!!!
85 As the Harts Turn!
86 What Almost Was...
87 Upset!!!
88 The King of Harts!!!
89 Sorry, Mom!
90 Hart to Heart With Yokozuna!
91 A Hart-Breaking Day For Shawn!
92 Crime of the Century!
93 Keep It In the Family!
94 Davey Boy and The Dynamite Kid!
95 Davey's Way in the UK!
96 That's What Family is For!
97 The Bulldog Bites Diesel!
98 Beware of the Angry Dog!
99 When Harts are Thicker Than Water!
100 The European Champion!
101 Tempers Explode on Raw Is War!

102 The "New" Hart Foundation!
103 Friend or Foe?
104 Playing a "Beat" on Jarrett!
105 Taking the Plunge into WrestleMania XII!
106 Feeling the Bite of the Bulldog!
107 Sleeping Giant Wakes!
108 Polishing Off the Goldust!
109 The First Attack!
110 Revenge at the Rumble!
111 Everything and the Kitchen Sink!
112 What A Body...Donna!
113 The Greatest Ever?
114 Sunny Unleashes Some Gloom!
115 The Guiding Light!
116 Don't Touch the Goods!
117 The Coming Out!
118 Sable Snubs the Snob!
119 Splitsville?!
120 Karate Fightin' to the Top!
121 The "Loose Cannon" Takes Aim!
122 The Sophomore Jinx?
123 Living the American Dream!
124 Mrs. Foley's Little Boy!
125 The Stone Cold Kliq!
126 Get to Steppin'!!!
127 The Rise of a New Nation!
128 Hell on Wheels!
129 Kane is Alive!!!
130 A Change of Face!
131 The Dead Man Cometh!
132 The Dark Days Begin!
133 The First Fight!
134 My Brother...My Enemy?!
135 I Love You, Man...Not!!!
136 What Goes Around Comes Around!
137 The Third Time's The Charm!
138 The Rise of Austin 3:16?
139 Get to Steppin'
140 A Common Bond?
141 R-E-S-P-E-C-T
142 Hell on Wheels!
143 Equal Opportunity @#$ Kickers!
144 Built Titan Tough!
145 Hey...I Got My License!
146 An Unlikely Hand in Victory
147 You Want it? Come and Get It!
148 Boiler Room Brawl!
149 Match of the Year Candidate!
150 Paying Homage to His Idol!
151 OWWWW...Have Mercy!
152 The Groupies!
153 United They Stand, Divided they Fall
154 Choose Your Weapon!
155 The Man For the Job!
156 Snap, Cracle and Pop!
157 Studd Gets the Big Win!
158 Hulk and Warrior Collide!
159 Hogan Continues His Streak!
160 A Flair for the Gold!
161 Yoko Makes it Look Easy!
162 Two Winners?!
163 Shawn Shatters the Record!
164 Heartbreak for Diesel!
165 A Cold Day for the "Hit Man"!
166 Hell on Earth!
167 The Hardy Boys Get "Kaned"!
168 Flash Gets Funked Up!
169 Love Hurts!

170 Ahmed Takes the Plunge!
171 The Brawl in Montreal!
172 Bang your Heads-Literally!
173 Apocalypse Falls on Crush!
174 Taylor-Made for Destruction!
175 The Tradition Begins!
176 Over 93,000 Strong!
177 The Ultimate Challenge!
178 Stars and Stripes Forever!
179 A Savage Ending for Flair!
180 A Hart-Felt Revenge!
181 Heartbreak for Shawn!
182 Marathon Men!
183 The Dark Side Reigns!
184 The King of Pain!
185 A Texas Homecoming!
186 Give Up?! Hell, Nooo!
187 The Dawn of Dude!
188 One Tough S.O.B.!!
189 Austin 3:16 vs Owen 3:16
190 Mobile Whoop-@#$!
191 The Marked Man!
192 Who's the Baddest?
NNO Taking the Bite Out of the Dog!
NNO Payback for a Rocker!
NNO Royal in the Rumble!
NNO Climbing to New Heights!
NNO Third Time's A Charm!
NNO Royal Again!
NNO Revenge!
NNO Champion!
NNO Big Daddy Dead!

1996-98 WWF Magazine Trading Cards Oversized

All cards are 10 1/2 X 5 inches.
COMPLETE SET (10)

NNO The Undertaker
NNO Shawn Michaels
NNO Ahmed Johnson
NNO Sycho Sid
NNO Vader
NNO Bret Hart
NNO Goldust
NNO Steve Austin
NNO Mankind
NNO Hunter Hearst-Helmsley

2019-20 WWE Bray Wyatt Collector's Boxes

Box 1	Firefly Funhouse/500*	125.00	250.00
Box 2	Wyatt Gym/1000*	30.00	75.00
Box 3	Holidays with R.Rabbit	30.00	75.00
Box 4	Mercy the Buzzard		

1995 WWF/WCW Bravo Sport Magazine

COMPLETE SET (9)

NNO 123 Kid
NNO Alex Wright
NNO Bret Hart
NNO Diesel
NNO Hulk Hogan
NNO Razor Ramon
NNO Shawn Michaels
NNO Sting
NNO Undertaker

Action Figures & Figurines

2017 Bleacher Creatures WWE

NNO	AJ Styles	12.50	25.00
NNO	Bayley	12.50	25.00
NNO	Braun Strowman		
NNO	Finn Balor	7.50	15.00
NNO	Jeff Hardy		
NNO	Kevin Owens	12.50	25.00
NNO	Seth Rollins	10.00	20.00
NNO	Shinsuke Nakamura		
NNO	Stone Cold Steve Austin		

2013-18 Bleacher Creatures WWE Shop Exclusives

NNO	Hulk Hogan		
NNO	John Cena		
NNO	Roman Reigns		
NNO	Ultimate Warrior		

2013 Bleacher Creatures WWE Series 1

NNO	CM Punk		
NNO	Daniel Bryan		
NNO	John Cena		
NNO	Kane		
NNO	Ryback		
NNO	Sheamus		

2013 Bleacher Creatures WWE Series 2

NNO	CM Punk		
NNO	John Cena		
NNO	Randy Orton		

2014 Bleacher Creatures WWE WrestleMania 30

NNO	New Orleans Bear		

2010 Burger King WWEKids.com Plush 6-Inch

NNO	John Cena		
NNO	Triple H		
NNO	Undertaker		

2015 Funko Mystery Minis WWE Series 1

COMPLETE SET (15)		55.00	110.00
UNOPENED CASE (12 BOXES)			
UNOPENED BOX (1 MINI)			
NNO	Andre the Giant	3.00	6.00
NNO	Brie Bella	3.00	6.00
NNO	Daniel Bryan	3.00	6.00
NNO	George The Animal Steele	6.00	12.00
NNO	Hacksaw Jim Duggan WM	10.00	20.00
NNO	Hulk Hogan	12.50	25.00
NNO	Iron Sheik	6.00	12.00
NNO	John Cena	3.00	6.00
NNO	Nikki Bella	4.00	8.00
NNO	Randy Savage WM	12.50	25.00
NNO	Ric Flair	12.50	25.00
NNO	Rock	7.50	15.00
NNO	Rowdy Roddy Piper WM	15.00	30.00
NNO	Ultimate Warrior	6.00	12.00
NNO	Undertaker	4.00	8.00

2016 Funko Mystery Minis WWE Series 2

COMPLETE SET (15)		50.00	100.00
UNOPENED CASE (12 BOXES)			
UNOPENED BOX (1 MINI)			
NNO	Bret Hitman Hart	3.00	6.00
NNO	Brock Lesnar	4.00	8.00
NNO	Dusty Rhodes	3.00	6.00
NNO	Goldust	3.00	6.00

(continued)

NNO	Jake The Snake Roberts TAR	20.00	40.00
NNO	John Cena	4.00	8.00
NNO	Kevin Nash	3.00	6.00
NNO	Million Dollar Man Ted Dibiase	3.00	6.00
NNO	Randy Orton	3.00	6.00
NNO	Razor Ramon TAR	15.00	30.00
NNO	Roman Reigns	3.00	6.00
NNO	Seth Rollins	3.00	6.00
NNO	Sgt. Slaughter TAR	10.00	20.00
NNO	Sting	3.00	6.00
NNO	Stone Cold Steve Austin	6.00	12.00

2017 Funko Pint Size Heroes WWE

COMPLETE SET (19)		75.00	150.00
NNO	Andre the Giant	10.00	20.00
NNO	Big E	4.00	8.00
NNO	Bray Wyatt	4.00	8.00
NNO	Brock Lesnar	3.00	6.00
NNO	Enzo Amore	5.00	10.00
NNO	Finn Balor TRU	10.00	20.00
NNO	John Cena	3.00	6.00
NNO	Kevin Owens	4.00	8.00
NNO	Kofi Kingston	5.00	10.00
NNO	Macho Man Randy Savage	15.00	30.00
NNO	Nikki Bella	4.00	8.00
NNO	Ric Flair TRU	7.50	15.00
NNO	Roman Reigns	4.00	8.00
NNO	Sasha Banks	4.00	8.00
NNO	Seth Rollins	3.00	6.00
NNO	Stone Cold Steve Austin TRU	10.00	20.00
NNO	Ultimate Warrior	7.50	15.00
NNO	Undertaker	4.00	8.00
NNO	Xavier Woods	3.00	6.00

2011-20 Funko Pop Vinyl Freddy Funko

COMMON FUNKO POP		12.50	25.00
34A	Hulk Hogan/500* FD	500.00	1000.00
34B	Hulk Hogan Injured /500* FD	500.00	1000.00
52	Sting/500* FD	500.00	750.00

2015-19 Funko Pop Vinyl Pocket Pop Keychains WWE

NNO	Hulk Hogan	7.50	15.00
NNO	John Cena V	7.50	15.00
NNO	John Cena WM DVD	6.00	12.00
NNO	Macho Man WM DVD	6.00	12.00
NNO	The Rock WM DVD	6.00	12.00
NNO	Sting WM DVD	5.00	10.00
NNO	Ultimate Warrior WM DVD	7.50	15.00
NNO	Undertaker WM DVD	10.00	20.00

2011-20 Funko Pop Vinyl WWE

1A	John Cena	12.50	25.00
1B	J.Cena Black Pants WWE.com	200.00	350.00
1C	J.Cena Green-Orange	12.50	25.00
1D	J.Cena Green Hat WWE.com	500.00	1000.00
2A	CM Punk V	75.00	150.00
2B	CM Punk Pink Trunks HT	250.00	500.00
3	The Rock V	30.00	75.00
4	Sheamus V	50.00	100.00
5A	Stone Cold Steve Austin V	30.00	75.00
5B	SC Steve Austin 2K16 GS	25.00	50.00
6A	Rey Mysterio V	150.00	300.00
6B	R.Mysterio Bright Blue 7-11	250.00	500.00
6C	Rey Mysterio Dark SDCC	400.00	800.00
7A	Daniel Bryan V	30.00	60.00

(continued)

7B	Daniel Bryan Red Trunks HT/UT	30.00	60.00
7C	Daniel Bryan Patterned WWE.com	200.00	350.00
8	Undertaker	50.00	100.00
9	Triple H V	25.00	50.00
10A	Macho Man Randy Savage V	25.00	50.00
10B	Savage Pink WWE.com	500.00	1000.00
10C	Macho Man Randy Savage Purple FYE	30.00	75.00
11A	Hulk Hogan	25.00	50.00
11B	Hogan Hulk Rules WWE.com	375.00	750.00
11C	Hollywood Hogan WWE 2K15	100.00	200.00
12	AJ Lee WWE.com	250.00	500.00
13	Brock Lesnar WM	25.00	50.00
14	Brie Bella	12.50	25.00
15	Nikki Bella	12.50	25.00
16	Paige V	30.00	75.00
17	Ric Flair TAR	20.00	40.00
18	Roddy Piper TAR	25.00	50.00
19A	Sting	30.00	75.00
19B	Wolfpac Sting GS	60.00	120.00
20	Ultimate Warrior	30.00	60.00
21	Andre the Giant	12.50	25.00
23	Roman Reigns	50.00	100.00
24A	Seth Rollins V	25.00	50.00
24B	Seth Rollins White Attire FYE	12.50	30.00
25	Bret Hart	20.00	40.00
26	Eva Marie	5.00	10.00
27	Kevin Owens V	10.00	20.00
28	Bray Wyatt V	20.00	40.00
29	Big E	7.50	15.00
30	Xavier Woods	5.00	10.00
31	Kofi Kingston	7.50	15.00
32	Shawn Michaels WG	6.00	12.00
33	Kane WG	20.00	40.00
34A	Finn Balor	7.50	15.00
34B	Finn Balor Demon Mask CH	50.00	100.00
35	Mick Foley	25.00	50.00
36	Goldberg	15.00	30.00
37	AJ Styles	25.00	50.00
38	The Demon Finn Balor FYE	25.00	50.00
39	Bayley TRU	25.00	50.00
40A	Chris Jericho Red	12.50	25.00
40B	Chris Jericho Blue FYE	12.50	25.00
41A	Million Dollar Man Black	7.50	15.00
41B	Million Dollar Man White CH	17.50	35.00
42	Sasha Banks	20.00	40.00
43A	Iron Sheik White	5.00	10.00
43B	Iron Sheik Red CH	17.50	35.00
44A	Zack Ryder NYCC	7.50	15.00
44B	Zack Ryder FCE	6.00	12.00
44C	Zack Ryder Green Tights/500* FHQ	400.00	600.00
45	Shinsuke Nakamura TRU	30.00	60.00
46A	The Rock	12.50	25.00
46B	The Rock Black Jacket CH	25.00	50.00
46C	The Rock Gold NYCC/TAR	25.00	50.00
46D	The Rock Gold TAR	12.50	25.00
47A	Razor Ramon	12.50	25.00
47B	Razor Ramon nWo Trunks CH	60.00	120.00
48	Braun Strowman	6.00	12.00
49	Alexa Bliss	30.00	60.00
50	Shawn Michaels	7.50	15.00
51A	Jake The Snake Robers Green	7.50	15.00
51B	Jake The Snake Roberts Blue CH	17.50	35.00
52A	Triple H	5.00	10.00
52B	Triple H Masked CH	30.00	75.00
53A	Vince McMahon	5.00	10.00

53B	Vince McMahon Pink Jacket CH	15.00	30.00
54	Sgt. Slaughter	12.50	25.00
55	Kurt Angle	6.00	12.00
56A	Asuka SDCC	30.00	75.00
56B	Asuka SCE	12.50	25.00
56C	Asuka w/Mask WM	30.00	60.00
56D	Asuka w/Mask TAR	15.00	30.00
57	Ric Flair Classic 2K19	75.00	150.00
58	Ronda Rousey	6.00	12.00
59	John Cena Clear AMZ	15.00	30.00
60	Randy Orton	12.50	25.00
61	Batista	7.50	15.00
62A	Charlotte Flair	20.00	40.00
62B	Charlotte Flair Blue Robe FL	10.00	20.00
63	Ric Flair Red Robe	10.00	20.00
64	Andre the Giant 6" WM	12.50	25.00
65	Becky Lynch	6.00	12.00
66	Trish Stratus	7.50	15.00
67	Elias	6.00	12.00
68	Bret Hit Man Hart Pink	6.00	12.00
69A	Undertaker Hooded	12.50	25.00
69B	Undertaker Hooded Purple Translucent AMZ	15.00	30.00
70	Becky Lynch The Man AMZ	15.00	30.00
71	Hulk Hogan Python Power WM	15.00	30.00
72	The Miz	6.00	12.00
73	Mean Gene Okerlund	7.50	15.00
74A	Diesel	5.00	10.00
74B	Kevin Nash CH	30.00	75.00
75A	Naomi	6.00	12.00
75B	Naomi GITD CH	15.00	30.00
76	John Cena Thuganomics	6.00	12.00
77	The Fiend Bray Wyatt AMZ	25.00	50.00
78	The Rock w/Microphone	10.00	20.00
79	Macho Man Randy Savage DC GS	12.50	25.00
80	Mr. T	6.00	12.00
81	Undertaker ABA AMZ	12.50	25.00
82	Ric Flair '92 Royal Rumble GS		
83	Macho Man Randy Savage Checkered Glasses GS		

1991 Galoob WCW Superstars 14-Inch

NNO	Lex Luger	50.00	100.00
NNO	Ric Flair	60.00	120.00
NNO	Sid Vicious	50.00	100.00
NNO	Sting	100.00	200.00

1991 Galoob WCW Superstars 14-Inch (loose)

NNO	Lex Luger	20.00	40.00
NNO	Ric Flair	30.00	75.00
NNO	Sid Vicious	30.00	75.00
NNO	Sting	30.00	60.00

1991 Galoob WCW Superstars Accessories

NNO	12-Figure Collector's Case	30.00	75.00
NNO	Championship Belt	75.00	150.00
NNO	Slam Action Wrestling Arena	125.00	250.00

1991 Galoob WCW Superstars Series 1

NNO	Arn Anderson	30.00	60.00
NNO	Barry Windham	25.00	50.00
NNO	Brian Pillman	30.00	60.00
NNO	Butch Reed	20.00	40.00
NNO	Lex Luger	15.00	30.00
NNO	Ric Flair	50.00	90.00
NNO	Rick Steiner	20.00	40.00
NNO	Ron Simmons	20.00	40.00
NNO	Scott Steiner	20.00	40.00
NNO	Sid Vicious	30.00	60.00
NNO	Sting/Blue Tights	30.00	60.00
NNO	Sting/Orange Tights	150.00	300.00
NNO	Tom Zenk	20.00	40.00

1991 Galoob WCW Superstars Series 1 (loose)

NNO	Arn Anderson	7.50	15.00
NNO	Barry Windham	7.50	15.00
NNO	Brian Pillman	7.50	15.00
NNO	Butch Reed	10.00	20.00
NNO	Lex Luger	7.50	15.00
NNO	Ric Flair	10.00	20.00
NNO	Rick Steiner	7.50	15.00
NNO	Ron Simmons	7.50	15.00
NNO	Scott Steiner	7.50	15.00
NNO	Sid Vicious	10.00	20.00
NNO	Sting/Blue Tights	12.50	25.00
NNO	Sting/Orange Tights	25.00	50.00
NNO	Tom Zenk	6.00	12.00

1991 Galoob WCW Superstars Series 2

NNO	Arn Anderson/Red Trunks	125.00	250.00
NNO	Barry Windham/Blue Trunks	125.00	250.00
NNO	Brian Pillman/Lt Blue Trunks	100.00	200.00
NNO	Lex Luger/Green Trunks	125.00	250.00
NNO	Ric Flair/Red Trunks	150.00	300.00
NNO	Rick Steiner/Green Tights	100.00	200.00
NNO	Ron Simmons/Blue Tights	25.00	50.00
NNO	Scott Steiner/ Red & Blue Tights	125.00	250.00
NNO	Sid Vicious/Pink Tights	100.00	200.00
NNO	Sting/Black Tights	150.00	300.00

1991 Galoob WCW Superstars Series 2 (loose)

NNO	Arn Anderson/Red Trunks	15.00	30.00
NNO	Barry Windham/Blue Trunks	12.50	25.00
NNO	Brian Pillman/Lt Blue Trunks	25.00	50.00
NNO	Lex Luger/Green Trunks	20.00	40.00
NNO	Ric Flair/Red Trunks	15.00	30.00
NNO	Rick Steiner/Green Tights	15.00	30.00
NNO	Ron Simmons/Blue Tights	20.00	40.00
NNO	Scott Steiner/ Red & Blue Tights	25.00	50.00
NNO	Sid Vicious/Pink Tights	20.00	40.00
NNO	Sting/Black Tights	20.00	40.00

1991 Galoob WCW Superstars UK

NNO	Big Josh	500.00	1000.00
NNO	Dustin Rhodes	100.00	200.00
NNO	El Gigante	150.00	300.00
NNO	Jimmy Garvin	150.00	300.00
NNO	Lex Luger/Robe		
NNO	Michael Hayes	200.00	350.00
NNO	Sting/Robe	250.00	400.00

1991 Galoob WCW Superstars UK (loose)

NNO	Big Josh	150.00	300.00
NNO	Dustin Rhodes	75.00	150.00
NNO	El Gigante	30.00	75.00
NNO	Jimmy Garvin	20.00	40.00
NNO	Lex Luger/Robe	75.00	150.00
NNO	Michael Hayes	20.00	40.00
NNO	Sting/Robe	60.00	120.00

1991 Galoob WCW Tag Team Superstars UK

NNO	Lex Luger/Sting		
NNO	Michael Haynes/Jimmy Garvin		
NNO	Ric Flair/Arn Anderson		
NNO	Rick & Scott Steiner		

1990 Galoob WCW Tag Team Superstars US

NNO	Lex Luger/Sting	75.00	150.00
NNO	Ric Flair/Arn Anderson	75.00	150.00
NNO	Rick & Scott Steiner	60.00	120.00
NNO	Ron Simmons/Butch Reed	100.00	200.00

1990 Hasbro WWF Series 1

NNO	Akeem	200.00	350.00
NNO	Andre the Giant	150.00	300.00
NNO	Ax	125.00	250.00
NNO	Big Boss Man	75.00	150.00
NNO	Brutus The Barber Beefcake	60.00	120.00
NNO	Hulk Hogan	150.00	300.00
NNO	Jake The Snake Roberts	100.00	200.00
NNO	Macho Man Randy Savage	300.00	600.00
NNO	Million Dollar Man Ted DiBiase	125.00	250.00
NNO	Ravishing Rick Rude	125.00	250.00
NNO	Smash	60.00	120.00
NNO	Ultimate Warrior	200.00	350.00

1990 Hasbro WWF Series 1 (loose)

NNO	Akeem	10.00	20.00
NNO	Andre the Giant	25.00	50.00
NNO	Ax	12.50	25.00
NNO	Big Boss Man	10.00	20.00
NNO	Brutus The Barber Beefcake	12.50	25.00
NNO	Hulk Hogan	15.00	30.00
NNO	Jake The Snake Roberts	12.50	25.00
NNO	Macho Man Randy Savage	20.00	40.00
NNO	Million Dollar Man Ted DiBiase	10.00	20.00
NNO	Ravishing Rick Rude	7.50	15.00
NNO	Smash	7.50	15.00
NNO	Ultimate Warrior	10.00	20.00

1991 Hasbro WWF Series 2

NNO	Dusty Rhodes	600.00	1000.00
NNO	Hacksaw Jim Duggan	75.00	150.00
NNO	Honky Tonk Man	60.00	120.00
NNO	Hulk Hogan	75.00	150.00
NNO	Macho King	150.00	300.00
NNO	Million Dollar Man	75.00	150.00
NNO	Rowdy Roddy Piper	75.00	150.00
NNO	Superfly Jim Snuka	60.00	120.00
NNO	Ultimate Warrior	125.00	250.00

1991 Hasbro WWF Series 2 (loose)

NNO	Dusty Rhodes	50.00	100.00
NNO	Hacksaw Jim Duggan	10.00	20.00
NNO	Honky Tonk Man	15.00	30.00
NNO	Hulk Hogan	12.50	25.00
NNO	Macho King	25.00	50.00
NNO	Million Dollar Man	7.50	15.00
NNO	Rowdy Roddy Piper	7.50	15.00
NNO	Superfly Jim Snuka	7.50	15.00
NNO	Ultimate Warrior	15.00	30.00

1991 Hasbro WWF Series 2 Tag Teams

NNO	The Bushwhackers	60.00	120.00
NNO	Demolition	150.00	300.00
NNO	The Rockers	60.00	120.00

1991 Hasbro WWF Series 2 Tag Teams (loose)

NNO	Butch	12.50	25.00
NNO	Crush	10.00	20.00
NNO	Luke	12.50	25.00
NNO	Marty Janetty	10.00	20.00
NNO	Shawn Michaels	10.00	20.00
NNO	Smash	10.00	20.00

1992 Hasbro WWF Series 3

NNO	Big Boss Man	60.00	120.00
NNO	Brutus Beefcake/Zebra Tights	200.00	400.00
NNO	Earthquake	75.00	150.00
NNO	Greg The Hammer Valentine	50.00	100.00
NNO	Hulk Hogan	100.00	200.00
NNO	Koko B. Ware	75.00	150.00
NNO	Macho Man Randy Savage	90.00	175.00
NNO	Mr. Perfect	60.00	120.00
NNO	Sgt. Slaughter	60.00	120.00
NNO	Texas Tornado	60.00	120.00
NNO	Typhoon	50.00	100.00
NNO	Ultimate Warrior	125.00	250.00

1992 Hasbro WWF Series 3 (loose)

NNO	Big Boss Man	10.00	20.00
NNO	Brutus The Barber Beefcake	30.00	60.00
NNO	Earthquake	12.50	25.00
NNO	Greg The Hammer Valentine	10.00	20.00
NNO	Hulk Hogan	15.00	30.00
NNO	Koko B. Ware	15.00	30.00
NNO	Macho Man Randy Savage	10.00	20.00
NNO	Mr. Perfect	15.00	30.00
NNO	Sgt. Slaughter	15.00	30.00
NNO	Texas Tornado	12.50	25.00
NNO	Typhoon	10.00	20.00
NNO	Ultimate Warrior	25.00	50.00

1992 Hasbro WWF Series 3 Tag Teams

NNO	Legion of Doom	125.00	250.00
NNO	Nasty Boys	125.00	250.00

1992 Hasbro WWF Series 3 Tag Teams (loose)

NNO	Animal	20.00	40.00
NNO	Hawk	20.00	40.00
NNO	Knobbs	10.00	20.00
NNO	Sags	10.00	20.00

1992 Hasbro WWF Series 4

NNO	Bret Hart	200.00	350.00
NNO	British Bulldog	75.00	150.00
NNO	Ricky The Dragon Steamboat	50.00	100.00
NNO	Undertaker	75.00	150.00

1992 Hasbro WWF Series 4 (loose)

NNO	Bret Hart	20.00	40.00
NNO	British Bulldog	12.50	25.00
NNO	Ricky The Dragon Steamboat	12.50	25.00
NNO	Undertaker	20.00	40.00

1993 Hasbro WWF Series 5

NNO	Hulk Hogan	75.00	150.00
NNO	IRS	50.00	100.00
NNO	Jim Neidhart	60.00	120.00
NNO	Macho Man	100.00	200.00
NNO	Mountie	50.00	100.00
NNO	Rick Martel	50.00	100.00
NNO	Sid Justice	60.00	120.00
NNO	Skinner	50.00	100.00
NNO	Virgil	30.00	75.00
NNO	Warlord	60.00	120.00

1993 Hasbro WWF Series 5 (loose)

NNO	Hulk Hogan	12.50	25.00
NNO	IRS	10.00	20.00
NNO	Jim Neidhart	10.00	20.00
NNO	Macho Man	20.00	40.00
NNO	Mountie	20.00	40.00
NNO	Rick Martel	12.50	25.00
NNO	Sid Justice	12.50	25.00
NNO	Skinner	12.50	25.00
NNO	Virgil	10.00	20.00
NNO	Warlord	15.00	30.00

1993 Hasbro WWF Series 6

NNO	Berzerker	75.00	150.00
NNO	El Matador	30.00	75.00
NNO	Papa Shango	75.00	150.00
NNO	Repo Man	60.00	120.00
NNO	Ric Flair	125.00	250.00
NNO	Tatanka	50.00	100.00

1993 Hasbro WWF Series 6 (loose)

NNO	Berzerker	20.00	40.00
NNO	El Matador	12.50	25.00
NNO	Papa Shango	15.00	30.00
NNO	Repo Man	12.50	25.00
NNO	Ric Flair	15.00	30.00
NNO	Tatanka	10.00	20.00

1993 Hasbro WWF Series 7

NNO	Crush	75.00	150.00
NNO	Kamala/Star on Belly	100.00	200.00
NNO	Kamala/Crescent Moon Belly	4000.00	8000.00
NNO	Nailz	125.00	250.00
NNO	Owen Hart	150.00	300.00
NNO	Razor Ramon	75.00	150.00
NNO	Shawn Michaels	75.00	150.00

1993 Hasbro WWF Series 7 (loose)

NNO	Crush	15.00	30.00
NNO	Kamala/Star on Belly	20.00	40.00
NNO	Kamala/Crescent Moon Belly	750.00	1500.00
NNO	Nailz	25.00	50.00
NNO	Owen Hart	25.00	50.00
NNO	Razor Ramon	25.00	50.00
NNO	Shawn Michaels	25.00	50.00

1993 Hasbro WWF Series 8

NNO	Bam Bam Bigelow	125.00	250.00
NNO	Bret Hart	200.00	400.00
NNO	Lex Luger	75.00	150.00
NNO	Mr. Perfect	100.00	200.00
NNO	Undertaker	250.00	500.00
NNO	Yokozuna	100.00	200.00

1993 Hasbro WWF Series 8 (loose)

NNO	Bam Bam Bigelow	25.00	50.00
NNO	Bret Hart	30.00	75.00
NNO	Lex Luger	15.00	30.00
NNO	Mr. Perfect	15.00	30.00
NNO	Undertaker	60.00	120.00
NNO	Yokozuna	30.00	75.00

1993 Hasbro WWF Series 9

NNO	Doink the Clown	100.00	200.00
NNO	Hacksaw Jim Duggan	100.00	200.00
NNO	Million Dollar Man	75.00	150.00
NNO	Rick Steiner	60.00	120.00
NNO	Scott Steiner	50.00	100.00
NNO	Tatanka	60.00	120.00

1993 Hasbro WWF Series 9 (loose)

NNO	Doink the Clown	25.00	50.00
NNO	Hacksaw Jim Duggan	30.00	75.00
NNO	Million Dollar Man	20.00	40.00
NNO	Rick Steiner	20.00	40.00
NNO	Scott Steiner	15.00	30.00

1993 Hasbro WWF Series 10

NNO	Butch	50.00	100.00
NNO	Fatu	50.00	100.00
NNO	Giant Gonzalez	60.00	120.00
NNO	Luke	50.00	100.00
NNO	Marty Jannetty	30.00	75.00
NNO	Razor Ramon/Purple Shorts	125.00	250.00
NNO	Razor Ramon/Red Shorts	150.00	300.00
NNO	Samu	30.00	75.00
NNO	Shawn Michaels/Black Tights	200.00	400.00
NNO	Shawn Michaels/White Tights	150.00	300.00

1993 Hasbro WWF Series 10 (loose)

NNO	Butch	15.00	30.00
NNO	Fatu	10.00	20.00
NNO	Giant Gonzalez	12.50	25.00
NNO	Luke	15.00	30.00
NNO	Marty Jannetty	15.00	30.00
NNO	Razor Ramon/Purple Shorts	50.00	100.00
NNO	Razor Ramon/Red Shorts	15.00	30.00
NNO	Samu	10.00	20.00
NNO	Shawn Michaels/Black Tights	50.00	100.00
NNO	Shawn Michaels/White Tights	10.00	20.00

1994 Hasbro WWF Series 11

NNO	1-2-3 Kid	500.00	1000.00
NNO	Adam Bomb	125.00	250.00
NNO	Bart Gunn	150.00	300.00
NNO	Billy Gunn	150.00	300.00
NNO	Crush	300.00	600.00
NNO	Ludvig Borga	150.00	300.00
NNO	Yokozuna	300.00	600.00

1994 Hasbro WWF Series 11 (loose)

NNO	1-2-3 Kid	200.00	400.00
NNO	Adam Bomb	100.00	200.00
NNO	Bart Gunn	100.00	200.00
NNO	Billy Gunn	125.00	250.00
NNO	Crush	125.00	250.00
NNO	Ludvig Borga	75.00	150.00
NNO	Yokozuna	75.00	150.00

1993 Hasbro WWF Magazine Series

NNO	Bret Hart	600.00	1200.00
NNO	Hulk Hogan	600.00	1200.00
NNO	Undertaker	1500.00	2500.00

1993 Hasbro WWF Magazine Series (loose)

NNO	Bret Hart	50.00	100.00
NNO	Hulk Hogan	400.00	800.00
NNO	Undertaker	1000.00	1500.00

1992 Hasbro WWF Mini Wrestlers

NNO	Brutus Beefcake/Butch/Luke/Greg Valentine	30.00	75.00
NNO	Mr. Perfect/Jim Duggan/Roddy Piper/Texas Tornado	30.00	75.00
NNO	Typhoon/Earthquake/Animal/Hawk	25.00	60.00

1992 Hasbro WWF Mini Wrestlers Playset

NNO	Royal Rumble Wrestling Ring (w/Hogan/Slaughter/Roberts/DiBiase/Boss Man/Savage	

1992 Hasbro WWF Mini Wrestlers Playset Figures (loose)

NNO	Big Boss Man	10.00	20.00
NNO	Hulk Hogan	20.00	40.00
NNO	Jake The Snake Roberts	15.00	30.00
NNO	Macho Man Randy Savage	20.00	40.00
NNO	Million Dollar Man Ted DiBiase	10.00	20.00
NNO	Sgt. Slaughter	20.00	40.00

2019 HeroClix WWE Series 1 Mixed Match Challenge

107	Charlotte Flair
108	Sasha Banks
109	Finn Balor
110	AJ Styles
111	WWE Ring

2019 HeroClix WWE Series 1 Mixed Match Challenge Maps

M001	WWE Backstage Area
M001	WWE Arena

2019 HeroClix WWE Series 1 Rock 'N Sock Starter Set

101	The Rock
102	Mankind
103	Stone Cold Steve Austin
104	Triple H
105	Ric Flair
106	Shawn Michaels

2019 HeroClix WWE Series 1 Rock 'N Sock Starter Set Maps

M001	WWE Training Center
M002	WWE War Games

2017 Jada Toys WWE Metalfigs 2.5-Inch

M228	John Cena
M229	Brock Lesnar
M230	Triple H
M231	Finn Balor
M232	Paige
M243	Sasha Banks

2017 Jada Toys WWE Metalfigs 4-Inch

M200	Finn Balor
M202	Paige
M203	Brock Lesnar
M205	John Cena
M206	Sami Zayn
M207	Sasha Banks
M210	Seth Rollins
M211	The Rock
M212	Charlotte Flair
M213	Kevin Owens
M218	AJ Styles
M220	The Rock
M242	John Cena
M275	Finn Balor

2017 Jada Toys WWE Metalfigs 6-Inch

M209	Triple H

2017 Jada Toys WWE Nano Metalfigs

W1	John Cena
W2	Triple H

W3 The Rock
W4 Roman Reigns
W5 Charlotte Flair
W6 Bayley
W7 Sami Zayn
W8 Chris Jericho
W9 Dean Ambrose
W10 Macho Man Randy Savage
W11 Sting
W12 Undertaker
W13 AJ Styles
W14 Kevin Owens
W15 Seth Rollins
W16 Finn Balor
W17 Sasha Banks
W18 Brock Lesnar
W19 Becky Lynch
W20 Kalisto
W21 Bray Wyatt
W22 Nikki Bella
W23 Ultimate Warrior
W24 Rowdy Roddy Piper

2017 Jada Toys WWE Nano Metalfigs 20-Pack

NNO Cena/Triple H/Rock/Reigns/Charlotte
Bayley/Zayn/Jericho/Ambrose/Savage/Sting/Undertaker/Styles/Owens/Rollins/Balor/Banks/Lesnar/Kalisto/Wyatt/(2017 Toys R Us Exclusive)

2007-08 Jakks Pacific ECW Wrestling Series 1

NNO CM Punk	20.00	40.00
NNO Kevin Thorn	25.00	50.00
NNO Rob Van Dam	15.00	30.00
NNO Sandman	25.00	50.00
NNO Tommy Dreamer	25.00	50.00

2007-08 Jakks Pacific ECW Wrestling Series 2

NNO Ariel	15.00	30.00
NNO Balls Mahoney	12.50	25.00
NNO Elijah Burke	25.00	50.00
NNO Joey Styles	20.00	40.00
NNO Kelly Kelly	25.00	50.00
NNO Mike Knox	15.00	30.00

2007-08 Jakks Pacific ECW Wrestling Series 3

NNO Layla	12.50	25.00
NNO Marcus Cor Von		
NNO Matt Striker	7.50	15.00
NNO Nunzio	6.00	12.00
NNO Snitsky		
NNO Stevie Richards		
NNO Tazz		

2007-08 Jakks Pacific ECW Wrestling Series 4

NNO Boogeyman		
NNO CM Punk	7.50	15.00
NNO Elijah Burke	15.00	30.00
NNO John Morrison	10.00	20.00
NNO Matt Striker		
NNO Tommy Dreamer		

2007-08 Jakks Pacific ECW Wrestling Series 5

NNO Christian	12.50	25.00
NNO Evan Bourne		
NNO Fit Finlay	12.50	25.00
NNO Jack Swagger		
NNO Mark Henry		
NNO Tyson Kidd	6.00	12.00

2010 Jakks Pacific TNA Wrestling Cross the Line Series 1

NNO James Storm/Bobby Roode	30.00	75.00
NNO Samoa Joe/Mick Foley	30.00	60.00
NNO Scott Steiner/Kevin Nash	25.00	50.00

2010 Jakks Pacific TNA Wrestling Cross the Line Series 2

NNO AJ Styles/Jeff Jarrett		
NNO Alex Shelley/Chris Sabin	30.00	75.00
NNO Brother Ray/Brother Devon		

2010 Jakks Pacific TNA Wrestling Cross the Line Series 3

NNO AJ Styles/Jeff Hardy		
NNO Kurt Angle/Mr. Anderson	20.00	40.00
NNO Stevie Richards/Daffney	12.50	25.00

2010 Jakks Pacific TNA Wrestling Cross the Line Series 4

NNO Eric Young/Kevin Nash	15.00	30.00
NNO Hulk Hogan/Abyss	30.00	75.00
NNO Sting/Rob Van Dam	20.00	40.00

2010 Jakks Pacific TNA Wrestling Deluxe Impact Series 1

NNO AJ-Styles/No Stubble		
NNO AJ Styles/Stubble		
NNO Jeff Jarrett/Dk Blonde Hair	10.00	20.00
NNO Jeff Jarrett/Lt Blonde Hair		
NNO Kurt Angle	10.00	20.00
NNO Samoa Joe	15.00	30.00
NNO Sting		
NNO Suicide		

2010 Jakks Pacific TNA Wrestling Deluxe Impact Series 1 Slammin' Celebration Exclusives

NNO AJ Styles
NNO Jeff Jarrett
NNO Kurt Angle
NNO Samoa Joe
NNO Sting
NNO Suicide

2010 Jakks Pacific TNA Wrestling Deluxe Impact Series 2

NNO AJ Styles		
NNO Amazing Red		
NNO Eric Young		
NNO Hernandez	25.00	50.00
NNO Hulk Hogan	40.00	80.00
NNO Mick Foley		

2010 Jakks Pacific TNA Wrestling Deluxe Impact Series 3

NNO Jay Lethal	15.00	30.00
NNO Kevin Nash	12.50	25.00
NNO Matt Morgan	20.00	40.00
NNO Shark Boy	15.00	30.00
NNO Sting		
NNO Velvet Sky	20.00	40.00

2010 Jakks Pacific TNA Wrestling Deluxe Impact Series 4

NNO Abyss	50.00	100.00
NNO D'Angelo Dinero		
NNO Desmond Wolfe	25.00	50.00
NNO Hulk Hogan	30.00	60.00
NNO Jeff Hardy		
NNO Rob Van Dam		

2010 Jakks Pacific TNA Wrestling Deluxe Impact Series 5

NNO Angelina Love	20.00	40.00
NNO Jeff Hardy		
NNO Mr. Anderson		
NNO Raven LOTR		
NNO Rob Terry	10.00	20.00
NNO Samoa Joe	20.00	40.00

2011 Jakks Pacific TNA Wrestling Deluxe Impact Series 6

NNO Doug Williams		
NNO Kazarian	12.50	25.00
NNO Kurt Angle	15.00	30.00
NNO Madison Rayne	20.00	40.00
NNO Sting	15.00	30.00
NNO Terry Taylor LOTR	17.50	35.00

2012 Jakks Pacific TNA Wrestling Deluxe Impact Series 7

NNO Bobby Roode	10.00	20.00
NNO James Storm		
NNO James Storm/Belt	30.00	75.00
NNO Jeff Hardy	30.00	60.00
NNO Mr. Anderson	10.00	20.00
NNO Velvet Sky	12.50	25.00

2012 Jakks Pacific TNA Wrestling Deluxe Impact Series 8

NNO AJ Styles		
NNO Hulk Hogan	30.00	60.00
NNO Matt Morgan	7.50	15.00
NNO Rob Van Dam		
NNO Rob Van Dam/Belt		
NNO Sting		

2013 Jakks Pacific TNA Wrestling Deluxe Impact Series 9

NNO Austin Aries
NNO Christopher Daniels
NNO Gail Kim
NNO Jeff Hardy
NNO Jeff Hardy/Belt
NNO Magnus

2013 Jakks Pacific TNA Wrestling Deluxe Impact Series 10

NNO Crimson
NNO Kurt Angle
NNO Miss Tessmacher
NNO Rob Terry
NNO Rob Van Dam

2013 Jakks Pacific TNA Wrestling Deluxe Impact Series 11

NNO AJ Styles
NNO Austin Aries
NNO Jeff Hardy
NNO Velvet Sky

2014 Jakks Pacific TNA Wrestling Deluxe Impact Series 12

NNO Bully Ray	12.50	25.00
NNO Chris Sabin	20.00	40.00
NNO Hernandez	12.50	25.00
NNO Magnus		

2014 Jakks Pacific TNA Wrestling Deluxe Impact Series 13

NNO Angelina Love	12.50	25.00
NNO Mr. Anderson	7.50	15.00

2010 Jakks Pacific TNA Wrestling Genesis

NNO AJ Styles
NNO AJ Styles/Belt
NNO Jeff Jarrett
NNO Jeff Jarrett/Belt
NNO Kurt Angle
NNO Kurt Angle/Belt
NNO Samoa Joe
NNO Samoa Joe/Belt
NNO Sting
NNO Sting/Belt
NNO Suicide
NNO Suicide/Belt

2010 Jakks Pacific TNA Wrestling Genesis 3-Packs

NNO AJ Styles/Kurt Angle/Suicide
NNO Jeff Jarrett/Samoa Joe/Sting

2010 Jakks Pacific TNA Wrestling Genesis 4-Packs

NNO AJ Styles/Kurt Angle/
Sting/Suicide

NNO Jeff Jarrett/Kurt Angle/
Samoa Joe/Sting

2010 Jakks Pacific TNA Wrestling Impact Series 1

NNO	Abyss	15.00	30.00
NNO	Jay Lethal	10.00	20.00
NNO	Kevin Nash	7.50	15.00
NNO	Kurt Angle	7.50	15.00
NNO	Sting	12.50	25.00
NNO	Suicide	20.00	40.00

2010 Jakks Pacific TNA Wrestling Legends of the Ring

NNO Hulk Hogan
NNO Jeff Jarrett
NNO Kevin Nash
NNO Kurt Angle
NNO Sting
NNO Sting USA Gear RSC

2010 Jakks Pacific TNA Wrestling Micro Impact Series 1

NNO Abyss/Shark Boy/Suicide
NNO AJ Styles/Jeff Jarrett/Mick Foley
NNO C. Daniels/Creed/Jay Lethal
NNO Kevin Nash/Kurt Angle/Sting

2010 Jakks Pacific TNA Wrestling Micro Impact Series 1 10-Pack

NNO Sting/Shark Boy/Jeff Jarrett/Suicide/Abyss
Jay Lethal/AJ Styles/Mick Foley/Kurt Angle/Kevin Nash

2010 Jakks Pacific TNA Wrestling Micro Impact Series 2

NNO	Abyss/Hulk Hogan/Jeff Hardy		
NNO	Eric Young/Lethal/Nash		
NNO	James Storm/Morgan/Roode	15.00	30.00
NNO	Jeff Jarrett/RVD/Sting		

1998 Jakks Pacific WWF 2 Tuff Series 1

NNO	Chyna/HHH	12.50	25.00
NNO	D.O.A.	7.50	15.00
NNO	Goldust/Marlena	10.00	20.00
NNO	Truth Commission	7.50	15.00

1998 Jakks Pacific WWF 2 Tuff Series 2

NNO	B. Christopher/J. Lawler	7.50	15.00
NNO	Kama Mustafa/D'Lo Brown	10.00	20.00
NNO	Kurrgan/Jackal	7.50	15.00
NNO	Road Dogg/B.A. Billy Gunn	12.50	25.00

1999 Jakks Pacific WWF 2 Tuff Series 3

NNO	Kane/Corporate Mankind	10.00	20.00
NNO	LOD 2000	15.00	30.00
NNO	Steve Austin/Undertaker	12.50	25.00
NNO	The Rock/Owen Hart	15.00	30.00

1999 Jakks Pacific WWF 2 Tuff Series 4

Also known as SummerSlam '99 2 Tuff Series 4.

NNO	Big Boss Man vs. Steve Austin	12.50	25.00
NNO	The Rock vs. Mankind	10.00	20.00
NNO	Undertaker vs. Kane	12.50	25.00
NNO	Val Venis vs. B.A. Billy Gunn	7.50	15.00

1999 Jakks Pacific WWF 2 Tuff Series 5

Also known as SummerSlam '99 2 Tuff Series 5.

NNO	Billy Gunn vs. Road Dogg	10.00	20.00
NNO	Debra McMichaels vs. Double J	7.50	15.00
NNO	Stone Cold Steve Austin vs. The Rock	12.50	25.00
NNO	Viscera vs. Undertaker	10.00	20.00

2003 Jakks Pacific WWE Adrenaline Series 1

NNO	Big Show/Brock Lesnar	25.00	50.00
NNO	Shawn Michaels/RVD	15.00	30.00
NNO	Tommy Dreamer		
	Jeff Hardy		

2003 Jakks Pacific WWE Adrenaline Series 2

NNO	Johnny Stamboli	15.00	30.00
	Chavo Guerrero		

NNO	Rey Mysterio/Matt Hardy	20.00	40.00
NNO	Test/Stacy Keibler	20.00	40.00

2003 Jakks Pacific WWE Adrenaline Series 3

NNO	Kurt Angle/Brock Lesnar	20.00	40.00
NNO	Shawn Michaels/Y2J		
NNO	Steve Austin/Eric Bischoff	20.00	40.00

2003 Jakks Pacific WWE Adrenaline Series 4

NNO	Billy Gunn/Torrie Wilson	12.50	25.00
NNO	Chris Benoit/Rhyno	17.50	35.00
NNO	Undertaker/John Cena	25.00	50.00

2003 Jakks Pacific WWE Adrenaline Series 5

NNO	Eddie Guerrero	25.00	50.00
	John Cena		
NNO	Rey Mysterio	15.00	30.00
	Billy Kidman		
NNO	Shelton Benjamin	10.00	20.00
	Charlie Haas		

2003 Jakks Pacific WWE Adrenaline Series 6

NNO	Eddie and Chavo Guerrero	15.00	30.00
NNO	Faarooq/Bradshaw	10.00	20.00
NNO	The Hurricane/Rosey	10.00	20.00

2004 Jakks Pacific WWE Adrenaline Series 7

NNO	Batista/Randy Orton	17.50	35.00
NNO	Chris Jericho/Christian		
NNO	Scott Steiner/Test	12.50	25.00

2004 Jakks Pacific WWE Adrenaline Series 8

NNO	Bubba Ray/D-Von Dudley	10.00	20.00
NNO	Rene Dupree	12.50	25.00
	Rob Conway		
NNO	Steven Richards/Victoria	15.00	30.00

2004 Jakks Pacific WWE Adrenaline Series 9

NNO	Charlie Haas/Rico	12.50	25.00
NNO	Eddie Guerrero	20.00	40.00
	John Bradshaw Layfield		
NNO	Matt Hardy/Lita	20.00	40.00

2004 Jakks Pacific WWE Adrenaline Series 10

NNO	Christian/Trish Stratus	20.00	40.00
NNO	Doug and Danny Basham	12.50	25.00
NNO	Triple H/Randy Orton	20.00	40.00

2005 Jakks Pacific WWE Adrenaline Series 11

NNO	Billy Kidman/Paul London	12.50	25.00
NNO	Heidenreich/Paul Heyman	12.50	25.00
NNO	John Cena/Funaki	20.00	40.00

2005 Jakks Pacific WWE Adrenaline Series 12

NNO	Batista/Triple H	15.00	30.00
NNO	JBL/Orlando Jordan	12.50	25.00
NNO	RVD/Rey Mysterio	15.00	30.00

2005 Jakks Pacific WWE Adrenaline Series 13

NNO	Luther Reigns/Kurt Angle	12.50	25.00
NNO	Rey Mysterio/Teddy Long	15.00	30.00
NNO	Rob Conway	12.50	25.00
	Sylvain Grenier		

2005 Jakks Pacific WWE Adrenaline Series 14

NNO	Eddie Guerrero/Booker T	15.00	30.00
NNO	M. Hassan/Daivari	20.00	40.00
NNO	William Regal/Tajiri	12.50	25.00

2005 Jakks Pacific WWE Adrenaline Series 15

NNO	John Cena/JBL	15.00	30.00
NNO	Kane/Edge	20.00	40.00
NNO	Rey Mysterio	25.00	50.00
	Eddie Guerrero		

2005 Jakks Pacific WWE Adrenaline Series 16

NNO	Batista/JBL	15.00	30.00
NNO	Chris Jericho/John Cena	20.00	40.00
NNO	Johnny Nitro	12.50	25.00
	Joey Mercury		

2006 Jakks Pacific WWE Adrenaline Series 17

NNO	John Cena/Kurt Angle	12.50	25.00
NNO	Matt Hardy/Edge	12.50	25.00
NNO	Super Crazy/Psicosis	15.00	30.00

2006 Jakks Pacific WWE Adrenaline Series 18

NNO	Bobby Lashley	17.50	35.00
	Orlando Jordan		
NNO	Lance Cade	15.00	30.00
	Trevor Murdoch		
NNO	Johnny Nitro		
	Road Warrior Animal		

2006 Jakks Pacific WWE Adrenaline Series 19

NNO	John Cena/Edge	15.00	30.00
NNO	Johnny Nitro	10.00	20.00
	Joey Mercury		
NNO	Rey Mysterio/Mark Henry	20.00	40.00

2006 Jakks Pacific WWE Adrenaline Series 20

NNO	Triple H/John Cena		
NNO	Trish Stratus/HBK	15.00	30.00
NNO	William Regal	12.50	25.00
	Paul Burchill		

2006 Jakks Pacific WWE Adrenaline Series 21

NNO	Booker T/Boogeyman	12.50	25.00
NNO	Gymini	12.50	25.00
NNO	Mikey vs. Big Show	15.00	30.00

2006 Jakks Pacific WWE Adrenaline Series 22

NNO	Johnny/Mitch	10.00	20.00
NNO	Psicosis/Super Crazy	15.00	30.00
NNO	Umaga/Armando Estrada	15.00	30.00

2007 Jakks Pacific WWE Adrenaline Series 23

NNO	Booker T vs. Batista	12.50	25.00
NNO	Elijah Burke	15.00	30.00
	Sylvester Terkay		
NNO	Jeff Hardy vs. Johnny Nitro	20.00	40.00

2007 Jakks Pacific WWE Adrenaline Series 24

NNO	Brian Kendrick/Paul London	12.50	25.00
NNO	HHH/Shawn Michaels	17.50	35.00
NNO	Undertaker/Kane	15.00	30.00

2007 Jakks Pacific WWE Adrenaline Series 25

NNO	Charlie Haas/Shelton Benjamin	12.50	25.00
NNO	John Cena vs. The Great Khali	20.00	40.00
NNO	MVP vs. Kane	15.00	30.00

2007 Jakks Pacific WWE Adrenaline Series 26

NNO	Cryme Tyme	12.50	25.00
NNO	The Highlanders	12.50	25.00
NNO	King Booker/Queen Sharmell	15.00	30.00

2007 Jakks Pacific WWE Adrenaline Series 27

NNO	Deuce/Domino	15.00	30.00
NNO	Jeff and Matt Hardy	17.50	35.00
NNO	Lance Cade/Trevor Murdoch	12.50	25.00

2007 Jakks Pacific WWE Adrenaline Series 28

NNO	CM Punk/Elijah Burke	15.00	30.00
NNO	Mr. Kennedy/Edge	12.50	25.00
NNO	Umage/Vince McMahon	12.50	25.00

2008 Jakks Pacific WWE Adrenaline Series 29

NNO	Cody & Dusty Rhodes	12.50	25.00
NNO	Miz/Layla	12.50	25.00
NNO	MVP/Matt Hardy	15.00	30.00

2008 Jakks Pacific WWE Adrenaline Series 30

NNO	Balls Mahoney/Kelly Kelly	20.00	40.00
NNO	HHH/Umaga	15.00	30.00
NNO	Rey Mysterio/Finlay		

2008 Jakks Pacific WWE Adrenaline Series 31

NNO	Big Daddy V/Matt Striker	12.50	25.00
NNO	Chuck Palumbo	15.00	30.00
	Michelle McCool		
NNO	The Highlanders	12.50	25.00

2008 Jakks Pacific WWE Adrenaline Series 32

NNO Jesse/Festus	10.00	20.00
NNO John Morrison/The Miz	15.00	30.00
NNO Santino Marella/Maria	15.00	30.00

2008 Jakks Pacific WWE Adrenaline Series 33

NNO Chavo Guerrero/Kane	15.00	30.00
NNO Katie Lea/Paul Burchill	15.00	30.00
NNO Vickie Guerrero/Edge	20.00	40.00

2008 Jakks Pacific WWE Adrenaline Series 34

NNO Hornswoggle/Finlay	30.00	60.00
NNO Randy Orton/JBL		
NNO Tommy Dreamer	20.00	40.00
Joey Styles		

2009 Jakks Pacific WWE Adrenaline Series 35

NNO Cody Rhodes/Ted DiBiase Jr.		
NNO Curt Hawkins/Zach Ryder	15.00	30.00
NNO Evan Bourne/Rey Mysterio		

2009 Jakks Pacific WWE Adrenaline Series 36

NNO Brian Kendrick/Ezekiel Jackson	15.00	30.00
NNO Mark Henry/Tony Atlas	15.00	30.00
NNO Shad Gaspard/JTG	20.00	40.00

2009 Jakks Pacific WWE Adrenaline Series 37

NNO Jeff Hardy/The Undertaker	20.00	40.00
NNO Million Dollar Man/DiBiase Jr.		
NNO Triple H/Randy Orton	12.50	25.00

2009 Jakks Pacific WWE Adrenaline Series 38

NNO Edge vs. Big Show		
NNO Finlay/Hornswoggle	25.00	50.00
NNO Jack Swagger vs. Christian		

2009 Jakks Pacific WWE Adrenaline Series 39

NNO Undertaker/HBK	12.50	25.00
NNO Triple H/Stephanie		
NNO Natalya/Tyson Kidd		

2000 Jakks Pacific WWF Back Talkin' Crushers Exclusive

NNO Stone Cold Steve Austin TF	10.00	20.00

1999 Jakks Pacific WWF Back Talkin' Crushers Series 1

NNO Big Show	6.00	12.00
NNO The Rock	7.50	15.00
NNO Steve Austin	10.00	20.00
NNO Undertaker	7.50	15.00

2000 Jakks Pacific WWF Back Talkin' Crushers Series 2

NNO Mankind	7.50	15.00
NNO Road Dogg	6.00	12.00
NNO The Rock	10.00	20.00

2000 Jakks Pacific WWF Back Talkin' Crushers Series 3

NNO Chris Jericho	10.00	20.00
NNO Steve Austin	10.00	20.00
NNO Triple H	7.50	15.00

2001 Jakks Pacific WWF Back Talkin' Slammers Series 1

NNO The Rock	12.50	25.00
NNO Stone Cold Steve Austin	12.50	25.00
NNO Triple H	10.00	20.00

2001 Jakks Pacific WWF Back Talkin' Slammers Series 2

NNO Chris Jericho	10.00	20.00
NNO Kurt Angle	12.50	25.00
NNO Undertaker		

2001 Jakks Pacific WWF Back Talkin' Slammers Series 3

NNO Chris Jericho	10.00	20.00
NNO Kurt Angle	12.50	25.00

NNO Stone Cold Steve Austin	10.00	20.00
NNO The Rock	10.00	20.00
NNO Triple H	7.50	15.00
NNO Undertaker		

2002 Jakks Pacific WWF Back Talkin' Slammers Series 4

NNO Chris Jericho		
NNO Kurt Angle		
NNO Triple H		

2000 Jakks Pacific WWF Backlash Series 1

NNO Al Snow	12.50	25.00
NNO Kane	6.00	12.00
NNO Shawn Michaels	15.00	30.00
NNO Stone Cold Steve Austin	10.00	20.00
NNO The Rock	12.50	25.00
NNO Triple H	10.00	20.00
NNO Undertaker	10.00	20.00
NNO X-Pac	7.50	15.00

2000 Jakks Pacific WWF Backlash Series 2

NNO Big Boss Man		
NNO Edge		
NNO Hardcore Holly		
NNO Road Dogg		
NNO The Rock		
NNO Stone Cold Steve Austin		
NNO Triple H	7.50	15.00
NNO X-Pac	6.00	12.00

2000 Jakks Pacific WWF Backlash Series 3

NNO Billy Gunn	7.50	15.00
NNO Edge	10.00	20.00
NNO Kane	7.50	15.00
NNO The Rock		
NNO Stone Cold Steve Austin		
NNO Test		
NNO Triple H		
NNO Undertaker		

2000 Jakks Pacific WWF Backlash Series 4

NNO Big Boss Man	6.00	12.00
NNO Billy Gunn	7.50	15.00
NNO Edge	10.00	20.00
NNO Kane	10.00	20.00
NNO The Rock		
NNO Stone Cold Steve Austin	12.50	25.00
NNO Triple H		
NNO Undertaker	15.00	30.00

2000 Jakks Pacific WWF Backlash Series 5

NNO Al Snow		
NNO Hardcore Holly	6.00	12.00
NNO Rock		
NNO Stone Cold Steve Austin	12.50	25.00
NNO Test		
NNO Undertaker	15.00	30.00
NNO Val Venis		
NNO X-Pac		

2005 Jakks Pacific WWE Backlash Series 7

NNO Batista	12.50	25.00
NNO Chris Benoit	12.50	25.00
NNO Kurt Angle	10.00	20.00
NNO Undertaker	15.00	30.00

2005 Jakks Pacific WWE Backlash Series 8

NNO Batista	12.50	25.00
NNO Edge	10.00	20.00
NNO Kurt Angle	12.50	25.00
NNO Triple H	10.00	20.00

2005 Jakks Pacific WWE Backlash Series 9

NNO Carlito	12.50	25.00
NNO Kurt Angle	20.00	40.00
NNO Randy Orton	7.50	15.00
NNO Rob Van Dam	12.50	25.00

NNO Shawn Michaels		
NNO Undertaker		

2005 Jakks Pacific WWE Backlash Series 10

NNO Batista	12.50	25.00
NNO Chris Benoit	7.50	15.00
NNO John Cena	12.50	25.00
NNO Rob Van Dam	7.50	15.00
NNO Shawn Michaels	15.00	30.00
NNO Triple H	10.00	20.00

2007 Jakks Pacific WWE Backlash Series 11

NNO Bobby Lashley	12.50	25.00
NNO Edge	15.00	30.00
NNO Finlay	15.00	30.00
NNO Jeff Hardy	15.00	30.00
NNO Rey Mysterio	20.00	40.00
NNO Undertaker	20.00	40.00

2008 Jakks Pacific WWE Backlash Series 12

NNO Kane		
NNO Matt Hardy		
NNO Miz		
NNO Mr. Kennedy		
NNO Randy Orton		
NNO Triple H		

2009 Jakks Pacific WWE Backlash Series 13

NNO Batista		
NNO Chavo Guerrero		
NNO Chris Jericho		
NNO Elijah Burke		
NNO John Cena		
NNO Nunzio		

2009 Jakks Pacific WWE Backlash Series 14

NNO Chavo Guerrero		
NNO Cody Rhodes		
NNO Matt Hardy	10.00	20.00
NNO Stone Cold Steve Austin		
NNO Triple H		

2009 Jakks Pacific WWE Backlash Series 15

NNO Chris Jericho	15.00	30.00
NNO CM Punk		
NNO John Cena	10.00	20.00
NNO Rey Mysterio	20.00	40.00
NNO Shawn Michaels	12.50	25.00
NNO Triple H	15.00	30.00

2008 Jakks Pacific WWE Best of Classic Superstars

NNO Andre the Giant	20.00	40.00
NNO Bret Hit Man Hart	20.00	40.00
NNO Eddie Guerrero	12.50	25.00
NNO Rowdy Roddy Piper		
NNO Shawn Michaels	12.50	25.00

2009 Jakks Pacific WWE Best of Deluxe Aggression

NNO Chris Jericho		
NNO John Cena		
NNO Randy Orton		
NNO Rey Mysterio		
NNO Triple H		
NNO Undertaker		

2006 Jakks Pacific WWE Best of Deluxe Aggression

NNO Batista	7.50	15.00
NNO John Cena	15.00	30.00
NNO Kane	10.00	20.00
NNO Rey Mysterio	10.00	20.00
NNO Triple H	7.50	15.00
NNO Undertaker	20.00	40.00

2008 Jakks Pacific WWE Best of Deluxe Aggression

NNO Chris Jericho	15.00	30.00
NNO CM Punk		

NNO John Cena	10.00	20.00
NNO Rey Mysterio	17.50	35.00
NNO Shawn Michaels	12.50	25.00
NNO Undertaker	20.00	40.00

2005 Jakks Pacific WWE Best of ECW

NNO Bubba Ray Dudley	15.00	30.00
NNO D-Von Dudley	12.50	25.00
NNO Rey Mysterio	12.50	25.00
NNO Rhyno	7.50	15.00
NNO Rob Van Dam	15.00	30.00
NNO Stevie Richards	7.50	15.00

2005 Jakks Pacific WWE Best of WCW

NNO Billy Kidman	10.00	20.00
NNO Chris Benoit	15.00	30.00
NNO Chris Jericho	12.50	25.00
NNO Eddie Guerrero	10.00	20.00
NNO Rey Mysterio	15.00	30.00
NNO Ric Flair	20.00	40.00

1998 Jakks Pacific WWF Bone Crunchin' Buddies

NNO Animal
NNO Dude Love
NNO Hawk
NNO Shawn Michaels

1999 Jakks Pacific WWF Bone Crunchin' Buddies

NNO Kane		
NNO The Rock		
NNO Steve Austin/Ring Gear	20.00	40.00
NNO Steve Austin/Street Clothes		
NNO Triple H	20.00	40.00
NNO Undertaker		

2001 Jakks Pacific WWF Bone Crunchin' Buddies

NNO Animal
NNO Hawk
NNO The Rock
NNO Stone Cold Steve Austin
NNO Undertaker

1999 Jakks Pacific WWF Break Down In Your House

NNO D'Lo Brown	7.50	15.00
NNO Droz	6.00	12.00
NNO Goldust	6.00	12.00
NNO Mankind	12.50	25.00
NNO Steve Austin	10.00	20.00
NNO X-Pac	6.00	12.00

1999 Jakks Pacific WWF Break Down In Your House Multi-Packs

NNO Steve Austin/D'Lo Brown/Droz BJ
NNO Steve Austin/Droz/Goldust/X-Pac SC
NNO X-Pac/Mankind/Goldust BJ

2003 Jakks Pacific WWE Bring the Noise

NNO Matt Hardy	10.00	20.00
NNO Shawn Michaels	7.50	15.00
NNO The Rock	20.00	40.00
NNO Tommy Dreamer	12.50	25.00
NNO Triple H	12.50	25.00
NNO Undertaker		

2008 Jakks Pacific WWE Build N' Brawl Playset

NNO Wrestling Ring
(w/HHH & Orton TRU

2008 Jakks Pacific WWE Build N' Brawl Series 1

NNO Batista
NNO Bobby Lashley
NNO Edge
NNO John Cena
NNO Triple H
NNO Undertaker

2008 Jakks Pacific WWE Build N' Brawl Series 2

NNO Batista
NNO Kane

NNO Mr. Kennedy
NNO Randy Orton
NNO Rey Mysterio
NNO Shawn Michaels

2008 Jakks Pacific WWE Build N' Brawl Series 3

NNO Boogeyman
NNO CM Punk
NNO Jeff Hardy
NNO Matt Hardy
NNO MVP
NNO Umaga

2008 Jakks Pacific WWE Build N' Brawl Series 4

NNO Chris Jericho
NNO Deuce
NNO Domino
NNO The Miz
NNO John Morrison
NNO Stone Cold Steve Austin

2008 Jakks Pacific WWE Build N' Brawl Series 5

NNO Chavo Guerrero
NNO Elijah Burke
NNO Finlay
NNO JBL
NNO Razor Ramon
NNO William Regal

2008 Jakks Pacific WWE Build N' Brawl Series 6

NNO Curt Hawkins
NNO Kofi Kingston
NNO Rey Mysterio
NNO Santino Marella
NNO Sgt. Slaughter
NNO Zack Ryder

2008 Jakks Pacific WWE Build N' Brawl Series 7

NNO Bret Hart
NNO John Cena
NNO Mark Henry
NNO Matt Hardy
NNO Rey Mysterio
NNO Undertaker

2008 Jakks Pacific WWE Build N' Brawl Series 8

NNO Batista
NNO Big Show
NNO Rey Mysterio
NNO The Rock
NNO Roddy Piper
NNO Shawn Michaels

2008 Jakks Pacific WWE Build N' Brawl Series 9

NNO John Cena
NNO Rey Mysterio
NNO Undertaker

2008 Jakks Pacific WWE Build N' Brawl WrestleMania

NNO John Cena		
NNO Rey Mysterio	12.50	25.00
NNO Triple H	10.00	20.00

1999 Jakks Pacific WWF Camo Carnage

NNO B.A. Billy Gunn	6.00	12.00
NNO Billy Gunn SI	7.50	15.00
NNO Billy Gunn w/Gun	7.50	15.00
NNO Chyna	6.00	12.00
NNO Chyna SI	7.50	15.00
NNO Chyna w/Gun	7.50	15.00
NNO HHH	6.00	12.00
NNO HHH SI	7.50	15.00
NNO HHH w/Gun	7.50	15.00
NNO Road Dogg	5.00	10.00
NNO Road Dogg SI	6.00	12.00
NNO Road Dogg w/Gun	6.00	12.00
NNO Stone Cold Steve Austin	7.50	15.00
NNO Steve Austin SI	10.00	20.00

NNO Steve Austin w/Gun	10.00	20.00
NNO X-Pac	5.00	10.00
NNO X-Pac SI	6.00	12.00
NNO X-Pac w/Gun	6.00	12.00

2004 Jakks Pacific WWE Classic Superstars Series 1

NNO Andre the Giant	20.00	40.00
NNO Bret Hart	30.00	75.00
NNO Hunter Hearst Helmsley	10.00	20.00
NNO Shawn Michaels	25.00	50.00
NNO Ultimate Warrior	15.00	30.00
NNO Undertaker	15.00	30.00

2004 Jakks Pacific WWE Classic Superstars Series 2

NNO Big John Studd Chair & Microphone	12.50	25.00
NNO Big John Studd Ring Bell & Stretcher	20.00	40.00
NNO Dude Love Tye-Dye Wrist Bands	15.00	30.00
NNO Dude Love Yellow Wrist Bands	12.50	25.00
NNO George The Animal Steele Painted Body Hair	15.00	30.00
NNO George The Animal Steele Synthetic Body Hair	25.00	50.00
NNO Mankind	20.00	40.00
NNO Ric Flair	20.00	40.00
NNO Sgt. Slaughter/Jacket Off		
NNO Sgt. Slaughter/Jacket On	15.00	30.00

2004 Jakks Pacific WWE Classic Superstars Series 3

NNO Ultimate Warrior		
NNO Bret Hit Man Hart	15.00	30.00
NNO Jake The Snake Roberts	15.00	30.00
NNO Million Dollar Man Ted DiBiase	25.00	50.00
NNO Superfly Jimmy Snuka	15.00	30.00
NNO Undertaker	12.50	25.00

2004 Jakks Pacific WWE Classic Superstars Series 4

NNO Hacksaw Jim Duggan	20.00	40.00
NNO Hillbilly Jim	15.00	30.00
NNO Junkyard Dog	12.50	25.00
NNO Rowdy Roddy Piper	15.00	30.00
NNO Tito Santana	12.50	25.00
NNO Yokozuna Smooth Belt Strap		
NNO Yokozuna Textured Belt Strap	20.00	40.00

2004 Jakks Pacific WWE Classic Superstars Series 5

NNO Brutus The Barber Beefcake	15.00	30.00
NNO Iron Sheik	15.00	30.00
NNO King Kong Bundy	20.00	40.00
NNO Mr. Wonderful Paul Orndorff	15.00	30.00
NNO Nikolai Volkoff	20.00	40.00
NNO Terry Funk	25.00	50.00

2005 Jakks Pacific WWE Classic Superstars Series 6

NNO Andre the Giant	15.00	30.00
NNO Bobby The Brain Heenan	12.50	25.00
NNO Doink	15.00	30.00
NNO Earthquake Painted Chest Hair	10.00	20.00
NNO Earthquake Synthetic Chest Hair	12.50	25.00
NNO Koko B. Ware	25.00	50.00
NNO One Man Gang	20.00	40.00
NNO Road Warrior Animal	20.00	40.00
NNO Road Warrior Hawk	15.00	30.00
NNO Shawn Michaels	12.50	25.00

2005 Jakks Pacific WWE Classic Superstars
Series 7

NNO	Andre the Giant	15.00	30.00
NNO	British Bulldog	12.50	25.00
NNO	Don Muraco	15.00	30.00
NNO	Eddie Guerrero	10.00	20.00
NNO	Gorilla Monsoon	12.50	25.00
NNO	Jimmy Hart	15.00	30.00
NNO	King Harley Race	20.00	40.00
NNO	Superstar Billy Graham	12.50	25.00
NNO	The Ultimate Warrior	15.00	30.00

2005 Jakks Pacific WWE Classic Superstars
Series 8

NNO	Bruiser Brody	25.00	50.00
NNO	Chief Jay Strongbow	15.00	30.00
NNO	Classy Freddie Blassie	10.00	20.00
NNO	Cowboy Bob Orton	20.00	40.00
	Ace on Boots		
NNO	Cowboy Bob Orton	15.00	30.00
	Plain Boots		
NNO	Hollywood Hogan	20.00	40.00
	Large World Title		
NNO	Hollywood Hogan	15.00	30.00
	Small World Title		
NNO	Hulk Hogan/'80s WWF Title	30.00	75.00
NNO	Hulk Hogan/'90s WWF Title	20.00	40.00
NNO	Jerry The King Lawler	15.00	30.00
NNO	Vader	25.00	50.00

2006 Jakks Pacific WWE Classic Superstars
Series 9

NNO	Akeem	12.50	25.00
NNO	Bam Bam Bigelow	25.00	50.00
NNO	The Godfather	15.00	30.00
NNO	Kamala	15.00	30.00
NNO	Papa Shango	20.00	40.00
NNO	Paul Bearer/Bow Tie	15.00	30.00
NNO	Paul Bearer/Windsor Tie	15.00	30.00
NNO	Ric Flair/Smooth Wrists	15.00	30.00
NNO	Ric Flair/Taped Wrists	10.00	20.00
NNO	Road Warrior Animal	10.00	20.00
NNO	Road Warrior Hawk	10.00	20.00

2006 Jakks Pacific WWE Classic Superstars
Series 10

NNO	Bruno Sammartino	12.50	25.00
NNO	Dusty Rhodes	20.00	40.00
NNO	Gorilla Monsoon	25.00	50.00
NNO	Greg The Hammer Valentine	20.00	40.00
NNO	Harley Race	15.00	30.00
NNO	Mr. Perfect	15.00	30.00
NNO	Rocky Maivia	20.00	40.00
NNO	Sabu	20.00	40.00

2006 Jakks Pacific WWE Classic Superstars
Series 11

NNO	123 Kid	20.00	40.00
NNO	Barry Windham	10.00	20.00
NNO	Diesel	15.00	30.00
NNO	Fabulous Moolah	10.00	20.00
NNO	Hulk Hogan	12.50	25.00
	Black Weightlifting Belt		
NNO	Hulk Hogan	20.00	40.00
	Yellow Weightlifting Belt		
NNO	Irwin R. Schyster	15.00	30.00
NNO	Ken Shamrock	12.50	25.00
NNO	Rick Steiner	15.00	30.00

2006 Jakks Pacific WWE Classic Superstars
Series 12

NNO	Arn Anderson	12.50	25.00
NNO	Brooklyn Brawler	15.00	30.00
NNO	Captain Lou Albano	15.00	30.00
NNO	Dean Malenko	12.50	25.00
NNO	Handsome Jimmy Valiant	20.00	40.00
NNO	Hollywood Hulk Hogan	30.00	60.00

NNO	Killer Kowalski	12.50	25.00
NNO	Nasty Boy Brian Knobbs	12.50	25.00
NNO	Nasty Boy Jerry Sags	12.50	25.00
NNO	Ultimate Warrior	15.00	30.00
	Facing Back		
NNO	Ultimate Warrior	15.00	30.00
	Facing Forward		

2006 Jakks Pacific WWE Classic Superstars
Series 13

NNO	Al Snow	15.00	30.00
NNO	Bad News Brown	10.00	20.00
NNO	Bret Hit Man Hart	15.00	30.00
NNO	Brother Love	25.00	50.00
NNO	Droz	10.00	20.00
NNO	Dusty Rhodes	15.00	30.00
NNO	Ernie Ladd	15.00	30.00
NNO	Luna Vachon	20.00	40.00
NNO	The Mountie	25.00	50.00
NNO	Mr. Perfect	15.00	30.00
NNO	Ravishing Rick Rude	20.00	40.00
NNO	Undertaker/LJN Style	25.00	50.00

2007 Jakks Pacific WWE Classic Superstars
Series 14

NNO	Abdullah The Butcher	30.00	60.00
NNO	Bob Backlund	20.00	40.00
NNO	Demolition Ax	20.00	40.00
NNO	Demolition Smash	20.00	40.00
NNO	Diamond Dallas Page	20.00	40.00
NNO	Honky Tonk Man	17.50	35.00
NNO	Mean Gene Okerlund	30.00	60.00
NNO	Rick The Model Martel	25.00	50.00
NNO	Sensational Sherri	15.00	30.00
NNO	Steve Austin/LJN Black Card	15.00	30.00
NNO	Steve Austin/LJN Blue Card		
NNO	The Ultimate Warrior	15.00	30.00

2007 Jakks Pacific WWE Classic Superstars
Series 15

NNO	The Genius	20.00	40.00
NNO	Johnny Rodz	12.50	25.00
NNO	Lex Luger	15.00	30.00
NNO	Outlaw Ron Bass	12.50	25.00
NNO	Razor Ramon	20.00	40.00
NNO	The Rock/LJN Style	12.50	25.00
NNO	Shawn Michaels	15.00	30.00
	w/Entrance Gear		
NNO	Shawn Michaels	15.00	30.00
	w/o Entrance Gear		
NNO	Tank Abbott w/Chair+Barbell	15.00	30.00
NNO	Tank Abbott w/Chair	20.00	40.00
NNO	Tully Blanchard	15.00	30.00
NNO	Zeus w/Chain+Pipe	40.00	80.00
NNO	Zeus w/Chain	20.00	40.00

2007 Jakks Pacific WWE Classic Superstars
Series 16

NNO	Barbarian	20.00	40.00
NNO	Giant Gonzalez/Painted Fur	25.00	50.00
NNO	Giant Gonzalez	60.00	120.00
	Synthetic Fur/500*		
NNO	Shawn Michaels/LJN Style	12.50	25.00
NNO	Sycho Sid w/Knee Pads &	15.00	30.00
	{WWF Belt by Feet		
NNO	Sycho Sid w/Knee Pads &	20.00	40.00
	{WWF Belt by Waist		
NNO	Sycho Sid w/o Knee Pads &	20.00	40.00
	{WWF Belt by Feet		
NNO	Sycho Sid w/o Knee Pads &	12.50	25.00
	{WWF Belt by Waist		
NNO	Vince McMahon	20.00	40.00
NNO	Warlord	20.00	40.00
NNO	The Ultimate Warrior	25.00	50.00
NNO	X-Pac/Belt by Feet	12.50	25.00
NNO	X-Pac/Belt by Waist		

2007 Jakks Pacific WWE Classic Superstars
Series 17

NNO	Eddie Guerrero	17.50	35.00
NNO	Ivan Putski	15.00	30.00
NNO	Ken Patera	25.00	50.00
NNO	Repo Man	17.50	35.00
NNO	The Rock	20.00	40.00
NNO	Rocky Johnson	15.00	30.00
NNO	Shane McMahon	15.00	30.00
	Centered Jersey Logo		
NNO	Shane McMahon		
	Off-Centered Jersey Logo		
NNO	Triple H/LJN Style	15.00	30.00
NNO	Typhoon	17.50	35.00

2007 Jakks Pacific WWE Classic Superstars
Series 18

NNO	Honky Tonk Man	15.00	30.00
NNO	Jim Ross	30.00	75.00
NNO	Kane	25.00	50.00
NNO	King Mabel	30.00	75.00
NNO	Mae Young	30.00	60.00
NNO	Ric Flair/LJN Style	15.00	30.00
NNO	Rikishi	15.00	30.00
NNO	Stone Cold Steve Austin	15.00	30.00
NNO	Sunny	20.00	40.00
NNO	Val Venis		
	Cruiserweight Torso		
NNO	Val Venis	20.00	40.00
	Heavyweight Torso		

2008 Jakks Pacific WWE Classic Superstars
Series 19

NNO	Adam Bomb	30.00	75.00
NNO	Cactus Jack	12.50	25.00
NNO	Eddie Guerrero	15.00	30.00
NNO	Evil Doink	20.00	40.00
NNO	Howard Finkel	20.00	40.00
NNO	Kevin Sullivan	15.00	30.00
NNO	Mankind/LJN Style	17.50	35.00
NNO	Nikita Koloff	30.00	60.00
NNO	The Rock	15.00	30.00
NNO	Tatanka	15.00	30.00

2008 Jakks Pacific WWE Classic Superstars
Series 20

NNO	Dynamite Kid	20.00	40.00
NNO	John Cena/LJN Style	12.50	25.00
NNO	Rey Mysterio	17.50	35.00
NNO	Ric Flair	25.00	50.00
NNO	The Rock	15.00	30.00
NNO	Ron Simmons	15.00	30.00
NNO	Tony Atlas	20.00	40.00

2008 Jakks Pacific WWE Classic Superstars
Series 21

NNO	Brian Pillman	12.50	25.00
NNO	Buff Bagwell	30.00	60.00
NNO	Chris Jericho	15.00	30.00
NNO	Jeff Hardy	20.00	40.00
NNO	Jesse The Body Ventura	15.00	30.00
NNO	Rey Mysterio/LJN Style	20.00	40.00
NNO	Tazz	12.50	25.00

2008 Jakks Pacific WWE Classic Superstars
Series 22

NNO	Andy Kaufman	50.00	100.00
NNO	Bob Spark Plugg Holly	15.00	30.00
NNO	Chainsaw Charlie	15.00	30.00
NNO	Earthquake	17.50	35.00
NNO	Eddie Guerrero/LJN Style	15.00	30.00
NNO	Matt Hardy	20.00	40.00
NNO	Mr. McMahon	15.00	30.00
NNO	Stone Cold Steve Austin	25.00	50.00

2009 Jakks Pacific WWE Classic Superstars Series 23

NNO	The Berzerker	25.00	50.00
NNO	Big Boss Man	30.00	60.00
NNO	Billy Kidman	15.00	30.00
NNO	Lance Storm	25.00	50.00
NNO	Road Warrior Animal	15.00	30.00
NNO	Road Warrior Hawk	15.00	30.00
NNO	Rob Van Dam	17.50	35.00
NNO	Spike Dudley	25.00	50.00
NNO	Trish Stratus/LJN Style	25.00	50.00

2009 Jakks Pacific WWE Classic Superstars Series 24

NNO	B. Brian Blair	20.00	40.00
NNO	Davey Boy Smith	15.00	30.00
NNO	Dynamite Kid	15.00	30.00
NNO	Hunter-Hearst-Helmsley	15.00	30.00
NNO	Jim Brunzell	15.00	30.00
NNO	Rey Mysterio	20.00	40.00
NNO	Rob Van Dam/LJN Style	15.00	30.00
NNO	Stephanie McMahon	15.00	30.00
NNO	Trish Stratus	30.00	60.00

2009 Jakks Pacific WWE Classic Superstars Series 25

NNO	Bastion Booger	30.00	75.00
NNO	Big Boss Man	15.00	30.00
NNO	Big Show	15.00	30.00
NNO	Goldberg	50.00	100.00
NNO	Haku	50.00	100.00
NNO	Jack Brisco	30.00	60.00
NNO	Jeff Hardy/LJN Style	20.00	40.00
NNO	Jerry Brisco	30.00	75.00
NNO	Jesse The Body Ventura	40.00	80.00

2009 Jakks Pacific WWE Classic Superstars Series 26

NNO	Bret Hit Man Hart	15.00	30.00
NNO	Dangerous Danny Davis	20.00	40.00
NNO	Dr. Death Steve Williams	30.00	60.00
NNO	Giant Machine/Andre	20.00	40.00
NNO	The Iron Sheik	20.00	40.00
NNO	Junkyard Dog	12.50	25.00
NNO	Matt Hardy/LJN Style	12.50	25.00
NNO	Meng	15.00	30.00
NNO	Mr. Fuji	20.00	40.00
NNO	The Sheik	25.00	50.00
NNO	The Shockmaster	25.00	50.00

2009 Jakks Pacific WWE Classic Superstars Series 27

NNO	The Barbarian	15.00	30.00
NNO	Bill Goldberg	50.00	100.00
NNO	Evil Doink	15.00	30.00
NNO	The Giant		
NNO	Kona Crush	50.00	100.00
NNO	Sgt. Slaughter	15.00	30.00
NNO	Steve Blackman	25.00	50.00
NNO	The Warlord	15.00	30.00

2009 Jakks Pacific WWE Classic Superstars Series 28

NNO	Bret Hit Man Hart	20.00	40.00
NNO	Rey Mysterio/LJN Style	30.00	60.00
NNO	Rowdy Roddy Piper	20.00	40.00
NNO	Shawn Michaels	12.50	25.00
NNO	Triple H	12.50	25.00
NNO	The Undertaker	25.00	50.00

2004 Jakks Pacific WWE Classic Superstars 2-Packs Series 1

NNO	Hart Foundation Black Knee Pads on Bret UK	75.00	150.00
NNO	Hart Foundation Pink Knee Pads	30.00	75.00
NNO	Road Warriors		
NNO	Rockers	30.00	75.00

2005 Jakks Pacific WWE Classic Superstars 2-Packs Series 2

NNO	Jake Roberts/Steve Austin	30.00	75.00
NNO	Mankind/Undertaker	30.00	60.00
NNO	Roddy Piper/Jimmy Snuka	30.00	60.00

2005 Jakks Pacific WWE Classic Superstars 2-Packs Series 3

NNO	Bushwhackers	25.00	50.00
NNO	Steve Austin/Roddy Piper	25.00	50.00
NNO	Wild Samoans	20.00	40.00

2006 Jakks Pacific WWE Classic Superstars 2-Packs Series 4

NNO	Hulk Hogan/Freddie Blassie	25.00	50.00
NNO	Sgt. Slaughter/Col. Mustafa	20.00	40.00
NNO	Undertaker/Paul Bearer	25.00	50.00

2006 Jakks Pacific WWE Classic Superstars 2-Packs Series 5

NNO	Demolition	40.00	80.00
NNO	Hulk Hogan/Ultimate Warrior	60.00	120.00
NNO	Hulk Hogan/Ultimate Warrior Head Variant		
NNO	Ted DiBiase/Virgil	20.00	40.00

2007 Jakks Pacific WWE Classic Superstars 2-Packs Series 6

NNO	Hollywood Blondes	30.00	60.00
NNO	Midnight Express	50.00	75.00
NNO	Strike Force	30.00	60.00

2007 Jakks Pacific WWE Classic Superstars 2-Packs Series 7

NNO	Arn Anderson/Tully Blanchard	25.00	50.00
NNO	Lex Luger/Dean Malenko	25.00	50.00
NNO	Ric Flair/Barry Windham	25.00	50.00

2008 Jakks Pacific WWE Classic Superstars 2-Packs Series 8

NNO	Giant Gonzales Harvey Wippleman	30.00	75.00
NNO	Jerry Lawler vs. {Andy Kaufman	50.00	100.00
NNO	Killer Bees	40.00	80.00

2008 Jakks Pacific WWE Classic Superstars 2-Packs Series 9

NNO	British Bulldogs	75.00	150.00
NNO	Ivan & Nikita Koloff	30.00	75.00
NNO	Rock 'n Roll Express	60.00	120.00

2009 Jakks Pacific WWE Classic Superstars 2-Packs Series 10

NNO	Tony Atlas/Rocky Johnson		
NNO	Too Cool		
NNO	Yokozuna vs. Bret Hart	30.00	60.00

2009 Jakks Pacific WWE Classic Superstars 2-Packs Series 11

NNO	Jake Roberts vs. Rick Martel		
NNO	Jake Roberts vs. Rick Martel/Blindfolds		
NNO	Rob Van Dam vs. Tazz	25.00	50.00
NNO	Rowdy Roddy Piper vs. Mr. Fuji	40.00	80.00

2009 Jakks Pacific WWE Classic Superstars 2-Packs Series 12

NNO	Cowboy Bob Orton/Randy Orton	30.00	60.00
NNO	Jim Neidhart/Natalya	30.00	75.00
NNO	Million Dollar Man/DiBiase Jr.	20.00	40.00

2009 Jakks Pacific WWE Classic Superstars 2-Packs Series 13

NNO	Steve Austin vs. Rock	30.00	60.00
NNO	Triple H/X-Pac	20.00	40.00
NNO	Bobby Heenan/Abe Schwartz	30.00	60.00

2004 Jakks Pacific WWE Classic Superstars 3-Packs Series 1

NNO	Jake Roberts/Andre Single Strap	150.00	300.00

John Studd

NNO	Jake Roberts/Andre Double Strap	30.00	75.00

John Studd

2005 Jakks Pacific WWE Classic Superstars 3-Packs Series 2

NNO	Bret Hart/Rock/HBK	30.00	75.00

2005 Jakks Pacific WWE Classic Superstars 3-Packs Series 3

NNO	3 Faces of Undertaker	60.00	120.00
NNO	Jim Neidhart/Tito Santana Marty Janetty	20.00	40.00

2005 Jakks Pacific WWE Classic Superstars 3-Packs Series 4

NNO	King Kong Bundy Volkoff & Sheik	45.00	90.00
NNO	Hart Foundation w/J. Hart	30.00	75.00

2006 Jakks Pacific WWE Classic Superstars 3-Packs Series 5

NNO	Fabulous Freebirds	30.00	60.00
NNO	Fabulous Freebirds Taped Wrists		
NNO	Mega-Maniacs w/Jimmy Hart	25.00	50.00

2006 Jakks Pacific WWE Classic Superstars 3-Packs Series 6

NNO	Captain Lou Albano Wild Samoans	20.00	40.00
NNO	Rowdy Roddy Piper/Cowboy Bob Orton/Mr. Wonderful	25.00	50.00

2006 Jakks Pacific WWE Classic Superstars 3-Packs Series 7

NNO	Terry Funk/Cactus Jack/Sabu	25.00	50.00
NNO	Undertaker/Kane/Paul Bearer	25.00	50.00

2007 Jakks Pacific WWE Classic Superstars 3-Packs Series 8

NNO	Jake Roberts/British {Bulldog/Koko B. Ware	40.00	80.00
NNO	Ric Flair/Perfect/Heenan	25.00	50.00

2008 Jakks Pacific WWE Classic Superstars 3-Packs Series 9

NNO	Rhythm & Blues {w/Jimmy Hart	30.00	75.00
NNO	Rocky Johnson/Peter Maivia/The Rock	40.00	80.00

2009 WWE Classic Superstars 3-Packs Series 10

NNO	Brainbusters w/Bobby Heenan	25.00	50.00
NNO	Demolition/Ax/ Smash/Crush	75.00	150.00

2009 Jakks Pacific WWE Classic Superstars 3-Packs Series 11

NNO	LOD 2000 w/Sunny	75.00	150.00
NNO	Nasty Boys w/Jimmy Hart	30.00	60.00

2009 Jakks Pacific WWE Classic Superstars 3-Packs Series 12

NNO	Powers of Pain w/Mr. Fuji		
NNO	Tito Santana/HBK w/Sherri		

1999 Jakks Pacific WWF Deadly Games

Also known as SummerSlam '99 Deadly Games.

NNO	Droz	6.00	12.00
NNO	HHH	6.00	12.00
NNO	Stone Cold Steve Austin	7.50	15.00

2005 Jakks Pacific WWE Deluxe Aggression Series 1

NNO	Batista	20.00	40.00
NNO	Kurt Angle	12.50	25.00
NNO	John Cena	30.00	60.00
NNO	Randy Orton	15.00	30.00
NNO	Rey Mysterio	20.00	40.00
NNO	Triple H	15.00	30.00

2006 Jakks Pacific WWE Deluxe Aggression
Series 2

NNO	Booker T	10.00	20.00
NNO	Carlito Cool	10.00	20.00
NNO	Edge	10.00	20.00
NNO	Kane	15.00	30.00
NNO	Rey Mysterio	15.00	30.00
NNO	Undertaker	25.00	50.00

2006 Jakks Pacific WWE Deluxe Aggression
Series 3

NNO	Batista	12.50	25.00
NNO	Chris Benoit	15.00	30.00
NNO	John Cena		
NNO	Kurt Angle	12.50	25.00
NNO	Lashley	7.50	15.00
NNO	Shawn Michaels		

2006 Jakks Pacific WWE Deluxe Aggression
Series 4

NNO	Boogeyman	12.50	25.00
NNO	Chris Masters	10.00	20.00
NNO	JBL	7.50	15.00
NNO	Mr. Kennedy		
NNO	Randy Orton	10.00	20.00
NNO	Rob Conway	7.50	15.00
NNO	Shelton Benjamin		

2006 Jakks Pacific WWE Deluxe Aggression
Series 5

NNO	Batista	10.00	20.00
NNO	Big Show	15.00	30.00
NNO	John Cena	20.00	40.00
NNO	Matt Hardy	10.00	20.00
NNO	Rob Van Dam	10.00	20.00
NNO	Triple H		

2007 Jakks Pacific WWE Deluxe Aggression
Series 6

NNO	Booker T
NNO	Edge
NNO	Finlay
NNO	John Cena
NNO	Kenny
NNO	Rob Van Dam

2007 Jakks Pacific WWE Deluxe Aggression
Series 7

NNO	Carlito
NNO	Chris Benoit
NNO	Mr. Kennedy
NNO	Jeff Hardy
NNO	Sabu
NNO	Rey Mysterio

2007 Jakks Pacific WWE Deluxe Aggression
Series 8

NNO	Bobby Lashley
NNO	CM Punk
NNO	Sandman
NNO	Gregory Helms
NNO	Undertaker
NNO	Johnny Nitro

2007 Jakks Pacific WWE Deluxe Aggression
Series 8 (loose)

NNO	Bobby Lashley
NNO	CM Punk
NNO	Sandman
NNO	Gregory Helms
NNO	Undertaker
NNO	Johnny Nitro

2007 Jakks Pacific WWE Deluxe Aggression
Series 9

NNO	Mr. McMahon
NNO	Kenny Dykstra
NNO	Kevin Thorn

NNO	John Cena
NNO	Jimmy Wang Yang
NNO	Tommy Dreamer

2007 Jakks Pacific WWE Deluxe Aggression
Series 10

NNO	Batista
NNO	Daivari
NNO	JBL
NNO	Matt Hardy
NNO	Randy Orton
NNO	Shawn Michaels

2007 Jakks Pacific WWE Deluxe Aggression
Series 11

NNO	Chavo Guerrero
NNO	Elijah Burke
NNO	John Cena
NNO	MVP
NNO	Snitsky
NNO	William Regal

2007 Jakks Pacific WWE Deluxe Aggression
Series 12

NNO	Batista
NNO	Boogeyman
NNO	CM Punk
NNO	Paul London
NNO	Shawn Michaels
NNO	Umaga

2008 Jakks Pacific WWE Deluxe Aggression
Series 13

NNO	Cody Rhodes	12.50	25.00
NNO	John Cena	12.50	25.00
NNO	Miz	10.00	20.00
NNO	Rey Mysterio	12.50	25.00
NNO	Stone Cold Steve Austin	15.00	30.00
NNO	Triple H	17.50	35.00

2008 Jakks Pacific WWE Deluxe Aggression
Series 14

NNO	John Morrison	20.00	40.00
NNO	Armando Estrada	10.00	20.00
NNO	Brian Kendrick	10.00	20.00
NNO	MVP	10.00	20.00
NNO	Randy Orton	12.50	25.00
NNO	Undertaker	20.00	40.00

2008 Jakks Pacific WWE Deluxe Aggression
Series 15

NNO	Chris Jericho		
NNO	Finlay		
NNO	Matt Striker	15.00	30.00
NNO	Mr. Kennedy		
NNO	Tazz		
NNO	Undertaker		

2008 Jakks Pacific WWE Deluxe Aggression
Series 16

NNO	Batista		
NNO	Edge	15.00	30.00
NNO	JBL	10.00	20.00
NNO	Nunzio		
NNO	Randy Orton		
NNO	Shelton Benjamin		

2008 Jakks Pacific WWE Deluxe Aggression
Series 17

NNO	Curt Hawkins		
NNO	DH Smith	12.50	25.00
NNO	Kofi Kingston	15.00	30.00
NNO	Paul Burchill	10.00	20.00
NNO	Santino Marella	10.00	20.00
NNO	Zack Ryder		

2008 Jakks Pacific WWE Deluxe Aggression
Series 18

NNO	Chris Jericho	15.00	30.00

NNO	Festus	10.00	20.00
NNO	Hardcore Holly	10.00	20.00
NNO	Jesse	10.00	20.00
NNO	John Morrison	10.00	20.00
NNO	The Miz		

2009 Jakks Pacific WWE Deluxe Aggression
Series 19

NNO	Chris Jericho		
NNO	John Cena	15.00	30.00
NNO	JTG	10.00	20.00
NNO	Matt Hardy	15.00	30.00
NNO	Shad	10.00	20.00
NNO	Ted DiBiase	12.50	25.00

2009 Jakks Pacific WWE Deluxe Aggression
Series 20

NNO	Big Show	10.00	20.00
NNO	Evan Bourne		
NNO	Shawn Michaels		
NNO	Stone Cold Steve Austin		
NNO	R-Truth	10.00	20.00
NNO	Rey Mysterio	17.50	35.00

2009 Jakks Pacific WWE Deluxe Aggression
Series 21

NNO	Edge	12.50	25.00
NNO	Goldust		
NNO	Jeff Hardy	25.00	50.00
NNO	John Cena	12.50	25.00
NNO	Rey Mysterio	20.00	40.00
NNO	Vladimir Kozlov	10.00	20.00

2009 Jakks Pacific WWE Deluxe Aggression
Series 22

NNO	Batista		
NNO	Christian	25.00	50.00
NNO	CM Punk	30.00	60.00
NNO	Jack Swagger	12.50	25.00
NNO	Randy Orton		
NNO	Triple H		

2009 Jakks Pacific WWE Deluxe Aggression
Series 23

NNO	Batista		
NNO	Big Show	10.00	20.00
NNO	John Cena	10.00	20.00
NNO	Randy Orton		
NNO	Rey Mysterio		
NNO	Triple H	15.00	30.00

2009 Jakks Pacific WWE Deluxe Aggression
Series 24

NNO	Kofi Kingston		
NNO	Matt Hardy		
NNO	MVP		
NNO	Rey Mysterio	15.00	30.00

2007 Jakks Pacific WWE Deluxe Aggression 2-Packs

NNO	Edge/Batista
NNO	Undertaker/Kane
NNO	Shawn Michaels/Triple H

2006 Jakks Pacific WWE Deluxe Aggression 3-Packs Series 1

NNO	Triple H/John Cena/Edge	15.00	30.00
NNO	Rey Mysterio/Randy Orton/Kurt Angle	25.00	50.00

2007 Jakks Pacific WWE Deluxe Aggression 3-Packs Series 2

NNO	DX & The Big Show
NNO	Rey Mysterio
	Lashley/Batista

2007 Jakks Pacific WWE Deluxe Aggression 3-Packs Series 3

NNO	Lashley/Sabu/RVD
NNO	Randy Orton/Edge/Jeff Hardy

2008 Jakks Pacific WWE Deluxe Aggression 3-Packs Series 4

NNO Shawn Michaels/John Cena/Edge		
NNO Mr. Kennedy/Undertaker/Fit Finlay	20.00	40.00

2008 Jakks Pacific WWE Deluxe Aggression 3-Packs Series 5

NNO Umaga/Triple H/Randy Orton	25.00	50.00
NNO Rey Mysterio/Undertaker/Fit Finlay	25.00	50.00

2009 Jakks Pacific WWE Deluxe Aggression 3-Packs Series 6

NNO Chris Jericho/Kane/Shawn Michaels		
NNO CM Punk/Edge/Chavo Guerrero		

2006 Jakks Pacific WWE Deluxe Classic Superstars Series 1

NNO Hulk Hogan	25.00	50.00
NNO Ric Flair	25.00	50.00
NNO Rowdy Roddy Piper (black tape)	15.00	30.00
NNO Rowdy Roddy Piper (gold tape)		
NNO Stone Cold Steve Austin	15.00	30.00
NNO The Rock	20.00	40.00

2007 Jakks Pacific WWE Deluxe Classic Superstars Series 2

NNO Bret Hart		
NNO British Bulldog		
NNO Kevin Nash		
NNO Mr. Perfect		
NNO Shawn Michaels		

2007 Jakks Pacific WWE Deluxe Classic Superstars Series 3

NNO Jake The Snake Roberts		
NNO Lex Luger		
NNO Ravishing Rick Rude		
NNO Scott Hall		
NNO Undertaker		

2007 Jakks Pacific WWE Deluxe Classic Superstars Series 4

NNO Brutus Beefcake		
NNO Honky Tonk Man		
NNO Iron Sheik		
NNO Million Dollar Man Ted DiBiase		
NNO Shawn Michaels		

2008 Jakks Pacific WWE Deluxe Classic Superstars Series 5

NNO Buff Bagwell	12.50	25.00
NNO Diamond Dallas Page		
NNO Jim The Anvil Neidhart	20.00	40.00
NNO Jimmy Superfly Snuka	12.50	25.00

2008 Jakks Pacific WWE Deluxe Classic Superstars Series 6

NNO Eddie Guerrero	25.00	50.00
NNO Hillbilly Jim	20.00	40.00
NNO Kane	30.00	60.00
NNO Sgt. Slaughter	17.50	35.00
NNO Triple H	12.50	25.00

2009 Jakks Pacific WWE Deluxe Classic Superstars Series 7

NNO Bret Hart	20.00	40.00
NNO Shawn Michaels	15.00	30.00
NNO The Rock	15.00	30.00
NNO Tito Santana	12.50	25.00
NNO Undertaker	20.00	40.00

2009 Jakks Pacific WWE Deluxe Classic Superstars Series 8

NNO Big John Studd	30.00	40.00
NNO British Bulldog	12.50	25.00
NNO Chainsaw Charlie	10.00	20.00
NNO Dynamite Kid	20.00	40.00
NNO Stone Cold Steve Austin	25.00	50.00

2000 Jakks Pacific WWF Double Slam Series 1

NNO Edge/Christian	17.50	35.00
NNO Kane/X-Pac	10.00	20.00
NNO Stone Cold Steve Austin Shane McMahon	15.00	30.00
NNO Vince McMahon/Undertaker	10.00	20.00

2000 Jakks Pacific WWF Double Slam Series 2

NNO Big Show Stone Cold Steve Austin	12.50	25.00
NNO HHH/X-Pac		
NNO The Rock/Billy Gunn	10.00	20.00
NNO Undertaker/Kane		

2000 Jakks Pacific WWF Double Slam Series 3

NNO Big Show/Test	7.50	15.00
NNO Billy Gunn/Hardcore Holly	7.50	15.00
NNO Debra/Stone Cold Steve Austin	15.00	30.00
NNO Mankind/Undertaker	15.00	30.00

2000 Jakks Pacific WWF Double Slam Series 4

NNO Chyna/Chris Jericho	17.50	35.00
NNO Matt Hardy/Jeff Hardy	17.50	35.00
NNO Triple H/Billy Gunn	10.00	20.00

2000 Jakks Pacific WWF Double Slam Series 5

NNO Bradshaw/Faarooq	10.00	20.00
NNO Edge/Christian	12.50	25.00
NNO Triple H/The Rock		

1998 Jakks Pacific WWF DTA Tour Series 1

NNO 8-Ball	6.00	12.00
NNO Chainz	7.50	15.00
NNO Dude Love	7.50	15.00
NNO Faarooq	6.00	12.00
NNO HHH	6.00	12.00
NNO Kane	12.50	25.00
NNO Shawn Michaels	10.00	20.00
NNO Vader	6.00	12.00

1999 Jakks Pacific WWF DTA Tour Series 2

NNO Double J Jeff Jarrett	6.00	12.00
NNO Al Snow	6.00	12.00
NNO Blue Blazer	15.00	30.00
NNO Edge	7.50	15.00
NNO Steve Blackman	6.00	12.00
NNO Undertaker	10.00	20.00

1999 Jakks Pacific WWF DTA Tour Series 3

NNO Christian	5.00	10.00
NNO Godfather	5.00	10.00
NNO HHH	7.50	15.00
NNO Ken Shamrock	7.50	15.00
NNO Stone Cold Steve Austin	12.50	25.00
NNO X-Pac	6.00	12.00

2004 Jakks Pacific WWE Exclusives

NNO Legion of Doom (Ringside Collectibles Exclusive)	150.00	300.00
NNO Roddy Piper/100* TFM	1000.00	2000.00
NNO Roddy Piper/1800* RSF	60.00	120.00
NNO Roddy Piper/3000* TFM	50.00	100.00
NNO Ultimate Warrior/100* NYC TF		

2005 Jakks Pacific WWE Exclusives

NNO Hillbilly Jim/5000*	30.00	75.00
NNO Hulk Hogan vs. Shawn Michaels/3000* RSC	75.00	150.00
NNO Mankind vs. Terry Funk KM	25.00	50.00
NNO Sgt. Slaughter/100* TFM	500.00	1000.00
NNO Sgt. Slaughter/3000* TFM	30.00	60.00
NNO Superstar B. Graham/3000* TRU CAN		
NNO Superstar B.Graham Blue Jeans/14000* TRU		
NNO Superstar B. Graham Green Gear/7000* TRU		
NNO Superstar B. Graham Pink Suit/7000 TRU		

2006 Jakks Pacific WWE Exclusives

NNO Superstar B. Graham Red Suit/400* TRU Orland		
NNO Terry Funk/100* NYC TF		

2006 Jakks Pacific WWE Exclusives

NNO Bobby Heenan Weasel/100* NYC TF	300.00	500.00
NNO Bret Hart vs. Shawn Michaels RSF	125.00	250.00
NNO British Bulldog & William Regal	50.00	100.00
NNO Diesel & Shawn Michaels 2 Dudes with Attitudes RSC	60.00	120.00
NNO Dusty Rhodes/3000* OL	50.00	100.00
NNO Hulk Hogan/Blue Trunks & {White Boots WM CAN	30.00	75.00
NNO Hulk Hogan/Blue Trunks & {White Boots WM US	25.00	60.00
NNO Hulk Hogan/Tye Dye & {Knee Brace WM US		
NNO Hulk Hogan/Tye Dye & {No Knee Brace WM US	30.00	75.00
NNO Hulk Hogan/Tye Dye WM CAN		
NNO Hulk Hogan 2-in-1 MANIA TIX	75.00	150.00
NNO Hulk Hogan vs. {Andre the Giant ARGO/BL	60.00	120.00
NNO Hulk Hogan/100* TFM	1500.00	3000.00
NNO Hulk Hogan/3000* TFM	60.00	120.00
NNO Jimmy Hart/100* NYC TF	600.00	1200.00
NNO Steve Austin WWE SZ	30.00	75.00
NNO Tazz/Towel Around Waist RSC		
NNO Tazz/Towel in Package RSC	60.00	120.00

2007 Jakks Pacific WWE Exclusives

NNO Bret Hart vs. Jeff Hardy OL	100.00	200.00
NNO Razor Ramon vs. HBK RSC	60.00	120.00
NNO Roddy Piper Deluxe/100* NYC TF	1000.00	2000.00
NNO Scott Hall & Kevin Nash	75.00	150.00
NNO Steve Austin vs. Bret Hart RSF	150.00	300.00
NNO Ultimate Warrior Classic Superstars Marble Finish/20*		
NNO Ultimate Warrior Classic Superstars One Warrior Nation/20*	2000.00	3500.00
NNO Ultimate Warrior Classic Superstars Warrior America/5*		
NNO Ultimate Warrior Classic Superstars WCW 1998/20*		
NNO Ultimate Warrior Ring Giant Warrior America/25*	1800.00	3000.00
NNO Ultimate Warrior Unmatched Fury Warrior America Gear/15*	4000.00	6000.00

2008 Jakks Pacific WWE Exclusives

NNO Undertaker vs. Kane RSC	300.00	600.00
NNO Undertaker GITD/100* TFM	1000.00	2000.00
NNO Undertaker/3000* TFM	75.00	150.00
NNO Cactus Jack/3000* TFM	50.00	100.00
NNO D-Generation X RSC	75.00	150.00
NNO Eddie Guerrero vs. Rey Mysterio	400.00	750.00
NNO Eddie Guerrero/100* NYC TF	1000.00	2000.00
NNO Hardy Boys RSC		
NNO Hardy Boys WWE SZ		
NNO Hart Foundation PROFIG		
NNO Ric Flair/3000* WWE 24/7	30.00	75.00
NNO Stephanie & Triple H RSC	60.00	120.00

2009 Jakks Pacific WWE Exclusives

NNO Edge/3000* TFM	125.00	250.00
NNO Goldust Shattered RSC	125.00	250.00
NNO Kane vs. Vader OL	30.00	60.00
NNO Rey Mysterio/100* TFM	300.00	600.00
NNO Shawn Michaels/ Multi-Belts PROFIG	125.00	250.00
NNO Shawn Michaels vs. {Steve Austin WWE SZ	75.00	150.00
NNO Shawn Michaels vs.	100.00	200.00
NNO Sunny/100* TFM	300.00	500.00
NNO Sunny/3000* TFM	30.00	75.00
NNO Undertaker vs. {Triple H WWE SZ	100.00	200.00

2005 Jakks Pacific WWE Face Flippin' Fighters

NNO Batista 12.50 25.00
NNO Chris Benoit 10.00 20.00
NNO Eddie Guerrero 12.50 25.00
NNO John Cena 20.00 40.00
NNO Randy Orton 12.50 25.00
NNO Undertaker 20.00 40.00

2001 Jakks Pacific WWF Famous Scenes Series 1

NNO Jeff Hardy/Matt Hardy 15.00 30.00
NNO Mick Foley/Undertaker 20.00 50.00
NNO The Rock/Triple H 12.50 25.00

2001 Jakks Pacific WWF Famous Scenes Series 2

NNO Chris Benoit/Chris Jericho 12.50 25.00
NNO HHH/Cactus Jack 20.00 40.00
NNO Kurt Angle/Rikishi 15.00 30.00

2001 Jakks Pacific WWF Famous Scenes Series 3

NNO Bubba Ray Dudley/D-Von Dudley 15.00 30.00
NNO Stone Cold Steve Austin
Vince McMahon

2001 Jakks Pacific WWF Famous Scenes Series 4

NNO Lita/Test 15.00 30.00
NNO The Rock/Billy Gunn
NNO Stone Cold Steve Austin 12.50 25.00
Undertaker

1998 Jakks Pacific WWF Fantasy Warfare

NNO Stone Cold Steve Austin vs. Andre the Giant 12.50 25.00
NNO Undertaker vs. Mankind 15.00 30.00

2002 Jakks Pacific WWF Fatal 4-Way Series 1

NNO Bubba Ray Dudley 6.00 12.00
NNO Edge 10.00 20.00
NNO Jeff Hardy 15.00 30.00
NNO Lita 12.50 25.00

2002 Jakks Pacific WWF Fatal 4-Way Series 2

NNO Chris Jericho 20.00 40.00
NNO Christian 7.50 15.00
NNO Stone Cold Steve Austin 12.50 25.00
NNO Undertaker 20.00 40.00

2002 Jakks Pacific WWF Fatal 4-Way Series 3

NNO Bubba Ray Dudley 6.00 12.00
NNO Chris Jericho 10.00 20.00
NNO Christian 10.00 20.00
NNO Jeff Hardy 12.50 25.00

1999 Jakks Pacific WWF Federation Fighters

NNO Kane
(two sleeves)
NNO Stone Cold Steve Austin 15.00 30.00
NNO Steve Austin/Jumpsuit 20.00 40.00

1999 Jakks Pacific WWF Federation Fighters Series 2

NNO Big Show 15.00 30.00
NNO Rock 25.00 50.00
NNO Stone Cold Steve Austin 15.00 30.00
NNO Undertaker 20.00 40.00

2001 Jakks Pacific WWF-WWE Final Count Series 1

NNO Billy Gunn vs. Edge
Downward Spiral
NNO Billy Gunn vs. Edge
Famous-er
NNO Lita vs. Matt Hardy
Litacanrana
NNO Lita vs. Matt Hardy
Twist of Fate
NNO Undertaker vs. Steve Austin
The Last Ride
NNO Undertaker vs. Steve Austin
Stone Cold Stunner

2002 Jakks Pacific WWF-WWE Final Count Series 2

NNO Kane vs. Steve Austin
NNO Kurt Angle vs. Triple H 12.50 25.00
NNO The Rock vs. Chris Jericho 20.00 40.00

2002 Jakks Pacific WWF-WWE Final Count Series 3

NNO Billy Gunn/Jeff Hardy 12.50 25.00
NNO Chris Jericho/Steve Austin
NNO Rikishi/Bubba Ray Dudley

2002 Jakks Pacific WWF-WWE Final Count Series 4

NNO Albert/Scotty Too Hotty
NNO The Rock/Kurt Angle 15.00 30.00
NNO Test/Christian

2002 Jakks Pacific WWF-WWE Final Count Series 5

NNO Bradshaw/Undertaker
NNO Jeff Hardy/Trish Stratus 12.50 25.00
NNO Rob Van Dam 25.00 50.00
Eddie Guerrero

2002 Jakks Pacific WWF-WWE Final Count Series 6

NNO Billy vs. Chuck 10.00 20.00
Famous-er
NNO Billy vs. Chuck 10.00 20.00
Jungle Kick
NNO C.Jericho vs. C.Benoit 15.00 30.00
Crippler Crossface
NNO C.Jericho vs. C.Benoit 15.00 30.00
Walls of Jericho
NNO Hulk Hogan vs. HHH 12.50 25.00
Pedigree
NNO Hulk Hogan vs. HHH 12.50 25.00
Running Leg Drop

2002 Jakks Pacific WWF-WWE Final Count Series 7

NNO Batista
NNO Billy Kidman
NNO Hurricane

2001 Jakks Pacific WWF Finishing Moves Series 1

NNO Chris Jericho/Kurt Angle
NNO The Hardy Boyz
NNO Triple H/The Rock

2001 Jakks Pacific WWF Finishing Moves Series 2

NNO Chris Jericho/The Rock
NNO Kane/Undertaker
NNO Rikishi/Triple H

2001 Jakks Pacific WWF Finishing Moves Series 3

NNO Chris Benoit/Chris Jericho
NNO Eddie Guerrero/Billy Gunn
NNO The Hardy Boyz

2001 Jakks Pacific WWF Finishing Moves Series 4

NNO Kane/Edge
NNO Lita/Buh Buh Dudley
NNO The Rock/Stone Cold Steve Austin

2002 Jakks Pacific WWE Flex 'Ems Series 1

NNO Chris Jericho 7.50 15.00
NNO Edge 7.50 15.00
NNO Hulk Hogan 10.00 20.00
NNO Kurt Angle 7.50 15.00
NNO The Rock 10.00 20.00
NNO Triple H 7.50 15.00

2002 Jakks Pacific WWE Flex 'Ems Series 2

NNO Batista 10.00 20.00
NNO Booker T 7.50 15.00
NNO Brock Lesnar 6.00 12.00
NNO Chris Benoit 6.00 12.00
NNO Hurricane 7.50 15.00
NNO Rob Van Dam 7.50 15.00

2002 Jakks Pacific WWE Flex 'Ems Series 3

NNO Batista 7.50 15.00
NNO Chris Benoit 7.50 15.00
NNO Chris Jericho 7.50 15.00
NNO Hurricane 7.50 15.00
NNO Rob Van Dam 7.50 15.00
NNO The Rock 10.00 20.00

2003 Jakks Pacific WWE Flex 'Ems Series 4

NNO Booker T
NNO Kane
NNO Kurt Angle
NNO Rey Mysterio
NNO Triple H
NNO Undertaker

2003 Jakks Pacific WWE Flex 'Ems Series 5

NNO Booker T
NNO Brock Lesnar
NNO Chris Benoit
NNO Chris Jericho
NNO Rey Mysterio
NNO Rob Van Dam

2003 Jakks Pacific WWE Flex 'Ems Series 8

NNO Chris Jericho
NNO Eddie Guerrero
NNO Kurt Angle
NNO Matt Hardy
NNO Randy Orton
NNO Rey Mysterio

2003 Jakks Pacific WWE Flex 'Ems Series 9

NNO Batista
NNO Chris Benoit
NNO Eddie Guerrero
NNO Randy Orton
NNO Rey Mysterio
NNO Rob Van Dam

2003 Jakks Pacific WWE Flex 'Ems Series 10

NNO Batista
NNO Booker T
NNO Chris Benoit
NNO Chris Jericho
NNO Eddie Guerrero
NNO Rey Mysterio

2003 Jakks Pacific WWE Flex 'Ems Series 11

NNO Batista
NNO Kurt Angle
NNO Randy Orton
NNO Rey Mysterio
NNO Triple H
NNO Undertaker

2003 Jakks Pacific WWE Flex 'Ems Series 12

NNO Kane
NNO Rey Mysterio
NNO Shawn Michaels
NNO Triple H

2003 Jakks Pacific WWE Flex 'Ems Series 13

NNO Batista
NNO Chris Benoit
NNO Randy Orton
NNO Rob Van Dam

2003 Jakks Pacific WWE Flex 'Ems Series 14

NNO Rey Mysterio
NNO Shawn Michaels
NNO Triple H
NNO Undertaker

1998 Jakks Pacific WWF Fully Loaded Series 1

NNO Al Snow 6.00 12.00
NNO B.A. Billy Gunn 7.50 15.00

NNO HHH	6.00	12.00
NNO Kane	7.50	15.00
NNO Road Dogg	5.00	10.00
NNO The Rock	10.00	20.00

1999 Jakks Pacific WWF Fully Loaded Series 2

Also known as SummerSlam '99 Fully Loaded 2.

NNO Road Dogg Jesse James	6.00	12.00
NNO The Rock	10.00	20.00
NNO Shane McMahon	12.50	25.00
NNO Stone Cold Steve Austin	10.00	20.00
NNO Test		
NNO X-Pac	7.50	15.00

2003 Jakks Pacific WWE Grudge Brawlers

NNO Christian		
NNO Chris Jericho		
NNO Kurt Angle		
NNO Jeff Hardy	30.00	60.00
NNO Triple H		
NNO Undertaker		

1997 Jakks Pacific WWF Grudge Match

NNO Bret Hitman Hart vs. Stone Cold Steve Austin	10.00	20.00
NNO Goldust vs. Savio Vega	6.00	12.00
NNO Shawn Michaels vs. Owen Hart	7.50	15.00
NNO Sycho Sid vs. Vader	10.00	20.00
NNO The Undertaker vs. Mankind	15.00	30.00
NNO Yokozuna vs. Ahmed Johnson	6.00	12.00

1998 Jakks Pacific WWF Grudge Match Series 1

NNO HHH vs. Owen Hart	7.50	15.00
NNO Ken Shamrock vs. Dan Severn	7.50	15.00
NNO Luna vs. Sable	20.00	40.00
NNO Marvelous Marc Mero vs. Lethal Weapon Steve Blackman		
NNO Stone Cold Steve Austin vs. Shawn Michaels	10.00	20.00
NNO Undertaker vs. Kane	10.00	20.00

1998 Jakks Pacific WWF Grudge Match Series 2

NNO HHH vs. Shawn Michaels	7.50	15.00
NNO Road Dogg Jesse James vs. Al Snow		
NNO Stone Cold Steve Austin vs. Vince McMahon	12.50	25.00

1998 Jakks Pacific WWF Grudge Match Series 3

NNO Stone Cold Steve Austin vs. The Rock	7.50	15.00
NNO X-Pac vs. Double J Jeff Jarrett	10.00	20.00

2005 Jakks Pacific WWE Havoc Unleashed Series 1

NNO Booker T	10.00	20.00
NNO Chris Benoit	7.50	15.00
NNO Edge	7.50	15.00
NNO Kurt Angle	12.50	25.00
NNO Scotty 2 Hotty	10.00	20.00
NNO Triple H	10.00	20.00

2006 Jakks Pacific WWE Havoc Unleashed Series 2

NNO Batista	10.00	20.00
NNO JBL	7.50	15.00
NNO RVD	12.50	25.00
NNO Shawn Michaels	12.50	25.00

2007 Jakks Pacific WWE Havoc Unleashed Series 3

NNO Bobby Lashley		
NNO Edge		
NNO HHH		
NNO John Cena		
NNO Kane		
NNO Matt Hardy		

2009 Jakks Pacific WWE Havoc Unleashed Series 4

NNO Batista	10.00	20.00
NNO HHH	6.00	12.00
NNO JBL	7.50	15.00
NNO Matt Hardy	7.50	15.00
NNO Undertaker	10.00	20.00

1997 Jakks Pacific WWF Heroes of Wrestling

NNO Sycho Sid	10.00	20.00
NNO Undertaker	12.50	25.00

2000 Jakks Pacific WWF House of Pain

NNO HHH	7.50	15.00
NNO Rock	12.50	25.00
NNO Stone Cold Steve Austin	12.50	25.00
NNO Tori	7.50	15.00
NNO Undertaker	12.50	25.00
NNO X-Pac	6.00	12.00

2000 Jakks Pacific WWF House of Pain (loose)

NNO HHH		
NNO The Rock		
NNO Stone Cold Steve Austin		
NNO Tori		
NNO Undertaker		
NNO X-Pac		

1998 Jakks Pacific WWF Jakk'd Up

NNO Sable		
NNO Stone Cold Steve Austin		
NNO Kane		
NNO Undertaker		

1998 Jakks Pacific WWF Jakk'd Up (loose)

NNO Sable		
NNO Stone Cold Steve Austin		
NNO Kane		
NNO Undertaker		

1999 Jakks Pacific WWF Boxed Sets

NNO Buried Alive	30.00	75.00
HHH/Vince/Undertaker/Austin		
NNO Championship Title Series	20.00	40.00
Austin/X-Pac/Kane/The Rock TRU		
NNO Hardcore Champions	20.00	40.00
Big Boss Man/Mankind/Al Snow/Hardcore Holly		
NNO Mick Foley's Triple Threat	25.00	50.00
Mankind/Dude Love/Cactus Jack KB		
NNO No Chance	20.00	40.00
Vince/Austin/Paul Wight		
NNO Over the Edge	15.00	30.00
Austin/Rock/HHH/Kane		
NNO Perfect 10		
Austin/Rock/Kane/Undertaker/Mankind/Big Show/X-Pac/HHH/Road Dogg/Billy Gunn TRU		
NNO SummerSlam '99 Camo Carnage	17.50	35.00
HHH/Billy Gunn/Ausin		
NNO SummerSlam Expect No Mercy		
Austin/Rock/Vince/Undertaker		
NNO SummerSlam '99 Last Man Standing	20.00	40.00
Austin/Rock/Vince/Shane		
NNO Survivor Series Mayhem	17.50	35.00
HHH/Rock/Austin		
NNO WWF Attitude	20.00	40.00
HBK/Animal/Austin/Hawk KM		

2001 Jakks Pacific WWF Boxed Sets

NNO 2 Extreme	30.00	75.00
Lita & The Hardys		
NNO Back in the Ring/Undertaker	25.00	50.00
Stone Cold Steve Austin/Mick Foley KM		
NNO Brothers of Destruction		
Austin/Undertaker/Kane TRU		
NNO Cold Day in Dudleyville	30.00	60.00
Rock/D-Von/Buh Buh Ray TRU		
NNO Get in the Groove	50.00	100.00
(Scottie/Rikishi/Sexay MEI		
NNO Insurrextion		
HHH/Austin/Bubba/Edge/Kane/Rock/Test/Jeff Hardy/Y2J/Regal UK		
NNO KOTR Lead Me to My Throne		
D-Von/Edge/Austin/Angle/Hardys		
NNO Picture Perfect	20.00	40.00
Edge/Christian KM		
NNO Renegades		
Raven/Austin/Shane McMahon KM		

##		
NNO Team Extreme	20.00	40.00
Matt & Jeff Hardy/Lita		
NNO Triple Threat	12.50	25.00
Y2J/Rock/HHH		

2002 Jakks Pacific WWE Boxed Sets

NNO nWo Federation Poison	25.00	50.00
Nash/X-Pac/Hall		
NNO RAW Draft		
Bubba Ray/Undertaker/Flair/Austin		
NNO Rock Solid	20.00	40.00
Rock/Scorpion King		
NNO SmackDown Draft		
Y2J/Hogan/Vince/Rock		

2004 Jakks Pacific WWE Employee Gift Exclusives

NNO Ric Flair/25*	
NNO Rowdy Roddy Piper/20*	
NNO Sgt. Slaughter/20*	

2002 Jakks Pacific WWF-WWE King of the Ring Series 1

NNO D-Von Dudley	7.50	15.00
NNO Edge	20.00	40.00
NNO Jeff Hardy	12.50	25.00
NNO Kurt Angle	10.00	20.00
NNO Matt Hardy	7.50	15.00
NNO Stone Cold Steve Austin		

2002 Jakks Pacific WWF-WWE King of the Ring Series 2

NNO Brock Lesnar	15.00	30.00
NNO Chris Jericho	12.50	25.00
NNO Hardcore Holly	12.50	25.00
NNO Rob Van Dam	15.00	30.00
NNO Test	10.00	20.00
NNO X-Pac	10.00	20.00

1998 Jakks Pacific WWF Legends

NNO Andre the Giant	20.00	40.00
NNO Captain Lou Albano	7.50	15.00
NNO Classy Freddie Blassie	7.50	15.00
NNO Jimmy Superfly Snuka	10.00	20.00

1999 Jakks Pacific WWF Live Wire Series 1

NNO Chyna	10.00	20.00
NNO Ken Shamrock	7.50	15.00
NNO Mankind	10.00	20.00
NNO Stone Cold Steve Austin	12.50	25.00
NNO Undertaker	15.00	30.00
NNO Vader	7.50	15.00

1999 Jakks Pacific WWF Live Wire Series 2

NNO Mark Henry	7.50	15.00
NNO Marvelous Marc Mero	6.00	12.00
NNO Rock	10.00	20.00
NNO Shawn Michaels	7.50	15.00
NNO Val Venis	6.00	12.00
NNO X-Pac	7.50	15.00

2003 Jakks Pacific WWE Main Event

NNO Hulk Hogan	12.50	25.00
NNO Shawn Michaels		
NNO Spike Dudley	15.00	30.00
NNO Stacy Keibler	10.00	20.00
NNO Tazz		
NNO Torrie Wilson	10.00	20.00
NNO Triple H		

1997 Jakks Pacific WWF Managers Series 1

NNO Bob Backlund/Sultan	12.50	25.00
NNO Clarence Mason/Crush	10.00	20.00
NNO Paul Bearer/Mankind	12.50	25.00
NNO Sable/Marc Mero	10.00	20.00

2002 Jakks Pacific WWE Match Champs

NNO Booker T	10.00	20.00
NNO Jeff Hardy	10.00	20.00
NNO Ric Flair	7.50	15.00
NNO Rob Van Dam	7.50	15.00

NNO The Rock	10.00	20.00
NNO Triple H	7.50	15.00

2002 Jakks Pacific WWF Match Enders

NNO Billy Gunn/Famous-er
NNO Edge/Downward Spiral
NNO Lita/Litacanrana
NNO Matt Hardy/Twist of Fate
NNO Triple H/Pedigree

NNO Undertaker/Last Ride	12.50	25.00

2007 Jakks Pacific WWE Maximum Aggression Series 1

NNO Bobby Lashley
NNO Carlito
NNO CM Punk
NNO Rey Mysterio
NNO Triple H

2008 Jakks Pacific WWE Maximum Aggression Series 2

NNO Carlito	20.00	40.00
NNO Chris Jericho		
NNO Elijah Burke	25.00	50.00
NNO Undertaker	20.00	40.00

2008 Jakks Pacific WWE Maximum Aggression Series 3

NNO Edge	20.00	40.00
NNO John Cena	15.00	30.00
NNO John Morrison		
NNO Randy Orton	15.00	30.00

2008 Jakks Pacific WWE Maximum Aggression Series 4

NNO Matt Hardy
NNO Kane
NNO Mr. Kennedy
NNO Shelton Benjamin

2009 Jakks Pacific WWE Maximum Aggression Series 5

NNO CM Punk	15.00	30.00
NNO John Cena	20.00	40.00
NNO Matt Hardy		
NNO Triple H	15.00	30.00

2009 Jakks Pacific WWE Maximum Aggression Series 6

NNO Rey Mysterio	25.00	50.00
NNO Shawn Michaels		
NNO Triple H	15.00	30.00
NNO Undertaker	20.00	40.00

1999 Jakks Pacific WWF Maximum Sweat Series 1

NNO Hunter Hearst-Helmsley	6.00	12.00
NNO Kane/Mask Off	10.00	20.00
NNO Kane/Mask On	12.50	25.00
NNO Rock The People's Champion	15.00	30.00
NNO Shawn Michaels	12.50	25.00
NNO Stone Cold Steve Austin	10.00	20.00
NNO Undertaker	15.00	30.00

1999 Jakks Pacific WWF Maximum Sweat Series 2

NNO B.A. Billy Gunn	10.00	20.00
NNO Edge	7.50	15.00
NNO Ken Shamrock	7.50	15.00
NNO Road Dogg	10.00	20.00
NNO Stone Cold Steve Austin	12.50	25.00
NNO Undertaker	10.00	20.00

1999 Jakks Pacific WWF Maximum Sweat Series 3

NNO Big Show	10.00	20.00
NNO Gangrel/Blue Shirt		
NNO Gangrel/Lt. Blue Shirt	12.50	25.00
NNO Mankind	7.50	15.00

NNO The Rock	10.00	20.00
NNO Stone Cold Steve Austin	10.00	20.00

1999 Jakks Pacific WWF Maximum Sweat Series 4

NNO Billy Gunn	7.50	15.00
NNO Droz	7.50	15.00
NNO Kane	7.50	15.00
NNO Road Dogg	7.50	15.00
NNO Stone Cold Steve Austin	10.00	20.00
NNO Undertaker		

1999 Jakks Pacific WWF Maximum Sweat Special Series

NNO B.A. Billy Gunn
NNO Edge
NNO Ken Shamrock
NNO Road Dogg

2008 Jakks Pacific WWE Micro Aggression 10-Packs

NNO Batista/Jeff Hardy/HBK/Kennedy/Cena
Mysterio/Undertaker/Carlito/HHH/Kane
NNO John Cena/Kennedy/HBK/CM Punk/Batista
Kane/HHH/Carlito/Undertaker/Mysterio
NNO John Cena/Matt Hardy/Orton/MVP/Primo
Kane/HHH/Carlito/Undertaker/Mysterio

2006 Jakks Pacific WWE Micro Aggression Playset

NNO Crash and Bash Playset	30.00	75.00
Chris Benoit/Triple H/Kane/Rey Mysterio		

2007 Jakks Pacific WWE Micro Aggression Playset

NNO Crash and Bash Arena
w/John Cena/HBK/Lashley/Edge

2008 Jakks Pacific WWE Micro Aggression Playsets

NNO Crash and Bash Cell	60.00	120.00
w/Cena/Undertaker/HBK/CM Punk		
NNO Crash and Bash El. Chamber	30.00	75.00
w/Cena/Rey Mysterio/Umaga/Kane		

2006 Jakks Pacific WWE Micro Aggression Series 1

NNO Kane/Undertaker/Chris Benoit	15.00	30.00
NNO Rey Mysterio/John Cena/Rob Van Dam	12.50	25.00
NNO Triple H/Shawn Michaels/John Cena	12.50	25.00

2007 Jakks Pacific WWE Micro Aggression Series 2

NNO Edge/Cena/RVD
NNO Rey Mysterio/Batista/Hogan
NNO Triple H/HBK/Orton

2007 Jakks Pacific WWE Micro Aggression Series 3

NNO Jeff Hardy/Cena/Carlito
NNO Jimmy Wang Yang/Undertaker/
Kennedy
NNO Shawn Michaels/CM Punk/
Tommy Dreamer

2007 Jakks Pacific WWE Micro Aggression Series 4

NNO Batista/Finlay/Rey Mysterio
NNO CM Punk/Lashley/
Hardcore Holly
NNO Edge/Cena/Orton

2008 Jakks Pacific WWE Micro Aggression Series 5

NNO CM Punk/Lashley/T.Dreamer
NNO Jeff Hardy/Cena/HBK
NNO Undertaker/Kennedy/Batista

2008 Jakks Pacific WWE Micro Aggression Series 6

NNO Carlito/King Booker/HHH
NNO Chris Masters/MVP/Edge
NNO Hardcore Holly/Burke/
Boogeyman

2008 Jakks Pacific WWE Micro Aggression Series 7

NNO John Cena/Umaga/Kennedy
NNO John Morrison/CM Punk/
Tommy Dreamer
NNO Matt Hardy/Batista/
Rey Mysterio

2008 Jakks Pacific WWE Micro Aggression Series 8

NNO Edge/Kane/Finlay
NNO Miz/Boogeyman/Burke
NNO Triple H/Jeff Hardy/Lashley

2008 Jakks Pacific WWE Micro Aggression Series 9

NNO CM Punk/Finlay/Morrison
NNO Rey Mysterio/MVP/Undertaker
NNO Shawn Michaels/Cena/Kennedy

2008 Jakks Pacific WWE Micro Aggression Series 10

NNO Chris Jericho/John Cena/JBL
NNO CM Punk/Elijah Burke/Domino
NNO Great Khali/Undertaker/Deuce

2008 Jakks Pacific WWE Micro Aggression Series 11

NNO Chavo/Big Daddy V/Benjamin
NNO Edge/Ric Flair/Kane
NNO Triple H/Cody Rhodes/Umaga

2008 Jakks Pacific WWE Micro Aggression Series 12

NNO Carlito/Santino/Orton
NNO Matt Hardy/Ryder/Hawkins
NNO Tommy Dreamer/Kofi/Miz

2009 Jakks Pacific WWE Micro Aggression Series 13

NNO Kane/Mysterio/Cena	10.00	20.00
NNO MVP/Undertaker/Jeff Hardy		
NNO Shawn Michaels/CM Punk/Y2J	12.50	25.00

2009 Jakks Pacific WWE Micro Aggression Series 14

NNO Carlito/Ryder/Hawkins	7.50	15.00
NNO Cody Rhodes/DiBiase/JBL	7.50	15.00
NNO Finlay/Dreamer/Matt Hardy		

2009 Jakks Pacific WWE Micro Aggression Series 15

NNO Cody Rhodes/Mysterio/Cena	10.00	20.00
NNO Edge/Jeff Hardy/HHH	7.50	15.00
NNO MVP/Matt Hardy/Morrison		

Jakks Pacific WWE Micro Aggression Series 16

NNO John Cena/Mysterio/ Undertaker	12.50	25.00
NNO Randy Orton/Rhodes/DiBiase		
NNO Triple H/MVP/Edge	10.00	20.00

2009 Jakks Pacific WWE Micro Aggression Series 17

NNO Finlay/Dreamer/Morrison		
NNO John Cena/Mysterio/Kane	12.50	25.00
NNO Undertaker/Hawkins/Ryder		

2001 Jakks Pacific WWF No Way Out Series 1

NNO Chris Jericho	10.00	20.00
NNO Grandmaster Sexay	7.50	15.00
NNO Kurt Angle		

NNO	The Rock	15.00	30.00
NNO	Scotty 2 Hotty	7.50	15.00
NNO	Stone Cold Steve Austin	12.50	25.00

2001 Jakks Pacific WWF No Way Out Series 2

NNO	Chris Benoit	15.00	30.00
NNO	Chris Jericho	15.00	30.00
NNO	Christian	10.00	20.00
NNO	Kurt Angle	12.50	25.00
NNO	Lita	10.00	20.00
NNO	Matt Hardy	12.50	25.00
NNO	Raven	10.00	20.00
NNO	Undertaker	15.00	30.00

2002 Jakks Pacific WWE nWo

NNO	Hulk Hogan/Tights	15.00	30.00
NNO	Hulk Hogan/T-Shirt	12.50	25.00
NNO	Kevin Nash/Tights	12.50	25.00
NNO	Kevin Nash/T-Shirt	10.00	20.00
NNO	Scott Hall/Tights	12.50	25.00
NNO	Scott Hall/T-Shirt	10.00	20.00

2002 Jakks Pacific WWE nWo 2-Packs

NNO	Hulk Hogan vs. The Rock	12.50	25.00
NNO	Kane vs. Kevin Nash	20.00	40.00
NNO	Steve Austin vs. Scott Hall	20.00	40.00

2002 Jakks Pacific WWE nWo Playset

NNO	Metal Match	30.00	60.00

2002 Jakks Pacific WWE Off the Ropes Series 1

NNO	Booker T	7.50	15.00
NNO	Brock Lesnar	10.00	20.00
NNO	Edge	7.50	15.00
NNO	Hollywood Hulk Hogan	15.00	30.00
NNO	Triple H	10.00	20.00
NNO	Trish Stratus	20.00	40.00

2003 Jakks Pacific WWE Off the Ropes Series 2

NNO	Chris Benoit	12.50	25.00
NNO	Hurricane	15.00	30.00
NNO	Kurt Angle	10.00	20.00
NNO	Matt Hardy		
NNO	Rikishi		

2003 Jakks Pacific WWE Off the Ropes Series 2 (loose)

NNO	Brock Lesnar	12.50	25.00
NNO	Chris Jericho	10.00	20.00
NNO	Christian	10.00	20.00
NNO	Rey Mysterio	15.00	30.00

2003 Jakks Pacific WWE Off the Ropes Series 4

NNO	Jamie Noble	7.50	15.00
NNO	Rob Van Dam	10.00	20.00
NNO	Scott Steiner	4.00	15.00
NNO	Undertaker		

2003 Jakks Pacific WWE Off the Ropes Series 5

NNO	Billy Gunn	10.00	20.00
NNO	Brock Lesnar	12.50	25.00
NNO	Eddie Guerrero	10.00	20.00
NNO	Ric Flair	7.50	15.00
NNO	Stone Cold Steve Austin	12.50	25.00
NNO	Triple H	10.00	20.00

2003 Jakks Pacific WWE Off the Ropes Series 6

NNO	Al Snow	12.50	25.00
NNO	A-Train	10.00	20.00
NNO	Big Show	7.50	15.00
NNO	Spike Dudley	10.00	20.00
NNO	Tajiri	12.50	25.00

2004 Jakks Pacific WWE Off the Ropes Series 7

NNO	Brock Lesnar	10.00	20.00
NNO	Chris Benoit	10.00	20.00
NNO	Lance Storm	7.50	15.00
NNO	Matt Hardy	12.50	25.00
NNO	Rob Van Dam	12.50	25.00
NNO	Triple H	10.00	20.00

2004 Jakks Pacific WWE Off the Ropes Series 8

NNO	JBL	10.00	20.00
NNO	Maven	10.00	20.00
NNO	Rob Van Dam	10.00	20.00
NNO	The Rock	15.00	30.00
NNO	Stacy Keibler	20.00	40.00
NNO	Steven Richards	7.50	15.00

2005 Jakks Pacific WWE Off the Ropes Series 9

NNO	Chris Benoit	12.50	25.00
NNO	Rey Mysterio	10.00	20.00
NNO	Triple H	10.00	20.00

2006 Jakks Pacific WWE Off the Ropes Series 10

NNO	Batista	7.50	15.00
NNO	Chris Masters	7.50	15.00
NNO	John Cena	10.00	20.00
NNO	Kurt Angle	10.00	20.00
NNO	Shawn Michaels	12.50	25.00

2007 Jakks Pacific WWE Off the Ropes Series 11

NNO	Boogeyman	
NNO	JBL	
NNO	John Cena	
NNO	Randy Orton	
NNO	Ric Flair	
NNO	Shawn Michaels	

2007 Jakks Pacific WWE Off the Ropes Series 12

NNO	Batista	
NNO	Elijah Burke	
NNO	The Great Khali	
NNO	Jeff Hardy	
NNO	Mr. Kennedy	
NNO	Tommy Dreamer	

2009 Jakks Pacific WWE Off the Ropes Series 13

NNO	Big Show	10.00	20.00
NNO	Chris Jericho	15.00	30.00
NNO	Festus	7.50	15.00
NNO	Hornswoggle		
NNO	JBL	7.50	15.00
NNO	Kofi Kingston	7.50	15.00

2003 Jakks Pacific WWE Pay Per View Series 1

Also known as First RAW Pay Per View Winners (Bad Blood).

NNO	Booker T	12.50	25.00
NNO	Goldberg	20.00	40.00
NNO	Ric Flair	10.00	20.00
NNO	Scott Steiner	30.00	75.00
NNO	Stone Cold Steve Austin		
NNO	Triple H		

2003 Jakks Pacific WWE Pay Per View Series 2

Also known as SummerSlam Elimination Chamber.

NNO	Eddie Guerrero	
NNO	Goldberg	
NNO	Kurt Angle	
NNO	Stone Cold Steve Austin	
NNO	Triple H	
NNO	Undertaker	

2003 Jakks Pacific WWE Pay Per View Series 3

Also known as Survivor Series.

NNO	Kane	
NNO	Kurt Angle	
NNO	Randy Orton	
NNO	Eric Bischoff	
NNO	Goldberg	
NNO	John Cena	

2004 Jakks Pacific WWE Pay Per View Series 4

Also known as WWE Backlash.

NNO	Chris Benoit	10.00	20.00
NNO	Chris Jericho	15.00	30.00
NNO	Edge	10.00	20.00
NNO	Hurricane	12.50	25.00

NNO	Randy Orton	15.00	30.00
NNO	Shelton Benjamin	12.50	25.00

2004 Jakks Pacific WWE Pay Per View Series 6

Also known as Bad Blood/Great American Bash. The Bad Blood set contained Chris Jericho, Edge, and Kane while the Great American Bash set contained JBL, John Cena, and Torrie Wilson.

NNO	Chris Jericho	10.00	20.00
NNO	Edge	15.00	30.00
NNO	JBL	10.00	20.00
NNO	John Cena	12.50	25.00
NNO	Kane	7.50	15.00
NNO	Torrie Wilson	20.00	40.00

2004 Jakks Pacific WWE Pay Per View Series 7

Also known as WWE SummerSlam.

NNO	Eddie Guerrero	10.00	20.00
NNO	Edge	7.50	15.00
NNO	JBL	6.00	12.00
NNO	Randy Orton	12.50	25.00
NNO	Trish Stratus	15.00	30.00
NNO	Undertaker	12.50	25.00

2005 Jakks Pacific WWE Pay Per View Series 8

Also known as WWE New Year's Revolution.

NNO	Batista	12.50	25.00
NNO	Eugene	10.00	20.00
NNO	Kane	15.00	30.00
NNO	Maven	7.50	15.00
NNO	Shawn Michaels/Ref Gear	15.00	30.00
NNO	Triple H	7.50	15.00

2005 Jakks Pacific WWE Pay Per View Series 9

Also known as ECW PPV The Return of ECW.

NNO	Bubba Ray Dudley	12.50	25.00
NNO	D-Von Dudley	10.00	20.00
NNO	Eric Bischoff		
NNO	JBL	7.50	15.00
NNO	Kurt Angle/Referee Gear		
NNO	Paul Heyman	10.00	20.00
NNO	Rey Mysterio	15.00	30.00
NNO	Rob Van Dam	10.00	20.00
NNO	Stone Cold Steve Austin		
NNO	Tajiri	12.50	25.00
NNO	Tazz	7.50	15.00
NNO	Tommy Dreamer	15.00	30.00

2006 Jakks Pacific WWE Pay Per View Series 10

Also known as Great American Bash.

NNO	Animal	7.50	15.00
NNO	Batista	7.50	15.00
NNO	JBL/Vest		
NNO	Orlando Jordan	12.50	25.00
NNO	Rey Mysterio	12.50	25.00
NNO	Undertaker	15.00	30.00

2006 Jakks Pacific WWE Pay Per View Series 11

Also known as Survivor Series.

NNO	Batista	15.00	30.00
NNO	Daivari/Ref Gear		
NNO	John Cena		
NNO	Kurt Angle	7.50	15.00
NNO	Randy Orton	10.00	20.00
NNO	Undertaker		

2006 Jakks Pacific WWE Pay Per View Series 12

Also known as No Way Out.

NNO	Gregory Helms	10.00	20.00
NNO	Kurt Angle	12.50	25.00
NNO	Matt Hardy	12.50	25.00
NNO	Randy Orton	15.00	30.00
NNO	Rey Mysterio	15.00	30.00
NNO	Undertaker	12.50	25.00

2006 Jakks Pacific WWE Pay Per View Series 13

Also known as WWE Backlash.

NNO	Carlito	

NNO Edge — 15.00 / 30.00
NNO John Cena — 20.00 / 40.00
NNO Ric Flair — 12.50 / 25.00
NNO Rob Van Dam — 10.00 / 20.00
NNO Shawn Michaels

2007 Jakks Pacific WWE Pay Per View Series 14

Also known as Cyber Sunday.

NNO Carlito
NNO Eric Bischoff/Ref Gear
NNO Jeff Hardy
NNO John Cena
NNO King Booker
NNO Umaga

2007 Jakks Pacific WWE Pay Per View Series 15

Also known as No Way Out.

NNO Batista
NNO Brian Kendrick
NNO Finlay
NNO John Cena
NNO Johnny Nitro
NNO Kane

2007 Jakks Pacific WWE Pay Per View Series 16

Also known as Vengeance.

NNO Bobby Lashley
NNO Deuce
NNO Edge
NNO John Cena
NNO Mark Henry
NNO Matt Hardy

2008 Jakks Pacific WWE Pay Per View Series 17

Also known as No Mercy.

NNO Batista
NNO CM Punk
NNO Randy Orton
NNO Rey Mysterio
NNO Triple H
NNO Umaga

2008 Jakks Pacific WWE Pay Per View Series 18

Also known as No Way Out.

NNO Chavo Guerrero
NNO Edge
NNO JBL
NNO John Cena
NNO Triple H
NNO Undertaker

2008 Jakks Pacific WWE Pay Per View Series 19

Also known as WWE One Night Only.

NNO Batista
NNO Big Show
NNO JBL
NNO Triple H
NNO Umaga
NNO Undertaker

2008 Jakks Pacific WWE Pay Per View Series 20

Also known as Cyber Sunday.

NNO Batista
NNO Jeff Hardy
NNO Matt Hardy
NNO Rey Mysterio
NNO Triple H
NNO Undertaker

2008 Jakks Pacific WWE Pay Per View Series 21

Also known as No Way Out.

NNO Edge
NNO Jack Swagger
NNO Randy Orton
NNO Shane McMahon
NNO Shawn Michaels
NNO Triple H

2001 Jakks Pacific WWF Playsets

NNO Attitude Ring — 25.00 / 50.00
NNO Hardcore Action Ring — 20.00 / 40.00
w/Ref/Jim Ross
NNO Hardcore Action Ring — 20.00 / 40.00
w/Ref/Jim Ross/Mick Foley

2016-17 Jakks Pacific WWE Plush Hangers

NNO AJ Styles
NNO Brock Lesnar
NNO Dean Ambrose
NNO Finn Balor
NNO John Cena
NNO Roman Reigns
NNO Seth Rollins
NNO Undertaker

2000 Jakks Pacific WWF Prop Boxes

NNO Back Alley Street Fight — 12.50 / 25.00
NNO Break Room Brawl
NNO House of Pain — 20.00 / 40.00

2004 Jakks Pacific WWE Pump 'N Flex Series 1

NNO Chris Benoit — 7.50 / 15.00
NNO Eddie Guerrero — 15.00 / 30.00
NNO John Cena — 20.00 / 40.00
NNO Kane — 12.50 / 25.00
NNO Kurt Angle — 10.00 / 20.00
NNO Triple H — 10.00 / 20.00

2004 Jakks Pacific WWE Pump 'N Flex Series 2

NNO Batista
NNO Booker T — 12.50 / 25.00
NNO John Cena — 12.50 / 25.00
NNO Randy Orton — 7.50 / 15.00
NNO Rene Dupree

2003 Jakks Pacific WWE RAW 10th Anniversary

NNO Goldust — 10.00 / 20.00
NNO Jeff Hardy — 15.00 / 30.00
NNO Jerry Lawler — 12.50 / 25.00
NNO Kurt Angle — 10.00 / 20.00
NNO The Rock — 15.00 / 30.00
NNO RVD — 12.50 / 25.00
NNO Shane McMahon — 15.00 / 30.00
NNO Shawn Michaels — 12.50 / 25.00
NNO Steve Austin — 20.00 / 40.00
NNO Triple H — 10.00 / 20.00
NNO Trish Stratus — 15.00 / 30.00
NNO Undertaker — 17.50 / 35.00

2002 Jakks Pacific WWE RAW Draft

1 Undertaker/27,500* — 12.50 / 25.00
2A Kevin Nash/8,750* — 12.50 / 25.00
2B Scott Hall/8,750* — 12.50 / 25.00
2C X-Pac/10,000* — 7.50 / 15.00
3 Kane/25,000* — 12.50 / 25.00
4 Rob Van Dam/21,250* — 10.00 / 20.00
5 Booker T/20,000* — 12.50 / 25.00
6 Big Show/18,750* — 10.00 / 20.00
7 Bubba Ray/18,750* — 12.50 / 25.00
8 Brock Lesnar
9 William Regal/16,250* — 10.00 / 20.00
10 Lita/16,250* — 15.00 / 30.00
11 Bradshaw/13,750* — 7.50 / 15.00
12 Steven Richards/12,500*
13 Matt Hardy/11,250* — 10.00 / 20.00
14 Raven/8,750* — 12.50 / 25.00
15 Jeff Hardy/7,500* — 20.00 / 40.00
16 Mr. Perfect
17 Spike Dudley/5,000*
18 D'Lo Brown
19 Shawn Stasiak
20 Terri

1999 Jakks Pacific WWF RAW Is War

NNO Mankind — 7.50 / 15.00
NNO The Rock — 15.00 / 30.00

NNO Stone Cold Steve Austin — 7.50 / 15.00
NNO Undertaker — 10.00 / 20.00

2003 Jakks Pacific WWE RAW Uncovered

NNO Jeff Hardy — 20.00 / 40.00
NNO Kane — 50.00 / 100.00
NNO Kurt Angle — 15.00 / 30.00
NNO Matt Hardy — 15.00 / 30.00
NNO Rey Mysterio — 20.00 / 40.00
NNO Rob Van Dam — 12.50 / 25.00

2002 Jakks Pacific WWF Real Reaction R-3 Tech Series 1

NNO Chris Benoit — 12.50 / 25.00
NNO Chris Jericho — 10.00 / 20.00
NNO Kane — 15.00 / 30.00
NNO Matt Hardy — 10.00 / 20.00
NNO The Rock — 10.00 / 20.00
NNO Stone Cold Steve Austin — 12.50 / 25.00

2002 Jakks Pacific WWF Real Reaction R-3 Tech Series 2

NNO Big Show — 12.50 / 25.00
NNO Edge — 10.00 / 20.00
NNO Jeff Hardy — 15.00 / 30.00
NNO Rock — 10.00 / 20.00
NNO Stone Cold Steve Austin — 10.00 / 20.00
NNO Undertaker — 15.00 / 30.00

2002 Jakks Pacific WWF Real Reaction R-3 Tech Series 3

NNO Big Show — 12.50 / 25.00
NNO Jeff Hardy — 15.00 / 30.00
NNO Kane
NNO Matt Hardy — 7.50 / 15.00
NNO Stone Cold Steve Austin
NNO Undertaker — 10.00 / 20.00

2002 Jakks Pacific WWF Real Reaction R-3 Tech Series 4

NNO Billy Gunn — 7.50 / 15.00
NNO Chuck Palumbo — 7.50 / 15.00
NNO Kurt Angle — 7.50 / 15.00
NNO Rikishi — 7.50 / 15.00
NNO Test — 6.00 / 12.00
NNO Triple H — 12.50 / 25.00

2002 Jakks Pacific WWF Real Reaction R-3 Tech Series 5

NNO Booker T — 7.50 / 15.00
NNO Chris Benoit — 7.50 / 15.00
NNO Jeff Hardy — 10.00 / 20.00
NNO Kevin Nash — 7.50 / 15.00
NNO Rob Van Dam — 6.00 / 12.00
NNO Undertaker — 12.50 / 25.00

2000 Jakks Pacific WWF Rebellion Series 1

Also known as WrestleMania XVII.

NNO Chris Benoit — 10.00 / 20.00
NNO Chris Jericho — 12.50 / 25.00
NNO Jeff Hardy — 7.50 / 15.00
NNO The Rock — 12.50 / 25.00
NNO Undertaker — 15.00 / 30.00
NNO X-Pac — 7.50 / 15.00

2001 Jakks Pacific WWF Rebellion Series 2

NNO Chris Benoit — 10.00 / 20.00
NNO Chris Jericho — 7.50 / 15.00
NNO Crash Holly — 10.00 / 20.00
NNO Kurt Angle — 10.00 / 20.00
NNO The Rock — 15.00 / 30.00

2001 Jakks Pacific WWF Rebellion Series 3

NNO D-Von Dudley — 7.50 / 15.00
NNO Jeff Hardy — 12.50 / 25.00
NNO Kurt Angle — 10.00 / 20.00
NNO Stone Cold Steve Austin — 20.00 / 40.00
NNO The Rock — 12.50 / 25.00

NNO	Triple H	7.50	15.00
NNO	Undertaker	12.50	25.00

2001 Jakks Pacific WWF Rebellion Series 4

NNO	Billy Gunn	7.50	15.00
NNO	Chris Benoit	10.00	20.00
NNO	Edge	10.00	20.00
NNO	HHH	10.00	20.00
NNO	Lita	10.00	20.00
NNO	X-Pac	7.50	15.00

2002 Jakks Pacific WWE Relentless

NNO	Booker T		
NNO	Edge	10.00	20.00
NNO	Rob Van Dam	15.00	30.00
NNO	Triple H		

2005 Jakks Pacific WWE Ring Giants Classic Series 1

NNO	Rowdy Roddy Piper	30.00	60.00
NNO	Ted DiBiase	25.00	50.00
NNO	Ultimate Warrior	30.00	75.00

2005 Jakks Pacific WWE Ring Giants Series 1

NNO	Chris Benoit	20.00	40.00
NNO	Eddie Guerrero	15.00	30.00
NNO	John Cena	15.00	30.00
NNO	Triple H	15.00	30.00

2005 Jakks Pacific WWE Ring Giants Series 2

NNO	Batista	12.50	25.00
NNO	Booker T	15.00	30.00
NNO	Kurt Angle	20.00	40.00
NNO	Randy Orton	15.00	30.00

2005 Jakks Pacific WWE Ring Giants Series 3

NNO	Carlito/Hair	20.00	40.00
NNO	Carlito/No Hair		
NNO	Kane	12.50	25.00
NNO	Rey Mysterio	30.00	75.00
	Red White Blue Pants		
NNO	Shawn Michaels	20.00	40.00

2005 Jakks Pacific WWE Ring Giants Series 4

NNO	Batista	15.00	30.00
NNO	John Cena	20.00	40.00
NNO	Rey Mysterio	15.00	30.00
NNO	Undertaker	20.00	40.00

2006 Jakks Pacific WWE Ring Giants Series 5

NNO	Batista		
NNO	John Cena		
NNO	Kurt Angle		
NNO	Rey Mysterio		

2006 Jakks Pacific WWE Ring Giants Series 6

NNO	Bobby Lashley		
NNO	Boogeyman		
NNO	Kurt Angle		
NNO	Rey Mysterio		

2006 Jakks Pacific WWE Ring Giants Series 7

NNO	Batista		
NNO	Hulk Hogan		
NNO	John Cena		
NNO	Rob Van Dam		

2007 Jakks Pacific WWE Ring Giants Series 8

NNO	Edge		
NNO	John Cena		
NNO	Rey Mysterio		
NNO	Shawn Michaels		

2007 Jakks Pacific WWE Ring Giants Series 9

NNO	Carlito		
NNO	Shawn Michaels		
NNO	Triple H		
NNO	Undertaker		

2007 Jakks Pacific WWE Ring Giants Series 10

NNO	Batista		
NNO	Jeff Hardy		
NNO	Mr. Kennedy		
NNO	Randy Orton		

2007 Jakks Pacific WWE Ring Giants Series 11

NNO	Boogeyman		
NNO	Edge		
NNO	Fit Finlay		
NNO	Matt Hardy		

2007 Jakks Pacific WWE Ring Giants Series 12

NNO	Jeff Hardy		
NNO	John Cena		
NNO	Rey Mysterio		
NNO	Triple H		

2007 Jakks Pacific WWE Ring Giants Series 13

NNO	Boogeyman		
NNO	Finlay		
NNO	Matt Hardy		
NNO	Randy Orton		

1997 Jakks Pacific WWF Ring Masters

NNO	Bret Hit Man Hart	10.00	20.00
NNO	Goldust	6.00	12.00
NNO	Shawn Michaels	10.00	20.00
NNO	Sycho Sid	6.00	12.00
NNO	Undertaker	7.50	15.00
NNO	Yokozuna		

2002 Jakks Pacific WWE Ringleader Collection

NNO	Chris Jericho	10.00	20.00
NNO	Hollywood Hulk Hogan	17.50	35.00
NNO	The Rock	10.00	20.00
NNO	Triple H	15.00	30.00
NNO	Undertaker	15.00	30.00

2002 Jakks Pacific WWE Ringside Rebels Series 1

NNO	The Rock	20.00	40.00
NNO	Stone Cold Steve Austin		
NNO	Undertaker	25.00	50.00

2002 Jakks Pacific WWE Ringside Rebels Series 2

NNO	Chris Jericho	15.00	30.00
NNO	The Rock	15.00	30.00
NNO	Triple H	12.50	25.00

2002 Jakks Pacific WWE Ringside Rebels Series 3

NNO	Booker T	10.00	20.00
NNO	Rob Van Dam	15.00	30.00
NNO	Triple H	12.50	25.00

2002 Jakks Pacific WWE Ringside Rebels Series 4

NNO	Hulk Hogan	20.00	40.00
NNO	Jeff Hardy	15.00	30.00

2002 Jakks Pacific WWE Ringside Rivals Fatal Showdown

NNO	Chris Jericho vs. Triple H		
NNO	Jeff Hardy vs. Eddie Guerrero		
NNO	Undertaker vs. Hollywood Hogan		

2002 Jakks Pacific WWE Ringside Rivals Head to Head

NNO	Edge vs. Kurt Angle		
NNO	Rob Van Dam vs. Booker T		
NNO	Test vs. Tajiri		

2002 Jakks Pacific WWE Ringside Rivals New Series

NNO	Billy Gunn vs. Chuck Palumbo		
NNO	Matt Hardy vs. Jeff Hardy		
NNO	The Rock vs. Brock Lesnar		

2002 Jakks Pacific WWE Ringside Rivals Raging Tempers

NNO	Rob Van Dam vs. Test		
NNO	The Rock vs. Booker T		
NNO	Vince McMahon vs. Ric Flair		

2001 Jakks Pacific WWF Ringside Rivals Series 1

NNO	Bradshaw vs. Test	10.00	20.00
NNO	Father (Vince) vs. Son (Shane)	12.50	25.00
NNO	The Rock vs. Stone Cold Steve Austin	15.00	30.00

2001 Jakks Pacific WWF Ringside Rivals Series 2

NNO	Edge vs. Christian	25.00	50.00
NNO	Kurt Angle vs. Undertaker	15.00	30.00
NNO	Matt Hardy vs. Bubba Ray Dudley	12.50	25.00
NNO	The Rock vs. Chris Jericho	25.00	50.00
NNO	Triple H vs. Stone Cold Steve Austin	20.00	40.00
NNO	William Regal vs. Mick Foley	20.00	40.00

2002 Jakks Pacific WWF Ringside Rivals Series 3

NNO	D-Von vs. Spike		
NNO	Edge vs. William Regal		
NNO	Triple H vs. Kurt Angle		

1998 Jakks Pacific WWF Ringside Collection Series 1

NNO	Referee	5.00	10.00
NNO	Sable	7.50	15.00
NNO	Sunny	10.00	20.00
NNO	Vince McMahon	6.00	12.00

1998 Jakks Pacific WWF Ringside Collection Series 2

NNO	Honky Tonk Man	6.00	12.00
NNO	Jim Cornette	15.00	30.00
NNO	Jim Ross	12.50	25.00
NNO	Referee	5.00	10.00
NNO	Sgt. Slaughter	7.50	15.00
NNO	Vince McMahon	7.50	15.00

1997 Jakks Pacific WWF Ripped and Ruthless Series 1

NNO	Goldust	5.00	10.00
NNO	Mankind	7.50	15.00
NNO	Stone Cold Steve Austin	10.00	20.00
NNO	Undertaker	12.50	25.00

1998 Jakks Pacific WWF Ripped and Ruthless Series 2

NNO	Kane	15.00	30.00
NNO	Sable	12.50	25.00
NNO	Shawn Michaels	10.00	20.00
NNO	Triple H	10.00	20.00

1998 Jakks Pacific WWF Ripped and Ruthless 2-Pack

NNO	Undertaker/Stone Cold Steve Austin		

1999 Jakks Pacific WWF Road Rage

Also known as SummerSlam '99 Road Rage.

NNO	Al Snow	7.50	15.00
NNO	Gangrel	7.50	15.00
NNO	Godfather	10.00	20.00
NNO	Hardcore Holly	6.00	12.00
NNO	The Rock	12.50	25.00
NNO	Test	6.00	12.00

2002 Jakks Pacific WWF Road to WrestleMania

NNO	Bubba Ray Dudley		
NNO	Chris Benoit		
NNO	Chris Jericho		
NNO	D-Von Dudley		
NNO	Jeff Hardy		
NNO	Undertaker		

2006 Jakks Pacific WWE Road to WrestleMania 22 Gear and Figure Sets

NNO	Kane/Glove & Elbow Pad		
NNO	Rey Mysterio/Mask		
NNO	Triple H/Crown		

2006 Jakks Pacific WWE Road to WrestleMania 22 Series 1

NNO	Chris Benoit		
NNO	Eddie Guerrero		

NNO John Cena
NNO Kurt Angle
NNO Rey Mysterio
NNO Shawn Michaels
NNO Shawn Michaels
Hulk Hogan Costume

2006 Jakks Pacific WWE Road to WrestleMania 22
2-Packs Series 1

NNO Batista/JBL
NNO Edge/Matt Hardy
NNO Undertaker/Randy Orton

2006 Jakks Pacific WWE Road to WrestleMania 22
Series 2

NNO Batista
NNO Carlito
NNO Chris Masters
NNO John Cena
NNO Kurt Angle
NNO Shawn Michaels

2006 Jakks Pacific WWE Road to WrestleMania 22
2-Packs Series 2

NNO Kane/Big Show
NNO Rey Mysterio/Matt Hardy
NNO Rob Conway/Tyson Tomko

2006 Jakks Pacific WWE Road to WrestleMania 22
Series 3

NNO Bobby Lashley
NNO Finlay
NNO Matt Hardy
NNO Ric Flair
NNO RVD
NNO Shelton Benjamin

2006 Jakks Pacific WWE Road to WrestleMania 22
2-Packs Series 3

NNO John Cena/Edge
NNO Kurt Angle/Rey Mysterio
NNO Undertaker/Mark Henry

2007 Jakks Pacific WWE Road to WrestleMania 23
Series 1

NNO Batista
NNO King Booker
NNO Rey Mysterio
NNO Ric Flair
NNO Shawn Michaels
NNO Triple H

2007 Jakks Pacific WWE Road to WrestleMania 23
2-Packs Series 1

NNO John Cena/Edge
NNO Randy Orton/Hulk Hogan
NNO Sabu/Big Show

2007 Jakks Pacific WWE Road to WrestleMania 23
Series 2

NNO Batista
NNO Chris Benoit
NNO CM Punk
NNO Ron Simmons
NNO Triple H

2007 Jakks Pacific WWE Road to WrestleMania 23
2-Packs Series 2

NNO Bobby Lashley/John Cena
NNO Matt Hardy/Jeff Hardy
NNO Undertaker/Mr. Kennedy

2007 Jakks Pacific WWE Road to WrestleMania 23
Series 3

NNO CM Punk
NNO Elijah Burke
NNO Jeff Hardy

NNO Matt Hardy
NNO Mr. Kennedy
NNO MVP

2007 Jakks Pacific WWE Road to WrestleMania 23
2-Packs Series 3

NNO Batista/Undertaker
NNO Bobby Lashley/Umaga
NNO John Cena/Shawn Michaels

2008 Jakks Pacific WWE Road to WrestleMania 24
Series 1

NNO Batista
NNO Carlito
NNO CM Punk/Blue Trunks
NNO Kane
NNO Mr. Kennedy
NNO Umaga

2008 Jakks Pacific WWE Road to WrestleMania 24
Series 1 2-Packs

NNO Randy Orton/John Cena
NNO Rey Mysterio/Chavo Guerrero   15.00   30.00
NNO Triple H/Mr. McMahon

2008 Jakks Pacific WWE Road to WrestleMania 24
Series 2

NNO Batista
NNO CM Punk/Red Trunks
NNO Kane
NNO Triple H
NNO Umaga
NNO Undertaker

2008 Jakks Pacific WWE Road to WrestleMania 24
Series 2 2-Packs

NNO Finlay & Mysterio
NNO Mr. Kennedy & Jeff Hardy
NNO Shawn Michaels & Randy Orton

2008 Jakks Pacific WWE Road to WrestleMania 24
Series 3

NNO Chris Jericho
NNO CM Punk/Black Trunks
NNO Finlay
NNO John Cena
NNO Kane
NNO Randy Orton

2008 Jakks Pacific WWE Road to WrestleMania 24
Series 3 2-Packs

NNO Batista & Umaga
NNO Edge & Undertaker
NNO Ric Flair & Shawn Michaels

2008 Jakks Pacific WWE Road to WrestleMania 24
Best of WrestleMania

NNO Batista
NNO John Cena
NNO Kane
NNO Rey Mysterio
NNO Shawn Michaels
NNO Triple H

2008 Jakks Pacific WWE Road to WrestleMania 24
Mask and Figure Sets

NNO Rey Mysterio
Black and Green Pants
NNO Rey Mysterio/Blue Pants
NNO Rey Mysterio/Silver Pants

2002 Jakks Pacific WWE Rollin' Rebels

NNO Hulk Hogan   30.00   75.00
NNO Undertaker   30.00   60.00

2002 Jakks Pacific WWE Royal Rumble

NNO Chris Jericho   7.50   15.00
NNO Referee Earl Hebner   6.00   12.00
NNO Ric Flair   10.00   20.00

NNO Tazz   6.00   12.00
NNO Triple H   7.50   15.00
NNO William Regal   6.00   12.00

2006 Jakks Pacific WWE Royal Rumble

NNO Carlito
NNO Randy Orton
NNO Rey Mysterio
NNO Rob Van Dam   12.50   25.00
NNO Shawn Michaels
NNO Triple H

2007 Jakks Pacific WWE Royal Rumble

NNO Batista
NNO Bobby Lashley
NNO John Cena
NNO Mr. Kennedy
NNO Shawn Michaels
NNO Undertaker

2008 Jakks Pacific WWE Royal Rumble

NNO Chris Jericho
NNO Edge
NNO JBL
NNO John Cena
NNO Randy Orton
NNO Ric Flair

2009 Jakks Pacific WWE Royal Rumble

NNO Cody Rhodes
NNO Great Khali
NNO Kane
NNO Mark Henry
NNO Ted DiBiase
NNO Vladimir Kozlov

2008 Jakks Pacific WWE Royal Rumble Playset

NNO Deluxe Ring
{w/Cena/Y2J/Mysterio/Edge}

2000 Jakks Pacific WWF Rulers of the Ring Series
1

NNO Al Snow   6.00   12.00
NNO Buh Buh Ray   7.50   15.00
NNO D-Von   7.50   15.00
NNO Edge   6.00   12.00
NNO Ivory   10.00   20.00
NNO Tazz   10.00   20.00

2000 Jakks Pacific WWF Rulers of the Ring Series
2

NNO Big Boss Man   7.50   15.00
NNO Brian Christopher   7.50   15.00
NNO Crash Holly   6.00   12.00
NNO Rikishi   7.50   15.00
NNO Scotty 2 Hotty   6.00   12.00
NNO Steve Blackman   10.00   20.00

2001 Jakks Pacific WWF Rulers of the Ring Series
3

NNO Eddie Guerrero   12.50   25.00
NNO Perry Saturn   10.00   20.00
NNO Prince Albert   10.00   20.00
NNO Raven   12.50   25.00
NNO Stephanie McMahon-Helmsley   10.00   20.00
NNO Steven Richards   7.50   15.00

2001 Jakks Pacific WWF Rulers of the Ring Series
4

NNO Bob Holly   10.00   20.00
NNO Christian   7.50   15.00
NNO Justin Credible   10.00   20.00
NNO Molly Holly   10.00   20.00
NNO Shane McMahon   15.00   30.00

2003 Jakks Pacific WWE Ruthless Aggression
Best of 2003

NNO A-Train
NNO Chavo Guerrero

NNO Eric Bischoff
NNO Goldust
NNO Rey Mysterio
NNO Rico
NNO Scott Steiner

2006 Jakks Pacific WWE Ruthless Aggression
Best of 2006

NNO Boogeyman
NNO Carlito
NNO Chris Masters
NNO Edge
NNO John Cena
NNO Kurt Angle
NNO Rey Mysterio
NNO Rob Van Dam
NNO Shawn Michaels

2007 Jakks Pacific WWE Ruthless Aggression
Best of 2007

NNO Great Khali	15.00	30.00
NNO John Cena	10.00	20.00
NNO Rey Mysterio	12.50	25.00
NNO Shawn Michaels	10.00	20.00
NNO Umaga		
NNO Undertaker		

2008 Jakks Pacific WWE Ruthless Aggression
Best of 2008

NNO Batista		
NNO John Cena	10.00	20.00
NNO Ric Flair	12.50	25.00
NNO Triple H	10.00	20.00
NNO Umaga	10.00	20.00
NNO Undertaker		

2009 Jakks Pacific WWE Ruthless Aggression
Best of 2009

NNO Batista		
NNO Hornswoggle		
NNO John Cena		
NNO Randy Orton		
NNO Rey Mysterio	15.00	30.00
NNO Triple H		

2002 Jakks Pacific WWE Ruthless Aggression
Series 1

NNO Brock Lesnar	15.00	30.00
NNO Chavo Guerrero	7.50	15.00
NNO Eric Bischoff	20.00	40.00
NNO John Cena	15.00	30.00
NNO Randy Orton	10.00	20.00
NNO Rey Mysterio		

2003 Jakks Pacific WWE Ruthless Aggression
Series 2

NNO Batista	6.00	12.00
NNO Billy Kidman	7.50	15.00
NNO Jamie Noble	6.00	12.00
NNO Rico	6.00	12.00
NNO Scott Steiner	7.50	15.00
NNO Tommy Dreamer	15.00	30.00

2003 Jakks Pacific WWE Ruthless Aggression
Series 3

NNO A-Train		
NNO Goldust	10.00	20.00
NNO John Cena	15.00	30.00
NNO Rey Mysterio	12.50	25.00
NNO Rob Van Dam	12.50	25.00
NNO Scott Steiner	25.00	50.00

2003 Jakks Pacific WWE Ruthless Aggression
Series 3.5

NNO Chavo Guerrero		
NNO Eric Bischoff	12.50	25.00
NNO Goldust		
NNO Rey Mysterio		

NNO Rico
NNO Scott Steiner

2003 Jakks Pacific WWE Ruthless Aggression
Series 4

NNO Bill Goldberg	25.00	50.00
NNO Chris Benoit	15.00	30.00
NNO Eddie Guerrero	10.00	20.00
NNO The Hurricane	15.00	30.00
NNO The Rock	25.00	50.00
NNO Undertaker	12.50	25.00

2003 Jakks Pacific WWE Ruthless Aggression
Series 5

NNO Billy Kidman	7.50	15.00
NNO John Cena	15.00	30.00
NNO Kane	15.00	30.00
NNO Kevin Nash	7.50	15.00
NNO Shawn Michaels	12.50	25.00
NNO Tajiri	7.50	15.00

2003 Jakks Pacific WWE Ruthless Aggression
Series 6

NNO Bill Goldberg	30.00	60.00
NNO Kurt Angle	7.50	15.00
NNO Maven	6.00	12.00
NNO Rey Mysterio	12.50	25.00
NNO Rob Van Dam	6.00	12.00
NNO Triple H	20.00	40.00

2003 Jakks Pacific WWE Ruthless Aggression
Series 7

NNO Brock Lesnar	15.00	30.00
NNO Chris Benoit	25.00	50.00
NNO Chris Jericho	12.50	25.00
NNO Kane/Unmasked	10.00	20.00
NNO Matt Hardy	10.00	20.00
NNO Randy Orton	10.00	20.00

2003 Jakks Pacific WWE Ruthless Aggression
Series 7.5

NNO Bill Goldberg		
NNO Chris Jericho		
NNO Goldust		
NNO Rey Mysterio	6.00	12.00
NNO Rob Van Dam		
NNO Stone Cold Steve Austin		

2004 Jakks Pacific WWE Ruthless Aggression
Series 8

NNO Bill Goldberg	30.00	75.00
NNO Christian (long sleeves)	12.50	25.00
NNO Christian (short sleeves)		
NNO Kurt Angle	6.00	12.00
NNO Test		
NNO The Rock	15.00	30.00
NNO Ultimo Dragon	20.00	40.00

2004 Jakks Pacific WWE Ruthless Aggression
Series 8.5

NNO A-Train		
NNO Big Show	6.00	12.00
NNO Eddie Guerrero	7.50	15.00
NNO John Cena	6.00	12.00
NNO Rey Mysterio		
NNO Undertaker		

2004 Jakks Pacific WWE Ruthless Aggression
Series 9

NNO Booker T SE	15.00	30.00
NNO Jamie Noble	7.50	15.00
NNO Kane	10.00	20.00
NNO Matt Hardy	12.50	25.00
NNO Matt Morgan	10.00	20.00
NNO Rob Van Dam	10.00	20.00
NNO Stone Cold Steve Austin	12.50	25.00

2004 Jakks Pacific WWE Ruthless Aggression
Series 10

NNO Chris Benoit	10.00	20.00
NNO Chris Jericho	7.50	15.00
NNO Edge	15.00	30.00
NNO Kurt Angle	10.00	20.00
NNO Rey Mysterio	12.50	25.00
NNO Ultimo Dragon	12.50	25.00

2004 Jakks Pacific WWE Ruthless Aggression
Series 10.5

NNO Charlie Haas		
NNO Jamie Noble	7.50	15.00
NNO John Bradshaw Layfield		
NNO Matt Hardy	10.00	20.00
NNO Shelton Benjamin		
NNO Tajiri		

2004 Jakks Pacific WWE Ruthless Aggression
Series 11

NNO Batista	7.50	15.00
NNO Booker T	12.50	25.00
NNO Eugene	7.50	15.00
NNO John Cena	7.50	15.00
NNO Rene Dupree	6.00	12.00
NNO Undertaker	10.00	20.00

2004 Jakks Pacific WWE Ruthless Aggression
Series 11.5

NNO Charlie Haas		
NNO John Cena		
NNO Randy Orton	10.00	20.00
NNO Rene Dupree		
NNO Rob Conway		
NNO Shelton Benjamin		

2004 Jakks Pacific WWE Ruthless Aggression
Series 12

NNO Booker T	7.50	15.00
NNO Chris Jericho	7.50	15.00
NNO Eric Bischoff	10.00	20.00
NNO Kurt Angle	12.50	25.00
NNO Randy Orton	7.50	15.00
NNO Rey Mysterio	12.50	25.00

2004 Jakks Pacific WWE Ruthless Aggression
Series 12.5

NNO Chris Benoit		
NNO Edge		
NNO Eric Bischoff		
NNO Randy Orton		
NNO Shelton Benjamin		
NNO Triple H		

2005 Jakks Pacific WWE Ruthless Aggression
Series 13

NNO Chavo Guerrero	7.50	15.00
NNO Kurt Angle	10.00	20.00
NNO Rosey	12.50	25.00
NNO Shelton Benjamin	10.00	20.00
NNO Tyson Tomko	7.50	15.00
NNO William Regal	10.00	20.00

2005 Jakks Pacific WWE Ruthless Aggression
Series 14

NNO John Cena	15.00	30.00
NNO Ric Flair	10.00	20.00
NNO Shelton Benjamin	7.50	15.00
NNO Triple H	10.00	20.00
NNO Trish Stratus	12.50	25.00
NNO Undertaker	7.50	15.00

2005 Jakks Pacific WWE Ruthless Aggression
Series 15

NNO Big Show	17.50	35.00
NNO Carlito	7.50	15.00
NNO Christian	12.50	25.00
NNO Gene Snitsky	15.00	30.00

NNO	Johnathan Coachman	7.50	15.00
NNO	Mark Jindrak	7.50	15.00

2005 Jakks Pacific WWE Ruthless Aggression
Series 15.5

NNO	Chris Masters		
NNO	Eric Bischoff		
NNO	Heidenreich		
NNO	Scotty 2 Hotty		
NNO	Shannon Moore		
NNO	Simon Dean		

2005 Jakks Pacific WWE Ruthless Aggression
Series 16

NNO	Batista	10.00	20.00
NNO	Kurt Angle	12.50	25.00
NNO	Rey Mysterio	12.50	25.00
NNO	Stone Cold Steve Austin	10.00	20.00
NNO	Triple H	10.00	20.00
NNO	Undertaker	12.50	25.00

2005 Jakks Pacific WWE Ruthless Aggression
Series 16.5

NNO	Chris Jericho		
NNO	John Cena		
NNO	Rob Van Dam		
NNO	Shawn Michaels		
NNO	Undertaker		
NNO	Viscera	15.00	30.00

2005 Jakks Pacific WWE Ruthless Aggression
Series 17

NNO	Hardcore Holly	10.00	20.00
NNO	Nunzio	7.50	15.00
NNO	Orlando Jordan	7.50	15.00
NNO	Paul London	7.50	15.00
NNO	Steven Richards	10.00	20.00
NNO	Tajiri	6.00	12.00

2005 Jakks Pacific WWE Ruthless Aggression
Series 17.5

NNO	Batista	10.00	20.00
NNO	The Hurricane	20.00	40.00
NNO	John Cena	7.50	15.00
NNO	Rey Mysterio	10.00	20.00
NNO	Shawn Michaels		
NNO	Undertaker		

2006 Jakks Pacific WWE Ruthless Aggression
Series 18

NNO	Batista		
NNO	Carlito	20.00	40.00
NNO	Eddie Guerrero	10.00	20.00
NNO	Heidenreich	12.50	25.00
NNO	John Cena	20.00	40.00
NNO	Shawn Michaels		

2006 Jakks Pacific WWE Ruthless Aggression
Series 18.5

NNO	Batista		
NNO	Chris Benoit		
NNO	Edge		
NNO	John Cena		
NNO	Matt Hardy		
NNO	Randy Orton		

2006 Jakks Pacific WWE Ruthless Aggression
Series 19

NNO	Chris Benoit		
NNO	Ken Kennedy		
NNO	Kurt Angle	15.00	30.00
NNO	Randy Orton	7.50	15.00
NNO	Rey Mysterio		
NNO	Rob Conway		

2006 Jakks Pacific WWE Ruthless Aggression
Series 20

NNO	Boogeyman	10.00	20.00
NNO	Booker T		

NNO	Chris Masters	7.50	15.00
NNO	Kid Kash		
NNO	Ric Flair	15.00	30.00

2006 Jakks Pacific WWE Ruthless Aggression
Series 20.5

NNO	Batista		
NNO	Ken Kennedy		
NNO	Randy Orton		
NNO	Rey Mysterio		
NNO	Undertaker		

2006 Jakks Pacific WWE Ruthless Aggression
Series 21

NNO	Carlito		
NNO	Chavo Guerrero		
NNO	Edge		
NNO	John Cena		
NNO	Rob Van Dam		
NNO	Triple H		

2006 Jakks Pacific WWE Ruthless Aggression
Series 22

NNO	Kurt Angle	15.00	30.00
NNO	Matt Striker	12.50	25.00
NNO	Nicky	6.00	12.00
NNO	Rey Mysterio		
NNO	Torrie Wilson	12.50	25.00
NNO	Victoria		20.00

2006 Jakks Pacific WWE Ruthless Aggression
Series 22.5

NNO	Big Show		
NNO	Edge		
NNO	Lita		
NNO	Psicosis		
NNO	Rey Mysterio		
NNO	Shawn Michaels		
NNO	Undertaker		

2006 Jakks Pacific WWE Ruthless Aggression
Series 23

NNO	John Cena		
NNO	Paul London		
NNO	Rey Mysterio	15.00	30.00
NNO	Shelton Benjamin		
NNO	Tatanka		
NNO	Triple H		

2006 Jakks Pacific WWE Ruthless Aggression
Series 23.5

NNO	Carlito		
NNO	Chris Masters		
NNO	Edge		
NNO	John Cena		
NNO	Rob Van Dam		
NNO	Shawn Michaels		

2006 Jakks Pacific WWE Ruthless Aggression
Series 24

NNO	Big Show		
NNO	Booker T		
NNO	Kane		
NNO	Kenny	10.00	20.00
NNO	Sabu	15.00	30.00
NNO	The Great Khali	20.00	40.00

2006 Jakks Pacific WWE Ruthless Aggression
Series 24.5

NNO	Batista		
NNO	John Cena		
NNO	Paul Heyman	15.00	30.00
NNO	Tommy Dreamer		
NNO	Triple H		
NNO	Undertaker		

2006 Jakks Pacific WWE Ruthless Aggression
Series 25

NNO	Batista		

NNO	Brian Kendrick		
NNO	Carlito		
NNO	Rey Mysterio	6.00	12.00
NNO	Shawn Michaels		
NNO	Test		

2007 Jakks Pacific WWE Ruthless Aggression
Series 26

NNO	Candice Michelle	12.50	25.00
NNO	Chris Benoit	15.00	30.00
NNO	Finlay	10.00	20.00
NNO	Hardcore Holly	7.50	15.00
NNO	John Cena	7.50	15.00
NNO	William Regal	15.00	30.00

2007 Jakks Pacific WWE Ruthless Aggression
Series 27

NNO	Batista	6.00	12.00
NNO	Bobby Lashley	15.00	30.00
NNO	Chris Masters	7.50	15.00
NNO	John Cena	6.00	12.00
NNO	Mr. Kennedy	7.50	15.00
NNO	Rey Mysterio	6.00	12.00

2007 Jakks Pacific WWE Ruthless Aggression
Series 28

NNO	Kenny Dykstra		
NNO	Miz	10.00	20.00
NNO	Mr. McMahon		
NNO	Rey Mysterio	12.50	25.00
NNO	Super Crazy	10.00	20.00
NNO	Torrie Wilson	20.00	40.00
NNO	Victoria	15.00	30.00

2007 Jakks Pacific WWE Ruthless Aggression
Series 29

NNO	Batista	7.50	15.00
NNO	Candice Michelle	12.50	25.00
NNO	Edge	12.50	25.00
NNO	Ken Kennedy	10.00	20.00
NNO	Matt Hardy	12.50	25.00
NNO	Melina	15.00	30.00
NNO	Shawn Michaels	12.50	25.00

2007 Jakks Pacific WWE Ruthless Aggression
Series 30

NNO	Boogeyman	12.50	25.00
NNO	John Cena	7.50	15.00
NNO	Mark Henry	10.00	20.00
NNO	MVP	10.00	20.00
NNO	Sandman	12.50	25.00
NNO	Triple H	10.00	20.00

2007 Jakks Pacific WWE Ruthless Aggression
Series 31

NNO	Batista	6.00	12.00
NNO	Jillian Hall	12.50	25.00
NNO	John Cena	7.50	15.00
NNO	John Morrison	10.00	20.00
NNO	Kelly Kelly	12.50	25.00
NNO	Kevin Thorn	10.00	20.00
NNO	Ric Flair	12.50	25.00

2007 Jakks Pacific WWE Ruthless Aggression
Series 31.5

NNO	Batista	10.00	20.00
NNO	Boogeyman	10.00	20.00
NNO	CM Punk	12.50	25.00
NNO	John Morrison	10.00	20.00
NNO	Matt Hardy	10.00	20.00
NNO	Randy Orton	12.50	25.00

2007 Jakks Pacific WWE Ruthless Aggression
Series 32

NNO	Carlito	12.50	25.00
NNO	John Morrison	12.50	25.00
NNO	Randy Orton	10.00	20.00
NNO	Triple H	10.00	20.00

NNO Umaga	10.00	20.00
NNO Undertaker	12.50	25.00

2008 Jakks Pacific WWE Ruthless Aggression Series 33

NNO Candice Michelle	15.00	30.00
NNO CM Punk	15.00	30.00
NNO John Cena	7.50	15.00
NNO Melina	20.00	40.00
NNO Randy Orton	7.50	15.00
NNO Rey Mysterio	15.00	30.00
NNO Triple H	12.50	25.00

2008 Jakks Pacific WWE Ruthless Aggression Series 34

NNO Chris Jericho	10.00	20.00
NNO Funaki	7.50	15.00
NNO Great Khali		
NNO Lilian Garcia	12.50	25.00
NNO Mickie James	15.00	30.00
NNO Nunzio		
NNO Shelton Benjamin		

2008 Jakks Pacific WWE Ruthless Aggression Series 34.5

NNO Batista		
NNO Cody Rhodes		
NNO Jamie Noble		
NNO The Miz		
NNO Ric Flair	10.00	20.00
NNO Great Khali		

2008 Jakks Pacific WWE Ruthless Aggression Series 35

NNO Beth Phoenix	6.00	12.00
NNO Edge	7.50	15.00
NNO Hornswoggle	15.00	30.00
NNO Joey Styles	6.00	12.00
NNO Rey Mysterio		
NNO Santino		
NNO Victoria	15.00	30.00

2008 Jakks Pacific WWE Ruthless Aggression Series 35.5

NNO Carlito	10.00	20.00
NNO Edge	7.50	15.00
NNO Elijah Burke	10.00	20.00
NNO Matt Hardy	10.00	20.00
NNO Ken Kennedy		
NNO Triple H	15.00	30.00

2008 Jakks Pacific WWE Ruthless Aggression Series 36

NNO Big Show	12.50	25.00
NNO Charlie Haas	10.00	20.00
NNO David Hart Smith	15.00	30.00
NNO Kofi Kingston	15.00	30.00
NNO Maryse	12.50	25.00
NNO Mickie James	15.00	30.00
NNO Umaga	12.50	25.00

2008 Jakks Pacific WWE Ruthless Aggression Series 37

NNO Cherry	17.50	35.00
NNO Colin Delaney	15.00	30.00
NNO Festus	7.50	15.00
NNO Katie Lee Burchill	20.00	40.00
NNO MVP		
NNO Paul Burchill		
NNO Santino Marella	12.50	25.00

2008 Jakks Pacific WWE Ruthless Aggression Series 38

NNO Batista	10.00	20.00
NNO The Brian Kendrick	15.00	30.00
NNO Hornswoggle	12.50	25.00
NNO Jesse		

NNO John Cena	10.00	20.00
NNO Rey Mysterio	15.00	30.00

2008 Jakks Pacific WWE Ruthless Aggression Series 38.5

NNO Big Show		
NNO Chris Jericho		
NNO Festus	10.00	20.00
NNO Jesse		
NNO Kane		
NNO Kofi Kingston	12.50	25.00

2009 Jakks Pacific WWE Ruthless Aggression Series 39

NNO Evan Bourne	10.00	20.00
NNO Jeff Hardy	15.00	30.00
NNO Mark Henry		
NNO Rey Mysterio	15.00	30.00
NNO Ted DiBiase	15.00	30.00
NNO Vladimir Kozlov	10.00	20.00

2009 Jakks Pacific WWE Ruthless Aggression Series 40

NNO Chris Jericho	20.00	40.00
NNO Edge	17.50	35.00
NNO Matt Hardy	12.50	25.00
NNO Randy Orton	12.50	25.00
NNO R-Truth		
NNO Undertaker	12.50	25.00

2009 Jakks Pacific WWE Ruthless Aggression Series 40.5

NNO Cody Rhodes	10.00	20.00
NNO Matt Hardy	10.00	20.00
NNO Ted DiBiase		
NNO Triple H	12.50	25.00
NNO Undertaker	20.00	40.00
NNO Vladimir Kozlov	10.00	20.00

2009 Jakks Pacific WWE Ruthless Aggression Series 41

NNO The Brian Kendrick	20.00	40.00
NNO CM Punk	20.00	40.00
NNO Goldust	15.00	30.00
NNO Hornswoggle	25.00	50.00
NNO John Cena	25.00	50.00
NNO Rey Mysterio	20.00	40.00

2009 Jakks Pacific WWE Ruthless Aggression Series 42

NNO Christian	20.00	40.00
NNO CM Punk	20.00	40.00
NNO The Great Khali		
NNO Jack Swagger		
NNO Shawn Michaels	25.00	50.00
NNO Triple H	10.00	20.00

2009 Jakks Pacific WWE Ruthless Aggression Series 43

NNO Batista	15.00	30.00
NNO John Cena	20.00	40.00
NNO Randy Orton	20.00	40.00
NNO Rey Mysterio	25.00	50.00
NNO Triple H		
NNO Undertaker		

2009 Jakks Pacific WWE Ruthless Aggression Series 44

NNO Edge	15.00	30.00
NNO John Cena	12.50	25.00
NNO Kane	15.00	30.00
NNO Matt Hardy		
NNO MVP		
NNO Rey Mysterio		

1998 Jakks Pacific WWF Shotgun Saturday Night Series 1

NNO Animal	7.50	15.00
NNO Hawk	7.50	15.00

NNO Henry Godwinn	6.00	12.00
NNO Phineas Godwinn	6.00	12.00
NNO Rocky Maivia	12.50	25.00
NNO Savio Vega	10.00	20.00
NNO Steve Austin	12.50	25.00
NNO Undertaker	7.50	15.00
NNO Stone Cold Steve Austin/Kane		
Shawn Michaels/Rocky Maivia		

1998 Jakks Pacific WWF Shotgun Saturday Night Series 2

NNO B.A. Billy Gunn	7.50	15.00
NNO Jeff Jarrett	6.00	12.00
NNO Jesse James	7.50	15.00
NNO Kane	10.00	20.00
NNO Sable	7.50	15.00
NNO Shawn Michaels	7.50	15.00

1999 Jakks Pacific WWF Shotgun Saturday Night Series 3

NNO Droz	5.00	10.00
NNO Edge	7.50	15.00
NNO Kurgann	6.00	12.00
NNO Road Dogg Jesse James	6.00	12.00
NNO Stone Cold Steve Austin	10.00	20.00
NNO Triple H	7.50	15.00

1999 Jakks Pacific WWF Shotgun Saturday Night Series 4

NNO Al Snow	6.00	12.00
NNO Gangrel	6.00	12.00
NNO Godfather	6.00	12.00
NNO Hardcore Holly	5.00	10.00
NNO Rock	7.50	15.00
NNO Test		

2001 Jakks Pacific WWF Signature Jams Series 1

NNO Billy Gunn	7.50	15.00
NNO Chris Jericho	12.50	25.00
NNO Jeff Hardy	15.00	30.00
NNO Kurt Angle	7.50	15.00
NNO The Rock	12.50	25.00
NNO Triple H	7.50	15.00

2001 Jakks Pacific WWF Signature Jams Series 2

NNO Chris Benoit		
NNO D-Von Dudley	7.50	15.00
NNO Kane		
NNO Matt Hardy	12.50	25.00
NNO Stone Cold Steve Austin		
NNO Undertaker		

2002 Jakks Pacific WWF Signature Jams Series 3

NNO Kane		
NNO Matt Hardy		
NNO Stone Cold Steve Austin		
NNO Undertaker		

2002 Jakks Pacific WWF Signature Jams Slam Grooves

NNO Billy Gunn		
NNO Jeff Hardy		
NNO Stone Cold Steve Austin		
NNO Undertaker		

1997 Jakks Pacific WWF Signature Series 1

NNO Goldust	7.50	15.00
NNO HHH	6.00	12.00
NNO Mankind	10.00	20.00
NNO Road Warrior Animal	7.50	15.00
NNO Road Warrior Hawk	7.50	15.00
NNO Steve Austin	7.50	15.00

1998 Jakks Pacific WWF Signature Series 2

NNO B.A. Billy Gunn	5.00	10.00
NNO Dude Love	10.00	20.00
NNO Kane	10.00	20.00
NNO Road Dogg	5.00	10.00

NNO Shawn Michaels	7.50	15.00
NNO Undertaker	7.50	15.00

1998 Jakks Pacific WWF Signature Series 3

NNO Edge	6.00	12.00
NNO HHH	7.50	15.00
NNO Jacqueline	10.00	20.00
NNO The Rock	10.00	20.00
NNO Stone Cold Steve Austin	7.50	15.00
NNO Undertaker	12.50	25.00

1999 Jakks Pacific WWF Signature Series 4

NNO Big Show	10.00	20.00
NNO Edge	7.50	15.00
NNO Ken Shamrock	7.50	15.00
NNO Rock	10.00	20.00
NNO Stone Cold Steve Austin	7.50	15.00
NNO X-Pac	6.00	12.00

1999 Jakks Pacific WWF Signature Series 5

NNO Al Snow	7.50	15.00
NNO Big Bossman	6.00	12.00
NNO Billy Gunn	6.00	12.00
NNO Kane	10.00	20.00
NNO Road Dogg	6.00	12.00
NNO Stone Cold Steve Austin	10.00	20.00

1999 Jakks Pacific WWF Signature Series 6

NNO Hardcore Holly	5.00	10.00
NNO HHH	7.50	15.00
NNO Mankind	7.50	15.00
NNO Stone Cold Steve Austin	10.00	20.00
NNO Undertaker	7.50	15.00
NNO Vince McMahon	7.50	15.00

1998 Jakks Pacific WWF Slammers Series 1

NNO Bret Hart	7.50	15.00
NNO Faarooq	6.00	12.00
NNO Goldust	6.00	12.00
NNO Mankind	6.00	12.00
NNO Steve Austin	7.50	15.00
NNO Undertaker	7.50	15.00

1998 Jakks Pacific WWF Slammers Series 2

NNO Brian Pillman	6.00	12.00
NNO Dude Love	7.50	15.00
NNO Kane	7.50	15.00
NNO Patriot	6.00	12.00
NNO Shawn Michaels	7.50	15.00
NNO Taka	6.00	12.00

2002 Jakks Pacific WWE SmackDown Draft

1 The Rock/26,250*	10.00	20.00
2 Kurt Angle/25,000*	12.50	25.00
3 Chris Benoit/23,750*	10.00	20.00
4 Hollywood Hogan/22,500*	15.00	30.00
6 Edge/18,750*	10.00	20.00
7 Rikishi/17,500*		
8 D-Von Dudley/16,250*	12.50	25.00
9 Mark Henry		
10 Maven/15,000*		
11 Billy Kidman		
12 Tajiri/13,750*	15.00	30.00
13 Chris Jericho/11,250*	15.00	30.00
14 Ivory/11,250*	15.00	30.00
15 Albert/8,750*	20.00	40.00
16 The Hurricane/7,500*	25.00	50.00
17 Al Snow/6,250*	12.50	25.00
18 Lance Storm/5,000*	25.00	50.00
19 DDP/3,750*	30.00	75.00
20 Torrie Wilson		
5A Billy/11,250*	15.00	30.00
5B Chuck/11,250*	15.00	30.00

2002 Jakks Pacific WWF Snappin' Bashers

NNO Chris Benoit	12.50	25.00
NNO Chris Jericho		
NNO Jeff Hardy	15.00	30.00
NNO The Rock		

NNO Stone Cold Steve Austin	7.50	15.00
NNO Undertaker		

1997 Jakks Pacific WWF Special Edition Series 1

NNO Ahmed Johnson	6.00	12.00
NNO British Bulldog	6.00	12.00
NNO Rocky Maivia	10.00	20.00
NNO Sunny	7.50	15.00
NNO Undertaker	7.50	15.00
NNO Vader	12.50	25.00
NNO Yokozuna/18000*	15.00	30.00

1998 Jakks Pacific WWF Special Edition Series 2

NNO Faarooq	6.00	12.00
NNO Goldust	6.00	12.00
NNO HHH	7.50	15.00
NNO Sable	10.00	20.00
NNO Savio Vega	6.00	12.00
NNO Stone Cold Steve Austin	7.50	15.00

1998 Jakks Pacific WWF Special Edition Series 3

NNO Animal	10.00	20.00
NNO Dan Severn	12.50	25.00
NNO Hawk	10.00	20.00
NNO Hunter Hearst-Helmsley	7.50	15.00
NNO Marvelous Marc Mero	7.50	15.00
NNO Shamrock	6.00	12.00

1999 Jakks Pacific WWF Special Edition Series 4

NNO B.A. Billy Gunn	7.50	15.00
NNO Chyna	10.00	20.00
NNO Mankind	12.50	25.00
NNO Road Dogg	7.50	15.00
NNO Stone Cold Steve Austin	10.00	20.00
NNO Undertaker		

1999 Jakks Pacific WWF Special Edition Series 5

NNO Al Snow	6.00	12.00
NNO Edge	7.50	15.00
NNO Mark Henry		
NNO Shamrock		
NNO Val Venis	6.00	12.00
NNO X-Pac		

1999 Jakks Pacific WWF Special Edition Series 6

NNO Double J	7.50	15.00
NNO Hardcore Holly	6.00	12.00
NNO HHH	7.50	15.00
NNO Stone Cold Steve Austin	10.00	20.00
NNO Test		
NNO The Rock	10.00	20.00

1997 Jakks Pacific WWF S.T.O.M.P. Series 1

NNO Ahmed Johnson	7.50	15.00
NNO Brian Pillman	5.00	10.00
NNO Crush	6.00	12.00
NNO Ken Shamrock	7.50	15.00
NNO Stone Cold Steve Austin	10.00	20.00
NNO Undertaker	7.50	15.00

1998 Jakks Pacific WWF S.T.O.M.P. Series 2

NNO Chyna	10.00	20.00
NNO Headbanger Mosh	7.50	15.00
NNO Headbanger Thrash	7.50	15.00
NNO Owen Hart	10.00	20.00
NNO Rocky Maivia	12.50	25.00
NNO Stone Cold Steve Austin	10.00	20.00

1998 Jakks Pacific WWF S.T.O.M.P. Series 3

NNO Animal	7.50	15.00
NNO Hawk	7.50	15.00
NNO Kane	7.50	15.00
NNO Marc Mero	15.00	30.00
NNO Sable	10.00	20.00
NNO Undertaker	10.00	20.00

2000 Jakks Pacific WWF S.T.O.M.P. Series 4

NNO B.A. Billy Gunn		
NNO Chyna		
NNO Road Dogg Jesse James		

NNO Stone Cold Steve Austin		
NNO Triple H		
NNO X-Pac		

1997 Jakks Pacific WWF Stretchin'

NNO Bret Hit Man Hart	12.50	25.00
NNO Shawn Michaels		
NNO Sycho Sid	10.00	20.00
NNO Undertaker	12.50	25.00

2001 Jakks Pacific WWF Stunt Action Superstars Series 1

NNO Jeff Hardy	12.50	25.00
NNO Kurt Angle	10.00	20.00
NNO Rikishi	7.50	15.00
NNO Stephanie McMahon	15.00	30.00
NNO Triple H	10.00	20.00
NNO X-Pac	7.50	15.00

2005 Jakks Pacific WWE SummerSlam Limited Edition

NNO Chris Benoit		
NNO Chris Jericho		
NNO Kane		
NNO Matt Hardy		
NNO Stone Cold Steve Austin		
NNO Test		
NNO The Rock		
NNO X-Pac		

1999 Jakks Pacific WWF Sunday Night Heat

NNO B.A. Billy Gunn	7.50	15.00
NNO Road Dogg		
NNO The Rock		
NNO Sable	7.50	15.00
NNO Stone Cold Steve Austin		
NNO Undertaker		

2016-17 Jakks Pacific WWE Superstar Buddies

NNO AJ Styles		
NNO John Cena		
NNO The Rock		

1997 Jakks Pacific WWF Superstars Best of 1997

NNO Bret Hart		
NNO British Bulldog	7.50	15.00
NNO Owen Hart	10.00	20.00

1997 Jakks Pacific WWF Superstars Best of 1997 Tag Teams

NNO Godwinns	12.50	25.00
NNO Headbangers	15.00	30.00
NNO Legion of Doom		
NNO New Blackjacks	10.00	20.00

1998 Jakks Pacific WWF Superstars Best of 1998 Series 1

NNO 8-Ball	6.00	12.00
NNO Blackjack Bradshaw	10.00	20.00
NNO Brian Christopher	6.00	12.00
NNO Chyna	12.50	25.00
NNO Shawn Michaels	10.00	20.00
NNO Skull	6.00	12.00
NNO Stone Cold Steve Austin	12.50	25.00
NNO Vader	6.00	12.00

1998 Jakks Pacific WWF Superstars Best of 1998 Series 2

NNO Dan Severn	5.00	10.00
NNO Dude Love	6.00	12.00
NNO HHH	7.50	15.00
NNO Jeff Jarrett	6.00	12.00
NNO Ken Shamrock	6.00	12.00
NNO Mark Henry	6.00	12.00
NNO Stone Cold Steve Austin	10.00	20.00
NNO Undertaker	7.50	15.00

1998 Jakks Pacific WWF Superstars Best of 1998 Tag Teams

NNO	Headbangers	
NNO	LOD 2000	
NNO	New Age Outlaws	

1996 Jakks Pacific WWF Superstars Series 1

NNO	Bret Hart	20.00	40.00
NNO	Diesel	15.00	30.00
NNO	Goldust	15.00	30.00
NNO	Razor Ramon	20.00	40.00
NNO	Shawn Michaels	12.50	25.00
NNO	Undertaker	15.00	30.00

1996 Jakks Pacific WWF Superstars Series 2

NNO	Bret Hart	12.50	25.00
NNO	Owen Hart	20.00	40.00
NNO	Shawn Michaels	15.00	30.00
NNO	Ultimate Warrior	20.00	40.00
NNO	Undertaker GITD	25.00	50.00
NNO	Vader	10.00	20.00

1997 Jakks Pacific WWF Superstars Series 3

NNO	Ahmed Johnson	10.00	20.00
NNO	Bret Hart	12.50	25.00
NNO	British Bulldog	7.50	15.00
NNO	Mankind	10.00	20.00
NNO	Shawn Michaels	10.00	20.00
NNO	Sycho Sid	7.50	15.00

1997 Jakks Pacific WWF Superstars Series 4

NNO	Faarooq	5.00	10.00
NNO	Hunter Hearst Helmsley	6.00	12.00
NNO	Jerry Lawler	7.50	15.00
NNO	Justin Hawk Bradshaw	12.50	25.00
NNO	Stone Cold Steve Austin	7.50	15.00
NNO	Vader	7.50	15.00

1997 Jakks Pacific WWF Superstars Series 5

NNO	Flash Funk	10.00	20.00
NNO	Ken Shamrock	6.00	12.00
NNO	Rocky Maivia	12.50	20.00
NNO	Savio Vega	7.50	15.00
NNO	Stone Cold Steve Austin	12.50	25.00
NNO	Sycho Sid	6.00	12.00

1998 Jakks Pacific WWF Superstars Series 6

NNO	Mark Henry	7.50	15.00
NNO	Owen Hart	12.50	25.00
NNO	Steve Blackman	12.50	25.00
NNO	Triple H	7.50	15.00
NNO	Jeff Jarrett	10.00	20.00
NNO	Marc Mero	6.00	12.00

1998 Jakks Pacific WWF Superstars Series 7

NNO	Dr. Death Steve Williams	12.50	25.00
NNO	Edge	7.50	15.00
NNO	Steve Austin	7.50	15.00
NNO	Undertaker	7.50	15.00
NNO	Val Venis	7.50	15.00
NNO	X-Pac	6.00	12.00

1999 Jakks Pacific WWF Superstars Series 8

NNO	Big Boss Man	6.00	12.00
NNO	Kane	7.50	15.00
NNO	Ken Shamrock		
NNO	The Rock	7.50	15.00
NNO	Shane McMahon	7.50	15.00
NNO	Shawn Michaels	7.50	15.00

1999 Jakks Pacific WWF Superstars Series 9

NNO	Bob Holly	6.00	12.00
NNO	Christian	6.00	12.00
NNO	Gangrel	10.00	20.00
NNO	Paul Wight	7.50	15.00
NNO	Undertaker	7.50	15.00
NNO	Vince McMahon	7.50	15.00

2006 Jakks Pacific WWE Superstars Series 1

NNO	Hulk Hogan	

NNO	The Rock	
NNO	Ric Flair	
NNO	Roddy Piper	
	Black Wrist Tape	
NNO	Roddy Piper	
	White Wrist Tape	
NNO	Stone Cold Steve Austin	

2007 Jakks Pacific WWE Superstars Series 2

NNO	Bret Hit Man Hart	
NNO	British Bulldog	
NNO	Kevin Nash	
NNO	Mr. Perfect	
NNO	Shawn Michaels	

2007 Jakks Pacific WWE Superstars Series 3

NNO	Jake The Snake Roberts	
NNO	Lex Luger	
NNO	Ravishing Rick Rude	
NNO	Scott Hall	
NNO	Undertaker	

2008 Jakks Pacific WWE Superstars Series 4

NNO	Brutus The Barber Beefcake	
NNO	Honky Tonk Man	
NNO	Iron Sheik	
NNO	Million Dollar Man	
NNO	Shawn Michaels	

2008 Jakks Pacific WWE Superstars Series 5

NNO	Buff Bagwell	
NNO	Diamond Dallas Page	
NNO	Jim The Anvil Neidhart	
NNO	Superfly Jimmy Snuka	

2009 Jakks Pacific WWE Superstars Series 6

NNO	Eddie Guerrero	
NNO	Hillbilly Jim	
NNO	Hunter Hearst Helmsley	
NNO	Kane	
NNO	Sgt. Slaughter	

2009 Jakks Pacific WWE Superstars Series 7

NNO	Bret Hit Man Hart	
NNO	Shawn Michaels	
NNO	El Matador	
NNO	The Rock	
NNO	Undertaker	

2009 Jakks Pacific WWE Superstars Series 8

NNO	Big John Studd	
NNO	Chainsaw Charlie	
NNO	Davey Boy Smith	
NNO	Dynamite Kid	
NNO	Stone Cold Steve Austin	

2003 Jakks Pacific WWE Superstars Uncovered

NNO	Hulk Hogan	20.00	40.00
NNO	Kurt Angle	12.50	25.00
NNO	Rob Van Dam	12.50	25.00
NNO	The Rock	30.00	60.00
NNO	Triple H	10.00	20.00
NNO	Undertaker	15.00	30.00

2004 Jakks Pacific WWE Talkin' Pounders

NNO	The Hurricane	
NNO	John Cena	
NNO	Randy Orton	
NNO	Rey Mysterio	

1997 Jakks Pacific WWF Talking Undertaker 14-Inch

NNO	Undertaker	25.00	50.00

1997 Jakks Pacific WWF Thumb Wrestlers

NNO	Bulldog vs. Shamrock	10.00	20.00
NNO	HHH vs. Mankind	10.00	20.00
NNO	Steve Austin vs. Owen Hart	12.50	25.00
NNO	Undertaker vs. HBK	15.00	30.00

1999 Jakks Pacific WWF Titan Tron Live Series 1

NNO	Kane	7.50	15.00
NNO	Mankind	7.50	15.00
NNO	Road Dogg	6.00	12.00
NNO	Rock	10.00	20.00
NNO	Stone Cold Steve Austin	15.00	30.00
NNO	Undertaker	15.00	30.00

2000 Jakks Pacific WWF Titan Tron Live Series 2

NNO	Big Show	6.00	12.00
NNO	Kane	17.50	35.00
NNO	Ken Shamrock	7.50	15.00
NNO	The Rock	12.50	25.00
NNO	Stone Cold Steve Austin	7.50	15.00
NNO	X-Pac	6.00	12.00

2000 Jakks Pacific WWF Titan Tron Live Series 3

NNO	Big Boss Man	7.50	15.00
NNO	Chris Jericho	7.50	15.00
NNO	Chyna	12.50	25.00
NNO	The Rock	7.50	15.00
NNO	Stone Cold Steve Austin	10.00	20.00
NNO	Test	6.00	12.00

2000 Jakks Pacific WWF Titan Tron Live Series 4

NNO	Big Show		
NNO	Cactus Jack	10.00	20.00
NNO	Road Dogg		
NNO	The Rock		
NNO	Triple H		
NNO	X-Pac		

2000 Jakks Pacific WWF Titan Tron Live Series 5

NNO	Chris Jericho	6.00	15.00
NNO	Kurt Angle	6.00	15.00
NNO	The Rock	10.00	20.00
NNO	Stone Cold Steve Austin	10.00	20.00
NNO	Test	6.00	12.00
NNO	Undertaker	10.00	20.00

2000 Jakks Pacific WWF Titan Tron Live Series 6

NNO	Big Show	
NNO	Edge	
NNO	Jeff Hardy	
NNO	Rock	
NNO	Tazz	
NNO	Triple H	

2000 Jakks Pacific WWF Titan Tron Live Series 7

NNO	Chris Jericho	
NNO	Kane	
NNO	Kurt Angle	
NNO	Stephanie McMahon	
NNO	Triple H	
NNO	Undertaker	

2000 Jakks Pacific WWF Titan Tron Live Series 8

NNO	Bubba Ray Dudley	
NNO	Jeff Hardy	
NNO	Matt Hardy	
NNO	Rikishi	
NNO	Road Dogg	
NNO	The Rock	

2001 Jakks Pacific WWF Titan Tron Live Series 9

NNO	Chyna	
NNO	Kurt Angle	
NNO	Mick Foley	
NNO	Rikishi	
NNO	The Rock	
NNO	Triple H	

2001 Jakks Pacific WWF Titan Tron Live Series 10

NNO	Billy Gunn	7.50	15.00
NNO	Kane	7.50	15.00
NNO	Matt Hardy	7.50	15.00
NNO	Rikishi	7.50	15.00
NNO	Stone Cold Steve Austin	10.00	20.00
NNO	Triple H	10.00	20.00

2001 Jakks Pacific WWF Titan Tron Live Series 11

NNO	Jeff Hardy	7.50	15.00
NNO	Kurt Angle	7.50	15.00
NNO	Rikishi	7.50	15.00
NNO	Stephanie McMahon	10.00	20.00
NNO	Stone Cold Steve Austin	10.00	20.00
NNO	Triple H	10.00	20.00

2001 Jakks Pacific WWF Titan Tron Live Series 12

NNO	Big Show	6.00	12.00
NNO	Chris Jericho	7.50	15.00
NNO	Kurt Angle	6.00	12.00
NNO	Rock	10.00	20.00
NNO	Stone Cold Steve Austin	10.00	20.00
NNO	Undertaker	12.50	25.00

2001 Jakks Pacific WWF Titan Tron Live Series 13

NNO	Chris Jericho	6.00	12.00
NNO	Lita	7.50	15.00
NNO	Rock	10.00	20.00
NNO	Stone Cold Steve Austin	12.50	25.00
NNO	Triple H	7.50	15.00
NNO	Undertaker	12.50	25.00

2000 Jakks Pacific WWF ToyFare Exclusives

NNO	Big Show	12.50	25.00
NNO	Debra	15.00	30.00
NNO	The Rock	20.00	40.00

2002 Jakks Pacific WWE Trash Talkin' Champions

NNO	Chris Jericho	20.00	40.00
NNO	Kurt Angle	10.00	20.00

2005 Jakks Pacific WWE Treacherous Trios Series 1

NNO	Kurt Angle/Eddie Guerrero/Big Show		
NNO	Triple H/Ric Flair/Batista	12.50	25.00
NNO	Undertaker/JBL/Heidenreich	15.00	30.00

2005 Jakks Pacific WWE Treacherous Trios Series 2

NNO	Mark Jindrak/Booker T/Kurt Angle	15.00	30.00
NNO	Orlando Jordan/Danny Basham/Doug Basham	12.50	25.00
NNO	Trish Stratus/Tyson Tomko/Christian	15.00	30.00

2005 Jakks Pacific WWE Treacherous Trios Series 3

NNO	Edge/Lita/Matt Hardy	30.00	60.00
NNO	Randy Orton/Undertaker Cowboy Bob Orton Jr.	25.00	50.00
NNO	Rey Mysterio/Chris Benoit/Batista	25.00	50.00

2006 Jakks Pacific WWE Treacherous Trios Series 4

NNO	Chris Benoit/Booker T/Randy Orton
NNO	Melina/Johnny Nitro/Joey Mercury
NNO	Kurt Angle/Daivari/Mark Henry

2007 Jakks Pacific WWE Treacherous Trios Series 5

NNO	Randy Orton/Edge/Carlito
NNO	Rey Mysterio/Booker T/Chavo
NNO	Shawn Michaels/HHH/Coachman

2007 Jakks Pacific WWE Treacherous Trios Series 6

NNO	Batista/Long/Undertaker
NNO	Brian Kendrick/Yang/London
NNO	Umaga/Cena/Armando Estrada

2008 Jakks Pacific WWE Treacherous Trios Series 7

NNO	Elijah Burke/CM Punk/Tommy Dreamer	25.00	50.00
NNO	Great Khali/Batista/Undertaker		
NNO	Randy Orton/John Cena/Jonathan Coachman		

2008 Jakks Pacific WWE Treacherous Trios Series 8

NNO	Curt Hawkins/Edge/Zack Ryder		
NNO	Deuce/Cherry/Domino	30.00	75.00
NNO	Triple H/John Cena/Orton	15.00	30.00

2009 Jakks Pacific WWE Treacherous Trios Series 9

NNO	Finlay/JBL/Hornswoggle		
NNO	JTG/John Cena/Shad	20.00	40.00
NNO	Miz/Matt Hardy/Morrison	25.00	50.00

2009 Jakks Pacific WWE Treacherous Trios Series 10

NNO	Big Show/Undertaker/Khali
NNO	Chris Jericho/Cena/CM Punk
NNO	Matt Hardy/Edge/Jeff Hardy

2002 Jakks Pacific WWE Unchained Fury Series 1

NNO	Booker T	10.00	20.00
NNO	Hurricane Helms	12.50	25.00
NNO	Lance Storm	10.00	20.00
NNO	Ric Flair	12.50	25.00

2002 Jakks Pacific WWE Unchained Fury Series 1 2-Packs

NNO	Booker T/Steve Austin	20.00	40.00
NNO	Ric Flair/Vince McMahon	25.00	50.00
NNO	Rob Van Dam/Chris Jericho		

2002 Jakks Pacific WWE Unchained Fury Series 2

NNO	Booker T	10.00	20.00
NNO	Kevin Nash	15.00	30.00
NNO	Kurt Angle	10.00	20.00
NNO	Rhyno	12.50	25.00
NNO	Rob Van Dam	15.00	30.00
NNO	Tajiri	10.00	20.00

2002 Jakks Pacific WWE Unchained Fury Series 2 2-Packs

NNO	Christian/DDP	12.50	25.00
NNO	Chuck Palumbo/Billy Gunn	15.00	30.00
NNO	Kurt Angle/Edge	15.00	30.00

2003 Jakks Pacific WWE Unlimited Series 1

NNO	Chris Jericho	12.50	25.00
NNO	Edge	12.50	25.00
NNO	Hulk Hogan	15.00	30.00
NNO	Kurt Angle	10.00	20.00
NNO	Rob Van Dam	7.50	15.00
NNO	The Rock	12.50	25.00

2003 Jakks Pacific WWE Unlimited Series 2

NNO	Batista	15.00	30.00
NNO	Billy Kidman	10.00	20.00
NNO	Booker T	12.50	25.00
NNO	Brock Lesnar	15.00	30.00
NNO	Eddie Guerrero	12.50	25.00
NNO	Triple H	10.00	20.00

2003 Jakks Pacific WWE Unlimited Series 3

NNO	Booker T	12.50	25.00
NNO	Brock Lesnar	20.00	40.00
NNO	Chris Benoit	10.00	20.00
NNO	Chris Jericho	10.00	20.00
NNO	Hulk Hogan	15.00	30.00
NNO	The Rock	15.00	30.00

2003 Jakks Pacific WWE Unlimited Series 4

NNO	Chris Benoit		
NNO	Kurt Angle		
NNO	Rob Van Dam	10.00	20.00
NNO	The Rock	15.00	30.00
NNO	Triple H	12.50	25.00

2006 Jakks Pacific WWE Unmatched Fury Series 1

NNO	Batista
NNO	Hulk Hogan
NNO	John Cena
NNO	Rey Mysterio

2007 Jakks Pacific WWE Unmatched Fury Series 2

NNO	Rob Van Dam	20.00	40.00
NNO	Shawn Michaels	30.00	60.00
NNO	Triple H	12.50	25.00
NNO	Undertaker	20.00	40.00
NNO	Undertaker GITD 100* NYC TF	300.00	500.00

2007 Jakks Pacific WWE Unmatched Fury Series 3

NNO	Carlito	15.00	30.00
NNO	Jeff Hardy	20.00	40.00
NNO	John Cena	15.00	30.00
NNO	Sabu	15.00	30.00

2007 Jakks Pacific WWE Unmatched Fury Series 4

NNO	Ken Kennedy	12.50	25.00
NNO	Mr. Perfect	20.00	40.00
NNO	Ric Flair	15.00	30.00
NNO	Umaga	12.50	25.00

2007 Jakks Pacific WWE Unmatched Fury Series 5

NNO	Bobby Lashley	25.00	50.00
NNO	Mick Foley	15.00	30.00
NNO	The Rock	20.00	40.00
NNO	Undertaker		

2007 Jakks Pacific WWE Unmatched Fury Series 6

NNO	Eddie Guerrero	15.00	30.00
NNO	Kane	12.50	25.00
NNO	Randy Orton	25.00	50.00
NNO	Rowdy Roddy Piper	30.00	60.00

2008 Jakks Pacific WWE Unmatched Fury Series 7

NNO	British Bulldog
NNO	Edge
NNO	Ravishing Rick Rude
NNO	Undertaker

2008 Jakks Pacific WWE Unmatched Fury Series 8

NNO	Boogeyman
NNO	Iron Sheik
NNO	Matt Hardy
NNO	Shawn Michaels

2008 Jakks Pacific WWE Unmatched Fury Series 9

NNO	Bret Hitman Hart	30.00	60.00
NNO	Finlay	12.50	25.00
NNO	Hornswoggle	20.00	50.00
NNO	Hornswoggle LE (Green/Gold/500*	200.00	350.00
NNO	Undertaker		

2008 Jakks Pacific WWE Unmatched Fury Series 10

NNO	Great Khali
NNO	Junk Yard Dog
NNO	MVP
NNO	Ultimate Warrior

2008 Jakks Pacific WWE Unmatched Fury Series 11

NNO	Chris Jericho
NNO	CM Punk
NNO	Honkytonk Man
NNO	Million Dollar Man

2008 Jakks Pacific WWE Unmatched Fury Series 12

NNO	Big Show
NNO	JBL
NNO	Razor Ramon
NNO	Undertaker

2009 Jakks Pacific WWE Unmatched Fury Series 14

NNO	Bret Hitman Hart	30.00	60.00
NNO	Hornswoggle	20.00	40.00
NNO	John Cena	15.00	30.00
NNO	Rey Mysterio	20.00	40.00

2009 Jakks Pacific WWE Unmatched Fury Series 15

NNO	CM Punk	60.00	120.00
NNO	Eddie Guerrero	25.00	50.00
NNO	Rowdy Roddy Piper	30.00	60.00
NNO	Stone Cold Steve Austin	20.00	40.00

2003 Jakks Pacific WWE Unrelenting

NNO	Booker T	7.50	15.00
NNO	Chris Jericho	10.00	20.00
NNO	Edge		
NNO	Jeff Hardy		
NNO	Rob Van Dam		
NNO	Triple H		

2008 Jakks Pacific WWE Vinyl Aggression Exclusive

NNO	Bret Hart RSC	20.00	40.00

2009 Jakks Pacific WWE Vinyl Aggression Exclusive

NNO Jesse Ventura/100* NYC TF

2008 Jakks Pacific WWE Vinyl Aggression Series 1

NNO Carlito
NNO ECW Stylized
NNO Hornswoggle
NNO John Cena
NNO Mankind
NNO Umaga
NNO Undertaker

2008 Jakks Pacific WWE Vinyl Aggression Series 2

NNO Batista
NNO Chris Jericho
NNO CM Punk
NNO DX Stylized
NNO Finlay
NNO Honkytonk Man
NNO Mr. Kennedy
NNO MVP
NNO Rey Mysterio
NNO Rock
NNO Shawn Michaels
NNO Tommy Dreamer
NNO Triple H Stylized

2008 Jakks Pacific WWE Vinyl Aggression Series 3

NNO Batista
NNO Chris Jericho
NNO Shawn Michaels
NNO Rock
NNO Tommy Dreamer
NNO Triple H

2008 Jakks Pacific WWE Vinyl Aggression Series 4

NNO Edge
NNO Jimmy Wang Yang
NNO Miz
NNO Randy Orton
NNO Santino
NNO Ted DiBiase

2008 Jakks Pacific WWE Vinyl Aggression Series 5

NNO Big Show
NNO DX Stylized
NNO Jake Roberts
NNO Kane
NNO Kofi Kingston
NNO Matt Hardy

2008 Jakks Pacific WWE Vinyl Aggression Series 6

NNO Festus
NNO Jesse
NNO John Morrison
NNO JTG
NNO Rowdy Roddy Piper
NNO Shad

2008 Jakks Pacific WWE Vinyl Aggression Series 7

NNO Beth Phoenix
NNO Boogeyman
NNO Great Khali
NNO Kane/Classic Mask
NNO Ricky Ortiz
NNO Triple H

1999 Jakks Pacific WWF White's Exclusives

NNO Sable
NNO Undertaker

1998 Jakks Pacific WWF WrestleMania XIV

NNO	Headbanger Mosh	6.00	12.00
NNO	Headbanger Thrasher	6.00	12.00
NNO	HHH	10.00	20.00
NNO	Rocky Maivia	7.50	15.00
NNO	Shawn Michaels	10.00	20.00
NNO	Stone Cold Steve Austin	7.50	15.00

2001 Jakks Pacific WWF WrestleMania X-7

NNO	Chris Jericho	7.50	15.00
NNO	Chyna	10.00	20.00
NNO	Eddie Guerrero	7.50	15.00
NNO	Edge	7.50	15.00
NNO	Kane	10.00	20.00
NNO	Stone Cold Steve Austin	12.50	25.00

2002 Jakks Pacific WWE WrestleMania X-8

NNO	Billy Gunn	7.50	15.00
NNO	Chuck Palumbo	7.50	15.00
NNO	Diamond Dallas Page	7.50	15.00
NNO	HHH	15.00	30.00
NNO	Maven	7.50	15.00
NNO	Rob Van Dam	12.50	25.00

2002 Jakks Pacific WWE WrestleMania X-8 2-Packs

NNO	Booker T/Edge	15.00	30.00
NNO	Kurt Angle/Kane	12.50	25.00
NNO	The Rock vs. Hollywood Hogan	30.00	60.00
NNO	Undertaker vs. Ric Flair	30.00	75.00

2004 Jakks Pacific WWE WrestleMania 19 Winners

NNO Chris Benoit
NNO Chris Jericho
NNO Kane
NNO Kurt Angle
NNO The Rock

2004 Jakks Pacific WWE WrestleMania 19 Winners 2-Packs

NNO D-Von and Bubba Ray Dudley
NNO La Resistance
Conway/Dupree
NNO Team Angle
Benjamin/Haas

2004 Jakks Pacific WWE WrestleMania 20 Series 1

NNO Edge
NNO Hardcore Holly
NNO Rob Van Dam
NNO Shane McMahon
NNO Stone Cold Steve Austin
NNO Triple H

2004 Jakks Pacific WWE WrestleMania 20 Series 3

NNO Booker T
NNO Chris Benoit
NNO Chris Jericho
NNO Kane
NNO Kurt Angle
NNO The Rock

2004 Jakks Pacific WWE WrestleMania 20 Series 3 2-Packs

NNO Bubba Ray & D-Von
NNO Rob Conway & Rene Dupree
NNO Shelton Benjamin & Charlie Haas

2004 Jakks Pacific WWE WrestleMania 20 Mask and Figure Sets Series 1

NNO Hurricane
NNO Kane
NNO Mankind
NNO Rey Mysterio

2004 Jakks Pacific WWE WrestleMania 20 Mask and Figure Sets Series 2

NNO Rey Mysterio
NNO Rosey
NNO Ultimo Dragon

2004 Jakks Pacific WWE WrestleMania 20 Playset

NNO Stage Entrance and Stunt Ring

2004 Jakks Pacific WWE WrestleMania 20 Times Square Limited Edition

NNO Ric Flair/600*
NNO Triple H/600*

2004 Jakks Pacific WWE WrestleMania 20 Series 2

Also known as WrestleMania 20 Winners.

NNO Chavo Guerrero
NNO Chris Benoit
NNO Christian
NNO Eddie Guerrero
NNO John Cena
NNO Undertaker

2004 Jakks Pacific WWE WrestleMania 20 Series 2 2-Packs

NNO Booker T/Rob Van Dam
NNO Ric Flair/Randy Orton
NNO Rikishi/Scotty 2 Hotty

2004 Jakks Pacific WWE WrestleMania 20 Series 1 2-Packs

Also known as WrestleMania 20 WrestleMania Recall.

NNO Brock Lesnar/Kurt Angle
NNO Edge/Christian
NNO Steve Austin/HBK

2005 Jakks Pacific WWE WrestleMania 21 Series 1

NNO	Eddie Guerrero	12.50	25.00
NNO	Rey Mysterio		
NNO	Triple H		
NNO	Victoria		

2005 Jakks Pacific WWE WrestleMania 21 Series 1 2-Packs

NNO Chris Jericho vs. Shawn Michaels
NNO John Cena vs. Big Show
NNO Kane vs. Kurt Angle

2005 Jakks Pacific WWE WrestleMania 21 Series 2

NNO Batista
NNO Booker T
NNO Charlie Haas
NNO Chris Benoit

NNO Eddie Guerrero 12.50 25.00
NNO Lita

2005 Jakks Pacific WWE WrestleMania 21 Series 2 2-Packs

NNO Maven/Eugene
NNO Rey Mysterio/Rene Dupree
NNO Rob Conway/William Regal

2005 Jakks Pacific WWE WrestleMania 21 Series 3

NNO Booker T
NNO Carlito
NNO Edge
NNO Randy Orton
NNO Stone Cold Steve Austin
NNO Undertaker

2005 Jakks Pacific WWE WrestleMania 21 Series 3 2-Packs

NNO John Cena/John Bradshaw Layfield
NNO Kurt Angle/Shawn Michaels
NNO Triple H/Batista

2005 Jakks Pacific WWE WrestleMania 21 Gear and Figure Sets Series 1

NNO Edge 10.00 20.00
NNO Hurricane
NNO JBL
NNO Kurt Angle
NNO Rey Mysterio 12.50 25.00
NNO Undertaker

2005 Jakks Pacific WWE WrestleMania 21 Gear and Figure Sets Series 2

NNO John Cena
NNO Rey Mysterio 12.50 25.00
NNO Undertaker 10.00 20.00

2005 Jakks Pacific WWE WrestleMania 21 Gear and Figure Sets Series 3

NNO Edge 10.00 20.00
NNO JBL
NNO Kurt Angle

2005 Jakks Pacific WWE WrestleMania 21 Gear and Figure Sets Series 4

NNO Hurricane
NNO John Cena
NNO Rey Mysterio 12.50 25.00

2005 Jakks Pacific WWE WrestleMania 21 Gear and Figure Sets 2-Packs

NNO Rey Mysterio/Rey Mysterio
NNO Rosey/Hurricane

2002 Jakks Pacific WWE Wrestling's Most Wanted

NNO Rock n' Roll Rivals
Edge/Y2J
NNO Ultimate Hardcore Match
RVD/Hardcore Holly
NNO Iron Man Match
HHH/Chris Benoit

2020 Jazwares AEW Unrivaled Collection Playsets

NNO Action Ring 30.00 75.00
NNO Action Ring w/Cody UK 75.00 150.00
NNO Authentic Scale Ring (w/Kenny Omega) 100.00 200.00

2020 Jazwares AEW Unrivaled Collection Series 1

NNO Brandi Rhodes 75.00 150.00
NNO Chris Jericho 25.00 50.00
NNO Chris Jericho/1000* CH 250.00 500.00
NNO Cody Rhodes 25.00 50.00
NNO Cody Rhodes/500* CH 600.00 1200.00
NNO Kenny Omega 30.00 75.00
NNO Matt Jackson 20.00 40.00
NNO Nick Jackson 25.00 50.00

1990 JusToys WCW Bend-Ems

NNO Arn Anderson 20.00 40.00
NNO Barry Windham 20.00 40.00
NNO Brian Pillman 15.00 30.00
NNO Butch Reed 15.00 30.00
NNO Lex Luger 15.00 30.00
NNO Ric Flair 30.00 60.00
NNO Rick Steiner 12.50 25.00
NNO Ron Simmons 15.00 30.00
NNO Scott Steiner 20.00 40.00
NNO Sid Vicious 15.00 30.00
NNO Sting 25.00 50.00
NNO Tom Zenk 30.00 75.00

1990 JusToys WCW Bend-Ems Challenge 2-Pack

NNO The Steiner Brothers

2001 JusToys WWF Bend-Ems Gear

NNO Chris Jericho
NNO Jeff Hardy 20.00 40.00
NNO Kane 25.00 50.00
NNO Matt Hardy 20.00 40.00
NNO Road Dogg 15.00 30.00
NNO Rock (black & white) 12.50 25.00
NNO Rock (blue & yellow) 15.00 30.00
NNO Steve Austin 12.50 25.00
NNO Triple H 20.00 40.00

1998 JusToys WWF Bend-Ems Playsets

NNO Super Slam Wrestling Ring (w/Austin & Michaels)
NNO Super Slam Wrestling Ring (w/Paul Bearer) 30.00 60.00

1994 JusToys WWF Bend-Ems Series I

NNO Bret Hitman Hart 12.50 25.00
NNO Diesel 7.50 15.00
NNO Doink 7.50 15.00
NNO Lex Luger 10.00 20.00
NNO Razor Ramon 10.00 20.00

1995 JusToys WWF Bend-Ems Series II

NNO 1-2-3 Kid 6.00 12.00
NNO British Bulldog 7.50 15.00
NNO Mabel 6.00 12.00
NNO Undertaker 7.50 15.00

1996 JusToys WWF Bend-Ems Series III

NNO Ahmed Johnson 5.00 10.00
NNO Goldust 6.00 12.00
NNO Shawn Michaels 7.50 15.00
NNO Yokozuna 6.00 12.00

1996 JusToys WWF Bend-Ems Series IV

NNO Sunny 7.50 15.00
NNO Sycho Sid 6.00 12.00
NNO Vader 6.00 12.00
NNO Wildman Marc Mero 5.00 10.00

1997 JusToys WWF Bend-Ems Series V

NNO Faarooq 6.00 12.00
NNO Mankind 10.00 20.00
NNO Rocky Maivia 12.50 25.00
NNO Stone Cold Steve Austin 6.00 12.00

1997 JusToys WWF Bend-Ems Series VI

NNO Animal 6.00 12.00
NNO Hawk 6.00 12.00
NNO Hunter Hearts Helmsley 5.00 10.00
NNO Undertaker 10.00 20.00

1997 JusToys WWF Bend-Ems Series VII

NNO Crush 7.50 15.00
NNO Ken Shamrock 7.50 15.00
NNO Owen Hart 12.50 25.00
NNO The Patriot 10.00 20.00

1998 JusToys WWF Bend-Ems Series IX

NNO Brian Christopher 6.00 12.00
NNO Cactus Jack 7.50 15.00
NNO Sable 10.00 20.00
NNO X-Pac 6.00 12.00

1998 JusToys WWF Bend-Ems Series VIII

NNO Chyna 7.50 15.00
NNO Jeff Jarrett 6.00 12.00
NNO Kane 7.50 15.00
NNO Taka 5.00 10.00

1998 JusToys WWF Bend-Ems Series X

NNO B.A. Billy Gunn 6.00 12.00
NNO Edge 7.50 15.00
NNO Road Dogg 6.00 12.00
NNO Steve Blackman 5.00 10.00

1999 JusToys WWF Bend-Ems Series XI

NNO Al Snow 6.00 12.00
NNO Godfather 7.50 15.00
NNO Mr. McMahon 7.50 15.00
NNO Val Venis 5.00 10.00

1999 JusToys WWF Bend-Ems Series XII

NNO Big Boss Man 5.00 10.00
NNO Mankind 7.50 15.00
NNO Paul Wight 5.00 10.00
NNO Steve Austin 10.00 20.00
NNO Undertaker 7.50 15.00

1999 JusToys WWF Bend-Ems Series XIII

NNO Droz 5.00 10.00
NNO D'Lo Brown 5.00 10.00
NNO Hardcore Holly 5.00 10.00
NNO Shane McMahon 6.00 12.00
NNO Steve Austin 7.50 15.00

2000 JusToys WWF Bend-Ems Series XIV

NNO Chris Jericho 6.00 12.00
NNO Jeff Hardy 6.00 12.00
NNO Matt Hardy 5.00 10.00
NNO The Rock 7.50 15.00

2001 JusToys WWF Bend-Ems Series XV

NNO Tazz
NNO Grandmaster Sexay
NNO Rikishi
NNO The Rock/Repack
NNO Scotty 2 Hotty

1994 Kelian AAA Wrestling Figures

NNO Blue Panther
NNO Cien Caras 30.00 60.00
NNO Fuerza Guerrera
NNO Heavy Metal 50.00 100.00
NNO Hijo Del Santo 60.00 120.00
NNO Konnan
NNO La Parka 60.00 120.00
NNO Mascara Sagrada
NNO Octagon
NNO Perro Aguayo 40.00 80.00
NNO Psicosis
NNO Rey Misterio

1994 Kelian AAA Wrestling Figures (loose)

NNO Blue Panther
NNO Cien Caras
NNO Fuerza Guerrera
NNO Heavy Metal
NNO Hijo Del Santo
NNO Konnan
NNO La Parka
NNO Mascara Sagrada
NNO Octagon
NNO Perro Aguayo
NNO Psicosis
NNO Rey Misterio

2019 Kidrobot Collectible Vinyl Mini Series WWE

NNO AJ Styles 6.00 12.00
NNO Alexa Bliss 7.50 15.00
NNO Andre the Giant 4.00 8.00
NNO Charlotte Flair 6.00 12.00
NNO John Cena 7.50 15.00

NNO Ric Flair	6.00	12.00
NNO Roman Reigns	5.00	10.00
NNO Ronda Rousey	5.00	10.00
NNO Sasha Banks	7.50	15.00
NNO Shawn Michaels	5.00	10.00
NNO The Rock	7.50	15.00
NNO Triple H Mystery CH		
NNO Ultimate Warrior	20.00	40.00
NNO Undertaker	7.50	15.00

1985 LJN WWF Wrestling Superstars 16-Inch

NNO Hulk Hogan	225.00	450.00
NNO Rowdy Roddy Piper	175.00	350.00

1985 LJN WWF Wrestling Superstars 16-Inch (loose)

NNO Hulk Hogan	60.00	120.00
NNO Rowdy Roddy Piper	75.00	150.00

1985 LJN WWF Wrestling Superstars Bendies

NNO Andre the Giant	50.00	100.00
NNO Big John Studd	30.00	75.00
NNO Bobby Heenan	50.00	100.00
NNO Brutus Beefcake	20.00	40.00
NNO Captain Lou Albano	50.00	100.00
NNO Corporal Kirchner	20.00	40.00
NNO George Steele	30.00	75.00
NNO Hillbilly Jim	30.00	75.00
NNO Hulk Hogan/Blue Knee Pads	25.00	50.00
NNO Hulk Hogan/Red Knee Pads	25.00	50.00
NNO Iron Sheik	25.00	60.00
NNO Jesse Ventura	30.00	60.00
NNO Junk Yard Dog	30.00	75.00
NNO King Kong Bundy	20.00	40.00
NNO Mr. Wonderful	25.00	60.00
NNO Nikolai Volkoff	25.00	60.00
NNO Randy Macho Man Savage	75.00	150.00
NNO Ricky The Dragon Steamboat	30.00	75.00
NNO Rowdy Roddy Piper	50.00	100.00

1985 LJN WWF Wrestling Superstars Bendies (loose)

NNO Andre the Giant	10.00	20.00
NNO Big John Studd	10.00	20.00
NNO Bobby Heenan	10.00	20.00
NNO Brutus Beefcake	7.50	15.00
NNO Captain Lou Albano	12.50	25.00
NNO Corporal Kirchner	6.00	12.00
NNO George Steele	7.50	15.00
NNO Hillbilly Jim	6.00	12.00
NNO Hulk Hogan/Blue Knee Pads	10.00	20.00
NNO Hulk Hogan/Red Knee Pads	10.00	20.00
NNO Iron Sheik	6.00	12.00
NNO Jesse Ventura	7.50	15.00
NNO Junk Yard Dog	7.50	15.00
NNO King Kong Bundy	5.00	10.00
NNO Mr. Wonderful	7.50	15.00
NNO Nikolai Volkoff	6.00	12.00
NNO Randy Macho Man Savage	20.00	40.00
NNO Ricky The Dragon Steamboat	15.00	30.00
NNO Rowdy Roddy Piper	15.00	30.00

1985 LJN WWF Wrestling Superstars Bendies Playset

NNO Cage Match Challenge w/Hogan Blue Knee Pads	150.00	300.00

1985 LJN WWF Wrestling Superstars Bendies Playset (loose)

NNO Cage Match Challenge	50.00	100.00

1985 LJN WWF Wrestling Superstars Bendies Tag Teams

NNO Hulk Hogan/Junk Yard Dog		
NNO Iron Sheik/Nikolai Volkoff	25.00	50.00
NNO George Steele/Captain Lou Albano	25.00	50.00
NNO King Kong Bundy/Big John Studd	50.00	100.00
NNO Randy Savage/Jesse Ventura	50.00	100.00
NNO Ricky Steamboat/Corporal Kirchner	60.00	120.00

1989 LJN WWF Wrestling Superstars Black Card Re-Release

NNO Adrian Adonis		
NNO Bam Bam Bigelow	50.00	100.00
NNO Big John Studd		
NNO Bret Hitman Hart		
NNO Brutus The Barber Beefcake		
NNO Demolition Ax		
NNO Elizabeth/Gold Skirt		
NNO Elizabeth/Purple Skirt		
NNO Hacksaw Jim Duggan	350.00	500.00
NNO Honky Tonk Man	450.00	900.00
NNO Hulk Hogan/Red Shirt		
NNO Hulk Hogan/White Shirt	1000.00	2000.00
NNO Jake The Snake Roberts	150.00	300.00
NNO Randy Macho Man Savage		
NNO Ted DiBiase		

1984 LJN WWF Wrestling Superstars Series 1

NNO Andre the Giant/Long Hair	250.00	500.00
NNO Big John Studd	125.00	250.00
NNO Hillbilly Jim	150.00	300.00
NNO Hulk Hogan	350.00	700.00
NNO Iron Sheik	200.00	400.00
NNO Jimmy Snuka	125.00	250.00
NNO Junk Yard Dog/Red Chain	125.00	250.00
NNO Junk Yard Dog/Silver Chain	150.00	300.00
NNO Nikolai Volkoff	125.00	250.00
NNO Rowdy Roddy Piper/Brown Boots		
NNO Rowdy Roddy Piiper/Red Boots	125.00	250.00

1984 LJN WWF Wrestling Superstars Series 1 (loose)

NNO Andre the Giant/Long Hair	25.00	50.00
NNO Big John Studd	15.00	40.00
NNO Hillbilly Jim	15.00	40.00
NNO Hulk Hogan	30.00	60.00
NNO Iron Sheik	15.00	30.00
NNO Jimmy Snuka	15.00	40.00
NNO Junk Yard Dog/Red Chain	25.00	50.00
NNO Junk Yard Dog/Silver Chain	15.00	30.00
NNO Nikolai Volkoff	15.00	30.00
NNO Rowdy Roddy Piper/Brown Boots		
NNO Rowdy Roddy Piper/Red Boots	30.00	60.00

1985 LJN WWF Wrestling Superstars Series 2

NNO Andre the Giant/Short Hair	300.00	600.00
NNO Brutus Beefcake	200.00	400.00
NNO George Steele	100.00	200.00
NNO Greg Valentine/Dk. Blonde Hair		
NNO Greg Valentine/Lt. Blonde Hair	100.00	200.00
NNO King Kong Bundy	100.00	200.00
NNO Mr. Wonderful	150.00	300.00

1985 LJN WWF Wrestling Superstars Series 2 (loose)

NNO Andre the Giant/Short Hair	50.00	100.00
NNO Brutus Beefcake	15.00	30.00
NNO George Steele	15.00	30.00
NNO Greg Valentine/Dk Blond Hair	12.50	25.00
NNO Greg Valentine/Lt. Blonde Hair	10.00	20.00
NNO King Kong Bundy	20.00	40.00
NNO Mr. Wonderful	15.00	30.00

1986 LJN WWF Wrestling Superstars Series 3

NNO Bobby Heenan/No Scrolls		
NNO Bobby Heenan/Scrolls	75.00	150.00
NNO Bruno Sammartino	60.00	120.00
NNO Captain Lou Albano/Red Lapel	50.00	100.00
NNO Captain Lou Albano/White Lapel	75.00	150.00
NNO Classy Freddie Blassie	60.00	120.00
NNO Corporal Kirchner/Beard		
NNO Corporal Kirchner/No Stubble	60.00	120.00
NNO Corporal Kirchner/Stubble		
NNO Don Muraco	100.00	200.00
NNO Jesse Ventura	125.00	250.00
NNO Jimmy Hart/Hearts on Megaphone	60.00	120.00
NNO Jimmy Hart/No Hearts on Megaphone	60.00	120.00

1986 LJN WWF Wrestling Superstars Series 3 (loose)

NNO Bobby Heenan/No Scrolls	30.00	60.00
NNO Bobby Heenan/Scrolls	20.00	50.00
NNO Bruno Sammartino	20.00	40.00
NNO Captain Lou Albano/Red Lapel	12.50	25.00
NNO Captain Lou Albano/White Lapel	15.00	30.00
NNO Classy Freddie Blassie	30.00	60.00
NNO Corporal Kirchner/Beard		
NNO Corporal Kirchner/No Stubble	15.00	30.00
NNO Corporal Kirchner/Stubble	15.00	30.00
NNO Don Muraco	20.00	40.00
NNO Jesse Ventura	20.00	40.00
NNO Jimmy Hart/Hearts on Megaphone	20.00	40.00
NNO Jimmy Hart/No Hearts on Megaphone	10.00	20.00
NNO Randy Savage	30.00	60.00
NNO Ricky Steamboat	15.00	30.00
NNO SD Jones/Hawaiian Shirt	20.00	40.00
NNO SD Jones/Red Shirt	12.50	25.00
NNO Terry Funk	30.00	75.00
NNO Tito Santana	20.00	40.00

1987 LJN WWF Wrestling Superstars Series 4

NNO Adrian Adonis	75.00	150.00
NNO Billy Jack Haynes	200.00	350.00
NNO Bret Hart/Pink Tights	300.00	600.00
NNO Bret Hart/Purple Tights		
NNO Brian Blair/Non-Tan	75.00	150.00
NNO Brian Blair/Tan	125.00	250.00
NNO Cowboy Bob Orton	100.00	200.00
NNO Elizabeth/Gold Skirt	125.00	250.00
NNO Elizabeth/Purple Skirt	1200.00	1800.00
NNO Hercules Hernandez	100.00	200.00
NNO Jake the Snake Roberts	200.00	400.00
NNO Jim Brunzell/Non-Tan	125.00	250.00
NNO Jim Brunzell/Tan	150.00	300.00
NNO Jim Neidhart/Pink Tights	300.00	600.00
NNO Jim Neidhart/Purple Tights		
NNO Kamala	150.00	300.00
NNO King Harley Race	300.00	500.00
NNO Koko B. Ware	200.00	350.00
NNO Mean Gene Okerlund	100.00	200.00
NNO Mr. Fuji	125.00	250.00
NNO Outback Jack	100.00	200.00
NNO Ted Arcidi	150.00	300.00

1987 LJN WWF Wrestling Superstars Series 4 (loose)

NNO Adrian Adonis	25.00	50.00
NNO Billy Jack Haynes	50.00	100.00
NNO Bret Hart/Pink Tights	50.00	100.00
NNO Bret Hart/Purple Tights		
NNO Brian Blair/Non-Tan	20.00	40.00
NNO Brian Blair/Tan		
NNO Cowboy Bob Orton	30.00	60.00
NNO Elizabeth/Gold Skirt	50.00	100.00
NNO Elizabeth/Purple Skirt	200.00	350.00
NNO Hercules Hernandez	20.00	40.00
NNO Jake the Snake Roberts	50.00	100.00
NNO Jim Brunzell/Non-Tan	15.00	30.00
NNO Jim Brunzell/Tan		
NNO Jim Neidhart/Pink Tights	30.00	75.00
NNO Jim Neidhart/Purple Tights		
NNO Kamala	30.00	60.00
NNO King Harley Race	60.00	120.00
NNO Koko B. Ware	30.00	75.00
NNO Mean Gene Okerlund	20.00	40.00
NNO Mr. Fuji	30.00	60.00
NNO Outback Jack	30.00	75.00
NNO Ted Arcidi	20.00	40.00

1988 LJN WWF Wrestling Superstars Series 5

NNO	Ax	300.00	600.00
NNO	Bam Bam Bigelow	200.00	400.00
NNO	Hacksaw Jim Duggan	300.00	450.00
NNO	Honky Tonk Man	300.00	500.00
NNO	Hulk Hogan/Red Shirt		
NNO	Hulk Hogan/White Shirt		
NNO	Johnny V	90.00	175.00
NNO	Ken Patera	150.00	300.00
NNO	One Man Gang	200.00	400.00
NNO	Referee/Blue Shirt	200.00	400.00
NNO	Referee/White Shirt	400.00	750.00
NNO	Rick Martel	300.00	600.00
NNO	Slick	150.00	300.00
NNO	Ted Dibiase	300.00	500.00
NNO	Tito Santana/White Trunks	200.00	350.00
NNO	Vince McMahon	150.00	300.00

1988 LJN WWF Wrestling Superstars Series 5 (loose)

NNO	Ax	50.00	100.00
NNO	Bam Bam Bigelow	50.00	100.00
NNO	Hacksaw Jim Duggan	100.00	200.00
NNO	Honky Tonk Man	50.00	100.00
NNO	Hulk Hogan/Red Shirt	125.00	250.00
NNO	Hulk Hogan/White Shirt	125.00	250.00
NNO	Johnny V	20.00	40.00
NNO	Ken Patera	30.00	60.00
NNO	One Man Gang	30.00	75.00
NNO	Referee/Blue Shirt	50.00	100.00
NNO	Referee/White Shirt	60.00	120.00
NNO	Rick Martel	30.00	60.00
NNO	Slick	30.00	75.00
NNO	Ted Dibiase	60.00	120.00
NNO	Tito Santana	25.00	50.00
NNO	Vince McMahon	60.00	120.00

1989 LJN WWF Wrestling Superstars Series 6

NNO	Andre the Giant	2000.00	4000.00
NNO	Big Boss Man	1250.00	2500.00
NNO	Haku	500.00	1000.00
NNO	Rick Rude	500.00	1000.00
NNO	Ultimate Warrior	3000.00	6000.00
NNO	Warlord	1500.00	3000.00

1984 LJN WWF Wrestling Superstars Accessories

NNO	Hulkamania Barbell Workout Set		
NNO	Hulkamania Deluxe Workout Set	200.00	400.00

1986 LJN WWF Wrestling Superstars Stretch Wrestlers

NNO	George The Animal Steele	125.00	250.00
NNO	Hulk Hogan	300.00	600.00
NNO	Junkyard Dog	125.00	250.00
NNO	King Kong Bundy	125.00	250.00
NNO	Macho Man Randy Savage	250.00	400.00
NNO	Mr. Wonderful Paul Orndorff	75.00	150.00
NNO	Ricky The Dragon Steamboat	150.00	300.00
NNO	Rowdy Roddy Piper	250.00	500.00

1985 LJN WWF Wrestling Superstars Tag Teams

NNO	British Bulldogs	400.00	800.00
NNO	Greg Valentine & Brutus Beefcake	200.00	400.00
NNO	Hart Foundation	1000.00	1500.00
NNO	Hillbilly Jim & Hulk Hogan	250.00	500.00
NNO	Iron Sheik & Nikolai Volkoff	150.00	300.00
NNO	Killer Bees	200.00	400.00
NNO	Strike Force	300.00	500.00

1986 LJN WWF Wrestling Superstars Thumb Wrestlers

NNO	Hillbilly Jim/Big John Studd	75.00	150.00
NNO	Hillbilly Jim/Macho Man Randy Savage	15.00	30.00
NNO	Hillbilly Jim/Nikolai Volkoff	12.50	25.00
NNO	Hillbilly Jim/Rowdy Roddy Piper	30.00	60.00
NNO	Hillbilly Jim/The Iron Sheik	30.00	75.00
NNO	Hulk Hogan/Big John Studd	25.00	50.00
NNO	Hulk Hogan/Jake The Snake Roberts	30.00	75.00

NNO	Hulk Hogan/King Kong Bundy	20.00	40.00
NNO	Hulk Hogan/Macho Man Randy Savage	25.00	50.00
NNO	Hulk Hogan/Nikolai Volkoff	30.00	75.00
NNO	Hulk Hogan/Rowdy Roddy Piper	60.00	120.00
NNO	Hulk Hogan/The Iron Sheik	20.00	40.00
NNO	Junkyard Dog/Big John Studd	15.00	30.00
NNO	Junkyard Dog/Nikolai Volkoff	30.00	75.00
NNO	Junkyard Dog/Rowdy Roddy Piper	100.00	200.00
NNO	Junkyard Dog/The Iron Sheik	15.00	30.00
NNO	Mr. Wonderful Paul Orndorff/Big John Studd	30.00	75.00
NNO	Mr. Wonderful Paul Orndorff/King Kong Bundy	15.00	30.00
NNO	Mr. Wonderful Paul Orndorff/Rowdy Roddy Piper	50.00	100.00
NNO	Ricky The Dragon Steamboat/Jake The Snake Roberts	30.00	75.00
NNO	Ricky The Dragon Steamboat Macho Man Randy Savage	25.00	50.00
NNO	Ricky The Dragon Steamboat/Nikolai Volkoff	12.50	25.00
NNO	Ricky The Dragon Steamboat/Rowdy Roddy Piper	15.00	30.00

1986 LJN WWF Wrestling Superstars Thumb Wrestlers (loose)

NNO	Big John Studd	5.00	10.00
NNO	Hillbilly Jim	5.00	10.00
NNO	Hulk Hogan	7.50	15.00
NNO	Iron Sheik	3.00	8.00
NNO	Jake The Snake Roberts	5.00	10.00
NNO	Junkyard Dog	3.00	8.00
NNO	King Kong Bundy	6.00	12.00
NNO	Macho Man Randy Savage	7.50	15.00
NNO	Mr. Wonderful Paul Orndorff	3.00	8.00
NNO	Nikolai Volkoff	3.00	8.00
NNO	Ricky The Dragon Steamboat	5.00	10.00
NNO	Rowdy Roddy Piper	6.00	12.00

2018 The Loyal Subjects Action Vinyls WWE

NNO	AJ Styles		
NNO	Brock Lesnar	10.00	20.00
NNO	Demon King Finn Balor	12.50	25.00
NNO	Demon King Finn Balor Black and White		
NNO	Finn Balor/Blue Trunks	30.00	75.00
NNO	John Cena	7.50	15.00
NNO	Macho Man Randy Savage/Gold/2*		
NNO	Macho Man Randy Savage	12.50	25.00
NNO	Macho Man Randy Savage/American Flag	30.00	75.00
NNO	Referee		
NNO	Referee/GITD		
NNO	Roman Reigns	10.00	20.00
NNO	Sasha Banks CH	40.00	80.00
NNO	Shinsuke Nakamura	7.50	15.00
NNO	Shinsuke Nakamura/Black Pants	15.00	30.00
NNO	Sting	15.00	30.00
NNO	Undertaker	12.50	25.00
NNO	RAW Ring/Bottom Left	10.00	20.00
NNO	RAW Ring/Bottom Right	10.00	20.00
NNO	RAW Ring/Top Left	10.00	20.00
NNO	RAW Ring/Top Right	10.00	20.00

2018 The Loyal Subjects Action Vinyls WWE SDCC Exclusives

NNO	AJ Styles vs. Shinsuke Nakamura	20.00	40.00
NNO	Brock Lesnar vs. Roman Reigns	12.50	25.00
NNO	John Cena vs. Undertaker	30.00	75.00

2015 Mattel Create A WWE Superstar Series 1

NNO	Bray Wyatt	10.00	20.00
NNO	Hulk Hogan	20.00	40.00
NNO	John Cena	12.50	25.00
NNO	The Rock	15.00	30.00

2015 Mattel Create A WWE Superstar Series 1 Sets

NNO	Gladiator Set	10.00	20.00
NNO	Lucha Set	10.00	20.00
NNO	Rocker Set	10.00	20.00

2015 Mattel Create A WWE Superstar Series 2

NNO	Kane	12.50	25.00
NNO	Randy Orton	10.00	20.00

NNO	Sheamus	10.00	20.00
NNO	Stone Cold Steve Austin		

2015 Mattel Create A WWE Superstar Series 2 Sets

NNO	Samurai Set		
NNO	Special Ops Set	20.00	40.00
NNO	Zombie Set	15.00	30.00

2015 Mattel Create A WWE Superstar Series 3

NNO	Goldust	25.00	50.00
NNO	John Cena	15.00	30.00
NNO	Rusev		
NNO	Triple H		
NNO	Ultimate Warrior	12.50	25.00

2015 Mattel Create A WWE Superstar Series 3 Sets

NNO	Enforcer Set	10.00	20.00
NNO	Hip Hop Set	10.00	20.00
NNO	Vigilante Set	15.00	30.00

2015 Mattel Create A WWE Superstar Series Playset

NNO	Ring Builder	30.00	75.00

2019 Mattel Masters of the WWE Universe

NNO	Finn Balor	10.00	20.00
NNO	Sting	12.50	25.00
NNO	Triple H	12.50	25.00
NNO	Ultimate Warrior	15.00	30.00

2019 Mattel Masters of the WWE Universe Playsets

NNO	Grayskull Mania (w/John Cena & Terror Claws Triple H)	25.00	50.00
NNO	Grayskull Ring	25.00	50.00

2020 Mattel Masters of the WWE Universe Series 2

NNO	Macho Man	20.00	40.00
NNO	John Cena	15.00	30.00
NNO	Roman Reigns	12.50	25.00
NNO	Rey Mysterio	12.50	25.00

2010 Mattel WWE Battle Packs Series 1

NNO	Santino/Beth Phoenix	15.00	30.00
NNO	Shawn Michaels vs. {Chris Jericho	20.00	40.00
NNO	Ted DiBiase/Cody Rhodes	30.00	75.00

2010 Mattel WWE Battle Packs Series 2

NNO	Carlito/Primo	12.50	25.00
NNO	Finlay/Hornswoggle	20.00	40.00
NNO	John Morrison/The Miz	15.00	30.00

2010 Mattel WWE Battle Packs Series 3

NNO	Edge/Big Show		
NNO	Rey Mysterio/Evan Bourne	25.00	50.00
NNO	Shad/JTG	30.00	60.00

2010 Mattel WWE Battle Packs Series 4

NNO	Chavo vs. Hornswoggle	7.50	15.00
NNO	Christian/Tommy Dreamer	40.00	80.00
NNO	Hart Dynasty	20.00	40.00

2010 Mattel WWE Battle Packs Series 5

NNO	Carlito/Primo	20.00	40.00
NNO	D-Generation X	25.00	50.00
NNO	Ricky Steamboat vs. Y2J	15.00	30.00

2010 Mattel WWE Battle Packs Series 6

NNO	Mark Henry & MVP		
NNO	Undertaker vs. Batista		
NNO	Vladimir Kozlov & Ezekiel Jackson	7.50	15.00

2010 Mattel WWE Battle Packs Series 7

NNO	CM Punk & Luke Gallows	20.00	40.00
NNO	Dolph Ziggler vs. John Morrison		
NNO	The Miz & Big Show		

2011 Mattel WWE Battle Packs Series 8

NNO John Cena vs. Randy Orton
NNO Matt Hardy/Great Khali
NNO Ted DiBiase/Cody Rhodes

2011 Mattel WWE Battle Packs Series 9

NNO Christian/Heath Slater	7.50	15.00
NNO Hart Dynasty	15.00	30.00
NNO Sheamus/Triple H	12.50	25.00

2011 Mattel WWE Battle Packs Series 10

NNO Darren Young/Justin Gabriel	15.00	30.00
NNO David Otunga/ Michael Tarver	15.00	30.00
NNO Randy Orton vs. Edge	40.00	80.00

2011 Mattel WWE Battle Packs Series 11

NNO Drew McIntyre/ Cody Rhodes	75.00	150.00
NNO Jimmy Uso/Jey Uso	25.00	50.00
NNO Undertaker/Kane	30.00	75.00

2011 Mattel WWE Battle Packs Series 13

NNO John Cena vs. R-Truth	15.00	30.00
NNO The Miz vs. Alex Riley	20.00	40.00
NNO Rey Mysterio vs. Cody Rhodes	30.00	60.00

2012 Mattel WWE Battle Packs Series 14

NNO Heath Slater/Justin Gabriel	12.50	25.00
NNO Macho Man Randy Savage vs. CM Punk	25.00	50.00
NNO Randy Orton vs. Mason Ryan	12.50	25.00

2012 Mattel WWE Battle Packs Series 15

NNO Brie Bella/Nikki Bella	30.00	60.00
NNO Sin Cara vs. Daniel Bryan	25.00	50.00
NNO The Rock vs. John Cena	12.50	25.00

2012 Mattel WWE Battle Packs Series 16

NNO Alberto Del Rio vs. Big Show		
NNO David Otunga/ Michael McGillicutty	12.50	25.00
NNO Randy Orton vs. Christian	15.00	30.00

2012 Mattel WWE Battle Packs Series 17

NNO John Cena vs. CM Punk	15.00	30.00
NNO Mark Henry vs. Trent Barreta	15.00	30.00
NNO Rey Mysterio vs. The Miz	25.00	50.00

2012 Mattel WWE Battle Packs Series 18

NNO CM Punk vs. Triple H	20.00	40.00
NNO Randy Orton vs. Wade Barrett		
NNO Zack Ryder vs. Dolph Ziggler	15.00	30.00

2012 Mattel WWE Battle Packs Series 19

NNO Daniel Bryan vs. Big Show	15.00	30.00
NNO Epico/Primo	25.00	50.00
NNO John Cena vs. Kane		

2013 Mattel WWE Battle Packs Series 20

NNO Brock Lesnar vs. Triple H	15.00	30.00
NNO Brodus Clay vs. Curt Hawkins	10.00	20.00
NNO Kofi Kingston/R-Truth	15.00	30.00

2013 Mattel WWE Battle Packs Series 21

NNO Darren Young/Titus O'Neil	12.50	25.00
NNO Kane vs. Daniel Bryan	20.00	40.00
NNO Sheamus vs. Randy Orton	15.00	30.00

2013 Mattel WWE Battle Packs Series 22

NNO Dolph Ziggler/ Vickie Guerrero	12.50	25.00
NNO Ryback vs. Jinder Mahal	12.50	25.00
NNO Sin Cara/Rey Mysterio	7.50	15.00

2013 Mattel WWE Battle Packs Series 23

NNO CM Punk vs. Mr. McMahon	20.00	40.00
NNO Rey Mysterio vs. Kofi Kingston	15.00	30.00
NNO Sin Cara vs. Cody Rhodes	15.00	30.00

2013 Mattel WWE Battle Packs Series 24

NNO Naomi/Cameron	20.00	40.00

NNO The Rock vs. John Cena	17.50	35.00
NNO Seth Rollins/Roman Reigns	15.00	30.00

2013 Mattel WWE Battle Packs Series 25

NNO Brock Lesnar/Paul Heyman	15.00	30.00
NNO CM Punk vs. Undertaker	25.00	50.00
NNO Mark Henry vs. Ryback	20.00	40.00

2014 Mattel WWE Battle Packs Series 26

NNO Nikki Bella/Brie Bella	20.00	40.00
NNO Seth Rollins/Dean Ambrose	15.00	30.00
NNO Triple H vs. Curtis Axel	12.50	25.00

2014 Mattel WWE Battle Packs Series 27

NNO Big Show/Mark Henry	12.50	25.00
NNO Brodus Clay/Tensai	10.00	20.00
NNO Daniel Bryan/Randy Orton	12.50	25.00

2014 Mattel WWE Battle Packs Series 28

NNO Big E/AJ Lee	20.00	40.00
NNO Jimmy Uso/Jey Uso	10.00	20.00
NNO Luke Harper/Erick Rowan	15.00	30.00

2014 Mattel WWE Battle Packs Series 29

NNO CM Punk vs. Ryback	25.00	50.00
NNO Goldust/Cody Rhodes	20.00	40.00
NNO Los Matadores	12.50	25.00

2014 Mattel WWE Battle Packs Series 30

NNO Brock Lesnar vs. Undertaker	15.00	30.00
NNO Jake Roberts/Dean Ambrose	15.00	30.00
NNO Xavier Woods/R-Truth	12.50	25.00

2014 Mattel WWE Battle Packs Series 31

NNO John Cena/Ultimate Warrior	12.50	25.00
NNO Luke Harper/Erick Rowan	12.50	30.00
NNO Sin Cara/Alberto Del Rio	10.00	20.00

2015 Mattel WWE Battle Packs Series 32

NNO Daniel Bryan/Triple H	15.00	30.00
NNO Jimmy Uso/Jey Uso	20.00	40.00
NNO Road Dogg/Billy Gunn	15.00	30.00

2015 Mattel WWE Battle Packs Series 33

NNO Andre the Giant/Big Show	25.00	50.00
NNO Rey Mysterio/RVD	15.00	30.00
NNO Shawn Michaels/Undertaker	7.50	15.00

2015 Mattel WWE Battle Packs Series 34

NNO Animal/Hawk	30.00	75.00
NNO Hornswoggle/El Torito	30.00	60.00
NNO Lana/Rusev	15.00	30.00

2015 Mattel WWE Battle Packs Series 35

NNO Kane/Roman Reigns	12.50	25.00
NNO Ryback/Curtis Axel	15.00	30.00
NNO Zeb Colter/Jack Swagger	12.50	25.00

2015 Mattel WWE Battle Packs Series 36

NNO Big E/Kofi Kingston	15.00	30.00
NNO Dean Ambrose/Seth Rollins	10.00	20.00
NNO Kevin Nash/Scott Hall	15.00	30.00

2015 Mattel WWE Battle Packs Series 37

NNO Jamie Noble/Joey Mercury	12.50	25.00
NNO Jey Uso/Jimmy Uso	12.50	25.00
NNO Konnor/Viktor	10.00	20.00

2015 Mattel WWE Battle Packs Series 38

NNO Adam Rose/Bunny	10.00	20.00
NNO Bray Wyatt/Undertaker	15.00	30.00
NNO Nikki Bella/Brie Bella	20.00	40.00

2016 Mattel WWE Battle Packs Series 39

NNO Darren Young/Titus O'Neill	10.00	20.00
NNO John Cena/Kevin Owens	7.50	15.00
NNO Tyson Kidd/Cesaro	7.50	15.00

2016 Mattel WWE Battle Packs Series 40

NNO Bushwhackers	10.00	20.00
NNO Enzo Amore/Big Cass	15.00	30.00
NNO Steve Austin/Mr. McMahon	15.00	30.00

2016 Mattel WWE Battle Packs Series 41

NNO Bubba Ray/Devon Dudley	15.00	30.00
NNO Charlotte/Ric Flair	12.50	25.00
NNO Simon Gotch/Aiden English		

2016 Mattel WWE Battle Packs Series 42

NNO Edge/Christian	10.00	20.00
NNO Sin Cara/Kalisto	15.00	30.00
NNO Triple H/Stephanie	12.50	25.00

2016 Mattel WWE Battle Packs Series 43A

NNO Big E/Kofi Kingston	15.00	30.00
NNO Nikki Bella/Brie Bella	20.00	40.00
NNO Undertaker/Kane	12.50	25.00

2016 Mattel WWE Battle Packs Series 43B

NNO Dean Ambrose/Brock Lesnar	12.50	25.00
NNO Finn Balor/Samoa Joe	20.00	40.00
NNO John Cena/Seth Rollins	10.00	20.00
NNO Roman Reigns/Sheamus	12.50	25.00

2016 Mattel WWE Battle Packs Series 44

NNO American Alpha	10.00	20.00
NNO Sami Zayn/Kevin Owens	12.50	25.00
NNO The Usos	15.00	30.00

2017 Mattel WWE Battle Packs Series 45

NNO AJ Styles/Roman Reigns	15.00	30.00
NNO Enzo Amore/Big Cass	20.00	40.00
NNO Scott Dawson/Dash Wilder	15.00	30.00
NNO Triple H/Road Dogg	15.00	30.00

2017 Mattel WWE Battle Packs Series 46

NNO Dean Ambrose/Shane McMahon	15.00	30.00
NNO Karl Anderson/Luke Gallows	25.00	50.00
NNO The Miz & Maryse	15.00	30.00
NNO The New Day (Kingston/Woods)	15.00	30.00

2017 Mattel WWE Battle Packs Series 47

NNO Bray Wyatt/Luke Harper	12.50	25.00
NNO The Hart Foundation	12.50	25.00
NNO Roman Reigns vs. Rusev	12.50	25.00
NNO Sasha Banks vs. Charlotte Flair	15.00	30.00

2017 Mattel WWE Battle Packs Series 48

NNO American Alpha	12.50	25.00
NNO Hype Bros.	10.00	20.00
NNO Shawn Michaels/Diesel	12.50	25.00

2017 Mattel WWE Battle Packs Series 49

NNO Daniel Bryan/The Miz	12.50	25.00
NNO Sheamus/Cesaro	12.50	25.00
NNO Stephanie McMahon/Mick Foley	10.00	20.00

2017 Mattel WWE Battle Packs Series 50

NNO Konnor/Viktor	10.00	20.00
NNO Luke Gallows/Karl Anderson	20.00	40.00
NNO Randy Orton/Bray Wyatt	12.50	25.00

2017 Mattel WWE Battle Packs Series 51

NNO Big E/Xavier Woods	12.50	25.00
NNO The Miz/Maryse	10.00	20.00
NNO Scott Dawson/Dash Wilder	15.00	30.00

2018 Mattel WWE Battle Packs Series 52

NNO Jey Uso/Jimmy Uso	30.00	60.00
NNO Roman Reigns/Brock Lesnar	12.50	25.00
NNO Sheamus/Cesaro	15.00	30.00

2018 Mattel WWE Battle Packs Series 53

NNO Carmella/James Ellsworth	12.50	25.00
NNO Matt Hardy/Jeff Hardy	25.00	50.00
NNO S. Nakamura/D. Ziggler	12.50	25.00

2018 Mattel WWE Battle Packs Series 54

NNO B. Strowman/R. Reigns	15.00	30.00
NNO Bray Wyatt/Finn Balor	12.50	25.00
NNO Nia Jax/Alexa Bliss	25.00	50.00
NNO Tyler Breeze/Fandango	10.00	20.00

2018 Mattel WWE Battle Packs Series 55

NNO	Big Show/Big Cass	17.50	35.00
NNO	Charlotte Flair/Becky Lynch	20.00	40.00
NNO	Seth Rollins/Dean Ambrose	15.00	30.00

2018 Mattel WWE Battle Packs Series 56

NNO	Miztourage
NNO	Roman Reigns vs. John Cena
NNO	Kurt Angle/Jason Jordan

2019 Mattel WWE Battle Packs Series 57

NNO	Braun Strowman vs. Kane
NNO	Sunil &Samir Singh
NNO	Finn Balor vs. Shinsuke Nakamura

2019 Mattel WWE Battle Packs Series 58

NNO	Kevin Owens/Sami Zayn
NNO	S. Benjamin/C. Gable
NNO	Triple H/HBK

2019 Mattel WWE Battle Packs Series 59

NNO	The Hardy Boyz
NNO	Jinder Mahal vs. AJ Styles
NNO	The Shield (Ambrose/Rollins)

2019 Mattel WWE Battle Packs Series 60

NNO	The Bar (Cesaro/Sheamus)
NNO	Goldberg vs. Stone Cold Steve Austin
NNO	Sasha Banks vs. Alexa Bliss

2019 Mattel WWE Battle Packs Series 61

NNO	AJ Styles/Daniel Bryan
NNO	The Iiconics (Billie Kay/Peyton Royce)
NNO	Jimmy and Jey Uso

2019 Mattel WWE Battle Packs Series 62

NNO	Akam & Rezar
NNO	Andrade/Zelina Vega
NNO	Rey Mysterio/Shinsuke Nakamura

2019 Mattel WWE Battle Packs Series 63

NNO	Bobby Lashley vs. Finn Balor
NNO	The New Day (Big E/Xavier Woods)
NNO	Seth Rollins vs. Brock Lesnar

2020 Mattel WWE Battle Packs Series 64

NNO	Daniel Bryan vs. AJ Styles	15.00	30.00
NNO	Lita & Trish Stratus	30.00	75.00
NNO	The Usos	60.00	120.00

2020 Mattel WWE Battle Packs Series 65

NNO	Ali & Kevin Owens	20.00	40.00
NNO	The Hardy Boyz	25.00	50.00
NNO	Ricochet & Velveteen	20.00	40.00

2020 Mattel WWE Battle Packs Series 66

NNO	Seth Rollins & Becky Lynch	25.00	50.00
NNO	Roman Reigns & Undertaker	30.00	60.00
NNO	Shane McMahon & Drew McIntyre	15.00	30.00

2016 Mattel WWE Battle Packs SummerSlam Heritage

NNO	John Cena/Brock Lesnar	12.50	25.00
NNO	Roman Reigns/Dean Ambrose	10.00	20.00

2017 Mattel WWE Battle Packs SummerSlam Heritage

NNO	Brock Lesnar/Randy Orton	15.00	30.00
NNO	Ultimate Warrior/Honkytonk Man	15.00	30.00

2016 Mattel WWE Battle Packs Then Now Forever

These figures were exclusive to Walmart.

NNO	Dean Ambrose/Brian Pillman	10.00	20.00
NNO	John Cena/Steve Austin	15.00	30.00
NNO	Ultimate Warrior/Sting	12.50	25.00

2010 Mattel WWE Battle Packs WrestleMania 26

NNO	John Cena/Batista		
NNO	The Miz/Big Show	20.00	40.00
NNO	R-Truth/John Morrison		

2014 Mattel WWE Battle Packs WrestleMania 30 Heritage

NNO	Batista vs. Brock Lesnar	15.00	30.00
NNO	Sheamus vs. Ultimate Warrior	12.50	25.00

2015 Mattel WWE Battle Packs WrestleMania 31 Heritage

NNO	Daniel Bryan vs. Rey Mysterio	20.00	40.00
NNO	Triple H vs. Roman Reigns	20.00	40.00

2016 Mattel WWE Battle Packs WrestleMania 32 Heritage

NNO	Bret Hart vs. Steve Austin	15.00	30.00
NNO	Ric Flair & The Rock	12.50	25.00

2016 Mattel WWE Battle Packs WrestleMania 33 Heritage

NNO	Andre the Giant/ Ted DiBiase	10.00	20.00
NNO	The Rock/John Cena	12.50	25.00

2018 Mattel WWE Battle Packs WrestleMania 34 Heritage

NNO	Sting/Triple H	10.00	20.00
NNO	John Cena/Nikki Bella	15.00	30.00
NNO	Roman Reigns/Undertaker	12.50	25.00

2018 Mattel WWE Battle Packs WrestleMania 35 Heritage

NNO	AJ Styles vs. Shinsuke Nakamura	15.00	30.00
NNO	Jeff Hardy vs. Edge	15.00	30.00
NNO	The Miz vs. Seth Rollins	12.50	25.00

2020 Mattel WWE Beast Mode

NNO	AJ Styles	7.50	15.00
NNO	Becky Lynch	7.50	15.00
NNO	Braun Strowman	5.00	10.00
NNO	Daniel Bryan	6.00	12.00
NNO	Finn Balor	7.50	15.00
NNO	The Rock	5.00	10.00
NNO	Roman Reigns	10.00	20.00
NNO	Triple H	7.50	15.00

2010 Mattel WWE Best of 2010

NNO	Batista	12.50	25.00
NNO	Evan Bourne	7.50	15.00
NNO	Hornswoggle	20.00	40.00
NNO	John Cena	10.00	20.00
NNO	Mark Henry	7.50	15.00
NNO	Rey Mysterio	12.50	25.00

2011 Mattel WWE Best of 2011

NNO	Big Show	12.50	25.00
NNO	John Cena	6.00	12.00
NNO	Kofi Kingston		
NNO	Randy Orton	7.50	15.00
NNO	Rey Mysterio	25.00	50.00
NNO	Santino Marella	7.50	15.00

2012 Mattel WWE Best of 2012

NNO	Alberto Del Rio		
NNO	Brodus Clay		
NNO	Daniel Bryan	15.00	30.00
NNO	Great Khali	40.00	80.00
NNO	Rey Mysterio	12.50	25.00
NNO	Sin Cara	25.00	50.00

2013 Mattel WWE Best of 2013

NNO	Brock Lesnar
NNO	Great Khali
NNO	Kaitlyn
NNO	Rey Mysterio
NNO	Tensai
NNO	Undertaker

2014 Mattel WWE Best of 2014

NNO	Cesaro	7.50	15.00
NNO	El Torito	12.50	25.00
NNO	John Cena	10.00	20.00

NNO	Roman Reigns	20.00	40.00
NNO	Sin Cara	25.00	50.00
NNO	Undertaker	10.00	20.00

2012 Mattel WWE Best of PPV Series 1

Also known as Best of PPV 2012. These figures were exclusive to Toys R Us.

NNO	Christian
NNO	John Cena
NNO	Mark Henry
NNO	Rey Mysterio	30.00	75.00

2012 Mattel WWE Best of PPV Series 2

Also known as Best of WrestleMania 28. These figures were exclusive to Toys R Us.

NNO	John Cena
NNO	The Rock
NNO	Sheamus
NNO	Triple H

2013 Mattel WWE Best of PPV Series 3

Also known as Best of PPV 2013. These figures were exclusive to Toys R Us.

NNO	Alberto Del Rio
NNO	John Cena
NNO	Mark Henry
NNO	Rey Mysterio

2013 Mattel WWE Best of PPV Series 4

Also known as Best of WrestleMania 29. These figures were exclusive to Toys R Us.

NNO	Alberto Del Rio	7.50	15.00
NNO	Sheamus	7.50	15.00
NNO	The Rock	12.50	25.00
NNO	Undertaker	10.00	20.00

2014 Mattel WWE Best of PPV Series 5

Also known as the Best of PPV 2014. These figures were exclusive to Toys R Us.

NNO	Damien Sandow
NNO	Daniel Bryan
NNO	Dolph Ziggler
NNO	Kofi Kingston

2016 Mattel WWE Best of PPV

NNO	Chris Jericho	10.00	20.00
NNO	Neville		
NNO	Rusev		
NNO	Undertaker		

2015 Mattel WWE Big Reveal 12-Inch

NNO	Rey Mysterio
NNO	Triple H
NNO	Ultimate Warrior
NNO	Undertaker

2012 Mattel WWE Brawlin' Buddies

NNO	John Cena
NNO	Randy Orton
NNO	Rey Mysterio
NNO	Sheamus

2013 Mattel WWE Brawlin' Buddies

NNO	John Cena
NNO	Kofi Kingston
NNO	Rey Mysterio
NNO	Zack Ryder

2012 Mattel WWE Brawlin' Buddies 2-Pack

NNO Rey Mysterio/John Cena
(Toys R Us Exclusive)

2013 Mattel WWE Brawlin' Buddies Championship Buddies

NNO	Brodus Clay
NNO	John Cena
NNO	The Rock
NNO	Sheamus

2014 Mattel WWE Dollar Store Series 1

NNO CM Punk
NNO John Cena
NNO Kane
NNO Randy Orton
NNO Rey Mysterio
NNO Sheamus

2014 Mattel WWE Dollar Store Series 2

NNO Alberto Del Rio
NNO Big Show
NNO Brodus Clay
NNO Daniel Bryan
NNO John Cena
NNO Undertaker

2017 Mattel WWE Dollar Store

NNO Brock Lesnar
NNO John Cena
NNO Roman Reigns
NNO Undertaker

2019 Mattel WWE Dollar Store

NNO AJ Styles
NNO Finn Balor
NNO John Cena
NNO The Rock
NNO Roman Reigns

2019 Mattel WWE Dollar Store 5-Pack

NNO Cena/Rock/Styles/Balor/Reigns

2010 Mattel WWE Elite Collection Best of 2010

NNO John Cena	20.00	40.00
NNO Kane	50.00	100.00
NNO Randy Orton	50.00	90.00
NNO Rey Mysterio	60.00	120.00
NNO Triple H	25.00	50.00
NNO Undertaker	30.00	60.00

2011 Mattel WWE Elite Collection Best of 2011

NNO John Cena	25.00	50.00
NNO John Morrison	60.00	120.00
NNO Randy Orton	20.00	40.00
NNO Rey Mysterio	30.00	75.00
NNO Sheamus		

2018 Mattel WWE Elite Collection Best of Attitude Era

NNO Chris Jericho	10.00	20.00
NNO The Rock	20.00	40.00
NNO Stone Cold Steve Austin	20.00	40.00
NNO Triple H	12.50	25.00

2012 Mattel WWE Elite Collection Best of PPV Series 1

Also known as Best of PPV 2012. These figures were exclusive to Toys R Us.

NNO Bret Hart
NNO Daniel Bryan
NNO John Cena
NNO Triple H

2012 Mattel WWE Elite Collection Best of PPV Series 2

Also known as Best of WrestleMania 28. These figures were exclusive to Toys R Us.

NNO Undertaker EXCL
NNO Big Show
NNO CM Punk
NNO The Miz
NNO Shawn Michaels

2013 Mattel WWE Elite Collection Best of PPV Series 3

Also known as Best of PPV 2013. These figures were exclusive to Toys R Us.

NNO Christian	60.00	120.00
NNO John Cena	25.00	50.00

NNO Sheamus	15.00	30.00
NNO Sin Cara	30.00	75.00

2013 Mattel WWE Elite Collection Best of PPV Series 4

Also known as Best of WrestleMania 29. These figures were exclusive to Toys R Us.

NNO Brock Lesnar	15.00	30.00
NNO CM Punk	30.00	60.00
NNO Daniel Bryan	15.00	30.00
NNO John Cena	12.50	25.00

2014 Mattel WWE Elite Collection Best of PPV Series 5

Also known as Best of PPV 2014. These figures were exclusive to Toys R Us.

NNO Alberto Del Rio	20.00	40.00
NNO CM Punk	30.00	60.00
NNO Curtis Axel	25.00	50.00
NNO Paul Bearer	15.00	30.00
NNO Randy Orton	17.50	35.00

2014 Mattel WWE Elite Collection Best of PPV Series 6

Also known as Best of WrestleMania 30. These figures were exclusive to Toys R Us.

NNO Bray Wyatt	12.50	25.00
NNO Daniel Bryan	20.00	40.00
NNO John Cena	12.50	25.00
NNO Undertaker	20.00	40.00

2017 Mattel WWE Elite Collection Booty-O's 3-Pack

NNO The New Day	25.00	50.00

2011 Mattel WWE Elite Collection Defining Moments Series 1

NNO Macho Man Randy Savage	50.00	100.00
NNO Shawn Michaels	75.00	150.00

2011 Mattel WWE Elite Collection Defining Moments Series 2

NNO The Rock	100.00	200.00
NNO Ultimate Warrior	60.00	120.00

2011 Mattel WWE Elite Collection Defining Moments Series 3

NNO Ricky Steamboat	40.00	80.00
NNO Triple H	125.00	250.00

2011 Mattel WWE Elite Collection Defining Moments Series 4

NNO Stone Cold Steve Austin	40.00	80.00
NNO Undertaker	100.00	200.00

2011 Mattel WWE Elite Collection Defining Moments Series 5

NNO Bret Hart	100.00	200.00
NNO John Cena	30.00	60.00

2014 Mattel WWE Elite Collection Defining Moments Series 6

NNO Hulk Hogan	30.00	75.00
NNO Ric Flair	40.00	80.00

2015 Mattel WWE Elite Collection Defining Moments Series 7

NNO Hulk Hogan
NNO Razor Ramon
NNO Sting
NNO Undertaker

2016 Mattel WWE Elite Collection Defining Moments Series 8

NNO John Cena
NNO Ric Flair/Retirement
NNO Stone Cold Steve Austin
NNO Sting/Surfer Gear
NNO Ultimate Warrior

2017 Mattel WWE Elite Collection Defining Moments Series 9

NNO Chris Jericho	15.00	30.00
NNO Macho Man Randy Savage	20.00	40.00
NNO Shinsuke Nakamura	20.00	40.00

2018 Mattel WWE Elite Collection Entrance Greats

NNO Bobby Roode	20.00	40.00
NNO Elias		
NNO Finn Balor		
NNO Goldberg	25.00	50.00
NNO Jeff Hardy	30.00	60.00
NNO Kurt Angle		

2010 Mattel WWE Elite Collection Entrance Greats Series 1

NNO Rey Mysterio	50.00	100.00
NNO Shawn Michaels	25.00	50.00
NNO Triple H	20.00	40.00

2010 Mattel WWE Elite Collection Entrance Greats Series 2

NNO Chris Jericho	30.00	60.00
NNO Million Dollar Man	20.00	40.00
NNO Rowdy Roddy Piper	25.00	50.00

2010 Mattel WWE Elite Collection Entrance Greats Series 3

NNO The Rock	30.00	75.00
NNO Undertaker	50.00	100.00

2018 Mattel WWE Elite Collection Epic Moments

NNO Festival of Friendship	30.00	75.00
Chris Jericho/Kevin Owens		
NNO Milk-O-Mania	25.00	50.00
Kurt Angle/Stone Cold Steve Austin/Stephanie McMahon		
NNO Shield Reunion	50.00	100.00
Seth Rollins/Roman Reigns/Dean Ambrose		
NNO Team Xtreme	30.00	60.00
Matt & Jeff Hardy		
NNO Undisputed Era	60.00	120.00
Adam Cole/Bobby Fish/Kyle O'Reilly		

2010 Mattel WWE Elite Collection Exclusives

NNO Rey Mysterio Flash RSC	150.00	300.00

2011 Mattel WWE Elite Collection Exclusives

NNO Bret Hart P&B Attack RSC	150.00	300.00
NNO CM Punk Straight Edge RSC	200.00	350.00
NNO Macho King RSC	150.00	300.00
NNO Undertaker SDCC	75.00	150.00
NNO Vince McMahon MA	60.00	120.00

2012 Mattel WWE Elite Collection Exclusives

NNO Macho Man nWo RSC	75.00	150.00
NNO Steve Austin Rattlesnake RSC		
NNO Triple H COO MA	20.00	40.00

2013 Mattel WWE Elite Collection Exclusives

NNO Brock Lesnar Pain RSC	30.00	75.00
NNO Cactus Jack Bang RSC	30.00	60.00
NNO Undertaker 21-0 TRU		

2014 Mattel WWE Elite Collection Exclusives

NNO CM Punk ECW	60.00	120.00
{Flashback RSC		
NNO Edge Rated R RSC	100.00	200.00
NNO Kane Hardcore RSC	125.00	250.00
NNO Kane Unmasked RSC		
NNO The Rock IC Champ RSC	25.00	50.00
NNO Mankind AMZ	25.00	50.00
NNO Rocky Maivia TAR	30.00	75.00
NNO Brock Lesnar 21-1 TRU	25.00	50.00

2015 Mattel WWE Elite Collection Exclusives

NNO Hulk Hogan American RSC	60.00	120.00
NNO John Cena TRU	50.00	100.00
NNO Scott Hall nWo RSC	50.00	100.00
NNO Seth Rollins TRU	30.00	60.00
NNO Shawn Michaels DX SE WG	30.00	60.00

NNO	Shawn Michaels SS RSC	50.00	100.00
NNO	Triple H DX SE WG	30.00	60.00
NNO	Virgil Convention Sign	30.00	60.00

2016 Mattel WWE Elite Collection Exclusives

NNO	Chris Jericho WM XIX RSC	25.00	50.00
NNO	Finn Balor Balor Club RSC	30.00	75.00
NNO	Kevin Nash nWo RSC	75.00	150.00
NNO	Nation of Domination KM OL	60.00	120.00
NNO	Sting nWo Wolfpac RSC	60.00	120.00
NNO	Brock Lesnar/	25.00	50.00
NNO	Shockmaster SDCC	60.00	120.00

2017 Mattel WWE Elite Collection Exclusives

NNO	AJ Styles WRMS	25.00	50.00
NNO	Andre the Giant AMZ	30.00	75.00
NNO	Becky Lynch WG	20.00	40.00
NNO	Bret Hit Man Hart KOTR RSC	60.00	120.00
NNO	Chris Jericho List GS	30.00	75.00
NNO	Hardy Boyz WWE SZ		
NNO	Isaac Yankem DDS TRU	60.00	120.00
NNO	Macho Man Wolfpack RSC	75.00	150.00
NNO	Maryse WG	20.00	40.00
NNO	Samoa Joe GS	20.00	40.00
NNO	Sasha Banks Title WG	25.00	50.00
NNO	Shano Mac RSC	30.00	75.00

2018 Mattel WWE Elite Collection Exclusives

NNO	AJ Styles TRU	25.00	50.00
NNO	The Brian Kendrick RSC	20.00	40.00
NNO	Hardy Boyz Brood RSC	50.00	100.00
NNO	Kurt Angle Shield RSC	15.00	30.00
NNO	Matt Hardy ECW RSC	25.00	50.00
NNO	Pete Dunne	30.00	75.00
NNO	The Shark SDCC	20.00	40.00

2019 Mattel WWE Elite Collection Exclusives

NNO	Alexa Bliss WG	25.00	50.00
NNO	Alexander Wolfe TAR	20.00	40.00
NNO	Andrade Cien Almas (NXT TakeOver) RSC	30.00	60.00
NNO	Bob Backlund WM	20.00	40.00
NNO	Gorilla Monsoon WM	60.00	120.00
NNO	Kassius Ohno TAR	75.00	150.00
NNO	Liv Morgan TAR	60.00	120.00
NNO	Macho Man Randy Savage (Slim Jim) SDCC	75.00	150.00
NNO	Paige TAR	50.00	100.00
NNO	Pat Patterson WM	20.00	40.00
NNO	Red Rooster TAR	50.00	100.00
NNO	Rock (SmackDown Live) WM	20.00	40.00
NNO	Sensational Sherri WG	20.00	40.00
NNO	Sonya Deville TAR	50.00	100.00
NNO	Tyler Bate (UK Champion)	25.00	50.00
NNO	Undertaker as Kane (Deadman's Revenge) RSC	30.00	75.00

2020 Mattel WWE Elite Collection Exclusives

NNO	Finn Balor/AJ Styles	25.00	50.00
NNO	Rey Mysterio/Samoa Joe (WrestleMania Moment)	30.00	75.00

2021 Mattel WWE Elite Collection Exclusives

NNO	Bray Wyatt Firefly Funhouse (Ringside Collectibles Exclusive)	50.00	100.00
NNO	Ultimate Warrior WrestleMania 12 (Ringside Collectibles Exclusive)		
NNO	Walter (Ringside Collectibles Exclusive)	60.00	120.00

2018 Mattel WWE Elite Collection Fan Central

NNO	Carmella	25.00	50.00

2019 Mattel WWE Elite Collection Fan Central

NNO	Akira Tozawa	20.00	40.00
NNO	Big Show	25.00	50.00
NNO	Bobby The Brain Heenan	20.00	40.00
NNO	Daniel Bryan	15.00	30.00
NNO	Mark Henry	25.00	50.00
NNO	Mojo Rawley	15.00	30.00
NNO	Triple H	15.00	30.00

2018 Mattel WWE Elite Collection Flashback Series 1

NNO	Mean Gene Okerlund	30.00	75.00
NNO	Syxx	25.00	50.00
NNO	Ultimate Warrior	25.00	50.00
NNO	Yokozuna	20.00	40.00

2018 Mattel WWE Elite Collection Flashback Series 2

NNO	Alundra Blayze	15.00	30.00
NNO	Razor Ramon	15.00	30.00
NNO	Shawn Michaels	20.00	40.00

2018 Mattel WWE Elite Collection Hall of Champions Series 3

NNO	Billy Gunn	15.00	30.00
NNO	Paul Bearer	25.00	50.00
NNO	Road Dogg	15.00	30.00
NNO	Ultimate Warrior	25.00	50.00

2016 Mattel WWE Elite Collection Hall of Fame 2-Packs

These figures were exclusive to Target.

NNO	Papa Shango/Ultimate Warrior	25.00	50.00
NNO	Wild Samoans	20.00	40.00

2017 Mattel WWE Elite Collection Hall of Fame 4-Pack

NNO	Eddie Guerrero/Kevin Nash/ Scott Hall/Larry Zybysko	25.00	50.00

2015 Mattel WWE Elite Collection Hall of Fame Four Horsemen 4-Pack

NNO	Ric Flair/Arn Anderson Barry Windham/Tully Blanchard	30.00	75.00

2015 Mattel WWE Elite Collection Hall of Fame Series 1

These figures were exclusive to Target.

NNO	Sgt. Slaughter	20.00	40.00
NNO	Stone Cold Steve Austin	25.00	50.00
NNO	Trish Stratus	25.00	50.00
NNO	Ultimate Warrior	20.00	40.00

2015 Mattel WWE Elite Collection Hall of Fame Series 2

These figures were exclusive to Target.

NNO	Eddie Guerrero	15.00	30.00
NNO	Hulk Hogan	25.00	50.00
NNO	Tito Santana	10.00	20.00
NNO	Yokozuna	20.00	40.00

2016 Mattel WWE Elite Collection Hall of Fame Series 3

These figures were exclusive to Target.

NNO	Jimmy Hart	20.00	40.00
NNO	Macho Man Randy Savage	25.00	50.00
NNO	Million Dollar Man Ted DiBiase	17.50	35.00

2016 Mattel WWE Elite Collection Hall of Fame Series 4

These figures were exclusive to Target.

NNO	Edge	25.00	50.00
NNO	Jerry Lawler	15.00	30.00
NNO	King Booker	20.00	40.00
NNO	Sting	20.00	40.00

2017 Mattel WWE Elite Collection Hall of Fame Series 5

These figures were exclusive to Target.

NNO	Diesel	17.50	35.00
NNO	George The Animal Steele		
NNO	Jake Roberts	12.50	25.00
NNO	Roddy Piper	12.50	25.00

2019 Mattel WWE Elite Collection Ghostbusters

NNO	John Cena	12.50	25.00
NNO	The Rock	15.00	30.00

NNO	Shawn Michaels	12.50	25.00
NNO	Stone Cold Steve Austin	12.50	25.00
NNO	Undertaker	15.00	30.00

2010 Mattel WWE Elite Collection Legends Hall of Fame Series

These figures were exclusive to K-Mart.

NNO	Am. Dream Dusty Rhodes	25.00	50.00
NNO	Jimmy Superfly Snuka	25.00	50.00
NNO	Ricky Steamboat	30.00	75.00
NNO	Sgt. Slaughter		
NNO	Stone Cold Steve Austin	50.00	100.00
NNO	Terry Funk	25.00	50.00

2010 Mattel WWE Elite Collection Legends Series 1

NNO	Am. Dream Dusty Rhodes	30.00	75.00
NNO	Ricky Steamboat	30.00	75.00
NNO	Road Warrior Animal	50.00	100.00
NNO	Road Warrior Hawk	50.00	100.00
NNO	Sgt. Slaughter	25.00	50.00
NNO	Stone Cold Steve Austin	40.00	80.00

2010 Mattel WWE Elite Collection Legends Series 1 2-Packs

These figures were exclusive to Toys R Us.

NNO	Bushwhackers	30.00	75.00
NNO	Iron Sheik/Nikolai Volkoff	50.00	100.00
NNO	Rowdy Roddy Piper/Cowboy Bob Orton	50.00	100.00

2010 Mattel WWE Elite Collection Legends Series 2

NNO	Iron Sheik	30.00	60.00
NNO	Jake The Snake Roberts	30.00	60.00
NNO	Jimmy Superfly Snuka	50.00	100.00
NNO	Kamala	20.00	40.00
NNO	Ravishing Rick Rude	30.00	75.00
NNO	Terry Funk	20.00	40.00

2010 Mattel WWE Elite Collection Legends Series 2 2-Packs

These figures were exclusive to Toys R Us.

NNO	Kerry and Kevin Von Erich		
NNO	Marty Jannetty/HBK		

2010 Mattel WWE Elite Collection Legends Series 3

NNO	Brian Pillman	60.00	120.00
NNO	British Bulldog	30.00	75.00
NNO	Hacksaw Jim Duggan	50.00	100.00
NNO	Mr. Perfect	30.00	75.00
NNO	The Rock	25.00	50.00
NNO	Vader/Black Mask	75.00	150.00
NNO	Vader/Red Mask	50.00	100.00

2011 Mattel WWE Elite Collection Legends Series 4

NNO	Ax	60.00	120.00
NNO	George The Animal Steele	30.00	60.00
NNO	Hillbilly Jim	30.00	75.00
NNO	Paul Orndorff	75.00	150.00
NNO	Smash	60.00	120.00
NNO	Ultimate Warrior	30.00	60.00

2011 Mattel WWE Elite Collection Legends Series 5

NNO	Akeem	100.00	200.00
NNO	Bam Bam Bigelow	30.00	60.00
NNO	Macho Man Randy Savage	30.00	75.00
NNO	Rick Martel	100.00	200.00

2011 Mattel WWE Elite Collection Legends Series 6

NNO	Eddie Guerrero	75.00	150.00
NNO	Kerry Von Erich	100.00	200.00
NNO	Kevin Von Erich	125.00	250.00
NNO	Texas Tornado	75.00	150.00
NNO	Ultimate Warrior	30.00	75.00

2015 Mattel WWE Elite Collection Network Spotlight

NNO	The Ringmaster Steve Austin	15.00	30.00
NNO	Big Boss Man	20.00	40.00
NNO	Hunter Hearst Helmsley	15.00	30.00

2016 Mattel WWE Elite Collection Network Spotlight

These figures were exclusive to Toys R Us.

NNO	Bayley	17.50	35.00
NNO	Roman Reigns	20.00	40.00
NNO	Shawn Michaels	25.00	50.00

2017 Mattel WWE Elite Collection Network Spotlight

NNO	Dean Ambrose	17.50	35.00
NNO	Finn Balor	20.00	40.00
NNO	TJ Perkins	25.00	50.00
NNO	Undertaker	25.00	50.00
NNO	Vince McMahon	15.00	30.00

2019 Mattel WWE Elite Collection Network Spotlight

NNO	Asuka	20.00	40.00
NNO	Diesel	17.50	35.00
NNO	Jinder Mahal	15.00	30.00
NNO	Rey Mysterio	25.00	50.00

2020 Mattel WWE Elite Collection Network Spotlight

NNO	Kurt Angle	25.00	50.00
NNO	Matt Hardy	20.00	40.00
NNO	Ricochet	20.00	40.00
NNO	Wendi Richter	12.50	25.00

2017 Mattel WWE Elite Collection NXT Series 1

NNO	Austin Aries	20.00	40.00
NNO	No Way Jose	30.00	60.00
NNO	Seth Rollins	20.00	40.00

2017 Mattel WWE Elite Collection NXT Series 2

NNO	Asuka	25.00	50.00
NNO	Dash Wilder	17.50	35.00
NNO	Scott Dawson	17.50	35.00
NNO	Shinsuke Nakamura	15.00	30.00

2018 Mattel WWE Elite Collection NXT Series 3

NNO	Alexander Rusev	15.00	30.00
NNO	Bobby Roode	20.00	40.00
NNO	Ember Moon	20.00	40.00
NNO	Roman Reigns	20.00	40.00

2010 Mattel WWE Elite Collection Series 1

NNO	CM Punk	75.00	150.00
NNO	Edge	30.00	75.00
NNO	MVP		
NNO	Rey Mysterio	75.00	150.00
NNO	Undertaker	50.00	100.00

2010 Mattel WWE Elite Collection Series 2

NNO	Batista		
NNO	Matt Hardy		
NNO	R-Truth	30.00	75.00
NNO	Randy Orton	60.00	120.00
NNO	Ted Dibiase	40.00	80.00
NNO	Triple H	30.00	75.00
NNO	Triple H (bottle pack)		

2010 Mattel WWE Elite Collection Series 3

NNO	Christian	60.00	120.00
NNO	Cody Rhodes	30.00	60.00
NNO	John Cena	40.00	80.00
NNO	The Miz	25.00	50.00
NNO	Santino Marella		
NNO	Shawn Michaels	60.00	120.00

2010 Mattel WWE Elite Collection Series 4

NNO	Big Show	25.00	50.00
NNO	Chris Jericho/Blue Gear	40.00	80.00

2010 Mattel WWE Elite Collection Series 4 (continued)

NNO	Chris Jericho/Purple Gear	50.00	100.00
NNO	Finlay		
NNO	John Morrison/ Bright Red Robe		
NNO	John Morrison/ Dk Red Robe	125.00	250.00
NNO	Kane	60.00	120.00
NNO	Kofi Kingston		

2010 Mattel WWE Elite Collection Series 5

NNO	Chavo Guerrero	25.00	50.00
NNO	Dolph Ziggler	20.00	40.00
NNO	Jack Swagger/No Singlet	20.00	40.00
NNO	Jack Swagger/Singlet	30.00	60.00
NNO	Mark Henry	20.00	40.00
NNO	Rey Mysterio	75.00	150.00
NNO	Vladimir Kozlov/ Jacket Sleeves		
NNO	Vladimir Kozlov/ No Jacket Sleeves		

2010 Mattel WWE Elite Collection Series 6

NNO	Batista	50.00	100.00
NNO	CM Punk	60.00	120.00
NNO	Goldust	30.00	75.00
NNO	JTG	45.00	90.00
NNO	Matt Hardy	50.00	100.00
NNO	Shad	45.00	90.00

2011 Mattel WWE Elite Collection Series 7

NNO	David Hart Smith	25.00	50.00
NNO	Hornswoggle	60.00	120.00
NNO	John Cena	30.00	75.00
NNO	Shawn Michaels	75.00	150.00
NNO	Triple H	30.00	75.00
NNO	Tyson Kidd	25.00	50.00

2011 Mattel WWE Elite Collection Series 8

NNO	Drew McIntyre	30.00	60.00
NNO	Edge	30.00	75.00
NNO	Evan Bourne	50.00	100.00
NNO	Sheamus	25.00	50.00
NNO	Undertaker	30.00	60.00
NNO	William Regal	40.00	80.00

2011 Mattel WWE Elite Collection Series 9

NNO	Kofi Kingston		
NNO	Luke Gallows	25.00	50.00
NNO	The Miz	30.00	75.00
NNO	MVP	60.00	120.00
NNO	Randy Orton	25.00	50.00
NNO	Zack Ryder	25.00	50.00

2011 Mattel WWE Elite Collection Series 10

NNO	Big Show	30.00	75.00
NNO	John Morrison	50.00	100.00
NNO	Kane	50.00	100.00
NNO	R-Truth	25.00	50.00
NNO	Ted Dibiase	30.00	60.00
NNO	Yoshi Tatsu	30.00	75.00

2011 Mattel WWE Elite Collection Series 11

NNO	Christian	30.00	60.00
NNO	CM Punk	50.00	100.00
NNO	John Cena		
NNO	The Miz	40.00	80.00
NNO	Rey Mysterio	60.00	120.00
NNO	Wade Barrett	40.00	80.00

2011 Mattel WWE Elite Collection Series 12

NNO	Alberto Del Rio	15.00	30.00
NNO	Daniel Bryan	20.00	40.00
NNO	Justin Gabriel	30.00	60.00
NNO	Kane FB	50.00	100.00
NNO	Papa Shango FB	25.00	50.00
NNO	Randy Orton	20.00	40.00

2012 Mattel WWE Elite Collection Series 13

NNO	Big Show	25.00	50.00
NNO	Cody Rhodes	45.00	90.00

2012 Mattel WWE Elite Collection Series 13 (continued)

NNO	Dolph Ziggler	20.00	40.00
NNO	Edge FB	30.00	75.00
NNO	Rey Mysterio	75.00	150.00
NNO	Sheamus	20.00	40.00

2012 Mattel WWE Elite Collection Series 14

NNO	Alberto Del Rio	20.00	40.00
NNO	Big Boss Man FB	30.00	75.00
NNO	John Cena	30.00	75.00
NNO	King Booker FB	25.00	50.00
NNO	The Rock	20.00	40.00
NNO	Undertaker	30.00	60.00

2012 Mattel WWE Elite Collection Series 15

NNO	Evan Bourne	30.00	75.00
NNO	Mark Henry	25.00	50.00
NNO	R-Truth	30.00	75.00
NNO	Rey Mysterio		
NNO	Sin Cara	30.00	60.00
NNO	Yokozuna FB	20.00	40.00

2012 Mattel WWE Elite Collection Series 16

NNO	CM Punk	50.00	100.00
NNO	Diesel FB	30.00	60.00
NNO	Ezekiel Jackson	30.00	75.00
NNO	Heath Slater	20.00	40.00
NNO	Kevin Nash FB	60.00	120.00
NNO	Randy Orton	15.00	30.00
NNO	The Rock	30.00	60.00

2012 Mattel WWE Elite Collection Series 17

NNO	John Cena	20.00	40.00
NNO	Kelly Kelly	30.00	60.00
NNO	Kofi Kingston	20.00	40.00
NNO	Mankind FB	30.00	75.00
NNO	Sheamus	15.00	30.00
NNO	Zack Ryder	30.00	60.00

2012 Mattel WWE Elite Collection Series 18

NNO	Brodus Clay	10.00	20.00
NNO	Jerry Lawler FB	15.00	30.00
NNO	Rey Mysterio	50.00	100.00
NNO	Sin Cara	75.00	150.00
NNO	Undertaker FB	30.00	75.00
NNO	Wade Barrett	15.00	30.00

2013 Mattel WWE Elite Collection Series 19

NNO	Brock Lesnar	20.00	40.00
NNO	Daniel Bryan	20.00	40.00
NNO	Dolph Ziggler	15.00	30.00
NNO	Kane	30.00	60.00
NNO	Miss Elizabeth FB	20.00	40.00
NNO	Shawn Michaels	20.00	40.00

2013 Mattel WWE Elite Collection Series 20

NNO	Chris Jericho	20.00	40.00
NNO	Christian FB	30.00	60.00
NNO	CM Punk	50.00	100.00
NNO	Cody Rhodes	20.00	40.00
NNO	John Cena	25.00	50.00
NNO	Santino Morella	30.00	75.00

2013 Mattel WWE Elite Collection Series 21

NNO	AJ Lee	25.00	50.00
NNO	Alberto Del Rio	15.00	30.00
NNO	Honky Tonk Man FB	25.00	50.00
NNO	Randy Orton	17.50	35.00
NNO	Rey Mysterio	60.00	120.00
NNO	Ryback	15.00	30.00

2013 Mattel WWE Elite Collection Series 22

NNO	Big Show	25.00	50.00
NNO	Damien Sandow	12.50	25.00
NNO	The Giant FB	50.00	100.00
NNO	Kane	20.00	40.00
NNO	The Rock	30.00	60.00
NNO	Tensai	15.00	30.00

2013 Mattel WWE Elite Collection Series 23

NNO	Antonio Cesaro	15.00	30.00

NNO	JBL FB	25.00	50.00
NNO	John Cena	20.00	40.00
NNO	Macho Man Randy Savage	25.00	50.00
NNO	Triple H FB	15.00	30.00
NNO	Undertaker FB	20.00	40.00

2013 Mattel WWE Elite Collection Series 24

NNO	Dolph Ziggler	20.00	40.00
NNO	The Miz	12.50	25.00
NNO	Rey Mysterio	30.00	75.00
NNO	Ryback	15.00	30.00
NNO	Trish Stratus FB	30.00	75.00
NNO	Wade Barrett	15.00	30.00

2013 Mattel WWE Elite Collection Series 25

NNO	Brodus Clay	12.50	25.00
NNO	Bruno Sammartino FB	30.00	60.00
NNO	Dean Ambrose	20.00	40.00
NNO	Seth Rollins	20.00	40.00
NNO	Sheamus	15.00	30.00
NNO	Sin Cara	25.00	50.00

2014 Mattel WWE Elite Collection Series 26

NNO	Big E Langston	12.50	25.00
NNO	Jack Swagger	25.00	50.00
NNO	Mark Henry	20.00	40.00
NNO	Road Dogg FB	25.00	50.00
NNO	Roman Reigns	20.00	40.00
NNO	Ultimate Warrior FB	15.00	30.00

2014 Mattel WWE Elite Collection Series 27

NNO	Billy Gunn FB	25.00	50.00
NNO	Fandango	12.50	25.00
NNO	Kofi Kingston	12.50	25.00
NNO	Rikishi FB/Gear on Side	25.00	50.00
NNO	Rikishi FB/Wearing Gear	20.00	40.00
NNO	Rob Van Dam	30.00	75.00
NNO	Undertaker	20.00	40.00

2014 Mattel WWE Elite Collection Series 28

NNO	Big Show	20.00	40.00
NNO	Bray Wyatt	20.00	40.00
NNO	Daniel Bryan	20.00	40.00
NNO	Demolition Crush FB	20.00	50.00
NNO	John Cena	20.00	40.00
NNO	Triple H	15.00	30.00

2014 Mattel WWE Elite Collection Series 29

NNO	Andre the Giant FB	30.00	60.00
NNO	CM Punk	30.00	75.00
NNO	Damien Sandow	15.00	30.00
NNO	Erick Rowan	20.00	40.00
NNO	Goldust	15.00	30.00
NNO	Luke Harper	20.00	40.00

2014 Mattel WWE Elite Collection Series 30

NNO	Batista	20.00	40.00
NNO	Brock Lesnar	15.00	30.00
NNO	Lex Luger FB	20.00	40.00
NNO	Road Warrior Animal FB	60.00	120.00
NNO	Road Warrior Hawk FB	60.00	120.00
NNO	Ryback	15.00	30.00

2014 Mattel WWE Elite Collection Series 31

NNO	Dean Ambrose	25.00	50.00
NNO	Jey Uso	15.00	30.00
NNO	Jimmy Uso	15.00	30.00
NNO	Kane	30.00	75.00
NNO	The Rock FB	25.00	50.00
NNO	Vader FB	50.00	100.00

2014 Mattel WWE Elite Collection Series 32

NNO	Big E Langston	12.50	25.00
NNO	Cody Rhodes	25.00	50.00
NNO	Daniel Bryan	17.50	35.00
NNO	Mark Henry	20.00	40.00
NNO	Rey Mysterio FB	50.00	100.00
NNO	Sin Cara	40.00	80.00

2015 Mattel WWE Elite Collection Series 33

NNO	Batista	25.00	50.00
NNO	Cesaro	12.50	25.00
NNO	Junkyard Dog FB	15.00	30.00
NNO	Roman Reigns	15.00	30.00
NNO	Seth Rollins	12.50	25.00
NNO	X-Pac FB	20.00	40.00

2015 Mattel WWE Elite Collection Series 34

NNO	Bad News Barrett	12.50	25.00
NNO	Doink the Clown FB	20.00	40.00
NNO	Hulk Hogan	25.00	50.00
NNO	John Cena	20.00	40.00
NNO	Paige	25.00	50.00
NNO	Rusev	12.50	25.00

2015 Mattel WWE Elite Collection Series 35

NNO	Diego	10.00	20.00
NNO	Earthquake FB	17.50	35.00
NNO	Fernando	15.00	30.00
NNO	Luke Harper	20.00	40.00
NNO	Randy Orton	15.00	30.00
NNO	Triple H	12.50	25.00

2015 Mattel WWE Elite Collection Series 36

NNO	Bo Dallas	12.50	25.00
NNO	Bray Wyatt	12.50	25.00
NNO	Dean Ambrose	15.00	30.00
NNO	DDP FB	25.00	50.00
NNO	Goldust	17.50	35.00
NNO	Stardust	20.00	40.00

2015 Mattel WWE Elite Collection Series 37

NNO	Brock Lesnar	15.00	30.00
NNO	Dean Malenko FB	17.50	35.00
NNO	John Cena	15.00	30.00
NNO	The Miz	12.50	25.00
NNO	Seth Rollins	25.00	50.00
NNO	Stephanie McMahon	12.50	25.00

2015 Mattel WWE Elite Collection Series 38

NNO	Adam Rose	10.00	20.00
NNO	Bradshaw FB	15.00	30.00
NNO	Daniel Bryan	30.00	60.00
NNO	Faarooq FB	15.00	30.00
NNO	Macho Man Randy Savage FB	15.00	30.00
NNO	Roman Reigns	20.00	40.00

2015 Mattel WWE Elite Collection Series 39

NNO	British Bulldog FB	15.00	30.00
NNO	Damien Mizdow	10.00	20.00
NNO	Dolph Ziggler	25.00	50.00
NNO	Godfather FB	15.00	30.00
NNO	Sting	20.00	40.00
NNO	Sycho Sid FB	12.50	25.00

2016 Mattel WWE Elite Collection Series 40

NNO	Irwin R. Schyster FB	10.00	20.00
NNO	John Cena	25.00	50.00
NNO	Ravishing Rick Rude FB	15.00	30.00
NNO	Sami Zayn	10.00	20.00
NNO	Tyson Kidd	12.50	25.00
NNO	Umaga FB	12.50	25.00

2016 Mattel WWE Elite Collection Series 41

NNO	123 Kid FB	15.00	30.00
NNO	Dean Ambrose	15.00	30.00
NNO	Finn Balor	15.00	30.00
NNO	Lita FB	12.50	25.00
NNO	Ryback	15.00	30.00
NNO	Terry Funk FB	20.00	40.00

2016 Mattel WWE Elite Collection Series 42

NNO	Kalisto	20.00	40.00
NNO	Nasty Boy Brian Knobbs FB	12.50	25.00
NNO	Nasty Boy Jerry Sags FB	12.50	25.00
NNO	Neville	10.00	20.00
NNO	Triple H	12.50	25.00
NNO	Xavier Woods	10.00	20.00

2016 Mattel WWE Elite Collection Series 43

NNO	Alberto Del Rio	7.50	15.00
NNO	Bret Hart FB	25.00	50.00
NNO	Jim Neidhart FB	12.50	25.00
NNO	Kevin Owens	10.00	20.00
NNO	Kofi Kingston	10.00	20.00
NNO	Samoa Joe	10.00	20.00

2016 Mattel WWE Elite Collection Series 44

NNO	Big E	10.00	20.00
NNO	Braun Strowman	20.00	40.00
NNO	Randy Savage FB	15.00	30.00
NNO	Sasha Banks	15.00	30.00
NNO	Sin Cara	30.00	75.00
NNO	Tugboat FB	10.00	20.00

2016 Mattel WWE Elite Collection Series 45

NNO	Bubba Ray Dudley	25.00	50.00
NNO	D-Von Dudley	25.00	50.00
NNO	Lord Steven Regal FB	12.50	25.00
NNO	Narcissist Lex Luger FB	10.00	20.00
NNO	Roman Reigns	15.00	30.00
NNO	Seth Rollins	20.00	40.00

2016 Mattel WWE Elite Collection Series 46

NNO	Booker T FB	15.00	30.00
NNO	Finn Balor	12.50	25.00
NNO	John Cena	12.50	25.00
NNO	Rusev	10.00	20.00
NNO	Sheamus	10.00	20.00
NNO	Stevie Ray FB	12.50	25.00

2016 Mattel WWE Elite Collection Series 47A

NNO	AJ Styles	15.00	30.00
NNO	Asuka	20.00	40.00
NNO	Big Boss Man FB	12.50	25.00
NNO	Cesaro	15.00	30.00
NNO	Kevin Owens	10.00	20.00
NNO	Tatanka FB	12.50	25.00

2016 Mattel WWE Elite Collection Series 47B

NNO	Brian Pillman FB
NNO	Demon Kane
NNO	Goldust FB
NNO	Konnor
NNO	The Rock FB
NNO	Viktor

2017 Mattel WWE Elite Collection Series 48

NNO	Boogeyman FB	25.00	50.00
NNO	Cactus Jack FB	25.00	50.00
NNO	Dean Ambrose	20.00	40.00
NNO	Dolph Ziggler	20.00	40.00
NNO	Erick Rowan	15.00	30.00
NNO	Kalisto	25.00	50.00

2017 Mattel WWE Elite Collection Series 49

NNO	Apollo Crews	15.00	30.00
NNO	Becky Lynch	12.50	25.00
NNO	Big Cass	10.00	20.00
NNO	Brutus Beefcake FB	10.00	20.00
NNO	Enzo Amore	10.00	20.00
NNO	Randy Orton FB	20.00	40.00

2017 Mattel WWE Elite Collection Series 50

NNO	Baron Corbin	7.50	15.00
NNO	John Cena	12.50	25.00
NNO	Rhyno	10.00	20.00
NNO	Shane McMahon	15.00	30.00
NNO	Stephanie McMahon	15.00	30.00
NNO	Warlord FB	12.50	25.00

2017 Mattel WWE Elite Collection Series 51

NNO	AJ Styles	12.50	25.00
NNO	Berzerker FB	7.50	15.00
NNO	Mankind FB	12.50	25.00
NNO	Roman Reigns	12.50	25.00
NNO	Sami Zayn	7.50	15.00
NNO	Scott Hall FB	12.50	25.00

2017 Mattel WWE Elite Collection Series 52

NNO	Braun Strowman	20.00	40.00
NNO	D'Lo Brown FB	12.50	25.00
NNO	Ken Shamrock FB	12.50	25.00
NNO	Kofi Kingston	10.00	20.00
NNO	Seth Rollins	12.50	25.00
NNO	Xavier Woods	7.50	15.00

2017 Mattel WWE Elite Collection Series 53

NNO	Alexa Bliss	15.00	30.00
NNO	Big E	10.00	20.00
NNO	Chris Jericho	10.00	20.00
NNO	Heath Slater	12.50	25.00
NNO	Kevin Owens	10.00	20.00
NNO	The Miz	10.00	20.00

2017 Mattel WWE Elite Collection Series 54

NNO	Bray Wyatt	15.00	30.00
NNO	Charlotte Flair	15.00	30.00
NNO	Jey Uso	12.50	25.00
NNO	Jimmy Uso	12.50	25.00
NNO	John Cena	15.00	30.00
NNO	Rich Swann	15.00	30.00

2017 Mattel WWE Elite Collection Series 55

NNO	Big Cass	10.00	20.00
NNO	Brock Lesnar	25.00	50.00
NNO	Enzo Amore	30.00	60.00
NNO	James Ellsworth	15.00	30.00
NNO	Neville FB	25.00	50.00
NNO	Undertaker	25.00	50.00

2017 Mattel WWE Elite Collection Series 56

NNO	AJ Styles	15.00	30.00
NNO	Jack Gallagher	10.00	20.00
NNO	Karl Anderson	15.00	30.00
NNO	Luke Gallows	15.00	30.00
NNO	Roman Reigns	20.00	40.00
NNO	Samoa Joe	10.00	20.00

2017 Mattel WWE Elite Collection Series 57

NNO	Baron Corbin	10.00	20.00
NNO	Jeff Hardy	30.00	75.00
NNO	Scotty 2 Hotty	12.50	25.00
NNO	Seth Rollins	15.00	30.00
NNO	Shinsuke Nakamura	15.00	30.00
NNO	Tye Dillinger	15.00	30.00

2017 Mattel WWE Elite Collection Series 58

NNO	Braun Strowman	15.00	30.00
NNO	Cesaro	12.50	25.00
NNO	Dean Ambrose	12.50	25.00
NNO	Matt Hardy	25.00	50.00
NNO	Mickie James	17.50	35.00
NNO	Sheamus	12.50	25.00

2017 Mattel WWE Elite Collection Series 59

NNO	Chad Gable	15.00	30.00
NNO	Finn Balor	15.00	30.00
NNO	Jason Jordan	15.00	30.00
NNO	Kurt Angle	12.50	25.00
NNO	The Miz	12.50	25.00
NNO	Zack Ryder	10.00	20.00

2017 Mattel WWE Elite Collection Series 60

NNO	Andre/Giant Machine	20.00	40.00
NNO	Elias	20.00	40.00
NNO	John Cena	15.00	30.00
NNO	Kofi Kingston	12.50	25.00
NNO	Triple H	20.00	40.00
NNO	Xavier Woods	12.50	25.00

2018 Mattel WWE Elite Collection Series 61

NNO	AJ Styles	15.00	30.00
NNO	Big E	12.50	25.00
NNO	Fandango	12.50	25.00
NNO	Kevin Owens	12.50	25.00
NNO	Shane McMahon	15.00	30.00
NNO	Tyler Breeze	12.50	25.00

2018 Mattel WWE Elite Collection Series 62

NNO	Roman Reigns	17.50	35.00
NNO	Braun Strowman	20.00	40.00
NNO	Dude Love	15.00	30.00
NNO	Akam	12.50	25.00
NNO	Rezar	12.50	25.00
NNO	Sting/Surfer Gear	17.50	35.00

2018 Mattel WWE Elite Collection Series 63

NNO	Dean Ambrose	12.50	25.00
NNO	Dusty Rhodes	17.50	35.00
NNO	Kane	12.50	25.00
NNO	Sami Zayn	12.50	25.00
NNO	Shelton Benjamin	20.00	40.00
NNO	Shelton Benjamin Gold Tights CH		
NNO	Shinsuke Nakamura	12.50	25.00

2018 Mattel WWE Elite Collection Series 64

NNO	Curt Hawkins	25.00	50.00
NNO	Curt Hawkins Black Gear CH		
NNO	Jey Uso	15.00	30.00
NNO	Jimmy Uso	15.00	30.00
NNO	John Cena	20.00	40.00
NNO	Samoa Joe	20.00	40.00
NNO	Seth Rollins	25.00	50.00

2018 Mattel WWE Elite Collection Series 65

NNO	Aiden English		
NNO	Aiden English Black Scarf CH		
NNO	Eric Young	17.50	35.00
NNO	Nia Jax	15.00	30.00
NNO	Roman Reigns	15.00	30.00
NNO	Ronda Rousey	20.00	40.00
NNO	Rusev		

2018 Mattel WWE Elite Collection Series 66

NNO	AJ Styles	20.00	40.00
NNO	Erick Rowan	15.00	30.00
NNO	Kevin Owens	10.00	20.00
NNO	Kevin Owens (KO Mania) (CHASE)		
NNO	Kurt Angle	15.00	30.00
NNO	Luke Harper	15.00	30.00
NNO	Nikki Cross	25.00	50.00

2019 Mattel WWE Elite Collection Series 67

NNO	Cedric Alexander FP	12.50	25.00
NNO	Jeff Hardy	12.50	25.00
NNO	Jeff Hardy USA Face Paint CH		
NNO	Randy Orton	10.00	20.00
NNO	Rey Mysterio	15.00	30.00
NNO	Shayna Baszler FP	15.00	30.00
NNO	Velveteen Dream FP	12.50	25.00

2019 Mattel WWE Elite Collection Series 68

NNO	Braun Strowman	12.50	25.00
NNO	Brie Bella	12.50	25.00
NNO	Daniel Bryan	12.50	25.00
NNO	King Mabel FP	10.00	20.00
NNO	King Mabel FP Lightning CH		
NNO	Roman Reigns	12.50	25.00
NNO	Undertaker	20.00	40.00

2019 Mattel WWE Elite Collection Series 69

NNO	Bobby Lashley	10.00	20.00
NNO	Miz	10.00	20.00
NNO	Mustafa Ali	12.50	25.00
NNO	Mustafa Ali (orange pants) (CHASE)		
NNO	Rey Mysterio	12.50	25.00
NNO	Ricochet	15.00	30.00
NNO	Tommaso Ciampa	12.50	25.00

2019 Mattel WWE Elite Collection Series 70

NNO	Demon Finn Balor	15.00	30.00
NNO	Dolph Ziggler	12.50	25.00
NNO	Dolph Ziggler Pink CH	25.00	50.00
NNO	EC3	10.00	20.00
NNO	Johnny Gargano	15.00	30.00

NNO	Seth Rollins/Shield Fatigues	15.00	30.00
NNO	Vince McMahon	15.00	30.00

2019 Mattel WWE Elite Collection Series 71

NNO	Adam Cole
NNO	Big Show
NNO	Drew McIntyre
NNO	Jeff Hardy
NNO	John Cena
NNO	Nikki Bella
NNO	Nikki Bella Red Gear CH

2019 Mattel WWE Elite Collection Series 72

NNO	Batista
NNO	Becky Lynch
NNO	Buddy Murphy
NNO	Buddy Murphy Black Shorts CH
NNO	Rey Mysterio
NNO	Roderick Strong
NNO	Velveteen Dream

2019 Mattel WWE Elite Collection Series 73

NNO	Aleister Black
NNO	Daniel Bryan
NNO	Elias
NNO	Gran Metalik
NNO	Gran Metalik Black Shirt CH
NNO	Kairi Sane
NNO	Triple H

2019 Mattel WWE Elite Collection Series 74

NNO	AJ Styles
NNO	Andrade
NNO	Finn Balor
NNO	Goldberg
NNO	Lince Dorado
NNO	Lince Dorado Gold CH
NNO	Natalya

2020 Mattel WWE Elite Collection Series 75

NNO	Hurricane	20.00	40.00
NNO	Hurricane White Boots CH	30.00	60.00
NNO	Jeff Hardy	15.00	30.00
NNO	Kalisto	30.00	60.00
NNO	Mandy Rose	20.00	40.00
NNO	Pete Dunne	20.00	40.00
NNO	Seth Rollins	20.00	40.00

2020 Mattel WWE Elite Collection Series 76

NNO	Braun Strowman	20.00	40.00
NNO	Christian Black Shirt CH	20.00	40.00
NNO	Christian White Shirt	20.00	40.00
NNO	John Cena	25.00	50.00
NNO	Lacey Evans	20.00	40.00
NNO	Tucker	15.00	30.00

2020 Mattel WWE Elite Collection Series 77

NNO	AJ Styles	20.00	40.00
NNO	Classy Freddie Blassie RSC	30.00	60.00
NNO	The Fiend Bray Wyatt	25.00	50.00
NNO	Miss Elizabeth	20.00	40.00
NNO	Ravishing Rick Rude Ult. Warrior Tights	20.00	40.00
NNO	Ravishing Rick Rude Yellow Tights CH	30.00	60.00
NNO	Ronda Rousey	15.00	30.00
NNO	Viscera	20.00	40.00

2020 Mattel WWE Elite Collection Series 78

NNO	Drake Maverick	15.00	30.00
NNO	Kofi Kingston	20.00	40.00
NNO	Matt Riddle	25.00	50.00
NNO	Naomi	15.00	30.00
NNO	Naomi Glow CH	20.00	40.00
NNO	Randy Orton	25.00	50.00
NNO	R-Truth	15.00	30.00
NNO	Superstar Billy Graham TAR	20.00	40.00

2020 Mattel WWE Elite Collection Series 79

NNO	Big E	15.00	30.00
NNO	Bobby Fish	20.00	40.00
NNO	Bobby Fish Black Gear CH	25.00	50.00

NNO Daniel Bryan	15.00	30.00
NNO Io Shirai	20.00	40.00
NNO Roman Reigns	15.00	30.00
NNO Xavier Woods	15.00	30.00

2020 Mattel WWE Elite Collection Series 80

NNO Bayley	25.00	50.00
NNO Erik	15.00	30.00
NNO Ivar	15.00	30.00
NNO Kevin Owens	20.00	40.00
NNO Kyle O'Reilly	20.00	40.00
NNO Kyle O'Reilly Black Gear CH	25.00	50.00
NNO Ricochet	15.00	30.00
NNO Rocky Johnson TAR	20.00	40.00

2020 Mattel WWE Elite Collection Series 81

NNO Angelo Dawkins	15.00	30.00
NNO Bianca Belair	30.00	60.00
NNO Mae Young WM	25.00	50.00
NNO Montez Ford	15.00	30.00
NNO The Rock	20.00	40.00
NNO Shinsuke Nakamura	20.00	40.00
NNO S.Nakamura Black CH	25.00	50.00
NNO Stunning Steve Austin	25.00	50.00

2021 Mattel WWE Elite Collection Series 82

NNO Alexa Bliss	30.00	60.00
NNO Finn Balor	25.00	50.00
NNO Jerry The King Lawler	25.00	50.00
NNO John Morrison	25.00	50.00
NNO Keith Lee	25.00	50.00
NNO Keith Lee White Gear CH	30.00	60.00
NNO Rob Gronkowski	40.00	80.00

2021 Mattel WWE Elite Collection Series 83

NNO Drew McIntyre	25.00	50.00
NNO Dusty Rhodes	25.00	50.00
NNO Edge	20.00	40.00
NNO Edge Black Gear CH	30.00	75.00
NNO King Baron Corbin	20.00	40.00
NNO Michael PS Hayes TAR	30.00	75.00
NNO Sasha Banks	30.00	60.00

2021 Mattel WWE Elite Collection Series 84

NNO Angel Garza		
NNO Jeff Hardy		
NNO Jeff Hardy CH		
NNO Murphy		
NNO Rhea Ripley		
NNO Roman Reigns		
NNO Sheamus		

2018 Mattel WWE Elite Collection SummerSlam 2018

NNO Dean Ambrose	20.00	40.00
NNO Edge	12.50	25.00
NNO Matt Hardy	10.00	20.00
NNO Seth Rollins	15.00	30.00

2019 Mattel WWE Elite Collection Survivor Series

NNO Alicia Fox		
NNO Don Muraco		
NNO Jeff Hardy		
NNO Shinsuke Nakamura		

2017 Mattel WWE Elite Collection Then Now Forever 3-Packs

These figures were exclusive to Walmart.

NNO Lex Luger/Randy Savage/Sting	30.00	60.00
NNO The Shield - Seth Rollins/Dean Ambrose/Roman Reigns	75.00	150.00

2016 Mattel WWE Elite Collection Then Now Forever Series 1

These figures were exclusive to Walmart.

NNO Bam Bam Bigelow FB	25.00	50.00
NNO Rusev	15.00	30.00
NNO The Rock FB	20.00	40.00
NNO Tyler Breeze	15.00	30.00

2017 Mattel WWE Elite Collection Then Now Forever Series 2

These figures were exclusive to Walmart.

NNO Earthquake FB	15.00	30.00
NNO Macho Man Randy Savage FB	17.50	35.00
NNO Sami Zayn	7.50	15.00
NNO Typhoon FB	15.00	30.00

2017 Mattel WWE Elite Collection Then Now Forever Series 3

These figures were exclusive to Walmart.

NNO Chad Gable	12.50	25.00
NNO Jason Jordan	10.00	20.00
NNO Miss Elizabeth	15.00	30.00
NNO Seth Rollins	12.50	25.00

2020 Mattel WWE Elite Collection Top Picks 2020

NNO Braun Strowman	20.00	40.00
NNO Ricochet	20.00	40.00
NNO Roman Reigns	20.00	40.00
NNO Seth Rollins	20.00	40.00

2021 Mattel WWE Elite Collection Top Picks 2021

NNO Drew McIntyre	20.00	40.00
NNO The Fiend Bray Wyatt	30.00	60.00
NNO Kofi Kingston	20.00	40.00
NNO Roman Reigns	25.00	50.00

2018 Mattel WWE Elite Collection Top Talent 2018

NNO AJ Styles	20.00	40.00
NNO Braun Strowman	15.00	30.00
NNO Finn Balor	15.00	30.00
NNO Seth Rollins	15.00	30.00

2019 Mattel WWE Elite Collection Top Talent 2019

NNO AJ Styles	15.00	30.00
NNO Braun Strowman	12.50	25.00
NNO Finn Balor	12.50	25.00
NNO Seth Rollins	10.00	20.00

2017 Mattel WWE Elite Collection Women's Division

These figures were exclusive to Walgreens.

NNO Alexa Bliss	20.00	40.00
NNO Becky Lynch	20.00	40.00
NNO Maryse	15.00	30.00
NNO Sasha Banks	17.50	35.00

2010 Mattel WWE Elite Collection WrestleMania 26

These figures were exclusive to Toys R Us.

NNO Jack Swagger	25.00	50.00
NNO Rey Mysterio	30.00	60.00
NNO Triple H		
NNO Undertaker	30.00	60.00

2011 Mattel WWE Elite Collection WrestleMania 27

These figures were exclusive to Toys R Us.

NNO Kofi Kingston	17.50	35.00
NNO The Miz	20.00	40.00
NNO The Rock	30.00	75.00
NNO Stone Cold Steve Austin	30.00	60.00
NNO Undertaker	30.00	75.00

2014 Mattel WWE Elite Collection WrestleMania 30 Heritage

Also known as WrestleMania XXX Heritage.

NNO Bret Hart	25.00	50.00
NNO Shawn Michaels	30.00	60.00

2015 Mattel WWE Elite Collection WrestleMania 31 Heritage

NNO Kane	30.00	75.00
NNO Undertaker	25.00	50.00

2016 Mattel WWE Elite Collection WrestleMania 32 Heritage

NNO Brock Lesnar	20.00	40.00
NNO Undertaker	20.00	40.00

2017 Mattel WWE Elite Collection WrestleMania 33 Heritage

NNO Shawn Michaels	25.00	50.00
NNO Triple H	15.00	30.00

2018 Mattel WWE Elite Collection WrestleMania 34 Heritage

NNO Brutus Beefcake FB	7.50	15.00
NNO John Cena	12.50	25.00
NNO Kevin Owens	10.00	20.00
NNO Randy Orton	20.00	40.00

2018 Mattel WWE Elite Collection WrestleMania 35 Heritage

NNO Sasha Banks	15.00	30.00
NNO Scott Hall	15.00	30.00
NNO Triple H	12.50	25.00
NNO Undertaker	17.50	35.00

2020 Mattel WWE Elite Collection WrestleMania 36 Heritage

NNO Booker T	20.00	40.00
NNO Kofi Kingston	15.00	30.00
NNO Mick Foley	20.00	40.00
NNO Woken Matt Hardy	12.50	25.00

2011 Mattel WWE Elite Collection WWE All-Stars 2-Packs

These figures were exclusive to Toys R Us.

NNO Jake The Snake Roberts vs. Randy Orton	60.00	120.00
NNO Macho Man Randy Savage vs. John Morrison	50.00	100.00
NNO Stone Cold Steve Austin vs. CM Punk	125.00	250.00

2012 Mattel WWE Fan Central

These figures were exclusive to K-Mart.

NNO Big Show		
NNO John Cena		
NNO Kane		
NNO Kofi Kingston		

2014 Mattel WWE Fan Central

These figures were exclusive to K-Mart. Also known as Champions Collection.

NNO Daniel Bryan	30.00	60.00
NNO The Rock		

2014-15 Mattel WWE Fan Central

These figures were exclusive to K-Mart.

NNO Dean Ambrose	12.50	25.00
NNO John Cena	10.00	20.00
NNO Randy Orton	10.00	20.00

2015 Mattel WWE Fan Central

These figures were exclusive to K-Mart.

NNO Bad News Barrett		
NNO Daniel Bryan		
NNO Ultimate Warrior		

2016 Mattel WWE Fan Central

These figures were exclusive to K-Mart.

NNO Finn Balor	10.00	20.00
NNO John Cena	7.50	15.00
NNO Ryback	7.50	15.00
NNO Triple H	6.00	12.00

2018 Mattel WWE Fan Central

NNO Finn Balor	12.50	25.00
NNO Kevin Nash	15.00	30.00
NNO Randy Orton	10.00	20.00
NNO Rusev	7.50	15.00

2018 Mattel WWE Flashback Series 1

NNO	Cowboy Bob Orton	7.50	15.00
NNO	The Million Dollar Man	7.50	15.00
NNO	Ravishing Rick Rude	7.50	15.00
NNO	Sgt. Slaughter	10.00	20.00

2018 Mattel WWE Flashback Series 2

NNO	Booker T	12.50	25.00
NNO	Lex Luger	10.00	20.00
NNO	Ric Flair	12.50	25.00
NNO	Sting	15.00	30.00

2018 Mattel WWE Flextremes

NNO Finn Balor
NNO John Cena
NNO The Rock
NNO Roman Reigns

2018 Mattel WWE Flextremes 4-Pack

NNO	Cena/Rock/Balor/Reigns	15.00	30.00

2011 Mattel WWE Heritage Series

NNO CM Punk
NNO John Cena
NNO Kane
NNO Melina
NNO Randy Orton
NNO Triple H

2011-12 Mattel WWE Legends Mattyshop Exclusives

NNO	Andre the Giant	125.00	250.00
NNO	Arn Anderson	100.00	200.00
NNO	Diamond Dallas Page	60.00	120.00
NNO	King Kong Bundy	125.00	250.00
NNO	The Rockers (Jannetty/Michaels)	200.00	350.00
NNO	Tully Blanchard	100.00	200.00

2017 Mattel WWE Make-A-Wish Foundation

NNO	John Cena	15.00	30.00

2015 Mattel WWE Mighty Minis Series 1

NNO	Bret Hart (blue)		
NNO	Bret Hart (pink)		
NNO	Daniel Bryan	2.50	5.00
NNO	Dolph Ziggler	2.00	4.00
NNO	John Cena	3.00	6.00
NNO	Roman Reigns	2.00	4.00
NNO	Rusev	2.50	5.00
NNO	Seth Rollins	2.00	4.00
NNO	Ted DiBiase	2.00	4.00
NNO	Undertaker	3.00	6.00

2015 Mattel WWE Mighty Minis Series 2

NNO	Brock Lesnar		
NNO	Dean Ambrose		
NNO	Goldust		
NNO	John Cena		
NNO	Kane	2.00	4.00
NNO	The Rock	4.00	8.00
NNO	Stone Cold Steve Austin		
NNO	Triple H		
NNO	Ultimate Warrior (orange)		
NNO	Ultimate Warrior (white)		

2016 Mattel WWE Mighty Minis SDCC Exclusive

NNO	Dean Ambrose	5.00	10.00

2017 Mattel WWE Monsters

NNO	Asuka as The Phantom	7.50	15.00
NNO	Braun Strowman as Frankenstein	12.50	25.00
NNO	Chris Jericho as The Mummy	7.50	15.00
NNO	Jake Roberts as The Creature	12.50	25.00
NNO	Roman Reigns as The Werewolf	10.00	20.00
NNO	Undertaker as The Vampire	12.50	25.00

2018 Mattel WWE M.U.S.C.L.E. SDCC Exclusives

NNO Andre the Giant
NNO Hacksaw Jim Duggan
NNO Iron Sheik
NNO Jake The Snake Roberts
NNO Junkyard Dog
NNO Macho Man Randy Savage
NNO Mean Gene Okerlund
NNO Million Dollar Man
NNO Ric Flair
NNO Rowdy Roddy Piper
NNO Sgt. Slaughter
NNO Ultimate Warrior

2018 Mattel WWE M.U.S.C.L.E. SDCC Exclusives 3-Pack

NNO	WWE Figurines	3.00	6.00

2016 Mattel WWE Mutants

NNO	Bray Wyatt	6.00	12.00
NNO	Brock Lesnar	20.00	40.00
NNO	Finn Balor	12.50	25.00
NNO	John Cena	7.50	15.00
NNO	Stardust	6.00	12.00
NNO	Sting	7.50	15.00

2017 Mattel WWE Network Spotlight

These figures were exclusive to Toys R Us.

NNO	Big Cass	6.00	12.00
NNO	Brock Lesnar	7.50	15.00
NNO	Enzo Amore	12.50	25.00
NNO	Sting Surfer Gear FB	10.00	20.00

2017 Mattel WWE NXT Series 1

These figures were exclusive to Target.

NNO	Andrade Cien Almas	15.00	30.00
NNO	Hideo Itami	7.50	15.00
NNO	Kevin Owens	6.00	12.00
NNO	Sami Zayn	6.00	12.00
NNO	Samoa Joe	7.50	15.00
NNO	Tye Dillinger	6.00	12.00

2017 Mattel WWE NXT Series 2

These figures were exclusive to Target.

NNO	Akam	12.50	25.00
NNO	Bobby Roode	10.00	20.00
NNO	Eva Marie	20.00	40.00
NNO	Johnny Gargano		
NNO	Rezar	12.50	25.00
NNO	Tommaso Ciampa		

2017 Mattel WWE NXT Series 3

These figures were exclusive to Target.

NNO	Johnny Gargano	15.00	30.00
NNO	Tommaso Ciampa	15.00	30.00

2018 Mattel WWE NXT Series 4

These figures were exclusive to Target.

NNO Billie Kay
NNO Paige
NNO Roderick Strong
NNO Triple H
NNO Xavier Woods

2012 Mattel WWE Power Slammers

NNO	Brodus Clay	10.00	20.00
NNO	John Cena		
NNO	Kofi Kingston		
NNO	Rey Mysterio	12.50	25.00
NNO	Sheamus		
NNO	The Miz		
NNO	Zack Ryder		

2010 Mattel WWE PPV Series 1

Also known as WrestleMania Heritage.

NNO Batista
NNO Edge
NNO John Cena
NNO Randy Orton
NNO Steve Austin
NNO Undertaker

2010 Mattel WWE PPV Series 2

Also known as Survivor Series 2009.

NNO John Cena
NNO John Morrison
NNO Kofi Kingston
NNO The Miz
NNO Rey Mysterio
NNO Undertaker

2010 Mattel WWE PPV Series 3

Also known as Royal Rumble 2010.

NNO Beth Phoenix
NNO Chris Jericho
NNO CM Punk
NNO Cody Rhodes
NNO Edge
NNO Triple H

2010 Mattel WWE PPV Series 4

Also known as Elimination Chamber 2010.

NNO Batista
NNO Chris Jericho
NNO Drew McIntyre
NNO John Cena
NNO Rey Mysterio
NNO Undertaker

2010 Mattel WWE PPV Series 5

Also known as Over the Limit 2010.

2010 Mattel WWE PPV Series 5

NNO Big Show
NNO CM Punk
NNO Jack Swagger
NNO John Cena
NNO Rey Mysterio
NNO R-Truth

2010 Mattel WWE PPV Series 6

Also known as Royal Rumble Heritage.

2010 Mattel WWE PPV Series 6

NNO Christian
NNO John Cena
NNO Randy Orton
NNO Rey Mysterio
NNO Sheamus
NNO Undertaker

2011 Mattel WWE PPV Series 7

Also known as WrestleMania Heritage II.

NNO CM Punk
NNO John Cena
NNO Kane
NNO Melina
NNO Randy Orton
NNO Triple H

2011 Mattel WWE PPV Series 8

Also known as TLC 2010.

NNO	Edge		
NNO	John Cena	20.00	40.00
NNO	John Morrison		
NNO	Rey Mysterio		
NNO	Sheamus		
NNO	Wade Barrett		

2011 Mattel WWE PPV Series 9

Also known as SummerSlam Heritage 2008.

NNO	Edge	15.00	30.00
NNO	Great Khali	20.00	40.00
NNO	John Cena		

NNO Randy Orton
NNO Rey Mysterio
NNO Triple H

2011 Mattel WWE PPV Series 10

Also known as Extreme Rules 2011.

NNO Alberto Del Rio
NNO Christian
NNO John Cena
NNO Rey Mysterio
NNO R-Truth
NNO Sheamus

2011 Mattel WWE PPV Series 11

Also known as Survivor Series Heritage.

NNO Big Show
NNO Chris Masters
NNO Evan Bourne
NNO John Cena
NNO The Rock
NNO Sheamus

2016 Mattel WWE Retro Series 1

NNO Brock Lesnar	15.00	30.00
NNO John Cena	20.00	40.00
NNO Kevin Owens	20.00	40.00
NNO Roman Reigns	75.00	150.00
NNO Ultimate Warrior	15.00	30.00
NNO Undertaker	25.00	50.00

2017 Mattel WWE Retro Series 2

NNO Kane	20.00	40.00
NNO Mankind	20.00	40.00
NNO The Rock	12.50	25.00
NNO Sting	15.00	30.00
NNO Stone Cold Steve Austin	15.00	30.00
NNO Triple H	15.00	30.00

2017 Mattel WWE Retro Series 3

NNO AJ Styles	6.00	12.00
NNO Dean Ambrose	7.50	15.00
NNO Goldberg	6.00	12.00
NNO Seth Rollins	10.00	20.00

2017 Mattel WWE Retro Series 4

NNO Finn Balor	15.00	30.00
NNO Kevin Owens	10.00	20.00
NNO Ric Flair	30.00	60.00
NNO Sami Zayn	7.50	15.00

2017 Mattel WWE Retro Series 5

NNO Big E	7.50	15.00
NNO Kofi Kingston	10.00	20.00
NNO Macho Man Randy Savage	12.50	25.00
NNO Macho Man/Arms Down	12.50	25.00
NNO Xavier Woods	6.00	12.00

2018 Mattel WWE Retro Series 6

NNO Bray Wyatt	7.50	15.00
NNO Daniel Bryan	10.00	20.00
NNO Shinsuke Nakamura	7.50	15.00
NNO Sting/Wolfpac	12.50	25.00

2018 Mattel WWE Retro Series 7

NNO Chris Jericho	7.50	15.00
NNO Kurt Angle	7.50	15.00
NNO Shawn Michaels	10.00	20.00
NNO Sheamus	7.50	15.00

2019 Mattel WWE Retro Series 8

NNO Braun Strowman	7.50	15.00
NNO Iron Sheik	7.50	15.00
NNO Jeff Hardy	7.50	15.00
NNO Zack Ryder	7.50	15.00

2019 Mattel WWE Retro Series 9

NNO Goldust	7.50	15.00
NNO Macho Man Randy Savage	12.50	25.00
NNO Randy Orton	7.50	15.00
NNO Samoa Joe	12.50	25.00

2019 Mattel WWE Retro Series 10

NNO Diesel	10.00	20.00
NNO Elias	7.50	15.00
NNO Junkyard Dog	15.00	30.00
NNO Matt Hardy	6.00	12.00

2018 Mattel WWE Retro Series Playset

NNO Collectible Retro Ring

2018-19 Mattel WWE Retrofest

NNO Hacksaw Jim Duggan	10.00	20.00
NNO Honky Tonk Man	10.00	20.00
NNO Macho Man Randy Savage	12.50	25.00
NNO Mr. Perfect	15.00	30.00
NNO Ric Flair	10.00	20.00
NNO Shawn Michaels	12.50	25.00

2010 Mattel WWE Series 1

Figures that include title belt are serial numbered to 1000.

NNO Batista
NNO Batista w/Title Belt/1000
NNO Big Show
NNO Big Show w/Title Belt/1000
NNO Evan Bourne
NNO Evan Bourne w/Title Belt/1000
NNO John Cena
NNO John Cena w/Title Belt/1000
NNO Kofi Kingston
NNO Kofi Kingston w/Title Belt/1000
NNO Triple H
NNO Triple H w/Title Belt/1000

2010 Mattel WWE Series 2

NNO CM Punk		
NNO CM Punk w/Title Belt/1000		
NNO Jack Swagger		
NNO Jack Swagger w/Title Belt/1000		
NNO Kane		
NNO Kane w/Title Belt/1000		
NNO Mark Henry	10.00	20.00
NNO Mark Henry w/Title Belt/1000		
NNO Rey Mysterio/Dk Blue		
NNO Rey Mysterio (light blue w/title belt)/1000		
NNO Rey Mysterio/Lt Blue	25.00	50.00
NNO Vladimir Kozlov		
NNO Vladimir Kozlov w/Title Belt/1000		

2010 WWE Series 3

NNO Chris Jericho	10.00	20.00
NNO Chris Jericho w/Title Belt/1000		
NNO Great Khali		
NNO Great Khali w/Title Belt/1000		
NNO Mickie James	12.50	25.00
NNO Mickie James w/Title Belt/1000		
NNO Randy Orton		
NNO Shelton Benjamin		
NNO Shelton Benjamin w/Title Belt/1000		
NNO Undertaker		
NNO Undertaker w/Title Belt/1000		

2010 Mattel WWE Series 4

NNO Dolph Ziggler	12.50	25.00
NNO Dolph Ziggler w/Title Belt/1000		
NNO Goldust	12.50	25.00
NNO Goldust w/Title Belt/1000		
NNO Matt Hardy	12.50	25.00
NNO Matt Hardy w/Title Belt/1000		
NNO MVP	15.00	30.00
NNO MVP w/Title Belt/1000		
NNO Shawn Michaels	17.50	35.00
NNO Shawn Michaels w/Title Belt/1000		
NNO William Regal	10.00	20.00
NNO William Regal w/Title Belt/1000		

2010 Mattel WWE Series 5

NNO Batista	12.50	25.00
NNO Hurricane	12.50	25.00
NNO Hurricane w/Title Belt/1000		

(continued)

NNO John Cena	10.00	20.00
NNO Melina	20.00	40.00
NNO Melina w/Title Belt/1000		
NNO Mike Knox	25.00	50.00
NNO Mike Knox w/Title Belt/1000		
NNO R-Truth		
NNO R-Truth w/Title Belt/1000		

2010 Mattel WWE Series 6

NNO Big Show	10.00	20.00
NNO Drew McIntyre	15.00	30.00
NNO Edge		
NNO Kelly Kelly	20.00	40.00
NNO The Miz		
NNO Ted DiBiase	12.50	25.00

2010 Mattel WWE Series 7

NNO Kofi Kingston		
NNO Michelle McCool	25.00	50.00
NNO Rey Mysterio	25.00	50.00
NNO Sheamus		
NNO Undertaker		
NNO Yoshi Tatsu	12.50	25.00
NNO Yoshi Tatsu w/Title Belt/1000		
NNO Sheamus w/Title Belt/1000		
NNO Michelle McCool w/Title Belt/1000		

2011 Mattel WWE Series 8

NNO Chris Masters	15.00	30.00
NNO Christian	10.00	20.00
NNO Finlay	12.50	25.00
NNO Kane	12.50	25.00
NNO Kofi Kingston	15.00	30.00
NNO Maryse	30.00	60.00

2011 Mattel WWE Series 9

NNO Evan Bourne	7.50	15.00
NNO Jack Swagger	6.00	12.00
NNO JTG	10.00	20.00
NNO Mark Henry		
NNO Natalya	20.00	40.00
NNO Rey Mysterio		

2011 Mattel WWE Series 10

NNO Dolph Ziggler	10.00	20.00
NNO John Cena	12.50	25.00
NNO Kofi Kingston	10.00	20.00
NNO Triple H		
NNO Wade Barrett	7.50	15.00
NNO Zack Ryder	10.00	20.00

2011 Mattel WWE Series 11

NNO Big Show	12.50	25.00
NNO Daniel Bryan	7.50	15.00
NNO Eve	12.50	25.00
NNO Sheamus	6.00	12.00
NNO Skip Sheffield	12.50	25.00

2011 Mattel WWE Series 12

NNO Alberto Del Rio	7.50	15.00
NNO Evan Bourne	7.50	15.00
NNO John Morrison		
NNO Randy Orton	7.50	15.00
NNO Rey Mysterio		
NNO Wade Barrett	7.50	15.00

2012 Mattel WWE Series 13

1 Rey Mysterio		
2 Vickie Guerrero	15.00	30.00
3 John Morrison		
4 R-Truth	15.00	30.00
5 Ezekiel Jackson		
6 Undertaker		

2012 Mattel WWE Series 14

Also known as Royal Rumble Heritage.

7 Bret Hit Man Hart
8 Shawn Michaels
9 Goldust

10 Rey Mysterio
11 John Morrison
12 Alberto Del Rio

2012 Mattel WWE Series 15

13 Layla	30.00	75.00
14 Kofi Kingston	15.00	30.00
15 John Cena	7.50	15.00
16 Wade Barrett	20.00	40.00
17 Brodus Clay		
18 Kane		

2012 Mattel WWE Series 16

Also known as WrestleMania Heritage.

19 Ultimate Warrior	15.00	30.00
20 John Cena	10.00	20.00
21 Eddie Guerrero	17.50	35.00
22 Triple H		
23 Undertaker		
24 Jack Swagger	7.50	15.00

2012 Mattel WWE Series 17

25 Rey Mysterio	15.00	30.00
26 Dolph Ziggler	10.00	20.00
27 Zack Ryder	10.00	20.00
28 The Miz	7.50	15.00
29 Alex Riley	7.50	15.00
30 Mark Henry	10.00	20.00

2012 Mattel WWE Series 18

Also known as RAW Supershow.

31 Kelly Kelly	12.50	25.00
32 Sin Cara		
33 Hunico	15.00	30.00
34 CM Punk	10.00	20.00
35 John Cena	7.50	15.00
36 Cody Rhodes		

2012 Mattel WWE Series 19

37 Hornswoggle		
38 Evan Bourne	10.00	20.00
39 Kofi Kingston	7.50	15.00
40 Justin Gabriel	6.00	12.00
41 Jinder Mahal	7.50	15.00
42 Randy Orton	7.50	15.00

2012 Mattel WWE Series 20

Also known as Global Superstars.

43 Natalya		
44 Rey Mysterio		
45 Yoshi Tatsu	7.50	15.00
46 John Cena	7.50	15.00
47 Sheamus	10.00	20.00
48 Wade Barrett		

2012 Mattel WWE Series 21

49 Beth Phoenix	25.00	50.00
50 R-Truth		
51 The Miz		
52 Mason Ryan		
53 Jack Swagger		
54 Big Show		

2012 Mattel WWE Series 22

55 Booker T	12.50	25.00
56 Mark Henry		
57 Chris Jericho	6.00	12.00
58 Christian	10.00	20.00
59 John Cena	7.50	15.00
60 Zack Ryder	7.50	15.00

2012 Mattel WWE Series 23

61 Rey Mysterio	15.00	30.00
62 Alicia Fox	15.00	30.00
63 Hunico	10.00	20.00
64 Santino Marella	7.50	15.00
65 Triple H		
66 Kane		

2013 Mattel WWE Series 24

1 John Cena		
2 CM Punk		
3 Zack Ryder	15.00	30.00
4 Drew McIntyre	15.00	30.00
5 Sheamus		
6 AJ	20.00	40.00

2013 Mattel WWE Series 25

7 Big Show		
8 Brock Lesnar		
9 Randy Orton		
10 The Miz	12.50	25.00
11 Eve	20.00	40.00
12 David Otunga	10.00	20.00

2013 Mattel WWE Series 26

Also known as WrestleMania Heritage.

13 Macho Man Randy Savage	12.50	25.00
14 Shawn Michaels	12.50	25.00
15 Undertaker	10.00	20.00
16 Kane	25.00	50.00
17 Mark Henry		
18 Daniel Bryan	10.00	20.00

2013 Mattel WWE Series 27

19 Cody Rhodes		
20 Kofi Kingston		
21 Wade Barrett		
22 Ryback	12.50	25.00
23 Brodus Clay		
24 Antonio Cesaro	10.00	20.00

2013 Mattel WWE Series 28

25 Rey Mysterio		
26 R-Truth	10.00	20.00
27 Heath Slater	10.00	20.00
28 Sin Cara	20.00	50.00
29 Tensai	7.50	15.00
30 Damien Sandow	7.50	15.00

2013 Mattel WWE Series 29

Also known as World Champions.

31 Ultimate Warrior		
32 Eddie Guerrero	15.00	30.00
33 Stone Cold Steve Austin		
34 Big Show		
35 John Cena	7.50	15.00
36 CM Punk		

2013 Mattel WWE Series 30

37 The Miz		
38 Hornswoggle	30.00	60.00
39 Santino Marella		
40 Sheamus	10.00	20.00
41 Daniel Bryan	10.00	20.00
42 AJ Lee	20.00	40.00

2013 Mattel WWE Series 31

43 Kane		
44 R-Truth	10.00	20.00
45 Zack Ryder		
46 Rosa Mendes	10.00	20.00
47 Wade Barrett	7.50	15.00
48 Alberto Del Rio	7.50	15.00

2013 Mattel WWE Series 32

Also known as Royal Rumble 2013.

49 Chris Jericho	10.00	20.00
50 The Rock	12.50	25.00
51 Randy Orton	12.50	25.00
52 John Cena	7.50	15.00
53 Ryback		
54 Antonio Cesaro	7.50	15.00

2013 Mattel WWE Series 33

55 Big Show		
56 Dolph Ziggler	10.00	20.00
57 Great Khali		

58 CM Punk	12.50	25.00
59 Tamina Snuka	10.00	20.00
60 Dean Ambrose		

2013 Mattel WWE Series 34

61 John Cena	7.50	15.00
62 The Miz		
63 Rey Mysterio		
64 Sin Cara	20.00	40.00
65 Ricardo Rodriguez	12.50	25.00
66 Brodus Clay	7.50	15.00

2014 Mattel WWE Series 35

1 Kane		
2 Damien Sandow	7.50	15.00
3 Daniel Bryan	17.50	35.00
4 Triple H		
5 Cody Rhodes	7.50	15.00
6 Jinder Mahal	10.00	20.00

2014 Mattel WWE Series 36

7 CM Punk	15.00	30.00
8 Big E Langston	7.50	15.00
9 Christian		
10 Jack Swagger		
11 Fandango		
12 Kaitlyn	12.50	25.00

2014 Mattel WWE Series 37

Also known as WrestleMania Heritage.

13 Mr. Perfect		
14 Batista		
15 Roman Reigns		
16 Ryback		
17 Zeb Colter		
18 Randy Orton		

2014 Mattel WWE Series 38

19 Chris Jericho		
20 Dolph Ziggler	7.50	15.00
21 Vickie Guerrero	10.00	20.00
22 Sheamus		
23 The Miz		
24 Kofi Kingston	7.50	15.00

2014 Mattel WWE Series 39

25 Bray Wyatt	7.50	15.00
26 Rob Van Dam	12.50	25.00
27 Justin Gabriel	10.00	20.00
28 John Cena		
29 Christian		
30 Heath Slater	10.00	20.00

2014 Mattel WWE Series 40

Also known as Local Heroes.

31 CM Punk	17.50	35.00
32 Alberto Del Rio	7.50	15.00
33 Rey Mysterio		
34 The Great Khali		
35 Zack Ryder	7.50	15.00
36 Edge	12.50	25.00

2014 Mattel WWE Series 41

37 Daniel Bryan	10.00	20.00
38 Santino Marella		
39 Cesaro		
40 Drew McIntyre		
41 Bray Wyatt		
42 Fandango		

2014 Mattel WWE Series 42

43 Natalya	12.50	25.00
44 Batista		
45 El Torito	10.00	20.00
46 Big Show		
47 Roman Reigns	10.00	20.00
48 Sin Cara		

2014 Mattel WWE Series 43

49 Mark Henry		
50 Eva Marie	10.00	20.00
51 Rob Van Dam	17.50	35.00
52 John Cena	7.50	15.00
54 Dolph Ziggler	7.50	15.00
55 Rey Mysterio		

2014 Mattel WWE Series 44

53 Kane	20.00	40.00
56 Big E		
57 Randy Orton		
58 Seth Rollins	10.00	20.00
59 Titus O'Neil		
60 Goldust	10.00	20.00

2015 Mattel WWE Series 45

Also known as World Champions.

1 Triple H	6.00	12.00
2 Chris Jericho	10.00	20.00
3 Mankind	10.00	20.00
4 The Miz	7.50	15.00
5 Ricky The Dragon Steamboat	10.00	20.00
6 Daniel Bryan	15.00	30.00

2015 Mattel WWE Series 46

8 Big Show	12.50	25.00
9 Kofi Kingston	10.00	20.00
10 Bad News Barrett	7.50	15.00
11 Jerry The King Lawler	20.00	40.00
12 Batista	17.50	35.00

2015 Mattel WWE Series 47

13 Alicia Fox	7.50	15.00
14 Rusev	6.00	12.00
15 Brock Lesnar	10.00	20.00
16 Kane	20.00	40.00
17 Christian	10.00	20.00
18 Cesaro	10.00	20.00

2015 Mattel WWE Series 48

Also known as WrestleMania Heritage.

19 Ric Flair	10.00	20.00
20 Hulk Hogan	12.50	25.00
21 Brie Bella	10.00	20.00
22 John Cena	7.50	15.00
23 Booker T	15.00	30.00
24 Randy Orton		

2015 Mattel WWE Series 49

25 Ryback		
26 Bray Wyatt	7.50	15.00
27 Roman Reigns	10.00	20.00
28 Bret Hart	12.50	25.00
29 Bo Dallas	7.50	15.00
30A Emma FP	12.50	25.00
30B Emma FP/Legs Variant		

2015 Mattel WWE Series 50

Sami Zayn has no number on the package.

31 Daniel Bryan	10.00	20.00
32 Adam Rose	6.00	12.00
33 Seth Rollins	7.50	15.00
34 Goldust	10.00	20.00
35 Summer Rae FP	15.00	30.00
36 Sami Zayn FP	6.00	12.00

2015 Mattel WWE Series 51

37 Dolph Ziggler	7.50	15.00
38 Dean Ambrose	10.00	20.00
39 Stardust	25.00	50.00
40 Stephanie McMahon	10.00	20.00
41 Stone Cold Steve Austin FB	12.50	25.00
42 Heath Slater	7.50	15.00

2015 Mattel WWE Series 52

43 John Cena		
44 Chris Jericho	6.00	12.00
45 The Miz	7.50	15.00
46 Nikki Bella	7.50	15.00
47 Mark Henry		
48 Adrian Neville FP	10.00	20.00

2015 Mattel WWE Series 53

49 Brock Lesnar	7.50	15.00
50 The Rock	10.00	20.00
51 Triple H	7.50	15.00
52 Damien Mizdow	6.00	12.00
53 AJ Lee	30.00	75.00
54 Tyler Breeze FP	6.00	12.00

2015 Mattel WWE Series 54

55 Roman Reigns	10.00	20.00
56 The Rock	10.00	20.00
57 Rusev	6.00	12.00
58 Big Show	12.50	25.00
59 Dolph Ziggler	7.50	15.00
60 Tyson Kidd	6.00	12.00

2015 Mattel WWE Series 55

60 Sting FB	10.00	20.00
61 John Cena	7.50	15.00
62 El Torito	20.00	40.00
63 Kane	7.50	15.00
64 Randy Orton	10.00	20.00
65 Bray Wyatt	10.00	20.00
66 Undertaker	12.50	25.00
67 Charlotte FP	15.00	30.00

2015 Mattel WWE Series 56

NNO Dean Ambrose	7.50	15.00
NNO Dean Ambrose/WWE Title		
NNO Hideo Itami FP	6.00	12.00
NNO John Cena	10.00	20.00
NNO John Cena/WWE Title	15.00	30.00
NNO Naomi	7.50	15.00
NNO Naomi/WWE Title	12.50	25.00
NNO Ultimate Warrior FB	12.50	25.00
NNO Ultimate Warrior FB/WWE Title		
NNO Xavier Woods	6.00	12.00
NNO Xavier Woods/WWE Title		

2015 Mattel WWE Series 57

NNO Big Show		
NNO Big Show/WWE Title	15.00	30.00
NNO Daniel Bryan	7.50	15.00
NNO Daniel Bryan/WWE Title	12.50	25.00
NNO Erick Rowan	6.00	12.00
NNO Erick Rowan/WWE Title	10.00	20.00
NNO Finn Balor FP	10.00	20.00
NNO Paige	12.50	25.00
NNO Paige/WWE Title	20.00	40.00
NNO Ryback	6.00	12.00
NNO Ryback/WWE Title		

2015 Mattel WWE Series 58

NNO Bad News Barrett	7.50	15.00
NNO Bad News Barrett/WWE Title		
NNO Bayley	10.00	20.00
NNO Bayley/WWE Title		
NNO Edge FB	7.50	15.00
NNO Edge FB/WWE Title		
NNO Fandango	6.00	12.00
NNO Fandango/WWE Title		
NNO Kevin Owens	7.50	15.00
NNO Kevin Owens/WWE Title		
NNO Lana	7.50	15.00
NNO Lana/WWE Title	15.00	30.00
NNO Paul Orndorff FB	7.50	15.00
NNO Paul Orndorff FB/WWE Title		
NNO Stardust	10.00	20.00
NNO Stardust/WWE Title		
NNO Undertaker	12.50	25.00
NNO Undertaker/WWE Title	20.00	40.00

2016 Mattel WWE Series 59

NNO Bray Wyatt	7.50	15.00
NNO Bray Wyatt/WWE Title		
NNO Eva Marie	10.00	20.00
NNO Eva Marie/WWE Title	12.50	25.00
NNO Honky Tonk Man FB	6.00	12.00
NNO Honky Tonk Man FB/WWE Title		
NNO Iron Sheik FB	10.00	20.00
NNO Iron Sheik FB/WWE Title		
NNO R-Truth	12.50	25.00
NNO R-Truth/WWE Title		
NNO Sasha Banks FP	10.00	20.00
NNO Sasha Banks FP/WWE Title		
NNO Sheamus	6.00	12.00
NNO Sheamus/WWE Title	7.50	15.00
NNO Triple H	6.00	12.00
NNO Triple H/WWE Title		

2016 Mattel WWE Series 60

NNO Brock Lesnar	7.50	15.00
NNO Brock Lesnar/WWE Title		
NNO John Cena	10.00	20.00
NNO John Cena/WWE Title		
NNO Kalisto FP	12.50	25.00
NNO Kalisto FP/WWE Title		
NNO Kofi Kingston	7.50	15.00
NNO Kofi Kingston/WWE Title		
NNO Luke Harper	6.00	12.00
NNO Luke Harper/WWE Title		
NNO Randy Orton	7.50	15.00
NNO Randy Orton/WWE Title		
NNO Renee Young	7.50	15.00
NNO Renee Young/WWE Title	10.00	20.00
NNO Seth Rollins	7.50	15.00
NNO Seth Rollins/WWE Title		

2016 Mattel WWE Series 61

NNO Big E	7.50	15.00
NNO Dean Ambrose	6.00	12.00
NNO Dolph Ziggler	7.50	15.00
NNO Finn Balor	10.00	20.00
NNO John Cena	7.50	15.00
NNO Natalya	10.00	20.00
NNO Neville	6.00	12.00
NNO Sami Zayn	6.00	12.00
NNO Zack Ryder	7.50	15.00

2016 Mattel WWE Series 62

NNO Becky Lynch FP	20.00	40.00
NNO The Miz	7.50	15.00
NNO Roman Reigns	10.00	20.00
NNO Sin Cara	20.00	40.00
NNO Sting FB	15.00	30.00

2016 Mattel WWE Series 63

NNO Alberto Del Rio	10.00	20.00
NNO Baron Corbin FP	7.50	15.00
NNO Paul Heyman	12.50	25.00
NNO Rusev	10.00	20.00
NNO Ryback	10.00	20.00
NNO Seth Rollins	7.50	15.00
NNO Sid Justice FB	10.00	20.00
NNO Undertaker	12.50	25.00

2016 Mattel WWE Series 64

NNO Apollo Crews FP	10.00	20.00
NNO Braun Strowman	15.00	30.00
NNO Brock Lesnar	12.50	25.00
NNO Dolph Ziggler	7.50	15.00
NNO John Cena	7.50	15.00
NNO Lana	10.00	20.00
NNO Xavier Woods	6.00	12.00

2016 Mattel WWE Series 65

NNO Emma	10.00	20.00
NNO Kane	10.00	20.00
NNO Kevin Owens	7.50	15.00
NNO The Rock	12.50	25.00
NNO Roman Reigns	7.50	15.00
NNO Samoa Joe	7.50	15.00
NNO Sheamus	7.50	15.00

2016 Mattel WWE Series 66

NNO	Alberto Del Rio	7.50	15.00
NNO	Big Show		
NNO	Daniel Bryan	12.50	25.00
NNO	Dean Ambrose	7.50	15.00
NNO	Paige	15.00	30.00
NNO	Roman Reigns	12.50	25.00
NNO	Tyler Breeze	6.00	12.00

2016 Mattel WWE Series 67

NNO	Cesaro	6.00	12.00
NNO	Cesaro/Slammy		
NNO	Goldust	10.00	20.00
NNO	Goldust/Slammy	12.50	25.00
NNO	JBL	7.50	15.00
NNO	JBL/Slammy		
NNO	John Cena	7.50	15.00
NNO	John Cena/Slammy	12.50	25.00
NNO	Luke Harper	7.50	15.00
NNO	Luke Harper/Slammy	7.50	15.00
NNO	Naomi	10.00	20.00
NNO	Naomi/Slammy	7.50	15.00
NNO	Randy Orton	7.50	15.00
NNO	Randy Orton/Slammy	12.50	25.00
NNO	Xavier Woods	7.50	15.00
NNO	Xavier Woods/Slammy		

2016 Mattel WWE Series 68A

NNO	Bo Dallas	7.50	15.00
NNO	Bo Dallas/Slammy	7.50	15.00
NNO	Dana Brooke	12.50	25.00
NNO	Dana Brooke/Slammy	7.50	15.00
NNO	DDP FB	10.00	20.00
NNO	Diamond Dallas Page/Slammy	7.50	15.00
NNO	Finn Balor	7.50	15.00
NNO	Finn Balor/Slammy	7.50	15.00
NNO	Kalisto	15.00	30.00
NNO	Kalisto/Slammy	12.50	25.00
NNO	Neville	6.00	12.00
NNO	Neville/Slammy	6.00	12.00

2016 Mattel WWE Series 68B

NNO	AJ Styles	6.00	12.00
NNO	AJ Styles/Slammy	6.00	12.00
NNO	Alexa Bliss FP	20.00	40.00
NNO	Alexa Bliss FP/Slammy	12.50	25.00
NNO	Chris Jericho	7.50	15.00
NNO	Chris Jericho/Slammy	7.50	15.00
NNO	The Rock	10.00	20.00
NNO	The Rock/Slammy	15.00	30.00
NNO	Seth Rollins	7.50	15.00
NNO	Seth Rollins/Slammy	7.50	15.00
NNO	Sting FB	7.50	15.00
NNO	Sting FB/Slammy		

2016 Mattel WWE Series 69

NNO	Bray Wyatt	7.50	15.00
NNO	Bray Wyatt/Slammy	10.00	20.00
NNO	John Cena	6.00	12.00
NNO	John Cena/Slammy	7.50	15.00
NNO	Sami Zayn	6.00	12.00
NNO	Sami Zayn/Slammy	6.00	12.00
NNO	Sgt. Slaughter FB	6.00	12.00
NNO	Sgt. Slaughter FB/Slammy	10.00	20.00
NNO	Tamina	7.50	15.00
NNO	Tamina/Slammy	7.50	15.00
NNO	Triple H	7.50	15.00
NNO	Triple H/Slammy	7.50	15.00

2017 Mattel WWE Series 70

NNO	Apollo Crews	7.50	15.00
NNO	Brie Bella	10.00	20.00
NNO	Carmella FP	12.50	25.00
NNO	Ric Flair	7.50	15.00
NNO	The Rock FB	12.50	25.00
NNO	Roman Reigns	10.00	20.00
NNO	Samoa Joe	12.50	25.00
NNO	Ultimate Warrior	15.00	30.00

2017 Mattel WWE Series 71

NNO	Austin Aries FP	6.00	12.00
NNO	Baron Corbin	6.00	12.00
NNO	Charlotte Flair	10.00	20.00
NNO	Finn Balor	12.50	25.00
NNO	John Cena	7.50	15.00
NNO	Seth Rollins	7.50	15.00
NNO	Undertaker	20.00	40.00

2017 Mattel WWE Series 72

NNO	Dean Ambrose	10.00	20.00
NNO	Dolph Ziggler	7.50	15.00
NNO	Nia Jax FP	7.50	15.00
NNO	Sheamus	10.00	20.00
NNO	Shinsuke Nakamura	7.50	15.00
NNO	Zack Ryder	10.00	20.00

2017 Mattel WWE Series 73

NNO	AJ Styles	10.00	20.00
NNO	Big E	10.00	20.00
NNO	Cesaro	7.50	15.00
NNO	Kevin Owens	10.00	20.00
NNO	Seth Rollins	7.50	15.00
NNO	Triple H	6.00	12.00

2017 Mattel WWE Series 74

NNO	Bayley	10.00	20.00
NNO	John Cena	7.50	15.00
NNO	Kane	20.00	40.00
NNO	Neville	7.50	15.00
NNO	Roman Reigns	7.50	15.00
NNO	Samoa Joe	10.00	20.00

2017 Mattel WWE Series 75

NNO	Braun Strowman	12.50	25.00
NNO	Brock Lesnar	10.00	20.00
NNO	Chris Jericho	6.00	12.00
NNO	Finn Balor	6.00	12.00
NNO	Lana	7.50	15.00
NNO	Randy Orton	15.00	30.00

2017 Mattel WWE Series 76

NNO	AJ Styles	6.00	12.00
NNO	Dolph Ziggler	7.50	15.00
NNO	John Cena	7.50	15.00
NNO	Macho King Randy Savage FB	10.00	20.00
NNO	The Rock FB	12.50	25.00
NNO	Sami Zayn	6.00	12.00

2017 Mattel WWE Series 77

NNO	Corey Graves	6.00	12.00
NNO	Dean Ambrose	6.00	12.00
NNO	Finn Balor	10.00	20.00
NNO	Roman Reigns	10.00	20.00
NNO	Seth Rollins	12.50	25.00

2017 Mattel WWE Series 78

NNO	AJ Styles	10.00	20.00
NNO	AJ Styles/Case	7.50	15.00
NNO	Braun Strowman	20.00	40.00
NNO	Braun Strowman/Case		
NNO	Kevin Owens	7.50	15.00
NNO	Kevin Owens/Case		
NNO	Natalya	10.00	20.00
NNO	Natalya/Case	7.50	15.00
NNO	The Rock FB	12.50	25.00
NNO	The Rock FB/Case	12.50	25.00
NNO	Shane McMahon	10.00	20.00
NNO	Shane McMahon/Case	10.00	20.00

2017 Mattel WWE Series 79

NNO	Baron Corbin	7.50	15.00
NNO	Baron Corbin/Case	7.50	15.00
NNO	Neville	7.50	15.00
NNO	Neville/Case		
NNO	Nia Jax	7.50	15.00
NNO	Nia Jax/Case	7.50	15.00
NNO	Samoa Joe	7.50	15.00
NNO	Samoa Joe/Case	10.00	20.00

NNO	Stone Cold Steve Austin	10.00	20.00
NNO	Steve Austin/Case	15.00	30.00
NNO	TJ Perkins	10.00	20.00
NNO	TJ Perkins/Case		

2017 Mattel WWE Series 80

NNO	Brock Lesnar	7.50	15.00
NNO	Chris Jericho	7.50	15.00
NNO	Chris Jericho/Case	7.50	15.00
NNO	Rich Swann	6.00	12.00
NNO	Rich Swann/Case	6.00	12.00
NNO	Roman Reigns	7.50	15.00
NNO	Roman Reigns/Case	10.00	20.00
NNO	Sasha Banks	10.00	20.00
NNO	Sasha Banks/Case	12.50	25.00

2017 Mattel WWE Series 81

NNO	Dana Brooke	7.50	15.00
NNO	Dana Brooke/Case	7.50	15.00
NNO	Kofi Kingston	7.50	15.00
NNO	Kofi Kingston/Case	7.50	15.00
NNO	Rhyno	10.00	20.00
NNO	Rhyno/Case	10.00	20.00
NNO	Sami Zayn	7.50	15.00
NNO	Sami Zayn/Case	7.50	15.00
NNO	Seth Rollins	7.50	15.00
NNO	Seth Rollins/Case	7.50	15.00

2017 Mattel WWE Series 82

NNO	AJ Styles	10.00	20.00
NNO	AJ Styles/Case	10.00	20.00
NNO	Becky Lynch	15.00	30.00
NNO	Becky Lynch/Case	10.00	20.00
NNO	John Cena	6.00	12.00
NNO	John Cena/Case	6.00	12.00
NNO	Luke Harper	7.50	15.00
NNO	Luke Harper/Case	7.50	15.00
NNO	Shinsuke Nakamura	7.50	15.00
NNO	Shinsuke Nakaura/Case		

2017 Mattel WWE Series 83

NNO	Alicia Fox	7.50	15.00
NNO	Alicia Fox/Case	7.50	15.00
NNO	Kurt Angle	7.50	15.00
NNO	Kurt Angle/Case	7.50	15.00
NNO	Randy Orton	12.50	25.00
NNO	Randy Orton/Case	10.00	20.00
NNO	Triple H	7.50	15.00
NNO	Triple H/Case	7.50	15.00
NNO	Tye Dillinger	6.00	12.00
NNO	Tye Dillinger/Case	7.50	15.00

2017 Mattel WWE Series 84

NNO	Dean Ambrose	7.50	15.00
NNO	Dean Ambrose/Case	7.50	15.00
NNO	Finn Balor	7.50	15.00
NNO	Finn Balor/Case	10.00	20.00
NNO	Kevin Owens	10.00	20.00
NNO	Kevin Owens/Case		
NNO	Naomi	7.50	15.00
NNO	Naomi/Case		
NNO	Rusev	7.50	15.00
NNO	Rusev/Case		

2017 Mattel WWE Series 85

NNO	AJ Styles	10.00	20.00
NNO	AJ Styles/Case	10.00	20.00
NNO	Alexa Bliss	10.00	30.00
NNO	Alexa Bliss/Case		
NNO	Bobby Roode	12.50	25.00
NNO	Bobby Roode/Case		
NNO	John Cena	7.50	15.00
NNO	John Cena/Case	7.50	15.00
NNO	Seth Rollins	10.00	20.00
NNO	Seth Rollins/Case	10.00	20.00

2018 Mattel WWE Series 86

NNO	Akira Tozawa	6.00	12.00
NNO	Charlotte Flair	7.50	15.00

NNO	Dolph Ziggler	12.50	25.00
NNO	The Rock	15.00	30.00
NNO	Roman Reigns	12.50	25.00

2018 Mattel WWE Series 87

NNO	AJ Styles	10.00	20.00
NNO	Bayley	7.50	15.00
NNO	Dean Ambrose	10.00	20.00
NNO	Jason Jordan	6.00	12.00
NNO	The Miz	7.50	15.00

2018 Mattel WWE Series 88

NNO	Baron Corbin	7.50	15.00
NNO	Chad Gable	6.00	12.00
NNO	Elias	7.50	15.00
NNO	John Cena	7.50	15.00
NNO	Sasha Banks	10.00	20.00

2018 Mattel WWE Series 89

NNO	Carmella	10.00	20.00
NNO	Cesaro	6.00	12.00
NNO	Kalisto	12.50	25.00
NNO	Kurt Angle	7.50	15.00
NNO	Sheamus	10.00	20.00

2018 Mattel WWE Series 90

NNO	Aiden English	6.00	12.00
NNO	Kane	12.50	25.00
NNO	The Miz	7.50	15.00
NNO	Roman Reigns	7.50	15.00
NNO	Roman Reigns/Shield Shirt	10.00	20.00
NNO	Ronda Rousey	15.00	30.00

2018 Mattel WWE Series 91

NNO	Alexa Bliss	10.00	20.00
NNO	Dean Ambrose	7.50	15.00
NNO	Dean Ambrose/Shield Shirt		
NNO	Drew Gulak	10.00	20.00
NNO	Finn Balor	7.50	15.00
NNO	Shinsuke Nakamura	7.50	15.00

2018 Mattel WWE Series 92

NNO	Jeff Hardy	10.00	20.00
NNO	John Cena	7.50	15.00
NNO	Mandy Rose	15.00	30.00
NNO	Samoa Joe	12.50	25.00
NNO	Seth Rollins	6.00	12.00
NNO	Seth Rollins/Shield Shirt		

2019 Mattel WWE Series 93

NNO	Bayley	7.50	15.00
NNO	Jinder Mahal	6.00	12.00
NNO	Macho Man Randy Savage	7.50	15.00
NNO	Macho Man/White Lightning CH	12.50	25.00
NNO	Triple H	6.00	12.00
NNO	Undertaker	7.50	15.00

2019 Mattel WWE Series 94

NNO	Big E	6.00	12.00
NNO	Kofi Kingston	10.00	20.00
NNO	Matt Hardy	6.00	12.00
NNO	Matt Hardy Mower of Lawn CH	12.50	25.00
NNO	Randy Orton		
NNO	Xavier Woods	6.00	12.00

2019 Mattel WWE Series 95

NNO	AJ Styles		
NNO	Bray Wyatt	7.50	15.00
NNO	Kurt Angle	7.50	15.00
NNO	Rusev	6.00	12.00
NNO	Sonya Deville	6.00	12.00
NNO	Sonya Deville Black Attire CH	10.00	20.00

2019 Mattel WWE Series 96

NNO	Bobby Roode		
NNO	Daniel Bryan	7.50	15.00
NNO	Kevin Owens	6.00	12.00
NNO	Sami Zayn	6.00	12.00
NNO	Sami Zayn Arabic CH		
NNO	Sasha Banks	10.00	20.00

2019 Mattel WWE Series 97

NNO	AJ Styles	7.50	15.00
NNO	Bret Hitman Hart	7.50	15.00
NNO	Jeff Hardy	7.50	15.00
NNO	Miz White Trunks	6.00	12.00
NNO	Miz Black Trunks CH	10.00	20.00
NNO	Razor Ramon	7.50	15.00

2019 Mattel WWE Series 98

NNO	Finn Balor	10.00	20.00
NNO	Elias	6.00	12.00
NNO	Ruby Riott	10.00	20.00
NNO	Tony Nese White Tights FP	7.50	15.00
NNO	Tony Nese Gray Tights FP CH	12.50	25.00
NNO	Ultimate Warrior	7.50	15.00

2019 Mattel WWE Series 99

NNO	Ariya Daivari White Tights CH	6.00	12.00
NNO	Ariya Daivari Black Tights CH	7.50	15.00
NNO	Becky Lynch	10.00	20.00
NNO	Drew McIntyre	10.00	20.00
NNO	Rey Mysterio	7.50	15.00
NNO	Shinsuke Nakamura	10.00	20.00

2019 Mattel WWE Series 100

NNO	John Cena	10.00	20.00
NNO	The Rock	10.00	20.00
NNO	Stone Cold Steve Austin	12.50	25.00
NNO	Shawn Michaels	10.00	20.00
NNO	Shawn Michaels Red & White CH	20.00	40.00
NNO	Undertaker	12.50	25.00

2019 Mattel WWE Series 101

NNO	AJ Styles		
NNO	Bobby Lashley		
NNO	Ali		
NNO	Ali Green Tights CH		
NNO	Ronda Rousey		
NNO	Sarah Logan		

2019 Mattel WWE Series 102

NNO	Constable Baron Corbin		
NNO	Drake Maverick		
NNO	Drake Maverick (black gear) (CHASE)		
NNO	Jeff Hardy		
NNO	The Miz		
NNO	Seth Rollins		

2019 Mattel WWE Series 103

NNO	AJ Styles		
NNO	Becky Lynch		
NNO	Becky Lynch Orange Shirt CH		
NNO	Brock Lesnar		
NNO	Kofi Kingston		
NNO	Matt Riddle		

2019 Mattel WWE Series 104

NNO	Alexa Bliss		
NNO	Daniel Bryan		
NNO	Keith Lee		
NNO	Keith Lee Black Tights CH		
NNO	Randy Orton		
NNO	Rey Mysterio		

2019 Mattel WWE Series 105

NNO	John Cena		
NNO	Lars Sullivan		
NNO	Paige GM		
NNO	Roman Reigns		
NNO	Ronda Rousey		
NNO	Ronda Rousey (CHASE)		

2020 Mattel WWE Series 106

NNO	Carmella	15.00	30.00
NNO	Carmella Orange/Purple CH	15.00	30.00
NNO	Finn Balor	7.50	15.00
NNO	Johnny Gargano	10.00	20.00

NNO	R-Truth	10.00	20.00
NNO	Triple H	7.50	15.00

2020 Mattel WWE Series 107

NNO	Bianca Belair	10.00	20.00
NNO	Braun Strowman	12.50	25.00
NNO	EC3	12.50	25.00
NNO	The Rock	15.00	30.00
NNO	Shinsuke Nakamura Black Gear	7.50	15.00
NNO	Shinsuke Nakamura Blue Gear CH	12.50	25.00

2020 Mattel WWE Series 108

NNO	AJ Styles Red/Gray	15.00	30.00
NNO	AJ Styles White/Gold CH	25.00	50.00
NNO	Aleister Black	12.50	25.00
NNO	Angelo Dawkins		
NNO	Montez Ford	7.50	15.00
NNO	Roman Reigns	15.00	30.00

2020 Mattel WWE Series 109

NNO	Becky Lynch	10.00	20.00
NNO	Lana Blue Gear CH	12.50	25.00
NNO	Lana Red Gear	7.50	15.00
NNO	Ricochet	10.00	20.00
NNO	Seth Rollins	7.50	15.00
NNO	Undertaker	12.50	25.00

2020 Mattel WWE Series 110

NNO	Finn Balor	7.50	15.00
NNO	John Cena	10.00	20.00
NNO	Kofi Kingston	7.50	15.00
NNO	Liv Morgan	15.00	30.00
NNO	Mike Kanellis Barbed Wire Tights	7.50	15.00
NNO	Mike Kanellis Name on Tights CH	12.50	25.00

2020 Mattel WWE Series 111

NNO	Bray Wyatt	12.50	25.00
NNO	Erick Rowan	7.50	15.00
NNO	Jeff Hardy	10.00	20.00
NNO	Kevin Owens	12.50	25.00
NNO	Nikki Cross	10.00	20.00
NNO	Nikki Cross Gray Pants CH	12.50	25.00

2020 Mattel WWE Series 112

NNO	Adam Cole	10.00	20.00
NNO	Bobby Lashley	10.00	20.00
NNO	Bobby Lashley Red CH	12.50	25.00
NNO	Braun Strowman	12.50	25.00
NNO	Sasha Banks	20.00	40.00
NNO	Seth Rollins	10.00	20.00

2020 Mattel WWE Series 113

NNO	Buddy Murphy	15.00	30.00
NNO	Drew McIntyre	15.00	30.00
NNO	Edge	12.50	25.00
NNO	Edge Silver Boots CH	15.00	30.00
NNO	John Cena	12.50	25.00
NNO	Mia Yim	15.00	30.00

2020 Mattel WWE Series 114

NNO	The Fiend Bray Wyatt	20.00	40.00
NNO	Kofi Kingston	7.50	15.00
NNO	Rhea Ripley	15.00	30.00
NNO	Ricochet	10.00	20.00
NNO	Ricochet (yellow gear) (CHASE)	12.50	25.00
NNO	Shorty G	7.50	15.00

2021 Mattel WWE Series 115

NNO	Becky Lynch	10.00	20.00
NNO	Big E	6.00	12.00
NNO	Braun Strowman	10.00	20.00
NNO	Humberto Carrillo	7.50	15.00
NNO	Humberto Carrillo Blue/White CH	12.50	25.00
NNO	Tegan Nox	10.00	20.00

2021 Mattel WWE Series 116

NNO	Dakota Kai	15.00	30.00
NNO	Kevin Owens	12.50	25.00
NNO	Roderick Strong	10.00	20.00

NNO Roderick Strong Black Gear CH		
NNO Seth Rollins	12.50	25.00
NNO Sheamus	7.50	15.00

2021 Mattel WWE Series 117

NNO Otis		
NNO Roman Reigns		
NNO Toni Storm		
NNO Toni Storm Red Gear CH		
NNO Tucker		
NNO Undertaker		

2021 Mattel WWE Series 118

NNO Austin Theory		
NNO Austin Theory (CHASE)		
NNO Erik		
NNO Finn Balor		
NNO Ivar		
NNO Jeff Hardy		

2020 Mattel WWE Showdown 2-Packs Series 1

NNO Roman Reigns vs. Finn Balor	15.00	30.00
NNO Sasha Banks vs. Alexa Bliss	25.00	50.00
NNO Undertaker vs. Jeff Hardy	20.00	40.00

2020 Mattel WWE Showdown 2-Packs Series 2

NNO Bobby Lashley vs. King Booker	20.00	40.00
NNO Randy Orton vs. John Cena	25.00	50.00
NNO The Rock vs. Triple H	20.00	40.00

2020 Mattel WWE Showdown 2-Packs Series 3

NNO The Fiend Bray Wyatt vs. Daniel Bryan		
NNO The Giant vs. Ric Flair		
NNO Kane vs. Edge		

2010 Mattel WWE Signature Series

NNO Chris Jericho		
NNO Dave Batista	12.50	25.00
NNO John Cena	10.00	20.00
NNO Shawn Michaels		

2011 Mattel WWE Signature Series

NNO Edge		
NNO Edge/Black		
NNO John Cena	7.50	15.00
NNO Randy Orton	10.00	20.00
NNO Rey Mysterio	7.50	15.00
NNO Triple H		
NNO Undertaker		

2012 Mattel WWE Signature Series

NNO Big Show		
NNO CM Punk		
NNO John Cena/Dk Shorts		
NNO John Cena/ Green Wristbands		
NNO John Cena/Lt Shorts		
NNO Kane		
NNO Randy Orton		
NNO Rey Mysterio/Gray		
NNO Rey Mysterio Red and White		
NNO Rey Mysterio/Red		
NNO Sheamus		
NNO Sin Cara		
NNO The Miz		
NNO The Rock		

2015 Mattel WWE Signature Series

NNO Bray Wyatt	7.50	15.00
NNO Daniel Bryan	15.00	30.00
NNO Dave Batista	7.50	15.00
NNO Dean Ambrose	7.50	15.00
NNO Hulk Hogan	15.00	30.00
NNO John Cena	7.50	15.00

2013 Mattel WWE Slam City Series 1

NNO Alberto Del Rio		
NNO Big Show	15.00	30.00
NNO Brock Lesnar		

NNO John Cena	7.50	15.00
NNO Kane	20.00	40.00
NNO Rey Mysterio	15.00	30.00

2018 Mattel WWE Sound Slammers Playset

NNO Destruction Zone	50.00	100.00

2018 Mattel WWE Sound Slammers Series 1

NNO Dean Ambrose	12.50	25.00
NNO John Cena	20.00	40.00
NNO Kevin Owens	12.50	25.00
NNO Roman Reigns	12.50	25.00
NNO Seth Rollins	12.50	25.00

2018 Mattel WWE Sound Slammers Series 2

NNO AJ Styles	10.00	20.00
NNO Bobby Roode	10.00	20.00
NNO Finn Balor	20.00	40.00
NNO Kurt Angle	10.00	20.00
NNO The Miz	10.00	20.00

2018 Mattel WWE SummerSlam Heritage

NNO John Cena	6.00	12.00
NNO Kurt Angle	6.00	12.00
NNO Ric Flair	7.50	15.00
NNO Roman Reigns	7.50	15.00
NNO Shane McMahon	7.50	15.00
NNO Shinsuke Nakamura	12.50	25.00

2014 Mattel WWE SummerSlam Heritage

NNO CM Punk	15.00	30.00
NNO Million Dollar Man Ted DiBiase	12.50	25.00
NNO Rey Mysterio		
NNO Shawn Michaels	12.50	25.00
NNO Triple H	10.00	20.00
NNO Undertaker	12.50	25.00

2016 Mattel WWE SummerSlam Heritage

NNO British Bulldog FB	6.00	12.00
NNO Dave Batista FB	6.00	12.00
NNO Jim Duggan FB	7.50	15.00
NNO Undertaker FB	12.50	25.00

2017 Mattel WWE SummerSlam Heritage

NNO Dusty Rhodes FB	7.50	15.00
NNO Nikki Bella	12.50	25.00
NNO The Rock FB	10.00	20.00
NNO Seth Rollins	7.50	15.00

2013 Mattel WWE Super Strikers

NNO Alberto Del Rio		
NNO Big Show	7.50	15.00
NNO Brock Lesnar		
NNO CM Punk	10.00	20.00
NNO Daniel Bryan	12.50	25.00
NNO Dolph Ziggler		
NNO John Cena		
NNO Kofi Kingston	7.50	15.00
NNO The Miz		
NNO Randy Orton	10.00	20.00
NNO The Rock		
NNO Roman Reigns	15.00	30.00
NNO Ryback		
NNO Sheamus	10.00	20.00
NNO Undertaker	12.50	25.00

2012 Mattel WWE Superstar Entrances Series 1

These figures were exclusive to Walmart.

NNO CM Punk	20.00	40.00
NNO Dolph Ziggler		
NNO John Cena	12.50	25.00
NNO The Miz	7.50	15.00
NNO R-Truth	7.50	15.00
NNO Randy Orton	12.50	25.00
NNO Triple H	10.00	20.00

2013 Mattel WWE Superstar Entrances Series 2

These figures were exclusive to Walmart.

NNO Daniel Bryan	15.00	30.00
NNO John Cena	10.00	20.00

NNO Ryback		
NNO Santino Marella		
NNO The Rock	10.00	20.00
NNO Zack Ryder		

2014 Mattel WWE Superstar Entrances Series 3

These figures were exclusive to Walmart.

NNO Brock Lesnar	10.00	20.00
NNO CM Punk	20.00	40.00
NNO Cody Rhodes	15.00	30.00
NNO John Cena	10.00	20.00
NNO Macho Man Randy Savage	15.00	30.00
NNO Sheamus	10.00	20.00
NNO The Rock	10.00	20.00

2014 Mattel WWE Superstar Entrances Series 4

These figures were exclusive to Walmart.

NNO AJ Lee	30.00	60.00
NNO Daniel Bryan	15.00	30.00
NNO Dolph Ziggler		
NNO John Cena	10.00	20.00
NNO Rob Van Dam	15.00	30.00
NNO The Rock	7.50	15.00

2015 Mattel WWE Superstar Entrances Series 5

These figures were exclusive to Walmart.

NNO Daniel Bryan	15.00	30.00
NNO John Cena	10.00	20.00
NNO Randy Orton	10.00	20.00
NNO Rowdy Roddy Piper	15.00	30.00
NNO Triple H	7.50	15.00

2015 Mattel WWE Superstar Entrances Series 6

These figures were exclusive to Walmart.

NNO Bo Dallas	7.50	15.00
NNO Hulk Hogan	20.00	40.00
NNO John Cena	10.00	20.00
NNO Kofi Kingston	7.50	15.00
NNO Wade Barrett	6.00	12.00

2011 Mattel WWE Superstar Matchups Series 4

NNO Rey Mysterio/ Blue and White		
NNO Rey Mysterio/Black and Blue		
NNO Sin Cara		

2017 Mattel WWE Superstars Dolls 12-Inch

NNO Alicia Fox		
NNO Asuka		
NNO Bayley		
NNO Becky Lynch	15.00	30.00
NNO Carmella		
NNO Charlotte Flair	12.50	25.00
NNO Eva Marie	10.00	20.00
NNO Lana		
NNO Natalya		

2017 Mattel WWE Superstars Dolls 12-Inch Fashions

NNO Alexa Bliss		
NNO Bayley		
NNO Becky Lynch		
NNO Brie Bella	12.50	25.00
NNO Natalya	12.50	25.00
NNO Nikki Bella	15.00	30.00
NNO Sasha Banks	12.50	25.00

2017 Mattel WWE Superstars Dolls 12-Inch Multi-Packs

NNO Charlotte Flair/Sasha Banks SDCC		
NNO Natalya/Becky Lynch/Sasha Banks/Bellas		

2017 Mattel WWE Superstars Dolls Action Figures Playset

NNO Ultimate Entrance Playset (w/Nikki Bella)		

2017 Mattel WWE Superstars Dolls Action Figures Series 1

NNO Brie Bella		

NNO Charlotte Flair
NNO Nikki Bella

2017 Mattel WWE Superstars Dolls Action Figures Series 2

NNO Alexa Bliss
NNO Brie Bella
NNO Natalya
NNO Nikki Bella

2017 Mattel WWE Superstars Dolls Action Figures Ultimate Fan Packs

NNO Bayley
NNO Charlotte Flair
NNO Sasha Banks

2017 Mattel WWE Surf's Up 2 WaveMania Action Figure DVD Combo

NNO Batista
NNO Big Show
NNO Bray Wyatt
NNO Daniel Bryan
NNO Dean Ambrose (black shirt)
NNO Dean Ambrose (white shirt)
NNO Dolph Ziggler
NNO El Torito
NNO Goldust
NNO John Cena (black shorts)
NNO John Cena (blue shorts)
NNO John Cena (green shorts)
NNO John Cena (tan shorts/blue armband)
NNO John Cena (tan shorts/red armband)
NNO Justin Gabriel
NNO Kane
NNO Mankind
NNO Miz
NNO Randy Orton
NNO Rey Mysterio
NNO Ric Flair
NNO Ricky "The Dragon" Steamboat
NNO Roman Reigns
NNO Rusev
NNO Ryback
NNO Santino Marella
NNO Seth Rollins
NNO Titus O'Neill
NNO Triple H

2013 Mattel WWE Survivor Series 2013

These figures were exclusive to K-Mart.

NNO CM Punk
NNO Ryback

2019 Mattel WWE Tag Team Buddies Plush Dolls 14"

NNO Bayley
NNO Becky Lynch
NNO Sasha Banks

2016 Mattel WWE Teenage Mutant Ninja Turtles Ninja Superstars Series 1

NNO Donatello as Undertaker	15.00	30.00
NNO Leonardo as John Cena	10.00	20.00
NNO Michelangelo as Macho Man Randy Savage	12.50	25.00
NNO Raphael as Sting	12.50	25.00

2017 Mattel WWE Teenage Mutant Ninja Turtles Ninja Superstars Series 2

NNO Donatello as Ultimate Warrior	12.50	25.00
NNO Leonardo as Finn Balor	10.00	20.00
NNO Michelangelo as Rowdy Roddy Piper	7.50	15.00
NNO Raphael as The Rock	15.00	30.00

2016 Mattel WWE Then Now Forever Series 1

These figures were exclusive to Walmart.

NNO Chris Jericho	6.00	12.00
NNO Seth Rollins	10.00	20.00
NNO Sin Cara	40.00	80.00
NNO Undertaker	15.00	30.00

2017 Mattel WWE Then Now Forever Series 2

These figures were exclusive to Walmart.

NNO Neville	6.00	12.00
NNO Sheamus	10.00	20.00
NNO Stone Cold Steve Austin FB	10.00	20.00
NNO Ultimate Warrior FB	12.50	25.00

2017 Mattel WWE Then Now Forever Series 3

These figures were exclusive to Walmart.

NNO Bray Wyatt	7.50	15.00
NNO Kevin Owens	6.00	12.00
NNO Seth Rollins	10.00	20.00
NNO Triple H	12.50	25.00
NNO X-Pac	12.50	25.00

2013 Mattel WWE TLC 2013

These figures were exclusive to Toys R Us.

NNO Alberto Del Rio
NNO Kofi Kingston
NNO Mark Henry
NNO Sheamus

2020 Mattel WWE Top Picks 2020

NNO John Cena	15.00	30.00
NNO Kofi Kingston	15.00	30.00
NNO The Rock	20.00	40.00
NNO Roman Reigns	12.50	25.00

2021 Mattel WWE Top Picks 2021

NNO Braun Strowman
NNO John Cena
NNO The Rock
NNO Roman Reigns

2018 Mattel WWE Top Talent 2018

NNO AJ Styles	15.00	20.00
NNO John Cena	7.50	15.00
NNO Roman Reigns	7.50	15.00
NNO Seth Rollins	6.00	12.00

2019 Mattel WWE Top Talent 2019

NNO AJ Styles		
NNO Jeff Hardy	7.50	15.00
NNO John Cena	12.50	25.00
NNO Seth Rollins	7.50	15.00

2020 Mattel WWE Top Talent 2020

NNO AJ Styles		
NNO Braun Strowman	15.00	30.00
NNO Finn Balor		
NNO John Cena	12.50	25.00

2017 Mattel WWE Tough Talkers Series 1

NNO Bray Wyatt	15.00	30.00
NNO Dean Ambrose	12.50	25.00
NNO John Cena	15.00	30.00
NNO Kevin Owens	10.00	20.00
NNO Roman Reigns	12.50	25.00
NNO Seth Rollins	12.50	25.00

2017 Mattel WWE Tough Talkers Series 2

NNO Big E	7.50	15.00
NNO Brock Lesnar	12.50	25.00
NNO Dean Ambrose	12.50	25.00
NNO John Cena	20.00	40.00
NNO Kofi Kingston	10.00	20.00
NNO Xavier Woods	10.00	20.00

2017 Mattel WWE Tough Talkers 2-Packs Series 1

NNO The Rock/Stone Cold Steve Austin	25.00	50.00
NNO Undertaker/Brock Lesnar	25.00	50.00

2017 Mattel WWE Tough Talkers 2-Packs Series 2

NNO AJ Styles/Seth Rollins	20.00	40.00
NNO Triple H/Roman Reigns	17.50	35.00

2017 Mattel WWE Tough Talkers Hall of Fame Series

NNO Macho Man Randy Savage	12.50	25.00
NNO Ric Flair	12.50	25.00
NNO Rowdy Roddy Piper	12.50	25.00

2017 Mattel WWE Tough Talkers Total Tag Team

NNO AJ Styles	15.00	30.00
NNO Randy Orton	12.50	25.00
NNO Sting	12.50	25.00
NNO Xavier Woods	10.00	20.00

2017 Mattel WWE Tough Talkers Total Tag Team 2-Packs

NNO Big E/Kofi Kingston	17.50	35.00
NNO Kevin Owens & Chris Jericho	15.00	30.00

2012 Mattel WWE Tribute to the Troops

These figures were exclusive to K-Mart.

NNO Big Show/Brown Hat		
NNO Big Show/Green Hat		
NNO John Cena	12.50	25.00
NNO Randy Orton/Brown Vest	10.00	20.00
NNO Randy Orton/Green Vest	10.00	20.00
NNO Rey Mysterio	20.00	40.00

2010 Mattel WWE Triple Threat 3-Packs

These figures were exclusive to K-Mart.

NNO Evan Bourne/Swagger/Kozlov
NNO John Cena/Batista/Y2J
NNO Kane/John Cena/Big Show
NNO Kane/Triple H/Great Khali
NNO Sheamus/John Cena/Triple H

2018 Mattel WWE True Moves 12-Inch

NNO AJ Styles	12.50	25.00
NNO Kane	10.00	20.00
NNO Randy Orton	10.00	20.00
NNO Kevin Owens	12.50	25.00
NNO Kurt Angle	10.00	20.00
NNO Kalisto	15.00	30.00
NNO Seth Rollins	12.50	25.00

2019 Mattel WWE Ultimate Edition Series 1

NNO Ultimate Warrior	20.00	40.00
NNO Ronda Rousey	25.00	50.00

2019 Mattel WWE Ultimate Edition Series 2

NNO Bret "Hitman" Hart	25.00	50.00
NNO Shinsuke Nakamura	20.00	40.00

2019 Mattel WWE Ultimate Edition Series 3

NNO Finn Balor
NNO Triple H

2020 Mattel WWE Ultimate Edition Series 4

NNO Brock Lesnar	30.00	60.00
NNO Shawn Michaels	60.00	120.00

2020 Mattel WWE Ultimate Edition Series 5

NNO Becky Lynch	30.00	60.00
NNO John Cena	40.00	80.00

2020 Mattel WWE Ultimate Edition Series 6

NNO Charlotte Flair	30.00	60.00
NNO The Rock	60.00	120.00
(Amazon Exclusive)		

2020 Mattel WWE Ultimate Edition Series 7

NNO The Fiend Bray Wyatt	30.00	75.00
NNO Hollywood Hulk Hogan	50.00	100.00

2021 Mattel WWE Ultimate Edition Series 8

NNO Edge
NNO Macho Man Randy Savage

2017 Mattel WWE Undertaker 5-Pack

NNO 1990/1994/1998/2014/2016	30.00	75.00

2019 Mattel WWE Wrekkin' Playsets

NNO Entrance Stage Playset	40.00	80.00
NNO Performance Center Playset	30.00	75.00
NNO Slam Mobile (w/Braun Strowman)	20.00	40.00

2019 Mattel WWE Wrekkin' Series 1

NNO AJ Styles	10.00	20.00
NNO John Cena	12.50	25.00
NNO Seth Rollins	10.00	20.00
NNO Undertaker	15.00	30.00

2019 Mattel WWE Wrekkin' Series 2

NNO Miz
NNO Woken Matt Hardy

2019 Mattel WWE Wrekkin' Series 3

NNO Daniel Bryan
NNO Rey Mysterio

2020 Mattel WWE Wrekkin' Playsets

NNO Collision Cage	60.00	120.00
NNO Slambulance	50.00	100.00
NNO Slamcycle (w/Drew McIntyre)	30.00	60.00
NNO Slamcycle (w/Undertaker)	30.00	60.00

2020 Mattel WWE Wrekkin' Series 4

NNO Elias	20.00	40.00
NNO Roman Reigns	25.00	50.00

2010 Mattel WWE WrestleMania 26

These figures were exclusive to Toys R Us.

NNO Chris Jericho		
NNO Christian	15.00	30.00
NNO Drew McIntyre	12.50	25.00
NNO Kane		
NNO Matt Hardy		
NNO Shawn Michaels		
NNO Shelton Benjamin		

2011 Mattel WWE WrestleMania 27

These figures were exclusive to Toys R Us.

NNO Alberto Del Rio	6.00	12.00
NNO Christian	20.00	40.00
NNO John Cena	12.50	25.00
NNO John Morrison	10.00	20.00
NNO Randy Orton	10.00	20.00
NNO Triple H	12.50	25.00

2021 Mattel WWE WrestleMania 37 Celebration

NNO Andre the Giant	20.00	40.00
NNO Macho Man Randy Savage	20.00	40.00

2014 Mattel WWE WrestleMania 30 Heritage

Also known as WrestleMania XXX Heritage.

NNO Brock Lesnar		
NNO John Cena	12.50	25.00
NNO The Rock	12.50	25.00
NNO Undertaker	10.00	20.00

2015 Mattel WWE WrestleMania 31 Heritage

NNO Hulk Hogan	15.00	30.00
NNO John Cena		
NNO The Rock	12.50	25.00
NNO Shawn Michaels	10.00	20.00

2016 Mattel WWE WrestleMania 32 Heritage

NNO Cesaro	6.00	12.00
NNO Eddie Guerrero	10.00	20.00
NNO Razor Ramon	17.50	35.00
NNO Roman Reigns	7.50	15.00

2017 Mattel WWE WrestleMania 33 Heritage

NNO Chris Jericho	12.50	25.00
NNO Roman Reigns	15.00	30.00
NNO Stone Cold Steve Austin	10.00	20.00
NNO Undertaker	15.00	30.00

2018 Mattel WWE WrestleMania 34 Heritage

NNO AJ Styles	7.50	15.00
NNO Bayley	7.50	15.00
NNO Big Show	20.00	40.00
NNO Dean Ambrose	7.50	15.00
NNO Mojo Rawley	6.00	12.00
NNO Seth Rollins	7.50	15.00

2018 Mattel WWE WrestleMania 35 Heritage

NNO Charlotte Flair	12.50	25.00
NNO Elias	7.50	15.00
NNO John Cena		
NNO Kevin Nash	10.00	20.00
NNO Matt Hardy	7.50	15.00
NNO Trish Stratus	12.50	25.00

2020 Mattel WWE WrestleMania 36 Heritage

NNO Batista	20.00	40.00
NNO Becky Lynch	12.50	25.00
NNO The Rock	15.00	30.00
NNO Seth Rollins	10.00	20.00
NNO Shane McMahon	15.00	30.00
NNO Stephanie McMahon	12.50	25.00

2021 Mattel WWE WrestleMania 37 Heritage

NNO Andrade	6.00	12.00
NNO Drew McIntyre	12.50	25.00
NNO The Fiend Bray Wyatt	12.50	25.00
NNO Ricochet	6.00	12.00

2016 Mattel WWE Zombies Series 1

NNO Bray Wyatt	7.50	15.00
NNO Dean Ambrose	15.00	30.00
NNO John Cena	15.00	30.00
NNO Paige	7.50	15.00
NNO The Rock	12.50	25.00
NNO Roman Reigns	12.50	25.00
NNO Triple H	7.50	15.00
NNO Undertaker	12.50	25.00

2017 Mattel WWE Zombies Series 2

NNO Stone Cold Steve Austin	12.50	25.00
NNO AJ Styles	7.50	15.00
NNO Brock Lesnar	7.50	15.00
NNO Kevin Owens	6.00	12.00
NNO Sasha Banks	12.50	25.00
NNO Seth Rollins	7.50	15.00

2018 Mattel WWE Zombies Series 3

NNO Charlotte Flair	10.00	20.00
NNO Finn Balor	12.50	25.00
NNO Jeff Hardy	10.00	20.00
NNO Kane	20.00	40.00
NNO Matt Hardy	10.00	20.00
NNO Shinsuke Nakamura	10.00	20.00

1990 Multi Toys WWF Power Grip Squirts

NNO Big Boss Man
NNO Hulk Hogan
NNO Jake The Snake Roberts
NNO Macho King Randy Savage
NNO Million Dollar Man Ted Dibiase
NNO Ultimate Warrior

1990 Multi Toys WWF Power Grip Squirts Tag Teams

NNO Bushwhackers
NNO Legion of Doom
NNO The Rockers

1990 Multi Toys WWF Squirt Heads

NNO Big Boss Man
NNO Hulk Hogan
NNO Jake The Snake Roberts
NNO Macho King Randy Savage
NNO Million Dollar Man Ted Dibiase
NNO Ultimate Warrior

2017 Ooshies WWE Series 1

NNO Asuka R
NNO Booker T R
NNO Booker T Black Trunks R
NNO Bray Wyatt C
NNO Brie Bella R
NNO Brock Lesnar C
NNO Cesaro C
NNO Charlotte Flair R
NNO Dean Ambrose C
NNO Dolph Ziggler C
NNO Finn Balor R
NNO Finn Balor (hologram) LE
NNO Jey Uso R
NNO Jimmy Uso R
NNO John Cena C
NNO John Cena Never Give Up R

NNO Junkyard Dog R
NNO Kalisto R
NNO Kalisto (golden) LE
NNO Kane R
NNO Kevin Owens C
NNO Kofi Kingston R
NNO Kofi Kingston Green Tights R
NNO Macho Man Randy Savage C
NNO Macho Man Randy Savage (glow-in-the-dark) R
NNO The Miz C
NNO Nikki Bella R
NNO Randy Orton C
NNO Randy Orton (glow-in-the-dark) R
NNO The Rock C
NNO The Rock (glow-in-the-dark) R
NNO Roman Reigns C
NNO Seth Rollins C
NNO Sheamus C
NNO Sting R
NNO Sting Wolfpack LE
NNO Stone Cold Steve Austin C
NNO Ultimate Warrior C
NNO Ultimate Warrior (glow-in-the-dark) R
NNO Undertaker R

1991 Original San Francisco Toymakers CMLL Luchadores

NNO Atlantis	25.00	50.00
NNO Lizmark	30.00	75.00
NNO Pierroth		
NNO Rayo de Jalisco		
NNO Ultimo Dragon	50.00	100.00
NNO Vampiro Canadiense	60.00	120.00

1999-00 Original San Francisco Toymakers ECW Wrestling Accessories

NNO Hardcore Grapple Gear
NNO Wrestling Ring Gift Set (w/Rob Van Dam & Sabu)
(Toys R Us Exclusive)

1999-00 Original San Francisco Toymakers ECW Wrestling Series 1

NNO Chris Candido	25.00	50.00
NNO Justin Credible	15.00	30.00
NNO Rob Van Dam	30.00	60.00
NNO Sabu	20.00	40.00
NNO Shane Douglas	15.00	30.00
NNO Taz	25.00	50.00

1999-00 Original San Francisco Toymakers ECW Wrestling Series 2

NNO Buh Buh Ray Dudley	20.00	40.00
NNO D-Von Dudley	20.00	40.00
NNO Lance Storm	15.00	30.00
NNO New Jack	30.00	75.00
NNO Tommy Dreamer	15.00	30.00

1999-00 Original San Francisco Toymakers ECW Wrestling Series 3

NNO Justin Credible
NNO New Jack
NNO Taz

1999-00 Original San Francisco Toymakers ECW Wrestling Series 4

NNO Axl Rotten	20.00	40.00
NNO Balls Mahoney	20.00	40.00
NNO Jerry Lynn	30.00	75.00
NNO Raven	25.00	50.00
NNO Rhino	30.00	60.00
NNO Rob Van Dam	30.00	60.00
NNO Taz	20.00	40.00
NNO Yoshihiro Tajiri	30.00	60.00

1999-00 Original San Francisco Toymakers ECW Wrestling Series 5

NNO Justin Credible	15.00	30.00
NNO Little Guido		

NNO	Mike Awesome	60.00	120.00
NNO	Nova	25.00	50.00
NNO	Sabu	30.00	60.00
NNO	Sandman	30.00	75.00
NNO	Steve Corino		
NNO	Super Crazy		

1999-00 Original San Francisco Toymakers ECW Wrestling Series 6

NNO	Balls Mahoney	25.00	50.00
NNO	Chris Candido	30.00	60.00
NNO	Lance Storm	20.00	40.00
NNO	New Jack	30.00	75.00
NNO	Raven	30.00	75.00
NNO	Rhino	50.00	100.00
NNO	Rob Van Dam	30.00	60.00
NNO	Tommy Dreamer	20.00	40.00

1998 Original San Francisco Toymakers WCW

NNO	Bret Hart	10.00	20.00
NNO	Chris Benoit	12.50	25.00
NNO	Diamond Dallas Page	20.00	40.00
NNO	Goldberg	15.00	30.00
NNO	Raven	7.50	15.00
NNO	Rey Mysterio	12.50	25.00
NNO	Ric Flair	10.00	20.00
NNO	Sting	10.00	20.00

1998 Original San Francisco Toymakers WCW 12-Inch

NNO	Bill Goldberg	20.00	40.00
NNO	Hollywood Hulk Hogan	15.00	30.00
NNO	Macho Man Randy Savage	20.00	40.00
NNO	Sting/Black & White	15.00	30.00
NNO	Sting/Red & Black	12.50	25.00

1998 Original San Francisco Toymakers WCW 4.5-Inch

NNO	Goldberg	7.50	15.00
NNO	Ric Flair	7.50	15.00
NNO	Rick Steiner	6.00	12.00
NNO	Sting	7.50	15.00

1997-98 Original San Francisco Toymakers WCW Boxed Sets

NNO	Clash of the Champions	25.00	50.00
NNO	Fall Brawl	10.00	20.00
	Sting/Giant		
NNO	Fearsome Foursome	20.00	40.00
NNO	Halloween Havoc	20.00	40.00
NNO	Live on Forever	30.00	75.00
	Hogan/Bagwell/Giant/Scott Steiner		
NNO	No Retreat No Surrender	25.00	50.00
	Nash/Sting/Savage/Luger		
NNO	Starrcade	20.00	40.00
NNO	We Are the Champions	25.00	50.00
	Goldberg/Giant/Hall/Hart		
NNO	World War 3	12.50	25.00

1997 Original San Francisco Toymakers WCW Fly Buddies

NNO	Giant	10.00	20.00
NNO	Hollywood Hulk Hogan	15.00	30.00
NNO	Sting	10.00	20.00

1998 Original San Francisco Toymakers WCW nWo 4.5-Inch

NNO	Giant	5.00	10.00
NNO	Hollywood Hogan	6.00	12.00
NNO	Kevin Nash	5.00	10.00
NNO	Lex Luger	3.00	8.00
NNO	Macho Man Randy Savage	5.00	10.00
NNO	Scott Hall	5.00	10.00
NNO	Scott Steiner	3.00	8.00

1998 Original San Francisco Toymakers WCW nWo Series

NNO	Curt Henning UER	6.00	12.00
NNO	The Giant	6.00	12.00

NNO	Hollywood Hogan	7.50	15.00
NNO	Kevin Nash	6.00	12.00
NNO	Lex Luger	5.00	10.00
NNO	Macho Man Randy Savage	7.50	15.00
NNO	Marcus Bagwell	3.00	8.00
NNO	Scott Hall	6.00	12.00
NNO	Scott Steiner	5.00	10.00
NNO	Sting	6.00	12.00

1995 Original San Francisco Toymakers WCW Playsets

NNO	Wrestling Ring & Cage	25.00	50.00

1998 WCW Playsets

NNO	Battle Royal Wrestling Ring & Cage		
	Hogan/Nash/Savage/Sting/Rick Steiner/Luger		
NNO	Thunder Wrestling Ring & Cage	30.00	60.00
	Nash/Giant/Luger/Sting		
NNO	Wrestling Ring & Cage w/Action Sounds	20.00	40.00
NNO	Wrestling Ring & Cage w/Giant/Luger	30.00	75.00
NNO	Wrestling Ring & Cage w/Sting KMART		
NNO	Wrestling Ring & Cage	20.00	40.00
	Hogan/Rick Steiner/Savage/Sting		

1995 Original San Francisco Toymakers WCW Series 1

1	Brian Knobbs	12.50	25.00
2	Hulk Hogan	30.00	75.00
3	Jerry Sags	10.00	20.00
4	Jimmy Hart ERR/Dk. Skin	150.00	300.00
5	Jimmy Hart/Lt. Skin	12.50	25.00
6	Johnny B. Badd	20.00	40.00
7	Kevin Sullivan	12.50	25.00
8	Ric Flair/Blue Tights	15.00	30.00
9	Ric Flair/Purple Tights	15.00	30.00
10	Sting	25.00	50.00
11	Vader	20.00	40.00

1995 Original San Francisco Toymakers WCW Series 1 (loose)

NNO	Brian Knobbs		
NNO	Hulk Hogan		
NNO	Jerry Sags		
NNO	Jimmy Hart		
NNO	Johnny B. Badd		
NNO	Kevin Sullivan		
NNO	Ric Flair/Blue Tights		
NNO	Ric Flair/Purple Tights		
NNO	Sting		
NNO	Vader		

1996 Original San Francisco Toymakers WCW Series 2

NNO	Hulk Hogan	20.00	40.00
NNO	Jimmy Hart	12.50	25.00
NNO	Johnny B. Badd	15.00	30.00
NNO	Kevin Sullivan	10.00	20.00
NNO	Macho Man Randy Savage	50.00	100.00
NNO	Ric Flair/Green Tights	15.00	30.00
NNO	Ric Flair/Purple Tights	15.00	30.00
NNO	Sting	20.00	40.00
NNO	Vader	25.00	50.00

1996 Original San Francisco Toymakers WCW Series 3

NNO	Alex Wright	12.50	25.00
NNO	Big Bubba Rogers	10.00	20.00
NNO	Booker T	7.50	15.00
NNO	Craig Pittman	7.50	15.00
NNO	Giant	12.50	25.00
NNO	Hulk Hogan	15.00	30.00
NNO	Macho Man Randy Savage	15.00	30.00
NNO	Ric Flair	12.50	25.00
NNO	Stevie Ray	10.00	20.00
NNO	Sting	15.00	30.00

1998 Original San Francisco Toymakers WCW Special Edition

NNO	Sting/Diamond Dallas Page

NNO	Diamond Dallas Page		
NNO	nWo Wolfpack Sting		
NNO	Sting/nWo Wolfpack Sting		
NNO	Sting	15.00	30.00

1995 Original San Francisco Toymakers WCW Tag Teams Series 1

NNO	Harlem Heat	25.00	50.00
NNO	Hulk Hogan/Sting	60.00	120.00
NNO	Nasty Boys/Black	15.00	30.00
NNO	Nasty Boys/Green	75.00	150.00

1995 Original San Francisco Toymakers WCW Tag Teams Series 1 (loose)

NNO	Booker T
NNO	Brian Knobbs/Black
NNO	Brian Knobbs/Green
NNO	Hulk Hogan
NNO	Jerry Sags/Black
NNO	Jerry Sags/Green
NNO	Stevie Ray
NNO	Sting

1996 Original San Francisco Toymakers WCW Tag Teams Series 2

NNO	Harlem Heat	30.00	60.00
NNO	Hulk Hogan/Sting	75.00	150.00
NNO	Nasty Boys	25.00	50.00

1996 Original San Francisco Toymakers WCW Tag Teams Series 3

NNO	Blue Bloods	25.00	50.00
NNO	Harlem Heat	20.00	40.00
NNO	Hollywood Hogan/Macho Man	20.00	40.00

1997 Original San Francisco Toymakers WCW Vibrating Action Figures

NNO	Chris Benoit	7.50	15.00
NNO	Giant	7.50	15.00
NNO	Hollywood Hulk Hogan	12.50	25.00
NNO	Lex Luger	6.00	12.00
NNO	Scott Hall	7.50	15.00
NNO	Sting	10.00	20.00
NNO	Taskmaster Kevin Sullivan	6.00	12.00

2016 Playmates WWE Nitro Machines

NNO	Dean Ambrose	3.00	8.00
NNO	John Cena	6.00	12.00
NNO	The Rock	7.50	15.00
NNO	Undertaker	7.50	15.00

2016 Playmates WWE Nitro Machines (loose)

NNO	Brock Lesnar	7.50	15.00
NNO	John Cena	7.50	15.00
NNO	The Rock	10.00	20.00
NNO	Undertaker	7.50	15.00

1985 Remco AWA Wrestling Accessories and Playsets

NNO	Battle Royal Playset (w/7 figures)	400.00	600.00
NNO	Battle Royal Playset 2 (w/7 figures)	500.00	800.00
NNO	Championship Belt Figure Holder	200.00	400.00
NNO	Regular Ring Playset	125.00	200.00
NNO	Steel Cage Match	300.00	600.00

1986 Remco AWA Wrestling Mini-Mashers

NNO	Animal
NNO	Barbarian
NNO	Boris Zhukov
NNO	Curt Henning
NNO	Hawk
NNO	Larry Zbyszko
NNO	Marty Jannetty
NNO	Nick Bockwinkel
NNO	Ric Flair
NNO	Scott Hall
NNO	Shawn Michaels
NNO	Stan Hansen

1986 Remco AWA Wrestling Mini-Mashers Green

NNO	Animal

NNO Barbarian
NNO Boris Zhukov
NNO Curt Henning
NNO Hawk
NNO Larry Zbyszko
NNO Marty Jannetty
NNO Nick Bockwinkel
NNO Ric Flair
NNO Scott Hall
NNO Shawn Michaels
NNO Stan Hansen

1986 Remco AWA Wrestling Mini-Mashers Packs

NNO	4-Pack	25.00	50.00
NNO	8-Pack	50.00	100.00
NNO	12-Pack	60.00	120.00

1986 Remco AWA Wrestling Mini-Mashers Purple

NNO Animal
NNO Barbarian
NNO Boris Zhukov
NNO Curt Henning
NNO Hawk
NNO Larry Zbyszko
NNO Marty Jannetty
NNO Nick Bockwinkel
NNO Ric Flair
NNO Scott Hall
NNO Shawn Michaels
NNO Stan Hansen

1986 Remco AWA Wrestling Mini-Mashers Red

NNO Animal
NNO Barbarian
NNO Boris Zhukov
NNO Curt Henning
NNO Hawk
NNO Larry Zbyszko
NNO Marty Jannetty
NNO Nick Bockwinkel
NNO Ric Flair
NNO Scott Hall
NNO Shawn Michaels
NNO Stan Hansen

1985 Remco AWA Wrestling Series 1

NNO	Fabulous Ones	100.00	200.00
NNO	High Flyers	100.00	200.00
NNO	Ric Flair/Larry Zbyszko	125.00	250.00
NNO	Rick Martel/Baron von Raschke w/AWA Ring	125.00	250.00
NNO	Rick Martel/Baron von Raschke w/AWA Sticker	75.00	150.00
NNO	Road Warriors	200.00	400.00
NNO	Road Warriors	150.00	300.00

1985 Remco AWA Wrestling Series 1 (loose)

NNO	Animal	6.00	12.00
NNO	Baron von Raschke	7.50	15.00
NNO	Greg Gagne	7.50	15.00
NNO	Hawk	6.00	12.00
NNO	Jim Brunzell	6.00	12.00
NNO	Larry Zbyszko	6.00	12.00
NNO	Ric Flair	15.00	30.00
NNO	Rick Martel	12.50	25.00
NNO	Stan Lane	6.00	15.00
NNO	Steve Keirn	6.00	12.00

1985 Remco AWA Wrestling Series 2

NNO	Fabulous Freebirds	100.00	200.00
NNO	Gagne's Raiders	125.00	250.00
NNO	Jimmy Garvin/Precious/Steve Regal	75.00	150.00
NNO	Long Riders	100.00	200.00
NNO	Road Warriors	150.00	300.00

1985 Remco AWA Wrestling Series 2 (loose)

NNO	Animal	10.00	20.00
NNO	Buddy Roberts	12.50	25.00
NNO	Curt Henning	10.00	20.00
NNO	Greg Gagne	6.00	12.00
NNO	Hawk	10.00	20.00

NNO	Jimmy Garvin	10.00	20.00
NNO	Michael Hayes	12.50	25.00
NNO	Paul Ellering	12.50	25.00
NNO	Precious	10.00	20.00
NNO	Scott Hog Irwin	7.50	15.00
NNO	Steve Regal	6.00	12.00
NNO	Terry Gordy	12.50	25.00
NNO	Wild Bill Irwin	7.50	15.00

1985 Remco AWA Wrestling Series 2 Fight to the Finish 2-Pack

NNO	Steve Regal vs. Curt Hennig (w/VHS Tape)	50.00	100.00

1985 Remco AWA Wrestling Series 3

NNO	Nick Bockwinkel vs. Larry Zbyszko	150.00	300.00
NNO	Scott Hall vs. Gorgeous Jimmy Garvin	150.00	300.00
NNO	Stan Hansen vs. Jerry Blackwell	100.00	200.00
NNO	Carlos Colon vs. Abdullah the Butcher	150.00	300.00

1985 Remco AWA Wrestling Series 3 (loose)

NNO	Abdullah the Butcher	20.00	40.00
NNO	Carlos Colon	7.50	15.00
NNO	Gorgeous Jimmy Garvin	5.00	10.00
NNO	Jerry Blackwell	10.00	20.00
NNO	Larry Zbyszko	15.00	30.00
NNO	Nick Bockwinkel	20.00	40.00
NNO	Referee Curley Brown	12.50	25.00
NNO	Referee Nasty Ned	15.00	30.00
NNO	Scott Hall	30.00	75.00
NNO	Stan Hansen	20.00	40.00

1986 Remco AWA Wrestling Series 4

Also known as Mat Mania. The Bockwinkel, Ellering, and Flair figures are from previous series and were re-released on Mat Mania cards.

NNO	Boris Zhukov	300.00	600.00
NNO	Buddy Rose	250.00	500.00
NNO	Doug Somers	200.00	400.00
NNO	Marty Jannetty	400.00	800.00
NNO	Nick Bockwinkel		
NNO	Nord the Barbarian	250.00	500.00
NNO	Paul Ellering		
NNO	Referee Dick Woehrle	200.00	350.00
NNO	Ric Flair	500.00	1000.00
NNO	Shawn Michaels	750.00	1500.00
NNO	Sheik Adnan Al-Kaissie	200.00	400.00

1986 Remco AWA Wrestling Series 4 (loose)

NNO	Boris Zhukov	125.00	250.00
NNO	Buddy Rose	125.00	250.00
NNO	Doug Somers	100.00	200.00
NNO	Marty Jannetty	150.00	300.00
NNO	Nord the Barbarian	150.00	300.00
NNO	Referee Dick Woehrle	60.00	120.00
NNO	Shawn Michaels	250.00	400.00
NNO	Sheik Adnan Al-Kaissie	250.00	500.00

1985 Remco AWA Wrestling Thumbsters

NNO	Greg Gagne vs. Hawk	30.00	75.00
NNO	Ric Flair vs. Larry Zbyszko	50.00	100.00
NNO	Rick Martel vs. Animal	30.00	75.00

1985 Remco AWA Wrestling Thumbsters (loose)

NNO	Animal	7.50	15.00
NNO	Greg Gagne	5.00	10.00
NNO	Hawk	7.50	15.00
NNO	Larry Zbyszko	5.00	10.00
NNO	Ric Flair	10.00	20.00
NNO	Rick Martel	7.50	15.00

1998 Ringside Supplies WWF Squirt Heads Cellophane Package

NNO The Rock
NNO Stone Cold Steve Austin
NNO Undertaker

1998 Ringside Supplies WWF Squirt Heads Mesh Package

NNO The Rock
NNO Stone Cold Steve Austin
NNO Undertaker

2017 S.H. Figuarts WWE

NNO	Kane	30.00	75.00
NNO	The Rock	30.00	60.00
NNO	Stone Cold Steve Austin	20.00	40.00
NNO	Triple H	12.50	25.00
NNO	Undertaker	30.00	75.00
NNO	Vince McMahon		

1990 Spectra Star WWF Rad Rollers Collection

NNO Hulk Hogan/Jake The Snake Roberts/Macho King Randy Savage
Big Boss Man/Million Dollar Man Ted DiBiase/Ultimate Warrior

1990 Spectra Star WWF Rad Rollers Collection (loose)

NNO Big Boss Man
NNO Hulk Hogan
NNO Jake The Snake Roberts
NNO Macho King Randy Savage
NNO Million Dollar Man Ted DiBiase
NNO Ultimate Warrior

2019 Super 7 ReAction Wrestling Figures

NNO Andre the Giant (singlet)
NNO Andre the Giant (w/vest)

2017 TeenyMates WWE Collector Sets

NNO WWE Hall of Fame Inductees
NNO WWE Superstars (w/Andre the Giant GITD)

2016 TeenyMates WWE Series 1

NNO Big Show C
NNO Bray Wyatt C
NNO Bret Hart C
NNO Brie Bella C
NNO Brock Lesnar C
NNO Daniel Bryan C
NNO Dean Ambrose C
NNO Dolph Ziggler C
NNO Goldust C
NNO Jey Uso C
NNO Jimmy Uso C
NNO John Cena (crystal clear) R
NNO John Cena C
NNO Kane C
NNO Kofi Kingston C
NNO Macho Man Randy Savage (orange) C
NNO Macho Man Randy Savage (glow-in-the-dark) R
(Collector Tin Exclusive)
NNO Macho Man Randy Savage (purple) R
NNO Nikki Bella C
NNO Randy Orton C
NNO The Rock C
NNO The Rock (metallic gold) UR
NNO Roman Reigns C
NNO Seth Rollins C
NNO Sheamus C
NNO Sin Cara C
NNO Stardust C
NNO Sting C
NNO Stone Cold Steve Austin C
NNO Triple H C
NNO Ultimate Warrior C
NNO Undertaker (glow-in-the-dark) R
NNO Undertaker C

2017 TeenyMates WWE Series 2

NNO AJ Styles C
NNO Andre the Giant C
NNO Andre the Giant (glow-in-the-dark) R
(Collector's Set Exclusive)
NNO Becky Lynch C
NNO Big E C
NNO Bray Wyatt C
NNO Brock Lesnar C
NNO Chris Jericho C
NNO Dean Ambrose C
NNO Finn Balor C
NNO Finn Balor (glow-in-the-dark) R
NNO Jake the Snake Roberts C

NNO	John Cena (ice blue) R	
NNO	John Cena C	
NNO	Kane C	
NNO	Kevin Owens C	
NNO	Kofi Kingston C	
NNO	Macho Man Randy Savage C	
NNO	Mankind C	
NNO	Ric Flair (blue robe) UR	
NNO	Ric Flair (pink robe) C	
NNO	The Rock C	
NNO	Roman Reigns C	
NNO	Rowdy Roddy Piper C	
NNO	Sasha Banks C	
NNO	Seth Rollins C	
NNO	Sgt. Slaughter R	
NNO	Shawn Michaels C	
NNO	Sting C	
NNO	Triple H C	
NNO	Ultimate Warrior C	
NNO	Ultimate Warrior (metallic gold) UR	
NNO	Xavier Woods C	

2019 Tomy WWE Blitz Brawlers

NNO	AJ Styles	
NNO	John Cena	

1990 Tonka WWF Wrestling Buddies

NNO	Big Boss Man	100.00	200.00
NNO	Hulk Hogan	250.00	500.00
NNO	Jake "The Snake" Roberts	325.00	650.00
NNO	Macho King Randy Savage	150.00	300.00
NNO	Million Dollar Man Ted DiBiase	400.00	800.00
NNO	Ultimate Warrior	250.00	500.00

1990 Tonka WWF Wrestling Buddies (loose)

NNO	Animal (Legion of Doom)	
NNO	Big Boss Man	
NNO	Hawk (Legion of Doom)	
NNO	Hulk Hogan	
NNO	Jake "The Snake" Roberts	
NNO	Macho King Randy Savage	
NNO	Million Dollar Man Ted DiBiase	
NNO	Ultimate Warrior	

1990 Tonka WWF Wrestling Buddies Tag Team

NNO	Legion of Doom	

2005 Toy Biz Best of TNA Series 1

NNO	AJ Styles	
NNO	Elix Skipper	
NNO	Jeff Hardy	
NNO	Ron Killings	

2006 Toy Biz Best of TNA Series 2

NNO	AJ Styles	
NNO	Chris Sabin	
NNO	Jeff Hardy	
NNO	Monty Brown	
NNO	Raven	
NNO	Ron Killings	

2005 Toy Biz TNA Wrestling 2-Packs Series 1

NNO	BG James/Konnan	15.00	30.00
NNO	Elix Skipper/C. Daniels	12.50	25.00
NNO	James Storm/Chris Harris	30.00	75.00

2006 Toy Biz TNA Wrestling 2-Packs Series 2

NNO	AJ Styles vs. Samoa Joe	20.00	40.00
NNO	Jeff Hardy vs. Abyss	50.00	100.00
NNO	Jeff Jarrett vs. Monty Brown	20.00	40.00

2006 Toy Biz TNA Wrestling 2-Packs Series 3

NNO	BG James/Kip James	20.00	40.00
NNO	Raven vs. Sabu	30.00	75.00
NNO	Sting vs. Jeff Jarrett	25.00	50.00

2007 Toy Biz TNA Wrestling 2-Packs Series 4

NNO	Christian Cage/Rhyno	20.00	40.00
NNO	Christopher Daniels	15.00	30.00
Homicide			
NNO	Kevin Nash/Chris Sabin	20.00	40.00

2007 TNA Wrestling Bashin' Brawlers Series 1

NNO	Samoa Joe	12.50	25.00
NNO	Sting	15.00	30.00

2007 TNA Wrestling Bashin' Brawlers Series 2

NNO	Christian Cage	10.00	20.00
NNO	Kevin Nash	10.00	20.00

2007 Toy Biz TNA Wrestling Collector's Edition 12-Inch Series 1

NNO	AJ Styles	30.00	60.00
NNO	Sting	30.00	75.00

2007 Toy Biz TNA Wrestling Collector's Edition 12-Inch Series 2

NNO	Christopher Daniels	15.00	30.00
NNO	Kurt Angle	25.00	50.00

2006 Toy Biz TNA Wrestling Masked Fury

NNO	Abyss	20.00	40.00
NNO	Shark Boy	20.00	40.00
NNO	Sting	25.00	50.00

2005 Toy Biz TNA Wrestling Playsets

NNO	6-Sided Wrestling Ring w/AJ Styles	75.00	150.00

2006 Toy Biz TNA Wrestling Playsets

NNO	Lockdown Six Sides of Steel w/Christian Cage		
NNO	Champion X Ring w/AJ Styles		
NNO	Championship Belt w/AJ Styles & Jeff Jarrett/Blue Package		
NNO	Championship Belt w/AJ Styles & Jeff Jarrett/Red Package		

2007 Toy Biz TNA Wrestling Playsets

NNO	Ultimate X Ring w/Christopher Daniels	50.00	100.00

2005 Toy Biz TNA Wrestling Series 1

NNO	Abyss	15.00	30.00
NNO	AJ Styles	20.00	40.00
NNO	Jeff Jarrett	12.50	25.00
NNO	Raven	12.50	25.00

2005 Toy Biz TNA Wrestling Series 2

NNO	Christopher Daniels	12.50	25.00
NNO	Jeff Hardy	20.00	40.00
NNO	Ron The Truth Killings	15.00	30.00
NNO	Shark Boy	12.50	25.00

2005 Toy Biz TNA Wrestling Series 3

NNO	AJ Styles	15.00	30.00
NNO	Alpha Male Monty Brown	20.00	40.00
NNO	Chris Sabin	20.00	40.00
NNO	Raven/Straight Jacket	12.50	25.00

2006 Toy Biz TNA Wrestling Series 4

NNO	Kevin Nash		
NNO	Petey Williams	12.50	25.00
NNO	Rhino	20.00	40.00
NNO	Wildcat Chris Harris Mustache	7.50	15.00
NNO	Wildcat Chris Harris No Mustache		

2006 Toy Biz TNA Wrestling Series 5

NNO	James Cowboy Storm	10.00	20.00
NNO	Kip James	10.00	20.00
NNO	Kip James/Black Trunks		
NNO	Lance Hoyt	15.00	30.00
NNO	Lance Hoyt/White Pants		
NNO	Samoa Joe	12.50	25.00
NNO	Samoa Joe Blue and Black Trunks		
NNO	Sting	15.00	30.00

2007 Toy Biz TNA Wrestling Series 6

NNO	Alex Shelley	10.00	20.00
NNO	Alex Shelley		
Green on Shorts			
NNO	Christian Cage	12.50	25.00
NNO	Jay Lethal	12.50	25.00
NNO	Jay Lethal/Green Gear		
NNO	Sonjay Dutt	7.50	15.00
NNO	Sonjay Dutt/Green Gear		

2007 Toy Biz TNA Wrestling Series 7

NNO	Brother Devon	10.00	20.00
NNO	Matt Bentley	10.00	20.00
NNO	Robert Roode	12.50	25.00
NNO	Robert Roode/Team Canada		
NNO	Scott Steiner	15.00	30.00
NNO	Scott Steiner/Black Pants		

2007 Toy Biz TNA Wrestling Series 8

NNO	Chase Stevens	15.00	30.00
NNO	Chase Stevens Headband and Jacket		
NNO	Eric Young	12.50	25.00
NNO	Eric Young/Team Canada	20.00	40.00
NNO	James Mitchell CH	20.00	40.00
NNO	Kurt Angle	10.00	20.00
NNO	Senshi	20.00	40.00
NNO	Senshi/Black Pants	25.00	50.00

2000 Toy Biz WCW Bash at the Beach

NNO	Bret Hitman Hart		
NNO	Diamond Dallas Page		
NNO	Goldberg	10.00	20.00
NNO	Lex Luger	6.00	12.00
NNO	Sting		

1998 Toy Biz WCW Bashin' Brawlers

NNO	Big Poppa Pump Scott Steiner		
NNO	Diamond Dallas Page	30.00	75.00
NNO	Goldberg	60.00	120.00
NNO	Hollywood Hogan	75.00	150.00
NNO	Kevin Nash		
NNO	Macho Man Randy Savage	50.00	100.00
NNO	Sting	60.00	120.00
NNO	Sting (Wolfpac)		

2000 Toy Biz WCW Battle Arms

NNO	Sting	12.50	25.00
NNO	Goldberg	15.00	30.00
NNO	Bret Hitman Hart	12.50	25.00

1999 Toy Biz WCW Bend 'N Flex

NNO	Booker T	7.50	15.00
NNO	Bret Hart	6.00	12.00
NNO	Diamond Dallas Page	6.00	12.00
NNO	Goldberg	10.00	20.00
NNO	Kevin Nash	12.50	25.00
NNO	Scott Hall	7.50	15.00
NNO	Scott Steiner	6.00	12.00
NNO	Sting	7.50	15.00

1999 Toy Biz WCW Bend 'N Flex 6-Pack

NNO	Sting/Goldberg/DDP Hall/Steiner/Nash	25.00	50.00

1999 Toy Biz WCW Brawlin' Bikers

NNO	DDP		
NNO	Goldberg	7.50	15.00
NNO	Hulk Hogan	20.00	40.00
NNO	Sting	10.00	20.00

2001 Toy Biz WCW Bruisers

NNO	Bam Bam Bigelow	7.50	15.00
NNO	DDP	12.50	25.00
NNO	Disco Inferno	10.00	20.00
NNO	Goldberg	20.00	40.00
NNO	Kevin Nash	10.00	20.00
NNO	Kidman	10.00	20.00
NNO	Randy Macho Man Savage	12.50	25.00
NNO	Raven	7.50	15.00
NNO	Rey Mysterio Jr.	15.00	30.00
NNO	Stevie Ray	10.00	20.00
NNO	Sting	15.00	30.00
NNO	Wrath	7.50	15.00

1999 Toy Biz WCW Collector's Edition 8-Inch Figures

NNO	Hollywood Hogan TAR		
NNO	Kevin Nash TAR		
NNO	Sting KB		

2000 Toy Biz WCW Grip 'N Flip Series 2

NNO	Kevin Nash vs. Konnan	10.00	20.00
NNO	Scott Steiner vs. Rick Steiner	7.50	15.00
NNO	Sting vs. Buff Bagwell	7.50	15.00

2000 Toy Biz WCW Gross-Out Wrestlers

NNO	Goldberg	30.00	75.00
NNO	Sid Vicious	25.00	50.00
NNO	Sting	50.00	100.00

1999 Toy Biz WCW Head Ringers

NNO	Bret Hart	
NNO	Buff Bagwell	
NNO	Diamond Dallas Page	
NNO	Goldberg	
NNO	Hulk Hogan	
NNO	Kevin Nash	
NNO	Konnan	
NNO	Sting	

1999 Toy Biz WCW Head Ringers (loose)

NNO	Bret Hart	
NNO	Buff Bagwell	
NNO	Diamond Dallas Page	
NNO	Goldberg	
NNO	Hulk Hogan	
NNO	Kevin Nash	
NNO	Konnan	
NNO	Sting	

2000 Toy Biz WCW Main Event 2-Packs

NNO	Goldberg/Sid Vicious		
NNO	Hulk Hogan/Ric Flair	40.00	80.00
NNO	Sting/The Total Package	30.00	60.00

2000 Toy Biz WCW Nitro Active Wrestlers

NNO	Buff Bagwell/Black Pants	
NNO	Buff Bagwell/Red Pants	
NNO	Goldberg	
NNO	Jeff Jarrett	
NNO	Kevin Nash	

2000 Toy Biz WCW Power Slam

NNO	Buff Bagwell	7.50	15.00
NNO	Dennis Rodman/Blue Hair	10.00	20.00
NNO	Dennis Rodman/Green Hair		
NNO	Dennis Rodman/Orange Hair	15.00	30.00
NNO	Goldberg	25.00	50.00
NNO	Hak	15.00	30.00
NNO	Hollywood Hogan	12.50	25.00
NNO	Hulk Hogan	12.50	25.00
NNO	Kanyon	6.00	12.00
NNO	Kevin Nash	10.00	20.00
NNO	Rowdy Roddy Piper	10.00	20.00
NNO	Sid Vicious	7.50	15.00
NNO	Sting	7.50	15.00

1999 Toy Biz WCW Ring Announcers

NNO	Mean Gene	30.00	60.00
	{w/Nash & Goldberg)		
NNO	Michael Buffer	15.00	30.00
	{w/Scott Steiner & DDP)		

2001 Toy Biz WCW Ring Fighters

NNO	Booker T/Dk Tights	12.50	25.00
NNO	Booker T/White Tights	10.00	20.00
NNO	Bret Hart	7.50	15.00
NNO	Chris Benoit/Red Tights	7.50	15.00
NNO	Chris Benoit/Blue Tights	10.00	20.00
NNO	Goldberg	10.00	20.00
NNO	Scott Steiner/Black Tights		
NNO	Scott Steiner/White Tights	10.00	20.00
NNO	Sting	12.50	25.00

1999 Toy Biz WCW Ring Masters

NNO	Bret Hart	10.00	20.00
NNO	Chris Jericho	10.00	20.00
NNO	Goldberg	15.00	30.00
NNO	Hulk Hogan	12.50	25.00
NNO	Lex Luger	7.50	15.00
NNO	Rick Steiner	10.00	20.00

2000 Toy Biz WCW Road Rebels

NNO	Goldberg	
NNO	Hulk Hogan	
NNO	Sting	

1999 Toy Biz WCW Road Wild Wrestlers

NNO	Goldberg	25.00	50.00
NNO	Hollywood Hogan	30.00	60.00
NNO	Kevin Nash	15.00	30.00
NNO	Sting	20.00	40.00

1999 Toy Biz WCW Rumble 'N Roar

NNO	Goldberg	25.00	50.00
NNO	Sting	30.00	60.00

1999 Toy Biz WCW Slam 'N Crunch

NNO	Buff Bagwell	10.00	20.00
NNO	Goldberg	15.00	30.00
NNO	Kevin Nash	10.00	20.00
NNO	Konnan	15.00	30.00
NNO	Saturn		
NNO	Sting	12.50	25.00

2001 Toy Biz WCW Slam Force

NNO	Bret Hart	20.00	40.00
NNO	Goldberg		
NNO	Hollywood Hogan		
NNO	Kevin Nash	12.50	25.00
NNO	Lex Luger		

1999 Toy Biz WCW Smash 'N Slam

NNO	DDP/No Vest	12.50	25.00
NNO	DDP/Vest	6.00	12.00
NNO	Giant w/Luchadore	10.00	20.00
NNO	Goldberg KB		
NNO	Goldberg w/Blue {Masked Lucha	10.00	20.00
NNO	Goldberg w/Red Masked Lucha	15.00	30.00
NNO	Hollywood Hogan/ No Tank Top	10.00	20.00
NNO	Hollywood Hogan/ Tank Top	12.50	25.00
NNO	Kevin Nash w/Referee/ No Red Pants	7.50	15.00
NNO	Kevin Nash w/Referee/ Red Pants	7.50	15.00
NNO	Lex Luger/No Shirt	6.00	12.00
NNO	Lex Luger/Shirt	12.50	25.00
NNO	Macho Man/Black and Red	15.00	30.00
NNO	Macho Man/Black and White	10.00	20.00
NNO	Scott Hall/Black and Red	12.50	25.00
NNO	Scott Hall/Black and White	12.50	25.00
NNO	Sting/Black and Red	10.00	20.00
NNO	Sting/Black and White	15.00	30.00

1999 Toy Biz WCW Smash 'N Slam 2-Packs

NNO	The Giant/Kevin Nash		
NNO	Macho Man/Miss Elizabeth		
NNO	Sting/Hulk Hogan	15.00	30.00

2001 Toy Biz WCW Target Exclusives

NNO	Hollywood Hogan	20.00	40.00
NNO	Kevin Nash	12.50	25.00

2000 Toy Biz WCW Thunder Slam

NNO	Bagwell/Jarrett/Vampiro		
NNO	Goldberg/Bam Bam Bigelow	10.00	20.00
NNO	Scott Hall/KevinNash	20.00	40.00
NNO	Sting/Bret Hart	10.00	20.00

2001 Toy Biz WCW TNT

NNO	Goldberg	17.50	35.00

NNO	Jeff Jarrett	12.50	25.00
NNO	Scott Steiner	15.00	30.00
NNO	Vampiro	12.50	25.00

2000 Toy Biz WCW Tuff Talkin' Wrestlers

NNO	Scott Steiner	15.00	30.00
NNO	Buff Bagwell	15.00	30.00
NNO	Macho Man Randy Savage	25.00	50.00
NNO	Konnan	12.50	25.00

2000 Toy Biz WCW Tuff Talkin' Wrestlers 2-Packs

NNO	Goldberg/Kevin Nash	30.00	75.00
NNO	Sting/Diamond Dallas Page	30.00	60.00

2000 Toy Biz WCW Unleashed

NNO	Franchise (Shane Douglas)	15.00	30.00
NNO	Kidman	15.00	30.00
NNO	Mike Awesome	10.00	20.00
NNO	Vampiro	12.50	25.00

2000 Toy Biz WCW Whiplashers

NNO	Kidman vs. Rey Mysterio	
NNO	Scott Steiner vs. Buff Bagwell	
NNO	Sting vs. Goldberg	

2000 Toy Biz WCW Window Crashers

NNO	Goldberg	
NNO	Hulk Hogan	
NNO	Kevin Nash	
NNO	Sting	

1991 Toymax WCW Wrestling Champs

NNO	Lex Luger	
NNO	Ric Flair	
NNO	Rick Steiner	
NNO	Sid Vicious	
NNO	Sting	

2019 Wicked Cool Toys WWE Micro Maniax Battle Game On!

NNO	Wrestling Ring	

2019 Wicked Cool Toys WWE Micro Maniax Series 1

NNO	Alexa Bliss	
NNO	Braun Strowman	
NNO	Daniel Bryan	
NNO	Finn Balor	
NNO	John Cena	
NNO	Macho Man Randy Savage	
NNO	Roman Reigns	
NNO	Ronda Rousey	

1985 Winston Toys WWF Hulk Hogan Rock 'n' Wrestling Figurine Erasers

NNO	Hulk Hogan	75.00	150.00
NNO	Iron Sheik	100.00	200.00
NNO	Jimmy "Superfly" Snuka	30.00	75.00
NNO	Junkyard Dog		
NNO	Rowdy Roddy Piper		
NNO	Wendi Richter		

1985 Winston Toys WWF Hulk Hogan Rock 'n' Wrestling Figurine Erasers (loose)

NNO	Hulk Hogan	
NNO	Iron Sheik	
NNO	Jimmy "Superfly" Snuka	
NNO	Junkyard Dog	
NNO	Rowdy Roddy Piper	
NNO	Wendi Richter	

2019 Zag Toys Domez WWE

NNO	Andre the Giant	
NNO	Jake The Snake Roberts	
NNO	Macho Man Randy Savage	
NNO	Ric Flair	
NNO	Rowdy Roddy Piper	
NNO	Sting	
NNO	Stone Cold Steve Austin	
NNO	Undertaker	
NNO	Undertaker Clear CH	